World Scientific – Nobel Laureate Series: Vol 2

WILLIAM F. SHARPE

Selected Works

World Scientific — Nobel Laureate Series

Vol. 1 Harry Markowitz: Selected Works
edited by Harry M Markowitz

Vol. 2 William F Sharpe: Selected Works
edited by William F Sharpe

World Scientific – Nobel Laureate Series: Vol 2

WILLIAM F. SHARPE

Selected Works

edited by

WILLIAM F. SHARPE

Stanford University, USA

World Scientific

NEW JERSEY • LONDON • SINGAPORE • BEIJING • SHANGHAI • HONG KONG • TAIPEI • CHENNAI

Published by

World Scientific Publishing Co. Pte. Ltd.
5 Toh Tuck Link, Singapore 596224
USA office: 27 Warren Street, Suite 401-402, Hackensack, NJ 07601
UK office: 57 Shelton Street, Covent Garden, London WC2H 9HE

British Library Cataloguing-in-Publication Data
A catalogue record for this book is available from the British Library.

Cover art by Kathy Sharpe

World Scientific — Nobel Laureate Series: Vol. 2
WILLIAM F SHARPE
Selected Works

ISBN-13 978-981-4329-95-8
ISBN-10 981-4329-95-9

Printed in Singapore by B & Jo Enterprise Pte Ltd

INTRODUCTION

When World Scientific Publishing first asked me if I would be willing to prepare a volume of selected works, I was reluctant to agree. Like most researchers, I am more interested in new ideas and results than old ones. But over the course of time I was persuaded that some people might find such a volume useful. Hence this book.

My first task was to select a subset of the work that I have done over many years. The second was to organize the papers in some helpful fashion. This required a number of iterations and the result may or may not be the best possible. Assuming that readers will have varied backgrounds and interests, I have tried to find a reasonable middle ground. Given limited space, I have concentrated on papers in my main lines of research, leaving out scattered work in computer economics, algorithms, programming languages, operations research and banking.

I have grouped the material in six broad subject areas. Within each of the resulting sections, the papers are in chronological order. I have also included comments about each of the papers. Some of these include information about the circumstances surrounding the preparation of the material and connections with other parts of my work and that of others. The readers indulgence is begged for the frequent references to the first person. Please do not assume that I mean to imply that I was the only or even the first person to have discovered or described a theory or empirical result. Such comments are simply intended to refer to the fact of authorship without using unnecessarily stuffy or stilted constructions.

The first section includes papers that deal with portfolio choice. These follow the seminal work of Harry Markowitz, whom I count as my mentor and who continues to be a close friend. Harry's fundamental research assumed that an investor has inputs about some aspects of the joint probability distribution of the returns on a number of individual securities (usually common stocks) and wishes to find one or more portfolios that are efficient (not dominated by other portfolios). Most of the papers included here explore ways to provide economical approximations of results using the standard Markowitz formulation. Several present algorithms and their implementation in computer programs. While some of the papers mention equilibrium aspects in passing, the focus is on the formation of efficient portfolios given estimates of security risks, returns and correlations, however they might be obtained.

The second section deals with the determination of asset prices when capital markets have reached equilibrium. Most of the papers rely on a mean/variance setting but one uses only an assumption of no arbitrage and some of the results in other papers are derived directly from this premise. The early work focuses on what is sometimes called the traditional Capital Asset Pricing Model, while a number of the others deal with extensions to include additional aspects of the capital markets. Index funds, which are to an extent motivated by equilibrium asset pricing theories, are discussed in two short pieces addressed to practitioners. The section ends with a paper that addresses equilibrium issues using the Arrow–Debreu time-state model of asset pricing.

The third section deals with the allocation of an overall fund among major asset classes. Over the course of time, practitioners found that mean/variance optimization was not especially practical when choosing a mix of individual securities such as the stocks to include in a portfolio. On the other hand, it seemed to represent a way to adopt a scientific approach to the allocation of a multi-asset fund among key asset classes such as domestic stocks, foreign stocks, government bonds and the like. For such tasks. a number of consultants as well as managers of pension and other institutional funds use some of the approaches described in the first two sections of this book, although often with constraints on formal optimizations and inputs adjusted judgmentally to reflect market conditions. This section addresses a number of issues relating to asset allocation, from early applications of mean/variance approaches to more recent approaches involving expected utility maximization and alternative ways to adapt a policy to reflect changing asset market values.

The fourth section includes papers that deal with the measurement of a fund's performance and risk. In this area, mean/variance analyses drawn from both portfolio choice and asset pricing theories have had substantial impact on the world of practical asset management. The section starts with my first attempt to provide a useful measure that combines both portfolio risk and return in a single number and employs it to analyze the performances of a set of mutual funds and possible factors contributing to differences among them. Subsequent papers further examine the properties of this measure (now generally termed the Sharpe Ratio) and other measures designed to take into account aspects of both risk and return. In later papers, the role of factor models is discussed, and the technique often described as "returns-based style analysis" introduced and applied. The section ends with analyses of methods for using measures of risk and correlation in budgeting and monitoring a pension fund's allocations of funds among investment managers.

The fifth section includes papers which emphasize empirical analyses. Many focus on factors causing differences in the performance of groups of stocks with different attributes. In many of these, the emphasis is on risks and correlations, where the importance of a number of factors is well established. However, some papers deal with average returns and the possibility that securities exposed to some factors may have higher or lower expected returns than those predicted by variants of the Capital Asset Pricing Model (which provides a reference point for many of the analyses). One paper estimates the likely costs of pursuing a socially desirable goal by divesting stocks doing business in a country (South Aftrica) until it changes an undesirable policy (apartheid). Not all the papers deal solely with stock returns; one analyzes the effects of differences in societal wealth on the premium for a market portfolio that includes stocks and bonds. The common aspect across the papers, however, is an emphasis on data analysis and tests of theories with less attention paid to their derivation.

The sixth and final section focuses on issues relating to the manner in which individuals finance their lives. Two papers, based on academic talks, deal with key decisions made both before and after retirement. The remaining papers focus on decisions made at or after retirement, including strategies for spending and investing savings and immediate or planned purchases of annuities. Although much of my work over the years has been devoted to issues faced by those saving for retirement, I am now focusing most of my research and writing on the issues that arise after retirement. These are increasingly important both for society and individuals; moreover, they are challenging both practically and theoretically. The papers included in this section provide more questions than answers, but reflect the unsettled state of the work in this difficult, yet important and fascinating area.

Acknowledgements

Many people helped make this book possible. My thanks to the publishers of the original versions of the works included here; each is listed with the relevant material below. Thanks also to the coauthors of the jointly-authored papers. I learned much from them, and they made major direct contributions to our joint works. I would also like to express my appreciation for the work done by Sandhya Venkatesh of World Scientific Publishing in bringing the disparate pieces of this volume together.

Finally I wish to thank my wife, Kathy Sharpe, who encouraged me to collect and comment on this material; she supports me in so many ways while maintaining a very busy life as a professional artist. Kathy provided the cover art for this volume, making it a joint work — much to our mutual surprise.

Section 1

The Diagonal Security Model

Reprinted with permission of the author from Chapter II in William F. Sharpe, *Portfolio Analysis based on a Simplified Model of the Relationships Among Securities*, A dissertation submitted in partial satisfaction of the requirements for the degree Doctor of Philosophy in Economics, University of California, Los Angeles, June 1961, pp. 9–23.

A Simplified Model for Portfolio Analysis

Reprinted by permission, William F. Sharpe, *Management Science*, Vol. 9, No. 2, January 1963, pp. 277–293. Copyright 1963, the Institute for Operations Research and the Management Sciences, 7240 Parkway Drive, Suite 300, Hanover, MD 21076 USA.

Mathematical Investment Portfolio Selection — Some Early Results

Reprinted by permission of the University of Washington Foster School of Business from the *University of Washington Business Review*, April 1963, pp. 14–27.

Portfolio Analysis (excerpt)

William F. Sharpe. *The Journal of Financial and Quantitative Analysis*, Vol. II, No. 1, June 1967, pp. 76–81, Copyright © 1967 School of Business Administration, University of Washington. Reprinted with the permission of Cambridge University Press.

Mean-Absolute Deviation Characteristic Lines for Securities and Portfolios

Reprinted by permission, William F. Sharpe, "Mean-Absolute Deviation Characteristic Lines for Securities and Portfolios," *Management Science*, October 1971, Volume 18 No. 2, pages B1-B13, Copyright 1971, the Institute for Operations Research and the Management Sciences, 7240 Parkway Drive, Suite 300, Hanover, MD 21076.

Imputing Expected Returns From Portfolio Composition

William F. Sharpe, *The Journal of Financial and Quantitative Analysis*, June 1974, pp. 463–472. Copyright © 1974 School of Business Administration, University of Washington. Reprinted with the permission of Cambridge University Press.

An Algorithm for Portfolio Improvement

Reprinted from K. D. Lawrence, J. B. Guerard, Jr., and Gary D. Reeves, Editors, **Advances in Mathematical Programming and Financial Planning**, JAI Press, Inc., 1987, "An Algorithm for Porfolio Improvement, pp. 155–170. Copyright Elsevier, 1987.

Section 2

A Positive Theory of Security Market Behavior

Reprinted with permission of the author from Chapter V in William F. Sharpe, *Portfolio Analysis Based on a Simplified Model of the Relationships Among Securities*, A dissertation submitted in partial satisfaction of the requirements for the degree Doctor of Philosophy, in Economics, University of California, Los Angeles, June 1961, pp. 76–100.

Capital Asset Prices — A Theory of Market Equilibrium Under Conditions of Risk

Reprinted with permission from *The Journal of Finance*, Vol. XIX, No. 3, September 1964, pp. 425–442.

The Capital Asset Pricing Model: Traditional and 'Zero-Beta' Versions

Reprinted with, permission from the *Journal of the Midwest Finance Association*, 1973, pp. 1–12.

The Parable of the Money Managers

Copyright 1976, CFA Institute. Reproduced and republished from the *Financial Analysts Journal*, July/August 1976, p. 4 with permission from CFA Institute. All rights reserved.

The Capital Asset Pricing Model: A 'Multi-Beta' Interpretation

Reprinted from Haim Levy and Marshall Sarnat, Editors, **Financial Decision Making Under Uncertainty**, Academic Press (New York), 1977, "The Capital Asset Pricing Model: A 'Multi-Beta' Interpretation, pp. 127–136, Copyright 1977.

Valuation of a Call Option on a Stock with Simple Price Changes

Reprinted with permission from William F. Sharpe, **Investments**, Prentice-Hall, Inc. 1978, pp. 366–371.

Security Codings: Measuring Relative Attractiveness in Perfect and Imperfect Markets

From William F. Sharpe and Cathryn M. Cootner, Editors, **Financial Economics, Essays in Honor of Paul Cootner**, 1st edition, © 1982, pp. 216–229. Reprinted by permission of Pearson Education, Inc., Upper Saddle River, NJ.

Factor Models, CAPMs, and the APT

Reprinted from "Factor Models, CAPMs and the APT", William F. Sharpe, *The Journal of Portfolio Management*, Fall 1984, Volume 11, Number 1, pp. 21–25. Copyright © 1984, Institutional Investor, Inc.

Market Equilibrium with no Short Sales

Reprinted with permission of the author from Financial Research Luncheon Seminar (FRILLS) Stanford University, Nov. 10, 1989.

The Arithmetic of Active Management

Copyright 1991, CFA Institute. Reproduced and republished from the *Financial Analysts Journal*, January/February 1991, pp. 7–9 with permission from CFAInstitute. All rights reserved.

Capital Asset Prices with and without Negative Holdings

Reprinted with permission from *The Journal of Finance*, The American Finance Association, June 1991, pp. 489–509.

Nuclear Financial Economics

Reprinted from **Risk Management: Problems & Solutions**, (William H. Beaver and George Parker, editors), McGraw-Hill, 1995, pp. 17–35. Reproduced with permission of the McGraw-Hill Companies.

Section 3

Bonds Versus Stocks: Some Lessons From Capital Market Theory

Copyright 1973, CFA Institute. Reproduced and republished from the *Financial Analysts Journal*, November/December 1973, pp. 74–80 with permission from CFA Institute. All rights reserved.

Likely Gains From Market Timing

Copyright 1975, CFA Institute. Reproduced and republished from the *Financial Analysts Journal*, March/April 1975, pp. 60–69 with permission from CFA Institute. All rights reserved.

Corporate Pension Funding Policy

Reprinted from the *Journal of Financial Economics*, Volume 3, Number 3, June 1976, pp. 183–193. Copyright 1976 with permission from Elsevier.

Major Investment Styles

Decentralized Investment Management

Optimal Funding and Asset Allocation Rules for Defined-Benefit Pension Plans (with J. Michael Harrison)

Integrated Asset Allocation

Dynamic Strategies for Asset Allocation (with André Perold)

Liabilities — A New Approach

Expected Utility Asset Allocation

Adaptive Asset Allocation Policies

Section 4

Mutual Fund Performance

Adjusting for Risk in Portfolio Performance Measurement

Asset Allocation: Management Style and Performance Measurement

The Sharpe Ratio

Morningstar's Risk-Adjusted Ratings

Budgeting and Monitoring Pension Fund Risk

Section 5

Risk-Aversion in the Stock Market — Some Empirical Evidence

Reprinted with permission from *The Journal of Finance*, Vol. XX, No. 3, September 1965, pp. 416–422.

Risk-Return Classes of New York Stock Exchange Common Stocks, 1931–1967 (with Guy M. Cooper)

Risk, Return and Yield: New York Stock Exchange Common Stocks, 1928–1969 (with Howard B. Sosin)

Duration and Security Risk

Ronald Lanstein and William F. Sharpe, *Journal of Financial and Quantitative Analysis*, November 1978, pp. 663–668.

Factors in New York Stock Exchange Security Returns, 1931–1979

Financial Implications of South African Divestment (with Blake R. Grossman)

Investor Wealth Measures and Expected Return

International Value and Growth Stock Returns (with Carlo Capaul and Ian Rowley)

Section 6

Financial Planning in Fantasyland

Reprinted with permission of the author from www.wsharpe.com, October 1997.

Retirement Financial Planning: A State/Preference Approach

Reprinted with permission of the author from www.wsharpe.com, February 2006.

Financing Retirement: Saving, Investing, Spending and Insuring

Reprinted with permission of the author from www.wsharpe.com, October 2006.

Lockbox Separation

Reprinted with permission of the author from www.wsharpe.com, June, 2007.

Efficient Retirement Financial Strategies (with Jason S. Scott and John G. Watson)

In **Recalibrating Retirement Spending and Saving**, 2008, edited by John Ameriks and Olivia Mitchell, pp. 440–456. By permission of Oxford University Press, Inc.

Choosing Outcomes versus Choosing Products: Consumer-focused Retirement Investment Advice (with D. G. Goldstein and E. J. Johnson)

Journal of Consumer Research, Vo. 35, No. 5, October, 2008, pp. 440–456,

The 4% Rule — At What Price? (with Jason S. Scott and John G. Watson)

Reprinted with permission from the *Journal of Investment Management*, Vol. 7, No. 3, Third Quarter 2009, pp. 31–48.

Contents

Section 1: Portfolio Choice

1-1 "The Diagonal Security Model," Chapter II in William F. Sharpe, *Portfolio Analysis based on a Simplified Model of the Relationships Among Securities*, A dissertation submitted in partial satisfaction of the requirements for the degree Doctor of Philosophy in Economics, University of California, Los Angeles, June 1961, pp. 9–23.

This paper is reprinted from Chapter II of my dissertation, completed in June of 1961. It was based on research done in the fall of 1960 and the spring of 1961. During this period, I worked with Harry Markowitz, who was at the RAND Corporation, as was I. Although Harry was not on the faculty at U.C.L.A., my Chairman, Armen Alchian, agreed to let him serve as a *de facto* adviser. The dissertation explored a number of aspects of a simple model of security returns suggested in Harry's *Portfolio Selection* book. In the literature, this was subsequently termed the single index or one-factor model. The chapter describes the model and shows how efficient portfolios can be obtained using an algorithm that requires little computer memory and processing time (a crucial aspect at the time when both were in limited supply and very expensive). The approach relies on a transformation of the security covariance matrix to one with elements along the principal diagonal, leading me to use the term "diagonal security model". While I propose here that the index represent the market in general, no assumption is made that this is related to any sort of equilibrium in the capital market — a subject that I took up later in the dissertation in a chapter reprinted in Section 2.

1-2 "A Simplified Model for Portfolio Analysis," *Management Science*, Vol. 9, No. 2, January 1963, pp. 277–293.

This paper was submitted to *Management Science* in December 1961 (as indicated in a footnote) although it was not published until January 1963. It presents the diagonal model, shows how a portfolio can be characterized as investment in a common factor and in security residual returns, and provides estimates of the efficacy of simplifying the relationships among securities in this manner. The first part of the paper is based on my dissertation but there is additional discussion of the effects of the ability to borrow and/or lend at fixed rates of interest on the solution to the portfolio optimization problem and ways to take such opportunities into account when finding efficient portfolios. Since the time required to solve a portfolio optimization problem will be affected by both the number of securities considered and the number of "corner portfolios" obtained, the paper uses Monte Carlo simulations to estimate the relationships between these attributes and their effects on computer processing time.

The final part of the paper describes empirical tests included in the dissertation that suggest relatively small differences between the compositions of efficient portfolios based on a full covariance matrix and those obtained using a single index approximation. However, the samples included relatively few securities and relatively few periods of historic data. Appropriately, the final paragraph cautions that they are "far too fragmentary to be considered conclusive". Not discussed was the fact that the optimal portfolios included only a minority of the securities in the sample, calling into question the inputs, whether taken directly or simplified using a single index model – a subject covered in later papers in this volume. Here, as in my dissertation, I chose to plot portfolio risk/return combinations with expected return on the horizontal axis and standard deviation on the vertical axis. In this, I followed the graph using expected return and variance in Markowitz' 1959 book. I also used "B" for the concept later termed "beta" due primarily to the lack of greek letters on my typewriter.

1-3 "Mathematical Investment Portfolio Selection — Some Early Results," *University of Washington Business Review*, April 1963.

This paper is based on a presentation that I gave at a joint meeting of the Econometric Society and the Institute of Management Sciences in September 1962. Shortly before, IBM had produced a program designed to solve the portfolio optimization problem. It was designed for formulations with full covariance matrices although pre-processing algorithms could be invoked for those who wished to use inputs from a single-index or multi-index model. In this paper, I argued that a single index model, if employed with a special-purpose algorithm of the sort that I had designed, could not only reduce computer costs but also was more amenable to use with subjective inputs obtained from security analysts. The latter part of the paper is devoted to the results of an experiment that I conducted in 1961, described in one of the chapters of my dissertation. In it, a practicing security analyst provided estimates of the sensitivities of the prices of a set of securities to changes in the security market (measured by the Dow-Jones average) as well as the probability distributions of returns if the overall market remained at its present level. From these, I computed the parameters needed for estimates based on the diagonal model and derived efficient portfolios. The analyst also provided three portfolios that he would recommend for investors with different degrees of conservatism. The results were encouraging in two respects. The recommended portfolios had increasing expected returns and standard deviations, given the security estimates. Moreover, they dominated a majority of portfolios of comparable diversification that had been selected randomly. However, none of the three recommended portfolios were on the (purportedly) efficient frontier. The final sections of the paper ruminate on the implications of these results, suggesting that Markowitz's approach with or without index model assumptions, may be too powerful for use with inputs derived from security analysts but that it provides a powerful way to think about and teach some of the key principles of investment management.

1-4 "Portfolio Analysis," (excerpt) *The Journal of Financial and Quantitative Analysis*, Vol. II, No. 1, June 1967, pp. 76–81.

Paper 1–4 is the general portion of my introduction to a special issue of the *Journal of Financial and Quantitative Analysis* devoted to Portfolio Analysis. It shows some of the elements of the impact of the subject on academic and, to a considerably lesser extent, practical finance. Concern with returns that are not normally distributed was substantial at the time and many were considering other probability distributions, including some with infinite variance. By 1967, normative (prescriptive) applications had been joined by positive (descriptive) theories and a few researchers were considering the impact of equilibrium on investment practice. The Arrow–Debreu state-preference model of equilibrium had at the time been little noticed in the area of financial economics but I indicated that it might have greater influence in the future. Finally, I suggested (rather prophetically, as it turned out) that the broader area of business finance would adopt many of the ideas that started with and were derived from those of portfolio analysis.

1-5 "Mean-Absolute Deviation Characteristic Lines for Securities and Portfolios," *Management Science*, October 1971, pp. B-1–B-13.

This paper was written after I completed my 1970 book, *Portfolio Theory* and *Capital Markets*, published by McGraw-Hill. The paper was motivated by considerable interest at the time in the possibility that *ex ante* return distributions of security returns might be "fat-tailed". Following ideas put forth by Mandelbrot, Fama and others argued that the best representation of such distributions might be taken from members of the stable Paretian class which have infinite variances. This had led some to argue that the mean absolute deviation of returns should be used as a measure of risk, rather than the standard deviation or variance. At the time, the importance of a security's characteristic line had been recognized in both normative and positive applications. Such relationships had typically been estimated from historic data using traditional least-squares analysis in which a line is chosen to minimize the sum of the squared deviations of the observations from the fitted relationship. The statistical literature left open the question of whether linear relationships might better be estimated by minimizing the mean absolute deviation of the differences between actual and fitted values. In this paper, I provided a simple algorithm for doing this with a two-variable relationship such as that utilized for security and portfolio characteristic lines. I then compared results using this approach with traditional least-squares for both a sample of individual securities and another of mutual funds. The results showed that the slope (beta) estimates obtained using the two methods were very similar. The intercepts differed substantially for individual securities, but much less so for diversified mutual fund portfolios. My conclusion was that traditional least-squares methods were probably sufficient for the majority of applications in this area.

1-6 "Imputing Expected Returns From Portfolio Composition," *Journal of Financial and Quantitative Analysis*, June 1974, pp. 463–472.

This paper introduced the idea of inferring an investment organization's predictions from its portfolio choice. The idea was to start with an estimate of the covariance matrix, then make inferences about the set of expected returns that would make the current holdings optimal. The key relationships are those from the first-order conditions for maximizing a quadratic function (including the mean and variance of portfolio return) subject to linear constraints (the full-investment constraint and possibly upper and lower bounds). Without bounds, this leads to the derivatives of a Lagrangean function; with bounds the associated Kuhn–Tucker conditions are relevant. If a riskless security is available, these conditions allow one to infer the relative expected excess returns of the portfolio components. This approach is, in effect, the basis for procedures widely used today for risk measurement and management, as I showed in a later paper on budgeting and measuring portfolio risk (included in Section 4). This paper also shows that if security markets are assumed to be consistent with the equilibrium conditions of the Capital Asset Pricing Model, one can infer expected measures of abnormal performance (here, denoted "A" but now commonly called "alpha") for the positions. An empirical analysis of the holdings of a large institutional investor showed that actual holdings were consistent with relatively small expected departures from equilibrium values — a result that has been found over and over again as this procedure has been applied in the investment industry.

1-7 "An Algorithm for Portfolio Improvement," in K. D. Lawrence, J. B. Guerard, Jr., and G. D. Reeves, Editors, *Advances in Mathematical Programming and Financial Planning*, JAI Press, Inc., 1987, pp. 155–170.

In 1978, when I published the first edition of my textbook, *Investments*, programs had been developed to solve general quadratic programming problems (most notably the one that I had used at the RAND Corporation). There were also programs designed to efficiently solve portfolio choice problems using the single index model, including one produced by IBM for use on its 1401 business computer (since the program was based on my diagonal model algorithm, I was asked to meet with the developers for a morning but my input was minimal, at best). Another program had been developed at Dartmouth College and my own program was available at the University of Washington and elsewhere. But a simple algorithm for a problem with a general covariance matrix, a full-investment constraint and upper and lower bounds on security holdings was not widely available. To fill the gap, and to provide an approach that could be used to help others better understand the economics of mean/variance portfolio optimization, I developed the gradient method described in this paper.

In the later 1970's, I was also serving as a consultant for the Investment Systems Group of Wells Fargo Investment Advisors, members of which provided valuable input and an opportunity to test the procedures in a real-world setting. I provided the results in this paper which was submitted for publication in *Management Science.* I then included the essence of the algorithm in the second edition of my textbook, published in 1981, indicating that the source was the paper, forthcoming in *Management Science.* Unfortunately, confusion among the journal's editorial board members led to years of delay. At some point I was asked by John Guerard to contribute a paper to the book that he and others were editing. I asked the journal for a release of my submission and the paper finally was published in the cited volume (in excellent company).

The algorithm takes advantage of the fact that with a single linear equality constraint and upper and lower bounds on holdings, a two-security swap is locally optimal for improving the objective function in a traditional mean/variance optimization. Moreover, the optimal magnitude for such a swap can be computed very quickly. By determining a series of such swaps, one can efficiently come extremely close to the formally optimal portfolio composition. The result is intuitive, extremely simple to program, and economizes on both computer memory and processing time. The algorithm was subsequently employed by a number of academic and investment organizations. In my own classes, I found it effective to present the algorithm as soon as I had introduced the concept of mean/variance portfolio efficiency, then let the students reach their own conclusions about optimality. With the first-order conditions firmly established, it was then easy to move to equilibrium in capital markets characterized by mean/variance investors, methods for risk budgeting and monitoring, as well as other aspects of then-traditional financial economics. Now that most students and practitioners have access to spreadsheet programs such as Microsoft's Excel that can solve general quadratic programming problems this algorithm's primary advantage would seem to be more pedagogical than practical.

II. THE DIAGONAL SECURITY MODEL

A. Important Attributes of Securities

Discussions with security analysts indicate that three aspects of the future performance of a security are usually considered explicitly. First, a security is classified as either high-yield or low-yield on the basis of the analyst's "best guess" concerning its future performance. Such an estimate corresponds to the expected-yield quantity (E) required for the portfolio-analysis problem.

The second aspect which receives attention in most security analyses is the risk that the most likely return may not be realized. Securities are considered more speculative, the greater is this risk. The variance parameter required by portfolio analysis makes explicit this notion of risk.

The third aspect of the performance of a security which is often considered explicitly is its relationship to the security market (and/or the economy) in general. Securities which rise and fall with the market are considered more sensitive or cyclical than those which are little affected by such broad movements. Thus the risk of a security is often considered to be due to two factors: the risk associated with the firm itself, and the risk of a market (or general business) decline with an associated effect on the firm in question.

In the diagonal model these three attributes -- expected yield, risk, and dependence on the market -- are made explicit. The simplicity of the model derives from the fact that these attributes are the only ones taken into account. Evidence presented in the next chapter suggests that any loss in precision due to this simplicity is likely to be small. It is shown below that the cost of portfolio analysis can be greatly reduced when the diagonal model is used. For these reasons the model appears worthy of the detailed examination it receives in this dissertation.

B. The Diagonal Model[1]

The basic equation of the diagonal model relates the yield of a security to its own attributes and to the performance of some index of market activity:

$$Y_i = A_i + B_i \cdot I + w_i \tag{1}$$

where A_i and B_i are parameters, and w_i is a random variable with an expected value of zero and a variance of Q_i. The parameter (I) represents the level of an index of some activity considered to be of major importance in determining the yields of most securities. In this study we use the level of the security market for this index. A number of alternative attributes are of interest and may be incorporated into future work.[2] Such measures can be substituted for the market level without altering the formulation of the

[1]This model is one of a number suggested by Markowitz; see his Portfolio Selection, pp. 96-101.

[2]A particularly interesting candidate is the general price

diagonal model presented here; on the other hand, if they are to be incorporated in addition to the market index, the model will have to be expanded. Models which relate the yield of a security to more than one such factor will undoubtedly prove valuable; however, in this study we will restrict our attention to the simple model in which but one element of this type influences the yields of most securities.

For a number of problems it is convenient to measure (I) in terms of deviations (either relative or absolute) from its expected value. However, we will formulate the model for the general case in which the expected value of (I) is non-zero, so that any desired measurement can be used.

Equation (1) constitutes the basic assumption of the diagonal model. Security analysis, in this model, involves the specification of three parameters for each security: A_i, B_i, and Q_i. These

---

level of the economy. The wealth of a firm can be shown to be affected by the price level and the relative importance of real and monetary assets and liabilities in its financial structure. In particular, if (M) is the firm's net monetary creditor position (monetary assets less monetary liabilities) and (R) its net real asset position (real assets less real liabilities), then the effect of changes in the price level on the firm's wealth can be shown to be proportional to R/(R+M). The diagonal model can be utilized to reflect this relationship by using R/(R+M) as an estimate of B_i for each security, with (I) representing an index of the general price level in the economy. For the general model of the effects of inflation on the wealth position of a firm, see R. Kessel, "Inflation-caused Wealth Redistribution," American Economic Review, XLVI (March, 1956), 128-141.

parameters specify the expected return, responsiveness to the market, and risk attributes discussed in the previous section. The only additional analysis required concerns the probable future course of the market. The analyst must specify an expected value and a variance for (I). Let:

$$A_{n+1} = \text{the expected value of I } (=\bar{I})$$

$$Q_{n+1} = \text{the variance of I } (=V_I)$$

The reason for this notation will become clear later in the chapter.

The diagonal model assumes that securities are unrelated except through their common dependence on the market; further, the random elements (w_i) are not related to the level of the index (I). Thus:

$$\text{Covariance } (w_i, w_j) = 0 \quad \text{for all i and j}$$

$$\text{Covariance } (w_i, I) = 0 \quad \text{for all i.}$$

These assumptions complete the information necessary for obtaining the elements required by the Markowitz portfolio-analysis technique from the parameters of the diagonal model.

The expected return of a security (E_i) and its variance (V_i) are simply:

(2) $$E_i = A_i + B_i \cdot A_{n+1}$$

and

(3) $$V_i = (B_i)^2 \cdot Q_{n+1} + Q_i$$

The diagonal model does not explicitly specify covariances among securities, but they are implied by common relationships with (I). If a fall in the market would reduce the returns on two securities, ceteris paribus, then their returns are correlated. Let C_{ij} be the covariance between Securities i and j. Then:

(4) $$C_{ij} = B_i \cdot B_j \cdot Q_{n+1}$$

The derivation of this relationship is shown in the footnote.[3]

To summarize, the diagonal model requires specifications of three parameters for each security, and two parameters for the level of the market in general. From these, the required inputs for the portfolio-analysis problem can be derived. If there are N securities, the N expected values can be computed according to Eq. (2), the N variance terms computed using Eq. (3), and the $(N^2-N)/2$ covariance terms calculated according to Eq. (4). Once these terms are derived, the portfolio analysis can proceed.

---

[3]If z is the divergence of (I) from its expected value, Y_i would be expected to diverge from its expected value by an amount $B_i z$. Similarly, Y_j would be expected to diverge from its expected value by an amount $B_j z$. The cross-product of the two divergences is $(B_i z \cdot B_j z)$ or $(B_i B_j z^2)$. The covariance between i and j is the sum of all such cross-products, divided by the number of occurrences (N). Thus:

$$C_{ij} = \frac{1}{N} \sum_z B_i B_j z^2$$

$$= B_i B_j \frac{1}{N} \sum_z z^2$$

But: $$\frac{1}{N} \sum_z z^2 = V_I = Q_{n+1}$$

Therefore: $$C_{ij} = B_i \cdot B_j \cdot Q_{n+1}$$

C. The Associated Portfolio-Analysis Problem

Portfolio analysis involves repeated minimization of the variance of a portfolio for various expected returns. In the general case, the variance of a portfolio of N securities is given by:

$$V = \sum_{i=1}^{N} \sum_{j=1}^{N} X_i X_j C_{ij} ,$$

while its mean is:

$$E = \sum_{i=1}^{N} E_i$$

We have shown above that all the terms required for the general portfolio-analysis can be derived from the parameters of the diagonal model. However, considerable effort is required to derive $(N^2-N)/2$ covariances and then to prepare and perform the associated quadratic programming problem. In this section we will develop an alternative approach which greatly reduces the effort involved in performing portfolio analysis based on the diagonal model.

An investor devoting his funds to a security can be considered to be purchasing two separate investments. First, he acquires the unique characteristics of the security in question. Second, he acquires a portion of the security market in general. This is the case if the return on the security is at all connected with the performance of the market. This relationship can be seen if we rewrite Eq. (1). The basic formula of the model then becomes:

$$Y_i = (A_i + w_i) + B_i \cdot I \tag{5}$$

The yield of a security is determined by three factors. A_i and w_i are unique to the security and are in no way related to the market. The third factor is not unique to the security; it is composed of two elements: B_i, the responsiveness of Y_i to the market level; and (I), the market level itself. Thus we can think of the investor who purchases a dollar's worth of Security i as having invested one dollar in $(A_i + w_i)$ and one dollar in $(B_i \cdot I)$.

Assume that an investor purchases two securities, i and j, dividing the total value of his portfolio between them in the proportions X_i and X_j, where $(X_i + X_j) = 1$. The yield on such a portfolio would be merely the weighted average of the yields of the two securities, with the relative amounts of the securities used as weights:

$$Y_p = X_iY_i + X_jY_j$$

Substituting the basic equation of the diagonal model, we have:

$$Y_p = X_i(A_i + B_i \cdot I + w_i) + X_j(A_j + B_j \cdot I + w_j)$$

Rearranging terms:

$$Y_p = X_i(A_i + w_i) + X_j(A_j + w_j) + (X_iB_i + X_jB_j)I$$

This formulation shows that the purchase of two securities can be viewed as an investment in three different media: the unique characteristics of Security i, the unique characteristics of Security j, and the influence of the market in general. The influence of the market on the yield of the portfolio partly depends on the influence which the market exerts on the securities in the portfolio. The effect of the market on the yield of Security i is shown by B_i; since X_i of the portfolio is invested in that security, the total influence of the market on the portfolio due to the holdings of Security i is given by $(X_i B_i)$. Holdings of Security j give rise to an additional market influence of $X_j B_j$ on the yield of the portfolio.

In the case of two securities, the total "investment" in the market is $(X_i B_i + X_j B_j)$. Let this total investment in the market be represented by X_{n+1}. In the general case we define this parameter as follows:

$$(6) \qquad X_{n+1} = \sum_{i=1}^{N} X_i B_i$$

(X_{n+1}) may be viewed as a weighted-average responsiveness to the market level. (B_i) is the responsiveness of Security i to the market. The responsiveness of a portfolio is merely the weighted-average responsiveness of the individual securities, where the appropriate weights are the relative amounts invested. Note that this investment in the market results from investment in securities; it is not possible to devote a portion of a portfolio directly to

X_{n+1}. The portfolio is divided among the N securities ($\sum_{i=1}^{N} X_i = 1$); such a division implies a particular value for X_{n+1}.

We have separated the influence of the market level on securities from their unique characteristics. We now need to revise our notation to account for the remaining effects on the yield of a security.

Let i* be the "basic security" whose yield is given by:

$$Y_{i*} = A_i + w_i$$

The mean and variance of such a security are given by:

$$E_{i*} = A_i$$

$$V_{i*} = Q_i$$

By assumption, the only relationships among securities arise from their common dependence on the market. "Basic securities" of the type defined above do not depend on the market; thus their covariances are zero. For all such securities:

$$C_{i*j*} = 0$$

Since we have assumed no correlation between the w parameters and (I), the covariance between each basic security and the $(n+1)^{st}$ security -- the market index -- is also zero:

$$C_{i*,n+1} = 0$$

We are now able to restate the portfolio-analysis problem in a manner which leads to a considerable reduction in effort. We have shown that an allocation of X_i of a portfolio to Security i can be considered an investment of X_i in the Basic Security i* and an additional investment of $(X_i B_i)$ in the market. For consistency in notation, let X_{i*} represent the investment in the Basic Security i*. Then:

$$X_{i*} = X_i \qquad \text{for } i \leq N$$

Recall that the sum of such investments represents the full portfolio, thus:

$$\sum_{i=1}^{N} X_{i*} = 1$$

The devotion of X_i of a portfolio to Security i brings about two effects. The first, an investment of X_{i*} in the Basic Security i*, has been described; the second, an investment of $(X_i B_i)$ in the market, is included in X_{n+1}, the term used to summarize the entire effect of the market on the portfolio. Again, for consistency in notation, we define:

$$X_{(n+1)*} = \sum_{i=1}^{N} X_i B_i$$

We have used A_{n+1} to represent the expected value of (I); the advantage of this notation can be seen in the following simple formula for the expected yield of a portfolio:

(7) $$E = \sum_{i=1}^{N+1} X_i A_i$$

The expected yield of a portfolio is simply the expected return of each basic security weighted with its importance in the portfolio, plus the expected market level times the parameter which relates the yield of the portfolio to that level. Proof of the validity of this formulation is given in the footnote.[4]

The variance of a portfolio can be expressed in a similar manner. Variance arises from investments in basic securities and from the effects of the market in general. Since none of these investment media are correlated with each other, the variance-covariance matrix for N basic securities and one $(N+1)^{st}$ security -- the market level -- contains non-zero entries only along the diagonal. It is this property which gives rise to the name used to

---

[4] $$E_i = A_i + B_i \cdot A_{n+1}$$

$$E = \sum_{i=1}^{N} X_i E_i$$

Therefore: $$E = \sum_{i=1}^{N} X_i (A_i + B_i \cdot A_{n+1})$$

$$= \sum_{i=1}^{N} X_i A_i + A_{n+1} \sum_{i=1}^{N} X_i B_i$$

But: $$X_{n+1} \equiv \sum_{i=1}^{N} X_i B_i$$

Therefore: $$E = \sum_{i=1}^{N} X_i A_i + X_{n+1} A_{n+1} = \sum_{i=1}^{N+1} X_i A_i$$

describe the model. The general formula for the variance of a portfolio is given by:

(8) $$V = \sum_{i=1*}^{(N+1)*} \sum_{j=1*}^{(N+1)*} X_i X_j C_{ij}$$

But: $$C_{ij} = 0 \quad \text{if } i \neq j$$

And, since we have defined (Q_{n+1}) as the variance of I:

$$C_{ij} = Q_i \quad \text{if } i = j$$

Thus the formula for the variance of a portfolio can be written:

$$V = \sum_{i=1}^{N+1} (X_i)^2 \cdot Q_i$$

Proof of the validity of this formulation is shown in the footnote.[5]

---

[5] $$C_{ii} = V_i = Q_i + (B_i)^2 Q_{n+1}$$

$$C_{ij} = B_i B_j Q_{n+1} \quad \text{if } i \neq j$$

$$V = \sum_{i=1}^{n} \sum_{j=1}^{n} (X_i X_j C_{ij})$$

$$= \sum_{i=1}^{n} \sum_{j=1}^{n} (X_i X_j B_i B_j Q_{n+1}) + \sum_{i=1}^{n} (X_i^2 Q_i)$$

$$= Q_{n+1} \left[\sum_{i=1}^{n} (X_i B_i) \sum_{j=1}^{n} (X_j B_j) \right] + \sum_{i=1}^{n} (X_i^2 Q_i)$$

But: $$\sum_{i=1}^{n} (X_i B_i) = \sum_{i=1}^{n} (X_j B_j) \equiv X_{n+1}$$

Therefore: $$V = Q_{n+1} (X_{n+1})^2 + \sum_{i=1}^{n} X_i^2 Q_i = \sum_{i=1}^{n+1} X_i^2 Q_i$$

This completes our re-formulation of the portfolio-analysis problem associated with the diagonal model. By defining a new variable -- X_{n+1} -- according to Eq. (6), it is possible to represent the mean and variance of a portfolio with relatively simple functions of the original parameters of the model. The advantages of these are indicated in the next section.

D. The Diagonal Model Portfolio-Analysis Code

A number of computer codes are now available for the solution of quadratic programming problems. One such program, the RAND Quadratic Programming Code,[6] was used to solve some of the portfolio analysis problems in this study. While the program is relatively efficient, its use is rather expensive -- analysis of 100 securities costs about $300 (a case involving 96 securities required 33 minutes on an IBM 7090 computer); moreover, no more than 253 securities can be analyzed with the code. Although new programs which are being prepared specifically for the portfolio-analysis problem[7] will

---

[6]The RAND code is described by Leola Cutler, Arthur E. Speckhard, and Philip Wolfe in "The RAND Quadratic Programming Code" (The RAND Corporation, Santa Monica, California, August, 1960) (mimeographed). The manner in which the code is applied to the portfolio-analysis problem is given by Neil R. Paine in "Mathematical Programming in Portfolio Selection" (Unpublished Ph.D. dissertation, School of Business Administration, University of Texas), pp. 92-95.

[7]Such a program is being written for the International Business Machines Corporation (letter from Robert T. Mertz, Data Systems Division, International Business Machines Corporation, May 12, 1961).

undoubtedly bring lower costs and greater capacity, portfolio analysis using a program which must provide for a full variance-covariance matrix will continue to be expensive and limited in capacity.

As indicated in the previous section, the diagonal model can be formulated in a manner which leaves only the diagonal of the variance-covariance matrix non-zero. This allows a considerable reduction in the computation required for solving the portfolio-analysis problem (thus decreasing machine time and cost), and also greatly reduces the amount of data which must be stored in the computer (thus increasing the maximum number of securities which can be analyzed). In order to take full advantage of these characteristics of the diagonal model, a special-purpose portfolio-analysis code was written in the Fortran language for use with IBM computing equipment.[8] The derivation of the solution technique, which uses Markowitz's critical line method,[9] is given in Appendix A; the program itself, with required inputs, is shown in Appendix B. The advantages of the code are considerable: analysis of 100 securities costs only $5 (the 96-security case which required 33 minutes with the RAND QP Code was completed in 30 seconds with this code) and as many as 2000 securities can be analyzed.

---

[8]The Fortran language is described by the International Business Machines Corporation in their Reference Manual: 709 Fortran Automatic Coding System (New York: International Business Machines Corporation, 1959).

[9]Markowitz, Portfolio Selection, Appendix.

It is interesting to note that the possibility of such a substantial reduction in cost was foreseen by Miller in his review of Markowitz's book. After discussing the concept of semi-variance he suggests:

> Of greater immediate promise for those concerned with concrete application is the suggestion in chapter iv to obtain the necessary covariance inputs not by estimating each separately (which would involve n(n-1)/2 such calculations) but by deriving them indirectly from only n regressions of each security on a single "index" return. This suggestion, which can be further refined in a variety of useful ways, undoubtedly will help to break through what has been one of the major cost barriers to the use of the E-V approach.[10]

Having accomplished this anticipated reduction in cost, we are ready to investigate the value of the diagonal model in various applications.

---

[10] Merton H. Miller, Review of Portfolio Selection, Efficient Diversification of Investments, by Harry M. Markowitz, The Journal of Business, The Graduate School of Business of the University of Chicago, XXXIII (October, 1960), 391-393.

Reprinted from MANAGEMENT SCIENCE
Vol. 9, No. 2, January, 1963
Printed in U.S.A.

A SIMPLIFIED MODEL FOR PORTFOLIO ANALYSIS*

WILLIAM F. SHARPE†

University of Washington

This paper describes the advantages of using a particular model of the relationships among securities for practical applications of the Markowitz portfolio analysis technique. A computer program has been developed to take full advantage of the model: 2,000 securities can be analyzed at an extremely low cost—as little as 2% of that associated with standard quadratic programming codes. Moreover, preliminary evidence suggests that the relatively few parameters used by the model can lead to very nearly the same results obtained with much larger sets of relationships among securities. The possibility of low-cost analysis, coupled with a likelihood that a relatively small amount of information need be sacrificed make the model an attractive candidate for initial practical applications of the Markowitz technique.

1. Introduction

Markowitz has suggested that the process of portfolio selection be approached by (1) making probabilistic estimates of the future performances of securities, (2) analyzing those estimates to determine an *efficient set* of portfolios and (3) selecting from that set the portfolios best suited to the investor's preferences [1, 2, 3]. This paper extends Markowitz' work on the second of these three stages —*portfolio analysis*. The preliminary sections state the problem in its general form and describe Markowitz' solution technique. The remainder of the paper presents a simplified model of the relationships among securities, indicates the manner in which it allows the portfolio analysis problem to be simplified, and provides evidence on the costs as well as the desirability of using the model for practical applications of the Markowitz technique.

2. The Portfolio Analysis Problem

A security analyst has provided the following predictions concerning the future returns from each of N securities:

$E_i \equiv$ the expected value of R_i (the return from security i)
C_{i1} through C_{in} ; C_{ij} represents the covariance between R_i and R_j (as usual, when $i = j$ the figure is the variance of R_i)

* Received December 1961.

† The author wishes to express his appreciation for the cooperation of the staffs of both the Western Data Processing Center at UCLA and the Pacific Northwest Research Computer Laboratory at the University of Washington where the program was tested. His greatest debt, however, is to Dr. Harry M. Markowitz of the RAND Corporation, with whom he was privileged to have a number of stimulating conversations during the past year. It is no longer possible to segregate the ideas in this paper into those which were his, those which were the author's, and those which were developed jointly. Suffice it to say that the only accomplishments which are unquestionably the property of the author are those of authorship—first of the computer program and then of this article.

The portfolio analysis problem is as follows. Given such a set of predictions, determine the set of *efficient portfolios*; a portfolio is efficient if none other gives either (a) a higher expected return and the same variance of return or (b) a lower variance of return and the same expected return.

Let X_i represent the proportion of a portfolio invested in security i. Then the expected return (E) and variance of return (V) of any portfolio can be expressed in terms of (a) the basic data (E_i-values and C_{ij}-values) and (b) the amounts invested in various securities:

$$E = \sum_i X_i E_i$$

$$V = \sum_i \sum_j X_i X_j C_{ij} .$$

Consider an objective function of the form:

$$\begin{aligned}\phi &= \lambda E - V \\ &= \lambda \sum_i X_i E_i - \sum_i \sum_j X_i X_j C_{ij} .\end{aligned}$$

Given a set of values for the parameters (λ, E_i's and C_{ij}'s), the value of ϕ can be changed by varying the X_i values as desired, as long as two basic restrictions are observed:

1. The entire portfolio must be invested:[1]

$$\sum_i X_i = 1$$

and 2. no security may be held in negative quantities:[2]

$$X_i \geqq 0 \quad \text{for all} \quad i.$$

A portfolio is described by the proportions invested in various securities—in our notation by the values of X_i. For each set of admissable values of the X_i variables there is a corresponding predicted combination of E and V and thus of ϕ. Figure 1 illustrates this relationship for a particular value of λ. The line ϕ_1 shows the combinations of E and V which give $\phi = \phi_1$, where $\phi = \lambda_k E - V$; the other lines refer to larger values of ϕ ($\phi_3 > \phi_2 > \phi_1$). Of all possible portfolios, one will maximize the value of ϕ;[3] in figure 1 it is portfolio C. The relationship between this solution and the portfolio analysis problem is obvious. The E, V combination obtained will be on the boundary of the set of attainable combinations; moreover, the objective function will be tangent to the set at that point. Since this function is of the form

$$\phi = \lambda E - V$$

[1] Since cash can be included as one of the securities (explicitly or implicitly) this assumption need cause no lack of realism.

[2] This is the standard formulation. Cases in which short sales are allowed require a different approach.

[3] This fact is crucial to the critical line computing procedure described in the next section.

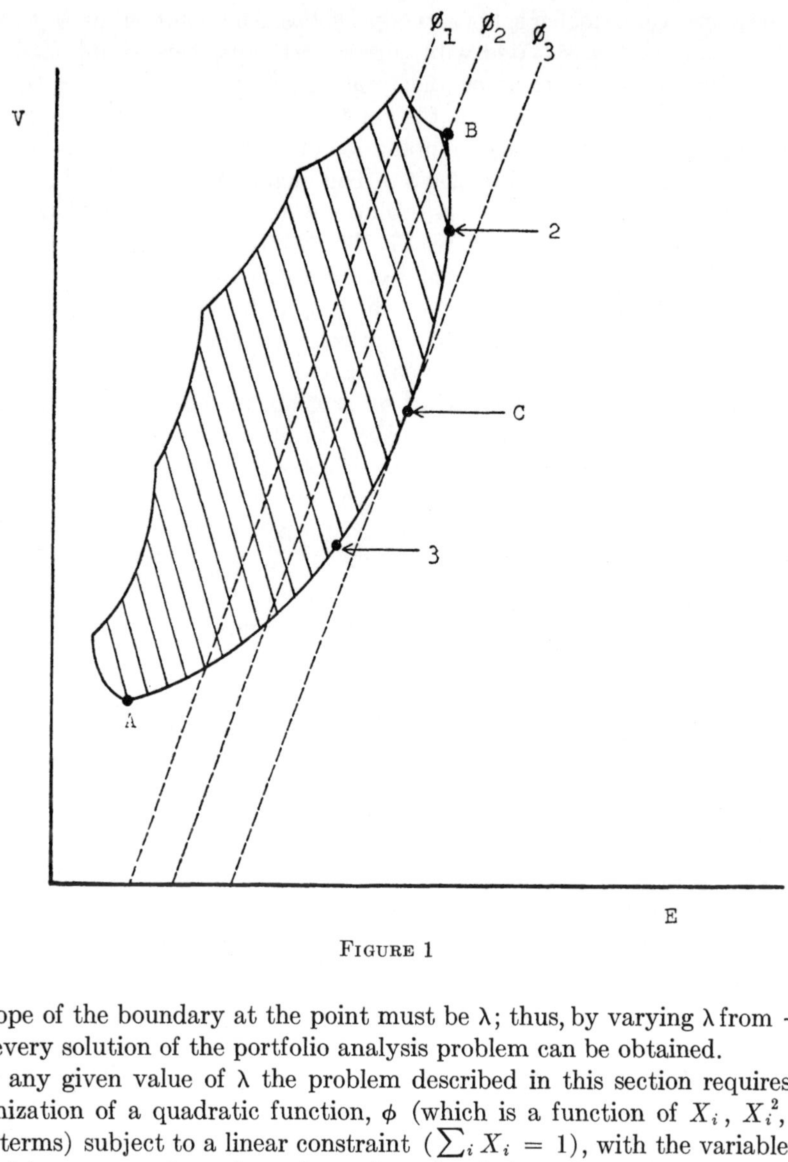

FIGURE 1

the slope of the boundary at the point must be λ; thus, by varying λ from $+\infty$ to 0, every solution of the portfolio analysis problem can be obtained.

For any given value of λ the problem described in this section requires the maximization of a quadratic function, ϕ (which is a function of X_i, X_i^2, and X_iX_j terms) subject to a linear constraint ($\sum_i X_i = 1$), with the variables restricted to non-negative values. A number of techniques have been developed to solve such *quadratic programming problems.* The critical line method, developed by Markowitz in conjunction with his work on portfolio analysis, is particularly suited to this problem and was used in the program described in this paper.

3. The Critical Line Method

Two important characteristics of the set of efficient portfolios make systematic solution of the portfolio analysis problem relatively straightforward. The first concerns the relationships among portfolios. Any set of efficient portfolios can be described in terms of a smaller set of *corner portfolios*. Any point on the E, V curve (other than the points associated with corner portfolios) can be obtained with a portfolio constructed by dividing the total investment between the two adjacent corner portfolios. For example, the portfolio which gives E, V combination C in Figure 1 might be some linear combination of the two corner portfolios with E, V combinations shown by points 2 and 3. This characteristic allows the analyst to restrict his attention to corner portfolios rather than the complete set of efficient portfolios; the latter can be readily derived from the former.

The second characteristic of the solution concerns the relationships among corner portfolios. Two corner portfolios which are adjacent on the E, V curve are related in the following manner: one portfolio will contain either (1) all the securities which appear in the other, plus one additional security or (2) all but one of the securities which appear in the other. Thus in moving down the E, V curve from one corner portfolio to the next, the quantities of the securities in efficient portfolios will vary until either one drops out of the portfolio or another enters. The point at which a change takes place marks a new corner portfolio.

The major steps in the critical line method for solving the portfolio analysis problem are:

1. The corner portfolio with $\lambda = \infty$ is determined. It is composed entirely of the one security with the highest expected return.[4]
2. Relationships between (a) the amounts of the various securities contained in efficient portfolios and (b) the value of λ are computed. It is possible to derive such relationships for any section of the E, V curve between adjacent corner portfolios. The relationships which apply to one section of the curve will not, however, apply to any other section.
3. Using the relationships computed in (2), each security is examined to determine the value of λ at which a change in the securities included in the portfolio would come about:
   a. securities presently in the portfolio are examined to determine the value of λ at which they would drop out, and
   b. securities not presently in the portfolio are examined to determine the value of λ at which they would enter the portfolio.
4. The next largest value of λ at which a security either enters or drops out of the portfolio is determined. This indicates the location of the next corner portfolio.
5. The composition of the new corner portfolio is computed, using the relationships derived in (2). However, since these relationships held only for the section of the curve between this corner portfolio and the preceding one, the solution process can only continue if new relationships are derived. The method thus returns to step (2) unless $\lambda = 0$, in which case the analysis is complete.

The amount of computation required to complete a portfolio analysis using

[4] In the event that two or more of the securities have the same (highest) expected return, the first efficient portfolio is the combination of such securities with the lowest variance.

this method is related to the following factors:

1. The number of securities analyzed

   This will affect the extent of the computation in step (2) and the number of computations in step (3).

2. The number of corner portfolios

   Steps (2) through (5) must be repeated once to find each corner portfolio.

3. The complexity of the variance-covariance matrix

   Step (2) requires a matrix be inverted and must be repeated once for each corner portfolio.

The amount of computer memory space required to perform a portfolio analysis will depend primarily on the size of the variance-covariance matrix. In the standard case, if N securities are analyzed this matrix will have $\frac{1}{2}(N^2 + N)$ elements.

4. The Diagonal Model

Portfolio analysis requires a large number of comparisons; obviously the practical application of the technique can be greatly facilitated by a set of assumptions which reduces the computational task involved in such comparisons. One such set of assumptions (to be called the diagonal model) is described in this article. This model has two virtues: it is one of the simplest which can be constructed without assuming away the existence of interrelationships among securities and there is considerable evidence that it can capture a large part of such interrelationships.

The major characteristic of the diagonal model is the assumption that the returns of various securities are related only through common relationships with some basic underlying factor. The return from any security is determined solely by random factors and this single outside element; more explicitly:

$$R_i = A_i + B_i I + C_i$$

where A_i and B_i are parameters, C_i is a random variable with an expected value of zero and variance Q_i, and I is the level of some index. The index, I, may be the level of the stock market as a whole, the Gross National Product, some price index or any other factor thought to be the most important single influence on the returns from securities. The future level of I is determined in part by random factors:

$$I = A_{n+1} + C_{n+1}$$

where A_{n+1} is a parameter and C_{n+1} is a random variable with an expected value of zero and a variance of Q_{n+1}. It is assumed that the covariance between C_i and C_j is zero for all values of i and j $(i \neq j)$.

Figure 2 provides a graphical representation of the model. A_i and B_i serve to locate the line which relates the expected value of R_i to the level of I. Q_i indicates the variance of R_i around the expected relationship (this variance is assumed to be the same at each point along the line). Finally, A_{n+1} indicates the expected value of I and Q_{n+1} the variance around that expected value.

The diagonal model requires the following predictions from a security analyst:

1) values of A_i, B_i and Q_i for each of N securities
2) values of A_{n+1} and Q_{n+1} for the index I.

The number of estimates required from the analyst is thus greatly reduced: from 5,150 to 302 for an analysis of 100 securities and from 2,003,000 to 6,002 for an analysis of 2,000 securities.

Once the parameters of the diagonal model have been specified all the inputs required for the standard portfolio analysis problem can be derived. The relationships are:

$$E_i = A_i + B_i(A_{n+1})$$

$$V_i = (B_i)^2(Q_{n+1}) + Q_i$$

$$C = (B_i)(B_j)(Q_{n+1})$$

A portfolio analysis could be performed by obtaining the values required by the diagonal model, calculating from them the full set of data required for the standard portfolio analysis problem and then performing the analysis with the derived values. However, additional advantages can be obtained if the portfolio analysis problem is restated directly in terms of the parameters of the diagonal model. The following section describes the manner in which such a restatement can be performed.

5. The Analogue

The return from a portfolio is the weighted average of the returns from its component securities:

$$R_p = \sum_{i=1}^{N} X_i R_i$$

The contribution of each security to the total return of a portfolio is simply $X_i R_i$ or, under the assumptions of the diagonal model:

$$X_i(A_i + B_i I + C_i).$$

The total contribution of a security to the return of the portfolio can be broken into two components: (1) an investment in the "basic characteristics" of the security in question and (2) an "investment" in the index:

$$\begin{aligned} &(1) \qquad X_i(A_i + B_i I + C_i) = X_i(A_i + C_i) \\ &(2) \qquad\qquad\qquad\qquad\qquad + X_i B_i I \end{aligned}$$

The return of a portfolio can be considered to be the result of (1) a series of investments in N "basic securities" and (2) an investment in the index:

$$R_p = \sum_{i=1}^{N} X_i(A_i + C_i) + \left[\sum_{i=1}^{N} X_i B_i\right] I$$

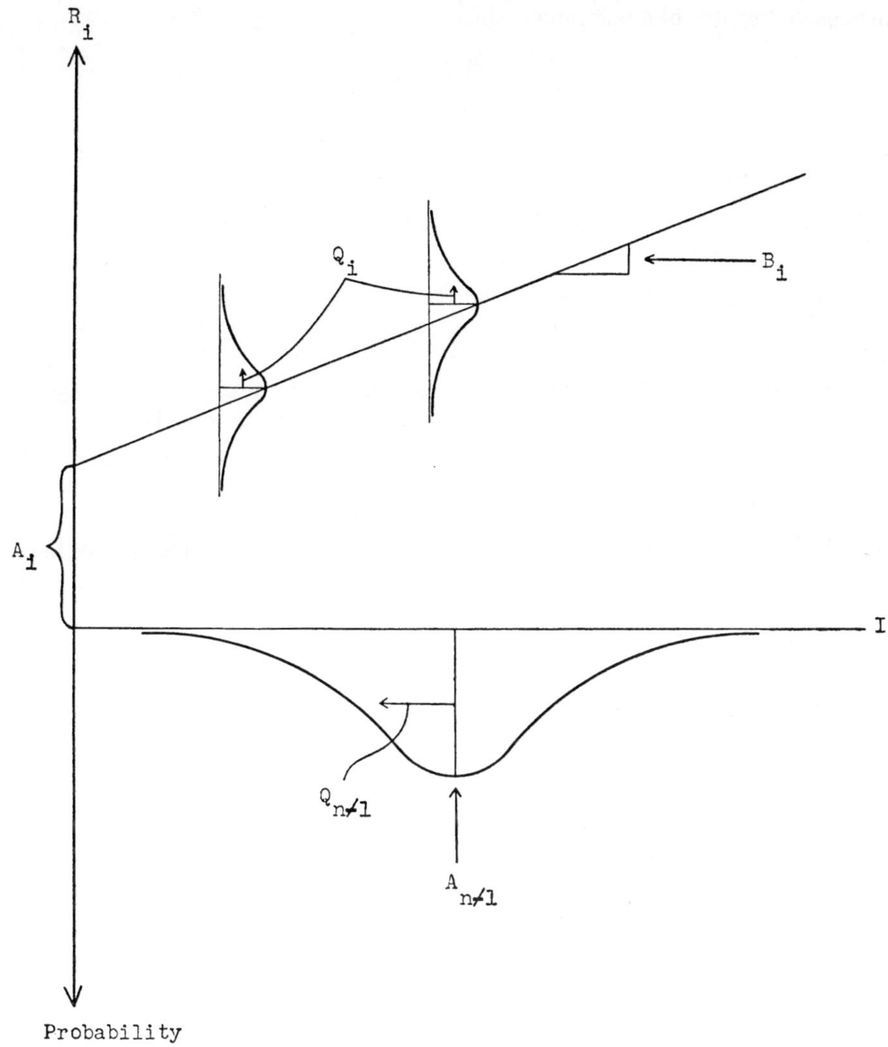

FIGURE 2

Defining X_{n+1} as the weighted average responsiveness of R_p to the level of I:

$$X_{n+1} \equiv \sum_{i=1}^{N} X_i B_i$$

and substituting this variable and the formula for the determinants of I, we obtain:

$$\begin{aligned} R_p &= \sum_{i=1}^{N} X_i(A_i + C_i) + X_{n+1}(A_{n+1} + C_{n+1}) \\ &= \sum_{i=1}^{N+1} X_i(A_i + C_i). \end{aligned}$$

The expected return of a portfolio is thus:

$$E = \sum_{i=1}^{N+1} X_i A_i$$

while the variance is:[5]

$$V = \sum_{i=1}^{N+1} X_i^2 Q_i$$

This formulation indicates the reason for the use of the parameters A_{n+1} and Q_{n+1} to describe the expected value and variance of the future value of I. It also indicates the reason for calling this the "diagonal model". The variance-covariance matrix, which is full when N securities are considered, can be expressed as a matrix with non-zero elements only along the diagonal by including an $(n + 1)$st security defined as indicated. This vastly reduces the number of computations required to solve the portfolio analysis problem (primarily in step 2 of the critical line method, when the variance-covariance matrix must be inverted) and allows the problem to be stated directly in terms of the basic parameters of the diagonal model:

$$\text{Maximize: } \lambda E - V$$

$$\text{Where: } E = \sum_{i=1}^{N+1} X_i A_i$$

$$V = \sum_{i=1}^{N+1} X_i^2 Q_i$$

$$\text{Subject to: } X_i \geqq 0 \text{ for all } i \text{ from 1 to } N$$

$$\sum_{i=1}^{N} X_i = 1$$

$$\sum_{i=1}^{N} X_i B_i = X_{n+1} .$$

6. The Diagonal Model Portfolio Analysis Code

As indicated in the previous section, if the portfolio analysis problem is expressed in terms of the basic parameters of the diagonal model, computing time and memory space required for solution can be greatly reduced. This section describes a machine code, written in the FØRTRAN language, which takes full advantage of the characteristics of the diagonal model. It uses the critical line method to solve the problem stated in the previous section.

The computing time required by the diagonal code is considerably smaller than that required by standard quadratic programming codes. The RAND QP

[5] Recall that the diagonal model assumes $\text{cov}(C_i, C_j) = 0$ for all i and j $(i \neq j)$.

code[6] required 33 minutes to solve a 100-security example on an IBM 7090 computer; the same problem was solved in 30 seconds with the diagonal code. Moreover, the reduced storage requirements allow many more securities to be analyzed: with the IBM 709 or 7090 the RAND QP code can be used for no more than 249 securities, while the diagonal code can analyze up to 2,000 securities.

Although the diagonal code allows the total computing time to be greatly reduced, the cost of a large analysis is still far from insignificant. Thus there is every incentive to limit the computations to those essential for the final selection of a portfolio. By taking into account the possibilities of borrowing and lending money, the diagonal code restricts the computations to those absolutely necessary for determination of the final set of efficient portfolios. The importance of these alternatives, their effect on the portfolio analysis problem and the manner in which they are taken into account in the diagonal code are described in the remainder of this section.

A. The "lending portfolio"

There is some interest rate (r_l) at which money can be lent with virtual assurance that both principal and interest will be returned; at the least, money can be buried in the ground ($r_l = 0$). Such an alternative could be included as one possible security ($A_i = 1 + r_l$, $B_i = 0$, $Q_i = 0$) but this would necessitate some needless computation.[7] In order to minimize computing time, lending at some pure interest rate is taken into account explicitly in the diagonal code.

The relationship between lending and efficient portfolios can best be seen in terms of an E, σ curve showing the combinations of expected return and standard deviation of return ($= \sqrt{V}$) associated with efficient portfolios. Such a curve is shown in Figure 3 (FBCG); point A indicates the E, σ combination attained if all funds are lent. The relationship between lending money and purchasing portfolios can be illustrated with the portfolio which has the E, σ combination shown by point Z. Consider a portfolio with X_z invested in portfolio Z and the remainder $(1 - X_z)$ lent at the rate r_l. The expected return from such a portfolio would be:

$$E = X_z E_z + (1 - X_z)(1 + r_l)$$

and the variance of return would be:

$$V = X_z^2 V_z + (1 - X_z)^2 V_l + 2X_z(1 - X_z)(\text{cov}_{zl})$$

[6] The program is described in [4]. Several alternative quadratic programming codes are available. A recent code, developed by IBM, which uses the critical line method is likely to prove considerably more efficient for the portfolio analysis problem. The RAND code is used for comparison since it is the only standard program with which the author has had experience.

[7] Actually, the diagonal code cannot accept non-positive values of Q_i; thus if the lending alternative is to be included as simply another security, it must be assigned a very small value of Q_i. This procedure will give virtually the correct solution but is inefficient.

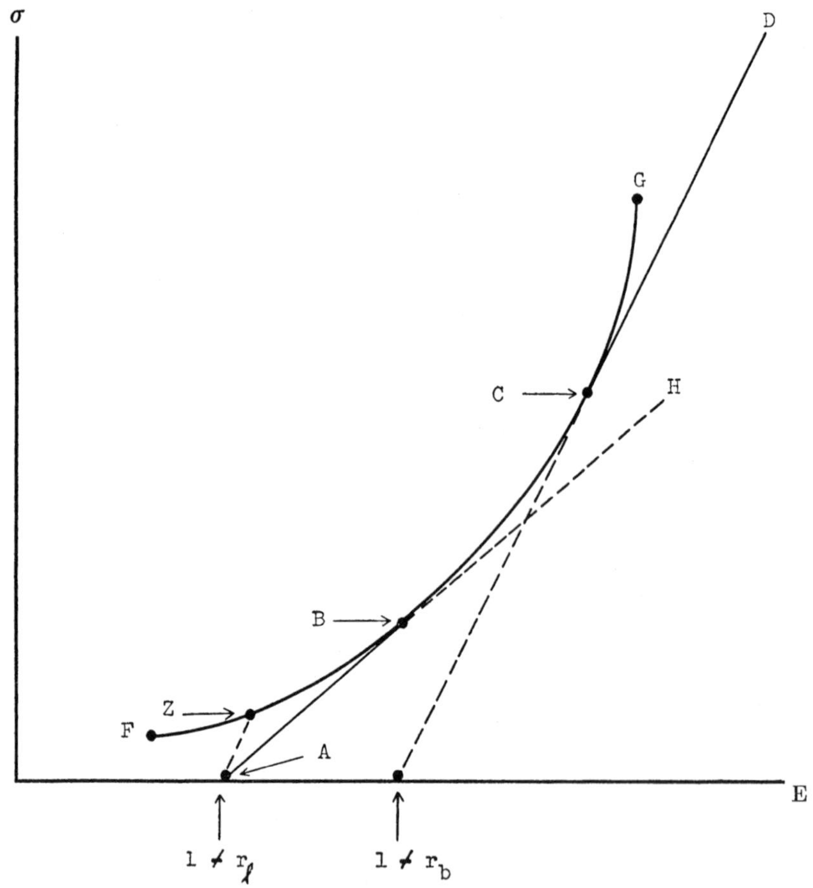

FIGURE 3

But, since V_l and cov_{zl} are both zero:

$$V = X_z^2 V_z$$

and the standard deviation of return is:

$$\sigma = X_z \sigma_z .$$

Since both E and σ are linear functions of X_z, the E, σ combinations of all portfolios made up of portfolio Z plus lending must lie on a straight line connecting points Z and A. In general, by splitting his investment between a portfolio and lending, an investor can attain any E, σ combination on the line connecting the E, σ combinations of the two components.

Many portfolios which are efficient in the absence of the lending alternative becomes inefficient when it is introduced. In Figure 3, for example, the possibility of attaining E, σ combinations along the line AB makes all portfolios along the original E, σ curve from point F to point B inefficient. For any desired level of

E below that associated with portfolio B, the most efficient portfolio will be some combination of portfolio B and lending. Portfolio B can be termed the "lending portfolio" since it is the appropriate portfolio whenever some of the investor's funds are to be lent at the rate r_l. This portfolio can be found readily once the E, σ curve is known. It lies at the point on the curve at which a ray from ($E = 1 + r_l$, $\sigma = 0$) is tangent to the curve. If the E, σ curve is not known in its entirety it is still possible to determine whether or not a particular portfolio is the lending portfolio by computing the rate of interest which *would* make the portfolio in question the lending portfolio. For example, the rate of interest associated in this manner with portfolio C is r_b, found by extending a tangent to the curve down to the E-axis. The diagonal code computes such a rate of interest for each corner portfolio as the analysis proceeds; when it falls below the previously stated lending rate the code computes the composition of the lending portfolio and terminates the analysis.

B. The "borrowing portfolio"

In some cases an investor may be able to borrow funds in order to purchase even greater amounts of a portfolio than his own funds will allow. If the appropriate rate for such borrowing were r_b, illustrated in figure 3, the E, σ combinations attainable by purchasing portfolio C with both the investor's funds and with borrowed funds would lie along the line CD, depending on the amount borrowed. Inclusion of the borrowing alternative makes certain portfolios inefficient which are efficient in the absence of the alternative; in this case the affected portfolios are those with E, σ combinations along the segment of the original E, σ curve from C to G. Just as there is a single appropriate portfolio if any lending is contemplated, there is a single appropriate portfolio if borrowing is contemplated. This "borrowing portfolio" is related to the rate of interest at which funds can be borrowed in exactly the same manner as the "lending portfolio" is related to the rate at which funds can be lent.

The diagonal code does not take account of the borrowing alternative in the manner used for the lending alternative since it is necessary to compute all previous corner portfolios in order to derive the portion of the E, σ curve below the borrowing portfolio. For this reason all computations required to derive the full E, σ curve above the lending portfolio must be made. However, the code does allow the user to specify the rate of interest at which funds can be borrowed. If this alternative is chosen, none of the corner portfolios which will be inefficient when borrowing is considered will be printed. Since as much as 65% of the total computer time can be spent recording (on tape) the results of the analysis this is not an insignificant saving.

7. The Cost of Portfolio Analysis with the Diagonal Code

The total time (and thus cost) required to perform a portfolio analysis with the diagonal code will depend upon the number of securities analyzed, the number of corner portfolios and, to some extent, the composition of the corner portfolios. A formula which gives quite an accurate estimate of the time required to perform an analysis on an IBM 709 computer was obtained by analyzing a series of runs during which the time required to complete each major segment of the program was recorded. The approximate time required for the analysis will be:[8]

Number of seconds = .6
+ .114 × number of securities analyzed
+ .54 × number of corner portfolios
+ .0024 × number of securities analyzed × number of corner portfolios.

Unfortunately only the number of securities analyzed is known before the analysis is begun. In order to estimate the cost of portfolio analysis before it is performed, some relationship between the number of corner portfolios and the number of securities analyzed must be assumed. Since no theoretical relationship can be derived and since the total number of corner portfolios could be several times the number of securities analysed, it seemed desirable to obtain some crude notion of the typical relationship when "reasonable" inputs are used. To accomplish this, a series of portfolio analyses was performed using inputs generated by a Monte Carlo model.

Data were gathered on the annual returns during the period 1940–1951 for 96 industrial common stocks chosen randomly from the New York Stock Exchange. The returns of each security were then related to the level of a stock market index and estimates of the parameters of the diagonal model obtained. These parameters were assumed to be samples from a population of A_i, B_i and Q_i triplets related as follows:

$$A_i = \bar{A} + r_1$$

$$B_i = \bar{B} + \psi A_i + r_2$$

$$Q_i = \bar{Q} + \theta A_i + \gamma B_i + r_3$$

where r_1, r_2 and r_3 are random variables with zero means. Estimates for the parameters of these three equations were obtained by regression analysis and estimates of the variances of the random variables determined.[9] With this information the characteristics of any desired number of securities could be generated. A random number generator was used to select a value for A_i; this value, together with an additional random number determined the value of B_i; the value of Q_i was then determined with a third random number and the previously obtained values of A_i and B_i.

Figure 4 shows the relationship between the number of securities analyzed

[8] The computations in this section are based on the assumption that no corner portfolios prior to the lending portfolio are printed. If the analyst chooses to print all preceding portfolios, the estimates given in this section should be multiplied by 2.9; intermediate cases can be estimated by interpolation.

[9] The random variables were considered normally distributed; in one case, to better approximate the data, two variances were used for the distribution—one for the portion above the mean and another for the portion below the mean.

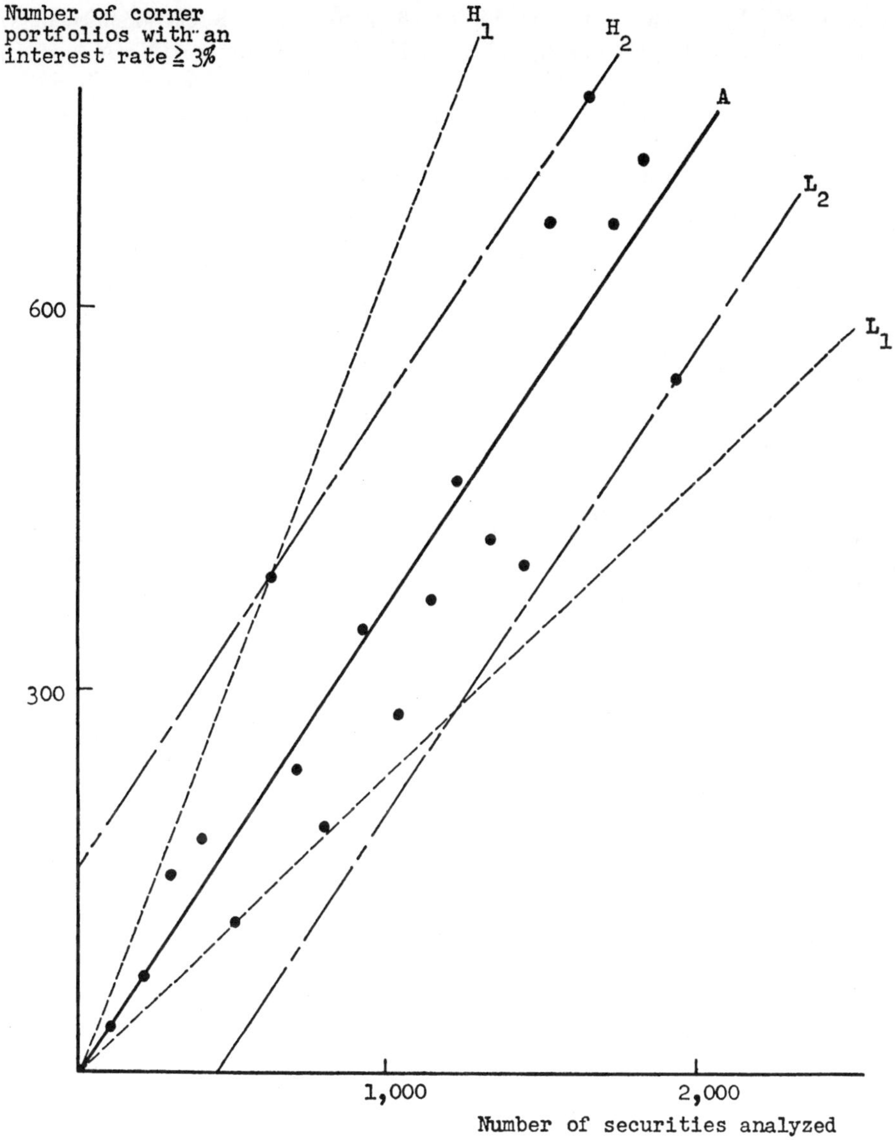

FIGURE 4

and the number of corner portfolios with interest rates greater than 3% (an approximation to the "lending rate"). Rather than perform a sophisticated analysis of these data, several lines have been used to bracket the results in various ways. These will be used subsequently as extreme cases, on the presumption that most practical cases will lie within these extremes (but with no presumption that these limits will never be exceeded). Curve *A* indicates the average relationship between the number of portfolios and the number of securities:

average $(N_p/N_s) = .37$. Curve H_1 indicates the highest such relationship: maximum $(N_p/N_s) = .63$; the line L_1 indicates the lowest: minimum $(N_p/N_s) = .24$. The other two curves, H_2 and L_2, indicate respectively the maximum deviation above (155) and below (173) the number of corner portfolios indicated by the average relationship $N_p = .37\ N_s$.

In Figure 5 the total time required for a portfolio analysis is related to the number of securities analyzed under various assumptions about the relationship

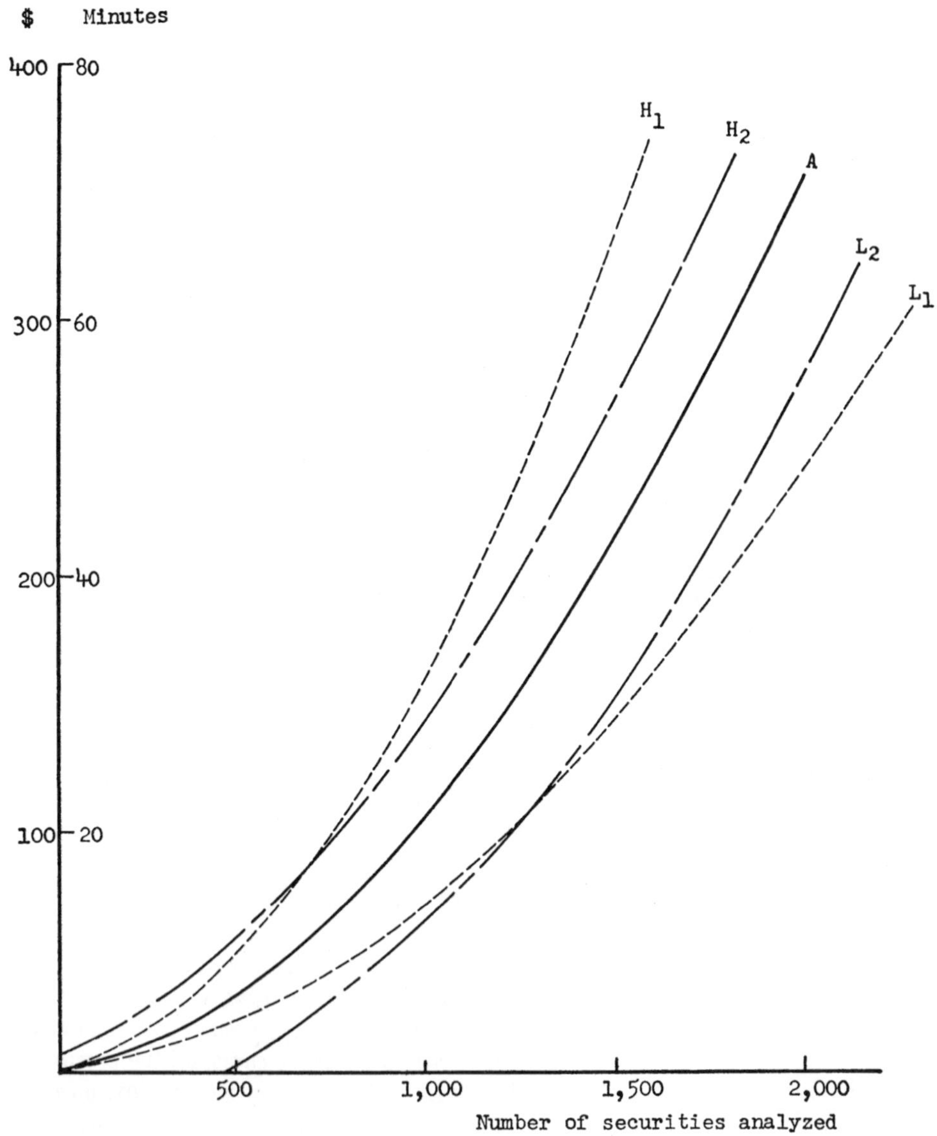

FIGURE 5

between the number of corner portfolios and the number of securities analyzed. Each of the curves shown in Figure 5 is based on the corresponding curve in Figure 4; for example, curve *A* in Figure 5 indicates the relationship between total time and number of securities analyzed on the assumption that the relationship between the number of corner portfolios and the number of securities is that shown by curve *A* in Figure 4. For convenience a second scale has been provided in Figure 5, showing the total cost of the analysis on the assumption that an IBM 709 computer can be obtained at a cost of $300 per hour.

8. The Value of Portfolio Analysis Based on the Diagonal Model

The assumptions of the diagonal model lie near one end of the spectrum of possible assumptions about the relationships among securities. The model's extreme simplicity enables the investigator to perform a portfolio analysis at a very small cost, as we have shown. However, it is entirely possible that this simplicity so restricts the security analyst in making his predictions that the value of the resulting portfolio analysis is also very small.

In order to estimate the ability of the diagonal model to summarize information concerning the performance of securities a simple test was performed. Twenty securities were chosen randomly from the New York Stock Exchange and their performance during the period 1940–1951 used to obtain two sets of

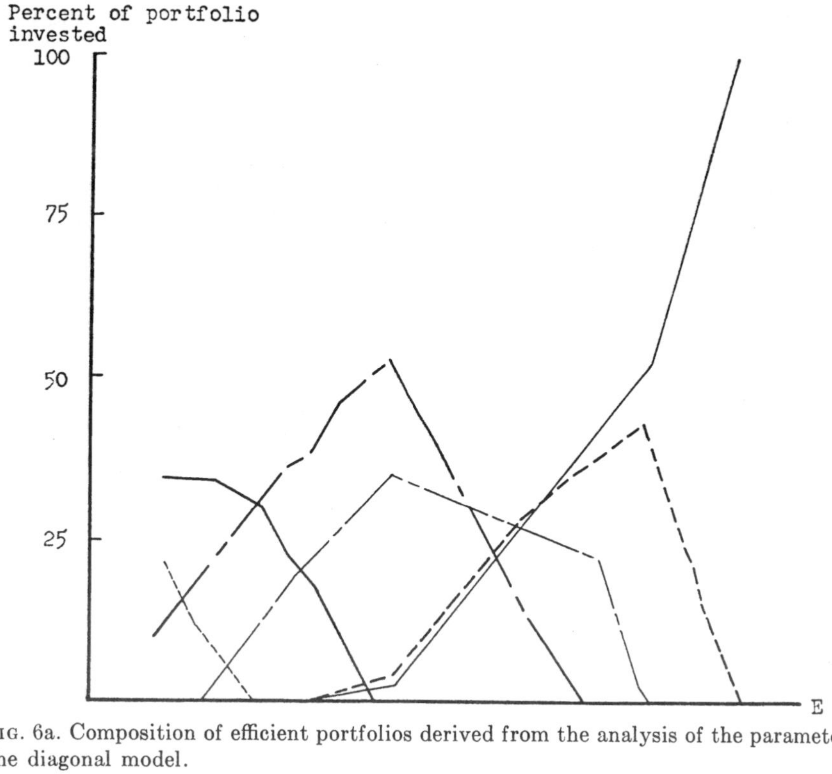

Fig. 6a. Composition of efficient portfolios derived from the analysis of the parameters of the diagonal model.

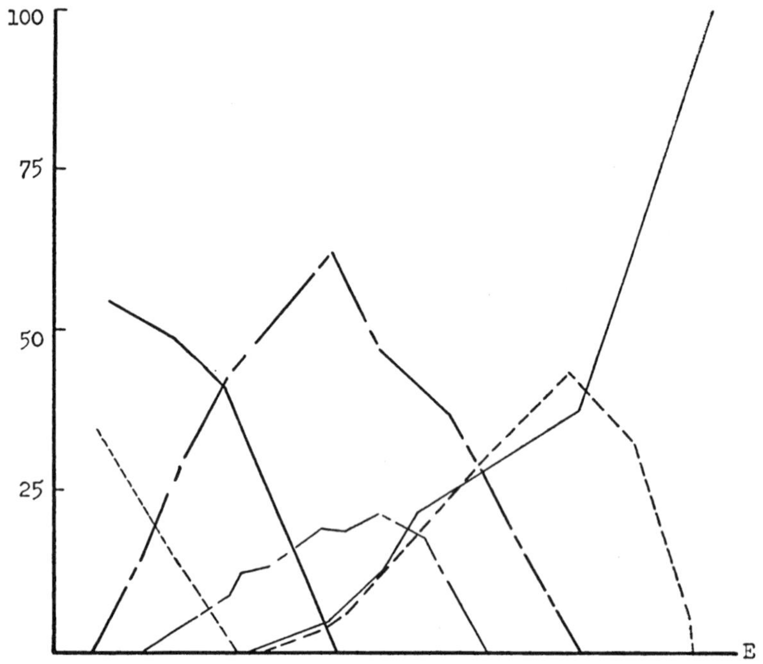

FIG. 6b. Composition of efficient portfolios derived from the analysis of historical data

data: (1) the actual mean returns, variances of returns and covariances of returns during the period and (2) the parameters of the diagonal model, estimated by regression techniques from the performance of the securities during the period. A portfolio analysis was then performed on each set of data. The results are summarized in Figures 6a and 6b. Each security which entered any of the efficient portfolios in significant amounts is represented by a particular type of line; the height of each line above any given value of E indicates the percentage of the efficient portfolio with that particular E composed of the security in question. The two figures thus indicate the compositions of all the efficient portfolios chosen from the analysis of the historical data (Figure 6b) and the compositions of all the portfolios chosen from the analysis of the parameters of the diagonal model (Figure 6a). The similarity of the two figures indicates that the 62 parameters of the diagonal model were able to capture a great deal of the information contained in the complete set of 230 historical relationships. An additional test, using a second set of 20 securities, gave similar results.

These results are, of course, far too fragmentary to be considered conclusive but they do suggest that the diagonal model may be able to represent the relationships among securities rather well and thus that the value of portfolio analyses based on the model will exceed their rather nominal cost. For these reasons it appears to be an excellent choice for the initial practical applications of the Markowitz technique.

References

1. MARKOWITZ, HARRY M., *Portfolio Selection, Efficient Diversification of Investments*, New York, John Wiley and Sons, Inc., 1959.
2. MARKOWITZ, HARRY M., "Portfolio Selection", *The Journal of Finance*, Vol. 12, (March 1952), 77–91.
3. MARKOWITZ, HARRY M., "The Optimization of a Quadratic Function Subject to Linear Constraints," *Naval Research Logistics Quarterly*, Vol. 3, (March and June, 1956), 111–133.
4. WOLFE, PHILIP, "The Simplex Method for Quadratic Programming," *Econometrica*, Vol. 27, (July, 1959), 382–398.

Quadratic programming is an extremely powerful technique. What are the prospects for the practical application of quadratic programming to investment portfolio analysis?

Mathematical Investment Portfolio Selection: Some Early Results

WILLIAM F. SHARPE

SEVERAL YEARS AGO, Harry M. Markowitz[1] suggested that the problem of selecting a portfolio of securities was very similar to a mathematical problem for which a proven solution technique existed. This technique—parametric quadratic programming—is, however, extremely complex, making it necessary to solve any realistically large problem with a high-speed digital computer.

Until recently, no computer program designed explicitly for the portfolio selection problem was generally available; thus, Markowitz' technique has been given no extensive practical test (although it has been widely accepted on the theoretical level). Very recently, however, two programs designed for portfolio selection have become generally available: IBM's long-awaited general Portfolio Selection Program,[2] and a program designed specifically for a particular kind of problem.[3]

[1] Harry M. Markowitz, "Portfolio Selection," *The Journal of Finance,* XII (March, 1952), pp. 77-91. A more comprehensive treatment is given in his *Portfolio Selection, Efficient Diversification of Investments* (New York: John Wiley and Sons, Inc., 1959).

[2] The program is described in the *General Information Manual, Portfolio Selection: A New Mathematical Approach to Investment Planning,* International Business Machines, 1962.

[3] The program is described in the author's "A Simplified Model for Portfolio Analysis," *Management Science,* IX, January 1963.

The author—

William F. Sharpe is Assistant Professor of Finance and Quantitative Analysis, College of Business Administration, University of Washington. Material included in this article was presented at the joint meeting of the Econometric Society and the Institute of Management Sciences, Ann Arbor, Michigan, September 11, 1962.

As IBM indicates, the availability of such programs "... permits testing of the mathematical theory on a practical scale"[4]—testing which will undoubtedly prove to be of considerable interest to many people outside the investment business, in addition to those within the field. While a large number of questions remain unanswered concerning the practicability of the technique, some early results are available to guide the experimentation about to begin. This article summarizes the author's work which has been completed to date.

The portfolio selection problem

The fundamentals of Markowitz' formulation of the portfolio selection problem can be summarized briefly. Basic to the approach are certain assumptions concerning the behavior of investors:

(1) Investors are assumed to view the future performance of securities or combinations of securities as subject to risk; in other words, they do not think in terms of only one possible outcome, but many.

(2) They are willing, however, to portray the prospects of a security (or combination of securities) with two summary measures—an *expected* rate of return on investment and the *risk* that the actual outcome will diverge from this expected result. The statistician's concept of variance (or the standard deviation, its square root) provides a useful measure of this latter element.[5]

(3) Among alternatives with equal expected rates of return, investors are assumed to prefer the one with the smallest risk.

(4) Among alternatives with equal risk, they are assumed to prefer the one with the greatest expected rate of return.

Figure I indicates the major implications of Markowitz' assumptions about investors' preferences. Each point on the diagram represents the predicted performance of a security or portfolio (i.e., a combination of securities). Line XY indicates maximum returns available with a given variance in particular portfolios; the reader may note that variance rises as return increases. Since expected return (E) and variance of return (V) are assumed to be satisfactory summaries of the prospects, this graph provides all the necessary data to enable an investor to make his choice.

On the other hand, much of this information need not be presented to the investor at all. For example, the assumptions imply that *of all* the portfolios which are plotted along the horizontal line, portfolio A will be preferred by any informed investor. Similarly, *of all* those along the vertical line, portfolio B will be preferred. In short, all portfolios which do not plot on the

[4] IBM, *op. cit.*, p. 1.

[5] Actually, Markowitz prefers semi-variance, which uses the deviations below the mean instead of all deviations, but he acknowledges the advantages of the variance from a computational standpoint.

FIGURE I
Portfolio Variance and Return

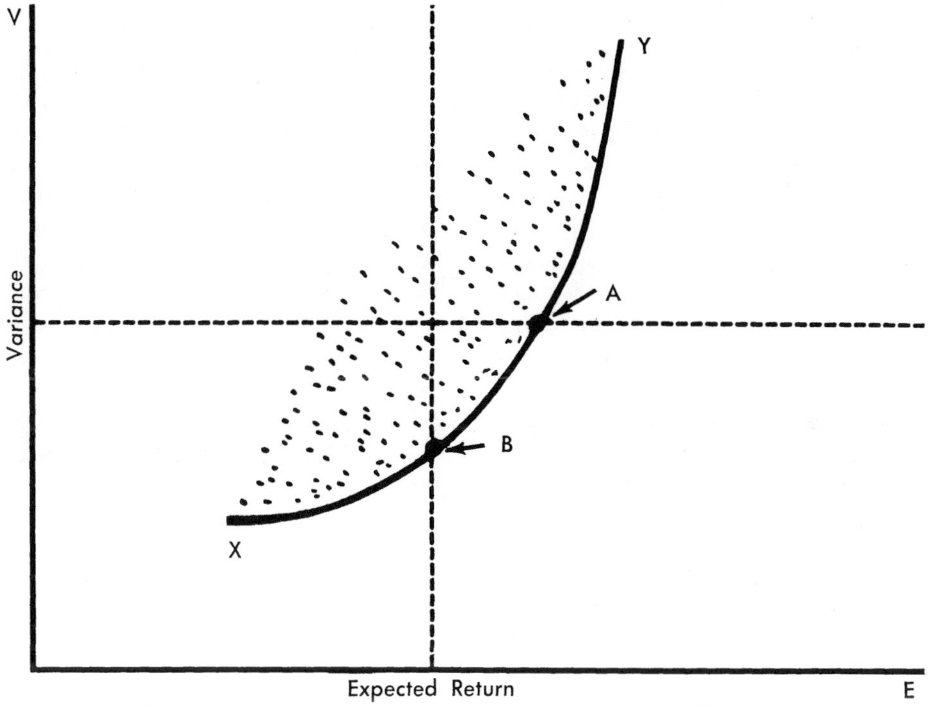

right-hand boundary of the space are dominated by at least one portfolio which does.

This leads to the concept of the *efficient portfolio.* Such a portfolio is simply one which plots on this boundary (XBAY in the diagram). All other portfolios are *inefficient*; they would never be selected and the investor need not be concerned with them at all. This relationship allows considerable division of labor. The only information required by the investor is:

(1) The location of the boundary of E, V combinations obtained with efficient portfolios (called the E, V curve).

(2) The composition of the efficient portfolios, or, more explicitly, the composition of the one which he chooses on the basis of the E, V curve.

The task of the investment adviser

The investment adviser (or advisers) can thus take on the tasks of:

(1) Making predictions about security performance.

(2) Incorporating these into predictions about the performance of portfolios.

(3) Determining the efficient portfolios.

(4) Determining the E, V combinations attainable from the efficient portfolios.

Markowitz' approach deals with the last three steps of this process—moving from the predictions about securities to the determination of efficient portfolios and their E, V combinations.

The mathematics of the manner in which the Markowitz technique determines the efficient portfolios from a set of predictions about the future performance of securities need not concern us here. Of more importance is the nature of the information required by the technique. In its most general form, the Markowitz approach requires the following information for each security to be analyzed:

(1) The security analyst's estimate of the expected rate of return on the security.

(2) His estimate of the risk (or variance) that the security's actual rate of return will diverge from that expected amount.

(3) A whole series of estimates, each one indicating the extent to which the prospects for this security are "tied" to (correlated with) the prospects for some other security. Thus, for GM stock one such estimate would be provided for the correlation between GM and Ford, another for GM and IBM, a third for GM and U.S. Steel, etc.

Application can be expensive

Not only does the technique, in its fullest form, require a great many inputs, but its application can be quite expensive. IBM indicates typical running times of 10 to 20 minutes for a 7090 computer with 12 tape units, although particularly complicated problems may take much longer. At commercial rental rates, a single analysis might thus average $250, certainly not an inconsiderable amount.

Even this very brief description of the Markowitz formulation should serve to indicate the power of the full technique; on the other hand, it may well have raised some doubts as to the practicality of the method, at least when used to process the subjective feelings of the typical practicing security analyst. There are two obvious problems here. The lesser concerns the cost of a full analysis, and the requirement of a fairly large computer to perform it. The more important problem concerns the inputs required for a full analysis. For an analysis of only 50 securities, 1325 separate parameters would be required. Obviously, some simplifying model of the relationships among securities is needed in order to reduce the number of required inputs.

Need for model recognized

The need for such a model was recognized by Markowitz and is provided for in the IBM code. The basic element of such a model is the use of one or more *indices,* and the notion of *tied* relationships between securities and such indices. The concept is simple. Most of the correlation between securities is due to some common dependence on a third factor or factors. Thus, Ford and GM stock are tied, partly because both are tied to the overall level of automobile sales. In addition, Ford and IBM are tied, most likely due to a common relationship with the overall level of the economy. Finally, the capital gains portion of the return on a security is undoubtedly tied, to a major extent, with the overall level of the security market.

By including one or more indices of activity (in an industry, the economy, or the stock market), and indicating the strength of the ties between securities and such indices, the resulting correlation between securities can be left to be determined by the computer.

There are two advantages to such a formulation. First, the number of predictions required from the security analyst can be reduced significantly. Second, if advantage is taken of the reduction in the size of the problem when designing a computer program, the cost of the analysis can be reduced. The IBM code, although designed to handle such indices, apparently does not attempt to modify the solution technique to take full advantage of the simplification. The other portfolio selection code, designed for the simplest possible model of this sort, does. The reduction in cost is substantial—analysis of 100 securities on an IBM 7090 (with only two tape units required) typically requires 30 seconds, reducing the cost to less than $10 per case. Perhaps more important, analysis of somewhat smaller problems can be performed on much smaller computers, making repeated experimentation a practical possibility.[6]

Simplest model

The model of the relationships among securities required by the simpler program is virtually the simplest one might possibly adopt, using but one index, and requiring all interrelationships among securities to be limited to those resulting from common ties to the index.

Figure II illustrates the relationship assumed for each security. The horizontal axis shows I, the level of the index, while the verticle axis indicates R, the rate of return on the security (including both income and capital gains, if any). The basic relationship between these two measures is linear, the position of the line being indicated by E—the expected rate of return of the security—and B—the response of its return to changes in the index (this latter can be zero or negative, if desired).

This relationship is not certain, however, and a third measure—Q—indicates the extent to which the actual rate of return might diverge from the line. This model, which is called the diagonal model for reasons having to

[6] The author's code, initially written for the IBM 709/7090, has been adapted for use on the IBM 1620 by Prof. Pao Lun Cheng at the University of Massachusetts.

FIGURE II
Analysis of a Security

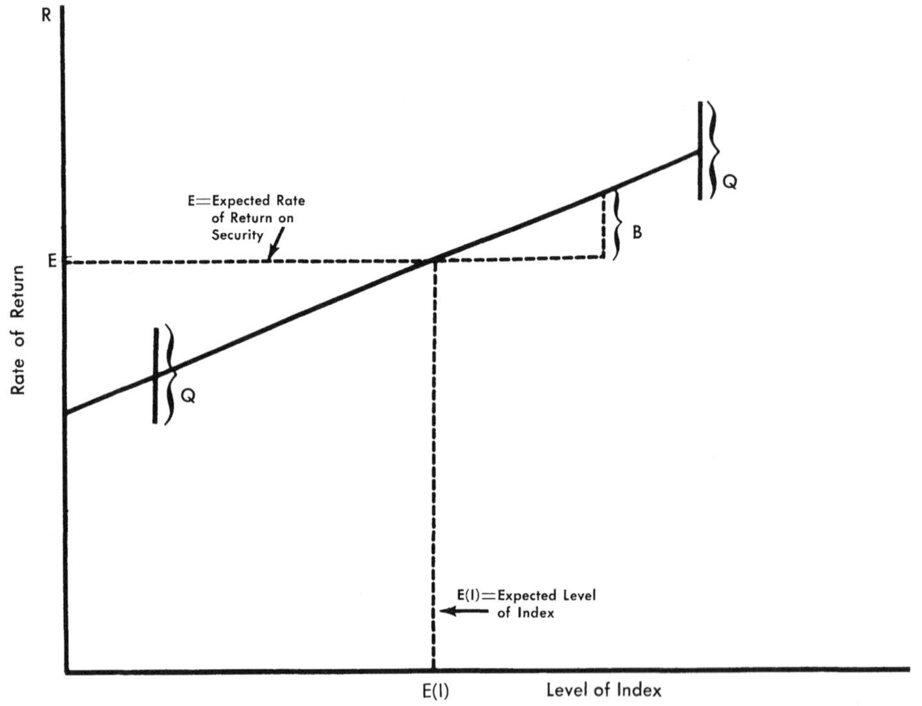

do with the technique used to solve the related portfolio selection problem, obviously requires relatively few inputs from the security analyst. For 50 securities, for example, only 152 estimates would be required—three for each security and two for the index (its expected level and the risk that it might diverge from this level).

The other advantage of the diagonal model, the substantial reduction in the cost of the portfolio selection process, has already been indicated. These are both highly desirable attributes. On the other hand, the drastic simplification of the relationships among securities might make results obtained from such a model quite worthless. There are, however, three rather diverse reasons why this may not be the case.

Usefulness of model

First, the diagonal model accords with the views of many practicing security analysts. A very common classification of securities is based on their responsiveness to overall movements in the economy or in the market—

FIGURE

Composition of

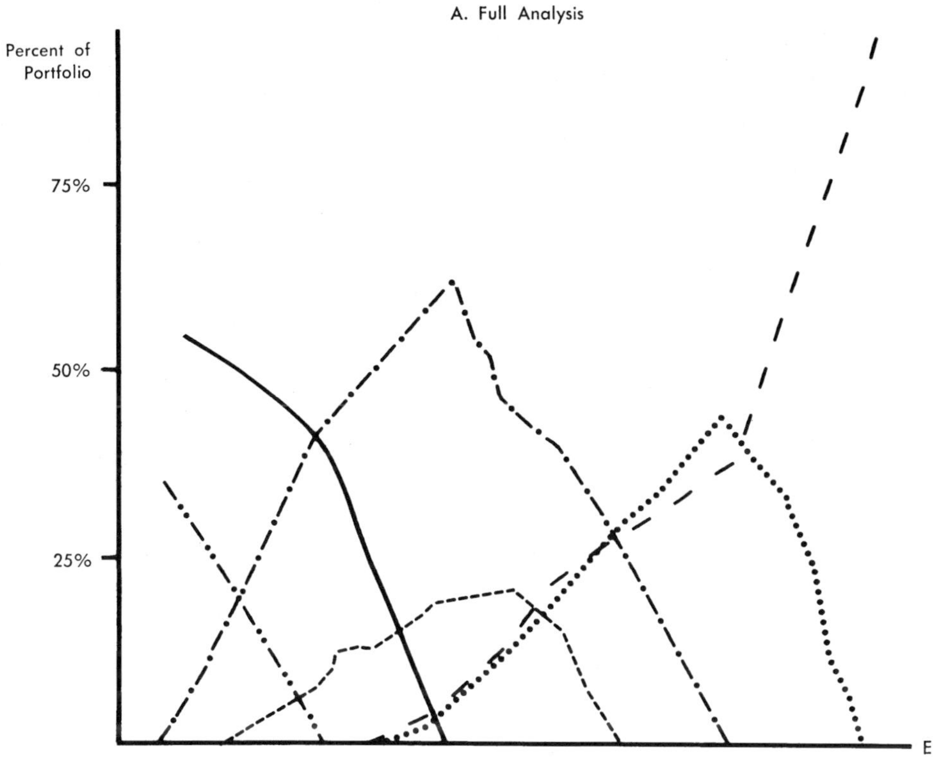

responsive securities are classed as aggressive, those responding only slightly being considered defensive. Defensive securities are considered more attractive than aggressive securities, if their expected rates of return are similar. In other words, investors are willing to accept a lower expected rate of return from defensive securities than they require from aggressive securities.

A second reason for suspecting that the diagonal model may be a satisfactory picture of reality is its apparent ability to summarize reality. Figure III shows the composition of various efficient portfolios (with differing E's) based on two portfolio analyses. The first involved a full analysis of 20 securities, using the actual historical data for the required estimates. The second analysis used only the inputs of the diagonal model, estimated by a statistical analysis of the actual data. While there are certainly differences between comparable portfolios produced by the two analyses, the similarities are rather striking. The diagonal model, with 62

III
Efficient Portfolios

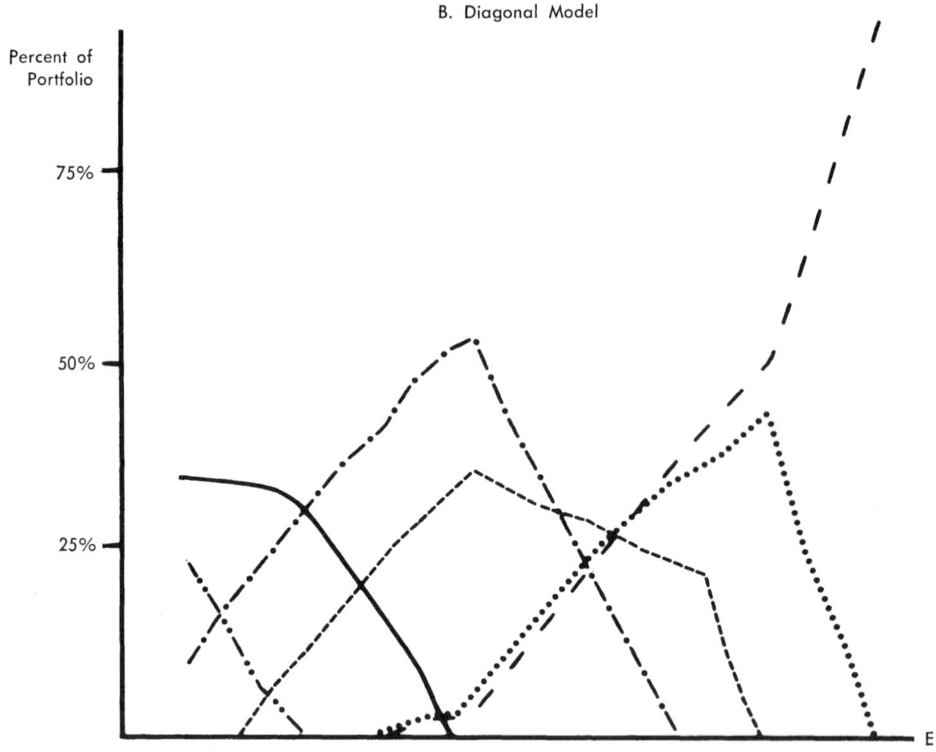

different estimates, was able to communicate most of the information contained in the 230 estimates used for the full analysis. A second test, using a different sample of securities, yielded similar results.

The third justification can only be alluded to here. If one makes certain assumptions about investor behavior, including the assumption that each investor acts as Markowitz suggests he act, it is possible to derive a market equilibrium theory which implies that the diagonal model does in fact represent reality. While a number of problems remain to be investigated in connection with this theory, it does lend additional support to the argument that the diagonal model deserves consideration.

Practical application

This discussion should serve to indicate that the diagonal model is worthy of an attempted practical application. Unfortunately, the results of some early attempts along this line have been disappointing. The experiments performed were of two types. The first involved a practicing security analyst, who not only provided data but also helped design an intermediate model to facilitate the transition from his analysis to the inputs required by the diagonal model. Subsequent applications involved university students, often with little background in either security analysis or portfolio analysis, using the intermediate model designed by the security analyst.

As indicated above, all of the experiments relied on an intermediate model which transformed the results of the security analysis into the inputs of the diagonal model. The nature of this model can be seen from the form used to record the analyst's predictions, shown in Figure IV. Notice that this analyst chose the Dow-Jones average as the underlying index, that he preferred to concentrate on the behavior of the price of the security, relegating dividends to a subsidiary role, that he chose a three-year horizon, and, perhaps most interesting of all, that he preferred to use a probability distribution to indicate the remaining risk.[7] In addition to filling out one such form for each security, the analyst provided a graph showing the likelihood of various levels of the Dow-Jones average.

[7] This latter choice was not the author's. A number of questions had been proposed to the analyst instead (e.g., what is the chance of a 10% rise, a 50% rise, etc.?), to which he replied, "It's too bad you won't just let me draw you a graph showing the chances of various prices." It should be pointed out, however, that this preference is obviously not universal, as subsequent discussions with other security analysts have shown.

Interpretation difficulties

Before assessing the results of this portfolio analysis, something should be said about the difficulties associated with interpreting such results. There is no sense in which the portfolio analysis technique itself can be shown to be "wrong," since it is an obviously valid mathematical procedure.

The only sense in which the procedure can be wrong is for the inputs to fail to reflect the true feelings of the security analyst, either because the underlying models are not adequate representations of the security market or investor behavior, or simply because he does not assign the appropriate values to the required inputs. But how can the results of the analysis shed any light on the adequacy of the inputs in performing this function? The obvious choice is to compare portfolios selected by the analysis with those selected by the analyst. If one is willing to assume that the security analyst is in fact a good *portfolio* analyst, then any major inconsistency would indicate that the inputs were inadequate.

This assumption raises considerable doubts concerning the reason for performing the portfolio analysis in the first place. If one makes the alternative assumption that the security analyst is not necessarily a good portfolio analyst, then inconsistency between the portfolios tells us nothing about the inputs.

Experiment with security analyst

Having raised (but not solved) the problem of interpretation, let us turn

FIGURE IV

Analyst's Prediction of Security Values

Name of Security: ....

Date of Analysis: ....

Analyst: ....

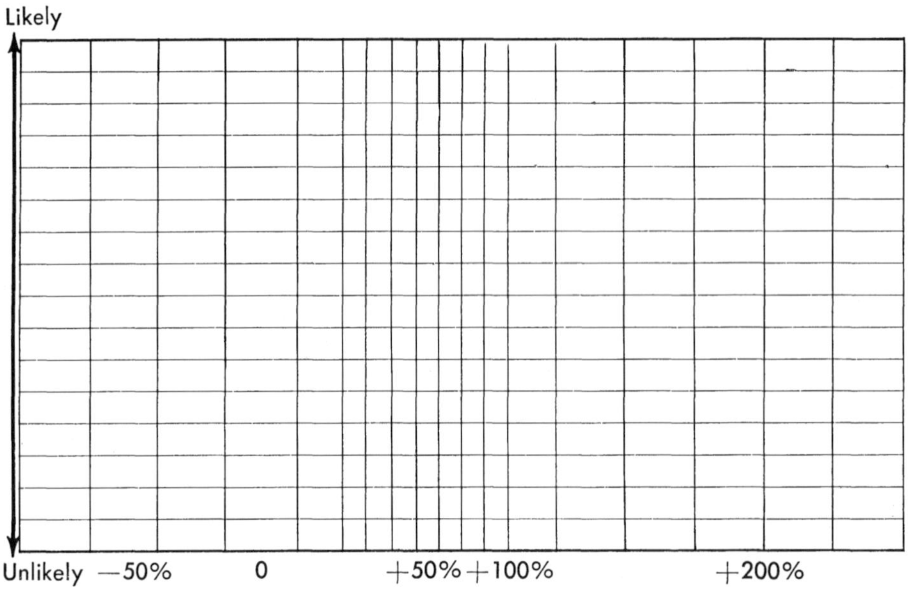

Total change in market price of the security over three years, if the Dow-Jones average remains at its present level.

(1) Total change in market price of the security over three years, if the Dow-Jones average rises to 25% more than its current value: ....% more/less than this security's current price.

(2) Total change in the market price of the security over three years, if the Dow-Jones average falls to 25% less than its current value: ....% more/less than this security's current price.

(3) Annual dividend yield of the security: ....%.

Notes: Interpret the graph as follows: if a security is now priced at \$50, and in three years it is priced at \$60, this is a change of +20%. If it is now priced at \$50, and in three years it is priced at \$40, this would be a change of —20%.

In questions (1) and (2), give your best single estimate, using the same measuring technique used in the graph. If you expect the price to rise 15%, show +15%; if you expect it to fall 15%, show —15%. If you expect it to remain at its present level, show 0%.

to the results obtained in the experiment with the security analyst. Prior to seeing any of the results of the portfolio analysis, he provided three recommended portfolios, ranked in order of conservatism. Figure V shows their predicted performance based on the inputs to the portfolio analysis program (points A, B, and C). One extremely low order test of these inputs is met—the relative conservatism attributed to the portfolios by the analyst agrees with their positions on the graph: portfolio A, rated most conservative, has the lowest expected return and risk; portfolio C, rated least conservative, has the greatest expected return and risk; and portfolio B falls between the two extremes.

A second test is also met. The other points in the diagram show the predicted performance of 50 portfolios of comparable diversification selected using random numbers. Of these 50 portfolios, 39 are worse (according to the inputs) than portfolios made up from the three selected portfolios.

These two tests indicate that the inputs are *relatively* satisfactory reflections of the analyst's feelings. But notice that the three portfolios which he selected are, according to the inputs, considerably inferior to comparable efficient portfolios whose predicted performances are shown by points on the line FF. Moreover, the efficient portfolios are much less diversified than the ones selected by the analyst. This might be interpreted as an indication that the analyst failed to realize that the advantages of a few of the securities outweighed the disadvantages of relatively little diversification. The alternative interpretation, to which both he and the author subscribe, is that the inputs were not sufficiently accurate to lead to the correct results.

Tests summarized

The tests performed with students using this model can be summarized quite succinctly: the results failed to meet even the two low order tests met in the experiment with the security analyst, and, thus, were even more negative.

It is quite clear that there was something wrong with the technique utilized in the experiments conducted to date. Perhaps the diagonal model is, after all, too extreme a simplification. If so, a less severe model, involving several indices, should provide considerable improvement, warranting the substantial increase in cost.[8] On the other hand, this increase may not be necessary, if the fault lay only in the intermediate model used. This latter possibility seems a likely cause of some of the difficulties encountered in the student tests, since, in this case, it was not designed by the participants. Neither of these possibilities, it should be noted, provides an argument against the Markowitz technique itself—only

[8] This increase exists at present because of the requirement that one shift from the diagonal code to the IBM code. In the near future, the required change may be less expensive; the possibility of a code capable of handling cases involving several indices, but designed to take advantage of the simplicity of such problems (in the manner used in the diagonal code), is under active investigation.

FIGURE V

Predicted Performance of Three Recommended Portfolios

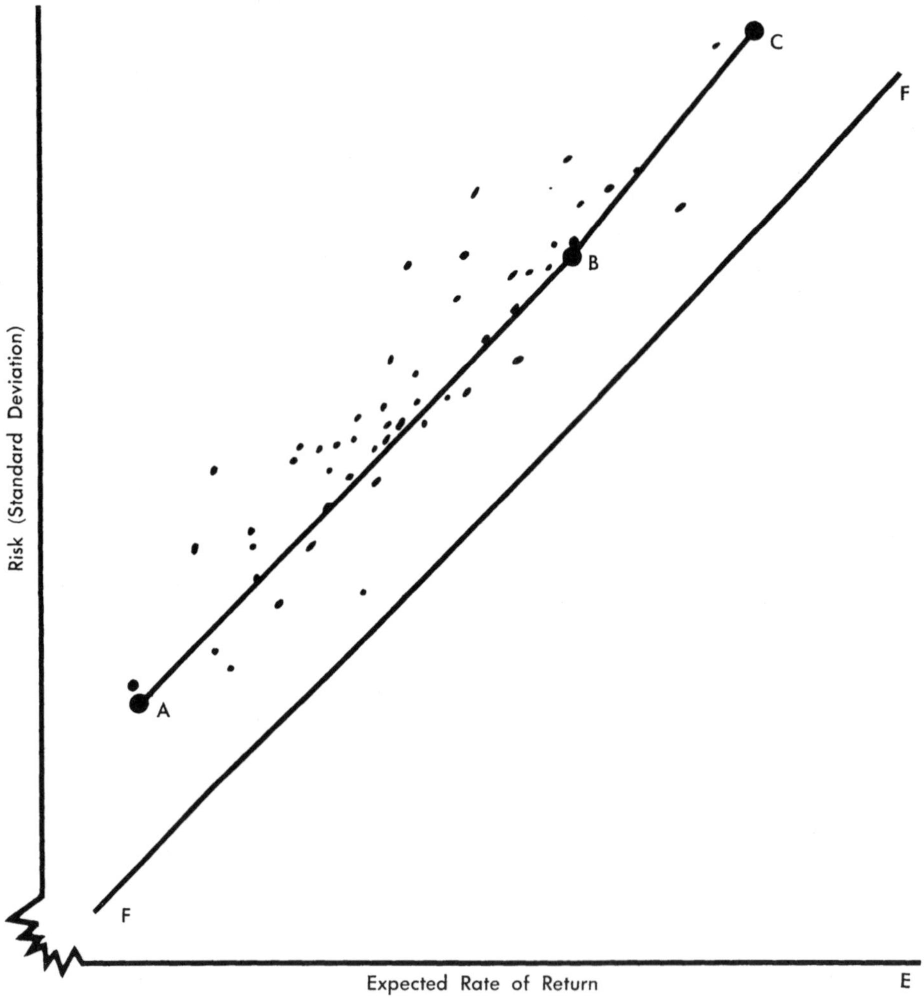

the particular simplifications used in the experiments described here.

There are, however, two other possible reasons for the failure which are more worrisome. First, the assumptions about investor behavior may not be valid—perhaps the expected return and a variance measure of risk do not provide sufficient information for an investment decision. The second possibility would be equally difficult to overcome. Markowitz' formulation acknowledges risk in one sense; it allows one to make predictions about the future in terms of a variance as well as an expected rate of return. But the quadratic programming technique then operates on this information with a high degree of precision, as if *these predictions* were known with certainty.

Uncertainty

It seems quite likely that most security analysts are not even certain about their measures of risk—in short, there is still uncertainty attached to the measures used in the mathematical solution.[9] The security analyst who participated in the experiment reflected this; he said that he was not absolutely certain where he should draw his graphs, that they were really rather fuzzy in his mind. Under these conditions, a relatively high-powered mathematical technique may lose much of its value.[10]

It is obviously far too early in the process of experimentation to attempt to form any conclusions about the practicality of the Markowitz technique for portfolio selection. On the other hand, it might prove interesting to those who are about to perform this experimentation to provide some guesses about the eventual conclusions. In that spirit, the following suggestions are offered as hypotheses to be tested in the experiments which are now beginning.

It seems entirely possible that the major value of Markowitz' technique for portfolio analysis may prove to be pedagogical. The author has found it extremely valuable in the classroom. It provides a concise, rigorous description of the portfolio selection problem, which certainly merits inclusion in an investment course, whether or not an actual analysis is to be run. In courses at the University of Washington, the theoretical treatment is supplemented with an actual computer run based on security analyses performed by the class, and, most important of all, a post mortem in which the relationship between the inputs and the results of the analysis is examined. One might expect this use of the technique to become increasingly important as computer programs and computers become more accessible to those teaching investment courses.

Practical use of technique

As far as use of the technique in practical situations is concerned, it may be that here, too, the main advantage is pedagogical.

Because of the many difficulties involved, the usefulness of the technique will probably be greatest where a rather close relationship between the security analyst and the facility for performing the portfolio analysis is main-

[9] This latter uncertainty is what Marschak has called the *degree of ignorance;* he also suggested that this is really what Knight meant when using the term *uncertainty*. See Helen Makower and Jacob Marschak, "Assets, Prices and Monetary Theory," *Economica,* V (1938), pp. 261-228.

[10] A similar problem often arises when using the related (and much more popular) technique of linear programming.

tained. Such a relationship would allow many iterations between man and machine, leading to better outputs, and enhancing the understanding of the security analysts. The ability to perform an analysis of a reasonable number of securities on computers as inexpensive as the IBM 1620 makes this a thoroughly practical objective.

Simple techniques such as pre-printed forms on port-a-punch cards, or more complex ones using special input panels could facilitate such an arrangement. It is not inconceivable to envision a staff of security analysts plus one small computer, loaded with the portfolio analysis program and operating as an integral part of the staff. Whenever an analyst wished to explore the implications of some change in predictions, he would merely enter the change into the computer and obtain the new portfolio analysis results directly.

Conclusion

To sum up, it would appear that the prospects for practical application of quadratic programming to portfolio analysis are good, but that considerable caution needs to be exercised in its application. Quadratic programming is, after all, an extremely powerful technique; security analysis, on the other hand, is a very crude art form, and even the use of a measure of risk cannot completely compensate for this difficulty. Nevertheless, one might venture the opinion that while it will certainly never supplant other methods of portfolio selection, the Markowitz technique is likely to prove a useful and inexpensive supplement to such methods.

PORTFOLIO ANALYSIS

William F. Sharpe*

Someone has said that maternity is a matter of fact, while paternity is, at best, a matter of opinion. Concerning the field to which this issue of the Journal is devoted, however, there is little difference of opinion -- Harry Markowitz is almost universally considered to be the father of portfolio analysis. The essence of the theory appeared in his 1952 article[1], although the full exposition was not available until several years later.[2]

The Background

Formally, portfolio analysis theory deals with the selection of a set of investments. Markowitz suggested that the investor should be interested in the probability distribution of his future wealth, and that the selection process should deal, at the very least, with some measure of dispersion of this distribution as well as with its central tendency. For purposes of computation, the standard deviation (or variance) is an attractive candidate for the former, and the expected value for the latter.

Assuming these measures are sufficient, the investor's problem can usefully be separated into three tasks. First, he must obtain estimates of future outcomes for individual securities; this is the task of security analysis. However, these should not be simply point-

---

*University of Washington

[1] Harry M. Markowitz, "Portfolio Selection," The Journal of Finance, March, 1952, pp. 77 - 91.

[2] ________________, Portfolio Selection: Efficient Diversification of Investments (New York: John Wiley and Sons, Inc., 1959).

estimates; explicit account should be taken of the risk of each security and, even more important, the extent to which its outcome is likely to be related to those of other securities. Given a suitable set of such estimates, the investor needs to determine the set of efficient portfolios. A portfolio is defined as efficient if (and only if) it offers a higher overall expected return than any other portfolio with comparable risk (i.e. standard deviation of return). This second task, portfolio analysis, cannot be performed by simply enumerating possible portfolios. One of Markowitz' major contributions was an algorithm specifically designed to perform this task -- formally, a problem in parametric quadratic programming. The final problem facing the investor is portfolio selection -- given the set of efficient portfolios, which one should he hold? This may depend entirely on his feelings towards risk vis-a-vis expected return. On the other hand, market mechanisms may play a part in the decision.

It seems almost incredible now, but until Markowitz suggested this approach to portfolio analysis, no rigorous basis existed to justify diversification; arguments were ad hoc at best. Moreover, the concept of risk, although a major element of finance (as opposed to economic) literature, was rarely even defined rigorously, let alone treated analytically. Markowitz both specified a framework that met these issues directly and provided a workable algorithm for employing that framework for practical problems. The intent was primarily normative, however. Markowitz did not suggest that people actually do select portfolios as if they had solved complicated problems in parametric quadratic programming; rather he suggested that they should select them in this manner. It is also important to note that he did not suggest a preferred technique for security analysis nor the appropriate method for portfolio selection. His interest lay in proposing a general structure for the overall process and providing an algorithm for performing the task of portfolio analysis.

As might have been expected, there was little evidence during the first few years after its initial publication that Markowitz' contribution would have a major impact. Now, however, it is becoming apparent that this was only the top of the iceberg. Articles on portfolio analysis and related subjects are becoming commonplace in such journals as Management Science, The Journal of Business, The Journal of Finance and, of course, this Journal. And the number of doctoral candidates in finance writing dissertations in the area gives the appearance of approaching infinity. In short, academic interest in the theory is intense. Needless to say, applications to real-world situations have lagged behind (as they undoubtedly should). But the first hesitant steps are now being taken by some of the more venturesome individuals and institutions. One can easily predict that these efforts will be greatly expanded in the future.

It is difficult to briefly describe the many paths down which portfolio analysis theory has led investigators, but some attempt may prove worthwhile. To keep the discussion brief, I will omit many names and all references; the interested reader will find most of the key articles referenced in the papers that follow.

An extremely important application and extension of the theory was made in 1958 by Tobin, who cast it in a positive role, suggesting that the theory offered a plausible explanation for liquidity preference. He also showed that the portfolio selection problem could be partly solved by considering the market for risk-free funds. Given the unpalatable, but perhaps acceptable, assumption that an investor can borrow or lend money at a single "pure" interest rate, there exists a preferred efficient combination of risky investments; the investor need only lever himself up or down by borrowing or lending to obtain the position consistent with his particular attitude towards risk vis-a-vis expected return. This "Tobin effect" has been proven to have major implications for both positive and normative applications of the theory.

A number of investigators have considered the question of the utility of the Markowitz procedure in a normative role. Given some method of security analysis and some rule for portfolio selection, does the Markowitz approach provide portfolios that outperform those selected in other ways? This is, of course, an empirical question; and all the usual problems associated with such questions arise. What is the appropriate test of performance? Are the methods reproducible in the future? And, if the test shows the Markowitz technique to be inferior, doesn't this simply suggest that the security analysis method utilized was poor? The majority of the tests performed to date have utilized past performance to derive (probabilistic) estimates of future performance. The alternative is usually a randomly-selected portfolio or the actual performance of a mutual fund. Surprisingly, even under these conditions, the Markowitz approach appears to stand up well. The evidence, although limited, is thus comforting to the theory's proponents.

A related line of investigation has dealt with simplified versions of the Markowitz approach. The objective is to economize on the number of inputs required for portfolio analysis (and thus necessary as outputs from the security analysis process) as well as the computer time required to perform the portfolio analysis. Some of the work has been theoretical, dealing primarily with efficient solution algorithms. But more recent investigations have been primarily empirical. Granted a simplified method should cost less to implement; is the (presumed) loss in performance small enough to make its selection worthwhile? Two types of tests have been employed. It is possible that the simplified method will produce portfolios virtually identical to those produced by a full analysis. If so, the test is over and the victory complete. If the portfolios do differ however, the argument is not settled; a second test must be employed. Do the portfolios selected by the simple method perform as well in the future as those selected with a full analysis (or at least well enough to make it worthwhile to reduce the cost of implementation accordingly)? Of course, hundreds of simplified methods can be imagined. Some have been tested already -- many more will be in the future.

The Markowitz approach as a normative theory of investment selection is increasingly being investigated empirically rather than theoretically. However, much theoretical work is being done along related lines. A number of investigators have rejected one or more of the bases on which the Markowitz theory is constructed. Many have argued that the mean and variance of future wealth are not sufficient parameters for decision making. Others have suggested that the probability distribution of a single security's rate of return is best approximated by a distribution with an infinite variance; under these conditions (a fortiori), a calculus based on variance has no meaning. Surprisingly, however, many of the conclusions of the Markowitz approach (especially those obtained with some of the simplified versions) hold even under these conditions. Other investigators have suggested that the investor should attempt to maximize expected wealth subject to constraints on the probability of losses of specified types. Although such chance-constrained programming approaches are formally competitive to the Markowitz theory, in spirit they have much in common with an extension of the latter suggested by Baumol.

Yet another school prefers to view the investor as considering his position under various states of the world, without simply assigning probabilities to such states and then proceeding along the lines of the Markowitz theory. It is far too early to suggest the final outcome, but it may well be that this state-preference theory will eventually coexist peacefully with the Markowitz theory as do the quantum and wave theories of light -- i.e. each will be considered applicable for a specified range of problems.

In finance and economics, models developed for normative purposes are often used for positive theories, and vice-versa. Portfolio analysis is no exception. Tobin's application has already been mentioned; much additional work is being done. As in traditional economic theory, it is assumed that individual decision makers act as if they were investigating alternatives, selecting efficient strategies, and trading on a relatively efficient market to the extent desirable, given their preferences. The difference is that risk is included explicitly. Given these assumptions, what kind of equilibrium conditions are to be expected? And, most important, how will key elements of the economy respond to changes of various types?

Most of the work in the area of positive theory has been both theoretical and concerned with capital (investment) markets per se. Empirical results are only now beginning to appear. By and large, they suggest that the world is reasonably consistent with the implications of the theory. But it is far too early to render any final judgement.

A fascinating line of inquiry along theoretical lines has been virtually untapped thus far, and it promises to be the more important. One of the major characteristics that distinguishes finance (and, indeed, business administration generally) from traditional economics is its insistence that risk permeates the business world and must be dealt with explicitly. If the Markowitz approach is useful in the context of security selection then it must be useful in almost all areas of finance (and probably most other areas of business administration). The textbooks in business finance need to be rewritten just as badly as do those dealing with investments. Some of the major theoretical contributions of the future will come, I predict, from those applying and extending the Markowitz approach to cover this broader field. Meanwhile, the continuing decrease in the cost of computer time, the continuing increase in the size of high-speed computer memory, the increasing availability of equipment allowing interaction between an investigator and his data, and the availability of large amounts of security data in machine-sensible form will lead to extensive empirical investigations in the areas of security analysis and portfolio analysis.

MANAGEMENT SCIENCE
Vol. 18, No. 2, October, 1971
Printed in U.S.A.

MEAN-ABSOLUTE-DEVIATION CHARACTERISTIC LINES FOR SECURITIES AND PORTFOLIOS*

WILLIAM F. SHARPE†

Stanford University

The characteristic line of a security or portfolio relates its rate of return to that of a "market portfolio." Several investigators have suggested the desirability of obtaining such a line by minimizing the sum of the absolute deviations rather than the sum of the squared deviations around the line. This paper presents a new algorithm for such a regression problem. The procedure has at least two virtues: it is simple, and it produces useful information as a byproduct of the solution process. Empirical evidence is also presented on the differences in the values obtained with the two regression methods (i.e., mean-absolute-deviation and least-squares). The differences appear to be relatively slight, at least for well-diversified portfolios.

Introduction

The *characteristic line* of a security or portfolio relates its rate of return to the rate of return of some broadly-based portfolio considered representative of the market as a whole. The notion of such a characteristic line is used in positive theories of capital market equilibrium (e.g., [8], [16], [18]). It also plays a key role in practical applications of normative portfolio theory (e.g., [6], [11], [17], [18]). And, characteristic lines are often fit to data on past returns to measure actual performance (e.g., [8], [13], [18], [22]).

Several years ago, Mandelbrot [10] suggested that distributions of security returns might be "fat-tailed"—i.e., have more outliers than would be expected from a normal distribution. Empirical work by Fama [6] confirmed the hypothesis: restricting attention to the class of stable Paretian distributions, the best results were obtained when distributions with characteristic exponents between 1.7 and 1.9 were used to summarize past returns. Under such conditions, sample variance (or standard deviation, its square root) is not likely to be stable over time.

The characteristics of empirical distributions of security returns have led some (e.g., [7]) to advocate the mean absolute deviation as a preferred measure of dispersion. The mean absolute deviation accords less importance to outliers than does the standard deviation—presumably a desirable attribute when substantial outliers may occur in one sample but not in another. Recently, the mean absolute deviation has been given official status as a recommended measure of dispersion by the Bank Administration Institute [1].

The choice of a measure of dispersion generally implies the use of a corresponding measure of central tendency. For example, if the standard deviation is considered an appropriate measure of dispersion, the arithmetic mean (average) is usually chosen to measure central tendency, since the standard deviation around the mean is less than that around any other value. In other words, the mean minimizes the sum of the squared deviations. On the other hand, if the mean absolute deviation is considered an appropriate measure of dispersion, the median is usually chosen to measure central

* Received October 1970; revised April 1971.

† The author is grateful to Stewart Hodges of the London Graduate School of Business Studies for introducing him to much of the literature on mean-absolute-deviation regression and to Marc Bogue of Stanford University for helpful comments.

tendency, since the mean absolute deviation around the median is less than that around any other value. In other words, the median minimizes the sum of the absolute deviations. (This is, in fact, the appropriate *definition* of the median.)

Similar arguments apply to curve-fitting. If dispersion around a characteristic line is to be measured in terms of the standard deviation of the residuals (i.e., "unexplained" components of return), the least-squares regression line is usually selected, since the sum of the squared deviations around such a line is smaller than that around any other line. The normal equations used to determine the parameters of a least-squares regression line are derived from this criterion. On the other hand, if dispersion is to be measured in terms of the mean absolute deviation of the residuals, a characteristic line which minimizes the sum of the absolute deviations is usually advocated.

Fama [6] first suggested the assumption that residuals from a security or portfolio's characteristic line follow a stable Paretian distribution with (formally) an infinite variance. Blume [3] subsequently provided empirical support: restricting attention to the class of stable Paretian distributions, the best results were obtained when a distribution with a characteristic exponent between 1.7 and 1.8 was used to summarize past residuals. These results have led some to advocate the mean absolute deviation as a preferred measure of dispersion of residuals around the characteristic line and the selection of a characteristic line that minimizes this measure. In a study by Wiginton [25], such an approach provided predictions that were no worse than those obtained using standard least-squares regression methods.

As Wise [26] has shown, when residuals follow a stable Paretian distribution with a characteristic exponent between 1 and 2, neither least-squares nor mean-absolute-deviation regression will provide the best linear unbiased estimators. A simulation study by Sargent [15] indicates that for distributions with characteristic exponents greater than 1.7, least-squares regression may be preferable to the mean-absolute-deviation approach. The choice between the two measures is therefore far from obvious.

This paper does not attempt to assess the relative merits of the two approaches. Instead it describes a particularly simple algorithm for fitting mean-absolute-deviation characteristic lines, then provides some empirical evidence on the differences in results obtained with the two methods.

Method

Edgeworth [5] advocated the use of mean-absolute-deviation regression in the 1880's, and provided an algorithm. In 1930, Rhodes [14] suggested an improved method. In 1940, Singleton [19] showed that the surface relating the sum of the absolute deviations to the values of the parameters of the regression equation is piecewise linear and convex; he also suggested that the method of steepest descent be used to iterate towards the minimum point. In 1955, Charnes, Cooper and Ferguson [4] showed that the problem could be formulated directly as one of linear programming. In 1959, Wagner [23] presented a method for obtaining a solution more rapidly by treating a slightly transformed version of the dual problem, using a linear programming algorithm designed to accommodate upper bounds directly.

All these methods can fit linear functions in N dimensions—i.e., they can handle problems with more than one independent variable. In 1958, Karst [9] suggested a method for the case of two dimensions—i.e., "simple" regression. The method is iterative, following an essentially arbitrary path; thus the information generated along the way is of little or no interest.

This section describes a new algorithm. Like Karst's, it can only solve problems in

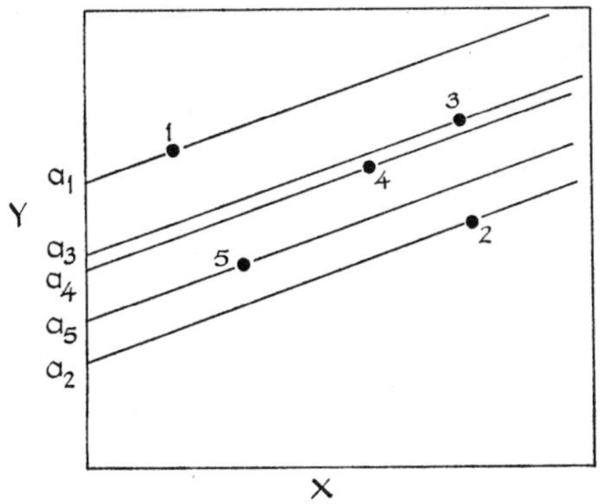

FIGURE 1

two dimensions but is particularly simple to describe, understand and use. Unlike Karst's, it follows a specified path to the solution—one designed to generate information of considerable interest along the way. The algorithm is simple to program, and requires little computer time.

Given a set of N observations of two variables, the objective is to select parameters a and b to minimize:

$$S = \sum_{i=1}^{N} | Y_i - (a + bX_i) | ,$$

where a and b are the intercept and slope, respectively, of the mean-absolute-deviation regression line: $Y = a + bX$.

It is convenient to restrict attention to cases in which N is odd. This guarantees that the median value of Y will be unique. It also simplifies the exposition of the algorithm. Define: $n = (N + 1)/2$. Then the median is the nth value of Y_i, when the values are ordered from largest to smallest. In other words, it is possible to assign $(n - 1)$ values of Y_i to be *above* the median, one value to equal the median, and the other $(n - 1)$ values to be *below* the median. In this context, the terms have the following meanings:

$$[Y_i \textit{ above } M] \rightarrow [Y_i \geqq M],$$

$$[Y_i \textit{ below } M] \rightarrow [Y_i \leqq M].$$

A simple extension provides a solution for the following problem: given some value of b (say, b'), what is the best (minimum-S) intercept? The answer is virtually obvious. The minimum-S line has the characteristics of the median—it must be possible to assign $(n - 1)$ points to be *above* it, one point to be *on* it, and the other $(n - 1)$ points to be *below* it. In this context, the terms have the following meanings:

$$[\text{point } i \textit{ above} \text{ the line}] \rightarrow [Y_i \geqq (a' + b'X_i)],$$

$$[\text{point } i \textit{ on} \text{ the line}] \rightarrow [Y_i = (a' + b'X_i)],$$

$$[\text{point } i \textit{ below} \text{ the line}] \rightarrow [Y_i \leqq (a' + b'X_i)],$$

where a', b' are the parameters of the line.

To find the optimal intercept, a, given a slope b', one could draw a line through each point with the desired slope, as shown in Figure 1. Let a_i be the intercept of the line through point i. Obviously, $a_i = Y_i - b'X_i$, and the desired intercept is simply the median of the a_i-values.

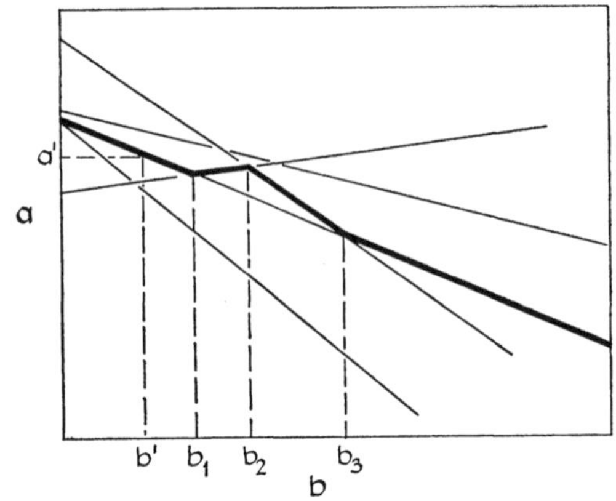

FIGURE 2

It will prove convenient to calculate the value of S associated with such a line by segregating the points. Thus,

$$S = \sum_{i\ above} [Y_i - (a + bX_i)] + \sum_{i\ below} [(a + bX_i) - Y_i]. \quad (1)$$

Rearranging:

$$S = \sum_{i\ above} Y_i - \sum_{i\ below} Y_i + b\Big[\sum_{i\ below} X_i - \sum_{i\ above} X_i\Big] + (N_{below} - N_{above})a,$$

where N_{below} = the number of points below the line, N_{above} = the number of points above the line. But the intercept has been chosen to allow as many points above the line as below. Thus $N_{above} = N_{below} = (n - 1)$, and the final term in equation (1) equals zero, giving

$$S = K_1 + K_2 b, \quad (2)$$

where

$$K_1 = \sum_{i\ above} Y_i - \sum_{i\ below} Y_i\,,$$
$$K_2 = \sum_{i\ below} X_i - \sum_{i\ above} X_i\,.$$

This is, of course, only part of the overall procedure. It remains to determine the optimal value of b. To facilitate this, a diagram of the type shown in Figure 2 can be used. Each point is represented by a line relating a_i to b. Thus the line for point i has the equation: $a_i = Y_i - X_i b$. The optimal intercept for any given value of b is that associated with the nth line from the top. For example, in Figure 2, if $b = b'$, the appropriate value of a is a'. Now, define the *border line* for any given value of b as the nth line from the top. The *border* is simply the set of border lines (in Figure 2, it has been shaded for emphasis). Clearly, the border shows the relationship between a and b when the optimal value of a is selected for each value of b. Moreover, the points associated with lines above the border will be above the associated regression line, while those associated with lines below the border will be below the associated regression line. Thus the terms *above* and *below* in the context of Figure 2 are equivalent to those used in Equation (2).

Over substantial ranges of b, the border line will not change (e.g., from b_1 to b_2 in Figure 2). Within such a range of values, the points *above* and *below* will also be the

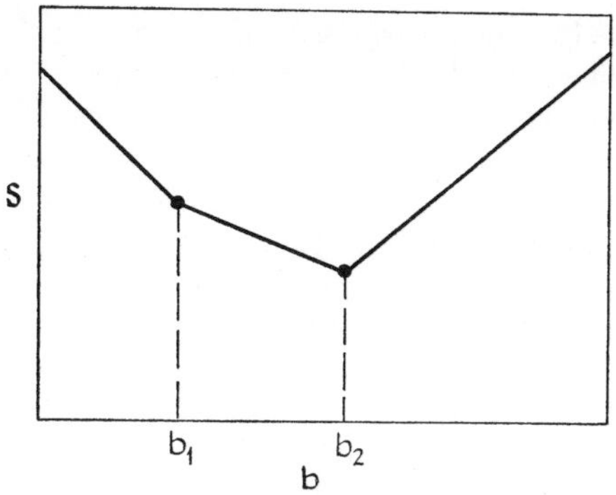

FIGURE 3

same, and the relationship between S and b will be linear, as given by Equation (2). Over the entire range of values, the relationship will be piecewise linear and convex, with each vertex corresponding to a point at which the border line changes, as illustrated in Figure 3.[1]

The overall solution strategy can now be formulated. Any value of b may be chosen at the outset. The associated values of a_i are calculated, the median value found, and all other points assigned to be either *above* or *below*. Then the equation of the corresponding segment of the S, b relationship is calculated, using Equation (2). The sign of K_2 indicates the appropriate direction for the next iteration: if K_2 is positive, only smaller values of b need be considered. If K_2 is negative, only larger values of b need be considered. If K_2 is zero, the initial value of b is a (nonunique) solution.

Having determined a border line and a direction of search, the nearest intersection of the present border line with another should be found. The calculations can be reduced by comparing slopes (i.e., X_i values) to determine whether or not two lines intersect in the region of interest (thus avoiding needless division operations). When the nearest intersection is found, new values of K_1 and K_2 must be computed. This requires little effort: the previous values need only be altered to account for the change in status of two points. If this alteration causes K_2 to change sign, the solution has been obtained and the algorithm can be terminated. If it does not, the nearest intersection of a line with the new border line should be found and the procedure repeated.

To obtain the mean-absolute-deviation regression line as rapidly as possible, it is desirable to begin with a good estimate of the slope (the slope of the least-squares regression line is a likely candidate). But for other reasons it may be desirable to start elsewhere and also to continue the procedure for several iterations after the solution has been found.

In many contexts, the slope of the regression line is of paramount interest. This is generally the case when a characteristic line is being fit to a set of data on security or

[1] Each point in Figure 3 is associated with a particular regression line. Consider any two arbitrary points (b_1, S_1) and (b_2, S_2). The corresponding lines must intersect, since their slopes differ. Now consider all lines which have slopes between the two values and also pass through the point of intersection. Singleton [19] has shown that for such a set of lines, the relationship between S and b will be convex. It follows that for any intermediate value $b' = b_1 + c(b_2 - b_1)$, it is possible to construct a regression line giving a value of S at least as small as $S' = S_1 + c(S_2 - S_1)$. Thus the relationship in Figure 3, which is the lower border of the set of feasible (b, S) values, must be convex.

portfolio returns, since the slope (variously called "volatility," "market sensitivity," or simply "beta") may remain fairly stable over time, while any deviation of the intercept from a specific value dictated by equilibrium conditions is likely to be transitory in nature. To put the matter in terms of curve-fitting, one would like to know how well lines of different slopes fit the available data. In other words, it is useful to consider a sensitivity analysis of the relationship between "fit" and slope.

The algorithm provides this for the case in which degree of fit is measured in terms of absolute deviations. Since the value of S indicates the "unexplained" deviation, a diagram such as Figure 3 presents the desired sensitivity analysis directly.

To see the value of such a procedure, it is useful to consider the manner in which least-squares regression results are reported. The "degree of fit" is usually summarized by a correlation coefficient or its square, the coefficient of determination. The latter is the ratio of (1) "explained" variation in Y at the optimal value of b to (2) the total variation in Y around its mean. The proportion of unexplained variation is, of course, one minus the coefficient of determination, and may be interpreted as:[2]

$$R_{\mathrm{lsr}} = \frac{SSD_{b=b'}}{SSD_{b=0}},$$

where

R_{lsr} = the ratio of unexplained variation for least-squares regression,

$SSD_{b=b'}$ = the sum of the squared deviations around the best (minimum-SSD) line with slope b',

$SSD_{b=0}$ = the sum of the squared deviations around the best (minimum-SSD) line with zero slope,

b' = the slope of the (minimum-SSD) least-squares regression line.

Since the objective in least-squares regression is to minimize the sum of the squared deviations, it is interesting to relate this sum to the value of the slope, assuming that the optimal intercept is chosen in each instance. The relationship will, in fact, be quadratic as illustrated in Figure 4. If the vertical axis is rescaled, with the intercept set equal to one, the minimum point on the curve will equal R_{lsr}, as shown.

Curves such as this are virtually never drawn. The reason is simple: the coefficient of determination and the optimal slope summarize all the relevant information. In terms of the rescaled version of Figure 4, point (0, 1) lies on the curve, as does point (b', R_{lsr}). Moreover, the latter lies at the minimum. These relationships suffice to determine the entire curve.[3] Thus the suggested sensitivity analysis is redundant in the case of least-squares regression.

[2] Since the mean is the value obtained for the intercept in the degenerate case in which the slope (b) is set to zero and the sum of the squared deviations minimized.

[3] Let the equation of the curve be: $R = \alpha + \beta b + \gamma b^2$, since (0, 1) lies on the curve: $\alpha = 1$. And since b' gives the minimum value of R: $b' = -\beta/2\gamma$. Thus, at b': $R = 1 - 2\gamma(b')^2 + \gamma(b')^2$. But at $b = b'$, $R = R_{\mathrm{lsr}}$. Thus:

$$R_{\mathrm{lsr}} = 1 - \gamma(b')^2$$

and

$$\gamma = \frac{1 - R_{\mathrm{lsr}}}{(b')^2}$$

from which it follows that:

$$\gamma = -\frac{2(1 - R_{\mathrm{lsr}})}{b'}$$

and all the parameters are determined.

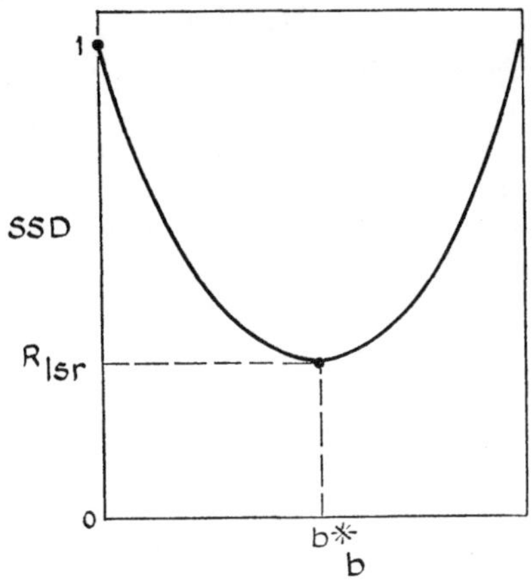

FIGURE 4

This is not the case with mean-absolute-deviation. Since the curve relating S to b is piecewise linear, no single ratio can, in general, provide all the required information. For this reason, examination of at least a portion of the curve in the neighborhood of the optimum slope may prove worthwhile.

The inability of a single ratio to summarize the entire relationship hardly implies that none should be calculated. The appropriate value is obviously:

$$R_{\text{mad}} = \frac{S_{b=b^*}}{S_{b=0}},$$

where

R_{mad} = the ratio of unexplained variation for mean-absolute-deviation regression,
$S_{b=b^*}$ = the sum of the absolute deviations around the best (minimum-S) line with slope b^*,
$S_{b=0}$ = the sum of the absolute deviations around the best (minimum-S) line with zero slope,
b^* = the slope of the (minimum-S) mean-absolute-deviation regression line.

The denominator in this ratio equals the sum of the absolute deviations around the median. Since it must be calculated anyway, it may prove worthwhile to begin the algorithm with $b = 0$, then proceed to the optimal value (b^*). To investigate the behavior of S on both sides of b^*, the procedure can be continued for a few iterations after the optimal point is reached.

Little more need be said about computational methods, except that one must be prepared to deal with cases in which the current border line is intersected by two or more lines at precisely the same point; a simple solution is to merely alter the value of b sufficiently to obtain a unique new border line. It is interesting to note, however, that this algorithm is very similar to one suggested for the selection of portfolios of securities in certain situations [17], and that another variant can determine the line that minimizes the maximum absolute deviation.[4] A computer program able to perform all three tasks could be written without great difficulty.[5]

[4] If the objective is to minimize the maximum absolute deviation, two borders must be considered—one made up of the top-most lines, the other of the bottom-most. The optimal value of b will lie at the point where the borders are closest to one another; the optimal value of a will

Results

At the practical level, two questions arise. First, how much do characteristic lines obtained using mean-absolute-deviation regression differ from those obtained using least-squares regression? Second, in those instances in which substantial differences do arise, which line is better? This section provides evidence on the first question (and thus on the importance of the second). However, the analysis required to answer the second question is beyond the scope of this paper.

Two sets of data were analyzed. The first included returns on each of the 30 common stocks used to compute the Dow-Jones Industrial Average. The second included returns on each of 30 open-end mutual funds (selected randomly from the set of all funds for which data were reported during the period 1964–1970). Returns were computed on a quarterly basis, beginning with the first quarter of 1965 and ending with the first quarter of 1970 (i.e., 21 observations in all).[6]

Standard and Poor's index of 425 common stocks was employed to represent the market. Both dividends and price changes were used to determine returns from the first quarter, 1965 through the first quarter, 1970 inclusive.[7]

Before performing the regression analyses, each value was converted to an *excess return* by subtracting the return on a 90-day treasury bill covering the same period.[8] Excess return is thus the return above (for positive values) or below (for negative values) the return on a riskless investment. In equilibrium, any characteristic line relating excess return on a security or a portfolio to the excess return on the market portfolio is expected to pass through the origin [18]. In practice, of course, nonzero intercepts will occur. But if the market is highly efficient, such occurrences will be random, and none can be expected to persist over a long period of time. For purposes of prediction, the slope of such a characteristic line fit to past data is likely to be far more relevant than the intercept. For purposes of performance measurement, both are relevant. Of course, the importance accorded to either value depends on the extent to which the line fits the data (in statistical terms: the "significance" of the coefficients).

The results of the analyses are shown in Figures 5 through 7. To facilitate the comparison, a 45-degree line has been drawn in each figure.

Figure 5a and 5b show the relationship between the slope of the characteristic line

lie midway between the borders at that point. The objective function will be convex with respect to b, so solution strategies similar to those described here may be employed.

[5] Most of the discussion in [17] and [18] applies to both cases. However, the distinction between a *basis* change and a *border* change is not relevant in the context of mean-absolute-deviation regression. Every border change should be checked to see if a solution has been obtained.

[6] The return for a quarter was based on the closing price (for a stock) or net asset value (for a fund) on the last trading day of the previous quarter. Both dividends and other distributions (e.g., capital gains distributions for funds, the market value of rights for stocks) were included, as well as the difference between the closing price (or net asset value) on the last trading day of the quarter and that on the last trading day of the previous quarter. Stock splits and stock dividends were taken into account by adjusting the data to reflect retention of the new stock. Prices and net asset values were obtained from [24] and [2]. Distributions were obtained from [21] and [12].

[7] The return for a quarter was based on the closing value of the index on the last trading day of the previous quarter. The dividends reported for the index during the quarter were used to determine return as well as the difference between the closing value of the index on the last trading day of the quarter and that on the last trading day of the previous quarter. All data were obtained from [20].

[8] The treasury bill which came due on the day closest to the last trading day of the quarter was used in each case. The return was based on the average of the bid and ask prices on the last trading day of the previous quarter. All data were obtained from [2].

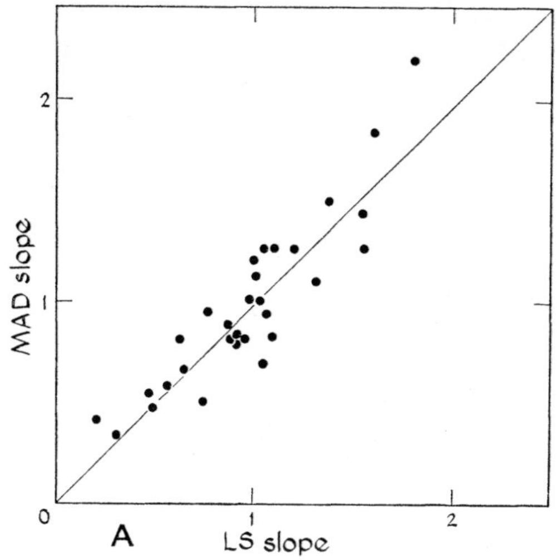

FIGURE 5a. (30 stocks).

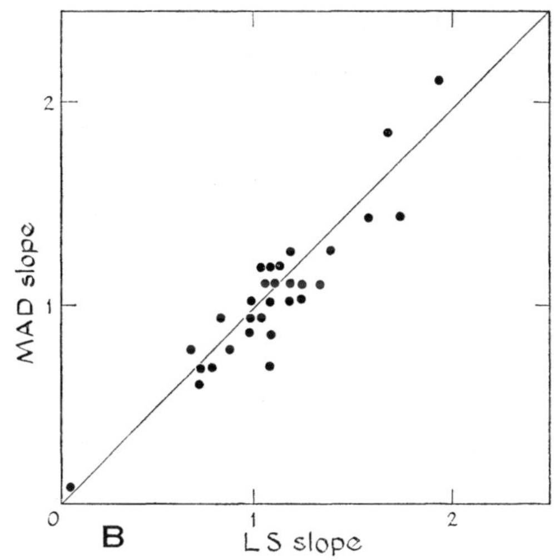

FIGURE 5b. (30 funds).

obtained using least-squares regression (horizontal axis) and that of the line obtained using mean-absolute-deviation regression (vertical axis). The figures show quite clearly that the two methods produce similar results and that the relationship is slightly stronger for the 30 mutual funds (Figure 5b) than for the 30 common stocks (Figure 5a). This is not surprising. Diversification should reduce the variation in return around the characteristic line. Thus the returns for a mutual fund should fall more closely along a line than the returns for a single security, reducing the likelihood that the two regression methods will give substantially different results (if all returns fell precisely along a line, the two methods would give identical results).

Figures 6a and 6b show the relationship between the intercept of the characteristic line obtained using least-squares regression (horizontal axis) and that of the line obtained using mean-absolute-deviation regression (vertical axis). For securities (Figure

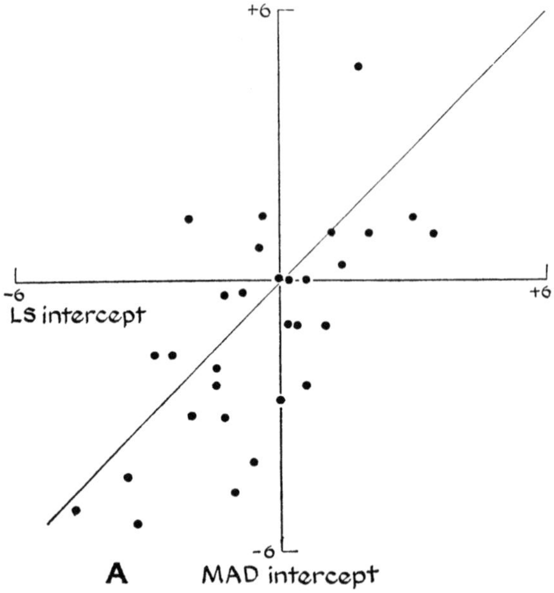

FIGURE 6a. (30 stocks).

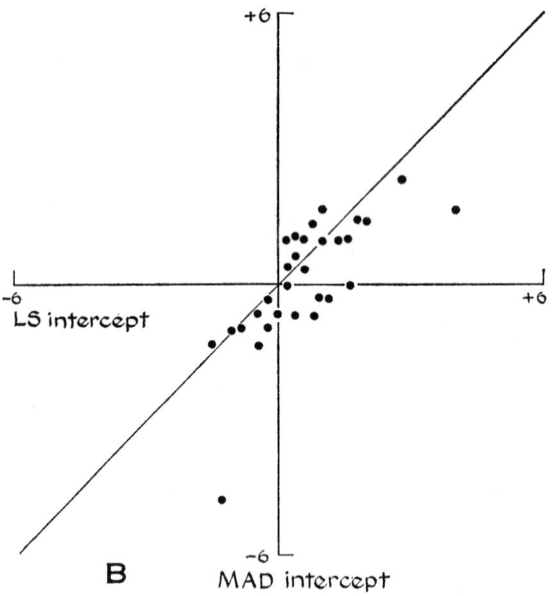

FIGURE 6b. (30 funds).

6a), the relationship is clearly positive, though by no means precise. For funds (Figure 6b), the differences are smaller, as expected.[9]

[9] The lowest point in the third quadrant is clearly an outlier. It represents a speculative fund dealing exclusively in insurance shares, with returns only slightly related to those of the market. Thus it behaves more like a stock than a fund. In statistical terms: the value of the intercept would not be considered significant in this case.

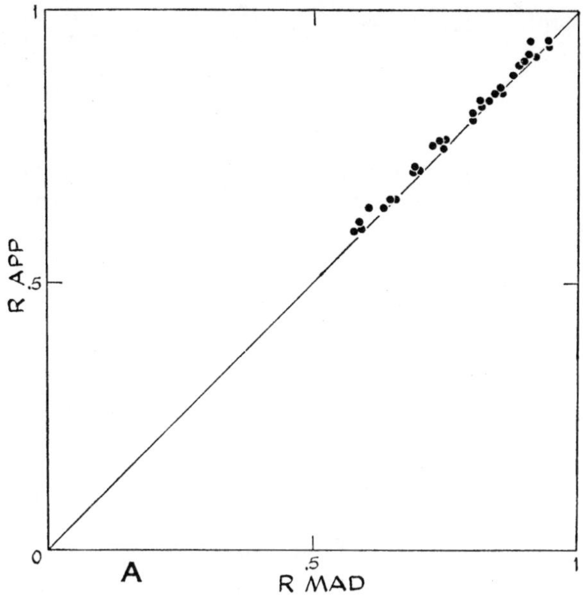

FIGURE 7a. (30 stocks).

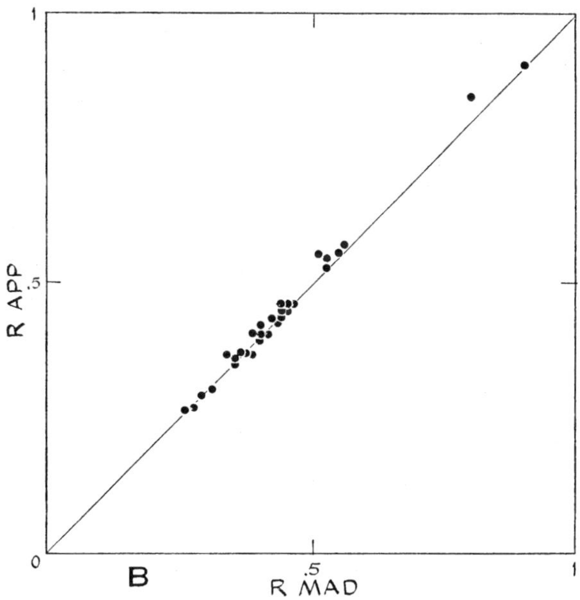

FIGURE 7b. (30 funds).

Figures 7a and 7b provide another view of the slopes obtained using mean-absolute-deviation and least-squares regressions. Assume that mean-absolute-deviation regression is, in fact, the appropriate procedure. In other words: the best slope is the one that minimizes the sum of the absolute deviations. What if one were to use instead the slope obtained with least-squares regression? How much worse would it be? Consider the following measure:

$$R_{\text{app}} = \frac{S_{b=b'}}{S_{b=0}},$$

where

R_{app} = the ratio of unexplained variation measured in terms of the sum of the absolute deviations around the best (minimum-S) line with slope equal to that obtained using least-squares regression,

$S_{b=b'}$ = the sum of the absolute deviations around the best (minimum-S) line with slope b',

$S_{b=0}$ = the sum of the absolute deviations around the best (minimum-S) line with zero slope,

b' = the slope of the (minimum-SSD) least-squares regression line.

Figures 7a and 7b show the relationship between R_{mad} (horizontal axis) and R_{app} (vertical axis). In no case is the latter more than 8 per cent larger than the former; on the average, it is only 1.5 per cent larger. Obviously, the least-squares regression slope is an excellent surrogate for the mean-absolute-deviation regression slope.

Conclusions

The algorithm presented here makes it relatively easy to fit characteristic lines to data on the past returns of securities or portfolios and to evaluate the sensitivity of the fit to the value chosen for the slope of the line. However, the empirical evidence suggests that the need to do this may not be as great as some have supposed. Even if the slope of the mean-absolute-deviation regression line is in some sense the correct one, the slope of the least-squares regression line is a close substitute. With regard to the intercept, the case is not as clear-cut. Values differ substantially when the two methods are used for individual securities. However, the differences are generally much smaller when highly-diversified portfolios are considered. In this connection it is important to note that characteristic lines for individual securities are usually computed in order to determine the characteristic lines for combinations of those securities (either explicitly, for a particular portfolio, or implicitly, for all feasible portfolios, as part of an overall portfolio analysis). Moreover, the intercept of a characteristic line is not likely to be considered significant unless the line fits the data rather well, and in such a case, the two methods generally give similar results.

The observations suggest that the computational advantages[10] of the least-squares procedure may make it the preferred method in this context. No definitive answer can be given at this point, but the evidence indicates that the gains to be derived by obtaining characteristic lines with mean-absolute-deviation regression instead of least-squares regression may be relatively modest.

References

1. *Bank Administration Institute*, "Measuring the Investment Performance of Pension Funds for the Purpose of Inter-Fund Comparison," Bank Administration Institute, Park Ridge, Ill. (1968).

[10] Fitting a line to given data is, of course, somewhat simpler using least-squares. Perhaps more important, the characteristic line obtained for a portfolio will be related in a simple manner to the lines obtained for the component securities. The intercept of the portfolio's characteristic line will be a weighted average of the intercepts of the lines of the component securities, with the proportions invested used as weights. A similar relationship will hold for the slopes. No such simple relationships hold for mean-absolute-deviation characteristic lines.

2. *Bank and Quotation Record*, various dates.
3. BLUME II, MARSHALL E., "The Assessment of Portfolio Performance: An Application of Portfolio Theory," Doctoral Dissertation, University of Chicago, March 1968.
4. CHARNES, A., COOPER, W. W. AND FERGUSON, R. O., "Optimal Estimation of Executive Compensation by Linear Programming," *Management Science* (1955), pp. 138–151.
5. EDGEWORTH, F. Y., "A New Method for Reducing Observations Relating to Several Quantities," *Philosophical Magazine* (5th Ser.), Vol. 24 (1887), pp. 222–223; Vol. 25 (1888), pp. 184–191.
6. FAMA, EUGENE F., "Portfolio Analysis in a Stable Paretian Market," *Management Science* (January 1965), pp. 404–419.
7. ——, "The Behavior of Stock Market Prices," *Journal of Business* (January 1965), pp. 34–105.
8. JENSEN, MICHAEL C., "Risk, the Pricing of Capital Assets, and the Evaluation of Investment Portfolios," *Journal of Business* (April 1969), pp. 167–247.
9. KARST, OTTO J., "Linear Curve Fitting Using Least Deviations," *Journal of the American Statistical Association* (March 1958), pp. 118–132.
10. MANDELBROT, BENOIT, "The Variation of Certain Speculative Prices," *Journal of Business* (1963), pp. 394–419.
11. MARKOWITZ, HARRY, *Portfolio Selection: Efficient Diversification of Investments*, John Wiley and Sons, New York, 1959.
12. *Moody's Dividend Record*, various dates.
13. O'BRIEN, JOHN W., "Practical Applications of Market Theory," *Financial Analysts' Journal* (July–August 1970), pp. 91–103.
14. RHODES, E. C., "Reducing Observations by the Method of Minimum Deviations," *Philosophical Magazine* (7th Ser.), Vol. 9 (1930), pp. 974–992.
15. SARGENT, THOMAS J. "Regressions in the Context of Stable Disturbances," *National Bureau of Economic Research Forty-Ninth Annual Report* (October 1969), pp. 107–108.
16. SHARPE, WILLIAM F., "Capital Asset Prices: A Theory of Market Equilibrium Under Conditions of Risk," *Journal of Finance* (September 1964), pp. 425–442.
17. ——, "A Linear Programming Algorithm for Mutual Fund Portfolio Selection," *Management Science* (March 1967), pp. 499–510.
18. ——, *Portfolio Theory and Capital Markets*, McGraw-Hill Book Company, New York, 1970.
19. SINGLETON, ROBERT R., "A Method for Minimizing the Sum of Absolute Values of Deviations," *Annals of Mathematical Statistics*, Vol. 11 (1940), pp. 301–310.
20. *Standard and Poor's Analyst's Handbook: Supplement*, various dates.
21. *Standard and Poor's Dividend Record*, varous dates.
22. TREYNOR, JACK L., "How to Rate Management of Investment Funds," *Harvard Business Review* (January–February 1965), pp. 63–75.
23. WAGNER, H. M., "Linear Programming Techniques for Regression Analysis," *Journal of the American Statistical Association* (March 1959), pp. 206–212.
24. *The Wall Street Journal*, various dates.
25. WIGINTON, JOHN C., "Portfolio Analysis Under the Stable Paretian Hypothesis: An Empirical Evaluation," York University Capital Markets Research Programme working paper.
26. WISE, JOHN, "Linear Estimators for Linear Regression Systems Having Infinite Residual Variances," *Berkeley-Stanford Mathematical Economics Seminar* (October 1963).

JOURNAL OF FINANCIAL AND QUANTITATIVE ANALYSIS
June 1974

IMPUTING EXPECTED SECURITY RETURNS FROM PORTFOLIO COMPOSITION

William F. Sharpe*

I. Introduction

The normative procedures of Markowitz [4], Sharpe [6], and others can be utilized to determine an optimal portfolio (set of security holdings) given estimates of risk, relevant constraints, and expected returns on securities. Building on these foundations, the positive models of Sharpe [7], Lintner [3], Mossin [5], and others assume that investors form portfolios as if they were following such procedures. We observe considerable differences in portfolio composition, some of which undoubtedly stem from differences in expectations. Yet the predictions of most investors are either made implicitly or, if made explicitly, are jealously guarded and hence cannot be observed by outsiders.

This paper shows how some crude estimates of an investment organization's expected returns might be imputed from its holdings of securities. Such values could prove interesting to others if in fact they represent the true expectations reasonably well. Alternatively, the organization could utilize such estimates itself in an iterative manner to improve its portfolio. Given a set of holdings, the implicit expected returns could be computed, then shown to the organization's analysts. Discrepancies could be used to suggest modifications in relative holdings. The revised portfolio could then be subjected to the same analysis, leading to a new set of implicit expected returns with the process repeated as many times as appears useful.

---

*Timken Professor of Finance, Stanford University. Extremely helpful comments on an earlier draft of this paper were provided by an anonymous referee a and by Professor Robert Litzenberger of Stanford University.

II. The Procedure

The standard portfolio selection problem can be stated as follows:

Select $X_1, X_2, \ldots, X_n$

to maximize $E_P - \lambda V_P$

where $$E_P = \sum_{i=1}^{N} X_i E_i$$

$$V_P = \sum_{i=1}^{N} \sum_{j=1}^{N} X_i X_j C_{ij}$$

subject to $$\sum_{j=1}^{N} a_{kj} X_j = b_k \quad \text{for } k = 1, \ldots, M.$$

X_i represents the proportion of the portfolio's initial value invested in security i; E_i is the expected return on security i; C_{ij} is the covariance between the returns on securities i and j; and the values of a_{kj} and b_k define M linear constraints.

In general, portfolio selection problems involve inequality constraints, including nonnegativity constraints on the X_i's. Moreover, the value of λ is usually varied parametrically through all nonnegative values. However, the *solution*, once determined, can be characterized as the solution to a problem of the form given here, with λ interpreted as a constant. Inequality constraints not binding in the solution are simply omitted from the expression of the problem; those that were binding are included as equalities. Variables selected to be zero due to nonnegativity constraints are omitted from the expression of the problem.

Rewriting the statement of the problem as a Lagrangean function:

$$Z = E_P - \lambda V_P + \sum_{k=1}^{M} \lambda_k \left(b_k - \sum_{j=1}^{N} a_{kj} X_j\right)$$

where λ_k represents the shadow-price of the k'th constraint.

The partial derivative of Z with respect to each of the X_i values must, of course, be zero at the solution:

$$\frac{\partial Z}{\partial X_1} = E_i - \frac{\partial V_p}{\partial X_i}\lambda - \sum_{k=1}^{M} a_{ki}\lambda_k = 0.$$

Thus,

$$E_i = \frac{\partial V_p}{\partial X_i}\lambda + \sum_{k=1}^{M} a_{ki}\lambda_k.$$

Given estimates of $\partial V_p/\partial X_i$, λ, the a_{ki}'s and λ_k's at the solution, the implied value of E_i is readily determined.

Securities not included in the portfolio may not have been analyzed by the organization at all. If so, no implied expected return may be appropriate. However, it may still be worthwhile to compute a bound on the expected return that would have led to zero holdings (assuming negative holdings or short sales were precluded). This result is consistent with the solution if:

$$\frac{\partial Z}{\partial X_i} \leq 0.$$

It follows that the implied expected return must satisfy:

$$E_i \leq \frac{\partial V_p}{\partial X_i}\lambda + \sum_{k=1}^{M} a_{ki}\lambda_k.$$

III. A Special Case

Consider the following special case. Each security's return is assumed to conform to a simple "market model":

$$\tilde{R}_i = \alpha_i + \beta_{im}\tilde{R}_m + \tilde{c}_i$$

where $\tilde{R}_i$ is the return on security i; $\tilde{R}_m$ is the return on a market portfolio[1];

[1]Under the conditions assumed in this section $\tilde{R}_m$ cannot in fact be the return on a portfolio composed of all securities in the market, since the residual terms $\tilde{c}_i$ would then have to be slightly negatively correlated on

α_i and β_{im} are constants; and $\tilde{c}_i$ is a random variable. Moreover, assume that:

$$\exp(\tilde{c}_i) = 0 \qquad \text{for every } i,$$

$$\text{cov}(\tilde{c}_i, \tilde{R}_m) = 0 \qquad \text{for every } i,$$

$$\text{cov}(\tilde{c}_i, \tilde{c}_j) = 0 \qquad \text{for every } i \neq j.$$

This implies that:

$$\tilde{R}_p = \sum_{i=1}^{N} X_i \tilde{R}_i = \sum_{i=1}^{N} X_i (\alpha_i + \beta_{im}\tilde{R}_m + \tilde{c}_i)$$

$$= \left(\sum_{i=1}^{N} X_i \alpha_i\right) + \left(\sum_{i=1}^{N} X_i \beta_{im}\right) \tilde{R}_m + \sum_{i=1}^{N} X_i \tilde{c}_i, \text{ and}$$

$$\text{var}(\tilde{R}_p) = \beta_{pm}^2 \, \text{var}(\tilde{R}_m) + \sum_{i=1}^{N} X_i^2 \, \text{var}(\tilde{c}_i)$$

where $\beta_{pm} \equiv \sum_{i=1}^{N} X_i \beta_{im}$.

Therefore,

$$\frac{\partial V_p}{\partial X_i} = 2\beta_{pm}\beta_{im} \, \text{var}(\tilde{R}_m) + 2X_i \, \text{var}(\tilde{c}_i).$$

Now, assume that only the "full investment" constraint is binding at the solution (except possibly nonnegativity constraints on variables omitted from the problem as stated):

$$\sum_{i=1}^{N} X_i = 1.$$

---

average. Formally, $\tilde{R}_m$ may be considered the value of some "market factor." Alternatively, the assumed lack of correlation among the $\tilde{c}_i$'s can be regarded as a useful approximation. On this point, see Fama [2] and Beja [1].

Then,

$$E_i = [2\beta_{pm}\beta_{im} \operatorname{var}(\tilde{R}_m) + 2X_i \operatorname{var}(\tilde{c}_i)]\,\lambda + \lambda_1.$$

Assume further that holdings include some amount invested in a riskless asset with (observable) return π. For this asset:

$$E_i = \pi = 0\lambda + \lambda_1.$$

Thus,

$$\lambda_1 = \pi.$$

It follows that for every asset held:

$$E_i - \pi = [2\beta_{pm}\beta_{im} \operatorname{var}(\tilde{R}_m) + 2X_i \operatorname{var}(\tilde{c}_i)]\,\lambda.$$

Historical values of β_{im}, $\operatorname{var}(\tilde{c}_i)$, and $\operatorname{var}(\tilde{R}_m)$ might be employed to obtain crude estimates of the relevant *ex ante* values. The only value required to complete the analysis would then be λ: the magnitude of the trade-off between expected return and variance at the solution. Multiplying the previous equation by X_i and summing:

$$\sum_i X_i (E_i - \pi) = \lambda \left\{ \sum_i X_i [2\beta_{pm}\beta_{im} \operatorname{var}(\tilde{R}_m) + 2X_i \operatorname{var}(\tilde{c}_i)] \right\}.$$

The term to the left of the equal sign is, of course, the portfolio's expected excess return, while the term to the right is (under the assumed conditions) simple λ times $2V_p$. Thus,

$$\lambda = \frac{E_p - \pi}{2V_p}.$$

Substituting:

$$E_i - \pi = [\beta_{pm}\beta_{im} \operatorname{var}(\tilde{R}_m) + X_i \operatorname{var}(\tilde{c}_i)] \left(\frac{E_p - \pi}{V_p} \right)$$

Rearranging, and substituting the formula for V_p:

$$\frac{E_i - \pi}{E_p - \pi} = \frac{\beta_{pm}\beta_{im}\operatorname{var}(\tilde{R}_m) + X_i \operatorname{var}(\tilde{c}_i)}{\beta_{pm}^2 \operatorname{var}(\tilde{R}_m) + \sum_{j=1}^{N} X_j^2 \operatorname{var}(\tilde{c}_j)} \equiv F_i .$$

As shown, using estimates for the key components of risk and the composition of the portfolio, it is possible to obtain an estimate of F_i: the expected excess return of a security relative to that of the chosen portfolio, assuming of course that the holdings are in fact optimal and that all other assumed conditions apply.[2]

To obtain an absolute measure of expected excess return, one must also assign a value to $(E_p - \pi)$.

It is also possible to compare the implied expected return for a security with that consistent with an efficient market (e.g., "correct" pricing of the security). According to the Capital Asset Pricing Model of Sharpe [7], Lintner [3], and Mossin [5], the expected return, E_i^*, should satisfy:

$$E_i^* - \pi = \beta_{im}(E_m - \pi).$$

While the implied expected excess return is:

$$E_i - \pi = F_i(E_p - \pi).$$

Subtracting the former equation from the latter yields:

$$E_i - E_i^* \equiv A_i = F_i E_p - \beta_{im} E_m - (F_i - \beta_{im})\pi.$$

This is the implicit expected *abnormal* return, i.e., that attributable to the degree of mispricing expected to be corrected within the prediction period. To calculate such a value, of course, one must assume values for both E_p and E_m.

---

[2] It is a simple matter to prove that the weighted average, $\sum_{i=1}^{N} X_i F_i$, will equal one.

An alternative formulation is the following:

$$A_i = \left[(F_i \beta_{pm} - \beta_{im}) \; (E_m - \pi) \right] + F_i A_p$$

where A_i is the "abnormal" expected return for security i and A_p is the abnormal expected return for the selected portfolio. The weighted average value for the first term is zero, while that of the second is A_p. In general, the second term will dominate the first and account for the majority of expected abnormal performance.

Figure I illustrates the use of this formula. Holdings of a large institution at the end of 1971 were analyzed, using historical values of price-relatives over the previous 60 months as estimates of the key components of risk.[3] The expected excess return on the market portfolio was assumed to be 5 percent per year, and the expected abnormal performance on the portfolio to be 1 percent per year. As shown, there was little correlation between imputed abnormal performance and proportion invested. Rankings of securities on the basis of imputed abnormal performance, using the method given here, are likely to differ significantly from rankings based solely on amount invested.

Some further notion of the magnitudes involved may be obtained by rewriting the basic relationship:

$$\frac{E_i - \pi}{E_p - \pi} = F_i = \frac{\beta_{pm}\beta_{im}\mathrm{var}(\tilde{R}_m) + X_i \; \mathrm{var}(\tilde{c}_i)}{\mathrm{var}(\tilde{R}_p)}$$

$$= \frac{\beta_{pm}^2 \mathrm{var}(\tilde{R}_m)}{\mathrm{var}(\tilde{R}_p)} \cdot \frac{\beta_{im}}{\beta_{pm}} + X_i \frac{\mathrm{var}(\tilde{c}_i)}{\mathrm{var}(\tilde{R}_p)}$$

Let r represent the correlation coefficient between $\tilde{R}_p$ and $\tilde{R}_m$. Under the assumed conditions:

---

[3]Values were obtained from the December 1971 "Beta Book" published by Merrill Lynch, Pierce, Fenner and Smith.

FIGURE I

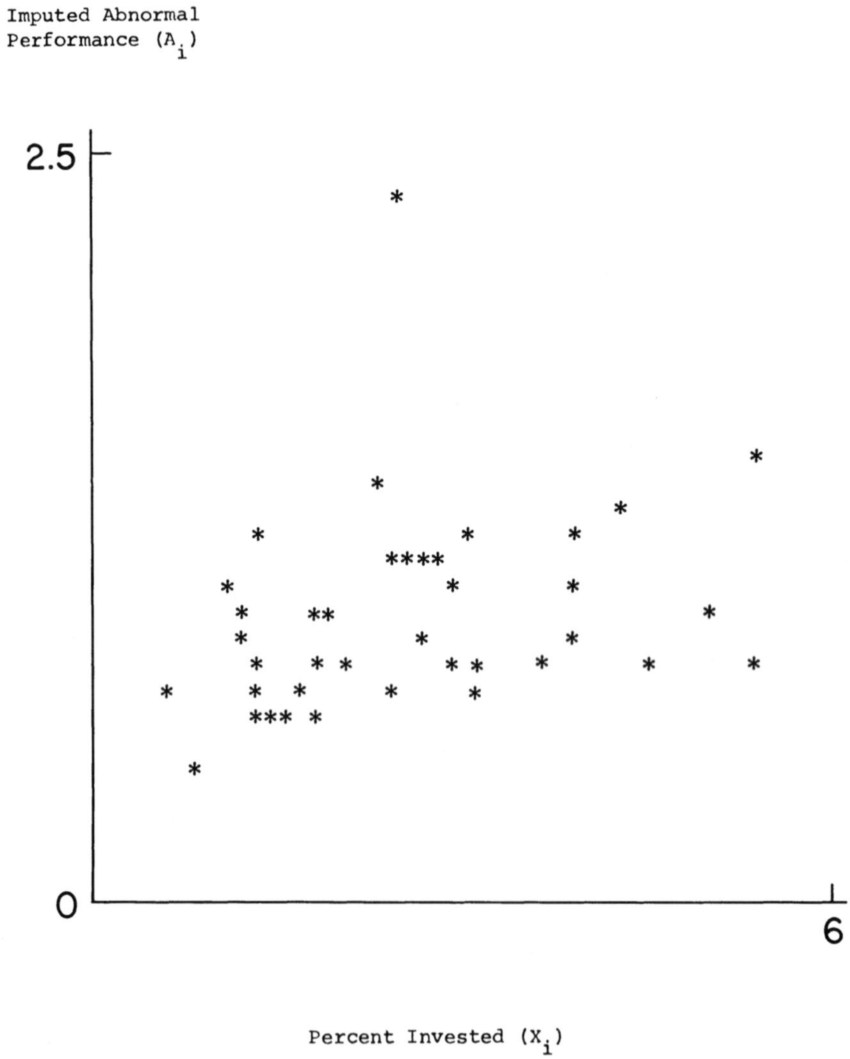

$$r^2 = \frac{\beta_{pm}^2 \ \mathrm{var}(\tilde{R}_m)}{\mathrm{var}(\tilde{R}_p)} .$$

Thus,[4]

$$F_i = r^2 \frac{\beta_{im}}{\beta_{pm}} + X_i \frac{\mathrm{var}(\tilde{c}_i)}{\mathrm{var}(\tilde{R}_m)} \cdot \frac{r^2}{\beta_{pm}^2}$$

For a typical common stock $\mathrm{var}(\tilde{c}_i)$ might be approximately twice as large as $\mathrm{var}(\tilde{R}_m)$. For a highly diversified portfolio with β_{pm} close to 1, the ratio (r^2/β_{pm}^2) will be relatively close to one. Thus the second term might be twice the size of the holdings. Under these conditions:

$$F_i \simeq r^2 \frac{\beta_{im}}{\beta_{pm}} + 2X_i .$$

Note that the first term is r^2 times the efficient market equilibrium value for the ratio of $(E_i - \pi)$ to $(E_p - \pi)$. The second term indicates the major departure from equilibrium pricing implied by the portfolio composition. This term will generally be small for securities in a well-diversified portfolio[5]. Extensive diversification implies relatively small differences between the relative expected security returns implied by market efficiency and those expected by the organization's analysts (or, as suggested by Treynor and Black [8], estimates of expected return obtained by multiplying analysts' predicted abnormal returns by a figure reflecting their predictive accuracy, then adding the result to the value consistent with market efficiency).

---

[4] Note that $\mathrm{var}(\tilde{c}_i)$ and $\mathrm{var}(\tilde{R}_m)$ need not be estimated separately in this connection; an estimate of the ratio of the former to the latter will suffice.

[5] Note that the value of F_i will, under these conditions, be relatively insensitive to minor deviations of X_i from its intended value.

IV. Conclusions

These procedures are hardly likely to unlock all the secrets of professional investment organizations, or to vastly improve their efficiency in portfolio selection. However, some modest gains may be facilitated on one or both fronts.

REFERENCES

[1] Beja, Avraham. "On Systematic and Unsystematic Components of Risk." *Journal of Finance*, March 1972.

[2] Fama, Eugene F. "Risk, Return and Equilibrium, Some Clarifying Comments." *Journal of Finance*, March 1968.

[3] Lintner, John. "The Valuation of Risk Assets and the Selection of Risky Investments in Stock Portfolios and Capital Budgets." *Review of Economics and Statistics*, February 1965.

[4] Markowitz, Harry. *Portfolio Selection: Efficient Diversification of Investments.* New York: John Wiley and Sons, Inc., 1959.

[5] Mossin, Jan. "Equilibrium in a Capital Asset Market." *Econometrica*, October 1966.

[6] Sharpe, William F. "A Simplified Model for Portfolio Analysis." *Management Science*, January 1963.

[7] ________________. "Capital Asset Prices: A Theory of Market Equilibrium under Conditions of Risk." *Journal of Finance*, September 1964.

[8] Treynor, Jack L., and Fischer Black. "How to Use Security Analysis to Improve Portfolio Selection." *Journal of Business*, January 1973.

AN ALGORITHM FOR PORTFOLIO IMPROVEMENT

W. F. Sharpe

I. THE PORTFOLIO IMPROVEMENT PROBLEM

The portfolio selection problem (as described in, e.g., [8, 15]) can be written:

$$\max_{X_1,\ldots,X_N} \quad z = E - \lambda V \tag{1a}$$

subject to

$$\sum_{i=1}^{N} X_i = 1 \tag{1b}$$

$$L_i \le X_i \le U_i \qquad \text{for} \quad i = 1, \ldots, N \tag{1c}$$

Advances in Mathematical Programming and Financial Planning,
Vol. 1, pages 155–169.

ISBN: 0-89232-582-8

where

$$E = \sum_{i=1}^{N} X_i E_i$$

$$V = \sum_{i=1}^{N} \sum_{j=1}^{N} X_i X_j C_{ij}$$

X_i = the proportion of the portfolio invested in security i
N = the number of securities to be considered
E_i = the expected return on security i
E = the expected return on the portfolio
C_{ij} = the covariance between the returns on securities i and j
V = the variance of the return on the portfolio
λ = a coefficient indicating the investor's risk aversion
z = the portfolio's certainty-equivalent return
L_i = a lower bound (typically, zero) on the proportion of the portfolio invested in security i
U_i = an upper bound on the proportion of the portfolio invested in security i (in some cases, not used or set to a large number)

In many applications, additional linear constraints are included.

In practice most portfolio problems require the revision of a preexisting portfolio. Moreover, some sort of penalty (e.g., for transactions costs) is associated with changes in holdings. This can be represented by expanding the objective function to

$$Z = z - \sum_{i=1}^{N} \{|X_i - H_i| t_i\} \tag{2}$$

where H_i = the initial proportion of the portfolio invested in security i
t_i = the "turnover penalty" per unit of change in the proportion of the portfolio invested in security i

Such a formulation can be represented without the explicit use of absolute values by adding new variables and linear constraints, as shown in [9].

Portfolio problems are special cases of the more general class of quadratic programming problems. However, three attributes are important. In their natural form, such problems involve a very dense matrix of quadratic coefficients (i.e., most or all of the C_{ij}'s are nonzero). Moreover, the constraints are extremely simple [e.g., (1b) and (1c)]. Finally, such problems are large: in practical applications it is common for as many as 500 securities to be considered eligible for inclusion in a portfolio.

II. PREVIOUS APPROACHES

Some practitioners have employed general-purpose quadratic programming codes [7, 10, 11, 18] for portfolio problems of modest size (e.g., up to 100 securities). However, much effort has been devoted to simplifying the quadratic portion of the problem to allow the use of algorithms designed to take advantage of the resulting structure.

Most security returns are correlated, thus $C_{ij} \neq 0$ for the vast majority of pairs i, j. However, it is not a simple matter to estimate the $(N^2 + N)/2$ values of *future* covariances that are relevant in this context. Historic data may yield unbiased estimates but such values may still be subject to sampling errors which can be exacerbated when operated upon by an optimizing algorithm. This suggests the need to employ simplified models of the relationships among security returns to provide useful estimates of the C_{ij}s, even if all such values are to be employed explicitly in the optimization phase. A number of analyses of the stochastic behavior of security returns, which can meet this need, have been reported (see, e.g., [1, 5, 6, 12]).

Given a simplified model of the relationships among security returns, it is generally possible to replace (1a) with a simpler relationship (usually, accompanied by the introduction of new variables and constraints), and then to design an algorithm that can efficiently solve the resulting special case of the portfolio problem. A number of approaches of this sort have been developed (see, e.g., [2, 3, 4, 13, 14, 16, 17]).

Unfortunately, many of these special-purpose algorithms are just that—they do not adapt easily to accommodate a different model of covariance relationships. Since some of the underlying models (most notably, [14]) are excessively limiting, practitioners have tended to invoke side constraints on holdings (e.g., tight upper bounds on individual security holdings, range limits on the amounts invested in particular economic sectors, and/or industries) to compensate for known or suspected inadequacies in the representation of return covariances.

We propose a different approach, choosing to exploit the simplicity of the constraints, while accepting as much complexity as desired in the covariance matrix. Although our general approach can easily be adapted to exploit simplified covariance models, in this paper we will deal only with a version designed to handle a full covariance matrix. We also emphasize the revision problem [as in [2)] although our algorithm solves the selection problem as a special case in which all $t_i = 0$. Only constraints (1b) and (1c) are accommodated but, as will be shown, additional aspects of practical problems can be handled by prior adjustment of the coefficients in the objective function. We will show that the approach, like some recent algorithms developed by Elton and Gruber [2, 3, 4] has desirable properties in terms of user acceptance and can also be adapted for interactive use by portfolio managers. Preliminary tests suggest that computer cost should be relatively small, making the algorithm well worth consideration.

III. THE BASIC APPROACH

The general idea behind the algorithm is embarrassingly simple—so much so that there can be no doubt that it has occurred to others and possibly been implemented in this context. However, the continuing stream of papers describing approaches requiring highly simplified models of return covariances suggests that the efficiency with which the approach can be implemented is not widely known.

Each iteration of the algorithm is designed to improve a previous feasible portfolio. Most cases begin with an actual portfolio meeting constraints (1b) and (1c). In the rare instance in which the initial portfolio is infeasible, straightforward procedures can usually be designed to obtain an initial feasible portfolio with minimum transactions costs.

Given a feasible portfolio $(X_1, \ldots, X_N)$ it is a simple matter to determine the locally optimal revision. Constraint (1b) requires that every decrease in one or more of the X_is be offset by an equal increase in one or more of the others. All securities for which $X_i < U_i$ are candidates for increased holdings while all securities for which $X_i > L_i$ are candidates for decreased holdings. If security i is increased from X_i to $X_i + \Delta$, where Δ is small, the objective function will be changed by an amount:

$$\Delta Z \approx \frac{\partial Z}{\partial X_i} \Delta$$

Similarly, if security i is decreased from X_i to $X_i - \Delta$, where Δ is small, the objective function will be changed by an amount

$$\Delta Z \approx -\frac{\partial Z}{\partial X_i} \Delta$$

Given constraint (1b), for small changes, the maximum improvement in Z will be obtained by (1) increasing X_i for the security among those eligible for an increase that gives the largest value of $\partial Z/\partial X_i$ and (2) decreasing X_i for the security among those eligible for a decrease that gives the (algebraically) smallest value of $\partial Z/\partial X_i$. If the value of $\partial Z/\partial X_i$

for the former security is less than or equal to that for the latter, no further improvement is possible and the optimal portfolio has been found. Otherwise the portfolio can be improved by changing the holdings of the two securities in the selected directions.

While this procedure selects the locally optimal change for each iteration, there remains the issue of the appropriate magnitude for the actual change. We adopt the following rule: Select Δ to maximize the increment ΔZ, subject to limits imposed by upper and lower bounds on holdings and the requirements of continuity. More explicitly, note from (2) that:

$$\Delta Z = \begin{cases} \Delta z - t_i\Delta & \text{for} \quad X_i > H_i \quad \text{(3a)} \\ \Delta z + t_i\Delta & \text{for} \quad X_i < H_i \quad \text{(3b)} \end{cases}$$

where $\Delta Z =$ the increment in Z
$\Delta z =$ the increment in z
$\Delta =$ the increment in X_i

Although Δz is continuous in Δ, relations (3) restrict the range over which ΔZ is continuous in Δ. This can be handled by imposing a bound, Δ_i, on the change as follows:

Current value of X_i	X_i to be	Δ_i	
$H_i \le X_i < U_i$	increased	$U_i - X_i$	(4a)
$H_i < X_i \le U_i$	decreased	$X_i - H_i$	(4b)
$L_i \le X_i < H_i$	increased	$H_i - X_i$	(4c)
$L_i < X_i \le H_i$	decreased	$X_i - L_i$	(4d)

Assume that in the selection phase, security $\imath$ has been chosen for increased holdings and security $\jmath$ has been chosen for decreased holdings. Formulas (3) can be utilized to find the value of Δ that would maximize the net increment ΔZ, disregarding bounds and continuity requirements. Formula (3a) is applicable if $X_i > H_i$ or if $X_i = H_i$ and X_i is to be increased. Formula (3b) is applicable if $X_i < H_i$ or if $X_i = H_i$ and X_i is to be decreased. Let Δ^* be the value of Δ that maximizes ΔZ, disregarding bounds and continuity. Then the actual increment is determined by

$$\Delta = \min(\Delta^*, \Delta_\imath, \Delta_\jmath) \tag{5}$$

After Δ is determined, the portfolio is revised accordingly

$$X_i \leftarrow X_i + \Delta$$

$$X_{\mathcal{J}} \leftarrow X_{\mathcal{J}} - \Delta$$

completing the iteration.

V. THE ALGORITHM

Figure 1 shows the main steps of the algorithm. The remainder of this section provides additional details concerning some of the procedures.

A. Computing $S_1, \ldots, S_N$

Since the covariance matrix is large, it is important to avoid its repeated use. Moreover, in many computer systems the matrix must be stored in slow-speed (e.g., disk) storage due to limited space in high-speed storage. For these reasons, the algorithm relies on a series of sums of the form[1]

$$S_i = \sum_{j=1}^{N} X_j C_{ij} \tag{6}$$

These are computed once at the beginning of the procedure, using the entire covariance matrix, a row at a time. They are revised after each iteration, but as will be seen, only two rows of the covariance matrix are needed to perform this task.

B. Selecting Securities for the Revision

Note that

$$\partial V/\partial X_i = 2S_i$$

Thus

$$\partial z/\partial X_i = E_i - 2\lambda S_i$$

The selection criteria can thus be written

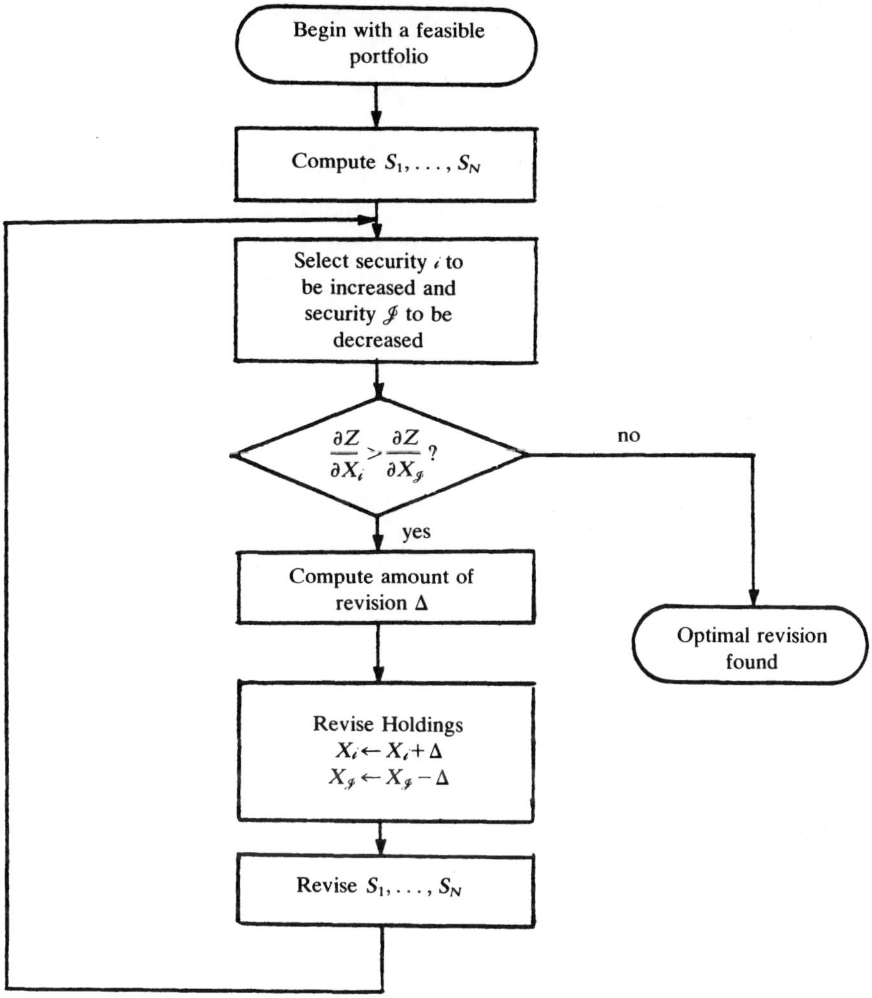

Figure 1.

For the security to be *increased*:

- for all i such that $X_i < U_i$
- select i to maximize: (7a)

$$\partial Z/\partial X_i = \begin{cases} E_i - 2\lambda S_i - t_i & \text{for} \quad X_i \geq H_i \\ E_i - 2\lambda S_i + t_i & \text{for} \quad X_i < H_i \end{cases}$$

For the security to be *decreased*:

- for all j such that $X_j > L_j$ (7b)

- select $\mathcal{J}$ to minimize:

$$\partial Z/\partial X_{\mathcal{J}} = \begin{cases} E_{\mathcal{J}} - 2\lambda S_{\mathcal{J}} - t_{\mathcal{J}} & \text{for} \quad X_{\mathcal{J}} > H \\ E_{\mathcal{J}} - 2\lambda S_{\mathcal{J}} + t_{\mathcal{J}} & \text{for} \quad X_{\mathcal{J}} \leq H \end{cases}$$

C. Computing the Amount of the Revision

Assume that the test for revision is met, that is, $\partial Z/\partial X_{\mathcal{i}} > \partial Z/\partial X_{\mathcal{J}}$. For the revision, we consider changes of the form

$$X_{\mathcal{i}} \leftarrow X_{\mathcal{i}} + \Delta$$

$$X_{\mathcal{J}} \leftarrow X_{\mathcal{J}} - \Delta$$

The change in z will be

$$\Delta z = \Delta(E_{\mathcal{i}} - E_{\mathcal{J}}) - 2\lambda\Delta \sum_{k=1}^{N} X_k C_{\mathcal{i}k} + 2\lambda\Delta \sum_{k=1}^{N} X_k C_{\mathcal{J}k}$$
$$- \Delta^2\lambda(C_{\mathcal{i}\mathcal{i}} - 2C_{\mathcal{i}\mathcal{J}} + C_{\mathcal{J}\mathcal{J}})$$

Substituting (6),

$$\Delta z = \Delta(E_{\mathcal{i}} - E_{\mathcal{J}}) - 2\lambda\Delta S_{\mathcal{i}} + 2\lambda\Delta S_{\mathcal{J}} - \Delta^2(C_{\mathcal{i}\mathcal{i}} - 2C_{\mathcal{i}\mathcal{J}} + C_{\mathcal{J}\mathcal{J}}) \tag{8}$$

Now, let

$$T_{\mathcal{i}} = \begin{cases} t_{\mathcal{i}} & \text{if} \quad X_{\mathcal{i}} \geq H_{\mathcal{i}} \\ -t_{\mathcal{i}} & \text{if} \quad X_{\mathcal{i}} < H_{\mathcal{i}} \end{cases}$$

$$T_{\mathcal{J}} = \begin{cases} t_{\mathcal{J}} & \text{if} \quad X_{\mathcal{J}} > H_{\mathcal{J}} \\ -t_{\mathcal{J}} & \text{if} \quad X_{\mathcal{J}} \leq H_{\mathcal{J}} \end{cases}$$

From (3)

$$\Delta Z = \Delta z - T_{\mathcal{i}}\Delta + T_{\mathcal{J}}\Delta$$

Substituting (7) and rewriting:

$$\Delta Z = \Delta[(E_{\mathcal{i}} - E_{\mathcal{J}}) - 2\lambda(S_{\mathcal{i}} - S_{\mathcal{J}}) - (T_{\mathcal{i}} - T_{\mathcal{J}})] - \Delta^2\lambda(C_{\mathcal{i}\mathcal{i}} - 2C_{\mathcal{i}\mathcal{J}} + C_{\mathcal{J}\mathcal{J}})$$

To maximize ΔZ, we set $\partial(\Delta Z)/\partial\Delta$ to zero, giving[2]

$$\Delta^* = \frac{(E_{\mathcal{i}} - E_{\mathcal{J}}) - 2\lambda(S_{\mathcal{i}} - S_{\mathcal{J}}) - (T_{\mathcal{i}} - T_{\mathcal{J}})}{2\lambda(C_{\mathcal{i}\mathcal{i}} - 2C_{\mathcal{i}\mathcal{J}} + C_{\mathcal{J}\mathcal{J}})} \tag{9}$$

The magnitude of the revision is then determined using (5), with values of $\Delta_{\mathcal{i}}$ and $\Delta_{\mathcal{J}}$ computed in accordance with (4).

D. Revising $S_1, \ldots, S_N$

After revising $X_{\mathcal{i}}$ and $X_{\mathcal{J}}$, each iteration is completed by revising the sums $S_1, \ldots, S_N$ to account for the changed holdings. The values are altered as follows:

$$S_i \leftarrow S_i + \Delta(C_{i\imath} - C_{i\mathscr{J}}) \qquad \text{for} \quad i = 1, \ldots, N$$

As indicated earlier, only two rows ($\imath$ and $\mathscr{J}$) from the original covariance matrix are required for this step. Moreover, after the initial computation of $S_1, \ldots, S_N$ only this procedure requires any use of the original covariance matrix.[3]

V. EXTENSIONS

Many problems that arise in practice can be solved directly using this algorithm, and modifications of the procedure and/or the use of supplementary procedures can allow a larger range of problems to be handled.

A. Targets and Penalties

As indicated earlier, many portfolio analysis problems involve linear constraints in addition to (1b) and (1c): portfolio yield may be restricted to lie within a specified range, the proportion invested in "growth stocks" may be limited, etc. Many such constraints are imposed to counteract (albeit crudely) inadequacies in the representation of the covariance matrix. Such constraints are, of course, unnecessary if the algorithm described here is used. However, some constraints may well reflect the undesirable consequences of divergence of some linear relationship from a given value or set of values.

A range constraint on a linear function of the X_is is equivalent to the addition of a penalty function to the objective function. Let

$$v_k = \sum_{i=1}^{N} a_{ik} X_i \tag{10}$$

where

v_k = the value of attribute k of the portfolio

a_{ik} = the contribution of security i to attribute k

The restriction

$$l_k \leq v_k \leq u_k$$

is equivalent to augmenting the objective function to obtain

$$z' = z - P_k$$

where

$$P_k = \begin{cases} \infty & \text{if} \quad v_k < l_k \\ 0 & \text{if} \quad l_k \leq v_k \leq u_k \\ \infty & \text{if} \quad v_k > u_k \end{cases}$$

Figure 2a shows this relationship.

While the algorithm described here cannot handle this type of restriction, it can accommodate a penalty function of the form shown in Figure 2b. Here the penalty is of the form:

$$P_k = p_k(v_k - t_k)^2$$

where

$$t_k = \text{the "target" for attribute } k$$

$$p_k = \text{the "penalty" for divergence of } v_k \text{ from } t_k$$

In many cases this type of quadratic penalty function will better reflect the reality of the practical problem than will a function of the form shown in Figure 2a.

Assume that there are K attributes in all. Then

$$z' = z - \sum_{k=1}^{K} p_k(v_k - t_k)^2 \tag{11}$$

$$= E - \lambda V - \sum_{k=1}^{K} [p_k v_k^2 - 2p_k t_k v_k + p_k t_k^2]$$

Substituting (10)

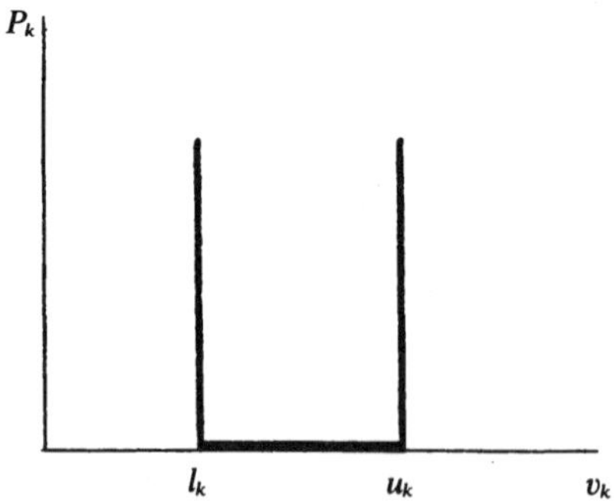

Figure 2a.

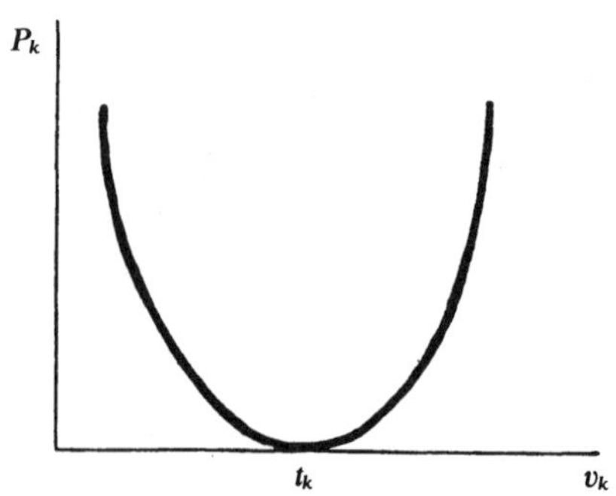

Figure 2b.

$$
\begin{aligned}
z' = \sum_{i=1}^{N} X_iE_i - \lambda \sum_{i=1}^{N}\sum_{j=1}^{N} (X_iX_jC_{ij}) \\
- \sum_{i=1}^{N}\sum_{j=1}^{N}\sum_{k=1}^{N} (a_{ik}a_{jk}p_k)X_iX_j \\
+ \sum_{i=1}^{N}\left[2\sum_{k=1}^{K}(a_{ik}p_kt_k)\right]X_i \\
- \sum_{k=1}^{K} p_kt_k^2
\end{aligned}
$$

Rearranging

$$z' = \sum_{i=1}^{N} X_iE_i - 1\left[\sum_{i=1}^{N}\sum_{j=1}^{N}(X_iX_jC'_{ij})\right] - \sum_{k=1}^{K}(p_kt_k^2) \tag{12}$$

where

$$E'_i = E_i + 2\left[\sum_{k=1}^{K}(a_{ik}p_kt_k)\right]$$

$$C'_{ij} = \lambda C_{ij} + \sum_{k=1}^{K}(a_{ik}a_{jk}p_k)$$

Note that the third term in (12) is not a function of the decision variables (the X_is). Thus its omission will not affect the solution. This gives

$$z' = \sum_{i=1}^{N} X_iE'_i - 1\left[\sum_{i=1}^{N}\sum_{j=1}^{N}(X_iX_jC'_{ij})\right]$$

which is of the form for which the algorithm is designed.

To handle targets and penalties, only a preprocessor is required to adjust the coefficients to be used for the optimization. Moreover, this need be done only once for all portfolios for which the same set of targets and penalties is applicable.[4]

B. Expanded Turnover Penalty Functions

Figure 3a portrays the algorithm's assumption concerning the total turnover penalty associated with variations in holdings of security *i*. On either side of the initial holding, the function is linear. This may well reflect the relevant turnover costs for highly liquid stocks. However, for less liquid securities the total cost (explicit transactions cost and possible price impact) may increase at an increasing rate, as shown in Figure 3b.

Such a relationship can easily be incorporated in the algorithm. Let the

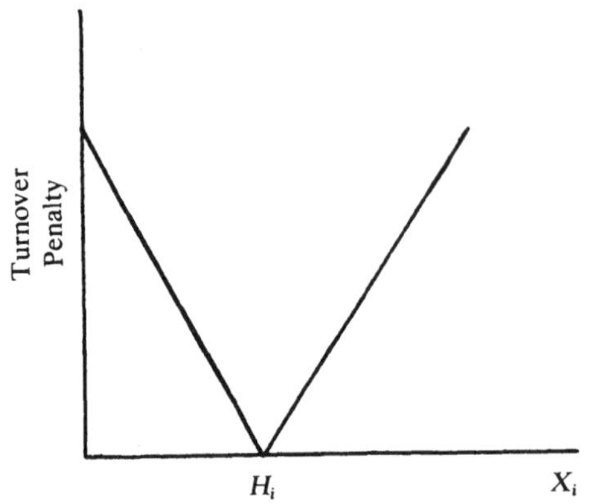

Figure 3a.

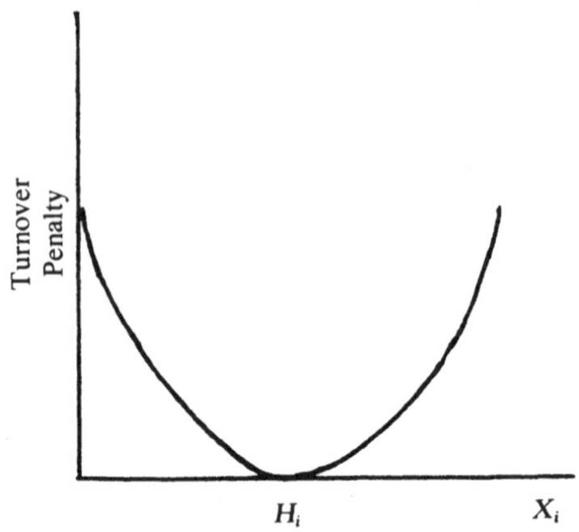

Figure 3b.

total turnover penalty for security i be

$$|X_i - H_i|t_i + (X_i - H_i)^2 t_i'$$

Such a function can be accommodated by making the appropriate changes in the selection procedure [Eq. (7)] and in the computation of the amount of the revision [Eq. (9)].

Another extension allows for asymmetry in the turnover penalty. Let the function be

$$(X_i - H_i)t_i^+ + (X_i - H_i)^2 t_i^{+'} \quad \text{if} \quad X_i > H_i$$
$$(H_i - X_i)t_i^- + (X_i - H_i)^2 t_i^{-'} \quad \text{if} \quad X_i < H_i$$

As before, Eqs. (7) and (9) are altered to deal with this case. Asymmetric turnover penalty functions can be used to handle, for example, the asymmetric tax treatment of realized capital gains and losses.

C. Interactive Use

It is possible to design a program so that the algorithm simply proceeds until an optimal solution is found, then prints the recommended changes. A portfolio manager using such a program could either accept the recommendations *in toto* or make adjustments in a fairly *ad hoc* manner to take into account any factors not adequately represented in the problem formulation (e.g., the need to hold only integral numbers of shares or preferences for trading in round lots of 100 shares[5]).

An alternative approach would involve the manager as part of the solution process. For example, after a selected number of iterations (one or more) the manager could decide whether or not to accept the buy/sell recommendations in whole, in part, or not at all. Moreover, at any time the manager would be able to alter one or more of the inputs (upper and lower bounds, turnover penalties, etc.) before any further revisions were analyzed by the algorithm.

Since each iteration selects the "best" security for purchase and the "worst" for sale, and since feasibility is maintained throughout, the procedure corresponds closely to that followed intuitively by many managers, and should thus enjoy considerable acceptance as well as (potentially) direct involvement. In fact, security traders might even become involved in the process, with actual transactions costs reflected directly from iteration to iteration.

ACKNOWLEDGMENT

This research was motivated by discussions with members of the Investment Systems Group of Wells Fargo Investment Advisors. Valuable comments and suggestions were made by Bob Fuhrman, Kelly Haughton, Cary Martin, Leland Robinson, Polly Shouse, and Larry Tint. This research was sponsored by the Stanford Program in Finance. Major contributors to the Stanford Program in Finance are Bank America Foundation, The First Boston Corporation, The Chase Manhattan Bank, Continental Bank Foundation, The Dean Witter Foundation, General Electric Company, Goldman, Sachs & Co., Morgan Guaranty Trust Company, Morgan Stanley & Co., Inc., Salomon Brothers, Security Pacific National Bank, and Wells Fargo Bank.

NOTES

1. Note that $S_i = C_{ip}$, the covariance of the return on security i with the return on the current portfolio. To exploit simplified models of covariances, this relationship can be used to greatly simplify the required computations. In many cases a special-purpose algorithm of this sort will operate more efficiently if sums related directly to the underlying determinants of covariance are maintained, with the C_{ip} values computed from these sums as needed.

2. Note also, from (7a) and (7b), that

$$\Delta^* = \frac{(\partial Z/\partial X_{\imath}) - (\partial Z/\partial X_{\mathcal{J}})}{2\lambda(C_{\imath\imath} - 2C_{\imath\mathcal{J}} + C_{\mathcal{J}\mathcal{J}})}$$

The denominator of (9) will be nonnegative in all cases and will equal 0 only if securities $\imath$ and $\mathcal{J}$ are perfectly correlated and have equal variances. In such a case, the security with the higher expected return net of transactions costs would dominate the other. This situation can be determined by checking the denominator of (9) and setting Δ^* at an appropriately large value if the denominator does in fact equal zero.

Note that the inclusion of a riskless asset causes no problem. Indeed several such assets may be included (with different rates and appropriate bounds) to represent, for example, different borrowing and lending rates. The ability to include risky and riskless assets obviates the need for the two-stage solutions, required with most quadratic programming codes.

3. Experience suggests that rounding errors are not very serious with this algorithm; thus complex procedures to avoid numeric errors are not needed. However, after many iterations, some errors may cumulate in the values of the S_is. To control for this, a count can be kept of the number of iterations since the initial computation of the sums. When the count exceeds a specified amount, the sums are recomputed using the original covariance matrix (i.e., the next iteration simply starts one step earlier than usual).

4. The objective function can be expanded trivially to allow for proportional utility or disutility associated with a linear function of the X_is. The coefficients are simply added to the expected returns of the securities. Thus to accommodate:

$$z' = z + P_k \sum_{i=1}^{N} a_{ik} X_i$$

simply define

$$E_i' = E_i + P_k a_{ik}$$

5. These factors can only be handled exactly by an (expensive) integer quadratic programming algorithm. However, interactive use and/or the incorporation of simple heuristic procedures in the algorithm described here should prove acceptable.

REFERENCES

1. E. J. Elton and M. J. Gruber, "Estimating the Dependence Structure of Share Prices—Implications for Portfolio Selection," *Journal of Finance* (Vol. 28, December 1973), pp. 1203–1232.
2. E. J. Elton, M. J. Gruber, and M. W. Padberg, "Portfolio Selection—The Exploitation of Special Structures," *Bulletin of the Operations Research Society of America* (Vol. 22, Spring 1974), p. B88 (Abstract).
3. E. J. Elton, M. J. Gruber, and M. W. Padberg, "Simple Criteria for Optimal Portfolio Selection," *Journal of Finance* (Vol. 31, December 1976), pp. 1341–1357.
4. E. G. Elton, M. J. Gruber, and M. W. Padberg, "Simple Rules for Optimal Portfolio Selection—the Multi-group Case," *Journal of Financial and Quantitative Analysis* (Vol. 12, September 1977), pp. 329–345.
5. J. L. Farrell, Jr., "Analyzing Covariation of Return to Determine Homogeneous Stock Groupings," *Journal of Business* (Vol. 47, April 1974), pp. 186–207.
6. B. F. King, "Market and Industry Factors in Stock Price Behavior," *Journal of Business* (Vol. 39, January 1966), pp. 139–190.
7. H. M. Markowitz, "The Optimization of a Quadratic Function Subject to Linear Constraints," *Naval Research Logistics Quarterly* (Vol. 3, March–June 1956), pp. 111–133.
8. H. M. Markowitz, *Portfolio Selection: Efficient Diversification of Investments* (New York: John Wiley & Sons, 1959).
9. J. A. Pogue, "An Extension of the Markowitz Portfolio Selection Model to Include Variable Transactions Costs, Short Sales, Leverage Policies and Taxes," *Journal of Finance* (Vol. 25, December 1970), pp. 1005–1027.

10. The RAND Corporation, "Quadratic Programming Code QP4."
11. A. Ravindran, "A Computer Routine for Quadratic and Linear Programming Problems," *Communications of the ACM* (Vol. 15, September 1972), pp. 818–820.
12. B. Rosenberg and V. Marathe, "Common Factors in Security Returns: Microeconomic Determinants and Macroeconomic Correlates," *Proceedings of the Seminar of the Analysis of Security Prices* (Chicago: University of Chicago Press, 1976).
13. B. Rosenberg and A. Rudd, "Portfolio Optimization Algorithms: A Progress Report," University of California Research Program in Finance working paper No. 42 (May 1976).
14. W. F. Sharpe, "A Simplified Model for Portfolio Analysis," *Management Science* (Vol. 9, 1963), pp. 277–293.
15. W. F. Sharpe, *Portfolio Theory and Capital Markets* (New York: McGraw-Hill, 1970).
16. W. F. Sharpe, "A Linear Programming Approximation for the General Portfolio Analysis Problem," *Journal of Financial and Quantitative Analysis* (Vol. 6, December 1971), pp. 1263–1275.
17. B. K. Stone, "A Linear Programming Formulation of the General Portfolio Selection Problem," *Journal of Financial and Quantitative Analysis* (Vol. 8, September 1973), pp. 621–636.
18. B. Van Hohenbalken, "Simplicial Decomposition in Nonlinear Programming Algorithms," University of Alberta Department of Economics Research Paper No. 21, 1974.

Section 2: Asset Prices

2-1 "A Positive Theory of Security Market Behavior," Chapter V in William F. Sharpe, *Portfolio Analysis Based on a Simplified Model of the Relationships Among Securities*, A dissertation submitted in partial satisfaction of the requirements for the degree Doctor of Philosophy in Economics, University of California, Los Angeles, June 1961, pp. 76–100.

In this, the penultimate chapter (before the conclusion section) of my dissertation, I turned from portfolio choice to the determination of asset prices in equilibrium and the associated relationship between risk and expected return. This was natural for one trained, as I had been by Armen Alchian at U.C.L.A., to consider the effects on prices when an equilibrium is reached between optimizing buyers and sellers. As in the rest of the dissertation, I assumed that security returns are consistent with a single index model. Moreover, I posited the existence of a riskless interest rate at which one could borrow or lend. The equilibrium conditions are shown in Figures 24 and 25. In Figure 24, all securities and portfolios lie along a straight line in a graph with expected return on the horizontal axis and the slope coefficient of the single index model (here, B, later termed beta) on the vertical axis. The line implies an expected return equal to the riskless interest rate when B (beta) equals zero and a constant premium in expected return per unit of beta for other securities. This relationship, which later became known as the security market line, is one of the key implications of the more general Capital Asset Pricing Model. Figure 26 shows that in equilibrium, all efficient portfolios lie on a straight line with expected return on the horizontal axis and standard deviation on the vertical axis. In the diagram, there are multiple portfolios of risky assets plotting on the efficient frontier. While this is possible, if securities have non-zero residual security risks that are uncorrelated with the single index returns, mathematically there will be only one efficient portfolio of risky securities. However, in practice, other portfolios of risky securities may plot very close to the linear efficient frontier, giving a picture similar to that shown in Figure 25.

The derivation relies primarily on a no-arbitrage condition for equilibrium and is similar to that made subsequently by Stephen Ross when deriving his Arbitrage Pricing Theory in a setting in which returns are generated by a multi-index (-factor) model. The chapter concludes with empirical tests using both *ex ante* predictions provided by an investment analyst and ex post security and mutual fund returns.

Based on these results, I concluded that it would be premature to reject the theory and that more empirical tests should be performed to assess its true value.

2-2 "Capital Asset Prices — A Theory of Market Equilibrium Under Conditions of Risk," *The Journal of Finance*, Vol. XIX, No. 3, September 1964, pp. 425–442.

This now well-known paper resulted from my attempt to generalize the results of the equilibrium theory in my dissertation. After completing my degree in June of 1961, I left the RAND Corporation to take a position on the faculty of the Business School at the University of Washington. I started almost immediately to adapt and improve the two main parts of my dissertation for publication in academic journals. The normative material appeared in *Management Science* (paper 1–2, submitted in late 1961 but not published until January 1963) with relatively little new material. Rather than do the same for the positive theory, I began work to generalize the results to a world in which security returns are not generated by a single-index model. Surprisingly, the conclusions were almost the same. Making the key assumption that investors agree on predicted security expected returns and covariances, chosen portfolios will lie along the linear efficient frontier shown in Figure 5. As in my dissertation, I assumed (erroneously) that multiple portfolios of risky securities might lie along this line, as shown in Figures 6 and 7. This complicated some of the derivations but had no effect on the conclusion (as shown in footnote 26). The key relationship, shown in Figure 7 and footnote 22, relies on the first-order conditions for optimization. As in my dissertation, the main result is the linear relationship between expected return and B (beta) shown in Figure 9. However, in this case no assumptions are made about the return-generating process. The value of B is simply the ratio of a (a) security's covariance with an efficient portfolio of risky securities divided by (b) the variance of that portfolio (or the equivalent form shown in footnote 25).

I obtained these results at some point in the fall of 1961 or early 1962 and submitted the paper to the *Journal of Finance.* As I have written elsewhere, the paper was initially rejected due to the argument that the assumption that investors agree on investment prospects — which a referee termed "homogeneity of investor expectations" — was unrealistic. I requested another review, and with minimal revisions the paper was finally published in 1964. After I had completed the paper, someone who had presumably seen it sent me a mimeographed paper by Jack Treynor that reached similar conclusions, as I acknowledged in footnote 7. I no longer have that paper. However, a copy of a mimeographed rough draft was apparently circulated in 1962 and eventually published in 1999. In it, Treynor says: "The assumptions required for the model we are about to introduce have much in common with the assumptions of the portfolio theorists (e.g. Markowiz, Tobin, Sharpe and Farrar)", but no references are cited.

After the paper became more widely read, others termed this approach the Capital Asset Pricing Model, or CAPM. Figure 8 showed a way to estimate B via a regression analysis of the type that I had used in my dissertation; this undoubtedly led others to use the term "beta" for the resulting coefficient. The equation at the end of footnote 25, when rearranged, shows that an investment's expected return is equal to the riskless interest rate plus the product of its beta times the difference between the expected return on an efficient portfolio of risk securities (g) and the riskless interest rate — a relationship now termed the Security Market Line. Here, I suggested that the relevant risk for determining expected returns was the risk resulting from swings in economic activity. I also argued that diversification enables the investor to escape all but the risk resulting from such swings. Finally, I suggested that the results were broadly consistent with investment counselors' willingness "... to accept a lower expected return from defensive" securities (those which respond little to changes in the economy) than they require from aggressive securities (which exhibit significant response)."

2-3 "The Capital Asset Pricing Model: Traditional and 'Zero-Beta' Versions," *Journal of the Midwest Finance Association*, 1973, pp. 1–12.

This paper was prepared at the request of the Midwest Finance Association. At the time, the basic features of the Capital Asset Pricing Model were well established. Here, I describe the model briefly and term it the "traditional CAPM". Many empirical analyses had been performed to test the model's security market line relationship plus the additional assumption that statistical properties of historical returns are adequate surrogates for the *ex ante* predictions of future expected returns and covariances in the CAPM. Many of these empirical analyses had found that there was a positive relationship between average returns and historic beta values, but that the slope coefficient was smaller and the intercept larger than implied by the CAPM. A number of authors had posed an alternative theory that provided implications more consistent with these results. This paper addresses such "zero-beta" approaches, which relied on the assumption that investors are unable to borrow at the same riskless rate of interest at which they can lend (as assumed in the CAPM). I attempted to clarify some properties of such models which had not been fully and/or correctly described in the existing literature. I then suggested that even under the heroic assumption that *ex post* relationships are sufficient surrogates for the *ex ante* characteristics of the theories, use of a portion of the overall market portfolio rather than a broader measure could lead to an underestimate of the slope of the true security market line.

2-4 "The Parable of the Money Managers," *Financial Analysts Journal*, July/August 1976, p. 4.

This was written partly in jest but I did intend to make a strong case for index funds which by 1976 were being marketed to both institutional and individual investors. Such funds, inspired by the CAPM, offered a cross-section of stocks using market value proportions. Such funds were not received with gratitude by most professional money managers, one of whom ran full-page ads suggesting that indexing was un-American. My parable, published in the official journal of the Financial Analysts Federation, was intended to suggest that a traditional fund that "picks stocks" is, in effect, making bets with the managers of other such funds and that on net, investors in such funds must pay the costs of such activities. My conclusion that over time, index funds would grow in importance turned out to be prescient. However, a number of years later I still found it useful to make the basic point more directly (in paper 2–10, below).

2-5 "The Capital Asset Pricing Model: A 'Multi-Beta' Interpretation," H. Levy and M. Sarnat, Editors, *Financial Decision Making Under Uncertainty*, Academic Press (New York), 1977, pp. 127–136.

This paper was published in a volume inspired by an important seminar on Financial Decision Making Under Uncertainty held at Ein Bokek, Israel in March 1975. The seminar included many of the leading thinkers in the field at the time and greatly influenced my later work. I participated in the seminar but did not present a paper. Afterwards, Haim Levy and Marshall Sarnat invited me to contribute to their book and I happily did so. In this paper I approach the issue of the sensitivities of security returns to multiple factors and do so without making any special assumptions about the return covariances. In particular, I do not assume that returns follow a multiple factor model with residual returns uncorrelated with the factors and each other. Instead, I decompose the general security covariance matrix into a set of sub-portfolios, then investigate the relationships between securities' overall beta values and their covariances with the sub-portfolio returns. In the latter part of the paper, I then briefly consider the effects of assuming a multi-factor model of security returns. I also explore these relationships in a discrete-state model. I conclude with exhortations to exercise caution when using historic data to estimate *ex ante* expectations and to insure that one does not attempt to estimate beta values by comparing changes in expectations for one variable with realized changes in another (as had some papers at the time). In re-reading the paper, I was surprised to see no references to the 1976 paper by Stephen Ross on his Arbitrage Pricing Theory. It is possible that I completed the paper before I became aware of Steve's work. Otherwise the lack of a reference was a very serious omission. In any event, except for the brief section on multifactor models, the paper does not make any assumptions about the return-generating process and differs in this respect from the APT.

2-6 "Valuation of a Call Option on a Stock with Simple Price Changes," in W. F. Sharpe, *Investments*, Prentice-Hall, Inc. 1978, pp. 366–371.

This is taken from the first edition of my textbook, *Investments*, published in 1978. Earlier, when discussing options in my investment class at Stanford, I had typically provided arbitrage arguments for the relationships among the prices of a stock, the riskless rate of interest and the prices of call and put options on that stock, then moved to the justly famous 1973 Black-Scholes option pricing model. However, students found the latter somewhat mysterious and failed to appreciate the underlying economics. To provide a simple example, I developed a case in which a security's price changed in very simple ways, moving to either a higher or a lower value in each of a series of discrete periods. I was working on this approach during the Ein Bokek conference and showed my results to Mark Rubenstein one afternoon on the beach by the Dead Sea. When I returned to Stanford, I continued work on the subject and found that the model converges to give the Black-Scholes results as the lengths of the intervals for the jump process become shorter (as I indicated in a footnote later in the chapter from which this excerpt is taken and as is hinted in Figure 14–7 here). While working on the book, I showed this relationship to John Cox, who was a colleague at Stanford at the time. He, Steve Ross and Mark Rubenstein then further developed and applied the binomial approach, resulting in the deservedly influential 1979 Cox-Ross-Rubenstein paper, which graciously cited my suggestions and this section of my textbook.

The approach that I employ here relies on the fact that in a discrete time interval with two future states of the world, a combination of any two sufficiently diverse securities can replicate the payoffs of a third. If there is to be no opportunity for riskless arbitrage, the price of the third security must equal that of the replicating portfolio of the other two. Thus, given the prices and payoffs of a stock and a riskless security, one can derive the value of an option written on that stock at any given time. Starting with the date of expiration, it is then possible to work backwards (use recursion) to find the current value of the option. While the numeric example used here is a bit tedious, the general calculation method is explicit. Only after writing this did I come to fully appreciate the similarities of this derivation with the Arrow–Debreu model of price determination in markets with discrete outcomes.

In later years, this approach came to be known as the binomial option pricing model. A few years ago, Mark Rubenstein told a conference audience that option pricing models using discrete stock price changes were more frequently used in practice than models of continuous price changes such as that of Black and Scholes. In any event, the values of a great many complex securities and derivative are now estimated using models based on discrete price models and security replication.

While such computations are vastly more complex than the simple one that I used in 1978, they share at least a common underlying economic premise.

2-7 "Security Codings: Measuring Relative Attractiveness in Perfect and Imperfect Markets," in W. F. Sharpe and C. M. Cootner, Editors, *Financial Economics, Essays in Honor of Paul Cootner*, Prentice-Hall, Inc., 1982, pp. 216–229.

This paper was prepared for a volume of essays in honor of my Stanford colleague and close friend Paul Cootner. Paul, who died suddenly at a very early age, made major contributions to the field just beginning then to be widely termed Financial Economics. His 1964 book of papers, *The Random Character of Stock Market Prices*, set the stage for all that came afterwards in this area. Paul was widely known for his path-breaking work on commodity futures; I was fortunate to have been able to audit his class on the subject. At the time of his death, he was working on a very broad theory of equilibrium. In his honor, his wife Cathryn and I edited a series of papers contributed by his friends and colleagues — a virtual who's who of the field.

In this paper, I attempted to parse out the ingredients that might logically form an investment firm's assignment of traditional codes for relative attractiveness to individual securities. Following some other work, I assumed that investors would be concerned with three elements of a portfolio's future performance: its expected return, variance of return and, due to differential taxation, dividend yield. This led to the possibility of an equilibrium characterized by a *security market plane*, with expected return on the vertical axis and variance (or standard deviation) and dividend yield on the horizontal axes. I considered two aspects of the equilibrium: first, differences between an investor's preferences and those of the market as a whole (implicit in market prices) and second, differences between an investment organization's predictions and those reflected in market values. While the results are complex, they do point to the need to differentiate between "tailoring" a portfolio to take into account a specific investor's situation vis-à-vis that of the market (or "average investor) and taking positions based on differences between an investment organization's predictions and those implicit in market prices (via "active management").

2-8 "Factor models, CAPMs, and the APT," *The Journal of Portfolio Management*, Fall 1984, Volume 11, Number 1, pp. 21–25.

This paper was written as attempt to reduce the considerable confusion at the time about versions of the CAPM, the Arbitrage Pricing Theory (APT) and the use of factor models. It was published in a journal read by both academics and practitioners and was designed to appeal to both audiences. I started with a general linear factor model in which the key assumption is that security residual returns are uncorrelated with one another. The initial section concluded with a warning that statistical methods for estimating such models, no matter how sophisticated, may miss some important possibilities for future returns that other information might identify. I next discussed equilibrium models that make statements about security expected returns, arguing that various versions of both the CAPM and the APT should be considered such models. I then argued that versions of the CAPM rely on assumptions about investor preferences but do not require assumptions that returns are generated by any type of factor model (hopefully clearing the air for those who conflated my work on the single-index model with that on the CAPM). Next, I showed that in contrast, the APT relies on the prior assumption that returns are generated by a multi-factor model and assumes only that investors prefer more money to less. The argument is similar to that I used in Chapter Five of my dissertation (reprinted in Section 1) and might better be called a no-(almost) arbitrage theory, although I do not use this term in the paper. In the penultimate Section, I discussed a world in which returns are (1) generated by a multi-factor model and (2) the CAPM equilibrium holds, using results from my 1977 "Multi-beta" paper, reprinted earlier in this section. I concluded with some rather philosophical remarks on the testability of all these approaches.

2-9 "Market Equilibrium with no Short Sales," Financial Research Luncheon Seminar (FRILLS) Stanford University, Nov. 10, 1989.

This is a handout that I prepared for a presentation to my Finance colleagues at the Stanford Financial Research Luncheon Seminar (FRILLS) in November 1989. I later presented similar material at the Nikko Securities Multi-University Finance Faculty Seminar in Tokyo in January 1990. My goal was to examine the properties of market equilibrium in world in which no investor could take a short position in any security, including the riskless asset. I assumed that investors had traditional mean/variance preferences and agreed on security expected returns and covariances. The approach was fairly straightforward. I assumed that in equilibrium, all investors agreed upon a set of security covariances and expected returns and that the former but not the latter were known to an outside observer. To keep the analysis simple, I also assumed that investors had equal amounts of wealth, although a more realistic version could replace this assumption, using observable values of investors' portfolios.

The first page sets up the inputs for the overall problem then states the observer's task as one of finding a set of expected returns that clear the markets, given an observed set of security covariances and investor risk tolerances. The maximand for an "uber-optimization", shown at the bottom of the first page, is the sum of the investors "utilities", measured by the functions of expected return and variance given near the top of the page. The constraints include each investor's full-investment constraint and a constraint that the holdings of each security equal the available amount.

The second page of the handout shows the algorithm, assuming that some arbitrary set of expected returns has been selected. First, form a Lagrangean function and derive the first-order conditions for the N*K partial derivatives of the objective with respect to each of the variables. These will be zero for variables in the solution and negative for those at their lower bounds of zero. The solution to this optimization will also provide a set of shadow prices for the full-investment constraint (here, λ_{ci}, one for each security i). Note that in the equation for the first-order conditions neither the first nor the last term is subscripted with k, the identifier for an individual investor. The final step is for each security (i) replace the initially-assumed expected return with that value minus 1/K times its full-investment constraint shadow price, as shown in the first line under "Alteration". This is all that need be done, since re-optimization will give the same set of holdings and clear the market for each security, making the shadow price for each of the full-investment constraints equal to zero. More importantly, the markets will clear so that no constraints are required to equate the supply and demand of each security. The last portion of the second page of the handout discusses some possible variations of the approach.

At the time I developed this procedure, I headed a small research and consulting firm that had several large pension and endowment funds as clients. Each month, I used this approach to produce a set of expected returns for a number of asset classes, based on estimates of risk tolerances for groups of investors derived from the holdings of large pension funds. While the estimated expected returns differed from those obtained with a standard Capital Asset Pricing Model, the deviations were not great and had relatively small effects on the optimal portfolios obtained when analyzing the specific circumstances of each of the clients. After the firm was closed in the early 1990's so that I could return to Stanford, I ceased producing monthly estimates of asset expected returns and have not used the algorithm since.

2-10 "The Arithmetic of Active Management," *Financial Analysts Journal*, January/February 1991, pp. 7–9.

I was fortunate to be able to publish this short piece in the *Financial Analysts Journal*, so that it would be exposed to as many investment professionals as possible. My goal was to make the case for the superior after-cost performance of the average passively-managed dollar (suitably defined) over that of the average actively-managed dollar (again, suitably defined). In a sense, this was a return to the argument for index funds that I made in 1976 in my Parable of the Money Managers, published in the same journal. By 1991, however, index funds had become a significant part of the investment industry and were being attacked on a number of grounds, some of which were simply specious. I started here by carefully defining my terms, then arguing that only simple arithmetic is needed to make the key point. The second part of the paper shows that purported counterexamples to the thesis typically use inappropriate measures. In the latter paragraphs I argued that when assessing an investment manager's performance one should use a "comparable passive alternative", identified in advance, rather than the then-common use of an equally-weighted peer group return or the performance of a "median manager" selected from such a group.

At an industry conference some years after this was published, a respected investment professional told the audience that this paper deserved another Nobel Prize. I am sure that he spoke in jest, since its point should be trivially obvious to most (moreover, his organization was a major vendor of index funds). That said, statements regarding passive management that are inconsistent with simple principles of arithmetic continue to appear, so it is useful to repeat the argument made here from time to time.

2-11 "Capital Asset Prices with and without Negative Holdings," reprinted in *The Journal of Finance*, The American Finance Association, June 1991, pp. 489–509.

This paper was prepared rather hurriedly for presentation in Stockholm in conjunction with the Nobel Prize award ceremonies in December, 1990. In that year, the Swedish Royal Academy of Sciences awarded the Sveriges Riksbank Prize in Economic Sciences in Memory of Alfred Nobel jointly to Harry Markowitz, Merton Miller and myself "*for their pioneering work in the theory of financial economics*". As the Nobel Foundation web site very appropriately says: "The shared Prize to Markowitz, Miller and Sharpe was ... an award for complementary contributions, in this case in financial economics, though the latter two had the advantage of standing on the shoulders of Markowitz."

In my case, the committee focused on the Capital Asset Pricing Model so, by convention, I chose to do so in this paper. The exposition is in many ways a summary of my work in the area but differs from earlier publications in some important ways. I explicitly treat equilibrium in markets in which negative holdings are not possible, incorporating the shadow prices that arise from such constraints in the asset pricing equations. I show that when there are no such constraints, the standard CAPM results are easily obtained by aggregating the properties of individuals' optimizations. This also makes obvious the economic meaning of key attributes of a capital market in equilibrium, such as the societal marginal utility of wealth, societal risk tolerance and the effects of the distribution of risk in an economy. I then explore cases in which non-negativity constraints are binding, showing that all three of the major conclusions of the CAPM may be affected: the market portfolio may not be efficient, some efficient strategies will include risky securities in non-market proportions and some securities and portfolios may plot below a security market line in expected return/beta space. This said, I argue that these results may be less important than they may have been when the CAPM was first derived. By 1990 stock index futures had made it far easier than before to take levered positions in the equity markets at low borrowing rates. Rather ironically, a theory that unrealistically assumed the availability of limitless borrowing at the riskless rate may have encouraged the investment industry to provide instruments that made this assumption closer to reality. This, in turn, might have made the original CAPM more relevant than it was when first derived.

Reviewing this paper after many years, I was struck by my unqualified enthusiasm for the financial innovations of the time, as evidenced in the concluding sentence ("... the combined effects of theoreticians, empiricists and practitioners are increasing the efficiency with which risk is allocated among individuals, leading to improvements in social welfare.") After the failure of financial markets worldwide from 2007 through 2009, due in considerable part to the widespread use of complex financial derivatives, this statement rings somewhat hollow. However, the derivatives that I discussed were futures products, traded on exchanges, marked to market daily and backed by clearing houses. These were not the culprits during the financial meltdown. Rather, problems were caused by "over-the-counter" derivative contracts and their ilk that were not marked to market and turned out to be insufficiently collateralized. To be sure, in the years after 1990, Financial Economics played a role in spawning Financial Engineering, which led to a plethora of innovations which may or may not have lowered expected social welfare *ex ante*, but certainly played a major role in leading to events that greatly decreased overall welfare *ex post*. Hopefully, more sophisticated regulations and better informed investors will decrease the magnitude of the mischief that the financial industry will cause in the future.

2-12 "Nuclear Financial Economics," in *Risk Management: Problems & Solutions*, (William H. Beaver and George Parker, editors), McGraw-Hill, 1995, pp. 17–35.

This was published in a book edited by two of my Stanford colleagues in conjunction with the activities of the Stanford Program in Finance. By the time I prepared this piece I had become convinced that the fundamental economics of most of the principles of Finance could best be understood and communicated using the Arrow-Debreu discrete time-state model. After a solid grounding in this setting one could then move to continuous models such as the Markowitz mean/variance approach to portfolio choice and the CAPM, both of which can be treated as special cases of the more general setting. I have continued to rely more and more on discrete time-state models, as can be seen in my 2007 book, *Investors and Markets: Portfolio Choice, Asset Prices and Investment Advice.*

Here I use the simplest possible setting that can include elements of both time and uncertainty — the two most important aspects of Financial Economics. I use an agrarian example (apple trees) to develop financial concepts and relationships. Assuming no previous exposure to finance on the part of the reader, I derive and define concepts such as discounting, interest rates, present values, forward prices, derivative valuation, replicating portfolios, and Modigliani–Miller's Proposition I. The first portion (and majority) of the paper relies only on a lack of arbitrage opportunities, obtaining the theorem that Stephen Ross, in his 2005 book, *Neoclassical Finance*, terms the "Fundamental Theorem of Finance". In the later sections I broaden the discussion to include the effects of individuals' probability estimates and preferences on the determination of state prices and the possible implications for equilibrium asset prices and expected returns. I show (rather casually) that in the general Arrow–Debreu setting, the key result of the CAPM can easily be obtained — that risk may be rewarded with higher expected return but "... it is not risk *per se* that is likely to be rewarded in [a] well-functioning capital market — only the *risk of doing badly in bad times*." In subsequent years I continued to develop and use this overall approach in my teaching and research, leading to the extensive treatment in *Investors and Markets*, a major goal of which was to encourage faculty to teach the first principles of Financial Economics using a discrete time-state setting. As I write this, the goal seems as distant as it was in 1995, but I realize that inertia is a powerful force in the academy and remain ever hopeful.

V. A POSITIVE THEORY OF SECURITY MARKET BEHAVIOR

A. The Theory

In this chapter we turn from normative applications of portfolio analysis to an attempt to construct a positive theory of security market behavior. The basic assumptions of this theory are: (1) investors act as if they were applying the Markowitz portfolio-analysis technique to probability beliefs about securities, and (2) their beliefs are expressed in terms of the diagonal model.

A number of relationships must be established before the market equilibrium conditions which result from these assumptions can be described. The first concerns the effect of portfolio size on variance. This can best be illustrated by considering alternative portfolios, each of which contains N securities, with (1/N) of the value of the portfolio invested in each security.[1] The variance of such a portfolio would be:

$$V = (X_{n+1})^2 \cdot V_I + \sum_{i=1}^{N} \left(\frac{1}{N}\right)^2 \cdot Q_i$$

$$= (X_{n+1})^2 \cdot V_I + \frac{\sum_{i=1}^{N} Q_i}{N^2}$$

---

[1]The results we will obtain can be shown to hold in the general case, where the amounts invested in different securities are unequal.

where:

$$X_{n+1} = \sum_{i=1}^{N} \left(\frac{1}{N}\right) B_i = \frac{\sum_{i=1}^{N} B_i}{N}$$

Letting $\bar{B}$ be the average value of B_i and Q the average value of Q_i for the N securities, the formula becomes:

$$V = (\bar{B})^2 \cdot V_I + \frac{\bar{Q}}{N} .$$

This formulation indicates that the larger the number of securities in a portfolio, the less significant is the portion of variance due to the Q_i parameters. With sufficiently large portfolios, this latter type of risk can be virtually disregarded since the variance of the portfolio will be due almost entirely to the B_i parameters. This is intuitively plausible. The parameter Q_i reflects a risk unique to a security which is in no way correlated with the performance of any other security; diversification can reduce this type of risk to negligible proportions. On the other hand, the parameter B_i refers to risk which is related to the performance of other securities; it is an implicit statement of the covariance between the yield of the security and that of all others. This type of risk cannot be offset by diversification and remains important regardless of the size of a portfolio.

Figure 22 illustrates the typical relationship between V and N, using median values of the 96-security sample during the period 1940-51 for $\bar{B}$ (=0.9) and $\bar{Q}$ (=0.05); the performance of the

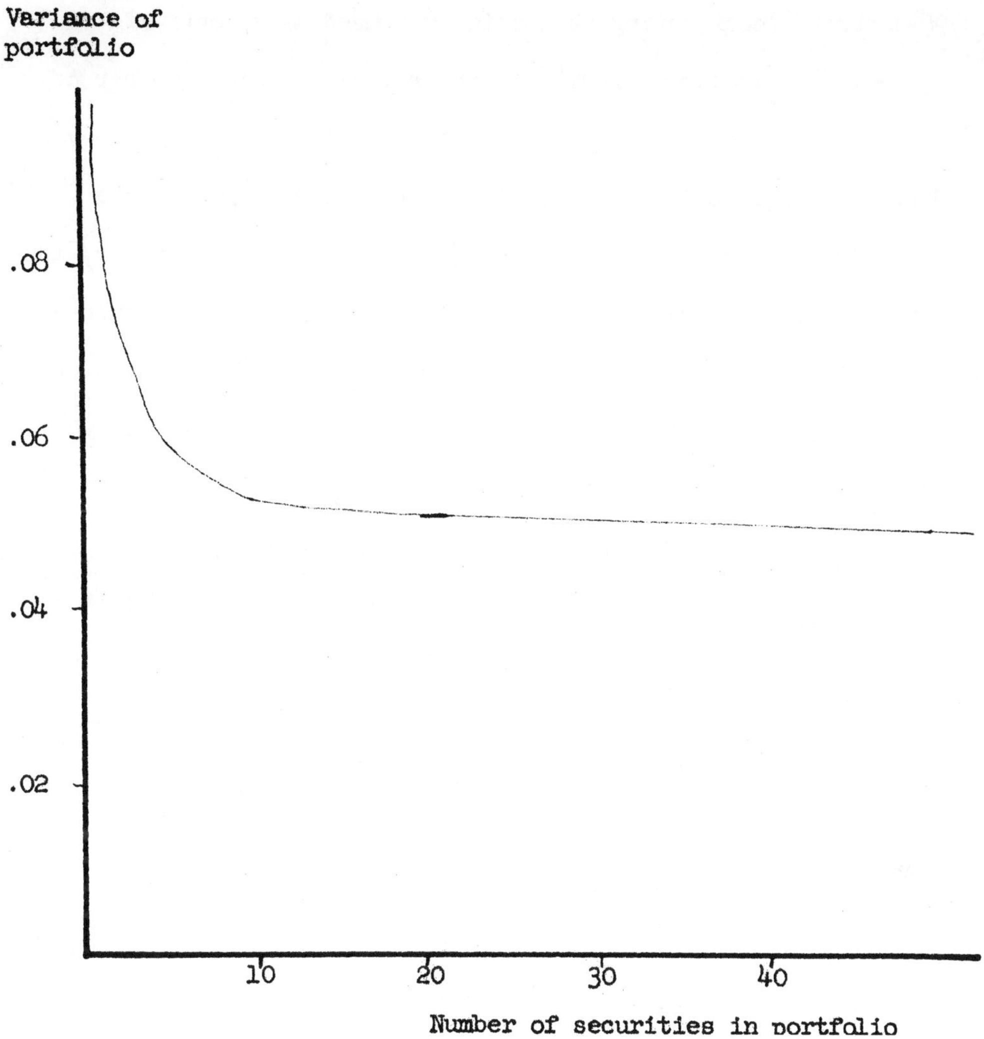

Fig. 22. - Predicted relationship between the number of securities in a portfolio and its variance

96-security index during the period was used as an estimate of V_I (=0.06). The curve indicates the relatively small number of securities required to reduce variance to nearly its minimum value. Since so few securities are typically required to reduce the variance of a portfolio to the amount due to the $\bar{B}$ parameter, and since so many securities are available to investors, we would expect to find that investors place primary emphasis on B_i when assessing the risk of a security, devoting much less attention to the Q_i parameter.

Consider next the effects of changes in the price of a security on the parameters B_i and E_i. Assume that investment in one share of a particular security will result in a value of $\$Z_i$ at the end of one year, where $\$Z_i$ includes both the price of the security at the time and all dividends paid during the year. Assume further that the value of Z_i will be determined by the formula:

(11) $$Z_i = F_i + G_i \cdot I + h_i$$

where (I) represents the deviation of the market index from its expected value (so that $E(I) = 0$), F_i and G_i are parameters, and h_i is a random variable with a zero mean. In this discussion we will assume that the initial price of the security will not affect the determination of Z_i. A number of alternative assumptions could be presented, but since they typically affect only the adjustment process, yielding the same equilibrium condition, we will limit our discussion to this case.

If Z_i is the total dollar value at the end of the year resulting from the purchase of one share of a security, and P_i is the price paid for that share at the beginning of the year, then, by our definition, the yield is:

$$Y_i = \frac{Z_i}{P_i}$$

Substituting Eq. (11) for Z_i:

$$Y_i = \frac{(F_i + G_i \cdot I + h_i)}{P_i}$$

Or:

$$Y_i = \frac{F_i}{P_i} + \frac{G_i}{P_i} \cdot I + \frac{h_i}{P_i}$$

Compare this formulation with the basic equation of the diagonal model:

$$Y_i = A_i + B_i \cdot I + w_i$$

Obviously:

$$A_i = \frac{F_i}{P_i}$$

$$B_i = \frac{G_i}{P_i}$$

$$w_i = \frac{h_i}{P_i}$$

We have defined (I) so that its expected value is zero. Thus:

$$E_i = A_i = \frac{F_i}{P_i}$$

These equations indicate that a change in the price of a security will affect both E_i, its expected yield, and B_i, the relationship between its yield and the market index. E_i and B_i will both move inversely with the price of the security; note, however, that their ratio is independent of the price:

$$\frac{B_i}{E_i} = \frac{\frac{G_i}{P_i}}{\frac{F_i}{P_i}} = \frac{G_i}{F_i}$$

These relationships are illustrated in Fig. 23. As the price of security R rises, the point showing its characteristics will move to the left along line 1; as its price falls, the point will move to the right along the same line.

Another relationship of importance in this analysis concerns the effects of combining portfolios. Since both B and E are linear functions of the quantities of the various securities included in a portfolio, the values of E and B pertaining to a portfolio formed by investing partly in one portfolio and partly in another will lie on the line connecting the values of E and B of the original portfolios. Thus, in Fig. 23, point T could represent an investment divided between portfolios W and U.

We have considered the characteristics of securities; we now

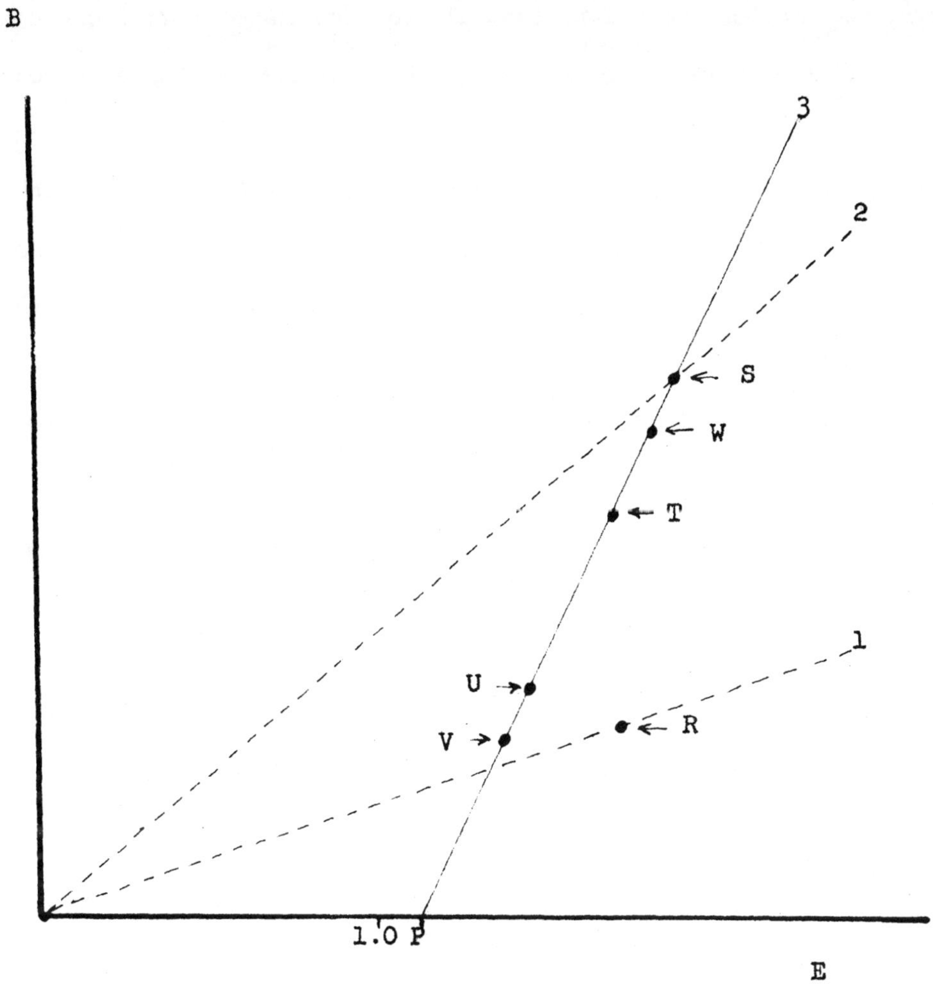

Fig. 23. - Disequilibrium in the security market

must consider one very important alternative investment: lending money at the "pure" interest rate. This alternative has an expected return equal to the pure interest rate ($E_i = 1 + r$), but there is no associated risk; thus B_i and Q_i are both zero. Since this can be considered merely another portfolio, combinations of lending money and regular portfolios will have predicted values of B and E which lie on the line connecting the two investments. Thus point U in Fig. 23 could be obtained by investing some portion of a fund in portfolio T and lending the remainder at the pure interest rate, shown by point P.

One additional characteristic of the pure-interest-rate alternative is important. It is possible to "disinvest" in a security (or portfolio) by borrowing rather than lending money at this rate;[2] thus it would be possible to obtain point U in Fig. 23 by borrowing money to purchase portfolio V. In general, by borrowing or lending, it is possible to obtain any combination of B and E falling on a line passing through point P in Fig. 23 and any point representing some portfolio or security.

The equilibrium process can now be shown. In Fig. 23 the points S, U, and V are a few of many securities which lie along line 3, which originates at point P. We have shown that the values of E and B associated with any portfolio composed of these securities will

[2]We assume equal borrowing and lending rates. The implications of differential rates are of considerable interest but will not be discussed here.

lie along line 3; of all such portfolios, one will have the smallest variance due to the Q_i parameters. Let this portfolio be represented by point W. Since there will be many securities along line 3, the variance of this portfolio which is caused by the Q_i parameters will be so close to zero that it can be disregarded.

Next consider the effects of borrowing and lending at the pure interest rate. Any combination of B and E along the line PW can be obtained by some combination of portfolio W and lending money. Since the variance due to the Q parameter is zero for both components of such an investment, its entire variance will be due to the B parameter. On the other hand, any combination of B and E along line 3 above point W can be obtained by borrowing money to purchase additional amounts of portfolio W; again, the variance will be due entirely to the B parameter.

Now assume that some security, such as R, lies to the right of line 3. Compare it with the combination of W and P represented by point T: both have the same expected yield but R has a smaller B-parameter and a greater Q-parameter. Under these conditions it would be profitable for investors to include security R in their portfolios; the proper amount would depend on the relationship between the parameters: the larger the difference in the B parameters relative to the Q parameter of R, the larger the proportion of the portfolio which should be devoted to R.[3]

---

[3]Assume that portfolio T has a B-parameter of $\bar{B}$ and no variance due to Q_i parameters. Then if B_R and Q_R are the parameters of

What would be the market response to a security which (temporarily) had characteristics similar to those described for

---

security R, and X_R is the amount of a portfolio invested in R, the variance due to Q_R will be:

$$V_Q = (X_R)^2 \cdot Q_R$$

$$\frac{d(V_Q)}{d(X_R)} = 2Q_R \cdot X_R$$

Letting $\triangle B$ be the difference $(\bar{B}-B_R)$, the B parameter of the new portfolio will be:

$$B = \bar{B} - X_R \cdot \triangle B$$

and the variance due to this parameter will be given by:

$$V_B = (\bar{B} - X_R \cdot \triangle B)^2 \cdot V_I$$

$$\frac{d(V_B)}{d(X_R)} = 2V_I(\triangle B)\left[X_R \triangle B - \bar{B}\right]$$

The optimum amount of security R can be found by equating the increase in variance due to Q_R with the absolute value of the decrease due to B_R as X_R is increased:

$$2Q_R X_R = -\left|2V_I\ (\triangle B)\left[X_R \cdot \triangle B - \bar{B}\right]\right|$$

The optimum is thus:

$$X_R = \frac{V_I \bar{B} \triangle B}{(\triangle B)^2 \cdot V_I + Q_R}$$

Rewriting:

$$X_R = \frac{V_I \bar{B}}{\triangle B \cdot V_I + \frac{Q_R}{\triangle B}}$$

This formulation shows that, ceteris paribus, the higher is Q_R relative to $\triangle B$, the larger the amount of the portfolio which should be invested in security R, thus proving the statement in the text.

security R? People would desire to buy more of this security and less of those securities with higher values of B, causing an increase in the price of R and a decrease in the prices of all securities along line 3. In Fig. 23 point R would move to the left along line 1, while points S, U, and V would move to the right along their respective lines from the origin, establishing a new line from point P lying to the right of line 3. If point R remained below this new line, similar incentives would exist for increased purchase of R and decreased purchases of S, U, and V, resulting in further movements of the prices of the securities.

Figure 24 indicates the equilibrium condition in the security market. All securities will lie along one straight line which cuts the E-axis at the pure interest rate. When a security temporarily moves to the right of the line, forces are set in motion which move the line to the right and the point representing the security to the left. On the other hand, when a security temporarily moves above the line, its price will fall, moving its point to the right, while the prices of securities on the line will rise, moving the line to the left. Only when conditions are as pictured in Fig. 24 will equilibrium be achieved.

Figure 24 indicates the combinations of B and E for individual securities which will occur when the market is in equilibrium; Fig. 25 illustrates the relationship between standard deviation of yield and average yield for portfolios under these conditions. We have shown that any combination of B and E on line PP' in Fig. 24

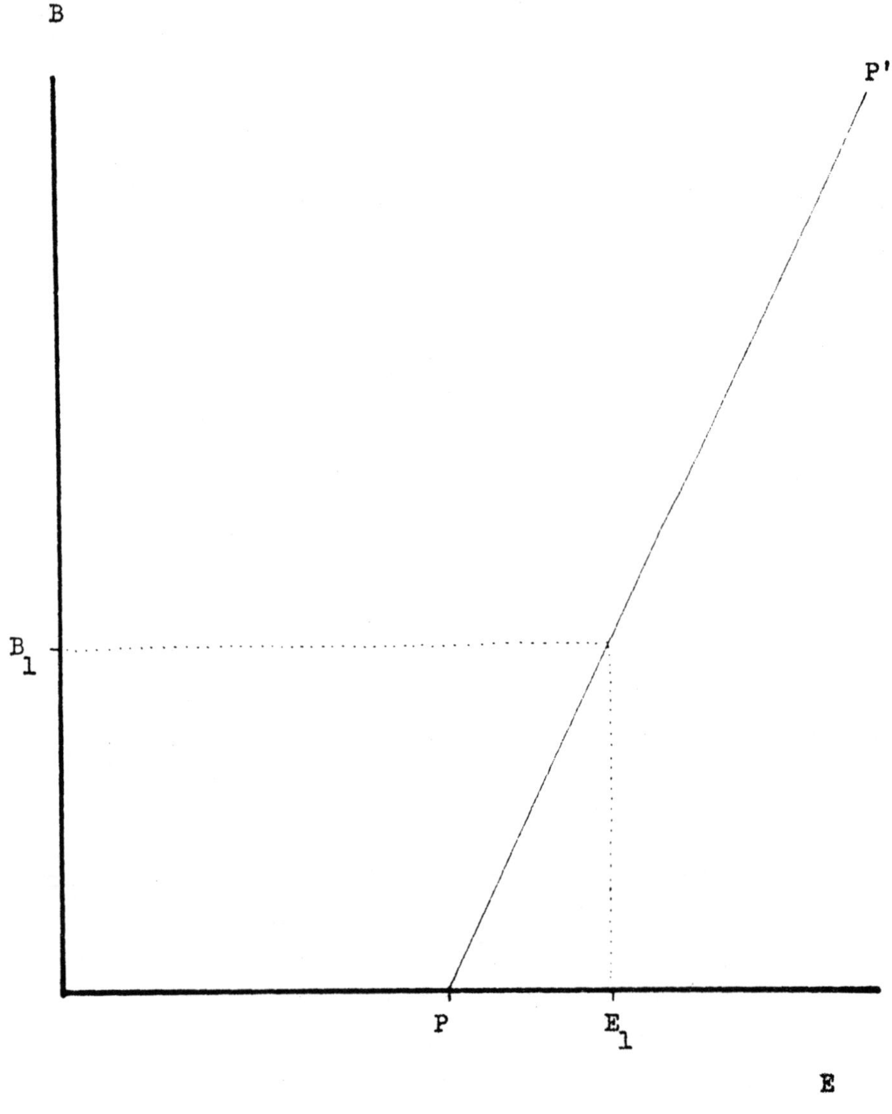

Fig. 24. - Equilibrium in the security market

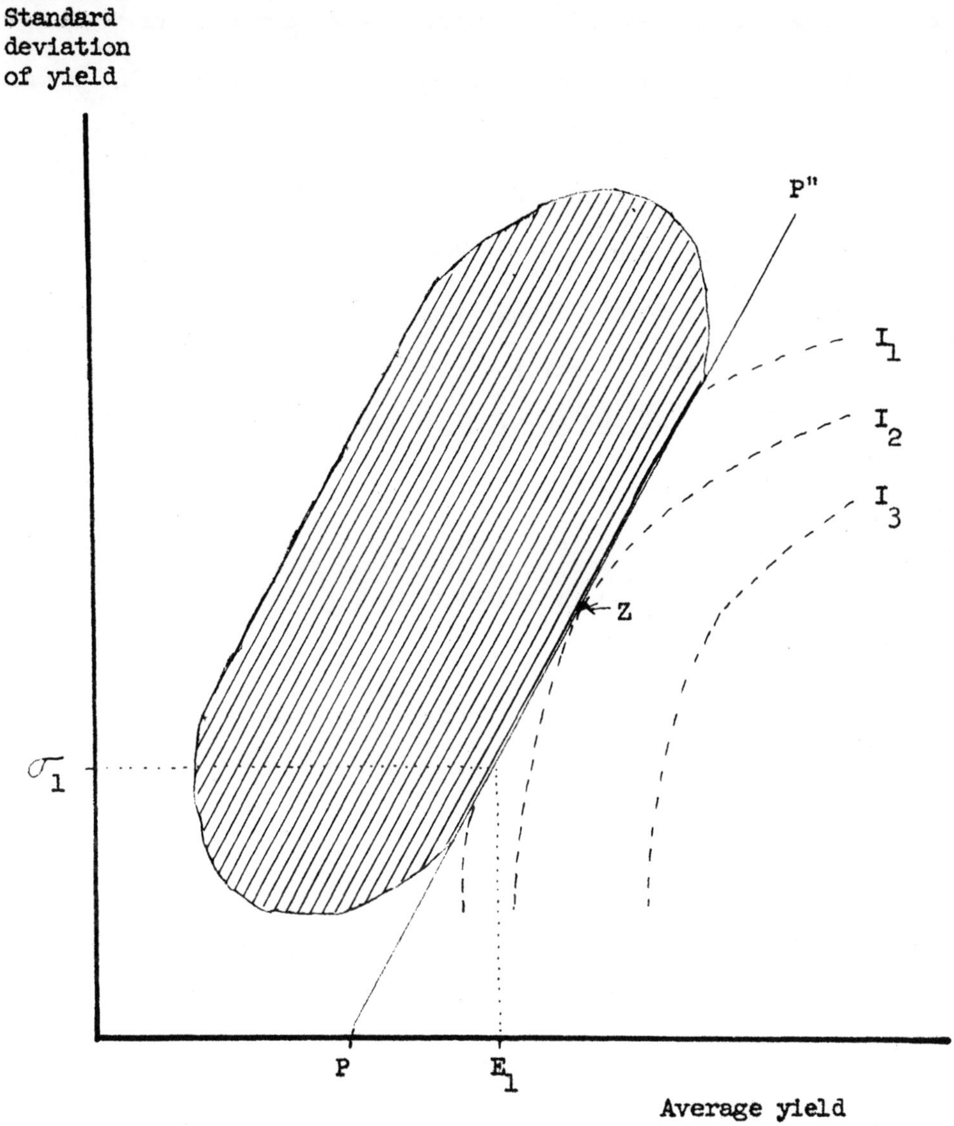

Fig. 25. - Equilibrium relationship between average yield and standard deviation of yield for portfolios

can be attained by some portfolio with zero variance due to Q. For example, there is a portfolio with an expected yield of E_1, a market response of B_1, and a variance due to non-market factors of zero. The total variance of such a portfolio is $(B_1)^2 V_I$ and its standard deviation $B_1 \sigma_I = \sigma_1$. For all portfolios with zero variance due to Q, B is a linear function of E -- line PP' in Fig. 24 -- and σ is a linear function of B; thus σ will be a linear function of E -- line PP" in Fig. 25. Note that this line also cuts the E-axis at the pure interest rate.[4]

We have shown that all portfolios for which the variance due to Q is zero will lie along line PP" in Fig. 25. But many possible portfolios (in particular, one-security portfolios) do not have zero variance due to Q; they will lie above the line, since they have as much variance due to B as do comparable efficient portfolios plus an additional variance due to Q. Such portfolios will lie within a space similar to that shown in Fig. 25. When the market has reached equilibrium, no quadratic program is required to distinguish between inefficient and efficient portfolios; the set of efficient portfolios is merely the set of diversified portfolios.

The investor who assumes that the security market is in equilibrium approaches the problem of portfolio selection in much

---

[4] Since B and σ for securities are likely to be correlated, the relationship between σ and E for single securities may also be a straight line intersecting the E-axis at the pure interest rate. This was the case for the estimates provided by the investment counselor, as can be seen in Fig. 20.

the same manner as the consumer approaches the problem of allocating his income between two goods. Having determined the attainable combinations of average yield and standard deviation of yield (line PP" in Fig. 25, the investor selects the combination which will maximize his utility. In Fig. 25 this combination is shown by point Z, where indifference curve I_2 touches line PP". In reading this figure, remember that since higher values of σ are less desirable than lower values, higher levels of utility lie to the right and downward.[5] An alternative interpretation of the portfolio-selection problem characterizes each investor as adjusting his holdings until his marginal rate of substitution of risk for earnings equals the common market rate. Of course the market rate is itself determined by the preferences of investors.

B. Arbitrage in the Security Market

We have described a process through which equilibrium in the security market can be attained. Instrumental in this process are arbitragers -- investors who attempt to discover securities which are temporarily undervalued or overvalued, and who, through their purchases and sales of such securities, bring about the price changes which restore equilibrium. The arbitrager does not believe

[5] This discussion assumes, of course, that investors wish to avert risk. For an excellent discussion of this problem (in a somewhat different context) see James Tobin, "Liquidity Preference as Behavior Towards Risk," The Review of Economics and Statistics, XXV (February, 1958), 65-86. Tobin derives a linear relationship between σ and E using a highly simplified model in which the alternative investments are cash and consols.

that all securities lie along a line similar to PP' in Fig. 24; he believes that some overvalued securities lie above such a line and that some undervalued securities lie below it. He rejects the former from consideration entirely, leaving only the undervalued securities plus those which he considers to be priced correctly in the set of securities from which efficient portfolios will be constructed.

Figure 26 serves as a convenient illustration of this process; it shows the values of B and E for the twenty securities selected by the investment counselor in the experiment described in the previous chapter. Notice that all but three of the securities (numbers 6, 10, and 12) lie along a line which passes through the pure interest rate;[6] the three exceptional securities are the ones which entered the set of efficient portfolios in such large amounts. Figure 26 indicates the reason. As indicated previously, when securities lie below the line, it will prove profitable to include them in portfolios, the amount depending on the magnitude of their Q-parameters relative to the distance from the line. All three of these securities had high Q-parameters but lay so far below the line (especially number 10) that the portfolio-analysis technique relied heavily on them in forming the set of efficient portfolios.

---

[6]The line was fitted free-hand. It passes through 1.12 at its intersection with the E-axis. This corresponds to an annual interest rate of 3.9% since all values refer to a three-year period.

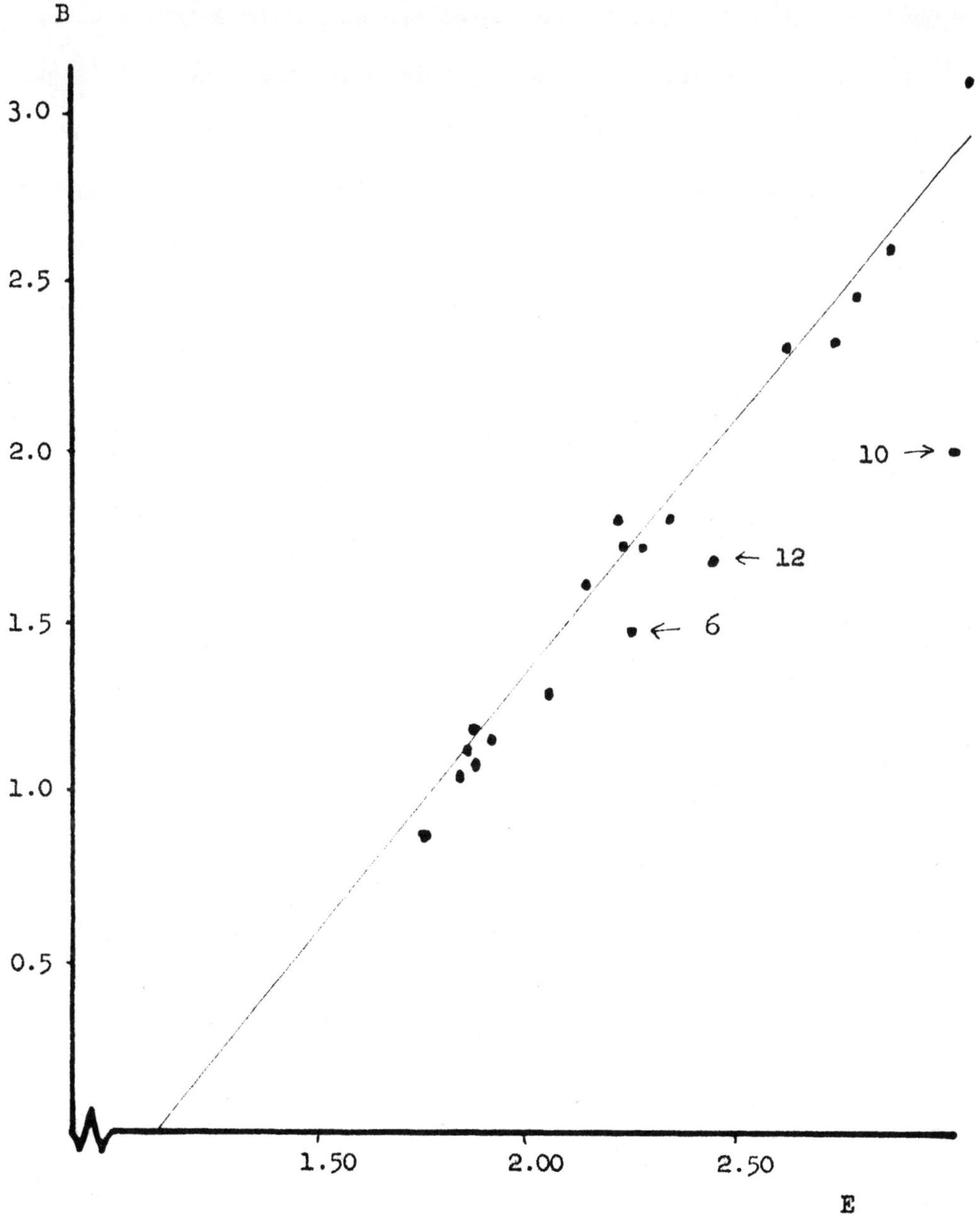

Fig. 26. - Predicted values of E and B for individual securities: subjective prediction experiment

Obviously these estimates overstated the counselor's true feelings concerning the distance of these points below the line. It is quite possible that the failure of these data to portray the absolute magnitudes of these distances correctly may have been the only major error which arose in the process of translating the investment counselor's beliefs into quantitative estimates. If this is the case, the consistency between the description of an arbitrager's views implied by our theory and the parameters obtained in the experiment provides a successful test of the positive theory.

C. Evidence on the Validity of the Theory

The theory of security market behavior presented here concerns the relationships among predicted values of various parameters. Since the test described in the previous section used _ex ante_ values it constituted a direct test of the theory. Unfortunately, the majority of available data deals with _ex post_ values, which describe not the predicted values of the parameters, but their actual magnitudes. Since prediction in the security market is an imperfect art, considerable differences between _ex post_ and _ex ante_ values of such parameters must occur; nonetheless, relationships which hold for _ex ante_ values should also prove valid for _ex post_ magnitudes, although with considerably less significance. This reduction in accuracy should be kept in mind in evaluating the tests reported in this section, all of which use _ex post_ values as estimates of the corresponding _ex ante_ magnitudes.

One implication of the theory concerns the relationship between average yield and standard deviation of yield for diversified portfolios: all such portfolios should lie along a straight line in the (σ, E) plane passing through the point at which $E = (1 + r)$ and $\sigma = 0$.

To test this implication, the performance of 23 open-end mutual funds was examined; this sample includes all common stock and balanced funds for which yield data were given in Wiesenberger's Investment Companies for all years from 1940 through 1959.[7]

Figure 27 shows the average yield and standard deviation of yield for the 23 mutual funds during the period 1940-51. The performance of two other large portfolios is also shown: the first, indicated by the point SP, comprises the common stocks which constitute the Standard and Poor's 90-stock index; the second, designated by point R, is a portfolio which includes equal amounts of the 96 industrial common stocks analyzed in this study. A line intersecting the horizontal axis at 1.03 (which corresponds to a 3% interest rate) has been drawn free-hand in Fig. 27; while there is considerable dispersion around this line, the data do not appear to be strongly inconsistent with the theory.

Figure 28 shows the performance of the 23 mutual funds during

---

[7]With one exception: Affiliated Fund was excluded from the analysis since its operations during some of the years were unusual for a mutual fund. Yields for the 23 companies were measured in accordance with the rules specified in Investment Companies (New York: Arthur Wiesenberger and Company, 1946-1960).

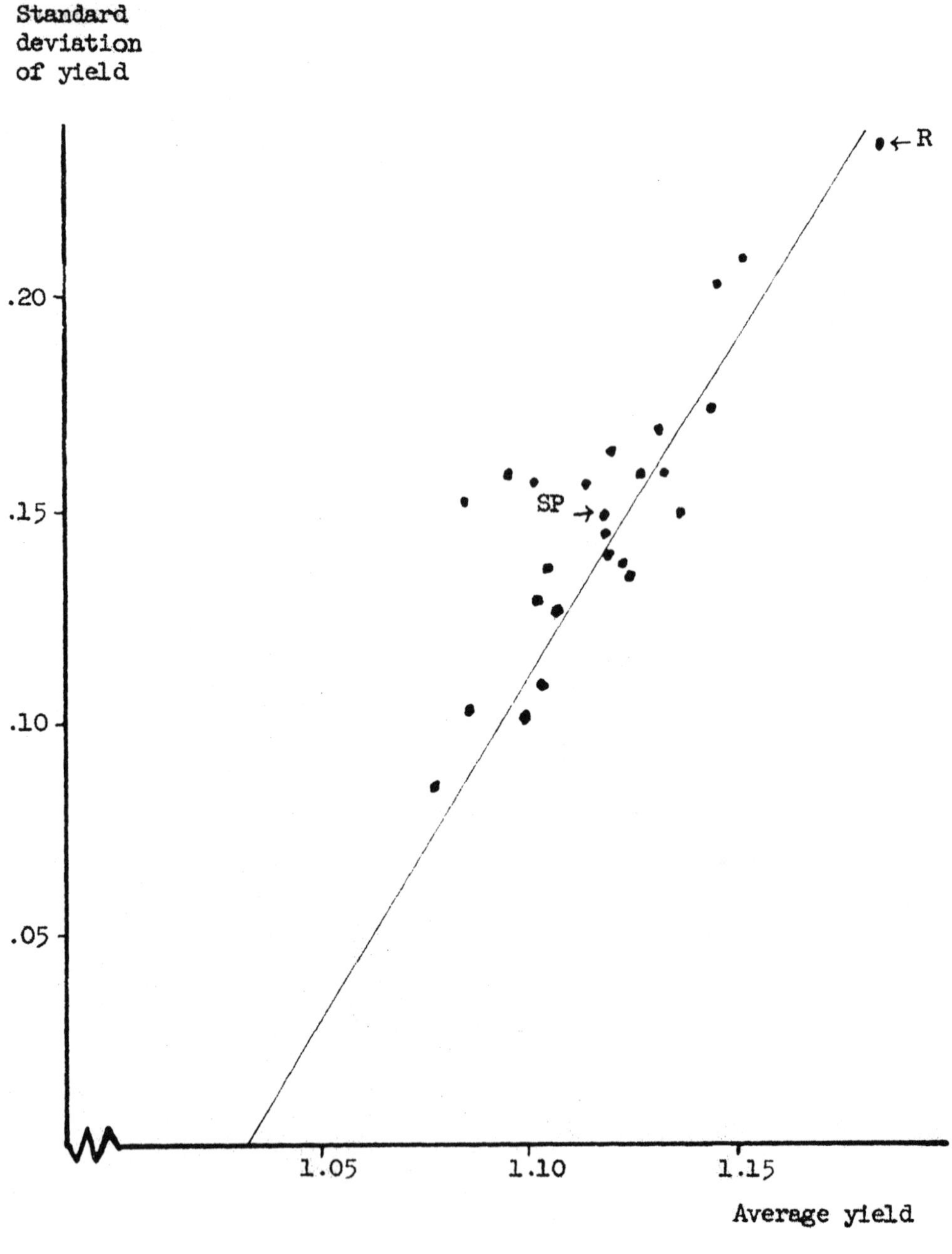

Fig. 27. - Average yield and standard deviation of yield: 23 investment companies and two indices, 1940-1951

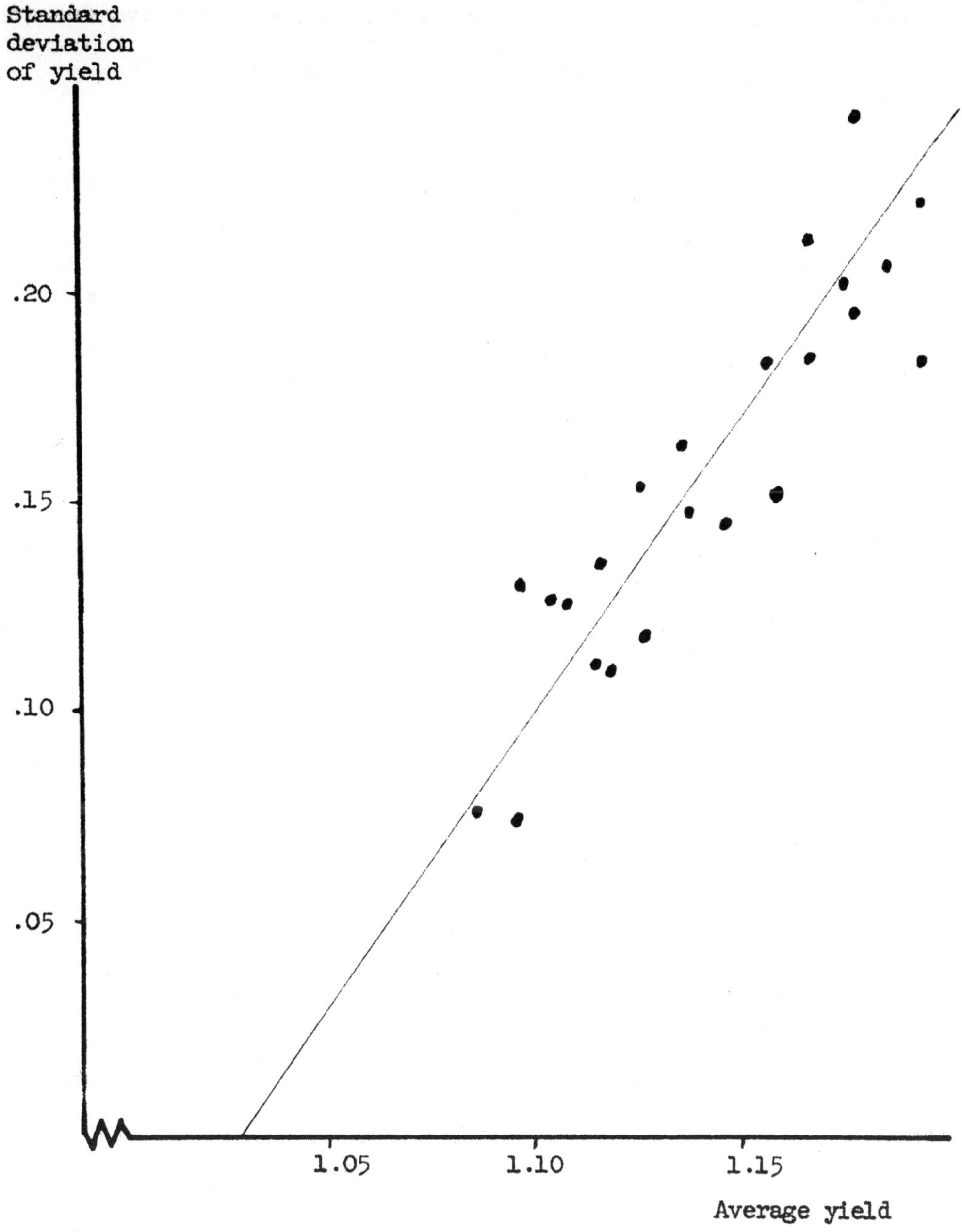

Fig. 28. - Average yield and standard deviation of yield: 23 investment companies, 1952-1959

the period 1952-59. Again a free-hand line has been drawn through 1.03 on the horizontal axis. These data also appear to be consistent with the implications of the theory.

A second implication of the theory concerns the relationship between B_i and E_i for individual securities; the model implies a linear relationship, with the value of E_i equal to (one plus the pure interest rate) when B_i is zero. To test this hypothesis, two periods were examined: 1940-51 and 1946-59. For each period, the correlation coefficient between B_i and E_i was calculated and two regression lines fitted by the least-squares technique.[8] Since both B_i and E_i are affected by price adjustments (the forces which bring about the implied relationship between these two parameters), the true relationship between B_i and E_i lies between the line obtained by the regression of B_i on E_i and that obtained by regressing E_i on B_i. Table 6 presents the results of the analysis.

The data in Table 6 are consistent with the hypothesis. The relationship between B_i and E_i is significant in both periods (a correlation coefficient of 0.26 would be significant at the 1% level). Moreover, the true line which relates B_i to E_i appears to

---

[8] For the early period the parameters were estimated in the manner described earlier. For the second period a different measure was used for (I) in estimating the B_i parameters. The index adopted was Moody's 200-common stock index; yearly figures were based on annual averages of the weekly level of the index. Data are given in Moody's Industrial Manual, (New York: Moody's Investors Service, 1940-1960).

Table 6

RELATIONSHIP BETWEEN B_i AND E_i FOR
96 INDUSTRIAL COMMON STOCKS

	1940-51	1946-59
Correlation coefficient between B_i and E_i	0.511	0.283
Value of E_i when $B_i = 0$:		
(1) Based on regression of B_i on E_i	0.942	0.934
(2) Based on regression of E_i on B_i	1.122	1.133
(3) Arithmetic mean of (1) and (2)	1.032	1.034

cut the average-yield axis at nearly the pure interest rate.[9]

Another implication of the theory concerns the relationship between Q_i and E_i. In equilibrium, the average yield of a security should depend entirely on its B_i parameter; there is no necessary reason for correlation between the average yield of a security and its Q_i parameter. Nonetheless, since the security market is not always in equilibrium, the value of Q_i may influence the yield of a security; if a security becomes undervalued, the rapidity with which

[9] One method for fitting a straight line to data under these circumstances was proposed by Abraham Wald, "The Fitting of Straight Lines if Both Variables Are Subject to Error," The Annals of Mathematical Statistics, XI (September, 1940), 284-300. When applied to the data of the 1940-51 period, Wald's method gave a regression line which intersected the E-axis at a value of 1.056.

its price will increase depends on the extent to which investors will wish to add it to their portfolios. We have shown that the larger is Q_i, the smaller will be the amount of such a security included in efficient portfolios; thus securities with high Q_i parameters will move more slowly toward equilibrium, causing an observed positive correlation between Q_i and E_i. In addition, securities for which Q_i is high tend to have large values of B_i; thus Q_i and E_i are likely to be related due to the correlation between B_i and E_i. In spite of these factors, however, the correlation between B_i and E_i should prove more significant than that between Q_i and E_i; a contrary finding would clearly be inconsistent with the theory.

The evidence of the two periods is contradictory. In the first period, the correlation between Q_i and E_i exceeded that between B_i and E_i -- the simple correlation coefficients were 0.606 and 0.511. On the other hand, the data from the second period were consistent with the hypothesis; the simple correlation coefficient between B_i and E_i was 0.283, more than twice 0.130, the coefficient for the correlation between Q_i and E_i.

Few conclusions can be reached from the evidence presented in this section; although the majority of the data proved to be consistent with the theory, one important set clearly contradicted one of its major implications. However, these data indicate that it would be premature to reject the theory at this time; extensive empirical tests are required in order to assess its true value as a tool of positive economics.

Reprinted from THE JOURNAL OF FINANCE, Vol. XIX, No. 3, September, 1964

CAPITAL ASSET PRICES: A THEORY OF MARKET EQUILIBRIUM UNDER CONDITIONS OF RISK*

WILLIAM F. SHARPE†

I. INTRODUCTION

ONE OF THE PROBLEMS which has plagued those attempting to predict the behavior of capital markets is the absence of a body of positive microeconomic theory dealing with conditions of risk. Although many useful insights can be obtained from the traditional models of investment under conditions of certainty, the pervasive influence of risk in financial transactions has forced those working in this area to adopt models of price behavior which are little more than assertions. A typical classroom explanation of the determination of capital asset prices, for example, usually begins with a careful and relatively rigorous description of the process through which individual preferences and physical relationships interact to determine an equilibrium pure interest rate. This is generally followed by the assertion that somehow a market risk-premium is also determined, with the prices of assets adjusting accordingly to account for differences in their risk.

A useful representation of the view of the capital market implied in such discussions is illustrated in Figure 1. In equilibrium, capital asset prices have adjusted so that the investor, if he follows rational procedures (primarily diversification), is able to attain any desired point along a *capital market line*.[1] He may obtain a higher expected rate of return on his holdings only by incurring additional risk. In effect, the market presents him with two prices: the *price of time*, or the pure interest rate (shown by the intersection of the line with the horizontal axis) and the *price of risk*, the additional expected return per unit of risk borne (the reciprocal of the slope of the line).

* A great many people provided comments on early versions of this paper which led to major improvements in the exposition. In addition to the referees, who were most helpful, the author wishes to express his appreciation to Dr. Harry Markowitz of the RAND Corporation, Professor Jack Hirshleifer of the University of California at Los Angeles, and to Professors Yoram Barzel, George Brabb, Bruce Johnson, Walter Oi and R. Haney Scott of the University of Washington.

† Associate Professor of Operations Research, University of Washington.

1. Although some discussions are also consistent with a non-linear (but monotonic) curve.

At present there is no theory describing the manner in which the price of risk results from the basic influences of investor preferences, the physical attributes of capital assets, etc. Moreover, lacking such a theory, it is difficult to give any real meaning to the relationship between the price of a single asset and its risk. Through diversification, some of the risk inherent in an asset can be avoided so that its total risk is obviously not the relevant influence on its price; unfortunately little has been said concerning the particular risk component which is relevant.

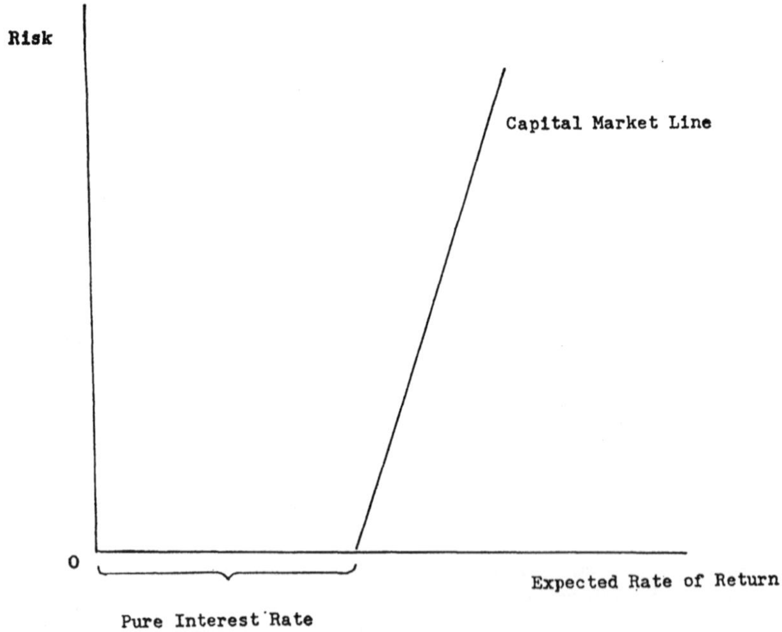

FIGURE 1

In the last ten years a number of economists have developed ***normative*** models dealing with asset choice under conditions of risk. Markowitz,[2] following Von Neumann and Morgenstern, developed an analysis based on the expected utility maxim and proposed a general solution for the portfolio selection problem. Tobin[3] showed that under certain conditions Markowitz's model implies that the process of investment choice can be broken down into two phases: first, the choice of a unique optimum combination of risky assets; and second, a separate choice concerning the allocation of funds between such a combination and a single riskless

2. Harry M. Markowitz, *Portfolio Selection, Efficient Diversification of Investments* (New York: John Wiley and Sons, Inc., 1959). The major elements of the theory first appeared in his article "Portfolio Selection," *The Journal of Finance*, XII (March 1952), 77-91.

3. James Tobin, "Liquidity Preference as Behavior Towards Risk," *The Review of Economic Studies*, XXV (February, 1958), 65-86.

asset. Recently, Hicks[4] has used a model similar to that proposed by Tobin to derive corresponding conclusions about individual investor behavior, dealing somewhat more explicitly with the nature of the conditions under which the process of investment choice can be dichotomized. An even more detailed discussion of this process, including a rigorous proof in the context of a choice among lotteries has been presented by Gordon and Gangolli.[5]

Although all the authors cited use virtually the same model of investor behavior,[6] none has yet attempted to extend it to construct a *market* equilibrium theory of asset prices under conditions of risk.[7] We will show that such an extension provides a theory with implications consistent with the assertions of traditional financial theory described above. Moreover, it sheds considerable light on the relationship between the price of an asset and the various components of its overall risk. For these reasons it warrants consideration as a model of the determination of capital asset prices.

Part II provides the model of individual investor behavior under conditions of risk. In Part III the equilibrium conditions for the capital market are considered and the capital market line derived. The implications for the relationship between the prices of individual capital assets and the various components of risk are described in Part IV.

II. Optimal Investment Policy for the Individual

The Investor's Preference Function

Assume that an individual views the outcome of any investment in probabilistic terms; that is, he thinks of the possible results in terms of some probability distribution. In assessing the desirability of a particular investment, however, he is willing to act on the basis of only two para-

4. John R. Hicks, "Liquidity," *The Economic Journal*, LXXII (December, 1962), 787-802.

5. M. J. Gordon and Ramesh Gangolli, "Choice Among and Scale of Play on Lottery Type Alternatives," College of Business Administration, University of Rochester, 1962. For another discussion of this relationship see W. F. Sharpe, "A Simplified Model for Portfolio Analysis," *Management Science*, Vol. 9, No. 2 (January 1963), 277-293. A related discussion can be found in F. Modigliani and M. H. Miller, "The Cost of Capital, Corporation Finance, and the Theory of Investment," *The American Economic Review*, XLVIII (June 1958), 261-297.

6. Recently Hirshleifer has suggested that the mean-variance approach used in the articles cited is best regarded as a special case of a more general formulation due to Arrow. See Hirshleifer's "Investment Decision Under Uncertainty," *Papers and Proceedings of the Seventy-Sixth Annual Meeting of the American Economic Association*, Dec. 1963, or Arrow's "Le Role des Valeurs Boursieres pour la Repartition la Meilleure des Risques," *International Colloquium on Econometrics*, 1952.

7. After preparing this paper the author learned that Mr. Jack L. Treynor, of Arthur D. Little, Inc., had independently developed a model similar in many respects to the one described here. Unfortunately Mr. Treynor's excellent work on this subject is, at present, unpublished.

meters of this distribution—its expected value and standard deviation.[8] This can be represented by a total utility function of the form:

$$U = f(E_w, \sigma_w)$$

where E_w indicates expected future wealth and σ_w the predicted standard deviation of the possible divergence of actual future wealth from E_w.

Investors are assumed to prefer a higher expected future wealth to a lower value, ceteris paribus ($dU/dE_w > 0$). Moreover, they exhibit risk-aversion, choosing an investment offering a lower value of σ_w to one with a greater level, given the level of E_w ($dU/d\sigma_w < 0$). These assumptions imply that indifference curves relating E_w and σ_w will be upward-sloping.[9]

To simplify the analysis, we assume that an investor has decided to commit a given amount (W_i) of his present wealth to investment. Letting W_t be his terminal wealth and R the rate of return on his investment:

$$R \equiv \frac{W_t - W_i}{W_i},$$

we have

$$W_t = R\,W_i + W_i.$$

This relationship makes it possible to express the investor's utility in terms of R, since terminal wealth is directly related to the rate of return:

$$U = g(E_R, \sigma_R).$$

Figure 2 summarizes the model of investor preferences in a family of indifference curves; successive curves indicate higher levels of utility as one moves down and/or to the right.[10]

8. Under certain conditions the mean-variance approach can be shown to lead to unsatisfactory predictions of behavior. Markowitz suggests that a model based on the semi-variance (the average of the squared deviations below the mean) would be preferable; in light of the formidable computational problems, however, he bases his analysis on the variance and standard deviation.

9. While only these characteristics are required for the analysis, it is generally assumed that the curves have the property of diminishing marginal rates of substitution between E_w and σ_w, as do those in our diagrams.

10. Such indifference curves can also be derived by assuming that the investor wishes to maximize expected utility and that his total utility can be represented by a quadratic function of R with decreasing marginal utility. Both Markowitz and Tobin present such a derivation. A similar approach is used by Donald E. Farrar in *The Investment Decision Under Uncertainty* (Prentice-Hall, 1962). Unfortunately Farrar makes an error in his derivation; he appeals to the Von-Neumann-Morgenstern cardinal utility axioms to transform a function of the form:

$$E(U) = a + bE_R - cE_R^2 - c\sigma_R^2$$

into one of the form:

$$E(U) = k_1E_R - k_2\sigma_R^2.$$

That such a transformation is not consistent with the axioms can readily be seen in this form, since the first equation implies non-linear indifference curves in the E_R, σ_R^2 plane while the second implies a linear relationship. Obviously no three (different) points can lie on both a line and a non-linear curve (with a monotonic derivative). Thus the two functions must imply different orderings among alternative choices in at least some instance.

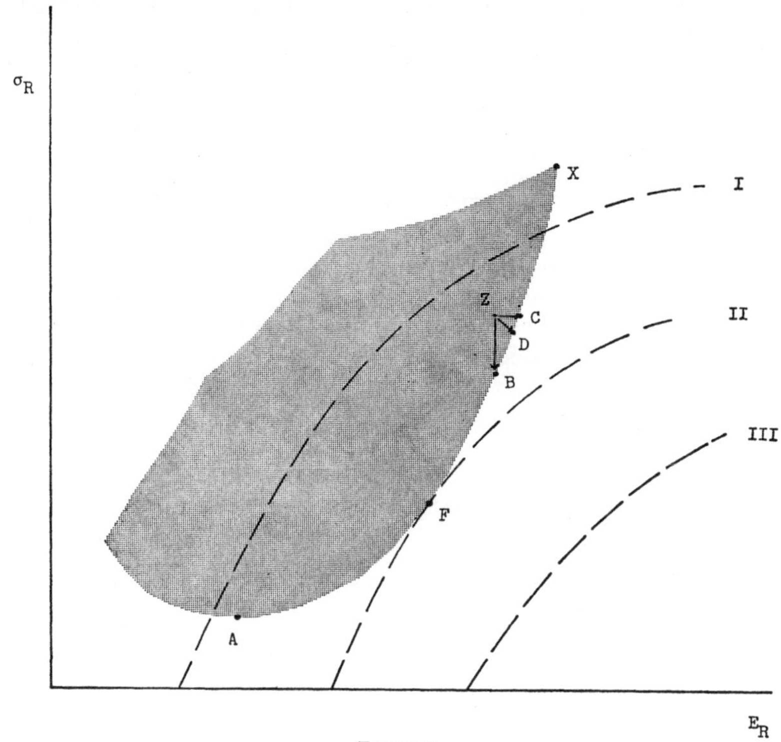

FIGURE 2

The Investment Opportunity Curve

The model of investor behavior considers the investor as choosing from a set of investment opportunities that one which maximizes his utility. Every investment plan available to him may be represented by a point in the E_R, σ_R plane. If all such plans involve some risk, the area composed of such points will have an appearance similar to that shown in Figure 2. The investor will choose from among all possible plans the one placing him on the indifference curve representing the highest level of utility (point F). The decision can be made in two stages: first, find the set of efficient investment plans and, second choose one from among this set. A plan is said to be efficient if (and only if) there is no alternative with either (1) the same E_R and a lower σ_R, (2) the same σ_R and a higher E_R or (3) a higher E_R and a lower σ_R. Thus investment Z is inefficient since investments B, C, and D (among others) dominate it. The only plans which would be chosen must lie along the lower right-hand boundary (AFBDCX)—the *investment opportunity curve.*

To understand the nature of this curve, consider two investment plans —A and B, each including one or more assets. Their predicted expected values and standard deviations of rate of return are shown in Figure 3.

If the proportion α of the individual's wealth is placed in plan A and the remainder (1-α) in B, the expected rate of return of the combination will lie between the expected returns of the two plans:

$$E_{Rc} = \alpha E_{Ra} + (1 - \alpha) E_{Rb}$$

The predicted standard deviation of return of the combination is:

$$\sigma_{Rc} = \sqrt{\alpha^2\sigma_{Ra}{}^2 + (1 - \alpha)^2 \sigma_{Rb}{}^2 + 2r_{ab}\,\alpha(1 - \alpha)\,\sigma_{Ra}\sigma_{Rb}}$$

Note that this relationship includes r_{ab}, the correlation coefficient between the predicted rates of return of the two investment plans. A value of +1 would indicate an investor's belief that there is a precise positive relationship between the outcomes of the two investments. A zero value would indicate a belief that the outcomes of the two investments are completely independent and —1 that the investor feels that there is a precise inverse relationship between them. In the usual case r_{ab} will have a value between 0 and +1.

Figure 3 shows the possible values of E_{Rc} and σ_{Rc} obtainable with different combinations of A and B under two different assumptions about

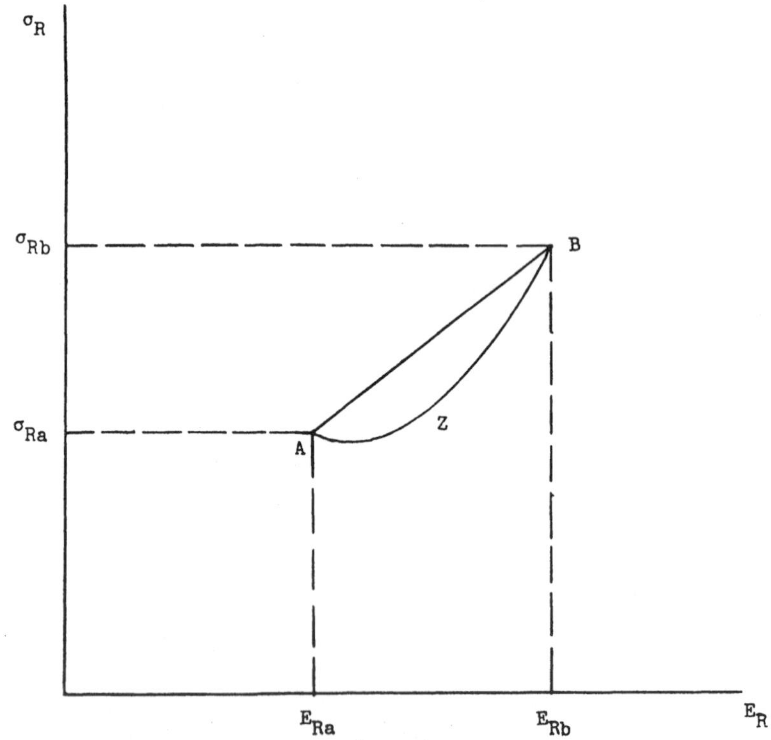

FIGURE 3

the value of r_{ab}. If the two investments are perfectly correlated, the combinations will lie along a straight line between the two points, since in this case both E_{Rc} and σ_{Rc} will be linearly related to the proportions invested in the two plans.[11] If they are less than perfectly positively correlated, the standard deviation of any combination must be less than that obtained with perfect correlation (since r_{ab} will be less); thus the combinations must lie along a curve below the line AB.[12] AZB shows such a curve for the case of complete independence ($r_{ab} = 0$); with negative correlation the locus is even more U-shaped.[13]

The manner in which the investment opportunity curve is formed is relatively simple conceptually, although exact solutions are usually quite difficult.[14] One first traces curves indicating E_R, σ_R values available with simple combinations of individual assets, then considers combinations of combinations of assets. The lower right-hand boundary must be either linear or increasing at an increasing rate ($d^2 \sigma_R/dE^2_R > 0$). As suggested earlier, the complexity of the relationship between the characteristics of individual assets and the location of the investment opportunity curve makes it difficult to provide a simple rule for assessing the desirability of individual assets, since the effect of an asset on an investor's over-all investment opportunity curve depends not only on its expected rate of return (E_{Ri}) and risk (σ_{Ri}), but also on its correlations with the other available opportunities ($r_{i1}, r_{i2}, \ldots, r_{in}$). However, such a rule is implied by the equilibrium conditions for the model, as we will show in part IV.

The Pure Rate of Interest

We have not yet dealt with riskless assets. Let P be such an asset; its risk is zero ($\sigma_{Rp} = 0$) and its expected rate of return, E_{Rp}, is equal (by definition) to the pure interest rate. If an investor places α of his wealth

11.
$$E_{Rc} = \alpha E_{Ra} + (1 - \alpha) E_{R_b} = E_{Rb} + (E_{R_a} - E_{R_b}) \alpha$$
$$\sigma_{R_c} = \sqrt{\alpha^2 \sigma_{R_a}{}^2 + (1-\alpha)^2 \sigma_{Rb}{}^2 + 2 r_{ab}\, \alpha(1-\alpha)\, \sigma_{Ra}\, \sigma_{Rb}}$$
but $r_{ab} = 1$, therefore the expression under the square root sign can be factored:
$$\sigma_{Rc} = \sqrt{[\alpha \sigma_{Ra} + (1-\alpha)\, \sigma_{R_b}]^2}$$
$$= \alpha\, \sigma_{Ra} + (1-\alpha)\, \sigma_{Rb}$$
$$= \sigma_{Rb} + (\sigma_{Ra} - \sigma_{Rb})\, \alpha$$

12. This curvature is, in essence, the rationale for diversification.

13. When $r_{ab} = 0$, the slope of the curve at point A is $-\dfrac{\sigma_{Ra}}{E_{Rb} - E_{Ra}}$, at point B it is $\dfrac{\sigma_{Rb}}{E_{Rb} - E_{Ra}}$. When $r_{ab} = -1$, the curve degenerates to two straight lines to a point on the horizontal axis.

14. Markowitz has shown that this is a problem in parametric quadratic programming. An efficient solution technique is described in his article, "The Optimization of a Quadratic Function Subject to Linear Constraints," *Naval Research Logistics Quarterly*, Vol. 3 (March and June, 1956), 111-133. A solution method for a special case is given in the author's "A Simplified Model for Portfolio Analysis," *op. cit.*

in P and the remainder in some risky asset A, he would obtain an expected rate of return:

$$E_{Rc} = \alpha E_{Rp} + (1 - \alpha) E_{Ra}$$

The standard deviation of such a combination would be:

$$\sigma_{Rc} = \sqrt{\alpha^2 \sigma^2_{Rp} + (1 - \alpha)^2 \sigma_{Ra}{}^2 + 2 r_{pa}\, \alpha (1 - \alpha)\, \sigma_{Rp} \sigma_{Ra}}$$

but since $\sigma_{Rp} = 0$, this reduces to:

$$\sigma_{Rc} = (1 - \alpha)\, \sigma_{Ra}.$$

This implies that all combinations involving any risky asset or combination of assets plus the riskless asset must have values of E_{Rc} and σ_{Rc} which lie along a straight line between the points representing the two components. Thus in Figure 4 all combinations of E_R and σ_R lying along

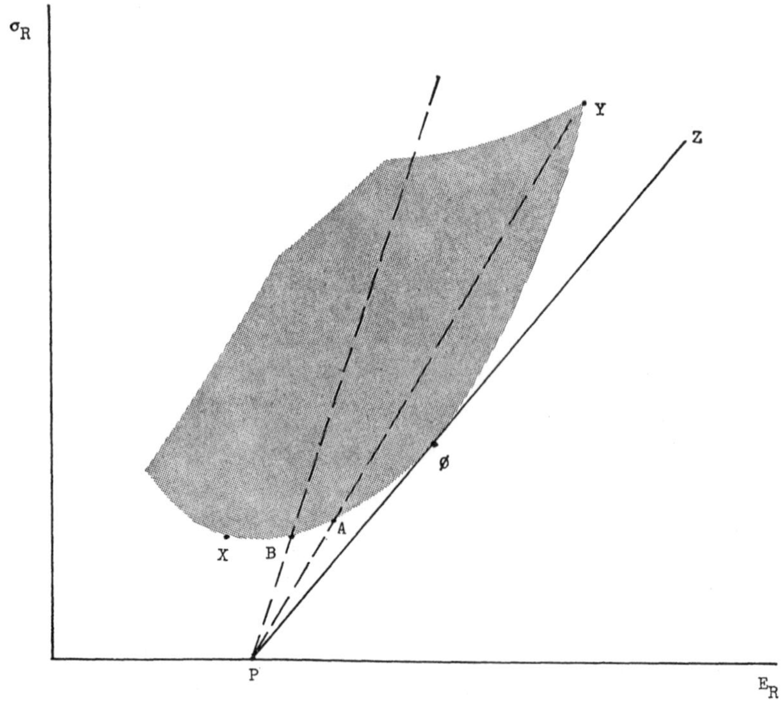

FIGURE 4

the line PA are attainable if some money is loaned at the pure rate and some placed in A. Similarly, by lending at the pure rate and investing in B, combinations along PB can be attained. Of all such possibilities, however, one will dominate: that investment plan lying at the point of the original investment opportunity curve where a ray from point P is tangent to the curve. In Figure 4 all investments lying along the original curve from X to ϕ are dominated by some combination of investment in ϕ and lending at the pure interest rate.

Consider next the possibility of borrowing. If the investor can borrow at the pure rate of interest, this is equivalent to disinvesting in P. The effect of borrowing to purchase more of any given investment than is possible with the given amount of wealth can be found simply by letting α take on negative values in the equations derived for the case of lending. This will obviously give points lying along the extension of line PA if borrowing is used to purchase more of A; points lying along the extension of PB if the funds are used to purchase B, etc.

As in the case of lending, however, one investment plan will dominate all others when borrowing is possible. When the rate at which funds can be borrowed equals the lending rate, this plan will be the same one which is dominant if lending is to take place. Under these conditions, the investment opportunity curve becomes a line (PϕZ in Figure 4). Moreover, if the original investment opportunity curve is not linear at point ϕ, the process of investment choice can be dichotomized as follows: first select the (unique) optimum combination of risky assets (point ϕ), and second borrow or lend to obtain the particular point on PZ at which an indifference curve is tangent to the line.[15]

Before proceeding with the analysis, it may be useful to consider alternative assumptions under which only a combination of assets lying at the point of tangency between the original investment opportunity curve and a ray from P can be efficient. Even if borrowing is impossible, the investor will choose ϕ (and lending) if his risk-aversion leads him to a point below ϕ on the line Pϕ. Since a large number of investors choose to place some of their funds in relatively risk-free investments, this is not an unlikely possibility. Alternatively, if borrowing is possible but only up to some limit, the choice of ϕ would be made by all but those investors willing to undertake considerable risk. These alternative paths lead to the main conclusion, thus making the assumption of borrowing or lending at the pure interest rate less onerous than it might initially appear to be.

III. Equilibrium in the Capital Market

In order to derive conditions for equilibrium in the capital market we invoke two assumptions. First, we assume a common pure rate of interest, with all investors able to borrow or lend funds on equal terms. Second, we assume homogeneity of investor expectations:[16] investors are assumed

15. This proof was first presented by Tobin for the case in which the pure rate of interest is zero (cash). Hicks considers the lending situation under comparable conditions but does not allow borrowing. Both authors present their analysis using maximization subject to constraints expressed as equalities. Hicks' analysis assumes independence and thus insures that the solution will include no negative holdings of risky assets; Tobin's covers the general case, thus his solution would generally include negative holdings of some assets. The discussion in this paper is based on Markowitz' formulation, which includes non-negativity constraints on the holdings of all assets.

16. A term suggested by one of the referees.

to agree on the prospects of various investments—the expected values, standard deviations and correlation coefficients described in Part II. Needless to say, these are highly restrictive and undoubtedly unrealistic assumptions. However, since the proper test of a theory is not the realism of its assumptions but the acceptability of its implications, and since these assumptions imply equilibrium conditions which form a major part of classical financial doctrine, it is far from clear that this formulation should be rejected—especially in view of the dearth of alternative models leading to similar results.

Under these assumptions, given some set of capital asset prices, each investor will view his alternatives in the same manner. For one set of prices the alternatives might appear as shown in Figure 5. In this situa-

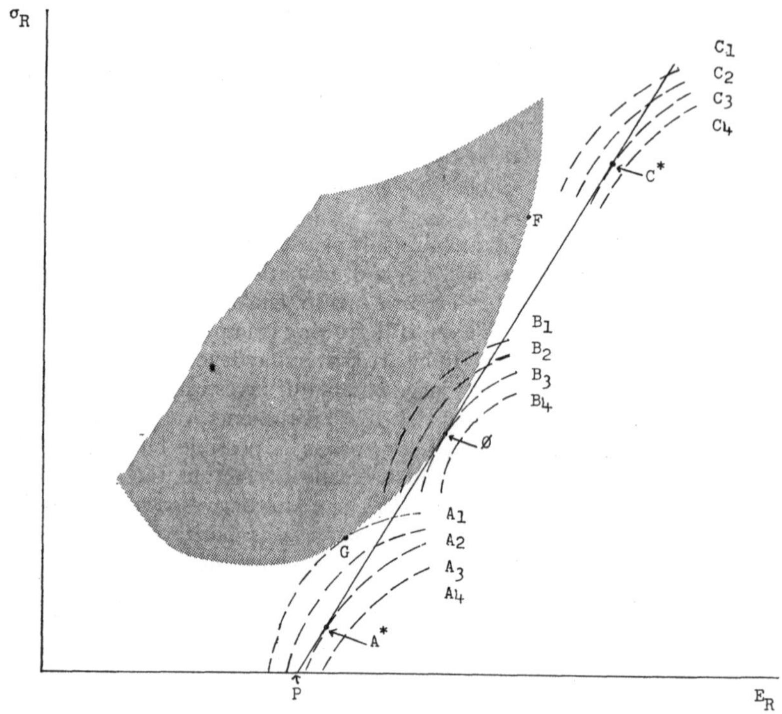

FIGURE 5

tion, an investor with the preferences indicated by indifference curves A_1 through A_4 would seek to lend some of his funds at the pure interest rate and to invest the remainder in the combination of assets shown by point ϕ, since this would give him the preferred over-all position A*. An investor with the preferences indicated by curves B_1 through B_4 would seek to invest all his funds in combination ϕ, while an investor with indifference curves C_1 through C_4 would invest all his funds plus additional (borrowed) funds in combination ϕ in order to reach his preferred position (C*). In any event, all would attempt to purchase only those risky assets which enter combination ϕ.

The attempts by investors to purchase the assets in combination ϕ and their lack of interest in holding assets not in combination ϕ would, of course, lead to a revision of prices. The prices of assets in ϕ will rise and, since an asset's expected return relates future income to present price, their expected returns will fall. This will reduce the attractiveness of combinations which include such assets; thus point ϕ (among others) will move to the left of its initial position.[17] On the other hand, the prices of assets not in ϕ will fall, causing an increase in their expected returns and a rightward movement of points representing combinations which include them. Such price changes will lead to a revision of investors' actions; some new combination or combinations will become attractive, leading to different demands and thus to further revisions in prices. As the process continues, the investment opportunity curve will tend to become more linear, with points such as ϕ moving to the left and formerly inefficient points (such as F and G) moving to the right.

Capital asset prices must, of course, continue to change until a set of prices is attained for which every asset enters at least one combination lying on the capital market line. Figure 6 illustrates such an equilibrium condition.[18] All possibilities in the shaded area can be attained with combinations of risky assets, while points lying along the line PZ can be attained by borrowing or lending at the pure rate plus an investment in some combination of risky assets. Certain possibilities (those lying along PZ from point A to point B) can be obtained in either manner. For example, the E_R, σ_R values shown by point A can be obtained solely by some combination of risky assets; alternatively, the point can be reached by a combination of lending and investing in combination C of risky assets.

It is important to recognize that in the situation shown in Figure 6 many alternative combinations of risky assets are efficient (i.e., lie along line PZ), and thus the theory does not imply that all investors will hold the same combination.[19] On the other hand, all such combinations must be perfectly (positively) correlated, since they lie along a linear border of

17. If investors consider the variability of future dollar returns unrelated to present price, both E_R and σ_R will fall; under these conditions the point representing an asset would move along a ray through the origin as its price changes.

18. The area in Figure 6 representing E_R, σ_R values attained with only risky assets has been drawn at some distance from the horizontal axis for emphasis. It is likely that a more accurate representation would place it very close to the axis.

19. This statement contradicts Tobin's conclusion that there will be a unique optimal combination of risky assets. Tobin's proof of a unique optimum can be shown to be incorrect for the case of perfect correlation of efficient risky investment plans if the line connecting their E_R, σ_R points would pass through point P. In the graph on page 83 of this article (*op. cit.*) the constant-risk locus would, in this case, degenerate from a family of ellipses into one of straight lines parallel to the constant-return loci, thus giving multiple optima.

the E_R, σ_R region.[20] This provides a key to the relationship between the prices of capital assets and different types of risk.

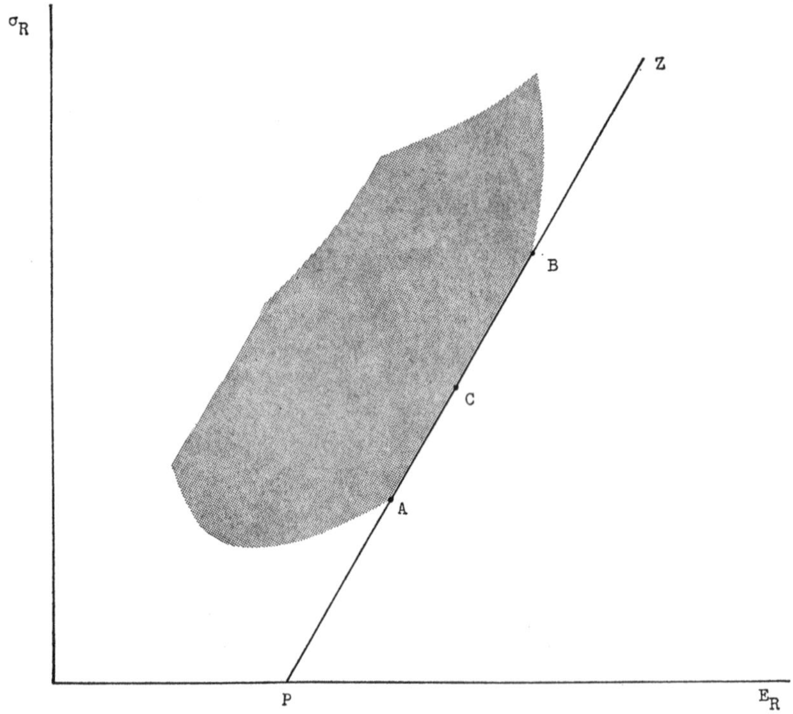

FIGURE 6

IV. THE PRICES OF CAPITAL ASSETS

We have argued that in equilibrium there will be a simple linear relationship between the expected return and standard deviation of return for efficient combinations of risky assets. Thus far nothing has been said about such a relationship for individual assets. Typically the E_R, σ_R values associated with single assets will lie above the capital market line, reflecting the inefficiency of undiversified holdings. Moreover, such points may be scattered throughout the feasible region, with no consistent relationship between their expected return and total risk (σ_R). However, there will be a consistent relationship between their expected returns and what might best be called *systematic risk*, as we will now show.

Figure 7 illustrates the typical relationship between a single capital

20. E_R, σ_R values given by combinations of any two combinations must lie within the region and cannot plot above a straight line joining the points. In this case they cannot plot below such a straight line. But since only in the case of perfect correlation will they plot along a straight line, the two combinations must be perfectly correlated. As shown in Part IV, this does not necessarily imply that the individual securities they contain are perfectly correlated.

asset (point i) and an efficient combination of assets (point g) of which it is a part. The curve igg′ indicates all E_R, σ_R values which can be obtained with feasible combinations of asset i and combination g. As before, we denote such a combination in terms of a proportion α of asset i and $(1 - \alpha)$ of combination g. A value of $\alpha = 1$ would indicate pure invest-

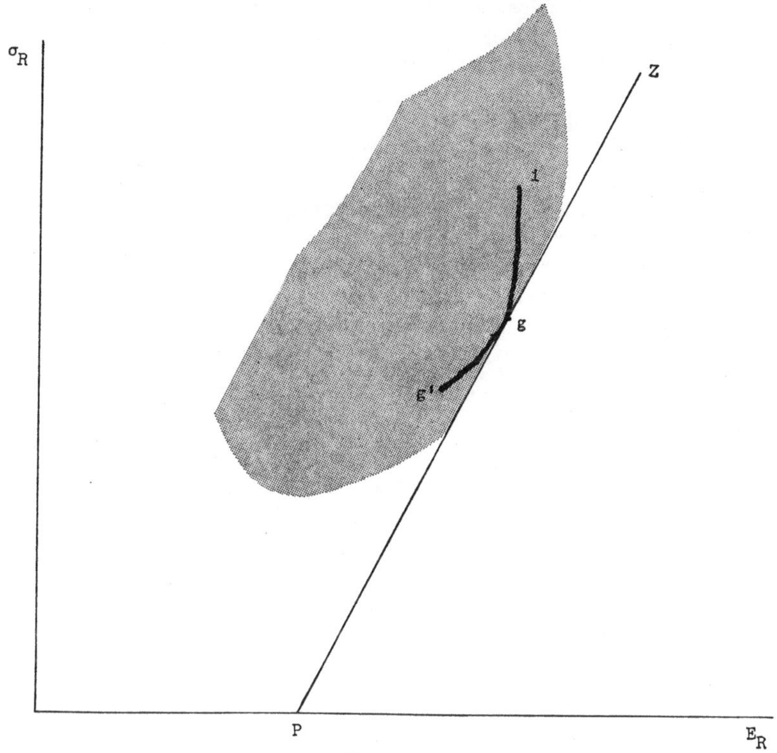

FIGURE 7

ment in asset i while $\alpha = 0$ would imply investment in combination g. Note, however, that $\alpha = .5$ implies a total investment of more than half the funds in asset i, since half would be invested in i itself and the other half used to purchase combination g, which also includes some of asset i. This means that a combination in which asset i does not appear at all must be represented by some negative value of α. Point g′ indicates such a combination.

In Figure 7 the curve igg′ has been drawn tangent to the capital market line (PZ) at point g. This is no accident. All such curves must be tangent to the capital market line in equilibrium, since (1) they must touch it at the point representing the efficient combination and (2) they are continuous at that point.[21] Under these conditions a lack of tangency would

21. Only if $r_{ig} = -1$ will the curve be discontinuous over the range in question.

imply that the curve intersects PZ. But then some feasible combination of assets would lie to the right of the capital market line, an obvious impossibility since the capital market line represents the efficient boundary of feasible values of E_R and σ_R.

The requirement that curves such as igg′ be tangent to the capital market line can be shown to lead to a relatively simple formula which relates the expected rate of return to various elements of risk for all assets which are included in combination g.[22] Its economic meaning can best be seen if the relationship between the return of asset i and that of combination g is viewed in a manner similar to that used in regression analysis.[23] Imagine that we were given a number of (ex post) observations of the return of the two investments. The points might plot as shown in Fig. 8. The scatter of the R_i observations around their mean (which will approximate E_{Ri}) is, of course, evidence of the total risk of the asset — σ_{Ri}. But part of the scatter is due to an underlying relationship with the return on combination g, shown by B_{ig}, the slope of the regression line. The response of R_i to changes in R_g (and variations in R_g itself) account for

22. The standard deviation of a combination of g and i will be:

$$\sigma = \sqrt{\alpha^2\sigma_{Ri}^2 + (1-\alpha)^2\sigma_{Rg}^2 + 2r_{ig}\alpha(1-\alpha)\sigma_{Ri}\sigma_{Rg}}$$

at $\alpha = 0$:

$$\frac{d\sigma}{d\alpha} = -\frac{1}{\sigma}[\sigma_{Rg}^2 - r_{ig}\sigma_{Ri}\sigma_{Rg}]$$

but $\sigma = \sigma_{Rg}$ at $\alpha = 0$. Thus:

$$\frac{d\sigma}{d\alpha} = -[\sigma_{Rg} - r_{ig}\sigma_{Ri}]$$

The expected return of a combination will be:

$$E = \alpha E_{Ri} + (1-\alpha)E_{Rg}$$

Thus, at all values of α:

$$\frac{dE}{d\alpha} = -[E_{Rg} - E_{Ri}]$$

and, at $\alpha = 0$:

$$\frac{d\sigma}{dE} = \frac{\sigma_{Rg} - r_{ig}\sigma_{Ri}}{E_{Rg} - E_{Ri}}.$$

Let the equation of the capital market line be:

$$\sigma_R = s(E_R - P)$$

where P is the pure interest rate. Since igg′ is tangent to the line when $\alpha = 0$, and since (E_{Rg}, σ_{Rg}) lies on the line:

$$\frac{\sigma_{Rg} - r_{ig}\sigma_{Ri}}{E_{Rg} - E_{Ri}} = \frac{\sigma_{Rg}}{E_{Rg} - P}$$

or:

$$\frac{r_{ig}\sigma_{Ri}}{\sigma_{Rg}} = -\left[\frac{P}{E_{Rg} - P}\right] + \left[\frac{1}{E_{Rg} - P}\right]E_{Ri}.$$

23. This model has been called the diagonal model since its portfolio analysis solution can be facilitated by re-arranging the data so that the variance-covariance matrix becomes diagonal. The method is described in the author's article, cited earlier.

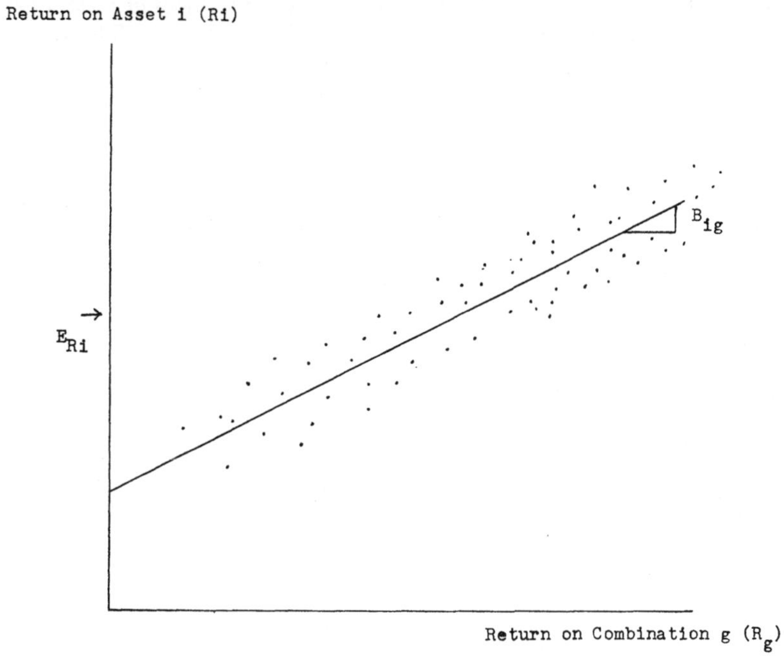

FIGURE 8

much of the variation in R_i. It is this component of the asset's total risk which we term the *systematic* risk. The remainder,[24] being uncorrelated with R_g, is the unsystematic component. This formulation of the relationship between R_i and R_g can be employed *ex ante* as a predictive model. B_{ig} becomes the *predicted* response of R_i to changes in R_g. Then, given σ_{Rg} (the predicted risk of R_g), the systematic portion of the predicted risk of each asset can be determined.

This interpretation allows us to state the relationship derived from the tangency of curves such as igg′ with the capital market line in the form shown in Figure 9. All assets entering efficient combination g must have (predicted) B_{ig} and E_{Ri} values lying on the line PQ.[25] Prices will

24. ex post, the standard error.

25.

$$r_{ig} = \sqrt{\frac{B_{ig}{}^2\sigma_{Rg}{}^2}{\sigma_{Ri}{}^2}} = \frac{B_{ig}\sigma_{Rg}}{\sigma_{Ri}}$$

and:

$$B_{ig} = \frac{r_{ig}\sigma_{Ri}}{\sigma_{Rg}}.$$

The expression on the right is the expression on the left-hand side of the last equation in footnote 22. Thus:

$$B_{ig} = -\left[\frac{P}{E_{Rg}-P}\right] + \left[\frac{1}{E_{Rg}-P}\right] E_{Ri}.$$

adjust so that assets which are more responsive to changes in R_g will have higher expected returns than those which are less responsive. This accords with common sense. Obviously the part of an asset's risk which is due to its correlation with the return on a combination cannot be diversified away when the asset is added to the combination. Since B_{ig} indicates the magnitude of this type of risk it should be directly related to expected return.

The relationship illustrated in Figure 9 provides a partial answer to the question posed earlier concerning the relationship between an asset's risk

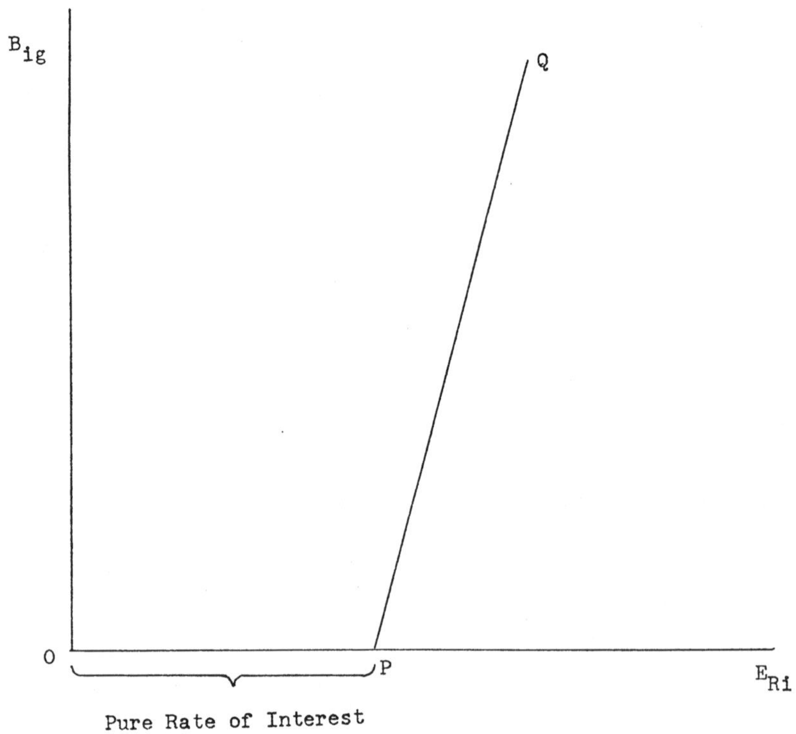

FIGURE 9

and its expected return. But thus far we have argued only that the relationship holds for the assets which enter some particular efficient combination (g). Had another combination been selected, a different linear relationship would have been derived. Fortunately this limitation is easily overcome. As shown in the footnote,[26] we may arbitrarily select *any* one

26. Consider the two assets i and i*, the former included in efficient combination g and the latter in combination g*. As shown above:

$$B_{ig} = -\left[\frac{P}{E_{Rg} - P}\right] + \left[\frac{1}{E_{Rg} - P}\right] E_{Ri}$$

and:

of the efficient combinations, then measure the predicted responsiveness of *every* asset's rate of return to that of the combination selected; and these coefficients will be related to the expected rates of return of the assets in exactly the manner pictured in Figure 9.

The fact that rates of return from all efficient combinations will be perfectly correlated provides the justification for arbitrarily selecting any one of them. Alternatively we may choose instead any variable perfectly correlated with the rate of return of such combinations. The vertical axis in Figure 9 would then indicate alternative levels of a coefficient measuring the sensitivity of the rate of return of a capital asset to changes in the variable chosen.

This possibility suggests both a plausible explanation for the implication that all efficient combinations will be perfectly correlated and a useful interpretation of the relationship between an individual asset's expected return and its risk. Although the theory itself implies only that rates of return from efficient combinations will be perfectly correlated, we might expect that this would be due to their common dependence on the over-all level of economic activity. If so, diversification enables the investor to escape all but the risk resulting from swings in economic activity—this type of risk remains even in efficient combinations. And, since all other types can be avoided by diversification, only the responsiveness of an asset's rate of return to the level of economic activity is relevant in

---

$$B_{i^*g^*} = -\left[\frac{P}{E_{Rg^*} - P}\right] + \left[\frac{1}{E_{Rg^*} - P}\right] E_{Ri^*}.$$

Since R_g and R_{g^*} are perfectly correlated:

$$r_{i^*g^*} = r_{i^*g}$$

Thus:

$$\frac{B_{i^*g^*}\sigma_{Rg^*}}{\sigma_{Ri^*}} = \frac{B_{i^*g}\sigma_{Rg}}{\sigma_{Ri^*}}$$

and:

$$B_{i^*g^*} = B_{i^*g}\left[\frac{\sigma_{Rg}}{\sigma_{Rg^*}}\right].$$

Since both g and g* lie on a line which intercepts the E-axis at P:

$$\frac{\sigma_{Rg}}{\sigma_{Rg^*}} = \frac{E_{Rg} - P}{E_{Rg^*} - P}$$

and:

$$B_{i^*g^*} = B_{i^*g}\left[\frac{E_{Rg} - P}{E_{Rg^*} - P}\right]$$

Thus:

$$-\left[\frac{P}{E_{Rg^*} - P}\right] + \left[\frac{1}{E_{Rg^*} - P}\right] E_{Ri^*} = B_{i^*g}\left[\frac{E_{Rg} - P}{E_{Rg^*} - P}\right]$$

from which we have the desired relationship between R_{i^*} and g:

$$B_{i^*g} = -\left[\frac{P}{E_{Rg} - P}\right] + \left[\frac{1}{E_{Rg} - P}\right] E_{Ri^*}$$

B_{i^*g} must therefore plot on the same line as does B_{ig}.

assessing its risk. Prices will adjust until there is a linear relationship between the magnitude of such responsiveness and expected return. Assets which are unaffected by changes in economic activity will return the pure interest rate; those which move with economic activity will promise appropriately higher expected rates of return.

This discussion provides an answer to the second of the two questions posed in this paper. In Part III it was shown that with respect to equilibrium conditions in the capital market as a whole, the theory leads to results consistent with classical doctrine (i.e., the capital market line). We have now shown that with regard to capital assets considered individually, it also yields implications consistent with traditional concepts: it is common practice for investment counselors to accept a lower expected return from defensive securities (those which respond little to changes in the economy) than they require from aggressive securities (which exhibit significant response). As suggested earlier, the familiarity of the implications need not be considered a drawback. The provision of a logical framework for producing some of the major elements of traditional financial theory should be a useful contribution in its own right.

THE CAPITAL ASSET PRICING MODEL: TRADITIONAL AND "ZERO-BETA" VERSIONS*

William F. Sharpe[(a)]

Introduction

Recent papers by Black, Jensen and Scholes [4] and Blume and Friend [6] have suggested that the traditional capital asset pricing model of Sharpe [21], Lintner [12] and Mossin [18] is inconsistent with empirical evidence. Black [3] has suggested its replacement with the so-called zero-beta model, while Blume and Friend [6] have rejected both formulations in favor of an unspecified model of market segmentation.

This paper provides a relatively simple and succinct derivation of the two models and compares their major features. It then considers the arguments of Blume and Friend concerning the relationship between empirical findings and the implications of the zero-beta version. It is shown that the evidence is not inconsistent with this version of the model. Finally, it is suggested that the evidence may also be consistent with the traditional version.

Key elements of this paper can be found in published work by Lintner [13], Black [3], Fama [8], Brennan [7], and Jensen [11]. However,it seems worthwhile to bring the material together in the present form to highlight some of the important relationships and correct some current misunderstandings.

A Generalized Security Risk-Return Theorem

Throughout, the following assumptions will be made: investors choose among alternative combinations of assets on the basis of expected return (E) and standard deviation of return (σ) alone, assets are perfectly divisible, and there are no transactions costs. The first assumption can be taken as given; alternatively, it can be derived from the assumption that all returns are jointly normal, as shown by Tobin [25]. Moreover, the assumption that transactions costs are zero implies that the appropriate period, during which normality is assumed to hold, is instantaneous, as shown by Jensen [10].

---

* This paper was presented at the 1973 annual meeting of the Midwest Finance Association. I am grateful to Professor David West of the University of Missouri-Columbia, who suggested its preparation, and to Professor Robert Litzenberger of Stanford University for helpful comments and suggestions.

(a) Professor of Business, Stanford University

Consider an investor facing an opportunity set such as that shown in Fig. 1. He will choose the point on the upper left-hand border at which one of his indifference curves is tangent to the opportunity set. Denote the chosen portfolio m. Define a security as <u>in</u> m if the amount selected is not due to any bound placed by institutional or other factors. The practical consequence of this definition is that the investor is free to alter the proportion of any or all such securities, at least slightly, in either direction from the amount represented in the chosen portfolio m. This implies the results, first shown in Sharpe [21], in Fig. 2: altering the proportion of any asset i in portfolio m, with compensating changes in all other assets, must give opportunities interior to the original set, as shown by the dashed curve. Moreover, this curve must itself be tangent to the frontier of the set at point m.

As first shown in Sharpe [21], the slope of the dashed curve in Fig. 2 at point m is:

$$\frac{(E_i - E_m)\,\sigma_m}{C_{im} - \sigma_m^2}$$

where: C_{im} = the co-variance between the return on asset i and the return on portfolio m.

Now construct a line tangent to the opportunity set at the chosen point m, as shown in Fig. 2. Denote its intercept π. Clearly the slope of this line, which is also the slope of the frontier at point m, will be:

$$\frac{E_m - \pi}{\sigma_m}$$

As indicated, these slopes must be equal. Thus:

$$\frac{(E_i - E_m)\,\sigma_m}{C_{im} - \sigma_m^2} = \frac{E_m - \pi}{\sigma_m}$$

Simplifying:

$$E_i - \pi = \beta_{im}(E_m - \pi)$$

$$\text{Where: } \beta_{im} = \frac{C_{im}}{\sigma_m^2}$$

This generalized relationship shows that for any security in m, expected return in excess of π will be proportional to the security's

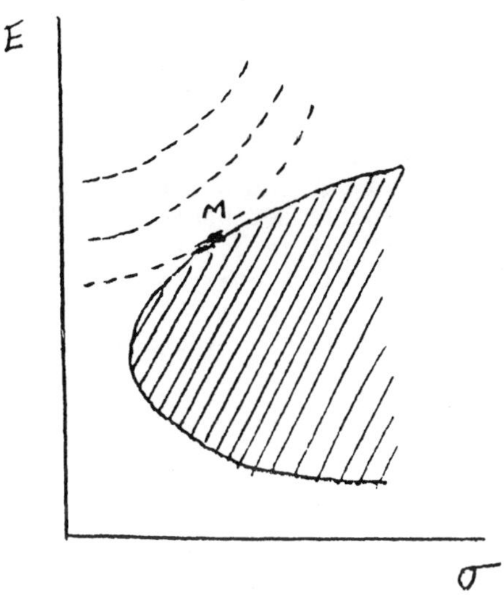

Fig. 1

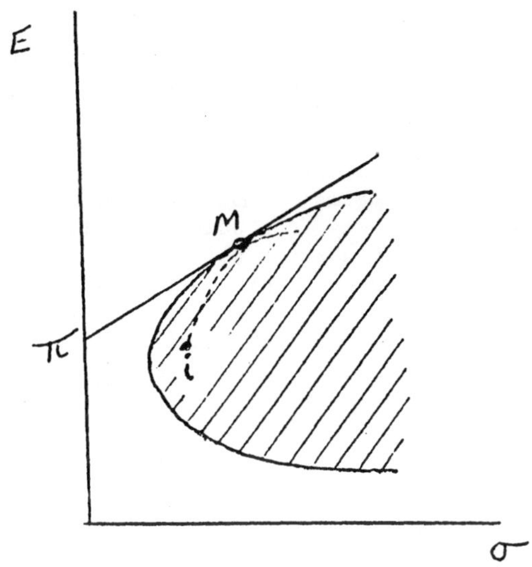

Fig. 2

marginal contribution to the risk of portfolio m, measured by β_{im}, its covariance with m, rescaled by dividing by the variance of m.

Fama [8] provides an expanded proof of this relationship for the general class of stable Paretian distributions, while Lintner [13] derives the relationship shown here, with the important interpretation of the intercept π as the marginal contribution of present wealth to the investor's certainty-equivalent future wealth.

The Traditional Captial Asset Pricing Model

To obtain the traditional version of the capital asset pricing model we add two assumptions to those already utilized. First, investors are assumed to agree on the joint probability distribution of future returns. Second, every investor is assumed to be able to borrow or lend at a common pure rate of interest, p, without limit.

As shown by Tobin [25], the availability of borrowing and lending opportunities at a common rate leads to the identification of an optimal combination of risky assets, plotting at the point at which a ray from point p is tangent to the opportunity set based only on risky assets, as shown in Fig. 3. However, if all investors agree on prospects, this must be the market portfolio in which every security is held in proportion to its share of total outstanding market value, or else the market will not clear. For this reason, the relevant point is labeled m in Fig. 3.

It follows immediately that the line tangent to the shaded region in Fig. 3 at point m must have an intercept of p. Substituting p for π in the equation of the previous section, we thus have the traditional result:

$$E_i - p = \beta_{im} (E_m - p)$$

where β_{im} is now defined relative to the market portfolio and $(E_i - p)$ and $(E_m - p)$ are expected excess returns over and above the pure interest rate.

Issuance of Securities

Most models of equilibrium in capital asset markets implicitly allow issuance (negative holdings) of assets by individual investors. As shown by Hirshleiffer [9] and Beja [2], this is likely to lead to inconsistent results, since the amount of a security which can be issued at the going market price depends on the uses to which the proceeds and the issuer's initial capital are to be devoted. Unfortunately, there is no completely satisfactory way to reflect this in any model using the simplifying assumptions of choice based only on mean and standard deviation of return.

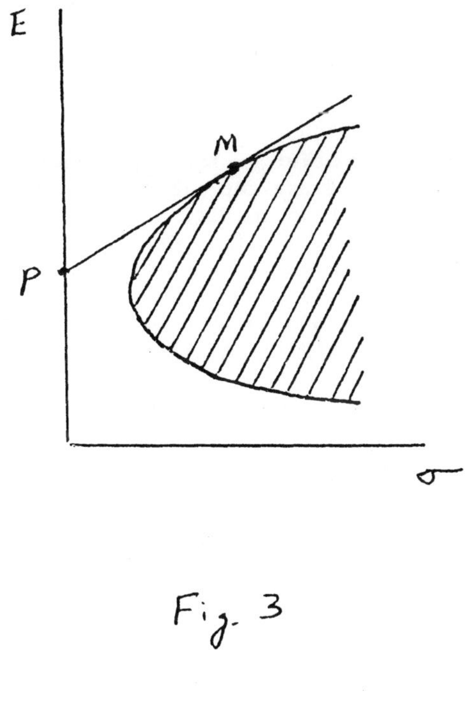

Fig. 3

The traditional capital asset pricing model allows equilibrium solutions in which some investors issue riskless securities, and thus may well violate this requirement for internal consistency.* However, in equilibrium everyone holds the same proportionate shares of risky securities. For markets to clear, all holdings of risky securities must thus be positive, so no problem arises in this connection. On the other hand, the zero-beta formulation will be seen to imply just the opposite results.

The Zero-Beta Model

Black [3], Vasicek [26] and Brennan [7] have proposed a model differing from the traditional version in at least one respect: investors are precluded from issuing riskless securities.** On the other hand, they are allowed to issue risky securities without limit, and the equilibrium solution will, in general, involve such issuance on the part of some investors.

As shown, e.g. in Sharpe [22], if investors are free to issue shares, every portfolio on the frontier of the opportunity set can be regarded as a linear combination of any two arbitrarily chosen portfolios on the frontier. This is shown in Fig. 4. The opportunity set is an hyperbola, assymptotic to the two lines drawn at point C, and riskless lending is available at some rate p, less than C.***

The efficient opportunities available under these assumptions lie along the line from p to L (the point at which a ray from p is tangent to the frontier of the risky asset opportunity set), then along the original frontier to the right of point L. Portfolio L is the optimal combination of risky assets for (only) those who choose to also lend some of their money--i.e. hold the riskless security. Others will choose different portfolios along the curve LmQ.

Where will the market portfolio plot? Any combination along the frontier can be considered a linear combination of, say, portfolios L and Q. When all portfolios are aggregated into the market portfolio, the result must therefore be a portfolio which is also a linear combination of L and Q. Thus the market portfolio must plot on the frontier, as indicated by point m.

---

* Fama [8] has proposed a portfolio-sharing company as an artifact to get around this objection. However, careful consideration of the argument shows that the original problem remains even in this case, as shown by Black [3].

** Black also considers a model with no riskless asset at all, as does Brennan. Here we focus on the case in which an asset that is riskless in nominal terms can be purchased, and investors are concerned only with nominal returns. Lintner [13] provides a detailed analysis of the case in which investors are concerned with real returns and there is no truly riskless asset.

*** Merton [16] has shown that these relationships must hold in equilibrium.

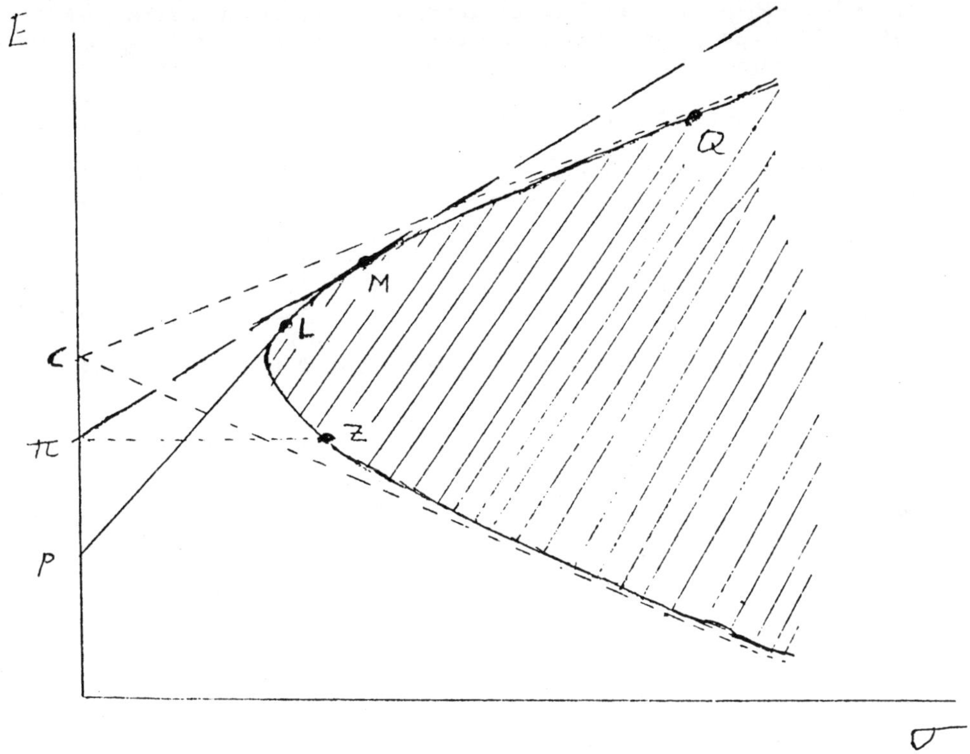

Fig. 4

Constructing the tangent at point m yields an intercept, π, which must be greater than or equal to p (and less than C). The disparity between p and π will be greater, the farther is m from portfolio L. In any event, this model implies a linear relationship between expected return and β_{im}, with a positive slope less than or equal to $(E_m - p)$. Its implications are thus weaker than those of the traditional model, which implies a slope of $(E_m - p)$ with intercept p.

Although portfolio m will involve only positive holdings of risky securities, except in a region in the neighborhood of m, efficient portfolios will include issuance of risky securities, with the attendant likelihood of internal inconsistency in the solution, since various investors may choose portfolios all along the frontier above point L. It is far from obvious whether it is more objectionable to assume issuance of one riskless security (as does the traditional model) or issuance of many risk securities (as does this version).

Black [3] has termed the intercept of the tangent line the expected return on the "zero-beta portfolio." Obviously, if $\beta_{im} = 0$:

$$E_i - \pi = 0\ (E_m - \pi) \qquad \text{and} \qquad E_i = \pi$$

While there will be many such portfolios, Black concentrates on the one which has the minimum variance of all those made up entirely of risky assets. It is the portfolio on the original frontier with expected return equal to π, as shown by point Z in Fig. 4. Note that it must be inefficient in the Markowitz [14] sense. Moreover, it is not directly identifiable and thus has no empirical counterpart, as do the market portfolio and the riskless asset.

It is important to recognize that the riskless security in this model does not enter the market portfolio.* Thus it will not conform to the equilibrium pricing relationship. Indeed, it will have an expected (certain) rate of return below that of a risky security of comparable market risk (in this case, zero-β_{im}) in equilibrium because investors are not allowed to take on the negative holdings they would prefer under such circumstances.

Empirical Evidence

Empirical work by Black, Jensen and Scholes [4], Blume and Friend [6] and others has attempted to test the capital asset pricing model using *ex post* results as surrogates for the *ex ante* variables of the theory. Average return is used to represent expected return, and historical covariances and variances to compute surrogates for beta values. Cross-sectional regression analysis is then performed, to determine

---

* Unless the market portfolio is also the optimal lending portfolio (i.e. points L and m coincide). But this gives the traditional capital asset pricing model results in any event.

the empirical relationship between average return and beta. To reduce measurement errors, grouping and instrumental variable procedures are usually employed as well.

As pointed out by many authors, such procedures can test only an expanded model involving the capital asset pricing model augmented by a number of assumptions regarding return-generating processes and stability of predictions. Negative results are therefore not necessarily inconsistent with the capital asset pricing model per se.

Tests to date seem to show a positive and linear relationship between average return and historic beta value. In some cases the intercept appears to be below the pure interest rate, and in others, roughly equal to it. But the more common result finds an intercept that exceeds the pure interest rate.*

Such results led Black, Jensen and Scholes [4] to suggest the rejection of the traditional model in favor of the weaker zero-beta formulation. However, Blume and Friend [6] argue that the results are inconsistent with both the traditional and the zero-beta versions. This conclusion stems from their interpretation of the zero-beta return as the return on the zero-beta portfolio with minimum variance considering all possible investments. If riskless assets may be purchased, this will of course equal the pure interest rate. But the intercept of the expected return-beta relationship will be greater than this under the assumed conditions of the zero-beta model as we have interpreted it. Thus the empirical results are not inconsistent with this version. Blume and Friend's error lies in their interpretation of the zero-beta portfolio. As Black states, it is the minimum-variance zero-beta portfolio of risky assets [3, p. 453]. Since this portfolio is unobservable, its return can only be estimated by the intercept of the empirical relationship between average return and beta for risky securities. Any value equal to or greater than the pure interest rate is thus consistent with the zero-beta model.

Does this mean that the traditional model must be rejected? Not necessarily, for all the measures employed in such tests are at best surrogates for the variables of the theory. Roll [20], Miller and Scholes [17] and Mayers [15] have analyzed the effects of errors arising from these sources. Perhaps most important, empirical studies have almost uniformly utilized an index of the returns on New York Stock Exchange stocks as a surrogate for the return on the market portfolio.** Implicitly this assumes that the weighted average return

---

* Many studies use excess return as the variable of interest, to accommodate changes in the pure interest rate. In such cases, the most common result finds a positive intercept--i.e. an average value of (return less the pure interest rate) which exceeds zero. This is comparable to finding that the intercept obtained by regressing average return on beta exceeds the (average) pure interest rate. Only the estimates of beta will differ under the two procedures, and the differences will be slight.

** Notable exceptions are the recent studies of international diversification by e.g. Agmon [1] and Solnik [24].

(using market value weights) on the remaining assets is perfectly positively correlated with the return on New York Stock Exchange stocks. This is simply incorrect. Whether the market portfolio is defined in terms of marketable securities or, as Mayers [15] has suggested, to include both marketable and non-marketable assets, New York Stock Exchange stocks constitute a relatively small proportion of the total. Moreover, Robichek, Cohn and Pringle [19], Solnik [24], Blume and Husic [5], Sharpe [23], and others have shown that returns on the omitted assets are at best imperfectly correlated with the returns on New York Stock Exchange stocks. The implication is that β_{im} will be measured subject to potentially large error, some of which may remain even after grouping securities on the basis of the measured values. It is well known that in any regression analysis the slope coefficient will generally be biased downward if the independent variable is measured subject to random error. Under such conditions errors in measured beta values will lead to too flat a slope when average return is regressed on beta. The measured slope can thus be less than $(E_m - p)$, even if the true slope is precisely $(E_m - p)$.

While this may not be the full explanation, it suggests that the news of the death of the traditional Capital Asset Pricing Model may be somewhat premature. To state the obvious: more research is needed.

REFERENCES

1. Agmon, Tamir, "Country Risk: The Significance of the Country Factor for Share-Price Movements in the United Kingdom, Germany and Japan," Journal of Business, Jan. 1973.

2. Beja, Avraham, "On Systematic and Unsystematic Components of Risk," Journal Finance, March 1972.

3. Black, Fischer, "Capital Market Equilibrium with Restricted Borrowing," Journal of Business, July 1972.

4. Black, Fischer, Jensen, Michael C. and Scholes, Myron, "The Capital Asset Pricing Model: Some Empirical Tests," in Jensen, Michael C., Studies in the Theory of Capital Markets, (Praeger: New York) 1972.

5. Blume, Marshall, and Husic, Frank J., "Risk and Return on the American Stock Exchange," paper presented at the Rodney L. White seminar on Feb. 19, 1971.

6. Blume, Marshall E. and Friend, Irwin, "A New Look at the Capital Asset Pricing Model," Journal of Finance, March 1973.

7. Brennan, Michael J., "Capital Market Equilibrium with Divergent Borrowing and Lending Rates," Journal of Financial and Quantitative Analysis, Dec. 1971.

8. Fama, Eugene F., "Risk, Return and Equilibrium," Journal of Political Economy, Jan.-Feb. 1971.

9. Hirshleifer, J., Investment, Interest and Capital, (Prentice-Hall: New Jersey) 1970.

10. Jensen, Michael C., "Risk, and Pricing of Capital Assets, and the Evaluation of Investment Portfolios," Journal of Business, April 1969.

11. Jensen, Michael C., "Capital Markets: Theory and Evidence," Bell Journal of Economics and Management Science, Autumn 1972.

12. Lintner, John, "The Valuation of Risk Assets and Selection of Risky Investments in Stock Portfolios and Capital Budgets," Review of Economics and Statistics, Feb. 1965.

13. Lintner, John, "The Aggregation of Investors' Diverse Judgment and Preferences in Purely Competitive Securities Markets," Journal of Financial and Quantitative Analysis, Dec. 1969.

14. Markowitz, Harry, "Portfolio Selection," Journal of Finance, March 1952.

15. Mayers, David, "Nonmarketable Assets and Capital Market Equilibrium," in Jensen, Michael C., Studies in the Theory of Capital Markets, (Praeger: New York) 1972.

16. Merton, Robert C., "An Analytic Derivation of the Efficient Portfolio Frontier," Journal of Financial and Quantitative Analysis, Sept. 1972.

17. Miller, Merton H. and Scholes, Myron, "Rates of Return in Relation to Risk: A Re-Examination of some Recent Findings," in Jensen, Michael C., Studies in the Theory of Capital Markets, (Praeger: New York) 1972.

18. Mossin, Jan, "Equilibrium in a Capital Asset Market," Econometrica, Oct. 1966.

19. Robichek, Alexander A., Cohn, Richard A., and Pringle, John J., "Returns on Alternative Investment Media and Implications for Portfolio Construction," Journal of Business, July 1972.

20. Roll, Richard, "Bias in Fitting the Sharpe Model to Time Series Date," Journal of Financial and Quantitative Analysis, Sept. 1969.

21. Sharpe, William F., "Capital Asset Prices: A Theory of Market Equilibrium Under Conditions of Risk," Journal of Finance,Sept. 1964.

22. Sharpe, William F., Portfolio Theory and Capital Markets, (McGraw-Hill: New York) 1970.

23. Sharpe, William F., "Bonds Versus Stocks: Some Lessons from Capital Market Theory," Graduate School of Business, Stanford University Research Paper No. 140, Feb. 1973.

24. Solnik, Bruno, "An International Market Model of Security Price Behavior," unpublished, Oct. 1972.

25. Tobin, James, "Liquidity Preference as Behavior Towards Risk," Review of Economic Studies, Feb. 1958.

26. Vasicek, Oldrich A., "Capital Market Equilibrium with no Riskless Borrowing," unpublished, March 1971.

Editor's Comment

The Parable of the Money Managers

Some years ago, in a land called Indicia, revolution led to the overthrow of a socialist regime and the restoration of a system of private property. Former government enterprises were reformed as corporations, which then issued stocks and bonds. These securities were given to a central agency, which offered them for sale to individuals, pension funds, and the like (all armed with newly printed money).

Almost immediately a group of *money managers* came forth to assist these investors. Recalling the words of a venerated elder, uttered before the previous revolution ("Invest in Corporate Indicia"), they invited clients to give them money, with which they would buy a cross-section of all the newly issued securities. Investors considered this a reasonable idea, and soon everyone held a piece of Corporate Indicia.

Before long the money managers became bored because there was little for them to do. Soon they fell into the habit of gathering at a beachfront casino where they passed the time playing roulette, craps, and similar games, for low stakes, with their own money.

After a while, the owner of the casino suggested a new idea. He would furnish an impressive set of rooms which would be designated the *Money Managers' Club*. There the members could place bets with one another about the fortunes of various corporations, industries, the level of the Gross National Product, foreign trade, etc. To make the betting more exciting, the casino owner suggested that the managers use their clients' money for this purpose.

The offer was immediately accepted, and soon the money managers were betting eagerly with one another. At the end of each week, some found that they had won money for their clients, while others found that they had lost. But the losses always exceeded the gains, for a certain amount was deducted from each bet to cover the costs of the elegant surroundings in which the gambling took place.

Before long a group of professors from Indicia U. suggested that investors were not well served by the activities being conducted at the Money Managers' Club. "Why pay people to gamble with your money? Why not just hold your own piece of Corporate Indicia?" they said.

This argument seemed sensible to some of the investors, and they raised the issue with their money managers. A few capitulated, announcing that they would henceforth stay away from the casino and use their clients' money only to buy proportionate shares of all the stocks and bonds issued by corporations.

The converts, who became known as managers of *Indicia funds,* were initially shunned by those who continued to frequent the Money Managers' Club, but in time, grudging acceptance replaced outright hostility. The wave of puritan reform some had predicted failed to materialize, and gambling remained legal. Many managers continued to make their daily pilgrimage to the casino. But they exercised more restraint than before, placed smaller bets, and generally behaved in a manner consonant with their responsibilities. Even the members of the Lawyers' Club found it difficult to object to the small amount of gambling that still went on.

And everyone but the casino owner lived happily ever after.

—William F. Sharpe
Timken Professor of Finance
Stanford University

FINANCIAL ANALYSTS JOURNAL® is published bi-monthly by The Financial Analysts Federation, a non-profit corporation devoted to the advancement of investment management and security analysis. Neither the Federation nor its publication's editorial staff is responsible for facts or opinions contained in articles therein. Indexed in the Business Periodicals Index. Second class postage paid at the Post Office at New York, N.Y. and additional offices.

SUBSCRIPTIONS. Domestic: one-year $16, two-year $28, three-year $36, single copy (prepaid only) $3.00; Outside U.S.A.: one-year $18, two-year $30, three-year $38, single copy (prepaid only) $3.50; Educational Institutions: 10 or more annual subscriptions to the same address $8 each. Copies will be airmailed to foreign subscribers at their request. They will be required, however, to prepay airmail postage (currently $4.40 *per copy* to Europe and Japan).

CHANGE OF ADDRESS: Send old label and new address with Zip Code six weeks before moving.

REPRINTS of articles published in the Journal are available at a nominal cost. Payment must accompany orders of $10 or less. Address requests to Reprint Department, FAJ.

Vol. 32, No. 4 : July/August 1976

Address all communications to: 219 East 42nd Street, New York, N. Y. 10017

THE CAPITAL ASSET PRICING MODEL

A "Multi-Beta" Interpretation

William F. Sharpe

Stanford University

I. Introduction

In recent years, considerable attention has been accorded the Capital Asset Pricing Model of Sharpe [10], Lintner [4], and Mossin [7]. It suggests that in equilibrium the expected excess return on a security over and above the pure interest rate will equal some constant times its *ex ante* risk, measured by the security's so-called "beta coefficient." The latter equals the covariance of the security's return with that of the market portfolio (consisting of all assets, each in proportion to total value outstanding) divided by the variance of the return on the market portfolio, where all measures refer to *ex ante* probability distributions.

Many have used these ideas for practical investment policies. Moreover, a number of tests have been performed to determine the extent to which *ex post* results conform to the relationships predicted by the theory for *ex ante* values. In the light of empirical work to date, Black [1] has suggested a

I am indebted to Professor Marcus C. Bogue of Carnegie-Mellon University for a number of suggestions on this subject. Helpful comments were also provided by Professors Paul Cootner and Robert Litzenberger of Stanford University and Professor Alan Kraus of the University of British Columbia.

"zero-beta" model, while Blume and Friend [3] have argued in favor of an unspecified model of market segmentation.

Given this interest, it seems worthwhile to examine carefully the nature of the beta measure of risk. The following section shows that a security's beta relative to the market portfolio can be expressed as a weighted average of beta values relative to any desired number of portfolios, the collection of which equals the market portfolio. When the beta values are scaled appropriately, the applicable weights represent the relative contributions of the portfolios to the uncertainty of the market portfolio, and will sum to equal one. In the following section these results are reinterpreted in the context of a general multifactor model. Finally, some possible uses for the approach are suggested.

The model given here provides a general setting for the special cases discussed by Mayers [5], Roll [9], Pettit and Westerfield [8], Miller and Scholes [6], and Blume and Husic [2] in different contexts. Although many elements of this analysis can be found in these papers, the present version appears to be sufficiently general to provide new insights, as well as more complete proofs of earlier results.

II. The Multi-Beta Interpretation

To begin, assume that there are N securities, which constitute the market portfolio m. Let X_i be the proportion of total value of m invested in security i. The return on security i is $\tilde{r}_i$ (tildes are used to represent random variables). Let $\tilde{R}_m$ be the return on the market portfolio.

$$\tilde{R}_m = \sum_{i=1}^{N} X_i \tilde{r}_i$$

The beta value for security i relative to the market portfolio is defined as

$$\beta_{im} = \text{cov}(\tilde{r}_i, \tilde{R}_m)/\text{var}(\tilde{R}_m) \tag{1}$$

where "cov" is covariance and "var" is variance.

Now, assume that the market portfolio is used to form M portfolios, with x_{ij} representing the proportion of the total market value of m invested in security i in portfolio j. All securities are allocated to one or more of the M portfolios. Thus,

$$X_i = \sum_{j=1}^{M} x_{ij} \qquad \text{for} \quad i = 1, \ldots, N$$

Let the total proportion of market value invested in portfolio j be represented by w_j:

$$w_j = \sum_{i=1}^{N} x_{ij} \qquad \text{for} \quad j = 1, \ldots, M$$

The return on the jth portfolio will be

$$\tilde{R}_j = \sum_{i=1}^{N} \left(\frac{x_{ij}}{w_j}\right)\tilde{r}_i$$

and the return on the market portfolio can be viewed simply as a weighted average of the returns on the M portfolios:

$$\tilde{R}_m = \sum_{j=1}^{M} w_j \tilde{R}_j \tag{2}$$

Substituting (2) into (1), we obtain

$$\beta_{im} = \text{cov}\left(\tilde{r}_i\,,\ \sum_{j=1}^{M} w_j \tilde{R}_j\right)\Big/\text{var}(\tilde{R}_m)$$

Rearranging, we have

$$\beta_{im} = \sum_{j=1}^{M} w_j\ \text{cov}(\tilde{r}_i\,,\ \tilde{R}_j)/\text{var}(\tilde{R}_m) \tag{3}$$

Multiplying both numerator and denominator of (3) by $\text{cov}(\tilde{R}_m, \tilde{R}_j)$ gives

$$\beta_{im} = \sum_{j=1}^{M} \left[\frac{w_j\ \text{cov}(\tilde{R}_m\,,\ \tilde{R}_j)}{\text{var}(\tilde{R}_m)} \cdot \frac{\text{cov}(\tilde{r}_i\,,\ \tilde{R}_j)}{\text{cov}(\tilde{R}_m\,,\ \tilde{R}_j)}\right] \tag{4}$$

Note, however, that

$$\text{cov}(\tilde{R}_m\,,\ \tilde{R}_j) = \text{cov}\left(\sum_{k=1}^{M} w_k \tilde{R}_k\,,\ \tilde{R}_j\right) = \sum_{k=1}^{M} w_k\ \text{cov}(\tilde{R}_k\,,\ \tilde{R}_j) \tag{5}$$

Denote the first term in (4) by u_j. Substituting (5) in the numerator yields

$$u_j \equiv \frac{w_j\ \text{cov}(\tilde{R}_m\,,\ \tilde{R}_j)}{\text{var}(\tilde{R}_m)} = \frac{w_j \sum_{k=1}^{M} w_k\ \text{cov}(\tilde{R}_k\,,\ \tilde{R}_j)}{\text{var}(\tilde{R}_m)} \tag{6}$$

Note, however, that

$$\text{var}(\tilde{R}_m) = \text{cov}\left(\sum_{j=1}^{M} w_j \tilde{R}_j\,,\ \sum_{k=1}^{M} w_k \tilde{R}_k\right) = \sum_{j=1}^{M}\sum_{k=1}^{M} w_j w_k\ \text{cov}(\tilde{R}_j\,,\ \tilde{R}_k)$$

Thus, $\sum_{j=1}^{M} u_j = 1$. The value of u_j can be interpreted as the proportion of the total variance of $\tilde{R}_m$ attributed to portfolio j. It takes into account not only the portfolio's own variance, but also any covariance with the other $J - 1$ portfolios. It is, of course, an *ex ante* concept, as developed here. In other words, u_j is the relative *uncertainty* of portfolio j.

An alternative interpretation of u_j may prove more useful for subjective estimation. Note first that

$$\partial\ \text{var}(\tilde{R}_m)/\partial w_j = 2\ \text{cov}(\tilde{R}_j\,,\ \tilde{R}_m)$$

Since $\sigma(\tilde{R}_m)$, the standard deviation of $\tilde{R}_m$, is the square root of $\text{var}(\tilde{R}_m)$,

$$\partial\sigma(\tilde{R}_m)/\partial w_j = \text{cov}(\tilde{R}_j, \tilde{R}_m)/\sigma(\tilde{R}_m)$$

It follows that

$$u_j = \frac{w_j \,\text{cov}(\tilde{R}_j, \tilde{R}_m)}{\text{var}(\tilde{R}_m)} = \frac{\partial\sigma(\tilde{R}_m)}{\partial w_j}\cdot\frac{w_j}{\sigma(\tilde{R}_m)} = \frac{\partial\sigma(\tilde{R}_m)/\sigma(\tilde{R}_m)}{\partial w_j/w_j} \tag{7}$$

The value of u_j may thus be interpreted as an *elasticity*, measuring the percentage change in the risk of the market portfolio per unit percentage change in w_j. Not surprisingly, the sum of such values must equal one, since under the assumed conditions an equal percentage change in all values of w_j will cause an equivalent percentage change in $\sigma(\tilde{R}_m)$.

Turning next to the second term of (4), we divide both numerator and denominator by $\text{var}(\tilde{R}_j)$ to obtain[1]

$$\frac{\text{cov}(\tilde{r}_i, \tilde{R}_j)/\text{var}(\tilde{R}_j)}{\text{cov}(\tilde{R}_m, \tilde{R}_j)/\text{var}(\tilde{R}_j)} \tag{8}$$

These may be defined as the beta values of the security and the market, respectively, relative to portfolio j:

$$\beta_{ij} \equiv \text{cov}(\tilde{r}_i, \tilde{R}_j)/\text{var}(\tilde{R}_j), \qquad \beta_{mj} \equiv \text{cov}(\tilde{R}_m, \tilde{R}_j)/\text{var}(\tilde{R}_j) \tag{9}$$

Thus, (8) may be written as

$$\beta_{ij}/\beta_{mj} \tag{10}$$

Combining (4), (6), and (10) gives the important relationship

$$\beta_{im} = \sum_{j=1}^{M} u_j \frac{\beta_{ij}}{\beta_{mj}} \tag{11}$$

That is, a security's beta relative to the market will be a weighted average of its betas relative to the M portfolios, where the weights represent the relative degrees of uncertainty associated with the portfolios, and the beta values are scaled relative to corresponding values for the market as a whole.[2]

The values of beta used in (11) are, of course, those defined in Eqs. (9). They correspond to the slope coefficients in a *simple* regression. In other words, β_{ij} captures the entire sensitivity of $\tilde{r}_i$ to variations in $\tilde{R}_j$, including any arising through induced effects on the variations of other portfolios.

Another form that may prove useful for subjective estimation can be

[1] This operation can only be performed when the return on portfolio j is uncertain (i.e., $\text{var}(\tilde{R}_j) \neq 0$).

[2] The scaling can be considered to apply to the value of β_{im} as well, since $\beta_{mm} = 1$.

obtained by multiplying each term on the right-hand side of (3) by $\text{var}(\tilde{R}_j)/\text{var}(\tilde{R}_j)$:

$$\beta_{im} = \sum_{j=1}^{M} \frac{w_j \, \text{cov}(\tilde{r}_i, \tilde{R}_j)}{\text{var}(\tilde{R}_m)} \cdot \frac{\text{var}(\tilde{R}_j)}{\text{var}(\tilde{R}_j)} \tag{12}$$

then substituting the definition of β_{ij} to obtain

$$\beta_{im} = \sum_{j=1}^{M} \frac{w_j \, \text{var}(\tilde{R}_j)}{\text{var}(\tilde{R}_m)} \beta_{ij} \tag{13}$$

In this version, β_{im} is seen to be a weighted average of the β_{ij}'s, with the weight for β_{ij} dependent on the contribution of $\tilde{R}_j$ to $\tilde{R}_m$ (i.e., w_j) and the uncertainty concerning the value of $\tilde{R}_j$ [i.e., $\text{var}(\tilde{R}_j)$].

III. A Multifactor Model

Assume that f key factors, $\tilde{F}_1$ through $\tilde{F}_f$, influencing security returns have been identified, and that the return on the market portfolio can be expressed as

$$\tilde{R}_m = \sum_{k=1}^{f} b_{mk} \tilde{F}_k + \tilde{c}_m \tag{14}$$

where $\tilde{c}_m$ represents the (random) difference between $\tilde{R}_m$ and the proportion of $\tilde{R}_m$ attributable to the factors.

Denote the proportion of the market return determined by the factors by $\tilde{M}$:

$$\tilde{M} = \sum_{k=1}^{f} b_{mk} \tilde{F}_k \tag{15}$$

Now assume that the chosen factors "explain" a large proportion of the uncertainty about $\tilde{R}_m$, that is,

$$\text{var}(\tilde{R}_m) \approx \text{var}(\tilde{M}) \tag{16}$$

A special case arises when $\text{var}(\tilde{c}_m)$ is zero. This can be obtained by the choice of n factors, each of which corresponds to the return on one of the securities. It can also be obtained with one factor, defined as $\tilde{R}_m$. However, neither of these cases is particularly instructive for present purposes. Nor is one in which factor-analytic techniques are applied to the full covariance matrix to determine a few factors with high explanatory power. Far more important are cases in which the factors represent anticipations about important economic variables affecting more than one firm. If enough appropriate factors of this type are chosen, (16) will hold only approximately, but can be employed for most practical purposes.

While variations in $\tilde{M}$ may serve as an adequate explanation of variations in $\tilde{R}_m$, they need not, of course, explain a large part of the variation in the return on any single security. However, variations in $\tilde{M}$ should prove adequate for explaining the covariance of a security's return with that of $\tilde{R}_m$, since

$$\begin{aligned}\operatorname{cov}(\tilde{r}_i, \tilde{R}_m) &= \operatorname{cov}(\tilde{r}_i, \tilde{M} + \tilde{c}_m) = \operatorname{cov}(\tilde{r}_i, \tilde{M}) + \operatorname{cov}(\tilde{r}_i, \tilde{c}_m) \\ &= [\operatorname{var}(\tilde{r}_i)]^{1/2}\{\operatorname{corr}(\tilde{r}_i, \tilde{M})[\operatorname{var}(\tilde{M})]^{1/2} \\ &\quad + \operatorname{corr}(\tilde{r}_i, \tilde{c}_m)[\operatorname{var}(\tilde{c}_m)]^{1/2}\}\end{aligned} \tag{17}$$

where "corr" denotes correlation coefficient. Under the assumed conditions, $\operatorname{var}(\tilde{c}_m)$ is small, allowing the approximation

$$\operatorname{cov}(\tilde{r}_i, \tilde{R}_m) \approx \operatorname{cov}(\tilde{r}_i, \tilde{M}) \tag{18}$$

The results obtained earlier can now be applied. In (2), interpret $\tilde{R}_j$ as the value of factor j and w_j as the sensitivity of $\tilde{R}_m$ to a change in factor j [e.g., as b_{mj} in (15)]. In (11), u_j then represents the percentage change in the uncertainty of the market portfolio per unit percentage change in the sensitivity of $\tilde{R}_m$ to factor j; the value of β_{ij} equals the covariance of $\tilde{r}_i$ with factor j, divided by the variance of the factor; and β_{mj} equals the covariance of $\tilde{R}_m$ with factor j divided by the variance of the factor. Of course, each beta value captures the entire sensitivity of a return to changes in a factor, including any arising through induced effects on the variations of other factors.

A similar interpretation can be given formula (13). Again, β_{im} is a weighted average of the β_{ij}'s, with the weight for β_{ij} dependent on the sensitivity of $\tilde{R}_m$ to a change in factor j (i.e., w_j) and the uncertainty about the factor [i.e., $\operatorname{var}(\tilde{R}_j)$].

IV. A Discrete-State Model

A particularly simple version of the result obtained earlier can be derived if possible future values are assumed to depend entirely on the occurrence of mutually exclusive and exhaustive states of the world.

Let there be S such states; denote the return on the market portfolio and security i in state s by R_{ms} and R_{is}, respectively. Let π_s be the probability that state s will occur. Expected returns will be

$$\bar{R}_m = \sum_{s=1}^{S} \pi_s R_{ms}, \qquad \bar{R}_i = \sum_{s=1}^{S} \pi_s R_{is} \tag{19}$$

If state s occurs, security i's return will diverge from its expected value by the amount $(R_{is} - \bar{R}_i)$, while the market portfolio's return diverges from its expectation by $(R_{ms} - \bar{R}_m)$. The ratio of the former to the latter can be defined as the security's beta if state i occurs:[3]

$$\beta_{is} = (R_{is} - \bar{R}_i)/(R_{ms} - \bar{R}_m) \tag{20}$$

The overall beta value of the security will, of course, be

$$\beta_i = \sum_{s=1}^{S} \pi_s(R_{is} - \bar{R}_i)(R_{ms} - \bar{R}_m) / \sum_{s=1}^{S} \pi_s(R_{ms} - \bar{R}_m)^2 \tag{21}$$

Rearranging,

$$\beta_i = \sum_{s=1}^{S} \left[\frac{\pi_s(R_{ms} - \bar{R}_m)^2}{\sum_{s=1}^{S} \pi_s(R_{ms} - \bar{R}_m)^2} \cdot \frac{R_{is} - \bar{R}_i}{R_{ms} - \bar{R}_m} \right] \tag{22}$$

or

$$\beta_i = \sum_{s=1}^{S} u_s \beta_{is} \tag{23}$$

where

$$u_s = \pi_s(R_{ms} - \bar{R}_m)^2 / \sum_{s=1}^{S} \pi_s(R_{ms} - \bar{R}_m)^2 \tag{24}$$

Clearly, u_s is the relative contribution of state s to the overall uncertainty of the market portfolio; and all the u_s values sum to equal one.

V. Expected Returns

Thus far, no use has been made of equilibrium relationships between expected return and risk. We now introduce the standard result obtained from the Capital Asset Pricing Model of Sharpe, Lintner, and Mossin, with homogeneous expectations and equal borrowing and lending rates. In this model, prices adjust until the expected excess return of any security or portfolio, over and above the pure interest rate, will equal the expected excess return on the market portfolio, times the security's beta relative to the market. Since the one-period pure interest rate is known with certainty *ex ante*, we can simply assume all returns are stated as excess returns. Letting $E(\tilde{R}_m)$ denote the expected excess return on the market portfolio, and $E(\tilde{r}_i)$ the expected excess return on security or portfolio i,

$$E(\tilde{r}_i) = E(\tilde{R}_m)\beta_{im} \tag{25}$$

[3] If $R_{ms} = \bar{R}_m$, this value is undefined; for purposes of formula (23), to follow, any value may be used.

Substituting (11),

$$E(\tilde{r}_i) = E(\tilde{R}_m) \sum_{j=1}^{M} \left(u_j \frac{\beta_{ij}}{\beta_{mj}} \right) \tag{26}$$

Now consider a security or portfolio with $\beta_{ij} = \beta_{mj}$ for one j, say j', and $\beta_{ij} = 0$ for all other j's. Then,

$$E(\tilde{r}_i) = E(\tilde{R}_m) u_{j'} \tag{27}$$

This is the expected return associated with the markets' average sensitivity to $\tilde{R}_j$. Since (25) holds for any security or combination of securities, it holds for the market portfolio as well. Thus,

$$E(\tilde{R}_m) = \sum_{j=1}^{M} [u_j E(\tilde{R}_m)] \tag{28}$$

That is, each portfolio or factor j contributes to the market's expected excess return in proportion to the market's overall risk.

VI. Historic Betas, *Ex Ante* Betas, and Actual Returns

As shown previously, the key *ex ante* measure of a security's risk, β_{im}, depends on current *ex ante* estimates of the security's sensitivity to various factors (its β_{ij} values) and the current relative uncertainties associated with those factors (the u_j values). Historic betas, measured via regression analysis using data from previous periods, can be decomposed in precisely the same manner, but the relevant values will be the security's historic sensitivities to the factors and the relative degrees of variation in anticipations about the major economic variables measured by those factors during the period studied. Historic betas may thus be poor surrogates for *ex ante* betas. This is most likely to occur when current relative uncertainties about major factors differ considerably from relative variations in anticipations about those factors in the historic period. Subjective estimates of appropriate u_j values, even if combined with historic β_{ij} values, may, under such circumstances, produce superior *ex ante* estimates of risk and thus expected return. To estimate the u_j's, one need not predict the level of each factor, only its current relative contribution to uncertainty—a difficult, but not necessarily impossible, task.

VII. Measurement of Factors

It should be emphasized that the relevant factors for the approach described here measure *anticipations* about key economic variables. Thus measures of, say, $\text{cov}(\tilde{r}_i, \tilde{R}_j)$, and hence the associated β_{ij} value, must be obtained by measuring a change in the factor with the simultaneous effect on the security. For example, a security's sensitivity to inflation might be measured by determining a company's accounting return's sensitivity to actual inflation, or by measuring the sensitivity of the stock's market return to some measure of change in anticipated inflation. Attempts to regress market return on actual inflation (with or without arbitrarily chosen lags) are likely to result in poor or meaningless estimates of the relevant sensitivity.

This emphasizes the need to try to measure anticipations. A fruitful line of inquiry involves the use of surrogates for initial estimates of the beta values for various securities (e.g., net debtor/creditor status for sensitivity to changes in anticipated inflation). Given such surrogates, one might construct a large portfolio (with both long and short positions of various stocks, if needed), attempting to maximize the portfolio's sensitivity to one factor while making it virtually insensitive to every other factor. The return on such a portfolio could then serve as a surrogate for changes in anticipations about the factor in question. By constructing similar portfolios for other factors, a multifactor model could be implemented using the more general multi-beta approach.

References

1. Black, F., "Capital Market Equilibrium with Restricted Borrowing," *Journal of Business* (July 1972).
2. Blume, M., and Husic, F. J., "Risk and Return on the American Stock Exchange," paper presented at the Rodney L. White seminar (February 19, 1971).
3. Blume, M., and Friend, I., "A New Look at the Capital Asset Pricing Model," *Journal of Finance* (March 1973).
4. Lintner, J., "The Valuation of Risk Assets and the Selection of Risky Investments in Stock Portfolios and Capital Budgets," *Review of Economics and Statistics* (February 1965).
5. Mayers, D., "Nonmarketable Assets and Capital Market Equilibrium," in *Studies in the Theory of Capital Markets* (M. C. Jensen, ed.). New York: Praeger, 1972.
6. Miller, M. H., and Scholes, M., "Rates of Return in Relation to Risk: A Re-Examination of Some Recent Findings," in *Studies in the Theory of Capital Markets* (M. C. Jensen, ed.). New York: Praeger, 1972.
7. Mossin, J., "Equilibrium in a Capital Asset Market," *Econometrica* (October 1966).
8. Pettit, R. R., and Westerfield, R., "A Model of Capital Asset Risk," *Journal of Financial and Quantitative Analysis* (March 1972).
9. Roll, R., "Bias in Fitting the Sharpe Model to Time Series Data," *Journal of Financial and Quantitative Analysis* (September 1969).
10. Sharpe, W. F., "Capital Asset Prices: A Theory of Market Equilibrium under Conditions of Risk," *Journal of Finance* (September 1964).

Valuation of a Call Option on a Stock with Simple Price Changes

To make concrete some further principles of option valuation it will prove helpful to deal with a rather simple kind of stock. Figure 14-6(a) shows the general nature of its behavior. In any given period its price will either jump
 up to some higher value ($P^+_{s,t+1}$) or down to some lower value ($P^-_{s,t+1}$). Look-

367 OPTION VALUATION ing forward from time t to time $t + 1$, there are thus two possible states of the world—up (+) and down (−). Associated with each state is a known stock price; the probabilities of the two states (p^+ and p^-) have also been estimated.

For every time and stock value there will be some corresponding value for a call option on the stock. These amounts are also indicated in Figure 14-6(a).

The final item in Figure 14-6(a) represents the results obtained by investing some amount of money, X, in the bank. It will grow to $(1 + r)$ times its initial value by the end of the period, and this return is certain.

All assumptions used previously will be retained. The option under study has an exercise price of $100, the stock pays no dividends prior to expiration, and the riskless rate of interest is fixed at r per period.

Figure 14-6(b) shows specific numeric values that will be used henceforth. The stock price is assumed to have a 60% chance of increasing 5% each period and a 40% chance of decreasing 5%; its expected return thus equals $(.6 \times +5) + (.4 \times -5)$, or 1% per period. The riskless interest rate is half this, .5% per period (i.e., $r = .005$).

Figure 14-6(c) fills in some more values. It covers the situation when the stock price is $100 one period prior to expiration. The time of expiration is denoted e, one period prior to expiration, $e - 1$, two periods prior, $e - 2$, etc.

There is a good reason for starting with the period prior to expiration. At expiration, the option value associated with every possible stock price is known: it is $(P_{s,e} - E)$ or zero, whichever is larger. In the situation shown in Figure 14-6(c), the end-of-period option value will be either $5 or $0.

What does this imply for the price of the option at the beginning of the period—i.e., how was the box for $P_{o,e-1}$ in Figure 14-6(c) filled in? Not surprisingly, by analogy, as we will see.

Figure 14-6(d) plots the end-of-period values for the stock and the option. Since there are only two possibilities, all (two) of the points lie on a straight line. The securities' returns are perfectly positively correlated. Whenever this is the case, it is possible to *hedge* one against the other and eliminate all risk.

The difference between the stock prices in the two states is $10; the difference between the option prices is $5. It is possible to hold stock and write a call option, and to arrange the proportions so that the differences in payoffs in the two positions are exactly equal. The investor's end-of-period net worth will then be the same in either event. In this case, the appropriate *hedge ratio* is .5; for every option written (sold), one-half a share of stock should be purchased. More generally, the appropriate hedge ratio, denoted h in Figure 14-6, is simply the difference between the end-of-period option values, divided by the difference between the end-of-period stock values:

$$h = \frac{P^+_{o,t+1} - P^-_{o,t+1}}{P^+_{s,t+1} - P^-_{s,t+1}} \tag{14-2}$$

Figure 14-6(e) shows how this can be employed. An investor buys half a share of stock and sells one call option. The initial investment required is $50 minus the (yet-to-be-determined) price received for writing the option. The value of the "portfolio" at the end of the period will be $47.50, *no matter which state occurs.* The investor has set up a *riskless hedge* by using the appropriate hedge ratio indicated by formula (14-2).

Figure 14-6
Stock and Option Prices

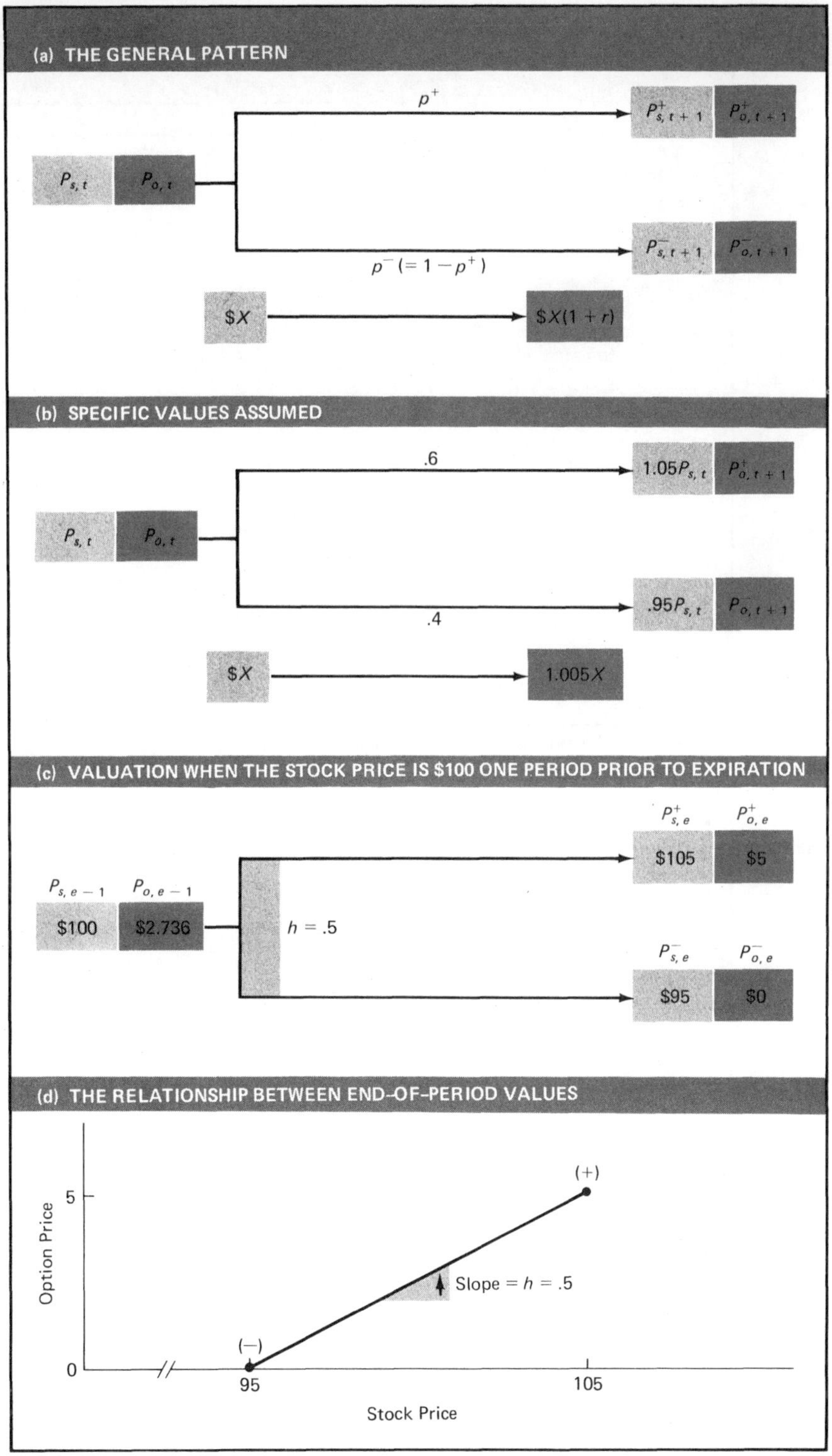

Figure 14-6 (continued)

(e) BALANCE SHEETS FOR A HEDGED POSITION

Time: $e-1$		Time: e, State: +		Time: e, State: −	
½ Share of Stock: \$50	1 Option: $P_{o,e-1}$ Net Worth: $50 - P_{o,e-1}$	½ Share of Stock: \$52.50	1 Option: \$5 Net Worth: \$47.50	½ Share of Stock: \$47.50	1 Option: \$0 Net Worth: \$47.50

(f) BALANCE SHEETS FOR A HEDGED POSITION WHEN THE OPTION IS CORRECTLY PRICED

Time: $e-1$		Time: e, State: +		Time: e, State: −	
½ Share of Stock: \$50	1 Option: \$2.736 Net Worth: \$47.264	½ Share of Stock: \$52.50	1 Option: \$5 Net Worth: \$47.50	½ Share of Stock: \$47.50	1 Option: \$0 Net Worth: \$47.50

$$\text{Return} = \frac{47.50 - 47.264}{47.264} = .005 = .5\%$$

(g) BALANCE SHEETS FOR A HEDGED POSITION WHEN THE OPTION IS OVERPRICED

Time: $e-1$		Time: e, State: +		Time: e, State: −	
½ Share of Stock: \$50	1 Option: \$2.80 Net Worth: \$47.20	½ Share of Stock: \$52.50	1 Option: \$5 Net Worth: \$47.50	½ Share of Stock: \$47.50	1 Option: \$0 Net Worth: \$47.50

$$\text{Return} = \frac{47.50 - 47.20}{47.20} = .006 = .6\%$$

(h) BALANCE SHEETS FOR A REVERSE HEDGE WHEN THE OPTION IS UNDERPRICED

Time: $e-1$		Time: e, State: +		Time: e, State: −	
1 Option: \$2.60 Bank Account: \$50	½ Share of Stock: \$50 Net Worth: \$2.60	1 Option: \$5 Bank Account: \$50.25	½ Share of Stock: \$52.50 Net Worth: \$2.75	1 Option: \$0 Bank Account: \$50.25	½ Share of Stock: \$47.50 Net Worth: \$2.75

$$\text{Return} = \frac{2.75 - 2.60}{2.60} = .058 = 5.8\%$$

Now for the analogy. The rate of interest on a riskless investment is .5% per period. The option should be priced so that a riskless strategy utilizing it also returns .5% per period. Since the ending value will be \$47.50, the required option value is that which satisfies:

369 $(50 - P_{o,e-1})1.005 = \$47.50$

Figure 14-6
(continued)

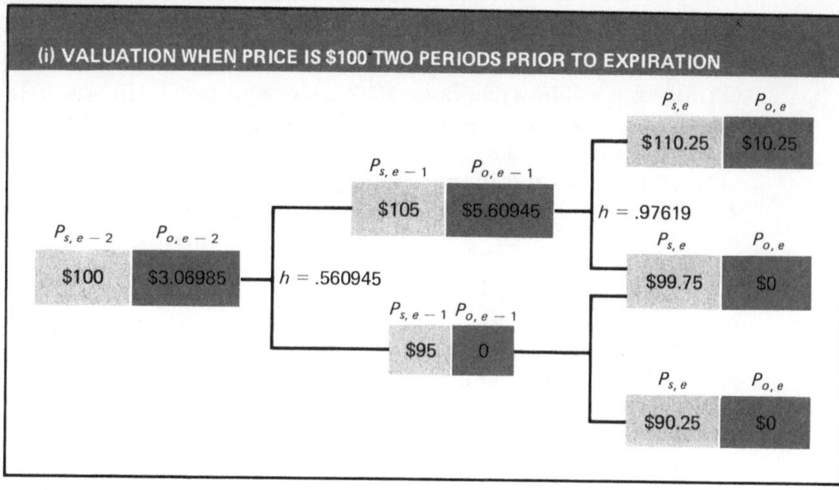

The solution is:

$$P_{o,e-1} = \$2.736$$

Figure 14-6(f) shows that the hedging strategy will in fact give a certain return equal to the riskless rate if the option price equals $2.736. Figure 14-6(g) shows that if the option were overpriced, at $2.80, the hedging strategy could give a certain return greater than the riskless rate. Such a situation would attract attention, bringing out would-be option sellers whose activities would shortly drive the price back down.

What if the option were underpriced, say at $2.60? Then clever investors could *reverse hedge,* buying options and selling stock. Figure 14-6(h) shows a case in which the stock is sold short and the proceeds placed in an interest-earnings bank account.[8] A certain 5.8% per period is returned on invested funds. Such a situation would attract would-be option buyers, driving the price back up.

Figure 14-6(f) thus portrays the likely situation, and we have an option pricing formula. The option price at time t must satisfy:

$$(hP_{s,t} - P_{o,t})(1 + r) = \begin{Bmatrix} [hP^{+}_{s,t+1} - P^{+}_{o,t+1}] \\ [hP^{-}_{s,t+1} - P^{-}_{o,t+1}] \end{Bmatrix} \tag{14-3}$$

where h is the hedge ratio required to give a riskless return. The first parenthesized expression on the left represents the funds invested at the beginning of the period. The brackets on the right indicate that either of the two included expressions can be used, for they are both equal to the certain end-of-period value. The formula simply requires the option to be priced so that a portfolio

[8]This is generally not possible in practice, lowering and/or eliminating the profit from such a hedge and raising the possibility that the option could sell at any price within a band limited by the prices at which hedging or reverse hedging would become profitable.

371 OPTION VALUATION

hedged to remove all risk will return the riskless rate on the funds invested.

Having established the principles summarized in formulas (14-2) and (14-3), it is possible to determine the option value for any time and stock price. Figure 14-6(i) does this for the case in which the stock price is $100 two periods prior to expiration. The option price boxes are filled in from right to left. Option values at expiration are simply (P_s − 100) or zero, whichever is larger. This takes care of the option values at time *e*. Turning to time *e* − 1, note that if a situation will lead to a worthless option no matter what, the option is already worthless. Thus if the stock price is $95 one period prior to expiration, the option will definitely expire worthless, and the option value is zero. This takes care of another box. Turning to the situation in which the stock price is $105 one period prior to expiration, formula (14-2) is used to determine the hedge ratio (.97619) and then formula (14-3) applied to determine the option price ($5.60945). To find the remaining hedge ratio (.560945) and option price ($3.06985), we again apply formulas (14-2) and (14-3), using the relevant stock values ($105 and $95) and the previously computed associated option values ($5.60945 and $0).

Figure 14-7 shows some values obtained with this kind of *recursive* calculation. Each curve plots option values associated with various stock prices at a specific time prior to expiration.

One characteristic of the curves in Figure 14-7 is quite general: if two options are otherwise identical but one has a longer time remaining before expiration, the latter will be worth at least as much as the former and generally will be worth more. This is obviously true of American options, for the one with a longer time to expiration can be used to do anything possible with the other, and more besides. Except in pathological cases caused by large dividend payments, the statement also applies to European options.

Figure 14-7 Option Values at Various Times Prior to Expiration (based on the numeric example in Figure 14-6)

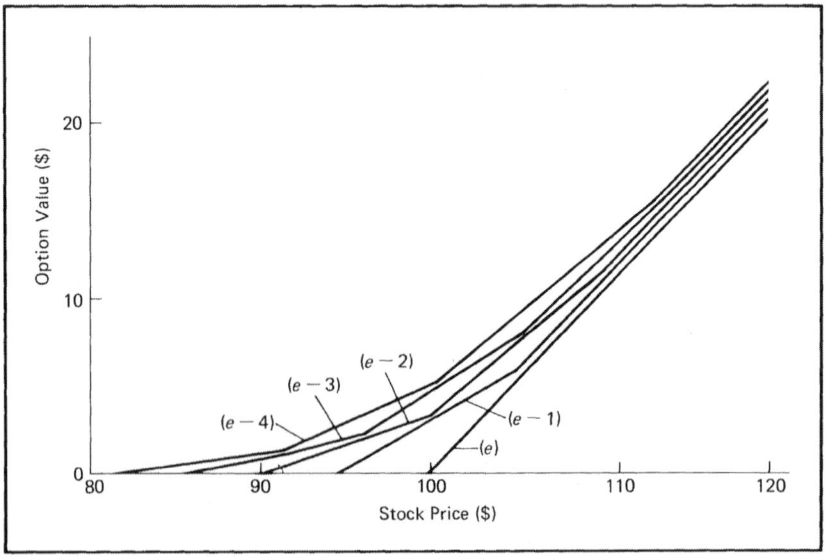

SECURITY CODINGS: MEASURING RELATIVE ATTRACTIVENESS IN PERFECT AND IMPERFECT MARKETS

W. F. SHARPE*
Stanford University

INTRODUCTION

It is a long-standing tradition for investment research departments to rate securities on the basis of "relative attractiveness." This is often done by assigning ordinal *codes*. A widely used scheme distinguishes five categories, with the following interpretations: (1) buy, (2) OK to buy, (3) hold, (4) OK to sell, and (5) sell.

As the titles indicate, the intent of such schemes is to provide information for the revision of clients' portfolios based on the research department's assessment of securities' prospects.

Security codings were first used in the early days of investment management before the development of portfolio theory and equilibrium theories such as the capital asset pricing model. At the very best they represent a simplistic approach

*Timken Professor of Finance. Valuable comments and suggestions were provided by William Fouse, Robert Fuhrman, Kelly Haughton, William Jahnke, Robert Litzenberger, Krishna Ramaswamy, Polly Shouse, and Lawrence Tint. The research was also supported by the Stanford Program in Finance. Major contributors to the Stanford Program in Finance are Bank America Foundation, The First Boston Corporation, The Chase Manhattan Bank, Continental Bank Foundation, The Dean Witter Foundation, General Electric Company, Goldman, Sachs & Co., Morgan Guaranty Trust Company, Morgan Stanley & Co., Inc., Salomon Brothers, Security Pacific National Bank, and Wells Fargo Bank.

to a complex problem. At worst they can be considered anachronisms which should be relegated to the shelf for historic curiosa.

In this paper we take a middle ground on the usefulness of such approaches. We assume that the desire of investment research departments is to produce measures of relative attractiveness. We therefore concentrate on the definition and calculation of measures of this sort that can take into account the lessons learned in the last 25 years. We focus on cardinal measures, but such values can, if desired, be mapped into ordinal codings (with a resultant loss of information).

Some of our results are conventional. However, the manner in which they are obtained is somewhat unconventional. In particular we provide motivation for using measures akin to the well-known "alpha" in both perfect and imperfect markets.

INVESTOR UTILITY FUNCTIONS

Any problem in optimization must include a specification of the objective function. Portfolio selection or revision is most assuredly an optimization problem, one in which the objective is to maximize the "utility" of the investor. An investor's utility function may have many arguments, but we will limit our discussion to three—two linear and one quadratic in the decision variables:

$$U_k = E_p - \lambda_k V_p - t_k y_p \qquad \textbf{(1)}$$

where U_k = the utility of investor k; E_p = the expected return of the portfolio; V_p = the variance of the portfolio's return; y_p = the yield of the portfolio; λ_k = investor k's *risk-aversion*; t_k = investor k's *yield-aversion;* and

$$\begin{aligned} E_p &= \sum_{i=1}^{N} x_i E_i \\ V_p &= \sum_{i=1}^{N}\sum_{j=1}^{N} x_i x_j C_{ij} \\ y_p &= \sum_{i=1}^{N} x_i y_i \end{aligned} \qquad \textbf{(1a)}$$

where x_i = the proportion of security i in the portfolio; E_i = the expected return on security i; C_{ij} = the covariance between the returns on securities i and j; y_i = the yield of security i; and N = the number of securities.

The parameters λ_k and t_k (respectively, the marginal rates of substitution between expected return and variance and between expected return and yield) can be considered local linear approximations in the region of the optimum to a more general nonlinear utility function. However, it is helpful for discussion purposes to give them a global interpretation so that U_k can be said to be measured in *certain gain-equivalent* units.

For virtually all investors $\lambda_k > 0$, reflecting aversion to risk. For some (for example, many tax-exempt investors), $t_k = 0$. For others (those in high tax brackets), $t_k > 0$. For a few (those allowed to spend only from yield) $t_k < 0$. Thus, there is reason to believe that investors differ in their attitudes towards risk and yield, and that they would do so even in a world in which all information were shared among all market participants.

Equation (1) differs from that implicit in the usual formulation of the capital asset pricing model (see, for example, Sharpe, 1964 and Lintner, 1965) but corresponds to the utility function implicit in Brennan's (1970) model of the impact of taxes on capital market equilibrium. There is some empirical evidence that many market participants are averse to yield; for recent studies see Litzenberger and Ramaswamy (1978) and Rosenberg and Marathe (1978). Other factors may also be relevant (for example, aversion to illiquidity, South African stocks, etc.). Equation (1) should thus be considered illustrative. As will be shown, the impact of the inclusion of additional attributes can be inferred from the results derived for this case.

PERFECT AND IMPERFECT MARKETS

Assume that each investor is advised by an investment research department concerning the values of the E_i's, C_{ij}'s, and y_i's.[1] We will define a *perfect market* as one in which (1) all advisers share the same information and thus agree on all E_i's, C_{ij}'s, and y_i's; and (2) there are neither limits on nor extra costs associated with short positions (negative x_i's).[2] An *imperfect market* lacks one or both these attributes.

EQUILIBRIUM IN A PERFECT MARKET

In a perfect market each investor will consider the same set of security attributes. Thus, we need not subscript such variables to indicate their source (the advisor in question). Investor k (or his or her advisor) solves the following problem:

$$\max U_k = E_p - \lambda_k V_p - t_k y_p \quad \text{subject to} \sum_{i=1}^{N} x_i = 1. \tag{2}$$

Forming the Lagrangean,

$$\max Z = E_p - \lambda_k V_p - t_k y_p + \lambda_f \left(1 - \sum_{i=1}^{N} x_i\right). \tag{3}$$

[1]Of course an investor can use multiple advisors or act as his or her own research department.

[2]Implicit in the discussion is the assumption that only return, risk, and yield matter—that is, that every investor has a utility function of the form $U_k = f(E\rho, V\rho, y\rho)$.

The first-order conditions (which are sufficient in this case) are

$$\frac{\partial Z}{\partial x_i} = 0 \qquad \text{(for all } i\text{)},$$
$$\frac{\partial Z}{\partial \lambda_f} = 1 - \sum_{i=1}^{N} x_i = 0. \tag{4}$$

Note that

$$\frac{\partial Z}{\partial x_i} = \frac{\partial U_k}{\partial x_i} - \lambda_f \tag{5}$$

where

$$\frac{\partial U_k}{\partial x_i} = E_i - 2\lambda_k \sum_{j=1}^{N} x_j C_{ij} - t_k y_i. \tag{5a}$$

Thus

$$2 \sum_{j=1}^{N} x_j C_{ij} + \frac{\lambda_f}{\lambda_k} = \frac{1}{\lambda_k} E_i - \frac{t_k}{\lambda_k} y_i \qquad \text{(for all } i\text{)}. \tag{6}$$

Let X_k = an $N + 1$ element column vector

$$\begin{bmatrix} x_1 \\ \cdot \\ \cdot \\ \cdot \\ x_N \\ \dfrac{\lambda_f}{\lambda_k} \end{bmatrix}$$

E = an $N + 1$ element column vector

$$\begin{bmatrix} E_1 \\ \cdot \\ \cdot \\ \cdot \\ E_N \\ 0 \end{bmatrix}$$

y = an $N + 1$ element column vector

$$\begin{bmatrix} y_1 \\ \cdot \\ \cdot \\ \cdot \\ y_N \\ 0 \end{bmatrix}$$

K = an $N + 1$ element column vector

$$\begin{bmatrix} 0 \\ \cdot \\ \cdot \\ \cdot \\ 0 \\ 1 \end{bmatrix}$$

C = an $N + 1$ by $N + 1$ element matrix

$$\begin{bmatrix} 2C_{11}, \ldots, 2C_{1N}, 1 \\ \cdot \quad\quad \cdot \\ \cdot \quad\quad \cdot \\ \cdot \quad\quad \cdot \\ 2C_{N1}, \ldots, 2C_{NN}, 1 \\ 1, \ldots, 1, \quad 0 \end{bmatrix}$$

Then the solution must satisfy

$$CX_k = K + \frac{1}{\lambda_k} E - \frac{t_k}{\lambda_k} y \qquad \text{or}$$
$$X_k = C^{-1}K + \frac{1}{\lambda_k} C^{-1}E - \frac{t_k}{\lambda_k} C^{-1}y. \tag{7}$$

This shows that X_k, the optimal set of holdings for investor k, is linear in $(1/\lambda_k)$ and (t_k/λ_k).[3] Moreover, three portfolios suffice to provide all investors with adequate opportunities to achieve optimality. For example, let $X_1 = C^{-1}k$, $X_2 = C^{-1}E$, and $X_3 = C^{-1}y$.

Then

$$X_k = X_1 + \frac{1}{\lambda_k} X_2 - \frac{t_k}{\lambda_k} X_3. \tag{7a}$$

Another form is

$$X_k = X_1 + \frac{1}{\lambda_k} [X_2 - t_k X_3] \tag{7b}$$

or

$$X_k = X_1 + \frac{1}{\lambda_k} X_t \tag{7c}$$

where

$$X_t = X_2 - tX_3. \tag{7d}$$

[3]Since X_k is an $N + 1$ element vector, it includes the holdings $x_1, \ldots, x_N$ and the value of λ_f/λ_k. Henceforth, the discussion should be assumed to apply to the first N rows of each of the X vectors.

Thus, the optimum portfolio can be considered a mix of (1) X_t (the optimal portfolio for the investor's yield-aversion and (2) X_1 (the minimum-variance portfolio with the appropriate mix depending on the investor's risk-aversion. If borrowing and lending at a single riskless rate is possible, X_1 will consist solely of the riskless asset, and the latter decision will reduce to the appropriate mix of this asset, and X_t—the optimal mix of risky securities for the investor's yield-aversion.

Similar separation theorems have been derived by others for cases involving factors in addition to risk and return; see, for example, Merton (1973).

Assume that the ratio of the market value of investor k's portfolio to the market value of all portfolios is w_k. Let X_m represent the vector of proportions of securities in the overall market. Clearly

$$\begin{aligned} X_m &= \sum_k w_k X_k \\ &= \sum_k w_k X_1 + \sum_k \frac{1}{\lambda_k} w_k X_2 - \sum_k w_k \frac{t_k}{\lambda_k} X_3 \\ &= X_1 + \left(\sum_k \frac{1}{\lambda_k} w_k\right) X_2 - \left(\sum_k w_k \frac{t_k}{\lambda_k}\right) X_3 \end{aligned} \quad \textbf{(8)}$$

Thus, the market portfolio will be a combination of these three (supporting) portfolios. Moreover, it will be a portfolio that would be optimal for an investor with

$$\frac{1}{\lambda_m} = \sum_k \frac{1}{\lambda_k} w_k \quad \textbf{(9)}$$

and

$$\frac{t_m}{\lambda_m} = \sum_k w_k \frac{t_k}{\lambda_k}. \quad \textbf{(9a)}$$

Thus, we can say that in a perfect market securities would be priced as if all investors had a common risk-aversion (λ_m) as given by (9) and a common yield-aversion t_m as implied (sequentially) by (9a). For discussion purposes, these may be termed *"the market's"* risk-aversion and yield-aversion, respectively.

Since the market portfolio would be optimal for an investor with risk-aversion λ_m and yield-aversion t_m, the first-order conditions insure (from (5)):

$$\frac{\partial Z}{\partial x_i} = E_i - 2\lambda_m \sum_{j=1}^{N} x_{jm} C_{ij} - t_m y_i - \lambda_f = 0 \quad \text{(for all } i\text{)} \quad \textbf{(10)}$$

where x_{jm} = the proportion of security j in the market portfolio. Thus

$$E_i = \lambda_f + 2\lambda_m \sum_{j=1}^{N} x_{jm} C_{ij} + t_m y_i \qquad \text{(for all } i\text{)} \quad \textbf{(11)}$$

As usual, we define

$$\beta_i = \frac{\sum_{j=1}^{N} x_{jm} C_{ij}}{V_m}$$

where V_m = the variance of return on the market portfolio. Equation (11) can accordingly be rewritten as

$$E_i = \lambda_f + 2\lambda_m V_m \beta_i + t_m y_i \qquad \text{(for all } i\text{).} \tag{12}$$

Equation (12) defines a *security market plane* relating E_i to β_i and y_i.[4] In a perfect market all securities would plot on such a plane, and all advisors would agree both on its location and on the fact that all securities plot on it.

EQUILIBRIUM IN AN IMPERFECT MARKET

In an imperfect market the situation could be quite different. Limits on holdings and/or costs associated with short positions require the replacement of the first-order conditions in (5) with Kuhn-Tucker conditions. Moreover, if advisors differ in their assessments of the E_i's, C_{ij}'s, and/or y_i's, the situation may be perceived differently by each advisor. Nonetheless, it seems likely that, given an advisor's opinions, there will appear to be some relationship among the values of the E_i's, β_i's, and y_i's. This could be determined by regressing the advisor's estimates of the E_i's on his or her estimates of the β_i's and y_i's.[5] Surpressing subscripts indicating the advisor whose opinions are indicated, such a relationship can be written

$$E_i = a + b\beta_i + cy_i + \alpha_i \tag{13a}$$

where a, b, c, and the α_i's are (potentially) unique for the advisor. The parameters a, b, and c can be said to represent the advisor's estimate of the structure of the market. Each value of α_i in Equation (13a) then represents the deviation of a security's expected return from that "normal" for its risk (β_i) and yield (y_i). If the advisor is prescient and the "appropriate" (equilibrium) pricing is characterized by the indicated security market plane, this may be due to "true" mispricing of the security. If not, it may simply be an error in the advisor's estimates of security prospects and/or the appropriate equilibrium relationship. Since an advisor is likely to adopt the former view, at least in part, we will term this a (perceived) *mispricing alpha*. In a perfect market, of course, all mispricing alphas would be zero.

[4] This is a generalization of the security market line described in Sharpe (1970). This is, in essence, the result first obtained by Brennan (1970). The term "security market plane" was introduced by Merton (1973) in a related context.

[5] Such a procedure is followed monthly by Wells Fargo Investment Advisors (see Wells Fargo Bank, 1978-). As suggested by Litzenberger and Ramaswamy (1979) a "clientele effect" may lead

Whatever the cause of nonzero alphas, Equation (13a) represents the advisor's notion of the structure of the market. Thus, b can be interpreted as the advisor's assessment of 2 times the market's risk-aversion times its estimate of risk, and c as his or her assessment of the market's yield-aversion. To highlight this interpretation, we will rewrite (13a) as

$$E_i = a + 2\lambda_m V_m \beta_i + t_m y_i + \alpha_i \tag{13b}$$

where, without loss of generality, λ_m, V_m, and t_m are understood to be the advisor's (possibly erroneous) assessment of these variables. Note also that

$$E_m = (a + 2\lambda_m V_m 1 + t_m y_m) \tag{13c}$$

since the relationship should be estimated so that $\alpha_m = 0$.

RELATIVE ATTRACTIVENESS

Assume that investor k holds a particular portfolio $X_p = [x_{1p}, \ldots, x_{Np}]$, which provides the level of utility $U_k(X_p)$. Now consider a change in which the holding of security i is increased by an amount Δ with all holdings of the securities in the portfolio decreased proportionately. Then the change in utility will be

$$\begin{aligned} \Delta U &\approx \frac{\partial U}{\partial x_{ip}} \Delta - \frac{\partial U}{\partial X_p} \Delta \\ &= \left[\frac{\partial U}{\partial x_{ip}} - \frac{\partial U}{\partial X_p} \right] \Delta. \end{aligned} \tag{14a}$$

We will define the term in the brackets in (14a) as security i's *relative attractiveness*. The larger it is, the greater the benefit associated with an increased holding of the security. A positive value implies that, all things being equal, the holding should be increased; a negative value, that the holding should be decreased. The term thus measures attractiveness and measures it relative to the current portfolio; hence the interpretation.

This concept of relative attractiveness is, of course, only local in nature. It does not indicate the appropriate magnitudes for the overall revisions in holdings. In a sense, the task of an investment advisor is to assess N E_i's, $(N^2 + N)/2$ different C_{ij}'s, and N y_i's. Given these estimates, an optimal revision can be found for the portfolio of any specific client. In general, no set of N values can summarize $[N + (N^2 + N)/2 + N]$ different values. Thus, N relative attractiveness measures cannot provide sufficient information for determining the optimal portfolios for all clients. But they can indicate appropriate directions and (local) magnitudes of improvement for clients holding similar portfolios, and our definition (14a) provides a measure that serves this function.

to a relationship which is quadratic in y_i; we limit the present discussion, however, to the simpler case in which the relationship is linear.

MEASURING ATTRACTIVENESS RELATIVE TO THE MARKET PORTFOLIO

If all investors had the same preferences and operated in a perfect market, all would hold the same portfolio; and for there to be equilibrium in the security market, it would have to be the market portfolio. And, of course, even in an imperfect market with differences in investor preferences, the market-value-weighted average portfolio must be the market portfolio.

In general, relative attractiveness can only be defined in terms of a specific portfolio.[6] The most obvious candidate for a general measure is the market portfolio. We thus define

$$A_{ik} \equiv \frac{\partial U_k}{\partial x_{im}} - \frac{\partial U_k}{\partial X_m} \tag{14b}$$

where A_i = security i's relative attractiveness for investor k; and $X_m = [x_{1m}, \ldots, x_{Nm}]$.

From (5a),

$$\frac{\partial U_k}{\partial x_{im}} = E_i - 2\lambda_k \sum_{j=1}^{N} x_{jm} C_{ij} - t_k y_i. \tag{15}$$

Substituting the definition of β_i ,

$$\frac{\partial U_k}{\partial x_{im}} = E_i - 2\lambda_k V_m \beta_i - t_k y_i. \tag{15a}$$

Similarly

$$\frac{\partial U_k}{\partial X_m} = E_m - 2\lambda_k V_m - t_k y_m. \tag{15b}$$

Thus

$$A_{ik} = [E_i - E_m] - (\beta_i - 1)\, 2\lambda_k V_m - (y_i - y_m)\, t_k \tag{16}$$

All values (the E_i's, C_{ij}'s, y_i's, and V_m) are assumed to be based on the predictions of investor k's advisor.

Equation (16) defines relative attractiveness, but it is useful to substitute (13b) and (13c) to highlight differences between the advisor's own predictions and his or her opinion about the structure of the market. This gives

$$\begin{aligned} A_{ik} = {} & [a + 2\lambda_m V_m \beta_i + t_m y_i + \alpha_i] - [a + 2\lambda_m V_m + t_m y_m] \\ & - 2\lambda_k V_m (\beta_i - 1) - (y_i - y_m) t_k \end{aligned} \tag{17a}$$

[6]This follows from the presence of a nonlinear term (V_p) in (1). If all terms were linear, $\partial U/\partial x_{ip}$ would not be a function of $[x_{1p}, \ldots, x_{Np}]$; but this is an uninteresting case.

or[7]

$$A_{ik} = (\beta_i - 1)(2\lambda_m V_m - 2\lambda_k V_m) + (y_i - y_m)(t_m - t_k) + \alpha_i \quad \textbf{(17b)}$$

Equation (17b) provides a number of insights into the notion of relative attractiveness. In the case analyzed here, the overall attractiveness of a security can be broken into three components, which can be termed, respectively, the *risk effect*, the *yield effect*, and the *mispricing effect*.

Consider the first two effects. Each is the product of (1) the difference between the partial derivative of the attribute with respect to the security and that with respect to the market; and (2) the difference between the "market's" aversion to that attribute and the investor's aversion. For an investor with an "average" aversion, there is no effect. But for an investor with an above average aversion, securities with below average characteristics will be relatively more attractive. The reverse is true for an investor with a below average aversion.[8]

Even in a perfect market, securities would differ in relative attractiveness (as defined here), since the market portfolio would not be optimal for any investor with nonaverage preferences. The first two terms of (17b) thus describe aspects that are relevant for "tailoring" portfolios to investor characteristics.[9]

The third term in (17b) is different in kind. To the extent that (13a–c) can be said to represent "appropriate" pricing, α_i indicates (perceived) mispricing. A security with a positive (negative) alpha would be considered by the advisor in question to be attractive (unattractive), all things being equal, for all investors.

The interpretation (and use) of the α_i terms in (17b) depends on one's assessment of market perfection and one's ability to correctly assess market structure. One view would consider the advisor's predictions correct as stated, and employ (16) directly. Equivalently, (13a–c) could be estimated and (17b) used without modification. Thus, the use of alphas as initially estimated is equivalent to an agnostic view on the structure of the market and any equilibrium position.

An alternative view would hold that (13a–c) represents an underlying equilibrium structure.[10] To the extent that the estimated α_i's contain measurement error, smaller (positive or negative) values might be employed when estimating relative attractiveness. On the other hand, to the extent that the estimated α's represent true mispricing, one might assume that short-term holding period returns would be larger (positive or negative) than indicated by the estimated

[7]Since b in (13a) can be interpreted as an estimate of $(2\lambda_m V_m)$, the advisor's estimate of V_m can be employed to estimate λ_m.

[8]Note that in the case of β_i, overall aversion depends on both the assessment of market risk (V_m) and the degree of aversion to such risk (λ_m).

[9]In the special case in which all investors have the same yield-aversion, two portfolios would suffice, as (7c) and (7d) show. Moreover, if investors could borrow or lend at a single riskless rate, one of the portfolios would contain only the riskless asset and the proportions of risky securities would be the same in all optimal mixes, since "tailoring" could be accomplished by simply combining such a portfolio with borrowing or lending (see, for example, Sharpe, 1970).

[10]One might, of course, utilize a more complex form, as suggested by Litzenberger and Ramaswamy (1979).

alphas, due to repricing of the securities to better conform to the appropriate equilibrium relationship.

In any event, only when alpha values are adjusted is a market equilibrium model being employed in a disequilibrium content. But even in this case, the relevance of (adjusted) alpha values can be justified as indications of appropriate modifications to a market portfolio, even though (and, to some extent, because) such a portfolio may not be efficient for *any* investor.[11]

As indicated in Equation (17b), a relative attractiveness measure of the type defined here can only be determined for a particular class of investors (for example, those with common values of $\lambda_k V_m$, and t_k). Moreover, due to the nature of the first two terms, a security with a positive relative attractiveness for some investors may have a negative relative attractiveness for others.

Note also that if the second term is omitted—as it is in the conventional security market line formulation—one may attribute to "mispricing" the effects of yield-aversion and, lacking the appropriate measure of this effect, fail to appropriately tailor portfolios for clients with different aversions to yield.

OTHER APPROACHES

We have argued that relative attractiveness should be defined in terms of a given portfolio. If a single portfolio is to be selected for this purpose, a surrogate for the overall market is the obvious candidate.

It is tempting to suggest a different approach in which attractiveness would be measured relative to a portfolio that would be optimal for a given class of investors if there were no mispricing. This would, however, be a far from straightforward procedure, for, as shown by equation (2c), such an optimal portfolio would depend on the entire structure of security covariances and returns.[12]

A simpler approach would concentrate on one attribute, assuming an average aversion toward the other. Thus, if $\lambda_k V_m = \lambda_m V_m$, equation (17b) simplifies to

$$A_{ik} = (t_m - t_k)(y_i - y_m) + \alpha_i. \qquad \textbf{(18)}$$

For any given yield-aversion (t_k) one can easily calculate the relative attractiveness of each security. And for different yield-aversions, one can calculate different values of relative attractiveness for a given security.[13]

EXTENSIONS

As indicated at the outset, other factors may be relevant, in the sense that investors hold different attitudes toward them. If so, the approach can (and should) be extended. The results that would be obtained can be inferred from

[11]At present, and possibly in the future.

[12]And for an investor with nonaverage yield aversion, this would be true even if there were a riskless asset, as equations (5d) and (5e) show.

[13]This is the procedure followed in Wells Fargo's Security Market Plane Report (1978).

those obtained here. Let A be a relevant portfolio attribute and a_k investor k's aversion to A. Then

$$A'_{ik} = A_{ik} + \left[\frac{\partial A}{\partial x_{im}} - \frac{\partial A}{X_m}\right](a_m - a_k) \quad \textbf{(18a)}$$

where a_m = the slope coefficient in a relationship of the form

$$E_i = a + b\beta_i + cy_i + \ . \ . \ . \ + a_m\left[\frac{\partial A}{\partial x_{im}}\right]. \quad \textbf{(18b)}$$

Equation (18b) represents a *security market hyperplane,*[14] while (18a) is the corresponding measure of relative attractiveness, including the "attribute-A" effect.

CONCLUSIONS

Given a proposed investor utility function (1) and a definition of relative attractiveness (14b), we derived in (16) a simple equation for relative attractiveness. This expression did not utilize any equation stating relationships among risks and returns and thus does not depend on any assumptions about market equilibrium. Next, by substituting values from (13b), we derived (17b), an equation for relative attractiveness that includes both investor and "market" attributes. However, this invoked no assumptions about market equilibrium and thus could be applicable in perfect or imperfect markets.

Why even go to the bother of estimating the "structure of the market" (13b)? Primarily because there is a presumption on the part of most investment advisors that divergences of returns from those suggested by such a structure may be due at least in part to estimation errors with the remainder likely to be "corrected" in relatively short order. If so, one might want to substitute for α_i in (17b) a value either smaller or larger than that obtained when fitting (13b).[15] This procedure, recommended by Ambachtsheer (1977) and Treynor and Black (1973) and followed implicitly by many advisors (and/or their clients), represents a middle ground between a belief in a simple perfect-market equilibrium and a world in which returns bear no relationship whatever to risks, yields, etc.

In any event, equation (17b) can encompass both approaches. The first two components are relevant in both perfect and imperfect markets: they reflect the desirability of "tailoring" portfolios to meet client preferences. The third component would not be relevant in a perfect market in which only return, risk, and yield matter. It arises from a difference of opinion between the advisor and the market,[16] and is the driving force behind "active" portfolio management.

[14]As indicated earlier, similar relationships have been derived from equilibrium models by Merton (1973) and others.

[15]Of course, in such a situation the best possible approximation to the "structure of the market" should be obtained.

[16]Sometimes it is the result of the advisor's error in estimating security prospects and/or the structure of the market.

No single measure can provide a complete guide for portfolio construction and revision. For this purpose, detailed estimates of risk and return are needed. However, our measure can provide useful information concerning the effects of moves away from average (market) holdings—moves designed to better tailor a portfolio to investor preferences and/or to take advantage of potential security mispricing. Moreover, it separates overall attractiveness into components, indicating the importance of each and making it possible for clients to weight them differently if desired.

References

Ambachtsheer, K. P., "Where Are the Customers' Alphas?" *Journal of Portfolio Management,* 4, no. 1 (Fall 1977), 52–56.

Brennan, M. J., "Taxes, Market Valuation and Corporate Financial Policy," *National Tax Journal,* 23 (Dec. 1970), 417–27.

Lintner, J., "The Valuation of Risk Assets and the Selection of Risky Investments in Stock Portfolios and Capital Budgets," *Review of Economics and Statistics,* 47 (Feb. 1965), 13–37.

Litzenberger, R., and **K. Ramaswamy,** "The Effect of Personal Taxes and Dividends on Capital Asset Prices: Theory and Empirical Evidence," *Journal of Financial Economics,* 7, no. 2 (June, 1979), 163–95.

Merton, R. C., "An Intertemporal Capital Asset Pricing Model," *Econometrica,* 41 (Sept. 1973), 867–87.

Rosenberg, B., and **V. Marathe,** "Tests of Capital Asset Pricing Hypotheses," University of California, Berkeley, Research Program in Finance, working paper no. 32, May 1975.

Sharpe, W. F., "Capital Asset Prices: A Theory of Market Equilibrium Under Conditions of Risks," *Journal of Finance,* 19 (Sept. 1964), 425–42.

———, *Portfolio Theory and Capital Markets.* New York: McGraw-Hill, 1970.

Treynor, J., and **F. Black,** "How to Use Security Analysis to Improve Portfolio Selection," *Journal of Business,* 46, no. 1 (Jan. 1973).

Wells Fargo Investment Advisors, *Security Market Plane Report* (monthly). San Francisco: Wells Fargo Bank N.A. 1978–.

Factor models, CAPMs, and the APT

Linking them together provides a valuable framework.

William F. Sharpe

Confusion reigns. Are they the same or are they different? Compatible or incompatible? Does one require another, and if so, which? Is peaceful coexistence among them possible, or must one take sides?

To address these issues, I will consider the three approaches in roughly the order of their introduction in the finance literature. After this "compare and contrast" exercise, I will discuss a synthesis, incorporating features of all three.

FACTOR MODELS

Factor models have been with us for many years. Earlier papers called them *index models*, but the alternative term has become fashionable of late. The change is a result of renewed interest in the use of factor *analysis* to obtain empirical estimates for such models. But there is no need to use factor analysis for this purpose. Factor models have been estimated using other techniques, and the pendulum may be swinging away from factor analysis but not away from factor models.

A factor model represents the behavior of security prices; it attempts to capture the major sources of *correlation* among security returns. The goal is to identify *pervasive factors* that affect significant numbers of securities.

A general representation of such a model is the following:

$$\tilde{R}_i = a_i + b_{i1}\tilde{F}_1 + b_{i2}\tilde{F}_2 + \ldots + b_{iM}\tilde{F}_M + \tilde{e}_i. \quad (1)$$

The tildes (squiggly lines) indicate variables not known with certainty in advance.

R_i is the return on security i, F_1 is the value of factor 1; F_2 is the value of factor 2, and so forth. There are M of these "pervasive factors." The last term (e_i) represents the portion of the return of security i that is unrelated to the specified factors. It is often termed the *security-specific* return or (more honestly) the *nonfactor-related return*.

The remaining values indicate the relationships between the return on the security and the values of the factors. If all the factors equaled zero, the return on the security would be a_i plus e_i. The values of b_{i1}, b_{i2}, etc., indicate the *sensitivities* of the return on the security to the values of factors 1, 2, etc. These are sometimes called *factor loadings* or, better, security *attributes*.

By convention, the *expected* value of e_i is taken to be zero. This means only that a_i is set to capture the expected nonfactor-related aspects of the return on the security. Also by convention, e_i is taken to be uncorrelated with the factors. This means only that the attributes (b_i values) are set so that all factor-related aspects are captured in the associated relationships.

There remains one assumption that makes a factor model less than vacuous. It is assumed that the e_i values are uncorrelated with one another. In other words, the returns of two securities will be correlated (move together) only through common reactions to one or more of the M factors. For this reason, e_i is sometimes termed security i's *idiosyncratic return*.

A factor model describes the *return-generating process*. Identification of the relevant factors should proceed from an analysis of the economics of the firms involved. Clearly, aspects of macroeconomics, microeconomics, industrial organization, and fundamental security analysis should play a major role in the process.

Markowitz [1959] proposed the use of a single-factor model. The idea was expanded upon by Sharpe [1963]. Multifactor models were discussed by Cohen and Pogue [1967] and Sharpe [1970]. Empirical papers that attempt to identify relevant factors and estimate the magnitudes of the associated values include those of King [1966], Feeney and Hester [1967], Elton and Gruber [1973], Fama and MacBeth [1973], Farrell [1974], Rosenberg and Marathe [1975], Roll and Ross [1980], Arnott [1980], Sharpe [1982], Estep, Hanson, and Johnson [1983], and Chen, Roll, and Ross [1983].

In an important sense, every large investment management organization represents an implicit factor model. Assignment of a certain group of stocks to one analyst and of another group to a different analyst suggests that stocks in the first group are related to one factor and stocks in the second group to another. The models implicit in investment organizations may be less than precise, but they exist, nonetheless.

As a practical matter, one *must* employ a factor model, either explicitly or implicitly. It is impossible to think separately about the interrelationship of every security with every other. Abstraction is essential. Good investment managers identify important factors in the economy and the marketplace and assess the extent to which different securities will respond to changes in these factors. Passive managers attempt to assess the market's predictions about the risks and returns associated with the factors and security-specific returns. Active managers also attempt to outguess the market on likely outcomes for factors and/or stocks.

There is no reason to assume or believe that a good factor model for one period will be a good one for the next period; key factors change — remember OPEC! So do the risks and returns associated with various factors and the sensitivities of securities to factors. Causes of change include mergers, new lines of business, changes in leverage, etc.

It would be convenient if neither the relevant factors nor the values of the relevant magnitudes were to change from month to month, or from year to year. If this were so, mechanical procedures could be applied to security returns over an extended past period and the relevant factor model inferred, along with all the needed magnitudes. Although procedures such as cluster analysis, principal components analysis, and factor analysis that assume such stability have provided useful results, it is likely that approaches that combine this type of econometric analysis with information about lines of business, political developments, or company-specific changes will prove even more useful.

EQUILIBRIUM THEORIES

A factor model can represent a market that is efficient or inefficient. There is nothing inherent in the approach that assumes any sort of *equilibrium* in the marketplace.

Equilibrium theories of security prices generally make statements about the relationship between (1) security-expected returns and (2) attributes of securities. A general representation of such an *equilibrium theory* is the following:

$$E_i = f(A_{i1}, A_{i2}, \ldots).$$

Here, E_i is the *expected* return on the security over the next period, while A_{i1}, A_{i2}, etc., are *attributes* of the security.

An equilibrium theory makes a statement about *expected* returns *across* securities. Thus it differs significantly from a factor model.

To see this, consider a simple (in fact, simplistic) *one-factor model*:

$$\tilde{R}_i = a_i + b_{i1} \tilde{F}_1 + \tilde{e}_i.$$

Now imagine that one security (i) has a sensitivity to the factor of 1.0 and that another (j) has a sensitivity of 2.0. Moreover, assume that the *expected* value of the factor is 12.

It might appear that the expected return on security j would be larger than that on security i since it is twice as sensitive to a factor with a positive expected value. But this is not necessarily so. What if the value of a_i were 16 and the value of a_j were 4? The expected returns would be:

$$i: 16 + 1 \times 12 = 28$$
$$j: 4 + 2 \times 12 = 28$$

If the non-factor-related expected return (a_i) can differ across securities, anything is possible. A factor model, per se, is not an equilibrium theory of security-expected returns.

Two major types of equilibrium theories have been advocated in the finance literature: *Capital Asset Pricing Theories* and the *Arbitrage Pricing Theory*.

CAPITAL ASSET PRICING THEORIES

The original Capital Asset Pricing Model was introduced by Sharpe [1964], Lintner [1965], and Mossin [1966]. Extensions were developed by Lintner [1969], Brennan [1970], Black [1972], Merton [1973], Kraus and Litzenberger [1976], Breeden [1979], and others.

All such theories make assumptions about *investor preferences*. They do not *require* a factor model. All are *consistent* with a world in which returns are generated by a one-factor model, a two-factor model, or an M-factor model; they are also consistent with a world in which there are as many factors as there are securities.

The original Capital Asset Pricing Model assumes that investors care only about portfolio *risk* and *expected return.* From these and other assumptions comes the conclusion that expected return will be related to one attribute — *beta* relative to the market portfolio:

$$E_i = R_f + (E_m - R_f)\,\beta_i. \qquad (2)$$

Here, E_i is the expected return on a security, R_f is the return on a risk-free security, and E_m is the return on the *market portfolio,* which includes all securities, each in proportion to total value outstanding.

β_i is a measure of the extent to which the return on a security is expected to "move with" the return on the market portfolio. Formally, it is a scaled, relative measure of the covariance between the two returns. The theory does not require that the relationship between the two returns be linear, although this is often assumed in empirical work.

Extended Capital Asset Pricing Models result from more general assumptions about markets and/or investor preferences. The "zero-beta CAPM" assumes that riskless borrowing is impossible; this results in a relationship similar to that of the original CAPM, but with a value greater than the riskless lending rate where R_f formerly appeared.

Other models assume that investors care about more than portfolio risk and return. For example, if the "average" investor likes liquidity, securities with greater liquidity (good news) will have lower expected returns (bad news), other things equal. More precisely:

$$E_i = a + b\,\beta_i - c\,L_i.$$

Here, L_i is the liquidity of security i. The three *parameters,* a,b, and c, have positive values. They do not carry subscripts since they are market-wide, not security-specific, values.

In this case, expected returns are related to two security attributes, beta and liquidity. Note that the relevant attributes are derived from assumptions about investor *preferences* (formally, the attributes that enter their utility functions). Note also that statements are made about the magnitudes involved. For example, higher liquidity leads to lower expected return for a given beta value, and a higher beta value leads to higher expected return for a given liquidity.

Preference-based equilibrium theories provide substantial guidance concerning relationships between expected return and security attributes. If this guidance is correct, well and good, but if not, not so good.

THE ARBITRAGE PRICING THEORY

The Arbitrage Pricing Theory (APT) of Ross [1976] is an equilibrium theory of security-expected returns. However, it takes an approach that is different from the Capital Asset Pricing Models. Few assumptions are made about investor preferences, but returns are assumed to be generated by a factor model. Thus the APT *requires* a factor model.

If returns are generated by an M-factor model of the sort described earlier, the APT — using a few more assumptions — concludes that:

$$E_i = \lambda_O + b_{i1}\lambda_1 + b_{i2}\lambda_2 + \ldots + b_{iM}\lambda_M. \qquad (3)$$

Here, λ_i is the *expected return per unit of sensitivity to factor 1,* λ_2 is the expected return per unit of sensitivity to factor 2, etc.

This result is not derived directly from the factor model. The no-arbitrage (equilibrium) assumption is reflected most directly in the first term on the right of the equal sign. It is the same for all securities (λ_O), not potentially different for each one (a_i in Equation 1). In the formal model it is approximately equal to the riskless rate of interest.

The APT makes statements neither about the magnitudes nor even about the signs of the λ's, except λ_O. The values can be positive, negative, or zero. Identification of the factor model and of the values of these "factor-related expected returns" is an empirical and/or judgmental task.

The APT makes relatively few assumptions, and, not surprisingly, it provides relatively little guidance concerning relationships between expected returns and security attributes. On the other hand, it can be consistent with a broad range of possibilities and is thus unlikely to be proven incorrect.

A SYNTHESIS

Since the Arbitrage Pricing Theory and Capital Asset Pricing Models are not inconsistent, it is natural to consider a world in which (1) returns are generated by a factor model, (2) the remaining assumptions of the APT hold, and (3) the assumptions of a CAPM hold. What conclusions can we reach by making assumptions about *both* the return-generating process *and* investor preferences?

The relationship between the beta of a security and its sensitivities to the factors is crucial. To an adequate approximation:

$$\beta_i = b_{i1}\,\beta_{F1} + b_{i2}\,\beta_{F2} + \ldots + b_{iM}\,\beta_{FM}. \qquad (4)$$

The new terms represent the beta values of the *factors* to changes in the return on the market portfolio. Thus β_{F1} is the change in factor 1 associated with a change in the market, β_{F2} is the change in factor 2 associated with a change in the market, and so on.

If the assumptions of the original Capital Asset

Pricing Model hold, expected returns must conform to the familiar to Equation (2). If returns are generated by an M-factor model, beta values must conform to Equation (4). Combining these two results in a manner similar to that used in Sharpe [1977] leads to:

$$E_i = R_f + (E_m - R_f)\,[\,b_{i1}\beta_{F1} + b_{i2}\,\beta_{F2} + \ldots + b_{iM}\beta_{FM}\,],$$

or:

$$E_i = R_f + b_{i1}\,[\,(E_m - R_f)\,\beta_{F1}\,] + b_{i2}\,[\,(E_m - R_f)\,\beta_{F2}\,] + \ldots + b_{iM}\,[\,(E_m - R_f)\,\beta_{FM}\,]. \quad (5)$$

If the conditions required for the Arbitrage Pricing Theory hold, its results (Equation 3) must also apply. Comparing Equations 3 and 5 leads to the conclusion that:

$$\lambda_O = R_f$$

$$\lambda_1 = (E_m - R_f)\,\beta_{F1}$$

$$\lambda_2 = (E_m - R_f)\,\beta_{F2}$$

$$\vdots$$

$$\lambda_M = (E_m - R_f)\,\beta_{FM}.$$

By making assumptions about investor preferences, we can say something about the factor-expected return premiums. For example, factors that move more with the market will provide higher expected return premiums; factors that move against (provide hedges for) the market will be associated with negative expected return premiums, etc.

Extended Capital Asset Pricing Models would add further terms, for instance, $-cL_i$, as in the earlier example. By including additional sources of investor utility, we can extend the Capital Asset Pricing Model *and* the Arbitrage Pricing Theory.

Combined theories provide more guidance than the APT can provide alone. The resulting predictions may be wrong — but they will be specific.

TESTABILITY

Roll [1977] has emphasized that definitive tests of Capital Asset Pricing Models can never be performed. As a practical matter, the definition of the market portfolio becomes somewhat fuzzy. Should owner-occupied real estate be included? What about foreign assets? Returns on a truly broadly based market portfolio, however defined, are not likely to be measured with any precision.

The situation is even worse for the Arbitrage Pricing Theory, because it specifies neither the number of important factors nor their definitions.

So, although Capital Asset Pricing Models are clear about the major item to be measured, it is unmeasurable. On the other hand, the Arbitrage Pricing Theory deals with items that might be easily measured but neglects to tell us what they are.

What to do?

It is comforting to consider the plight of the microeconomist. Since Alfred Marshall [1890], economists have approached the world secure in the belief that demand curves are downward-sloping. They continue to do so, even though one can never definitively establish that the theorem holds for a specific good, let alone identify the precise location of the relevant curve on a piece of graph paper.

The financial economist and the investment professional find themselves in a similar situation. It is undoubtedly true that relatively few key factors account for the most important aspects of portfolio risk and return. It is also undoubtedly true that most investors like high expected returns and dislike risk.It is undoubtedly true that the average investor prefers liquid assets to illiquid ones.

While the relative importance of various factors changes over time, as do the preferences of investors, we need not completely abandon a valuable framework within which we can approach investment decisions methodically. We have developed a useful set of tools and should certainly continue to develop them. Meanwhile, we can use the tools we have, as long as we use them intelligently, cautiously, and humbly.

REFERENCES

Arnott, Robert D. "Cluster Analysis and Stock Price Movement." *Financial Analysts Journal,* November-December 1980.

Black, Fischer. "Capital Market Equilibrium with Restricted Borrowing." *Journal of Business,* July 1972.

Breeden, Douglas T. "An Intertemporal Asset Pricing Model with Stochastic Consumption and Investment Opportunities." *Journal of Financial Economics,* September 1979.

Brennan, Michael J. "Taxes, Market Valuation and Corporate Financial Policy." *National Tax Journal,* December 1970.

Chen, Nai-fi; Richard Roll; and Stephen A. Ross. "Economic Forces and the Stock Market: Testing the APT and Alternative Asset Pricing Theories." Working Paper no. 20-83, Graduate School of Management, UCLA, December 1983.

Cohen, K. J., and J. A. Pogue. "An Empirical Evaluation of Alternative Portfolio-Selection Models." *Journal of Business,* April 1967.

Elton, E. J., and M. J. Gruber. "Estimating the Dependence Structure of Share Prices — Implications for Portfolio Selection." *Journal of Finance,* December 1973.

Estep, Tony; Nick Hanson; and Cal Johnson. "Sources of value and risk in common stocks." *The Journal of Portfolio Management,* Summer 1983.

Farrell, James. "Analyzing Covariation of Returns to Determine Homogeneous Stock Groupings." *Journal of Business,* April 1974.

Feeney, G. J., and D. D. Hester. *"Stock Market Indices: A Principal Components Analysis,"* in D. D. Hester and J. Tobin, eds., *Risk Aversion and Portfolio Choice.* New York: John Wiley & Sons, 1967.

Fama, Eugene, and James MacBeth. "Risk, Return and Equilibrium: Empirical Tests." *Journal of Political Economy,* May-June 1973.

King, Benjamin F., "Market and Industry Factors in Stock Price Behavior." *Journal of Business,* January 1966.

Kraus, Alan, and Robert Litzenberger. "Skewness Preference and the Valuation of Risky Assets." *Journal of Finance,* September 1976.

Lintner, John. "The Valuation of Risk Assets and the Selection of Risky Investments in Stock Portfolios and Capital Budgets." *Review of Economics and Statistics,* February 1965.

——. "The Aggregation of Investors' Diverse Judgements and Preferences in Purely Competitive Markets." *Journal of Financial and Quantitative Analysis,* November 1969.

Markowitz, Harry M. *Portfolio Selection: Efficient Diversification of Investments.* New York: John Wiley & Sons, 1959.

Marshall, Alfred. *Principles of Economics.* New York: Macmillan, 1890.

Merton, Robert C. "An Intertemporal Capital Asset Pricing Model." *Econometrica* 41, 1973.

Mossin, Jan. "Equilibrium in a Capital Asset Market." *Econometrica,* October 1966.

Roll, Richard. "A Critique of the Asset Pricing Theory's Tests — Part 1: On Past and Potential Testability of the Theory." *Journal of Financial Economics,* March 1977.

Roll, Richard, and Stephen A. Ross. "An Empirical Investigation of the Arbitrage Pricing Theory." *Journal of Finance,* December 1980.

Ross, Stephen A. "The Arbitrage Pricing Theory of Capital Asset Pricing." *Journal of Economic Theory,* December 1976.

Rosenberg, Barr, and Vinay Marathe. "The Prediction of Investment Risk: Systematic and Residual Risk." *Proceedings of the Seminar on the Analysis of Security Prices,* University of Chicago, November 1975.

Sharpe, William F. "A Simplified Model for Portfolio Analysis." *Management Science,* January 1963.

——. "Capital Asset Prices — A Theory of Market Equilbrium Under Conditions of Risk." *The Journal of Finance,* September 1964.

——. *Portfolio Theory and Capital Markets.* New York: McGraw Hill, 1970.

——. "The Capital Asset Pricing Model: A 'Multi-Beta' Interpretation," in Haim Levy and Marshall Sarant, eds. *Financial Decision Making Under Uncertainty.* New York: Academic Press, 1977.

——. "Some factors in New York Stock Exchange security returns, 1931-1979." *The Journal of Portfolio Management,* Summer 1982.

FRILLS
W.F. Sharpe
November 10, 1989

Market Equilibrium with no Short Sales

Assumptions

K investors with equal amounts of wealth
N assets
Mean-Variance Objective functions
No short positions

Individual Objective Functions (for k=1,K)

$$U_k = E_k - \frac{V_k}{t_k}$$

Expected return and Variance (for k=1,K)

$$E_k = \sum_i X_{ik} E_i$$

$$V_k = \sum_i \sum_j X_{ik} X_{jk} C_{ij}$$

Full Investment Constraints (for k=1,K)

$$\sum_i X_{ik} = 1$$

Market Clearing Constraints (for i=1,N)

$$\sum_k \frac{1}{K} X_{ik} = X_{im}$$

Problem

Given C_{ij}'s, t_k's, determine E_i's that will clear the markets.

Maximand

$$\sum_k U_k$$

Lagrangean

$$Z = \sum_k (E_k - \frac{V_k}{t_k}) + \sum_k \lambda_{fk}\left(1 - \sum_i X_{ik}\right) + \sum_i \lambda_{ci}\left(X_{im} - \frac{1}{K}\sum_k X_{ik}\right)$$

First order conditions (i=1,N; k=1,K)

$$\frac{\partial Z}{\partial X_{ik}} = E_i - \frac{2}{t_k}\sum_j X_{jk}C_{ij} - \lambda_{fk} - \frac{1}{K}\lambda_{ci}$$

Solution

if $X_{ik} > 0$:

$$\frac{\partial Z}{\partial X_{ik}} = 0$$

if $X_{ik} = 0$:

$$\frac{\partial Z}{\partial X_{ik}} < 0$$

Alteration (i=1,N)

$$E_i^* \Leftarrow E_i - \frac{1}{K}\lambda_{ci}$$

$$\lambda_{ci}^* \Leftarrow 0$$

Effects

First order conditions met without changing X_{ik} values

Market clearing constraints ineffective

E_i^* values clear markets

Variation

Distribution of relative risk tolerances known

Market Risk Premium known

Must alter absolute t_k values so that E_i^* values
are consistent with the given market risk premium

From the Board

The Arithmetic of Active Management

by William F. Sharpe, Timken Professor Emeritus of Finance, Stanford University, and Chairman, William F. Sharpe Associates

"Today's fad is index funds that track the Standard & Poor's 500. True, the average soundly beat most stock funds over the past decade. But is this an eternal truth or a transitory one?"

"In small stocks, especially, you're probably better off with an active manager than buying the market."

"The case for passive management rests only on complex and unrealistic theories of equilibrium in capital markets."

"Any graduate of the ____ Business School should be able to beat an index fund over the course of a market cycle."

Statements such as these are made with alarming frequency by investment professionals.[1] In some cases, subtle and sophisticated reasoning may be involved. More often (alas), the conclusions can only be justified by assuming that the laws of arithmetic have been suspended for the convenience of those who choose to pursue careers as active managers.

If "active" and "passive" management styles are defined in sensible ways, it *must* be the case that

(1) before costs, the return on the average actively managed dollar will equal the return on the average passively managed dollar and
(2) after costs, the return on the average actively managed dollar will be less than the return on the average passively managed dollar.

These assertions will hold for *any* time period. Moreover, they depend *only* on the laws of addition, subtraction, multiplication and division. Nothing else is required.

Of course, certain definitions of the key terms are necessary. First a *market* must be selected—the stocks in the S&P 500, for example, or a set of "small" stocks. Then each investor who holds securities from the market must be classified as either *active* or *passive*.

- A *passive investor* always holds every security from the market, with each represented in the same manner as in the market. Thus if security X represents 3 per cent of the value of the securities in the market, a passive investor's portfolio will have 3 per cent of its value invested in X. Equivalently, a passive manager will hold the same percentage of the total outstanding amount of each security in the market.[2]
- An *active investor* is one who is not passive. His or her portfolio will differ from that of the passive managers at some or all times. Because active managers usually act on perceptions of mispricing, and because such perceptions change relatively frequently, such managers tend to trade fairly frequently—hence the term "active."

Over any specified time period, the *market return* will be a weighted average of the returns on the securities within the market, using beginning market values as weights.[3] Each passive manager will obtain precisely the market return, before costs.[4] From this, it follows (as the night from the day) that the return on the average actively managed dollar *must* equal the market return. Why? Because the market return must equal a weighted average of the returns on the passive and active segments of the market. If the first two returns are the same, the third must be also.

This proves assertion number 1. Note that only simple principles of arithmetic were used in the process. To be sure, we have seriously belabored the obvious, but the ubiquity of statements such as those quoted earlier suggests that such labor is not in vain.

To prove assertion number 2, we need only rely on the fact that the costs of actively managing a given number of dollars will exceed those of passive management. Active managers must pay for more research and must pay more for trading. Security analysts (e.g., the graduates of prestigious business schools) must eat, and so must brokers, traders, specialists and other market-makers.

Because active and passive returns are equal before cost, and because active managers bear greater costs, it follows that the after-cost return from active management *must* be lower than that from passive management.

This proves assertion number 2. Once again, the proof is embarrassingly simple and uses only the most rudimentary notions of simple arithmetic.

Enough (lower) mathematics. Let's turn to the practical issues.

Why do sensible investment professionals continue to make statements that seemingly fly in the face of the simple and obvious relations we have described? How can presented evidence show active managers beating "the market" or "the index" or "passive managers"? Three reasons stand out.[5]

1. Footnotes appear at end of article.

- First, the passive managers in question may not be truly passive (i.e., conform to our definition of the term). Some index fund managers "sample" the market of choice, rather than hold all the securities in market proportions. Some may even charge high enough fees to bring their total costs to equal or exceed those of active managers.
- Second, active managers may not fully represent the "non-passive" component of the market in question. For example, the set of active managers may exclude some active holders of securities within the market (e.g., individual investors). Many empirical analyses consider only "professional" or "institutional" active managers. It is, of course, possible for the average professionally or institutionally actively managed dollar to outperform the average passively managed dollar, after costs. For this to take place, however, the non-institutional, individual investors must be foolish enough to pay the added costs of the institutions' active management via inferior performance. Another example arises when the active managers hold securities from outside the market in question. For example, returns on equity mutual funds with cash holdings are often compared with returns on an all-equity index or index fund. In such comparisons, the funds are generally beaten badly by the index in up markets, but sometimes exceed index performance in down markets. Yet another example arises when the set of active mangers excludes those who have gone out of business during the period in question. Because such managers are likely to have experienced especially poor returns, the resulting "survivorship bias" will tend to produce results that are better than those obtained by the average actively managed dollar.
- Third, and possibly most important in practice, the summary statistics for active managers may not truly represent the performance of the average actively managed *dollar*. To compute the latter, each manager's return should be weighted by the dollars he or she has under management at the beginning of the period. Some comparisons use a simple average of the performance of all managers (large and small); others use the performance of the median active manager. While the results of this kind of comparison are, in principle, unpredictable, certain empirical regularities persist. Perhaps most important, equity fund managers with smaller amounts of money tend to favor stocks with smaller outstanding values. Thus, *de facto*, an equally weighted average of active manager returns has a bias toward smaller-capitalization stocks vis-a-vis the market as a whole. As a result, the "average active manager" tends to be beaten badly in periods when small-capitalization stocks underperform large-capitalization stocks, but may exceed the market's performance in periods when small-capitalization stocks do well. In both cases, of course, the average actively managed *dollar* will underperform the market, net of costs.

To repeat: Properly measured, the average actively managed dollar must underperform the average passively managed dollar, net of costs. Empirical analyses that appear to refute this principle are guilty of improper measurement.

This need not be taken as a counsel of despair. It is perfectly possible for *some* active managers to beat their passive brethren, even after costs. Such managers must, of course, manage a minority share of the actively managed dollars within the market in question. It is also possible for an investor (such as a pension fund) to choose a set of active managers that, collectively, provides a total return better than that of a passive alternative, even after costs. Not all the managers in the set have to beat their passive counterparts, only those managing a majority of the investor's actively managed funds.

An important corollary is the importance of appropriate *performance measurement*. "Peer group" comparisons are dangerous. Because the capitalization-weighted average performance of active managers will be inferior to that of a passive alternative, the former constitutes a poor measure for decision-making purposes. And because most peer-group averages are not capitalization-weighted, they are subject to additional biases. Moreover, investing equal amounts with many managers is not a practical alternative. Nor, *a fortiori*, is investing with the "median" manager (whose identity is not even known in advance).

The best way to measure a manager's performance is to compare his or her return with that of a *comparable passive alternative*. The latter—often termed a "benchmark" or "normal portfolio"—should be a *feasible* alternative identified *in advance* of the period over which performance is measured. Only when this type of measurement is in place can an active manager (or one who hires active managers) know whether he or she is in the minority of those who have beaten viable passive alternatives.

Footnotes

1. The first two quotations can be found in the September 3, 1990 issue of *Forbes*.
2. When computing such amounts, "cross-holdings" within the market should be netted out.
3. Events such as mergers, new listings and reinvestment of dividends that take place during the period require more complex calculations but do not affect the basic principles stated here. To keep things simple, we ignore them.
4. We assume here that passive managers purchase their securities before the beginning of the period

in question and do not sell them until after the period ends. When passive managers do buy or sell, they may have to trade with active managers; at such times, the active managers may gain from the passive managers, because of the active managers' willingness to provide desired liquidity (at a price).

5. There are others, such as differential treatment of dividend reinvestment, mergers and acquisitions, but they are typically of less importance.

THE JOURNAL OF FINANCE • VOL. XLVI, NO. 2 • JUNE 1991

Capital Asset Prices with and without Negative Holdings

WILLIAM F. SHARPE*

Introduction

FOLLOWING TRADITION, I DEAL here with the Capital Asset Pricing Model, a subject with which I have been associated for over 25 years, and which the Royal Swedish Academy of Sciences has cited in honoring me with the award of the Prize in Economic Sciences in Memory of Alfred Nobel.

I first present the Capital Asset Pricing Model (hence, CAPM), incorporating not only my own contributions[1] but also the outstanding work of Lintner (1965, 1969) and the contributions of Mossin (1966) and others. My goal is to do so succinctly yet in a manner designed to emphasize the economic content of the theory.

Following this, I modify the model to reflect an extreme case of an institutional arrangement that can preclude investors from choosing fully optimal portfolios. In particular, I assume that investors are unable to take negative positions in assets. For this version of the model I draw heavily from papers by Glenn (1976), Levy (1978), Merton (1987), and Markowitz (1987, 1990).

Finally, I discuss the stock index futures contract—a major financial innovation of worldwide importance that postdates the development of the CAPM. Such contracts can increase the efficiency of capital markets in many ways. In particular, they can bring actual markets closer to the idealized world assumed by the Capital Asset Pricing Model.

The Capital Asset Pricing Model

The initial version of the CAPM, developed over 25 years ago, was extremely parsimonious. It dealt with the central aspects of equilibrium in capital markets and assumed away many important aspects of such markets as they

*Timken Professor Emeritus of Finance, Stanford University Graduate School of Business and Chairman, William F. Sharpe Associates. I am particularly grateful for the detailed comments and suggestions on the contents of this lecture provided by Robert Litzenberger and Andre' Perold. Subsequent comments and suggestions by Haim Levy and Harry Markowitz are also gratefully acknowledged. My longer-term debt to colleagues in many places is also substantial; I particularly wish to thank those at Stanford University and at William F. Sharpe Associates for their contributions to my work over the years.

[1]Beginning with Sharpe (1961) and Sharpe (1964).

existed at the time. In the last 25 years, theorists have extended and adapted the approach to incorporate some of these real-world phenomena. Important examples are Lintner's (1969) version, which focuses on returns in real terms; Brennan's (1970) version, which deals with the effects of taxation; Black's (1972) version in which there is no riskless asset; Merton's (1973) version, which incorporates investors' concern with future investment opportunities; Rubinstein's (1974) version, which deals with a more general class of utility functions; Kraus and Litzenberger's (1976) version, which takes into account the third moment of the return distribution; Levy's (1978) version, which incorporates transactions costs; Breeden's (1979) version, which focuses on investors' preferences for consumption; Merton's (1987) version, which deals with market segmentation; and Markowitz' (1990) version, which considers restrictions on short sales.

Throughout, empiricists have subjected variations of the model to tests of increasing power. Moreover, alternative models have been proposed, most notably Ross' (1976) Arbitrage Pricing Theory.

While theorists have been busy adapting the CAPM to incorporate real-world impediments to efficiency, practitioners have been equally busy reducing some of those impediments. Many of the financial instruments and institutions developed in the last decade serve to better "complete the markets"—in particular, to allow a more efficient distribution of risk among investors.

I will not attempt a general treatment of the institutional costs and constraints that can affect the efficiency with which risk is allocated, nor of the many recent financial innovations that serve to reduce such costs and constraints. Instead, I will focus on one prototypical example—restrictions on negative positions in securities, and one such innovation—stock index futures.

To facilitate the exposition, many formulas and proofs will be relegated to footnotes. In this I follow a long personal tradition, since a key proof in Sharpe (1964)—my first published paper on the Capital Asset Pricing Model—was contained in a footnote.[2]

The CAPM and Financial Economic Theory

A common taxonomy of work in financial economics differentiates between *normative* (prescriptive) and *positive* (descriptive) theories. Markowitz' (1952) path-breaking mean-variance portfolio theory falls cleanly into the former category, dealing as it does with rules for optimal portfolio choice by an individual. The CAPM can be neatly classified as belonging to the latter, since it is concerned with the determination of the prices of capital assets in a competitive market. But two such categories are not sufficient. Much of the work in the field can best be described as approaching *normative issues in a positive context.* The seminal Modigliani-Miller (1958) model is of this genre,

[2] More specifically, footnote 22.

since it prescribes optimal behavior of a corporation faced with a capital market in which security prices are determined by the actions of individual investors cognizant of opportunities for substitution.

Even this three-way taxonomy fails to capture the interrelationships among the alternative approaches. Most positive models in financial economics, like those in the broader field of economics, are built on normative foundations. Individuals engaging in maximizing behavior are assumed to interact with one another until an equilibrium condition is reached. This is clearly the case with the CAPM, which explicitly assumes that investors follow the prescriptions of Markowitz' portfolio theory. Moreover, as in traditional micro-economic theory, financial economic theories of equilibrium relationships are taken as prescriptions for decision in markets that may not strictly conform to the conditions of the theory.

The domain of positive financial economics theory is sometimes divided into a set of models that may be termed *utility-based* and a complementary set that may be termed *arbitrage-based*. Models that fall in the latter category derive implications from the assumption that capital asset prices will adjust until it is impossible to find a strategy that requires no initial investment, provides a positive cash flow in at least one state of nature, and requires no negative cash flow in any future state of nature.[3] Models that fall in the former category typically conform to the conditions required for the latter, but derive stronger implications due to added assumptions about the *utility functions* that investors are assumed to maximize.[4]

Much of the early work in financial economics dealt with markets in which the interaction of a large number of individuals, each equally informed, determined prices. In this sense the work followed the tradition of competitive equilibrium theory in economics. More recently, attention has focused on markets in which there are few participants and/or in which different individuals have different sets of information.

The CAPM is, of course, a theory in the earlier tradition of the field. It is a positive theory, incorporates assumptions about investors' utility functions, and assumes a market with a large number of participants, each of whom has access to the same set of information.

[3]Prominent arbitrage-based theories in financial economics are the Black-Scholes (1973) model, which deals with the prices of options vis-a-vis related securities, and Ross' (1976) Arbitrage Pricing Theory, which draws implications about the prices of capital assets when returns are generated by a specified factor model. While the monumental Arrow (1953) Debreu (1959) state-preference approach to uncertainty makes some assumptions about individuals' utility functions, many of its key results are arbitrage-based. A number of theories in financial economics have been constructed using the Arrow-Debreu "state of the world" paradigm, among them the binomial model of option pricing first presented in my textbook (1978) and then extended by Cox, Ross, and Rubinstein (1979) and many others.

[4]It is, or course, true that arbitrage-based models make some assumptions about investor preferences—for example, that investors prefer larger payoffs to smaller payoffs in any given state of the world. However, such assumptions are minimal, compared with the more detailed assumptions of utility-based models.

Capital Asset Prices with Negative Holdings

Assumptions

Assume that the economy consists of K investors. Investor k's invested wealth, expressed as a proportion of the total wealth invested by all investors is W_k. He or she wishes to maximize:

$$U_k = E_k - \frac{V_k}{\tau_k}. \tag{1}$$

For expository convenience, I will term U_k investor k's *utility*. It may be regarded as a primitive utility function. Alternatively, it may be considered an approximation to the investor's *expected utility* in the sense of Von Neumann and Morgenstern (1944). If the investor is assumed to have a negative exponential utility function over wealth and returns are jointly normally distributed, the approximation will be exact. Even if the investor has some other utility function and/or returns are not jointly normally distributed, U_k may provide an excellent approximation, as shown by Levy and Markowitz (1979).

In equation (1), E_k is the expected return on investors k's portfolio, V_k is the variance of the portfolio, and τ_k is his or her risk tolerance. Investors differ in risk tolerance.

This relationship can be interpreted in a number of useful ways. Clearly, risk tolerance measures an investor's *marginal rate of substitution of variance for expected return*. For convenience we assume that each investor's risk tolerance is constant over the feasible range of expected return and variance.[5]

The value obtained by dividing portfolio variance by an investor's risk tolerance can be characterized as a *risk penalty*, leading to the interpretation of U_k as a *risk-adjusted expected return*. Alternatively, U_k may be considered a *certainty-equivalent* return, since a portfolio with a return of U_k and zero risk would have the same utility for the investor as the portfolio in question.

This is the objective function of Markowitz' (1952) "mean-variance" approach to portfolio selection. It is a highly parsimonious characterization of investors' goals, employing a myopic view (i.e., "one period at a time") and focusing on only two aspects of the probability distribution of possible returns over that period.[6] Moreover, it assumes that the investor[7] can assess at least the first two moments of the probability distributions associated with alternative investment portfolios. The genius of the approach is its ability to

[5]This is not required. The results that follow can be obtained under more general conditions, with the resultants values of τ_k interpreted as investors' marginal rates of substitution, given their optimal holdings.

[6]Note, however, that this assumption will be less onerous, the shorter the time period under consideration. In continuous-time versions of the model, the time period is (in effect) infinitesimal in length. Under such conditions, two moments may serve as adequate representations even if the probability distribution of returns over a finite period and/or investors' preferences for returns over such a period are quite complex.

[7]aided, perhaps by an advisor

capture much of what matters to investors. Moreover, it serves well as a base for extensions and adaptations designed to accommodate additional aspects of investor's preferences.

As in Markowitz' work, the expected return on a portfolio depends on the expected returns on its component securities.[8] A portfolio's risk depends on both the risks of the component securities and on their correlations with one another. More succinctly: portfolio risk depends on the covariances among securities.[9]

All investors are in agreement concerning expected returns and covariances. Of course, these moments of the joint distribution of security returns will be a function of security prices. When equilibrium prices are attained, however, each investor will choose an optimal portfolio, given the current values of expected returns and covariances; moreover the resultant portfolio choices will cause the markets to clear.

Investors are allowed to take negative positions in one or more assets. Thus holdings may be positive, zero or negative. There are no transactions costs or other constraints and asset positions are fully divisible.

Portfolio Optimality

Investor k seeks to maximize U_k subject to a *full investment constraint* of the form:

$$\Sigma_i X_{ik} = 1.$$

where X_{ik} represents the proportion of investor k's portfolio invested in asset i.

To do so, he or she must select a portfolio in which the *marginal utility* of every security is the same. If this were not the case, it would be possible to reallocate funds from a security with a lower marginal utility to one with a higher one, thereby increasing utility without violating the full investment constraint.

The *first order condition* for portfolio optimality can be represented as follows:

$$E_i - \frac{2}{\tau_k} C_{ik} = \lambda_{fk} \qquad \text{for all } i. \tag{2}$$

[8]The expected return of investor k's portfolio is given by:

$$E_k = \Sigma_i X_{ik} E_i$$

where X_{ik} represents the proportion of investor k's portfolio invested in asset i.

[9]The variance of investor k's portfolio is given by:

$$V_k = \Sigma_i \Sigma_j X_{ik} X_{jk} C_{ij}$$

where C_{ij} represents the covariance between the returns on assets i and j.

Here C_{ik} is the covariance of security i with investor k's optimal portfolio and λ_{fk} is investor k's *marginal utility of wealth*.[10]

Aggregation

Assume that markets have cleared, so that all securities are held by the K investors in the economy. Relationships among key variables can be examined by aggregating the conditions that must hold when each investor obtains an optimal solution, taking into account the relative amounts of wealth that each has invested. To do so requires only a few straightforward operations. In effect, a wealth-weighted average is taken of the first-order conditions for each security. Not surprisingly, the result is similar to that obtained earlier.

$$E_i - \frac{2}{\tau_m} C_{im} = \lambda_{fm} \qquad \text{for all } i. \tag{3}$$

Here τ_m is the wealth-weighted risk tolerance of the investors in the market, or the *societal risk tolerance*. The value of C_{im} represents the covariance of security i with the *market portfolio*, which includes all securities in the market, with each represented in proportion to its outstanding value. The last term is a weighted average of the values of λ_{fk} for the K

[10]Incorporating U_k and the full investment constraint in a Lagrangean function to be maximized gives:

$$Z_k = U_k + \lambda_{fk}(1 - \Sigma_i X_{ik}).$$

Clearly λ_{fk} is the *marginal utility of wealth* for investor k, since it equals the partial derivative of Z_k with respect to the investors' wealth (in this metric, the value 1 in the parenthesized full investment constraint, since the X_{ik} values are expressed as proportions of the investor's total wealth).

Recall that:

$$E_k = \Sigma_{ik} X_{ik} E_i, \quad \text{and}$$
$$V_k = \Sigma_i \Sigma_j X_{ik} X_{jk} C_{ij}.$$

Hence, taking the partial derivative of Z_k with respect to investor k's holding of security i gives:

$$\frac{\partial Z_k}{\partial X_{ik}} = E_i - \frac{2}{\tau_k} \Sigma_j X_{jk} C_{ij} - \lambda_{fk}.$$

But note that the covariance of security i with any portfolio p will equal a weighted average of the covariances of the security with the securities in the portfolio, using relative portfolio holdings as weights. Here:

$$C_{ik} = \Sigma_j X_{jk} C_{ij}.$$

Substituting this relationship in the prior equation and rearranging terms gives equation (2).

investors, with the weights depending on the investors' influences in the marketplace, where influence depends on both invested wealth and risk tolerance. It can be interpreted as the *societal marginal utility of wealth.*[11]

Expected Returns

One of the key implications of the CAPM concerns the relationships among the expected returns of capital assets. It can be obtained by a minor rearrangement of the previous equation to give:

$$E_i = \lambda_{fm} + \frac{2}{\tau_m} C_{im} \qquad \text{for all } i. \tag{4}$$

This shows that in equilibrium there is a linear relationship between the expected returns on securities and their covariances with the market portfolio. Usually the relationship is expressed in terms of a security's *beta*, a scaled measure obtained by dividing a security's covariance with the market portfolio by the variance of the market portfolio (V_m). Substituting this measure gives:

$$E_i = \lambda_{fm} + \frac{2V_m}{\tau_m} \beta_{im} \qquad \text{for all } i, \text{ where } \beta_{im} \equiv \frac{C_{im}}{V_m}. \tag{5}$$

[11]To derive equation (3) begin by multiplying all terms in equation (2) by τ_k and rearranging slightly, giving:

$$\tau_k E_i - 2C_{ik} = \tau_k \lambda_{fk}.$$

Next, multiply all terms by W_k, then sum over all investors, giving:

$$\Sigma_k W_k \tau_k E_i - 2\Sigma_k W_k C_{ik} = \Sigma_k W_k \tau_k \lambda_{fk}.$$

Define τ_m as:

$$\tau_m \equiv \Sigma_k W_k \tau_k.$$

Now consider the second term. Note that:

$$C_{ik} = \mathrm{Cov}(\tilde{R}_i, \tilde{R}_k)$$

where $\tilde{R}_i$ and $\tilde{R}_k$ are, respectively, the returns on security i and investor k's portfolio. By the properties of covariance:

$$\Sigma_k W_k C_{ik} = \mathrm{Cov}(\tilde{R}_i, \Sigma_k W_k \tilde{R}_k).$$

But the summation on the right-hand side is simply a wealth-weighted average of the returns on the investors' portfolios or, more simply put, the return on the *market portfolio.* Hence the summation on the left-hand side is the covariance of the return on security i with that of the market portfolio, which can be denoted C_{im}.

Making these substitutions and dividing all terms by τ_m gives:

$$E_i - \frac{2}{\tau_m} C_{im} = \frac{\Sigma_k W_k \tau_k \lambda_{fk}}{\tau_m}.$$

The last term is a weighted average of the values of λ_{fk} for the K investors, with the weights given by the product of W_k and τ_k. Denoting this λ_{fm} gives equation (3).

Of course, equation (5) is also linear. Moreover, since portfolio expected returns and covariances with the market portfolio are simply value-weighted averages of the corresponding measures for the component securities, it follows that this relationship holds for all portfolios as well as for all securities.

The Risk Premium

Since the previous equation holds for any portfolio, it will hold for the market portfolio itself. Moreover, the beta value of the market portfolio with itself must equal 1. Letting E_m represent the expected return on the market portfolio, these relationships imply that:

$$\frac{E_m - \lambda_{fm}}{V_m} = \frac{2}{\tau_m}. \tag{6}$$

The term on the left-hand side is the *risk premium per unit of variance*. As the equation shows, it is inversely related to societal risk tolerance.

The Security Market Line

Substituting the risk premium per unit of variance for $2/\tau_m$ in the equation for security expected returns gives a more traditional form of the relationship:

$$E_i = \lambda_{fm} + (E_m - \lambda_{fm})\beta_{im} \qquad \text{for all } i. \tag{7}$$

A graphical portrayal is termed the *security market line*. The CAPM implies that all securities and portfolios will plot along such a line. Many would argue that this relationship is the most important single conclusion derived from the CAPM. It shows that expected returns will be linearly related to *market risk*, but not, as often believed, to *total risk*.

Riskless Borrowing and Lending

As can be seen from equation (7), λ_{fm} may be interpreted as the expected return on any "zero-beta" portfolio, including the zero-beta portfolio with minimum variance, as suggested by Black (1972). If a riskless asset is available, λ_{fm} will equal R_f, the riskless rate of return. Under these conditions, the Security Market Line relationship can be written:

$$E_i = R_f + (E_m - R_f)\beta_{im} \qquad \text{for all } i. \tag{8}$$

Henceforth, we assume that a riskless asset does exist and can be held in positive or negative amounts—i.e., that investors may either lend or borrow at the riskless rate R_f.

The Characteristic Line

The value of β_{im} may be given an interpretation similar to that found in regression analysis utilizing historic data, although in the context of the CAPM it is to be interpreted strictly as an ex ante value based on probabilistic beliefs about future outcomes. The relationship between $\tilde{R}_i$ and $\tilde{R}_m$, the stochastic returns on security i and the market portfolio, respectively, can be written as:

$$\tilde{R}_i = a_i + \beta_{im}\tilde{R}_m + \tilde{\varepsilon}_i. \tag{9}$$

Given the manner in which β_{im} is defined, it must be the case that $\tilde{\varepsilon}_m$ is uncorrelated with[12] $\tilde{R}_m$. Moreover, a_i can be defined so that the expected value of $\tilde{\varepsilon}_i$ is zero. However, there is no reason to expect that $\tilde{\varepsilon}_i$—the *residual return* or *non-market component of return* for security i—will be uncorrelated with the comparable component for security j.[13]

While the CAPM places no restrictions on the correlations of the residual terms, it does restrict the values of the intercept (a_i) terms. Since the expected value of ε_i is zero, the security market line relationship requires that each intercept be related directly to the security's beta value.[14] The CAPM thus implies that:

$$\tilde{R}_i = (1 - \beta_{im})R_f + \beta_{im}\tilde{R}_m + \tilde{\varepsilon}_i. \tag{10}$$

A graphical portrayal of this relationship is termed a security or portfolio's *characteristic line*.

Factor Models of Security Returns

Much confusion has arisen concerning the relationship between the equilibrium results of the CAPM and the underlying relationships among security returns. As can be seen, the CAPM make *no* assumptions about the "return generating process". Hence, its results are completely consistent with *any* such process.

Early approaches to portfolio selection[15], assumed that returns were generated by a model similar (but not identical) to that of equation (9), with the

[12]but not necessarily independent of

[13]In fact, this cannot strictly be the case except in economies with infinitely many securities. Since the market-value weighted sum of the left-hand sides of equation (9) equals $\tilde{R}_m$, the market-weighted sum of the $\tilde{\varepsilon}_i$ values must be zero. Thus at least two of the $\tilde{\varepsilon}_i$ values must be negatively correlated.

[14]Taking expectations of equation (9) gives:

$$E_i = a_i + \beta_{im}E_m.$$

Comparison with (8) implies that:

$$a_i = (1 - \beta_{im})R_f.$$

[15]such as that suggested by Markowitz (1959) that I further developed in Sharpe (1961, 1963, and 1970)

further condition that the residual values were uncorrelated across securities.[16] My initial approach to capital asset pricing in Sharpe (1961) made a similar assumption. Such a "single index" or "single factor" model represents a special case of a *factor model of security returns*. Multi-factor models have been explored by a number of researchers and currently enjoy widespread use in financial practice.

A factor model of security returns identifies a relatively few key factors to which a security's return is assumed to be linearly related, in the following manner:

$$\tilde{R}_i = a_i + \textstyle\sum_l b_{il}\tilde{F}_l + \tilde{\varepsilon}_i. \tag{11}$$

In such a model the $\tilde{\varepsilon}_i$ values are assumed to be uncorrelated across securities. Ross' (1976) Arbitrage Pricing Theory (APT) concludes that if returns are generated by such a model, expected returns must be approximately linearly related to the b_{il} values if opportunities to gain through arbitrage are to be precluded. However, the APT provides no implications concerning either the signs or the magnitudes of the coefficients in the associated pricing relationship.

It is entirely possible to augment the assumptions of the APT with those of the CAPM (most importantly, the assumption that investors maximize mean-variance utility functions). The resulting implications will then be consistent with both theories. Moreover, by making assumptions about investors' objectives one can obtain precise statements about the signs and magnitudes of the coefficients of the APT pricing relationship, as I have shown in Sharpe (1984).

The Efficiency of the Market Portfolio

A key concept due to Markowitz (1952) is that of the *efficiency* of a portfolio. In the present context a portfolio can be said to be *efficient* if it would be optimal for an investor with some (non-negative) risk tolerance. Comparison of equations (2) and (3) directly implies that the market portfolio is efficient in this sense.

Consider an investor who has a risk tolerance equal to τ_m and holds the market portfolio. Equation (3) shows that the first-order conditions for the maximization of his or her utility will be met for every security. Since the market portfolio will be optimal for such an investor, it must be efficient. More specifically, the market portfolio will be optimal for an investor with the average (societal) risk tolerance.

The Two-Fund Separation Theorem

Under the conditions assumed in the CAPM, every investor's optimal portfolio can be obtained by a suitably chosen combination of any two

[16] In such a model the "common factor" can be highly correlated with the return on the market portfolio, but not precisely equal to it if the assumption that the residual values are to be uncorrelated with one another is to be maintained.

arbitrarily selected efficient portfolios.[17] Two natural choices are those that would be optimal for investors with risk tolerances of zero and τ_m. The former is the minimum-variance portfolio. The latter is, of course, the market portfolio. Following Tobin (1969), this is generally termed the two-fund separation theorem.

When a riskless asset is available, the minimum-variance portfolio will be composed solely of that asset. Thus all investors will hold combinations of the riskless asset and the market portfolio. For investors with risk tolerance greater than τ_m, optimal investment will involve a negative position in the riskless asset and a positive position in the market portfolio—and hence all risky assets. Note, however, that the market portfolio will include the net positive supply of riskless assets in the economy; hence only investors with τ_k values considerably greater than τ_m will actually have to borrow money. Every other investor will select some combination of the riskless asset and the market portfolio, and thus require only non-negative holdings.

Key Implications

The key implications of the CAPM are that:

1. the market portfolio will be efficient,
2. all efficient portfolios will be equivalent to investment in the market portfolio plus, possibly, lending or borrowing, and
3. there will be a linear relationship between expected return and beta.

Practical applications of these relationships are many. Investors can easily identify efficient portfolio strategies and such strategies can be effectively implemented through mutual funds and other institutional vehicles. Corpo-

[17]To provide two-fund separation in this case, rewrite equation (2) as follows:

$$\Sigma_j 2C_{ij}X_{jk} + \tau_k \lambda_{fk} = \tau_k E_i.$$

Portfolio optimality requires that this relationship be satisfied for each of the N securities and that the full-investment constraint by met. This gives rise to a set of $N+1$ simultaneous equations that can be written as:

$$\begin{pmatrix} 2C_{11} & \cdots & \cdots & 2C_{1N} & 1 \\ \cdot & & & \cdot & \cdot \\ \cdot & & & \cdot & \cdot \\ 2C_{N1} & \cdots & \cdots & 2C_{NN} & 1 \\ 1 & \cdots & \cdots & 1 & 0 \end{pmatrix} \begin{pmatrix} X_{1k} \\ \cdot \\ \cdot \\ X_{NK} \\ \lambda_{fk}^* \end{pmatrix} = \begin{pmatrix} 0 \\ \cdot \\ \cdot \\ 0 \\ 1 \end{pmatrix} + \begin{pmatrix} E_1 \\ \cdot \\ \cdot \\ E_N \\ 0 \end{pmatrix} \tau_k$$

where λ_{fk}^* represents $\tau_k \lambda_{fk}$. Writing this in matrix notation gives:

$$DY = K + \tau_k F.$$

The solution, obtained by multiplying both sides by the inverse of D is thus:

$$Y = \{D^{-1}K\} + \tau_k \{D^{-1}F\}.$$

Note that the optimal portfolio is a linear function of τ_k. Thus it can be restated as a linear function of any two vectors satisfying the above equation associated with different values of t_k.

rate and governmental decision-makers can use the Security Market Line relationship to determine the desirability of an investment project by comparing its expected return with that available in the capital market for projects with similar beta values (i.e., with similar market risk or sensitivity to economic conditions).

In the frictionless world of the CAPM, each investor chooses a portfolio that maximizes his or her utility. This leads to an efficient distribution of risk in the economy, given, of course, the distribution of wealth among investors.

Negative Holdings

The CAPM assumes that investors can take negative positions in assets. For the riskless asset, the traditional manner in which such a position is achieved involves borrowing money. For a risky asset, the traditional method requires a *short sale*.

A "short position" is achieved by borrowing an asset such as a share of stock, with a promise the repay in kind, typically on demand. The borrowed asset is then sold, generating a cash receipt. If the proceeds of the sale may be used for other types of investment, the overall effect is equivalent to that of a negative holding of the asset in question. If, however, the proceeds are "impounded" to serve as collateral for the borrowed asset, such a short position may differ from a negative holding of the asset in question. In many countries, proceeds from some short sales are impounded in this manner, and the short seller receives little or no interest on the impounded amount.[18] Moreover, some institutional investors are precluded from the use of short positions, either through explicit rules or implicit threat of suit for violation of fiduciary standards. Other restrictions may apply—for example, exchanges may not allow a short sale following a previous decline in the price of the security in question.

Of necessity, arbitrage-based theories allow short positions. Whether such positions will be taken in equilibrium is usually unclear, since the models lack sufficient assumptions (i.e., those concerning utility functions) to characterize equilibrium holdings. More importantly, by the very nature of the arbitrage approach, multiple solutions in terms of holdings are possible in equilibrium due to the presence (or potential presence) of redundant securities.

While the CAPM assumes that investors can take negative positions in any asset, it implies that in equilibrium the only such positions taken will involve the minimum-variance portfolio. When a riskless asset is available, the only negative holdings in equilibrium will involve borrowing by investors with above-average risk tolerance who wish to finance added investment in a portfolio representing the overall capital market.

[18]Often additional collateral must be "posted" as "margin", but the short seller is generally allowed to receive the proceeds associated with the investment of this amount.

With costless monitoring of investors' positions, zero transactions costs, and equal information about securities available to all investors, the only restrictions on negative holdings would be those required to achieve payment of the requisite cash flows. An investor's overall portfolio must be such that in each state of the world the sum of the positive cash flows is at least as large as the sum of the negative cash flows required to match the payments made by the issuers of the securities held in negative amounts. If this condition is violated, such securities have not been fully replicated and the investor cannot expect to receive the full price when taking the associated negative positions.

Since all information is not fully public, and monitoring and transactions are costly, institutional arrangements for short selling have traditionally required the posting of separate collateral for each position, with little if any consideration given to the effects of diversification at the portfolio level. Under such conditions it is difficult or expensive for a high risk-tolerance investor to borrow money to finance added investment in a market-like portfolio. Stock index futures contracts now provide investors with a more efficient means for doing so. Before considering them, however, we investigate the characteristics of an extreme case in which no negative positions are allowed.

Capital Asset Prices without Negative Holdings

Assumptions

To explore the effects of constraints on asset holdings we retain all the assumptions of the CAPM and add N^*K non-negativity constraints of the form:

$$X_{ik} \geq 0 \qquad \text{for all } i \text{ and } k.$$

Portfolio Optimality

Investor k seeks to maximize U_k subject to a full investment constraint and the relevant non-negativity constraints. This is a *quadratic programming problem*. An exact solution to a portfolio optimization problem of this form can be obtained using the *critical line algorithm* developed by Markowitz (1956).

When the solution is obtained, some values of X_{ik} will be positive. The corresponding securities are said to be *in* the optimal portfolio. The remainder will be at their lower bounds of zero and are said to be *out* of the portfolio.

Each of the securities *in* the optimal portfolio must have the same marginal utility. If this were not the case, it would be possible to reallocate funds from one such security with a lower marginal utility to one with a higher marginal utility, thereby increasing utility without violating either the full investment constraint or any of the non-negativity constraints. The common value of marginal utility for such securities will be the investor's marginal utility of wealth, which we will again denote λ_{fk}.

Each of the securities *out* of the portfolio must have a marginal utility less than (or equal to) that of the securities in the portfolio. If this were not the case, it would be possible to reallocate funds from a security in the portfolio to one out of the portfolio, thereby increasing utility without violating any of the constraints.

These relationships, which derive from more general ones termed *Kuhn-Tucker conditions*, can be written conveniently as:

$$E_i - \frac{2}{\tau_k} C_{ik} = \lambda_{fk} - z_{ik} \qquad \text{for all } i \tag{12}$$

where z_{ik} will be zero for securities in the portfolio and greater than or equal to zero for securities out of the portfolio.

Aggregation

As with the CAPM, we take a wealth-weighted average of the conditions for the optimality of individual investors' portfolios. The result has a similar form:

$$E_i - \frac{2}{\tau_m} C_{im} = \lambda_{fm} - z_{im} \qquad \text{for all } i. \tag{13}$$

Not surprisingly, z_{im} is a weighted average of the z_{ik} values for the K investors, with the weights depending on the investors' influences in the marketplace, where influence depends on both wealth and risk tolerance.[19]

Expected Returns

The previous equation can be transformed simply to obtain:

$$E_i = \lambda_{fm} + \frac{2V_m}{\tau_m} \beta_{im} - z_{im} \qquad \text{for all } i. \tag{14}$$

Were it not for the last term, there would be a linear relationship between expected return and beta, as in the CAPM. But the last term implies that only securities that are in *every* investor's optimal portfolio will plot along such a line.[20] Every security that is *out* of at least one investor's optimal portfolio will plot below the line.[21] Moreover, the larger the number of investors for whom the lower bound for a security is binding, the larger is the corresponding value of z_{im} likely to be.

[19]That is,

$$z_{im} \equiv \frac{\sum_k W_k \tau_k}{\tau_m} z_{ik}.$$

[20]Only for such securities will all the z_{ik} values be zero, giving value of zero for z_{im} (their weighted average).

[21]At least one z_{ik} value will be positive; since the remainder will all equal zero, the value of z_{im} (their weighted average) will be positive.

It is important to note that the magnitudes of the z_{im} values will be affected by the distribution of risk tolerances across investors. In the special case in which all investors have the same risk tolerance, everyone will choose to hold the market portfolio and all the z_{im} values will equal zero, giving results identical to those of the original CAPM. Loosely speaking, the greater the variation in risk tolerances across investors, the more likely it is that some of the z_{im} values will be positive. Note, however, that in this connection each investor's influence will depend on both his or her wealth and risk tolerance. Unless there is substantial variation in the risk tolerances of the wealthiest investors, the z_{im} values may be very close to zero, giving results very similar to those of the original CAPM.

The Risk Premium

To determine the risk premium in this case, one must take a market value-weighted average of the equilibrium relationships in the previous equation. Doing so gives:

$$\frac{E_m - \lambda_{fm}}{V_m} = \frac{2}{\tau_m} - \frac{z_{mm}}{V_m}, \tag{15}$$

where z_{mm} represents the market value weighted average of the z_{im} values.[22]

Clearly, the risk premium per unit of variance will be a function of the extent to which investors' portfolios are affected by the non-negativity constraints.[23]

The Security Market Line Relationship

Given the final term in the previous equation, it is not particularly instructive to derive a counterpart to the security market line of the CAPM. However, equation (14) can stand as the analogue to a security market line for this case. As indicated earlier, the first two terms do indeed provide such a line. However, in this case the line serves as an upper boundary. Some or all of the securities may plot below the line, with the distances dependent on the degree to which the associated non-negativity constraints are binding. Thus there may not be a precise linear relationship between expected returns and beta values.

[22] Multiplying equation (13) by X_{im} and summing over i gives:

$$E_m = \lambda_{fm} + \frac{2V_m}{\tau_m}\beta_{mm} - \Sigma_i X_{im} z_{im}.$$

Rearranging terms gives equation (15).

[23] Moreover, the magnitude of λ_{fm} will be also be affected by such restrictions.

Riskless Securities

In this case no riskless borrowing is allowed, since negative positions are precluded. The net positive supply of riskless securities will, however, be included in the market portfolio. For any investor for whom the constraint on borrowing is binding, λ_{fk} will exceed R_f. For all others, the two values will be equal. Hence, λ_{fm} will equal or exceed R_f.

The Efficiency of the Market Portfolio

In the CAPM, the marginal utilities of all securities with respect to the holdings in the market portfolio are equal when evaluated using the societal risk tolerance. This is sufficient for the efficiency of the market portfolio. It is also necessary if the market portfolio is to be efficient for an investor with the societal risk tolerance.

More generally, for the market portfolio to be efficient, the marginal utilities of all securities measured relative to the market portfolio must be equal when evaluated using *some* positive risk tolerance. This follows from the fact that the market portfolio includes positive amounts of every security, hence all securities will be *in* such a portfolio.

For this condition to be met, there must be a linear relationship between security expected returns and their beta values.[24] With restrictions on negative holdings this may not be the case, due to the influences of the z_{im} values.[25] Hence the market portfolio may be inefficient. Of course, the extent of the inefficiency will depend on the magnitudes of the z_{im} values—if most are small, the degree of inefficiency of the market portfolio may be inconsequential.

Fund Separation

Markowitz (1959) showed that non-negativity constraints cause the efficient frontier to be piecewise linear in the space of holdings. Within each linear range, efficient portfolios can be obtained by combining any two other

[24]For all securities in the market portfolio to have the same marginal utilities requires that:

$$E_i - \frac{2}{\tau} C_{im} = \lambda,$$

where τ and λ are positive constants.

Rearranging terms and converting C_{im} to the equivalent value expressed in terms of β_{im} gives:

$$E_i = \lambda + \frac{2V_m}{\tau} \beta_{im}.$$

To meet the condition for efficiency of the market portfolio, there must thus be a strictly linear relationship between E_i and β_{im}. Moreover, the intercept and slope must both be positive, otherwise the implied values of λ and τ, respectively, will be negative.

[25]If all the z_{im} values are zero, of course, the linear relationship will obtain. In the highly unlikely event that there is a linear relationship between the z_{im} values and the corresponding beta values, there will also be a linear relationship between the E_i and β_{im} values.

portfolios within the range.[26] However, no two portfolios can, in general, be utilized to obtain *all* efficient portfolios. Hence two-fund separation may not strictly apply in this case.

Key Implications

When negative positions are precluded:

1. the market portfolio may not be efficient,
2. some efficient portfolios may not be equivalent to investment in the market portfolio plus, possibly, lending or borrowing, and
3. there may not be a linear relationship between expected return and beta.

All these implications suggest a diminution in the efficiency with which risk can be allocated in an economy. The choice of optimal portfolios becomes more difficult than in the simple setting of the CAPM. Calculations of cost of capital for corporate and governmental investment projects may require more than the determination of a simple relationship between expected return and market risk. More fundamentally, overall welfare may be lower than it would be if the constraints on negative holdings could be reduced or removed.

While the magnitudes of the departures from the implications of the original CAPM might be small even under the extreme conditions assumed in this case, it is clear that institutional arrangements to improve investor's abilities to take negative positions can increase the efficiency with which risk is allocated in an economy. Following some comments on financial innovation in general, I will discuss the stock index futures contract—an innovation that provides such an improvement.

Financial Innovation

More than most sciences, economics not only analyzes reality, it also alters it. Theory leads to empiricism which changes behavior. Nowhere is this more evident than in financial economics. The academic field of finance differs radically from that of three decades ago, due in large part to advances in financial economic theory and to the extensive empirical research that has flowed from those advances. At least as important, the practice of finance has been affected in fundamental ways by the progress in financial economics. Most notably, the last decade has been marked by unprecedented innovation in financial instruments, markets and institutions.

Given the bewildering pace of such innovation, it is not surprising that some individuals and organizations have at times found it difficult to fully understand the proper uses of some of the new instruments and procedures. Evidence abounds that those who fail to learn the principles of financial economics in more formal ways will do so through experience. Markets are

[26] Those lying at the end-points provide convenient choices.

effective although sometimes cruel teachers. In general, financial systems are self-correcting. Given time, participants learn to use new instruments and procedures to improve overall welfare, not just to reallocate wealth from one set of hands to another. It is usually best to wait until the forces of competition are able to regulate a market rather than to impose regulations prematurely.

Much financial innovation has been possible due to the remarkable advances in computation and communication technology. Moreover, increased global competition, with the accompanying dimuinution of monopoly power on the part of organizations and governments, has played an important role. Nonetheless, I cannot help but believe that discoveries in the science of financial economics have had a major influence. Stock index futures contracts appear to provide a clear example of this.

Stock Index Futures Contracts

Features

A traditional *forward contract* is an agreement on the part of the seller to deliver a stated amount of a commodity on a given future date to the buyer at a pre-specified price. A *futures contract* is a standardized forward contract with the further provision that the delivery price be reset at the end of each trading day to equal the price at which new agreements were struck. At the time of each such resetting, one of the two parties pays the other an amount equal to the difference between the new price and the old. This process is known as "posting variation margin" as a result of the "marking to market" of the price of the contract.

The seller of a futures contract is said to be *short* the contract; the buyer is said to be *long*.

Futures exchanges make it possible for the two parties in a contract to be "unlinked". Thus *A* may sell a contract to *B*. *B* may later sell it to *C* without *A*'s involvement. And later, *C* may sell it to *A*, extinguishing it before the final delivery date.

To protect the other party in such an arrangement, each party must post collateral as "margin". The amount need only cover potential losses between two trading days, however, due to the process of marking to market. Margins equal to 10% to 20% of the value of a position typically suffice. To insure that collateral is maintained, yet preserve the standardization of the contract, brokers representing those with positions utilize a *clearing house*, which provides assurance that obligations will be met.

A *financial futures contract* may call for the actual delivery of a stated financial instrument or one or more of a set of such instruments. Alternatively, it may call only for a final marking to market on the delivery day, with one party paying the other an amount equal to the difference between the prior futures price and the value of the underlying financial instrument on the delivery day. The latter is often termed *cash delivery*.

A *stock index futures contract* covers a pre-specified portfolio of stocks. It allows investors to take long or short positions in diversified portfolios. Most such contracts provide for *cash delivery*.

Effects

A key aspect of a stock index futures contract is its focus on a *diversified portfolio* rather than on an individual security or commodity. In this respect, such a contract is similar to a mutual fund, unit trust, commingled index fund or stock index option. All provide investors with "packages" of securities, substantially reducing the costs associated with diversification. Recent growth in investors' reliance on all such vehicles stands, at least in part, as testimony to the influence of financial economics on the process by which risk is borne in modern economies.

A second feature of a stock index futures contract is of particular interest in the present context. Such a contract provides an efficient method for simultaneously taking a positive position in a diversified stock portfolio and a negative position in a riskless asset. In effect, the purchaser of such a contract borrows money to purchase a stock portfolio while the seller lends money and takes a short position in the stock portfolio.[27] If the buyer of the contract posts as margin riskless securities with a value equal to that of the futures position, the net effect is similar to that of investing a comparable amount in the stocks in the associated index. If less than 100% margin is posted, the effect is similar to that of a levered purchase of the stocks in the index. While not precisely the same as borrowing at the riskless rate to purchase a portfolio of stocks, a long position in a futures contract can provide a very close approximation to such a strategy. Moreover, the upper limit on the borrowing implicit in the arrangement is sufficiently large to satisfy all but a potentially few investors with extremely high risk tolerances.

It is striking that a levered holding of a highly diversified portfolio (i.e., the market portfolio) is precisely the optimal investment strategy for high risk tolerance investors in the simple setting of the original CAPM. While no financial futures contract corresponds to the overall market portfolio, combinations of existing contracts (including those on bonds and other types of securities) may approximate such a strategy.

In a sense, the seller of a futures contract holds negative positions in the underlying securities, and the existence of such positions is inconsistent with the implications of the CAPM. However, when viewed more broadly, this inconsistency may be more apparent than real. Often the seller of a stock index futures contract also holds the individual securities that make up the index in question. The futures position thus provides a *hedge* against changes in the value of the portfolio of actual stocks. As a result, the hedged futures seller's *net* position is virtually risk-free and hence equivalent to investment

[27]For details see, for example, Duffie (1989).

in a riskless asset. Such a person can assemble the securities in an economical manner and, in effect, provide a means for others to buy or sell the package without incurring the costs associated with the purchase or sale of large numbers of individual stocks. In effect, he or she loans money to the high risk-tolerance investor to enable the latter to purchase added amounts of risky securities.

Futures contracts written on diversified portfolios require less margin than would a set of contracts on individual securities, each with its own required margin. Moreover, stock index contracts take advantage of economies of scale in transactions and recording-keeping.

In effect, stock index futures contracts provide those who might be limited by traditional constraints on borrowing with a means for achieving desirable investment strategies. Moreover, the strategies are similar to those that are optimal for high risk-tolerance investors in the setting of the original CAPM. Hence, the existence of such contracts may well bring actual capital markets closer to those of this simple equilibrium theory. If so, stock index futures contracts may significantly improve the efficiency with which risk is allocated in an economy.

Conclusions

Here I have explicitly considered only one type of impediment to the efficient allocation of risk. However, this case can serve as a representative of many others. The greater the costs and constraints associated with the purchase and sale of securities, the farther will an economy be from the goal of allocating risk to those most able and willing to bear it.

Happily, technological advances and greater understanding of the principles of financial economics are reducing costs and constraints of this type at a rapid pace. As a result, capital markets are moving closer the the conditions assumed in some of the simpler types of financial theory. Far more important: the combined efforts of theoreticians, empiricists and practitioners are increasing the efficiency with which risk is allocated among individuals, leading to improvements in social welfare.

REFERENCES

Arrow, K., 1953, Le role des valeurs boursiers pour la repartition la meilleure des risques, *Econometrie*, Colloques Internationaux du Centre National de la Recherche Scientifique, Vol. XI, Paris, 41-47.

Black, F., 1972, Capital market equilibrium with restricted borrowing *Journal of Business* 45, 444-454.

—— and M. Scholes, 1973, The pricing of options and corporate liabilities, *Journal of Political Economy* 81, 637-654.

Breeden, D., 1979, An intertemporal asset pricing model with stochastic consumption and investment opportunities, *Journal of Financial Economics* 7, 265-296.

Brennan, M. J., 1970, Taxes, market valuation and corporate financial policy, *National Tax Journal* December 1970, pp. 417-427.

Cox, J., S. Ross, and M. Rubinstein, 1979, Option pricing: A simplified approach, *Journal of Financial Economics* 7, 229-263

Debreu, G., 1959, *Theory of Value*, (John Wiley and Sons, Somerset, NJ).

Duffie, D., 1989, *Futures Markets*, (Prentice Hall, Englewood Cliffs, NJ).

Glenn, D., 1976, Super premium security prices and optimal corporate financing decisions, *Journal of Finance* 31, 507-524.

Kraus, A. and R. Litzenberger, 1976, Skewness preference and the valuation of risk assets, *Journal of Finance* 38, 1085-1100.

Levy, H., 1978, Equilibrium in an imperfect market: A constraint on the number of securities in a portfolio, *American Economic Review* 68, 643-658.

—— and H. Markowitz, 1979, Approximating expected utility by a function of mean and variance, *American Economic Review* 69, 308-317.

Lintner, J., 1965, The valuation of risk assets and the selection of risky investments in stock portfolios and capital budgets, *Review of Economics and Statistics* 47, 13-37.

——, 1969, The aggregation of investors' diverse judgements and preferences in purely competitive markets, *Journal of Financial and Quantitative Analysis* 4, 346-382.

Markowitz, H., 1952, Portfolio selection, *Journal of Finance* 7, 77-91.

——, 1956, The optimization of a quadratic function subject to linear constraints, *Naval Research Logistics Quarterly* 3, 111-133.

——, 1959, *Portfolio Selection: Efficient Diversification of Investments*, (John Wiley and Sons, Somerset, NJ).

——, 1987, *Mean-Variance Analysis in Portfolio Choice and Capital Markets*, (Basil Blackwell Inc., New York).

——, 1990, Risk adjustment, *Journal of Accounting, Auditing and Finance*, Forthcoming.

Merton, R., 1973, An intertemporal capital asset pricing model, *Econometrica* 41, 867-887.

——, 1987, A simple model of capital market equilibrium with incomplete information, *Journal of Finance* 52, 483-510.

Modigliani, F. and M. Miller, 1958, The cost of capital, corporation finance, and the theory of investment, *American Economic Review* 48, 261-297.

Mossin, J., 1966, Equilibrium in a capital asset market, *Econometrica* 35, 768-783.

Ross, S. 1976, Arbitrage theory of capital asset pricing, *Journal of Economic Theory* 13, 341-360.

Rubinstein, M., 1974, An aggregation theorem for securities markets, *Journal of Financial Economics* 1, 225-244.

Sharpe, W., 1961, Portfolio analysis based on a simplified model of the relationships among securities, PhD Dissertation, University of California at Los Angeles.

——, 1963, A simplified model for portfolio analysis, *Management Science* 9, 277-293.

——, 1964, Capital asset prices: A theory of market equilibrium under conditions of risk, *Journal of Finance* 19, 425-442.

——, 1970, *Portfolio Theory and Capital Markets*, (McGraw-Hill, New York).

——, 1978, *Investments*, Englewood Cliffs, (Prentice-Hall, NJ).

——, 1984, Factor models, CAPMs, and the APT, *Journal of Portfolio Management* Fall, 21-25.

Tobin, J., 1969, Liquidity preference as behavior towards risk, *Review of Economic Studies* 25, 65-86.

Von Neumann, J. and O. Morgenstern, 1944, *Theory of Games and Economic Behavior*, (Princeton University Press).

Nuclear Financial Economics

William F. Sharpe, Professor, Graduate School of Business, Stanford University

Introduction

An important subfield of physics—*Nuclear Physics*—deals with the smallest particles of which matter is composed. Constructs developed by Kenneth Arrow[1] and Gerard Debreu[2] provide a similar foundation for financial economics. With a bit of hyperbole, the approach may be termed *nuclear financial economics*.

In pioneering their work, Arrow and Debreu explored aspects of general equilibrium. After dealing with the economists' then–traditional world of certainty, they turned to issues related to *risk*.

Here we show how the Arrow–Debreu approach can be used to analyze risk in the domains of financial engineering, corporate finance, and investment analysis.[3] The simplest possible cases, involving only two time periods (the present and a future date) are employed. While the results are quite general, no attempt is made to prove generality nor to extend the analyses to cover more complex cases. The relatively modest goal of the paper is to interest readers in using "nuclear financial economics" to analyze issues involving risk in financial settings.

Contingent Contracts

To deal with risk, Arrow and Debreu introduced the concept of a *contingent contract*—a contract "for delivery of goods or money contingent on the occurrence of [a] state of affairs,"[4] equivalently: "a contract for the transfer of a commodity [specifying], in addition to its physical properties, its location and date, an event on the occurrence of which transfer is conditional."[5]

A special kind of contingent contract provides one unit of money or some notional commodity at one date if and only if one of the many possible states of the world at that date obtains. This may be termed a "pure" or "primitive" security, or simply a *time–state claim*. A *complete market* is one in which all such claims may be purchased or sold explicitly or synthetically at stated prices.

The *price* of a contingent contract or time–state claim is "...the amount paid...initially by...the agent who commits himself to accept...delivery of one unit of that commodity. Payment is irrevocably made although delivery does not take place if specified events do not obtain."[6]

The concept of a contingent contract allows for the analysis of risk in simple yet powerful ways, as we will show.

Financial Engineering

The International Association of Financial Engineers defines *financial engineering* as "...the development and the creative application of financial technology to solve problems in finance and to exploit financial opportunities."[7]

The Arrow–Debreu approach may seem too far removed from the real world to be used for such purposes. There are hundreds of millions of contingencies for which no specific contingent contracts exist, and it is difficult to imagine a way to synthesize most such contracts from securities that do exist. Nonetheless, the concept is in fact widely used in financial engineering under the assumption that markets are sufficiently complete for the states of the world that affect the securities being analyzed.

Those who employ so–called *binomial models of asset returns*[8] utilize contingent claims[9] explicitly. Those who employ continuous–time models, such as that of Black and Scholes, [10] do so implicitly. Curiously, however, many practitioners of financial engineering are unaware of the intellectual underpinnings of the methods that they employ.

Financial engineering is by no means the only area in which the Arrow–Debreu approach can be employed. In fact, it can address fundamental issues of corporate finance and investment analysis. It allows a very clear distinction between models that require only the assumption that markets are arbitrage–free and those that require additional assumptions about investor preferences and predictions.

In the field of investment analysis, both academics and practitioners tend to favor the *mean–variance* approach introduced by Markowitz[11] over that of Arrow and Debreu. While there are good reasons for doing so, it seems unfortunate that the latter is often entirely omitted from investment courses. A preferred strategy utilizes the Arrow–Debreu model to develop fundamental ideas, then turns to mean–variance analysis and its use in practice.

The Economy

To illustrate the power of the Arrow–Debreu approach, we consider an extremely simple economy in which there is no currency. Apples are the only good and all trades involve apples. There are two time periods—*now* and *next year*. The only source of risk is the uncertainty about next year's weather. More precisely, there are two possible states of the world concerning next year: *good weather* and *bad weather*.

There are three distinct goods available for trade at present: (1) apples now, (2) apples next year if the weather is good, and (3) apples next year if the weather is bad.

Note that the latter two are contingent contracts. For simplicity, we call these goods "present apples," "good–weather apples," and "bad–weather apples."

In this economy, *dealers* stand ready to trade any one of the three goods for any other. Competition is so fierce that bid and ask prices are the same.

Initially, we assume that dealers will *swap* 0.4 present apples for 1.0 good apple. More precisely, if an individual will give up 0.4 apples today, he or she will receive a certificate promising delivery of 1.0 apple next year if (but only if) the weather during the coming year has been good; if the weather has been bad, no apples will be delivered next year.

Dealers will also swap 0.5 present apples for 1.0 bad apple. More precisely, if an individual will give up 0.5 apples today, he or she will receive a certificate promising delivery of 1.0 apple by next year if (but only if) the weather during the coming year has been bad; if the weather has been good, no apples will be delivered next year.

Following convention, we call the terms of trade for swaps involving future and present goods *prices*. Thus the price of a good–weather apple is 0.4 (present apples) and the price of bad–weather apple is 0.5 (present apples). Equivalently, the *present values* of such contingent claims are 0.4 and 0.5, respectively. Note that the term *present value* is simply a convention for stating terms at which market transactions can be made to convert claims for future payments to current payments. Absent competitive markets in which such swaps can be made, the concept has no particular usefulness.

Production in this economy comes from apple trees, each of which will produce 100 apples next year if the weather is good and 70 apples if the weather is bad. This is illustrated (naturally) via a *tree diagram* in Figure 1. For convenience, prices are also shown.

Figure 1

Apple Tree Payoffs and Prices

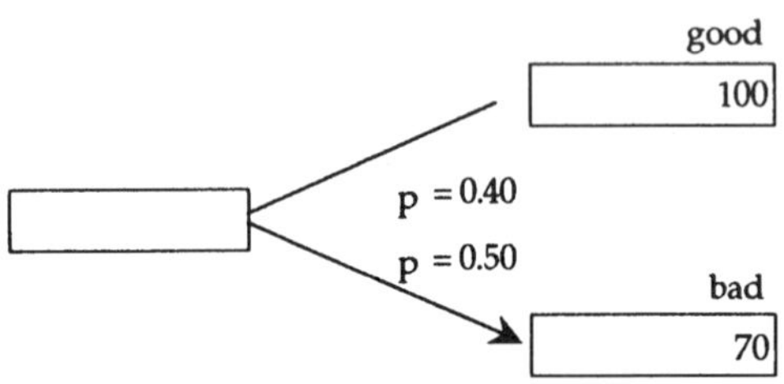

Arbitrage–Free Pricing

The two prices in Figure 1 show the terms of trade for swaps in which a present good is exchanged for a contingent future good. Not shown are the terms for a swap in which one contingent future good is exchanged for another. However, *arbitrage* will insure that such trades are made using terms consistent with those already shown. Consider someone who wishes to trade 1.0 good–weather apple for some number of bad–weather apples. One way to do this is to trade 1.0 good–weather apple for 0.4 present apples while at the same time trading 0.4 present apples for 0.8 bad–weather apples. The net result is to *swap* 1.0 good–weather apple for 0.8 bad–weather apples. Such a swap has zero *net present value* and thus can be said to be "fair." If any dealer were willing to swap good–weather and bad–weather apples at any other terms of trade, an astute individual could exploit the dealers by engaging in combinations of trades that could provide (1) net receipt of apples in at least one time and state and (2) no net payout of apples at any time and state. Such an opportunity, termed an *arbitrage,* is rare in a well-functioning, competitive capital market.

In an arbitrage-free economy with no transactions costs, any given time-state claim will sell for the same price, no matter how obtained. This will also be true for any "package" of time-state claims. This is known as the *law of one price.*

Most transactions involve complex combinations of present and future time-state claims. All are *swaps* in a broad sense. Those involving both present and future payments are often termed *investments,* with the term "swap" reserved for those that involve only future contingent payments. However, such terminology obscures the fact that all reflect trades of one set of valuable claims for another.

Valuation

How much is an apple tree worth? The answer is easily obtained by *valuing* each of the contingent claims that it provides. The 100 good-weather apples can be traded for 40 (0.4 x 100) present apples and the 70 bad-weather apples for 35 (0.5 x 70) present apples. Thus the (present) value of the tree is 75 (present) apples, as shown in Figure 2.

Figure 2

Apple Tree Payoffs and Prices

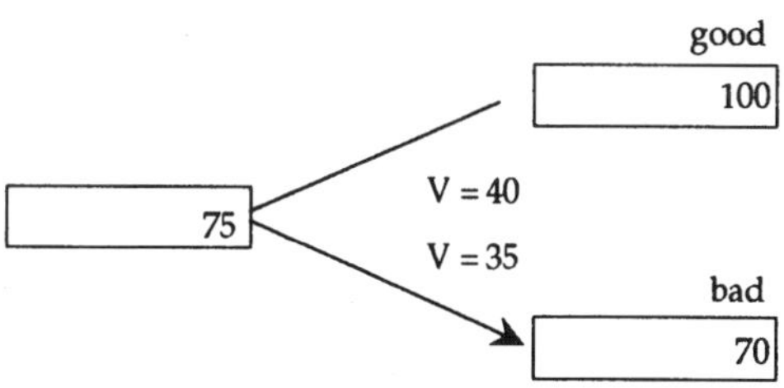

Note that valuation is designed to answer the question: "For how much in present goods (or money) can the asset in question be traded—either directly or indirectly." *In principle, all standard valuation methods rest on the use of market prices to answer such questions.*

Financing

Consider the apple–tree owner who issues two claims. The first promises the holder 60 apples next year. Since the amount promised is fixed, the associated *security* can be termed a *bond*. The other claim promises the holder all the apples left over after the bondholder has been paid. The associated security represents a *residual claim* and can be termed a (common) *stock*.

Table 1 provides the computations required to determine the value of the bond. Note that it is *riskless* since the promised amount can be paid no matter what the state of the world (weather) may be. An equivalent method for valuing a riskless security *discounts* the promised payment using the *riskless discount factor*. For a riskless security, the factor is simply the sum of the prices of all the time–state claims for the date in question; for this is the cost of obtaining one unit at that date, no matter what the state of the world. In this economy, the discount factor is 0.9 (0.4 + 0.5). This is sometimes stated in terms of a *rate of interest*. In this case, the rate of interest is equal to 0.1/0.9, or 11.11%, since 0.9 today can be converted to 1.0 next year (and vice–versa) with certainty.

Table 1

Time	State	Payment	Price	Present Value
1	good	60	0.4	24
1	bad	60	0.5	30
				54

Whichever method is employed, the result is the same. The value of the bond is 54 present apples.

Table 2 provides the computations required to determine the value of the stock. It is *worth* 21 present apples since the same set of contingent payments could be obtained with 21 apples by judiciously making swaps with dealers.

Table 2

Time	State	Payment	Price	Present Value
1	good	40	0.4	16
1	bad	10	0.5	5
				21

Note that the value of the bond plus the value of the stock is 75 present apples. Not surprisingly, this is the value computed earlier for the tree as a whole.

What if the tree had been financed by issuing "risky debt"? Consider a case in which the bondholder has been promised 80 apples next year. In fact, he or she will receive 80 apples if the weather is good but only 70 if the weather is bad. Clearly the bond cannot be valued by discounting the promised payment. Table 3 shows how this should be done. Note that the actual value (67 present apples) is considerably less than the value that the bond would command if the promised payments were guaranteed (0.9 x 80, or 72 present apples).

Table 3

Time	State	Payment	Price	Present Value
1	good	80	0.4	32
1	bad	70	0.5	35
				67

With this sort of financing (high leverage), the stock is risky indeed—it will pay 20 apples if the weather is good but nothing if the weather is bad (i.e., the firm will be bankrupt). Such a stock will be worth 8 apples, as shown in Table 4.

Table 4

Time	State	Payment	Price	Present Value
1	good	20	0.4	8
1	bad	0	0.5	0
				8

Note that the sum of the values remains the same as before (67 + 8 = 75). This reflects the *principle of value additivity*. In a complete market with no transactions costs, the value of the sum of the claim will be the same, no matter how those claims are structured. In this setting, "financing doesn't matter." This is the essence of the famous Modigliani–Miller Proposition Number I.[12]

In the real world, of course, transactions costs (broadly construed) do matter. Nonetheless, the principle of value additivity remains useful if a broad-enough view is taken of the set of claimants on a firm's prospects. In particular, governments (which impose taxes on firms and on those who receive income from firms) must be included, as must lawyers, accountants, investment bankers and others who may be more likely to absorb some of a firm's cashflows under certain financial arrangements than under others.

In a sense, the questions to be asked concerning alternative financing procedures have more to do with the division of the pie than with its overall size. The latter tends to be determined more by nonfinancial decisions than by financial ones. However, there are cases in which financial decisions can significantly alter incentives for those charged with "corporate governance" to maximize the size of the pie.

Synthetic Securities

In the real world, people rarely make explicit agreements for payments to be made if one and only state of the world obtains. Most traded securities represent patterns of payments over many states. Equivalently, they may be thought of as packages of pure time–state claims.

To illustrate this, we return to the case of a firm that has issued a riskless bond promising a payment of 60 apples (as described in Table 1) and a stock representing a claim for the remaining apples (as described in Table 2).

Consider an economy in which the only traded goods are this firm's bond and stock. We assume each can be divided into smaller holdings and that dealers are willing to trade the bond for 54 present apples and the stock for 21 present apples. No other markets exist.

Given the current price of a security and the payments it will provide in each state of the world, it is possible to determine the *value–relative*, or future payment per unit invested, that will be received if that state obtains. Tables 5 and 6 show these computations for the bond and stock, respectively. Note that the percentage *realized return* associated with a given state of the world is simply 100 times [the value–relative minus 1.0].

Table 5

Time	State	Bond Payment	Price	Value Relative	% Return
1	good	60	54	1.1111	11.11
1	bad	60	54	1.1111	11.11

Table 6

Time	Stock State	Payment	Price	Value Relative	% Return
1	good	40	21	1.9048	90.48
1	bad	10	21	0.4762	-52.38

Figure 3 plots the value–relatives for the two securities. Since the bond is riskless, it lies on a 45–degree line from the origin—indicating that the payoff per unit invested is the same, no matter what happens in the future. Any security that plots at a point not falling on such a line is *risky*—the payments differ in different states of the world, and hence the amount to be received is not fully predictable in advance. In this case, the stock is risky and the bond is not.

Figure 3

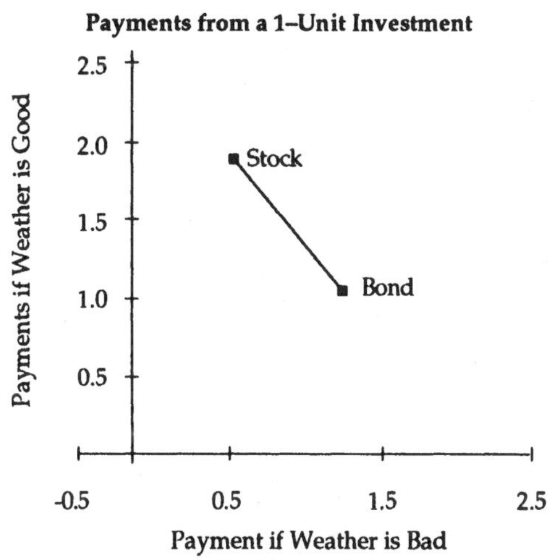

An *investor* may prefer the bond over the stock or vice versa. However, these are by no means the only alternatives. By choosing a *portfolio* that includes proportionate shares of the bond and the stock with a total present value of 1 (apple), an investor can obtain any point on the line connecting the two points in Figure 3.

It is helpful to write the relationships among portfolio *holdings*, payments in the two states of the world and portfolio *value*. Letting N_s and N_b represent the number of stocks and bonds held, P_G and P_B the payments received in good and bad weather, and V the present value of the portfolio:

$$40N_s + 60N_b = P_G$$
$$10N_s + 60N_b = P_B$$
$$21N_s + 54N_b = V$$

The equation of the line in Figure 3 is obtained by setting V equal to 1 and then varying N_s and N_b over the range in which neither is negative.

But these are not the alternatives in a well–functioning capital market. Directly or indirectly, it should be possible to take a *negative* position in a security (e.g. "sell it short") as long as an investor's overall portfolio does not involve commitments that would lead to obligations involving negative *net* payments in any state of the world. By judicious use of such positions, an investor should be able to obtain any point on the line through the two points extended to the axes, as shown in Figure 4.

Figure 4

Payments from a 1–Unit Investment

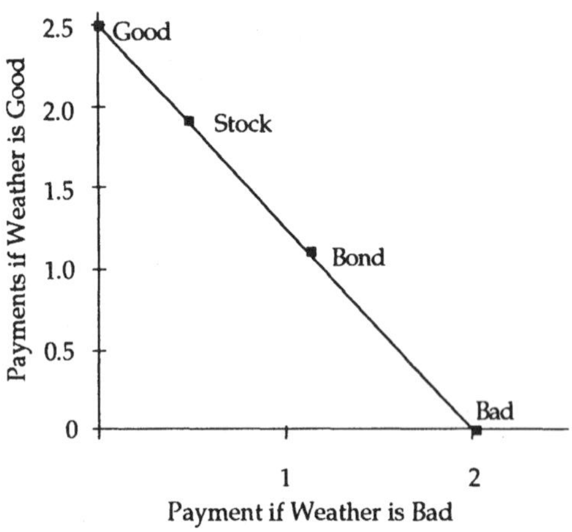

In practice, such arrangements require procedures to guarantee "counterparty creditworthiness." Frequent marking of positions to market, the use of impound accounts, the guaranteeing of credit, and the reliance on credit ratings made by outside agencies represent institutional approaches to this issue.

Note that by combining a "long" position in the stock with a short position in the bond in precisely the right proportions, one can *construct* a (pure) "good–weather claim." This is represented by the point labeled *good* in

Figure 4. Not surprisingly, it provides 2.5 good–weather apples per 1.0 present apple. Equivalently, the price of 1.0 good–weather apple, obtained in this manner, is 0.4 present apples (as in our earlier example). By combining *existing securities* (the bond and the stock), one can *synthesize* a security that does not exist (a good–weather security). The result is often termed a *derivative security* since it is derived from existing securities.

The point labeled "bad" shows the payments received from a synthetic bad–weather security with a present value of 1. Not surprisingly, the associated price of 1.0 bad–weather apple is 0.5 (again, as in our earlier example).

In principle, any desired set of payments in the two states of the world can be created using only the two "standard" securities. Given desired payments P_G and P_B, one simply solves the set of simultaneous equations:

$$40N_s + 60N_b = P_G$$

$$10N_s + 60N_b = P_B$$

The value (cost) of obtaining the payments can then be determined by "pricing out the portfolio" with the final equation:

$$21N_s + 54N_b = V$$

In financial engineering terms, the portfolio (N_s and N_b) is sometimes termed a *replicating strategy.*[13]

It is a simple matter to determine the prices of pure time–state claims implicit in a set of existing securities. First, the cost of a strategy for which $P_G = 1$ and $P_B = 0$ is determined. This is the price of a claim to receive 1 unit if and only if the " G" state obtains. In this economy it is 0.4. Then the cost of a strategy for which $P_G = 0$ and $P_B = 1$ is determined. This is the price of a claim to receive 1 unit if and only if the " B" state obtains. In this economy it is 0.5. Henceforth, any desired set of payments can be "priced" by simply multiplying the amounts to be paid by these prices and then summing. In this case:

$$V = 0.40P_G + 0.50P_B$$

Only when a replicating strategy needs to be employed will it be necessary to solve the original set of simultaneous equations.[14]

Forward Prices

A *forward price* can be defined as a price to be paid *with certainty* at a specified future date for delivery of one or more goods, where the amount delivered may be contingent on events occurring on or before that date. An important special case is the *forward price of a (pure) time–state claim.*

In our economy, the expenditure of 0.4 apples today will purchase a security promising delivery of 1.0 apple tomorrow if the weather during the forthcoming year is good. A forward contract for the same security would promise the payment of some amount f_G next year, *no matter what*. For example, one party might promise to pay 0.4444 apples next year (no matter what) in exchange for a promise from a counterparty that the latter will deliver 1.0 apple if the weather has been good and nothing if it has been bad. Equivalently, after netting, if the weather has been good, the counterparty will deliver 0.5556 apples; on the other hand, if the weather has been bad, the original party will deliver 0.4444 apples.

In the absence of any payments or receipts during the year (as in our example), a very simple relationship should hold between the present price and the associated forward price. The forward price will simply equal the present price plus associated interest. Equivalently, the present price will equal the forward price divided by the discount factor for the payment date. In this case:

$$0.4444 = 0.40 / 0.90$$

If this relationship does not hold, clever arbitrageurs can exploit others in the market. They literally "make something for nothing." Such opportunities are fleeting at best.

Forward prices for pure time–state claims can also be used to value desired payments. First, the *forward value* (F) for the set of payments is determined. Here:

$$F = f_G P_G + f_B P_B$$

This is the amount that one should be willing to commit to pay next year for the set of payments in question.

To find the present value, the forward value is simply discounted. Here:

$$V = .90F$$

This two–step procedure is widely used by financial engineers. Unfortunately, the underlying economics is obscured by the use of terms that are at best confusing and at worst misleading. Forward prices of time–state claims are termed *risk–neutral probabilities* (or just *probabilities*). The forward value of the set of payments is called the *expected future value*, and the present value is the *discounted expected future value.*

While the procedures employed by those who use such terms provide correct answers, it is dangerous to confuse forward prices with probabilities and forward values with expected values. In a world of risk–averse investors, probabilities and forward prices will generally differ, as will forward and expected values.

There is every reason to believe that investors are risk averse. This, in turn, gives rise to differences in expected returns. To construct an appropriate investment strategy, one must attempt to understand such differences.

Investment Choice

The astute reader will have noted that none of the conclusions reached thus far used the concept of *probability* in any way! Issues of valuation, replication, the construction of swaps, and so on, can in principle be addressed without assuming or measuring probabilities associated with various states of the world. All that is required is a sufficiently complete market and price information for enough securities to allow purchase of pure time–state claims, either directly or synthetically.[15]

In effect, once a tree representing the payments provided by a sufficient set of existing securities has been drawn, further analysis proceeds from the sole assumption that markets are arbitrage–free. This is the proper domain of financial engineering.[16]

Investment choice deals with the selection of a *portfolio* of investments. Fundamentally, it is concerned with choosing an appropriate combination of time–state claims given the investor's overall wealth. In the Arrow–Debreu framework, wealth (including potential future earnings from human capital) can be stated in present–value terms. The *consumption–investment* decision is to select the best combination of present and state–contingent future goods (for example, apples) from among all combinations that can be obtained given overall wealth. Letting P_N represent the payment now (that is, consumption of present apples), $EU()$ the investor's "expected utility" function, and W his or her wealth, the goal is to:

$$\text{maximize:} \quad EU(P_N, P_G, P_B)$$

$$\text{subject to:} \quad 1.00P_N + 0.50P_G + 0.40P_B \leq W.$$

Clearly, the utility that an investor expects to receive from holdings of contingent claims on future consumption will depend on his or her assessment of the probabilities that the associated state of the world will actually come about. Hence, investment choice must deal with probabilities.

Moreover, while the financial engineer may be able to take security prices as given, investors will wish to consider their determinants, including productive opportunities and the opinions and preferences of others. In a sense, the current price of a time–state claim reflects a consensus of all investors' *predictions* of the *probability* of the associated state and their *feelings* about the *desirability* of obtaining goods in that state. A specific investor will, in the first instance, compare his or her own assessment of the probability of a state and the desirability of obtaining goods in it with the price that must be paid for the associated contingent contract. At a deeper level, however, the investor is comparing his or her own probability assessment and utility with that of the consensus of other investors.

Space precludes a detailed analysis of these relationships here. Instead we focus on two central aspects of investment analysis: the existence of *risk premiums* and *type* of risk that is likely to be rewarded with such premiums.

Consensus Probabilities

There is no reason to believe that individuals agree on the probabilities associated with various future states of the world. Thus the very notion of, say, "the probability" of good weather is ill defined. As a practical matter, it is frequently assumed that markets are "efficient" in a particular sense. A market can be said to be *efficient relative to a given set of information* if security prices are the same as they would be if all investors had carefully analyzed that information. The set of probabilities assessed by a "careful analyst" after having processed a body of information can be termed "fully informed" relative to that set of information. Theorists sometimes assume, for example, that prices "incorporate all publicly available information."

Roughly, this is equivalent to assuming that prices "reflect" probabilities that would be assigned by a sophisticated analyst after having studied all such information.

A modest set of assumptions holds that security prices reflect a set of "consensus probabilities" representing weighted averages of investors' predictions. In this process, the predictions of those with large amounts of wealth are generally weighted more heavily than the predictions of those with small amounts of wealth.

Formal models of investment behavior generally assume that all investors hold the same set of opinions concerning probabilities. Results are then derived concerning security prices, expected returns, and the like. Such results can be compared with the opinions of a particular investor who may assign different probabilities either due to the use of a different information set or a different analysis of the same information. Recommended consumption and investment decisions can arise from any of the three types of differences between the investor and "average investor": differences in *preferences*, in *circumstances*, or in *predictions*.

For the purposes of this paper, we assume that there are no differences of opinion concerning the probabilities of possible states of the world. More precisely, everyone agrees that the probability of good weather is 0.5, as is the probability of bad weather.

Forward Prices, Probabilities, and Expected Returns

Properly constructed probabilities have two well-known properties: they are non-negative and sum to 1.0 when all possible states of the world are included.

Forward prices for pure time-state claims have precisely the same properties. As long as the goods in question are indeed "good," each forward price will be non-negative. Moreover, as argued earlier, the sum of all such forward prices will be 1.0 when all possible states of the world are included.

These two facts imply that either (1) every pure time-state claim forward price will equal its probability or (2) some forward prices will be greater and others less than the associated probabilities.

The *expected payment* from a pure time-state claim is simply the probability that the associated state will occur since an expected value is obtained by multiplying a payment (here, 1.0) by a probability. The ratio of the expected payment to the current price will equal the *expected value relative*, or [1 + the *expected return*] for the time–state claim in question.

Table 7 shows the calculations for our economy. The expected return for a good–weather apple contact is 25%; that for a bad–weather apple contract is 0%. Note that the former exceeds the riskless rate of interest (11.11%) while the latter falls below it.

Table 7

Time	State	Price	Payment	1 + Exp. Return
1	good	40	0.5	1.25
1	bad	50	0.5	1.00

Recall that arbitrage insures that a forward price will equal the present price times $(1+i)$, where i is the riskless rate of interest. It follows that if the probability of a state equals the forward price of a claim to receive one unit in that state, then the expected return on the claim will equal the riskless rate of interest. Using this as a watershed, we can easily conclude that for any pure time–state claim:

Probability	>	Forward Price	<==>	Expected Return	>	Riskless Rate
Probability	=	Forward Price	<==>	Expected Return	=	Riskless Rate
Probability	<	Forward Price	<==>	Expected Return	<	Riskless Rate

In our economy, the good–weather state represents a case of the first type, and the bad–weather state represents a case of the third type.

If all forward prices equaled probabilities, all time–state claims would have expected returns equal to the riskless rate of interest. But then, so would all securities! In such a world, there would be no reason to expect to do better with stocks, for example, than with Treasury securities.

We can define a *risk premium* as the difference between the expected return on a security and the riskless rate of interest. In a society in which all time–state claim forward prices equaled probabilities, there would be no risk premiums.

Simple experience, introspection and many empirical studies suggest that in actual economies, prices will be set so that some securities should be *expected* to outperform others. In the vernacular, such securities should provide better "long–term performance."

To offer a superior expected return, a security must provide disproportionate amounts of payments in the states of the world for which the probability exceeds the forward price of the associated time–

state claim. Such a security will have a *risk* for which there is a *reward* (risk premium). Our good–weather–apple security provides an example.

But, as we have argued, if there are states for which the probability exceeds the forward price, there must be states for which the reverse holds. Securities providing disproportionate amounts of payments in such states will produce what may be termed a *risk discount*—their expected returns will be less than the riskless rate. Such securities will have a risk for which there is a *penalty* rather than a reward. Our bad–weather–apple security provides an example.

The Societal Risk Premium

In our economy, good–weather apples are cheap—their forward price is less than the expected payment. Conversely, bad–weather apples are expensive—their forward price is greater than the expected payment. This is perfectly plausible. If the weather is bad, there will be fewer apples. In general, the greater the value of an additional apple, the fewer there are to consume. Investors will reduce present consumption to provide more "for a rainy day" than they will to provide for a sunny day. More to the point, an additional unit of a commodity is likely to be worth more in a *state of scarcity* than in a *state of plenty.*

In well–functioning economies, bad news generally accompanies good news. If there is good news about a security (high expected returns), there is likely to be bad news as well (very bad returns in states of scarcity). Securities with high expected returns are likely to be "fair–weather friends"; those with low expected returns are likely to be "foul–weather friends."

What of the *market portfolio*—made up of all securities representing claims for future goods and services? What will be the *societal risk premium* associated with investment in a portfolio that includes proportional shares of all securities?

Given the fact that some time–state claims must provide risk discounts if others are to provide risk premiums, one might erroneously conclude that the societal risk premium would equal zero. However, this is unlikely to be the case. The expected return on a portfolio will be a value–weighted average of the expected returns on the underlying securities. More fundamentally, it will equal a value–weighted average of the expected returns on the underlying time–state claims. In general, a greater amount of value will be associated with "states of plenty" than with "states of scarcity." Since the former provide risk premiums and the latter risk discounts, the value–weighted average expected return is likely to exceed the riskless rate of interest. There will be a societal risk premium to compensate those who hold proportionate shares in the market as a whole for their willingness to take on the risk of doing badly in bad times.

Conclusion

The main goal of this paper was to show the power of using contingent claims analysis to analyze the impact of risk on financial decisions. In the process, we reached some conclusions concerning a simple economy—conclusions that can be shown to hold for far more general economies.

Risk can usefully be characterized in terms of the pattern of payments obtained over different future states of the world. If markets are sufficiently complete, it is possible to transform any such set of payments into any other set that has the same present value. Moreover, the cost of obtaining any desired set of payments can be computed directly, and a strategy that will replicate the payments using existing securities can be constructed. The technology for doing this provides the backbone of the profession of financial engineering. The creation and valuation of derivative securities represent direct applications of the methods discussed here.

It is not enough, however, to know how to construct and value sets of payments. Ultimately, someone must select the best feasible payment set for a given investor. In general, one can expect to earn higher returns in the long run from certain strategies than from others. However, it is not risk *per se* that is likely to be rewarded in well–functioning capital market—only *the risk of doing badly in bad times.*

Financial engineers can reshape future contingencies into many different patterns. Investors are thus faced with larger and larger menus from which to choose. More than ever, it is important that they understand the determinants of security prices, which form the inputs for financial engineering. Nuclear financial economics, concerned as it is with "first principles," can provide a solid base for such an understanding.

Notes

[1] Arrow, K. J. "The Role of Securities in the Optimal Allocation of Risk-bearing." *The Review of Economic Studies*, XXXI(2):86 (April 1964): 91–96.

[2] Debreu, G. *Theory of Value*. The Cowles Foundation Monograph 17, 1959.

[3] This chapter is intended to be incorporated into the author's work-in-progress, tentatively titled *Financial Economics and the Management of Investments*. The comments and suggestions of Professors William Beaver, Ayman Hindy, and Paul Pfleiderer at the Stanford Graduate School of Business are gratefully acknowledged.

[4] Arrow, K. J. in William Breit and Roger W. Spencer, *Lives of the Laureates: Ten Nobel Economists*, Second Edition, Cambridge, Mass.: MIT Press, 1990, p. 55.

[5] Debreu, *Theory of Value, op. cit.*

[6] Debreu, *Theory of Value, op. cit.*

[7] *The Journal of Financial Engineering*, 1, 1 (June 1992).

[8] This concept was introduced in William F. Sharpe, *Investments*, First Edition, Prentice-Hall, Englewood Cliffs, N.J., 1978, 7:3, pp. 366–71, then expanded upon in John C. Cox, S. A. Ross and M. Rubenstein, "Option Pricing: A Simplified Approach," *Journal of Financial Economics*, September 1979, pp. 229–263.

[9] Some use the term *time–state claim* instead of *contingent claim*.

[10] Black, F. and M. Scholes, "The Pricing of Options and Corporate Liabilities." *Journal of Political Economy* (May–June 1973): 141–183.

[11] Markowitz, H. M. "Portfolio Selection." *Journal of Finance*, 7:2 (March 1952): 77–91.

[12] Modigliani, F. and M. H. Miller, "The Cost of Capital, Corporation Finance and the Theory of Investment." *American Economic Review* (June 1958): 261–297.

[13] This terminology is more appropriate when multiple time periods are involved. In such a situation, some of the decision variables represent investments that are programmed to take place at various dates in specific circumstances. The solution then determines not only the current set of investments but also investments to be undertaken over time. While such problems can be solved by determining the solution to a set of simultaneous equations, it is generally preferable to take advantage of special aspects of the structure of an assumed payment tree to reduce the computational burden.

[14] Alternatively, the solutions for the pure time–state claim replicating strategies can be mixed in the appropriate propositions.

[15] In general, as many "independent" securities as there are states of the world will suffice. In our economy, with two states of the world, only two are required. Formally, it must be possible to invert the matrix of payments from the securities in the various states of the world. This will not be possible, if, for example, the payments from one of the securities can be obtained from some combination of one or more of the others.

[16] In practice, the distinction is not this precise. Financial engineers usually construct payment trees based on assumptions about security attributes (for example, standard deviations of returns) that incorporate probabilities. In many cases, additional assumptions are employed (e.g., that each branch of a binomial tree is equally probable). If the collective set of such assumptions is in error, the resulting valuation and replication strategies may be incorrect. The potential magnitudes of such errors are basically empirical issues. In any event, the subject is beyond the scope of this paper.

Section 3: Asset Allocation

3-1 "Bonds Versus Stocks: Some Lessons From Capital Market Theory," *Financial Analysts Journal*, November/December 1973, pp. 74–80.

This paper is intended to remind readers that the market portfolio of the CAPM includes both bonds and stocks. This in turn implies that a portfolio of stocks alone may be inefficient, as may one of bonds alone. Providing empirical tests of the historic performance of the two asset classes and a market-valued combination at the time was difficult, to say the least. I was forced to use the Dow-Jones Industrial Average as a surrogate for a diversified portfolio of stocks and a bond mutual fund to represent the bond market. With these draconian choices I was able to produce quarterly returns from 1938 through 1971. To estimate the returns on a market portfolio, I combined the two return series using year-end market values of the bonds and stocks listed on the New York Stock Exchange. For the overall period, the market portfolio outperformed both the bond and stock portfolios when measured using the Reward/Variability ratio (described in a paper in a later section and now known as the Sharpe Ratio). However, for the sub-period from 1946 through 1971, the stock portfolio dominated the market portfolio using this measure, although by a relatively small magnitude. I conclude by suggesting that the postwar results are likely to have been due to a divergence between expectations and actual performance, then finish with the proposition that when examining an investment strategy one should ask: "Why not bonds and stocks, in proportion to market values?".

3-2 "Likely Gains From Market Timing," *Financial Analysts Journal*, March/April 1975, pp. 60–69.

This paper grew out of a series of discussions with a friend who managed investments for wealthy individuals, many of whom had positions in both bonds and stocks. In 1973 and 1974, major stocks markets had experienced wrenching changes, with the U.S. indices falling by up to 50% (and considerably more in real terms, due to very high inflation). A number of multi-asset investment managers had concluded that they could improve overall performance significantly if they were able to "time the market" by anticipating major stock market moves. My goal was to show that, absent significant predictive ability, such attempts could increase year-to-year variability without a commensurate increase in average return, resulting in inferior performance compared to a buy-and-hold strategy of comparable risk. The model was admittedly simplistic, involving annual decisions and 100% shifts between stocks and short-term liquid investments. Moreover, I included transactions costs of 2% — high by today's standards but not unreasonable at a time of no traded index funds and fixed commissions for stock transactions (abolished on "May day" in 1975, shortly after this was published). In the paper I take risk into account using two alternative measures: (1) the geometric return and (2) the average return of a mix of stocks and cash equivalents with the same standard deviation of return. Figure 2 in the paper shows that under the assumed conditions, a manager must have a predictive accuracy of 75 to 85% to produce superior performance via such market timing. Subsequent papers with more complex strategies and smaller transactions costs showed that the hurdle might be lower, but the challenge for market timers remains.

3-3 "Corporate Pension Funding Policy," *Journal of Financial Economics*, June 1976, pp. 183–193.

The passage in 1974 of the Employee Retirement Income Security Act (ERISA) rightfully attracted the attention of actuaries, labor economists and financial economists. A series of high profile corporate bankruptcies and the associated failures of their employees to receive promised pensions led to this legislation, designed to eliminate or mitigate such tragic consequences. When fully implemented after a few years, the legislation would require corporate pension plans to be insured completely or in large part by a quasi-governmental agency, the PBGC. In return, corporations sponsoring such plans would be required to pay insurance premiums. A number of authors had explored the possible implications of the legislation for corporate financial decisions, in particular the amount to invest to back such liabilities and the risk to be taken with such funds.

This paper addresses these issues using the strong assumptions that markets are complete and that all participants can hedge or complement financial positions resulting from their involvement in a pension plan, employment in a sponsoring company or ownership of a company's shares. These assumptions, in turn, imply that all parties will assign the same values to the options implicit in pension promises and any insurance thereof. I also assumed that taxes do not matter and that workers or their unions will negotiate compensation packages (including wages and pension benefits) so that the total market value is unaffected by the distribution of value among the components. With these assumptions, it follows that pension funding policy does not matter.

The conclusion states that "Absent tax effects ... If [PBGC] premiums reflect the values that would be placed on such obligations by a private insurance company acting in the best interests of public shareholders corporate funding policy cannot matter ... [but] if premiums ... are not set in this manner, there will be optional corporate pension funding policies." Subsequent history shows that premiums have not been set in this manner. Moreover, officers of corporate pension plans continue to worry about risks specific to their organization that can be greatly reduced through diversification by their shareholders. In retrospect, this paper serves best to establish a special case with which to contrast a real world that is very different indeed.

3-4 "Major Investment Styles," *Journal of Portfolio Management*, Winter 1978, pp. 68–75.

This material was taken from the first edition of my textbook, *Investments*. Someone had suggested that it might be useful to make the ideas available to the wider audience of investment professionals who read the *Journal of Portfolio Management*. The paper provides a taxonomy, however imperfect, of approaches to investment management. Most of the discussion concerns asset allocation, although the section on the optimal use of bets focuses on security selection, drawing heavily on the 1973 paper by Jack Treynor and Fischer Black. Somewhat novel is the discussion of changing expectations of risk and return and the associated concept of a supply of risk-bearing function such as that shown in Figure 18–3. I end with words of caution about the possible consequences of overestimation of one's predictive ability and the possible need to temper the actions of predictors who possess less than adequate humility

3-5 "Decentralized Investment Management," *Journal of Finance*, May 1981, pp. 217–234.

This paper was prepared for my Presidential Address to the American Finance Association, presented at the annual meeting in Denver in December 1980 and subsequently published in the association's *Journal of Finance*. I chose to tackle a difficult and puzzling problem — the use of multiple investment managers by large pension, endowment and foundation funds. Clearly, the practice is inconsistent with a world in which all investors and managers agree on security risks and returns unless the managers held ether the market portfolio or value-weighted subsets thereof. In today's parlance, the sponsor of an overall fund of this type must believe that the managers of its components have superior information and can successfully predict security "alphas".

To even begin to deal with this subject analytically, I made the extreme assumption that the investor and all the managers agree on security covariances, differing only in their estimates of expected returns. I then showed that the first-best solution would involve the selection of a single portfolio using an optimal set of expected returns that incorporate the estimates made by all of the managers, taking into account their relative predictive abilities. I then argued that the economics of the industry preclude this, since individual managers wish to keep their estimates secret and charge different clients different prices based on the perceived values of such estimates. The remainder of the paper deals with the phenomenon, given these institutional realities.

To keep the equations simple I relied heavily on matrix notation, which makes it easy to derive a number of separation results. Conceptually, I found it useful to differentiate "diversification of style" from "diversification of judgement". The former involves managers who focus on different portions of the securities market, while the latter involves managers who choose from the same set of securities but hold different opinions about expected returns. I also treated cases involving factor models and generalized some of the results of Treynor and Black. Perhaps most relevant: in some settings the use of benchmarks and assessment of managers' performance relative to such benchmarks is seen to have merits but this is not universally likely to be the case. For good or bad reasons, it seemed to me that for active multi-managed portfolios the gap between financial theory and practice was rather substantial. And, in my opinion it remains so today.

3-6 "Optimal Funding and Asset Allocation Rules for Defined-Benefit Pension Plans," (with J. Michael Harrison), in *Financial Aspects of the United States Pension System*, Z. Bodie and J. B. Shoven, Editors, The University of Chicago Press (Chicago), 1983, pp. 91–105.

This paper was prepared for a 1982 conference sponsored by the National Bureau of Economic Research and its project on the Economics of the United States Pension System. It was coauthored with my Stanford colleague Michael Harrison, who provided many of the ideas as well as the general mathematical results and a formal elegance absent from most of my other work.

In the years that followed the passage of ERISA in 1974, many had analyzed the problems facing the sponsor of a defined-benefit pension plan. Of particular interest were the decisions concerning the amount to put in a fund designed to serve as collateral for the liabilities and the combination of assets in that fund. Unlike my 1976 paper on the subject, this work considers the effects of tax policies and incorrectly priced insurance policies. More specifically, we assumed (alas, realistically) that the PBGC premiums were not affected by a plan's default risk and that holding bonds in a pension fund would provide after-tax advantages relative to stocks. Prior papers had analyzed these aspects independently. One had shown that fixed insurance premiums favored minimum funding and all-stock portfolios. Another had shown that differential taxation favored maximum funding and all-bond portfolios. Many practitioners had assumed that if both aspects were taken into account, the optimum strategy would involve an interior solution with both bonds and stocks and with fund levels between the minimum and maximum amounts allowed by law.

Assuming an objective of maximizing shareholder value and utilizing a state-preference approach, we showed this is not the case. Instead, the optimal policy will be at one of the two extreme ends of the allowable range for each variable. The discrepancy with actual practice is hinted at in footnote 3 which indicates that we ruled out the more realistic assumption that corporate managers impose their own risk-averse utility functions when choosing these policies — a phenomenon consistent with my observations in subsequent years.

3-7 "Integrated Asset Allocation," *Financial Analysts Journal*, September/October 1987, pp. 25–32.

In 1986, my wife and I started a financial research and consulting company. In its first two years it was named Sharpe-Russell Research Inc., reflecting an arrangement in which the Frank Russell Company provided both funds and clients. For the next two years, it was named Sharpe-Tint, Inc. since Lawrence Tint was a partner at the time. In the final two years we changed the name to William F. Sharpe Associates since neither the Frank Russell Company nor Lawrence Tint were still involved and we wished to acknowledge the work of a small but excellent group of employees. This paper was written as a manifesto of what we hoped to accomplish in the firm at its outset. It provides a general framework for asset allocation (Figure A), then deals with the special cases represented by practices of the time. More specifically, it describes strategic asset allocation (Figure B), tactical asset allocation (Figure C) and insured asset allocation (Figure D). For illustrations it provides examples using two assets with simplifying assumptions about relative and absolute risk tolerance functions.

In the firm, my goal was to incorporate elements of all three types of current practice, providing what I termed "integrated asset allocation". While not completely successful, we made significant progress for at least some of our clients. As the paper suggests, we wished to take liabilities into account, focusing on the surplus of our defined benefit plans. Unusual at the time, this did not really come into vogue until much later when accounting standards for corporations began to change to require reporting of liabilities at least partially marked to market values. Unfortunately, accounting for governmental pensions has not moved in this direction so measures of surplus for such plans continue to fail to reflect the economic value of liabilities.

In the paper, I illustrated some of the concepts using two assets and assuming constancy in an investors' absolute or relative risk tolerance. I also discussed some of the work of Merton and Perold with respect to portfolio insurance.

After this paper was published, I was asked to prepare an expanded version for a chapter on Asset Allocation in the 1990 edition of Maginn and Tuttle's CFA Association book, "*Managing Investment Portfolios: A Dynamic Process*". I was fortunate to have this opportunity for it made the material available to a broader readership, including those studying for their CFA exams.

3-8 "Dynamic Strategies for Asset Allocation" (with Andre Perold), *Financial Analysts Journal*, January/February 1988, pp. 16–27.

After completing the paper on integrated asset allocation, I continued to work on issues associated with portfolio insurance and other dynamic asset allocation formulas. At some point, Andre' Perold and I discovered that we had papers in draft form that addressed many of the same issues but with some differences in analyses and presentation. After exchanging the papers and discussing the subject further, we agreed that it made sense to combine our efforts. Hence this paper.

Our goal was to provide a classification of the major types of dynamic strategies, show what they assumed about an investor's risk tolerance function, and indicate how they would likely perform in oscillating or trending markets. We did this with both simulations (my contribution) and formulas (Andre's). One of us had been utilizing payoff diagrams such as the one in Figure A, while the other had emphasized exposure diagrams such as the one in Figure B. We agreed that each portrayal helped elucidate the subject, and used both.

Our major conclusion was that different strategies result in linear, concave or convex payoff functions and that the choice of any such strategy should ultimately depend on the investor's risk-aversion function. We make the point that only buy-and-hold strategies can be followed by everyone and that if some investors adopt convex strategies, others must choose concave ones. We also emphasize the point that for markets to be in equilibrium, prices must adjust until the return distributions from concave and convex strategies attract equal amounts of capital. An important part of the paper analyzes constant-mix strategies, in which the exposure to any asset class is a constant proportion of wealth, showing that such strategies are dynamic, provide concave payoff functions and cannot be followed by everyone.

At the time this paper was prepared there was widespread interest among both academics and practitioners in portfolio insurance strategies. However, in October 1987 stock markets experienced dramatic falls in value, with the U.S. Dow-Jones Industrial Average falling 22.6% on October 19th ("Black Monday") alone. Due to the rapid changes taking place, many following dynamic portfolio insurance strategies were unable to make the trades called for by their formulas and failed to obtain the promised results. Moreover, many observers felt that the trades made by those with portfolio insurance strategies may have exacerbated the market declines. For good or bad reasons, portfolio insurance fell into disrepute and with it much of the interest in dynamic strategies (and this paper).

3-9 "Liabilities — A New Approach," (with Lawrence G. Tint), *The Journal of Portfolio Management*, Winter 1990, pp. 5–10.

This paper grew out of some of the analyses developed for defined-benefit pension clients of the consulting firm then called Sharpe-Tint, Inc. For one client we had devoted a great deal of effort to the task of estimating the economic value of liabilities on a monthly basis, using the workforce demographics and accumulated benefits discounted with treasury bond yields. Our goal was to take into account both the fund's assets and liabilities, concentrating on asset expected returns and the risk of the surplus (difference between asset and liability values). The client was not ready to go this far but was amenable to considering a measure that partially took economic liabilities into account. To generalize, the paper considers a function equal to assets minus a constant times the liability value. In today's parlance, setting this to 1 would consider liabilities in full and lead to a strategy termed "liability-driven investment". Setting it to zero would lead to a traditional "asset only" analysis. After considerable testing, the client in question accepted a coefficient of 0.2, giving 20% emphasis to liabilities.

The key insight in the paper is that liabilities can be taken into account by adding to the expected return of each asset a "liability hedging credit", then performing a standard asset-only optimization. The liability hedging credit for an asset will depend on the relative magnitudes of the values of liabilities and assets, the emphasis to be placed on liabilities, the client's risk tolerance, and the correlation between the asset's return and that of the liability. This leads to some results that are expected and some that may be surprising. For example, in the case summarized in the paper, growth stocks were more effective in hedging liability risk than were intermediate government bonds. The best asset for this purpose was of course long government bonds — the one usually recommended today by consultants for this purpose.

Despite efforts in the later 1980's by myself and several others of like mind to encourage sponsors of defined-benefit plans to take the economic values of liabilities into account when choosing asset allocations, there was little acceptance of the idea. But, thanks to recent accounting changes, liability hedging is now in vogue. I am not aware that anyone is using the liability hedging credit formulas in this paper, but continue to feel that such calculations could be useful, if only to better understand the solutions obtained from standard asset/liability optimizations.

3-10 "Expected Utility Asset Allocation," *Financial Analysts Journal*, Vol. 63, Number 5, September/October 2007, pp. 18–30.

In 2003 I was asked to give a series of lectures at Princeton University in the spring of 2004. I chose to discuss portfolio choice, asset pricing and investment advice. Rather than use the traditional mean/variance approaches, I chose a setting with discrete-state opportunities and more general investor preferences, showing that mean/variance paradigms represented special cases. I also developed a simulation program to exhibit convergence to equilibrium. After completing the lectures, I continued to work on the material and to create a simulator that did not rely on the proprietary computer language that I had used for the lectures. The result was my

2007 book *Investors and Markets, Portfolio Choices, Asset Prices and Investment Advice*, published by the Princeton University Press. My goal was to encourage those who teach finance to do so using a similar framework. This paper grew out of that project and was intended to make a comparable case to practitioners.

My concern was with the asset allocation studies performed episodically by many institutional investors. Almost all used mean/variance approaches either explicitly (typically, in the optimization phases) or implicitly (more often, when estimating asset class risks, correlations and expected returns). At the time I prepared the paper, the security market cataclysm of 2007–2009 had not yet begun but there was already increasing concern with non-normal return distributions and the possibility of substantial "left-tail events". My goal in the paper was to show that a discrete-state approach could easily handle such possibilities as well as more general attitudes towards return than those assumed in mean/variance approaches. I also wanted to show that the traditional approaches could be partly or wholly adapted in this framework. Going beyond the material in the book, I provided a simple gradient algorithm for choosing a maximum expected utility asset allocation with any set of discrete combinations of asset returns. My hope was (and is) that institutional investors would consider this more general approach rather than use *ad hoc* procedures in which optimization is more honored in the breach than in the observance.

3-11 "Adaptive Asset Allocation Policies," *Financial Analysts Journal*, Vol. 66, Number 3, May/June 2010, pages. 45–59.

This paper arose out of my frustration with the way in which most institutional investors and multi-asset mutual funds set and follow their asset allocation policies. Traditionally, almost all had a policy in which the amount invested in each major asset class was expressed as a percentage of total value. To implement such a policy requires contrarian behavior — selling relative winners and buying relative losers. In practice, many institutional investors avoided such behavior by more or less ignoring their policies and adopting new ones when divergences were too great. But multi-asset mutual funds tended to adhere more to their policies, buying and selling securities in ways that were only consistent with a belief in market inefficiency or designed for investors with unusual utility functions. As such mutual funds were being used more and more for individuals' retirement savings, it seemed important to argue that a better approach should be taken and to provide a simple formula for approximating the results of the more complete combination of reverse optimization and optimization that I had advocated in earlier papers.

The paper quotes extensively from the article that Andre' Perold and I had published in 1988, making the point that a traditional asset allocation policy is a constant-mix strategy and that to follow it one must engage in a contrarian dynamic strategy. Here I suggested that many organizations and funds consider instead an alternative approach.

The procedure is very simple and only requires that an investment organization specifies a "normal" or "base" combination of asset class values for which their stated asset allocation policy is designed. The original policy can then be "adapted" to the actual market values of asset classes at any time using a very simple formula (18). The paper concludes with a plea for index providers to make market value data more widely available and for institution investors and mutual funds to use this important information when making (or not making) adjustments to their portfolio holdings.

by W. F. Sharpe

Bonds versus Stocks
Some lessons from capital market theory

The apparent end of the bear market in bonds and relatively high interest rates have led some investors to conclude that bonds are now the superior investment medium. On the other hand, stocks continue to command a large following. Theoretically, neither should completely dominate the other: some combinations of bonds and stocks should prove superior to either taken alone. We shall first summarize the theoretical argument, and then examine some relevant data.

In the last decade increasing use has been made in both academic and investment institutions of the "capital asset pricing model" of Sharpe [6], Lintner [2] and Mossin [4], developed from the portfolio selection model of Markowitz [3]. The theory is described in detail in Sharpe [8] and more concisely in Vasicek and McQuown [9]. Only the major implications will be summarized here.

The approach is based on a *portfolio view*. The investor is assumed to be concerned only with the prospects for his overall portfolio. Securities are evaluated in this context.

A key aspect of the theory is the treatment of *risk*. Only the risk of the overall portfolio is considered important. As a corollary, the appropriate measure of an individual security's risk is its contribution to portfolio risk.

William F. Sharpe is Professor of Business, Stanford University, and Advisor, Computer Applications Department, Merrill Lynch, Pierce, Fenner and Smith, Inc. *Comments and suggestions of Paul Cootner, Alan Kraus, Robert Litzenberger and James Van Horne of Stanford University and Guy Cooper, Gilbert Hammer and Lawrence Tint of Merrill Lynch are gratefully acknowledged.*

When evaluating alternative portfolios, investors are assumed to prefer those with the greatest expected return for given risk. The appropriate amount of risk and return will, of course, depend on an investor's personal circumstances. But a high-risk portfolio will not be considered unless it offers a high expected return as well. The formal theory measures risk by the standard deviation of portfolio return,[1] but under plausible assumptions, this can be shown to be closely related to more familiar measures of risk.

These considerations lead to a view of the future such as that shown in Figure I. Each point in the shaded region represents a portfolio of risky securities. Were only these alternatives available, the investor would select one of those along the upper left-hand border, depending on his tastes, circumstances, etc. However, other possibilities exist. Point P represents the (riskless) interest rate. By splitting his funds between the combination of risky securities plotted at point M and a security giving this interest rate, prospects along line PM can be attained. By borrowing funds to purchase combination M on margin at this rate, prospects along the segment MN can be attained. The preferred strategy is to select combination M of risky securities, with riskless investment or personal leverage used as required to obtain the most desirable risk-return combination along line PMN.

Figure I plots *prospects*. Different investors will view prospects differently and thus arrive at different conclusions regarding the composition of portfolio M. Some will choose to hold a disproportionately large amount of a given security, while

1. Footnotes and references appear at end of article.

others hold a disproportionately small amount, or none at all. However, since every security will be held by someone, the "average" portfolio will contain each security in proportion to its total market value outstanding.

In an efficient market, prices always fully reflect available information. An extreme case arises when all investors have the same information and process it in the same way. Under these conditions, everyone will reach the same conclusion concerning the composition of portfolio M in Figure I. For the market to clear, prices must then adjust until portfolio M contains every security, each in proportion to its total market value.

This is, of course, a highly abstract view of reality. However, it suggests that in an efficient market, a highly diversified portfolio containing many types of securities, each in proportion to total value outstanding, may be expected to outperform other possible combinations.

It is important that the term "security" as used here not be considered a synonym for a "common stock." Such an interpretation is neither intended nor desired. The theory is designed to apply to all types of traded securities, and may prove relevant for analyzing certain types of non-marketable securities as well.

There are, of course, many types of securities. New York Stock Exchange listed stocks are important, but not all-important. Bonds clearly deserve consideration, but so also do stocks listed on other exchanges, over-the-counter stocks and private placements. An even broader view would include certain types of real estate, privately-held corporate stock, etc. For present purposes, we concentrate on "bonds" and "stocks" assuming they are the only available investment media. Extensions to include other assets must await further research.

Figure II provides an example of the prospects of various alternatives from the viewpoint of a typical well-informed investor. For convenience, the prospects have been stated in terms of *excess return:* the return over and above the riskless interest rate. Thus point P, with zero expected excess return and zero risk, plotting at the origin, represents a riskless investment.

Point B in Figure II represents investment entirely in bonds; Point S represents investment entirely in stocks. The figure is drawn to show the typical relationship between the two media—stocks provide both higher expected return and

Figure I

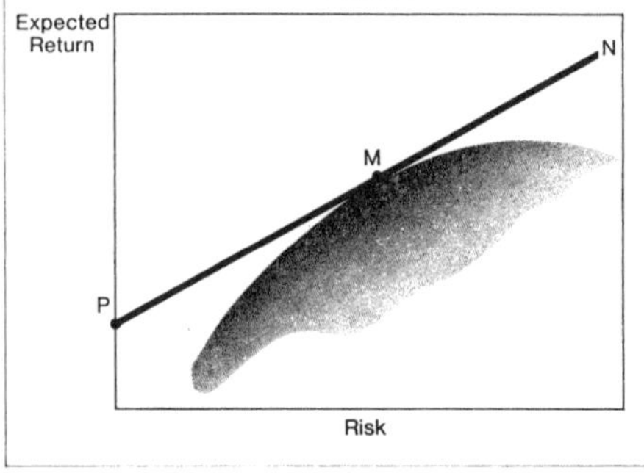

Figure II

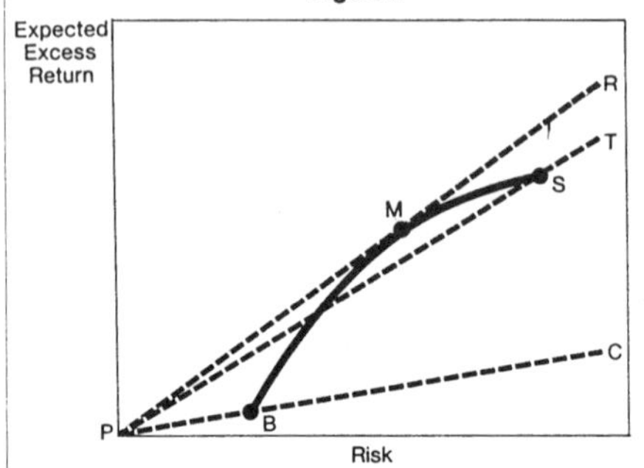

higher risk than do bonds. Each point on the curved line between points B and S represents the prospects of some combination of bonds and stocks. One of these, indicated by point M, includes the two investment media in proportion to their outstanding market values. It is the overall "market portfolio."

Implicit in the construction of a diagram such as that shown in Figure II is the specification of a *holding period.* Whatever the period selected, point P represents the total return on a security with absolutely certain prospects over the interval. When measuring the prospects for bonds or stocks, both cash received (e.g., interest payments on bonds and dividend payments on stocks) and the change in the owner's net worth resulting from changes in market value during the period must be considered. Hence, unless the holding period is very long, the typical corporate bond must be considered risky, since its total impact on the holder's net worth over the short term can rarely be predicted with certainty.

Expected Reward/Risk Ratios

Figure II illustrates the theoretical advantages of investment in bonds plus stocks. By combining riskless investment or personal leverage with the balanced portfolio M, prospects along line PMR can be obtained. By combining riskless investment or personal leverage with stocks alone, only prospects along line PST can be obtained. By combining riskless investment or personal leverage with bonds alone, only prospects along line PBC can be obtained. For any given level of risk, a strategy involving both bonds and stocks gives a higher expected return than one based exclusively on either bonds or stocks: line PMR lies above lines PST and PBC.

A convenient measure for such differences is the expected reward/risk ratio, which indicates the slope of a line from the origin through the point representing the prospects of an investment. The expected excess return is the expected reward. Dividing by risk gives the expected reward per unit of risk. The theory implies that in the consensus opinion, the greatest expected reward/risk ratio will be associated with a truly balanced portfolio — one in which investments are represented in proportion to their market values. Other portfolios will have lower ratios.

Theoretical versus Actual Results

Unhappily, actual results seem to differ from the consensus of well-informed opinion for surprisingly long periods of time. The long bear market in bonds in the post-World War II period is a prime example. Unanticipated inflation, coupled with governmental management of interest rates apparently led to serious differences between expected and actual returns on bonds. Such occurrences are, in the final analysis, merely manifestations of risk, hence in no way inconsistent with the overall theory. However, they raise serious difficulties for those attempting to test the theory against actual data. At best, actual values can be regarded as faint clues to underlying expectations (past, present or future). Nonetheless, a glimpse at the record seems worthwhile.

The Data

More or less arbitrarily, quarterly holding periods were chosen as a basis for the analysis that follows. Ninety-day prime bankers' acceptances were used for the riskless interest rates. For risky assets, changes in value plus interest or dividend payments were utilized to calculate total return for each quarter, then the return on a 90-day prime bankers' acceptance was subtracted to obtain the corresponding excess return. The average value of the quarterly excess returns was used as a surrogate for expected excess return, and the standard deviation of the quarterly excess returns as a surrogate for risk. The expected reward/risk ratio was measured by the ratio of average excess return to standard deviation of excess return — a measure often termed the *reward/variability ratio.*

The Dow-Jones Industrial Average was used to represent "stocks." Quarterly dividends for this index are available from 1938 to the present. For this reason, the period from 1938 through 1971 was selected for study. The postwar period, from 1946 through 1971, was also analyzed separately.

It is difficult to obtain a satisfactory index of total return on corporate bonds on a quarterly basis. Rather than use published indexes, or construct one, the total return on Keystone's B-2 bond fund was utilized. The fund has maintained a portfolio of about 40 "medium-grade" corporate bonds since the middle 1930's. Turnover is modest, and fund objectives seem to have been fairly constant throughout its existence: "the bonds . . . are selected and supervised with a two-fold long-term goal in view: (1) to produce relatively dependable income at as good a rate as may be prudently obtained; and (2) to maintain the relative stability of capital which is normally characteristic of good-grade bonds as a class."[2] Management fees and expenses averaged slightly more than one-half of one per cent of net asset value per year during the period studied. To adjust for this, the average value[3] (0.14125 per cent per quarter) was added back to fund returns. Load charges were not considered.

If Keystone management consistently selected superior or inferior bond positions, these results might overstate or understate the performance of naively or randomly selected bond portfolios. The evidence [1, 7] on mutual fund performance suggests that few if any funds are able to consistently outperform naive or random strategies. More serious, perhaps, is the possible divergence between the performance of medium-grade bonds and the overall performance of bonds, including the large number of high-grade issues. Additional problems may result from the use of the Dow-Jones Industrial Average to represent the overall performance of stocks, including the large number of lower-quality issues. For these and other reasons, the results that follow should be regarded as at best indicative of the performance of all bonds and stocks.

The proportion of the "market portfolio" invested in bonds each year was assumed to equal the ratio, at the end of the previous year, of: (1) the market value of non-U. S. Treasury bonds listed on the New York Stock Exchange to (2) the market value of all such bonds plus all stock listed on the New York Stock Exchange.[4] The proportion declined throughout most of the period: ranging between 35 and 40 per cent from 1938 to 1942 and between six and 10 per cent from 1960 to 1970.

Data were obtained from a number of sources.[5] Although some errors may remain, considerable effort was expended to obtain precise measures of the relevant quantities.

Results

Table I shows the performance of bonds and stocks. Both provided positive excess returns on average, but stocks outperformed bonds in this respect in both periods. For the overall period, bonds provided about 47 per cent as much excess return as stocks on average. During the postwar era alone, however, bonds produced only about 16 per cent of the average excess return of stocks.

The variability of bond returns was, as shown, smaller than that of stock returns in both periods: approximately 53 per cent overall and 42 per cent in the postwar era. As expected, bonds offered less reward *and* less risk.

The values of R^2 shown in Table I measure the extent to which excess returns on bonds and stocks moved together. A value of zero would indicate no correlation at all, while a value of 1.0 would indicate perfect correlation. Over the entire period, 46 per cent of the variation in bond returns was explained by the variation in stock returns; in the postwar period the figure was about 37 per cent. These values suggest that bond and stock returns are correlated, limiting but by no means eliminating the advantages to be obtained from holding both types of investment.

The final values shown in Table I provide another measure of the relationship between bonds and stocks. Over the entire period, bond excess returns had a "beta" of 0.356 relative to stock excess returns. In words: an excess return on stocks one per cent greater than average was typically accompanied by an excess return on bonds 0.356 per cent greater than average. For the postwar period, the beta was smaller (0.252), but still significantly greater than zero.[6]

Table II shows the average excess return and standard deviation of excess return for the "market portfolio" obtained by holding bonds and stocks each quarter in proportion to the market values outstanding at the close of the previous year. Not surprisingly, the values show that such a strategy provided more risk and return than bonds alone, and less risk and return than stocks alone.

Table III shows the results obtained when the excess returns on bonds and stocks were compared with the excess returns on the "market portfolio." The inclusion of bonds in the market portfolio accounts for the somewhat higher values of R^2 obtained when bond excess returns were compared with those of the market portfolio (Table III) in-

Table I. Performance: Bonds and Stocks

	Period	
Measure	1938-1971	1946-1971
Average quarterly excess return (% per quarter)		
(1) Bonds	1.069	.330
(2) Stocks	2.290	2.033
(3) Ratio: (1)/(2)	.467	.162
Standard deviation of quarterly excess returns (% per quarter)		
(4) Bonds	4.069	2.703
(5) Stocks	7.745	6.491
(6) Ratio: (4)/(5)	.525	.416
(7) R^2 of bond and stock excess returns	.46	.37
(8) Beta of bond excess returns on stock excess returns	.356	.252

Table II. Performance: "Market" Portfolio

	1938-1971	1946-1971
Average quarterly excess return (% per quarter)	2.132	1.788
Standard deviation of quarterly excess returns (% per quarter)	6.746	5.972

stead of the returns on stocks alone (Table I). The large proportion of the market portfolio invested in stocks accounts for the high values of R^2 obtained when stock excess returns were compared with those of the market portfolio. Table III also shows that when beta values are computed relative to the market portfolio, the appropriate values for bonds are substantially greater than zero while the appropriate values for stocks are greater than one.

Table III. Regression Results: Bonds and Stocks vs. the "Market" Portfolio

	1938-1971	1946-1971
R^2 of excess returns with excess returns on the market portfolio		
(1) Bonds	.52	.40
(2) Stocks	.98	.998
Beta of excess returns on market portfolio excess returns		
(1) Bonds	.436	.286
(2) Stocks	1.138	1.085

Table IV shows the reward-to-variability ratios for all three investment strategies. For the overall period, the results are consistent with expectations: the market portfolio provided more reward per unit of variability than investment in either bonds alone or stocks alone. In fact, the strategy in which bonds and stocks were held in proportion to the market values outstanding at the end of the previous year dominated any strategy employing a constant proportion of bonds and stocks throughout the overall period.

Table IV. Reward/Variability Ratios

Portfolio	1938-1971	1946-1971
Stocks	.2957	.3132
"Market" Portfolio	.3160	.2994
Bonds	.2627	.1221

In the postwar period alone, the results did not conform to expectations. An all-stock portfolio provided more reward per unit of variability than the market portfolio. Moreover, an all-stock portfolio dominated any strategy employing a constant proportion of bonds and stocks. This is not surprising in view of the low average excess return on bonds from 1946 through 1971. It seems unlikely that investors expected such results.

Figure III

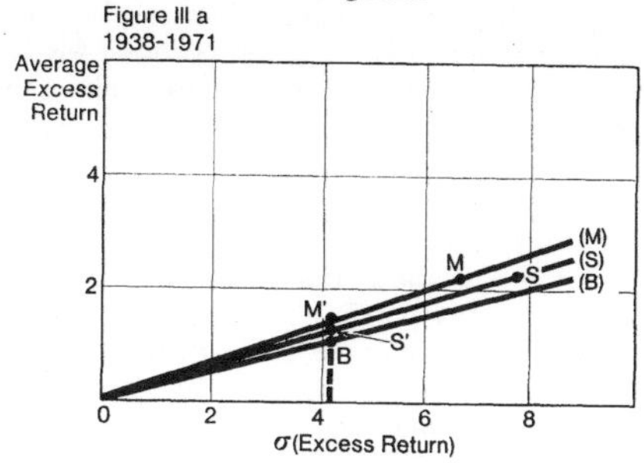

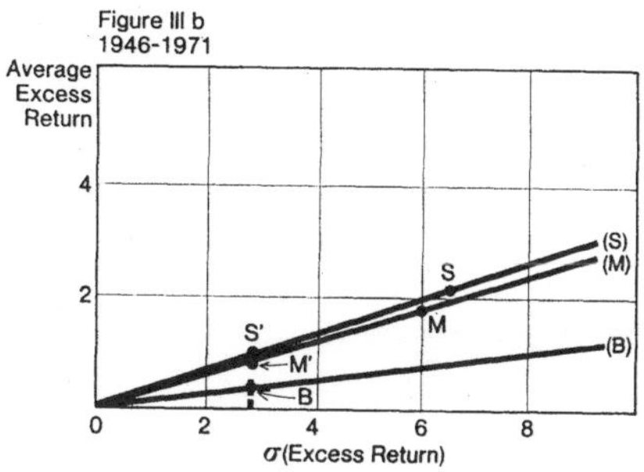

During the postwar period the average excess return on bonds was 0.330 per cent per quarter. Had the return each quarter been 0.7 per cent higher, the results for this period would have conformed to expectations: the reward/variability ratio of the market would have exceeded that of an all-stock portfolio.[7] This difference is small enough to be attributed to errors in expectations. In fact, there is even a small chance that such a difference could have arisen even if expectations had been unbiased.[8]

Figures III a and b plot the results for the three alternatives. Point B represents an all-bond portfolio, point S an all-stock portfolio and point M the "market" portfolio. The line drawn from the origin through a point indicates combinations of average excess return and standard deviation of excess return attainable by combining the portfolio with riskless investment or by using personal leverage to buy additional amounts of the portfolio. The slope of each line is, of course, the reward/variability ratio of the corresponding portfolio.

The lines in Figures III a and b can be used to determine the average excess return that could have been attained with a given portfolio for any specified level of variability. For example, point S′ indicates the average excess return associated with a strategy employing stocks and riskless investment in the proportion that gave overall returns with the same standard deviation of excess return as that of an all-bond portfolio. Point M′ represents a corresponding strategy employing the market portfolio and riskless investment. The actual values are shown in Table V. Riskless investment with bonds and stocks in market proportions (point M′) clearly dominated all-bond investment in both periods. For equal risk, a market based strategy provided 0.217 (1.286-1.069) per cent per quarter greater average excess return over the 1938-1971 period. While less than one per cent per year, the difference is by no means insignificant. The difference is even more striking in the postwar period: 0.479 per cent per quarter (.809 - .330); or almost two per cent per year.

Table V. Average Excess Returns (% Per Quarter) for Strategies With Variability Equal to That of an All-Bond Portfolio

	1938-1971	1946-1971
Bonds (point B)	1.069	.330
Riskless investment plus stocks (point S′)	1.203	.847
Riskless investment plus the "market" portfolio (point M′)	1.286	.809

Conclusions

The capital asset pricing model suggests that the mix with the best prospects for the future, considering both expected return and risk, will include bonds and stocks in proportion to outstanding market values. Our results for the 1938-1971, period are consistent with this assertion, while those obtained for the postwar period alone suggest either that the approach is in error or that there was a substantial divergence between expectations and actual performance. All things considered, it seems more appropriate to attribute the somewhat negative results in the postwar period to unanticipated events than to reject the theory. Overall, the record is reasonably consistent with the approach.

One should hardly conclude that every investor should hold a market-value balanced portfolio. Cash requirements, tax situations, legal and institutional restrictions, investment horizons and predictions differ, hence appropriate investment strategies also differ. But divergences from the standard mix of bonds and stocks should be justifiable in terms of these differences. The appropriate question is not "Why bonds?" or "Why stocks?". It is, rather, "Why not bonds *and* stocks, in proportion to market values?" ♦

Footnotes

1. The standard deviation is a measure of the likely dispersion around the expected value. If the distribution follows a normal (bell-shaped) curve, the chances are about two out of three that the actual value will lie within one standard deviation of the expected value.
2. Keystone B-2 Fund annual report for the fiscal year ended October 31, 1960, p. 2.
3. Based on the values given in Moody's manuals for 1940, 1950, 1960 and 1970.
4. The market value of all NYSE-listed stocks at year-end closing prices is given in the Exchange's Fact Books. The market value of listed non-U. S. Treasury bonds was estimated. First, the par value of U. S. Treasury bonds was subtracted from the par value of all bonds listed on the Exchange. This difference was then multiplied by the ratio of the market value of all NYSE-listed bonds to the par value of all NYSE-listed bonds to obtain an estimate of the market value of non-U. S. Treasury bonds listed on the Exchange. Market and par values for all listed bonds are given in the Exchange's Fact Books. Par values of U. S. Treasury bonds are given in the Federal Reserve Bulletin.
5. The Bank and Quotation Record, Barron's, the Commercial and Financial Chronicle, Dow-Jones' Investors Handbook, the Federal Reserve Bulletin, Moody's manuals, Moody's and Standard and Poor's Dividend Records, the New York Stock Exchange Fact Book, and the Statistical Abstract of the United States.
6. In each case the t-value was between 7.0 and 8.0.
7. When 0.7 per cent per quarter was added to each bond excess return, the reward/variability ratio for the market portfolio in the postwar period increased to 0.3133.
8. The standard deviation of quarterly bond excess returns during the period was 2.704, as shown in Table I. Assuming a process with this risk, and independent draws each quarter, the standard

deviation of a 104-quarter average would be approximately 0.265. Given this standard deviation, the probability that an actual value might differ from the expected value by 0.7 or more is approximately 0.01, assuming a normal distribution.

References

1. Jensen, Michael C., "The Performance of Mutual Funds in the Period 1945-1964," *Journal of Finance*, May 1968.
2. Lintner, John, "The Valuation of Risk Assets and the Selection of Risky Investments in Stock Portfolios and Capital Budgets," *Review of Economics and Statistics*, February 1965.
3. Markowitz, Harry, *Portfolio Selection: Efficient Diversification of Investments*, (New York: John Wiley and Sons, Inc.) 1959.
4. Mossin, Jan, "Equilibrium in a Capital Asset Market," *Econometrica*, October 1966.
5. Securities and Exchange Commission, *Institutional Investor Study Report*, Supplementary Volume I.
6. Sharpe, William F., "Capital Asset Prices: A Theory of Market Equilibrium Under Conditions of Risk," *Journal of Finance*, September 1964.
7. ———, "Mutual Fund Performance," *Journal of Business*, January 1966.
8. ———, *Portfolio Theory and Capital Markets*, (New York: McGraw-Hill) 1970.
9. Vasicek, Oldrich and McQuown, John A., "The Efficient Market Model," *Financial Analyst Journal*, September-October 1972.

Likely Gains from Market Timing

by William F. Sharpe

Reprinted from Financial Analysts Journal, March/April 1975—

by William F. Sharpe

Likely Gains from Market Timing

The investment manager who hopes to outperform his competitors usually expects to do so either by the selection of securities within a given class or by the allocation of assets to specific classes of securities. Potentially, one of the most productive forms of the latter strategy is to hold common stocks during bull markets and cash equivalents during bear markets ("market timing").

In a perfectly efficient market, any attempt to obtain performance superior to that of the overall "market portfolio" (taking into account both risk and return) by picking and choosing among securities would fail. Although few investment managers are ready to admit that U.S. security markets are completely efficient, there is a growing awareness that inefficiencies are few: Any divergence between the price of a security and the "intrinsic value" that would be assigned to it by well informed and highly skilled analysts is likely to be small, temporary and difficult to identify in advance. Empirical studies of the performance of professionally managed portfolios yield results consistent with this view: Few, if any, provide better-than-average return relative to risk year in and year out.

William F. Sharpe is Timken Professor of Finance, Stanford University and Advisor, Computer Applications Department, Merrill Lynch, Pierce, Fenner and Smith, Inc. *This paper resulted from discussions with R. Eliot King, of R. Eliot King, Associates. Lawrence Tint of Merrill Lynch, Pierce, Fenner and Smith, Inc., and Professor John McDonald of Stanford University provided a number of suggestions, including the model of unbiased predictions in the appendix. William Fouse, of the Wells Fargo Bank, provided valuable comments on an earlier version.*

Some have argued that abnormal gains from selection of individual stocks or even industry groups are likely to be too small to justify the costs associated with attempts to identify and take advantage of apparent inefficiencies. Instead, it is said, the big gains are to be made by successful market timing. This approach is sufficiently popular to be recognized as one of several major "management styles." When portfolio values shrink in extended bear markets, investors increasingly regard this style as a likely cure for their ills. Thus managers committed to timing strategies with the skill or luck to have moved to cash equivalents in the bear market of 1973-1974 were able to attract money in the latter part of 1974, while their competitors suffered both decreases in the market value of assets and often actual loss of accounts. Market efficiency implies that it should be at least as difficult to predict market turns as to identify specific securities that will perform abnormally well or poorly. Moreover, attempts to take advantage of such predictions entail non-recoverable transaction costs, and expose investment funds to larger losses when errors are made. On the average, stocks outperform short-term money market instruments. Without superior predictive ability, one is likely to forego return by shifting from stocks to cash equivalents. But this is to state the obvious. How superior must one's predictions be to implement a market timing style effectively?

This article explores the potential gains from market timing and shows how they relate to the manager's ability to make correct predictions. Counter to widely held beliefs, the results suggest that the gains are likely to be modest at best, and that only a manager with truly superior predictive ability should even attempt to time the market.

The Assumption of Annual Reviews

The aggressive investment manager would like to call every market turn. Whenever he foresees a change large enough to cover transaction costs, he can move all assets under management into stocks (in the case of a predicted rise in the market) or out of stocks and into, say, Treasury bills (in the case of a predicted fall in the market). An even more dramatic way to time the market is to implement bullish predictions by purchasing securities highly sensitive to market swings (i.e. with large beta values) or buying securities on margin, and to implement bearish predictions by selling such securities short.

The problem, of course, is that the top or bottom of a cycle is only obvious after the fact (and sometimes long after the fact). Moreover, different analysts will identify different points as "major" peaks and troughs of the market, even in retrospect.

To provide a rough assessment of the likely gains from virtually clairvoyant market timing, we begin this article by comparing two strategies. The first involves simply buying and holding the average; the second, buying at the low for a year, selling at the next annual high, buying at the next annual low, etc. It considers only capital gains and losses, under the simplifying assumption that dividends from fully invested positions and interest from cash-equivalent positions would be roughly equal and spent as received. For the three periods analyzed, each beginning at an annual low and ending at an annual high, the results (expressed in terms of equivalent constant annual rates of growth of capital) were as follows:

		Equivalent Annual Rate of Capital Growth	
From	To	Buy-and-hold Strategy	Timing Strategy
1929	1972	3.8%/year	19.9%/year
1934	1972	6.6	17.3
1946	1972	7.1	15.7

Of course no one could do this successfully over an extended period of time. To move from the realm of fantasy to that of at least potential reality, the remainder of the article considers only strategies involving scheduled annual reviews. The manager is assumed to assess the outlook for the market at the beginning of each year, then place the assets under management in either stocks of average risk or short-term money market instruments for the remainder of the year. The first alternative is represented by Standard and Poor's Composite Index, the second by prime bankers' acceptances (up to 1942) or U.S. Treasury bills (after 1942).[1]

To reflect the cost of shifting funds, transaction costs equal to two per cent of the value of the assets under management are assessed every time there is a shift from stocks to cash equivalents or vice versa. Readers who prefer a different assumption will find it a relatively simple matter to adjust our results. While better performance might be obtained by reviewing a portfolio more than once each year, increased transactions costs would reduce potential gains.

"Good" versus "Bad" Market Years

Consistent with the strategy considered, each year can be categorized as either a good or a bad (stock) market year. In a good year, the total return, including dividends, on stocks exceeds that on cash equivalents. In a bad year the reverse holds. In terms of bad and good years, successful investment timing can be defined as holding stocks in good market years and cash equivalents in bad market years.[2]

Table 1 shows the annual total returns for cash equivalents (prime bankers' acceptances or Treasury bills) and stocks (Standard and Poor's Composite Index) from 1929 through 1972. The third column indicates whether the market was good or bad in the year in question.

Gains from Perfect Timing

Table 2 summarizes the results for three investment strategies over three different periods. Table 1 provides us with the data from which to construct a third strategy—buying and holding cash equivalents. Not surprisingly, this strategy, investing solely in cash equivalents, provided the lowest average return and the lowest variability of return. The second strategy involves investment solely in stocks (i.e., a buy-and-hold stock policy), which produced higher returns on the average, but at the cost of greater variability. The third strategy involves market timing, but with perfect predictive ability. In each year, funds were placed with the higher return investment medium for that year. For good market years, the return utilized in the calculations was the return on Standard and Poor's Composite Index. For bad market years, the return on cash equivalents was used. In each year for which a switch was made, transaction costs were deducted from the return.[3]

Three measures of performance are shown in

1. Footnotes appear at end of article.

TABLE 1. Annual Total Returns: Cash Equivalents and Stocks, 1929 to 1972

Year	Return on Cash Equivalents	Return on Stocks	Type of Year	Year	Return on Cash Equivalents	Return on Stocks	Type of Year
1929	5.03%	-7.93%	Bad	1951	1.76%	23.37%	Good
1930	2.48	-23.92	Bad	1952	1.84	17.71	Good
1931	1.57	-41.72	Bad	1953	2.11	-1.17	Bad
1932	1.28	-8.99	Bad	1954	0.93	51.23	Good
1933	0.63	52.98	Good	1955	1.93	30.96	Good
1934	0.25	-1.49	Bad	1956	2.91	6.44	Good
1935	0.13	46.32	Good	1957	3.66	-10.48	Bad
1936	0.16	33.28	Good	1958	2.13	42.44	Good
1937	0.43	-33.93	Bad	1959	4.29	11.79	Good
1938	0.44	30.05	Good	1960	3.53	0.28	Bad
1939	0.44	-0.76	Bad	1961	2.89	26.60	Good
1940	0.44	-9.93	Bad	1962	3.10	-8.83	Bad
1941	0.44	-11.15	Bad	1963	3.41	22.50	Good
1942	0.44	19.22	Good	1964	3.89	16.30	Good
1943	0.76	25.69	Good	1965	4.23	12.27	Good
1944	0.80	19.28	Good	1966	5.34	-9.99	Bad
1945	0.82	35.69	Good	1967	4.94	23.73	Good
1946	0.83	-7.78	Bad	1968	5.78	10.84	Good
1947	0.89	5.49	Good	1969	7.28	-8.32	Bad
1948	1.15	5.42	Good	1970	6.94	3.51	Bad
1949	1.15	17.76	Good	1971	4.98	14.12	Good
1950	1.28	30.55	Good	1972	5.01	18.72	Good

Table 2. The first is simply the arithmetic average of the annual rates of return. The second, the standard deviation of return, measures the extent of the deviations of return around this average. The third is the geometric mean of the annual returns, i.e. the constant rate of return that would have produced the same value at the end of the period as the actual returns, assuming no withdrawals during the entire period.

TABLE 2. Overall Performance: Cash Equivalents, Stocks, and a Policy with Perfect Timing

	Cash Equivalents	Stocks	Perfect Timing
1929 to 1972			
Average Return	2.38%	10.64%	14.86%
Standard Deviation of Annual Returns	1.96	21.06	14.58
Geometric Mean Return	2.36	8.49	13.99
1934 to 1972			
Average Return	2.40%	12.76%	15.25%
Standard Deviation of Annual Returns	2.00	18.17	13.75
Geometric Mean Return	2.38	11.23	14.46
1946 to 1972			
Average Return	3.27%	12.79%	14.63%
Standard Deviation of Annual Returns	1.83	15.64	12.46
Geometric Mean Return	3.25	11.73	13.99

Obviously, perfect prediction of the four bad years from 1929 through 1932 and the extremely good year in 1933 would have paid handsomely. From 1929 through 1932, investment in stocks resulted in a loss of 62.85 per cent of the initial value, while investment in cash equivalents resulted in a gain of 10.72 per cent. On the other hand, stocks returned almost 53 per cent in 1933, while cash equivalents paid less than one per cent. These five years account for much of the superiority of the perfect prediction strategy relative to stocks over the period 1929 to 1972. As Table 2 shows, the differences between the buy-and-hold strategy and the perfect prediction strategy are considerably smaller from 1934 to 1972 and in the postwar period.

A policy involving accurate market timing has two advantages: It brings returns that are both higher on average and subject to less variability. As shown in Table 2, perfect timing gave an average annual return of 14.86 per cent per year from 1929 through 1972, while buying and holding stocks returned only 10.64 per cent—a difference of 4.22 per cent per year. The former policy brought less variable returns as well: The standard deviation of annual returns was 14.58 per cent per year, instead of 21.06 per cent.

To express the superiority of the perfect prediction strategy in a single number is, of course, a difficult task. Two measures will be provided here, and used in the subsequent analysis of less-than-perfect predictions. The first is the geometric mean return, which is generally smaller than the arithmetic average, with the disparity larger, the greater the variability of the annual returns. As shown in Table 2, for the 1929 to 1972 period, the geometric mean returns for the two strategies differ by 5.50 per cent per year (13.99 - 8.49).

The second measure compares arithmetic average returns, but with variability held roughly constant.[4] The results from the market timing strategy are compared with those of a policy in which a mixture of stocks and cash equivalents is held, with the particular mixture chosen to have the same standard deviation of annual returns as the timing strategy. Over the 1929 to 1972 period, such a strategy provided an average annual return of 8.10 per cent, or 6.76 per cent less than that provided by perfect timing.

The advantages of perfect timing are summarized in Table 3, using these two measures, for each of the three periods.

Barring truly devastating market declines similar to those of The Depression, it seems likely that gains of little more than four per cent per year from timing should be expected from a manager whose forecasts are truly prophetic. More human managers should expect even less satisfying results, with the actual gains depending, of course, on actual predictive abilities.

TABLE 3

Measure of Return	Alternative Used for Comparison	Period 1929-72	1934-72	1946-72
Geometric Mean Return	Buying and holding stocks	5.50	3.23	2.26
Annual Average Return	A mixture of stocks and cash equivalents with equal standard deviation of annual returns	6.76	5.01	3.78

Gains from Less-Than-Perfect Timing

To assess the likely performance of funds whose managers attempt to time the market and sometimes fail, we will use an extremely simple characterization of an admittedly complex process. Hopefully, it captures enough of the essence of the situation to provide useful insights. A different characterization giving similar results is described in the appendix.

At the beginning of each year the manager is assumed to predict either a good or a bad market year, then either leave his funds alone or move them to the alternative investment medium, depending on his prediction. As in the previous analysis, funds are assumed to be invested either in stocks or cash equivalents, with transaction costs of two per cent incurred whenever a change is made.

FIGURE 1. The Assumed Predictive Process

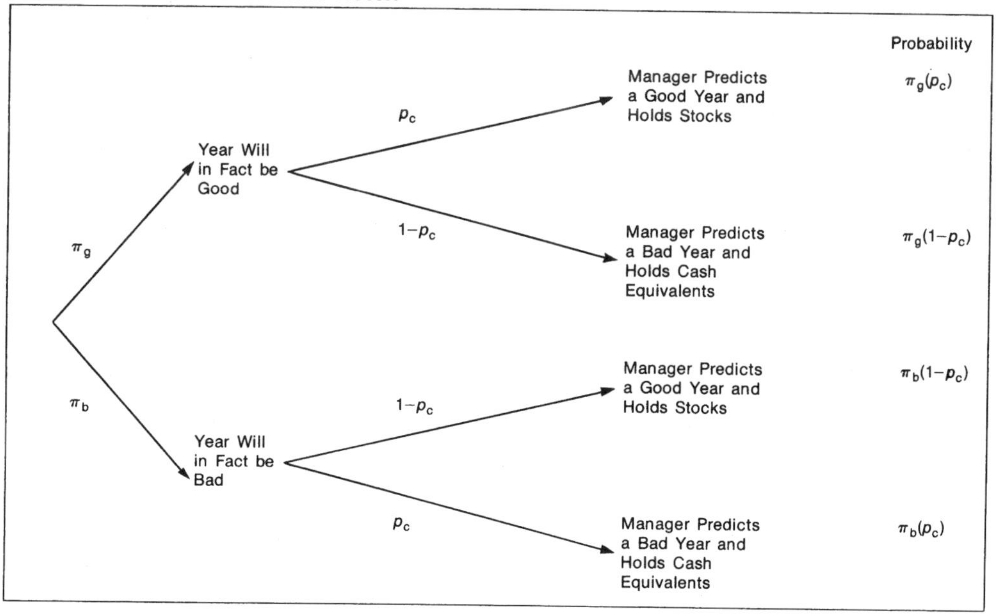

Figure 1 shows the essential difference between this and the previous analysis. The manager is assumed to be right only some of the time. Specifically, the proportion of correct predictions is represented by ρ_c. Thus the probability that he will predict a good year when in fact a good year is coming is ρ_c, while the probability is $(1-\rho_c)$ that he will predict a bad year when a good year is actually in store. His predictive ability when a bad year is in prospect is assumed to be of comparable accuracy, as shown. The actual probabilities of good and bad years are π_g and π_b, respectively, giving the overall probabilities for each of the four situations shown on the right of Figure 1.

We have already analyzed the special case in which $\rho_c=1$ (perfect prediction), using actual data. We now turn to an examination of the likely results obtained when ρ_c is less than 1.

To do this, assumptions must be made about the likelihood of good and bad years and the results associated with each possible combination. Table 4 presents historical values of the required variables. The proportion of good market years varied between 0.60 and 0.70. Returns on cash equivalents averaged slightly higher and varied slightly more in bad market years than in good, but these differences are relatively unimportant. Far more significant are the major differences between the returns on stocks in good and bad market years. Good years have been somewhat less good (smaller average returns on stocks, with roughly the same standard deviation) and bad market years have been somewhat less bad (smaller average losses on stocks, and smaller standard deviations) in recent periods. The overall expected return for any given degree of predictive accuracy is simply a weighted average of the expected values for the four outcomes, with the probabilities of the outcomes used as weights:

$$\mu \text{ (the overall expected return)} = \sum_i p_i\mu_i$$

where

p_i = the probability of outcome i, and

μ_i = the expected return for outcome i.

TABLE 4. Performance During Good and Bad Years

Measure	Period 1929-72	1934-72	1946-72
Proportion of Good Years	0.61	0.67	0.70
Return on Cash Equivalents in Good Years			
Mean	2.21%	2.27%	2.92%
Standard Deviation	1.72	1.72	1.57
Return on Cash Equivalents in Bad Years			
Mean	2.66%	2.68%	4.10%
Standard Deviation	2.26	2.45	2.12
Return on Stocks in Good Years			
Mean	24.10%	22.99%	20.43%
Standard Deviation	12.98	11.90	11.83
Return on Stocks in Bad Years			
Mean	−10.74%	− 7.70%	− 5.35%
Standard Deviation	11.64	8.94	5.03

Future values of these variables may differ substantially from those obtained in any one of these three historic periods. As shown in Table 3, the 1929 to 1972 period was the most favorable for a timing strategy, and the 1946 to 1972 period the least favorable.

Those observers who feel that recent events portend a future like the early years of The Great Depression are probably excessively pessimistic. On the other hand, the two decades following World War II may have been exceptionally favorable for holders of stocks. To get a balanced view of how a timing strategy might perform in the future, we have chosen the middle road, utilizing the values from the period 1934 to 1972. Readers who consider this choice unsatisfactory can easily substitute other values in our formulas.

Table 5 shows results based on the period 1934 to 1972. Each row corresponds to a different degree of predictive accuracy. The first shows the likely results for a manager who is right only half the time (ρ_c=0.50), and the last the likely outcomes for one who is right all the time (ρ_c=1).

The standard deviation of the overall return is slightly more difficult to calculate. The general formula is:[5]

$$\sigma^2 = \sum_i p_i\sigma_i^2 + \sum_i p_i(\mu_i-\mu)^2$$

where, in addition to symbols previously defined:

σ = the overall standard deviation, and

σ_i = the standard deviation of return for outcome i.

The resulting values are shown in column 3 of Table 5.

Thus far transaction costs have not been taken into account in the calculations. Although the overall standard deviation will also be affected, their major effect is to lower the overall expected return. For simplicity the latter effect will be ignored. However, the former can easily be handled. The respective probabilities that funds will be in

TABLE 5. Likely Results with Less-Than-Perfect Predictions

(1) p_c	(2) Expected Return	(3) Standard Deviation of Return	(4) Net Expected Return	(5) Geometric Mean Return	(6) Advantage: Geometric Mean Return vs Buying & Holding Stocks	(7) Advantage: Expected Return vs a Mixture of Stocks and Cash Equivalents of Equal Standard Deviation of Return
0.50	7.63%	13.93%	6.63%	5.72%	-5.68%	-3.79%
0.51	7.81	13.98	6.81	5.89	-5.51	-3.65
0.52	7.98	14.03	6.98	6.06	-5.34	-3.51
0.53	8.15	14.07	7.15	6.23	-5.17	-3.46
0.54	8.33	14.11	7.33	6.40	-5.00	-3.21
0.55	8.50	14.15	7.50	6.57	-4.83	-3.06
0.56	8.67	14.19	7.67	6.74	-4.66	-2.91
0.57	8.85	14.22	7.85	6.91	-4.49	-2.75
0.58	9.02	14.25	8.02	7.08	-4.32	-2.59
0.59	9.19	14.28	8.20	7.25	-4.15	-2.44
0.60	9.36	14.31	8.37	7.42	-3.98	-2.28
0.61	9.54	14.34	8.54	7.60	-3.81	-2.12
0.62	9.71	14.36	8.72	7.77	-3.63	-1.96
0.63	9.88	14.39	8.89	7.94	-3.46	-1.80
0.64	10.06	14.40	9.07	8.11	-3.29	-1.63
0.65	10.23	14.42	9.24	8.29	-3.11	-1.47
0.66	10.40	14.44	9.41	8.46	-2.94	-1.31
0.67	10.58	14.45	9.59	8.64	-2.77	-1.14
0.68	10.75	14.46	9.76	8.81	-2.59	-0.97
0.69	10.92	14.47	9.94	8.99	-2.42	-0.80
0.70	11.10	14.48	10.11	9.16	-2.24	-0.63
0.71	11.27	14.48	10.29	9.34	-2.06	-0.46
0.72	11.44	14.49	10.46	9.51	-1.89	-0.29
0.73	11.61	14.49	10.64	9.69	-1.71	-0.11
0.74	11.79	14.49	10.81	9.87	-1.54	0.06
0.75	11.96	14.48	10.99	10.04	-1.36	0.24
0.76	12.13	14.48	11.17	10.22	-1.18	0.42
0.77	12.31	14.47	11.34	10.40	-1.00	0.60
0.78	12.48	14.46	11.52	10.58	-0.82	0.78
0.79	12.65	14.45	11.69	10.76	-0.65	0.96
0.80	12.83	14.44	11.87	10.94	-0.47	1.14
0.81	13.00	14.42	12.04	11.12	-0.29	1.33
0.82	13.17	14.40	12.22	11.30	-0.11	1.52
0.83	13.35	14.38	12.40	11.48	0.07	1.71
0.84	13.52	14.36	12.57	11.66	0.25	1.89
0.85	13.69	14.34	12.75	11.84	0.43	2.08
0.86	13.86	14.31	12.92	12.02	0.61	2.28
0.87	14.04	14.28	13.10	12.20	0.80	2.47
0.88	14.21	14.25	13.28	12.38	0.98	2.66
0.89	14.38	14.22	13.45	12.56	1.16	2.86
0.90	14.56	14.19	13.63	12.75	1.34	3.05
0.91	14.73	14.15	13.81	12.93	1.53	3.25
0.92	14.90	14.11	13.98	13.11	1.71	3.45
0.93	15.08	14.07	14.16	13.29	1.89	3.65
0.94	15.25	14.02	14.34	13.48	2.08	3.86
0.95	15.42	13.98	14.52	13.66	2.26	4.06
0.96	15.60	13.93	14.69	13.85	2.44	4.26
0.97	15.77	13.88	14.87	14.03	2.63	4.47
0.98	15.94	13.83	15.05	14.22	2.81	4.68
0.99	16.11	13.77	15.23	14.40	3.00	4.89
1.00	16.29	13.71	15.40	14.59	3.19	5.10

cash equivalents or stocks in each of two consecutive years can be computed. The probability of a switch in any given year will equal (1) the probability that stocks will be held in year t and cash equivalents in year t+1, plus (2) the probability that cash equivalents will be held in year t and stocks in year t+1. Assuming that outcomes in successive years are uncorrelated, this probability can

FIGURE 2. Annual Return Advantage from Market Timing

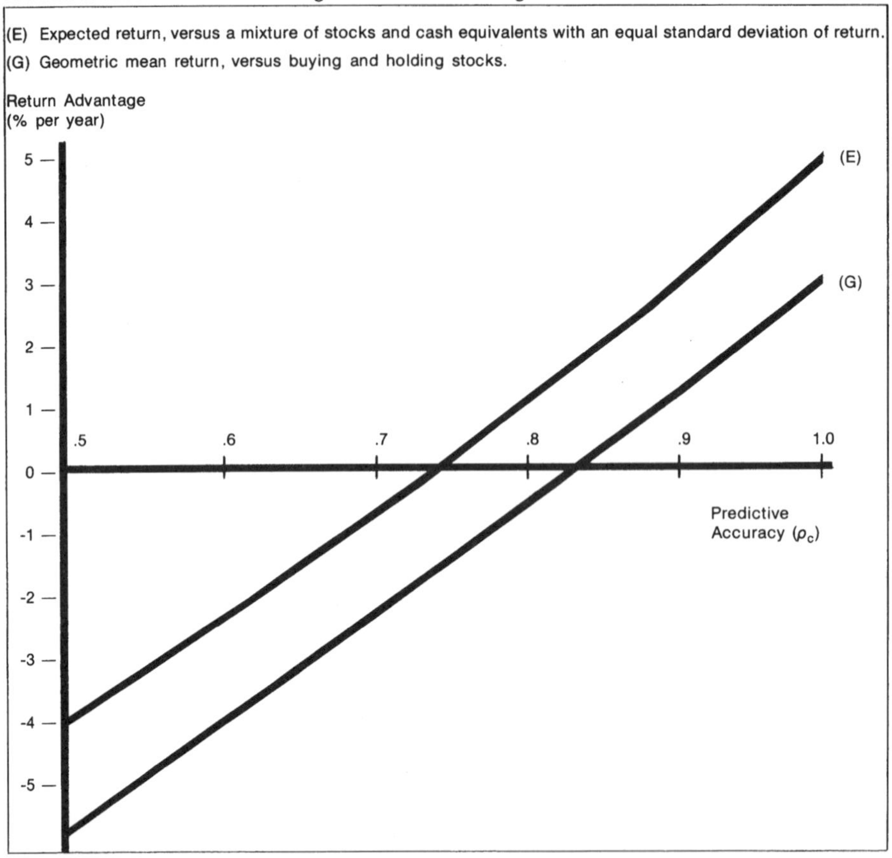

be determined directly. Expected transaction costs can then be computed by simply multiplying the assumed cost by the probability that it will be incurred in any given year. Column 4 of Table 5 shows the overall expected return after this amount has been subtracted. The result, the net expected return, is the predicted value of the average annual return. The correspondence can be seen by comparing the value in the final row of Table 5 (15.40) with the actual result for the 1934 to 1972 period (15.25) shown in Table 2.

The fifth column in Table 5 shows the estimated long-run return for each level of predictive ability. This is the predicted value of the geometric mean return after many years have passed.[6] Again, the correspondence can be seen by comparing the value in the final row of Table 5 (14.59) with the actual result for the 1934 to 1972 period (14.46) shown in Table 2.

Comparable values for a policy of buying and holding stocks can be estimated using the same formulas, with the probabilities adjusted appropriately. For the values assumed in Table 5, the resulting geometric mean return is 11.40 per cent per year. The sixth column in the table shows the difference between the geometric mean return for the market timing strategy and that likely to be obtained by simply buying and holding stocks.

The final column in Table 5 shows the difference between the expected net return for the market timing strategy and the expected return from a mixture of stocks and cash equivalents with a comparable standard deviation of return.

The values in columns 6 and 7 of Table 5 are plotted in Figure 2. They suggest that a manager who attempts to time the market must be right roughly three times out of four, merely to match the overall performance of those competitors who don't. If he is right less often, his relative performance will be inferior. There are two reasons for this. First, such a manager will often have his funds in cash equivalents in good market years, sacrificing the higher returns stocks provide in such years. Second, he will incur transaction costs in making switches, many of which will prove to be unprofitable.

Conclusion

The conclusion is fairly clear. Attempts to time the market are not likely to produce incremental returns of more than four per cent per year over the long run. Moreover, unless a manager can predict whether the market will be good or bad each year with considerable accuracy (e.g., be right at least seven times out of ten), he should probably avoid attempts to time the market altogether.

This pessimistic view will not appeal to those who feel that they can avoid the next bear market by judicious shifts of funds out of stocks and into short-term low-risk instruments. Some are now doing this, and others are actively considering it. Overall, of course, funds cannot be "shifted" beyond any changes in the market values of the relevant securities outstanding. But individual investors can and do make such shifts.

It is said that the military is usually well prepared to fight the previous war. A number of investors now engaging in active market timing appear to be preparing for the previous market. Unfortunately for the military, the next war may differ from the last one. And unfortunately for investors, the next market may also differ from the last one. ■

APPENDIX

A manager who keeps assets in stocks at all times is like an optimistic market timer. His actions are consistent with a policy of predicting a good year every year. While such a manager may know that such predictions will be wrong roughly one year out of three, such an attitude is nonetheless likely to lead to results superior to those achieved by most active market timers.

On the other hand, managers whose actions can be characterized by the model described in this article may be regarded as pessimistic. This is most obvious when p_c=0.50. A manager of this type with no predictive ability at all will make a gloomy prediction as often as a rosy one. He will not only make mistakes, but will also predict bad years too often.

Table A1 shows this, under the assumption that good years occur two-thirds of the time. As the table illustrates, a less-than-perfect predictor is likely to foresee only some of the good years: His probability of pre-

FIGURE A1. Unbiased Predictions

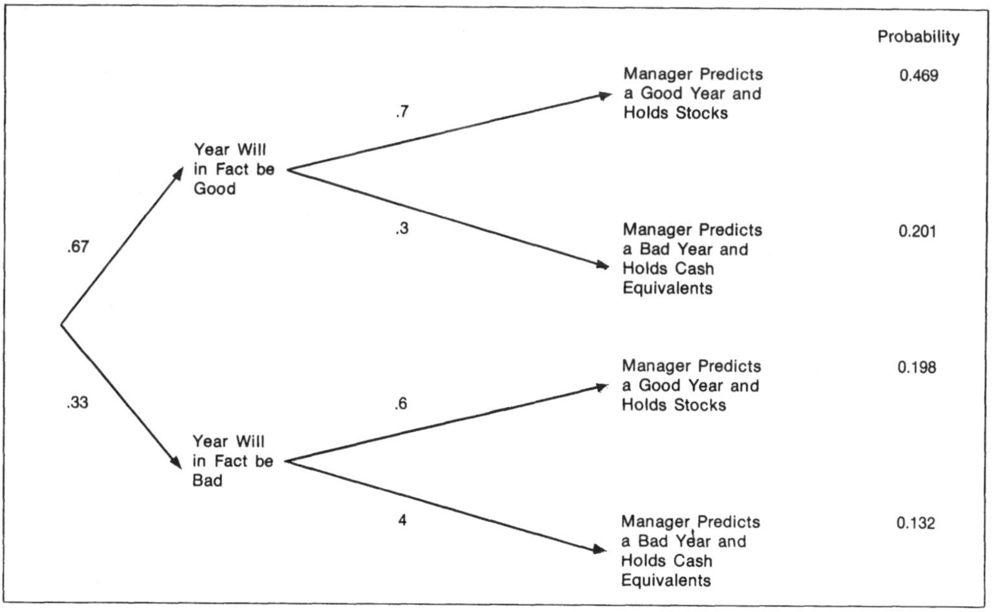

Table A1. Probability that a Manager Will Predict a Good Year, When the Actual Probability Is 0.67

Predictive Accuracy	Probability Manager Will Predict A Good Year
0.50	0.50
0.60	0.53
0.70	0.57
0.80	0.60
0.90	0.63
1.00	0.67

dicting a good year is less than the probability of its occurrence.

This suggests that a slightly different characterization of a market timer may be worth considering. Thus far we have assumed that the probability of predicting a good year prior to a good year equals the probability of predicting a bad year prior to a bad year. Since good years are more likely than bad ones, this makes such a predictor biased in the manner shown in Table A1.

To reduce or eliminate this bias, the predictor must be more accurate in good years than in bad years. This follows from the greater frequency of good years and is, of course, quite plausible. One who buys and holds stocks can be considered perfectly accurate in good years and perfectly inaccurate in bad years. A market timer with some predictive ability might provide greater than zero accuracy in bad years and less than perfect accuracy in good years, but the former might still fall below the latter.

The model in the text provides one extreme assumption: equal accuracy in both good and bad years. This appendix considers another: We assume that the manager's predictions are unbiased in the sense that the probability that he will predict a good year equals the probability that there will in fact be a good year.

FIGURE A2. Annual Return Advantage from Market Timing with Unbiased Predictions

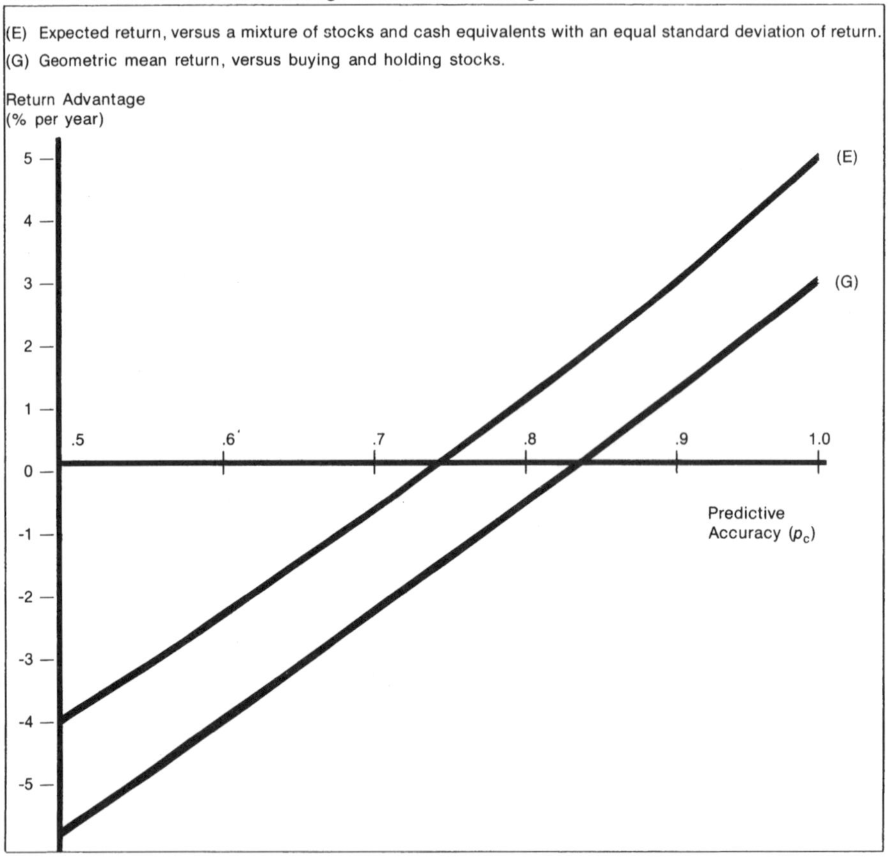

Figure A1 provides an example. The probability that such a manager will predict a good year is 0.469 + 0.198, or approximately 0.67, the probability that a good year will in fact occur. The probability that the prediction will be correct is 0.469 + 0.132, or approximately 0.60. The latter figure measures his overall predictive accuracy.

Figure A2 shows the advantage gained by such a manager for various levels of predictive accuracy, using the measures employed in Figure 2. Interestingly, the results do not differ significantly from those obtained earlier.

It should be noted that a manager with no predictive ability at all could provide a better than 50-50 predictive accuracy following an unbiased approach. Imagine a person throwing a die every year, then predicting a good year if numbers 1 through 4 turn up, and a bad year if numbers 5 or 6 turn up. Figure A3 portrays the resulting probabilities, assuming that the probability of a good year, like the probability of predicting one, is 0.67. The predictive accuracy of such a scheme is 0.449 + 0.109, or 0.558. But, as Figure A2 shows, the outcome is still substantially inferior to buy-and-hold strategies. ■

Footnotes

1. Dividends have been added to the relative change in the Standard and Poor's Composite Index to obtain the total annual returns. This is equivalent to assuming all dividends held in cash until the end of the year in which they are paid.
2. Consideration of transaction costs would alter this conclusion slightly, but this added factor will be ignored here. Transaction costs have, however, been taken into account in all calculations.
3. In each case, funds were assumed to be in the "right" investment at the beginning of the initial year of the period being analyzed.
4. This equalizes one measure of performance (variability) to allow concentration on the other (arithmetic average return). To accomplish this, a constant proportion of stocks relative to total assets (at market value) was used at the beginning of each year, with the proportion selected to give the same overall variability as that obtained from the relevant timing strategy.
5. This is a general relationship and requires no assumptions about normality, independence, etc.
6. The geometric mean return is estimated using the approximation:

$$100\left[\frac{\mu}{100} + \frac{\left(\frac{\sigma}{100}\right)^2}{2\left(1+\frac{\mu}{100}\right)}\right]$$

where:

μ = the overall net expected return (column 4)

σ = the overall standard deviation of return (column 5).

FIGURE A3. An Unbiased Predictor with no Predictive Ability

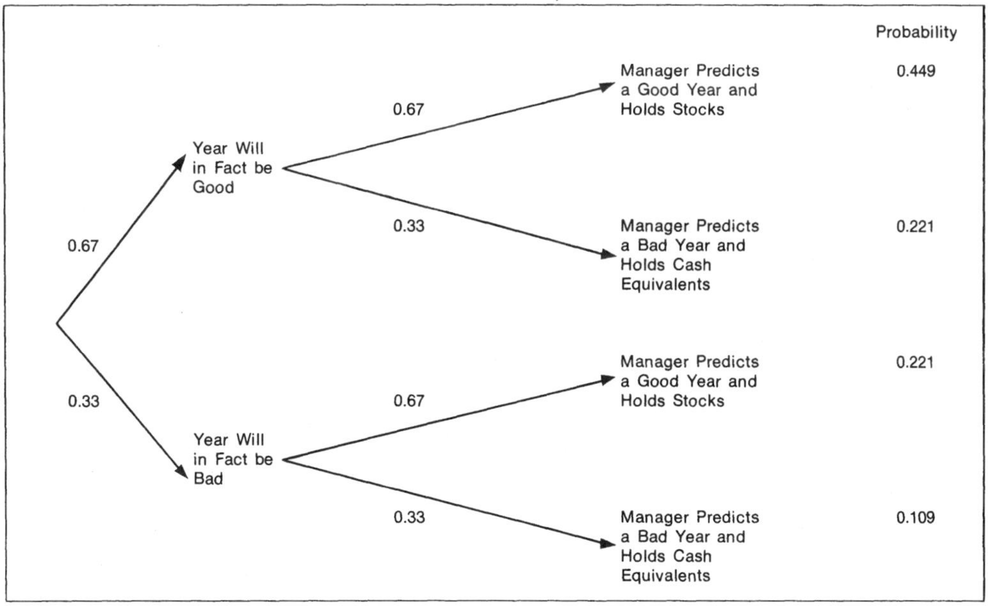

Journal of Financial Economics 3 (1976) 183–193. © North-Holland Publishing Company

CORPORATE PENSION FUNDING POLICY

William F. SHARPE

Stanford University, Stanford, CA 94305, U.S.A.

Received January 1976, revised version received January 1976

What policy should a corporation adopt concerning the funding of a defined-benefit pension plan and the investment of the assets held in trust for the plan? Until recently, pension plans did not have to be insured, and some risk could be borne by intended beneficiaries. Federal legislation has now mandated such coverage. This paper analyzes corporate policy under three conditions which correspond, roughly, to the earlier situation ('uninsured' loans), the current situation ('partially insured' loans), and the situation required by law to be implemented in the future ('completely insured' plans). We show that if insurance premiums are set correctly, corporate policy in this area may not matter; otherwise the optimal policy may simply be that which maximizes the difference between the value of the insurance and its cost.

1. Introduction

Despite its obvious social and economic importance, the area of corporate pension funding has only recently received theoretical attention in the finance literature. Tepper (1974) has proposed a framework for determining the optimal pattern of corporate contributions to a pension fund, Black (1976) has discussed both this issue and the optimal investment policy for the assets in the fund and Treynor [Treynor et al. (1976)] has analyzed aspects of both corporate and social policy.

Until recently many corporations tended to delegate the determination of pension fund contributions to actuaries and the choice of fund investment policy to professional money managers. However, corporate officers are devoting increasing attention to both matters. Several consulting services now use simulation analyses to estimate probability distributions of future contributions, based on assumptions concerning investment policy [for a description, see McLaughlin (1975)]. Procedures of this type assume that funding policy matters, and that the optimal policy depends in some way on the attitudes of corporate management.

Within the last few years increasing attention has been given to the social aspects of pension funding. The passage of the Employee Retirement Income Security Act of 1974 (ERISA) profoundly altered the private pension system in the United States. Most importantly, it mandated that plans[1] be insured.

[1] More precisely, most defined-benefit plans.

This paper analyzes corporate funding policy in three environments: first, the pre-ERISA situation in which a fund could, if desired, be completely uninsured; next, the situation which must, under ERISA, be fully implemented by the early 1980's, in which each fund is completely insured; and finally, the current situation in which a fund is insured only for amounts in excess of 30 percent of corporate net worth (a case that we will term one of 'partial' insurance).

The main analysis will utilize a simple one-period, no-tax environment. Following Black (1976) and Treynor et al. (1976), we explicitly recognize the implicit option contracts associated with pension funds. After discussing the three cases, current and proposed insurance premiums will be analyzed. Finally, possible extensions will be treated.

Most of the analysis is conducted on the assumption that the relevant parties (corporations, corporate stockholders, employees, insurance companies, insurance company stockholders) are rational and have access to the same capital market.[2] As usual in such conditions, corporate policy decisions do not matter – i.e., there is no single optimal funding policy. While this is not particularly surprising, it is instructive to see just how it comes about. The relevance of the results to the 'real world' is of course another matter. As will be seen, the post-ERISA situation may conform more to these assumptions than the pre-ERISA situation.

Thus one may conclude that while policy decisions in this area may once have mattered, they may matter less and less as the implementation of the legislation proceeds. In the future, if there is an optimal funding policy for a corporation, its determination will require explicit analysis of the differences between the conditions of the real world and the assumptions made here. The determination of such a policy should in all likelihood depend little if at all on attitudes of corporate officers (e.g., their personal degree of risk-aversion), unless the goal of the firm is not to maximize shareholder welfare. And, even if optimal policy exists, the cost (in the decreased value of the corporation's stock) associated with the choice of a different policy is likely to be small.

2. Uninsured funds

A corporation is obligated to pay its employees an amount L_1, presently known with certainty, at the end of the year.[3] To help meet this obligation, a *fund* with assets having a present market value of A_0 has been set aside. At the end of the year it will be worth the (presently uncertain) amount $\tilde{A}_1 = (1+\tilde{r})A_0$,

[2]This differs in major ways from Tepper's (1974) approach and in some respects from Black's (1976).

[3]L_1 may be paid as a lump sum or used to purchase annuity contracts from an insurance company, where each contract guarantees the benefits earned by an employee (subject only to mortality conditions). The amount, L_1, required to purchase such annuities is assumed to have been negotiated in advance, with only the quantity ($\leq L_1$) unknown.

where $\tilde{r}$ is the (uncertain) return on the assets in which A_0 is invested. At the end of the year, if $\tilde{A}_1 > L_1$, the liabilities will be paid in full, and the excess $(\tilde{A}_1 - L_1)$ refunded to the corporation. If there is a shortfall, the employees will receive only $\tilde{A}_1$, and the firm will not be liable for the deficiency.[4]

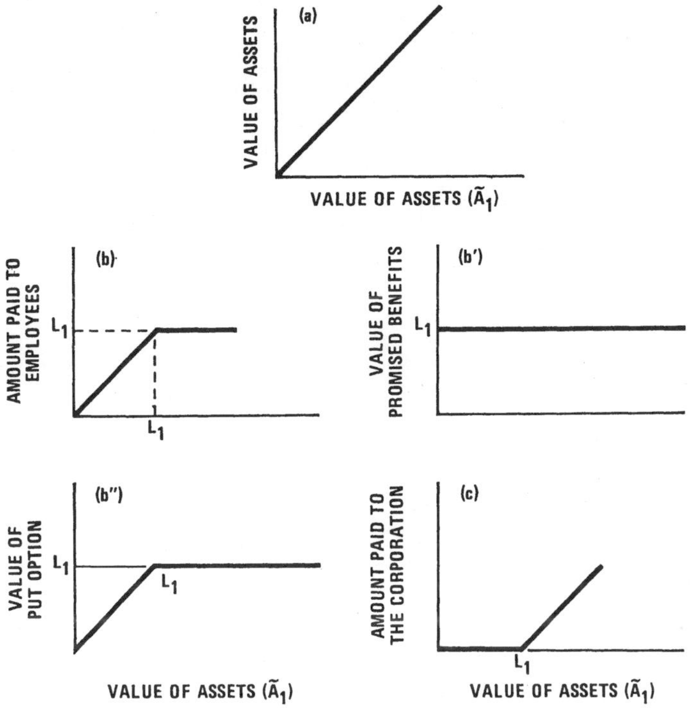

Fig. 1. Values of claims versus the value of fund assets.

Fig. 1 shows (a) the value of the assets, (b) the amount paid to employees, and (c) the amount paid to the corporation as a function of $\tilde{A}_1$. In effect, the corporation has a *call option* on the assets at an exercise price of L_1, as shown in fig. 1c. The employees' situation can be broken into two parts. They hold a contract to receive a *certain* payment of L_1, as shown in fig. 1b′, and have, in effect, sold a *put option* on the assets of the fund, with an exercise price of L_1, as shown in fig. 1b″.

The call (fig. 1c), put (fig. 1b″) and bond (fig. 1b′) collectively offer the same prospects at year-end as a portfolio invested in the assets (fig. 1a). In an efficient

[4]Legally, this would require the termination of the current pension plan, which would generally increase the liabilities since all accrued benefits become 'fully vested' in such a case; however, since assets would be insufficient to cover vested accrued benefits in this situation, the distinction need not be made here. In actuality, other costs (explicit and/or implicit) may be imposed on a corporation terminating a fund. These will also be ignored here. Treynor [in Treynor et al. (1976)] has suggested that in practice the firm may regard itself as implicitly liable for the shortfall. In this discussion we assume no such commitment exists.

market, investments or combinations of investments offering identical prospects sell at the same price.[5] Thus,

$$\mathrm{PV}\,[\mathrm{call}]-\mathrm{PV}\,[\mathrm{put}]+\mathrm{PV}\,[L_1] = \mathrm{PV}\,[\tilde{A}_1]. \tag{1}$$

We will assume that such instruments are available in the capital market or could be made available if desired. Moreover, all participants are assumed to have recourse to the market, where they can, if desired, take positions that will complement or offset those resulting from corporate funding decisions. Under these conditions, eq. (1) will hold, no matter how options or underlying assets are priced in the market.

Since PV $(\tilde{A}_1) = A_0$, the fund's assets valued at current market prices, we may re-write (1) as

$$\mathrm{PV}\,[\mathrm{put}]-\mathrm{PV}\,[\mathrm{call}] = \mathrm{PV}\,[L_1]-A_0. \tag{2}$$

The value on the right-hand side of (2) is the current level of 'unfunded liabilities'.[6]

Employees receive two types of payment in this situation: the present value of promised benefits (PV $[L_1]$) and the present value of wages, which we will denote W_0. On the other hand, they lose the present value of the put option (PV [put]). Assuming rational behavior on the part of employees (or their negotiating agents), this sum will be invariant to corporate pension funding decisions. In particular, let

$$\mathrm{PV}\,[L_1]+W_0-\mathrm{PV}\,[\mathrm{put}] = W, \tag{3}$$

where W is a constant fixed by employer–employee negotiations. Adding W_0 to both sides of (2),

$$W_0+\mathrm{PV}\,[\mathrm{put}]-\mathrm{PV}\,[\mathrm{call}] = \mathrm{PV}\,[L_1]-A_0+W_0. \tag{4}$$

Re-arranging, and substituting (3),

$$W_0+A_0-\mathrm{PV}\,[\mathrm{call}] = \mathrm{PV}\,[L_1]+W_0-\mathrm{PV}\,[\mathrm{put}] = W. \tag{5}$$

[5]Eq. (1), which uses the relationship first given by Stoll (1969), holds only for European options, as shown by Merton (1973). To avoid further discussion, it will be assumed that plan termination can take place only at year-end, and thus that all options are in fact European. Note also that all dividends and coupons are assumed to be retained in the fund, so there is no 'payout' during the year.

[6]The unfunded liabilities reported by firms typically differ from this. Here, assets are valued at market; in practice, book values are often used. Here also, liabilities are valued at market; in practice, future benefit payments are discounted using a single 'actuarial rate' of interest which may bear little if any relationship to the current term structure of interest rates.

In general, the value of any option will be a function of its remaining life (here, 1 year), the current value of the underlying asset (here, A_0), the exercise price (here, L_1), and the characteristics of the return distribution. The latter will be denoted $\sigma(\tilde{r})$; this could be interpreted as simply a characterization of the distribution or as its standard deviation of return (e.g., if the Black–Scholes option valuation formula were to be employed). For present purposes, we will consider it simply an (undefined) measure of risk with the characteristic that the value of an option will increase with increases in $\sigma(\tilde{r})$, *ceteris paribus*. As shown by Merton (1973), this relationship holds quite generally.

Re-writing (5) to highlight the determinants of option prices,

$$W_0+A_0-\mathrm{PV}\,[\mathrm{call}\,(A_0, L_1, \sigma(\tilde{r})] = W. \tag{6}$$

Eq. (6) shows that under the assumed conditions, corporate pension funding policy is irrelevant. There are two direct decision variables – A_0 and $\sigma(\tilde{r})$ – along with the related variables W_0 and L_1. Any change in funding (A_0) or investment policy [$\sigma(\tilde{r})$] will change the value of the corporation's call option and, in the case of A_0, its contribution. Offsetting changes in W_0, L_1, or the other funding variable must therefore be made to keep the left-hand side of (6) equal to the constant, W. But the left-hand side of (6) equals the present value of the corporation's outlays (W_0+A_0) less the value of its call option. Since this must be constant, any change in funding policy will change the *forms* in which employee wages and benefits affect the corporation's value, but not the total *amount*.

3. Fully insured funds

Consider a fully insured fund. The situation is as before, with one exception: when assets are insufficient to cover benefits, the difference is made up by an insurance company. To obtain such 'contingent liability' coverage, the corporation pays a premium, in advance.

The payoffs received by the various parties can be related to the ending asset value ($\tilde{A}_1$) using fig. 1. As before, fig. 1a shows the total value of the assets and fig. 1c the value obtained by the corporation. Now, however, the employees' situation is shown in fig. 1b′ – they will receive L_1 with certainty. In effect, the insurance company has sold the put option (shown in fig. 1b″), instead of the employees. If $\tilde{A}_1$ falls below L_1, the difference must be made up by the insurance company – an obligation for which it will charge the corporation a premium. Assuming that the insurance company is rational and has access to the capital market, the premium will equal the value of the associated put option.

Re-arranging (5) to highlight the situation,

$$W_0+A_0-\mathrm{PV}\,[\mathrm{call}]+\mathrm{PV}\,[\mathrm{put}] = \mathrm{PV}\,[L_1]+W_0. \tag{7}$$

The term on the right-hand side now represents the total present value of employee benefits (including wages). As before, we assume that via employee negotiations this must equal a constant, W. Expanding the notation as before to emphasize the determinants of option values,

$$W_0+A_0-\mathrm{PV}\,[\mathrm{call}\,(A_0,L_1,\sigma(\tilde{r})]+\mathrm{PV}\,[\mathrm{put}\,(A_0,L_1\,\sigma(\tilde{r}))]=W. \quad (8)$$

The term on the left-hand side of e.g. (8) equals (1) the total outlay by the corporation for its employees, including wages paid (W_0), assets placed in the pension fund (A_0) and the premium paid to the insurance company (PV [put $(A_0, L_1, \sigma(\tilde{r}))$], less (2) the present value of the resulting call option (PV [call $(A_0, L_1, \sigma(\tilde{r}))$]. But the total amount must equal a constant. Thus any change in corporate funding policy [i.e., A_0 and/or $\sigma(\tilde{r})$] cannot affect the present value of its outlay, since adjustments in other factors will keep the total constant.

As before, the results depend on rational behavior and the availability of market alternatives. In this instance, the case is especially strong. Employees need only negotiate the level of benefits and current wages. Since both are assumed to be known with certainty,[7] valuation is straightforward. The insurance company is given the task of valuing the required put option and charging an appropriate premium. If a private company is utilized, the valuation should not differ from that represented in eq. (8), for both the stockholders of the insurance company and the stockholders of the corporation operate in the same market. If the insurance company chooses to offset its options via transactions in the underlying assets and related options (e.g., by shorting the stocks and writing a call option) it can do so at standard market prices. Alternatively, it may pass its risk on to its stockholders, who may engage in offsetting transactions or not, as they wish. Whether the options are created by the corporation, to be 'sold' by the insurance company (directly or indirectly) or created by investors in the options market is irrelevant for the issue at hand.

4. Partially insured funds

Under the provisions of ERISA, the Pension Benefit Guarantee Corporation[8] (PBGC), a quasi-governmental agency, stands ready to make up any shortfall in the assets of a terminated pension fund. However, the corporation which sets up the plan is liable for the smaller of (1) the excess of liabilities over assets, or (2) 30 percent of corporate net worth (where the latter is to be determined by the PBGC). At present, employers with their own ('single-employer') plans pay an annual premium of $1 per employee per year for such coverage.

[7]In practice, any uncertainty due to 'private' risk (e.g., mortality) can be insured against and the expected value considered equivalent to an equal certain value.

[8]To avoid confusion, we will refer to this agency as the PBGC, reserving the term 'corporation' to indicate the employing firm which sets up a pension fund.

Within a few years, each employer must contract for 'contingent liability' coverage. While details are yet to be worked out, this may be offered by the PBGC, by private insurers, or by some combination thereof. If the PBGC writes both the 'basic' and the 'contingent liability' insurance, it will fill the role of the insurance company in the previous ('fully insured') case. Otherwise, both the PBGC and a private insurance company will, in effect, sell put options to a given corporation. In the interim, only the PBGC insures a fund's benefits, and the corporation bears the risk associated with the required contingent liability.

Analysis of this case is fairly straightforward. The situation would be obvious if the corporation were to increase its stock outstanding so that the new shares equal 30 percent of the total, and place these shares in its pension fund. At year-end such shares would be used to pay off liabilities only after all other investments had been utilized. Any excess would be returned to the corporation.

Of course the physical issue of stock would only dramatize the nature of the liability. In any event, the result is the same.[9]

Letting N_0 and $\tilde{N}_1$ represent the net worth of the corporation at the present and at year-end, respectively, the firm can be said to 'place' $A_0+0.3N_0$ in the fund. The total portfolio will then have a risk of $\sigma(\tilde{r})$, where

$$1+\tilde{r} = (\tilde{A}_1+0.3\tilde{N}_1)/(A_0+0.3N_0), \tag{9}$$

or

$$\tilde{r} = X_A\tilde{r}_A+X_N\tilde{r}_N, \tag{10}$$

where

$$\tilde{r}_A = (\tilde{A}_1-A_0)/A_0,$$

$$\tilde{r}_N = (\tilde{N}_1-N_0)/N_0,$$

$$X_A = A_0/(A_0+0.3N_0),$$

$$X_N = N_0/(A_0+0.3N_0).$$

5. Insurance premiums

Under the conditions assumed here, the appropriate premium for insurance coverage can be determined by estimating the market value of the relevant put option. This requires more than the assumption that equal prospects sell for equal prices (which is the only assumption utilized thus far). For example, assume that a fund's assets are invested in Standard and Poor's 500-stock index (or a similar portfolio), and that analysis of historic data can adequately estimate the future beta and residual standard deviation of the corporation's own stock, where

[9] Assuming, of course, that the PBGC evaluates net worth as the current (market) value of the corporation's equity – an assumption likely to only approximately correct (at best) in practice.

both measures are based on regressions of the stock's return on that of the SP500. Then from (10) the standard deviation of $\tilde{r}$ will equal

$$\sigma(\tilde{r}) = \sqrt{(X_A + X_N\beta)^2\sigma_m^2 + X_N^2\sigma_e^2}, \tag{11}$$

$\sigma(\tilde{r})$ = the standard deviation of r,

β = the beta of the corporation's stock,

σ_m = the standard deviation of the SP500 market index,

σ_e = the residual standard deviation of the corporation's stock.

Eq. (11) could be utilized along with the Black–Scholes (1973) formula for the valuation of a put option, and which is of the form

$$P_0/E = f(P/E, \sigma(\tilde{r}), t, \pi), \tag{12}$$

P = the current price of the underlying asset,

E = the exercise price of the option,

$\sigma(\tilde{r})$ = the (instantaneous) standard deviation of return, on the underlying asset,

t = the time to expiration,

π = the riskless rate of interest,

P_0 = the value of the option.

In the present context,

$$P_r/L_1 = f((A_0 + 0.3N_0)/L_1, \sigma(\tilde{r}), 1, \pi), \tag{13}$$

P_r = the premium for a one-year policy,

L_1 = the liabilities (benefits) covered by the policy,

$A_0 + 0.3N_0$ = the underlying assets.

As indicated earlier, the PBGC presently charges \$1 per covered employee per year for basic coverage, which is hardly appropriate. Given erroneous insurance premium schedules, there will be an optimal corporate funding policy, i.e., the one that maximizes the difference between the value of the put option and the premium charged for it. Currently, a corporation can increase its current market value by increasing liabilities, decreasing fund assets, or increasing the risk of the assets in the fund. Within the constraints set by law, all three should be done if stockholder welfare is to be maximized.

As long as insurance premiums are set incorrectly, some sort of subsidy will result. Some corporations may subsidize others, and corporations may on average subsidize or be subsidized by taxpayers.

ERISA provides three bases for premiums charged by the PBGC, which may be used singly or jointly. They are:

(1) the number of participants,

(2) the unfunded benefits (PV $(L_1)-A_0$),

(3) the total benefits (L_1).

None of these is sufficient for determining the appropriate premium. Under the assumptions used in the Black–Scholes formula, the premium *per dollar of liabilities* can be determined from the *ratio* of underlying assets to liabilities, along with the risk of the assets (and the length of time and riskless interest rate). However, the *difference* between the liabilities and the underlying assets cannot be used directly.[10]

6. Extensions

We have characterized pension funds as having one-year lives, when in fact most continue for long periods of time. However, the multi-period nature of funds can be accommodated within our framework. At the end of the first year of its operation, a fund can either be terminated or not. If it is not terminated, the assets and liabilities are 'bequeathed' to the next year. The new asset base will equal the market value of the old assets plus the amount of new contributions, less the amounts actually paid to pensioners. The liabilities at the end of the new year will equal those inherited from the previous year (i.e., the 'prior service' liabilities), less amounts actually paid out, plus non-forfeitable benefits (i.e., the 'current service' liabilities) that will be accrued during the forthcoming year. With these modifications, the overall problem can be viewed as a sequence of one-year problems.

We have also assumed that no additional cost is borne by a corporation that terminates a plan. In fact, many corporate officers will not consider an analysis that takes into account the possibility of voluntary plan termination, on the grounds that 'breaking faith' with employees could do irrepairable damage to the firm. As Treynor [in Treynor et al. (1976)] has pointed out, an implicit liability to beneficiaries appears to have been assumed. In the future the situation may be different, however, since termination of a plan only shifts the burden to an insurance company, and a corporation could well argue that it has paid for the right to do so.

It is of course possible that the PBGC will deter otherwise profitable voluntary

[10]That is, (12) cannot be transformed to another formula of the form: $P_0/E = g((P-E), \sigma(\tilde{r}), t, \pi)$.

plan terminations by a threat (implicit or explicit) to raise premiums for any new plan set up by the corporation. Alternatively, the Internal Revenue Service could refuse to qualify a new plan for favorable tax treatment.

A set of provisions in ERISA gives the PBGC the right to terminate a plan if any of several conditions is met. Some concern fraud, discriminatory treatment of corporate officers, etc. However, the PBGC may also terminate a plan whenever:

(1) the plan has not contributed the minimum amount required using an acceptable actuarial procedure,

(2) 'the plan is unable to pay benefits when due', or

(3) 'the possible long-run loss of the . . . (PBGC) . . . with respect to the plan may reasonably be expected to increase unreasonably if the plan is not terminated.'

One might interpret these statements as indicating that a double American option is involved, with either party able to force exercise at any time.[11] A more plausible interpretation – that the PBGC will force termination whenever $(A_0+3N_0) \leqq L_1$ – has been analyzed by Treynor [in Treynor et al. (1976)].

7. Conclusions

The basic ideas presented here can be stated fairly succinctly. Since pension benefits are now guaranteed, it is unlikely that employees or their negotiating agents will fail to properly value promises made by a corporation (and kept by it and/or one or more insurance companies). Absent tax effects, changes in corporate pension funding policy should only affect the distribution of obligations between the corporation and any insurance companies involved. If premiums reflect the values that would be placed on such obligations by a private insurance company acting in the best interests of public stockholders, corporate funding policy cannot matter. In effect, the corporation purchases an option from an insurance company. The value of that option to the public shareholders of the corporation should equal its value to the public shareholders of an insurance company. Any change in funding policy will change this amount, but the change in the value of the option to the corporation's stockholders will be precisely offset by the change in the premium that the corporation must pay, leaving the overall value of the corporation unaffected.

If premiums for pension fund insurance are not set in this manner, there will be optional corporate pension funding policies. In effect, the corporation should adopt those policies which maximize the difference between the market value of

[11]Such an option would always be worth precisely its value if exercised immediately. If it were priced at any other amount, one of the two parties could pay or receive the price, force an immediate exercise, and make a certain profit.

the option represented by the insurance contract and the premium charged for the contract.

On a social level, one could well criticize the provisions in ERISA concerning pension fund insurance (but not necessarily the requirement that such insurance be purchased).[12] Given these provisions, there are compelling reasons for hoping that private insurers will be relied upon to write contingent liability coverage, with competition allowed to bring about appropriate premium schedules. If this is done, corporate pension funding policy may in fact matter little if at all. Otherwise, corporate managers will undoubtedly wish to examine the premium schedule, and try to get as much advantage from it as possible.

[12]Since failure by employees to properly recognize the nature of their claim on an uninsured fund could lead to a type of exploitation and/or inefficient allocation of labor.

References

Black, F., 1976, The investment policy spectrum: Individuals, endowment funds, and pensions funds, Financial Analysts' Journal, Jan./Feb.

Black, F. and M. Scholes, 1973, The pricing of options and corporate liabilities, Journal of Political Economy, May/June.

McLaughlin, F., 1975, Using simulation to chart the way, Pension World, Sept.

Merton, R.C., 1973, The theory of rational option pricing, Bell Journal of Economics and Management Science, Spring.

Stoll, H.R., 1969, The relationship between put and call option prices, Journal of Finance, Dec.

Tepper, I., 1974, Optional financial policies for trusteed pension plans, Journal of Financial and Quantitative Analysis, June.

Treynor, J.L., P. Regan, W. Priest and J. Spiegelman, 1976, The financial implications of ERISA, forthcoming.

Major investment styles*

Some familiar concepts are more complex than they appear, but can also be used more systematically.

William F. Sharpe

68 WINTER 1978

There are many different ways to invest money, and few money managers adopt strategies that are either simple or extreme. Nonetheless, a few cases can be used to characterize the major approaches. The key styles are:

- *Passive*
- *Active:*
  Market timing
  Security selection
  Market timing and security selection

An investment portfolio can be formed from any or all of three essential components:

1. risk-free securities
2. the market portfolio (composed of all risky assets, in market proportions)
3. "bets" that, when added to the market portfolio, raise some proportions and lower others.

As will be shown, investment styles differ in their use of these components and the extent to which consensus opinions are adopted as correct.

PASSIVE MANAGEMENT

The simplest investment style is relatively *passive*. Only Treasury bills and the market portfolio are utilized, and the consensus opinion concerning the risk and return of the latter is considered to be correct. One decision is required: the appropriate mixture of the two components. The best combination will, of course, depend on the client's attitude toward risk and return.

Figure 18-2 provides an illustration. Point *T* plots the return offered by Treasury bills, and point *M* the risk and expected return of the market portfolio, using consensus estimates. Combinations of the two investments plot along line *TM*. The client's attitude toward risk and return is shown by the set of indifference curves, and the optimal position *(P)* lies at the point where an indifference curve is tangent to line *TM*. In this case the best mix uses both Treasury bills and the market portfolio. In other situations only one might be chosen, or the market portfolio might be levered up via borrowing.

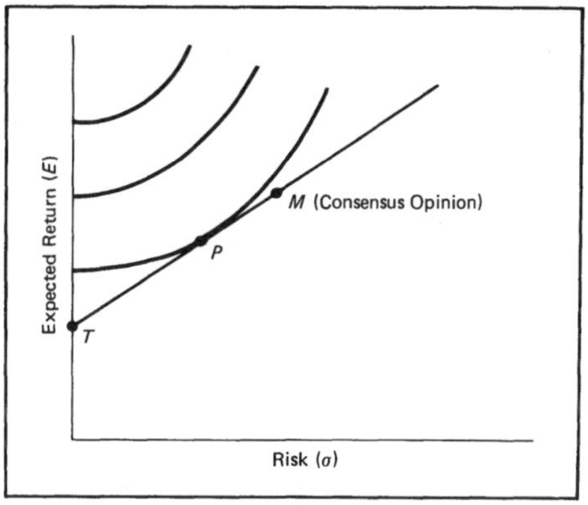

FIGURE 18-2. PASSIVE INVESTMENT MANAGEMENT

When management is passive, the overall mix will be altered only when (1) the client's preferences change and/or (2) the consensus opinion about the risk and return of the market portfolio changes. The manager must continue to assess the latter and keep in touch with the client concerning the former. But no additional activity is required.

THE SUPPLY OF RISK-BEARING

Every investment manager should have as accurate a view as possible concerning the current consensus opinion of the risk and return associated with investment in the market as a whole. For the active

* Reprinted with permission from William F. Sharpe, *Investments,* Prentice-Hall, 1978.

manager this is an important input; for the passive manager it is all-important.

When estimates of overall economic uncertainty increase, security prices will usually adjust so that the risk and expected return of the market portfolio both increase. But what about the return per unit of risk?

Figure 18-3 shows a likely situation. In Figure 18-3(a) the market's prospects are initially those shown by point *M*. Given this alternative, plus the ability to borrow and lend at the interest rate shown by point *T*, investors collectively choose to hold all available risky securities.

Now, imagine that some unforeseen event causes investors' opinions about market risk and return to change, so that the market portfolio plots at point *M'*. Since the excess return per unit of risk is unchanged, everyone will want the same amount of risk and return as before. But this will require the sale of some of everyone's now more risky securities. This cannot be done (who will buy?). Instead, the prices of risky securities will fall, increasing their expected returns.[1] Eventually the market portfolio will plot at a point such as *M"* on a line with a higher slope (excess return per unit of risk).

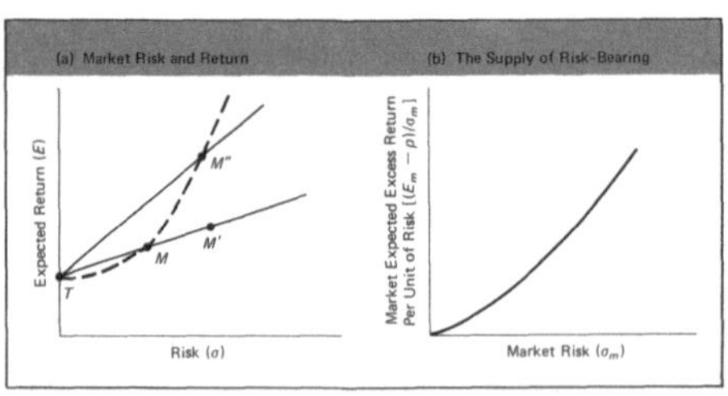

FIGURE 18-3. CHANGES IN MARKET RISK AND RETURN

The dashed line in Figure 18-3(a) shows the points at which the market portfolio is likely to plot as the assessment of risk changes, given investors' attitudes toward risk. Of course, changes in the society's average attitude toward risk and return can alter the relationship in any direction, but such variations are likely to be small and less frequent than changes in estimates of economic uncertainty.

Figure 18-3(b) summarizes the situation in a slightly different manner. It shows the premium per unit of risk (vertical axis) required to induce investors to accept various amounts of risk (horizontal axis). As shown, this *supply of risk-bearing curve* is upward-sloping.

(1) Footnotes appear at the end of the article.

Both the dashed line in Figure 18-3(a) and the curve in Figure 18-3(b) show that a change in the risk of the market portfolio is likely to be accompanied by a more-than-proportionate change in its expected excess return.

MARKET TIMING

Passive portfolio managers estimate the consensus opinion of market risk and return and accept it as correct. Market timers also estimate the consensus opinion but reserve the right to consider it incorrect. When selecting a mix of Treasury bills and the market portfolio, a market timer will use his or her own opinion and thus may choose a different combination than would be recommended to the same client by a passive manager.

This is illustrated in Figure 18-4. Point *M* plots the consensus opinion concerning the market's prospects and point *M** the manager's opinion. Given the latter, the optimal mix with Treasury bills for the client in question is that which plots at point *P** (in this case, a 50-50 combination of the two ingredients).

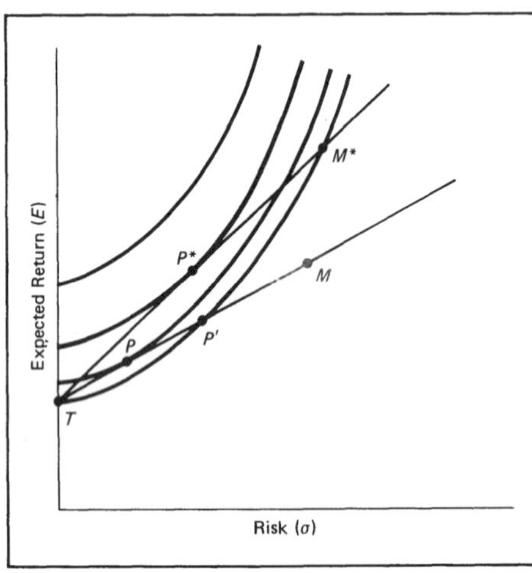

FIGURE 18-4. MARKET TIMING

If the manager is correct, all is well. But what if the consensus opinion is right? Then the appropriate mixture is that shown by point *P* (here, one with 30% stocks and 70% Treasury bills). The manager has made two mistakes. First, the mixture is inappropriate. Second, both the client and the manager are misinformed about the true prospects — here, they believe that the selected mix plots at point *P** when in fact it plots at point *P'*. This error might cause the client to make incorrect decisions in other domains (e.g., business, marriage, etc.) Of course, errors of the same type can arise when a passive manager misestimates the consensus opinion of the market, but they are likely to be less severe.

A market timer will generally alter a portfolio (i.e., the mix of risky and riskless securities) when his or her opinion about market prospects changes, even if there is no change in the consensus opinion or the client's attitude toward risk and return. The amount of the change will depend on the client's preferences; but the fact that such changes occur frequently and may be large makes market timing an *active* management style.

FORMULA TIMING

Mechanical methods are sometimes employed in an attempt to "beat the market" through timing. Some sort of formula is used to alter exposure to the market from time to time, in the hope of thereby taking advantage of market cycles. For example, one might periodically switch between stocks and Treasury bills to maintain a *constant dollar* value of stocks. Or one might adjust holdings periodically to maintain a *constant ratio* of stocks to Treasury bills, based on market values (i.e., sell stocks after the market rises, and buy stocks after the market falls). Or one might fit a trend line to some market index and alter the ratio of stocks to bonds, based on the relationship of the index to its trend line (this is called a *variable ratio* plan).

70 WINTER 1978

All these procedures are motivated by the assumption that recent moves in the stock market (either absolutely, or relative to a trend of some sort) are more likely to be reversed than continued. Neither economic logic nor empirical evidence supports this view. Formula timing alters holdings in ways that are likely to be both costly and inappropriate, given a client's circumstances and attitude toward risk.

DOLLAR AVERAGING

A related concept is that of *dollar averaging*. The idea is to invest a constant dollar amount at regular intervals. For example, one might buy a thousand dollars' worth of American Telephone and Telegraph stock each month. The higher the price, the smaller the number of shares purchased; and the lower the price, the larger the number of shares. When the price changes, a dollar averager gets both good news and bad news (one based on the change in the value of previous holdings, the other based on the price at which new holdings can be purchased). For an investor buying a portfolio of stocks a similar relationship would hold between the average level of "the market" and the average cost of his or her "shares" in the market.

It is a mathematical certainty that the average cost of shares purchased via dollar averaging will be less than the average price of such shares (unless the price never changes). More shares are purchased at low prices and thus the average cost, which is a weighted average using shares purchased as weights, will be less than the average price, which is an unweighted average.[2] Moreover, the difference between the two values will generally be greater, the greater the variation in price from period to period.

While this is interesting mathematically, it has no obvious economic significance. Two questions are relevant, however: (1) is dollar averaging better than some alternative? and (2) is variance in stock price actually good for one who is dollar averaging?

The first question can be answered only if another question is asked: if one did not invest $1,000 per month in stocks, what would happen to the money? For example, it could be used to buy Treasury bills until $12,000 (plus interest) is accumulated at year-end, the total then being invested in stocks. This would involve a different relative exposure to the market every month, with the differences more or less unrelated to the client's circumstances or attitude toward risk. Unless savings in transactions costs made possible by large stock purchases are significant, this is not likely to be as good an idea as dollar averaging.

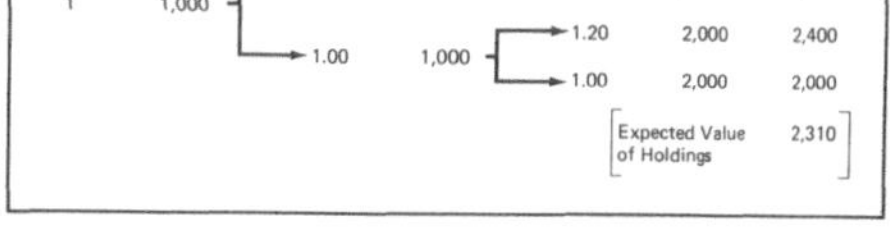

FIGURE 18-5. DOLLAR AVERAGING

The second question can be answered relatively easily, if the issue is posed carefully. Figure 18-5 shows two possible investments. The first earns 10% in each of two periods with certainty: its price goes from $1 per share to $1.10, and then to $1.21. The second investment is equally likely to earn either 20% or 0% each period. At each of the first two dates an investor buys $1,000 worth of shares. The ending values of the resulting holdings are shown in the figure. If the certain investment is chosen, a final value of $2,310 is obtained. If the other investment is selected, the outcome is uncertain. Its expected value is $2,310, but the actual value can be more or less.

The risky investment in Figure 18-5 is equivalent to buying the riskless investment and then betting each year's return (10%) on the flip of a fair coin to get double (20%) or nothing (0%). Adding risk without increasing expected return increases the uncertainty surrounding ending value without increasing the expected ending value, even for one who is dollar averaging. There is nothing inherently wrong with dollar averaging, but it has no magical properties and certainly does not change uncertainty per se from a vice to a virtue.

SECURITY SELECTION

A third major investment style concentrates on *security selection*. The consensus opinion of prospects for the market as a whole is accepted as correct, but the prices of individual securities are questioned. On average, security prices are assumed to equal intrinsic values, but the selector believes that he or she can identify at least a few securities that are overpriced and others that are underpriced. Barring special circumstances, the former will be held in less-than-market proportions; the latter, in more-than-market proportions. Putting it somewhat differently: a portfolio will be chosen that includes all securities in market proportions plus bets "against" overpriced securities and "for" underpriced securities.

Table 18-1
Dividing a Portfolio into Market Proportions Plus Bets

(1) Security (i)	(2) Security Beta (β_i)	(3) Proportion of Security in Market (X_i^M)	(4) Proportion of Security in Portfolio (X_i^P)	(5) = (4)/.80 Proportion of Security in Risky Portfolio $\left(= X_i^P / \sum_i X_i^P\right)$	(6) = (5) − (3) Bet on Security (X_i^B)
1	.7	.20	.32	.40	+.20
2	1.0	.50	.32	.40	−.10
3	1.2	.30	.16	.20	−.10
Sum of proportions $\left(= \sum_i X_i\right)$		1.00	.80	1.00	0
Beta of portfolio $\left(= \sum_i X_i \beta_i\right)$		1.00	.74	.92	−.08

Table 18-1 provides an example. The market is assumed to consist of three securities. Column (2) shows the beta values and column (3) the relative amounts outstanding (i.e., the market-value proportions). Column (4) indicates the relative amounts by value in the portfolio being analyzed. Note that these figures sum to only .80, indicating that the remaining 20% of the portfolio is invested in riskless securities. The figures in column (5) were obtained by dividing each value in column (4) by .80 to determine the proportion of funds "at risk" invested in each risky security. By design, these add to 1.0 and can thus be compared with the market proportions in column (3), which also add to 1.0. The figures in column (6), which show the bets placed on the securities, were obtained by determining the differences between the risky portfolio proportions [column (5)] and market proportions [column (3)]. By construction, these sum to zero: bets "for" securities must be offset by bets "against" others.

The bottom row in Table 18-1 shows the beta values for each of the portfolios, calculated by taking a weighted average of the security beta values, using relative proportions as weights. The overall portfolio has a beta value of .74, obtained by investing 80% of total funds in a risky portfolio with a beta of .92 [the beta of the risky portfolio is shown at the bottom of column (5), and $.8 \times .92 = .74$]. The beta value of the bets is $-.08$, which accounts for the difference between the market portfolio's beta (1.00) and that of the actual risky portfolio (.92).

What will be the portfolio's risk and return? The answer depends on the prospects for the market portfolio and the risk and return of the bets.

Adding bets to a market portfolio will add nonmarket risk as holdings are moved away from market proportions. If, on net, the bets are good, expected return will also increase.

Figure 18-6 illustrates this. As before, points *M* and *T* indicate the prospects of the market portfolio and Treasury bills, respectively. Passive strategies can be used to obtain any point on line 1. In this case, however, the manager has selected a set of bets that, when combined with the market portfolio, will give point $(M + B)$. By combining this risky portfolio with Treasury bills, points along line 2 can be obtained — a clear improvement.

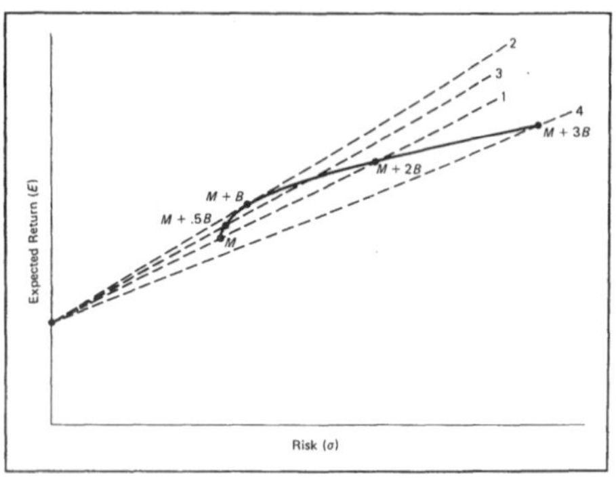

FIGURE 18-6. SECURITY SELECTION: OPTIMAL USE OF GOOD BETS

Since the bets shown in Figure 18-6 are good, why not increase them? This will increase expected return, but it will also increase risk. Moreover, expected return will increase at a slower rate than risk.[3] This is shown by the solid curve, which plots combinations of the market portfolio and the chosen set of bets, varying the size of the bets. For example, if the amount bet is doubled, point *(M + 2B)* will be obtained; when mixed with Treasury bills, this gives points along line 1 — no better than those available via passive management. If the bets are tripled, things will be even worse — line 4 lies below line 1. On the other hand, if the bets are halved, point *(M + .5B)* will be obtained; this can be combined with Treasury bills to give points on line 3 — worse than line 2, but better than line 1.

Figure 18-6 is typical of the situation when a series of good bets is being considered: the curve increases at a decreasing rate, with risk changing more rapidly than expected return.[4]

In the case shown in Figure 18-6 the manager has chosen the right amount to bet. This can be seen graphically — point *(M + B)* lies on the ray from point *T* tangent to the curve. If either less or more is bet, a poorer set of combinations will be obtained when the risky portfolio is mixed with Treasury bills.

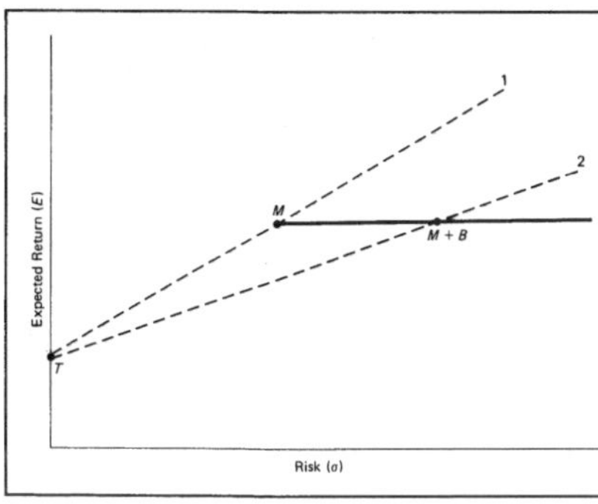

FIGURE 18-8. SECURITY SELECTION: AVERAGE BETS

Figure 18-8 shows a more gloomy situation. Here the bets are neither good nor bad. Security analysis is average. The recommended bets add nonmarket risk but do not change either the portfolio's beta value or its expected return. The curve of the previous figure becomes a horizontal line, and potential performance is lowered (from line 1 to line 2) if the manager's choice of bets is adopted. The situation will not be as bad if the bets are reduced. But the best approach involves no bets at all!

THE OPTIMAL USE OF BETS

In a perfectly efficient market no manager's diagram would look like Figure 18-6; in a nearly efficient market some might. If an organization has truly superior analysis, two questions arise: (1) what bets should be placed, and (2) how much should be bet? This section considers the latter question; the next treats the former.

The following estimates are needed:

- β_B = the beta value of the bets
- α_B = the alpha value (expected nonmarket return) of the bets
- σ_B^2 = the nonmarket risk of the bets
- E_M = the expected return on the market portfolio
- σ_M^2 = the risk of the market portfolio
- p = the return on a riskless asset (e.g., Treasury bills).

The optimal proportion to be invested in the bets (w) is that which satisfies:[5]

$$\frac{w}{1 + w\beta_B} = \frac{\alpha_B/\sigma_B^2}{(E_M - p)/\sigma_M^2} \tag{18-1}$$

The numerator of the left-hand side indicates the relative amount bet; the denominator indicates the relative amount invested in the market, both directly (= 1) and indirectly (= $w\beta_B$) via the implicit market component in the bets.[6] The left-hand side of the formula is thus the proportion of bets relative to the investment in the market.

Table 18-2
Determining the Optimal Set of Bets

a. Market Estimates

Expected excess return $(E_m - p) = 6$
Variance of return $= 600$
$\frac{E_m - p}{V_m} = .01$

b. Security Estimates

(1) security (i)	(2) α_i	(3) V_i	(4) = (2)/(3) α_i/V_i	(5) = (4)/.01 $X_i' = \frac{\alpha_i/V_i}{(E_m - p)/V_m}$	(6) β_i	(7) = (5) × (6) $X_i'\beta_i$
1	2	800	.0025	.25	.7	.175
2	−3	1500	−.0020	−.20	1.0	−.20
3	3	2400	.00125	.125	1.2	.15
						.125

(8) X_i^m	(9) = .875 × (8) $X_i^{m'} = \left(1 - \sum_i X_i'\beta_i\right)X_i^m$	(10) = (5) + (9) $X_i'' = X_i' + X_i^{m'}$	(11) = (10)/1.05 $X_i^h = X_i'' / \sum_i X_i''$	(12) = (11) − (8) $X_i^B = X_i^h - X_i^m$
.20	.175	.4250	.40476	.20476
.50	.4375	.2375	.22619	−.27381
.30	.2625	.3875	.36905	.06905
		1.05		

The right-hand side of the formula is the ratio of two measures of performance. The numerator $(\alpha_b/\sigma^2{}_B)$ indicates the expected return per unit of variance for the nonmarket component of the return from the bets. The denominator $[(E_M - p)/\sigma^2{}_M)]$ is the expected excess return per unit of variance for the market.[7] The greater the numerator relative to the denominator, the larger should be the relative amount bet.

A special case of formula (18-1) arises when the bets are neither good nor bad. In such an instance the optimal approach is to ignore them, as the formula indicates: if $\alpha_B = 0$, then $w = 0$.

THE OPTIMAL SET OF BETS

Any set of bets involves a nonmarket component, with expected return α_B and risk σ_B^2. It may also involve a market component: positive if β_B is positive, negative if β_B is negative.

To find the optimal set of bets generally requires the help of a computer.[8] Forecasts of returns (expected market return, security α's) and risks (market and nonmarket) plus all necessary constraints go in, and an optimal portfolio comes out. A comparison of the proportionate holdings of risky securities with those in the market portfolio indicates the bets that should be placed (assuming the forecasts were in fact relevant). Some organizations assume that each security's nonmarket risk is due entirely to factors unique to the firm. Under this useful but extreme assumption, if no restrictions are placed on holdings, a simple approach developed by Treynor and Black[9] can be employed.

The procedure is illustrated in Table 18-2. First, estimates of the market's expected excess return $(E_m - p)$ and variance of return (V_m) are obtained. Their ratio is then computed: this indicates the reward per unit of variance risk associated with investment in the market.

The remainder of the table shows the computations for the three securities used earlier in Table 18-1. The major ingredients are analysts' estimates of expected nonmarket returns (the α_i's) and nonmarket variances (the V_i's). Under the assumed conditions V_i measures security i's total contribution to the nonmarket risk of the bets, and the ratio α_i/V_i indicates its expected reward per unit of such risk. The greater a security's reward-to-risk contribution, the larger should be the amount bet. If a security is underpriced, alpha will be positive and a bet should be placed "for" the security. If a security is overpriced, alpha will be negative, and a bet should be placed "against" it.

The entries in column (5) of the table indicate the appropriate investment in the nonmarket characteristics of the securities per unit of investment in the market. Each is obtained by dividing the security's reward-to-risk ratio by that estimated for the market portfolio. The securities' estimated beta values, shown in column (6), are used in column (7) to determine the sum of the beta values times the amounts in column (5). This amount (.125) is the net beta value of a portfolio with the proportions shown in column (5).

Column (8) indicates the amounts of each security in the market portfolio. Since the proportions in column (5) provide some implicit exposure to the market, the explicit exposure need not be as large. The required amounts, shown in column (9), represent an investment of .875 (= 1 − .125) in the market portfolio.

Summing columns (5) and (9) gives the amounts shown in column (10). To convert these to proportions, each entry is divided by the sum, yielding the values in column (11). These are the relative proportions of the risky securities in the optimal combination of the market portfolio and bets. Comparison with the market proportions indicates the optimal bets, as shown in column (12).

It is tempting to adopt this approach, for it obviates the use of a computer.[10] But it is at best an approximation,[11] and at worst it can lead to bad performance, even when an organization has superior security analysis. Nonetheless, it does take nonmarket risk into account when choosing security holdings, thus avoiding the common mistake of entirely ignoring this important factor.

Tables comparing proportionate holdings of various securities in a portfolio with the proportions in a standard index are used by many investment management organizations for internal reporting and, increasingly, for external reporting to clients. Total holdings may be compared with a comprehensive index, or holdings in different sectors compared with market proportions, and holdings within each sector also compared with market proportions. In either case the goal is to show how the organization has placed its bets. The former approach does this on a security-by-security basis, while the latter separates overall bets placed on sectors from those placed on specific securities within each sector.

MARKET TIMING AND SECURITY SELECTION

Most managers combine styles, engaging in both market timing and security selection. Consensus estimates for both market and security prospects are considered, but not always adopted. Gains can be made via market timing, security selection, or both. On the other hand, erroneous forecasts on either front can reduce performance.

No new principles are required to guide the manager who engages in both security selection and market timing. The diagrams and computations used for security selection apply with only one modification: the manager's estimates of market risk and return are employed instead of consensus estimates. The portfolio of bets will be the same, but the mixture with the market (w) will be different, as will the mix with Treasury bills considered appropriate for any given client.

This type of manager is likely to be especially active. Whenever he or she has a change of heart concerning either the market or individual securities, a change in holdings will be considered, even when the client's attitudes and the consensus opinions concerning security prospects remain the same.

ADJUSTING PREDICTIONS

The rules for placing individual bets and for deciding the overall amount to bet [formula (18-1)] assume that the estimates of performance are neither optimistic nor pessimistic.

Many organizations use security analysis to estimate alpha values (in effect), leaving the estimation of security nonmarket risk to computer departments instructed to assume that the future will be more or less like the past. Such estimates of risk may be wrong, but they are as likely to err in one direction as another.

This is not likely to be the case for the estimates of alpha values. Any given analyst may be optimistic or pessimistic and likely to exaggerate or understate. Moreover, an entire organization may have similar attributes. The appropriate value to use for a security is not necessarily the estimated value of its prospective abnormal return (alpha) but, rather, the expected value of alpha when such an estimate is given.

The principle applies as well to estimates used for market timing. The appropriate values for market return (E_M) and risk ($\sigma^2{}_M$) are those which summarize the likely distribution of market returns, given the current estimate. For example, assume that an organization simply predicts each year's market as being "bullish" or "bearish." To know how to act, given such a prediction, one would like a century or two of data on such predictions, made by the same people, using the same procedures. If this information were available, all the market returns in years predicted to be bullish could be analyzed and a mean and standard deviation obtained. These values could be used to estimate market prospects when the organization feels bullish. Similarly, the mean and standard deviation of market returns in years previously predicted to be bearish could be used when the organization feels bearish.

It may be possible to obtain a record for calibrating security analysts, since predictions for many securities can be made at any time. But a comparable record for market analysts is out of the question, since there is only one market to predict.

Lacking a definitive record with which to assess predictive accuracy, it behooves any analyst to be humble about his or her ability to detect errors in the consensus opinion regarding either the market as a whole or specific securities. Overestimation of predictive ability leads to less-than-optimal performance and can lead to performance that is worse than that obtained via passive strategies. Underestimation also leads to less-than-optimal performance but better than passive performance. If predictors lack adequate humility, their enthusiasm can be tempered by directives from above reducing the size of the bets on individual securities and/or the amount of turnover allowed for the portfolio.

[1] And generally changing risk per dollar of price as well.

[2] The average cost will equal the *harmonic mean* of the prices (i.e., the reciprocal of the average of the reciprocals of the prices).

[3] This is generally the case when risky assets (such as *M* and *B*) with less-than-perfectly positively correlated returns are combined. For details, see W. F. Sharpe, *Portfolio Theory and Capital Markets* (New York: McGraw-Hill Book Company, 1970).

[4] In some cases the curve can move upward and to the left of point *M*, then turn to the right. In others it can move downward from point *M*. The major conclusions for action are the same, however; only the graphs are different.

[5] This formula is based on an analysis similar to that given in Jack Treynor and Fischer Black, "How to Use Security Analysis to Improve Performance," *The Journal of Business*, '46, no. 1 (January, 1973), 66–86. © 1973 by the University of Chicago. All Rights Reserved.

[6] The bets have a beta value of β_B and the proportion w has a proportionate beta value (and hence market exposure) of w times β_B.

[7] The return on Treasury bills is subtracted from E_M to reflect the fact that investment in the market portfolio uses up funds and thus should be assessed an opportunity cost. Increasing the size of the bets requires no new funds and thus incurs no cost.

[8] The need for a computer is especially great if any restrictions expressed as inequalities are relevant (e.g., no short sales allowed). Under such conditions, *quadratic programming methods* are required. For details see Sharpe, *Portfolio Theory and Capital Markets*.

[9] Jack L. Treynor and Fischer Black, "How to Use Security Analysis to Improve Portfolio Performance," *The Journal of Business*, 46, no. 1 (January, 1973) 66–86. © 1973 by the University of Chicago. All Rights Reserved.

[10] However, it may require negative holdings. This is generally impossible (short sales with required impounds are not the same as negative holdings). Simply changing negative values to zeros in this situation will not provide the generally best set of holdings; so a computer may be required after all.

[11] Among other things, the model underlying the approach is internally inconsistent (e.g., the market portfolio has nonmarket risk). This results in demonstrably suboptimal results in examples. When the technique is used with large numbers of securities, this source of error is less worrisome.

THE JOURNAL OF FINANCE • VOL. XXXVI, NO. 2 • MAY 1981

The Journal of FINANCE

VOL. XXXVI | MAY 1981 | NO. 2

Decentralized Investment Management

W. F. SHARPE*

Introduction

THE MARKOWITZ (12, 13) paradigm for mean-variance portfolio analysis involves two main components: (1) the preferences (indifference curves in mean-variance space) of the beneficiary of the portfolio's performance and (2) the oportunity set (feasible region in mean-variance space) based on someone's subjective estimates of security expected returns, risks and correlations. Most discussions assume that two people are involved—the "client" (beneficiary) and the "investment manager." The former's preferences and the latter's judgements are somehow brought together and an optimal portfolio selected.

In practice the situation is often more complex. Some investment funds (e.g. mutual funds) have many beneficiaries. Others (e.g. some pension funds) are managed by more than one investment firm. The problem of optimal portfolio selection in such a context is considerably more difficult than in the traditional setting.

We will not deal with the problems associated with more than one beneficiary here. Instead we will focus on situations in which more than one investment manager is employed in the process of selecting an investment portfolio. What might explain the use of such procedures? What types of objective functions should such managers be given? How should funds be allocated among managers? Under what circumstances can myopic decision rules lead to overall results that are optimal? These are the questions we address.

Current Practice

If security markets are perfectly efficient and correspond to the original capital asset pricing model of Sharpe (18), Lintner (10) and Mossin (14), the solution to

* Timken Professor of Finance, Graduate School of Business, Stanford University. Some of the ideas in this paper resulted from discussions with Keith Ambactsheer, David Howarth, Nancy Jacob, Jay Light, Robert Litzenberger, Barr Rosenberg, James Scott and Polly Shouse. This research was sponsored by the Stanford Program in Finance. Major contributors to the Stanford Program in Finance are: BankAmerica Foundation, The First Boston Corporation, the Chase Manhattan Bank, Continental Bank Foundation, The Dean Witter Foundation, General Electric Company, Goldman, Sachs & Co., Great Western Financial Corporation, E. F. Hutton and Co., Morgan Guaranty Trust Company, Morgan Stanley & Co., Inc., Salomon Brothers, Security Pacific National Bank and Wells Fargo Bank.

the investment management problem is straightforward: every client should invest in some combination of the "market portfolio" and a riskless asset. If markets are perfectly efficient but more complex (e.g. conform to a more complicated asset pricing model) the task is more difficult. Nonetheless, in such a world a single "consensus" set of predictions could be used for the management of a portfolio and such predictions would be relatively simple to obtain and use.

In fact, those in charge of large pools of money (e.g. corporate pension fund sponsors) act as if they do not believe that the market is perfectly efficient. They hire investment managers in the belief that the managers they select can make better predictions in at least some domains than can the average, or "consensus" investor.

Private pension funds now hold approximately $225 billion in assets; state and local retirement funds hold an additional $180 billion (25). Moreover, the typical large fund uses multiple investment managers. One survey (8) identified 18 funds, each of which used more than 15 managers. In 1980 the American Telephone and Telegraph Corporation employed 112 investment managers for its pension funds (8).

Another aspect of current practice seems puzzling: each manager of a multiply-managed portfolio is typically given an explicit or implicit objective function that is *myopic*—i.e. he or she is not expected to select securities that "fit well" with the remainder of the portfolio. Usually the manager does not even know the composition of the rest of the portfolio. In a recent survey of large pension funds only 23% of the respondents disagreed with the statement: "With multiple managers, the individual managers should not be held responsible for coordinating investments with the portfolios of other managers." (7).

How can this possibly be optimal? Portfolio theory holds that security covariances are crucial aspects of portfolio risk. Is it possible to ignore many of them and still obtain optimal results? If so, how? These questions are central in the analysis that follows.

Another aspect of current practice also appears to be contrary to first principles. Implicitly or explicitly clients often give their managers incentives to worry about *relative performance* as well as *absolute performance*. A manager might be told that a poor portfolio return is undesirable, but that a return below that of some reference such as Standard and Poor's 500-stock index is even worse.

There is much controversy about the actual efficiency of security markets. We will not deal with this issue. Rather, we take the phenomenon of decentralized investment management on its own ground. We assume that clients believe that they can find superior investment managers. Given that assumption, we then attempt to explain some of the key aspects of their behavior.

All the cases to be considered involve one "client" and one or more "managers." Moreover, we assume that the client has a well-defined objective which is a function of portfolio return and risk. While most pension fund sponsors behave as if this were the case, there are strong arguments for alternative approaches, as shown by Sharpe (20), Treynor, Priest and Regan (24), Tepper (21) and Black (3). Here too, we take the problem on its own ground.

Reasons for Decentralized Management

Investment managers perform many functions: trading, record-keeping, risk and return estimation and portfolio management. While special skills may exist in trading, record-keeping and management *per se*, we focus exclusively on the prediction function.

Rightly or wrongly, a client who employs several managers believes that the best predictions can be obtained by some appropriate blend of the predictions of the chosen managers. If so, why not have the managers provide their predictions, with the client blending them and performing the appropriate portfolio optimization? In other words, why not replace *decentralized management* with *decentralized prediction-making* and *centralized management*?

To answer this question one needs to consider the economics of the investment prediction industry. While the *average* cost of a set of predictions may be substantial, the direct *marginal* cost of providing them to another user is very small. Moreover, a good set of predictions should be worth more to a large investor than to a small one. More specifically—the value should be related to the amount of money that will be influenced by the predictions. The predictor has a (natural) monopoly on a set of predictions and, if desiring to maximize profit, will wish to employ price discrimination (or, to use a less perjorative term—value-based pricing).

For effective price discrimination resale must be precluded. The predictor will thus have an incentive to make it difficult for other managers to obtain his or her predictions. This is one reason why investment firms may not wish to provide their predictions to the client, since the latter might divulge them to competitors. But there is another, perhaps more important, reason. If several sets of predictions are used for a centralized decision it is difficult to determine the value of one set for the overall portfolio, reducing the scope for value-based pricing strategies.

Many managers refuse to "sell" their predictions. Instead they require clients to give them money to "manage." Their predictions are employed in the management of such money, with mangement fees based in whole or in part on the amount of money under management. Moreover, the total fee charged is almost always a monotonic increasing function of the amount of money managed, although the fee per dollar managed is typically a decreasing function of the money managed (another aspect consistent with the traditional model of price discrimination).

To represent such a situation we assume that the client cannot obtain a manager's predictions directly, nor infer them from the manager's investment decisions (as described by Sharpe (19) and Fisher (6)) and then use the inferred predictions to manage other money. We will, however, assume that the client knows what the best "blend" of the managers' predictions would be—i.e. has estimated a function relating the best prediction to the (unknown) predictions of the managers. This can be done via regression analysis of ex post results on ex ante predictions (using old data), as described by Ambachtsheer and Farrell (1) or judgementally. Both approaches are currently used.

Approaches to Decentralized Management

Why have more than one investment manager? In discussions of the practice, such as those of Ezra (5) and Williams (26) two themes dominate: diversification and specialization. For example, Williams (26) differentiates between "diversification of styles"—hiring experts on different sets of securities—and "pure diversification"—based on a desire "... to have more than one manager in case a manager makes a large error."

To make these concepts more rigorous, we will use the term *diversification of style* to cover a polar case in which each manager analyzes a completely different subset of the universe of securities. The term *diversification of judgement* will be used to cover the other polar case in which two or more managers analyze the same subset of securities. Of course most situations involve both aspects, but as will be seen, these can be treated as combinations of the two extreme cases.

Previous Research

Decentralized investment management has received little direct attention, but much of the theory of investment is, of course, relevant. Markowitz' (12, 13) mean-variance approach constitutes the basic structure to be used here. Although the assumption of unlimited risk-free borrowing and lending will not be invoked, much of the analysis relies on separation results similar to that obtained initially under this assumption by Tobin (22). Separation has been employed in other contexts by Lintner (11), Black (2), Brennan (4), Kraus and Litzenberger (9), and others. In part of the analysis we will utilize the idea of "consensus" forecasts; these could (but need not) be related to the key attributes of an efficient market model such as the original capital asset pricing model of Sharpe (18), Lintner (10) and Mossin (14), the zero-beta model of Lintner (11) and Black (2), the tax-related model of Brennan (4), the arbitrage pricing theory of Ross (16), or any other equilibrium model. For generality we simply refer to "consensus estimates," leaving the interpretation open.

The first direct approach to separation in a nearly-efficient market context was the active/passive dichotomy of Treynor and Black (23). Their paper relied on the single-index model of return generation, but the important results are easily generalized (as will be shown).

In a seminal paper on multiple investment management, Rosenberg (15) dealt with the situation we term "diversification of judgement." A later paper by Rudd and Rosenerg (17), while concentrating on other issues, covers some aspects of the situation we term "diversification of style."

Much of this paper involves the restatement, generalization, and extension of previous work. No claim is made for complete originality.

Assumptions

The overall objective to be maximized is:

$$u_p = e_p - v_p/t_p \tag{1}$$

where:

u_p: the "utility" of the portfolio

e_p: the expected return of the portfolio, using "optimum" estimates of security expected returns

v_p: the variance of the portfolio

t_p: the risk tolerance for the portfolio (the client's marginal rate of substitution of variance for expected return)

The client's risk tolerance (t_p) is assumed to be constant over the likely range of decisions regarding e_p and v_p.

Unrestricted short sales are assumed to be possible with no required impounds. We also assume that neither management fees nor trading costs are affected by the client's allocation of funds among managers nor by the objective functions assigned to the managers. In addition, we assume that it is possible to provide appropriate incentives to lead each manager to maximize the objective function specified by the client.

All expected returns and covariances are assumed to be stated on an after-tax basis for the client in question. And, as indicated earlier, restrictions are assumed to exist so that one manager's predictions may not be used by another manager or by the client for "in-house" money management.

A major (and extreme) assumption relates to predictions: we assume that all managers analyzing a set of securities agree about the risks and correlations of those securities (i.e. the entries in that portion of the overall covariance matrix). Moreover, we assume that the client can, if needed, obtain such consensus estimates of covariances. On the other hand, we assume that different managers may make estimates of security expected returns that differ from the "consensus" estimates (which may or may not be derived from an equilibrium model). In such a world, one hires managers for (hopefully) superior predictions of expected returns, not risks.

This assumption involves a troublesome lack of symmetry. Presumably two analysts with different information will make different estimates of both risk and return. Two defenses are offered for our approach. First, it conforms to at least some current practice: a number of investment managers subscribe to an econometric service that provides security risk estimates, adding their own estimates of expected returns and then determining the implied "optimal" portfolios. Another reason is related to the main question addressed here. Under this assumption myopic decision-making can in some circumstances lead to optimal results. Our approach allows for different information sets (obviously necessary to justify decentralized decisions) yet provides a setting in which such procedures can sometimes prove competitive with centralized decision-making. In the presence of significant disagreement about risks as well as returns, decentralized decision-making is likely to be significantly less desirable. Since we analyze the procedure in its best possible setting, the practical implications of our results should be assessed accordingly.

The First-Best Solution

While (1) is the most natural form for the client's objective function, it is convenient to transform it from expected return equivalent units to variance equivalent units. Thus we assume that the objective is to maximize:

$$u_p = t_p e_p - v_p \tag{1 a}$$

subject only to the "full investment" constraint:

$$\textstyle\sum_{i=1}^{n} x_{ip} = 1 \tag{2}$$

where:

x_{ip}: the proportion of the portfolio invested in security i
n: the number of securities

To solve this problem one must maximize the Lagrangean function:

$$t_p e_p - v_p + z_p\,[1 - \textstyle\sum_{i=1}^{n} x_{ip}] \tag{3}$$

where:

z_p: a Lagrange multiplier for the portfolio (the marginal utility of money in variance equivalent terms)

The first-order conditions—which are both necessary and sufficient in this case—are:

$$\begin{bmatrix} 2c_{11} & \cdots & 2c_{1n} & 1 \\ \cdot & & \cdot & \cdot \\ \cdot & & \cdot & \cdot \\ \cdot & & \cdot & \cdot \\ 2c_{n1} & \cdots & 2c_{nn} & 1 \\ 1 & \cdots & 1 & 0 \end{bmatrix} \begin{bmatrix} x_{1p} \\ \cdot \\ \cdot \\ \cdot \\ x_{np} \\ z_p \end{bmatrix} = \begin{bmatrix} 0 \\ \cdot \\ \cdot \\ \cdot \\ 0 \\ 1 \end{bmatrix} + t_p \begin{bmatrix} e_{1p} \\ \cdot \\ \cdot \\ \cdot \\ e_{np} \\ 0 \end{bmatrix} \tag{3a}$$

where:

c_{ij}: the covariance between the returns of securities i and j
e_{ip}: the "optimum" estimate of the expected return of security i

This is more coveniently written in matrix form:

$$DY_p = K + t_p F_p \tag{3b}$$

where each upper-case letter represents the corresponding matrix or vector in (3a).

The solution to this system of equations is:

$$Yp = \underbrace{[GK]}_{\substack{\text{minimum-}\\ \text{variance}\\ \text{portfolio}}} + t_p \underbrace{[GF_p]}_{\substack{\text{divergences per}\\ \text{unit of risk}\\ \text{tolerance}}} \tag{4}$$

where:

$$G = \text{the inverse of } D$$

The vector Y_p represents the optimal portfolio (plus the associated value of z_p). Note that it can be considered to be the sum of two vectors. The first (GK) is a *portfolio* (in the sense that the values of the first n terms sum to 1), while the second is a constant (t_p) times a set of *divergences* (in the sense that the first n terms sum to 0). For a client with no tolerance for risk (GK) is the optimal portfolio—thus it must be the minimum-variance portfolio, as indicated. The second vector (GF_p) indicates the optimal divergence of each holding (from that of the minimum-variance portfolio) per unit of client risk tolerance.

This *separation* result is similar to that of Lintner (11) and Black (2); as in their "zero-beta" model, all clients can be served by mixtures of two actual portfolios—one based on $t_p = 0$, the other on an arbitrarily large value of t_p.

Active-Passive Management

We turn now to the first case in which a client wishes to choose a portfolio that is optimal for a specified "blend" of predictions. In this case the ingredients are the consensus forecasts of expected returns and those of a single "active" manager—i.e. one with beliefs that diverge in at least some respects from those of the consensus. The client is assumed to have determined an appropriate weight w_k such that the optimal etimate of a security's expected return is given by:

$$e_{ip} = e_{ic} + w_k \underbrace{[e_{ik} - e_{ic}]}_{\substack{\text{manager } k\text{'s "alpha"} \\ \text{estimate for security } i \\ (= \alpha_{ik})}} \tag{5}$$

where:

e_{ic}: the "consensus" estimate of the expected return of security i

w_k: the weight associated with manager k's estimate of expected return for a security in the equation for the optimum estimate of expected return when more than one manager's estimate is to be used

e_{ik}: manager k's estimate of the expected return of security i

α_{ik}: manager k's estimate of the alpha value for security i

As indicated, the client feels that the best estimate of a security's expected return is the consensus value plus a portion of manager k's "alpha" (defined as the difference between manager k's estimate and that of the consensus of investors).

Rewriting (5) gives:

$$e_{ip} = [l - w_k]e_{ic} + w_k e_{ik} \tag{5a}$$

and

$$e_{ip} = w_c e_{ic} + w_k e_{ik} \tag{5b}$$

where:

w_c: the weight associated with the consensus estimate of expected return for a security in the equation for the optimum estimate of expected return

The system of equations (5b) is more conveniently written in matrix notation:

$$F_p = w_c F_c + w_k F_k \tag{6}$$

where:

$$F_c = [e_{1c} \cdots e_{nc}\ 0]'$$

$$F_k = [e_{1k} \cdots e_{nk}\ 0]'$$

Note, from (5*a*) that the weights in (6) sum to 1.

Substituting (6) in (4) gives the solution for this case:

$$Y_p = [GK] + t_p\{G[w_c F_c + w_k F_k]\} \tag{7}$$

Rewriting:

$$Y_p = \underbrace{GK + t_p GF_c}_{\substack{\text{optimal passive} \\ \text{portfolio}}} + \underbrace{w_k t_p G[F_k - F_c]}_{\substack{\text{optimal active} \\ \text{divergences}}} \tag{7a}$$

This version of the solution shows that the optimal portfolio can be treated as composed of two portions: (1) an *optimal passive portfolio* for the client ($GK + t_p GF_c$) and a set of *optimal active divergences* ($w_k t_p G[F_k - F_c]$) due to the manager's private information. The greater the reliability of this information, the greater should be w_k and the divergences of holdings from optimal passive (consensus) amounts.

Another grouping of the terms in (7) is also of interest:

$$Y_p = \underbrace{w_c[GK + t_p GF_c]}_{\substack{\text{optimal passive} \\ \text{portfolio}}} + \underbrace{w_k[GK + t_p GF_k]}_{\substack{\text{optimal active} \\ \text{portfolio}}} \tag{7b}$$

This version shows that the portfolio can be broken into two parts—an optimal passive and an optimal active portfolio. The appropriate overall portfolio can be considered a combination of these components, with the weights dependent on the active manager's predictive ability.

This decomposition can also be used to determine an optimal decentralized investment policy. The client's investment funds can be allocated in accordance with predictive accuracy, with the portion w_c invested by a passive manager and the portion w_k invested by the active manager:

$$a_c = w_c$$

$$a_k = w_k$$

where:

a_c: the proportion of the portfolio managed passively
a_k: the proportion of the portfolio invested by manager k

Each manager can be instructed to maximize a myopic objective function (i.e. one requiring no information relating to the rest of the portfolio). The passive manager is told to maximize:

$$u_c = e_c - v_c/t_p$$

where

u_c: the "utility" to be maximized by the passive manager
e_c: the expected return of a passively-managed portfolio, using "consensus" estimates of security expected returns
v_c: the variance of the passively-managed portfolio

The active manager is told to maximize:

$$u_k = e_k - v_k/t_p$$

where

u_k: the "utility" to be maximized by manager k
e_k: the expected return of manager k's portfolio, using manager k's estimates of security expected returns
v_k: the variance of manager k's portfolio

This suffices, since $[GK + t_p GF_c]$ maximizes u_c and $[GK + t_p GF_k]$ maximizes u_k.

Note that the client's overall risk tolerance (t_p) is used in each case. Thus each manager is instructed to act as if his or her portion of the fund were the entire portfolio. In this situation decentralized management with myopic decision rules can give completely optimal results.

Relative Performance Objectives

The active/passive approach is completely feasible if w_k does not exceed 1. But what if a client wants a manager to be more aggressive than normal—i.e. assigns a w_k value greater than 1 to the manager's predictions? In such a case w_c in (7b) becomes negative, implying a short sale of the optimal passive portfolio in order to generate extra money for active management. As a practical matter, short sale of a passive portfolio is likely to be costly or precluded entirely. However, the desired result can be obtained in another way. In fact, the optimal portfolio can be achieved for any value of w_k without hiring a passive manager if the active manager is given an objective function that includes *relative performance.*

The decisions required to maximize portfolio expected return do not differ from those required to maximize the expected difference between the return on the portfolio and that of some standard portfolio. To represent "relative performance" as a separate objective thus requires modification of the treatment of risk. For our purposes the appropriate standard is the optimal passive portfolio for the client. A client "concerned about relative performance" is interested in the likely divergence of the portfolio's return from that of the standard portfolio. This can be reflected in an expanded objective function:

$$u_k = t_p e_k - v_k - s_k d_k \tag{8}$$

where

d_k: the variance of the difference between the return of manager k's portfolio and the return of the optimal passive portfolio

s_k: the weight attached to relative risk in manager k's objective function

In (8) d_k is the variance of the difference between the return on the portfolio and that of the specified "index fund." A positive value of s_k indicates that the client considers relative risk to be bad, other things equal. A negative value indicates that he or she considers it good, other things equal; more specifically, for a given absolute risk (v_k) the larger the relative risk (d_k) the better.

Note that (8) is a myopic decision rule. It relies on the composition of an optimal passive portfolio, but does not require information about any decisions made by the client or by other managers.

The solution to (8) is:

$$Y_k = \underbrace{[GK] + t_p[GF_c]}_{\text{optimal passive portfolio}} + \underbrace{\{1/[1 + s_k]\}t_pG[F_k - F_c]}_{\text{active divergences}} \tag{9}$$

The similarity to (7a) is obvious. Clearly there is a direct correspondence between s_k in (9) and w_k in (7a). By providing the manager with an objective function that includes relative performance, the client can induce the manager to choose a portfolio that is optimal, given the client's assessment of the latter's predictive ability. To induce behavior that is less aggressive than normal, relative risk is penalized. To induce behavior that is more aggressive than normal. relative risk is rewarded.

In practice most clients explicitly or implicitly consider relative risk undesirable (over and above its contribution to absolute risk). In the case of a single active manager this is consistent with a belief that the manager's predictions are poorer than the manager considers them to be. This may well be a healthy attitude.

Diversification of Style

We turn now to cases involving more than one active manager. To make the notation as simple as possible we will usually focus on situations involving only two managers. Extensions to cases with more than two managers are, however, straightforward.

We begin with the polar case in which each manager analyzes a completely separate subset of the universe of securities, with no concern for the remainder or for any interrelationships between securities in the domain analyzed and those in the remainder of the universe.

Portfolio Attributes

If the client's funds are allocated between two managers, with the portion a_1 given to the first manager and the portion a_2 ($= 1 - a_1$) given to the second, the expected return of the portfolio will be:

$$e_p = a_1e_1 + a_2e_2 \tag{10}$$

Note that the expected return of each of the active portfolios is assumed to equal the amount estimated by the manager of that portfolio.

The variance of the overall portfolio will be:

$$v_p = a_1^2 v_1 + a_2^2 v_2 + 2a_1 a_2 v_{12} \tag{11}$$

where

v_{kl}: the covariance between the returns of the portfolios of managers k and l

and its utility to the client will be:

$$u_p = a_1 e_1 + a_2 e_2 - [a_1^2 v_1 + a_2^2 v_2 + 2a_1 a_2 v_{12}]/t_p \tag{12}$$

The goal is, of course, to maximize (12).

Improvement Procedures

In general, the first-best solution cannot be obtained in one step with decentralized management since covariances between the returns of the active portfolios must be taken into account. However, an iterative process can be used. Two types of procedures can lead to an improvement in u_p. By alternating between them, an overall optimum can, in principle, be obtained.

One improvement procedure involves reallocation of the client's funds, on the assumption that the investment managers will not alter their relative holdings of securities:

$$\text{given } e_1,\ e_2,\ v_1,\ v_2,\ v_{12}$$

$$\text{select } a_1,\ a_2 \text{ to maximize } u_p.$$

In effect, the portfolios are treated as mutual funds in which more or less may be invested. Unfortunately, even with this limiting assumption the procedure requires estimates of the expected returns of the component portfolios—values that are not easily estimated.

The second improvement procedure singles out one manager for attention, assuming that the allocation of funds and the compositions of other managers' portfolios will remain unchanged. The manager in question is asked to maximize a function that includes his or her portfolio's expected return and variance plus its covariance with the remainder of the overall portfolio. Rewriting (12):

$$u_p = a_1[e_1 - a_1 v_1/t_p - 2a_2 v_{12}/t_p] + [a_2 e_2 - a_2^2 v_2/t_p] \tag{13}$$

Thus manager 1 can be instructed to maximize:

$$u_1 = e_1 - v_1/t_1 - 2a_2 v_{12}/t_p \tag{14}$$

with:

$$t_1 = t_p/a_1 \tag{14a}$$

Or manager 2 can be instructed to maximize:

$$u_2 = e_2 - v_2/t_2 - 2a_1 v_{12}/t_p \tag{15}$$

with:

$$t_2 = t_p/a_2 \tag{15a}$$

Note that this type of procedure does not utilize a truly myopic decision rule. In general, the selected manager must utilize information that depends on the composition of the remainder of the portfolio.

Modification for a Multi-Factor Return Generating Model

An interesting special case arises when security covariances can be attributed to covariances among a set of *factors*. Assume that returns are generated by the following process:

$$\tilde{r}_i = \sum_{j=1}^{nf} b_{ij}\tilde{f}_j + \tilde{h}_i \tag{16}$$

with:

$$\text{covariance } [\tilde{h}_i, \tilde{h}_j] = 0 \quad \text{for all} \quad i \neq j \tag{16a}$$

where:

$\tilde{r}_i$: the return on security i (a random variable)
b_{ij}: the sensitivity (beta) of security i to factor j
$\tilde{f}_j$: the value of factor j (a random variable)
$\tilde{h}_i$: security i's residual return (a random variable)
nf: the number of factors

Under these conditions the last term in (14) will be:

$$2[a_2/t_p]v_{12} = \underbrace{[X_1'B]}_{\text{portfolio 1 betas}}\underbrace{\underbrace{[QB'X_2]}_{\text{portfolio 2 betas}}2a_2/t_p}_{\text{penalty/rewards for portfolio 1 betas}} \tag{17}$$

where:

$X_k = [x_{1k} \cdots x_{nk}]'$

x_{ik} : the proportion of manager k's portfolio invested in security i

$$B = \begin{bmatrix} b_{11} & \cdots & b_{1,nf} \\ \vdots & & \vdots \\ b_{n,1} & \cdots & b_{n,nf} \end{bmatrix}$$

b_{kj}: the sensitivity (beta) of manager k's portfolio to factor j

nf : the number of factors

$$Q = \begin{bmatrix} cf_{11} & \cdots & cf_{1,nf} \\ \vdots & & \vdots \\ cf_{nf,1} & \cdots & cf_{nf,nf} \end{bmatrix}$$

cf_{ij}: the covariance between factors i and j

As indicated, the magnitude of this term involves the beta values of manager 1's portfolio relative to the factors and a set of penalties or rewards—one for each beta value. The latter are related to the beta values of the remainder of the portfolio and the covariance structure of the factors (Q).

Letting:

P_{kj}: the penalty for the sensitivity of manager k's portfolio to factor j

the objective function to be given a selected manager can be written as:

$$u_k = e_k - v_k/t_k - \sum_{k=1}^{nf} b_{kj}P_{kj} \tag{18}$$

where

b_{kj}: the sensitivity (beta) of manager k's portfolio to factor j

In effect, the manager is instructed to regard certain beta values as bad ($P_{k,j} > 0$) and others as good ($P_{k,j} < 0$), with relevant magnitudes indicated. The manager need not be told the actual composition of the remainder of the portfolio, but the decision rule is still not truly myopic since the beta value penalties depend on the holdings in the remainder of the portfolio.

A particularly interesting case occurs when all the securities in a manager's domain have the same beta value with respect to the first factor, the same beta value with respect to the second factor, etc. Then the portfolio beta values will be unaffected by the manager's security choices and (18) can be simplified to:

$$u_k = e_k - v_k/t_k \tag{19}$$

In this (very special) case the appropriate decision rule for each manager is myopic, although the rule for allocating funds *among* managers still requires estimates of covariances among the subsets of securities (and their expected returns).

As a practical matter myopic decision making in the case of nonoverlapping domains is likely to be desirable when the beta values of securities within a domain relative to any "important" factor do not differ substantially. A factor's importance will depend on the sensitivities of the remainder of the portfolio to the factors and on the factor's covariances with other factors.

Diversification of Judgement

We turn now to the other polar case, in which every manager analyzes the same subset of the universe of securities. We assume, of course, that due to different information sets, the managers reach different conclusions regarding security expected returns. As before, much of the discussion will employ a two-manager case for convenience.

As in the previous analysis of active and passive management we assume that the client has determined an optimal relationship between the predictions of the managers and an unbiased estimate of expected return, given all their available information. We will analyze two possibilities although they by no means exhaust the list of interesting alternatives.

If the client believes that the best estimate of a security's expected return is bounded by the managers' estimates, the equation for optimal estimates of expected returns can be written as:

$$e_{ip} = w_1 e_{i1} + w_2 e_{i2} \tag{20}$$

with:

$$w_1 + w_2 = 1 \tag{20a}$$

Note that we assume that a specific manager's predictive ability is the same for every stock analyzed. Note also that no use is made here of consensus predictions.

The set of equations (20) can be written more succinctly in matrix notation:

$$F_p = w_1 F_1 + w_2 F_2 \tag{21}$$

The optimal portfolio can be found by substituting (21) in (4):

$$Y_p = [GK] + t_p\{G[w_1 F_1 + w_2 F_2]\} \tag{22}$$

Re-arranging terms gives:

$$Y_p = w_1 \underbrace{[GK + t_p GF_1]}_{\text{optimal portfolio for manager 1}} + w_2 \underbrace{[GK + t_p GF_2]}_{\text{optimal portfolio for manager 2}} \tag{22a}$$

The similarity to our analysis of active and passive management is not surprising. And, as in that case, decentralized investment management with myopic decision rules can easily provide the first-best solution. Funds are allocated in accordance with predictive abilities:

$$a_1 = w_1$$

$$a_2 = w_2$$

with the following objective functions given to the managers:

$$u_1 = e_1 - v_1/t_p$$

$$u_2 = e_2 - v_2/t_p$$

Note that each manager is instructed to act as if he or she were managing the entire portfolio (i.e. the client's overall risk tolerance (t_p) is used in the objective functions).

The procedure may not be feasible in some cases. For example, consider a situation in which the client believes that there is a relationship between each security's alpha value and the alpha values estimated by the managers:

$$\alpha_{ip} = w_1 \alpha_{i1} + w_2 \alpha_{i2} \tag{23}$$

where:

α_{ip}: the "optimal" estimate of the alpha value for security i

There is no obvious reason for the weights to sum to 1 in this case. For example, if each manager makes unbiased estimates given his or her information, each value of w_k would be 1 if *only* that manager's predictions were used (i.e. it would correspond to a coefficient in a *simple* linear regression of alpha on predicted alpha). But the parameters in (23) correspond to coefficients in a *multiple* regression. Only if the predictions were completely uncorrelated with each other would they equal the corresponding coefficients from a simple linear regression. If this were the case, and if each manager's predictions were unbiased (given his or her information set) the sum of the w_k's would equal the number of managers—an amount clearly greater than 1. More realistic cases would generally lead to smaller sums, but the amount could easily exceed 1.

To determine the optimal estimate of a security's expected return in this case one must incorporate consensus predictions:

$$e_{ip} = e_{ic} + \alpha_{ip} \tag{24}$$

Given the definition of alpha, this can be written as:

$$e_{ip} = e_{ic} + w_1[e_{i1} - e_{ic}] + w_2[e_{i2} - e_{ic}] \tag{24a}$$

or:

$$e_{ip} = w_c e_{ic} + w_1 e_{i1} + w_2 e_{i2} \tag{24b}$$

As shown, the expected return can be considered a weighted average of three estimates; moreover, in this case the weights will sum to 1:

$$w_c = 1 - w_1 - w_2 \tag{25a}$$

$$w_c + w_1 + w_2 = 1 \tag{25b}$$

In principle one could treat this as an expanded version of the case previously analyzed and apply similar procedures to obtain the solution. However, if the weights for the managers' alpha predictions sum to more than 1, w_c will be negative. With the previous procedure this would require short sale of the optimal passive portfolio to finance the allocation of more than the client's total fund to the active managers. However, there is an alternative. The approach suggested for changing the "aggressiveness" of a single active manager can be used: i.e. relative risk can be included in the managers' assigned objective functions.

While many alternative combinations are possible, an interesting one involves the allocation of funds in accordance with the managers' predictive abilities:

$$a_k = w_k / \sum_{k=1}^{m} w_k \tag{26}$$

where

m: the number of managers

Each manager is then assigned an objective function including both relative and absolute risk:

$$u_k = e_k - v_k/t_p - [s_k/t_p]d_k \tag{27}$$

The attitude toward relative risk is given by:

$$s_k = [1/\sum_{k=1}^{m} w_k] - 1 \tag{28}$$

Note that each manager is given the same objective function. Relative risk *per* se is penalized ($s_k > 0$) if the sum of the weights for the managers' predictive abilities is less than 1; it is rewarded ($s_k < 0$) if the sum is greater than 1.

In practice many clients using more than one manager appear to explicitly or implicitly consider relative risk undesirable (over and above its impact on absolute risk). This is consistent with a belief that the investment managers consider their predictions better than they really are (i.e. their alpha values are biased away from zero)—a belief that may be well-founded.

Diversification of Style and Judgement

Often the investment managers hired by a client analyze different but not completely different sets of securities. In such a situation there are elements of both diversification of style and diversification of judgement.

Absent clever partitioning of the domains analyzed by the managers into subsets of securities with common values in the cells of the off-diagonal blocks of the covariance matrix, decentralized investment management with truly myopic decision rules cannot produce the first-best solution directly in such a situation. However, the optimal solution can be approached iteratively, by combining the approaches we have discussed.

First, one should partition the universe of securities into different domains in such a way that within each domain a single optimal estimation rule applies—e.g. one of the form:

$$e_{ip} = \sum_{k=1}^{m} w_k e_{ik} \tag{29}$$

The procedures described for *diversification of style* can then be applied directly, with each of these domains treated as a single "manager."

The funds allocated to a given domain can be divided among the managers who analyze that subset of securities using the procedures described for *diversification of judgement*—i.e. in accordance with the managers' predictive abilities for securities within that domain. For such securities, each manager can be assigned an objective function that takes into account covariance with all the securities in the portfolio that are not in the domain (using relationships of the form (14) or (18)). Such decisions are myopic in one sense—they do not take into account holdings of securities in the domain chosen by other managers. But they are not fully myopic—directly or indirectly they should, in general, take into account relationships with the securities in the portfolio that are not in the domain.

Conclusions

It is difficult to provide a useful summary of this rather complex topic. To a person schooled in portfolio theory, decentralized investment management with myopic decision rules seems likely to be a decidedly second-best approach to the problem. Moreover, the emphasis on relative performance seems misplaced, since it is difficult to see why this attribute should enter the client's utility function. The message of this paper for those with such feelings is simply that such practices may be sensible after all.

On the other hand, such practices may not be sensible. Some people involved in decisions to hire several investment managers may not fully appreciate the problems associated with security covariances and the rather limited conditions under which decentralized management with fully myopic decision rules can give desirable results.

At the very least, our analysis emphasizes the need to distinguish between cases in which one hires several managers to analyze one subset of securities (*diversification of judgement*) and cases in which different managers are hired to analyze different sets of securities (*diversification of style*). As we have shown these are quite different situations in terms of the potential efficiency of decentralized management and the procedures that can help attain that efficiency.

There is, of course, much more to this problem. We have assumed away many important aspects of the principal-agent relationship(s). We have also disregarded possibilities for Pareto-optimal procedures for combining the agents' information sets for use in a centralized decision without making any of the agents (or the client) worse off. Finally, we have sidestepped the entire issue of market efficiency and the potential value of the agents' information sets (including their analytic procedures).

In short, we have clearly provided necessary and sufficient conditions for the traditional final sentence in such a paper: More research on this subject is needed.

REFERENCES

1. Ambachtsheer, Keith P. and Farrell, James L., Jr., "Can Active Management Add Value?" *Financial Analysts' Journal*, November/December 1979.
2. Black, Fischer, "Capital Market Equilibrium with Restricted Borrowing," *Journal of Business*, July 1972.
3. Black, Fischer, "The Tax Consequences of Long-Run Pension Policy," *Financial Analysts' Journal*, July/August 1980.
4. Brennan, M. J., "Taxes, Market Valuation and Corporate Financial Policy," *National Tax Journal*, 23, 417–427.
5. Ezra, D. Don, *Understanding Pension Fund Finance and Investment*, Pagurian Press Limited, Toronto, 1980.
6. Fisher, L., "Analysts' Input and Portfolio Changes," *Financial Analysts' Journal*, May/June 1975.
7. Greenwich Research Associates, *Large Corporate Pension Funds*, 1980.
8. *Institutional Investor*, June 1980, pp. 57–58.
9. Kraus, Alan and Litzenberger, Robert H., "Skewness Preference and the Valuation of Risk Assets," *Journal of Finance*, September 1976.
10. Lintner, J., "The Valuation of Risk Assets and the Selection of Risky Investments in Stock Portfolios and Capital Budgets," *Review of Economics and Statistics*, February 1965.
11. Lintner, J., "The Aggregation of Investors' Diverse Judgements and Preferences in Purely Competitive Markets," *Journal of Financial and Quantitative Analysis*, December 1969.
12. Markowitz, H., "Portfolio Selection," *Journal of Finance*, March 1952.
13. Markowitz, H., *Portfolio Selection: Efficient Diversification of Investments*, Wiley, 1959.
14. Mossin, J., "Equilibrium in a Capital Asset Market," *Econometrica*, October 1966.
15. Rosenberg, B., "Institutional Investment Management with Multiple Portfolio Managers," University of California Berkeley Institute of Business and Economic Research, working paper #65, October 1977.
16. Ross, Stephen A., "The Arbitrage Theory of Capital Asset Pricing," *Journal of Economic Theory*, 13, 341–360.
17. Rudd, A. and Rosenberg, B., "The 'Market Model' in Investment Management," *Journal of Finance*, May 1980.

18. Sharpe, William F., "Capital Asset Prices: A Theory of Market Equilibrium under Conditions of Risk," *Journal of Finance*, September 1964.
19. Sharpe, William F., "Imputing Expected Security Returns from Portfolio Composition," *Journal of Financial and Quantitative Analysis*, June 1974.
20. Sharpe, William F., "Corporate Pension Funding Policy," *Journal of Financial Economics*, June 1976.
21. Tepper, Irwin, "Taxation and Corporate Pension Policy," unpublished.
22. Tobin, J., "Liquidity Preference as Behavior Toward Risk," *Review of Economic Studies*, February 1958.
23. Treynor, Jack L. and Black, Fischer, "How to Use Security Analysis to Improve Portfolio Selection," *Journal of Business*, January 1974.
24. Treynor, Jack L., Regan, Patrick and Priest, William, "Pension Claims and Corporate Assets," *Financial Analysts' Journal*, May/June 1978.
25. United States Securities and Exchange Commission, *Statistical Bulletin*, June 1980.
26. Williams, Arthur, III, *Managing Your Investment Manager*, Dow-Jones Irwin, 1980.

4 Optimal Funding and Asset Allocation Rules for Defined-Benefit Pension Plans

J. Michael Harrison and William F. Sharpe

4.1 Introduction

Considerable attention has been devoted to the funding of defined-benefit pension plans. Both the level of funding and the allocation of fund assets have been considered from the viewpoints of various interested parties (beneficiaries, corporate managers, corporate shareholders, and the Pension Benefit Guaranty Corporation). Both practical and theoretical investigations have tended to characterize the asset allocation decision as one of choosing an appropriate "bond-stock mix."

Sharpe (1976) showed that, in the absence of taxes, if the parties bearing the cost of possible default behave rationally, neither the asset allocation decision nor the funding decision may affect the wealth of corporate shareholders. On the other hand, if some parties do not require compensation for actions that increase the risk of default, the optimal policy from the viewpoint of corporate shareholders may involve funding as little as possible and using asset allocation to maximize default risk.

Two important papers, by Black (1980) and Tepper (1981), consider the effects of current tax law, assuming that there is no probability of default.[1] Under these conditions shareholder wealth may be maximized by funding to the greatest possible extent and holding assets (such as bonds) taxed highly for other investors. This chapter considers a world in which pension funds may default, the cost of the associated risk of default is not borne fully by the sponsoring corporation, and there are differential tax effects. We explore ways in which the wealth of the shareholders

J. Michael Harrison is professor of decision sciences, Stanford University Graduate School of Business. William F. Sharpe is professor of finance, Stanford University Graduate School of Business and research associate, National Bureau of Economic Research.

The comments and suggestions of Jeremy Bulow, Myron Scholes, and Robert Litzenberger are gratefully acknowledged.

of a corporation sponsoring a pension plan might be increased if the Internal Revenue Service (IRS) and the Pension Benefit Guaranty Corporation (PBGC) follow simple (and naive) policies. This analysis suggests that the two agencies may want to consider more complex rules. Optimal policy for the PBGC is discussed briefly in Sharpe (1976); Tepper (1982) describes some of the issues involved in setting tax policy. We do not explore such issues here. Instead, we hope to provide useful inputs for addressing these more fundamental questions.

4.2 The General Problem

Throughout we will deal with a defined-benefit plan. An initial decision must be made concerning the amount of assets in the plan. Following this decision, we assume that the plan will be frozen. That is, no further benefits will accrue and no further contributions will be made. In addition to the decision concerning the level of initial assets, decisions must be made in subsequent periods concerning the allocation of assets among alternative investment instruments. The former is termed the *funding decision*, the latter are *asset allocation decisions*. All may be constrained by legal, regulatory, or other restrictions.

The liabilities of a frozen defined-benefit plan can be described by a vector of benefit payments $B_1, B_2, \ldots, B_T$ to be paid from the fund at times $1, 2, \ldots T$ if possible. We assume these are known with certainty.[2] At each time t, the current market value of the fund's assets is compared with the benefits then due. If assets exceed required payments, the benefits are paid and the remaining assets reinvested. If not, no further benefits are paid by the fund. If all benefits have been paid at date T, the remaining assets revert to the sponsoring corporation. Beneficiaries may be insured in whole or in part against default, but we assume that neither insurance premia nor wages paid by the corporation are affected by the level of funding or the allocation of fund assets. Moreover, we assume that the goal of those making these decisions is to maximize the wealth of corporate shareholders.[3]

4.2.1 Valuation of Contingent Claims

To represent a market with "tax effects" we employ a modified version of the state-preference approach used by Litzenberger and Van Horne (1978). Individual investors can purchase claims to receive income contingent on the occurrence of alternative states of the world. However, different kinds of payments may be taxed differently for at least some investors. Thus a claim for a capital-gain dollar contingent on state s may be valued differently in the market than one for a dividend dollar contingent on the same state. Given M such types of dollars and N states of the world, we assume that it is possible, explicitly or implicitly, for individual investors to puchase all $M \times N$ primitive (Arrow-Debreu) contingent claims. This is similar to, but not the same as, the familiar complete-markets approach. The latter typically assumes that existing securities span the space of state-contingent claims and that unlimited short sales with no impounds and full use of the proceeds are possible. In a taxable world, if this were possible, riskless tax arbitrage between two investors in different tax brackets could occur, as shown by Schaefer (1978). Thus we implicitly assume the existence of boundaries on holdings and/or tax treatment.

We assume that at time T the residual value of the fund, R (which will be zero if the fund has defaulted), will be used to pay shareholders. The amount may be subject to corporate tax, leaving less than R to be paid out. Let $R(s)$ = the residual value if state s occurs; t^c = the corporate tax rate, assumed to be independent of s and $R(s)$; and $v^a(s)$ = the present value of a dollar paid to the corporation's shareholders in state s. If the residual is to be paid in the form of dividends, $v^a(s)$ will be the market price for a dividend dollar in state s; if the residual is to be paid in capital gains, $v^a(s)$ will be the market price of a capital-gains dollar in state s. We assume only that the form each distribution would take is known and that the $v^a(s)$ values are selected accordingly.

Letting $v(s) = v^a(s)(1 - t^c)$, the present value of $R(s)$ is $V(s) = v(s)R(s)$. Henceforth we will focus on the $v(s)$ values, with $v(1), \ldots, v(N)$ termed the *valuation function*.

Given a set of possible residual values $R(1), \ldots, R(N)$ the value of the pension fund for the corporate shareholders will be $V = \Sigma_s V(s) = \Sigma_s[v(s)R(s)]$. We assume that the objective of those making the decisions concerning the fund is to maximize V, given some valuation function $v(1), \ldots, v(N)$. A key ingredient in our analysis is the assumption that neither the corporate taxes nor the personal taxes paid on $R(s)$ will be related to the choice of investments made by the managers of the pension fund. For example, the eventual taxes paid if a dividend dollar is received within the pension fund in a given state of the world would be the same as those paid if a capital-gains dollar had been received within the fund in the same circumstances. A dollar received in the pension fund in a given state of the world thus has the same value for the corporation's shareholders, whatever its type. However, the present price of a claim to receive such a dollar may depend on its type. Thus the presence of differential tax treatment will influence the relative attractiveness of alternative instruments, even for a tax-exempt pension fund.

4.2.2 Choice of Assets

While individuals may have some flexibility in their choice of state-contingent payments, we assume that the pension fund must choose from a limited set of combinations of such claims. The fund manager's choice set thus does not span the set of state-contingent claims. In the next part of the chapter we consider a choice between two instruments (e.g. bonds and stocks) in a one-period setting. We show that in this case one of two extreme funding policies (fund either as much or as little as possible) will be optimal, as will one of two extreme asset allocation policies (invest either in bonds or in stocks but not in both). Later we obtain analogous results in a setting involving many periods and many assets. We then address the issue raised by Black and Tepper: given two instruments, bonds and stocks, with different tax status and different risks, we show that an all-bond, maximum-funding policy may not be optimal. The final section of the chapter provides suggestions for future research.

4.3 One Period and Two Assets

We begin with the asset allocation decision. Consider a pension plan with A dollars to invest. This may be used to purchase either or both of two types of assets. One unit of asset 1 can be purchased for one dollar and will pay $D^1(s)$ dollars one period hence if the state of the world is s. Similarly, one unit of asset 2 can be purchased for one dollar and will pay $D^2(s)$ dollars in one period if state s occurs. We assume a simple regulatory setting in which the plan's managers may select a value of X between X_{min} and X_{max}, where $X =$ the proportion of the fund's assets to be invested in asset 2. We also assume that there are no transactions costs.

The value of assets one period hence will be $(1-X)AD^1(s) + XAD^2(s)$. At the end of the period, a benefit of B dollars must be paid out of the fund's assets if possible. The amount (if any) left for taxes and payments to shareholders will be $R(A,X,s) = [(1-X)AD^1(s) + XAD^2(s) - B]^+$, where $[z]^+$ denotes z if $z \geq 0$ and zero if $z<0$. Assume that neither the firm's wage bill nor its insurance premium is a function of X or A.[4] The amount of the residual claim in state s is $R(A, X, s) = \{A[D^1(s) + X(D^2(s) - D^1(s))] - B\}^+$. The goal is to maximize the value of the residual claim $V = \Sigma_s\, v(s)\, R(A, X, s)$ by choosing feasible values of A and X.

Let

$$\begin{aligned} V(s) &= v(s)R(A, X, s) \\ &= v(s)\{A[D^1(s) + X(D^2(s) - D^1(s))] - B\}^+. \end{aligned}$$

Figure 4.1 plots $V(s)$ as a function of X, given A, for three cases: (1) a state in which asset 2 underperforms asset 1, (2) a state in which the two assets have equal payoffs, and (3) a state in which asset 2 outperforms asset 1. A key observation is that the function is (weakly) convex from above—going from left to right the slope never decreases. Note that V is simply the sum over states of such components of value: $V = \Sigma_s V(s)$. Thus it must also be weakly convex from above. It follows that, given A,

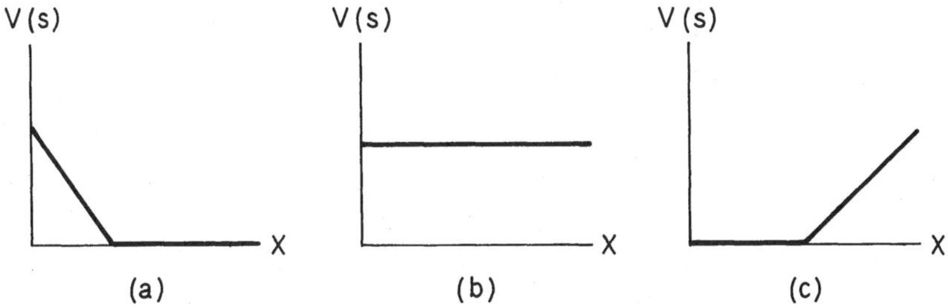

Fig. 4.1 Convexity of $V(s)$ as a function of X.

shareholder wealth will be maximized at either X_{min} or X_{max}, but every interior feasible value of X will be dominated. Depending on the situation, all funds should be invested in either asset 1 or asset 2. *No* mixed solutions will be optimal.

Now consider the question of the appropriate funding level. Assets invested in a pension fund must come from somewhere. Corporate projects must be forgone, funds must be raised from bondholders or stockholders, etc. For simplicity, assume that dollars not invested in the fund will be used to finance an investment that will pay $D^c(s)$ dollars one period hence if the state of the world is s, and that such payoffs will be taxed in the same manner as those obtained as residual values from the pension fund. Then the opportunity cost of an investment of A dollars in the fund will be $A\,\Sigma_s[v(s)\,D^c(s)] = A\,V^c$, where V^c = the present value of one dollar invested in corporate assets (at the margin, one dollar) and the net present value of the pension fund to the shareholders will be $V^n = \Sigma_s[V(s) - v(s)D^c(s)]$. Equivalently stated, $V^n = \Sigma_s\ V^n(s)$, where $V^n(s) = v(s)\{[Ar(s) - B]^+ - AD^c(s)\}$ and $r(s) = (1 - X)D^1(s) + XD^2(s)$. The value of V^n will typically be negative; thus $(-V^n)$ can be interpreted as the cost of the pension plan. We assume that the goal is to maximize the former value (i.e., to minimize the cost of the plan).

Figure 4.2 shows the assumed regulatory climate. The fund may choose a value of A between A_{min} and A_{max} and a value of X between X_{min} and X_{max}. The value of A_{max} might correspond to ERISA's full funding limitation and A_{min} to its minimum funding standard. The values of X_{min} and X_{max} are intended to represent a naive policy on the part of the PBGC concerning prudent management of the fund. In this simple case the feasible region has four corners. In Section 4.4 we consider a somewhat broader class of regulatory policies; however, the assumption is retained that the feasible region is convex, with linear borders.

Figure 4.3 plots $V^n(s)$ as a function of A, given X, for three cases: (1) a state in which pension assets do better than corporate assets, (2) a state in which the two types of assets do equally well, and (3) a state in which

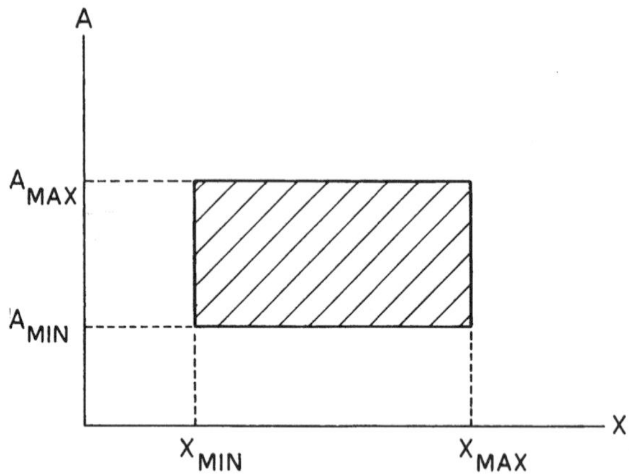

Fig. 4.2 The feasible region with simple regulatory constraints.

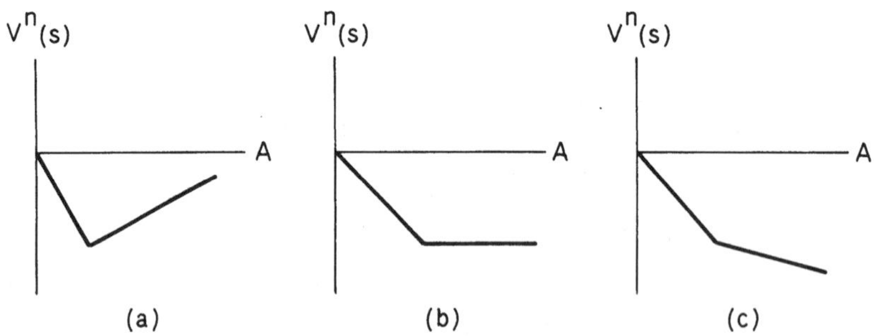

Fig. 4.3 Convexity of $V^n(s)$ as a function of A.

pension assets underperform corporate assets. This function is also (weakly) convex from above. And, since V^n is the sum over states of such components of value, it too must be weakly convex from above. It follows that, give X, shareholder wealth will be maximized at either $A_{\min}$ or $A_{\max}$ but every interior feasible value of A will be dominated. Depending on the situation, one should fund a plan as much or as little as possible.

Given A, an extreme value of X should be chosen. Given X, an extreme value of A should be chosen. The overall optimum thus involves an extreme value of A and an extreme value of X. In figure 4.2, all positions but those at the corners of the feasible region will be dominated.

4.4 Many Periods and Many Assets

Consider now a more general problem with defined benefits $B_1, \ldots, B_T$ payable at times $1, \ldots, T$. Further suppose that the pension plan can invest in K assets, indexed by $k = 1, \ldots, K$. Generalizing the notation used earlier, we denote by D_t^k the return at time t to a dollar invested at time $t-1$ in security k. Of course D_t^k further depends on the state s, but it will be convenient to suppress this dependence initially.

Next let X_t^k denote the fraction of the pension plan's wealth that is invested in security k between times $t-1$ and t, and define

$$M_t = \sum_{k=1}^{K} X_t D_t^k \quad \text{for } t = 1, \ldots, T. \tag{1}$$

If a total of Z dollars is invested at time $t-1$, the wealth of the pension fund at time t, before payment of benefits, will be ZM_t. We call M_t the pension fund's *investment multiplier* for period t. The portfolio proportions X_t^k are decision variables and can depend on the state s through information that is available at time $t-1$ (see below), but we suppress this dependence for the moment. The pension fund manager's other decision variable is the initial investment level A. We denote by W_t the wealth of the pension fund at time t, immediately after payment of benefits. These wealth levels W_t can be expressed in terms of the initial investment level A and portfolio proportions X_t^k by the recursive formula

$$W_t = (W_{t-1} M_t - B_t)^+ \quad \text{for } t = 1, \ldots, T \tag{2}$$

with $W_0 = A$ by convention.

PROPOSITION: The residual wealth $R = W_T$ is a convex function of each multiplier M_t alone, holding the other multipliers, the benefit obligations, and the initial investment level fixed. Furthermore, R is a convex function of the initial investment level A, holding all else fixed.

PROOF: Let t be arbitrary, let $M_t' \geqq = 0$ and $M_t'' \geqq = 0$ be two possible values for the multiplier in period t, and set $M_t = .5M_t' + .5M_t''$. Let $W_1', \ldots, W_T'$ be defined by (2), with M_t' in place of M_t (plus the convention $W_0' = A$), and let $W_0'', W_1'', \ldots, W_T''$ be defined similarly. To prove the first statement of the proposition, we need to show that $W_T \leqq .5W_T' + .5W_T''$. Obviously $W_i = W_i' = W_i''$ for $i = 0, \ldots, t-1$. Then

$$\begin{aligned} W_t &= (W_{t-1} M_t - B_t)^+ = [W_t(.5M_t' + .5M_t'') - B_t]^+ \\ &= [.5(W_{t-1} M_t' - B_t) + .5(W_{t-1} M_t'' - B_t)]^+ \\ &\leqq .5(W_{t-1} M_t' - B_t)^+ + .5(W_{t-1} M_t'' - B_t)^+ \\ &= .5W_t' + .5W_t'', \end{aligned} \tag{3}$$

because $(\cdot)^+$ is a convex function. But $(\cdot)^+$ is also an increasing function, so from (3) we have next that

$$\begin{aligned} W_{t+1} &= (W_t M_{t+1} - B_{t+1})^+ \\ &\leqq [(.5W_t' + .5W_t'') M_{t+1} - B_{t+1}]^+ \\ &= [.5(W_t' M_{t+1} - B_{t+1}) + .5(W_t'' M_{t+1} - B_{t+1})]^+. \end{aligned} \tag{4}$$

Using again the convexity of $(\cdot)^+$,

$$\begin{aligned}(5)\qquad &[.5(W_t' M_{t+1} - B_{t+1}) + .5(W_t'' M_{t+1} - B_{t+1})]^+ \\ &\leqq .5(W_t' M_{t+1} - B_{t+1})^+ + .5(W_t'' M_{t+1} - B_{t+1})^+ \\ &= .5W_{t+1}' + .5W_{t+1}''.\end{aligned}$$

Combining (4) and (5) gives $W_{t+1} \leqq .5W_{t+1}' + .5W_{t+1}''$, and one can obviously continue in this way to prove by induction that $W_T \leqq .5W_T' = .5W_T''$. This completes the proof of the first statement.

To prove that W_T is a convex function of the investment level, let $A' \geqq 0$ and $A'' \geqq 0$ be arbitrary, and set $A = .5A' + .5A''$. Set $W_0' = A'$ and $W_0'' = A''$ and define W_t, W_t', and W_t'' in the obvious way for $t = 1, \ldots, T$. We need to show that $W_T \leqq .5W_T' + .5W_T''$. Steps (4) and (5) above can be used inductively to prove the stronger result that $W_t \leqq .5W_t' + .5W_t''$ for all $t = 1, \ldots, T$. Thus the proof of the proposition is complete.

4.4.1 Formulation of the Fund Manager's Problem

We assume that the pension fund manager wants to select an initial funding level A and relative portfolio proportions X_t^k so as to maximize the valuation of the residual claim $R = W_T$ subject to regulatory limitations imposed on the initial funding level or fund allocation among assets. One must also specify the fund manager's capability to adjust the allocation dynamically in response to information received. The latter aspect makes formal representation to multiperiod problems fundamentally more complex than single-period problems. We will adopt a rather abstract representation of the manager's optimization problem, but one that is well suited to our objectives.

Let Ω be the set of all states s that might pertain at time T. A trading strategy will be formally defined as a collection $(A, X_1, \ldots, X_T)$ where A is a constant, $X_1 = (X_1^1, \ldots, X_1^K)$ is a vector whose components sum to one, and, for $t = 2, \ldots, T$, $X_t = [X_t^1(s), \ldots, X_t^K(s)]$ is a vector of functions whose components sum to one for every state s.

One interprets $X_t^k(s)$ as the fraction of the fund's wealth to be invested in security k during period t if state s prevails, and it is obviously necessary to restrict the way in which this fraction may depend on s. We take as given a sequence $P_1, \ldots, P_{T-1}$ of successively finer partitions of Ω, with cells of the partition P_t representing those events whose occurrence or nonoccurrence will be known at time t. In addition to the restrictions stated above, it is required that X_t (viewed as a vector-valued function of s) be measurable with respect to P_{t-1}, meaning that $X_t(s) = X_t(s')$ whenever s and s' lie in the same cell of the partition P_{t-1}.

To complete the formulation, we require that $A \varepsilon I$ and that $X_t(s) \varepsilon \Delta$ for all $t = 1, \ldots, T$ and $s \varepsilon \Omega$, where I is a compact interval and Δ is a set to be described shortly. As in the model of Section 4.2, I is the interval between a lower funding limit imposed by the PBGC and an upper limit imposed by the IRS, while Δ is the set of all asset distributions (relative portfolio proportions) that are judged by the PBGC to be prudent. For the two-asset model of Section 4.2 we took Δ to be the set of all pairs (X^1, X^2) such that $X_{min} \leqq X^1 \leqq X_{max}$ and $X^1 + X^2 = 1$. For the general setting we assume that Δ is the bounded solution set of some finite system of linear inequalities and equalities, including the requirement $X^1 + \ldots + X^K = 1$. (Thus Δ is a compact, convex, polyhedral set and has a finite number of extreme points.)

The preceding paragraph contains a strong assumption. We are assuming that the definition of a prudent asset distribution does not depend on the initial funding level A, and more generally does not depend on the success enjoyed by the fund's investments up to an intermediate decision point. This assumption is essential in all that follows, although Δ can be allowed to depend on t and even s (subject to measurability restrictions) without substantially changing our analysis.

For $t = 1, \ldots, T$, let Γ_t be the set of all functions X_t that map Ω into Δ and are measurable with respect to P_{t-1}. The preceding discussion may be summarized as follows. The pension fund manager must choose $A \varepsilon I$, $X_1 \varepsilon \Gamma_1, \ldots, X_T \varepsilon \Gamma_T$ so as to maximize

$$V = \sum_s v(s)\,[R(s) - AD^c(s)], \tag{6}$$

where $v(\cdot)$ is the valuation function discussed in Section 4.2 and $R(s)$ is defined in terms of A and the relative portfolio proportions $X_t^k(s)$ as at the beginning of this section. Ours is not a standard dynamic programming formulation of the fund manager's sequential decision problem. In particular, we have made no explicit mention of the way current portfolio decisions may depend on the fund wealth carried forward from previous periods. By coordinating the way successive portfolio descriptions $X_1, \ldots, X_T$ are made to depend on s, however, one can synthesize any desired dependency of current decisions on past success or failure. Our formulation is completely equivalent to the standard one. For future reference, we observe that this problem does have an optimal solution (the supremum is attained) because it amounts to maximization of a continuous function over a compact subset of a finite-dimensional Euclidean space.

4.4.2 Optimality of Extremal Strategies

Hereafter we denote by $x = (x^1, \ldots, x^K)$ a generic element of Δ, by $y = (y^1, \ldots, y^K)$ a generic extreme point of Δ, and by E the (finite) set of all such extreme points y. Since Δ is a compact, convex, polyhedral set by assumption, each point $x \varepsilon \Delta$ can be written as a convex combination of the extreme points $y \varepsilon E$. That is, there exist *nonnegative* weights $[a(y), y \varepsilon E]$ such that $\Sigma_y a(y) = 1$ and

(7) $$x = \sum_y a(y)\, y$$

or, equivalently,

(8) $$x^k = \sum_y a(y) y^k, \text{ for } k = 1, \ldots, K.$$

A strategy $(A, X_1, \ldots, X_T)$ for the fund manager's optimization problem is said to be extremal if A is an endpoint (extreme point) of the interval I *and* $X_t(s) \varepsilon E$ for each state s and each $t = 1, \ldots, T$. Incidentally, a single strategy component X_t will be called extremal if $X_t(s) \varepsilon E$ for all states s.

It is the pupose of this subsection to prove there exists an optimal strategy which is extremal. Toward that end, first let $(A, X_1, \ldots, X_T)$ be an arbitrary feasible strategy. Adding a notational dependence on A for emphasis, let $R(A, s) = W_T(A, s)$ be defined in terms of A and the relative portfolio proportions $X_t^k(s)$ as at the beginning of this section, and then let $V(A)$ be defined in terms of $R(A, s)$ by (6). The Proposition shows that $R(A, s)$ is a convex function of A for each fixed s, and it follows immediately, because the contingent claim valuations $v(s)$ are nonnegative, that $V(A)$ is convex. Thus $V(A)$ will be maximized by taking A to be an endpoint of the feasible interval I. To repeat, the valuation associated with an arbitrary feasible strategy can be increased (or at least not decreased) by moving A to one of the extreme points of I, leaving $X_1, \ldots, X_T$ fixed.

We now argue that a similar improvement can be effected by substituting for any of the strategy components X_t a well-chosen extremal strategy component. Again let $(A, X_1, \ldots, X_T)$ be arbitrary, fix a period t, and let S be any cell of the partition P_{t-1}. Then there exists a point $x \varepsilon \Delta$ such that $X_t(s) = x$ for all $s \varepsilon S$. Adding a notational dependence on x for emphasis, let us set

(9) $$M_t(s, x) = \sum_{k=1}^{K} X_t^k(s) D_t^k(s).$$
$$= \sum_{k=1}^{K} x^k D_t^k(s) \quad \text{for } s \varepsilon S.$$

Then $R(s, x) = W_T(s, x)$ is defined in terms of $M_t(s, x)$ for states $s \varepsilon S$ as at the beginning of this section, and we set $V(S, x) = \Sigma_{s\varepsilon S} v(s)[R(s, x) - AD^c(s)]$. Obviously $V(S, x)$ is the contribution to the total valuation V made by states in cell S, and it is only the contribution from these states that is affected by our choice of x.

Recall that x can be represented in terms of the extremal points y via (7), and we now consider how the partial valuation $V(S)$ would be affected if we were to replace x by some $y \varepsilon E$. By analogy with (9), let

(10) $$M_t(s, y) = \sum_{k=1}^{K} y D_t^k(s) \text{ for } y \varepsilon E \text{ and } s \varepsilon S,$$

and then let $R(s, y)$ and $V(S, y)$ be defined in terms of $M_t(s, y)$ in the obvious way. From (7), (9), and (10), we have

(11) $$M_t(s, x) = \Sigma_{y \varepsilon E} a(y) M_t(s, y) \text{ for } s \varepsilon S.$$

The Proposition says that $R = W_T$ is a convex function of M_t, so (11) implies

(12) $$R(s, x) \leqq \Sigma_{y \varepsilon E} a(y) R(s, y) \text{ for } s \varepsilon S,$$

and hence, because $\nu(s) \geqq 0$ for all $s \varepsilon S$,

(13) $$V(S, x) \leqq \Sigma_{y \varepsilon S} a(y) V(S, y).$$

Obviously (13) can only hold if $V(S, y) \geqq V(S, x)$ for at least one extreme point y, so we can increase (or at least not decrease) $V(s)$ by substituting this y for x in our specification of the strategy component X_t. Repeating this argument for each cell of the partition P_{t-1}, we come to the following: one can increase the overall valuation $V = \Sigma_s V(s)$, or at least not decrease it, by substituting for X_t an extremal strategy component X_t^*.

The proof that there exists an extremal optimal policy is now essentially complete. We know that there exists an optimal solution $(A, X_1, \ldots, X_T)$. But one can substitute for A an extremal investment level A^*, then substitute for X_1 a well-chosen extremal strategy component $X_1^*, \ldots$, then substitute for X_T a well-chosen extremal strategy component X_T^*, without ever decreasing the total valuation. Absolutely essential to this argument is the assumption that one can take A to be any point in the interval I and X_t to be any element of Γ_t, regardless of how the other componenets of the overall strategy have been selected.

4.5 Bonds versus Stocks

We turn now to the issues raised by Black (1980) and Tepper (1981). Given a choice between bonds and stocks and a range of permissible funding levels, what policies will be optimal for corporate shareholders? To analyze these issues, we will use the simple one-period, two-asset setting of Section 4.3.

Key to the Black-Tepper argument is the superiority of pension fund investment over corporate investment and, within the pension fund, the superiority of bonds (here, asset 1) over stocks (asset 2). In our notation this assumption takes the form

(14) $$\sum_s \nu(s) D^1(s) > \sum_s \nu(s) D^2(s) > \sum_s \nu(s) D^c(s).$$

From (14) it is easy to deduce the following: if all feasible (A, X) combinations provide adequate coverage to pay every beneficiary in full in every state of the world, the optimal solution will involve full funding $(A = A_{\max})$ and investment solely in bonds $(X = 0)$. The argument goes as follows. Since there will be no default in any state, the positive part

($[\cdot]^+$) notation becomes redundant and the value of the residual can be written as

$$V^n = \sum_s v(s)[Ar(s)] - \sum_s v(s)B - A\sum_s v(s)D^c(s)$$
$$= A[\sum_s v(s)r(s) - \sum_s v(s)D^c(s)] - B\sum_s v(s).$$

Note that at $X=0$, $\Sigma_s v(s)r(s) = \Sigma_s v(s)D^1(s)$ and at $X=1$, $\Sigma_s v(s)r(s) = \Sigma_s v(s)D^2(s)$. Given the tax effects, the expression in brackets is clearly maximized at $X=0$. Moreover, at $X=0$ this expression is positive. Conditional on the choice of an optimal X value, V^n is thus maximized at $A = A_{max}$. This is the conclusion reached by Black and Tepper. Our setting is different—we rely on a market structure, while they use arbitrage arguments that require explicit offsetting actions—but the conclusions are the same.

The Black-Tepper result involves the use of pension funding and investment in bonds to take advantage of an asymmetric tax structure. Policies that involve possible default by the fund provide a way to take advantage of possible asymmetric behavior on the part of the PBGC, the insurer of pension benefits. If stocks are more effective than bonds in this role, and if the feasible (A, X) region includes combinations that make default possible, the Black-Tepper strategy may not maximize shareholder wealth. The matter is not straightforward, even in this very simple setting. The value of the insurance depends on the relationship between the payoffs over states of fund assets and benefits. It is entirely possible that a risky bond might provide both tax benefits and a large value for the insurance. In effect, we are assuming that the manager will consider both the tax effect and the insurance effect of decisions concerning funding and investment. Our previous results indicate that in our setting, the optimal policy will involve an extreme point in the feasible (A, X) space, whether the choice of bonds versus stocks involves a trade-off of these two effects or not. It is instructive, however, to examine a very simple case in which there is such a trade-off.

Assume that the payoffs from the two instruments are $D^1(1) = 1.1$, $D^1(2) = 1.1$ (bonds) and $D^2(1) = 1.2$, $D^2(2) = .1$ (stocks). The valuation function is $v(1) = .85$, $v(2) = .10$. We assume that $\Sigma_s v(s)D^c(s) = 1$. Note that there is a tax effect, since $\Sigma_s v(s)D^1(s) = 1.045$, $\Sigma_s v(s)D^2(s) = 1.030$, and $\Sigma_s v(s)D^c(s) = 1.000$. Benefits are 110, regardless of state, and regulatory constraints are $A_{max} = 120$, $A_{min} = 100$, $X_{max} = 1.0$, and $X_{min} = 0.0$.[5] Note that investment solely in bonds will cover benefit payments in every state, even at the minimum feasible funding level. Thus the value of the insurance will increase with X.

Figure 4.4 shows the feasible region and the value of V^n at each corner (as indicated earlier, the absolute value can be interpreted as the cost of the pension plan). One might think that, given the trade-off between the insurance and tax effects, and our previous results, the optimal policy

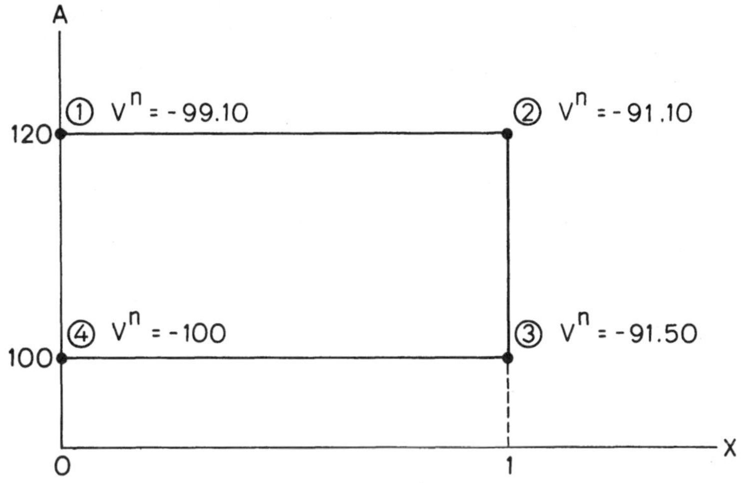

Fig. 4.4 Values of V^n at the four corners of the feasible region.

would involve either full funding plus investment in bonds (corner 1 in fig. 4.4) or minimum funding plus investment in stocks (corner 3 in fig. 4.4). However, as our example shows, this need not be the case. Here the cost of the plan is minimized by a policy involving full funding and investment solely in stocks (corner 2).

4.6. Summary and Conclusions

The main conclusion of this chapter is the indication that a fund manager should focus on extreme funding and investment strategies if our assumptions about regulatory constraints are valid. The IRS and the PBGC, on the other hand, may want to adopt regulatory policies such that the fund manager's optimal strategies will be more consistent with broader social objectives.

Notes

1. Tepper makes this assumption explicitly, Black implicitly.
2. Since the only source of uncertainty is mortality, appeal may be made to the law of large numbers for justification.
3. This rules out decisions made to maximize the utility of risk-averse managers or shareholders who are unable to diversify sufficiently to regard the decision as one of maximizing current wealth.
4. Realistically, given ERISA and the behavior of the PBGC.
5. Given the contingent liability of the corporate sponsor under ERISA, the values of A should include 30% of the corporation's net worth. With this interpretation, our numeric example is not overly fanciful.

by William F. Sharpe

Integrated Asset Allocation

Integrated asset allocation provides a framework for viewing the key elements of the important asset allocation decision. Its general perspective subsumes more traditional asset allocation procedures in current use, including strategic, tactical and insurance approaches.

Integrated asset allocation is concerned with the optimization of an investor's net worth. It thus deals with expected net worth (assets less liabilities) and standard deviation of future net worth, given the investor's willingness to take on added net worth risk in order to increase expected net worth.

The asset allocation procedure involves several major steps. The investor's current net worth is transformed, via a risk tolerance function, into the investor's risk tolerance. At the same time, current capital market conditions—prices, earnings, dividends—are transformed (via a heuristic or complex process) into expected returns, risks and correlations for various asset classes. Given these predictions and the investor's risk tolerance, an "optimizer" (ranging in complexity from a simple rule of thumb to a full-scale quadratic program) determines the most appropriate asset mix. The mix determines actual returns to the investor over the period. These returns feed back, via investor net worth and capital market conditions, into the next period's allocation procedure.

ASSET ALLOCATION ANALYSIS is hardly new. The first formal strategic allocation studies were performed well over a decade ago. Asset mixes have been managed using market timing models for several years. Portfolio insurance procedures have been used to allocate assets dynamically for at least three years.

This article provides an overview of a general approach to asset allocation—one that subsumes more traditional procedures as special cases. We begin with a description of the overall approach, termed *integrated asset allocation*. Next we discuss alternative objectives for asset allocation analyses. As many studies are limited to two asset classes, we treat such cases in some detail. Finally, we describe the three major types of asset allocation analysis currently being performed—*strategic, tactical* and *insured*.

William Sharpe is President of Sharpe-Russell Research, Inc.

The author thanks Keith Ambachtsheer, Ernest Bianco, George Chow, Peter Dietz, Don Ezra, Mark Friebel, Kelly Haughton, Martin Leibowitz, Douglas Love, André Perold, Andrew Turner and Jan Twardowski for their comments and suggestions.

Integrated Asset Allocation

Figure A illustrates the major steps involved in asset allocation. The boxes on the left are concerned with the capital markets; those on the right are specific to an investor. The boxes in the middle bring together aspects of the capital markets and the investor's circumstances to determine the investor's asset mix and its performance. The process begins at the top and proceeds downward, then repeats.

Box I1 represents the current values of the investor's assets and liabilities and, by implication, net worth. An individual investor's net worth is his or her *wealth*; a pension fund's net worth is the plan *surplus*. Net worth will generally determine the investor's current tolerance for risk, shown in box I3. The relation between the investor's circumstances (box I1) and risk tolerance (box I3) can be portrayed by a *risk tolerance function*. It is shown in box I2.

Box C1 represents the current state of the capital markets. Included are such things as

Figure A Integrated Asset Allocation

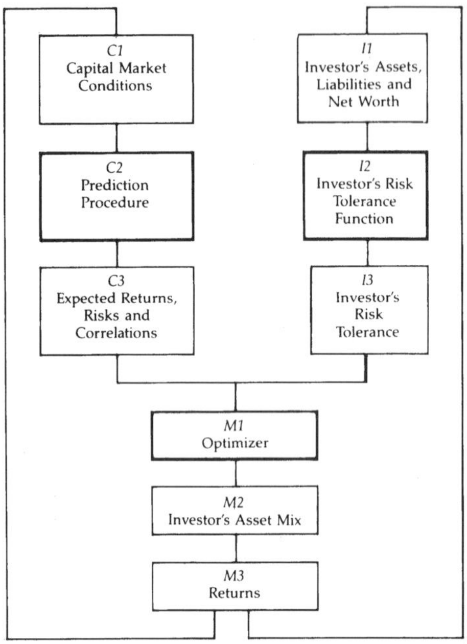

current and historical levels of stock and bond indexes, past and projected dividends and earnings. These data are the major inputs for predicting the expected returns and risks of various asset classes and the correlations of their returns (shown in box C3). Some procedure must be used to translate capital market conditions (box C1) into predictions about asset returns (box C3); it is represented by box C2.

Given an investor's risk tolerance (box I3) and predictions of assets' expected returns, risks and correlations (box C3), an optimizer can be employed to determine the most appropriate asset mix (box M2). Depending on such things as the number of assets, the optimizer (shown in box M1) may be a simple rule of thumb, a mathematical function or a full-scale quadratic program.

Box M3 represents actual returns to the investor. Given the investor's asset mix at the beginning of a period (box M2), the asset returns during the period (box M3) determine the value of the investor's assets at the beginning of the next period. Given the nature of the investor's liabilities at the beginning of a period, changes in capital markets (including returns on fixed income obligations) and accrual of new obligations determine the investor's liabilities at the beginning of the next period. Returns in one period thus influence the investor's assets, liabilities and net worth at the beginning of the next period, as shown by the "feedback loop" from box M3 to box I1.

Returns during a period also constitute part of the overall capital market conditions at the beginning of the next period. This is shown by the feedback loop from box M3 to box C1. As these loops show, the process is a continuing one, with decisions from one period affecting those of the next.

From period to period, any (or all) of the items in boxes C1, C3, I1, I3, M2 and M3 may change. However, the items in boxes C2, I2 and M1 should remain fixed, because they represent the *decision rules* (procedures). Thus the investor's risk tolerance (box I3) may change, but the risk tolerance *function* (box I2) should not. Predictions of returns (box C3) may change, but not the *procedure* (box C2) for making such predictions. The optimal asset mix (box M2) may change, but not the *optimizer* (box M1) that determines it.

Many investors make some or all of the decisions shown in boxes I2, C2 and M1 "by hand" (and/or heuristically). In an increasing number of organizations, however, some or all of these procedures have been automated, with decision rules specified in advance, then followed routinely. Portfolio insurance procedures fall clearly into this category, as do certain process-driven tactical asset allocation methods.

To implement a fully *integrated asset allocation* procedure, one only (!) has to fill in (or leave out) the boxes. Traditional approaches do so, but in rather extreme ways.

Asset Allocation Objectives

To arrive at an optimal asset mix, an optimizer must have an explicit *objective function*. Typically, this involves the risk and expected value of some key attribute.

In integrated asset allocation analysis, the attribute is the investor's *net worth* at some future date. Optimization thus deals with expected future net worth and the standard deviation of future net worth.

Traditional analyses usually concentrate on the value of the investor's *assets* at some point in the future. Optimization thus deals with the expected return and standard deviation of return on current assets.

The nature of the objective function must also be reflected in the measure of risk tolerance, which indicates the investor's willingness to accept greater risk in order to obtain a greater expected reward. In traditional analysis, risk tolerance is typically concerned with the trade-off between expected return and standard deviation of return. In integrated asset allocation analysis, risk tolerance measures the investor's willingness to take on added net worth risk in order to increase expected net worth.

"Asset only" analyses can be considered special cases of integrated asset allocation in which liabilities equal zero (or are positive, but not subject to uncertainty).

Two-Asset Allocation

The remainder of this article will focus on cases in which only two assets are considered and liabilities equal zero. Many traditional asset allocation analyses conform to these restrictions, and we will discuss such approaches in this context. The appendix analyzes conditions for an optimal asset mix when multiple asset classes and liabilities are considered.

When only two assets are involved, the relation between the inputs and the optimal asset mix is particularly simple. Let the assets be S (e.g., stocks) and B (e.g., bonds or bills). As shown in the appendix, the optimal (dollar) amount to be invested in S can be computed as:

$$D_S = k_0W + k_1ART,$$

where k_0 and k_1 are parameters, W is the investor's current net worth, and ART is his or her *absolute risk tolerance*.

To determine the proportion of assets to be invested in stocks, divide both sides of the equation by W, giving:

$$\frac{D_S}{W} = k_0 + k_1\frac{ART}{W}.$$

The latter ratio is termed the investor's *relative risk tolerance*. Representing this by RRT, and using the standard notation X_S to represent the relative amount invested in stocks gives:

$$X_S = k_0 + k_1RRT.$$

If asset B is riskless, the value of k_0 becomes zero, giving:

$$D_S = k_1ART$$

and

$$X_S = k_1RRT.$$

The appendix shows that the values of k_0 and k_1 depend on the expected returns and risks of the assets and on the estimated correlation between their returns. Of particular importance is the fact that k_1 is proportional to the difference between the assets' expected returns:

$$k_1 = \frac{E_S - E_B}{k_2},$$

where k_2 depends (as does k_0) solely on the risks of the two assets and on the estimated correlation between their returns.

To avoid excess notation, no indication of time has been included in the equations. Each value is assumed to be relevant for the single period over which a decision is to be made. As will be seen, traditional approaches to asset allocation make different assumptions concerning the constancy of various aspects of these relationships over time.

Strategic Asset Allocation

Figure B portrays a typical strategic asset allocation analysis in terms comparable to those used for the more general integrated asset allocation.[1]

Strategic asset allocation studies are usually done episodically (e.g., once every three years). Relatively few asset mixes are considered (e.g., bond/stock combinations with 0, 10, 20, . . . , 100 per cent invested in stocks). An analysis (typically using Monte Carlo simulation) is performed to determine the likely range of outcomes associated with each mix. The outcome analyzed may be pension contributions over the next five years, or pension surplus five years hence.

When the analysis is complete, the investor is asked to examine the ranges of outcomes associated with each of the mixes, then choose the preferred one. This constitutes the "policy," "long-run" or "strategic" asset mix.

In the vast majority of strategic analyses, each

1. Footnotes appear at end of article.

Figure B Strategic Asset Allocation

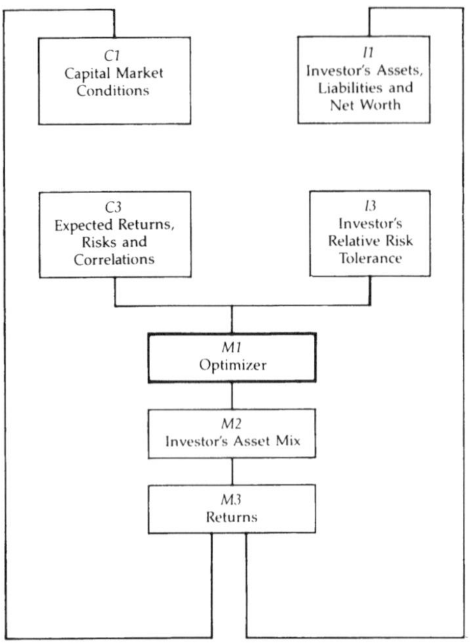

mix is expressed in terms of the percentage of total value invested in each asset class. Such an approach can be termed a *constant mix strategy*. It differs from a "buy-and-hold" strategy, because transactions required periodically to rebalance the mix after market moves change relative asset values. Although liabilities are usually included in the simulation results, no explicit attempt is made to alter the asset mix to take the nature of the liabilities into account.

Strategic studies almost always employ long-run capital market conditions. In particular, asset expected returns, risks and correlations remain constant throughout the simulation. Thus Figure B omits a connection between boxes C1 and C3. Changing capital market conditions from period to period do not influence predictions concerning asset returns.

If predictions are constant, the parameters k_0 and k_1 in our equations will remain the same from period to period. Letting the subscript t denote the time period, we can write the equation for the proportion to be invested in stocks over the period as:

$$X_t = k_0 + k_1 RRT_t.$$

For each set of simulations in a strategic study, the percentage asset mix is held constant. In the case of two assets, this implies that X_t remains the same from period to period. As the equation indicates, however, this can be optimal only if the investor's relative risk tolerance remains unchanged. Figure B portrays this condition by omitting a connection between boxes I1 and I3 and by using the term *relative risk tolerance* in box I3. Changing circumstances from period to period do not influence the investor's (relative) attitude toward risk.

Each of the possible strategies considered in a strategic study can be represented by a different level of relative risk tolerance. The lower the tolerance for risk, the more conservative the asset mix. The analysis is framed in terms of asset mix. By selecting one of the strategies analyzed, however, the investor provides information about his or her risk tolerance.

Tactical Asset Allocation

Tactical procedures are applied routinely, as part of continuing asset management. Their goal is to take advantage of inefficiencies in the relative prices of securities in different asset classes.

Until recently, tactical asset allocators switched funds between bonds and stocks.[2] Some tactical allocators now use bonds, stocks and cash equivalents. A few managers apply tactical approaches to multiple asset classes, including both domestic and international securities.[3]

Figure C portrays a typical tactical asset allocation analysis in terms comparable to those used earlier. Explicitly or implicitly, tactical procedures assume that the investor's relative risk tolerance is unaffected by changes in his or her circumstances. As in Figure B, this is portrayed in Figure C by the absence of a connection between boxes I1 and I3 and by the use of the term *relative* risk tolerance in box I3.

Tactical changes in asset mix are driven by changes in predictions concerning asset returns. In simpler systems, only predictions of expected returns on stocks and bonds change. In more complex systems, expected returns, risks and

Figure C Tactical Asset Allocation

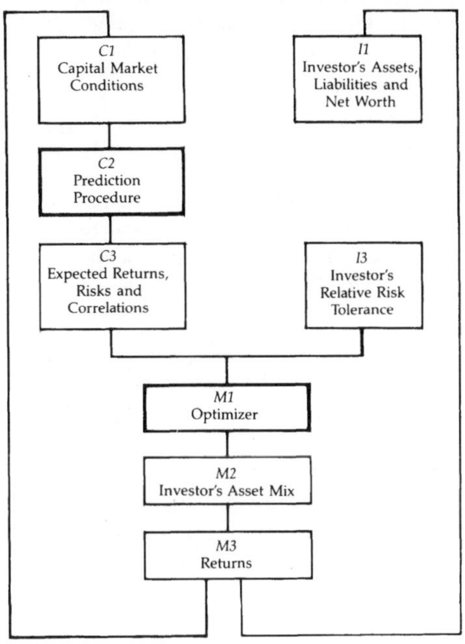

even correlations change.

In many systems, the percentage invested in stocks is related linearly to the spread between the expected returns of stocks and bonds. This can be seen to follow directly from the assumed conditions. Given constant estimates of risks and correlation, the parameters k_0 and k_2 in our equations remain the same from period to period. Assuming constant relative risk tolerance, and letting the subscript t denote time, we can write the equation for the proportion to be invested in stocks as:

$$X_{St} = k_0 + \frac{RRT}{k_2}(E_{St} - E_{Bt}).$$

In practice, tactical asset allocation systems are often "contrarian" in nature. Typically, the expected return on stocks is based on the relation between the current level of a stock market index and projections of dividends for its component stocks. Variations in projected dividends are usually smaller than the corresponding variations in stock prices. Expected returns thus tend to fall when prices rise, leading to a decrease in stock holdings.

Changes in asset expected returns, risks and correlations take place in even the most efficient security markets. However, tactical asset allocation procedures typically operate on the assumption that markets overreact to information. In this sense, they base decisions on deviant beliefs, rather than on the consensus of investors.

Insured Asset Allocation

Portfolio insurance procedures are applied routinely, as part of continuing asset management. In principle, they aim to improve the "fit" between long-run results and an investor's objectives, without attempting to "time" the market. In practice, they are sometimes used for "closet" market timing. We focus here on portfolio insurance in principle.

Figure D Insured Asset Allocation

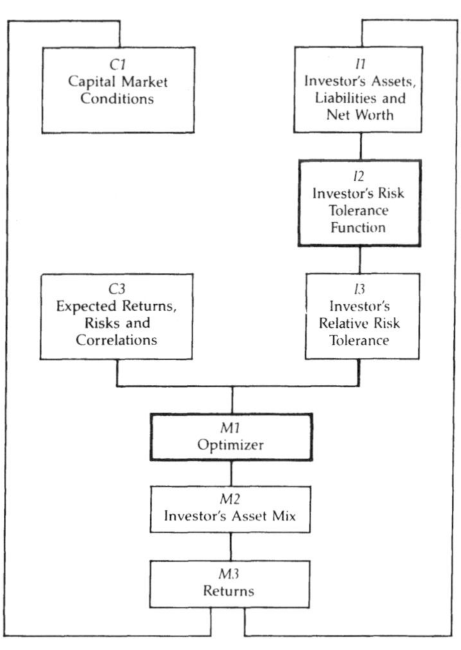

Figure E Option-Based Portfolio Insurance

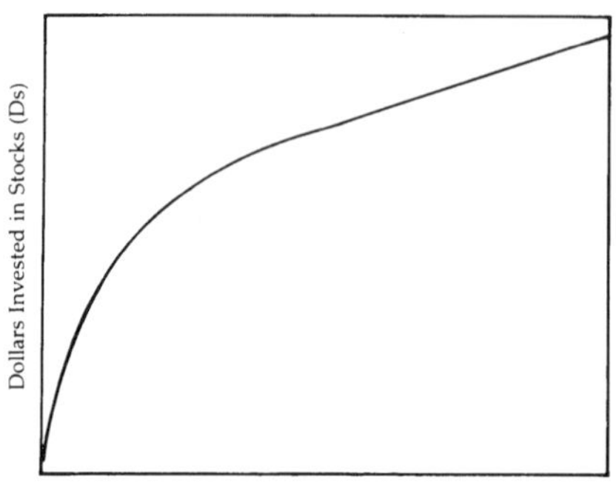

Figure D portrays an insured asset allocation procedure in the terms used earlier.

The earliest forms of portfolio insurance involved dynamic changes in asset allocation designed to replicate effects obtainable with certain option positions. For example, one might replicate the outcomes obtained by holding a portfolio plus a one-year put option written on that portfolio. Equivalently, one might replicate the outcomes obtained by holding a one-year Treasury bill plus a one-year call option on the portfolio. In either case, the striking price of the option represents a floor below which the value of the investor's assets at the specified horizon date should not fall.[4] We will call an approach of this type *option-based portfolio insurance.*

Most portfolio insurance strategies allocate assets between two major classes (e.g., stocks and Treasury bills). In essence, such an approach provides a rule that relates the appropriate asset mix to the excess of the current value of the investor's net worth over a desired *floor*. The relation is similar to that shown in Figure E. The horizontal axis plots the current value of the "cushion" (asset value minus floor value) and the vertical axis the dollar amount to be invested in the risky asset (e.g., stocks). In an option-based insurance procedure, the floor at any given time is the present value of the desired floor at the horizon date. When asset values fall to that floor, nothing is invested in the risky asset. As asset values increase, the amount invested in the risky asset can increase, reaching the total value of the assets as an upper limit.

Option-based portfolio insurance strategies require the amount invested in the risky asset to be a function of both the current value of the asset cushion and the time remaining until the horizon (i.e., the option's expiration date). As the horizon date approaches, the curve relating asset mix to the cushion moves toward an extreme; just before the horizon, assets are invested entirely in one class or the other, depending on whether assets are equal to the floor or above it.

Many have objected to this time-variant nature of option-based portfolio insurance strategies. In particular, such a characteristic seems inappropriate for an ongoing pension fund with a very long (or infinite) horizon. More recent approaches to portfolio insurance are time-invariant.[5] In particular, the curve relating the amount invested in the risky asset to the size of the cushion remains stationary from period to period. We call this approach *constant proportion portfolio insurance* (CPPI).[6]

CPPI uses a simple rule of the type shown in Figure F. The dollar amount invested in the risky asset equals a constant times the size of the cushion (asset value minus floor value), with the constant greater than one.

Formally, portfolio insurance approaches assume that asset expected returns, risks and correlations remain the same over the period during which the insurance is "in force" (although some *ad hoc* procedures have been de-

Figure F Constant Proportion Portfolio Insurance

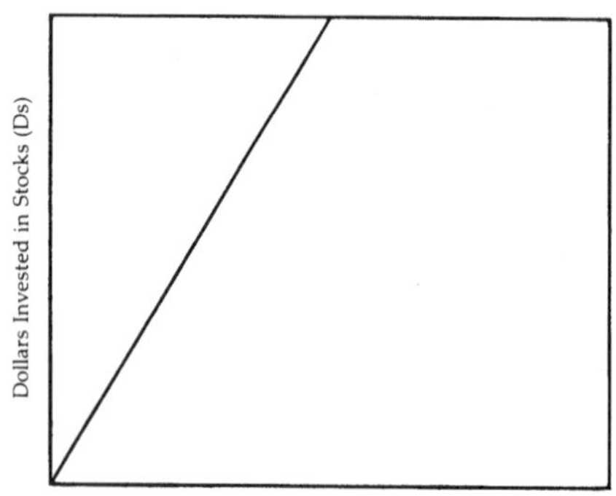

Figure G A Linear Risk-Tolerance Function

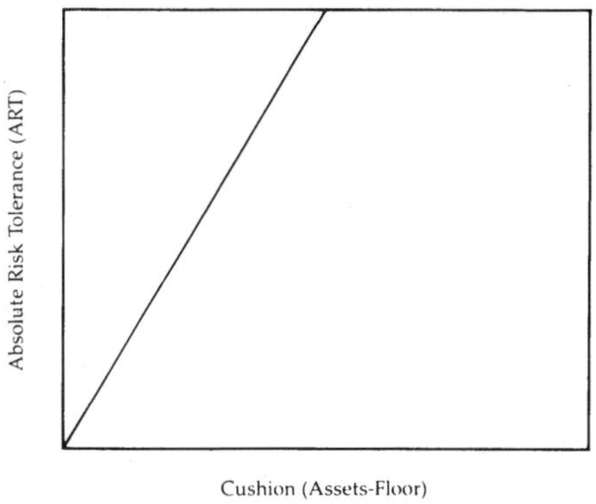

veloped to deal with unexpected changes in risk). Figure D portrays this assumption by omitting a connection between boxes C1 and C3.

While portfolio insurance strategies are normally *analyzed* in terms of a relation such as that shown in Figure F, they are *motivated* by a relation of the type shown in Figure G. As before, the horizontal axis plots the level of the asset cushion, but the vertical axis now indicates the investor's absolute risk tolerance. Risk tolerance is zero when assets reach the minimum value at which the floor can be assured. As asset value increases, so does the investor's risk tolerance.

The relation between the decision rule (e.g., Figure F) and the investor's underlying risk tolerance function (e.g., Figure G) is especially straightforward when one of the two assets is riskless. As shown earlier, in such a case:

$$D_S = k_I ART.$$

Thus Figures F and G differ only by the "scaling factor" k_I, because:

$$ART = \frac{D_S}{k_I}.$$

Figure G plots the basis for constant proportion portfolio insurance: The investor's one-period absolute risk tolerance is assumed to be proportional to the size of the asset cushion. Merton has shown that such a policy is optimal if the investor's overall utility function displays linear absolute risk tolerance relative to wealth at a specific horizon date or relative to consumption at many dates.[7]

Different portfolio insurance approaches imply different relations of the type shown in Figure G. Some are time-variant; some are not. Some give linear relationships; some do not. However, all can be viewed as implicit specifications of the investor's *risk tolerance function*.

Conclusions

Asset allocation is probably the most important task an investor undertakes.[8] The extensive effort that has been devoted to the development and application of procedures provides evidence that a number of practitioners recognize its importance. However, much of this work has been fragmented, and many of the models are subject to severe constraints. We hope the structure presented here can provide a more general framework for truly integrating the important aspects of this key investment activity. ■

Appendix

Conditions for an Optimal Asset Mix

Assume that an investor's utility is related to net worth at the end of a relatively short decision period by the function:

$$U = f(W),$$

where W represents net worth at the end of the period.

Pratt defines *absolute risk aversion* as follows:[9]

$$ARA = -\frac{dU/dW}{d^2U/dW^2}.$$

The reciprocal is termed *absolute risk tolerance*:

$$ART = -\frac{d^2U/dW^2}{dU/dW}.$$

Because the time period is short, the range of possible values of W will be small. Over a small range of values of W, the investor's actual utility function can be adequately approximated by another function displaying constant absolute risk tolerance. Such a function can be written as:

$$U = 1 - e^{-cW},$$

with

$$ART = \frac{1}{c}.$$

Because the time period is short, changes in net

worth can typically be assumed to follow a normal distribution without excessive loss of precision.

Following Von Neumann and Morgenstern, assume that the investor's objective is to maximize expected utility of wealth.[10] As shown by Lintner, if returns are normally distributed and the investor has constant absolute risk tolerance, expected utility can be written as:[11]

$$EU = -e^{-c(E_w - c/2(V_w))}.$$

To make this as large as possible, one should maximize:

$$E_W - \frac{c}{2} V_W$$

or

$$E_W - \frac{1}{2ART} V_W,$$

where E_W and V_W are the expected value and variance of end-of-period wealth, respectively.

Assume that the investor's current wealth is W_0. Let R_i be asset i's *value-relative*—the ratio of end-of-period value to current value. Let D_i represent the current (dollar) value of asset or liability i. (As a liability is a "negative asset," it will have a negative value of D_i.) Clearly, end-of-period wealth will equal:

$$W = \sum_i D_i R_i.$$

Because the sum of the D_i values must equal W_0, optimality requires that an additional dollar invested in asset i must contribute as much to the objective function as an additional dollar invested in asset j. That is:

$$\frac{\partial E_W}{\partial D_i} - \frac{1}{2\ ART} \frac{\partial V_W}{\partial D_i} = K \text{ for all assets i.}$$

Substituting equations for the partial derivatives gives:

$$E_i - \frac{1}{ART} \sum_j D_j \sigma_i \sigma_j \rho_{ij} = K \text{ for all assets i,}$$

where

E_i = the expected value of R_i,
σ_i = the standard deviation of R_i and
ρ_{ij} = the correlation between R_i and R_j.

Note that, although the equations hold only for assets, the summation (over j) includes assets and liabilities.

In the case of two assets (S and B), this implies:

$$D_S = k_0 W_0 + k_1 ART,$$

where

$$k_0 = \frac{V_B - C_{BS}}{V_S + V_B - 2C_{BS}},$$

$$k_1 = \frac{E_S - E_B}{V_S + V_B - 2C_{BS}},$$

and

$$V_B = \sigma_B^2$$

$$V_S = \sigma_S^2$$

$$C_{BS} = \sigma_B \sigma_S \rho_{BS}.$$

Note that, in the text, the value of W is written without a subscript, as the distinction between beginning and end-of-period values does not need to be emphasized there.

Footnotes

1. See L. Kingsland, "Projecting the Financial Condition of a Pension Plan Using Simulation Analysis," *Journal of Finance*, May 1982.
2. See W. L. Fouse, "The Evolution of Asset Allocation Theory and Practice," in *Asset Allocation for Institutional Portfolios* (Charlottesville, VA: Institute of Chartered Financial Analysts, 1987).
3. See G. B. Brinson, "Implementing and Managing the Asset Allocation Process," in *Asset Allocation for Institutional Portfolios* (Charlottesville, VA: Institute of Chartered Financial Analysts, 1987).
4. See M. Rubinstein, "Alternative Paths to Portfolio Insurance," *Financial Analysts Journal*, July/August 1985.
5. F. Black and R. Jones, "Simplifying Portfolio Insurance," *Goldman, Sachs Research Report*, August 1986. For the foundation of this approach, see R. C. Merton, "Optimum Consumption and Portfolio Rules in a Continuous Time Model," *Journal of Economic Theory* 3 (1971).
6. Following A. F. Perold, "Constant Proportion Portfolio Insurance" (Harvard Business School, August 1986).
7. Merton, "Optimum Consumption," *op. cit.*
8. See G. P. Brinson, L. R. Hood and G. L. Beebower, "Determinants of Portfolio Performance," *Financial Analysts Journal*, July/August 1986.
9. See J. W. Pratt, "Risk Aversion in the Small and in the Large," *Econometrica*, January-April 1964.
10. J. Von Neumann and O. Morgenstern, *Theory of Games and Economic Behavior*, 3rd ed. (Princeton, NJ: Princeton University Press, 1953).
11. J. Lintner, "The Market Price of Risk, Size of Market and Investor's Risk Aversion," *Journal of Business*, April 1968.

by André F. Perold and William F. Sharpe

Dynamic Strategies for Asset Allocation

As risky assets (e.g., stocks) fluctuate in value, the value of a portfolio containing them may change, as may their allocation relative to the safe assets (e.g., bills) within the portfolio. One must decide how to rebalance the portfolio in response to such changes. Dynamic strategies are explicit rules for doing so. Different strategies will produce different risk and return characteristics.

Buy-and-hold strategies are "do nothing" strategies. They have a minimum return proportional to the amount allocated to bills and an upside proportional to the amount allocated to stocks. Their performance is linearly related to the performance of the equity market.

Strategies that sell stocks as the market falls and buy stocks as the market rises represent the purchase of portfolio insurance. Particular examples are constant-proportion portfolio insurance and option-based portfolio insurance. These strategies have better downside protection and better upside potential than buy-and-hold strategies. They do worse in relatively trendless, volatile markets.

Constant-mix strategies—holding a constant fraction of wealth in stocks—buy stocks as the market falls and sell them as it rises. These and other such strategies effectively represent the sale of portfolio insurance. They have less downside protection than, and not as much upside as, buy-and-hold strategies. They do best in relatively trendless but volatile markets.

The greater the "popularity" of one type of strategy—be it the purchase or sale of portfolio insurance—the more costly it becomes, and the greater the rewards to those who follow the opposite strategy. Only buy-and-hold strategies can be followed by all investors.

"Good Heavens! For more than 40 years I have been speaking prose without knowing it."

—Moliere, *Le Burgeois Gentilhomme*

MOST PORTFOLIOS CONTAIN risky assets. Fluctuations in the values of such assets will generally cause the value of the portfolio in which they are held to change. The asset allocation of the portfolio will also change. If the risky assets increase in value, for example, the proportion of the portfolio they comprise is also likely to increase. One must decide how to rebalance the portfolio in response to such changes. *Dynamic strategies* are explicit rules for doing so.

This article examines and compares four dynamic strategies—

- buy-and-hold,

André Perold is Associate Professor of Business Administration at the Harvard Business School. William Sharpe is Timken Professor of Finance at the Stanford Graduate School of Business and President of Sharpe-Russell Research, Inc.

- constant mix,
- constant-proportion portfolio insurance and
- option-based portfolio insurance.

Buy-and-hold and *constant-mix* strategies are perhaps the most familiar of the four. *Option-based portfolio insurance* strategies (OBPI) replicate positions that can, in principle, be obtained with options. These were the strategies first used to implement portfolio insurance programs; their popularity has, in turn, attracted much attention to the general area of dynamic strategies. *Constant-proportion portfolio insurance* (CPPI) is much simpler to implement than OBPI.[1] It is, basically, a special case of a more general set of policies (constant-proportion strategies) that also embraces the constant-mix and buy-and-hold strategies as special cases. Just as Moliere's character found he had been speaking prose, many investment managers will find they have been using a type of constant-proportion strategy.

Different rules have different consequences in both the long term and short term. A rule preferred by one type of investor may not be preferred by another. For each strategy, we show how the portfolio performs in bull, bear and flat markets and in volatile and not-so-volatile markets. We discuss what risk tolerance an investor must have in order for a particular strategy to be the appropriate choice. To emphasize fundamentals, we focus on a choice between only two assets—stocks and bills. The concepts, however, are readily generalized to other asset classes.[2]

Payoff and Exposure Diagrams

This article makes extensive use of two types of diagrams. A *payoff diagram* for a given strategy relates the portfolio performance over a certain period of time to the performance of the stock market over the same period. An *exposure diagram* relates the dollars invested in stocks to total assets; it depicts the *decision rule* underlying a strategy.

Consider two extreme strategies—100 per cent bills and 100 per cent stocks. Among all possible dynamic strategies with neither borrowing nor short sales of stock, these are the minimum risk and maximum return strategies, respectively. Assume that the current level of the stock market is 100 and that the current value of total assets is $100.

Figure A is the payoff diagram for these two strategies. In the minimum risk (100 per cent bills) case, the value of the portfolio is unaffected by the level of the stock market. In the maximum return (100 per cent stocks) case, the value of the portfolio is related dollar for dollar to the level of the market.[3]

Figure B is the exposure diagram for the two strategies. In the minimum risk case, there is never any exposure to stocks; the value of stocks held is zero, no matter what the value of the portfolio may be. In the maximum return case there is 100 per cent exposure to stocks; the desired stock position equals the value of the portfolio at all times.

Figure A Payoff Diagram for Maximum Return and Minimum Risk Strategies

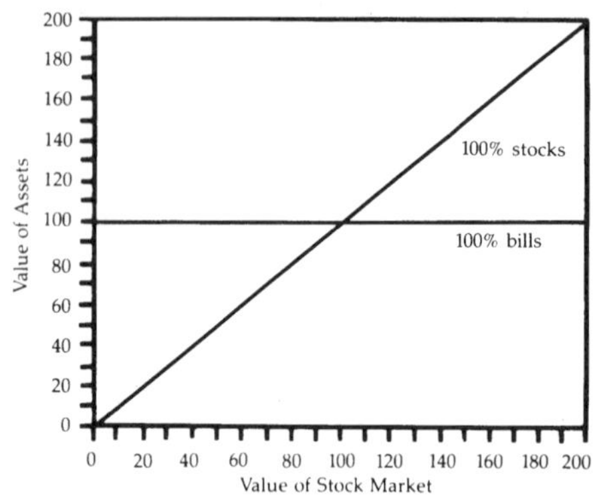

Figure B Exposure Diagram for Maximum Return and Minimum Risk Strategies

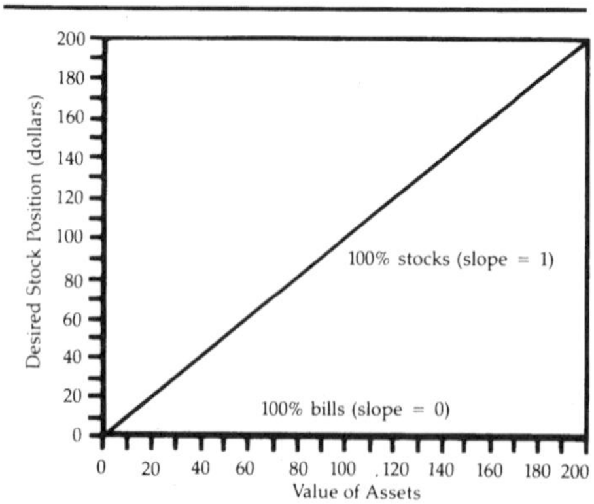

1. Footnotes appear at end of article.

The exposure diagram pertaining to a given strategy also depicts the risk tolerance an investor must have in order for that strategy to be optimal for him or her.[4] In a stock-bill allocation, the optimal amount to invest in stocks is proportional to the investor's risk tolerance. For example, the minimum risk strategy is optimal for an investor who has no tolerance for risk.

Buy-and-Hold Strategies

A buy-and-hold strategy is characterized by an initial mix (e.g., 60/40 stocks/bills) that is bought and then held. The minimum risk and maximum return strategies provide examples. Buy-and-hold strategies are "do nothing" strategies: No matter what happens to relative values, no rebalancing is required. Buy-and-hold strategies are easy to analyze. They also serve as anchor points for more complex approaches.

Figure C shows the payoff diagram for a buy-and-hold strategy with a 60/40 mix of stocks and bills. As before, we assume that the investor's portfolio is worth $100 and that the current level of the stock market is 100. The figure illustrates some general features of such strategies.

- The portfolio's value is linearly related to that of the stock market.
- Portfolio value increases as a function of stock market value, with a slope equal to the proportion in stocks in the initial mix. In the figure, every dollar of additional stock market value increases the value of the investor's portfolio by 60 cents.
- Portfolio value will never fall below the value of the initial investment in bills.
- Upside potential is unlimited.
- The greater the initial percentage invested in stocks, the better the performance of a buy-and-hold strategy when stocks outperform bills and the worse the performance of a buy-and-hold strategy when stocks underperform bills.

Figure C Payoff Diagram for 60/40 Stock/Bill Buy-and-Hold Strategy

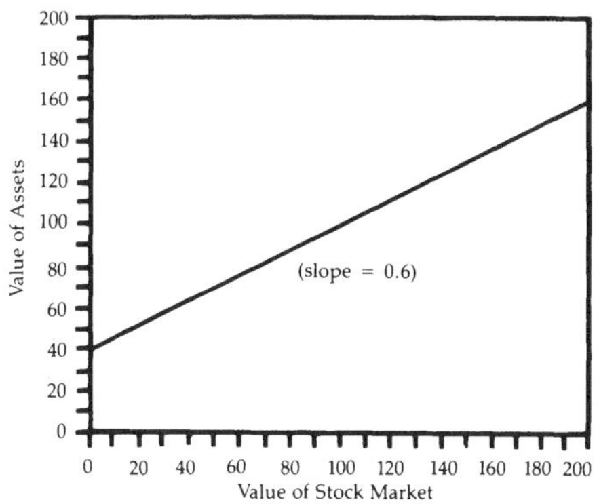

Figure D Exposure Diagram for 60/40 Stock/Bill Buy-and-Hold Strategy

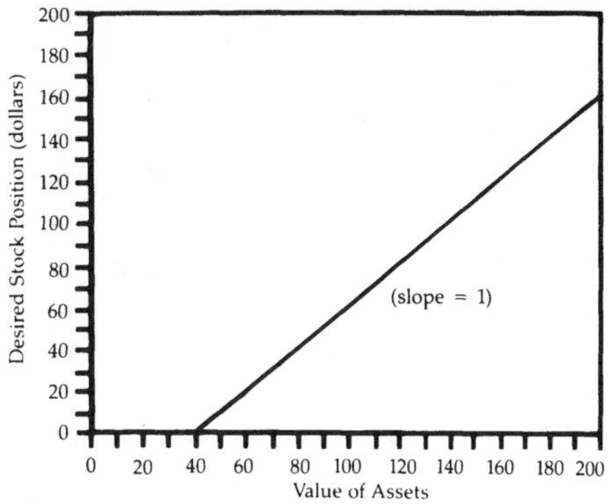

The payoff diagrams of other buy-and-hold strategies will differ from Figure C only in terms of the intercept (the point at which the line hits the vertical axis) and the slope.

Figure D shows the exposure diagram for a 60/40 buy-and-hold strategy. The investor's tolerance for risk becomes zero at asset levels below 60 per cent of initial wealth. The exposure diagrams of other buy-and-hold strategies all have a slope of one and differ only in terms of the asset level at which the investor's tolerance for risk (hence exposure to stocks) becomes zero.

Constant-Mix Strategies

Constant-mix strategies maintain an exposure to stocks that is a constant proportion of wealth. Figure E shows the exposure diagram for a 60/40 constant-mix policy. Investors who like constant-mix strategies have tolerances for risk that vary proportionately with their wealth. They will hold stocks at all wealth levels.

Constant-mix strategies are dynamic ("do something") approaches to investment decision-making. Whenever the relative values of

Figure E Exposure Diagram for 60/40 Stock/Bill Constant-Mix Strategy

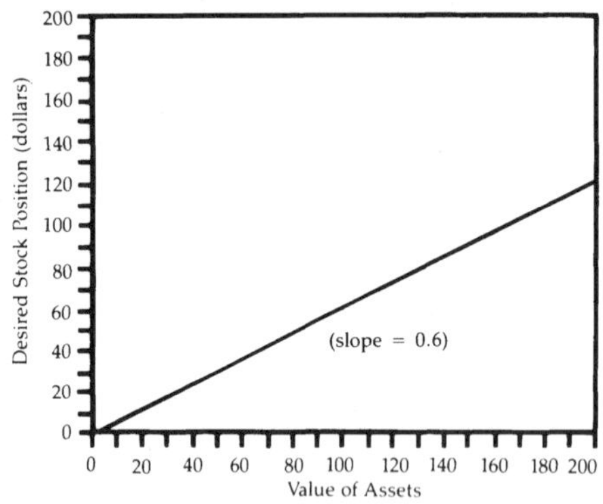

assets change, purchases and sales are required to return to the desired mix.

Consider an investor who has put $60 in stocks and $40 in bills and wishes to maintain a 60/40 constant mix. Now assume that the stock market declines by 10 per cent (from 100 to 90). The investor's stocks are now worth $54, giving a total portfolio value of $94. At this point, the stock proportion is $54/$94, or 57.4 per cent—well below the desired 60 per cent level. To achieve the desired level, the portfolio must have 60 per cent of $94, or $56.40, in stocks. Thus the investor must purchase $2.40 (=$56.40–$54.00) of stocks, obtaining the money by selling a comparable amount of bills. Table I outlines the steps involved.

In general, rebalancing to a constant mix requires **the purchase of stocks as they fall in value**, where, strictly speaking, changes in value are measured in relative terms.[5]

Implementation of any dynamic strategy requires a rule concerning the conditions under which rebalancing will actually be undertaken. Typical approaches avoid transactions until either the value of the portfolio or a portion of it (e.g., stocks) has changed by at least a given percentage. For purposes of illustration, we will assume that rebalancing occurs whenever the stock market changes by 10 points (as in the preceding example).

Table II shows what would happen if stocks fell from 100 to 90, then from 90 to 80, and so on

Table I Rebalancing to a Constant Mix—An Example

Case	*Stock Market*	*Value of Stock*	*Value of Bills*	*Value of Assets*	*Percentage in Stocks*
Initial	100	60.00	40.00	100.00	60.0%
After Change	90	54.00	40.00	94.00	57.4%
After Rebalancing	90	56.40	37.60	94.00	60.0%

Table II Rebalancing to a Constant Mix when Stock Value Falls

Case	*Stock Market*	*Value of Stock*	*Value of Bills*	*Value of Assets*	*Percentage in Stocks*
Initial	100	60.00	40.00	100.00	60.0%
After Change	90	54.00	40.00	94.00	57.4%
After Rebalancing	90	56.40	37.60	94.00	60.0%
After Change	80	50.13	37.60	87.73	57.1%
After Rebalancing	80	52.64	35.09	87.73	60.0%
After Change	70	46.06	35.09	81.15	56.8%
After Rebalancing	70	48.69	32.46	81.15	60.0%
After Change	60	41.74	32.46	74.20	56.3%
After Rebalancing	60	44.52	29.68	74.20	60.0%
After Change	50	37.10	29.68	66.78	55.6%
After Rebalancing	50	40.07	26.71	66.78	60.0%
After Change	40	32.05	26.71	58.76	54.5%
After Rebalancing	40	35.26	23.51	58.76	60.0%
After Change	30	26.44	23.51	49.95	52.9%
After Rebalancing	30	29.97	19.98	49.95	60.0%
After Change	20	19.98	19.98	39.96	50.0%
After Rebalancing	20	23.98	15.98	39.96	60.0%
After Change	10	11.99	15.98	27.97	42.9%
After Rebalancing	10	16.78	11.19	27.97	60.0%
After Change	0	0.00	11.19	11.19	0.0%
After Rebalancing	0	6.71	4.48	11.19	60.0%

Table III Rebalancing to a Constant Mix when Stock Value Rises

Case	*Stock Market*	*Value of Stock*	*Value of Bills*	*Value of Assets*	*Percentage in Stocks*
Initial	100	60.00	40.00	100.00	60.0%
After Change	110	66.00	40.00	106.00	62.3%
After Rebalancing	110	63.60	42.40	106.00	60.0%
After Change	120	69.38	42.40	111.78	62.1%
After Rebalancing	120	67.07	44.71	111.78	60.0%
After Change	130	72.66	44.71	117.37	61.9%
After Rebalancing	130	70.42	46.95	117.37	60.0%
After Change	140	75.84	46.95	122.79	61.8%
After Rebalancing	140	73.67	49.12	122.79	60.0%
After Change	150	78.94	49.12	128.05	61.6%
After Rebalancing	150	76.83	51.22	128.05	60.0%
After Change	160	81.95	51.22	133.17	61.5%
After Rebalancing	160	79.90	53.27	133.17	60.0%
After Change	170	84.90	53.27	138.17	61.4%
After Rebalancing	170	82.90	55.27	138.17	60.0%
After Change	180	87.78	55.27	143.04	61.4%
After Rebalancing	180	85.83	57.22	143.04	60.0%
After Change	190	90.59	57.22	147.81	61.3%
After Rebalancing	190	88.69	59.12	147.81	60.0%
After Change	200	93.35	59.12	152.48	61.2%
After Rebalancing	200	91.49	60.99	152.48	60.0%

until they became worthless.[6] Table III illustrates the more pleasant case in which stocks rise from 100 to 110, then to 120, and so. In this example, and in general, rebalancing to a constant mix requires **the sale of stocks as they rise in value**.

Figure F uses the results from these two examples to produce a payoff diagram. For comparison, the line showing results for a 60/40 buy-and-hold strategy is also shown. In this case, the buy-and-hold strategy clearly dominates the constant-mix strategy. Whether the stock market goes up or down, the buy-and-hold investor has more money than his constant-mix companion!

Figure F Payoff Diagram for 60/40 Constant-Mix Strategy

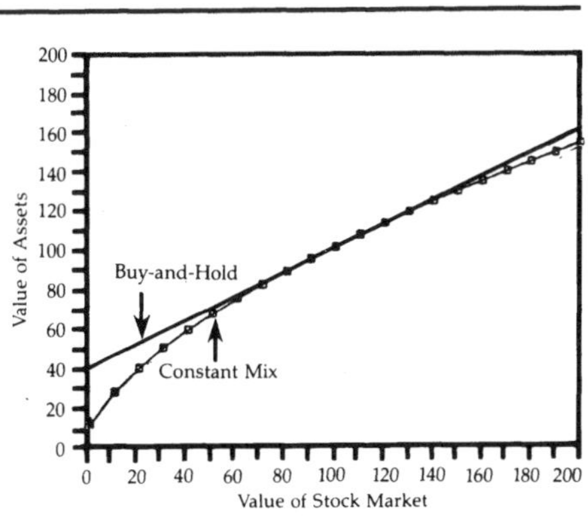

Why, then, would anyone want to adopt a constant-mix strategy? To find the answer, we must consider other ways in which the stock market might move.

Effects of Volatility

In our previous examples, once the stock market started moving it kept moving in the same direction. In such a world the choice of an investment strategy is simple indeed. But the real world is not so simple; the stock market is perfectly capable of reversing itself. And such reversals favor constant-mix strategies over buy-and-hold approaches.

Consider a case in which stocks fall from 100 to 90, then recover to 100. The market is *flat*, in the sense that it ends up where it started; in between, however, it *oscillates* back and forth. In such a case, someone following a buy-and-hold strategy will end up with exactly the same wealth he had at the beginning. Not so the constant-mix investor. Table IV gives his results, obtained by following the rules from the previous examples.

The constant-mix investor makes money ($0.27). Figure G shows why. When the stock market falls from 100 to 90, the value of the investor's assets falls to $94. In the figure, this is shown by the line from point a to point b. (The number of shares of stock held in the portfolio determines the slope of this line.) For the buy-

Table IV Constant-Mix Results with Market Volatility

Case	*Stock Market*	*Value of Stock*	*Value of Bills*	*Value of Assets*	*Percentage in Stocks*
Initial	100	60.00	40.00	100.00	60.0%
After Change	90	54.00	40.00	94.00	57.4%
After Rebalancing	90	56.40	37.60	94.00	60.0%
After Change	100	62.67	37.60	100.27	62.5%
After Rebalancing	100	60.16	40.11	100.27	60.0%

and-hold investor, further moves in the stock market will have proportionately similar effects. Thus, if the market falls to 80, the buy-and-hold investor's assets will fall to point c; if the market rises back to 100, this investor's assets will rise back to 100 (point a). A buy-and-hold investor simply travels up and down a single straight line in the payoff diagram.

This is not so for the constant-mix investor. Every rebalancing changes the number of shares of stock he holds, hence the slope of the line along which he will next travel in the payoff diagram. After a fall from point a to point b, he purchases more shares of stock. This increases the slope of the line. Thus, in Figure G, a further fall in the market to 80 will place the constant-mix investor at point d—below that of his buy-and-hold friend. But a subsequent rise in the market to 100 will place the constant-mix investor at point e—above that of the buy-and-hold investor. And, of course, after each such change, the constant-mix investor will rebalance, creating a new line for the next step of the journey.

Who will win overall? The answer depends on the pattern of market moves.

Figure G Payoff Diagram for 60/40 Constant-Mix and Buy-and-Hold Strategies

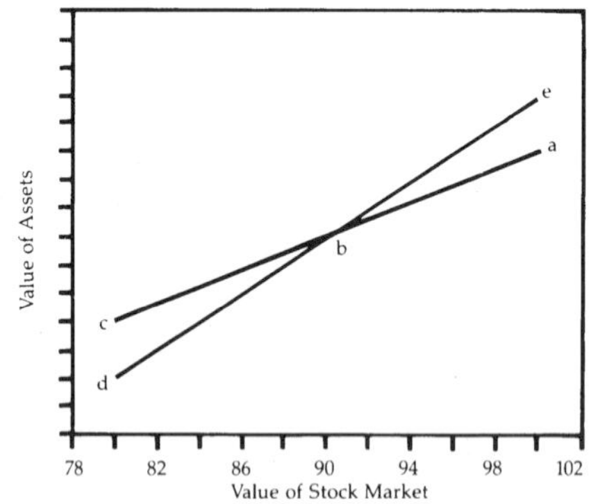

If the market moves from 100 to 90 and then back to 100, the constant-mix investor will end up ahead. In general, a strategy that buys stocks as they fall and sells as they rise will capitalize on reversals. The marginal purchase decisions will turn out to be good ones, as will the marginal sell decisions. A constant-mix strategy will thus outperform a comparable buy-and-hold strategy in a flat (but oscillating) market precisely because it trades in a way that exploits reversals. Greater volatility (i.e., more and/or larger reversals) will accentuate this effect.

Conversely, if the market moves from 100 to 90 and then to 80, both types of investors will lose, but the buy-and-hold investor will lose less. In general, a constant-mix approach will underperform a comparable buy-and-hold strategy when there are no reversals. This will also be the case in strong bull or bear markets, when reversals are small and relatively infrequent, because most of the marginal purchase and sell decisions will turn out to have been poorly timed.

The value of a constant-mix investor's assets after several rebalancings will depend on both the final level of the stock market and on the manner in which stocks move from period to period before reaching that final level. The relation depicted in the payoff diagram will thus be somewhat fuzzy. Cases in which the market ends up near its starting point are likely to favor constant-mix strategies, while those in which the market ends up far from its starting point are likely to favor buy-and-hold strategies.

Figure H provides an example. The horizontal axis plots the level of the stock market after a number of decisions (rebalancings) have been undertaken. The vertical axis shows the final value of the investor's assets. The straight line shows the value of a buy-and-hold investor's portfolio. Each of the squares represents one of 2,000 possible outcomes for a constant-mix investor who rebalances after any 10-point move in the stock market.[7]

Here, neither strategy dominates the other. A

Figure H Payoff Diagram for Constant-Mix and Buy-and-Hold Strategies

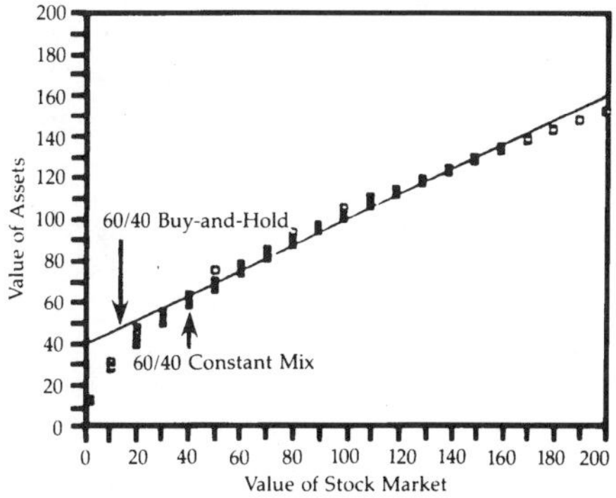

constant-mix policy tends to be superior if markets are characterized more by reversals than by trends. A buy-and-hold policy tends be superior if there is a major move in one direction.[8]

Constant-Proportion Strategies

Constant-proportion strategies take the following form:

Dollars in Stocks = m (Assets–Floor),

where m is a fixed multiplier. *Constant-proportion portfolio insurance* (CPPI) strategies are constant-proportion strategies with multipliers greater than one.[9]

Figure I Exposure Diagram for CPPI Strategy*

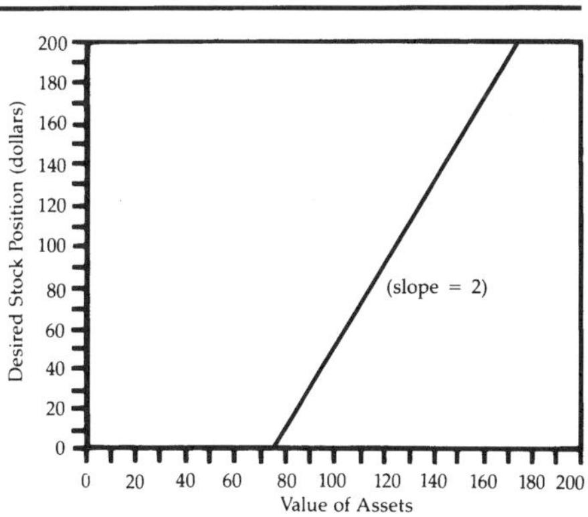

*Floor equals $75; multiplier equals two.

To implement a CPPI strategy, the investor selects the multiplier and a floor below which she does not want the portfolio value to fall. This floor grows at the rate of return on bills, and must initially be less than total assets. If we think of the difference between assets and the floor as a "cushion," then the CPPI decision rule is simply to keep the exposure to equities a constant multiple of the cushion.

Figure I shows the exposure diagram for a CPPI strategy with a floor of $75 and a multiplier of two. As with buy-and-hold strategies, investors who like CPPI strategies have zero tolerance for risk (hence no exposure to stocks) below a specified floor. However, with CPPI tolerance for risk increases more quickly above the floor than with buy-and-hold strategies.

Exposure diagrams for CPPI strategies are similar to those for buy-and-hold strategies. This is not surprising: Buy-and-hold strategies are constant-proportion strategies with a multiplier of one and a floor equal to the value invested in bills. Constant-mix strategies also represent special cases of the constant-proportion formula. They have floors of zero and multipliers with values between zero and one. For a constant-mix strategy, the multiplier corresponds to the percentage invested in stocks.

For the payoff diagram for a CPPI strategy, we assume $100 of wealth, a floor of $75 and a multiplier (m) of two. As the initial cushion is $25, the initial investment in stocks must be twice this, or $50. The initial mix is thus 50/50 stocks/bills.

Now imagine that the stock market falls from 100 to 90. The investor's stocks will fall 10 per cent, from $50 to $45. Total assets will then be $95, and the cushion will equal $20 (=$95–$75). According to the CPPI rule, the appropriate stock position is $40 (=2 × $20). This requires the sale of $5 of stocks and investment of the proceeds in bills. If stocks fall further, more should be sold. If they increase in value, stocks should be bought. And so on.

From this analysis, we see that a CPPI strategy **sells stocks as they fall and buys stocks as they rise.**

Under a CPPI strategy, the portfolio will do at least as well as the floor, even in a severe bear market. Such a strategy puts more and more into bills as stocks decline, reducing the exposure to stocks to zero as the assets approach the floor. The only scenario in which the portfolio might do worse than the floor is if the market

Figure J Payoff Diagram for CPPI and Two Buy-and-Hold Strategies

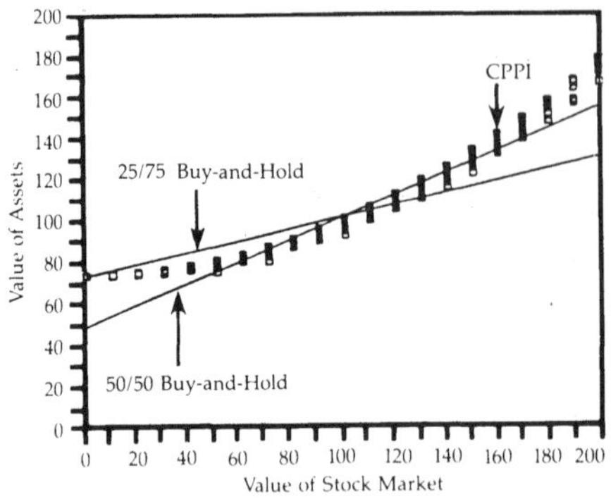

drops precipitously before one has had the chance to rebalance. Just how precipitous the decline must be depends on the multiplier. With a multiplier of two, the market can fall by as much as 50 per cent with no rebalancing before the floor is endangered. More generally, the market can fall by as much as 1/m with no rebalancing before the floor is endangered.

In a bull market, the CPPI strategy will do very well. It calls for buying stocks as they rise, with each marginal purchase paying off handsomely. In a flat market, a CPPI strategy will do relatively poorly, owing to the same phenomenon that makes constant-mix strategies perform so well—reversals. Reversals hurt CPPI strategies because they sell on weakness only to see the market rebound, and buy on strength only to see the market weaken.

Figure J illustrates these principles. The horizontal axis plots the level of the stock market after a number of decisions (rebalancings) have been undertaken. The vertical axis shows the final value of the investor's assets. Each of the squares represents one of 2,000 possible outcomes for a CPPI investor (with a floor of $75 and a multiplier of two) who rebalances after any 10-point move in the stock market.[10] (The appendix contains an exact formula for the payoff when rebalancing is continuous and costless.)

Figure J also gives the payoffs from two buy-and-hold strategies. The steeper of the two lines corresponds to a policy with the same initial asset mix (50/50) as used in the CPPI strategy. The second involves investment of $75 in bills and $25 in stocks to insure that the portfolio's value will never fall below the floor of $75.

Not surprisingly, none of the three strategies shown in Figure J completely dominates the others. The winner in any contest will be determined by the behavior of the market.

Concave versus Convex Strategies

From our analysis so far, it is apparent that the basic shape of the payoff diagram is not so much dependent on the specific decision rule underlying the strategy as it is on the kind of rebalancing required. We have looked at payoff curves for three kinds of rebalancing—

- do nothing;
- buy stocks as they fall, sell as they rise; and
- sell stocks as they fall, buy as they rise.

"Do nothing" strategies (buy-and-hold) give payoff diagrams that are *straight lines*.

Strategies that "buy stocks as they fall . . ." give rise to *concave* payoff curves (which increase at a decreasing rate as one moves from left to right). That is, they tend not to have much downside protection, and to do relatively poorly in up markets. They generally do very well, however, in flat (but oscillating) markets.

Strategies that "sell stocks as they fall . . ." give rise to *convex* payoff curves (which increase at an increasing rate as one moves from left to right). They tend to do very poorly in flat (but oscillating) markets. But they tend to give good downside protection, and to perform well in up markets.

Constant-mix and CPPI strategies are perhaps the simplest examples of concave and convex strategies, respectively.

Strategies giving convex payoff diagrams represent the *purchase* of portfolio insurance, while those giving concave diagrams represent its *sale*.[11] Concave and convex strategies may be seen as mirror images of one another on either side of buy-and-hold strategies. Every "buyer" of a convex strategy is a "seller" of a concave strategy, and vice versa. When the portfolio of one who buys a convex strategy is combined with the portfolio of the seller of that strategy, the result is a buy-and-hold position.

There is a simple and straightforward relationship between the *shape* of a payoff diagram and the *slope* of the exposure diagram (which here corresponds to the multiplier, m).[12] Strategies with slopes less than one give rise to concave payoff diagrams, while strategies with slopes greater than one give rise to convex payoff diagrams.

There are many ways to construct strategies with concave payoff diagrams. Any procedure that "buys stocks as they fall, sells as they rise" will do. And any procedure that "sells stocks as they fall, buys as they rise" will produce a convex payoff diagram.

That convex and concave strategies are mirror images of one another tells us that the more demand there is for one of these strategies, the more costly its implementation will become, and the less healthy it may be for markets generally. If growing numbers of investors switch to convex strategies, then markets will become more volatile, for there will be insufficient buyers in down markets and insufficient sellers in up markets at previously "fair" prices. In this setting, those who follow concave strategies may be handsomely rewarded. Conversely, if growing numbers of investors switch to concave strategies, then the markets may become too stable. Prices may be too slow to adjust to fair economic value. This is the most rewarding environment for those following convex strategies. Generally, whichever strategy is "most popular" will subsidize the performance of the one that is "least popular." Over time, this will likely swell the ranks of investors following the latter and contain the growth of those following the former, driving the market toward a balance of the two.[13]

Option-Based Portfolio Insurance

Option-based portfolio insurance (OBPI) strategies begin by specifying an investment *horizon* and a desired floor value at that horizon. While not stated explicitly, OBPI strategies implicitly involve a floor value at every time prior to the horizon. For example, if the horizon is one year, and the floor at year-end is $82.50, then the floor at any prior time is the present value of $82.50 discounted using the riskless rate of interest. At a 10 per cent bill rate, the initial floor is $75. The floor value grows at the riskless rate, as it does with CPPI and buy-and-hold strategies.

Once a floor is chosen and its present value calculated, the typical OBPI strategy consists of a set of rules designed to give the same payoff at the horizon as would a portfolio composed of bills and call options. Figure K provides an example. The bills have face value equal to the floor (e.g., $82.50). The cushion is invested in the calls. The appendix describes the method for choosing the parameters.

Figure K Payoff Diagram for OBPI

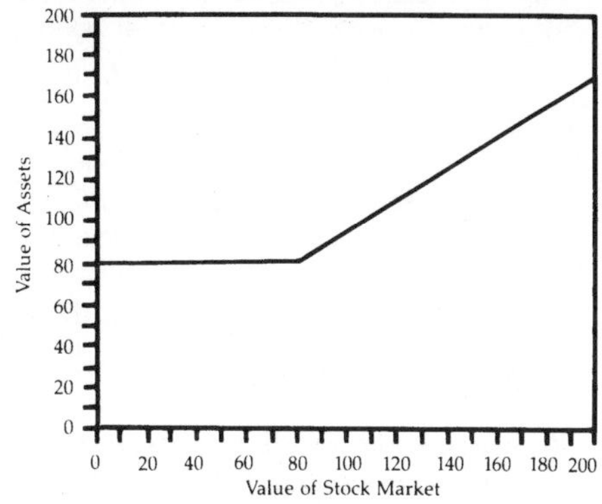

With OBPI, the exposure diagram (hence the decision rule) depends very much on the time remaining before the horizon is reached. One instant prior to the horizon, OBPI involves investing entirely in bills if the assets equal the floor, and entirely in stocks if the assets exceed the floor. With more than just an instant to go before "expiration," the exposure diagram is a curve. Figure L shows an example in which there is one year left before the horizon. To draw this curve, one must utilize a relatively

Figure L Exposure Diagram for OBPI

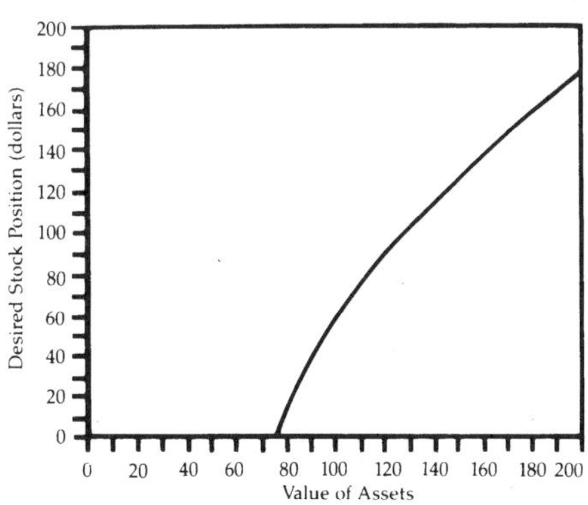

complex option pricing formula.[14] Moreover, new curves must be found as time passes.

Note in Figure L that the slope of the exposure curve is greater than one at all points. It begins at a value considerably greater than one and falls towards a value of one as the cushion becomes very large. This will be the case at any time prior to the horizon date. OBPI strategies are thus "sell stocks as they fall . . ." strategies. They must thus provide convex payoff diagrams. Over any period ending prior to the horizon, such payoff diagrams will plot as curves. At the horizon, as shown in Figure K, the diagram plots as two straight lines, but with a shape that is convex overall.

With a traditional OBPI strategy, for any given (positive) cushion, the exposure to stocks increases as time passes, reaching 100 per cent of the asset value at the horizon. Such approaches are thus calendar-time dependent. This contrasts with CPPI strategies, in which the exposure depends only on the size of the cushion.

The calendar-time dependence of OBPI is particularly acute when the strategy "expires" at the horizon, because a new set of rules must then be put in place. For the long-term investor whose true horizon extends beyond the horizon specified in the OBPI strategy, this is a drawback. The asset mix just before expiration (either 0/100 or 100/0) will typically be vastly different from the mix as reset just after expiration. It is difficult to imagine circumstances in which it is sensible to effect dramatic changes in mix merely because one calendar period has ended and another has begun.

Dynamic Strategies with Resetting

When, if ever, should one "reset" the parameters of a dynamic strategy? This answer depends not only on the rationale behind the choice of strategy, but also on the type of dynamic strategy chosen. For example, as just noted, with option-based portfolio insurance, one has no choice but to reset at the horizon.

It is important to be aware that the manner in which one resets the parameters of a dynamic strategy can dramatically alter its basic characteristics. For example, we saw in Figure L that, with OBPI, the multiplier is different at different levels of the cushion. Thus OBPI can be considered a variation of the CPPI approach in which the multiplier is changed as the cushion changes.

As a second example, consider the following "rolling" CPPI strategy. Begin as usual with a multiplier and a floor, but then, as total assets fluctuate in value, adjust the floor so that it is always a constant fraction of assets. (Keep the multiplier constant at, say, two.) If we keep the floor at, say, 80 per cent of assets, then it would appear that we will always be assured of losing no more than 10 per cent of current assets. But, by substituting into the CPPI formula the following:

$$\text{Floor} = 0.8 \times \text{Assets},$$

we see that all we have achieved is to transform the CPPI strategy into a constant-mix strategy.[15] As shown earlier, such strategies have no downside protection at all.

A rolling option-based portfolio insurance strategy that involves (1) rolling the horizon forward (e.g., one year) so that it always remains as far away as it was in the beginning, and (2) resetting the end-of-horizon floor so as to keep it in constant proportion to assets is also just a constant-mix strategy in disguise.[16]

One form of resetting that seems to be popular involves beginning with some portfolio insurance strategy (say, CPPI) and sticking to the rules if the market is flat or declines. If there is an appreciable up move, however, the floor is raised in order to "lock in" profits. Thus the floor is raised if assets increase but left intact otherwise. How "ratcheting up the floor" in this manner alters the basic character of the dynamic strategy will depend very much on exactly how it is implemented. Typically, however, it can cause stocks to be sold in both up and down markets. In down markets, the selling occurs because the floor is being held fixed, thus preserving the portfolio insurance nature of the strategy. In up markets, when the cushion would ordinarily increase and thus give rise to buying, the floor is raised and the cushion thus reduced. If the floor is raised far and or fast enough, the net effect will be to reduce the size of the cushion, giving rise to selling. Overall, the resulting strategy provides expected payoffs that are concave to the right and convex to the left.

Resetting can dramatically alter the character of a strategy. Resetting rules should thus be considered an integral part of the dynamic strategy, and their effects explicitly taken into account.

Option-based portfolio insurance strategies,

by their nature, require resetting. However, constant-proportion strategies (CPPI, buy-and-hold and constant-mix approaches) can be implemented in perpetuity with no change in the key parameters. For investors with long time horizons, these latter strategies are attractive candidates.

Selecting a Dynamic Strategy

Which dynamic strategy is demonstrably the best? The goal of this article is to emphasize that "best" should be measured by the degree of fit between a strategy's exposure diagram and the investor's risk tolerance (expressed as a function of an appropriate cushion).

Ultimately, the issue concerns the preferences of the various parties that will bear the risk and/or enjoy the reward from investment. There is no reason to believe that any particular type of dynamic strategy is best for everyone (and, in fact, only buy-and-hold strategies could be followed by everyone). Financial analysts can help those affected by investment results understand the implications of various strategies, but they cannot and should not choose a strategy without substantial knowledge of the investor's circumstances and desires.■

Footnotes

1. It has been advocated recently in F. Black and R. Jones, "Simplifying Portfolio Insurance," *Journal of Portfolio Management*, Fall 1987 and in A.F. Perold, "Constant Proportion Portfolio Insurance" (Harvard Business School, August 1986). The basic procedure is rooted in the work of R.C. Merton, "Optimum Consumption and Portfolio Rules in a Continuous Time Model," *Journal of Economic Theory* 3 (1971). With respect to the general subject matter of this article, see also M.J. Brennan and R. Solanki, "Optimal Portfolio Insurance," *Journal of Financial and Quantitative Analysis*, September 1981 and H. E. Leland, "Who Should Buy Portfolio Insurance?" *Journal of Fianance* 35 (1980).
2. As shown in W.F. Sharpe, "Integrated Asset Allocation," *Financial Analysts Journal*, September/October 1987.
3. For simplicity, all the payoff diagrams ignore the accrual over time of interest on any bills held. The appendix provides payoff curve formulas that include the interest earned on bills.
4. More precisely, it depicts absolute risk tolerance over the next short period of time.
5. Rebalancing is required only if the return on stocks differs from that on bills.
6. In this example, the value of assets does not fall to zero. This is because we rebalance after consecutive absolute market moves (of 10 points). If we were to rebalance after a never-ending stream of percentage declines, the value of assets would approach zero.
7. Each of the points shows the results of a simulation involving 20 periods in which the stock market could move up 10 points, down 10 points or stay the same. In performing the simulation, each of the three possible moves was considered equally probable.

   When rebalancing occurs continuously and costlessly, an exact formula can be obtained for the payoff under a constant-mix strategy. Details are given in the appendix.
8. No consideration has been given in this analysis to transaction costs, which would lower the points associated with any dynamic strategy.
9. When m is greater than one, the formula may call for investing more than total assets in stocks. If such leverage is not permitted, the CPPI rule becomes:

   Dollars in Stocks = Lesser of [m(Assets-Floor), Assets].
10. See footnote 7. In some cases, a market move of greater than 50 per cent (i.e., from 10 to 0) occurred before rebalancing. This explains the few instances in which ending asset value fell below the floor of $75.
11. This is a more general description of portfolio insurance than given in M. Rubinstein, "Alternative Paths to Portfolio Insurance," *Financial Analysts Journal*, July/August 1985.
12. The slope of the exposure diagram equals the multiplier (the ratio of dollars invested in stocks to the cushion) only when both are constant.
13. There are, of course, many other types of investors (and issuers of securities) following different implicit and explicit trading rules. More generally, markets must be balanced across all of these.
14. See the one developed in F. Black and M. Scholes, "The Pricing of Options and Corporate Liabilities," *Journal of Political Economy*, May–June 1973.
15. Dollars in Stocks = m(Assets-Floor)
    = 2(Assets–0.8 · Assets)
    = 0.4 · Assets
    = 40/60 stock/bill constant mix.
16. This is discussed in S. Benninga and M. Blume, "On the Optimality of Portfolio Insurance," *Journal of Finance* 40 (1985), pp. 1341–1352. Other forms of rolling OBPI preserve the portfolio insurance feature (convexity) of OBPI. For example, by rolling the horizon but keeping the floor at a fixed nominal level, the exposure curve no longer varies over time. It is simply one of the curves drawn in Figure L (corresponding to the length of the horizon), frozen for all time.

Appendix

This appendix gives the formulas for the payoff and exposure diagrams shown in the body of the article. The following notation is used:

A = total assets at t (payoff);
A_0 = initial assets;
S = stock market at t (total return index);
S_0 = initial level of stock market;
F = floor at t;
F_0 = initial floor;
E = desired stock position (exposure); and
r = bill rate.

Buy-and-Hold Strategies

Let x be the initial fraction invested in stocks. The initial floor is:

$$F_0 = (1 - x)A_0.$$

The floor at time t is:

$$F = (1 - x)A_0e^{rt} = F_0e^{rt}.$$

The payoff at t is:

$$A = F + x\, A_0S/S_0.$$

The exposure is:

$$E = A - F.$$

Constant-Proportion Strategies

Let m be the multiplier. The floor at t is:

$$F = F_0e^{rt}.$$

A constant-mix strategy corresponds to the following special case:

$$F = F_0 = O.$$

The payoff at t is:

$$A = F + (A_0 - F_0)\left(\frac{S}{S_0}\right)^m e^{(1-m)(r+0.5m\sigma^2)t}.$$

The exposure is:

$$E = m(A - F).$$

When no leverage is allowed, the exposure is limited to total assets, A. In this case:

$$E = min(A, m(A - F)),$$

and there is no simple formula for the payoff in terms of the level of the stock market.

Option-Based Portfolio Insurance

Let $B(S,K,r,\sigma,t,T)$ be the Black-Scholes formula for the value at time t of a European call option (on one unit of the market) with strike price K and expiration date T:

$$B = SN(d) - Ke^{-rt}N(d - \sigma t^{0.5}),$$

where

$$d = \frac{\log\left(\frac{S}{K}\right) + (r + 0.5\sigma^2 t)}{\sigma t^{0.5}}$$

and $N \cdot (\ \cdot\ )$ is the cumulative of the unit normal distribution and σ is the volatility of the market.

OBPI involves investing F_0 in bills and purchasing n call options, where n and K are determined jointly by the following equations:

$$n \cdot B(S,K,r,\sigma,O,T) = A_0 - F_0$$

and

$$n \cdot K = F_T,$$

where F_T is the floor at expiration, and the initial floor is

$$F_0 = F_Te^{-rT}.$$

The first equation indicates that the value of calls purchased equals the initial cushion. The second indicates that the total exercise price equals the floor. Thus there is always enough money to exercise the calls (the portfolio will never become levered).

At any t between o and T the payoff is:

$$A = F + n \cdot B(S,K,r,\sigma,t,T),$$

where the floor is:

$$F = F_Te^{-r(T-t)}.$$

At expiration:

$$A = F_T + n \cdot \max(S - K,O).$$

The exposure is

$$E = n \cdot N(d),$$

where d can be expressed as a function of the cushion $A - F$ by solving for S using:

$$B(S,K,r,\sigma,t,T) = (A - F)/n.$$

Convex and Concave Strategies

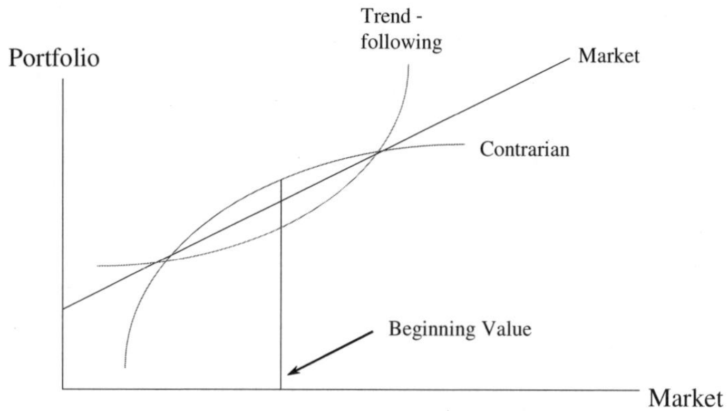

Dynamic Strategies for Asset Allocation
(illustration)

Liabilities—A new approach

An approach that avoids either asset only or full surplus optimization.

William F. Sharpe and Lawrence G. Tint

Pension fund managers have shown faint interest in consideration of liabilities in pension fund asset allocation strategies. There are a variety of reasons for their lack of enthusiasm. First, the decision to abandon return maximization as a goal strikes ERISA-conditioned pension officers as imprudent, illegal, or not in their own personal interest. Moreover, suggested methods require an all-or-nothing approach to liability consideration — investors maximize either return or surplus; they are not offered a middle ground. Finally, in practice, surplus optimization or portfolio dedication normally requires acceptance of the idea that the accounting characterization of liabilities is, in fact, an accurate reflection of the true corporate liability.

This article presents a new approach for dealing with liabilities. Our method allows the effect of liability and asset comovement to be seen as a utility benefit for the portfolio, exactly analogous to, but in the opposite direction from, a risk penalty. In just the way that a return with unwanted volatility can be considered to offer the same utility as a lower certainty-equivalent return, a return with desired liability and asset comovement can be considered to offer as much utility as a higher return without that comovement.

We call the degree to which a particular asset or asset class can provide utility for an investor with a particular set of liabilities the *liability hedging credit* of the asset. The liability hedging credit is positively related to the covariance between the asset and the liability, positively related to the ratio of current assets to current liabilities, and inversely related to the risk tolerance of the investor.

The liability hedging credit can be calculated in a way that permits full or partial emphasis on liabilities. Full consideration yields the same result as surplus optimization, while zero consideration yields the same result as asset-only optimization. Partial consideration of liabilities allows the portfolio to take on hedging characteristics without the requirement of full surplus optimization.

Most importantly, the measure allows optimization to be performed at various levels of emphasis. The end result is a series of optimum portfolios with different levels of expected return, risk, and hedging. Knowledgeable pension managers can see precisely what they must give up in terms of one of these characteristics for a gain in one or both of the others.

The analytical underpinnings of liability hedging credits can be expanded to apply to other assets held by the investor but beyond the range of normal asset allocation decisions. Such extension allows portfolio managers to take into account the impact of the relationships between assets not subject to immediate allocation, such as real estate, venture capital and leveraged buy-outs, and the more traditional market-valued assets.

SURPLUS OPTIMIZATION

We start by assuming that the pension fund has determined what liabilities it wishes to consider in determining its investment strategy. This, in itself,

WILLIAM F. SHARPE is Timken Professor of Finance at Stanford University (Stanford, CA 94305) and principal of Sharpe-Tint, Inc., in Los Altos. LAWRENCE G. TINT is a principal of the same firm.

THE JOURNAL OF PORTFOLIO MANAGEMENT 5

is a difficult and confusing task, but not the subject under consideration here.

Let L represent the value of the relevant liability concept (for example, an "economic value" for the projected benefit obligation) and k the importance to be attached to it (e.g., 1.0 for a full surplus optimization). The relevant measure of surplus is

$$S = A - kL,$$

where A represents the value of the fund's assets and S is the surplus.

For example, if A = \$100, L = \$70, and k = 1,

$$S = \$100 - 1 \times \$70 = \$30,$$

which conforms to a traditional notion of surplus.

If A = \$100, L = \$70, and k = 0,

$$S = \$100 - 0 \times \$70 = \$100.$$

Here the "surplus" is equivalent to the fund's total assets, because zero emphasis is placed on the liabilities.

Today's surplus is known. Next year's is not. Letting subscripts 0 denote today and 1 next year, and tildes represent uncertain quantities:

$$S_0 = A_0 - kL_0, \text{ and}$$
$$\tilde{S}_1 = \tilde{A}_1 - k\tilde{L}_1.$$

A pension fund is concerned with next year's surplus. This amount can be expressed relative to today's asset value, i.e., $(\tilde{S}_1/A_0)$. This calculation is similar to the procedure followed when liabilities are ignored (i.e., k = 0). In such circumstances, the relevant concern is next year's asset value relative to today's. Relating future surplus to today's asset value is thus a natural extension of "asset-only" practice. More importantly, it maintains the dimensions in which risk tolerance is measured.

Because $\tilde{S}_1 = \tilde{A}_1 - k\tilde{L}_1$, the goal is to maximize

$$\frac{\tilde{A}_1}{A_0} - k\frac{\tilde{L}_1}{A_0}.$$

For reasons that will be made clear below, it is convenient to multiply the last term by (L_0/L_0) and rearrange terms to give

$$\frac{\tilde{A}_1}{A_0} - k\frac{L_0}{A_0}\frac{\tilde{L}_1}{L_0}.$$

This permits conversion to the more familiar notion of returns. Next year's asset value over today's equals $1 + \tilde{R}_A$, where $\tilde{R}_A$ is the rate of return on assets. Equivalently, next year's liability value over today's equals $1 + \tilde{R}_L$, where $\tilde{R}_L$ is the growth rate of the liabilities, which is defined here as the rate of return on liabilities. Note that these calculations exclude net cash inflows or outflows for the fund and net new accruals or paydowns for the liabilities.

Given these relationships, the equation can be rewritten as:

$$1 + \tilde{R}_A - k\frac{L_0}{A_0}(1 + \tilde{R}_L)$$

or

$$\left[1 - k\frac{L_0}{A_0}\right] + \left[\tilde{R}_A - k\frac{L_0}{A_0}\tilde{R}_L\right].$$

The first bracketed expression involves no uncertainty, so asset allocation decisions cannot affect it. For purposes of decision-making, one can concentrate entirely on the second expression. For convenience, let us denote this term $\tilde{Z}$:

$$\tilde{Z} \equiv \tilde{R}_A - k\frac{L_0}{A_0}\tilde{R}_L.$$

Let t be the fund's risk tolerance. Surplus optimization is designed to choose the asset mix that will maximize utility, defined as

$$U \equiv \text{Expected}(\tilde{Z}) - [\text{Variance}(\tilde{Z})/t],$$

taking the current mix, relevant transaction costs, and upper and lower bounds on holdings into account.

When k equals zero the variable of interest is $\tilde{R}_A$:

$$\tilde{Z} = \tilde{R}_A - 0 \times \frac{L_0}{A_0}\tilde{R}_L = \tilde{R}_A.$$

When k equals one,

$$\tilde{Z} = \tilde{R}_A - 1 \times \frac{L_0}{A_0}\tilde{R}_L = \tilde{R}_A - \frac{L_0}{A_0}\tilde{R}_L.$$

The importance of the liability return is directly related to the magnitude of the liability value vis-à-vis the asset value (L_0/A_0). Only if a plan has no surplus $(L_0/A_0 = 1)$ should one simply subtract the liability return from the asset return.

The better a plan's funding (i.e., the lower the value of (L_0/A_0)), the smaller the effect of liabilities on asset allocation and the less the impact of a switch from an asset-only (k = 0) to a full surplus (k = 1) optimization.

Grouping terms somewhat differently:

$$\tilde{Z} = \tilde{R}_A - \left[k\frac{L_0}{A_0}\right]\tilde{R}_L.$$

The bracketed expression may be treated as the overall weight attached to the liability return. As can be seen, it will depend on the importance to be attached to liabilities (k) and their relative size (L_0/A_0).

LIABILITY HEDGING CREDITS

The goal of surplus optimization is to maximize utility, defined as

$$U \equiv \text{Expected}(\tilde{Z}) - [\text{Variance}(\tilde{Z})/t],$$

where

$$\tilde{Z} \equiv \tilde{R}_A - k\frac{L_0}{A_0}\tilde{R}_L.$$

The first term [Expected($\tilde{Z}$)] equals

$$\text{Expected}(\tilde{R}_A) - k\frac{L_0}{A_0}\text{Expected}(\tilde{R}_L).$$

Only the first term can be affected by asset allocation decisions. Thus only the expected return on assets needs to be considered — just as in a traditional asset allocation. The objective may thus be simplified to maximize:

$$\text{Expected}(\tilde{R}_A) - [\text{Variance}(\tilde{Z})/t]$$

without affecting the answer in any way.

This highlights an important point: Surplus optimization can be accomplished by changing only the risk that is considered, not the expected returns.

Standard formulas imply that the numerator of the second term, which represents risk, can be expressed as follows:

$$\text{Variance}(\tilde{Z}) = \text{Variance}(\tilde{R}_A) - 2k\frac{L_0}{A_0}$$

$$\text{Covariance}(\tilde{R}_A, \tilde{R}_L) + k^2\frac{L_0^2}{A_0^2}\text{Variance}(\tilde{R}_L),$$

where

Covariance ($\tilde{R}_A$, $\tilde{R}_L$) is the covariance between $\tilde{R}_A$ and $\tilde{R}_L$.

The last term includes only constants (the current liability and asset values and the importance attached to liabilities) and the risk associated with the future liability value. This term is unaffected by the asset allocation decisions and can be ignored without affecting the result.

This objective becomes:

$$\text{Maximize Expected}(\tilde{R}_A) - \left[\frac{\text{Variance}(\tilde{R}_A)}{t} - 2\frac{k}{t}\frac{L_0}{A_0}\text{Covariance}(\tilde{R}_A, \tilde{R}_L)\right],$$

or

$$\text{Maximize Expected}(\tilde{R}_A) - \frac{\text{Variance}(\tilde{R}_A)}{t} + 2\frac{k}{t}\frac{L_0}{A_0}\text{Covariance}(\tilde{R}_A, \tilde{R}_L).$$

The first two terms in these expressions are precisely equal to those employed for asset-only optimizations. The two together are often termed the risk-adjusted expected return — i.e., the expected return on assets less an appropriate risk penalty. Naming all three terms:

Utility = Expected Return − Risk Penalty
+ Liability Hedging Credit.

The risk penalty is equal to the variance (standard deviation squared) of the return on the assets divided by the investor's current risk tolerance. For example, if an asset mix has an expected return of 13% and a standard deviation of 10%, then for an investor with a (fairly typical) risk tolerance of 50:

Expected Return	13%	
Variance	$(10\%)^2$	= 100
Risk Penalty	100/50	= 2%

Risk-Adjusted
Expected Return 13% − 2% = 11%

For such an investor, this mix is as desirable as 11% for certain.

If the investor is concerned with liabilities (k > 0), the third term must be included to determine the overall desirability of an asset mix. This added term is called the liability hedging credit for the asset mix. Like the other two terms, it is stated in units of equivalent expected return per year. Thus an asset mix with a liability hedging credit of 1.5 would be equivalent to one offering 1.5% more in expected return but providing no liability hedging at all.

Extending the example above, assume that the asset mix in question has a liability hedging credit of 3%. Thus:

Expected Return	13%	
Variance	$(10\%)^2$	= 100
Risk Penalty	100/50	= 2%
Liability Hedging Credit	3%	

Risk-Adjusted
Expected Return 13% − 2% + 3% = 14%

For such an investor, this mix is as desirable as one offering 14% for certain but with no ability to serve as a hedge against fluctuations in liability values.

ASSET LIABILITY HEDGING CREDITS

Surplus optimization involves a willingness to accept lower expected return and/or greater asset risk in order to increase the ability of an asset mix to hedge against increases in liability values. Fund managers can find the best asset mix while taking liabilities into account to the desired extent by including the appropriate liability hedging credit in the calculation:

$$LHC_{mix} = \frac{2}{t}\frac{L_0}{A_0} \text{Covariance}(\tilde{R}_A, \tilde{R}_L),$$

where the subscript "mix" indicates that the value applies to the asset mix as a whole.

The greater the fund's tolerance for risk (t), the smaller the liability hedging credit. This conforms to intuition. The credit relates to the ability of an asset mix to reduce surplus risk. The greater one's tolerance for risk, the smaller the credit that should be awarded for reducing it. More importantly, the less the expected return that should be sacrificed to reduce such risk.

Conversely, the greater the value of the liabilities relative to assets, the greater the liability hedging credit. This also makes sense. The higher the relative magnitude of liabilities, the more credit should be awarded for a given percentage reduction in such risk. More importantly, the greater the expected return that should be sacrificed to achieve such a reduction.

The final term measures the covariance between the return on the asset mix and the return on the liabilities. If this equals zero, the return on the asset mix is uncorrelated with the return on the liabilities. Assets thus provide no hedging against liability increases, and the LHC is (appropriately) zero.

If, on the other hand, the covariance of $\tilde{R}_A$ with $\tilde{R}_L$ is positive, asset returns tend to be high when liability returns are high and low when liability returns are low. This provides some hedging against liability changes. The greater the covariance, the better this hedging ability, and the greater (appropriately) the LHC.

Most asset mixes have at least some tendency to hedge liability risks, but one could construct a mix with returns negatively correlated with liability returns. In such a case the LHC would be negative, indicating that the mix was worse than one with no hedging ability at all. Such a mix would tend to fall in value when liability values increase — exacerbating, not mitigating, the effect of the latter on the fund's surplus.

It is important to determine how the liability hedging credits for individual securities or asset classes combine to form the liability hedging credit for the portfolio mix. As the return on the asset mix is simply a weighted average of the returns on the assets, with the portfolio's relative market values as weights:

$$\tilde{R}_A = \sum_i X_i \tilde{R}_i,$$

where $\tilde{R}_i$, is the return on asset i, X_i is the proportion of the portfolio invested in asset i, and Σ denotes the summation of all such terms.

From this it follows that:

$$\text{Covariance}(\tilde{R}_A, \tilde{R}_L) = \sum_i X_i \text{Covariance}(\tilde{R}_i, \tilde{R}_L).$$

Thus the covariance of the return on the asset mix with the liabilities is simply the portfolio market-value-weighted average of the covariances of the component assets with the liabilities.

Finally, the liability hedging credit for any asset (i) can be defined as

$$LHC_i = \frac{2}{t}\frac{L_0}{A_0} \text{Covariance}(\tilde{R}_i, \tilde{R}_L).$$

The LHC of the entire mix will then be simply the portfolio market-value-weighted average of the LHCs of the asset classes:

$$LHC_{mix} = \sum_i X_i LHC_i.$$

COMPONENTS OF ASSET LIABILITY HEDGING CREDITS

The covariance of an asset with a liability is not particularly intuitive. Consideration of its components will permit further insight.

$$\text{Covariance}(\tilde{R}_i, \tilde{R}_L) = \rho_{iL}\sigma_i\sigma_L,$$

where

ρ_{iL} = the correlation between $\tilde{R}_i$ and $\tilde{R}_L$,

σ_i = the standard deviation (risk) of $\tilde{R}_i$, and

σ_L = the standard deviation (risk) of $\tilde{R}_L$.

Thus, other things equal, an asset class whose returns are highly correlated with liabilities will provide better liability hedging and receive a greater liability hedging credit; an asset with more risk will provide better liability hedging and receive a greater liability hedging credit; and the greater the liability risk, the greater all positive asset liability hedging credits.

Of course, other things are not always equal. For example, in the case of growth stocks and intermediate bonds, estimates of forward-looking risk and correlations relative to one plan's accumulated benefit obligation (ABO) liability were as in the Table.[1]

TABLE

Risk and Correlation Estimates

Asset Class	ρ_{iL}	σ_i	$\rho_{iL}\sigma_i$
Intermediate Bonds	0.87	4.20%	3.654%
Growth Stocks	0.21	19.75%	4.148%

In this case, growth stocks provided slightly more hedging ability than intermediate bonds. While their interest rate sensitivity was a smaller part of their total risk (witness the correlation coefficient of 0.21

versus 0.87), their total risk was much greater (19.75% versus 4.20%). The combined effect, obtained by multiplying the correlation coefficient by the standard deviation, is slightly greater for growth stocks. Here, intermediate bonds offered no advantage vis-à-vis growth stocks in terms of liability hedging.

USE OF LIABILITY HEDGING CREDITS

Our derivations show that those concerned with liabilities need add only one new component to measures they traditionally use for asset allocation: a liability hedging credit. The LHC for any asset mix equals a market-value-weighted average of the liability hedging credits of the assets:

$$LHC_{mix} = \sum_i X_i LHC_i.$$

The liability hedging credit for an asset will depend on the concept of liabilities chosen and the:

1. Fund's risk tolerance (t);
2. Importance to be attached to liabilities (k);
3. Current value of liabilities relative to assets (L_0/A_0);
4. Correlation of the asset's return with the liabilities (ρ_{iL});
5. Asset's risk (σ_i); and
6. Liability risk (σ_L).

More precisely,

$$LHC_i = \frac{2}{t} k \frac{L_0}{A_0} \rho_{iL}\sigma_i\sigma_L.$$

The Figure shows liability hedging credits for one fund's projected benefit obligation (PBO) at the end of March 1989, with full emphasis placed on liabilities (k = 1).[2] Note that long government bonds provide by far the best hedging ability and Japanese stocks the worst. Note also that some of the differences are quite large. For example, long government bonds provide an LHC of 4.3% compared to 1.5% for growth stocks — a difference of 2.8%.

To interpret these numbers, it is important to understand that the optimal asset mix is the same that

FIGURE 1

LIABILITY HEDGING CREDITS: PBO MARCH 1989

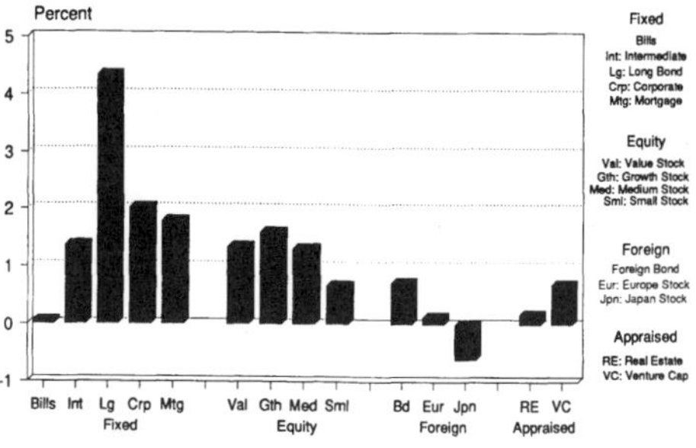

would be obtained if each of these values were added directly to the expected return for the asset in question, and a traditional mean/variance asset allocation optimization were then performed. This suggests how the liability hedging credits should be used. By adding them to the expected returns, the manager of the fund gives long bonds a "bonus" equivalent to 2.8% per year over growth stocks. This is appropriate if changes in PBO surplus really deserve full emphasis.

OTHER APPLICATIONS

We have focused so far on liability hedging. This technique for dealing with liabilities also can be applied to situations where liabilities are not necessarily involved, but where other assets beyond the asset allocator's decisions form part of the beneficial owner's net worth. An individual investor, for example, might wish to consider his or her house, social security benefits, and various other assets when determining the optimal asset allocation among securities.

The value of next period's "surplus" (net worth) in this case may be written:

$$\tilde{S}_1 = \tilde{A}_1 + k\tilde{O}_1$$

where $\tilde{O}_1$ represents the (uncertain) future value of the "other assets," and k represents the emphasis to be placed on these assets. As before, dividing by current asset value provides an objective that conforms to standard usage, giving:

$$\frac{\tilde{A}_1}{A_0} + k \frac{O_0}{A_0} \frac{\tilde{O}_1}{O_0}.$$

The derivation need not be continued beyond this point, as the equation differs from that for liabilities in only one respect: the terms are related by a plus sign rather than a minus sign. This makes sense, because an asset can be considered a negative liability. A "negative hedging credit" can be obtained simply by reversing the signs and altering the notation appropriately. Thus, from:

$$LHC_i = \frac{2}{t} k \frac{L_0}{A_0} \rho_{iL}\sigma_i\sigma_L$$

one can obtain:

$$OACP_i = \frac{2}{t} k \frac{O_0}{A_0} \rho_{iO}\sigma_i\sigma_O,$$

where $OACP_i$ represents the "Other Asset Covariance Penalty" for asset i and is to be subtracted from expected return when determining the asset's contribution to overall utility. Other things equal, the greater an asset's covariance with the "other assets," the less desirable it is.

Some cases will involve both "other assets" and liabilities, and some may involve multiple types of "other assets" and/or liabilities. It might seem that all such considerations must be grouped together and analyzed as a single entity, but this is not necessary. Rather, each can be analyzed in the manner shown above, and the relevant liability hedging credits and/or other asset covariance penalties simply added together.

We can show this in the case of a fund with other assets (O) and liabilities (L). For simplicity, it is assumed that full emphasis is to be placed on each.

In this case, next period's "surplus" (net worth) is:

$$\tilde{S}_1 = \tilde{A}_1 + \tilde{O}_1 - \tilde{L}_1.$$

Dividing by current assets gives:

$$\frac{\tilde{A}_1}{A_0} + \frac{O_0}{A_0}\frac{\tilde{O}_1}{O_0} - \frac{L_0}{A_0}\frac{\tilde{L}_1}{L_0}.$$

Note that only the first term can be affected by the asset allocation decision. To see the essence of the analysis, the three terms can be represented as:

$$\tilde{Z} = \tilde{a} + \tilde{b} + \tilde{c},$$

where the signs are included in the definitions of the new variables, and only $\tilde{a}$ can be affected by the asset allocation decision.

As always, the objective is to maximize:

$$U = \text{Expected}\ (\tilde{Z}) - [\text{Variance}(\tilde{Z})/t].$$

The expected value will be:

$$\text{Expected}\ (\tilde{a}) + \text{Expected}\ (\tilde{b}) + \text{Expected}\ (\tilde{c}).$$

Because the latter two terms are unaffected by asset allocation decisions, they may be dropped from the objective function without affecting the outcome. This leaves:

$$U = \text{Expected}\ (\tilde{a}) - [\text{Variance}\ (\tilde{Z})/t].$$

As before, only the expected return on the assets matters.

The variance of Z will have several terms:

$$\text{Variance}\ (\tilde{a}) + \text{Variance}\ (\tilde{b}) + \text{Variance}\ (\tilde{c}) + 2\text{Covariance}\ (\tilde{a},\tilde{b}) + 2\text{Covariance}\ (\tilde{a},\tilde{c}) + 2\text{Covariance}\ (\tilde{b},\tilde{c}).$$

Only three are affected by the asset allocation decision. Their sum is:

$$\text{Variance}\ (\tilde{a}) + 2\text{Covariance}\ (\tilde{a},\tilde{b}) + 2\text{Covariance}\ (\tilde{a},\tilde{c}).$$

The objective function can thus be written as:

$$\text{Maximize Expected}\ (\tilde{a}) - [\text{Variance}\ (\tilde{a})/t] - [2\text{Covariance}\ (\tilde{a}, \tilde{b})/t] - [2\text{Covariance}\ (\tilde{a}, \tilde{c})/t]$$

The first two terms constitute the usual measure of utility in an "asset only" context. The third and fourth correspond to the type of "other asset covariance penalty" or "liability hedging credit" derived earlier.

These principles are general. The only effects of other assets or liabilities on asset allocation arise as a result of covariances between the assets being allocated and the "outside" assets or liabilities. As covariances are additive, each such influence may be analyzed separately, and the results added to (or subtracted from) the asset's expected returns prior to performing the asset allocation analysis. The result will be an asset mix that provides the appropriate amount of utility, based on the chosen concept of the net worth of the beneficial owner.

SUMMARY

This article provides a procedure allowing proper incorporation of any coexisting assets or liabilities into the asset mix considerations for the remainder of a portfolio. The end result is an asset mix that is developed through a traditional mean/variance asset-only optimization but that maximizes utility for the beneficial owner of the portfolio while taking these other factors into account.

The liability hedging credits and other asset covariance penalties that form the basis for the procedure are calculated in a straightforward manner. They can be applied in a way that permits full or partial consideration of the movements of the other assets or liabilities. They can be developed separately and are additive across these other assets or liabilities. Once calculated, they have merely to be added to the expected returns on the assets to provide the proper values for the optimization.

This procedure permits the pension officer to avoid either asset-only or full surplus optimization. It allows for sensitivity analysis to determine the effects of greater or lesser emphasis on other assets or liabilities. It permits the use and development of liability descriptions that do not necessarily conform to traditional accounting and actuarial standards. Finally, it can be used to measure the exact relationships among expected returns, risks, and hedging characteristics.

Pension plan asset allocators can see exactly what must be sacrificed in terms of one or two of these characteristics to improve the third. The procedure allows them to make the appropriate investment choices for the asset classes under their control, yet take into consideration the impacts of others. This should lead, in the long run, to a fund optimally tailored for its intended purposes.

[1] The values of the estimated forward-looking standard deviations and correlations used in the table were developed through the use of the proprietary risk and liability estimation procedures of Sharpe–Tint, Inc.

[2] The figure is developed using the asset and liability values of a large defined-benefit pension plan and Sharpe-Tint, Inc.'s, estimates of that plan's risk tolerance and forward-looking asset class standard deviations and correlations.

FAJ Financial Analysts Journal
Volume 63 • Number 5
©2007, CFA Institute

Expected Utility Asset Allocation

William F. Sharpe

Most asset allocation analyses use the mean–variance approach for analyzing the trade-off between risk and expected return. Analysts use quadratic programming to find optimal asset mixes and the characteristics of the capital asset pricing model to determine reasonable optimization inputs. This article presents an alternative approach in which the goal of asset allocation is to maximize expected utility, where the utility function may be more complex than that associated with mean–variance analysis. Inputs for the analysis are based on the assumption of asset prices that would prevail if there were a single representative investor who desired to maximize expected utility.

Many institutional investors periodically adopt an asset allocation policy that specifies target percentages of value for each of several asset classes. Typically, a policy is set by a fund's board after evaluating the implications of a set of alternative policies. The staff is then instructed to implement the policy, usually by maintaining the actual allocation to each asset class within a specified range around the policy target level. Studies of the asset allocation (or asset/liability) policy are usually conducted every one to three years, or sooner if market conditions change radically.

Most asset allocation studies include at least some analyses that use standard mean–variance optimization procedures and incorporate at least some of the aspects of equilibrium asset-pricing theory based on mean–variance assumptions—typically, a standard version of the capital asset pricing model (CAPM), possibly augmented by assumptions about asset mispricing.

In a complete asset allocation study, a fund's staff (often with the help of consultants) typically does the following:

1. Selects desired asset classes and representative benchmark indices.
2. Chooses a representative historical period and obtains returns for the asset classes.
3. Computes historical asset average returns, standard deviations, and correlations.
4. Estimates future expected returns, standard deviations, and correlations. Historical data are typically used, with possible modifications, for standard deviations and correlations. Expected returns are often based more on current market conditions and/or typical relationships in capital markets.
5. Finds several mean–variance-efficient asset mixes for alternative levels of risk tolerance.
6. Projects future outcomes for the selected asset mixes, often over many years.
7. Presents to the board relevant summary measures of future outcomes for each of the selected asset mixes.
8. Finally, asks the board to choose, based on its views concerning the relevant measures of future outcomes, one of the candidate asset mixes to be the asset allocation policy.

The focus of this article is on the key analytical tools used in Steps 4 and 5. In Step 5, analysts typically use the technique of *portfolio optimization.* To provide reasonable inputs for such optimization, analysts often rely on informal methods but, in some cases, use the technique of *reverse portfolio optimization.*

For expository purposes, I begin with a discussion of portfolio optimization methods; I then turn to reverse optimization procedures. In each case, I review the standard analytical approach based on mean–variance assumptions and then describe a more general procedure that assumes investors seek to maximize expected utility. Importantly, mean–variance procedures are special cases of the more general expected utility formulations. For clarity, I term the more general approaches "expected utility optimization" and "expected utility reverse optimization," and I call the traditional methods "mean–variance optimization" and "mean–variance reverse optimization."

William F. Sharpe is STANCO 25 Professor of Finance, Emeritus, Stanford University, and founder of Financial Engines, Inc., Palo Alto, California.

Editor's Note: William F. Sharpe is a member of the *FAJ* Advisory Council.

The prescription to select a portfolio that maximizes an investor's expected utility is hardly new, nor are applications in the area of asset allocation. Particularly relevant in this respect is the work by Cremers, Kritzman, and Page (2005) and by Adler and Kritzman (2007), in which a "full-scale optimization" numerical search algorithm is used to find an asset allocation that maximizes expected utility under a variety of assumptions about investor preferences.

This article adds to the existing literature in three ways. First, it presents a new optimization algorithm for efficiently maximizing expected utility in an asset allocation setting. Second, it provides a straightforward reverse optimization procedure that adjusts a set of possible future asset returns to incorporate information contained in current market values. Finally, it shows that traditional mean–variance procedures for both optimization and reverse optimization are obtained if the new procedures are used with the assumption that all investors have quadratic utility.

In large part, this study applies and extends material covered in *Investors and Markets: Portfolio Choices, Asset Prices, and Investment Advice* (Sharpe 2007), to which readers interested in more detail are referred.

Mean–Variance Analysis

Much of modern investment theory and practice builds on the Markowitz (1959) assumption that an investor need be concerned in many cases solely with the mean and variance of the probability distribution of his or her portfolio return over a specified future period. Given this assumption, only portfolios that provide the maximum mean (expected) return for given variance of return (or standard deviation of return) warrant consideration. Analysts can thus consider a representative set of such mean–variance-efficient portfolios of asset classes in an asset allocation study and choose the one that best meets the board's preferences in terms of the range of relevant future outcomes over one or more future periods.

A focus on only the mean and variance of portfolio return can be justified in one of three ways. First, if all relevant probability distributions have the same form, mean and variance may be sufficient statistics to identify the full distribution of returns for a portfolio. Second, if an investor wishes to maximize the expected utility of portfolio return and considers utility a quadratic function of portfolio return, only mean–variance-efficient portfolios need be considered. Third, over the range of probability distributions to be evaluated, a quadratic approximation to an investor's true utility function may provide asset allocations that supply expected utility adequately close to that associated with a fully optimal allocation, as argued in Levy and Markowitz (1979).

Asset allocation studies often explicitly assume that all security and portfolio returns are distributed normally over a single period (for example, a year). If this were the case, the focus on mean–variance analysis would be appropriate, no matter what the form of the investor's utility function. But there is increasing agreement that at least some return distributions are not normally distributed, even over relatively short periods, and that explicit attention needs to be given to "tail risk" arising from greater probabilities of extreme outcomes than those associated with normal distributions. Furthermore, interest has been increasing in investment vehicles that are intentionally designed to have nonnormal distributions and substantial downside tail risk, such as hedge funds. For these reasons, in at least some cases, the first justification for mean–variance analysis as a reasonable approximation to reality may be insufficient.

The second justification may also not always suffice. Quadratic utility functions are characterized by a *satiation level* of return beyond which the investor prefers less return to more—an implausible characterization of the preferences of most investors. To be sure, such functions have a great analytical advantage and may serve as reasonable approximations for some investors' true utility functions. Nonetheless, many investors' preferences may be better represented by a different type of utility function. If so, that true utility function can be taken into account not only in choosing an optimal portfolio but also when making predictions about trade-offs available in the capital markets.

Finally, although mean–variance analysis may provide a sufficient approximation in a given setting to produce an adequate asset allocation, it would seem prudent to evaluate the efficacy of the traditional approach by at least conducting an alternative analysis based on detailed estimates of possible future returns and the best possible representation of the investor's preferences. To facilitate such an evaluation, I present more general approaches to optimization and reverse optimization. Specifically, I will assume that forecasts are made by enumerating an explicit set of discrete possible sets of asset returns over a period of choice, with the probability of each outcome estimated explicitly. Given such a set of forecasts, I first show how an optimal portfolio would be chosen if one used a traditional mean–variance analysis; then, I present the more general approach that can take into account an alternative form of an investor's utility function. Subsequently, I show how mean–variance methods are used to obtain forecasts consistent with capital market equilibrium and then present a more general approach that can take into account different aspects of the process by which asset prices are determined. For both optimization and reverse optimization, the expected utility approach can provide the same results as the mean–variance approach if the special assumptions of the latter are used.

Increased generality does not come without cost. The mean–variance approach can be used with continuous distributions (typically, jointly normal). The procedures I present here require *discrete* distributions, in which each possible scenario is included. At the very least, the procedures thus require that many alternative outcomes be enumerated. This article is limited to the presentation of the analytical approaches; I leave for future research an analysis of their practical aspect. Suffice it to say here that the potential advantages of discrete approaches include their ability to allow for more complex distributions than those associated with joint normality and the ability to take into account more aspects of investor preferences.

Mean–Variance Optimization

As shown by Markowitz (1959), quadratic programming algorithms can be used to find the portfolio that provides the maximum expected return for a given level of standard deviation of return. Solving such a quadratic programming problem for each of several different levels of standard deviation of return or variance (standard deviation squared) can provide a set of mean–variance-efficient portfolios for use in an asset allocation study.

A standard way to generate a mean–variance-efficient portfolio is to maximize a function of expected return and standard deviation of return of the form

$$d = e - \frac{v}{t}, \tag{1}$$

where

d = desirability of the portfolio for the investor

e = portfolio expected return

v = portfolio variance of return

t = investor's risk tolerance

Solving such a problem for various levels of risk tolerance provides a set of mean–variance-efficient portfolios for an asset allocation study. By choosing one portfolio from a candidate set of such portfolios, the board, in effect, reveals its risk tolerance.

For any given risk tolerance, a mean–variance optimization requires the following inputs:

- forecasts of asset return standard deviations,
- forecasts of correlations among asset returns,
- expected asset returns,
- the investor's risk tolerance, and
- any relevant constraints on asset holdings.

In practice, constraints are often incorporated in such analyses to avoid obtaining "unreasonable" or "infeasible" asset mixes. In many cases, however, such constraints reflect inadequate attention to ensuring that the asset forecasts used in the analysis are, taken as a whole, reasonable.

Although general quadratic programming algorithms or other procedures for handling nonlinear problems may be used to perform mean–variance optimization, problems in which the only constraints are bounds on the holdings of individual assets can be solved by using a simpler gradient method, such as that described in Sharpe (1987). In such a method, an initial feasible portfolio is analyzed to find the best asset that could be purchased and the best asset that could be sold, where "best" refers to the effect of a small change in holdings on the desirability of the portfolio for the investor. As long as the purchase of the best-to-buy security (financed by the sale of the best-to-sell asset) will increase the desirability of the portfolio, such a swap is desirable. Next, the amount of the swap is chosen so as to maximize the increase in the portfolio's desirability subject to constraints on feasibility. The process is then repeated until the best possible swap cannot increase the portfolio's desirability. As I will show, a similar approach can be used in a more general setting.

To illustrate both types of optimization, I use a simple example. In this case, there are three assets (cash, bonds, and stocks) and four possible future *states* of the world (or, *scenarios*). Based on history, current conditions, and equilibrium considerations, an analyst has produced the forecasts given in **Table 1**.[1] Each entry shows the total return per dollar invested for a specific asset if and only if the associated state of the world occurs. Each state has an equal probability of occurring, that is, 0.25. The investor's risk tolerance, t, equals 0.70.

Table 1. Forecasted Future Asset-Class Returns by State

State	Cash	Bonds	Stocks
State 1	1.0500	1.0388	0.8348
State 2	1.0500	0.9888	1.0848
State 3	1.0500	1.0888	1.2348
State 4	1.0500	1.1388	1.2848

The goal is thus to maximize $e - (v/0.70)$.

The first step in a mean–variance optimization is to compute the expected returns, standard deviations, and correlations of the assets from the forecasted returns (Table 1) and probabilities of states. **Table 2** provides these expected returns and standard deviations; **Table 3** shows the correlations.

Table 2. Expected Returns and Standard Deviations

Asset	Expected Return	Standard Deviation
Cash	1.0500	0.0000
Bonds	1.0638	0.0559
Stocks	1.1098	0.1750

Table 3. Correlations

	Cash	Bonds	Stocks
Cash	1.0000	0.0000	0.0000
Bonds	0.0000	1.0000	0.6389
Stocks	0.0000	0.6389	1.0000

In this example, there are no constraints on asset holdings other than that the sum of the proportions invested in the assets equal 1. The resulting mean–variance-optimal portfolio is composed as shown in the first column of **Table 4**. Had there been a lower bound on each asset holding of 0 and an upper bound of 1, the same portfolio would have been obtained because the constraints would not have been binding.

Table 4. Optimal Portfolios

Asset	Mean–Variance Portfolio	Expected Utility Portfolio: Quadratic Utility
Cash	0.0705	0.0705
Bonds	0.3098	0.3098
Stocks	0.6196	0.6196

Expected Utility Optimization

I now introduce the more general approach to optimization and illustrate its use with the same simple example. I show that the general procedure will produce the same results as mean–variance optimization if the investor is assumed to have a particular type of preference but that a different type of preference will give a different optimal portfolio.

Expected Utility. The key assumption is that the goal of an investor is to maximize the expected utility of the return from his or her portfolio. Associated with the portfolio return in each state of the world is a utility that measures the "happiness" associated with the total return in that state. The expected utility of the return in a state equals its utility times the probability that the state will occur. The expected utility of the portfolio is then the sum of the expected utilities of its returns in the states.

The utility of a total portfolio return, R_p, in state s is denoted $u(R_{ps})$. The investor's goal is to maximize expected utility eu, where[2]

$$eu = \sum_s \pi_s u(R_{ps}), \tag{2}$$

where π_s is the probability that state s will occur.[3]

Note that Equation 2 assumes that the utility function is the same for all states and that expected utility is separable and additive across states. These assumptions rule out some possible aspects of preferences but are considerably more general than the mean–variance assumptions.

The first derivative of utility, *marginal utility* of total portfolio return in state s, is denoted $m(R_{ps})$. I assume that marginal utility decreases with R_{ps}, which is equivalent to assuming that the investor is risk averse.

I assume that the only constraints are an upper bound, ub, and a lower bound, lb, on individual asset holdings of the form

$$lb_i \le x_i \le ub_i, \tag{3}$$

where x_i is the proportion of the fund invested in asset i; the x_i values sum to 1.

Maximizing Expected Utility. I now present an algorithm for solving the nonlinear programming problem described in the previous section.

First, note that the marginal expected utility, meu, of the portfolio return in state s is

$$meu(R_{ps}) = \pi_s m(R_{ps}). \tag{4}$$

Now consider the effect on portfolio expected utility of a small change in the amount invested in asset i. Because \$1 invested in the asset provides R_{i1} in State 1, R_{i2} in State 2, and so on, the marginal expected utility (per dollar) of asset i will be

$$meu_i = \sum_s R_{is} meu(R_{ps}). \tag{5}$$

This relationship will hold for any asset and for any portfolio because a portfolio's return is simply the weighted sum of asset returns, with the weights summing to 1.

Note that for each asset, the cost of obtaining its set of returns across states is \$1. Now consider a portfolio containing two assets, i and j, where (1) $meu_i > meu_j$ and the investor can (2) purchase additional units of asset i and (3) sell some units of asset j. Clearly, the portfolio can be "improved"—that is, its expected utility can be increased. The reason is straightforward. Because obtaining each asset's set of returns costs $1, if these three asset conditions are met, expected utility can be increased by selling some units of asset *j* and using the proceeds to buy units of asset *i*.

It is a simple matter to determine whether or not such a change is possible for a given portfolio. The marginal expected utility for each asset can be computed, and each asset can be classified as a potential buy (if $x_i < ub_i$) and/or a potential sell (if $x_i > lb_i$). The "best buy" is the asset among the potential buys with the largest marginal expected utility. The "best sell" is the one among the potential sells with the smallest marginal expected utility. If the marginal expected utility of the best buy exceeds that of the best sell, then the best swap involves selling units of the best sell and purchasing units of the best buy. If the marginal expected utility of the best buy does not exceed that of the best sell, or if there are no potential buys or no potential sells, then the portfolio cannot be improved.

Once a desirable swap has been identified, the optimal magnitude for the amount to be swapped can be determined. A simple procedure determines the largest feasible magnitude, which is given by the upper bound of the asset to be bought and the lower bound of the asset to be sold. The marginal expected utilities of the assets that would obtain were this swap undertaken are then determined. If the spread between the marginal utility of the asset being bought and that of the asset being sold would still be positive, the maximum swap should be made. Otherwise, an intermediate amount (for example, halfway between the minimum of zero and the maximum) should be considered; then, the marginal expected utilities that would obtain were *that* swap undertaken should be calculated. If the spread would still be positive, the range of swaps should be restricted to that between the intermediate amount and the maximum amount. Otherwise, the range should be restricted to that between the minimum and the intermediate amount. This procedure is continued until the marginal expected utility spread is lower than a desired threshold or a similar condition is met for the difference between the current maximum and minimum swap amounts.

The overall algorithm for finding the maximum expected utility portfolio is thus as follows:

1. Find a feasible portfolio.
2. Determine the best possible two-asset swap.
3. If no such swap is feasible, terminate the analysis.
4. If a swap is feasible, compute the best magnitude for the swap and revise the portfolio.
5. Repeat, starting at Step 2, until the condition in Step 3 is met.

Up to the precision used for the termination conditions, this procedure will find a portfolio that maximizes expected utility under the specified conditions—namely, only upper and lower bounds on asset holdings and marginal utility that decreases with portfolio return.

Quadratic Utility Functions. I first illustrate the use of the optimization procedure with a case in which the investor's utility is a quadratic function of portfolio return. I have chosen an investor with an attitude toward risk that is equal to that of the investor considered earlier ($t = 0.70$).

An investor with quadratic utility can be described as maximizing the expected value of a quadratic function of portfolio return of the form

$$u(R) = R - \frac{k}{2}R^2, \tag{6}$$

where k is the quadratic utility parameter.

The associated marginal utility function is

$$m(R) = 1 - kR. \tag{7}$$

The satiation level is that for which marginal utility equals $1/k$ because for higher levels of return, the marginal utility will be negative and total utility will be lower than that associated with a return of $1/k$. Other things being equal, the lower k is, the more risk an investor with quadratic utility will take.

For an investor with quadratic utility, expected utility will be a linear function of the expected portfolio return and the expected value of the return squared. But the expected value of the return squared is equal to the portfolio variance plus the expected return squared. Thus, expected utility will be a function of portfolio expected return and variance of return, although not of the linear form used in the mean–variance-optimization procedure described earlier. For any given expected return, an investor with quadratic utility will wish to minimize variance and hence will choose a mean–variance-efficient portfolio.

Now consider a quadratic utility investor with $k = 0.6938$ (to four decimal places) and a corresponding satiation return of 1.4413. The expected utility maximization algorithm gives the optimal portfolio shown in the second column of Table 4. It is precisely the same portfolio shown for the mean–variance-optimal portfolio. The reason is that quadratic utility parameter k was set to a value determined by riskless rate of return r, expected return e, and variance v of the optimal portfolio found earlier, as follows:[4]

$$k = \frac{e - r}{v + e^2 - re}. \tag{8}$$

In this case, the same portfolio is optimal for an investor maximizing $e\ -v/t$ where $t = 0.70$ and one maximizing expected utility where utility equals $R - (k/2)R^2$ and $k = 0.6938$. A lower value of k would result in a recommended portfolio with a greater mean and variance, and a higher value of k would result in a more conservative portfolio. In any event, the algorithm will produce a mean–variance-efficient portfolio whenever the utility function is quadratic. Thus, as I claimed, mean–variance optimization can be considered a special case of the more general expected utility optimization approach.

"HARA" Utility Functions. Although the optimization algorithm can be used for an investor with a quadratic utility function, its main advantage is the ability to find an optimal portfolio for an investor with another type of utility function. The only requirements are that the expected utility of the portfolio be a separable additive function of the expected utilities in the alternative states, that marginal utility be a decreasing function of portfolio return, and that the only constraints be upper and lower bounds on asset holdings.

To illustrate, consider a function of considerable generality known as a HARA function (because an investor with such a function exhibits "hyperbolic absolute risk aversion"). Specifically, the investor's utility is related to portfolio return as follows:

$$u(R) = \frac{(R-b)^{1-c}}{1-c}, \tag{9}$$

where c is the risk-aversion coefficient. The value of b can be considered the investor's *minimum required level of return* because the marginal utility of increasing return above this level is infinite. Thus, only values of R greater than b should be considered. Above this level, the investor's marginal utility will be related to portfolio return by

$$m(R) = (R-b)^{-c}. \tag{10}$$

In most cases, c will be greater than 1, although the marginal utility equation (which is the only one needed for the algorithm) may be used when c equals 1 (and utility is equal to the logarithm of return) or when c is less than 1 and positive.

An important special case arises when b is zero. In such a case, the investor is said to have *constant relative risk aversion*. For such an investor, a given percentage increase in return will cause a given percentage decrease in marginal utility, regardless of the initial level of return. More generally, a given percentage increase in return over and above the minimum required level $(R - b)$, regardless of the initial level of return, will cause a given percentage decrease in marginal utility. With respect to total return, R, an investor with $b > 0$ has decreasing relative risk aversion whereas an investor with $b < 0$ has increasing relative risk aversion.

The first column in Panel A of **Table 5** shows the results obtained from using the expected utility optimization (Max EU) method with the return data from Table 1 and the 0.25 probability of each return for an investor with constant relative risk aversion $(b = 0)$ and a risk-aversion coefficient, c, of 4. Upper and lower bounds on asset holdings were set to allow short positions in any asset, but none were binding. As can be seen, the optimal Max EU portfolio includes long holdings in all three assets, with a larger holding in bonds than in stocks. Panel B of Table 5 shows the returns on this portfolio in the four states of the world. The first column in Panel C of Table 5 provides key characteristics of the Max EU portfolio. The first characteristic is the *certainty-equivalent return* (CER) of this portfolio for the investor described. The CER is the return that, if obtained in every state, would provide the same expected utility as the portfolio itself. As can be seen, the portfolio derived by the Max EU method is as desirable for this investor as a return of 1.0654, which is considerably greater than the riskless rate of interest (1.050). Importantly, no other feasible portfolio can provide a greater CER for this investor.

The remaining characteristics in Table 5 are the conventional statistics for the portfolio: expected return, standard deviation of return, and Sharpe ratio (the ratio of expected return minus the riskless rate to standard deviation).

Table 5. Max EU and Equal-Risk Max MV Portfolios

Portfolio	Max EU Optimal	Max MV Optimal
A. Weight		
Cash	0.0885	0.2956
Bonds	0.5101	0.2347
Stocks	0.4014	0.4698
B. Returns		
State 1	0.9579	0.9463
State 2	1.0327	1.0520
State 3	1.1440	1.1459
State 4	1.1896	1.1811
C. Characteristics		
CER	1.0654	1.0651
Expected return	1.0810	1.0813
Standard deviation	0.0911	0.0911
Sharpe ratio	0.3406	0.3436

The second column in Table 5 shows the characteristics of a portfolio obtained with mean–variance optimization (Max MV) chosen to have the same standard deviation of return. As can be seen, its composition is considerably different, with a substantially smaller position in bonds than in stocks.

Table 5 also shows that the two approaches to optimization provide quite different returns in the states. In particular, the Max MV portfolio has a lower return in the worst state (State 1), a lower return in the best state, and higher returns in the intermediate states. By design, it has the same standard deviation of return as the Max EU portfolio and, given the manner of its derivation, a higher expected return and Sharpe ratio. But it is nonetheless inferior in terms of the expected utility for the investor in question: Its CER of 1.0651 is 3 basis points smaller than the Max EU CER of 1.0654.

Clearly, a mean–variance-optimal portfolio may not be optimal for an investor with nonquadratic utility. Such an investor might willingly accept a portfolio with a lower Sharpe ratio than is available at the same risk level as conventionally measured (by standard deviation of return). Similarly, an investor with quadratic utility might choose a portfolio with a lower CER as measured by an investor with some other type of utility function. Given diverse investor preferences, there should be diverse portfolio holdings. The expected utility optimization procedure allows one to find preferred asset holdings for investors whose utility functions differ in form as well as in parameters.

Reverse Optimization

Whether a mean–variance or expected utility approach is used for asset allocation optimization, the quality of the result depends crucially on the meaningfulness of the inputs. Such inputs should, at the very least, take into account historical returns, current asset market values, and the best possible assumptions about relationships among returns in capital markets.

Formal procedures for setting realistic inputs have been developed for use in mean–variance analyses. Some analysts use the procedures explicitly; others adopt judgmental approaches motivated by such considerations. This section begins by describing the standard reverse optimization procedure applied in a mean–variance context. Next, I provide a more general approach that uses expected utility and show that with the assumption of quadratic utility, the same results can be obtained as with the standard approach. Finally, I show that the more general approach can be used to reflect more general assumptions about equilibrium in capital markets.

Key to all these approaches is the goal that a set of return forecasts conform with or be based on a view of the nature of equilibrium in capital markets and with the current market values of the assets in question. In many cases, asset allocation studies are intended to find asset mixes that would be appropriate under the assumption that the markets for major asset classes are *informationally efficient*, in the sense that prices fully reflect available information about the uncertain future prospects for those asset classes. Such forecasts are sometimes termed "efficient market forecasts" or "passive forecasts." Investors who aspire to choose an asset allocation based on efficient market assumptions assume that asset classes are priced reasonably, although they may assume that within asset classes, some securities are mispriced.

In some cases, analysts prefer to use forecasts for an asset allocation study that incorporate an assumption that some or all asset classes are mispriced. This approach nonetheless requires an underlying set of forecasts consistent with correct pricing of all asset classes. I concentrate here on the derivation of efficient market forecasts and leave for later research the subject of possible adjustments to reflect perceived mispricing.

Mean–Variance Reverse Optimization. The standard mean–variance approach to reverse optimization assumes that the conditions of the CAPM hold—that is, that a particular relationship exists between each asset's expected return and a measure based on asset risks, correlations, and the current market values of the asset classes. In many cases, practitioners use historical standard deviations and correlations, either directly or with some modification, as predictions of the corresponding future risks and correlations. Asset expected returns are in these cases determined from current asset market values and the conditions of the CAPM.

The CAPM implies that in equilibrium, each asset's expected excess return over the riskless rate of interest is proportional to the asset's beta value, which is, in turn, based on the asset's covariance with the market portfolio of all asset classes. Given a set of asset standard deviations and correlations and the current market values of the asset classes, one can easily compute each asset's beta value. Then, given an assumed expected return for the market portfolio, one can compute each asset's expected return. The resultant set of return forecasts can then be considered *efficient market forecasts*.

This process is equivalent to solving a mean–variance optimization process in reverse; hence the name. As we have seen, a mean–variance optimization problem is of the form:

$$\text{Expected returns} + \text{Risks} + \text{Correlations} + \text{Risk tolerance} \rightarrow \text{Optimal portfolio.}$$

In reverse optimization, the market portfolio is assumed to be optimal for a "representative investor" with a particular risk tolerance. Risks and correlations are known, so the conditions for portfolio optimality are used to find the set of expected returns that would give the market portfolio as a solution to a mean–variance optimization problem. Thus,

$$\text{Risks} + \text{Correlations} + \text{Representative risk tolerance} + \text{Market portfolio} \rightarrow \text{Expected returns}.$$

The use of reverse optimization for obtaining inputs for asset allocation studies was advocated in Sharpe (1985). Subsequently, Black and Litterman (1992) extended this approach to show how views about asset mispricing can be used to modify the initial reverse optimization results. In each case, *current* market values of the asset classes are used to ensure that the forecasts as a whole are plausible.

Not every asset allocation study includes reverse optimization based on current asset market values. This accounts in large part for the relatively frequent use of *ad hoc* constraints or other methods to ensure plausibility for the results obtained in the optimization phase. The failure to use current asset market values is unfortunate because such values contain highly useful information about investors' collective assessments of the present values of the uncertain future prospects of asset classes. Failing to take this important information into account when making crucial policy decisions is foolish.

To illustrate mean–variance reverse optimization, I use the analysis that produced the forecasts in Table 1 together with the assumption that the states are equally probable.

Table 6 shows the historical returns for the three assets in four prior years (states). The return on the first asset, cash, in each year can be thought of as the yield on a one-year U.S. T-bill purchased at the beginning of the year. The second and third sets of returns can be considered the returns on index funds of, respectively, bonds and stocks. The Table 6 entries show the actual returns for each asset in each year in the historical period, although they are labeled State 1, State 2, and so on, to reflect the fact that the entries will be transformed to show outcomes in alternative possible future states of the world. To keep the analysis simple, each state is assumed to be equally probable.

Table 6. Historical Returns

State	Cash	Bonds	Stocks
State 1	1.0600	1.0200	0.7200
State 2	1.0700	0.9800	0.9800
State 3	1.0600	1.0700	1.1200
State 4	1.0500	1.1100	1.1600

The *relative values* for the assets at the end of the most recent year are as follows:

Cash	0.10
Bonds	0.30
Stocks	0.60

The information in Table 6 is based entirely on historical information. The relative values use current data to reflect market participants' current forecasts of the assets' future prospects.

The remaining information needed for the reverse optimization procedure also concerns the future. The first information is the current riskless rate of interest, 1.050, and the second is an estimate of the difference between the expected return of the market portfolio and the current riskless rate (or, the market risk premium), which is 0.040.

The goal of reverse optimization is to combine the information in Table 6 with the relative values, the riskless rate, and the risk premium to obtain relevant forecasts of possible future returns. The first step is to convert the returns in Table 6 to *excess* returns by subtracting from each one the return on the riskless asset in the year in question. The excess returns are then added to the current riskless rate of interest to obtain forecasts more consistent with current observed market information. The result is the returns in **Table 7**.

Table 7. Excess Returns + Current Riskless Rate

State	Cash	Bonds	Stocks
State 1	1.0500	1.0100	0.7100
State 2	1.0500	0.9600	0.9600
State 3	1.0500	1.0600	1.1100
State 4	1.0500	1.1100	1.1600

The next step is to compute the projected covariances of the assets. Because the covariance of assets i and j equals their correlation times the product of their standard deviations, this computation incorporates the historical risks and correlations of the assets' excess returns. As shown earlier, the standard deviations are 0, 0.0559, and 0.1750 for, respectively, cash, bonds, and stocks and the correlation between bonds and stocks is 0.6389. The covariance matrix is shown in **Table 8**.

Table 8. Covariance Matrix

	Cash	Bonds	Stocks
Cash	0.000000	0.000000	0.000000
Bonds	0.000000	0.003125	0.006250
Stocks	0.000000	0.006250	0.030625

To compute the beta of every security relative to the current market portfolio requires combining the information in Table 8 with the relative values. The beta value for an asset is its covariance with the market portfolio divided by the variance of the market portfolio. The covariance of an asset with the market portfolio is a weighted average of its covariances with the assets, where the market portfolio proportions are the weights. The variance of the market portfolio is the weighted average of the asset covariances with the market, where the market proportions are the weights. These formulas give the following beta values:

Cash	0.0000
Bonds	0.3458
Stocks	1.4938

Given these beta values, the market risk premium (0.040), and the riskless rate of interest (1.050), it is straightforward to compute a set of security expected returns consistent with the CAPM. The expected return on a security is simply the riskless rate of interest plus the security's beta value times the market risk premium. The results of these calculations are the following expected returns:

Cash	1.0500
Bonds	1.0638
Stocks	1.1098

Computation of efficient market forecasts for a standard mean–variance optimization is now complete. The information required for the optimization phase is the expected returns and the covariance matrix in Table 8. Importantly, these parameters take into account historical information about asset return variability and covariability, the current market values of the asset classes, the current riskless rate of interest, the estimated future market risk premium, and an assumed set of relationships that would obtain in a market conforming with the CAPM.

The covariance matrix in Table 8 and the expected returns were the inputs used for the mean–variance-optimization analysis in the earlier section of this article. The proportions in Table 4 for the optimal MV portfolio can thus be considered the appropriate strategy to be followed by a mean–variance investor with a risk tolerance of 0.70 operating in a market in which the market portfolio is mean–variance efficient and the risk premium is 4 percent.

The Representative Investor. When optimization inputs are created by using mean–variance reverse optimization, the solution for one specific level of risk tolerance will be the market portfolio. The risk tolerance in the objective function $e - v/t$ for which the market portfolio is optimal will equal twice the market portfolio's variance divided by the market risk premium. In this case, the resulting "market risk tolerance" equals 0.6778. In effect, the market prices of the assets are those that would prevail if there were a single investor with quadratic utility who wished to maximize $e - (v/0.6778)$. Such an investor is often termed the "representative investor." In a world of unconstrained investors with quadratic utility, this is a reasonable interpretation, with the market risk tolerance equal to a wealth-weighted average of the risk tolerances of the actual investors. In a more realistic setting, however, the relationship is likely to be more complex. Nonetheless, it is useful to characterize asset returns as consistent with a capital market with a single representative investor of a particular type.

Although I use the term "representative investor," I emphasize that the key ingredient in all that follows is the use of a marginal utility function consistent with market equilibrium. It will reflect the marginal utility functions of actual investors but may not be a simple weighted average of their individual marginal utility functions. A more appropriate term for the market function in question is the "asset pricing kernel," although for expository purposes, I will continue to refer to it as "the marginal utility function of the representative investor." For an in-depth discussion of this issue, see Sharpe (2007).

Obtaining Return Forecasts by Reverse Optimization

As previously, I assume that optimization will be based on a discrete set of possible future asset returns in alternative future states of the world and the probabilities associated with those states. The goal is to develop a reverse optimization procedure that can produce such a set of forecasts. I show first how this goal can be reached in a standard mean–variance setting; then, I provide a more general approach.

MV Reverse Optimization. In the previous example, the standard mean–variance reverse optimization procedure used the returns in Table 7 to generate the covariance matrix in Table 8. Then, the covariance matrix and the current market portfolio were used to determine asset beta values. Finally, the beta values were combined with the riskless return and the market risk premium to determine the expected returns: cash, 1.0500; bonds, 1.0638; and stocks,1.1098. The present goal is to provide a procedure that will produce a return table and set of probabilities consistent with the covariance matrix in Table 8 and these expected returns.

The approach is quite simple. Adding a (possibly zero or negative) constant to the return on an asset in every state will not affect its covariance with any other asset. Thus, for each asset class, a constant can be selected that will give the desired expected return without altering the asset risks, correlations, and covariances.

The goal is to select a set of differences, d_i, such that the new return, R_{is}, for each asset in each state is equal to the old return, R_{is}^0, plus the selected difference:

$$R_{is} = R_{is}^0 + d_i. \tag{11}$$

Taking expected values over states gives

$$E(R_i) = E(R_i^0) + d_i. \tag{12}$$

In this case, the old expected returns are probability-weighted averages of the four years for each of the assets shown in Table 7. The first column in **Table 9** shows those expected returns; the second column shows the desired expected returns listed previously; and the third column shows the constant d_i to be added to each asset's old return to give the desired expected return.

Table 9. MV Reverse Optimization: Constants for New Returns

Asset	Old Expected Return	New Expected Return	Difference
Cash	1.0500	1.0500	0.0000
Bonds	1.0350	1.0638	0.0288
Stocks	0.9850	1.1098	0.1248

Table 10 shows the set of returns obtained by adding these constants to the adjusted returns—that is, the excess returns plus the risk-free rate.[5] As intended, this set of returns will have the same covariance matrix as the returns in Table 7 and the desired expected returns as shown in Table 9.

Table 10. MV Reverse Optimization: New Security Returns

State	Cash	Bonds	Stocks
State 1	1.0500	1.0388	0.8348
State 2	1.0500	0.9888	1.0848
State 3	1.0500	1.0888	1.2348
State 4	1.0500	1.1388	1.2848

Note that Table 10 is the same as Table 1. In fact, Table 10 is the origin of Table 1 that was used for the optimization examples. The forecasted returns for the assets in alternative states were produced in the manner shown here from historical returns, the current riskless return, an assumption about the expected return on the market, the current values of the assets, and an assumption that equilibrium in the capital markets obtains and is consistent with a representative investor who cares only about portfolio mean and variance. The forecasts are thus efficient market forecasts with no alterations to reflect possible mispricing.

EU Reverse Optimization. Now consider the more general approach to reverse optimization. To preserve the information about return variation and covariation contained in historical returns, I take as a constraint the requirement that each new return for an asset in a state be equal to the old return in that state plus a constant. The constants, however, must be consistent with the requirement that the market portfolio provide the maximum expected utility for the representative investor.

Note first that when using the desired new returns, the market portfolio's return in a state will equal its return in that state when the old returns are used plus the market value–weighted sum of the asset constants:

$$R_{ms} = \sum_i x_{im} R_{is} = \sum_i x_{im} R_{is}^0 + \sum_i x_{im} d_i. \tag{13}$$

For each state, the new return on the *market* will equal the old return plus a constant, d_m, which will, in turn, equal a value-weighted sum of the asset constants:

$$d_m = \sum_i x_{im} d_i. \tag{14}$$

But this value must be set to produce the desired expected return on the market portfolio—the sum of the risk-free rate and the market risk premium:

$$E(R_m) = E(R_m^0) + d_m. \tag{15}$$

The old and new values and the constant to be added to each old market expected return are as follows:

Old value = 1.0065
New value = 1.0900
d_m = 0.0835

Adding 0.0835 to every market return gives the following new market returns:

State 1	0.9175
State 2	1.0525
State 3	1.1725
State 4	1.2175

I now turn to the conditions required for a portfolio to maximize expected utility. Recall first that the marginal expected utility of asset i will be related to its returns in the states and the marginal expected utilities for the states. For an investor who holds the market portfolio, the marginal expected utility of that portfolio will be

$$meu_m = \sum_s R_{ms}\pi_s m(R_{ms}). \quad (16)$$

Moreover, for such an investor, the marginal expected utility of the risk-free asset, which returns R_f in every state, will be

$$meu_f = R_f \sum_s \pi_s m(R_{ms}). \quad (17)$$

But each of these assets sells for the same price, \$1. Hence, for the market portfolio to be optimal, the assets' marginal expected utilities must be the same:

$$\sum_s R_{ms}\pi_s m(R_{ms}) = R_f \sum_s \pi_s m(R_{ms}). \quad (18)$$

All the values in Equation 18 are given; only the form and parameters of the representative investor's marginal utility function are free to be determined. I illustrate the manner in which this can be done in two cases.

EU Reverse Optimization with Quadratic Utility. In this section, I assume that the representative investor's utility function is quadratic; thus, the marginal utility function is linear. That is,

$$m(R_{ms}) = 1 - kR_{ms}. \quad (19)$$

Substituting Equation 19 in Equation 18 and simplifying gives

$$E(R_m) - kE(R_m^2) = R_f - kR_f E(R_m). \quad (20)$$

For Equation 20 to hold, the value of k must satisfy

$$k = \frac{E(R_m) - R_f}{E(R_m^2) - R_f E(R_m)}. \quad (21)$$

Using the new market returns—namely,

State 1	0.9175
State 2	1.0525
State 3	1.1725
State 4	1.2175

—gives a value of k equal to 0.6998. The market portfolio will be optimal for a quadratic utility investor with this value of k and hence a satiation return level, $1/k$, of 1.4289.

What remain to be determined are the constants to be added to the individual asset returns. This is easily accomplished. Because every asset costs \$1, the marginal expected utility for each asset must be the same. For example, the marginal utility of asset i must equal that of the riskless asset—that is,

$$\sum_s R_{is}\pi_s m(R_{ms}) = R_f \sum_s \pi_s m(R_{ms}). \quad (22)$$

But Equation 11 shows that the return on asset i in state s is its old return plus d_i. Thus, d_i must be set so that

$$\sum_s (R_{is}^o + d_i)\pi_s m(R_{ms}) = R_f \sum_s \pi_s m(R_{ms}). \quad (23)$$

The required value of d_i is thus

$$d_i = \frac{R_f \sum_s \pi_s m(R_{ms}) - \sum_s R_{is}^0 \pi_s m(R_{ms})}{\sum_s \pi_s m(R_{ms})}. \quad (24)$$

The resulting d_i values are

Cash	0.0000
Bonds	0.0288
Stocks	0.1248

The market value–weighted average of these d_i values is 0.0835, the value computed earlier to be added to each market return to obtain the desired expected return on the market portfolio.

The two procedures will always give the same value, whether the utility function is quadratic or not, as can be seen by multiplying either Equation 23 or Equation 24 by x_i and summing over the assets.

Table 11 shows the resulting new returns by asset class and state. Not surprisingly, they are the same as the ones shown in Table 10 and Table 1. Thus, this general approach gives the same results as the standard mean–variance optimization when the representative investor's utility function is quadratic.

Table 11. EU Reverse Optimization's New Returns: Quadratic Utility

State	Cash	Bonds	Stocks
State 1	1.0500	1.0388	0.8348
State 2	1.0500	0.9888	1.0848
State 3	1.0500	1.0888	1.2348
State 4	1.0500	1.1388	1.2848

EU Reverse Optimization with HARA Utility. Now consider the second case. Here, the representative investor is characterized by a HARA utility function. Thus,

$$m(R_{ms}) = (R_{ms} - b)^{-c}. \quad (25)$$

As before, the marginal expected utility of the market portfolio must equal that of the riskless asset, as in Equation 18. Thus, the goal is to find values of b and c that satisfy

$$\sum_s R_{ms}\pi_s\left[(R_{ms} - b)^{-c}\right] = R_f \sum_s \pi_s\left[(R_{ms} - b)^{-c}\right]. \quad (26)$$

There are multiple pairs of such values. To simplify, one can prespecify the value of b, then solve for c. Because the equation is nonlinear, a search over alternative values of c is required, but it can be done quickly by using any standard procedure. If desired, the procedure can be repeated for different values of b and then the most realistic combination chosen.

For this example, I assume that $b = 0$, so the representative investor will have constant relative risk aversion (an assumption frequently made when calibrating asset-pricing models). With historical returns from Table 6, the relative values of the current market portfolio (cash, 0.10; bonds, 0.30; stocks, 0.60), and the current forecasts for the riskless rate (1.050) and risk premium (0.040), the value for c is found to be 2.9868.

Once the values of b and c have been specified, it is straightforward to compute the marginal expected utility for each state. Then, the d_i values can be computed by using the procedure followed earlier. **Table 12** compares the results with those for the quadratic utility function. As can be seen, the data differ, but not by large amounts.

Table 12. EU Reverse Optimization: Portfolio Differences

Asset	For Quadratic Utility	For HARA Utility
Cash	0.0000	0.0000
Bonds	0.0288	0.0269
Stocks	0.1248	0.1257

Table 13 shows the forecasted returns obtained by adding the d_i values to the returns for the assets. Of course, these differ from the returns in Table 11, which were based on a quadratic utility function, but again, not by large amounts.

Table 13. EU Reverse Optimization's New Returns: HARA Utility

State	Cash	Bonds	Stocks
State 1	1.0500	1.0369	0.8357
State 2	1.0500	0.9869	1.0857
State 3	1.0500	1.0869	1.2357
State 4	1.0500	1.1369	1.2857

State Prices

In the discussions of both optimization and reverse optimization, I focused on the marginal expected utilities of states and assets. A closely related concept is the rate at which an investor would be willing to substitute one asset or state for another. This rate will equal the ratio of the associated marginal expected utilities. Of particular interest is mrs_s, the marginal rate of substitution of the riskless asset that pays \$1 in every state for a *state claim* paying \$1 in state s. Letting R_{ps} be the return on the investor's portfolio in state s, we find

$$mrs_s = \frac{\pi_s m(R_{ps})}{\sum_s \pi_s m(R_{ps})}. \tag{27}$$

Because the riskless asset costs \$1 and returns R_f, the marginal rate of substitution of present value for the riskless asset is $1/R_f$. Thus, the marginal rate of substitution of present value for a state claim paying \$1 in state s is equal to the product of the two marginal rates of substitution. This product can be considered p_s, the representative investor's *reservation price* or, more simply, the *state price* for the state claim:

$$p_s = \frac{\pi_s m(R_{ps})}{R_f \sum_s \pi_s m(R_{ps})}. \tag{28}$$

The state prices for the HARA example would be

State 1	\$0.3700
State 2	\$0.2456
State 3	\$0.1779
State 4	\$0.1589

Not surprisingly, they sum to 1/1.05.

In a reverse optimization, the reservation state prices can be used as estimates of the values of assets not included explicitly in the analysis. Any asset that is traded should sell for a price close to the value computed from the state prices. This allows evaluation of the extent to which the derived representative investor's utility function provides a reasonable characterization of equilibrium in the capital market and the returns on the assets in it.

To illustrate, assume that there is a traded put option on the stock index fund with an exercise price of \$1. It will be in the money only if State 1 occurs. Assuming that adjustments are made for dividends, it will pay \$0.0825 in State 1 and 0 in every other state. Its price should thus equal 0.3700 × \$0.0825, or \$0.0305. If the actual price differs significantly from this figure, the analyst may want to perform another reverse optimization with a different type of utility function or a different fixed parameter for the same type of utility function.

More generally, the values of traded derivative securities on underlying assets included in the reverse optimization can be used to improve the entire procedure. In this example, different values of b could be selected, with the results for each evaluated on the basis of the conformance of the actual prices of asset derivatives to the values computed by using the associated state prices.

Applications

This article was limited to the presentation of expected utility approaches to asset optimization and reverse optimization. Other research has the task of evaluating the practicality of such methods in actual applications. A necessary condition for success in applications is the creation of plausible discrete forecasts of alternative sets of asset returns.

The potential payoffs from this approach could be substantial. Complex distributions of possible future outcomes could be analyzed. Differences between an investor's views about the future and those reflected in asset prices could be incorporated by adding "alpha values" to asset returns and/or changing the probabilities associated with some or all of the states. A wide range of investor preferences could be considered. The optimization procedure could be extended to cover cases in which assets are to be allocated while liabilities are taken into account. And the procedures could also be applied in the area of risk management and budgeting. Perhaps most important is that expected utility asset allocation analysis could replace many *ad hoc* procedures currently used by investment staffs and boards. It would thus provide a single and consistent analytical approach. The practical challenges may be formidable, but the possible gains could be substantial.

The author is grateful to John Watson of Financial Engines and Jesse Phillips of the University of California for careful reviews of earlier drafts and a number of helpful comments.

This article qualifies for 1 PD credit.

Notes

1. The data in all the tables are rounded. For the calculations, however, the original values were used. The data in Table 1 were produced by using reverse optimization. For details, see the subsequent discussion and the description of Table 10.
2. In this and some subsequent formulas, I use two or more letters for some variable names. This convention is familiar to those who write computer programs but may cause consternation for some mathematicians. Hopefully, the meanings of the formulas will be plain in context.
3. The use of the symbol for *pi* for probability may cause some confusion, but the mnemonic value is considerable, and the presence of a subscript should serve as a reminder that this is not 3.14159 . . . .
4. The relationship in Equation 8 can be derived from the characteristics of the two optimization problems.
5. As indicated in Note 1, values shown in this article are rounded. For those wishing to replicate the results, the constants added to bonds and stocks to produce Table 10 were, respectively, 0.02883125864454 and 0.1247510373444.

References

Adler, Tim, and Mark Kritzman. 2007. "Mean–Variance versus Full-Scale Optimization." *Journal of Asset Management*, vol. 7, no. 5 (January):302–311.

Black, Fischer, and Robert Litterman. 1992. "Global Portfolio Optimization." *Financial Analysts Journal*, vol. 48, no. 5 (September/October):28–43.

Cremers, Jan-Hein, Mark Kritzman, and Sebastien Page. 2005. "Optimal Hedge Fund Allocations: Do Higher Moments Matter?" *Journal of Portfolio Management*, vol. 31, no. 3 (Spring):70–81.

Levy, Haim, and Harry M. Markowitz. 1979. "Approximating Expected Utility by a Function of Mean and Variance." *American Economic Review*, vol. 69, no. 3 (June):308–317.

Markowitz, H.M. 1959. *Portfolio Selection: Efficient Diversification of Investments*. New York: Wiley.

Sharpe, William F. 1985. *AAT: Asset Allocation Tools*. Redwood City, CA: Scientific Press.

———. 1987. "An Algorithm for Portfolio Improvement." In *Advances in Mathematical Programming and Financial Planning*. Edited by K.D. Lawrence, J.B. Guerard, and Gary D. Reeves. Greenwich, CT: JAI Press.

———. 2007. *Investors and Markets: Portfolio Choices, Asset Prices, and Investment Advice*. Princeton, NJ: Princeton University Press.

Financial Analysts Journal
Volume 66 • Number 3
©2010 CFA Institute
FAJ

Adaptive Asset Allocation Policies

William F. Sharpe

This article proposes an asset allocation policy that adapts to market movements by taking into account changes in the outstanding market values of major asset classes. Such a policy considers important information, reduces or avoids contrarian behavior, and can be followed by a majority of investors.

The third edition of *Managing Investment Portfolios: A Dynamic Process* states:

> Strategic asset allocation can be viewed as a process with certain well-defined steps. Performing those steps produces a set of portfolio weights for asset classes; we call this set of weights the strategic asset allocation (or the *policy portfolio*).[1]

This article is about such asset allocation policies.

Traditional Asset Allocation Policies

The March 2009 asset allocation report of the California Public Employees' Retirement System (CalPERS)[2] provides the example of a traditional asset allocation policy shown in **Table 1**. A key feature of such a policy is that the target for each asset class is stated as a *percentage of the total value* of the fund, with each asset target between 0 percent and 100 percent. An asset allocation policy is almost always stated in this manner. I use the term "traditional" for such a policy to differentiate it from the adaptive policies described later in the article.

Table 1. CalPERS' Asset Allocation Policy, March 2009

Asset Class	Policy Target
Global equity	66%
Global fixed income	19
Inflation-linked assets	5
Real estate	10
Cash	0

Source: CalPERS (2009).

William F. Sharpe is STANCO 25 Professor Emeritus of Finance, Stanford University, California.

A typical large institutional investor sets an asset allocation policy after considerable analysis, changing it only episodically. According to the CalPERS (2009) report:

> CalPERS follows a strategic asset allocation policy that identifies the percentage of funds to be invested in each asset class. Policy targets are typically implemented over a period of several years.

To accommodate disparities between policy proportions and actual portfolio holdings, most traditional asset allocation policies include acceptable ranges around each target weight within which the magnitude of the particular asset class is allowed to vary. For some investors, the deviations can become substantial. At the end of March 2009, the proportions held by CalPERS differed substantially from its policy target (adopted in the latter part of 2007 but still in effect at the time), as shown in **Table 2**.[3]

Table 2. CalPERS' Target and Actual Asset Allocations, March 2009

Asset Class	Policy Target	Current	Current–Target
Global equity	66%	53.5%	–12.5 pps
Global fixed income	19	25.2	+6.2
Inflation-linked assets	5	2.5	–2.5
Real estate	10	11.4	+1.4
Cash	0	7.3	+7.3

pps = percentage points.
Source: CalPERS (2009).

To restore the portfolio by conforming it with the asset allocation policy, CalPERS would have had to sell some of its holdings in three asset classes (global fixed income, real estate, and cash) and purchase additional amounts of two others (global equity and inflation-linked assets). This action was not taken immediately, however, because the CalPERS board was considering a new asset allocation policy at the time.

Although statistics are lacking, most large pension funds, endowments, and foundations appear to have traditional asset allocation policies. In many cases, considerable discrepancies between policy and actual asset proportions are allowed to develop. Some funds actively rebalance holdings to avoid substantial discrepancies, whereas others allow the proportions to change with market movements and then revisit their asset allocation policies when the differences between actual and policy weights become large. Relatively few institutional investors seem to engage in what some might term "slavish" adherence to a set of policy asset weights by engaging in frequent rebalancing transactions.

The majority of multi-asset mutual funds also have traditional asset allocation policies. Unlike many institutional investors, however, many such mutual funds allow only relatively small deviations of the actual asset proportions from those specified in the policy.

Many individual investors invest some or all of their retirement savings in multi-asset mutual funds, either directly or through a 401(k) or other type of retirement plan. Under the Pension Protection Act of 2006, the U.S. Department of Labor[4] includes only two types of mutual or collective funds as "qualified default investment alternatives" (QDIAs): *balanced* (sometimes called *life-stage*) and *target-date* (sometimes called *life-cycle*) funds.[5] At the end of December 2008, 9.1 percent of the $1.084 trillion invested in mutual funds offered by the top 25 providers of such funds to 401(k) plans was invested in balanced or life-stage funds and 8.9 percent was invested in target-date funds.[6]

To illustrate, I provide an example of each type of fund.

Vanguard Balanced Index Fund

With $7.5 billion under management in April 2009, the Vanguard Balanced Index Fund

> seeks—with 60 percent of its assets—to track the investment performance of a benchmark index that measures the investment return of the overall U.S. stock market. With 40 percent of its assets, the fund seeks to track the investment performance of a broad, market-weighted bond index.[7]

The Vanguard Balanced Index Fund compares its returns with those of a benchmark, with 60 percent invested in the MSCI US Broad Market Index and 40 percent in Barclays Capital U.S. Aggregate Bond Index. Over the 36 months ended March 2009, the R^2 value for a comparison of the fund's returns with those of the benchmark was 1.00 (rounded to two decimal places), indicating close conformance of the asset proportions with the 60/40 policy.[8]

Fidelity Freedom 2020 Fund

Fidelity Investments offers a series of target-date funds. Of those funds at the end of December 2008, the Fidelity Freedom 2020 Fund was the one most used by defined-contribution plans, with assets of more than $12 billion from such plans.[9] The next six funds in order of total assets from defined-contribution plans were Fidelity Freedom funds with other target dates.

An excerpt from the 2008 prospectus for the Fidelity family of funds is instructive:

> The following chart [**Figure 1**] illustrates each Freedom Fund's approximate asset allocation among equity, fixed-income, and short-term funds as of March 31, 2008. The chart also illustrates how these allocations may change over time. The Freedom Funds' target asset allocations may differ from this illustration. . . . [Moreover, the fund's adviser] intends to manage each Freedom Fund according to its target asset allocation strategy, and does not intend to trade actively among underlying Fidelity funds or intend to attempt to capture short-term market opportunities. However, [the fund's adviser] . . . may modify the target asset allocation strategy for any Freedom Fund and modify the selection of underlying Fidelity funds for any Freedom Fund from time to time.[10]

A comparison of the allocation for the Fidelity Freedom 2020 Fund at the end of March 2008[11] with that at the end of March 2009[12] is shown in **Table 3**. As intended, over the course of the year, the percentage of value invested in equity had fallen, providing overall asset allocations extremely close to those called for by the "glide paths" shown in Figure 1.

Although these funds provide only examples, their activities suggest that many active and passive multi-asset mutual funds choose to rebalance their holdings significantly after major market movements in order to minimize differences

Table 3. Fidelity Freedom 2020 Fund's Asset Allocations, 2008 and 2009

Asset	Actual, 31 March 2008	Actual, 31 March 2009
U.S. equity	52.6%	52.1%
Non-U.S. equity	13.7	12.9
Investment-grade fixed income	25.5	26.1
High-yield fixed income	7.6	7.6
Short-term funds	0.6	1.3

Source: Fidelity Investments (2008, 2009).

Figure 1. Fidelity Freedom Funds' Asset Allocations

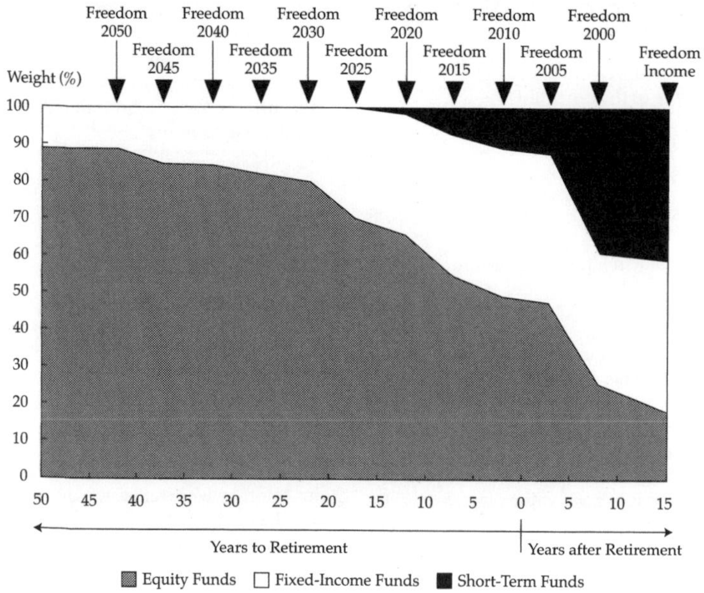

Note: On the *x*-axis, "0" refers to retirement.
Source: Fidelity Investments (2008).

between actual and policy asset allocations. Funds that do so follow traditional asset allocation policies: Balanced funds rebalance to conform with a constant asset allocation over time, and target-date funds rebalance to conform with an asset allocation that varies slowly over time as called for by a pre-specified glide path.

The Contrarian Nature of Traditional Asset Allocation Strategies

The term "contrarian" is used in many contexts. The following definition is closest to the meaning I intend in this article:

> An investment style that goes against prevailing market trends by buying assets that are performing poorly and then selling when they perform well.[13]

For purposes of this article, I consider investors contrarian if they buy assets that perform poorly relative to the other assets in the portfolio and sell assets that perform well relative to the others.

Consider an investor who attempts to keep the actual asset percentages of a portfolio consistent with a stated asset allocation policy. I define such a strategy as one that *follows an asset allocation policy* by rebalancing a portfolio frequently to conform it with a pre-specified set of asset proportional values. Assume that our investor rebalances a portfolio to conform it with a stated set of asset proportions at the end of every review period (e.g., every month or quarter). Given n asset classes, the dollar amounts initially invested in the assets are $X_1, \ldots, X_n$. The initial value of the portfolio is

$$V_0 = \sum_i X_i, \tag{1}$$

and the initial asset proportions are

$$\frac{X_1}{V_0}, \ldots, \frac{X_n}{V_0}. \tag{2}$$

We assume that these proportions are equal to the investor's asset allocation policy proportions.

Now imagine that a period has passed and that the *value relative* for asset i (the ratio of the ending value to the beginning value) is k_i. The new dollar values of the assets are

$$k_1X_1,...,k_nX_n. \tag{3}$$

The ending value of the portfolio is

$$V_1 = \sum_i k_iX_i, \tag{4}$$

and the new asset proportions are

$$\frac{k_1X_1}{V_1},...,\frac{k_nX_n}{V_1}. \tag{5}$$

We denote the value relative for portfolio K_p as

$$K_p \equiv \frac{V_1}{V_0}. \tag{6}$$

Now assume that the investor wishes to purchase and sell securities in amounts that will make the new asset proportions equal the initial policy proportions. Let $D_1, \ldots, D_n$ represent the dollar amounts of the assets purchased (if positive) or sold (if negative). The goal is to select a set of positive, negative, and possibly zero values for $D_1, \ldots, D_n$ such that

$$\frac{k_iX_i + D_i}{V_1} = \frac{X_i}{V_0} \tag{7}$$

for every asset i. This step requires that

$$D_i = \left(K_p - k_i\right)X_i. \tag{8}$$

Also of interest is the amount of an asset purchased as a proportion of the value before the transaction. We can denote this amount as Y_i:

$$Y_i \equiv \frac{D_i}{k_iX_i} = \frac{K_p}{k_i} - 1. \tag{9}$$

If an asset underperforms the portfolio as a whole, $(K_p - k_i)$ will be positive. As Equation 8 shows, the investor will purchase the asset because D_i will be positive. Such assets are *relative losers*. Moreover, the poorer such an asset's performance (i.e., the smaller its value relative, k_i), the greater will be Y_i, the amount purchased, as a percentage of the current holding.

Conversely, if an asset outperforms the portfolio as a whole, $(K_p - k_i)$ will be negative. The investor will sell the asset because D_i will be negative. Such assets are *relative winners*. Moreover, the better such an asset's performance (i.e., the larger its value relative, k_i), the greater will be Y_i, the amount sold, as a percentage of the current holding.

In this setting, an investor who follows an asset allocation policy is undoubtedly a contrarian. To repeat the obvious:

> Rebalancing a portfolio to a previously set asset allocation policy involves selling relative winners and buying relative losers.[14]

Contrarians All?

If I wish to buy a security, someone must sell it to me. If I wish to sell a security, someone must buy it. Anyone who rebalances a portfolio to conform with an asset allocation policy must trade with someone.

From time to time, companies and other entities issue new securities and purchase or redeem existing ones. But most security transactions involve trades of existing securities between two investors, which raises the question, can all investors be contrarians? The answer is no.

I illustrate with a simple example. Each of four investors follows an asset allocation policy with positive proportions of four asset classes, although the proportions differ. A period has passed, and the assets have performed differently. In **Table 4**, the assets are numbered in terms of their performance (i.e., $k_1 > k_2 > k_3 > k_4$). The investors differ in their initial allocations and thus have different overall portfolio returns (K_p values). Each investor wishes to make transactions to rebalance the portfolio to the particular asset allocation policy. In Table 4, a minus sign indicates an asset to be sold and a plus sign one to be purchased. The last three columns show the number of investors wishing to sell an asset, the number wishing to buy, and the difference between the two.

Because every investor holds the best performing asset, every portfolio return will be below the return of the best performing asset. Hence, every investor will wish to sell shares of Asset 1. Conversely, every portfolio return will be greater than the return of the worst performing asset, and

Table 4. Asset Allocation Trades for Four Investors

Assets in Decreasing Order of Return	Investor A	Investor B	Investor C	Investor D	No. of Sellers	No. of Buyers	Net No. of Sellers
1	–	–	–	–	4	0	4
2	–	–	–	+	3	1	2
3	+	+	–	+	1	3	–2
4	+	+	+	+	0	4	–4

thus every investor will wish to buy shares of Asset 4. With regard to the best and worst performing assets, every investor is indeed a contrarian, and the group as a whole must find some investors who do not follow asset allocation policies with whom to trade.

Note that in each investor's column, minus (sell) signs come first, followed by plus (purchase) signs because each investor will wish to sell all assets with performance (k_i) greater than that of the portfolio (K_p). Investor asset allocations, like portfolio returns, will differ, however, so the points at which minus signs stop and plus signs begin will vary—all of which leads to a key characteristic of the last column: The net number of sellers (number of sellers − number of buyers) will be smaller, the poorer an asset's performance.

To keep the example simple, I assume that each investor's portfolio performance differs from that of each asset. This assumption, however, need not be the case. If an asset's performance equals that of an investor's portfolio, the investor will not wish to buy or sell shares in it—a situation that could be represented with a zero in the table.

We could make another modification that would increase the realism of the example. Some investors may have an asset allocation policy that calls for zero exposure to one or more assets. This situation could also be represented with a zero in the table because no trades will be required.

Taking such possibilities into account would modify the characteristics of the table only slightly. The net number of sellers will either decrease or stay the same, the lower an asset's performance.

We should not read too much into this result. Although the net *number* of sellers will not increase the lower an asset's return, the difference between the *dollar value* of shares offered for sale and the dollar value of shares desired to be purchased by the group of investors that follows asset allocation policies may not share this characteristic because of differences in the values of an asset's holding across portfolios. Put somewhat differently, the relationship between (1) the net number of shares offered and (2) asset return may not be completely monotonic, especially for assets with returns close to that of the overall market.

Despite this caveat, those attempting to rebalance portfolios to asset allocation policies will, as a group, wish to sell shares of the best performing asset and purchase shares of the worst performing asset. This fact alone leads to two conclusions that should seem obvious at this point:

> Not all investors can be contrarians.

Thus:

> Not all investors can follow traditional asset allocation policies.[15]

More pragmatically, for a large number of investors to be able to follow traditional asset allocation policies, a large number of other investors must be willing to take the other sides of the requisite trades. Investors in the latter group must purchase assets that have performed well (relative winners) and sell assets that have performed poorly (relative losers). As I discuss later in the article, such a strategy will prove superior if security price trends persist; therefore, investors who pursue such a strategy are often termed *trend followers*. To oversimplify, for every contrarian there must be a trend follower. Not only is it impossible for all investors to follow contrarian strategies, but it is also impossible for those with a majority of capital assets to do so.

Identifying investors who have traditional asset allocation policies is easy. As indicated earlier, there are many such investors. But identifying investors who pursue trend-following policies is harder. This fact raises a more practical question: How many investors actually follow an asset allocation policy? The answer might well be relatively few. Although many investors have asset allocation policies, relatively few are likely to follow their policies by rebalancing their portfolios frequently. As suggested earlier, multi-asset mutual funds appear to be a major exception: They rebalance their portfolios frequently by buying relative losers and selling relative winners.

Why a Contrarian Strategy?

Why might an investor wish to adopt a contrarian strategy? There are two possible reasons. The investor might believe that markets are *efficient* and that the preferences and/or positions of the ultimate beneficiary or beneficiaries of a fund differ sufficiently from those of the average investor to warrant such a strategy. Alternatively, the investor might believe that markets are *inefficient* and that the majority of investors do not realize that a contrarian strategy can provide a better combination of risk and return than can conventional trend-following strategies.

Efficient-Market Views. Perold and Sharpe (1988) documented a key relationship between market returns and the performance of different asset allocation policies. They compared the payoffs provided by following a traditional asset allocation policy with those obtained by following a buy-and-hold strategy. Assuming investments in two asset classes (bills and stocks), they defined *constant-mix strategies* as those that "maintain an exposure to stocks that is a constant proportion of wealth" (p. 18). They noted:

> In general, rebalancing to a constant mix requires the purchase of stocks as they fall in value . . . and the sale of stocks as they rise in value . . . where, strictly speaking, changes in value are measured in relative terms. (pp. 19–20)

Perold and Sharpe (1988) further showed that the desirability of rebalancing to constant proportions of wealth depends on the movements of market prices:

> In general, a strategy that buys stocks as they fall and sells as they rise will capitalize on reversals. The marginal purchase decisions will turn out to be good ones, as will the marginal sell decisions. A constant-mix strategy will thus outperform a comparable buy-and-hold strategy in a flat (but oscillating) market precisely because it trades in a way that exploits reversals. . . . [But] a constant-mix approach will underperform a comparable buy-and-hold strategy when there are no reversals. This will also be the case in strong bull or bear markets when reversals are small and relatively infrequent, because most of the marginal purchase and sell decisions will turn out to have been poorly timed. . . .
>
> Cases in which the market ends up near its starting point are likely to favor constant-mix strategies, while those in which the market ends up far from its starting point are likely to favor buy-and-hold strategies. . . . Neither strategy dominates the other. A constant-mix policy tends to be superior if markets are characterized more by reversals than trends. A buy-and-hold policy tends to be superior if there is a major move in one direction. (pp. 21–22)
>
> Ultimately, the issue concerns the preferences of the various parties that will bear the risk and/or enjoy the reward from investment. There is no reason to believe that any particular type of dynamic strategy is best for everyone (and, in fact, only buy-and-hold strategies could be followed by everyone). (p. 26)

Roughly speaking, an efficient-market view holds that an investor is best served by adopting the average opinion of investors about the probabilities of possible future combinations of returns. Among investors who accept this premise, the return distribution associated with a rebalancing strategy will appeal to only a minority, with another group of investors taking the other sides of the rebalancing trades of the first group. Absent superior knowledge about the return-generating process, investors should follow a traditional asset allocation policy only if they are less concerned than the average investor about inferior returns in very bad or very good markets. This scenario seems an unlikely one for the typical small investor, for whom most balanced and target-date funds are designed.

From late 2007 through early 2009, returns on stock markets around the world were dismal, with many markets posting losses of 50 percent or more in real terms. Sobered by these results, some analysts changed their assumptions about stock returns. In some cases, positive serial correlations of returns were assumed. This assumption increased the probabilities of trends and thus extreme long-term returns. In other cases, some other process was included to provide a distribution with a "fat left tail," which increased the probabilities of large negative returns. Some analysts included both features in their models. In models with such assumptions, extreme markets are more likely, making traditional asset allocation policies even less appropriate for funds designed for small investors.

Inefficient-Market Views. Many advocates of rebalancing rationalize their position by assuming that markets are inefficient and that other investors with whom they can trade do not fully understand the nature of asset returns. As Arnott and Lovell (1990) opined:

> How many investors permit their asset mix to drift with the whims of the markets (assuring overweighting at market highs and underweighting at the lows). . . . Simple rebalancing can provide the necessary measure of control over a drifting mix. It is worthwhile if properly managed. (pp. 13, 18)

Note the reference to "market highs . . . and lows." The statement suggests that one can tell when an asset is at its market high or low before the fact—hardly an efficient-market concept.

Although Arnott, Burns, Plaxco, and Moor (2007) took a more nuanced approach, they still seemed to suggest that rebalancing can take advantage of market inefficiency:

> Not rebalancing may mean holding assets that have become overpriced, offering inferior future rewards. A commitment to rebalance to the strategic asset allocation offers an effective way to dissuade clients from abandoning policy at inauspicious moments. (p. 702)

To buttress their view, Arnott et al. (2007) reported the results of an empirical test that used monthly rebalancing from 1973 to 2003, which showed that a rebalanced portfolio would have provided a greater average return with a smaller standard deviation than would a "drifting mix." As discussed earlier, rebalancing to a constant mix typically outperforms a buy-and-hold strategy when reversals are more common than trends. In periods with more trends than reversals, the comparison is likely to yield the opposite conclusion. As is frequently the case, the outcomes of empirical tests with past data can be highly period dependent.

When adopting an investment strategy, one must make an assumption about the nature of future security markets. If one believes that markets are inefficient, taking advantage of investors who do not realize that this is so makes sense. Nonetheless, the task can be daunting, as Arnott (2009) argued:

> At its heart, rebalancing is a simple contrarian strategy. In ebullient times, this means taking money away from our biggest winners. In the worst of times, the process forces us to buy more of the assets that have caused us the greatest pain. Most investors acknowledge it as a critical part of the successful investor's toolkit. But recognition and action are two different things. Surrounded by bad news, pulling the trigger to buy securities down 50 percent, 75 percent, or even 90 percent is exceedingly difficult for even the staunchest of rebalancers. Many lose their nerve and blink, letting a healthy portion of the excess returns slip from their grasp. (p. 1)

Arnott's argument reflects some of the points I have made thus far. It recognizes that rebalancing is, in fact, a contrarian strategy. It acknowledges that such action involves buying losers and selling winners. It suggests that most investors believe rebalancing is desirable but that many "lose their nerve and blink." And it reflects Arnott's view that markets are sufficiently inefficient that by failing to rebalance, investors let "a healthy portion of the excess returns slip from their grasp."

Asset Allocation Policy and Market Efficiency

The vast majority of those who adopt an asset allocation policy heed the following recommendations:

> The expectations involved in strategic asset allocation are long term. "Long term" has different interpretations for different investors, but five years is a reasonable minimum reference point.[16]

Are markets efficient in the long run? That depends on what is meant by the term "efficient." In the current context, we need merely ask whether an investor wishes to assume that significant numbers of investors are foolish enough to take the other side of contrarian trades when doing so is undesirable. An investor who adopts a traditional asset allocation policy and rebalances frequently to conform with it must either (1) have an unusual set of preferences for returns in different markets (as described earlier) or (2) believe that markets will be inefficient in this sense more often than not over a period of several years.

I believe that the majority of institutional investors who adopt traditional asset allocation policies do so for neither of those two reasons. Rather, they adopt a policy designed to reflect both their preferences for risk vis-à-vis return and their special circumstances when they adopt a policy. As time passes and markets change, the policy no longer serves its original purpose. But neither a traditional rebalancing approach nor a "drifting mix" is appropriate. I suggest two possible alternatives later in the article. First, however, let us see how far a traditional policy can diverge from its original position.

Bond and Stock Values in the United States

Consider a simple asset allocation policy that involves only U.S. bonds and U.S. stocks. Assume that the former are represented by the Barclays Capital (formerly Lehman) U.S. Aggregate Bond Index and the latter by the Wilshire 5000 Total Market Index.[17] Now, consider a balanced mutual fund that has chosen an asset allocation policy with 60 percent invested in U.S. stocks and 40 percent in U.S. bonds and that uses these two indices as benchmarks. Its goal is to provide its investors with a portfolio representative of the broad U.S. market of stocks and bonds. Investments in each asset class are made via index funds in order to track the underlying returns closely.

The similarity of this fund to the Vanguard Balanced Index Fund is not coincidental. The two differ only with respect to the indices used for U.S. stock returns, but the two alternatives are highly correlated.

Figure 2 shows the ratio of (1) the total market capitalization of the stock index to (2) the sum of the total market capitalizations of the bond and stock indices over the period January 1976–June 2009. More succinctly, it shows the value of U.S. stocks as a percentage of the value of U.S. stocks and bonds over 33.5 years.

As Figure 2 shows, the relative values of U.S. stocks and bonds have varied substantially. This finding is not an exception—in other countries, security values have also varied substantially.

Figure 2. The Ratio of the Value of U.S. Stocks to U.S. Stocks plus Bonds, January 1976–June 2009

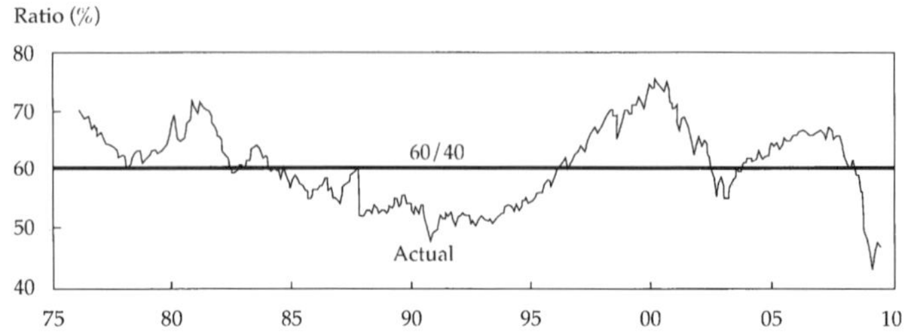

Over the entire period, the proportion of value of stocks averaged 60.7 percent—close to that of a traditional 60/40 strategy with monthly rebalancing, as shown in the figure. The average increase in the value of bonds was larger than that of stocks. But the total return on stock investments averaged more than that on bond investments, as one might expect over the long run as a reward for the greater risk of stock investments.

Table 5 shows the annualized monthly averages[18] of the total returns, the percentage changes in market value, and the differences between the two. Overall, investors neither extracted large amounts of cash from the bond and stock markets nor invested substantial amounts of new cash. They did, however, invest in new bonds in amounts that were close to the sum of coupon payments received from bonds and the dividends paid by their stocks.

Table 5. Returns and Changes in Market Value of U.S. Bonds and Stocks, January 1976–June 2009

	Return	Change in Market Value	Difference
Bonds	8.20%	10.82%	2.62 pps
Stocks	11.27	8.96	–2.31

pps = percentage points.

Assume that our balanced fund opened its doors in February 1984, when the value of U.S. stocks was 59.62 percent of the total value of stocks and bonds. At the time, the fund with 60 percent in stocks well represented an investment in the U.S. bond and stock markets and should have had a similar risk and expected return. Fast-forward to October 1990. The market value of stocks is now 47.99 percent of the total, but the fund has been rebalanced to maintain its policy target of 60 percent. It is no longer representative of the market's risk and return; instead, the fund is riskier, presumably with a higher expected return.

Figure 2 shows that from January 1976 through June 2009, our fund varied from being significantly riskier than the U.S. bond plus stock market to being considerably less risky. At the end of March 2000, the proportion of market value in stocks was 75.06 percent, leading to the lowest relative risk for the fund in the entire period. At the end of February 2009, the situation was just the opposite: The proportion of market value in stocks fell to its nadir of 43.18 percent, making the fund, at 60 percent, much riskier than the overall U.S. bond plus stock market.

In sum, our fund failed to meet its goal of providing a strategy representative of the overall U.S. bond and stock markets except in the very long run. And, as Keynes (1923) taught us, "in the long run we are dead" (ch. 3).

To accomplish its goal, our fund needs to *adapt* its allocation policy. Let us now consider two approaches that an investor might use: (1) optimization based on reverse optimization and (2) an approach that I call an adaptive asset allocation policy. We will assume that the investor is concerned with only the return on assets (ruling out cases in which liabilities are taken into account) and that the managed fund constitutes the entire portfolio (ruling out the use of balanced or target-date funds as components of a larger portfolio).

Optimization Based on Reverse Optimization

Many asset allocation policies are chosen after extensive analyses designed to determine a set of optimal strategies with different combinations of risk and return. In some cases, the analysis uses a standard Markowitz mean–variance approach. In others, the goal is to maximize an investor's expected utility. In many cases, these optimization analyses are conducted with constraints on asset holdings that are designed to reflect liquidity requirements or other factors. Moreover, the chosen policy may differ to some extent from the analytically "optimal" asset mixes.

Whatever the process, asset allocation policies are set after considering estimates of the risks and returns of major asset classes and the correlations among their returns. More generally, the relationship can be characterized as follows:

$$\text{Asset allocation}_t = f\left(\text{Investor characteristics}_t, \text{Market forecasts}_t\right). \quad (10)$$

The subscripts indicate that the appropriate asset allocation at time t depends on the investor's characteristics and the forecasts for asset returns and risks at the time. The notation $f()$ should be read as "is a function of" the items in parentheses.

Consultants and others who make market forecasts typically consider historical returns and some aspects of economic theory. Some forecasters, but by no means all, consider the current market values of major asset classes. The following rather crude equation represents the preferred approach:

$$\text{Market forecasts}_{>t} = f\left(\text{History}_{<=t}, \text{Economic theory}_t, \text{Market values}_t\right). \quad (11)$$

The subscripts indicate that market forecasts for outcomes occurring after time t are based on historical information for periods up to and including time t and on economic theory and market values at time t.[19]

Why should market values inform forecasts? Because an asset's current market value reflects the collective view of the probabilities of future prospects. This information is valuable and should be taken into account when managing a portfolio.

Analytic approaches for making market forecasts in this manner are generally termed *reverse optimization*.[20] Mean–variance approaches assume that capital markets provide unbiased estimates of future prospects (Sharpe 1974, 1985) or incorporate views about deviations from such estimates (Black and Litterman 1991). A comparable approach has been suggested for making forecasts to be used in expected utility analyses (Sharpe 2007).

Combining Equations 10 and 11 gives the following important relationship:

$$\text{Asset allocation}_t = f\left(\text{Investor characteristics}_t, \text{History}_{<=t}, \text{Economic theory}_t, \text{Market values}_t\right). \quad (12)$$

The inevitable conclusion is that an investor's asset allocation, expressed in the traditional manner as percentages of total value in each asset class, should change over time to reflect changing market values, even if the investor's characteristics are unchanged. This conclusion is the key tenet of this article.

Note that such an approach may not require substantial transactions over and above those associated with reinvesting dividends, interest payments, and other cash received from security issuers. Moreover, there is no reason to expect that such an approach will involve selling relative winners and buying relative losers, as must be done to conform with a traditional asset allocation policy.

Equation 12 also shows that a formal system could be set up to revise an investor's asset allocation policy frequently by conducting a reverse optimization analysis followed by optimization. This process, however, requires complex models in order to accommodate real-world aspects[21] and is apparently used by relatively few organizations.[22]

To provide an alternative, I offer a procedure that can be used to periodically adapt an organization's asset allocation policy in light of asset market values without requiring actions that are clearly contrarian in nature. The procedure is simple and can be implemented easily. Although I make no claim that it is the best possible approach, it should be better than either strict conformance with a traditional asset allocation policy or the adoption of such a policy followed by subsequent actions (or lack thereof) that treat the policy as irrelevant.

Adaptive Asset Allocation Policies

The term "adapt" can be defined as follows:

> To adjust oneself to different conditions, environment, etc.[23]

In this case, the "different conditions, environment, etc." are new asset market values.

Imagine that a fund investing in U.S. stocks and bonds established an asset allocation policy of 80 percent stocks and 20 percent bonds at the end of February 1984, with the Wilshire 5000 Total Market Index representing stocks and the Barclays Capital U.S. Aggregate Bond Index representing bonds (as shown in Figure 2, the market proportions were 59.62 percent and 40.38 percent, respectively). Assume that this information was taken into account in the study that led to the 80/20 policy.

A traditional approach would hold that the policy calls for adjustments in holdings to achieve an 80/20 allocation no matter what the subsequent market proportions might be. But as I have argued, this course is unlikely to be a wise one. Instead, the policy proportions should be adjusted as market values change. I propose instead a procedure that I call an adaptive asset allocation (AAA) policy.

Table 6 and **Table 7** show the required calculations for the appropriate allocation at the end of October 1990, when stocks were a substantially smaller portion of overall market value.

Table 6. Market Values of U.S. Bonds and Stocks, February 1984 and October 1990

	Stocks ($ billions)	Bonds ($ billions)	% Stocks
$V_{im,0}$ (Feb. 1984)	1,648.19	1,116.49	59.62
$V_{im,t}$ (Oct. 1990)	2,652.92	2,875.69	47.99
$k_i = V_{im,t}/V_{im,0}$	1.6096	2.5757	

Table 7. Adaptive Policy Allocations, February 1984 and October 1990

	Stocks	Bonds	Sum
$AA_{if,0}$	80.00%	20.00%	
$(AA_{if,0})(k_i)$	128.77	51.51	180.28%
$(AA_{if,0})(k_i)/\text{Sum}(AA_{if,0})(k_i)$	71.43	28.57	

Table 6 shows the total outstanding market capitalizations for each of the two indices at the two dates (February 1984 [time 0] and October 1990 [time t]) and the ratios of the ending values to the beginning values (denoted k_i, as before). Table 7 shows the calculations for the new asset allocation. For each asset, the initial proportion in the fund is multiplied by the ratio of the new total market value of the asset class as a whole to the old value. In this case, the outstanding values of both assets increased substantially. Hence, the sum of the adjusted proportions for the fund is much greater than 100 percent, as shown in the third column. To compute the new asset value proportions for the fund, the figures in the second row are divided by their sum, which gives the new asset allocation shown in the last row.

In this case, stocks fell from representing close to 60 percent of total market value to slightly less than 48 percent. Thus, the fund's asset allocation policy changed from one with 80 percent invested in stocks to one with 71.43 percent so invested.

Why is this procedure likely to be preferred to a traditional approach? Because it need not require that investors who have such policies transact with other investors whenever market prices change, as do traditional asset allocation policies.

Consider a world in which changes in asset market values result only from changes in security prices and reinvestment of cash flows from each asset in the same class. An investor who makes no withdrawals or additional investments and chooses to reinvest all cash flows from each asset class in the same class will be in compliance with the particular adaptive policy at all times and will not need to transact with other investors. This scenario follows from the fact that the value of the investor's holdings of each class will change by precisely the same percentage as the value of the market (k_i) will change. In such a setting, AAA policies are *macro-consistent* in the sense that all investors can follow such strategies.

Of course, the investment world is extremely complex. New issues of securities, buybacks, and redemptions occur frequently. Moreover, the total values of these transactions for an asset class rarely net to zero. Public companies go private and vice versa. Some investors have positive net cash flows that require purchases of new assets, whereas others must sell assets to raise cash. Despite these complications, a group of investors that follows AAA policies is unlikely to need to make large purchases or sales of assets with investors who do not follow such policies. This situation contrasts starkly with the situation of investors who attempt to comply with traditional asset allocation policies; such investors must frequently purchase assets that are relative losers and sell those that are relative winners.

Tables 6 and 7 use the following formula to compute the proportion invested in asset i in fund (f) at time t:

$$X_{if,t} = \frac{X_{if,0}\left(V_{im,t}/V_{im,0}\right)}{\sum_i X_{if,0}\left(V_{im,t}/V_{im,0}\right)}. \tag{13}$$

Here, $V_{im,t}$ and $V_{im,0}$ are the total outstanding market values of asset i at times t and 0, respectively. The proportion invested in asset i at time 0 is $X_{if,0}$, and the proportion to be invested at time t is $X_{if,t}$.

Note that the total market value of asset i at time 0 equals its proportion of total value ($X_{im,0}$) times the total value of all assets at the time ($V_{m,0}$). A similar relationship holds for time t. Thus,

$$\begin{aligned} V_{im,0} &= X_{im,0}V_{m,0} \\ V_{im,t} &= X_{im,t}V_{m,t}. \end{aligned} \tag{14}$$

Substituting these relationships in Equation 13 and canceling terms gives a formula for calculating the new proportion for the fund to invest in asset i

as a function solely of the proportions at time 0 and of the ratios of the proportions for the market portfolio at the two periods:

$$X_{if,t} = \frac{X_{if,0}\left(X_{im,t}/X_{im,0}\right)}{\sum_i X_{if,0}\left(X_{im,t}/X_{im,0}\right)}. \quad (15)$$

Table 8 shows the computations for February 1984 and October 1990.

Table 8. Adaptive Policy Allocations with Asset Proportions, February 1984 and October 1990

	Stocks	Bonds	Sum
$X_{im,0}$	59.62%	40.38%	
$X_{if,0}$	80.00	20.00	
$X_{im,t}$	47.99	52.01	
$(X_{if,0})(X_{im,t})/X_{im,0}$	64.39	25.76	90.15%
$X_{if,t}$	71.43	28.57	

In this example, the initial asset allocation set at time 0 is assumed to have been appropriate, given the market values of the asset classes at the time. This allocation is typically the case when an institutional investor selects an asset allocation policy. The adaptive formula (Equation 15), however, can be applied in other contexts. Key is the statement of an asset allocation policy in terms of base values for (1) the policy and (2) the market. A possible example would be the following:

> The fund's Asset Allocation Policy is to have 80 percent invested in stocks and the remainder in bonds when the market value of stocks is 60 percent of the total value of stocks and bonds, with the proportions to be determined each period by using the adaptive asset allocation formula.

Table 9 shows this asset allocation policy in terms of the formula (Equation 15).

Table 9. An Asset Allocation Policy

	Stocks	Bonds
$X_{im,0}$	60%	40%
$X_{if,0}$	80	20

More generally, we can denote the mixes of market and fund assets as

$$X_{m,0} = \left(X_{1m,0}, X_{2m,0}, \ldots, X_{nm,0}\right) \quad (16)$$

and

$$X_{f,0} = \left(X_{1f,0}, X_{2f,0}, \ldots, X_{nf,0}\right), \quad (17)$$

where there are n assets and $X_{m,0}$ and $X_{f,0}$ are vectors representing the *base* market and fund asset allocations, respectively.

With this interpretation, we can straightforwardly apply the adaptive approach to a wide range of investments. I illustrate with three prototypical types of funds.

Institutional Funds

As indicated earlier, most pension funds, endowments, and foundations conduct asset allocation studies that lead to the selection of a policy asset mix, which can be considered the base policy ($X_{f,0}$). Presumably, this asset allocation was considered appropriate given the market conditions ($X_{m,0}$) at the time, whether or not these market values were used explicitly when determining asset prospects. Under this assumption, the asset allocation policy can be converted to an adaptive policy by simply applying the adaptive formula (Equation 15) in subsequent periods.

As with the traditional approach, allowable deviations from the policy targets may be selected. For example, these deviations could be set to equal the currently allowed deviations of the holdings in each asset class. If the fund makes few, if any, trades, the resulting ranges are less likely to be violated under an adaptive policy than under a traditional approach.

Undoubtedly, many institutional funds would consider the conversion from a traditional to an adaptive asset allocation policy too dramatic to accept overnight. At the very least, I would suggest that the required computations for an adaptive asset allocation policy be performed periodically so that key decision makers could evaluate the fund's holdings in terms of both the traditional approach and this alternative approach. In time, such an exercise might lead to a greater acceptance of the latter.

Balanced Funds

As previously discussed, multi-asset mutual funds are likely to make transactions that are required by their traditional asset allocation policies. To a considerable extent, a multi-asset mutual fund's asset allocation policy will drive its investments, which makes the choice of the type of policy especially important.

Typically, a balanced fund is designed to provide a mix of two or more asset classes with a constant level of "conservatism" or "aggressiveness." Although some may think of these terms as absolute, a more pragmatic approach is to interpret them as relative. In this view, an "aggressive" fund should provide more risk than the market as a whole, whereas a "conservative" one should provide less. A "representative" fund could be designed to provide the same risk as the market as a whole.

Constructing an adaptive representative fund is easy. It would have the market proportions of the asset classes in every period. At the time of formation, the actual proportions ($X_{f,0}$) would be set to equal the market proportions ($X_{m,0}$). The adaptive formula (Equation 15) would subsequently lead the fund manager to hold assets in market proportions at each period. For example, a balanced fund designed to represent the U.S. stock and bond markets would follow the curve rather than the horizontal line in Figure 2.

An aggressive fund would begin with an asset mix that had greater risk than that of the market at the time and would then adjust its holdings by using Equation 15. **Figure 3** shows the actual proportions for a fund that wishes to hold an 80/20 mix of U.S. stocks and bonds when the market proportions are 60/40.

As intended, the fund remained more aggressive than the market throughout the period. Nevertheless, the ratio of the fund's proportion in stocks to that of the market varied, beginning at 1.333 (80 percent/60 percent) and ranging between 1.18 and 1.55.

Not surprisingly, at the four times when the total market value of stocks was close to 60 percent of the total value of stocks and bonds, the fund's asset allocation policy dictated a value close to the intended 80/20 mix. In this example, although the fund was started when the market mix was 60/40, it could have been started at any time with a policy stated in terms of a "normal mix" ($X_{f,0}$) when markets are "normal" ($X_{m,0}$).

This scenario suggests a simple way to convert an existing balanced fund to an adaptive one. The stated policy ($X_{f,0}$) need only be augmented by the "normal" market conditions ($X_{m,0}$) for which it is appropriate. The asset allocation policy for any period can then be determined by using the adaptive formula (Equation 15).

Target-Date Funds

As discussed earlier, a target-date fund has a policy "glide path" that indicates the appropriate asset allocation at each time in the future until the date at which money in the fund is to be transferred to another vehicle. In effect, the fund has a base allocation for every period, which can be straightforwardly accommodated in the adaptive asset allocation formula. Let $X_{ib,t}$ represent the "base" allocation for time t as specified in the current policy. This allocation replaces the constant allocation given by $X_{if,0}$ in Equation 15:

$$X_{if,t} = \frac{X_{ib,t}\left(X_{im,t}/X_{im,0}\right)}{\sum_i X_{ib,t}\left(X_{im,t}/X_{im,0}\right)}. \tag{18}$$

Equation 15 is more general than Equation 18, which can be considered a special case in which $X_{ib,t} = X_{if,0}$ for every period t.

Figure 4 illustrates an adaptive target-date fund. It assumes that the fund was started in January 1976 with a glide path calling for 90 percent in stocks initially, with the allocation decreasing by a constant percentage each month until it reaches 10 percent in June 2009. Figure 4 shows the base allocations that would be implemented by a traditional target-date fund, as well as the market proportions.

To convert this traditional fund to an adaptive target-date fund, we assume that the original glide path was chosen as appropriate when the market proportions in stocks and bonds are 60 percent and 40 percent, respectively. Using these proportions for the $X_{im,0}$ values in Equation 18, we can see the allocations for the adaptive target-date fund. Because the glide path is assumed to be optimal when the market proportions are 60/40, the adaptive proportions and the policy glide path coincide when stocks are 60 percent of the total value of bonds and stocks. Whenever the market proportion of stocks is below 60 percent, the fund's allocation to stocks is below that specified by the glide

Figure 3. Asset Allocations: Market and an Aggressive Balanced Fund

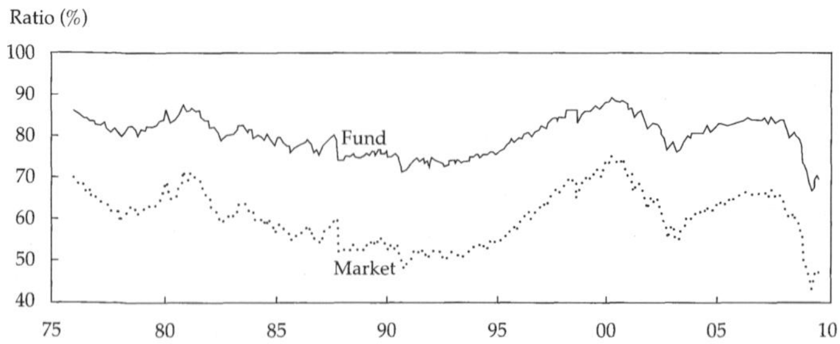

Figure 4. Asset Allocations: Market and an Adaptive Target-Date Fund

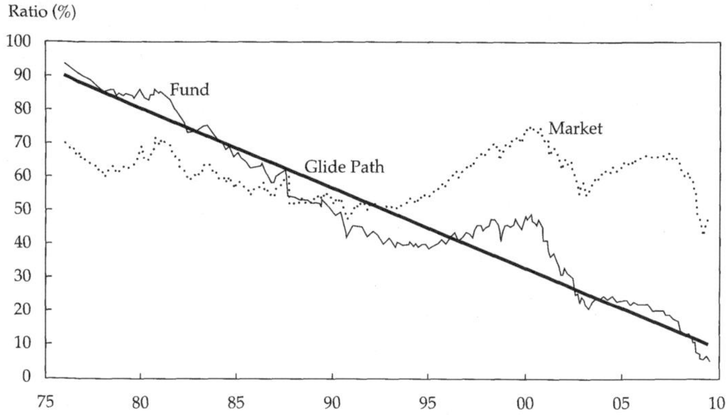

path. Conversely, when stocks represent more than 60 percent of the value of the market, the fund's allocation to stocks is greater than that called for by the glide path.

Conclusion

If my arguments have merit, a number of changes should be made by the investment industry.

First and foremost, more data will need to be made available about the market values of the securities in each of the benchmarks designed to represent major asset classes. Most such indices are computed by third parties. For example, Barclays Capital and Wilshire Associates calculate the two indices used in this article. Recent and historical monthly *returns* for most popular indices may be difficult but not totally impossible to obtain from such providers.[24] But obtaining data for the market *values* of the securities in an index is much harder. Clearly, the index provider has such information.[25] In cases where returns for the index are computed by using a subset of the securities in the represented universe, the provider should still have sufficient information to provide an estimate of the total market value of the class.

It is unclear whether the lack of widespread availability of asset class market values is a result of providers' desires to recover the costs of obtaining such information through subscription fees, a lack of sufficient interest on the part of investors and investment managers, or both. Of course, the thesis of this article is that asset market values are highly relevant for any decision concerning asset allocation, whether made episodically or adjusted routinely by using a procedure such as the one I have proposed. If more investment managers adopt my proposed procedure, market value data may become more widely available.

I cannot easily understand why funds do not routinely compare their asset allocations with current market proportions in order to ensure that any differences are commensurate with differences between their circumstances and those of "the average investor." Yet this comparison is rarely done. Perhaps the lack of easily obtained data on market values is the cause, with the absence of such comparisons the effect. Alternatively, the situation may be the reverse, with the lack of available data on market values caused by insufficient investor interest.

I would hope that readers of this article would request (or demand) that those who provide benchmark indices make the corresponding market values equally available. For publicly offered mutual funds or exchange-traded funds, this provision could be encouraged or required by regulatory authorities.

Second, it would be useful if institutional investors, armed with appropriate market value data, would at least compute the asset allocations that would result from an adaptive policy of the type described here. These computations could inform discussions between staff members and those charged with oversight, such as the members of investment committees and boards. In time, more investment organizations could become sufficiently comfortable with adaptive procedures to substitute them for the contrarian policies associated with the traditional approach.

Third, some mutual fund companies might offer adaptive balanced funds and/or adaptive target-date funds. In time, such vehicles might attract enough investors to represent a significant part of the market. A good first step would be to offer a balanced index fund designed to truly represent the mix of stocks and bonds in the United States. As shown in Figure 2, such a fund would differ significantly from such offerings as the Vanguard Balanced Index Fund. If successful, a representative balanced fund might pave the way for additional funds to follow adaptive asset allocation policies.

Although some will find the arguments in this article obvious and others will consider them radical, I hope that a sufficient number of readers will be convinced of the merit of these arguments to lead to changes in investment practice.

I thank Geert Bekaert of Columbia University, Steven Grenadier of Stanford University, Jesse Phillips of the University of California, Eamonn Dolan of C.M. Capital, Carlo Capaul of Julius Baer, and John Watson and Robert Young of Financial Engines, Inc., for their helpful comments.

This article qualifies for 1 CE credit.

Notes

1. Maginn, Tuttle, Pinto, and McLeavey (2007, p. 231).
2. CalPERS (2009).
3. CalPERS (2009).
4. U.S. Department of Labor (2009).
5. More specifically, the pertinent regulation provides for four types of QDIAs:

   > (1) A product with a mix of investments that takes into account the individual's age or retirement date (an example of such a product could be a life-cycle or targeted-retirement-date fund); (2) an investment service that allocates contributions among existing plan options to provide an asset mix that takes into account the individual's age or retirement date (an example of such a service could be a professionally managed account); (3) a product with a mix of investments that takes into account the characteristics of the group of employees as a whole, rather than each individual (an example of such a product could be a balanced fund); and (4) a capital preservation product for only the first 120 days of participation (an option for plan sponsors wishing to simplify administration if workers opt out of participation before incurring an additional tax).

   See U.S. Department of Labor (2009).
6. Appell (2009, pp. 11, 14).
7. Vanguard (2009).
8. Vanguard (2009).
9. Appell (2009, p. 12).
10. Fidelity Investments (2008, pp. 40–41).
11. Fidelity Investments (2008, p. 11).
12. Fidelity Investments (2009).
13. Investopedia.com, s.v. "Contrarian" (www.investopedia.com/terms/c/contrarian.asp).
14. This observation is true under the assumption made throughout the article that no asset proportions are negative. Funds with policies involving negative proportions (e.g., leverage) may buy relative winners and sell relative losers. For example, consider a fund with a policy of investing 150 percent in stocks and –50 percent in short-term bonds (loans). Assume that the initial position is \$150 in stocks and –\$50 in bonds, giving a net worth of \$100. If the value of the stock portfolio doubles, the new position will equal \$300 in stocks and –\$50 in bonds, giving a net worth of \$250. The new proportions will be 120 percent in stocks and –20 percent in bonds. To restore the fund to its policy proportions will require purchasing more stocks and selling more bonds (i.e., borrowing more money). Such a fund will thus purchase relative winners and sell relative losers.
15. That is, policies with non-negative asset proportions.
16. Maginn, Tuttle, Pinto, and McLeavey (2007, pp. 233–234).
17. Throughout the article, I use the "full-cap" version of the index rather than the "float-adjusted" alternative that uses weights for the securities based on estimates of the number of shares likely to be available for trading.
18. Each annualized monthly average is equal to 12 times the corresponding monthly average value.
19. For an early discussion of the need to account for changes in market values when making forecasts, see Rosenberg and Ohlson (1976).
20. An excellent example is described in EnnisKnupp (2009).
21. A mean–variance approach could be designed in which the asset allocation policy is characterized by a given ratio of the investor's risk tolerance to that of the market as a whole. I explored this possibility earlier (Sharpe 1990). To be practical, the reverse optimization procedure needs to be consistent with an equilibrium in which there are restrictions and/or costs associated with negative holdings—an issue that I have previously discussed (Sharpe 1991).
22. Full disclosure: I co-founded an investment management and advisory company (Financial Engines, Inc.) that uses asset market values and reverse optimization at least once a month to adjust forecasts of risks, returns, and correlations for such investment vehicles as mutual funds, followed by optimization analyses to make any appropriate changes in investor portfolios. Although no asset allocation policy per se is involved, the underlying philosophy is similar.
23. Dictionary.com, s.v. "Adapt" (http://dictionary.classic.reference.com/browse/adapt; retrieved 8 June 2009).
24. Some returns for the Barclays Capital U.S. Aggregate Bond Index can be obtained on the websites of mutual funds and exchange-traded funds that use it as a benchmark. Returns for the Wilshire 5000 Total Market Index can be obtained at www.wilshire.com/Indexes/calculator.
25. On its website, Wilshire (www.wilshire.com/Indexes/Broad/Wilshire5000/Characteristics.html) provides tables that include the total market values of the securities in its U.S. equity index at the end of the most recent month, but no historical data on market values are provided. The Barclays Capital website does not provide any data on the market values of the securities in the U.S. Aggregate Bond Index. I am grateful to both organizations for providing me with the historical data used in this article.
26. Fundamental Index is a registered trademark of Research Affiliates, LLC.

References

Appell, Douglas. 2009. "DC Mutual Funds." *Pensions and Investments*, vol. 37, no. 8 (20 April):11–16.

Arnott, Robert D. 2009. *Fundamental Index*[26] *Newsletter* (May).

Arnott, Robert D., and Robert M. Lovell, Jr. 1990. "Monitoring and Rebalancing the Portfolio." In *Managing Investment Portfolios: A Dynamic Process*. 2nd ed. Edited by John L. Maginn and Donald L. Tuttle. Charlottesville, VA: Association for Investment Management and Research.

Arnott, Robert D., Terence E. Burns, Lisa Plaxco, and Philip Moor. 2007. "Monitoring and Rebalancing." In *Managing Investment Portfolios: A Dynamic Process*. 3rd ed. Edited by John L. Maginn, Donald L. Tuttle, Jerald E. Pinto, and Dennis W. McLeavey. Hoboken, NJ: John Wiley & Sons.

Black, Fischer, and Robert B. Litterman. 1991. "Asset Allocation: Combining Investor Views with Market Equilibrium." *Journal of Fixed Income*, vol. 1, no. 2 (September):7–18.

CalPERS. 2009. "Investments, Asset Allocation" (31 March): www.calpers.ca.gov/index.jsp?bc=/investments/assets/assetallocation.xml; retrieved 21 May 2009.

EnnisKnupp. 2009. "EnnisKnupp Capital Market Modeling Assumptions: Updated July 2009" (www.ennisknupp.com/Portals/0/whitepapers/Capital%20Markets%20Modeling%20Assumptions_Updated%20July%2009.pdf).

Fidelity Investments. 2008. "Supplement to the Fidelity Freedom Funds Prospectus" (29 May).

———. 2009. "Fidelity Freedom 2020 Fund Composition."

Keynes, John Maynard. 1923. *A Tract on Monetary Reform*. London: Macmillan.

Maginn, John L., Donald L. Tuttle, Jerald E. Pinto, and Dennis W. McLeavey, eds. 2007. *Managing Investment Portfolios: A Dynamic Process*. 3rd ed. Hoboken, NJ: John Wiley & Sons.

Perold, André F., and William F. Sharpe. 1988. "Dynamic Strategies for Asset Allocation." *Financial Analysts Journal*, vol. 44, no. 1 (January/February):16–27.

Rosenberg, Barr, and James A. Ohlson. 1976. "The Stationary Distribution of Returns and Portfolio Separation in Capital Markets: A Fundamental Contradiction." *Journal of Financial and Quantitative Analysis*, vol. 11, no. 3 (September):393–401.

Sharpe, William F. 1974. "Imputing Expected Security Returns from Portfolio Composition." *Journal of Financial and Quantitative Analysis*, vol. 9, no. 3 (June):463–472.

———. 1985. *AAT: Asset Allocation Tools*. New York: The Scientific Press.

———. 1990. "Investor Wealth Measures and Expected Return." In *Quantifying the Market Risk Premium Phenomenon for Investment Decision Making*. Charlottesville, VA: Association for Investment Management and Research.

———. 1991. "Capital Asset Prices with and without Negative Holdings." *Journal of Finance*, vol. 46, no. 2 (June):489–509.

———. 2007. "Expected Utility Asset Allocation." *Financial Analysts Journal*, vol. 63, no. 5 (September/October):18–30.

U.S. Department of Labor. 2009. "Regulation Relating to Qualified Default Investment Alternatives in Participant-Directed Individual Account Plans" (www.dol.gov/ebsa/newsroom/fsqdia.html; retrieved 21 May 2009).

Vanguard. 2009. "Vanguard Balanced Index Fund Investor Shares: Portfolio & Management" (https://personal.vanguard.com/us/funds/snapshot?FundId=0002&FundIntExt=INT#hist=tab%3A2; retrieved 21 May 2009).

Section 4: Performance and Risk Analysis

4-1 "Mutual Fund Performance," *The Journal of Business*, Vol. XXXIX, No. 1, Part II, January 1966, pp. 119–138.

This was my first foray since the dissertation into portfolio performance analysis. I was interested in measuring and predicting the performance of funds designed to serve as an investor's overall portfolio which was the goal at the time of most mutual funds. The paper deals with the 34 funds for which annual rates of return were available for at least the twenty years ending in 1964. This small sample size seems at best charming and at most ludicrous when viewed from the present day. There are now thousands of U.S. mutual funds and data are widely available for their monthly returns. Now most funds specialize in a particular style and should thus be evaluated on their efficacy in providing a portion of investor's overall portfolio. But this paper was written in simpler times.

Drawing on the CAPM and with an appropriate attribution to Tobin's separation theorem, I argue that *ex ante*, all efficient strategies should lie along a (capital market) line in expected return/standard deviation space. An inefficient strategy would thus have a lower expected return than that of an equal-risk strategy lying on the line. If *ex post* values are adequate surrogates for *ex ante* values, this suggests a performance measure with the average excess return over a riskless rate in the numerator and the realized standard deviation of return in the denominator. I called this the "reward-to-variability ratio" (R/V) although others subsequently termed it the "Sharpe Ratio".

Figure 1 shows the results from 1954 through 1963 for the thirty-four funds. Since at the time I was still plotting expected return on the horizontal axis and variability (standard deviation) on the vertical axis, the *ex post* efficient line plotted below all but one of the funds. The remainder of the paper is concerned with the ability of various measures known before 1954 to explain the performance of the funds in the subsequent ten years shown in Figure 1. Given the small number of funds and the paucity of returns for each, the results are at best suggestive. There was some persistence in performance, with prior measures of the R/V Ratio providing considerable predictive power for future realizations. A measure previously proposed by Treynor, with beta in the denominator, correlated slightly better with future R/V Ratios, possibly because it focused more on the persistent portion of total risk. However, as shown in Figure 3, most of the funds were highly diversified, so the differences in the two ratios were slight. The most important results in the paper were that (1) many of the differences in net risk-adjusted performance were associated with differences in expense ratios, and that (2) the average fund underperformed an unmanaged diversified index (here, the Dow-Jones Industrials).

Since this study was published, there have been hundreds if not thousands of studies of mutual fund performance employing larger samples, more frequent measures of return and far more sophisticated measures of performance. But the vast majority of such studies have found, as did I, that after costs the average fund underperforms an appropriate passive index. I believe that many who have conducted such studies would still agree with my conclusion in 1966: "... the burden of proof may reasonably be placed on those who argue the traditional view — that the search for securities whose prices diverge from their intrinsic value is worth the expense required ..."

4-2 "Adjusting for Risk in Portfolio Performance Measurement," *Journal of Portfolio Management*, Winter 1975.

This was written to provide a practical summary of the rationale for and current state of development of risk-adjusted measures of performance. I argued that "Measures that account for risk (although perhaps imperfectly) are generally superior to those that do not [and that] ... this is widely recognized in the academic community and, increasingly in the investment community". I also pointed to the fact that at the time (in 1975) several firms offered performance measurement services similar to those described in the paper.

The focus is entirely on pragmatic measures of *ex post* performance, with no attention paid to efficient market motivations or likely empirical results. Reflecting the greater availability of data at the time, I suggest using quarterly returns and expressing all results as excess returns over and above the returns on 90-day treasury bills. I describe the attributes of the reward-to-variability ratio in this context, covering cases in which comparisons involve implicit leverage and historic periods in which average excess returns are negative. I pay considerable attention to comparisons with a market portfolio, suggesting the choice of Standard and Poor's 500 Stock Composite Index, which was then the gold standard in institutional practice. The latter portion of the paper suggests that for portfolios intended to constitute only a portion of an investor's overall holdings, a more appropriate measure would compare returns with those of a comparable-volatility (beta) portfolio rather than a comparable variability (standard deviation) one. This leads to the notion of alpha, introduced by Michael Jensen in 1968 (related to but different from Treynor's earlier measure). By the time this paper was written, the convention in risk/return diagrams was to plot expected or average return on the vertical axis and predicted or historical standard deviation on the horizontal axis, as I did in this paper and all my succeeding work.

By 1975 funds had begun to specialize, but there were few indices of returns in portions of the overall market so the idea of comparing a fund's returns with those of a benchmark with a comparable style was nascent at best. Not surprisingly, this paper concludes with Jensen's measure of alpha, in which the benchmark is taken to be a portfolio comprising a broad market index and a short-term riskless security.

4-3 "Asset allocation: Management Style and Performance Measurement," *The Journal of Portfolio Management*, Volume 18, Number 2, Winter 1992, pp. 7–19.

This paper has a complex past. I developed and applied the method here termed "style analysis" to deal with some of the problems faced by the boards and staffs of the large multi-manager funds with which my firm worked, beginning in 1986. We needed a way to apply a multi-factor model across all the asset classes in which such funds invested; moreover, we had little or no data on the holdings of the component funds so had to rely on the information contained in their monthly return data. At first, I thought that standard regression analyses would suffice, but some experimentation disabused me of that idea. I then thought of using constrained regressions, expressed as quadratic programming problems. The results, illustrated in Table 2 and most of the Figures, far exceeded expectations. Henceforth we applied the procedures routinely for the firm's clients; I continued to do so for a small number of funds after closing the firm in 1992 until shortly before this book went to press.

I first described these procedures in detail in a paper submitted in 1988 to a new journal, *The Investment Management Review.* The editors published a version in their September/October 1988 issue under the title "Determining a Fund's Effective Asset Mix." Unfortunately, the article was very garbled with paragraphs out of order, figures mislabeled and other egregious errors. I requested another try, resulting in publication of a "corrected version" in their November/December 1988 issue. This was better but still contained serious errors. Shortly thereafter, the publication (deservedly) went out of business. Undaunted, I continued to apply the procedures, described them in a presentation at the Darden School at the University of Virginia in October of 1990 and circulated a paper afterwards based on that material. Later I submitted this version to the *Journal of Portfolio Management*, which published it (perfectly) in late 1992. It summarized both the style analysis procedure and the related analyses that I and my colleagues at the firm (all of whom are listed on the initial page of the paper) had been using for years for a number of large multi-managed pension funds and endowments.

The paper makes the case that performance analysis should be based on comparisons with benchmarks chosen well in advance. This calls for truly out-of-sample analyses of a manager or fund's performance when using style analysis to obtain relevant combinations of passive indices to serve as benchmarks. In practical applications I always obeyed this stricture but others, alas, have not always done so.

From the time that I began this work, my goal was to make these ideas public. I briefly considered producing a commercial software product but soon concluded that the task was better left to others. Several firms now provide services based on the method (sometimes termed "returns-based style analysis") and one company — Zephyr Associates — has built a substantial business providing software and databases using the concept. In more recent years, a number of academics and practitioners have taken the idea considerably farther by including indices representing returns on option-like strategies and numerous other "rules-based" alternatives.

4-4 "The Sharpe Ratio," *Journal of Portfolio Management*, Fall 1994, pp. 49–58.

By 1994, the Sharpe Ratio (ne'e Reward to Variability Ratio) was widely used and probably even more widely misused. Moreover, many practitioners evidenced confusion about some of its properties and limitations. I felt that it was a propitious time to write a self-contained piece on the original measure and some of the variants then in use.

I defined the term "Sharpe Ratio" broadly, to include any measure using the ratio of the mean of a differential return to its standard deviation, where a differential return is computed by taking the difference between the return on the investment of interest and that of a relevant benchmark asset or combination of assets. Given this definition, the original Sharpe Ratio constitutes a special case in which the benchmark is a riskless asset; measures such as the "information ratio" implemented by BARRA and others then can be considered cases in which risky benchmarks are utilized.

With the concept so defined, it is straightforward to show that such a ratio measures the performance of a *zero-investment strategy* and that the value of the ratio is independent of the scale at which the strategy is undertaken. Moreover, if several such strategies, uncorrelated with an investor's other holdings and one another, are to be chosen, it follows that their scales should be set so the *ex ante* risks are proportional to the *ex ante* Sharpe Ratios (restating and generalizing the classic result obtained by Treynor and Black in 1973). More generally, when assessing positions that will constitute only a portion of an investor's overall portfolio, it is important to try to select benchmarks that capture as much of the correlation among different components as possible so the differential returns will be relatively uncorrelated. If this is done, measures that take only means and standard deviations of differential returns into account will be far more useful than otherwise. Not surprisingly, in the paper I recommend that readers consider returns-based style analysis procedures to help meet this objective.

4-5 "Morningstar's Risk-Adjusted Ratings," *Financial Analysts Journal*, July/August 1998, pp. 21–33.

By the time I started work on this paper, Morningstar, Inc. had become a major force in the mutual fund arena. Funds that received high "star" ratings from Morningstar experienced significantly larger inflows of new money than those that did not. The company's "risk-adjusted ratings" were thus of great practical import. It seemed worth devoting the considerable effort required to understand their computation and characteristics. I did so in two papers. One, that I posted to my web site (www.wsharpe.com) where it remains, reported the results of extensive empirical analyses. The other, reproduced here, dealt primarily with theoretical matters, but did include a graph from the empirical study showing that during the recent period, which had been characterized by high returns, values computed using Morningstar's risk-adjusted return (RAR) measure and those based on the traditional excess-return Sharpe Ratio were highly correlated. I did, however, suggest that this would likely not be the case after periods of low or negative returns.

The paper is rather daunting, for Morningstar's measure differs significantly from those arising from mean/variance models. To a close approximation, it appeared to be consistent with the maximization of expected utility by an investor with a bilinear utility function such as that in Figure 1. As I show in the paper, such an investor could be characterized by an extreme portfolio choice — selecting either a very high-risk alternative or a very low-risk one. This seemed an inappropriate characterization of the behavior of most investors, in contrast with the implications obtained from standard Markowitz models of portfolio choice.

In part, the Morningstar measures were used to rank funds within relatively narrowly-defined categories or styles, suggesting their use in selecting funds for inclusion in a multi-fund portfolio. I argued that for such a purpose, neither the RAR measure nor the excess return Sharpe Ratio would be appropriate, suggesting instead a measure based on differential returns relative to a benchmark appropriate for the fund's category or style. For this purpose, I concluded, a "selection Sharpe Ratio" (now usually called an *information ratio*) would be far more appropriate.

In 2002 Morningstar replaced the bilinear risk measure described in this paper with one that, according to their web site, is based on expected utility theory, taking all returns into account with more emphasis on downward variation. In preparing this commentary I was unable to easily find details. Nonetheless, I continue to wonder why one would wish to choose a fund from a category designed to constitute a portion of an overall portfolio using a criterion designed to maximize the expectation of a utility function on the assumption that the fund constituted the investor's total portfolio. In any event, no single utility function is likely to reflect the preferences of all the members of the investment community. There may be a case for using Morningstar's current measure rather than an information ratio but I have not seen it.

4-6 "Budgeting and Monitoring Pension Fund Risk," *Financial Analysts' Journal*, Vol. 58, No. 5 (September/October 2002), 74–86.

This paper was intended to provide both the details and economic interpretation of methods for budgeting and monitoring pension fund risk. At the time I wrote it, commercial firms were beginning to offer services designed to perform these tasks, often for considerable sums. The underlying procedures had grown from simpler methods designed to allocate funds among investments with uncorrelated risks. In such cases, portfolio variance can be decomposed into a set of additive terms, each equal to the square of the portion invested times its variance. With these assumptions, one could create "risk budgets" and compute "risk contributions". Moreover, the contribution of any portion of the portfolio could easily be changed by changing its risk, the amount of funds invested, or both. However, none of these relationships applied directly to portfolios whose components were correlated with one another. Vendors had dealt with this computationally, but the original terminology persisted and it appeared that some of those in charge of pension funds failed to understand the economics involved and/or the ways in which such systems could be utilized effectively. My goal was to show how the calculations could correctly be performed, interpreted and used. Moreover, I wanted to describe the manner in which the approach could be generalized to include the effects of liabilities.

The key insight is that in this setting the relevant measure for a portfolio component is its "marginal risk contribution", equal to twice its covariance with the overall portfolio, as shown in equation (2). It follows that under standard assumptions the first order conditions for portfolio optimality require that expected returns be proportional to these amounts, as shown in equation (7b). To emphasize the economic relevance of the results, I used the term "Implied Excess Return" which, despite my subsequent efforts, failed to catch on in the industry.

The paper's considerable discussion of practical aspects associated with the implementation of these approaches grew out of my work with some large pension and endowment funds. I continued to apply the procedures in the paper every quarter from 2002 through 2010. Unfortunately, I did so based solely on asset risks, since in no case did I have access to liability values based on market interest rates. Perhaps the most dramatic results from these analyses were the relatively small active management "alpha" values implied by the funds' actual holdings, as shown for an actual fund (XYZ) in Tables 6 and 7. This was not atypical for a large U.S, pension fund at the time and remains true for many today. Despite the allocation of considerable resources and expenditures to the selection of active managers, most funds choose to diversify extensively as if they expected very little more than the returns from the asset classes in which the managers invest. As the paper put it, "A high degree of diversification is consistent with relatively low expectations concerning managers' ability to add value." Nonetheless, those in charge of such funds often state that they expect their non-indexed managers to add between 200 and

400 basis points per year to performance via active management — an inconsistency that remains difficult to explain.

Reprinted from THE JOURNAL OF BUSINESS OF THE UNIVERSITY OF CHICAGO
Vol. XXXIX, No. 1, Part II, January 1966

MUTUAL FUND PERFORMANCE*

WILLIAM F. SHARPE†

I. INTRODUCTION

WITHIN the last few years considerable progress has been made in three closely related areas—the theory of portfolio selection,[1] the theory of the pricing of capital assets under conditions of risk,[2] and the general behavior of stock-market prices.[3] Results obtained in all three areas are relevant for evaluating mutual fund performance. Unfortunately, few of the studies of mutual funds have taken advantage of the substantial backlog of theoretical and empirical material made available by recent studies in these related areas. However, one paper pointing the direction for future studies of mutual fund performance has appeared. Drawing on results obtained in the field of portfolio analysis, Jack L. Treynor has suggested a new predictor of mutual fund performance[4]—one that differs from virtually all those used previously by incorporating the volatility of a fund's return in a simple yet meaningful manner.

This paper attempts to extend Treynor's work by subjecting his proposed measure to empirical test in order to evaluate its predictive ability. But we will also attempt to do something more—to make explicit the relationships between recent developments in capital theory and alternative models of mutual fund performance and to subject these alternative models to empirical test.

II. IMPLICATIONS OF RECENT DEVELOPMENTS IN CAPITAL THEORY

A. PORTFOLIO ANALYSIS THEORY[5]

The theory of portfolio analysis is essentially normative; it describes efficient techniques for selecting portfolios on the basis of predictions about the performance of individual securities. The key element in the portfolio analyst's view of the world is his emphasis on both expected return and risk. The selection of a preferred combination of risk and expected return must, in the final analysis, depend on the preferences of the investor and cannot be made solely by the tech-

* I am grateful to Norman H. Jones, of the RAND Corporation, and Eugene F. Fama, of the University of Chicago, for helpful comments and suggestions.

† Associate professor of economics and operations research, University of Washington, and consultant, the RAND Corporation. Any views expressed in this paper are those of the author. They should not be interpreted as reflecting the views of the RAND Corporation or the official opinion or policy of any of its governmental or private research sponsors.

[1] The original work in the field was that of H. Markowitz; see his "Portfolio Selection," *Journal of Finance*, XII (March, 1952), 71–91, or the subsequent expanded version, *Portfolio Selection, Efficient Diversification of Investments* (New York: John Wiley & Sons, 1959). For extensions see my "A Simplified Model for Portfolio Analysis," *Management Science*, IX (January, 1963), 277–93, and Eugene F. Fama, "Portfolio Analysis in a Stable Paretian Market," *Management Science*, XI (January, 1965), 404–19.

[2] See, e.g., my "Capital Asset Prices: A Theory of Market Equilibrium under Conditions of Risk," *Journal of Finance*, XIX (September, 1964), 425–42.

[3] For a summary of this work see Eugene F. Fama, "The Behavior of Stock-Market Prices," *Journal of Business*, XXXVIII (January, 1965), 34–105.

[4] "How To Rate Management of Investment Funds," *Harvard Business Review*, XLIII (January–February, 1965), 63–75.

[5] The material in this section is based on the references given in n. 1.

nician. However, the technician can (and should) attempt to find *efficient* portfolios—those promising the greatest expected return for any given degree of risk. The *portfolio analyst's* tasks are thus (1) translating predictions about security performance into predictions of portfolio performance, and (2) selecting from among the large number of possible portfolios those that are efficient. The *security analyst's* task is to provide the required predictions of security performance (including the interrelationships among the performances of securities). The *investor's* task is to select from among the efficient portfolios the one that he considers most desirable, based on his particular feelings regarding risk and expected return.

What tasks are implied for the mutual fund by this view of the investment process? Certainly those of security analysis and portfolio analysis. The emphasis in mutual fund advertising on diversification and the search for incorrectly priced securities reflects the importance accorded these aspects of the process. Portfolio analysis theory, unfortunately, does not make clear the manner in which the third function should be performed. A mutual fund cannot practically determine the preference patterns of its investors directly. Even if it could, there might be substantial differences among them. The process must work in the other direction, with the mutual fund management selecting an attitude toward risk and expected return and then inviting investors with similar preferences to purchase shares in the fund. At one extreme, the fund might attempt to describe an entire pattern of relative preference for expected return vis-à-vis risk (i.e., a pattern of indifference curves). A much more likely method, and one that seems to be followed in practice, involves merely a description of the general degree of risk planned for the fund's portfolio; the fund then simply attempts to select the efficient portfolio for that degree of risk (i.e., the one with the greatest expected return).

Portfolio analysis theory per se makes no assumptions about the pattern of security prices or the skill of investment managers. Thus few implications can be drawn concerning the results obtained by different mutual funds. Performance ex post might vary in two respects. First, different funds could exhibit different degrees of variability in return, due either to conscious selection of different degrees of risk or to erroneous predictions of the risk inherent in particular portfolios. Second, funds holding portfolios with similar variability in return might exhibit major differences in average return, due to the inability of some managers to select incorrectly priced securities and/or to diversify their holdings properly. In short, if sound mutual fund management requires the selection of incorrectly priced securities, effective diversification, and the selection of a portfolio in the chosen risk class, there is ample room for major and persisting differences in the performance of different funds.

B. THE BEHAVIOR OF STOCK-MARKET PRICES[6]

Recent work on the general behavior of stock-market prices has raised serious questions concerning the importance of one of the functions of mutual fund management. The theory of random walks asserts that the past behavior of a security's price is of no value in predicting its future price. The impressive evidence supporting this theory suggest that it

[6] The material in this section is based on Fama's "The Behavior of Stock-Market Prices," *op. cit.*

may be very difficult (and very expensive) to detect securities that are incorrectly priced. If so, it is not because security analysts are not doing their job properly, but because they are doing it very well. However, if this is the case, it may not pay the manager of a particular fund to devote extensive resources to the search for incorrectly priced securities; and the fund that does so may provide its investors a poorer net performance (after costs) than one that does not.

Under these conditions, what are the tasks of the mutual fund? Broadly defined, they still include security analysis, portfolio analysis, and the selection of a portfolio in the desired risk class. But the emphasis is changed. Security analysis is directed more toward evaluating the interrelationships among securities—the extent to which returns are correlated. And portfolio analysis is concerned primarily with diversification and the selection of a portfolio of the desired risk. In a perfect capital market, any properly diversified portfolio will be efficient; the mutual fund manager must select from among alternative diversified portfolios the one with the appropriate degree of risk.

Strictly speaking, the implications of this view of the world for mutual fund performance do not differ from those of the theory of portfolio analysis. Ex post, funds can be expected to exhibit differences in variability of return, due to intentional or unintentional selection of different risk classes. And the portfolios of some funds may be more efficient than others (i.e., give greater average return at the same level of variability) if managers differ in their ability to diversify effectively. However, the likelihood that persistent differences in efficiency will occur is greatly reduced. Recent work has shown that the task of diversification may be much simpler than formerly supposed, requiring only the spreading of holdings among standard industrial classes.[7] If so, most funds are likely to hold portfolios that are efficient ex ante. Any differences in efficiency ex post are thus probably transitory. The only basis for persistently inferior performance would be the continued expenditure of large amounts of a fund's assets on the relatively fruitless search for incorrectly valued securities.

C. THE THEORY OF CAPITAL-ASSET PRICES UNDER CONDITIONS OF RISK

Empirical work on the behavior of stock-market prices supports the view that the market responds very rapidly to new information affecting the value of securities. A natural reaction to these results is the construction of a model of a perfectly informed market in which each participant used his information in the manner suggested by portfolio analysis theory. Such an approach has been described elsewhere;[8] only the major features will be given here.

The predicted performance of a portfolio is described with two measures: the expected rate of return (E_i) and the predicted variability or risk, expressed as the standard deviation of return (σ_i). All investors are assumed to be able to invest funds at a common risk-free interest rate and to borrow funds at the same rate (at least to the desired extent). At any point of time, all investors share the same predictions concerning the future performance of securities (and thus portfolios). Under these conditions all ef-

[7] See Benjamin F. King, "Market and Industry Factors in Stock Price Behavior," *Journal of Business*, XXXIX, No. 1, Part II (Supplement, January, 1966).

[8] In my "Capital Asset Prices . . . ," *op. cit.*

ficient portfolios will fall along a straight line of the form[9]

$$E_i = p + b\sigma_i ,$$

where p is the pure (riskless) interest rate and b is the risk premium. Since investors are assumed to be risk-averse, b will be positive.

These results follow immediately from a relationship first described by James Tobin.[10] If an investor can borrow or lend at some riskless interest rate p and/or invest in a portfolio with predicted performance (E_i, σ_i), then by allocating his funds between the portfolio and borrowing or lending he can attain any point on the line

$$E = p + \left(\frac{E_i - p}{\sigma_i}\right) \sigma .$$

Any portfolio will thus give rise to a complete (linear) boundary of E,σ combinations. The best portfolio will be the one giving the best boundary; clearly it is the one for which $(E_i - p)/\sigma_i$ is the greatest. If more than one portfolio is to be efficient, all must lie along a common line and give identical values of this ratio.

The capital-market model described here deals with predictions of future performance. Since the predictions cannot be obtained in any satisfactory manner, the model cannot be tested directly. Instead, ex post values must be used—the average rate of return of a portfolio must be substituted for its expected rate of return, and the actual standard deviation of its rate of return for its predicted risk. We denote these measures by A_i and V_i (the latter for variability).

The capital-market model implies that ex post values for A_i and V_i for efficient portfolios should lie along a straight line, with higher values of V_i associated with higher values of A_i. Because there is risk in the stock market, the points will not lie precisely along such a line, even if the model is completely correct. But the relationship should be present, visible, and statistically significant.

The implications of this model for mutual fund performance are relatively straightforward. If all funds hold properly diversified portfolios and spend the appropriate amount for analysis and administration, they should provide rates of return giving A_i, V_i values lying generally along a straight line. Points that diverge from the underlying relationship should reflect only transitory effects and not persistent differences in performance. On the other hand, if some funds fail to diversify properly, or spend too much on research and/or administration, they will persistently give rates of return yielding inferior A_i, V_i values. Their performance will be poorer and can be expected to remain so.

III. PERFORMANCE OF 34 OPEN-END MUTUAL FUNDS, 1954–63

To test some of the implications drawn in the previous section, the annual rates of return for thirty-four open-end mutual funds[11] during the period 1954–63 were analyzed in the manner described above. The annual rate of return for a fund is based on the sum of dividend payments, capital gains distributions, and changes in net asset value; it is thus a measure of *net* performance—gross yield less the expenses of management and administration. The latter range from 0.25 per

[9] By definition, for inefficient portfolios: $E_i < p + b\sigma_i$.

[10] In his "Liquidity Preference as Behavior towards Risk," *Review of Economic Studies*, XXV (February, 1958), 65–86.

[11] The funds used for this and all subsequent analyses were those for which annual rates of return were given by Weisenberger for at least the last 20 years. All data are from Arthur Weisenberger & Co., *Investment Companies* (1953, 1962, 1964 eds.).

cent of net assets per year to 1.5 per cent per year. Most funds also charge an initial fee of approximately 8.5 per cent for selling costs when shares are purchased; annual rates of return are *not* net of such costs.

The average annual rate of return (A_i) and the standard deviation of annual rate of return (V_i) for each fund are shown in Figure 1; the values are listed in Table 1. The relationship predicted by the theory of capital asset prices is clearly present—funds with large average returns typically exhibit greater variability than those with small average returns. Moreover, the relationship is approximately linear and significant.[12] However, there are differences in efficiency; a number of funds are actually dominated (i.e., some other fund provided both a greater value of A_i and a smaller value of V_i). To analyze the differences, we need a single measure of performance; once such a measure is specified, any persistent differences can be investigated by testing alternative measures for predicting performance.

An intuitively appealing and theoretically meaningful measure of performance is easily derived from the Tobin effect. With substitution of the ex post measures (A and V) for the ex ante measures (E and σ), the formula described in Section II becomes

$$A = p + \left[\frac{A_i - p}{V_i}\right] V .$$

By investing in fund i and borrowing or lending at the riskless rate p, an investor could have attained any point along the line given by this formula. In 1953 it was possible to purchase a ten-year U.S. government bond at a price that would have guaranteed a return of slightly less than 3 per cent if held to maturity. Using 3 per cent as the estimate of p for the period, Boston Fund, shown by point Y in Figure 1, plus borrowing or lending could have provided any combination of average return and variability lying along line PYZ. Incorporated Investors, shown by point Q, could have provided any combination lying along line PQ. Clearly the former is better than the latter, since for *any* level of risk it offered a greater average return. Indeed, the steepness[13] of the line associated with a fund provides a useful measure of performance—one that incorporates both risk and average return. We define this as the reward-to-variability ratio: For Boston Fund the ratio is equal to the distance XP on Figure 1 divided by the distance XY. The larger the ratio, the better the performance.

An alternative interpretation of the ratio gives rise to the name—reward-to-variability ratio (R/V). The numerator shows the difference between the fund's average annual return and the pure interest rate; it is thus the *reward* provided the investor for bearing risk. The denominator measures the standard deviation of the annual rate of return; it shows the amount of risk actually borne. The ratio is thus the reward per unit of variability.

The final column of Table 1 shows the values of the R/V ratio for the thirty-four funds. They vary considerably—from almost 0.78 (the Boston Fund) to slightly over 0.43 (Incorporated Investors). Those who view the market as nearly perfect and managers as good diversifiers would argue that the differ-

[12] The results of statistical tests on these data are reported in my "Risk Aversion in the Stock Market: Some Empirical Evidence," *Journal of Finance*, September, 1965, pp. 416–22.

[13] The contangent of the angle made by the line with the horizontal axis is equal to the R/V ratio. Putting it another way, the reciprocal of the slope of the line (dA/dV) equals the R/V ratio.

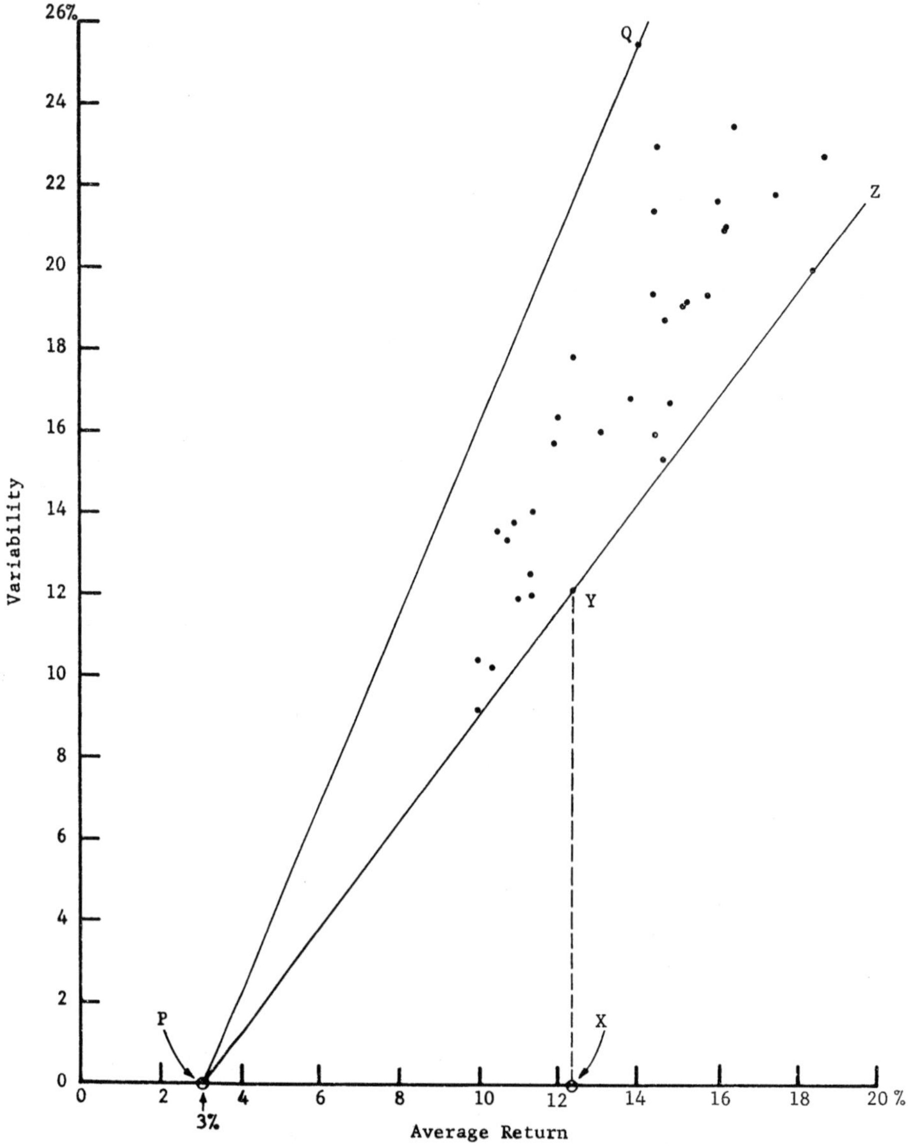

FIG. 1.—Average return and variability, 34 open-end mutual funds, 1954–63

ences are either transitory or due to excessive expenditures by some funds. Others would argue that the differences are persistent and can be attributed (at least partially) to differences in management skill. The remainder of this paper attempts to test these alternative explanations, using pre-1954 data to predict performance from 1954 to 1963, and in the tradition of empirical studies of mutual funds, provides comparisons with the performance of the securities used to compute the Dow-Jones Industrial Average.

IV. THE PERSISTENCE OF DIFFERENCES IN PERFORMANCE

To determine the extent to which differences in performance continue through time, the returns from the thirty-four funds during the period 1944–53 were used to compute R/V ratios for the decade preceding the one previously investigated.[14] The funds were ranked in each

[14] Since the long-term interest rate during this period was somewhat lower than that prevailing in the latter period, a pure interest rate of 2.5 per cent was used in the calculations (this was approximately the yield on a ten-year U.S. government bond in

TABLE 1

PERFORMANCE OF 34 MUTUAL FUNDS, 1954–63

Mutual Fund	Average Annual Return (Per Cent)	Variability of Annual Return (Per Cent)	Reward-to-Variability Ratio (R/V)*
Affiliated Fund	14.6	15.3	0.75896
American Business Shares	10.0	9.2	.75876
Axe-Houghton, Fund A	10.5	13.5	.55551
Axe-Houghton, Fund B	12.0	16.3	.55183
Axe-Houghton, Stock Fund	11.9	15.6	.56991
Boston Fund	12.4	12.1	.77842
Broad Street Investing	14.8	16.8	.70329
Bullock Fund	15.7	19.3	.65845
Commonwealth Investment Company	10.9	13.7	.57841
Delaware Fund	14.4	21.4	.53253
Dividend Shares	14.4	15.9	.71807
Eaton and Howard, Balanced Fund	11.0	11.9	.67399
Eaton and Howard, Stock Fund	15.2	19.2	.63486
Equity Fund	14.6	18.7	.61902
Fidelity Fund	16.4	23.5	.57020
Financial Industrial Fund	14.5	23.0	.49971
Fundamental Investors	16.0	21.7	.59894
Group Securities, Common Stock Fund	15.1	19.1	.63316
Group Securities, Fully Administered Fund	11.4	14.1	.59490
Incorporated Investors	14.0	25.5	.43116
Investment Company of America	17.4	21.8	.66169
Investors Mutual	11.3	12.5	.66451
Loomis-Sales Mutual Fund	10.0	10.4	.67358
Massachusetts Investors Trust	16.2	20.8	.63398
Massachusetts Investors—Growth Stock	18.6	22.7	.68687
National Investors Corporation	18.3	19.9	.76798
National Securities—Income Series	12.4	17.8	.52950
New England Fund	10.4	10.2	.72703
Putnam Fund of Boston	13.1	16.0	.63222
Scudder, Stevens & Clark Balanced Fund	10.7	13.3	.57893
Selected American Shares	14.4	19.4	.58788
United Funds—Income Fund	16.1	20.9	.62698
Wellington Fund	11.3	12.0	.69057
Wisconsin Fund	13.8	16.9	0.64091

* R/V ratio = (average return — 3.0 per cent)/variability. The ratios shown were computed from original data and thus differ slightly from the ratios obtained from the rounded data shown in the table.

period, from 1—the fund with the highest (best) R/V ratio, to 34—the fund with the lowest (worst) R/V ratio. Figure 2 plots the rankings in the two periods. Although the relationship is far from perfect, there is a general upward trend, suggesting that funds ranking low in the early period tend to rank low in the later period, while those ranking high in the early period tend to rank high in the later period. The value of Spearman's rank correlation coefficient (+.360) bears this out[15] as does the count of points in the four quadrants (shown in the lower

1943). Although different assumptions regarding the pure interest rates in the two periods would substantially affect the rankings of individual funds, the relative predictive ability of the measures considered in this paper is not significantly affected by altering the assumed rates over a considerable range.

[15] The standard error for the sample size used in this and all subsequent calculations is 0.174.

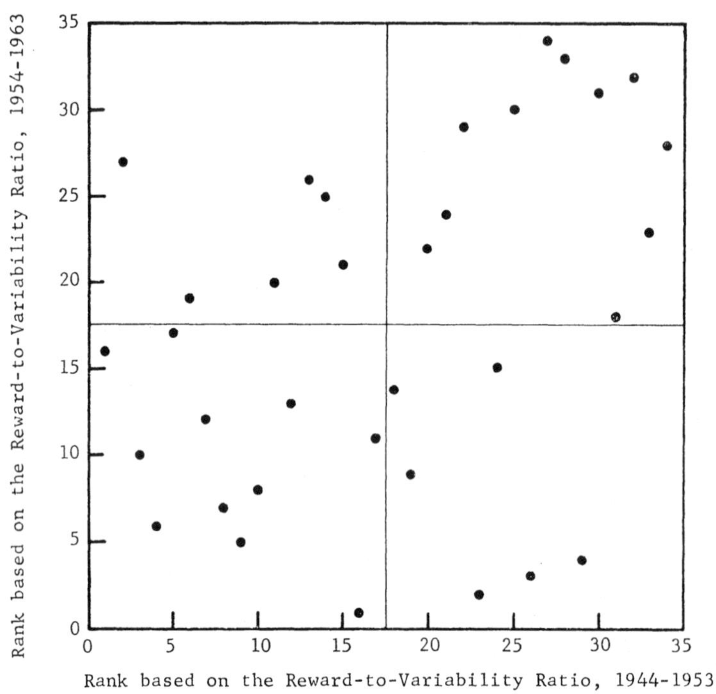

Rank correlation coefficient = .360

	best	worst
worst	6	11
best	11	6

FIG. 2.—Predictions based on the reward-to-variability ratio

portion of the figure). Put rather crudely, the latter shows that an investor selecting one of the seventeen best funds in the first period would have an 11:6 chance of holding one of the seventeen best in the second period. Conversely, if he had selected one of the seventeen worst in the first period he would have an 11:6 chance of holding one of the seventeen worst in the second period. Simple regression analysis using the actual values of the R/V ratios gives similar results: the correlation coefficient is +.3157 and the t-value for the slope coefficient +1.88.

These results show that differences in performance can be predicted, although imperfectly. However, they do not indicate the sources of the differences. Equally important, there is no assurance that past performance is the best predictor of future performance. We consider next the alternative measure proposed by Treynor.

V. THE TREYNOR INDEX

In a perfect capital market no securities would be incorrectly priced. Thus one function of the mutual fund (finding such securities) would be eliminated, leaving only the tasks of diversification and selecting the appropriate risk class. Moreover, under such conditions it has been shown[16] that all truly diversified portfolios will move with the over-all market, giving high returns when the market in general provides high returns and low returns when the market provides low returns. The data bear out this hypothesis. During the period 1954–63, almost 90 per cent of the variance of the return on the typical fund in our sample was due to its comovement with the return on the thirty securities used to compute the Dow-Jones Industrial Average· moreover, as shown in Figure 3, the percentage was quite similar for most of the thirty-four funds. Treynor has taken advantage of this relationship by using the *volatility* of a fund as a measure of its risk instead of the total *variability* used in the R/V ratio. Since the returns on all diversified portfolios move with the market, the extent to which changes in the market are reflected in changes in a fund's rate of return can stand as a good measure of the total variability of the fund's return over time. By observing this relationship over some past period, a reasonably good estimate of volatility—the change in the rate of return on a fund associated with a 1 per cent change in the rate of return on, say, the Dow-Jones portfolio—can be obtained. We will use B_i to represent this value for the ith fund.[17]

The measure that we will term the Treynor Index (TI) can be obtained by simply substituting volatility for variability in the formula for the R/V ratio:

$$TI = \frac{A_i - p}{B_i}.$$

Stated in this manner, the relationship between the two measures is clear. And the extent of the contribution of volatility to over-all variability makes the ranking of funds on the basis of the Treynor Index very close to that based on the R/V ratio. Figure 4 shows the rankings using the two measures for the period 1954–63. Since the mutual funds in our sample all hold highly diversified portfolios, the similarity of the rankings is not surprising. And the cost of using the Treynor Index as a measure of past

[16] In my "Capital Asset Prices . . . ," *op. cit.*

[17] To be consistent with the notation in my "A Simplified Model for Portfolio Analysis," *op. cit.*

performance is relatively slight[18] since it mirrors the R/V ratio quite well. However, if some relatively undiversified funds (or more likely, privately held portfolios) had been included, the results could have been significantly different, since the Treynor Index cannot capture the portion of variability that is due to lack of diversification. For this reason it is an inferior measure of *past* performance. But for this reason it may be a superior measure for predicting *future* performance.

If mutual funds hold well-diversified portfolios, any major discrepancies between the variability of their returns and that portion due to movements in the market are likely to be due to transitory effects. By concentrating on the systematic part of a fund's variability—that is, its volatility—we can avoid paying attention to these transitory effects and

[18] Treynor apparently intended that his index be used both for measuring a fund's performance after the fact and for predicting its performance in the future: "When one talks about the historical performance pattern of a fund, he is looking at the past; but when he considers the preferences of individual investors and their choices among funds, he is talking about their appraisal of the future. We shall continue to talk about the performance of funds in terms of historical performance patterns, even though actual investor choices among funds are necessarily based on expectations regarding future performance patterns. The implication is that a good historical performance pattern is one which, if continued into the future, would cause investors to prefer it to others" (Treynor, *op. cit.*, p. 67).

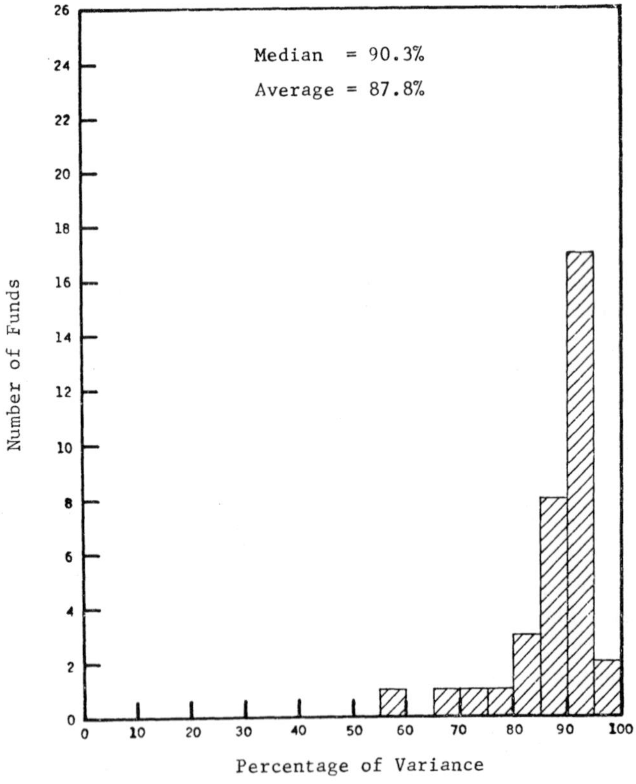

FIG. 3.—Percentage of variance due to comovement with the Dow-Jones Industrial Average, 34 open-end mutual funds, 1954–63.

concern ourselves with the more permanent relationships. Thus, given some reasonable assurance that a fund will perform its diversification function well, the Treynor Index may provide better predictions of future performance than the *R*/*V* ratio.

As Figure 5 shows, the data bear out this suspicion. Using the rankings of funds based on the Treynor Index computed from 1944–53 data to predict rankings based on the performance (measured by the *R*/*V* ratio) in the subsequent ten years gives somewhat better results than those obtained before. The odds of remaining in the selected half are now 12 to 5 (instead of 11 to 6) and the rank correlation coefficient is substantially higher—.454 instead of .360. Simple regression using actual values gives similar results—the correlation coefficient is +.4008 and the *t*-value for the slope co-

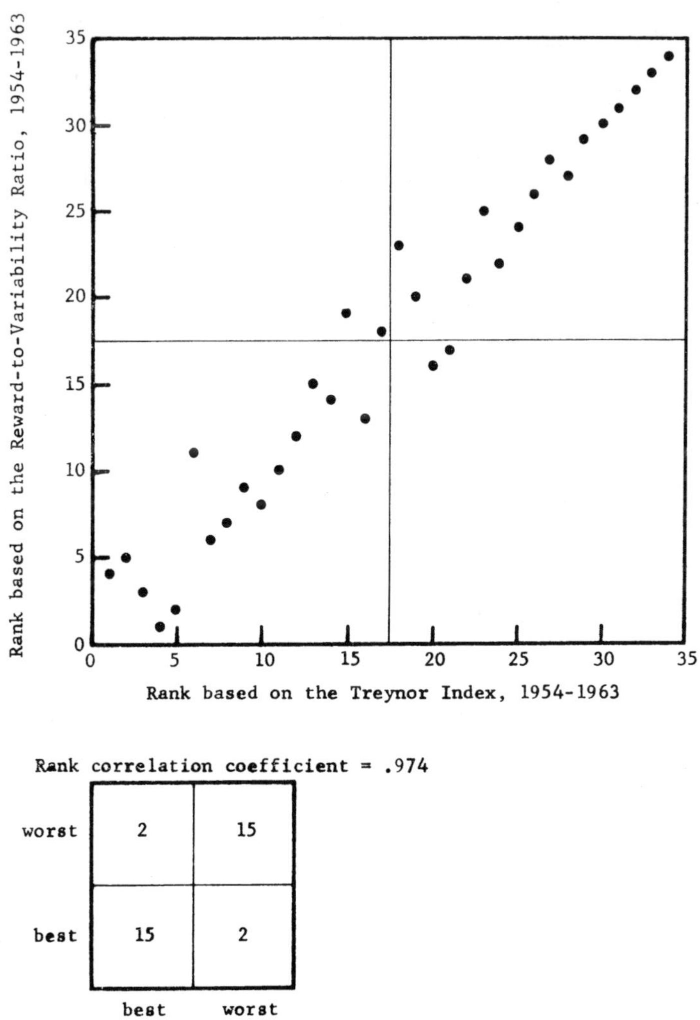

FIG. 4.—Correlation between ranks, reward-to-variability ratio versus Treynor Index

efficient +2.47. While the differences between these results and those based on the R/V ratio are far from overwhelming, the Treynor Index does appear to be the better predictor.

Before turning to other methods for predicting performance, the relationship between the measure we have termed the Treynor Index and that suggested by Treynor needs to be clarified. Our measure (TI) is similar in form to the R/V ratio. One measure proposed by Treynor[19] was simply the negative of ours:

$$\text{Slope angle} = -TI.$$

This form has a major advantage, since it can be transformed into a rather different quantity—the rate of return on a market portfolio (e.g., the Dow-Jones portfolio) that would cause the fund in

[19] Described on p. 69 in Treynor, *op. cit.*:

$$\text{tangent } \alpha = \frac{(\mu - \mu^*)}{\sigma}.$$

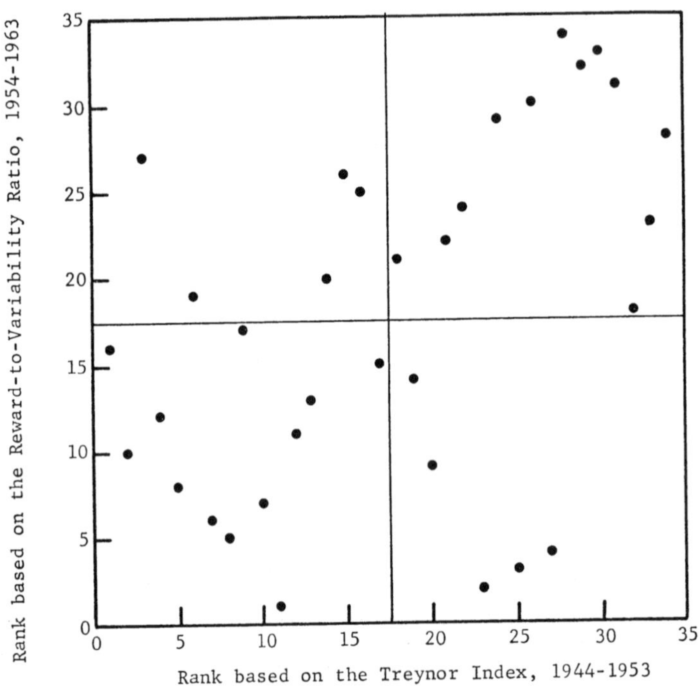

Rank correlation coefficient = .454

	best	worst
worst	5	12
best	12	5

Fig. 5.—Predictions based on the Treynor Index

question to provide a rate of return equal to the pure interest rate.[20] This substitute measure has considerable intuitive appeal. Moreover, if predictions are to be made subjectively (using some judgment) rather than objectively (solely on the basis of historical data), the advantages of this alternative index are substantial. For the purposes of this paper, however, such considerations are relatively unimportant, since we are dealing only with objective methods of prediction. Accordingly we will continue to state the Treynor Index in the form directly comparable to the R/V ratio.

[20] The original index ("*SA*" for slope angle) is

$$SA_i = -TI_i = -\left(\frac{A_i - p}{B_i}\right) = \frac{p - A_i}{B_i}.$$

If the relationship between the rate of return on the fund (r_i) and that on the Dow-Jones portfolio (D) is

$$r_i = a_i + B_i D\,,$$

then the average return on the fund is related to that on the Dow-Jones portfolio (D) by

$$A_i = a_i + B_i D\,.$$

Thus

$$SA_i = \frac{p - A_i}{B_i} = \frac{p - (a_i + B_i D)}{B_i}$$

$$= \left(\frac{p - a_i}{B_i}\right) - D\,.$$

D_i^*—the return on the Dow-Jones portfolio required to make the return on the fund equal to the pure interest rate (p) is

$$p = r_i = a_i + B_i D_i^*\,, \qquad D_i^* = \frac{p - a_i}{B_i}.$$

Therefore,

$$SA_i = D_i^* - \bar{D}\,.$$

Clearly, if the slope angle for one fund is higher than that of another, the return on the Dow-Jones required to make it yield the pure interest rate will be also. Since D_i^* is simply the slope angle plus a constant ($\bar{D}$), both measures will give the same ranking. The advantage of using D_i^* lies in its intuitive appeal and the fact that if future values are being estimated directly, no prediction about market performance is required. The insensitivity of Treynor's rankings (using either of the two measures) to predictions about market behavior follows directly from his assumption that variability is due *only* to the response of the fund's return to changes in the market. If there is another source of variability, the rankings of funds (using the R/V ratio) will depend to some extent on the behavior of the market.

VI. EXPENSE RATIOS AND SIZE

Past performance appears to provide a basis for predicting future performance, especially when measured with the Treynor Index. But this does not necessarily imply that differences in performance are due to differences in management skill. The high correlation among mutual fund rates of return suggests that most accomplish the task of diversification rather well. Differences in performance are thus likely to be due to either differences in the ability of management to find incorrectly priced securities or to differences in expense ratios. If the market is very efficient, the funds spending the least should show the best (net) performance. If it is not, funds devoting more resources to management may gain enough to more than offset the increased expenditure and thus show better net performance. Intimately related with such considerations is the impact of size. A fund with substantial assets can obtain a given level of security analysis by spending a smaller percentage of its income than can a smaller fund; alternatively, by spending the same percentage it can obtain more (and/or better) analysis. On the other hand, more analysis may be required for a large fund than for a small one. In any event, both influences should be considered.

Figure 6 shows the relationship between the expenses incurred by the thirty-four funds and their performance. Since we are concerned with prediction, the funds were ranked on the basis of the ratio of expenses to net assets during 1953 (needless to say, expense ratios changed somewhat during the subsequent ten years). Expenses ranged from 0.27 per cent of net assets (rank 1) to 1.49 per cent of net assets (rank 34).

The results tend to support the cynics: good performance is associated with low expense ratios. One of our summary measures (the rank correlation coefficient)[21] suggests that expense ratios provide somewhat better predictions than the Treynor Index; another suggests that the two are equally good (the odds of remaining in the selected half are 12 to 5 in both cases). The third suggests that the expense ratio is a slightly poorer predictor than the Treynor Index: Simple regression using actual values gave a

[21] Some of the funds had equal expense ratios (to the accuracy of two decimal places, as computed by Weisenberger). In such cases ranks were assigned alphabetically. For this reason the rank correlation coefficient is not as trustworthy as those computed for the other comparisons.

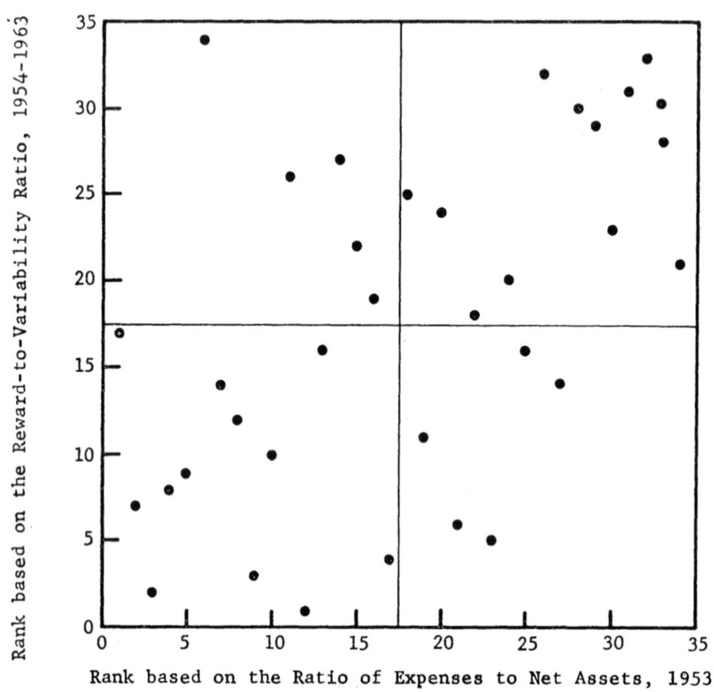

Rank correlation coefficient = .505

	lowest	highest
worst	5	12
best	12	5

FIG. 6.—Predictions based on the ratio of expenses to net assets

correlation coefficient of −.3746 (the Treynor Index gave +.4008) with a *t*-value of −.229 (instead of +2.47). Selecting a fund with a low ratio of expense to net assets may not be as foolish as some have suggested.

Figure 7 provides information concerning the predictive ability of the amount of a fund's assets. Size, measured by net asset value at the end of 1953, ranged from $522 million (rank 1) to $5.26 million (rank 34). Although the data show some correlation—with the larger funds exhibiting somewhat better performance—the relationship is marginal at best. This is borne out by the correlation coefficient based on actual values; it is +.1523, with a *t*-value of +0.87.

Multiple correlations, using actual values of the variables, gave the results shown in Table 2. The extremely small *t*-values for the slope coefficients relating

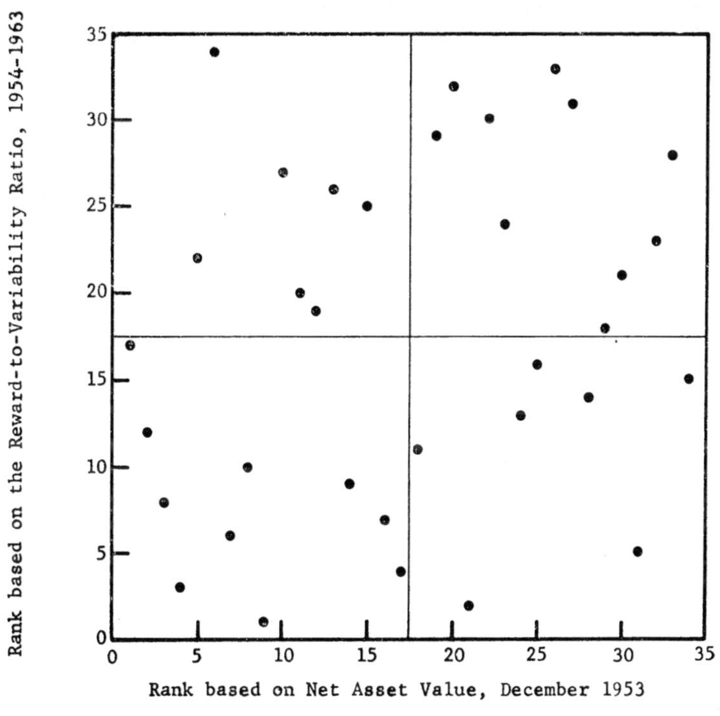

Rank correlation coefficient = .234

worst	7	10
best	10	7
	largest	smallest

FIG. 7.—Predictions based on size

R/V ratios to size, plus the fact that the signs differ from case to case, support the assertion that size per se is an unimportant factor in predicting future performance. The t-values for the Treynor Index and the exprense ratio support the assertion that both are useful for such predictions (although neither is highly significant).

Unfortunately, the results do not provide strong confirmation for either of the views of mutual fund management described in the earlier sections of this paper. Expense ratios account for a substantial portion of the differences in performance, but so does another measure (the Treynor Index). Thus differences in management skill may be important. However, one reservation is in order. Expense ratios as reported do not include all expenses; brokers' fees are omitted. Thus the expense ratio does not capture all the differences in expenses among funds. It is entirely possible that funds with performance superior to that predicted by the traditional expense ratio engage in little trading, thereby minimizing brokerage expense. It was not feasible to attempt to measure total expense ratios for this study; had such ratios been used, a larger portion of the difference in performance might have been explained in this manner, and the apparent differences in management skill might have been smaller. Clearly, more work is needed before the traditional view of the importance of the search for incorrectly priced securities can be accepted.

TABLE 2

DEPENDENT VARIABLE: R/V RATIO, 1953–63

Multiple Correlation Coefficients	t-Values for Slope Coefficients		
	Treynor Index, 1944–53	Expense/ NAV 1953	Size (NAV) Dec. 1953
.4633	+1.67	−1.43	−0.46
.4572	+1.64	−1.38	......
.4015	+2.26	......	+ .15
.3767	......	−2.07	−0.24

VII. THE RELATIVE RISK OF MUTUAL FUNDS

All the calculations presented thus far deal with a measure of performance (the R/V ratio) that disregards risk per se, concentrating instead on the relationship between the reward obtained from the fund and the risk actually experienced. As shown earlier, the investor should be most concerned with this relationship, if he can arrange his other commitments (either by borrowing additional funds or by investing in some riskless security) to complement the risk inherent in a particular fund in any manner he desires. However, to do this he must have some idea of the variability the fund will actually experience. If mutual fund managers do not perform the second of the three tasks we have outlined (staying in a selected risk class), investors will find it difficult to arrange their over-all holdings in the most desirable manner. Holders of mutual fund shares presumably expect that funds will show reasonable consistency over time with regard to the variability of returns.

Figure 8 provides some evidence on this point. The funds were ranked in each of the two periods studied (1944–53 and 1954–63) on the basis of variability —rank 1 indicating the smallest amount and rank 34 the largest. A reasonable amount of consistency between periods is evident, but a number of major shifts appear.[22] In some cases this may have been due to announced changes in man-

[22] Simple regression analysis using actual values gave a correlation coefficient of +.4518 and a t-value of +2.86.

agement philosophy; in others it was probably inadvertent. Whatever the cause, the prevalence of such shifts in our sample is likely to disappoint some investors. On the other hand, there is no well-defined standard against which the results can be compared; given the difficulties involved,[23] one might reasonably argue that the data show that mutual fund managers fulfil remarkably well the obligation to stay within their selected risk classes.

VIII. MUTUAL FUNDS VERSUS THE DOW-JONES INDUSTRIAL AVERAGE

We have dealt at length with comparisons among mutual funds but have not

[23] In "The Variation of Certain Speculative Prices," *Journal of Business*, XXXVI (October, 1963), 394–419, B. Mandelbrot has shown that predicting the variability of the changes in security prices is very difficult indeed. Presumably the law of large numbers cannot be relied upon to eliminate enough of the difficulty to make predictions of variability of the return on portfolios relatively simple.

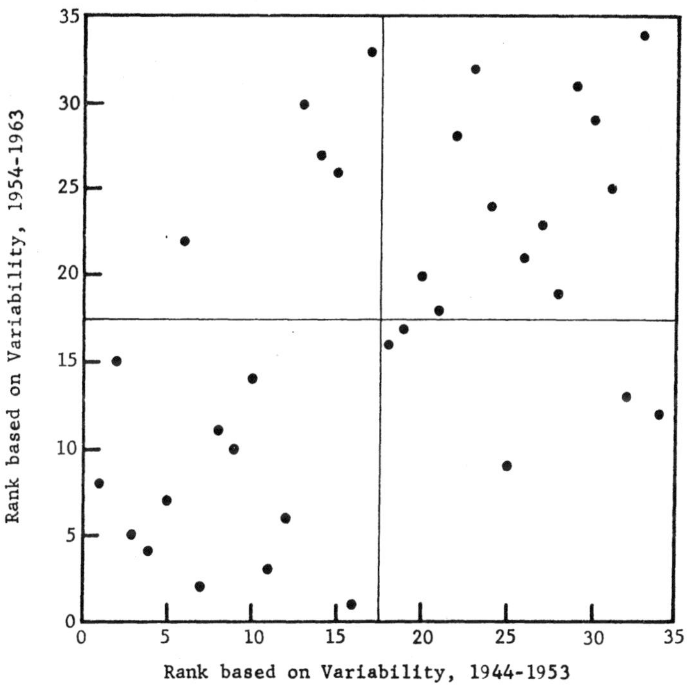

Rank correlation coefficient = .528

largest	5	12
smallest	12	5
	smallest	largest

FIG. 8.—Consistency of risk class

considered an alternative strategy—investing directly in a reasonably diversified group of securities. To investigate such an alternative we must specify the portfolio to be held; following tradition, the thirty securities used to compute the Dow-Jones Industrial Average will be used.

When calculating the returns from the Dow Jones portfolio, no costs (brokerage, management, or administrative) are deducted. To some extent this overstates the performance available from such a direct investment. On the other hand, the initial selling (load) charge is not deducted when determining the returns from mutual funds; thus the results from both types of investments are overstated. The magnitudes of the differences between the measures we use and those relevant for a particular investor depend on a number of factors,[24] but for most investors the comparison made here should give results similar to those obtained if all the relevant costs had been considered.

Figure 9 shows the distribution of the R/V ratios for the thirty-four funds (based on their performance during the

[24] For example, the amount to be invested, the number of years the portfolio is to be held, and the extent to which dividends are to be reinvested.

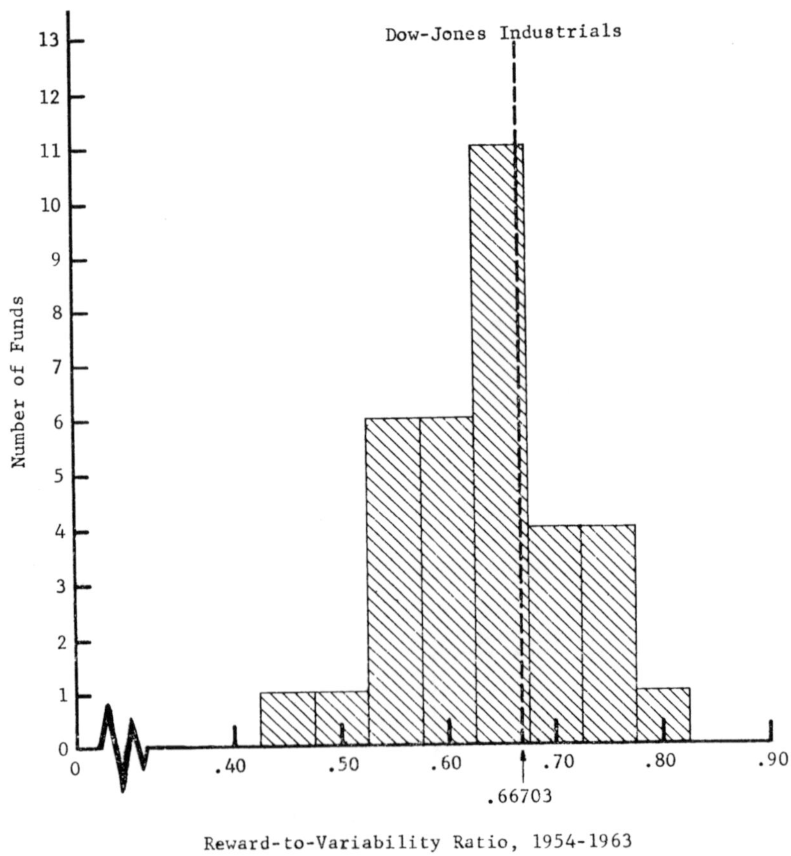

FIG. 9.—Mutual fund performance versus Dow-Jones Industrials, 1954–63

period 1954–63). The vertical line represents the R/V ratio for the Dow-Jones portfolio—its return average 16.3 per cent during the period with a variability of 19.94 per cent, giving an R/V ratio of 0.667. The average R/V ratio for the funds in our sample was 0.633—considerably smaller than that of the Dow-Jones Average. Although another group of mutual funds would give different results, the odds are greater than 100 to 1 against the possibility that the average mutual fund did as well as the Dow-Jones portfolio from 1954 to 1963.[25] In this group, only eleven funds did better than the Dow-Jones portfolio, while twenty-three did worse.

From the standpoint of the investor the comparison shown in Figure 9 is the most relevant. But to account for the relatively poor performance of most mutual funds it is instructive to compare *gross* performance (i.e., before deducting expenses) with that of the Dow-Jones portfolio. Such a comparison[26] shows that nineteen funds did better than the Dow-Jones portfolio, and only fifteen did worse. Although another group of funds would give different results, it is unlikely that the gross performance of the average mutual fund was worse than that of the Dow-Jones portfolio from 1954 to 1963.[27]

While it may be dangerous to generalize from the results found during one ten-year period, it appears that the average mutual fund manager selects a portfolio at least as good as the Dow-Jones Industrials, but that the results actually obtained by the holder of mutual fund shares (after the costs associated with the operation of the fund have been deducted) fall somewhat short of those from the Dow-Jones portfolio. This is consistent with our previous conclusion that, all other things being equal, the smaller a fund's expense ratio, the better the results obtained by its stockholders.

IX. CONCLUSIONS

This paper represents an attempt to bring to bear on the measurement and prediction of mutual fund performance some of the results of recent work in capital theory and the behavior of stock-market prices. We have shown that performance can be evaluated with a simple yet theoretically meaningful measure that considers both average return and risk. This measure precludes the "discovery" of differences in performance due solely to differences in objectives (e.g., the high average returns typically obtained by funds who consciously hold risky portfolios). However, even when performance is measured in this manner there are differences among funds; and such differences do not appear to be en-

[25] The standard deviation of the R/V values for the 34 funds was 0.08067. If the population of mutual funds had a mean of 0.667 and a standard deviation of 0.08067, the distribution of sample means for groups of 34 would have a standard deviation of 0.01383 ($=0.08067/\sqrt{34}$) and be roughly normally distributed. The observed mean of 0.633 is 2.46 standard deviations below the assumed mean of 0.667; the odds are 144 to 1 that under the hypothesized conditions a sample of 34 funds would have an average R/V value as low as 0.633.

[26] The comparison was made by assuming that each fund maintained its 1953 ratio of expenses to net assets throughout the subsequent ten years. Under these conditions the only change required to compute the R/V ratios for gross performance was to add each fund's expense ratio to its average return before the R/V ratio was computed.

[27] The standard deviation of the gross R/V values for the 34 funds was 0.08304. If the populatoin of mutual funds had a mean of 0.667 and a standard deviation of 0.08304, the distriubtion of sample means for groups of 34 would have a standard deviation of 0.01424 ($=0.08304/\sqrt{34}$) and be roughly normally distributed. The observed mean of 0.677 is 0.74 standard deviations above the assumed mean of 0.667; the odds are 3.36 to 1 that under the hypothesized conditions a sample of 34 funds would have an average gross R/V value as high as 0.677.

tirely transitory. To a major extent they can be explained by differences in expense ratios, lending support to the view that the capital market is highly efficient and that good managers concentrate on evaluating risk and providing diversification, spending little effort (and money) on the search for incorrectly priced securities. However, past performance per se also explains some of the differences. Further work is required before the significance of this result can be properly evaluated. But the burden of proof may reasonably be placed on those who argue the traditional view—that the search for securities whose prices diverge from their intrinsic values is worth the expense required, even for a mutual fund operating under severe constraints on the proportion of funds invested in any single security.[28] Fortunately many who hold this view have both the means and the data required to perform extensive analyses; we will all look forward to their results.

[28] By law, no more than 5 per cent of the assets of a fund may be invested in any given security, and no more than 10 per cent of the assets of a given firm may be held by the fund. Moreover, the very size of many mutual funds makes it impossible to invest even the legal maximum in a security without driving its price up to a point substantially above the original (bargain) amount.

Adjusting for risk in portfolio performance measurement

Measurable risk is the hallmark of accurate performance evaluations.

William F. Sharpe

A common human failing is the desire for simple answers to difficult questions. Evaluation of investment performance is no exception. How well did a security or portfolio do in the past? Most people would like to have such a question answered with a single number. Which security or portfolio did best? Most would like an unambiguous reply.

Faced with this kind of question, analysts have, until recently, tended to go to one of two extremes. Some provided direct answers using either: 1) a measure of average return over some period, or 2) a measure relating terminal value to initial value. Others simply rejected the question on the grounds that performance is far too complicated to measure in any simple way; that every portfolio has its own unique characteristics; and that one simply can't compare apples with oranges.

There is, of course, much truth in the latter position. Securities and portfolios really *are* different. Any attempt to measure performance with one number *must* involve some simplification. On the other hand, simplification is the essence of science. It is impossible to compare everything with everything. Some abstraction is necessary.

Take as given the assumption that performance is to be measured with only one number. Then one must consider the obvious question: Which number? Only the investigation of the best single measure can provide an adequate basis for answering the prior question: Is one enough?

Consider the problem of measuring the performance of a mutual fund from, say, January 1, 1969 through December 31, 1973. One traditional approach would be to compute the annual returns for each of the five years, then average them. Another would assume an investment of, say, \$10,000 on January 1, 1969, then compute the terminal value on December 31, 1973, assuming that all interim dividends and capital gains had been reinvested in the fund.

Numbers such as these are far from irrelevant, but they fail to take *risk* into account. We know that there is risk in the world, and that investors generally dislike it. There is substantial theoretical and empirical support for the assertion that security prices reflect this fact. As a result, there is a trade-off between risk and return. On the average, the best high-risk portfolio provides a greater return than the best low-risk portfolio. If this were not the case, the former would not be held by knowledgeable people. Because of the lack of large numbers of foolish investors, security prices must adjust so that anyone who takes the pains to be fairly well-diversified can obtain higher returns on average only by taking on more risk.

A reasonable goal is thus to find a measure of performance that takes risk into account. This article describes some of the leading candidates. Although all are based on a rather elegant theory of equilibrium capital asset prices, it is instructive to present them simply as useful measures of past performance. Thus no assumptions about market equilibrium, equality of *ex post* and *ex ante* values, etc., will be invoked. Nor will questions concerning the "significance" of differences in past performance be considered to avoid an extended discussion of statistical procedures.

EXCESS RETURNS

To begin, decisions must be made about the *period* to be covered and the *differencing interval* to be used. No simple prescription is available since the proper choice depends on the purpose for which performance is being measured. For concreteness, we will assume that a period of five years is to be covered, with

29 THE JOURNAL OF PORTFOLIO MANAGEMENT

a quarterly differencing interval. Of course, the procedures to be described can also be applied to other combinations of periods and intervals.

The first task is to compute the rate of return for each of the twenty quarters. If great precision seems desirable, the actual dates of the cash flows, plus information on interim values, can be used to compute the time-weighted rate of return for a quarter. Alternatively, an internal rate of return can be computed. It sometimes suffices to simply assume that all cash flows are held until the end of the quarter in which they are received.

This leads to the familiar formula whereby the return on a security or a portfolio in any given period is equal to the sum of the starting price, plus income received, less the price at the end of the period as a percent of the starting price.

While this calculation measures the performance of a security or a portfolio during a particular quarter, it fails to differentiate quarters in which interest rates were generally low. To measure the differences in return from prevailing interest rates, one must compute the *excess return*, which is of course the difference between the actual return and the return on a riskless security such as a 90-day Treasury bill over the same period of time.

All the measures described in this article will be defined in terms of excess returns. In some cases, definitions proposed in other sources have been modified slightly. When short-term interest rates did not vary significantly, there was less reason to use excess returns. Now, however, it is especially important for us to do so.

THE REWARD-TO-VARIABILITY RATIO

We consider first a measure designed to assess the performance of a portfolio representing most or all of an investor's capital. It is both simple and intuitively appealing. The "reward" provided by a portfolio is measured by its average quarterly excess return. This can be considered the reward obtained for bearing risk. The risk actually borne is measured by the "variability," or standard deviation of quarterly excess returns around the average value. This is computed by measuring the deviation of each quarter's excess return from the average, then squaring it; the resulting values are averaged and the square root taken. The final figure measures the extent to which the excess returns deviate from their average; in a typical case, approximately two thirds of the values will be within one standard deviation of the average.

Although the standard deviation of excess return may not completely accord with one's interpretation of the term "risk," it is generally highly correlated with more familiar measures and thus provides an adequate surrogate.

The reward-to-variability ratio is simply the ratio of reward (which is good) to variability (which is bad). It indicates the reward per unit of risk borne. The larger the ratio, the better the performance.

This seems an *ad hoc* argument at best, and it is. Fortunately, a much stronger case may be made. Consider Figure 1. Points i and j plot the average excess return and standard deviation of excess return for portfolios i and j. Point π shows the results for investment solely in 90-day Treasury bills. Since such a strategy results in an excess return of zero in every quarter, the point is located at the origin (i.e., both the average excess return as well as the standard deviation are zero).

FIGURE 1

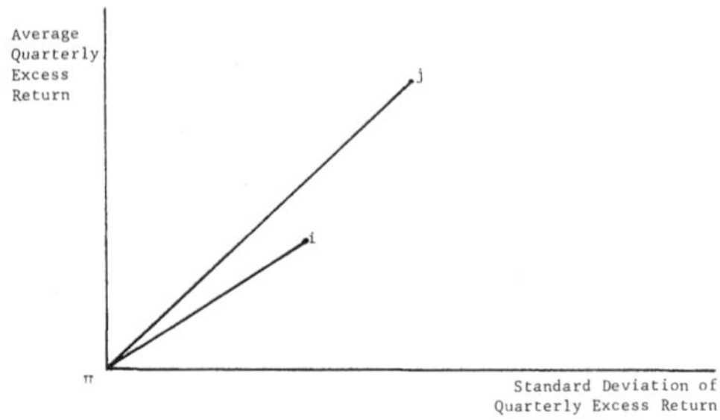

FIGURE 2

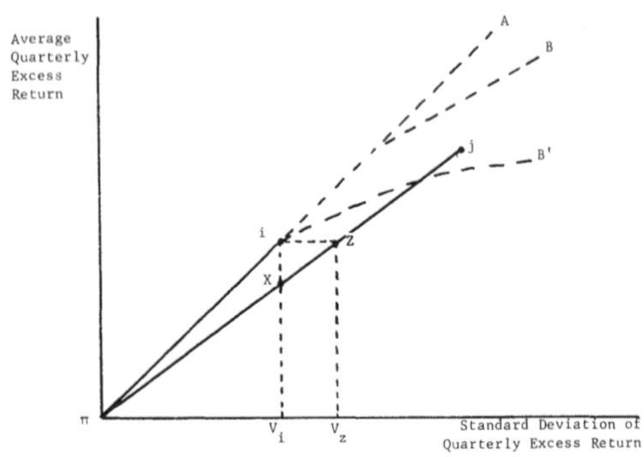

Now consider a strategy involving investment in portfolio i and Treasury bills. If half an investor's funds had been in Treasury bills each quarter and the other half in portfolio i, the average quarterly excess return on his account would have been half that of Treasury bills (zero) plus half that on portfolio i. A similar relationship holds for the standard deviation (but only because the standard deviation of the excess returns from Treasury bills is zero). Thus the performance of a 50-50 mix of Treasury bills and portfolio i would plot halfway between point π and point i. Similarly, an account with 70% in Treasury bills and 30% in portfolio i each quarter would plot 70% of the way between point i and point π. Thus portfolio i plus Treasury bills could have provided any desired point along line πi.

Similarly, portfolio j plus Treasury bills could have provided any desired point along line πj. By recognizing the opportunity to split funds between a portfolio and Treasury bills, we can replace the point associated with a portfolio by the line associated with strategies using only that portfolio plus treasury bills.

In the case shown in Figure 1, portfolio j is clearly superior to portfolio i. For any level of variability attainable with portfolio i plus Treasury bills, a higher average return could have been obtained with portfolio j plus Treasury bills. Moreover, some high-variability, high-average return alternatives are not even available with portfolio i plus Treasury bills. In this case, at least, the portfolio with the steeper line is clearly the better.

But note that the slope of such a line *is* the reward-to-variability ratio. The portfolio with the steeper line has the higher reward-to-variability ratio, and vice-versa.

The portfolio with the higher reward-to-variability ratio may not be better in all cases. Figure 2 provides a counterexample. Here, the portfolio with the smaller average excess return has the larger reward-to-variability ratio, but it is not unambiguously better.

Consider an investor who wanted an overall standard deviation below V_i. For such a person, portfolio i clearly was better. But what about a more adventuresome investor? Note that point i dominates all points from X to Z along line πj, since it gives more average return and less variability. Only in the range above V_z might portfolio j provide a more desirable investment strategy.

If the possibility of borrowing funds were taken into account, the case in favor of portfolio i in Figure 2 is likely to be even stronger. By investing his own funds, plus some borrowed money, in portfolio i, an investor could have attained a result lying to the right of point i. The actual location would depend on both the amount borrowed and the interest rate paid. If the investor could have borrowed without limit at the rate paid by the U.S. Treasury, points along line iA (the extension of π_i) could have been attained, and portfolio i would clearly have been superior to portfolio j. In fact, investors often "borrow" from themselves for such purposes, by withdrawing money from savings accounts or by paying off a mortgage at a slower rate.

Up to a point, then, the cost of "borrowed" funds may be close to the Treasury bill rate. Beyond that point, however, a loan must be obtained, and the interest rate for such a loan is likely to exceed the Treasury bill rate. Moreover, the rate may increase with the amount borrowed. All of this implies that the result may lie along a curve such as iB or iB′. Only in the latter case might portfolio j be a reasonable choice, and only then for adventuresome investors.

Despite the rather robust nature of the reward-to-variability ratio, it is wise to avoid comparisons involving portfolios with significantly different variabilities. But over a reasonable range of risk, the reward-to-variability ratio can provide an adequate risk-adjusted measure of portfolio performance.

COMPARISONS WITH THE MARKET

The reward-to-variability ratio provides an absolute measure of the performance of a portfolio. Subject to the qualifications mentioned earlier, two or more portfolios can be compared using it. Perhaps more important, the performance of a portfolio can be compared with that of one selected by a so-called "naive investor."

The usual model of a naive investor is someone who blindly "buys the averages." Thus a portfolio composed of the stocks used to compute the Standard and Poor's 500 Stock Composite Index might be selected for the comparison. In any event, some sort of *market portfolio* is used to represent the results obtained with virtually no investment management or skill.

FIGURE 3

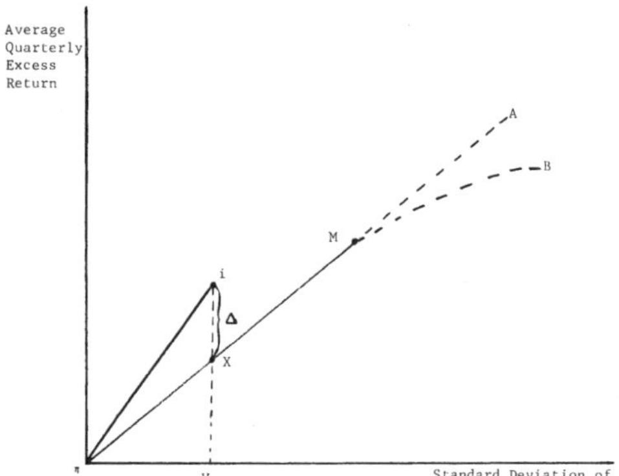

In Figure 3, point M represents the market portfolio and point i the portfolio to be evaluated. In this case, the portfolio's excess return was less variable than that of the market, so it is possible to compare portfolio i directly with a *combination* of the market portfolio and Treasury bills — a combination chosen to have the same variability as portfolio i.

Point X in Figure 3 represents such a *market based portfolio of comparable variability*. In this case, its average excess return was less than that of portfolio i. Portfolio i's *average quarterly differential return* (Δ) indicates how much better (for positive values) or worse (for negative values) portfolio i was on the average than a market-based portfolio of comparable variability.

The situation is more complex if the portfolio's excess return were more variable than that of the market. A naive investor who desired *less* variability than that provided by the market could clearly have divided his money between Treasury bills and the market portfolio. Neither more nor less than this was assumed in the previous case. But what results would have been obtained by the market? If he could have borrowed sufficient funds at the Treasury bill rate, of course, a point lying along line MA (the extension of πM) could have been attained. But what if this had not been possible? Could a portfolio plotting on MA have been found, or one along some curve such as MB?

No categorical answer is possible, since this is essentially an empirical question. One might plot the points representing a number of well-diversified portfolios of securities chosen more or less at random in an attempt to estimate the relevant curve. In practice, however, this is seldom done. Instead, the alternatives are assumed (sometimes implicitly) to lie along the straight line from the origin through the point M. For portfolios with returns that were substantially more variable than those of the market, this may be a questionable procedure. Little harm may be done however, if, in the final analysis, the resultant performance measures are compared with those of portfolios in roughly the same risk class.

VOLATILITY

Variability (standard deviation of excess returns) is an adequate measure of the risk of an entire portfolio. But it is not a satisfactory measure of the risk of a portion of that portfolio — be it a smaller portfolio or a single security — for the variability of the whole does not usually equal a weighted average of the variabilities of the parts.

The general relationship between the risk of an overall portfolio and that of its component securities is complex. Empirical evidence supports the assertion, however, that the most relevant single measure of risk is the *volatility* of a security or a portfolio.

From 30 to 40% of the variation in the typical stock's rate of return is attributable to the co-movement of its price with the overall level of the market. For well-diversified portfolios, the proportion is generally more than 90%. The responsiveness of rate of return to market swings is clearly the most important single measure of risk.

The idea is simple enough. The excess rate of return on a security or portfolio is regressed on the excess rate of return on a market portfolio to obtain a *characteristic line*.

The slope of this line is the *volatility* (more commonly termed *beta*). If the value is less than one, the security or portfolio was *defensive* — it tended to move less than the average security during market swings. If the volatility is more than one, the security or portfolio was *aggressive* — it tended to move more than the average security during market swings. Treasury bills always have a volatility of zero. And, by definition, the market portfolio always has a volatility of one.

No investor averse to risk is likely to invest all his money in a single security. Moreover, many portfolios constitute only a portion of their investor's overall wealth (for example, people combine mutual fund shares with other securities). For evaluating most securities and many portfolios, *volatility* is thus a more relevant measure of risk than *variability*.

It is an easy matter to redefine the performance measures described earlier to account for this. The reward-to-variability ratio is replaced with the *reward-to-volatility ratio*. All the arguments in its favor and questions regarding its universal applicability are similar to those presented earlier. The average differential return can also be computed, but with the comparison related to a market-based portfolio of equal *volatility*. The same line of reasoning applies as does the same line of reservations.

The real meaning of such comparisons can best be seen in conjunction with the characteristic line. Assume that portfolio i is to be evaluated. We begin with the quarter-by-quarter excess returns. The problem is to compare them with those of a relevant naive investment strategy. As before, the goal is to compare two alternatives of equal risk. In this case, the relevant naive strategy should have had the same volatility as the portfolio in question. This requires the determination of the portfolio's characteristic line, as shown in Figure 4. For concreteness, assume that the slope is 0.6. The "comparable-volatility market-based portfolio" will be based on a strategy of investing 60% of the total funds in the market portfolio and 40% in Treasury bills. Every quarter's excess return for such a portfolio will fall precisely along a straight line through the origin with a slope of 0.6 (as intended).

The two lines are parallel (by construction).

For each quarter, the excess return on portfolio i can be compared with that of the comparison portfolio and the *differential return* computed. For example, in Figure 4 the differential return is positive (d_1) in period 1 and negative (d_2) in period 2. By the nature of the least-squares regression procedure, the vertical intercept of portfolio i's characteristic line will equal its *average differential return* (Δ) over a market-based portfolio of comparable volatility. This important measure is also called *alpha*.

FIGURE 4

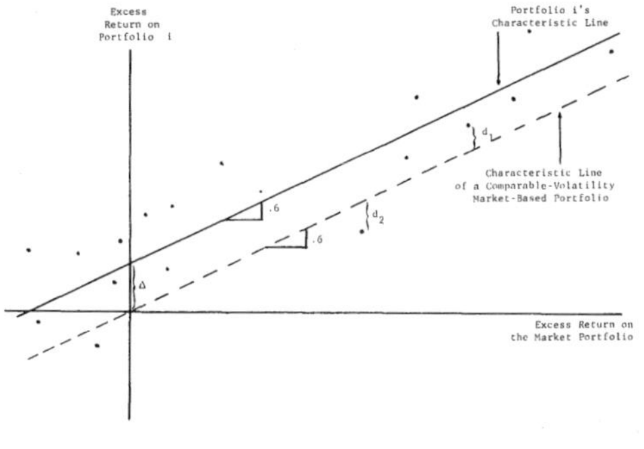

The vertical intercept of a security or portfolio's characteristic line can easily be interpreted as a measure of performance. It indicates the percent per quarter by which the excess return exceeded (for positive values) or fell below (for negative values) that obtainable to the investor from a market-based portfolio of comparable volatility.

Needless to say, this measure is subject to all the reservations mentioned earlier. It may thus be unwise to use it to compare the performance of securities and portfolios of markedly different volatilities. But over a reasonable range of variation, it should provide a good risk-adjusted measure of performance.

STOCK SELECTION AND DIVERSIFICATION

If a portfolio is highly diversified, its performance will be described almost perfectly by its characteristic line: all variation in its rate of return may be attributed to market swings and the portfolio's volatility. But if a portfolio is not highly diversified, its excess return will vary around its characteristic line, leading to additional overall variability. The average differential return over a market-based portfolio of comparable *volatility* provides a measure of the manager's superiority or inferiority vis-a-vis *stock selection*, disregarding the extent to which the portfolio is diversified. The average differential return over a market-based portfolio of comparable *variability* provides a measure that takes into account both the manager's ability to select stocks and his ability to provide diversification. For a perfectly diversified portfolio, the two measures will be the same; for an imperfectly diversified portfolio, the latter will generally be smaller. The difference can be considered the decline in performance resulting from lack of diversification.

In a real sense, *the* problem of portfolio management is to achieve an appropriate balance between stock selection and diversification. The answer is clearly not to select the one (supposedly) best stock. On the other hand, to achieve near perfect diversification, a manager would have to select hundreds of stocks — almost certainly resulting in average performance. Comparison of the two measures of average differential return can provide at least some insight into the way in which a portfolio manager has performed this delicate balancing act.

ABNORMAL PERIODS

In a "normal" period, the average excess return on a market portfolio of risky assets is positive. This is reflected in all the diagrams used thus far. And it accords with the expectations that *must* be held by the majority of (risk-averse) investors. But nature sometimes does the unexpected. It is possible for the average quarterly excess return on the market portfolio over a five-year period to be zero, or even negative. In the former case, adjustment for risk would be harmless, at best, since the average excess return of every market-based portfolio would equal zero. In the latter case, however, the average excess return of a market-based portfolio would be smaller (i.e., more negative), the larger the portfolio's variability or volatility, leading to somewhat different results.

Figure 5 provides an example. The market portfolio's average excess return was negative, so line πMA slopes downward. The "reward" for bearing the risk of portfolio M was negative; thus, both the reward-to-variability and the reward-to-volatility ratios were negative. Although one can easily explain this (abnormal times give abnormal results), the intuitive meaning of both measures is lost.

Average differential return fares somewhat better, as the figure shows. For example, portfolio i's performance is rated superior to that of a market-based portfolio of comparable variability, as is that of portfolio j. Moreover, portfolio j's performance was given a superior rating.

Why? Because it was compared with M_j — a market-based portfolio of greater variability than that of M_i, with which portfolio i was compared. Of course, during this abnormal period, one was penalized for taking on risk. But it is still important to assess performance relative to that achieved by a naive investor holding a portfolio of comparable risk. The measures of average differential return do this, even when the market is more perverse than usual.

FIGURE 5

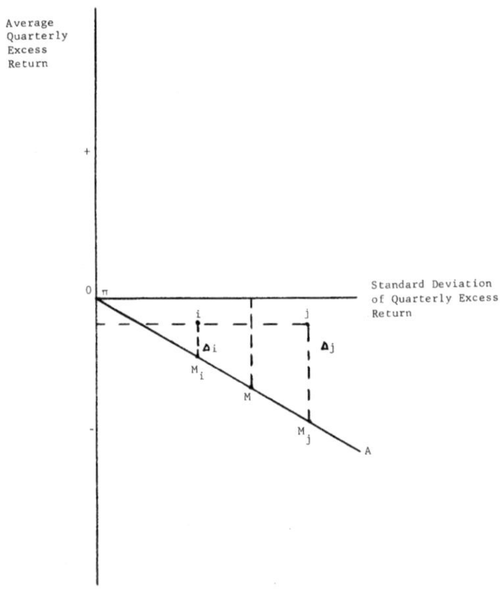

CONCLUSIONS

There is much more to be said about performance measurement. We have only provided an introduction to some of the modern approaches. The hallmark of all such procedures is the explicit consideration of risk. The evidence is, by now, almost overwhelming: Measures that account for risk (although perhaps imperfectly) are generally superior to those that do not. This is widely recognized in the academic community and, increasingly, in the investment community. Several firms now offer performance measurement services using procedures similar to those described here, and at least one has gone well beyond, to provide detailed diagnoses of the performance of components of each portfolio. Risk-adjusted performance is clearly here to stay.

REFERENCES

This paper draws from the previous work of a number of authors. The interested reader will find more details in the following references (arranged in chronological order):

Treynor, Jack L., "How to Rate Management of Investment Funds," *Harvard Business Review* (January-February, 1965) pp. 63-75.

Sharpe, William F., "Mutual Fund Performance," *Journal of Business* (January, 1966) pp. 119-138.

Jensen, Michael C., "The Performance of Mutual Funds in the Period 1945-1964," *The Journal of Finance* (May, 1968) pp. 389-416.

Fama, Eugene F., *Risk and the Evaluation of Pension Fund Portfolio Performance,* (Park Ridge, Ill.: Bank Administration Institute, 1968).

Jensen, Michael C., "Risk, the Pricing of Capital Assets and the Evaluation of Investment Portfolios," *Journal of Business* (April, 1969) pp. 167-247.

Sharpe, William F., *Portfolio Theory and Capital Markets,* (McGraw-Hill, 1970).

Williamson, J. Peter, *Investments: New Analytic Techniques* (Praeger Publishers, 1970).

Fama, Eugene F., "Components of Investment Performance," *The Journal of Finance* (June, 1972) pp. 551-567.

Merrill Lynch, Pierce, Fenner and Smith, Inc., "Merrill Lynch Presents IPA: Investment Performance Analysis," 1973.

Asset allocation: Management style and performance measurement

An asset class factor model can help make order out of chaos.

William F. Sharpe

It is widely agreed that asset allocation accounts for a large part of the variability in the return on a typical investor's portfolio. This is especially true if the portfolio is invested in multiple funds, each including a number of securities.

Asset allocation is generally defined as the allocation of an investor's portfolio across a number of "major" asset classes. Clearly such a generalization cannot be made operational without defining such classes.

Once a set of asset classes has been defined, it is important to determine the exposures of each component of an investor's overall portfolio to movements in their returns. Such information can be aggregated to determine the investor's overall effective asset mix. If it does not conform to the desired mix, appropriate alterations can then be made.

Once a procedure for measuring exposure to variations in returns of major asset classes is in place, it is possible to determine how effectively individual fund managers have performed their functions and the extent (if any) to which value has been added through active management. Finally, the effectiveness of the investor's overall asset allocation can be compared with that of one or more benchmark asset mixes.

An effective way to accomplish all these tasks is to use an asset class factor model. After describing the characteristics of such a model, we illustrate application of a model with twelve asset classes to analyze the performance of a set of open-end mutual funds between 1985 and 1989.

ASSET CLASS FACTOR MODELS

Factor models are common in investment analysis. Equation (1) is a generic representation:

$$\tilde{R}_i = [b_{i1}\tilde{F}_1 + b_{i2}\tilde{F}_2 + ... + b_{in}\tilde{F}_n] + \tilde{e}_i \quad (1)$$

$\tilde{R}_i$ represents the return on asset i, $\tilde{F}_1$ represents the value of factor 1, $\tilde{F}_2$ the value of factor 2, $\tilde{F}_n$ the value of the nth (last) factor, and $\tilde{e}_i$ the "non-factor" component of the return on i. All these values are (potentially) unknown before-the-fact, as indicated by the tildes. The remaining values (b_{i1} through b_{in}) represent the sensitivities of $\tilde{R}_i$ to factors $\tilde{F}_1$ through $\tilde{F}_n$.

A key assumption makes a model of this sort more than simply an exercise in data description: The non-factor return for one asset (e.g., $\tilde{e}_i$) is assumed to be uncorrelated with that of every other (e.g., $\tilde{e}_j$). In effect, the factors are the only sources of correlation among returns.

An asset class factor model can be considered a special case of the generic type. In such a model each factor represents the return on an asset class, and the sensitivities (b_{ij} values) are required to sum to 1

WILLIAM F. SHARPE is Timken Professor Emeritus of Finance, Stanford University Graduate School of Business, and Chairman of William F. Sharpe Associates in Los Altos (CA 94022). This article is adapted from the O'Neil Abbott Distinguished Lecture given at the Darden School of the University of Virginia on October 2, 1990. The author thanks Robert O'Neil, Mark Eaker, and the faculty of the Darden School for making the presentation possible. He also thanks Mark Friebel, Sharon Kitajima, Diana Lieberman, Anita Nanda, and Kathryn Sharpe, colleagues at William F. Sharpe Associates, for their contributions.

THE JOURNAL OF PORTFOLIO MANAGEMENT 7

(100%). In effect, the return on an asset i is represented as the return on a portfolio (shown by the sum of the terms in the bracketed expression) invested in the n asset classes plus a residual component ($\tilde{e}_i$). For expository convenience, the sum of the terms in the brackets can be termed as the return attributable to *style* and the residual component ($\tilde{e}_i$) as the return attributable to *selection*. Indeed, a key contribution of this approach is separation of return into these two main components.

EVALUATING ASSET CLASS FACTOR MODELS

The usefulness of an asset class factor model depends on the asset classes chosen for its implementation. While not strictly necessary, it is desirable that such asset classes be 1) mutually exclusive, 2) exhaustive, and 3) have returns that "differ." Pragmatically, each should represent a market capitalization-weighted portfolio of securities; no security should be included in more than one asset class; as many securities as possible should be included in the chosen asset classes; and the asset class returns should either have low correlations with one another or, in cases where correlations are high, different standard deviations.

While the appropriate measure of the efficacy of any specific implementation depends on the uses to which the model is to be put, factor models typically are evaluated on the basis of their ability to explain the returns of the assets in question (i.e., the R_is). A useful metric is the proportion of variance "explained" by the selected asset classes. Using the traditional definition, for asset i:

$$R^2 = 1 - \frac{\mathrm{Var}(\tilde{e}_i)}{\mathrm{Var}(\tilde{R}_i)}. \quad (2)$$

The right-hand side of Equation (2) equals 1 minus the proportion of variance "unexplained." The resulting R-squared value thus indicates the proportion of the variance of R_i "explained" by the n asset classes.[1]

It is important to recognize that this measure indicates only the extent to which a specific model fits the data at hand. A better test of the usefulness of any implementation is its ability to explain performance out-of-sample. It is necessary therefore to consider not only the ability of a model to explain a given set of data but also its parsimony. Other things equal (e.g., R-squared values), the fewer the asset classes, the more likely the model is to represent continuing fundamental relationships with predictive content.[2]

To evaluate the exposures of funds to changes in the returns of key asset classes, the appropriate measure is the collective ability of a set of such classes to explain the time series variability in the returns on a typical fund (e.g., mutual fund or separately managed institutional account). Note that this criterion differs from that often applied in evaluating factor models designed to describe specific portions of the overall capital market.

For example, when constructing an equity factor model, one might consider the ability of the selected factors to explain the time series variation in the returns of a typical stock. Most stock market models include factors representing returns on industry groups and/or economic sectors — factors that account for much of the typical security's return. If most managers diversify across industries and economic sectors, however, inclusion of factors related to differences in industry and sector returns will add little if any explanatory power to a model designed to explain fund returns.

A TWELVE-ASSET CLASS MODEL

The model we use has twelve asset classes. The return of each is represented by a market capitalization-weighted index of the returns on a large number of securities. For reasons that will become clear, it is important to note that each index represents a strategy that could be followed at low cost using an index fund. The composition of each index is specified in sufficient detail by its provider to enable an investor to track the returns with little error through a passive (index-like) investment strategy.

Table 1 describes the twelve asset classes and the indexes used for the associated return series. Most are widely used indexes that require no further description. The four less well-known are those employed to represent U.S. equity classes.

In effect, the institutional universe of U.S. equities has been divided into four mutually exclusive and exhaustive groups.[3] The first two represent a partition of the stocks in Standard & Poor's 500 stock index. Every six months the S&P 500 stocks are ranked according to the ratio of the most recently published book value per share to a previous month-end price per share. A dividing line is drawn so that approximately half the total value of the 500 stocks is placed on either side. Stocks with high book-to-price ratios are included in the "value" stock index; the remainder are in the "growth" stock index.

A similar procedure is followed in constructing the medium capitalization and small capitalization stock indexes. Non-S&P 500 stocks are ranked on the basis of total outstanding market capitalization every six months, and a dividing line drawn so that approximately 80% of the total value is above the line and

TABLE 1

Asset Classes

Bills
Cash-equivalents with less than 3 months to maturity
Index: Salomon Brothers' 90-day Treasury Bill Index

Intermediate-Term Government Bonds
Government bonds with less than 10 years to maturity
Index: Lehman Brothers' Long-Term Government Bond Index

Long-Term Government Bonds
Government bonds with more than 10 years to maturity
Index: Lehman Brothers' Long-Term Government Bond Index

Corporate Bonds
Corporate bonds with ratings of at least Baa by Moody's or BBB by Standard & Poor's
Index: Lehman Brothers' Corporate Bond Index

Mortgage-Related Securities
Mortgage-backed and related securities
Index: Lehman Brothers' Mortgage-Backed Securities Index

Large-Capitalization Value Stocks
Stocks in Standard & Poor's 500 stock index with high book-to-price ratios
Index: Sharpe/BARRA Value Stock Index

Large-Capitalization Growth Stocks
Stocks in Standard & Poor's 500 stock index with low book-to-price ratios
Index: Sharpe/BARRA Growth Stock Index

Medium-Capitalization Stocks
Stocks in the top 80% of capitalization in the U.S. equity universe after the exclusion of stocks in Standard & Poor's 500 stock index
Index: Sharpe/BARRA Medium Capitalization Stock Index

Small-Capitalization Stocks
Stocks in the bottom 20% of capitalization in the U.S. equity universe after the exclusion of stocks in Standard & Poor's stock index
Index: Sharpe/BARRA Small Capitalization Stock Index

Non-U.S. Bonds
Bonds outside the U.S. and Canada
Index: Salomon Brothers' Non-U.S. Government Bond Index

European Stocks
European and non-Japanese Pacific Basin stocks
Index: FTA Euro-Pacific Ex Japan Index

Japanese Stocks
Japanese stocks
Index: FTA Japan Index

20% below it. Most of the stocks in the first group are placed in the medium capitalization index, and most of the remaining stocks in the small capitalization index. To avoid excessive turnover in the composition of these indexes of relatively illiquid stocks (and an associated high cost for index tracking), any stock that has recently "crossed over the line" a relatively small distance is allowed to remain in its former index.[4]

FIGURE 1

COMPOSITION OF FOUR DOMESTIC EQUITY CLASSES

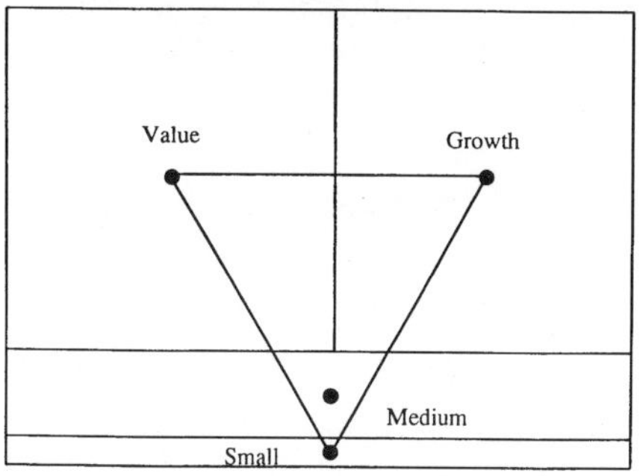

Many of the differences in returns of U.S. equity mutual funds can be attributed to differences in their exposures to these four asset classes. In effect, there appear to be two key dimensions along which such funds differ. One may loosely be termed "value/growth," the other "small/large." Figure 1 illustrates the composition of the four domestic equity asset classes. Each index can be considered a capitalization-weighted "center of gravity" of the securities in its associated class, as the dots in Figure 1 indicate. Note that any combination of the four indexes with non-negative holdings can be represented by a point in the area defined by the index locations (in this case, a triangle).[5]

Much has been written about both the small-stock and the value/growth phenomena. While the terms "value" and "growth" reflect common usage in the investment profession, they serve only as convenient names for stocks that tend to be similar in several respects. As is well known, across securities there is significant positive correlation among: book/price, earnings/price, low earnings growth, dividend yield, and low return on equity. Moreover, the industry compositions of the value and growth groups differ (e.g., companies with high research budgets tend to have low book values compared to their stock prices).

Those concerned with these distinctions have focused most of their research on long-run average return differences; that is, they have asked whether small stocks or value stocks "do better than they should" in the long run. Less attention has been paid to likely sources of short-run variability in returns among such groups. For present purposes, it suffices that such variability is substantial.

Figure 2 provides relevant evidence: The variability in returns across the four asset classes from year-to-year is far greater than would be encountered

FIGURE 2

ANNUAL EQUITY RETURNS
1986-1990

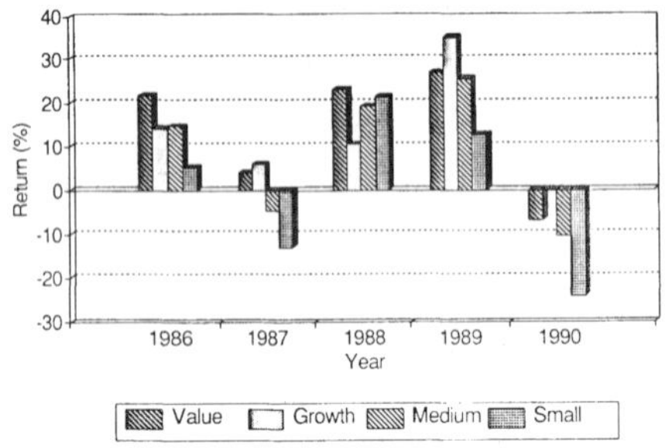

Note: Updated from lecture presentation date to include complete calendar year 1990 returns.

if groups with similar numbers of securities had been formed randomly. Fund exposures across these dimensions vary greatly. As a result, much of the variation in fund returns in any given period can be attributed to the combined effects of their exposures to these asset classes and the realized returns on those classes.

DETERMINING FUND EXPOSURES

The traditional view of asset allocation assumes that an investor allocates assets among (potentially many) funds, each of which includes (potentially many) securities. Ultimately one is interested in the investor's exposures to the key asset classes. These are a function of 1) the amounts of the investor's portfolio invested in the various funds, and 2) the exposures of each fund to the asset classes. The exposures of a fund to the various asset classes are, in turn, a function of 1) the amounts that the fund has invested in various securities, and 2) the exposures of the securities to the asset classes.

While it is possible to attempt to determine a fund's exposures from a detailed analysis of the securities held by the fund, a simpler approach typically provides more than enough information for purposes of asset allocation. Such a method uses only realized fund returns to establish the typical exposures of the fund to the asset classes. Because only easily obtained information is required, the approach may be termed "external," in comparison with methods that rely on information that may be available only from sources internal to the fund.

Inspection of Equation (1) suggests a procedure that might be used in this connection. Given, say, sixty monthly returns on a fund, along with comparable returns for a selected set of asset classes, one could simply use a multiple regression analysis with fund returns as the dependent variable and asset class returns as the independent variables. The resulting slope coefficients could then be interpreted as the fund's historic exposures to the asset class returns.

Table 2 provides an example for Trustees' Commingled U.S. Portfolio (an open-end mutual fund offered by the Vanguard Group). Monthly returns from January 1985 through December 1989 are used for the dependent variable, with the corresponding returns for the twelve asset classes serving as independent variables.

The column entitled "Unconstrained Regression" shows results obtained applying Equation (1). The first twelve rows show the resulting slope coefficients (b_{ij} values) expressed as percentages. The coefficient total is shown next, followed by the R-squared value (also expressed as a percentage). A substantial portion (95.20%) of the monthly variance in the fund's returns is explained by this equation. The coefficients, however, do not sum to 100%. What is more important, several are vastly inconsistent with the fund's

TABLE 2

Regression and Quadratic Programming Results
Trustees' Commingled Fund—U.S. Portfolio
January 1985 through December 1989

	Unconstrained Regression	Constrained Regression	Quadratic Programming
Bills	14.69	42.65	0
Intermediate Bonds	-69.51	-68.64	0
Long-Term Bonds	-2.54	-2.38	0
Corporate Bonds	16.57	15.29	0
Mortgages	5.19	4.58	0
Value Stocks	109.52	110.35	69.81
Growth Stocks	-7.86	-8.02	0
Medium Stocks	-41.83	-43.62	0
Small Stocks	45.65	47.17	30.04
Foreign Bonds	-1.85	-1.38	0
European Stocks	6.15	5.77	0.15
Japanese Stocks	-1.46	-1.79	0
Total	72.71	100.00	100.00
R-squared	95.20	95.16	92.22

actual policy (to invest in common stocks with no short positions).

The column in Table 2 entitled "Constrained Regression" reports the results of a multiple regression analysis similar to the first, with one added constraint: The coefficients are required to sum to 100%. The reduction in R-squared was slight (from 95.20% to 95.16%), but the inconsistency between the coefficients and the fund's investment policy remains.

The last column in Table 2 reports the results of an analysis where each coefficient is constrained to lie between 0 and 100%, and the sum is again required to be 100%. As in the previous cases, the objective of the analysis was to select a set of coefficients that minimizes the "unexplained" variation in returns (i.e., the variance of e_i), subject to the stated constraints. An equivalent goal was to maximize the associated value of R-squared, subject to the stated constraints. For this analysis the presence of inequality constraints ($0 \le b_{ij} \le 100\%$ for each j) required the use of a quadratic programming algorithm.

The addition of constraints reflecting the fund's actual investment policy causes a slight reduction in the fit of the resulting equation to the data at hand (i.e., a decrease in R-squared to 92.22%). Now, however, the coefficients conform far more closely to the reality of the fund's investment style, making the resulting characterization more likely to provide meaningful results with out-of-sample data.

As Table 2 shows, the analysis suggests that the fund traditionally invests so as to obtain returns similar to those achievable with a portfolio with roughly 70% invested in a market-representative portfolio of value stocks and 30% in a market-representative portfolio of small stocks. During the period investigated, over 92% of the month-to-month variation in the return on the fund could be explained by the concurrent variation in the return on this particular mix of value and small stocks.

STYLE ANALYSIS

The use of quadratic programming for the purpose of determining a fund's exposures to changes in the returns of major asset classes is termed *style analysis* (see Sharpe [1988]). The goal is to find the "best" set of asset class exposures (b_{ij} values) that totals to 100% and conforms with rudimentary information concerning the fund's policies (typically, no net short positions in any asset class; for funds known to employ short positions, other bounds may be invoked). In this context, the best such set of exposures is the one for which the variance of e_i is the least.

Rearranging Equation (1):

$$\tilde{e}_i = \tilde{R}_i - [b_{i1}\tilde{F}_1 + b_{i2}\tilde{F}_2 + \ldots + b_{in}\tilde{F}_n] \quad (3)$$

The term on the left can be interpreted as the difference between the return on the fund (the first term on the right-hand side) and that of a passive portfolio with the same style (shown by the sum of the terms in the brackets). The goal of style analysis is to select the style (set of asset class exposures) that minimizes the variance of this difference. Such a difference can be termed the fund's "tracking error" and its variance the fund's "tracking variance."

Note that the objective of this analysis is not to minimize either the average value of the difference or the sum of the squared differences. Thus the method is not designed to find a style that "makes the fund look bad" (or good). Rather, the goal is to infer as much as possible about the fund's exposures to variations in the returns of the asset classes during the period studied.

We have noted that a quadratic programming algorithm must be used for such an analysis. For an exact solution, one can implement Markowitz's critical line method (see Markowitz [1987]). This study uses the simpler gradient method described in Sharpe [1987]. Although in principle the latter produces only an approximate solution, differences between the results obtained with the two methods prove to be of no practical importance in this application.

MUTUAL FUND STYLES

Figure 3 provides a graphical summary of the results shown in the final column of Table 2. The bar chart indicates the estimated style of the fund, and the pie chart the associated R-squared value. In the latter the R-squared value is identified as attributable to the fund's *style* and the remainder (1 − R-squared) to *selection*.

It is important to note that the style identified in such an analysis is, in a sense, an average of potentially changing styles over the period covered. Month-to-month deviations of the fund's return from that of style itself can arise from selection of specific securities within one or more asset classes, rotation among asset classes, or both security selection and asset class rotation. For the sake of simplicity, we use the term selection to cover all such sources of tracking differences.

It is sometimes helpful to examine the behavior of a manager's average exposures to asset classes over time. To do so, one can perform a series of style analyses, using a fixed number of months for each analysis, rolling the window used for the analysis through time. Figure 4 shows the results from such a study for Trustees' Commingled U.S. Fund.

FIGURE 3

TRUSTEES' COMMINGLED—U.S. PORTFOLIO
JANUARY 1985-DECEMBER 1989

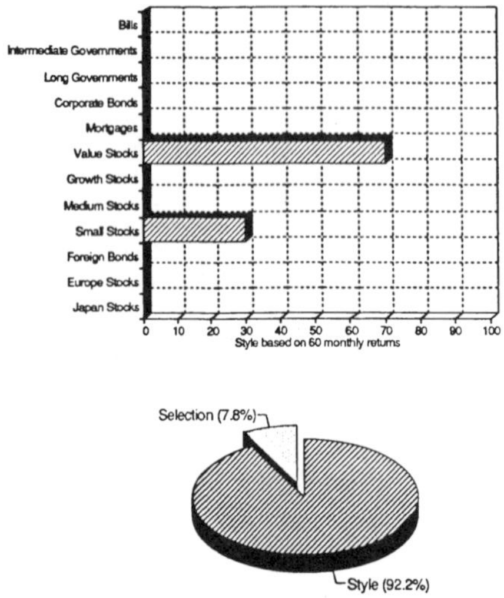

FIGURE 5

FIDELITY MAGELLAN FUND
JANUARY 1985-DECEMBER 1989

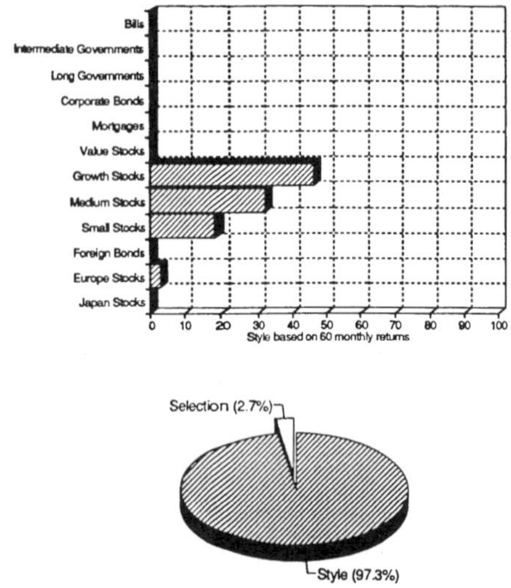

The point at the far right of the diagram represents the style described when the sixty months ending in December 1989 are analyzed. This corresponds to the style shown in Figure 3. Every other point represents the results of an analysis using a different set of sixty monthly returns (note, however, that each such set has fifty-eight months in common with its predecessor). As Figure 4 shows, this fund's style appeared to remain quite constant throughout the period analyzed.

Figures 5 and 6 show the results obtained when the same type of analysis is applied to the returns of Fidelity Magellan Fund — a highly popular open-end common stock fund. As Figure 5 shows, its style differs considerably from that of Trustees' Commingled U.S. Fund; the emphasis is on growth rather than value stocks and exposure to medium-capitalization stocks in addition to smaller ones.

The pie chart in Figure 5 shows that the fund is considerably more diversified (and/or engaged in

FIGURE 4

TRUSTEES' COMMINGLED—U.S. PORTFOLIO
STYLE COMPOSITION

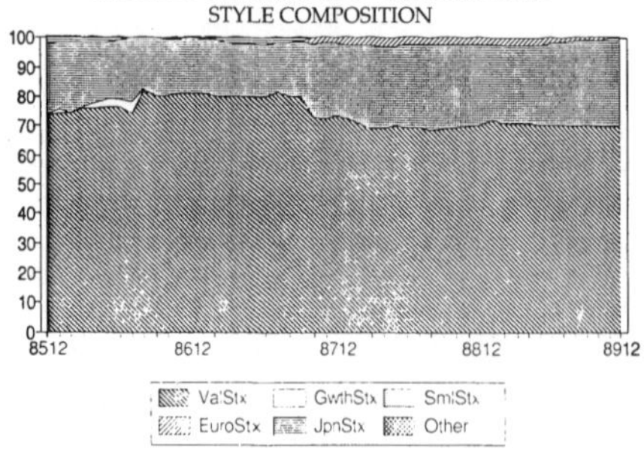

FIGURE 6

FIDELITY MAGELLAN FUND
STYLE COMPOSITION

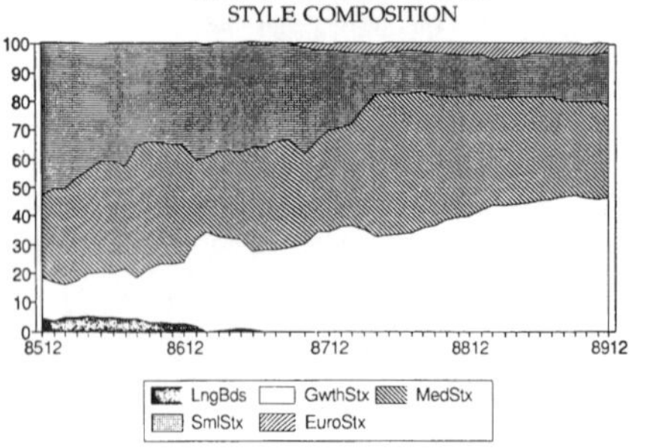

less rotation) than Trustees' Commingled U.S. Fund. During the period covered, over 97.3% of the monthly variation in Magellan returns could be attributed to the concurrent return on a passive portfolio with the style shown in the bar chart in Figure 5.

Figure 6 suggests that the Magellan Fund progressively increased its emphasis on large growth stocks and decreased its exposure to small-capitalization stocks during the 1980s. This is not surprising, as the fund grew to approximately $14 billion by the end of the period, making substantial investment in very small stocks increasingly difficult.

MUTUAL FUND TYPES

Figures 3 through 6 show results for two particular mutual funds. Here we provide a more representative view of the efficacy of the procedure, with style analysis performed for each of 395 funds using returns from January 1985 through December 1989. Averages are taken for both the styles and the R-squared values of all funds classified as being of the same "type" by Jaye C. Jarrett & Company, Inc., the providers of the data used for this study. In all, seven such types are represented. The results are shown in Figures 7 through 13

Each figure should be interpreted as representative of the style (bar chart) and variance attributable to style (pie chart) of a "typical" fund of the type. A portfolio invested in all the funds of a particular type would typically have a much higher R-squared (percent of variance attributable to style) than is shown in the figure in question. Moreover, there is typically considerable variation in both style and R-squared values among the funds within each type group. Given these caveats, the analyses provide useful illustrations of some of the features of the style analysis method.

Utility Stock Fund

Figure 7 shows the results for a typical utility stock fund. Such funds (atypically) concentrate their holdings in one industry. As a result, style accounts for an unusually small part (although still 59.3%) of the variance in return. Although such funds hold common stocks, their returns behave more like a passive portfolio invested in both stocks and bonds. That is, utility revenues are "sticky" because of the regulatory process, causing shares of such companies to have features that are both stock-like and bond-like.

The utility fund example emphasizes the fact that style analysis provides measures that reflect how returns act, rather than a simplistic concept of what the portfolios include. Note, finally, that all equity exposure is to value stocks, reflecting the high dividend yields typical of utility shares.

Growth Equity Fund

Figure 8 portrays a typical growth equity fund. Here the most prominent exposure is, as expected, to growth stocks, although the typical fund of this type

FIGURE 7

STYLES, 1985-1989
FOUR UTILITY FUNDS

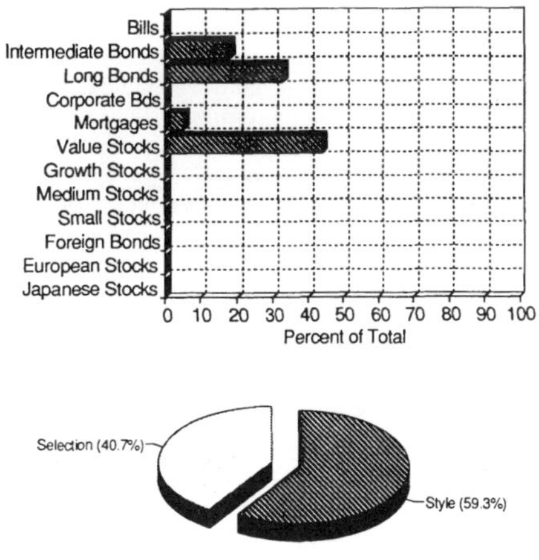

FIGURE 8

STYLES, 1985-1989
161 GROWTH EQUITY FUNDS

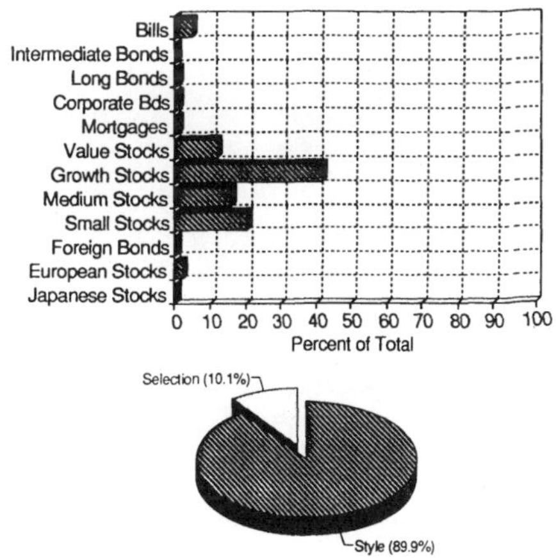

also responds to movements in the returns of other asset classes. Note the exposure to Bills, which probably results from the actual cash holdings that many such funds maintain to meet liquidity needs.

Overall, the results illustrate the fact that few funds are "pure" in the sense of responding only to movements in returns of one asset class. The style analysis procedure can detect some of the subtleties that exist in practice, instead of classifying each fund by a single (pure) style. Finally, note that almost 90% of the monthly variation in return of the typical growth equity fund can be attributed to its style — a result typical of common stock funds.

Growth and Income Equity Fund

Figure 9 shows the characteristics of a typical growth and income equity fund. Here too, style accounts for approximately 90% of the monthly variation in returns. The effects of a liquidity reserve are probably at least partly responsible for the exposure to Bills, although choice of stocks with lower beta values than those in the asset class indexes could also play a role.

Note the almost perfect balance between value and growth stocks, reflecting an "S&P 500-like" stance with respect to large-capitalization stocks. The exposures to small and medium stocks may reflect actual investment in such stocks and/or a preference for equal weighting rather than capitalization weighting within the large stock sector. In an important sense, the source of a set of exposures may not even need to be identified, as long as the exposures are representative of likely future results.

FIGURE 9

STYLES, 1985-1989
118 GROWTH AND INCOME EQUITY FUNDS

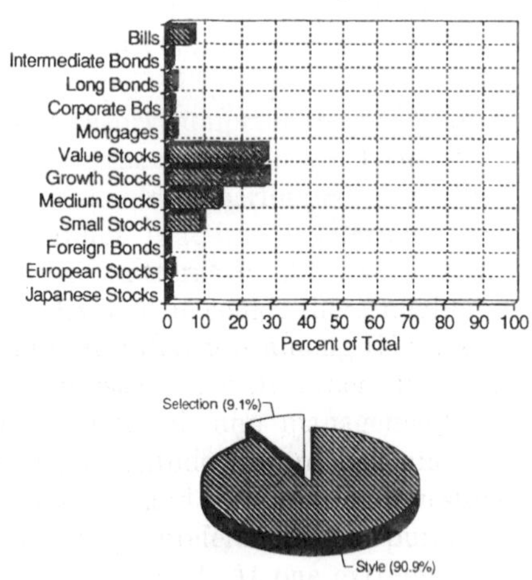

FIGURE 10

STYLES, 1985-1989
THIRTY-FOUR SMALL STOCK FUNDS

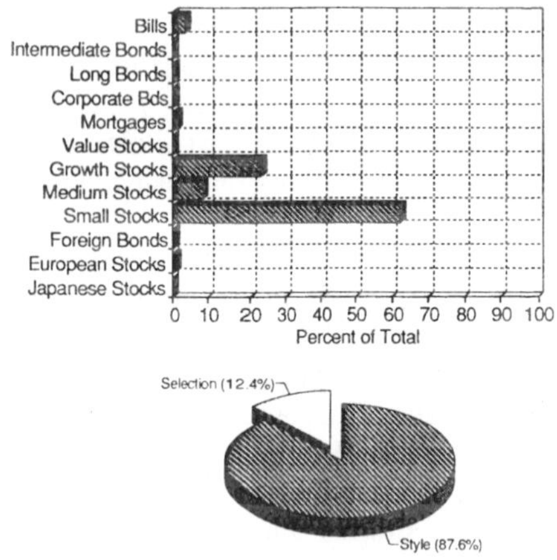

Small Stock Fund

Figure 10 indicates that small stock funds do indeed buy small stocks (as defined by the asset class used for this study). They also appear to buy somewhat larger ones. Moreover, there tends to be an emphasis on growth rather than value. This may reflect the actual purchase of large-capitalization growth stocks by some funds. It may also indicate a preference for medium-capitalization stocks with growth characteristics. As Figure 1 suggests, a point lying to the right of the point representing the medium stock index can be represented by a combination of the large growth stock index, the small stock index, and the medium stock index.

As before, the goal is to represent the behavior of the fund, not its precise composition. Finally, note that the R-squared value is slightly lower (87.6%) than for the other diversified funds — perhaps reflecting the lower liquidity of this sector of the equity market.

Balanced Fund

Figure 11 shows that balanced funds are precisely that. While any single fund may diverge substantially from the style shown in the figure, collectively balanced funds provide results similar to those obtained by holding all U.S. asset classes and small

FIGURE 11

STYLES, 1985-1989
NINETEEN BALANCED FUNDS

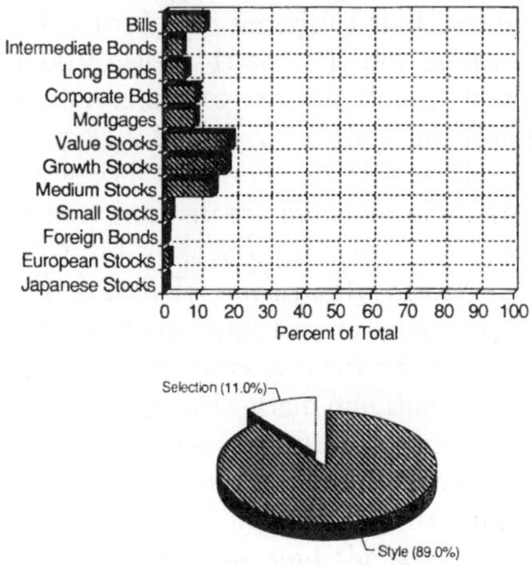

FIGURE 12

STYLES, 1985-1989
FIFTY-FOUR BOND HIGH-QUALITY FUNDS

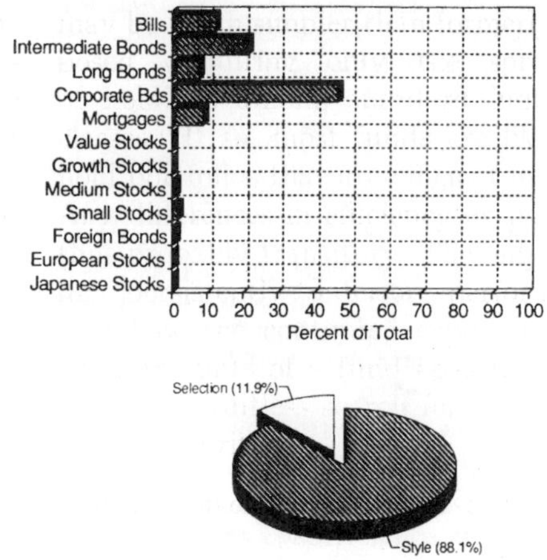

amounts of foreign ones. As with other diversified funds, style accounts for roughly 90% of the monthly variation in the returns for the typical fund of this type.

High-Quality Bond Fund

Figure 12 shows that the method works for bond funds as well as for stock and balanced ones. The typical high-quality bond fund provides exposure to corporate bonds, government bonds, and mortgage-related securities, with style accounting for slightly over 88% of monthly variance in return. In any given case, a mix of, e.g., intermediate government bonds and corporate bonds might reflect actual holdings or the average quality of the corporate bond portfolio.

Thus a portfolio with a higher average quality than that reflected in the Corporate Bond Index typically acts more like a mixture of corporate bonds (defined by the index) and intermediate government bonds. Similarly, a portfolio of corporate bonds with a longer duration than that of the Corporate Bond Index will "track" more closely with a mix of corporate bonds (defined by the index) and long-term government bonds. As always, behavior, not nomenclature, is relevant.

Convertible Bond Fund

Figure 13 shows a case where an asset class not explicitly represented in a model can be represented well by the classes that are included. In this case, 88.8% of the monthly variation in returns of a typical convertible bond fund can be attributed to the concurrent variation in the returns of a mix of stocks, bills, and bonds. This is not too surprising. A convertible bond has characteristics of both bonds and stocks.

FIGURE 13

STYLES, 1985-1989
FIVE CONVERTIBLE BOND FUNDS

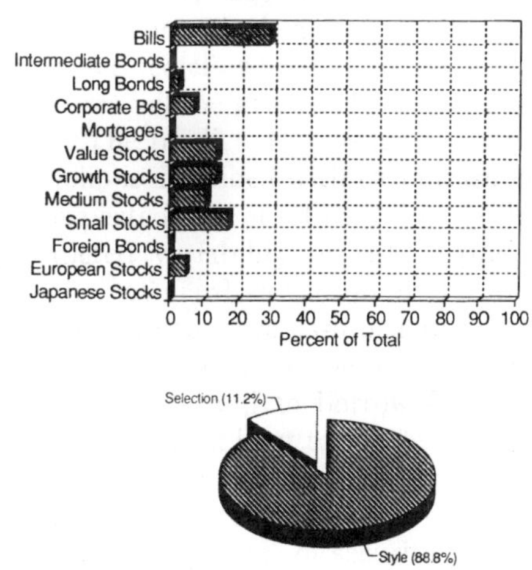

Of course, as bond and stock markets diverge, the relative sensitivities of any given convertible bond to the two markets will change, giving such an instrument its distinctive non-linear characteristic. Interestingly, managers of convertible bond funds appear to have preferred habitats, causing them to buy and sell convertible bonds so as to maintain fairly consistent exposures to asset classes of the type utilized in this study.

Fund Type Summary

As these examples show, a remarkable amount of information can be revealed from analysis of the returns provided by the manager of an investment fund. This is especially gratifying because in the final analysis return is the product the investor buys from such a manager.

THE INVESTOR'S EFFECTIVE ASSET MIX

Once the styles of an investor's funds have been estimated, it is a simple matter to determine the associated overall effective asset mix. Letting W_i represent the proportion of the investor's portfolio invested in fund i, overall portfolio return ($\tilde{R}_p$) will be:

$$\tilde{R}_p = \sum_i W_i \tilde{R}_i \tag{4}$$

As both Equations (1) and (4) are linear, substitution of the former in the latter will provide another linear equation:

$$\tilde{R}_p = \left[\sum_i W_i b_{i1}\right]\tilde{F}_1 + \left[\sum_i W_i b_{i2}\right]\tilde{F}_2 + \ldots + \left[\sum_i W_i b_{in}\right]\tilde{F}_n + \left[\sum_i W_i \tilde{e}_i\right] \tag{5}$$

or:

$$\tilde{R}_p = b_{p1}\tilde{F}_1 + b_{p2}\tilde{F}_2 + \ldots + b_{pn}\tilde{F}_n + \tilde{e}_p \tag{6}$$

where the b_{pj} values are the portfolio's exposures to the asset classes. As can be seen by comparing Equations (5) and (6), each b_{pj} is simply a value-weighted average of the exposures of the component funds to the asset class in question, with the relative amounts invested in the funds used as weights.

The resulting effective asset mix (specified by the values b_{p1}, b_{p2}, ..., b_{pn}) will account for a large portion of the month-to-month variation in returns for the typical portfolio invested in many funds. Under the assumption that the residual e_i terms are uncorrelated, diversification across funds will greatly reduce the variance of the final (non-factor) component and thus increase the portion of variance attributable to asset allocation. Even if some of the residuals are correlated, the use of multiple funds will typically lead to substantial reduction in selection risk.

The effective asset mix represents the style of the investor's overall portfolio. For a multiple-manager portfolio, style is even more important than for an individual fund.

PERFORMANCE MEASUREMENT

In a sense, a passive fund manager provides an investor with an investment style, while an active manager provides both style and selection. This statement can be used to define the terms "active" and "passive" management. In this taxonomy, the precise implementation of an asset class factor model plays a crucial role. This suggests that one may wish to select a set of asset classes so that only superior performance relative to a static mix of the chosen classes warrants the higher fees usually associated with "active" as opposed to "passive" management. This is the approach we take, focusing on a fund's *selection return*, defined as the difference between the fund's return and that of *a passive mix with the same style*.

There are several desiderata associated with the selection of a benchmark for performance measurement. A benchmark portfolio should be 1) a viable alternative, 2) not easily beaten, 3) low in cost, and 4) identifiable before the fact.

Style analysis provides a natural method for constructing benchmarks meeting these requirements. The return obtained by a fund in each month can be compared with the return on a mix of asset classes with the same estimated style, where the style is estimated prior to the month in question. Note that this differs from the use of the e_i values obtained as by-products of a style analysis, because the latter are in-sample, not out-of-sample values.

To illustrate this approach for Trustees' Commingled U.S. and Fidelity's Magellan Funds, for each month t:

1. The fund's style is estimated, using returns from months t-60 through t-1.[6]
2. The return on the resulting style is calculated for month t.
3. The difference between the fund's return in month t and that of the style benchmark determined in Steps 1) and 2) is computed. This difference is defined as the fund's Selection Return for month t.

Figure 14 shows the cumulative sum of the monthly selection returns from January 1986 through December 1989 for Trustees' Commingled U.S. Fund.[7]

FIGURE 14

TRUSTEES' COMMINGLED—U.S. PORTFOLIO
CUMULATIVE RETURN DIFFERENCE: FUND VERSUS STYLE

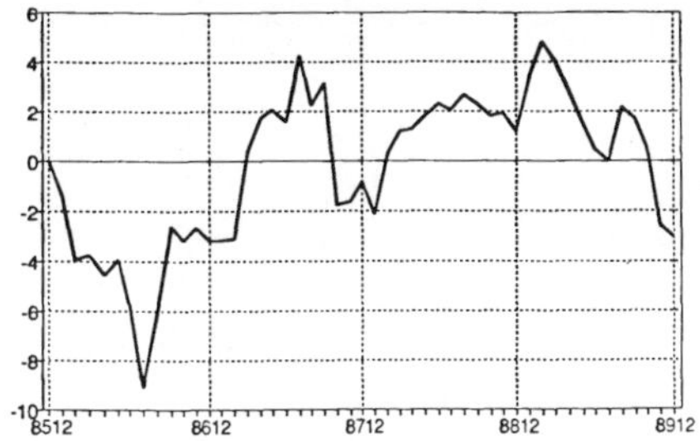

Return Difference

Average	-0.06%	per month
StdDev	1.69%	per month
T(Avg)	-0.26	

In such a graph, increases result from positive selection returns and decreases from negative ones.

The table below the graph in Figure 14 summarizes the results in a different manner. On average, the fund underperformed its style benchmarks by -0.06% (6 basis points) per month, with a standard deviation of 1.69% (169 basis points) per month. The t-statistic associated with the mean difference was, however, small in absolute value, suggesting that the average difference was not statistically significantly different from zero.[8]

Figure 15 emphasizes the advantages to be gained by analyzing performance the way we have described. It compares the return on Trustees' Commingled U.S. Fund with that of Standard & Poor's 500 stock index (commonly used to evaluate mutual fund performance). The fund's performance, so measured, was over three times as bad as that shown previously: The cumulative difference was -10% and the average difference -20 basis points per month.

But such a comparison includes results attributable to both style and selection. During the period in question the fund's style underperformed that of the S&P 500 (primarily because of its exposure to small stocks). Indeed, this accounts for approximately two-thirds of the fund's underperformance relative to the S&P 500.

An investor choosing Trustees' Commingled U.S. Fund could and should have known that its style favored value stocks and small stocks. The choice to expose some of the portfolio to these asset classes is the investor's. Results (good or bad) associated with the choice of such a style should be attributed to the

FIGURE 15

TRUSTEES' COMMINGLED—U.S. PORTFOLIO
CUMULATIVE RETURN DIFFERENCE:
FUND VERSUS BENCHMARK

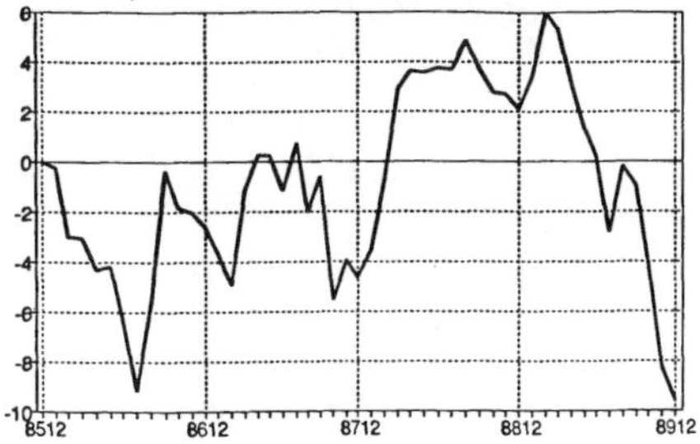

Return Difference

Average	-0.20%	per month
StdDev	2.13%	per month
T(Avg)	-0.65	

Benchmark: S&P500

investor, not to the manager of a fund following that style.

Figures 16 and 17 show the results of similar analyses for Fidelity Magellan Fund. As Figure 16 shows, the fund provided a positive but statistically insignificant outperformance when compared with the S&P 500 over the period.

FIGURE 16

FIDELITY MAGELLAN FUND
CUMULATIVE RETURN DIFFERENCE:
FUND VERSUS BENCHMARK

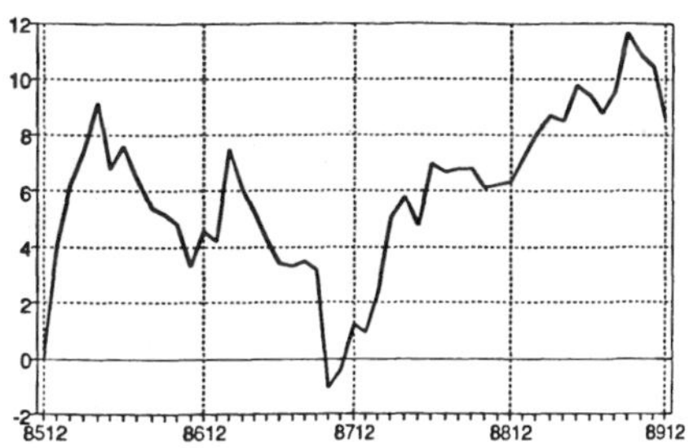

Return Difference

Average	0.18%	per month
StdDev	1.48%	per month
T(Avg)	0.84	

Benchmark: S&P500

FIGURE 17

FIDELITY MAGELLAN FUND
CUMULATIVE RETURN DIFFERENCE: FUND VERSUS STYLE

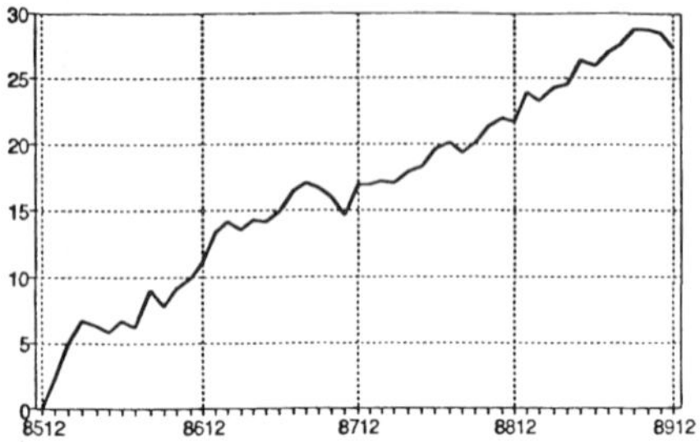

Return Difference

Average	0.57%	per month
StdDev	1.05%	per month
T(Avg)	3.76	

But Figure 17 shows that such a comparison masks Magellan's truly outstanding selection performance. During the period, the fund outperformed its style benchmarks by a cumulative amount of over 25%. Outperformance averaged 57 basis points per month, with a standard deviation of 105 basis points. The t-statistic of 3.76 shows that such differences are highly significant statistically. Two aspects account for the large t-value: the relatively large average return difference, and the relatively small variation in the difference from month to month.[9]

MUTUAL FUND PERFORMANCE

Fidelity Magellan's performance from 1985 through 1989 is far from typical. While only out-of-sample results can provide a definitive test of the collective performance of mutual funds, the average e_i values obtained as by-products of fund style analyses can provide at least some evidence on the matter.

Figure 18 shows the distribution of the average tracking errors obtained from the style analyses of 636 stock, bond, and balanced funds. Each value is the average e_i value obtained from a style analysis using returns for one fund covering the period from January 1985 through December 1989. Note that the distribution is roughly normal, with a mean of -0.074 (-7.4 basis points per month). This is roughly consistent with the hypothesis that the average mutual fund cannot "beat the market" before costs, because such funds constitute a large (and presumably representative) part of the market. Annualized, the mean underperformance is approximately 0.89% per year — a

FIGURE 18

AVERAGE TRACKING ERROR
636 MUTUAL FUNDS, 1985-1989

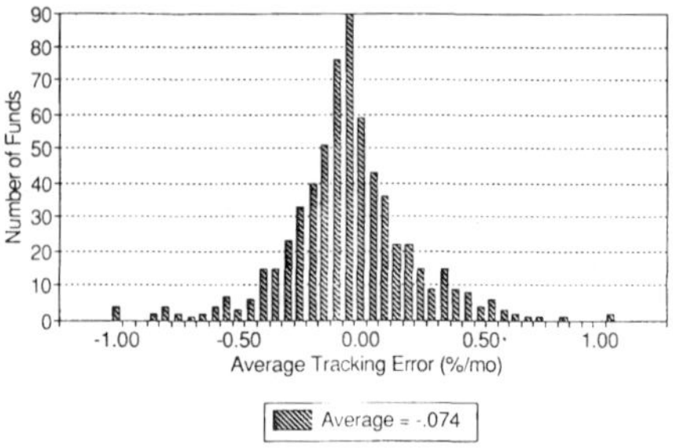

percentage that, if anything, may be slightly less than the non-transaction costs incurred by a typical mutual fund.

MEASURING AN INVESTOR'S PERFORMANCE

In the paradigm developed in this article, an investor makes decisions that result in an effective asset mix and a set of selection returns. In a sense, the investor selects a set of (passive or active) managers and a specific allocation of funds among such managers. Given the managers' styles, this determines the investor's effective asset mix.

The procedures described earlier can be applied directly to measure the efficacy with which the investor performs his or her functions. The performance of each month's effective asset mix can be compared with that of a predetermined benchmark asset mix to assess the value added or lost through asset allocation decisions (advertent or inadvertent). The remainder of the investor's return is attributable to the joint effects of 1) the fund managers' selection returns, and 2) the investor's allocation of money among the managers. The investor selection return ($\tilde{S}_p$) is simply:

$$\tilde{S}_p = \sum_i W_i \tilde{S}_i \quad (7)$$

where the $\tilde{S}_i$ values are determined out-of-sample, using procedures such as those described earlier.

CONCLUSION

An asset class factor model can help make order out of the chaos that often attends the investment process. It can provide a consistent view of investment decisions that investors make to economize on information flows and exploit comparative advantages. The style analysis procedure described in this article allows such a model to be implemented economically. At the very least it can serve as a valuable supplement to other methods designed to help investors achieve their goals in cost-effective ways.

[1]When an equation such as (1) is fit by regression analysis, the same value will be obtained whether Equation (2) is used or the proportion of variance explained is computed directly. This follows from the fact that the residual returns obtained from a regression analysis are guaranteed to be uncorrelated with each of the asset class returns. When quadratic programming is employed, it is possible that the residual returns will be correlated with the returns on one or more asset classes; hence the two procedures for computing R-squared may yield slightly different results. In practice, such differences are typically insignificant. This article uses Equation (2) for all calculations.

[2]If regression analysis is used to fit Equation (1), conventional tests of statistical significance can also be invoked to evaluate the likely performance of the model out-of-sample. When quadratic programming is employed, the assumptions that lie behind such tests are violated, making true out-of-sample tests the only reliable means of evaluating the efficacy of the approach.

[3]More precisely, BARRA's all-U.S. universe.

[4]That is, a security already placed in one class is not permitted to migrate to the other class unless it passes the capitalization requirement by 20% of the boundary value.

[5]More generally, the convex hull of the points.

[6]For a more operational procedure, returns for a period ending with month t-2 might be used.

[7]No compounding is done in Figure 14 (and the subsequent ones using similar portrayals). This makes it possible to compare vertical distances directly at any point in the figure. Because selection return represents the difference between the returns of two portfolios, compounding would not provide the difference in the cumulative values of the fund and the benchmark. This being said, it should be pointed out that as the logarithm of a monthly value relative will generally differ little from the corresponding monthly return, a graph where compounded selection returns are shown on a logarithmic scale appears similar to one where returns are summed and shown on an arithmetic scale, as in this article.

[8]The t-statistic is computed by dividing the average return difference by the standard error of the mean (here, the standard deviation of the return difference divided by the square root of 60).

[9]The t-statistic is closely related to the reward-to-variability ratio (sometimes termed the Sharpe Ratio) for the "active" component of a fund's return, which is simply the mean value divided by the standard deviation.

REFERENCES

Markowitz, Harry M. *Mean-Variance Analysis in Portfolio Choice and Capital Markets.* Oxford: Basil Blackwell, Inc., 1987.

Sharpe, William F. "An Algorithm for Portfolio Improvement," in Kenneth D. Lawrence, John B. Guerard, Jr., and Gary D. Reeves, eds., *Advances in Mathematical Programming and Financial Planning,* Vol. 1, pp. 155-170. Greenwich: JAI Press, Inc., 1987.

——. "Determining a Fund's Effective Asset Mix." *Investment Management Review,* December 1988, pp. 59-69.

The Sharpe Ratio

Properly used, it can improve investment management.

William F. Sharpe

Over twenty-five years ago, in Sharpe [1966] I introduced a measure for the performance of mutual funds and proposed the term *reward-to-variability ratio* to describe it (the measure is also described in Sharpe [1975]). While the measure has gained considerable popularity, the name has not. Other authors have termed the original version the Sharpe Index (Radcliff [1990, p. 286] and Haugen [1993, p. 315]), the Sharpe Measure (Bodie, Kane, and Marcus [1993, p. 804], Elton and Gruber [1991, p. 652], and Reilly [1989, p. 803]), or the Sharpe Ratio (Morningstar [1993, p. 24]). Generalized versions have also appeared under various names (see, for example, BARRA [1992, p. 21] and Capaul, Rowley, and Sharpe [1993, p. 33]).

Bowing to increasingly common usage, this article refers to both the original measure and more generalized versions as the Sharpe Ratio. My goal here is to go well beyond the discussion of the original measure in Sharpe [1966] and Sharpe [1975], providing more generality and covering a broader range of applications.

THE RATIO

Most performance measures are *computed* using historic data but *justified* on the basis of predicted relationships. Practical implementations use ex post results while theoretical discussions focus on ex ante values. Implicitly or explicitly, it is assumed that historic results have at least some predictive ability.

WILLIAM F. SHARPE is professor of finance at the Graduate School of Business of Stanford University in Stanford (CA 94035).

For some applications, it suffices for future values of a measure to be related monotonically to past values — that is, if fund X has a higher historic measure than fund Y, it is assumed it will have a higher future measure. For other applications, the relationship must be proportional — that is, it is assumed that the future measure will equal some constant (typically less than 1.0) times the historic measure.

To avoid ambiguity, we define here both ex ante and ex post versions of the Sharpe Ratio, beginning with the former. Elsewhere, however, we focus on the use of the ratio for making decisions, and hence are concerned with the ex ante version. The important issues associated with the relationships (if any) between historic Sharpe Ratios and unbiased forecasts of the ratio are left for other expositions.

Throughout, we build on Markowitz's mean-variance paradigm, which assumes that the mean and standard deviation of the distribution of one-period return are sufficient statistics for evaluating the prospects of an investment portfolio. Clearly, comparisons based on the first two moments of a distribution do not take into account possible differences among portfolios in other moments or in distributions of outcomes across states of nature that may be associated with different levels of investor utility.

When such considerations are especially important, return mean and variance may not suffice, requiring the use of additional or substitute measures. Such situations are, however, beyond the scope of this article. Our goal is simply to examine the situations in which two measures (mean and variance) can usefully be summarized with one (the Sharpe Ratio).

The Ex Ante Sharpe Ratio

Let $\tilde{R}_F$ represent the return on fund F in the forthcoming period and $\tilde{R}_B$ the return on a benchmark portfolio or security. The tildes over the variables indicate that the exact values may not be known in advance. Define $\tilde{d}$, the *differential return*, as:

$$\tilde{d} \equiv \tilde{R}_F - \tilde{R}_B \tag{1}$$

Let $\bar{d}$ be the *expected value* of $\tilde{d}$ and σ_d be the predicted standard deviation of $\tilde{d}$. The ex ante Sharpe Ratio (S) is:

$$S \equiv \frac{\bar{d}}{\sigma_d} \tag{2}$$

In this version, the ratio indicates the expected differential return per unit of risk associated with the differential return.

The Ex Post Sharpe Ratio

Let R_{Ft} be the return on the fund in period t, R_{Bt} the return on the benchmark portfolio or security in period t, and D_t the differential return in period t:

$$D_t \equiv R_{Ft} - R_{Bt} \tag{3}$$

Let $\bar{D}$ be the average value of D_t over the historic period from t = 1 through T:

$$\bar{D} \equiv \frac{1}{T}\sum_{t=1}^{T} D_t \tag{4}$$

and σ_D be the standard deviation over the period:[1]

$$\sigma_D \equiv \sqrt{\frac{\sum_{t=1}^{T}(D_t - \bar{D})^2}{T - 1}} \tag{5}$$

The ex post, or historic, Sharpe Ratio (S_h) is:

$$S_h \equiv \frac{\bar{D}}{\sigma_D} \tag{6}$$

In this version, the ratio indicates the historic average differential return per unit of historic variability of the differential return.

It is a simple matter to compute an ex post Sharpe Ratio using a spreadsheet program. The returns on a fund are listed in one column and those of the desired benchmark in the next column. The differences are computed in a third column. Standard functions are then used to compute the components of the ratio. For example, if the differential returns are in cells C1 through C60, a formula would provide the Sharpe Ratio using Microsoft's Excel spreadsheet program:

AVERAGE(C1:C60)/STDEV(C1:C60)

The historic Sharpe Ratio is closely related to the t-statistic for measuring the statistical significance of the mean differential return. The t-statistic will equal the Sharpe Ratio times the square root of T (the number of returns used for the calculation). If historic Sharpe Ratios for a set of funds are computed using the same number of observations, the Sharpe Ratios will thus be proportional to the t-statistics of the means.

Time Dependence

The Sharpe Ratio is not independent of the time period over which it is measured. This is true for both ex ante and ex post measures.

Consider the simplest possible case. The one-period mean and standard deviation of the differential return are, respectively, $\bar{d}_1$ and σ_{d_1}. Assume that the differential return over T periods is measured by simply summing the one-period differential returns, and that the latter have zero serial correlation. Denote the mean and standard deviation of the resulting T-period return, respectively, $\bar{d}_T$ and σ_{d_T}. Under the assumed conditions:

$$\bar{d}_T = T d_1 \qquad (7)$$

$$\sigma^2_{d_T} = T \sigma^2_{d_1} \qquad (8)$$

and:

$$\sigma_{d_T} = \sqrt{T}\, \sigma_{d_1} \qquad (9)$$

Letting S_1 and S_T denote the Sharpe Ratios for 1 and T periods, respectively, it follows that:

$$S_T = \sqrt{T}\, S_1 \qquad (10)$$

In practice, the situation is likely to be more complex. Multiperiod returns are usually computed taking compounding into account, which makes the relationship more complicated. Moreover, underlying differential returns may be serially correlated. Even if the underlying process does not involve serial correlation, a specific ex post sample may.

It is common practice to "annualize" data that apply to periods other than one year, using Equations (7) and (8). Doing so before computing a Sharpe Ratio can provide at least reasonably meaningful comparisons among strategies, even if predictions are initially stated in terms of different measurement periods.

To maximize information content, it is usually desirable to measure risks and returns using fairly short (e.g., monthly) periods. For purposes of standardization it is then desirable to annualize the results.

To provide perspective, consider investment in a broad stock market index, financed by borrowing. Typical estimates of the annual excess return on the stock market in a developed country might include a mean of 6% per year and a standard deviation of 15%. The resulting excess return Sharpe Ratio of "the stock market," stated in annual terms, would then be 0.40.

Correlations

The ex ante Sharpe Ratio takes into account both the expected differential return and the associated risk, while the ex post version takes into account both the average differential return and the associated variability. Neither incorporates information about the correlation of a fund or strategy with other assets, liabilities, or previous realizations of its own return. For this reason, the ratio may need to be supplemented in certain applications. Such considerations are discussed in later sections.

Related Measures

The literature surrounding the Sharpe Ratio has, unfortunately, led to a certain amount of confusion. To provide clarification, two related measures are described here. The first uses a different term to cover cases that include the construct that we call the Sharpe Ratio. The second uses the same term to describe a different but related construct.

Whether measured ex ante or ex post, it is essential that the Sharpe Ratio be computed using the mean and standard deviation of a *differential return* (or, more broadly, the return on what will be termed a zero investment strategy). Otherwise it loses its *raison d'être.* Clearly, the Sharpe Ratio can be considered a special case of the more general construct of the ratio of the mean of any distribution to its standard deviation.

In the investment arena, a number of authors associated with BARRA (a major supplier of analytic tools and data bases) have used the term *information ratio* to describe such a general measure. In some publications, the ratio is defined to apply only to differential returns and is thus equivalent to the measure that we call the Sharpe Ratio (see, for example, Rudd and Clasing [1982, p. 513] and Grinold [1989, p. 31]). In others, it also encompasses the ratio of the mean to the standard deviation of the distribution of the return on a single investment such as a fund or a benchmark (see, for example, BARRA [1993, p. 22]). While such a "return information ratio" may be useful as a descriptive statistic, it lacks a number of the key properties of what might be termed a "differential return information ratio" and may in some instances lead to wrong decisions.

For example, consider the choice of a strategy involving cash and one of two funds, X and Y. X has an expected return of 5% and a standard deviation of 10%. Y has an expected return of 8% and a standard deviation of 20%. The riskless rate of interest is 3%. According to the ratio of expected return to standard deviation, X (5/10, or 0.50) is superior to Y (8/20, or 0.40). According to the Sharpe Ratios using excess return, X (2/10, or 0.20) is inferior to Y (5/20, or 0.25).

Now, consider an investor who wishes to attain a standard deviation of 10%. This can be achieved with fund X, which will provide an expected return of 5.0%. It can also be achieved with an investment of 50% of the investor's funds in Y and 50% in the riskless asset. The latter will provide an expected return of 5.5% — clearly the superior alternative.

Thus the Sharpe Ratio provides the correct answer (a strategy using Y is preferred to one using X), while the "return information ratio" provides the wrong one.

In their seminal work, Treynor and Black [1973] define the term "Sharpe Ratio" as the *square* of the measure that we describe. Others, such as Rudd and Clasing [1982, p. 518] and Grinold [1989, p. 31], also use such a definition.

While interesting in certain contexts, this construct has the curious property that all values are positive — even those for which the mean differential return is negative. It thus obscures important information concerning performance. We prefer to follow more common practice and thus refer to the Treynor-Black measure as the *Sharpe Ratio squared* (SR^2).[2]

We focus here on the Sharpe Ratio, which takes into account both risk and return without reference to a market index. Sharpe [1966, 1975] discusses both the Sharpe Ratio and measures based on market indexes, such as Jensen's alpha and Treynor's average excess return to beta ratio.

SCALE INDEPENDENCE

Originally, the benchmark for the Sharpe Ratio was taken to be a riskless security. In such a case, the *differential return* is equal to the *excess return* of the fund over a one-period riskless rate of interest. Many of the descriptions of the ratio in Sharpe [1966, 1975] focus on this case.

More recent applications use benchmark portfolios designed to have a set of "factor loadings" or an "investment style" similar to that of the fund being evaluated. In such cases, the differential return represents the difference between the return on the fund and the return that would have been obtained from a "similar" passive alternative. The difference between the two returns may be termed an "active return" or "selection return," depending on the underlying procedure used to select the benchmark.

Treynor and Black [1973] cover the case in which the benchmark portfolio is, in effect, a combination of riskless securities and the "market portfolio." Rudd and Clasing [1982] describe the use of benchmarks based on factor loadings from a multifactor model. Sharpe [1992] uses a procedure termed *style analysis* to select a mix of asset class index funds that have a "style" similar to that of the fund. When such a mix is used as a benchmark, the differential return is termed the fund's *selection return*. The Sharpe Ratio of the selection return can then serve as a measure of the fund's performance over and above that due to its investment style.[3]

Central to the usefulness of the Sharpe Ratio is the fact that a differential return represents the result of a *zero-investment strategy*. This can be defined as any strategy that involves a zero outlay of money in the present and returns either a positive, negative, or zero amount in the future, depending on circumstances. A differential return clearly falls in this class, because it can be obtained by taking a long position in one asset (the fund) and a short position in another (the benchmark), with the funds from the latter used to finance the purchase of the former.

In the original applications of the ratio, where the benchmark is taken to be a one-period riskless asset, the differential return represents the payoff from a unit investment in the fund, financed by borrowing.[4] More generally, the differential return corresponds to the payoff obtained from a unit investment in the fund, financed by a short position in the benchmark. For example, a fund's *selection return* can be considered to be the payoff from a unit investment in the fund, financed by short positions in a mix of asset class index funds with the same style.

A differential return can be obtained explicitly by entering into an agreement in which a party and a counterparty agree to *swap* the return on the benchmark for the return on the fund and vice versa. A *forward contract* provides a similar result. Arbitrage will insure that the return on such a contract will be very close to the excess return on the underlying asset for the period ending on the delivery date.[5] A similar relationship holds approximately for traded contracts such as stock index futures, which clearly represent zero-investment strategies.[6]

To compute the return for a zero-investment strategy, the payoff is divided by a *notional value.* For example, the dollar payoff for a swap is often set to equal the difference between the dollar return on an investment of \$X in one asset and that on an investment of \$X in another. The net difference can then be expressed as a proportion of \$X, which serves as the notional value. Returns on futures positions are often computed in a similar manner, using the initial value of the underlying asset as a base. In effect, the same approach is utilized when the difference between two returns is computed.

Since there is zero net investment in any such strategy, the *percent* return can be made as large or small as desired by simply changing the notional value used in such a computation. The *scale* of the return thus depends on the more-or-less arbitrary choice of the notional value used for its computation.[7]

Changes in the notional value clearly affect the mean and the standard deviation of the distribution of return, but the changes are of the same magnitude, leaving the Sharpe Ratio unaffected. The ratio is thus *scale-independent.*[8]

THE INFLUENCE OF A ZERO-INVESTMENT STRATEGY ON ASSET RISK AND RETURN

Scale independence is more than a mathematical artifice. It is key to understanding why the Sharpe Ratio can provide an efficient summary statistic for a zero-investment strategy. To show this, we consider the case of an investor with a pre-existing portfolio who is considering the choice of a zero-investment strategy to augment current investments.

The Relative Position in a Zero-Investment Strategy

Assume that the investor has \$A in assets and has placed this money in an investment portfolio with a return of $\tilde{R}_I$. She is considering investment in a zero-investment strategy that will provide a return of $\tilde{d}$ per unit of notional value. Denote the notional value chosen as V (e.g., investment of V in a fund financed by a short position of V in a benchmark). Define the *relative position*, p, as the ratio of the notional value to the investor's assets:

$$p \equiv \frac{V}{A} \tag{11}$$

The end-of-period payoff will be:

$$A(1 + \tilde{R}_I) + Ap\tilde{d} \tag{12}$$

Let $\tilde{R}_A$ denote the total return on the investor's initial assets. Then:

$$\tilde{R}_A = \tilde{R}_I + p\tilde{d} \tag{13}$$

If $\overline{R}_A$ denotes the expected return on assets and $\overline{R}_I$ the expected return on the investment:

$$\overline{R}_A = \overline{R}_I + p\overline{d} \tag{14}$$

Now, let σ_A, σ_I, and σ_d denote the standard deviations of the returns on assets, the investment, and the zero-investment strategy, respectively, and ρ_{Id} the correlation between the return on the investment and the return on the zero-investment strategy. Then:

$$\sigma_A^2 = \sigma_I^2 + 2\rho_{Id}\sigma_I p\sigma_d + (p\sigma_d)^2 \tag{15}$$

or, rewriting slightly:

$$\sigma_A^2 = \sigma_I^2 + 2\,\sigma_I\,\rho_{Id}\,(p\sigma_d) + (p\sigma_d)^2 \quad (16)$$

The Risk Position in a Zero-Investment Strategy

The parenthesized expression ($p\sigma_d$) is of particular interest. It indicates the risk of the position in the zero-investment strategy relative to the investor's overall assets. Let k denote this *risk position*

$$k \equiv p\sigma_d \quad (17)$$

For many purposes it is desirable to consider k as the relevant decision variable. Doing so states the magnitude of a zero-investment strategy in terms of its risk relative to the investor's overall assets. In effect, one first determines k, the level of risk of the zero-investment strategy. Having answered this fundamental question, the relative (p) and absolute (V) amounts of notional value for the strategy can readily be determined, using Equations (17) and (11).[9]

Asset Risk and Expected Return

It is straightforward to determine the manner in which asset risk and expected return are related to the risk position of the zero-investment strategy, its correlation with the investment, and its Sharpe Ratio.

Substituting k in Equation (16) gives the relationship between 1) asset risk, and 2) the risk position and the correlation of the strategy with the investment:

$$\sigma_A^2 = \sigma_I^2 + 2\,\sigma_I\,\rho_{Id}\,k + k^2 \quad (18)$$

To see the relationship between asset expected return and the characteristics of the zero-investment strategy, note that the Sharpe Ratio is the ratio of $\bar{d}$ to σ_d. It follows that

$$\bar{d} = S\sigma_d \quad (19)$$

Substituting Equation (19) in Equation (14) gives:

$$\bar{R}_A = \bar{R}_I + pS\sigma_d \quad (20)$$

or:

$$\bar{R}_A = \bar{R}_I + kS \quad (21)$$

which shows that the expected return on assets is related directly to the product of the risk position times the Sharpe Ratio of the strategy.

By selecting an appropriate scale, any zero-investment strategy can be used to achieve a desired level (k) of relative risk. This level, plus the strategy's Sharpe Ratio, will determine asset expected return, as shown by Equation (21). Asset risk, however, will depend on both the relative risk (k) and the correlation of the strategy with the other investment (σ_{Id}). In general, the Sharpe Ratio, which does not take that correlation into account, will not by itself provide sufficient information to determine a set of decisions that will produce an optimal combination of asset risk and return, given an investor's tolerance of risk.

ADDING A ZERO-INVESTMENT STRATEGY TO AN EXISTING PORTFOLIO

Fortunately, there are important special cases in which the Sharpe Ratio will provide sufficient information for decisions on the optimal risk/return combination: one in which the pre-existing portfolio is riskless, the other in which it is risky.

Adding a Strategy to a Riskless Portfolio

Suppose first that an investor plans to allocate money between a riskless asset and a single risky fund (e.g., a "balanced" fund). This is, in effect, the case analyzed in Sharpe [1966, 1975].

We assume there is a pre-existing portfolio invested solely in a riskless security, to which is to be added a zero-investment strategy involving a long position in a fund, financed by a short position in a riskless asset (i.e., borrowing). Letting R_c denote the return on such a "cash equivalent," Equations (1) and (13) can be written as:

$$\tilde{d} = \tilde{R}_F - R_c \quad (22)$$

and

$$\tilde{R}_A = R_c + p\tilde{d} \quad (23)$$

Since the investment is riskless, its standard deviation of return is zero, so both the first and second terms on the right-hand side of Equation (18) become zero, giving:

$$\sigma_A = k \tag{24}$$

The investor's total risk will thus be equal to that of the position taken in the zero-investment strategy, which will in turn equal the risk of the position in the fund.

Letting S_F represent the Sharpe Ratio of fund F, Equation (21) can be written:

$$\overline{R}_A = R_c + kS_F \tag{25}$$

It is clear from Equations (24) and (25) that the investor should choose the desired level of risk (k), then obtain that level of risk by using the fund (F) with the greatest excess return Sharpe Ratio. Correlation does not play a role since the remaining holdings are riskless.

This is illustrated in the Exhibit. Points X and Y represent two (mutually exclusive) strategies. The desired level of risk is given by k. It can be obtained with strategy X using a relative position of p_X (shown in the figure at point PxX), or with strategy Y using a relative position of p_Y (shown in the figure at point PyY). An appropriately scaled version of strategy X clearly provides a higher mean return (shown at point MRx) than an appropriately scaled version of strategy Y (shown at point MRy). Strategy X is hence to be preferred.

The Exhibit shows that the mean return associated with *any* desired risk position will be greater if strategy X is adopted instead of strategy Y. But the slope of such a line *is* the Sharpe Ratio. Hence, as long as only the mean return and the risk position of the zero-investment strategy are relevant, the optimal solution involves maximization of the Sharpe Ratio of the zero-investment strategy.

Consider, for example, a choice between fund XX, with a risk of 10% and an excess return Sharpe Ratio of 0.20, and fund YY, with a risk of 20% and an excess return Sharpe Ratio of 0.25. Assume the investor has $100 to invest and desires a level of risk (here, k) equal to 15%.

The optimal strategy involves investment of $100 in the riskless asset plus a zero-investment strategy based on fund YY. To make the risk of the latter equal to 15%, a relative position (p) of 0.75 should be taken. This, in turn, requires an investment of $75 in the fund, financed by $75 of borrowing (i.e., a short position in the riskless asset). The net position in the riskless asset will thus be $25 ($100 – $75), with $75 invested in Fund YY.

In this case the investor's tasks include the selection of the fund with the greatest Sharpe Ratio and the allocation of wealth between this fund and borrowing or lending, as required to obtain the desired level of asset risk.

Adding a Strategy to a Risky Portfolio

Consider now the case in which a single fund is to be selected to complement a pre-existing group of risky investments. For example, an investor might have $100, with $80 already committed (e.g., to a group of bond and stock funds). The goal is to allocate the remaining $20 between a riskless asset ("cash") and a single risky fund (e.g., a "growth stock fund"), accepting the possibility that the amount allocated to cash might be positive, zero, or negative, depending on the desired risk and the risk of the chosen fund.

In this case the investment should be taken as the pre-existing investment plus a riskless asset (in the example, $80 in the initial investments plus $20 in cash equivalents). The return on this total portfolio will be $\tilde{R}_I$. The zero-investment strategy will again involve a long position in a risky fund and a short position in the riskless asset.

As stated earlier, in such a case it will not necessarily be optimal to select the fund with the largest possible Sharpe Ratio. While the ratio takes into account two key attributes of the predicted performance of a zero-investment strategy (its expected return and its risk), it does not include information about the correlation of its return with that of the investor's other holdings (ρ_{Id}). It is entirely possible that a fund with a smaller Sharpe Ratio could have a sufficiently smaller

EXHIBIT
MUTUALLY EXCLUSIVE INVESTMENTS

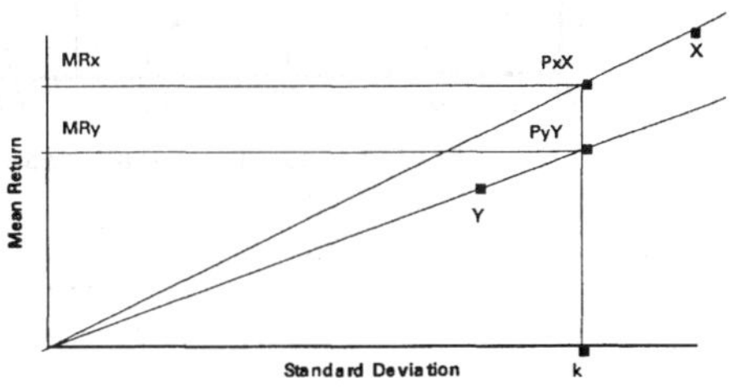

correlation with the investor's other assets that it would provide a higher expected return on assets for any given level of overall asset risk.

However, if the alternative funds being analyzed have similar correlations with the investor's other assets, it will still be optimal to select the fund with the greatest Sharpe Ratio. To see this, note that with ρ_{Id} taken as given, Equation (18) shows that there is a one-to-one correspondence between σ_A and k. Thus, for any desired level of asset risk, the investor chooses the corresponding risk position k given by Equation (18), regardless of the fund to be employed.

But, as before, the expected return on assets will be:

$$\overline{R}_A = \overline{R}_I + kS_F \tag{26}$$

which can be maximized by selecting the fund with the largest Sharpe Ratio.

The practical implication is clear. When choosing one from among a group of funds of a particular type for inclusion in a larger set of holdings, the one with the largest predicted excess return Sharpe Ratio may reasonably be chosen, if it can be assumed that all the funds in the set have similar correlations with the other holdings. If this condition is not met, some account should be taken of the differential levels of such correlations.

THE CHOICE OF A SET OF UNCORRELATED STRATEGIES

Suppose finally that an investor has a pre-existing set of investments and is considering taking positions in one or more zero-investment strategies, each of which is uncorrelated both with the existing investments and with each of the other such strategies. Such lack of correlation is generally assumed for residual returns from an assumed factor model and hence applies to strategies in which long and short positions are combined to obtain zero exposures to all underlying factors in such a model.

In particular, this is assumed to hold for the "non-market returns," which are the residual returns in one-factor "market models" of the type employed in Treynor-Black [1973]. It is also assumed to hold for the "active returns" that constitute the residual returns in a model of the type used by BARRA (described, for example, in Grinold [1989]).

Most germane, perhaps, for selecting funds, this is assumed to hold for the "selection returns" that constitute the residuals from the asset class factor model used in the style analysis procedure described in Sharpe [1992]. Note, however, that the key results apply to all three cases.[10]

Under the assumed conditions, the counterpart to Equation (13) is:

$$\tilde{R}_A = \tilde{R}_I + \sum_i p_i \tilde{d}_i \tag{27}$$

where p_i represents the relative position taken in strategy i, and $\tilde{d}_i$ represents its return.

Letting σ_{d_i} represent the risk of position i, asset risk is given by:

$$\sigma_A^2 = \sigma_I^2 + \sum_i p_i^2 \sigma_{d_i}^2 \tag{28}$$

and expected asset return by:

$$\overline{R}_A = \overline{R}_I + \sum_i p_i \overline{d}_i \tag{29}$$

Adding subscripts to Equations (21) and (18), and substituting the results, gives:

$$\overline{R}_A = \overline{R}_I + \sum_i k_i S_i \tag{30}$$

and

$$\sigma_A^2 = \sigma_I^2 + \sum_i k_i^2 \tag{31}$$

Now, assume that the investor's goal is to maximize a standard risk-adjusted expected return of the form:

$$\overline{R}_A - \tau^{-1} \sigma_A^2 \tag{32}$$

where τ represents risk tolerance (the marginal rate of substitution of variance for expected return). Substituting Equations (30) and (31) in (32) gives:

$$\overline{R}_I + \sum_i k_i S_i - \tau^{-1} (\sigma_I^2 + \sum_i k_i^2) \quad (33)$$

Since the terms involving the initial investment will be unaffected by the decisions (k_is) concerning the zero-investment strategies, it suffices to maximize:

$$\sum_i k_i S_i - \tau^{-1} \sum_i k_i^2 \quad (34)$$

To do so, the partial derivative with respect to each decision variable (k_i) should be set equal to zero:

$$S_i - 2\tau^{-1}k_i = 0 \quad (35)$$

The optimal risk position in strategy i is thus:

$$k_i = \frac{\tau}{2} S_i \quad (36)$$

Hence the risk levels of the strategies should be proportional to their Sharpe Ratios. Strategies with zero predicted Sharpe Ratios should be ignored. Those with positive ratios should be "held long," and those with negative ratios "held short." If strategy X has a positive Sharpe Ratio that is twice as large as that of strategy Y, twice as much risk should be taken with X as with Y. The overall scale of all the positions should, in turn, be proportional to the investor's risk tolerance.

An interesting application occurs when long and short positions can be taken (e.g., via financial futures) in the asset classes that underlie a style analysis model of the type described in Sharpe [1992]. In principle, funds should be selected only on the basis of their selection returns, with the respective amounts of selection risk set in proportion to the funds' selection return Sharpe Ratios. The net exposures to asset classes required to implement this mixture of zero-investment strategies can then be compared with the investor's desired passive asset mix to determine needed net positions.

SUMMARY

The Sharpe Ratio is designed to measure the expected return per unit of risk for a *zero-investment strategy*. The difference between the returns on two investment assets represents the results of such a strategy. The Sharpe Ratio does not cover cases in which only one investment return is involved.

Clearly, any measure that attempts to summarize even an unbiased prediction of performance with a single number requires a substantial set of assumptions for justification. In practice, such assumptions are, at best, likely to hold only approximately. Certainly, the use of unadjusted historic (ex post) Sharpe Ratios as surrogates for unbiased predictions of ex ante ratios is subject to serious question. Despite such caveats, there is much to recommend a measure that at least takes into account both risk and expected return over any alternative that focuses only on the latter.

For a number of investment decisions, ex ante Sharpe Ratios can provide important inputs. When choosing one from among a set of funds to provide representation in a particular market sector, it makes sense to favor the one with the greatest predicted Sharpe Ratio, as long as the correlations of the funds with other relevant asset classes are reasonably similar. When allocating funds among several such funds, it makes sense to allocate funds such that the selection (residual) risk levels are proportional to the predicted Sharpe Ratios for the selection (residual) returns. If some of the implied net positions are infeasible or involve excessive transaction costs, of course, the decision rules must be modified. Nonetheless, Sharpe Ratios may still provide useful guidance.

Whatever the application, it is essential to remember that the Sharpe Ratio does not take correlations into account. When a choice may affect important correlations with other assets in an investor's portfolio, such information should be used to supplement comparisons based on Sharpe Ratios.

All the same, the ratio of expected added return per unit of added risk provides a convenient summary of two important aspects of any strategy involving the difference between the return of a fund and that of a relevant benchmark. The Sharpe Ratio is designed to provide such a measure. Properly used, it can improve the process of managing investments.

ENDNOTES

[1]We use the formula for the standard deviation of a population, taking the observations as a sample. When the value of T is the same for all the funds being measured, the standard deviation of the historic data (in which the denominator is T rather than T − 1) can generally be used instead, as the relative magnitudes of the resulting measures would be the same.

[2]Treynor and Black show that if resources are allocated optimally, the SR^2 of a portfolio will equal the sum of the SR^2 values for its components. This follows from the fact that the optimal holding of a component will be proportional to the ratio of its mean differential return to the square of the standard deviation of its differential return. Thus, for example, components with negative means should be held in negative amounts. In this context, the product of the mean return and the optimal holding will always be positive. For completeness, it should be noted that Treynor and Black use the term *appraisal ratio* to refer to what we term here the SR^2 of a component and the term *Sharpe Ratio* to refer to the SR^2 of the portfolio, although other authors have used the latter term for both the portfolio and its components.

[3]This type of application is described in BARRA [1992, p. 21].

[4]In this context, maximization of the Sharpe Ratio is the normative equivalent to the separation theorem first put forth in Tobin [1958] in a positive context.

[5]To see this, note that by borrowing money to purchase the underlying asset, one can obtain precisely the same asset at the delivery date. The ending value of such a strategy will be perfectly correlated with the value of the forward contract, and neither will require any outlay. If the payoffs at the end of the period differ, one could take a long position in one combination (e.g., the forward contract or the asset/borrowing combination) and a short position in the other, and obtain a guaranteed payment at the end of the period with no outlay at any other time. This is unlikely to be the case in a market populated by astute investors. In practice, transaction costs limit the precision of this relationship.

[6]Futures contracts are often not protected against changes in value due to (for example) dividend payments. They also generally require daily marking to market. For these reasons, they differ from forward contracts with dividend protection, for which the arbitrage relationship will hold within the bounds of transaction costs. Futures contracts generally require that margin be posted. However, this is not an investment in the underlying asset.

[7]Despite this drawback, once a notional value has been selected, the actual rate of return can be used for comparison purposes.

[8]Indeed, a Sharpe Ratio can be computed without regard to notional value by simply using the mean and standard deviation of the distribution of the final payoff.

[9]To see the advantages of concentration on the risk position of a strategy, consider two funds. One (X) invests directly; the other (Y) borrows money at the riskless rate and invests in X, with a leverage ratio of 2 to 1. Let k_X be the optimal position in fund X. Clearly the optimal position in fund Y will be half as large. However, the standard deviation of return on fund Y will be twice that of fund X. Thus the optimal risk position in Y will be the same as that in X.

[10]In fact, the basic relationship on which this section builds was first obtained by Treynor and Black [1973].

REFERENCES

BARRA Newsletter, September/October 1992, May/June 1993, BARRA, Berkeley, CA.

Bodie, Zvi, Alex Kane, and Alan J. Marcus. *Investments*, 2d edition. Homewood, IL: Richard D. Irwin, 1993.

Capaul, Carlo, Ian Rowley, and William F. Sharpe. "International Value and Growth Stock Returns." *Financial Analysts Journal*, January/February 1993, pp. 27-36.

Elton, Edwin J., and Martin J. Gruber. *Modern Portfolio Theory and Investment Analysis*, 4th edition. New York: John Wiley & Sons, 1991.

Grinold, Richard C. "The Fundamental Law of Active Management." *Journal of Portfolio Management*, Spring 1989, pp. 30-37.

Haugen, Robert A. *Modern Investment Theory*, 3d edition. Englewood Cliffs, NJ: Prentice-Hall, 1993.

"Morningstar Mutual Funds User's Guide." Chicago: Morningstar Inc., 1993.

Radcliff, Robert C. *Investment Concepts, Analysis, Strategy*, 3d edition. New York: HarperCollins, 1990.

Reilly, Frank K. *Investment Analysis and Portfolio Management*, 3d edition. Chicago: The Dryden Press, 1989.

Rudd, Andrew, and Henry K. Clasing. *Modern Portfolio Theory: The Principles of Investment Management*. Homewood, IL: Dow-Jones Irwin, 1982.

Sharpe, William F. "Mutual Fund Performance." *Journal of Business*, January 1966, pp. 119-138.

——. "Adjusting for Risk in Portfolio Performance Measurement." *Journal of Portfolio Management*, Winter 1975, pp. 29-34.

——. "Asset Allocation: Management Style and Performance Measurement." *Journal of Portfolio Management*, Winter 1992, pp. 7-19.

Tobin, James. "Liquidity Preference as Behavior Toward Risk." *Review of Economic Studies*, February 1958, pp. 65-86.

Treynor, Jack L., and Fischer Black. "How to Use Security Analysis to Improve Portfolio Selection." *Journal of Business*, January 1973, pp. 66-85.

Morningstar's Risk-Adjusted Ratings

William F. Sharpe

The characteristics of the "risk-adjusted rating" (RAR) on which Morningstar bases its "star ratings" and "category ratings" are analyzed, and the RAR is compared with more traditional mean–variance measures. The RAR measure has characteristics similar to those of an expected utility function based on an underlying bilinear utility function. These characteristics are of some concern because strict adherence to maximizing expected utility with such a function could lead to extreme investment strategies. This study finds that Morningstar varies one of the parameters of this function in a manner that frequently produces results similar to the results of using the excess-return Sharpe ratio. Finally, the argument is presented that neither Morningstar's measure nor the excess-return Sharpe ratio is an efficient tool for choosing mutual funds within peer groups for a multifund portfolio.

This decade's rapid, global growth of investment via mutual funds has led to a demand for simple measures of the performance of such funds. In the United States, the most popular such measure is the "risk-adjusted rating" (RAR) produced by Morningstar, Inc. Mutual fund families are proud to advertise that one or several of their funds have "received five stars from Morningstar." One study found that as much as 90 percent of new money invested in stock funds in 1995 went to funds with four-star or five-star ratings.[1] Although this percentage may or may not be correct for mid-1998, certainly few advertisements announce that a fund has received one star.

For better or worse, therefore, Morningstar's risk-adjusted measures greatly influence U.S. investor behavior. Because they differ significantly from traditional risk-adjusted performance measures, such as various forms of the Sharpe ratio, understanding the strengths and limitations of Morningstar's measures is important.

Ex Ante and *Ex Post* Measurement

Mutual fund performance measures are typically based on one or more summary statistics of past performance. Measures that attempt to take risk into account incorporate a measure of historical return and a measure of historical variability or loss. Because investment decisions affect only the future, the use of historical results involves an implicit assumption that the statistics derived from past performance have at least some predictive content for future performance. The evidence is ample that, although measures of historical variability can be useful for predicting future levels of risk, measures of average or cumulative return are, at best, highly imperfect predictors of expected future return. Nevertheless, leaving questions of predictability for other studies, the goal of this article is to examine the properties of Morningstar's and other measures under the assumption that statistics from historical frequency distributions are reliable predictors of corresponding statistics from a probability distribution of future returns.[2] In particular, the aim is to relate alternative performance measures to likely investment decisions; the rationale is that, even if the relationship between the past and the future is subject to a great deal of noise, one should attempt to select a performance measure that aligns well with the decision to be undertaken. Ultimately, of course, the intent is, first, to use all relevant information to make unbiased forecasts of expected returns, risks, and any other relevant characteristics of future fund performance and, then, to use such estimates to determine an optimal combination of investments in appropriate funds.

William F. Sharpe is the Stanco 25 Professor of Finance at the Stanford University Graduate School of Business. An earlier version of this article can be found at www.sharpe.stanford.edu/msrar.htm

This analysis of the Morningstar measures focuses on their key properties. The reader interested in empirical analyses of the Morningstar and more traditional measures, and analyses of the similarities and differences among them in practice, will find a relatively extensive treatment in Sharpe (1997).

Morningstar's Ratings

The analysis begins with a description of the computations used by Morningstar. The risk-adjusted rating (RAR) for a fund is calculated by subtracting a measure of the fund's relative risk (*RRisk*) from a measure of its relative return (*RRet*):

$$RAR_i = RRet_i - RRisk_i.$$

Each of the relative measures for a fund (relative returns and relative risks) is computed by dividing the corresponding measure for the fund by a denominator that is used for all the funds in a specified peer group. Morningstar assigns each fund to one (and only one) peer group. For its star ratings, Morningstar uses four such groups: domestic equity, international equity, taxable bond, and municipal bond. For its category ratings, peer groups are defined more narrowly. In mid-1997, for example, Morningstar had 20 domestic equity categories, 9 international equity categories, 10 taxable bond categories, and 5 municipal bond categories.

Letting $g(i)$ represent the peer group to which fund i is assigned,

$$RRet_i = \frac{Ret_i}{BRet_{g(i)}}$$

and

$$RRisk_i = \frac{Risk_i}{BRisk_{g(i)}},$$

where $BRet_{g(i)}$ and $BRisk_{g(i)}$ denote the bases used for the relative return and relative risk of all funds in the group in question.

Star and Category RARs. Morningstar calculates RAR values by taking load charges into account for determining its star ratings but omits load charges for the newer category ratings. The time periods also differ. Morningstar computes four sets of star ratings: The first three cover the last 3, 5, and 10 years, but the most popular (overall) measure is based on a combination of the 3-, 5-, and 10-year results. In contrast, the category ratings cover only the last 3 years (36 months).

For simplicity, this study concentrates on the calculations for the RAR values used for the category ratings. Sharpe (1997) provides considerable detail about the broader set of measures and a host of empirical analyses of their similarities and differences.

Return. Morningstar's measure of a fund's return is the difference between the cumulative value obtained by investing \$1 in the fund over the period, VR_i, and the cumulative value obtained by investing \$1 in U.S. T-bills, VR_b:

$$Ret_i = VR_i - VR_b.$$

Thus, if \$1 invested in the fund would have grown to \$1.50 in 36 months, assuming reinvestment of all distributions, and \$1 invested in T-bills with reinvestment would have grown to \$1.20, then

$$Ret_i = 1.50 - 1.20$$
$$= 0.30, \text{ or } 30\%.$$

Two steps are required to calculate the base to be used in calculating the relative returns for all the funds in a group. First, the returns for all the funds in the group are averaged. If the result is greater than the increase in value that would have been obtained with T-bills, the group average is used. Otherwise, the growth in value for T-bills is used. Thus,

$$BRet_{g(i)} = \max\,[\text{mean}_{i \text{ in } g(i)}(Ret_i),\ VR_b - 1].$$

Note that for the average value of Ret_i to be used, the funds must do at least twice as well as T-bills—that is,

$$\text{mean}_{i \text{ in } g(i)}\,(VR_i - 1) \geq 2(VR_b - 1).$$

As will be shown, the fact that $BRet_{g(i)}$ may have one of two distinct values makes it difficult to characterize the RAR measure in general terms.

Risk. To measure a fund's risk, Morningstar first computes the fund's excess return (*ER*) for each month by subtracting the return on a short-term T-bill from the fund's return. Next, it converts all the positive monthly excess returns to zeros. Finally, it takes a simple mean of the resulting "monthly losses" and reverses the sign to give a positive number.[3] Thus,

$$Risk_i = -\text{mean}_t[\min_t\,(ER_{it}, 0)].$$

The result is defined as a measure of the fund's "average monthly loss." Strictly, it is a measure of opportunity loss, where the forgone opportunity is investment in T-bills and months in which an opportunity gain occurred are counted as periods of zero opportunity loss.

The base used to calculate the relative returns for all the funds in a group is simply the average of all the risk measures for the funds in that group:

$BRisk_{g(i)} = \text{mean}_{i \text{ in } g(i)}(Risk_i)$.

Assigning Ratings. To assign ratings, Morningstar ranks the RARs for all the funds in a peer group. Funds that fall in the top 10 percent of the resulting distribution receive five stars (or a category rating of 5); those in the next 22.5 percent get four, the next 35 percent get three, the next 22.5 percent get two, and the bottom 10 percent get one.

Mean–Variance Measures

Most academic treatments of risk and return are based on the mean–variance approach developed in Markowitz (1952).

Expected Utility. Markowitz argued that the desirability of a probability distribution of portfolio returns should be summarized using the first two moments: the expected return and the standard deviation of return (or its square, the variance of return). The *ex post* counterparts are the arithmetic mean return, denoted M_i for fund i, and the standard deviation of historical returns, denoted S_i.

For an investor who chooses only one mutual fund, the fund's return will equal the investor's overall portfolio return. In this very special case, if the investor follows Markowitz's prescriptions, the expected utility, EU, of a portfolio invested solely in fund i can be written as

$$EU_i = M_i - r_k(S_i^2),$$

where r_k is a measure of investor k's risk aversion—reflecting the investor's marginal rate of substitution of mean return for variance of return. The goal of such an investor is to select the one fund for which this measure is the greatest.

Although this type of expected utility function is widely used for optimization analyses, it is rarely chosen for *ex post* performance measurement. Part of the reason is that it applies strictly only when all an investor's funds are to be allocated to one single risky investment. Even more limiting, however, is that, in principle, no universal measure of this type can be used by all investors. Rather, each investor must evaluate performance by using a measure designed for his or her degree of risk aversion, r_k.

The Excess-Return Sharpe Ratio. In an important contribution to investment theory, Tobin (1958) showed that combining a riskless investment with a risky one provides an opportunity set in which expected excess return is proportional to standard deviation of return. The implication is that an investor who is able to borrow or lend at a given rate and who is planning to hold only one mutual fund plus borrowing or lending should select the fund for which the ratio of expected excess return to standard deviation is the highest. This ratio is generally termed the Sharpe ratio, based on its introduction in Sharpe (1966). As shown in Sharpe (1994), the key properties of the original measure apply broadly to any "zero-investment strategy," such as that given by the difference between the returns on any two investments. To avoid confusion, I refer to the measure based on excess returns as the excess-return Sharpe ratio, denoted *ERSR*.

With R_{bt} representing the return on a riskless security, the excess-return Sharpe ratio for fund i is

$$ERSR_i = \frac{\text{mean}_t(R_{it} - R_{bt})}{\text{stdev}_t(R_{it} - R_{bt})}.$$

Ex ante, R_b is a fixed constant, so

$$ERSR_i = \frac{M_i - R_b}{S_i}.$$

Ex post, the more complete formula is typically used to account for any variation in R_b.

The goal of an investor who can borrow or lend at a fixed rate but is planning to hold only one risky mutual fund is to select the fund with the greatest *ex ante* $ERSR_i$, because a strategy that uses that fund with the appropriate amount of leverage can provide the greatest possible expected return for any desired level of risk. As with other measures, of course, selection of a fund with the highest *ex post* excess-return Sharpe ratio is only appropriate under the maintained assumption that the historical return distribution is a good predictor of the future probability distribution.

Excess-return Sharpe ratios are often used as measures of mutual fund performance, partly because they are less limited in applicability than mean–variance expected utility measures. An important consideration is that, under the assumptions on which the argument is based, the fund with the greatest Sharpe ratio is the best for any investor regardless of the investor's degree of risk aversion. In this sense, the measure is universal. Strictly, of course, the ratio is suitable only for cases in which an investor plans to invest in a single risky asset plus (possibly) borrowing or lending. Thus, the Sharpe ratio is slightly more general (two investments rather than one) than mean–variance expected utility measures, but it is still potentially inappropriate for the typical portfolio involving multiple risky funds.

RAR as an Expected Utility Function

As discussed, a fund's RAR is the difference between two relative measures:

$$RAR_i = \frac{Ret_i}{BRet_{g(i)}} - \frac{Risk_i}{BRisk_{g(i)}}.$$

Rearranging slightly gives

$$RAR_i = \left(\frac{1}{BRet_{g(i)}}\right)\left(Ret_i - \frac{BRet_{g(i)}}{BRisk_{g(i)}} \times Risk_i\right).$$

Note that $1/BRet_{g(i)}$ and $BRet_{g(i)}/BRisk_{g(i)}$ are the same for all the funds in a given group. Because the first term must be positive, both the rankings of funds within a group and the relative magnitudes of their ratings will be unaffected if this term is omitted. Denoting the second expression as $k_{g(i)}$ gives a rescaled RAR of the following form:

$$RRAR_i = Ret_i - k_{g(i)}\,(Risk_i).$$

It is tempting to interpret this modified function as a measure of the expected utility of fund i for an investor with a risk aversion of $k_{g(i)}$, where risk aversion is a measure of the investor's marginal rate of substitution of Ret_i for $Risk_i$. In such an interpretation, $k_{g(i)}$ would represent the risk aversion of each of the investors who selected funds in the group in question. This article addresses the relevance of such an assumption later. For now, *RRAR* can be considered a measure of expected utility.

Periodicity. Sharpe ratios use standard statistics from a frequency distribution of differential returns. For example, the first two moments of the probability distribution of next month's excess return might be assumed to be similar to the same moments from the frequency distribution of the last 36 months' excess returns. An important aspect is that the same time period (e.g., months) is to be used for both statistics.

Morningstar's risk measure has a similar character. Each monthly loss is given the same weight, with the average value presumably used as a surrogate for the expected value of next month's loss. The measure of return, however, is the difference between two cumulative values taken over the complete historical period. The properties of such a statistic are complex because it represents the difference between two value relatives, each of which can be considered to equal the result obtained by raising (one plus the geometric mean return) to the Tth power, where T is the number of months in the overall period. Because the geometric mean of a series of returns is a function of both the arithmetic mean and the variance of the series, the resulting return measure includes aspects of return and risk. This characteristic makes the statistical properties of Morningstar's measure highly complex, which seriously compromises the analyst's ability to estimate likely ranges of future performance given historical results.

In contrast, the Sharpe ratio is a simple transformation of the standard t-statistic for measuring the statistical significance of the difference between a realized mean value and zero; hence, the Sharpe ratio has familiar statistical properties.

Here, the analysis makes a modification that renders the RAR measure internally consistent. In particular, as a measure of return, this analysis uses the difference between the fund's arithmetic mean monthly return and the arithmetic mean return on T-bills and modifies the procedure used to calculate the relative return base accordingly. The modified RAR, *MRAR*, is calculated as

$$MRAR_i = MRet_i - mk_{g(i)}(Risk_i),$$

where

$$MRet_i = \text{mean}_t(R_{it} - R_{bt}).$$

In this measure, $mk_{g(i)}$ is the marginal rate of substitution of mean monthly excess return for mean loss, given by

$$mk_{g(i)} = \frac{MBRet_{g(i)}}{BRisk_{g(i)}},$$

where

$$MBRet_{g(i)} = \max\,[\text{mean}_{i \text{ in } g(i)}(MRet_i),\ \text{mean}_t(R_{bt})].$$

Except in extreme cases, the relative $MRAR_i$ values for the funds within a peer group will be similar to those obtained using Morningstar's actual procedures (that is, the corresponding $RRAR_i$ or RAR_i values). The following analysis assumes that $MRet_i$, $BRet_{g(i)}$, and $k_{g(i)}$ are computed using arithmetic monthly mean values. This assumption produces precise analytic results. Fortunately, the main qualitative conclusions apply also to the more complex measures used by Morningstar.

Maximizing Expected Utility with a Bilinear Utility Function. Consider an investor with a Von Neuman–Morgenstern utility function of the form

$$U = a(R_i - R_b) \text{ if } R_i \le R_b$$

and

$$U = R_i - R_b \text{ if } R_i > R_b,$$

where R_i is the return on fund i, R_b is the return on T-bills, and a is a constant greater than 1.

An example of such a function, in which $R_b = 5$ percent and $a = 3$, is shown in Figure 1. As can be seen, it is composed of two linear segments, with a greater slope to the left of R_b than to the right. Such a function exhibits risk aversion in the large, because the loss in utility associated with a return below R_b is greater than the gain in utility associated with a return equally far above R_b. Within return ranges that lie wholly above or wholly below R_b, however, the function is linear and thus reflects risk neutrality.

A bilinear function of this sort captures one of the three salient features of the prospect theory of decision making under uncertainty derived by Kahneman and Tversky (1979). An individual with such a function experiences loss aversion, where loss is measured from a reference point determined by the current riskless rate of return, R_b. More precisely, the function can be said to reflect opportunity loss aversion, with the value of the parameter a providing a measure of the degree of such aversion and the riskless rate acting as the reference point or alternative investment opportunity.

Consider an investor with a bilinear utility function who wishes to determine the expected utility of a given mutual fund over a future period. To begin, the formula for the utility function is rewritten as

$$U = R_i - R_b + (a-1)[(R_i - R_b) \text{ if } R_i \leq R_b \text{ and otherwise, } 0].$$

The expected value of U will thus be

$$E(U) = E(R_i - R_b) + (a-1) \times E(L_i),$$

where $L_i = R_i - R_b$ if $R_i \leq R_b$ and $L_i = 0$ if $R_i > R_b$. Note that L_i is exactly equal to Morningstar's monthly loss figure.

Next, let there be T possible future returns, each of which is equally likely to be realized. Now, the expected values are simply arithmetic means and

$$E(U) = \text{mean}(R_i - R_b) + (a-1) \times \text{mean}(L_i).$$

Substituting historical excess returns for future returns gives a measure that would be precisely equal to Morningstar's RAR if Morningstar used arithmetic mean monthly excess returns for its return calculations. Because the differences resulting from this disparity are likely to be small, Morningstar's RAR measure is highly similar, if not identical, to the measure that would be chosen by an investor who wishes to maximize a bilinear utility function but has decided to invest in only one mutual fund.

Loss Aversion. Compare the equation for expected utility with the modified version of Morningstar's RAR measure:

Figure 1. A Bilinear Utility Function

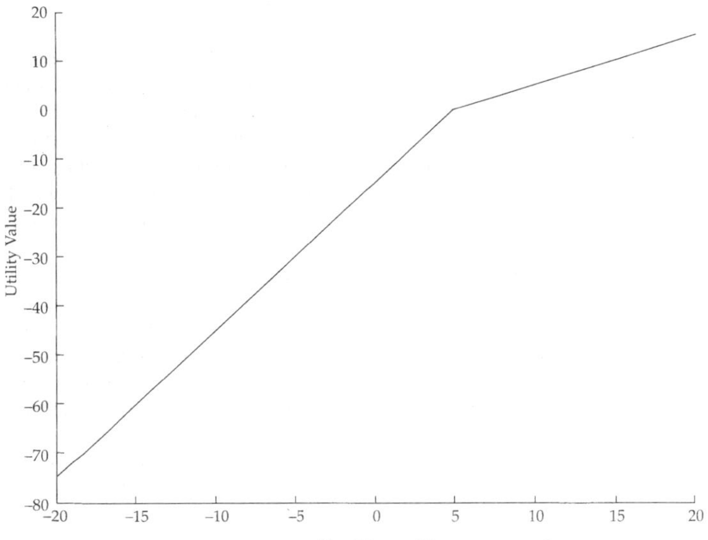

$$MRAR_i = Ret_i - k_{g(i)}(Risk_i).$$

Thus, it is approximately true that

$$a = 1 + k_{g(i)}.$$

Because $k_{g(i)}$ is positive, the investor will exhibit opportunity loss aversion, with the magnitude of aversion increasing as $k_{g(i)}$ increases.

Optimal Investment Choice for an Investor with a Bilinear Utility Function. Although the bilinear utility function has at least one attractive property, on closer examination it can be seen to imply extreme investment choices under plausible circumstances. Consider a strategy in which a proportion of an investor's wealth equal to x is placed in risky fund i and a proportion equal to $1 - x$ is placed in a riskless asset. The mean and standard deviation of the strategy's excess return will be given, respectively, by xM_i and xS_i. Because both these measures are proportional to scale, their ratio is scale independent. Thus, the excess-return Sharpe ratio for the strategy will equal that of the fund itself. Indeed, it is the property that Sharpe ratios are scale independent that makes them attractive as measures of performance.

For a strategy such as the one just described, both of Morningstar's measures are also proportional to scale: Recall that

$$Ret_i = VR_i - VR_b.$$

Letting TR_i and TR_b represent the total compound return for fund i and T-bills, respectively, over the period covered,

$$\begin{aligned} Ret_i &= (1 + TR_i) - (1 + TR_b) \\ &= TR_i - TR_b. \end{aligned}$$

For a strategy in which x is invested in fund i and $1 - x$ is invested in T-bills,

$$\begin{aligned} Ret_x &= [x(1 + TR_i) + (1 - x)(1 + TR_b)] - (1 + TR_b) \\ &= x(TR_i - TR_b) \\ &= x(Ret_i). \end{aligned}$$

A similar relationship holds for the average loss measure: In months for which $R_i \le R_b$,

$$L = x(R_i - R_b),$$

whereas in months for which $R_i > R_b$,

$$\begin{aligned} L &= 0 \\ &= x \times 0. \end{aligned}$$

Hence, for the strategy in which x is invested in fund i and $1 - x$ is in T-bills,

$$Risk_x = x(Risk_i).$$

The fact that both Morningstar's measures are proportional to scale implies that by combining a risky fund with borrowing or lending, an investor can attain any point on a linear opportunity set in $Ret_x - Risk_x$ space. Faced with such a trade-off, what choice will an investor with a bilinear utility function make?

Figure 2 shows possible outcomes for three investors with various degrees of risk aversion. In each case, the opportunity set is shown by the single solid line. The dotted lines are representative iso-expected utility lines. All combinations of risk and return along any iso-expected utility line provide the same expected utility; higher lines represent greater expected utility than lower lines. Each investor's objective is to find the feasible point (on the solid line) with the highest expected utility (on the highest attainable dotted line).

Note that for two of the three investors, the optimal choice is an extreme one. The conservative investor invests solely in T-bills; the aggressive investor puts as much as possible in the mutual fund, borrowing to the maximum allowable limit. Only for an investor with risk aversion precisely equal to the available risk–return trade-off is any "interior" strategy optimal, and any such investor is totally indifferent to the degree of leverage involved.

Such choices are clearly inconsistent with the observed behavior of the vast majority of investors, which calls into serious question the assumption that investors have utility functions as simple as that of the bilinear form. The problem is mitigated slightly in settings in which many investment options and multiple funds are available. Even in these cases, however, the efficient opportunity set is likely to be close to linear, which produces results very similar to Figure 2.

These objections apply also to a function in which expected utility is a linear function of the mean M_i and standard deviation S_i. The problem does not arise, however, when the Markowitz formulation is used. In it, expected utility is a linear function of mean and *variance*, so that the implied iso-expected utility curves increase at an increasing rate in mean–standard deviation space. As shown in Figure 3, preferences defined in the traditional manner lead to interior investment choices even when the efficient portion of the opportunity set is linear.

RAR as a Function of Mean and Variance

Although Morningstar's RAR measure differs considerably from a utility function based on a fund's

Figure 2. Investment Choice for Three Investors with Bilinear Utility Functions

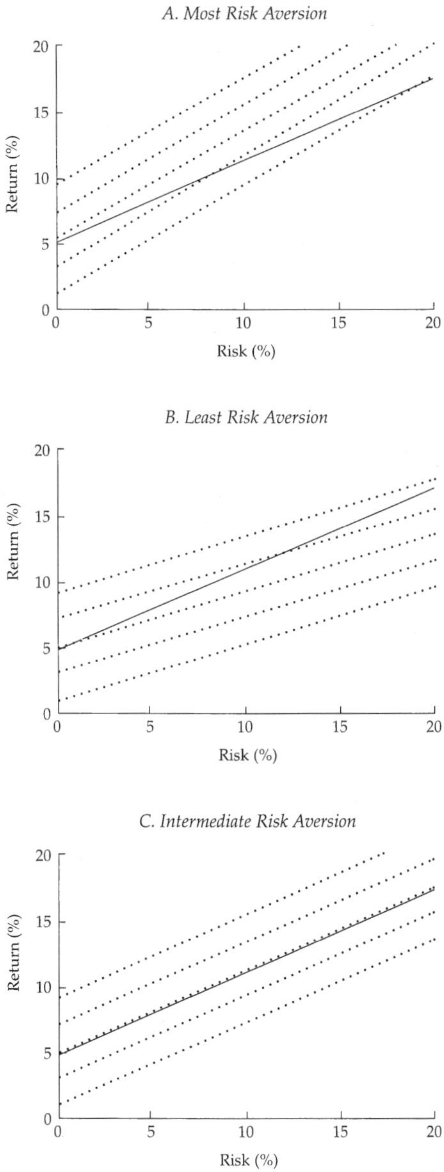

mean and variance of return, the measure is likely to be well approximated by a function of these more traditional measures.

To begin, consider return. Ret_i is the difference between the value relative for the fund and the value relative for T-bills. But the value relative over T periods will equal 1 plus the geometric mean return, G, to the Tth power. Thus,

$$Ret_i = (1 + G_i)^T - (1 + G_b)^T.$$

A close approximation for the geometric mean of a series is given by subtracting one-half the variance from the arithmetic mean. Thus,

$$Ret_i = \left(1 + M_i - \frac{S_i^2}{2}\right)^T - \left(1 + M_b - \frac{S_b^2}{2}\right)^T.$$

As can be seen, Morningstar's return measure incorporates aspects of both mean return and risk (standard deviation of return), with Ret_i increasing in M_i and decreasing in S_i. Given knowledge of M_i and S_i, one can clearly obtain a good estimate of Ret_i.

The situation is not as clear-cut for $Risk_i$. In general, it will depend on both the shape of the return distribution and its moments. Letting pr_x be the probability of state of the world x and ER_{ix} be the excess return on fund i in state x, the expected loss for fund i is defined as

$$Risk_i = -\text{sum}_x\,[pr_x \times \min_x(ER_{ix}, 0)].$$

Consider now the situation in which the mean and variance of the distribution of excess returns are sufficient statistics to identify the entire distribution—the case, for example, if returns are normally distributed. Under this assumption (where f means "is a function of"),

$$Risk_i = f[M_i - R_b, S_i]$$

because $M_i - R_b$ is the mean of the excess return distribution and S_i is its standard deviation (assuming R_b is known).

Using a relationship given in Triantis and Hodder (1990), it can be shown that for a normal distribution,

$$\begin{aligned} Risk_i &= f[M_i - R_b, S_i] \\ &= S_i \times n(-z) - (M_i - R_b) \times N(-z), \end{aligned}$$

where

$$z = \frac{M_i - R_b}{S_i},$$

$n(\,)$ = the standard normal density function

$N(\,)$ = the standard cumulative normal density function[4]

Empirical evidence given in Sharpe (1997) indicates that monthly return distributions for diversified mutual funds may be sufficiently close to normal to make this approximation quite accurate.

Figure 3. Investment Choice for an Investor with a Mean–Variance Utility Function

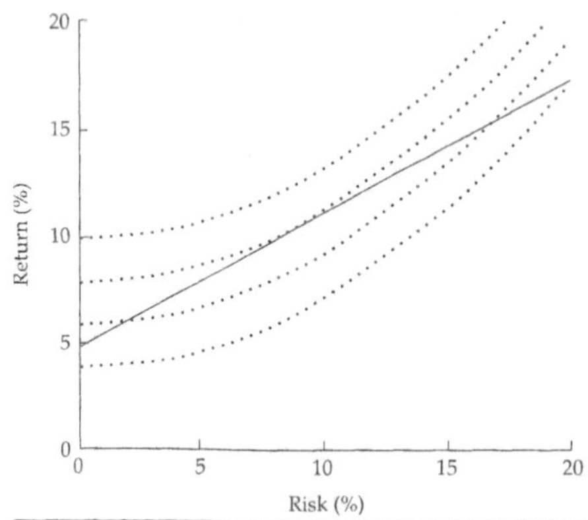

So, if both $Risk_i$ and Ret_i are well approximated as functions of M_i and S_i, then RAR_i will be also. Figure 4 shows the relationship between RAR and various combinations of expected annual excess return, *e*, and standard deviation of annual excess return, *sd*, using the approximations given for the case in which the riskless rate of interest is 5 percent a year, the holding period is three years, and the peer group has an average excess return of 5 percent and a standard deviation of 15 percent. As can be seen, the relationship is monotonic and close to linear in the region shown, which includes likely combinations for popular investment strategies.

The high degree of linearity of the relationship in Figure 4 can be seen more clearly in Figure 5,

Figure 4. RAR as a Function of Expected Excess Return and Standard Deviation

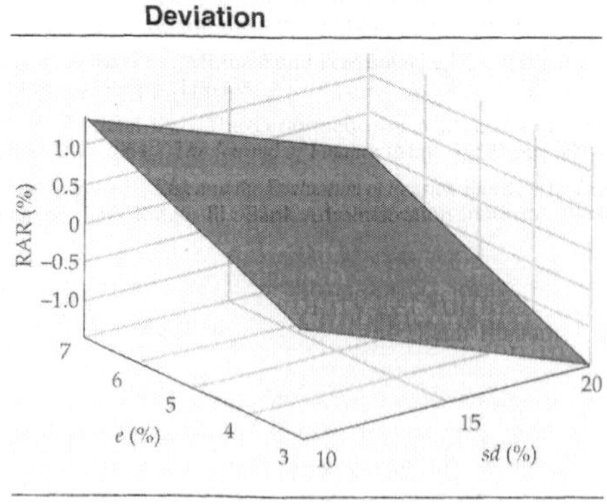

Figure 5. Iso-RAR Curves

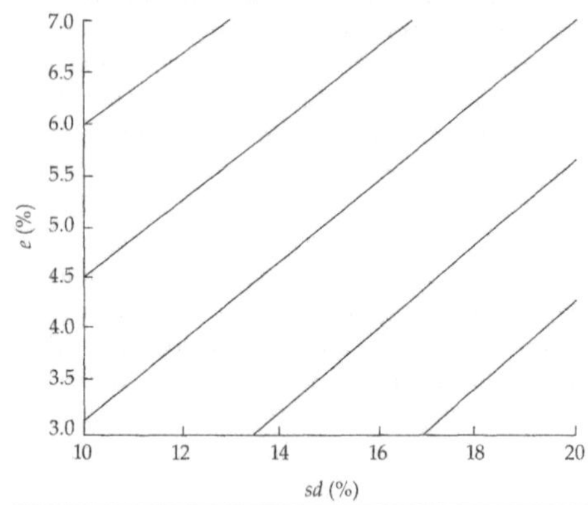

which shows a few of the associated iso-RAR curves. Clearly, an investor who wishes to maximize RAR is likely to select an extreme solution unless the opportunity set is highly nonlinear.

Recall that a portfolio is said to be mean–variance efficient if it provides the maximum possible mean for a given level of variance and the minimum possible variance for a given level of mean. Equivalently, Fund A is said to be inefficient if a Fund B exists with (1) the same expected return but less risk, (2) the same risk but more expected return, or (3) less risk and more expected return. With functions such as those shown in Figures 4 and 5, in each such case, if the approximations hold, Fund B will also have a higher RAR value than Fund A. Thus, excluding from consideration portfolios that are inefficient, using the mean–variance criterion is appropriate even if the ultimate goal is to select a portfolio with the largest possible RAR value.

These relationships imply that the key differences between Morningstar's measures and those used in more-traditional mean–variance analyses concern (1) the use of a linear combination of a return measure and a risk measure, rather than a ratio of the two, and/or (2) the use of risk *per se* rather than risk squared in the linear measure. The use of a multiperiod value relative and a measure of average loss is thus of secondary importance in terms of implications for fund selection.

These results illustrate the earlier assertion that Morningstar's actual RAR calculations give implications for investment choice very similar to those given by the simpler modified (*MRAR*) measure. Moreover, they suggest that if monthly returns are close to normally distributed, a choice based on RAR measures will differ from one based on the use

Morningstar's Risk-Adjusted Ratings

of a traditional mean–variance approach only in the selection of an extreme point rather than an interior point on the mean–variance efficient frontier. In effect, the RAR measure assumes that an investor's marginal rate of substitution of expected return for risk is the same no matter the level of his or her portfolio's return or risk. This assumption is unfortunate because it implies a preference for extreme risk–return combinations, which is inconsistent with investor behavior in this context and in more-general cases involving choices among competing alternatives.

RARs and Excess-Return Sharpe Ratios

Conceptually, fund rankings based on RAR values are different from rankings based on excess-return Sharpe ratios. This difference can be seen in Figure 6, which shows selected iso-excess-return Sharpe ratio (iso-SR for short) lines and selected mean–variance approximations of iso-RAR curves.

Figure 6. Iso-SR Lines and Approximate Iso-RAR Curves

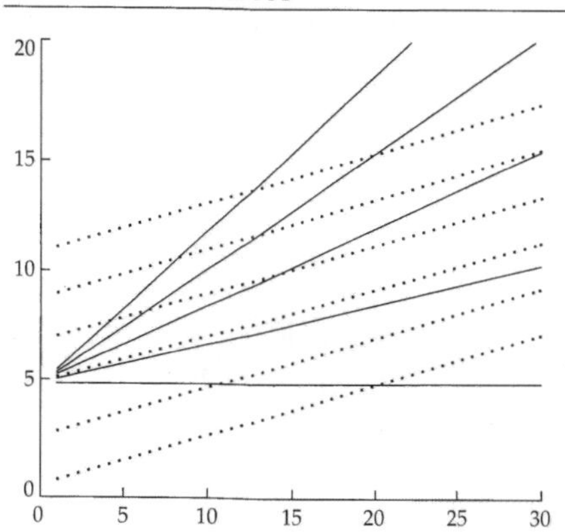

To assess the likely magnitudes of such differences, consider a selected mutual fund, Fund X, and the iso-RAR and iso-SR lines on which it lies. Figure 7 shows a case in which Fund X has an expected return of 10 percent and a standard deviation of 15 percent. The set of all funds that are better than Fund X based on the RAR criterion will lie above the dotted line in Figure 7, and the set of all funds that are worse than Fund X based on the RAR criterion will lie below the dotted line. The funds

Figure 7. The Iso-SR and Iso-RAR Lines for a Single Fund

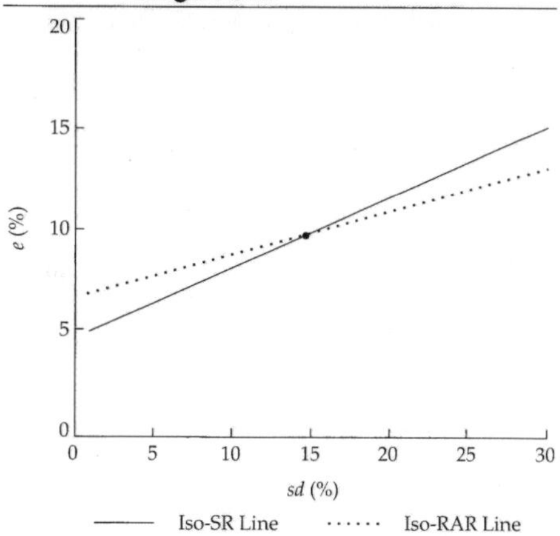

that are better than Fund X based on the excess-return Sharpe ratio will lie above the solid line, and those that are worse will lie below the solid line.

Obviously, the sets of funds rated better or worse than Fund X will differ depending on the criterion used, but the differences may be few. Figure 8 shows the regions in which the criteria give different results. Any fund plotting in the gray shaded area will have a higher RAR than Fund X but a lower excess-return Sharpe ratio. Any fund plotting in the black shaded area will have a lower RAR than Fund X but a higher excess-return Sharpe ratio. For all funds that plot above both lines or

Figure 8. Regions in Which the SR and RAR Criteria Conflict

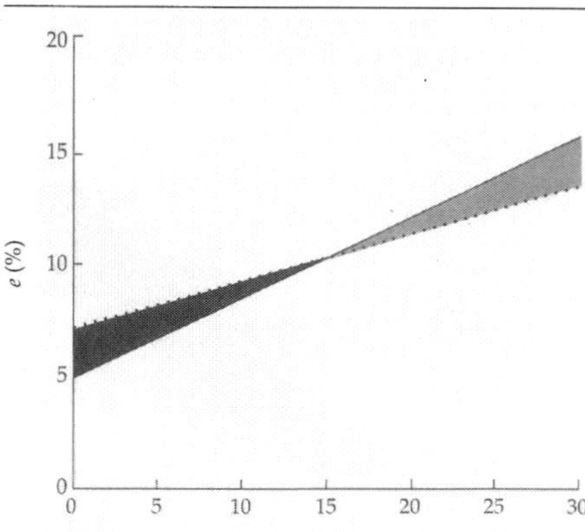

below both lines, however, the criteria will lead to the same conclusion. In general, the closer the slopes of the two lines, the fewer the disparities in rankings between the two criteria.

Now, recall the procedures used to compute Morningstar's RAR measures. The slope of the iso-RAR curves is given by the ratio of the return base to the risk base. If the period used for the computation is one in which the average return for the funds in the relevant peer group was sufficiently high (greater than two times the return on T-bills), the return base will equal the mean excess return for the funds in the peer group. In every case, the risk base is the mean risk for the funds in the peer group: Let Fund A have mean excess return and standard deviation of return equal, respectively, to the corresponding average values for all the funds in its peer group. *By construction*, then, the mean–variance approximation to the iso-RAR line for Fund A will be coincident with the iso-SR line for Fund A. In such circumstances, the sets of funds that are better and worse than Fund A will be the same no matter which criterion is used.

The same can be said about any fund that plots on Fund A's iso-SR (and iso-RAR) line—that is, any fund with the same excess-return Sharpe ratio as a fund with the average risk and return for the peer group. In practice, funds are likely to cluster reasonably closely around this line. Hence, peer groups with good average historical performance might be expected to have rankings based on Morningstar's RAR measure relatively similar to their rankings based on the excess-return Sharpe ratio. And Figure 9, taken from Sharpe (1997), shows that this expectation is supported.

Each point in Figure 9 represents the percentile rankings (by Morningstar on the x-axis and by the Sharpe ratio on the y-axis) of one of 1,286 diversified equity funds within its category peer group based on its performance from 1994 through 1996. The correlation coefficient was 0.986, showing that, despite substantial differences in computational procedures, Morningstar's approach and the simpler excess-return Sharpe ratio do give similar results in times of relatively high returns for U.S. equity funds.

These results are striking, but keep in mind that they were found during a high-return period and, therefore, Morningstar's procedure used the mean returns of the peer groups for the return bases in the calculations. Because *ex post* returns are used for the performance measures, there can be situa-

Figure 9. Rankings Based on Morningstar's Category RARs and Excess-Return Sharpe Ratios

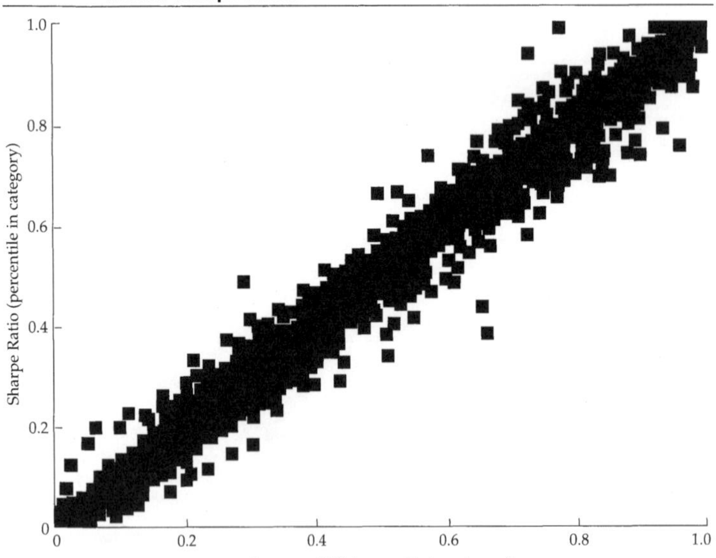

tions in which the average return for a peer group is small or even negative. In such cases, Morningstar sets the return base at the level obtained by T-bills, which could lead to greater disparity between rankings based on the Morningstar and the Sharpe ratio measures. Figure 10 shows an extreme version of such a situation.

In Figure 10, both Funds X and Y are shown to have performed poorly. But Fund Y had a better (algebraically greater, or less negative) excess-return Sharpe ratio than Fund X, as shown by its placement on a higher iso-SR (solid) line. Morningstar's RAR measure, however, assigns a better rating to Fund X than to Fund Y because Fund X provided a better average return and a lower risk, which resulted in Fund X plotting on a higher iso-RAR (dotted) line.

Figure 10. Performance of Two Funds in Bad Times

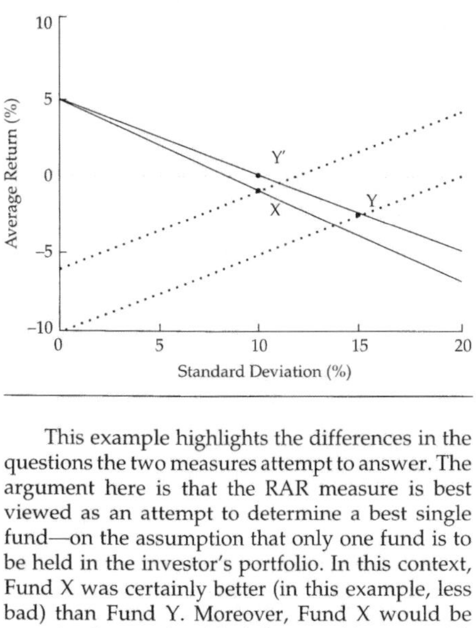

This example highlights the differences in the questions the two measures attempt to answer. The argument here is that the RAR measure is best viewed as an attempt to determine a best single fund—on the assumption that only one fund is to be held in the investor's portfolio. In this context, Fund X was certainly better (in this example, less bad) than Fund Y. Moreover, Fund X would be superior for any (positive) degree of investor risk aversion (any slope of the iso-RAR lines). An investor limited to one fund is not the setting, however, for which the excess-return Sharpe ratio was developed. It is intended for situations in which an investor can use borrowing or lending to achieve his or her desired level of risk. In this latter context, the excess-return Sharpe ratio gives the more appropriate answer: An investor who desired a level of risk of, say, 10 percent would have either held Fund X or followed a strategy of putting two-thirds of his or her wealth in Fund Y and lending the rest at the riskless rate (here, 5 percent). The latter strategy, shown by point Y′ in Figure 10, had a greater excess-return Sharpe ratio and was clearly better than investment solely in Fund X.

Multifund Portfolios

Morningstar's measure is best suited to answer questions posed by an investor who places all of his or her money in one fund. The excess-return Sharpe ratio is best suited to answer questions posed by an investor who allocates money to one fund and also to borrowing or lending. Neither type of investor should be interested in ranking funds within peer groups; indeed, such rankings conceal information about the relative magnitudes of the underlying variables—information that is crucial for such investors. Why, then, does Morningstar present its risk-adjusted ratings in terms of rankings of funds within peer groups?

The most plausible answer is that Morningstar assumes that investors have some other basis for allocating funds and plan to use Morningstar's rankings as at least an important input when deciding which fund or funds to choose from each peer group. In such a situation, however, neither Morningstar's measure nor the excess-return Sharpe ratio is an appropriate performance measure. The reason is simple: When evaluating the desirability of a fund in a multifund portfolio, the relevant measure of risk is the fund's contribution to the total risk of the portfolio. This contribution will depend on the fund's total risk and, more importantly in most cases, on its correlations with the other funds in the portfolio. Neither the Morningstar RAR measure nor the excess-return Sharpe ratio incorporates any information about correlations. Therefore, excessive reliance on either measure for selecting funds could seriously diminish the effectiveness of the resulting multifund portfolio.

In some very special cases, however, a different single measure of fund performance may be useful for constructing an optimal multifund portfolio. Sharpe (1994) showed that the "selection Sharpe ratio," based on the mean and standard deviation of the difference between a fund's return and that of an appropriate asset-class benchmark, may be used if the investor may take long and short positions in asset classes as needed. The preconditions for this special case are not met in many cases, however, and even if they are, significant differences can exist between rankings based on excess-return Sharpe ratios and rankings based on selection Sharpe ratios. Given the relationships between RARs and excess-return Sharpe ratios, rankings based on selection Sharpe ratios will also differ considerably from those based on RARs.

In short, in many cases, using any procedure to rank funds within peer groups and then using the rankings to select one or more funds from each of several peer groups is likely to be suboptimal. In some cases, the process will be highly suboptimal.

Conclusions

Morningstar's RAR measure has a number of drawbacks. It is complex, and it has poor statistical qualities. More importantly, it fails to capture an important aspect of investor preferences—the desire for portfolios that are neither the least nor most risky available.

Fortunately, the inherent disadvantages are considerably mitigated by Morningstar's practice of adjusting the risk aversion implicit in the measure to equal the ratio of return to risk for each peer group over the specific period covered, although this adjustment is made only if the peer group performance has been modest or poor. This adjustment increases the time and sample dependency of the measure, but it has the advantage of aligning the Morningstar rankings well with rankings that would be obtained by using the more familiar, less complex, and statistically more straightforward excess-return Sharpe ratio.

If the only choice for a measure by which to select funds is between Morningstar's RAR measure and the excess-return Sharpe ratio, the evidence favors selecting the Sharpe ratio. A more appropriate choice, however, is to use either a different performance measure or none at all. If the investor can separate fund selection from asset allocation without cost by taking long and short positions as needed in index funds representing "pure asset plays," the investor can usefully evaluate funds on the basis of their projected selection Sharpe ratios. Such measures take into account only a fund's non-asset-related expected return and risk. Typically, rankings based on selection Sharpe ratios will differ considerably from rankings based on Morningstar's measures or excess-return Sharpe ratios, and of course, the preferred portfolios that result will also differ.

Although it is tempting to conclude that investors constructing multifund portfolios should shift their focus from performance measures based on total or excess return to measures such as the selection Sharpe ratio that are based on differential or relative-to-benchmark return, the conclusions of this study do not lead to such counsel. The conditions under which the selection Sharpe ratio is appropriate are stringent and unlikely to hold for many investors. Rather than continue the search for the ideal universal performance measure, the preferable approach is to return to basics.

Markowitz taught that portfolio construction should take into account the best possible estimates of all relevant future risks and returns. This principle is as true for portfolios of mutual funds as it is for portfolios of individual securities. Asset allocation exercises, followed by selection of funds within peer groups based on simple rankings, are easy, but they may lead to inefficient overall portfolios. A better approach—one based on first principles—takes into account the complexity involved in portfolio decisions. The key information an investor needs to evaluate a mutual fund is (1) the fund's likely future exposures to movements in major asset classes, (2) the likely added (or subtracted) return over and above a benchmark with similar exposures, and (3) the likely risk vis-à-vis the benchmark. Investors should devote their efforts to obtaining the best possible estimates for future values of these key ingredients and to using the estimates optimally to determine efficient portfolios.

The author would like to thank John Watson of Financial Engines, Inc., for suggestions and comments and several members of the staff of Morningstar for reviewing the formulas in an earlier draft of this paper.

Notes

1. Described in Damato (1996).
2. Paul R. Pudaite, Morningstar's director of Quantitative Research, has pointed out that one does not need to make the assumption that future performance is related to past performance to justify the measurement of the latter: "I believe there's a place for achievement tests as well as aptitude tests of investment management. Independent of predictive ability, it's important to develop a grading system of past performance that provides today's investment managers with a clear and worthy goal for their future efforts." (Private correspondence, February 1998).
3. For the calculations used by Morningstar, whether the sign is reversed makes no difference because of the subsequent division by the risk base, which is an average of all the risk numbers. The sign is reversed here for ease of interpretation so that, as with standard deviation, a smaller absolute value of risk will be considered more desirable than a larger absolute value.
4. This function was obtained, while taking into account the relationship shown in Equation A1 in Triantis and Hodder, by integrating over negative values of the excess return.

References

Damato, Karen. 1996. "Morningstar Edges Toward One-Year Ratings." *Wall Street Journal* (April 5):C1.

Kahneman, Daniel, and Amos Tversky. 1979. "Prospect Theory: An Analysis of Decision under Risk." *Econometrica*, vol. 74, no. 2 (March):263–91.

Markowitz, Harry. 1952. "Portfolio Selection." *Journal of Finance*, vol. 7, no. 1 (March):77–91.

Sharpe, William F. 1966. "Mutual Fund Performance." *Journal of Business*, vol. 39, no. 1 (January):119–38.

———. 1994. "The Sharpe Ratio." *Journal of Portfolio Management*, vol. 21, no. 1 (Fall):49–59.

———. 1997. "Morningstar Performance Measures." http://www.sharpe.stanford.edu/stars0.htm

Tobin, James. 1958. "Liquidity Preference as Behavior towards Risk." *Review of Economic Studies*, vol. 26, no. 1 (February):65–86.

Triantis, Alexander J., and James E. Hodder. 1990. "Valuing Flexibility as a Complex Option." *Journal of Finance*, vol. 45, no. 2 (June):549–64.

Budgeting and Monitoring Pension Fund Risk

William F. Sharpe

This article describes a set of mean–variance procedures for setting targets for the risk characteristics of components of a pension fund portfolio and for monitoring the portfolio over time to detect significant deviations from those targets. Because of the significant correlations of the returns provided by the managers of a typical defined-benefit pension fund, the risk of the portfolio cannot be characterized as simply the sum of the risks of the individual components. Expected returns, however, can be so characterized. I show that the relationship between marginal risks and implied expected excess returns provides the economic rationale for the risk budgeting and monitoring being implemented by a number of pension funds. I then show how a fund's liabilities can be taken into account to make the analysis consistent with goals assumed in asset/liability studies. I also discuss the use of factor models and aggregation and disaggregation procedures. The article concludes with a short discussion of practical issues that should be addressed when implementing a pension fund risk-budgeting and -monitoring system.

Institutional investment portfolios are composed of individual investment vehicles that are generally run by individual managers. And traditionally, each of the components of a portfolio is an asset whose future value cannot fall below zero. In this environment, the total monetary value of the portfolio is typically considered an overall budget to be allocated among investments.

In a formal portfolio model, the decision variables are the proportions of total portfolio value allocated to the available investments. For example, in a portfolio-optimization problem, the "budget constraint" is usually written as

$$\sum_i X_i = 1, \qquad (1)$$

where X_i is the proportion of total value allocated to investment *i*.

This approach does not work well for portfolios that include investments that combine equal amounts of long and short positions. For example, a trading desk may choose to take a long position of \$100 million in one set of securities and a short position of \$100 million in another. The net investment is zero, but the same would be true of a strategy involving long positions of \$200 million and short positions of \$200 million. For this type of portfolio, some other budgeting approach may be desirable. One solution is to include a required margin, to be invested in a riskless security, and to state gains and losses as percentages of that margin. This approach may suffice for a fund that uses few such investments, but it is less than satisfactory for funds and institutions that use large short and long positions.

In recent years, hedge funds and financial institutions with multiple trading desks have developed and applied a different approach to this problem. Instead of (or in addition to) a dollar budget, they use a *risk budget*.[1] The motivation is straightforward: The goal of the organization is to achieve the most desirable risk–return combination. To obtain expected return, it must take on some risk. One may think of the optimal set of investments as maximizing expected return for a given level of overall portfolio risk. The level of portfolio risk provides the risk budget, and the goal is to allocate this budget across investments in an optimal manner. Once a risk budget is in place, the manager can monitor the portfolio components to assure that risk positions do not diverge from those stated in the risk budget by more than prespecified amounts.

Recently, managers of defined-benefit pension funds have taken an interest in using the techniques of risk budgeting and monitoring. To some extent, their interest has been motivated by a desire to

William F. Sharpe is STANCO 25 Professor of Finance, Emeritus, at Stanford University, California.

better analyze positions in derivatives, hedge funds, and other potentially zero-investment vehicles, but even a fund with traditional investment vehicles can achieve a greater understanding of its portfolio by analyzing the risk attributes of each of the components.

Pension Fund Characteristics

Much of the practice of risk management in financial institutions is concerned with short-term variations in values. For example, a firm with a number of trading desks may be concerned with the effect of each desk on the overall risk of the firm. Risk-management systems for such firms are designed to control the risk of each trading desk and to monitor each to identify practices that may be "out of control"—may be adding more risk to the portfolio than was intended. Often such systems use valuations made daily (or even more frequently). Moreover, the horizon over which risk is calculated is typically measured in days rather than weeks, months, or years.

Pension funds differ from such institutions in a number of respects. The components in a pension fund portfolio are typically accounts managed by other investment firms or by groups within the organization. Such accounts may or may not be valued daily, but major performance reports are typically produced monthly with end-of-month valuations. Horizons for risk and return projects are often measured in years, if not decades. Finally, for a pension fund to identify and control an external manager who is taking excessive risk can be difficult.

A pension fund can gather data on the individual securities held by its managers and establish a risk-measurement and -monitoring system by using daily data on a security-by-security level, and some funds have implemented systems designed to do this, thereby replicating the types of risk-management tools used by financial institutions. Such systems are complex, however, require a great deal of data, and are costly. For these reasons, a pension fund manager may choose a less ambitious approach by relying, instead, on data about the values of manager accounts provided on a less frequent basis. The focus in this article is on procedures that can be used in such a system, namely, a system in which investment managers are evaluated on the basis of returns on invested capital, as in standard performance reporting and analysis.

Another key attribute of a defined-benefit pension fund is its obligation to pay benefits in the future. This obligation gives rise to a liability, so its investment practices should, in principle, be viewed in terms of their impact on the difference between asset and liability values.

When allocating funds among investments, most large pension funds take a two-stage approach. The top stage involves a detailed study of the fund's allocation among major asset classes, usually (but not always) taking into account the liabilities associated with the fund's obligation to pay future pensions. For example, such an asset-allocation or asset/liability study might be performed every three years. Its result is a set of asset-allocation targets and a set of allowed ranges for investment in each asset class. Based on the asset-allocation analysis, the pension allocates funds among investment managers, subject to the constraint that each asset exposure fall within the specified range.

In many cases, the fund's asset-allocation analysis uses a standard one-period mean–variance approach, often coupled with Monte Carlo simulation to make long-term projections of the effects of each possible asset allocation on the fund's future funded status, required contributions, and so on. For most large funds, asset allocation typically accounts for more than 90 percent of total risk, which justifies the attention given it by management and the fund's investment board.

Estimating Risk

Central to any risk-budgeting and -monitoring system is a set of estimates of the impact of future events that can affect the value of the portfolio. In some systems, actual historical changes in values are used as estimates of possible future scenarios. In others, a portfolio is subjected to a "stress test" by assuming, for example, that the worst experiences of the past could come together in some future event, even though the past events actually occurred at different times.

Although such direct use of historical data provides useful information, a more common practice for longer-horizon projections is to consider a broad range of possible future scenarios based on models of the return-generating process. A standard approach uses estimates of risks and correlations together with assumptions about the shapes of possible probability distributions. Many analysts use a factor model to focus on the key sources of correlated risks. In this article, I assume that such an approach is being used. I also assume that only a single set of estimates for such a model is needed, although the procedures described here can be adapted relatively easily for use with alternative estimates as part of stress testing.

Factor Models. The world of investments is complex, with hundreds of thousands of possible investment vehicles. Thus, estimating risks and correlations on a security-by-security basis is virtually impossible. For this reason, almost all risk estimation systems use some sort of *factor model*, in which a relatively small number of factors are identified and their risks and correlations are estimated. The assumption is that the return on any individual investment component can be expressed as a function of one or more of these factors plus a residual return that is independent of the factors and of the residual returns on all other investments. This approach reduces the estimation problem to one requiring estimates of the factor risks and correlations plus, for each investment component, the estimation of the parameters in the function relating its return to the factors and the risk associated with its residual return. In some systems, factors are assumed to exhibit serial correlation over time, but a component's residual returns are generally assumed to be independent from period to period. One-period returns are generally assumed to be normally or lognormally distributed, with multiperiod return distributions determined by the characteristics of the underlying process.

Ideally, there should be a clear correspondence between the factors used in risk budgeting and monitoring and the asset classes used for the fund's asset-allocation studies. In practice, however, the two are likely to differ. For this reason, I allow for the possibility that the factor model and the risk and correlation estimates used in the risk-budgeting system may differ from the model and estimates used in the asset/liability analysis.

Following common practice in the pension fund industry, I assume that factor models used in the overall process are linear. More precisely, I assume that the return on any investment component can be expressed as a linear function of the returns on the factors (or asset classes) plus an independent residual.

The Fund and Its Components. This analysis deals with a pension fund that employs a number of investment managers. The fund has a fixed number of dollars in assets, A, and a liability, L, representing the present value of its accrued obligations. Ideally, both assets and liabilities should be measured in terms of market value. In practice, however, liabilities are often obtained as a byproduct of actuarial analyses designed to determine appropriate current fund contributions. Such liabilities are typically not (nor were they intended to be) equal to the market value of any particular definition of accrued liabilities. Such actuarial liability values tend to respond relatively slowly to changes in the values of assets, interest rates, and so on. For this reason, analyses that compare market values of assets with actuarial values of liabilities give results that are affected less by the inclusion of liabilities than would be the case if the market values of liabilities were used.

Ultimately, the decision variables for the fund's overall allocation are the amounts given to each of the investment managers (henceforth, "managers"). An assumption in this approach is that each manager's factor exposures and residual risk can be determined. This determination could be made by using a top-down approach, such as returns-based style analysis, or a bottom-up procedure based on the manager's security holdings. The best approach depends on the horizon over which risk is to be estimated, the costs and accuracies of alternative models, and other considerations. Here, we simply assume that such measures have been obtained.

■ *Asset allocation and expected excess returns.* To fix ideas firmly, we start with an extremely simple example: A fund has identified three asset classes—cash, bonds, and stocks. It plans to allocate its money ($100 million) among three managers in accordance with the results of an asset-allocation study. Each manager runs an index fund that tracks one of the classes exactly. Thus, the manager-selection problem and the asset-allocation problem are one and the same. For now, ignore the fund's liabilities and concentrate solely on the risk and return of the fund's assets.

To simplify the analysis, all calculations deal with *excess returns*, where the excess return on an asset is defined as its return minus the return on cash. Thus, we are concerned with expected excess return (*EER*), standard deviation of excess return (*SDER*), both of which are given in **Table 1**, and the correlation of excess returns, which is 0.4. For computational ease, the standard deviations and correlations are combined to produce a covariance matrix, which includes all the risk estimates. The covariance between two asset classes is simply their correlation times the product of their standard deviations. The covariances for cash, stocks, and bonds are given in **Table 2**.

Table 1. Example Expected Excess Returns and Risks

Asset	*EER*	*SDER*
Cash	0	0
Bonds	2	10
Stocks	6	18

Table 2. Example Covariances

	Cash	Bonds	Stocks
Cash	0	0	0
Bonds	0	100	72
Stocks	0	72	324

Given the estimated expected excess returns and covariances, a Markowitz-efficient portfolio can be found for any given level of risk. By definition, such a portfolio provides the greatest possible expected excess return for the level of risk. For our example, assume that, after considering the long-term effects of each of several such portfolios through the use of Monte Carlo simulation, the fund selects the allocation given in **Table 3**. This portfolio's expected excess return is 4.3650 percent, and its standard deviation of excess return is 12.7942 percent.

Table 3. Example Optimal Asset Allocation

Asset	Proportion
Cash	0.0741
Bonds	0.2976
Stocks	0.6283

In this case, each manager is given the specified amount for its asset class and each manager's return equals that of its asset class. Given these assumptions, we can compute the *dollar expected excess return* (*$EER*) for each manager and its proportion of the portfolio's *$EER*, as shown in **Table 4**. For example, the bond manager has 0.2976 (29.76 percent) of the total asset value of $100 million, or $29.76 million. The expected excess return on this part of the portfolio is 0.02 (2 percent) a year, so this manager is expected to add $595.2 thousand (or about $0.60 million) to the portfolio over and above the amount that could have been earned by putting the money in cash. Similar computations show that the stock manager is expected to add about $3.8 million over what cash would produce. The cash manager cannot contribute any expected excess return. Summing the three components gives the portfolio's total expected added value of about $4.4 million, which is consistent with the portfolio expected excess return obtained in the asset-allocation study.

The final column of Table 4 shows the proportion of total dollar expected excess return contributed by each manager, obtained by dividing each manager's *$EER* by the portfolio's total *$EER*. In this case, the bond manager is expected to contribute approximately 13.6 percent of the expected excess return and the stock manager to contribute 86.4 percent. Note that these percentages differ significantly from the amount of assets allocated to each (approximately 29.8 percent and 62.8 percent, respectively).

Manager risks. Computing the risk of each manager's position, in percentage or in dollar terms, would be straightforward. We could also compute a value-at-risk amount for each manager indicating, for example, what amount the manager's value could fall below with 1 chance out of 20. But such measures are not sufficient to determine the effect of a manager's investments on the risk or VAR of the portfolio as a whole because they do not take into account the correlations between managers' returns.

Indeed, the entire concept of risk budgeting seems to be doomed to failure in cases involving risks that are correlated because risks are not additive when they are correlated. Fortunately, a measure of *manager risk contribution* can serve as the foundation of a budgeting procedure in the following manner.

Define the *marginal risk* of a manager as the change in total portfolio risk per unit change in the amount allocated to the manager when that amount is small. More precisely, marginal risk is the derivative of portfolio risk, expressed as variance (standard deviation squared) with respect to the amount allocated to the manager. The marginal risk of a manager, MR_i, will equal twice its covariance with the portfolio as a whole, which is, in turn, a weighted average of the covariances of the manager's returns with those of the other managers,

Table 4. Example Manager Allocations and Expectations

Manager	Proportion of Total Asset Value	Dollars (millions)	*EER*	*$EER* (millions)	Proportion of *$EER*
Cash	0.0741	$ 7.41	0.00	$0.0000	0.0000
Bond	0.2976	29.76	0.02	0.5952	0.1364
Stock	0.6283	62.83	0.06	3.7698	0.8636
Portfolio	1.0000	$100.00		$4.3650	1.0000

with the current portfolio proportions used as weights:

$$MR_i = \frac{\partial V_i}{\partial X_i} = 2C_{i,p} = 2\sum_j X_j C_{i,j}, \quad (2)$$

where

V_p = variance of the portfolio's return

X_i and X_j = proportions of investment given to manager i and manager j

$C_{i,p}$ = covariance of manager i's returns with portfolio returns

$C_{i,j}$ = covariance of manager i's returns with manager j's returns

and ∂ denotes a partial derivative.

Applying Equation 2 to the case at hand gives marginal risks as follows: for the cash manager, none; for the bond manager, 150; for the stock manager, 450.

The stock manager has three times the marginal risk of the bond manager. Recall that the expected excess return of the stock manager is also three times that of the bond manager. As we will see, this is not a coincidence.

First-order conditions for an optimal portfolio. A Markowitz-efficient portfolio offers the greatest expected return for a given level of risk. To find a set of such portfolios, a computationally efficient approach is to solve the following problem for maximizing expected utility, *EU*:

$$\text{Maximize: } EU = EER_p - \frac{V_p}{rt} \qquad \text{Subject to: } \sum_i X_i = 1, \quad (3)$$

where EER_p is the expected value of portfolio excess return and rt is risk tolerance.

For a given level of risk tolerance, the solution will provide an efficient portfolio. By solving with different levels of rt, one can find all efficient portfolios and select the one with the most desirable risk and expected return based on the preferences of the decision makers. In our example, the selected portfolio maximizes expected utility for a risk tolerance of 75.

In practice, optimization problems are formulated with inequality constraints. The amounts invested in at least some asset classes are constrained to lie above a lower bound (e.g., 0) and/or below an upper bound (e.g., 25 percent of the portfolio). I will discuss the effect of constraints later; for now, assume that such constraints are absent or, if present, not binding in the solution.

Consider the *marginal expected utility* (*MEU*) of a position in a portfolio, which is defined as the rate of change of expected utility *EU* per unit change in the amount invested in that position. Marginal expected utility is calculated as

$$MEU_i = \frac{\partial EU}{X_i} = \frac{\partial EER_p}{\partial X_i} - \frac{\partial V_p/\partial X_i}{rt}. \quad (4)$$

But under the assumption that the expected return of an asset is the same regardless of the amount invested in it, the derivative of EER_p with respect to X_i will equal EER_i. Moreover, the derivative of V_p with respect to X_i is the value that we have defined as the manager's marginal risk, MR_i. So, we can write

$$MEU_i = EER_i - \frac{MR_i}{rt}. \quad (5)$$

Imagine a portfolio in which the marginal expected utilities of two managers differ. Clearly, the portfolio is not optimal. Why? Because one could take some money away from the manager with the lower *MEU* and give it to the manager with the higher *MEU* and thereby increase the expected utility of the portfolio. It thus follows that a condition for portfolio optimality in the absence of binding constraints is that marginal expected utility equal some constant; that is, for all i,

$$MEU_i = k, \quad (6)$$

where k is a constant.

Equation 6 is the first-order condition for portfolio optimality. It provides the economic basis for risk-management systems of the type studied in this article. To see why, consider cash, the risk-free asset. Its expected excess return is zero, as is its risk and marginal risk. Thus, its MEU_i value will equal zero. But then, k will equal zero. Thus, each manager's expected marginal utility will be zero, which means that each manager's expected excess return will equal the manager's marginal risk divided by the manager's risk tolerance:

$$MEU_i = EER_i - \frac{MR_i}{rt} = 0, \quad (7a)$$

so

$$EER_i = \frac{MR_i}{rt}. \quad (7b)$$

Optimization and reverse optimization. Equation 7b is central to the motivation for a risk-management system based on mean–variance analysis. One way to solve an optimization problem in the absence of inequality constraints is to find the set of proportions (the X_i's) summing to 1 for which each manager's marginal risk is equal to its expected return times the fund's risk tolerance. In other words, solve the set of simultaneous equations that will make

$$MR_i = rtEER_i \tag{8}$$

for every asset *i*. This process is termed *portfolio optimization*.

For our purposes, reversing this process is more instructive: Assume that a portfolio is optimal and that the covariances of its components are known, as is the risk tolerance of the fund. Then, one can find the expected excess returns for the components by using the first-order conditions of Equation 7b. That is, the expected excess return of every asset *i* is equal to the marginal risk of the asset divided by the fund's risk tolerance. This process is generally termed *reverse optimization*. It is also sometimes described as finding the *implied views* (of expected excess returns) for a portfolio.

■ *Estimating a fund's implied EER.* Assume that the covariance matrix for a fund's managers is known. To compute implied expected excess returns, one needs only an estimate of the fund's risk tolerance, *rt*, which can be found if one manager's expected excess return is known. Recall our example. In it, by using only the covariance matrix, we computed the marginal risks for the managers. To find the implied expected excess returns, we need only know the expected excess return of one component or combination of components. For example, the marginal risk of the example stock manager is 450. If the expected excess return on stocks is 6 percent, then $rt = 450/6$, or 75, and the implied expected excess returns are those shown in **Table 5**.

Table 5. Example Implied Expected Excess Returns

Manager	Marginal Risk	Implied *EER*
Cash	0	0
Bond	150	2
Stock	450	6

Not surprisingly, the implied values of the assets' *EERs* are identical to those that were used in the optimization process.

■ *Computing proportions of $EER.* Given expected excess returns, we can compute dollar expected excess returns as we did before, as well as the proportions of total *$EER* for each manager. The proportions will be the same, however, regardless of risk tolerance, and they can be computed solely from the covariance matrix and portfolio composition. Define $P\$EER_i$ as the proportion of dollar expected excess return provided by manager *i*; then,

$$\begin{aligned} P\$EER_i &= \frac{X_i EER_i}{\sum_i (X_i EER_i)} \\ &= \frac{X_i MR_i / rt}{\sum_i (X_i MR_i / rt)} \\ &= \frac{X_i MR_i}{\sum_i (X_i MR_i)}. \end{aligned} \tag{9}$$

This relationship both explains and justifies the computations that lie behind mean–variance risk budgeting and management. Marginal risks act as surrogates for expected excess returns. An overall fund should be managed so that the marginal risk of each of its components is commensurate with the expected excess return of that component. Given expectations about returns, a risk budget can be established that allows each component to have a marginal risk and fund allocation that give it an appropriate contribution, $P\$EER_i$.

■ *Portfolio risk decomposition.* Recall that the marginal risk of a portfolio component will equal twice its covariance with the portfolio. From the properties of covariance, we know that

$$\begin{aligned} \sum_i X_i MR_i &= \sum_i X_i 2C_{i,p} \\ &= 2\sum_i X_i C_{i,p} \\ &= 2V_p. \end{aligned} \tag{10}$$

Thus, the sum of the weighted marginal risks of the portfolio components will equal twice the variance of the overall portfolio. This relationship leads some to define the risk contribution of a component as half its marginal risk (that is, its covariance with the portfolio), so a weighted average of these values will equal the variance of the overall portfolio. Clearly, this approach will have no effect on the $P\$EER_i$ values, but it sometimes leads to an incorrect view that one can decompose portfolio risk into a set of additive components, and it leads to incorrect statements of the form "this manager contributed 15 percent to the total risk of the portfolio."

There is a case in which computations based on marginal risks do provide an additive decomposition of total portfolio risk. If all component returns are independent, the marginal risk of manager i will equal $2X_iV_i$ and the product X_iMR_i will equal $2X_i^2V_i$. Summing these values for all managers will give an amount equal to twice the portfolio variance. In this special case, defining a manager's risk contribution as half its marginal risk thus makes the product X_iMR_i equal precisely its contribution to total portfolio risk. We will see that the assumption of independence may be appropriate for the portion of a manager's return that is not related to the factors included in the underlying factor model and that this interpretation of risk decomposition can be applied to that portion of overall portfolio variance. Much of the literature on risk budgeting and monitoring focuses on such nonfactor risk and, therefore, is justified in claiming that the procedures provide an allocation of portfolio risk. Assuming additive decomposition of total portfolio risk is not applicable, however, for the *correlated* components of a pension fund, which generate most of its risk.

Humans best process information when relationships are linear. Expected returns are linear, and the expected return of a portfolio can be decomposed into portions provided by each of the portfolio components. But risk is generally not linear. For this reason, the computations I have described, which are used in many pension fund mean–variance risk-budgeting and -monitoring systems, are best viewed in terms of a budget of implied expected excess return and deviations from the budget.

Pension Fund Applications

In practice, pension fund risk budgeting and monitoring involves three related but somewhat separate phases—choosing a policy portfolio, establishing a risk budget, and monitoring.

In the first phase, the *policy phase,* the fund selects a *policy portfolio* in which dollar amounts are allocated to managers. As indicated previously, this step often involves two stages: (1) an asset-allocation or asset/liability study using optimization analysis that allocates funds among asset classes and (2) the subsequent allocation of funds among managers through the use of procedures that may be quantitative, qualitative, or a combination of both. Rarely is the policy portfolio determined entirely by mean–variance optimization, and even the optimization analysis used as part of the process often involves binding constraints that mean the first-order conditions I have described will not hold strictly for every component. In any event, in part of this policy phase, the fund manager will use expected returns, risks, and correlations, which I will term the *policy expected returns* and *policy risks and correlations.* This phase will also involve a (possibly implicit) factor model, which I will term the *policy factor model.* The output of this phase is the *policy portfolio,* which allocates specific amounts of capital to each of the components of the fund.

The second phase is the establishment of the fund's risk budget. In this phase, the fund managers make the (possibly heroic) assumption that the policy portfolio is optimal in a mean–variance sense at the time of its designation. Ideally, this risk budget would be interpreted in terms of the policy factor model and policy expected returns and covariances. The very nature of the policy phase may make this approach impossible, however, because there are typically insufficient estimates of risks and returns and, in most cases, the policy portfolio is not created directly from a formal unconstrained optimization. In practice, therefore, a more complete factor model and set of risks and correlations, typically provided by an outside vendor, are used to perform a reverse optimization based on the policy portfolio as of the date of its formation. This process yields a series of implied expected excess returns and proportions of the portfolio's dollar expected excess return attributable to each component. Such values represent the components' *risk budgets* (*RBs*). From the previous formulas, the risk budgets can be stated most directly as

$$RB_i = \frac{X_iC_{i,p}}{V_p} \tag{11}$$

for each manager i.

Even if the policy portfolio is implemented precisely, when the policy phase is completed, market movements, manager actions, and changing risks and correlations will lead to changes in many or all aspects of the situation. These changes lead to the third phase—monitoring and revision. In this phase, the fund managers use current estimates of risks and correlations, typically provided by the outside vendor, together with manager positions and/or return histories to compute a new set of values for investment proportions, covariances, and portfolio variance. This step provides a current set of *risk proportions* (*RP*). With primes denoting current values, the risk proportions are calculated as

$$RP_i = \frac{X_i'C_{i,p}'}{V_p'}. \tag{12}$$

The monitoring phase involves comparison of the current risk proportions with the risk budgets. Significant disparities lead to evaluation, analysis, and in some cases, action.

Not surprisingly, this process can easily be misunderstood and misused. The risk budget figures are actually surrogates for proportions of expected value added (over cash) at the time of the policy analysis. The risk proportion figures are surrogates for the proportions of implied expected value added, based on the current situation. The presumption is that large disparities need to be justified by changes in estimates of the abilities of a manager to add value. Lacking this justification, some sort of action should be taken. Note, however, that a change in a manager's *RP* value may be caused by events beyond a manager's control. Moreover, the fund managers have many ways to change a manager's *RP* value if such a change is needed. The amount invested in the manager, X_i, may be adjusted, as may the covariance of the manager's return with that of the portfolio. The covariance may, in turn, be changed by altering the manager's investment strategy or by changing the allocation of funds among other managers and/or the strategies of other managers.

In any event, the comparison of risk proportion values with risk budget values provides a discipline for monitoring an overall portfolio to ensure that it remains reasonably consistent with original or modified estimates of the abilities of the managers. Although the actions to be taken in the event of significant disparities are not immediately obvious, it is important for the fund managers to know when actions of some sort are desirable.

Figure 1 shows the three phases and their components. The policy phase is performed periodically, followed by the risk-budgeting phase. The monitoring phase is then performed frequently, until the process begins anew with another policy phase.

Figure 1. Phases for Budgeting and Monitoring Pension Fund Risk

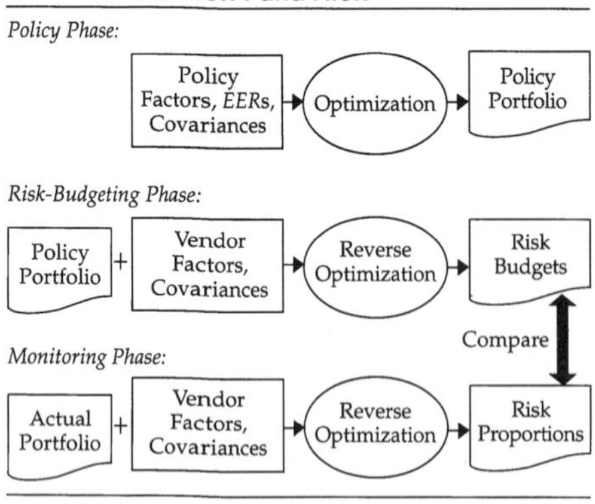

Incorporating Liabilities. Thus far, I have ignored the presence of liabilities and assumed that all three phases focus on the risk and return of the fund's assets. Such a focus may not be appropriate, however, for a fund designed to discharge liabilities. Fortunately, the procedures I have described can be adapted to take liabilities into account.

Continuing to use a one-period analysis, begin with current asset values, A_0, and current liability values, L_0. At the end of the period, the value of assets and liabilities will be, respectively, A_1 and L_1, neither of which is known with certainty at the beginning of the period. Define the fund's *surplus*, *S*, as assets minus liabilities. Thus, $S_0 = A_0 - L_0$ and $S_1 = A_1 - L_1$. Assume that the fund is concerned with the risk and return of its future surplus, expressed as a portion of current assets, that is, S_1/A_0. Equivalently,

$$\frac{S_1}{A_0} = \left(\frac{A_1}{A_0}\right) - \left(\frac{L_0}{A_0}\right)\left(\frac{L_1}{L_0}\right). \tag{13}$$

The first expression in parentheses equals 1 plus the return on assets, $1 + R_A$; the last expression in parentheses can be interpreted as 1 plus the return on liabilities, $1 + R_L$. Defining the current ratio of liabilities to assets, L_0/A_0, as the fund's *debt ratio, d*, means that S_1/A_0 may be written as

$$(1 - d) + R_A - dR_L.$$

The expression $1 - d$ is a constant; hence, it cannot be affected by the fund's investment policy. We thus consider only the difference between the asset return and the liability return multiplied by the debt ratio, dR_L.

We are now ready to write the expected utility of the portfolio as a function of the expected value and risk of $R_A - dR_L$. Let *rt* be the fund's risk tolerance for surplus risk. Then,

$$EU = E(R_A) - E(dR_L) - \frac{V(R_A - dR_L)}{rt}. \tag{14}$$

Expanding the variance term gives

$$EU = E(R_A) - E(dR_L) - \frac{V(R_A)}{rt} + \frac{2dC_{A,L}}{rt} - \frac{d^2V_L}{rt}. \tag{15}$$

Because the decision variables are the asset investments, we can ignore terms that are not affected by them. Neither the expected liability return nor the variance of the liability return is affected by investment decisions. Hence, for optimization and reverse optimization purposes, we can define expected utility as

$$EU = E(R_A) - \frac{V(R_A)}{rt} + \frac{2dC_{A,L}}{rt}. \quad (16)$$

Note that Equation 16 differs from expected utility in the case of an asset-only optimization only by the addition of the final term, which includes the covariance of the asset return with the liabilities, $C_{A,L}$. Moreover, covariances are additive, so the covariance of the asset portfolio with the liabilities will equal a value-weighted average of the covariances of the components with the liabilities. This relationship implies that the marginal expected utility of component i will be calculated as

$$MEU_i = EER_i - \frac{MR_i}{rt} + \frac{2dC_{i,L}}{rt}, \quad (17)$$

where $C_{i,L}$ is the covariance of the return of asset i with that of the liabilities.

We can now write the first-order condition for optimality in an asset/liability analysis as follows: For each asset i,

$$MEU_i = EER_i - \frac{MR_i}{rt} + \frac{2dC_{i,L}}{rt} = k. \quad (18)$$

But the risk-free asset (here, cash) has zero values for all three components. Hence, as before, $k = 0$, so

$$EER_i - \frac{MR_i}{rt} + \frac{2dC_{i,L}}{rt} = 0 \quad (19a)$$

and

$$EER_i = \frac{MR_i}{rt} - \frac{2dC_{i,L}}{rt}. \quad (19b)$$

To compute implied expected excess returns, we need only subtract the covariance of an asset with the liability from its marginal risk, then divide by risk tolerance. Alternatively, recalling that $MR_i = 2C_{i,p}$, we can write

$$EER_i = \left(\frac{2}{rt}\right)(C_{i,p} - dC_{i,L}). \quad (20)$$

All the procedures described in the asset-only case can be adapted in straightforward ways to incorporate liabilities. For example, the risk budgets and risk positions can be determined by using the following formulas:

$$RB_i = \frac{X_i(C_{i,p} - dC_{i,L})}{V_p - dC_{p,L}} \quad (21a)$$

and

$$RP_i = \frac{X_i'(C_{i,p}' - d'C_{i,L}')}{V_p' - d'C_{p,L}'}, \quad (21b)$$

where, as before, the variables without primes reflect values at the time of the policy analysis and the variables with primes reflect values at the current time. Due to the properties of variances and covariances, the values of RB_i will sum to 1, as will the values of RP_i.

Fund Use of Factor Models. As mentioned previously, most risk estimation procedures use a factor model to provide robust predictions. Generically, such a model has the form

$$R_i = b_{i1}F_1 + b_{i2}F_2 + \ldots + b_{in}F_n + e_i, \quad (22)$$

where $b_{i1}, b_{i2}, \ldots, b_{in}$ are the sensitivities of R_i to factors $F_1, F_2, \ldots, F_n$, respectively, and e_i is component i's residual return. Each e_i is assumed to be independent of each of the factors and of each of the other residual returns.

A risk model of this type requires estimates of the risks (standard deviations) of each of the factors and of each of the residual returns. It also requires estimates of the correlations of the factors with one another.

Note that in this model, each return is a linear function of the factors. We can thus aggregate by using the proportions held in the components to obtain the portfolio's return:

$$R_p = b_{p1}F_1 + b_{p2}F_2 + \ldots + b_{pn}F_n + e_p, \quad (23)$$

where each value of b_p is the value-weighted average of the corresponding b_i values and e_p is the value-weighted average of the e_i values.

It is convenient to break each return into a factor-related component and a residual component. Defining R_{Fi} as the sum of the first n terms on the right-hand side of Equation 22, we can write

$$R_i = R_{Fi} + e_i. \quad (24)$$

Similarly, for the portfolio, we can write

$$R_p = R_{Fp} + e_p. \quad (25)$$

Now, consider the covariance of component i with the portfolio. By the properties of covariance, it will be

$$\begin{aligned} C_{i,p} &= \text{cov}(R_{Fi} + e_i, R_{Fp} + e_p) \\ &= \text{cov}(R_{Fi}, R_{Fp}) + \text{cov}(R_{Fi}, e_p) + \text{cov}(e_i, R_{Fp}) \\ &\quad + \text{cov}(e_i, e_p). \end{aligned} \quad (26)$$

By the assumptions of the factor model, the second and third covariances are zero. Hence,

$$C_{i,p} = \text{cov}(R_{Fi}, R_{Fp}) + \text{cov}(e_i, e_p). \quad (27)$$

Recall that e_p is the value-weighted average of the e_i values. Because the residual returns are assumed to be uncorrelated with one another, the covariance of e_i with e_p is caused by only one term.

We let v_i be the variance of e_i (that is, component i's residual variance). Then,

$$\text{cov}(e_i, e_p) = X_i v_i \tag{28a}$$

and

$$C_{i,p} = \text{cov}(R_{Fi}, R_{Fp}) + X_i v_i. \tag{28b}$$

Substituting Equation 28b in Equation 20 for the implied excess return in the presence of liabilities produces

$$EER_i = \left(\frac{2}{rt}\right)[\text{cov}(R_{Fi}, R_{Fp}) + X_i v_i - dC_{i,L}]. \tag{29a}$$

This equation can be regrouped into two parts—one part that would be applicable were there no residual risk and one part that results from residual risk:

$$EER_i = \left(\frac{2}{rt}\right)\left[\text{cov}(R_{Fi}, R_{Fp}) - dC_{i,L}\right] + \left(\frac{2}{rt}\right)X_i v_i. \tag{29b}$$

The final term in Equation 29b is often termed "the manager's implied alpha value"—that is, the difference between overall expected return and that return resulting from the manager's exposures to the factors (and here, covariance with the fund's liability). Thus, we have

$$EER_i = \text{Factor-related } EER_i + \alpha_i, \tag{30a}$$

where

$$\text{Factor-related } EER_i = \left(\frac{2}{rt}\right)\left[\text{cov}(R_{Fi}, R_{Fp}) - dC_{i,L}\right] \tag{30b}$$

and

$$\alpha_i = \left(\frac{2}{rt}\right)X_i v_i. \tag{30c}$$

Just as implied expected returns can be decomposed into factor-related and residual components, so too can risk budgets and risk proportions. For example, a manager could be given a budget for factor-related contributions to risk and a separate budget for residual risk. Many systems concentrate on the residual-risk budget, which has substantial advantages because, as indicated earlier, the contributions to portfolio residual risk can, in fact, be added to give the total portfolio residual variance. However, the residual risks contribute only a small part of the total risk of a typical pension fund.

Aggregation. Expected excess returns are additive. Therefore, the expected excess return for a group of managers will equal a weighted average of their expected excess returns, with the relative values invested used as weights. Covariances are also additive. The marginal risk of a group of managers can thus be computed by weighting their marginal risks by relative values invested. So, a fund manager can aggregate risk budgets and risk proportions in any desired manner. For example, a fund may be organized in levels, with each level's risk budget allocated to managers or securities in the level below it. Thus, the fund could have a risk budget for equities, with subbudgets for domestic equities and international equities. Within each of these subbudgets, there might be budgets for individual managers, and so on.

Consider the following example for a large pension fund, Fund XYZ. **Table 6** provides the implied expected excess returns. (Note in Table 6 that alpha values are stated in basis points and *EER* values are stated in percentages.) The results shown in Table 6 were obtained by using an asset-class factor model with historical risk and correlation estimates. The relationships of the managers to the factors were found by using returns-based style analysis. Residual variances came from out-of-sample deviations from benchmarks based on previous returns-based style analyses. After the managers were analyzed, they were combined into groups based on the fund's standard classifications. Implied expected excess returns were calibrated so that a passive domestic equity portfolio would have the expected excess return used in the fund's most recent asset-allocation study. Although this fund does take liabilities into account when choosing its asset allocation, the figures shown in Table 6 are based solely on asset risks and correlations.

Table 6. Fund XYZ: Implied Expected Excess Returns

Asset	Factor-Related *EER*	Alpha	Total *EER*
Cash equivalents	0.02%	0 bps	0.02%
Fixed income	1.53	0	1.53
Real estate	4.01	36	4.36
Domestic equity	5.66	3	5.69
International equity	4.82	3	4.84
International fixed income	1.42	0	1.42
Global asset allocation	3.79	0	3.79
Special assets	3.13	26	3.40

Note that the implied alpha values are all small; four are less than half a basis point and are thus shown as zero. Such alphas are not unusual for funds with many managers. A high degree of diversification is consistent with relatively low expectations concerning managers' abilities to add value.

As shown in **Table 7**, the implied expected excess returns can be combined with the amounts allocated to the managers to determine the implied expected values added over a cash investment, *$EER*. These individual expectations can be divided by the total *$EER* for the portfolio to show the relative contribution to excess expected return of each manager or the aggregate. Table 7 shows the results for the Fund XYZ broken into the factor-related component and residual-related component (alpha).

In this case, by far the largest part of the implied added value (98.83 percent) is attributable to the managers' factor exposures. This result has a natural interpretation as the proportion of portfolio variance explained by factor risks and correlations plus the portfolio's exposures to those factors. This interpretation follows from the fact that the alpha values are derived from contributions to residual variance, each of which equals $X_i^2 v_i$, making the sum equal to the portfolio's residual variance.

Reports such as Table 7 can be valuable when the pension fund is allocating staff resources for manager oversight, selection, and monitoring. Note, for example, that the Fund XYZ has allocated slightly less than 45 percent of its money to its domestic equity managers, whereas this analysis indicates that such managers should be expected to provide more than 60 percent of the value added over investing the entire fund in cash. This difference might lead to the conclusion that 60 percent of staff resources should be assigned to this part of the portfolio rather than 45 percent.

I have presented the results of this analysis in terms of implied dollar expected excess returns, but in most risk-budgeting systems, the terms "risk budget" and "risk contribution" would typically be used instead of the "implied" terminology. For example, assume that the Table 7 report was produced by using the Fund XYZ's policy portfolio. Then, the percentages in the final column would constitute the risk budgets for the aggregate groups. At subsequent reporting periods, the same type of analysis could be performed, giving a new set of results that could be compared with those obtained at the time the policy phase was completed. The resulting report would look like **Table 8**, with the final two columns filled in on the basis of the current situation.

In many systems, each part of the portfolio is given both a risk budget and an accompanying set of ranges. The ranges are often broken into a "green zone" (acceptable) and a "red zone" (unacceptable) with a "yellow zone" (watch) in between.

Implementation Issues

Although risk-budgeting and -monitoring systems can prove very useful in a pension fund context, some issues associated with their implementation need to be addressed.

First, as I have shown, the central principle behind the use of risk budgets based on mean–variance analysis is the assumption that a particular portfolio is optimal in the sense of Markowitz, with no binding inequality constraints. This assumption may be inconsistent with the procedures the pension fund uses to allocate funds among managers at the time of a policy study (or at any time). It is true that asset-class allocations are typically made with the assistance of optimization analysis, but many formal optimization procedures include bounds on asset allocations, some of which are binding in the solution.

Moreover, the results of the optimization study provide guidance only on allocation across broad asset classes, and the study typically assumes that

Table 7. Fund XYZ: Portions of Implied Portfolio Dollar Expected Excess Returns

		Percent of *$EER*		
Asset	Percent of Dollars	Factor Related	Alpha	Total
Cash equivalents	1.72%	0.01%	0.00%	0.01%
Fixed income	21.30	7.69	0.02	7.71
Real estate	5.15	4.88	0.43	5.31
Domestic equity	44.74	59.84	0.31	60.14
International equity	19.11	21.77	0.11	21.88
International fixed income	3.15	1.06	0.00	1.06
Global asset allocation	0.00	0.00	0.00	0.00
Special assets	4.84	3.59	0.30	3.89
Total	100.00%	98.83%	1.17%	100.00%

Table 8. Fund XYZ Basic Risk-Management Report

Asset	Risk Budget	Risk Proportions	Difference
Cash equivalents	0.01%		
Fixed income	7.71		
Real estate	5.31		
Domestic equity	60.14		
International equity	21.88		
International fixed income	1.06		
Global asset allocation	0.00		
Special assets	3.89		
Total	100.00%		

all funds are invested in pure, zero-cost index funds, each of which tracks a single asset class precisely. Actual implementations involve managers that engage in active management and many that provide exposures to multiple asset classes. Because the eventual allocation of funds among managers is made by using a variety of procedures—some quantitative, others qualitative—the resulting allocation may not be completely optimal in mean–variance terms.

Potential problems may also arise when the asset-allocation model uses one set of factors (the asset-class returns) while the risk-budgeting and risk-monitoring system is using another. Even if the policy portfolio is optimal when the policy factor model and its assumptions about expected returns, risks, and correlations are used, it may not be optimal when the risk-budgeting system's factor model, manager factor exposures, manager risks, and correlation estimates are used. Yet, consistency may have been assumed when the risk budgets were set.

Finally, there is the problem of choosing an appropriate action when an *RP*, risk proportion, diverges unacceptably from a previously set *RB*, risk budget. For example, what if the risk proportion exceeds the risk budget? Should money be taken away from the manager, or should the manager be asked to reduce its contribution to portfolio risk? If the manager is to reduce its contribution to risk, what actions should the manager take? One way is to have the manager reduce residual risk, but doing so might not be sufficient and could lower the manager's chance of superior performance. An alternative is to ask the manager to change exposures to the underlying factors, but such changes could force a manager to move from its preferred "style" or investment habitat, with ill effects on overall performance.

Some of these problems are mitigated if the risk-budgeting and -monitoring system deals only with residual (nonfactor) risks. But for a typical pension fund, such risks constitute a small part of overall portfolio risk, which is consistent with low implied expectations for added return (alpha). A comprehensive view of a portfolio requires analysis of both the small (uncorrelated) part of its risk and the large (correlated) part.[2]

Conclusions

Many beneficial results can be obtained by combining a risk model with attributes of a fund's investments. A portfolio based on a policy study and its implementation can be used to set targets or risk budgets. These can be used to allocate effort for manager oversight, selection, and monitoring. Subsequently, actual portfolios can be analyzed to determine the extent to which risk computations based on current holdings differ from those obtained when using policy holdings. Significant differences can then be used to initiate changes as needed.

The use of risk budgeting and monitoring by defined-benefit pension funds is currently limited. As more funds implement such procedures, however, analysts and managers will discover the strengths and weaknesses of risk budgeting in this context and can deal with implementation issues. There is no doubt that risk budgeting and monitoring can produce large amounts of data. In time, we will learn how to ensure that they produce the most useful information.

Notes

1. In describing and interpreting some of the procedures used in risk-budgeting systems, I have drawn on a great deal of work done by others as well as some of my earlier results. The idea of computing implied views of expected excess returns based on portfolio composition and covariances can be found in Sharpe (1974), and the relationship between an asset's expected return and its covariance with a set of liabilities is described in Sharpe and Tint (1990).
2. The literature on risk budgeting and monitoring is extensive. An excellent source is Rahl (2000).

References

Rahl, Leslie, ed. 2000. *Risk Budgeting—A New Approach to Investing*. London, U.K.: Risk Books.

Sharpe, William F. 1974. "Imputing Expected Returns from Portfolio Composition." *Journal of Financial and Quantitative Analysis*, vol. 9, no. 2 (June):463–472.

Sharpe, William F., and Lawrence G. Tint. 1990 "Liabilities—A New Approach." *Journal of Portfolio Management*, vol. 16, no. 2 (Winter):5–10.

Section 5: Empirical Analyses

5-1 "Risk-Aversion in the Stock Market — Some Empirical Evidence," *The Journal of Finance*, Vol. XX, No. 3, September 1965, pp. 416–422.

This paper preceded my 1966 analysis of mutual fund performance (included in section 4) but utilized the same set of data on the returns of 34 mutual funds. Using this admittedly small number of funds and the few returns for each available at the time, I tested for evidence that conformed with the capital market line implied by the Capital Asset Pricing Model. As the paper shows, over the period covered the funds' mean returns and standard deviations of returns plotted close to a line with a slope of 0.58 (i.e. 5.8 percent added expected return per 1 percent of added standard deviation) and an intercept of 3.8% year. Moreover, most of the funds' returns were highly correlated with those of the Dow Jones Industrial Average, which I used as a surrogate for the market portfolio. The latter observation suggests that the funds were reasonably efficient in a mean/variance sense. This, combined with the fact that they plotted relatively close to an *ex post* realization of the *ex ante* capital market line predicted by the CAPM, provided some support for the joint hypothesis that (1) *ex post* results are at least indicative of *ex ante* predictions and (2) that the CAPM holds with respect to the latter.

5-2 "Risk-Return Classes of New York Stock Exchange Common Stocks, 1931–1967" (with Guy M. Cooper), *Financial Analysts Journal*, March/April 1972, 81, pp. 46–54.

This paper reports the results of an empirical test of the CAPM conducted in large part by Guy Cooper, then a PhD student in Finance at Stanford, who subsequently left the program for a successful career in the investment industry. The level of detail can be seen in Table IV which provides information concerning the historic characteristics of each of the included securities.

This is a study about the cross-section of stock returns (to use current jargon). It investigates differences in the performance of a number of portfolios, each formed using data available in advance based on a fixed set of rules. Unlike my earlier studies that used small numbers of investments and returns calculated infrequently over short periods of time, this used monthly returns for over a thousand stocks over decades thanks to the availability of high quality data gathered by the Center for

Research in Security Prices at the University of Chicago. CRISP forever changed the standards for empirical research on security markets, leading to a torrent of work produced by both academics and practitioners that continues to this day.

In this paper, we were careful to measure *ex post* returns by including both price changes and dividends. We used the by-then standard term *beta* to refer to the covariance of return with the market scaled by the variance of the market return (measured by the CRISP index of the overall market, designed by Lawrence Fisher). When forming portfolios, we used a measure based only on price changes which we called *market sensitivity* (possibly in homage to my earlier work).

Our goal was to see if a set of portfolios formed using historic relations with the overall market would subsequently differ in both beta values and long-term returns. We used 60 months of historic performance prior to the beginning of each calendar year to group securities into ten portfolios with equal numbers of securities based on prior market sensitivities, then computed the returns for the portfolios on the assumption that securities were held in equal weights at the beginning of each year. *Ex post* returns were computed in this manner for every year from 1931 through 1967. Figures IVa and IVb summarize the main results. With some exceptions, portfolios of stocks with higher historic market sensitivities had higher betas in the future and higher average returns. While a number of stocks migrated from one risk-return class to another (as shown in tables I, II and III), the results were broadly consistent with both a model of persistence and the equilibrium results of a CAPM in which the relevant holding period was one year. On the other hand, very long-term results gave a less dramatic picture, as shown by the geometric mean returns in Figure IVc.

These results were very comforting to those who considered the CAPM a useful approximation to reality. However, a plethora of subsequent studies using more information, different methods for portfolio formation and later time periods have found a number of "anomalies" from this simple and (for some) satisfying story. Practitioners continue to search for strategies that will allow them to gain business for stock funds that exploit one or more such anomalies. Virtually all have compelling characteristics when back-tested but when implemented, many fail to provide equally stellar performance.

5-3 "Risk, Return and Yield: New York Stock Exchange Common Stocks, 1928–1969" (with Howard B. Sosin), *Financial Analysts Journal*, March/April 1976, pp. 33–42.

This paper reports a study done with Howard Sosin, a PhD candidate at Stanford, who went on to a career involving many early and profitable uses of financial engineering. He and I had done previous research on closed-end investment companies, examining the behavior of the ratios of their market values to net asset values. We found that for the limited number of such funds for which data were available, such ratios varied substantially over time, were somewhat correlated with one another, and had beta values close to zero.

In this study, we examined the relationships among risks, returns and yields for groups of individual common stocks. Our goal was to determine the properties of portfolios with various "yield tilts". We then compared these with the market as a whole.

The paper begins with a set of reasons why, other things equal, some people might prefer dividends to capital gains or *vice-versa*. Presumably, market prices reflect the net result of such preferences. A question being addressed by others at the time was whether this resulted in equilibrium relationships that would make it desirable to tilt away from the yield of the market portfolio for an investor who considered a one dollar return from dividends as desirable as one from capital gains.

As with earlier work, the study utilized the CRISP database. It also used an early version of the now widespread Ibbotson/Sinquefield database. At the end of each year, we sorted stocks based on recent dividend yield, then used the list to form ten portfolios. This was done in two steps. First, each stock was assigned to one of ten provisional portfolios, each with an equal number of stocks, then groups were formed from these to obtain portfolios with different dividend yields but as much diversification as possible. The paper then examined the *ex post* performance of the ten portfolios, assuming reconstitution at the end of every year. Since the stocks in each portfolio were given equal weights at the beginning of each year, an equal-weighted index was constructed to represent the overall market, although as footnote 7 indicates, market weights would have been preferable had the requisite data been available.

The study showed that dividend yields are sufficiently persistent to make it possible to build portfolios with significantly different *ex post* yields. However, portfolios at the ends of the yield spectrum were poorly diversified. Over the long run, low-yield portfolios did better but they also had higher beta values and their long-run performance was no more than commensurate with this fact, given the performance of the market as a whole. The paper concludes that "Neither the magnitude nor the direction of performance measured by the alpha value [of a yield tilt] can be predicted in advance — only its uncertainty." A final analysis using total portfolio risk reached a similar conclusion.

In subsequent years, investigators have performed much more sophisticated analyses of the differences in performance of stocks with different fundamental characteristics, such as dividend yields, price/earnings ratios, and price/book ratios, often using such measures to separate securities into "value" and growth categories. Using this terminology, the low-yield groups used in this study could have been considered "growth stock portfolios" and the high-yield ones "value stock portfolios". The study showed, as did many after it, that over and above their correlations with the overall market, securities within each group tend to be correlated with one another. Among other things, this makes comparisons highly time-period dependent, counseling caution when attempting to predict the future efficacy of adopting either a value strategy or a growth strategy rather than investing in the market as a whole.

5-4 "Duration and Security Risk" (with Ronald Lanstein), *Journal of Financial and Quantitative Analysis*, November 1978, pp. 663–668.

This paper was written with Ronald Lanstein who was then consulting with Wells Fargo Investment Advisors, as was I. Ron provided much of the mathematics in the earlier part of the paper as well as some of the empirical work. While there, he and I had the opportunity to use a database of analysts' predictions of future dividends for a number of individual stocks. This allowed us to compute the duration of estimated cash flows for each stock, based on predictions made at the end of 1972. We then analyzed the returns on the stocks over the subsequent five years. Our goal was to examine the effects of differences in durations on the extra-market covariances of the securities. To do so, we focused on the correlations of the non-market (residual) returns of securities within and among 15 groups formed based on estimated durations. Figure 2 shows the key result. Stocks with similar durations tend to move together, over and above the effects of market movements. Those with very different durations tend to move differently once the effects of the market as a whole have been taken into account. The result was very regular and the absolute value of the t-statistic for the linear relationship in Figure 2 was over 15.

This result is not unlike that found in the earlier study with Howard Sosin. High yield stocks have lower durations than low-yield ones, and the two groups tend to move differently from time to time. But the use of detailed cash flow estimates to group securities provided a basis for at least a partial explanation of this and similar empirical phenomena. It is possible that movements in groups such as these and others formed on the basis of more easily computed indicators such as dividend yield, price/earnings ratios and the like could reflect, at least in part, differences in their responses to changes in expectations for near-term vis-à-vis longer-term economic conditions.

5-5 "Factors in New York Stock Exchange Security Returns, 1931–1979," *The Journal of Portfolio Management*, Summer 1982, pp. 5–19.

I undertook this very arduous empirical study in order to provide a general audience with results similar to those being sold commercially by firms such as BARRA, Wells Fargo Investment Advisors and Wilshire Associates. Moreover, I wanted to analyze returns over the long historic period from 1926 through 1979 for which data were available for academic and other research. Since I lacked sufficient balance sheet and income statement data, I could not replicate some of the aspects of the commercial models but was able to measure a number of the most important effects being examined at the time.

Key to this and similar work was the fitting of a multi-factor model (such as that shown in equation 1) to security returns for each month for which data were available. For some of the initial analyses, I used standard multiple regression but for the detailed results I employed a procedure in which securities that conformed more with the model in the past were assigned greater weights in subsequent regressions.

As shown in Table 5, the factors explained relatively little of the cross-sectional variation in the security returns in a typical month, although the results would have been considerably better had diversified portfolios been used. The time-series fit of the models, shown in Table 6, was considerably better. Market moves explained 25% of the time-series variation in the typical stock. Market moves plus historic beta values explained almost 34%. Common factors added a little over 4% and sector factors another 2%. While the results showed that close to 60% of the time series variation in the return of a typical stock were not attributable to the factors studied, the figure would have been much lower for a diversified portfolio.

Figures 3 through 22 show the cumulative returns on strategies that are long a high exposure to a factor and short a low exposure, as well as the rolling 24-month standard deviations of such strategies for the common factors. Today such approaches would be called hedge funds or zero-investment strategies. A similar construction is currently employed by Fama and French to compute factors widely used in academic studies.

Table 8 provides a recipe for estimating a security's future beta based on the empirical values obtained using the factor model. The approach is based on a procedure developed by Barr Rosenberg to produce "Barr's better betas".

Table 9 compares the average realization of each of the factors with the value expected if the CAPM held exactly. Most of the differences are statistically insignificant but there are three exceptions. High-yield ("value") stocks did unexpectedly better than low- or no-yield stocks, large (high-capitalization) stocks did unexpectedly worse than small (low-capitalization) stocks and energy stocks were unexpectedly good performers. In subsequent years, much has been written about the "value effect" and the "small stock effect" and many investment funds have been formed in attempts to exploit one or both of these "anomalies". However, the "yield factor" is frequently negative, as Figure 9 showed that it was in portions of this period and the size factor has also had periods in which large stocks outperformed small stocks, as Figure 11 showed happened (although infrequently) in this period. For good reasons, the U.S. Securities Exchange Commission requires funds to tell investors that past performance does not guarantee future results.

5-6 "Financial Implications of South African Divestment," (with Blake R. Grossman), *Financial Analysts Journal*, July/August 1986, pp. 15–29.

This was written with Blake Grossman, who was the top student (by far) in a large undergraduate class in Economics that I taught at Stanford. I soon introduced him to the people at Wells Fargo Investment Advisors where he was when we wrote this paper. Blake subsequently rose to be head of WFIA and its successors, leading one of the largest and most innovative investment managers in the world.

The paper was motivated by widespread interest in the possibility of changing the South African government's reprehensible policy of apartheid by divesting institutional portfolio holdings of stocks of companies doing business in South Africa. Student movements to do this started in 1977 at Stanford, then spread to many campuses in the United States. The University of California eventually divested $3 billion of South Africa related stocks, an action cited by Nelson Mandela as particularly significant in changing the apartheid policy. By 1986 much had been written about the financial impact on an institutional portfolio of such divestment; however, many of the analyses were simplistic and a number of the more careful ones utilized strategies that were chosen after the fact or could not be followed by a large number of investors. We felt that it was important to estimate the implications of divestment carefully to facilitate informed debate.

For most of the analyses, we examined a stringent policy that would have excluded over 37% of the value of stocks on the New York Stock Exchange, relegating less dramatic approaches to an Appendix. We also tested the divestment strategy using strictly out-of-sample analyses, with one exception: we chose the South Africa related (SAR) stocks using the relatively recent inception of the accepted list of such stocks. However, a check using an alternative source with a longer history showed similar results.

We compared a value-weighted portfolio of all the stocks on the New York Stock Exchange (NYSE) with a value-weighted portfolio of the "South Africa Free" stocks (SAF). As Figure G shows, the two portfolios would have had similar performance over the period from 1960 through 1983, although the SAF portfolio would have done somewhat better on average with a higher standard deviation (Table II). Adding treasury bills to the latter to provide equal risk, the SAF portfolio would still have outperformed the NYSE portfolio (Table III). Digging deeper, by using attributes such as those in my 1982 factor paper, we found (not surprisingly) that the SAF portfolio had a smaller average stock capitalization than the NYSE universe and different industry exposures (Figure B). We used a factor model similar to that in the prior paper, augmented with a "South Africa factor" in which all South Africa Related (SAR) stocks were assigned a value of 1 and SAF stocks a value of 0. The performance of the resulting factor over time provided a measure of the relative performance of SAR stocks, other things (exposures to the remaining factors) equal. The results, shown in Figure I, indicated that SAR stocks outperformed SAF stocks from 1960 through 1975, then underperformed through 1983 (though only the former was statistically significant). We speculated that this could have reflected high expected returns for SAR stocks due to a net aversion on the part of investors through 1975 followed by a repricing to obtain even higher expected returns in the future as investors' aversion to companies doing business in apartheid South Africa increased. Whether this was true or not, we argued that in the long run, if more investors were disgusted by the practice than not, divestment should lead to at least slightly inferior overall performance, other things equal, although our results suggested that historically, such differences had been very small.

The paper also estimated the costs of transitioning from a diversified portfolio to one of South Africa free stocks. We did so first using published results based on active trades, then again using a database provided by Wells Fargo documenting the costs of "informationless" trades made for their passive index funds. The estimated costs of divestment were much lower based on the latter data and considerably lower than many estimates then being made in the investment industry.

In the years after this paper was published, pressure on the South African government to end apartheid continued to increase. Negotiations within the country started in 1990 and the odious practice was well on the way to being abolished when F. W. de Klerk and Nelson Mandela were jointly awarded the Nobel Peace Prize in 1993. While the role of divestment of securities by American investors may have been small, it undoubtedly helped move the process forward.

5-7 "Investor Wealth Measures and Expected Return," *Quantifying the Market Risk Premium Phenomenon for Investment Decision Making*, The Institute of Chartered Financial Analysts, 1990, pp. 29–37.

This paper was presented at a conference sponsored by the Institute of Chartered Financial Analysts and subsequently included in a proceedings volume published by the Institute. The overall focus of the conference was on market risk premia and possible investment strategies related thereto. I chose to discuss a broader measure of the market than the usual index of stock returns and based the empirical work on the returns and values of a "U.S. Mix" of Treasury bills, bonds and stocks, although, had data been easily obtained, I would have used a global counterpart.

The initial part of the paper argues that as the overall wealth of a society increases, so should the "societal risk tolerance". To clear markets, it follows that the premium in expected return per unit of risk should be smaller, the greater the societal risk tolerance. This, in turn, implies some degree of mean reversion in security returns.

The next section of the paper uses variance ratio tests (Figure 2) and measures of significance based on Monte Carlo analyses (Figure 3) to show that over the period from 1946 through 1989, the U.S. Mix did in fact show some signs of mean-reversion — a result consistent with earlier analyses of the returns of stocks alone. An empirical test of the reduced-form equation (8) of the model gave statistically significant coefficients with the expected signs, providing at least some support for the approach.

The final section of the paper offers tests of a subset of possible dynamic strategies based on the earlier view of equilibria in the capital markets. Figure 8 suggests some possible approaches, each of which represents an investor's relative risk tolerance (via-a-vis that of the average investor) as a function of the relative risk premium (vis-à-vis that under normal market conditions). The results from empirical tests of a set of associated tactical asset allocation strategies are shown in Figures 9 through 11. While such strategies offered better reward/risk ratios, as the paper indicates this does not imply that they "offer something for nothing" since they "... require an investor to take on added risk at the hardest times — such as when investors are poorer than usual." Moreover, empirical tests of dynamic strategies which include transactions costs (omitted in this study) and cover other time periods and/or markets could well give considerably different results.

Looking back, I consider the important contributions of the paper to be its focus on the effects of wealth on the overall societal risk premium, the possible impacts of market swings on societal risk tolerance and hence risk premia per unit of risk, and the role of dynamic asset allocation policies in accommodating the minorities of investors whose risk tolerances change more or less than those of average investors when overall wealth rises or falls.

5-8 "International Value and Growth Stock Returns," (with Carlo Capaul and Ian Rowley), *Financial Analyst's Journal*, January/February 1993, pp. 27–36.

This paper was written during the first part of the period from 1987 through 2001 when I served as a Strategic Advisor to the Institutional Investment Management group at the Union Bank of Switzerland (UBS) in Zurich. Carlo Capaul and Ian Rowley were members of the group in the early 1990's and did the bulk of the required work. Our goal was to extend to other countries previous analyses of the performance of value and growth stocks in the United States. This required a great deal of careful analysis and the revision of extant databases as well as empirical analyses of the resulting information. Today high-quality databases of international stock returns and characteristics are easily obtained but such was not the case when we did this work.

For tractability we used price/book ratios to classify stocks into "value" and "growth" categories, justifying the approach with U.S., data (Table 1). For the U.S., we used the S&P/BARRA Value and Growth indices, each constructed to include half the value of the stocks in the S&P500 Index. Using detailed data provided by Morgan Stanley Capital International, we then constructed similar indices and market indices (including the stocks in both value and growth indices) for each of the five other countries, We converted all returns to U.S. dollars, computed the results for portfolios of European stocks and "Global" indices for all six countries, then computed excess returns over those of one-month U.S. Treasury bills for all the indices. Given the data available to us, we were only able to analyze monthly returns from January 1981 through June 1992. Today, using data now available for both earlier months and the substantial period following our study, a number of investigators have examined value/growth effects and similar phenomena.

Our first set of analyses confirmed that value and growth stocks behaved very differently in each of the six countries. Table III shows that in each country for which detailed data were available, the value and growth portfolios were considerably less correlated than would be expected if securities had been randomly chosen for inclusion.

We then analyzed the returns on "value-growth spreads", corresponding to zero-investment strategies with value stocks held long and growth stocks held short. In all six countries, value stocks outperformed growth stocks on average. Interestingly, the results for the U.S. were considerably smaller than in the period analyzed in the widely-cited study by Fama and French. Table IV shows that in none of the countries was the value-growth spread statistically significantly positive (using a t-statistic of 2.0 as the criterion). In this sense, the global spread was the most significant, with a t-statistic of 1.98. This was due to the fact that the spreads for individual countries were not highly correlated (Table V), resulting in benefits from diversifying value-tilted strategies across countries.

Table VI shows that value stocks had lower beta values in the majority of the countries and also globally, with the latter statistically significant, although less so than in the U.S., where the phenomenon had been previously observed. Thus, the superior performance of value stocks during this period could not be attributed to higher beta values. Table VII shows that the value stock portfolio provided a higher Sharpe Ratio than a market portfolio in every country as well as in the two regions. The differences were not huge — at a global level a decision to avoid all growth stocks and adjust leverage to achieve the same risk as the overall market would have provided an incremental return of 1.88% per year before added costs. As we indicated, this might reflect an equilibrium such as that driven by differential tax treatment of dividends and capital gains. Or it might be due to a preference for "household names". Of course, the period was short, and the results could have been atypical or transitory. In addition, value tilt strategies require added transactions costs, which we did not take into account.

Since this paper was published, there have been numerous analyses of value-tilted strategies and variations on the theme. These and other ways to concentrate on subsets of the overall stock market have been analyzed *ad nauseum.* Some would say that the jury is in and superior strategies have been identified. Others, myself among them, would counsel caution before adopting a strategy that assumes that in the future one can continue to exploit other investors who overprice some subset of securities easily identified before the fact.

Reprinted from THE JOURNAL OF FINANCE, Vol. XX, No. 3, September, 1965

RISK-AVERSION IN THE STOCK MARKET: SOME EMPIRICAL EVIDENCE

WILLIAM F. SHARPE*

A RECENT ARTICLE in this *Journal*[1] explored the conditions for equilibrium in the market for capital assets under the assumptions that investors are risk-averters, have similar (probabilistic) beliefs about the future performance of various assets, and can borrow or lend funds at a common (pure) interest rate. Briefly, the article showed that under such conditions market prices of capital assets will adjust so that the predicted risk of each efficient portfolio's rate of return is linearly related to its predicted expected rate of return. Letting σ_i stand for the standard deviation of the subjective probability distribution of the rate of return on an efficient portfolio, and E_i for the expected value of the distribution, the prices of capital assets will adjust until all efficient portfolios conform to the relationship:[2]

$$E_i = p + b\sigma_i$$

where p is the pure (riskless) interest rate and b (>0) is the risk-premium. An important corollary concerns the relationship among the predicted rates of return on efficient portfolios: under the assumed conditions they will be perfectly correlated.

Strictly speaking, the implications of this theory cannot be tested practically, since the relationships refer to predictions concerning expected returns from assets and the associated risks. Clearly, actual results may diverge considerably from the predictions made by investors at the time they purchase assets. Moreover, investor preferences and investment opportunities presumably change over time. This poses a major problem: if the equilibrium value of p (the price of time) and b (the price of risk) change from year, it may be dangerous to use data from several years to estimate their average values. But if the results from several years are not used, how can predicted values of E_i and σ_i be estimated? In many respects the problem is similar to that of measuring demand curves. If any empirical tests are to be performed, rather stringent assumptions must be made.

The remainder of this paper shows the results obtained by using *ex post* values of the means and standard deviations of return as surrogates for the corresponding *ex ante* predictions of investors. Section I provides evidence concerning the relationship between E_i and σ_i for the portfolios held by a

* Associate Professor of Economics and Operations Research, University of Washington, and Consultant, The RAND Corporation. The views expressed in this paper are those of the author. They should not be interpreted as reflecting the views of The RAND Corporation or the official opinion or policy of any of its governmental or private research sponsors.

1. W. F. Sharpe, "Capital Asset Prices: A Theory of Market Equilibrium Under Conditions of Risk," *The Journal of Finance,* Vol. XIX, No. 3 (September 1964), pp. 425-442.

2. By definition, for an inefficient portfolio $E_i < p + b\sigma_1$.

number of open-end mutual funds. With the additional assumption that such portfolios were efficient, the data can be used to test the assertion that for efficient portfolios, larger values of E_i are associated with larger values of σ_i—i.e., the risk-premium (b) is positive. The linearity of the relationship is discussed in Section II. Section III presents some results bearing on the corollary that the returns from efficient portfolios will be highly correlated with one another, and hence with some over-all index of performance. The results are summarized briefly in Section IV.

I

To provide some evidence concerning the behavior of the capital market, the annual returns from 34 open-end mutual funds[3] during the period from 1954 through 1963 were analyzed in the manner suggested by the theory. The average rate of return[4] for each fund over the ten-year period was used as an estimate of its expected rate of return (E_i). Similarly, the standard deviation[5] of the actual rate of return for each fund over the ten-year period was used as an estimate of its predicted risk (σ_i). Lacking any satisfactory test for reasonable diversification, all 34 funds were assumed to have chosen efficient combinations of securities.[6] Needless to say, the measures utilized cannot be expected to perfectly reflect investors' predictions and some mutual funds may hold rather inefficient portfolios; thus the relationship between the values of σ_i and E_i in the sample will be approximate at best. But if the theory is worth any consideration at all, there should be such a relationship, it should be significant, and funds experiencing greater variability should provide greater average returns.

Table 1 shows the results for the 34 funds in the sample; the E_i, σ_i combination for each fund is plotted as a point in Figure 1. The predicted relationship is clearly present. The correlation coefficient between σ and E is +.836, highly significant[7] and consistent with the assumption of risk-aversion.

It is not a simple matter to select appropriate estimates for the pure interest rate and the risk-premium from the sample data. The market process by which E_i and σ_i values are made to follow a linear relationship involves changes in the prices of capital assets; the price changes in turn alter the values of both E_i and σ_i.[8]

Since neither can properly be considered an independent variable, the

3. The funds selected were those for which annual rates of return were given by Wiesenberger for at least the last twenty years. All data are from Arthur Wiesenberger and Co., *Investment Companies,* 1962 and 1964 editions.

4. In all cases, rate of return is based on the sum of dividend payments, capital gains distributions, and changes in net asset value.

5. Derived from an estimate of variance computed by dividing the sums of the squared deviations by $(N-1)$.

6. The return on a fund is, of course, slightly less than the return on its portfolio, due to the expenses incurred by the fund's management. For the purposes of this analysis, the two are assumed to be equal.

7. A coefficient of .45 is significant at $P = .01$; the t-value of the slope of the regression line is 8.61.

8. Recall that E_i and σ_i refer to the mean and standard deviation of the rate of return.

appropriate line for estimating their relationship presumably lies between the one obtained by regressing σ on E and that obtained by regressing E on σ. Figure 1 shows the two regression lines and an intermediate one. The latter is simply the line passing through the intersection of the two regression lines[9]

TABLE 1

Mutual Fund	Average Annual Return 1954-1963 (E_i)	Standard Deviation of Annual Return 1954-1963 (σ_i)
1. Affiliated Fund	14.6%	15.3%
2. American Business Shares	10.0	9.2
3. Axe-Houghton, Fund A	10.5	13.5
4. Axe-Houghton, Fund B	12.0	16.3
5. Axe-Houghton, Stock Fund	11.9	15.6
6. Boston Fund	12.4	12.1
7. Broad Street Investing	14.8	16.8
8. Bullock Fund	15.7	19.3
9. Commonwealth Investment Company	10.9	13.7
10. Delaware Fund	14.4	21.4
11. Dividend Shares	14.4	15.9
12. Eaton and Howard, Balanced Fund	11.0	11.9
13. Eaton and Howard, Stock Fund	15.2	19.2
14. Equity Fund	14.6	18.7
15. Fidelity Fund	16.4	23.5
16. Financial Industrial Fund	14.5	23.0
17. Fundamental Investors	16.0	21.7
18. Group Securities, Common Stock Fund	15.1	19.1
19. Group Securities, Fully Administered Fund	11.4	14.1
20. Incorporated Investors	14.0	25.5
21. Investment Company of America	17.4	21.8
22. Investors Mutual	11.3	12.5
23. Loomis-Sayles Mutual Fund	10.0	10.4
24. Massachusetts Investors Trust	16.2	20.8
25. Massachusetts Investors—Growth Stock	18.6	22.7
26. National Investors Corporation	18.3	19.9
27. National Securities—Income Series	12.4	17.8
28. New England Fund	10.4	10.2
29. Putnam Fund of Boston	13.1	16.0
30. Scudder, Stevens and Clark Balanced Fund	10.7	13.3
31. Selected American Shares	14.4	19.4
32. United Funds—Income Fund	16.1	20.9
33. Wellington Fund	11.3	12.0
34. Wisconsin Fund	13.8	16.9

with a risk-premium (b) equal to the average of the values for the regression lines. The estimates of the pure interest rate and the risk-premium corresponding to the three lines are:

9. This point corresponds to the average values of E_i and σ_i for the funds in the sample. The values are:

$$\overline{E}_i = 13.64\% \text{ per annum}$$
$$\overline{\sigma}_i = 17.07\% \text{ per annum.}$$

	p	b
Regression line: σ on E	2.06	.678
Regression line: E on σ	5.55	.474
Intermediate line	3.81	.576

The values obtained from the intermediate line can be interpreted as follows. During this period investors required (and got) an annual rate of return of approximately 3.8 per cent on riskless assets. To take on risk, they required

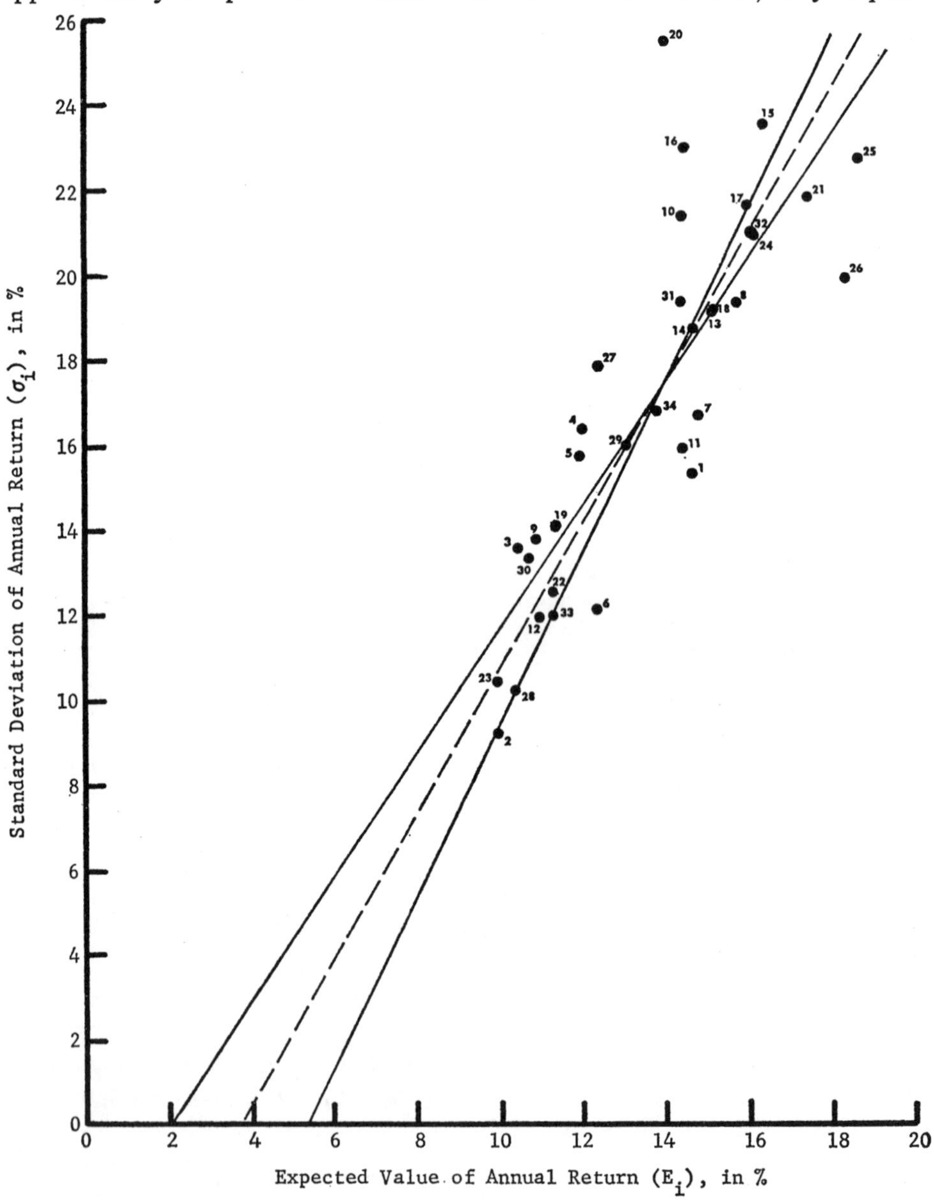

Figure 1

(and got) an additional .58 per cent of expected return per annum for each 1 per cent of predicted standard deviation of annual return (risk). These values may or may not properly characterize the conditions in the capital market during the period covered by the sample. Even if they do, there is no *a priori* reason to assume that they will characterize any future period. However, for purposes of prediction these results may be as useful as any others presently available.

II

Thus far we have shown that higher values of σ_i are associated with higher values of E_i, but we have not tested directly the implication of the theory that the relationship is linear. This conclusion is a direct result of the assumption that investors can either borrow or lend at a common pure interest rate. If an investor's funds can be divided between a risky portfolio and an investment at the pure interest rate, he can obtain any combination of E and σ on the line connecting the point representing the E, σ combination of the risky portfolio and the point representing the E, σ combination obtained with the pure interest rate.[10] If the investor is able to borrow funds at the same rate of interest, any point on the extension of the line to higher values of E and σ is also attainable. Under these conditions all efficient portfolios must lie along a straight line passing through the point representing the pure interest rate. If the assumptions are violated, of course, this relationship need not hold. Since investors are probably unable to borrow extensively at the pure interest rate in order to purchase risky assets, we should not be too surprised to find that the relationship between σ and E turns upward from a straight line as higher values of E (and σ) are reached.

There is some evidence of such curvature in the sample data. A quadratic regression equation gave a slightly higher correlation coefficient than did the linear regression equation—(+.852 instead of +.836)[11]—and the curvature was of the type anticipated. This result could be due to the presence of one or more relatively inefficient portfolios in the region of high risk,[12] but no satisfactory method for testing the validity of this explanation is available. In any event, although the implication of linearity is violated to some extent, it seems reasonable to assert that for purposes of characterizing the general nature of the capital market the relationship between σ and E for efficient portfolios can be assumed to be linear.

10. This relationship (and those in the remainder of the paragraph) can be found in Sharpe, *op. cit.*, pp. 431-433.

11. The regression equation was of the form: $E = a + b\sigma + c\sigma^2$. The t-values of the latter two coefficients were:

b : +2.87
c : —1.78.

The relative magnitudes of the two correlation coefficients given in the text overstate slightly the advantage of the quadratic equation since one more degree of freedom was lost in its estimation. A χ^2 test of the normality of the distribution of the residuals from the regression of σ on E shows that the assumption of linearity is significant at $p = .30$.

12. The fund with the highest standard deviation may well be guilty of this charge.

III

If all efficient portfolios lie along a straight line in the (E, σ) plane, their predicted rates of return will be perfectly correlated. Putting it another way, the predicted rate of return of any single portfolio should be linearly related to that of any other we might choose for the comparison. If each portfolio is compared with the same (standard) portfolio, the correlation coefficients should all equal +1. As before, we can only use actual results as surrogates

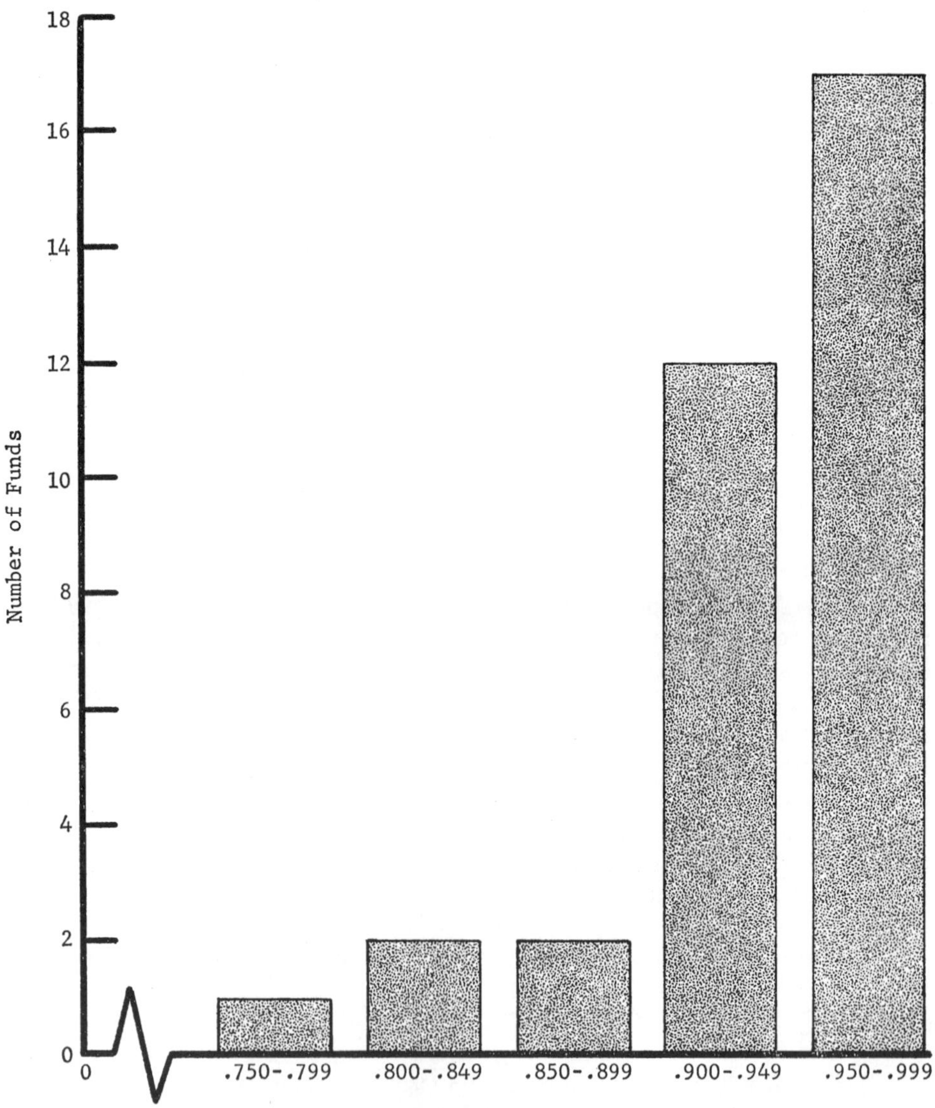

Correlation Coefficient: Rate of Return on Fund vs Rate of Return on Dow-Jones Portfolio, 1954-1963

Figure 2

for predicted performance, and thus cannot expect perfect correlations. However, if an appropriate standard is selected, relatively high values should be obtained.

To test this implication of the theory, a correlation coefficient was computed for each of the 34 funds—measuring the extent to which the values of the fund's actual rate of return during the ten-year period were correlated with those of the 30-security portfolio used to compute the Dow-Jones Industrial Average. Figure 2 shows the distribution of the correlation coefficients for the 34 funds. Needless to say, none was +1, and the sample size used to compute each coefficient was only ten (since just ten values of annual rate of return were employed). However, although no satisfactory test for consistency can be employed, the results certainly appear to be in substantial agreement with the theory.

IV

This concludes the evidence. Although fragmentary, and not even particularly novel,[13] the data do lend considerable support to the theory tested. Mutual fund portfolios that show substantial variability in annual return provide larger returns on the average than do those with less variable returns, as predicted by the risk-aversion hypothesis. And though the relationship between average yield and standard deviation does not appear to be perfectly linear, the differences are slight and in the expected direction. Finally, the portfolios exhibit the high correlations with the over-all market predicted by the theory.

Although these results are comforting, the issues surrounding the behavior of the capital market are far from settled. It is entirely possible that data obtained from different segments of the market and different time periods may not conform to the relationships predicted by the theory and found here.[14] Hopefully more detailed and extensive investigations will be made in the future; the importance of the subject certainly warrants the effort.

13. A similar analysis can be found in W. F. Sharpe, *Portfolio Analysis Based on a Simplified Model of the Relationships Among Securities,* Ph.D. Dissertation, UCLA, June 1961. A sample of 23 mutual funds showed similar relationships in two separate periods: 1940-1951 and 1951-1959. In the study leading to his recent article, "How to Rate Management of Investment Funds," *The Harvard Business Review,* January/February 1965, Vol. 43, No. 1, pp. 63-75, Jack L. Treynor apparently obtained results similar to those given here (although they are not stated explicitly in the article). The tests described here are sufficiently obvious that it seems reasonable to assume that they have been performed elsewhere as well, although no results appear to have been published.

14. In particular, a sample of portfolios with larger standard deviations might exhibit even greater non-linearity due to the greater importance of the discrepancy between borrowing and lending rates.

by William F. Sharpe and Guy M. Cooper

Risk-Return Classes of New York Stock Exchange Common Stocks, 1931-1967

Within the last decade economists have investigated rather thoroughly the nature of a "perfect" or "efficient" market for securities. A widely used model dealing with uncertainty is that developed by Sharpe [6]*, Lintner [3], Mossin [5], and Fama [2], based on the pioneering contributions of Markowitz [4] and Tobin [8]. Variously known as the "capital asset pricing model," "capital market theory," or the "market line theory," the approach deals with *ex ante* or predicted relationships. Briefly, it suggests that:

1) the appropriate measure of risk for a security or portfolio is the covariance of its rate of return with that of a portfolio composed of all risky assets, each held in proportion to its total value.

2) the expected return of any security or portfolio will equal a constant plus some other constant times its risk.

Derivation of these results can be found in Sharpe [7].

While the model provides important insights into the nature of actual capital markets, it is of limited value for the selection of an investment strategy unless additional specifications are made concerning the stability and/or predictability of key measures.

A number of investigators have performed tests of such expanded capital asset pricing models. The original specifications are augmented with assumptions about the stability of key variables through time. The expanded models suggest (1) that measurement of values during some previous period can be used to implement strategies that will in fact differ with respect to both risk and expected return; (2) that high-risk, high-return strategies will return more on the average than low-risk, low-return strategies; and (3) that high-risk, high-return strategies will bring greater losses in bear markets (i.e., have more risk) than will low-risk, low-return strategies.

An extensive study of this type was performed by Black, Jensen and Scholes [1]. They were concerned primarily with testing the validity of an expanded capital asset pricing model, and less directly with assessing the performance of alternative investment strategies. In this paper, the general approach of Black, Jensen and Scholes is followed with modifications designed to reduce its expense as a practical investment selection technique.

*References [ ] appear at end of article.

WILLIAM F. SHARPE *is Professor of Business, Stanford University, Graduate School of Business.*

GUY M. COOPER *is a student in the Doctoral Program, Stanford University, Graduate School of Business.*

Support for this research was provided by the Dean Witter Foundation under a grant to the Stanford Graduate School of Business. The authors wish to express their appreciation to Marcus C. Bogue for invaluable assistance in the course of the work.

Moreover, we report information particularly relevant to the selection of such a technique. Our focus is primarily on assessing alternative investment strategies; by and large, we bypass issues concerned with the adequacy of various expanded capital asset pricing models.[1]

Performance Measures

For any single period, a relevant measure of performance from the investor's point of view is return:

$$\text{return} = \frac{\text{ending value} + \text{dividends} - \text{beginning value}}{\text{beginning value}}$$

For securities, return can be calculated on a per-share basis, with appropriate adjustments for stock dividends and stock splits.

A related measure is appreciation:

$$\text{appreciation} = \frac{\text{ending value} - \text{beginning value}}{\text{beginning value}}$$

The other component of return is yield:

$$\text{yield} = \frac{\text{dividends}}{\text{beginning value}}$$

Obviously:

$$\text{return} = \text{appreciation} + \text{yield}$$

The data used in this study were taken from the CRISP (Center for Research in Security Prices) tapes developed at the University of Chicago. Monthly returns and appreciation figures for all New York Stock Exchange stocks over the period from January 1926 through June 1968 were utilized.

Performance over a number of periods can be measured by the average return. Let R_{pt} represent the return on a portfolio of stocks in time period t. The average return from period 1 through period T is:

$$\text{average return} = \frac{1}{T} \sum_{t+1}^{T} R_{pt}$$

(where $\sum$ denotes summation).

An alternative measure of performance is the geometric instead of the arithmetic mean. The result indicates the constant return in each period that would have provided the same terminal value as the actual series of returns. The value is:

$$\text{equivalent constant return} = \left[\prod_{t=1}^{T} (1 + R_{pt}) \right]^{1/T} - 1$$

(where $\prod$ denotes multiplication).

Risk can be measured in a great many ways. We focus on a measure that highlights the impact of swings in the market on the return from a security or portfolio. If there were no prospects of bear markets, there would be little risk in the common meaning of the term. Stocks are considered risky because they can go down. And typically, the more sensitive a security or portfolio is to swings in the market, the more it goes down in a bear market. To measure this, we use the slope of a regression line relating return on the portfolio to the return on a broadly-based portfolio used to represent "the market." Figure I provides an illustration.

We term the slope of such a line "beta." More formally:[2]

$$\beta_p \equiv \frac{\text{Cov}(R_p, R_m)}{\text{Var}(R_m)}$$

where:

$$\text{Cov}(R_p, R_m) = \text{covariance between } R_p \text{ and } R_m = \frac{1}{T} \left[\sum_{t=1}^{T} (R_{pt} - \bar{R}_p)(R_{mt} - \bar{R}) \right]$$

$$\text{Var}(R_m) = \text{variance of } R_m = \frac{1}{T} \left[\sum_{t=1}^{T} (R_{mt} - \bar{R}_m)^2 \right]$$

$\bar{R}_p$ = average return on portfolio p

$\bar{R}_m$ = average return on the market portfolio.

For purposes of this study, the Fisher market index included on the CRISP tape was used to measure R_m.

It is important to recognize that beta may not provide an adequate measure of the total risk of a portfolio. However, for well diversified portfolios, the majority of the variation in return is attributable to changes in the return on the market, and beta will thus provide a good measure of risk.

1. Footnotes appear at end of article.

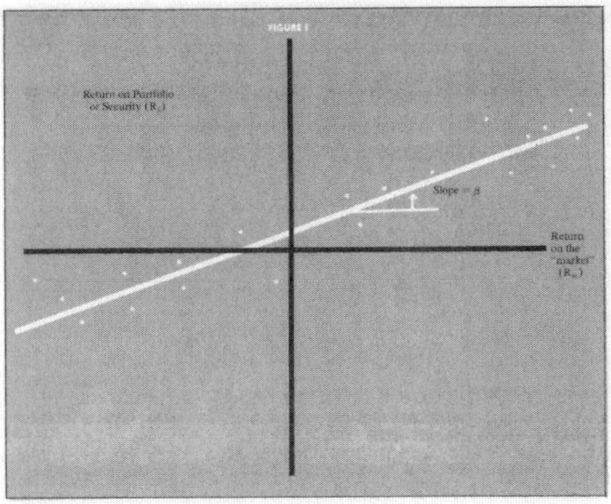

Risk-Return Classes

In an efficient market, one rarely gets something for nothing. If investors prefer high average returns to low average returns *and* prefer low risk to high risk, prices should adjust so that the best low risk strategy provides lower returns on the average than the best high risk strategy.

The average return of a portfolio is simply the weighted average of the average returns of its component securities, with the proportions of value used as weights. Moreover, the beta of a portfolio is a weighted average of the betas of its component securities, with the proportions of value used as weights. Finally, the beta of a well diversified portfolio provides a good surrogate for its total risk, since almost all fluctuations in the portfolio's value will follow market swings.

A well-diversified portfolio with a high beta value will be risky. In an efficient market, it will also provide a high average return. A portfolio of this type may be constructed by choosing a large number of stocks with high beta values. Such a strategy should provide high returns on the average, but with substantial risk.

A well-diversified portfolio with a low beta value will have relatively little risk. In an efficient market, it will also provide a relatively low average return. A portfolio of this type may be constructed by choosing a large number of stocks with low beta values. Such a strategy should provide relatively low returns on the average, but with little risk.

In a period in which the market goes up, high-beta stocks will go up more than low-beta stocks. Unless dividend yields are strongly inversely related to beta values, average return and beta will thus be positively correlated over periods in which the market goes up. And since both history and expectations of risk-averse investors indicate that the market is more likely to go up than down, over long periods average return should be positively related to beta.

Stocks with high beta values should have high returns on the average; they may be said to be in a high *risk-return class*. On the other hand, stocks with low beta values should have low returns on the average; they may be said to be in a low *risk-return class*.

To use this relationship as a basis for an investment strategy, some means must be found to select stocks that will, in fact, have high beta values *in the future*. An obvious possibility involves the measurement of beta in the past, on the assumption that beta is reasonably stable over time. This procedure was utilized by Black, Jensen and Scholes and will be adopted here, with minor modifications.

Market Sensitivity

To measure performance it is important to use return — i.e., appreciation plus dividend yield. However, most variation in return is due to changes in appreciation; dividend yield being relatively constant over time. This suggests that the value of beta would not change significantly if dividend yield were excluded. To avoid confusion, we continue to use the term "beta" for the slope of the regression line relating the return on a portfolio or security to that of the market. The term "market sensitivity" will be used to denote the slope of a regression line relating the appreciation on a portfolio or security to that of the market. Figure II provides an illustration.

To compare the two measures, the monthly returns and appreciation values for 1572 securities during the period from January 1960 through June

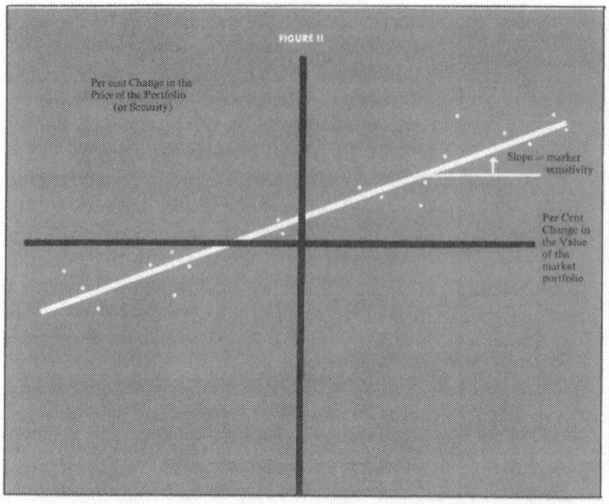

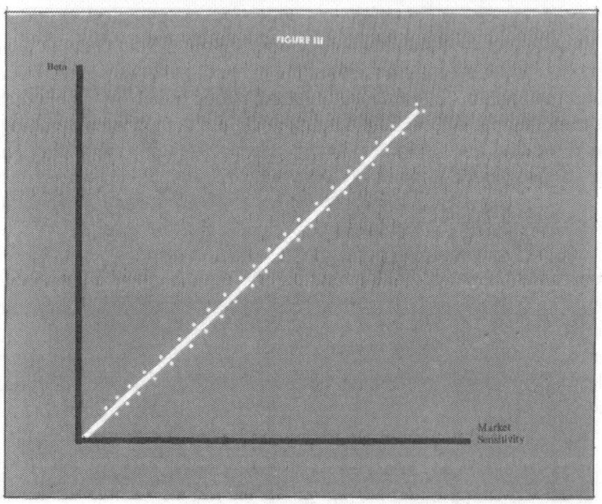

1968 were utilized. For each security the value of beta was calculated using returns; then the value of market sensitivity was calculated, using only price changes. The results were very similar. If each of the 1572 pairs were plotted, the points would lie almost exactly along a 45-degree line through the axis, as illustrated in Figure III. The similarity of the two measures is clear from the results obtained when the values of beta were regressed on the values of market sensitivity. The regression equation was:

$$\text{Beta} = .004 + .997 \text{ (Market sensitivity)}$$

$$\text{Coefficient of determination } (R^2) = .996$$

This suggests that as a practical matter, market sensitivity may be used instead of beta when classifying securities into risk-return classes. Since dividend information may be difficult to collect and verify, this makes it possible to lower the cost of implementing strategies based on risk-return classes.

Portfolio Selection Strategies

We have determined the outcomes obtained from each of ten investment strategies during the 37-year period from 1931 through 1967. For each security listed on the New York Stock Exchange, market sensitivity was calculated, based on the monthly price changes for the 60 months prior to the beginning of the investment calendar year (a security would not be included if a full 60 months of data were not available). The number of securities for which market sensitivity was calculated ranged from 478 (in 1931) to 985 (in 1967).

After the market sensitivity values were calculated, the numerical values were ranked. Based on this ranking, securities were divided into deciles. The securities in the top decile (i.e., those with the highest market sensitivities) were considered to be in risk-return class 10 at the time of classification. The securities in the next decile were considered to be in risk-return class 9, etc. The number of securities in a given risk-return class ranged from 47 (in 1931) to 99 (in 1967).

This procedure — calculation of market sensitivities, ranking of securities, and assignment to risk-return classes—was repeated for each of the possible investment years from 1931 through 1967.

Strategies are numbered from 10 to 1. Strategy 1 involves the purchase of equal dollar amounts of all stocks in risk-return class 1 at the beginning of each year. Every dividend received during the year is reinvested in the stock that pays it (at the beginning of the month following payment). On the first of the next year, stocks are bought and sold until the portfolio contains equal dollar amounts of all stocks in risk-return class 1 *at that time*. Rebalanc-

FIGURE IVa

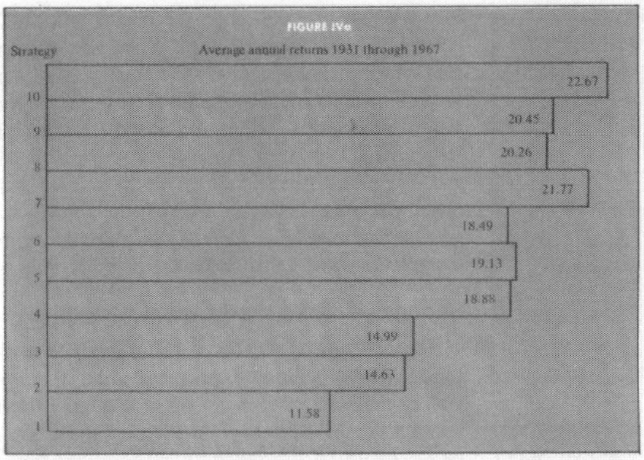

FIGURE IVb

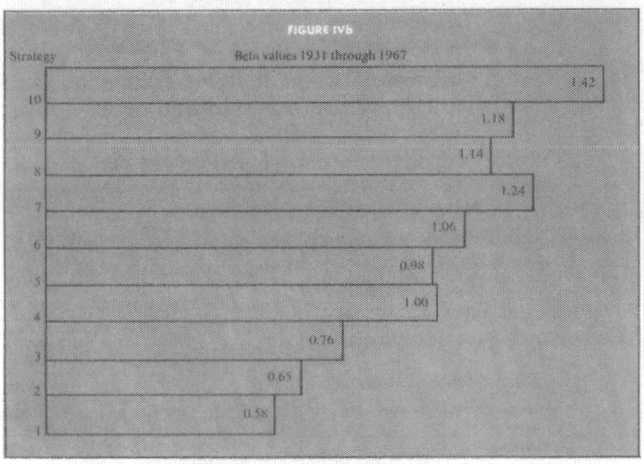

ing is thus required both to accommodate changes in the set of stocks in the specified risk-return class and to account for differential price changes.

To reduce the number of computations, the results have not been adjusted to account for transactions costs. However, these are relatively small and differ little among strategies since annual performance measures are being considered and rebalancing is done only once each year.

Performance

Figures IVa through IVd show the results obtained when each of the ten strategies was followed over the entire period studied (from 1931 through 1967). Figure IVa shows the average annual return for each strategy. On the average, strategy 10 provided a return of over 22 per cent per year, while strategy 1 provided less than 12 per cent. Although the values do not decrease uniformly, the general relationship is of the expected type—portfolios composed of securities in lower risk-return classes tend to provide lower average return.

Figure IVb shows the actual values of beta for the ten strategies. Returns obtained with strategy 10 moved 42 per cent more than the market as a whole; on the other hand, returns obtained with strategy 1 moved only 58 per cent as much as the market as a whole. Again, the values do not decrease uniformly, but the general relationship is of the expected type—portfolios composed of securities in lower risk-return classes tend to move less with swings in the market.[3]

Figure IVc shows the equivalent constant annual return for each of the ten strategies. Here the picture is far less clear. The investor concerned *only* with the very long run (in this case, 36 years) must take into account the impact of both risk and average return on his overall position. When returns vary, the geometric mean will always be smaller than the arithmetic mean, and the difference will typically be greater, the greater the variation. High risk-return classes typically offer a higher average return but also bring greater variability. The net effect over the very long term is thus relatively unpredictable. In this case, the best results would have been obtained with strategy 7. An investor who reinvested both capital and dividends every year while following strategy 7 would have accumulated as much wealth at the end of the period as if he had placed his money in a bank paying roughly 16 per cent interest per year, compounded annually. On the other hand, an investor following strategy 1 would have accumulated only as much wealth as if he had placed his funds in a bank paying roughly 10 per cent per annum, compounded annually.

Figure IVd summarizes the relationship between average return and the actual value of beta for each of the ten strategies during this period. As expected, the relationship is positive and quite significant (during this period the market rose on the

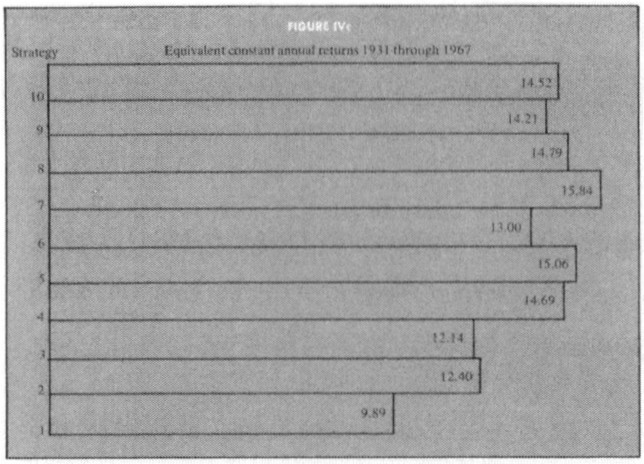

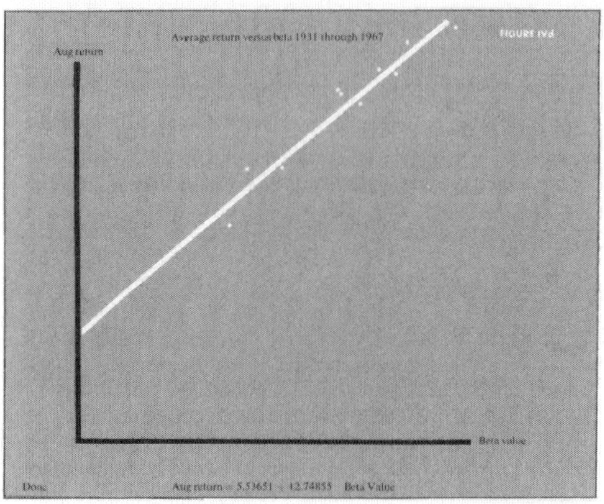

average). The intercept is somewhat higher than the return on relatively safe investments during the period — a result consistent with that of Black, Jensen and Scholes—and the relationship appears to be approximately linear.[4]

Figures IVa, b, c, and d were producing using the Tektronix T4002 display and the Hewlett-Packard 2000C computer at the Stanford Graduate School of Business. Users of this system can obtain results for any other period between 1931 and 1967 by calling for program $GRCC and running it. The program will give instructions, request the starting and ending year, and then provide the four graphs. By and large, the results will prove consistent with expectations. When the average market return is large, high risk-return classes tend to provide higher returns on the average than lower risk-return classes. When the average market return is small or negative, high risk-return classes tend to provide smaller returns on the average than lower risk-return classes. Finally, the shorter the time-period studied, the less the results conform to expectations due to the influence of other factors.

Changes in Risk-Return Classes

The investor who holds a well-diversified portfolio need not be unduly concerned about the possibility that one or more of his stocks may move into a different risk-return class in the future. Some of the securities that were formerly in risk-return class 5 may move to class 6 (or 7, 8, 9 or 10), while some of the others may move to class 4 (or 3, 2, or 1). But the effect on the total portfolio may nonetheless be negligible, as securities moving to higher classes can be offset by those moving to lower classes. Putting it somewhat differently: it is easier to predict an average (i.e., the portfolio's beta) than the value of any single component (i.e., a given security's beta).

But changes in risk-return class membership are not unimportant. They give rise to transactions costs for the strategies described here. They are particularly relevant for those who do not (and perhaps cannot) hold well-diversified portfolios—e.g., corporate officers. And they are important when risk-return class membership is used to estimate a firm's cost of capital.

To provide some evidence on such changes, the risk-return class of every security was determined for every year between 1931 and 1967 in which price and dividend data were available for the preceding 60 months. The risk-return class in each year was compared with first the class in the succeeding year, then the class five years hence. While the first comparison uses 48 months of common data, the second involves no overlap at all. Over 27,000 combinations were used for the first set of comparisons, and over 24,000 for the second.

Tables I and II summarize the results in transition matrices. For example, Table I shows that 74.2 per cent of the securities in risk-return class

TABLE I. Transition Matrix
Risk-Return Class in Year T vs. Risk-Return Class in Year T + 1

Risk-Return class in year t	Risk-Return class in year t + 1: 10	9	8	7	6	5	4	3	2	1
10	.7417	.1712	.0309	.0111	.0054	.0011	.0018	.0004	.0000	.0004
9	.1732	.4989	.2079	.0587	.0240	.0104	.0025	.0004	.0004	.0004
8	.0368	.2122	.4091	.2094	.0765	.0232	.0111	.0029	.0021	.0007
7	.0121	.0657	.2286	.3564	.1986	.0804	.0271	.0079	.0025	.0007
6	.0043	.0199	.0733	.2246	.3452	.2060	.0744	.0231	.0075	.0018
5	.0047	.0097	.0222	.0764	.2141	.3535	.2123	.0696	.0147	.0047
4	.0007	.0018	.0111	.0314	.0806	.2168	.3807	.2043	.0478	.0093
3	.0000	.0018	.0025	.0096	.0268	.0686	.2082	.4268	.2068	.0321
2	.0000	.0004	.0011	.0036	.0075	.0196	.0538	.2089	.5091	.1843
1	.0000	.0004	.0004	.0014	.0018	.0011	.0093	.0323	.1869	.7471

TABLE II. Transition Matrix
Risk-Return Class in Year T vs. Risk-Return Class in Year T + 5

Risk-Return class in year t	Risk-Return class in year t + 5: 10	9	8	7	6	5	4	3	2	1
10	.3517	.1929	.1153	.0568	.0494	.0373	.0203	.0120	.0083	.0079
9	.2051	.1835	.1487	.1272	.0808	.0601	.0414	.0228	.0116	.0128
8	.1324	.1593	.1638	.1303	.1047	.0890	.0612	.0393	.0219	.0149
7	.0794	.1310	.1579	.1327	.1186	.1083	.0930	.0583	.0310	.0149
6	.0523	.0977	.1121	.1343	.1389	.1195	.1137	.0820	.0445	.0293
5	.0423	.0647	.0855	.1041	.1361	.1361	.1448	.1112	.0763	.0336
4	.0326	.0491	.0759	.0994	.1106	.1254	.1320	.1448	.1023	.0611
3	.0203	.0289	.0488	.0715	.0951	.1146	.1286	.1588	.1584	.1084
2	.0087	.0161	.0268	.0384	.0499	.0771	.1139	.1630	.2145	.2314
1	.0042	.0087	.0104	.0203	.0303	.0419	.0722	.1133	.2183	.4047

TABLE III

Risk-Return Class in	Proportion in Same Risk-Return Class		Proportion Within One Risk-Return Class	
Year T	In Year t + 1	In Year t + 5	In Year t + 1	In Year t + 5
10	.7417	.3517	.9129	.6927
9	.4989	.1835	.8800	.5373
8	.4091	.1638	.8307	.4534
7	.3564	.1327	.7836	.4092
6	.3452	.1389	.7758	.3927
5	.3535	.1361	.7799	.4170
4	.3807	.1320	.8018	.4022
3	.4268	.1588	.8418	.4458
2	.5091	.2145	.9023	.6089
1	.7471	.4047	.9340	.6230

10 in year t were still in risk-return class 10 in year t + 1. Table II shows that only 35.2 per cent remained in risk-return class 10 in year t + 5.[5] Table III provides another summary, indicating the frequencies with which securities were in the same risk-return class or within one risk-return class one and five years later. As this Table shows, there is substantial stability over time, even at the level of individual securities. For portfolios, of course, the relationship would be considerably more stable.

Security Data

Table IV, which has subsections (a) to (j), shows the risk-return classes of all New York Stock Exchange stocks that could be assigned to a class on January 1, 1967. (Tables appear on pages 10 to 16). Table IVa includes securities in class 10, Table IVb, those in class 9, etc. Within a risk-return class, securities are arranged alphabetically (with minor exceptions). Beside the name of each security is a list of symbols indicating its status in each year, beginning with 1931 and ending with 1967. The symbols have the following meanings:

Years for which insufficient data for the prior 60 months was available are left blank.

9	risk-return class 10
8	risk-return class 9
7	risk-return class 8
6	risk-return class 7
5	risk-return class 6
4	risk-return class 5
3	risk-return class 4
2	risk-return class 3
1	risk-return class 2
0	risk-return class 1

The performance of simple strategies based on risk-return class membership suggests the usefulness of data of the type shown in Table IV. The classifications can be used to test investment strategies that might have been adopted in 1967 or earlier. Moreover, they provide at least some information concerning current risk-return classes, if the stability shown in Tables II and III is at all applicable at present. ♦

The risk-return class in which a portfolio falls may be determined by (1) taking a weighted average of the beta values of the component stocks, using relative market values as weights, then (2) finding the risk-return class whose range of security betas includes the value computed for the portfolio.

Lacking information on beta values of individual securities, a crude approximation may be obtained by (1) taking a weighted average of the risk-return classes of the component stocks, using relative market values as weights, then (2) rounding the result to the nearest whole number.

FOOTNOTES

1. This paper differs from that of Black, Jensen and Scholes (BJS) in a number of respects. The differences will be summarized here, although a full understanding may require a prior reading of the remainder of this paper. First, BJS require only 24 months of data to estimate a security's risk-return class (although they use up to 60 if available); we require 60 months. Second, BJS use beta to determine risk-return classes, while we use market sensitivity. Third, BJS measure performance in terms of monthly returns; we use annual values (both because an annual holding period seems more consistent with an annual review of risk-return classes and because annual rebalancing involves smaller transactions costs than monthly rebalancing of the portfolios). Finally, we report geometric means as well as arithmetic means for those interested in long-run performance and provide data concerning stability of risk-return classes for those interested in the characteristics of individual securities.
2. For a derivation of this relationship, see Sharpe [7].
3. In general, the value of beta describes the majority of the fluctuations in returns for these portfolios. The coefficients of determination for the regressions of portfolio return on market return were:

Strategy	Coefficient of Determination
10	.94
9	.94
8	.95
7	.95
6	.98
5	.98
4	.92
3	.94
2	.88
1	.87

4. This relationship can be derived from a model in which it is impossible to borrow without limit at the same rate of interest at which one can lend. If the portfolio used as a market surrogate is riskier than the optimal combination of risky securities for one who plans to lend part of his funds, the result follows directly as long as the market surrogate is on the efficient frontier. The true "market portfolio" (which includes all assets —e.g., corporate bonds, real estate, etc.) may well be less risky than the typical index of New York Stock Exchange common stocks such as that used in this study. It is entirely possible that if a better surrogate for the market portfolio could be obtained, the relationship between average return and beta would intercept the average return axis very near the interest rate on safe investments.
5. The sum of the figures in a row in either Table I or Table II will be less than 1; the difference represents cases in which the security could not be classified in the later period due to lack of adequate data.

References

[1] Black, Fischer, Michael C. Jensen, and Myron Scholes, "The Capital Asset Pricing Model: Some Empirical Tests," in *Studies in the Theory of Capital Markets*, M. C. Jensen, ed. (Praeger Publishing, forthcoming, 1971).

[2] Fama, Eugene F., "Risk, Return and Equilibrium: Some Clarifying Comments," *Journal of Finance*, March 1968 (pp. 29-40).

[3] Lintner, John, "The Valuation of Risk Assets and the Selection of Risky Investments in Stock Portfolios and Capital Budgets," *Review of Economics and Statistics*, February 1965, pp. 13-17.

[4] Markowitz, Harry, "Portfolio Selection," *Journal of Finance*, March, 1952, pp. 77-91.

[5] Mossin, Jan, "Equilibrium in a Capital Asset Market," *Econometrica*, Oct. 1966, pp. 768-783.

[6] Sharpe, William F., "Capital Asset Prices: A Theory of Market Equilibrium under Conditions of Risk," *Journal of Finance*, September 1964, pp. 425-442.

[7] Sharpe, William F., *Portfolio Theory and Capital Markets*, McGraw-Hill, 1970.

[8] Tobin, James, "Liquidity Preference as Behavior Towards Risk," *Review of Economic Studies*, February 1958, pp. 65-86.

Table IV. Risk-Return Classifications for NYSE Stocks, 1931-1967

(See article by Sharpe and Cooper in this issue)

TABLE IVa. Risk-Return Class 10

	1935	'40	'45	'50	'55	'60	'65	
AMP Incorporated								99
Admiral Corporation					7554	54899	99999	99
Alleghany Corp.	9	99999	99999	99999	98999	99999	99999	99
Allied Products Corp.							554	99
Alside Inc.								9
American Export Industries Inc.				122	21223	23555	34788	99
American Research & Development Corp.								9
American Ship Building Co.	001	12233	44452	11100	00012	21432	33889	99
Canteen Corp.					1233	22233	54999	99
Bell & Howell Co.					65324	54555	78999	99
Boston & Maine Corp.	44	56689	99999	99999	99999	99999	88999	9
Braniff Airways				6	78899	99998	89999	99
Bullard Co.	8	76777	77762	56689	87773	11599	99999	99
Calumet & Pecla Inc.	46788	87767	88874	45344	67899	99989	88888	89
J. I. Case Co.	88755	54233	45557	65433	57788	87657	78899	99
Cemco Instruments								9
Cerro Corp.	43676	66523	44432	22133	46889	99999	99899	99
Certainteed Products Corp.	78688	88997	77789	98998	89989	97543	4899	99
Cessna Aircraft Co.							9999	99
Chicago & Eastern Illinois RR.				9999	98899	99887	88999	99
Chicago & Great Western Ry. (Del).				9999	99999	99999	98989	89
Chicago Milwaukee St. Paul & Pacific					99999	99999	98999	99
Chicago Rock Island & Pacific Ry.					76	66888	88888	89
Chris-Craft Industries, Inc.				77799	99986	42334	56999	99
Servel Inc.	5	55764	44437	66667	89887	66455	78999	99
Collins Radio Co.								99
C.E. and I. Steel Corp.	99888	88899	98885	57788	99999	99998	88999	99
Colt Industries Inc.	50355	56758	99998	77733	54335	43799	99999	99
Commercial Solvents Corp.	7543	33245	56666	66667	78999	99889	99999	99
Congoleum Nairn Inc.	76322	11132	33334	34443	32222	22578	89988	99
Continental Airlines Inc.								9
Continental Copper & Steel Industries						8774	44566	89
Copper Range Co.					9	99999	98899	99
Diners Club Inc.							9	99
Douglas Aircraft Co. Inc.		4374	43342	32211	14458	88862	24999	99
Eastern Airlines			3	22122	13677	88778	88899	99
Elgin National Watch					123	58899	99999	99
Erie Lackawanna Railroad Co.	57888	87669	99956	77777	88899	97999	99999	99
Evans Products Co. Del.	9	98989	99998	88899	99998	88999	99988	89
Eversharp Inc.					6642	01233	56999	99
Fairchild Camera and Instruments								9
Fansteel, Inc.						987	77888	99
Federal Pacific Electric Co.							64688	89
First Charter Financial Corp.								99
Fluor Corp. Ltd.							999	99
Foote Mineral Co.							899	99
Gar Wood Industries			677	78887	88999	99999	99887	89
General Instrument Corp.					577	78899	99999	99
General Refractories Co.	55789	88878	88885	66766	77678	75655	66999	99
General Time Corp.			2257	77654	53346	77789	999 9	99
Hoffman Electronics Corp.							78999	99
I T E Circuit Breaker Co.							788	89
Indiana General Corp.								99
International Rectifier Corp.								9
Interstate Department Stores Inc.	78	88997	88767	66788	78856	52333	14799	99
Joy Manufacturing Co.				6665	53446	66755	65788	89
Missouri Kansas Texas RR.	77977	88689	88999	99999	99999	99999	88889	99
Leesona Corp.								9
Lionel Corp.						233	57999	99
Lukens Steel					98998	98968	98899	99
MCA Incorporated								99
Soo Line R.R.				8	88789	99998	78999	99
Monon Railroad					9999	99997	64999	99
National Airlines					67889	89998	88877	79
New York Central RR.	21444	55568	89988	88877	89999	99999	99989	99

CLASS 10 (cont'd)	1935	'40	'45	'50	'55	'60	'65	
Northwest Airlines				5678	76789	99999	99999	99
Philadelphia and Reading Corp.					44357	78767	89999	99
Northwest Industries				7	99999	98999	99999	99
Packard Bell Electronics Corp.							8	79
Pan American World Airways Inc.			6	65444	46788	88776	77999	99
Penn Central	11433	44245	66675	56545	67788	88898	88989	99
Piper Aircraft Corp.							999	99
Pittsburgh Steel			997	89999	99999	99998	99899	99
Plough Inc.					0001	11212	56999	99
Polaroid Corp.							77	89
Reading Co.	11655	56336	77786	56533	43344	44565	46889	99
Reynolds Metals		33424	45668	87899	89989	99999	99999	89
Roan Selection Trust, Ltd.							46656	69
Ryder System Inc.								99
SCM Corp.			346	56544	68887	63778	99999	99
Seagrave Corp.	14877	77533	43363	88853	56477	64589	89999	99
Sparton Corp.	9	99998	88888	99999	99999	89999	99999	99
Standard Kollsman Industries						6689	99999	99
Standard Packaging Corp.							99	89
Standard Pressed Steel Company								9
Rexall Drug and Chemical Co.		43	44457	67788	87755	54256	77999	99
Worthington Corporation	99666	65678	88875	55478	89988	67777	87778	89
Sunshine Mining			127	89987	78778	85787	78557	89
Telautograph Corp.	11000	00110	11125	44568	99985	33699	9999	99
Thiokol Chemical							9	99
Trans World Airlines Inc.			56545	65433	35799	99888	88999	99
Transitron Electronic								99
United Air Lines Inc.		5	55546	44434	45788	99988	87888	89
U.S. Industries Inc.	88999	99899	99998	78889	99999	98889	99999	99
Perfect Film and Chemical Corp.					98765	31122	03788	99
UMC Industries							9	99
Vendo Co.								99
Western Maryland Ry.	88977	77458	99899	99998	99999	99977	87999	99
White Consolidated Industries Inc.	788	78778	88888	88899	87646	88989	89999	99

TABLE IVb. Risk-Return Class 9

ABC Consolidated Corp.						21	25788	88
Adams Millis	1	11111	11101	01212	10012	33222	64888	88
General Bronze Corp.	7	66667	87767	67876	64353	46667	77766	88
Allis Chalmers Manufacturing Co.	66665	55434	33454	45556	77765	56666	65567	78
American Airlines			3	23233	33457	78788	88777	78
Ambac Industries, Inc.	98444	43688	77778	88898	99898	76643	78888	88
American Photocopy Equipment Co.								78
Ampex Corporation							8	78
Amphenol Corp.							998	98
Armour & Co.	70355	47856	77777	77789	98888	78877	76787	88
Arthur G. McKee Co.								78
Associated Brewing Co.			22213	53223	23332	10879	99876	58
Avnet, Inc.								8
Bausch & Lomb Inc.							76	78
Beckman Instruments							9999	98
Beech Aircraft				12	33278	88876	86676	68
Bell Intercontinental Corp.				764	32246	87533	45888	88
Divco Wayne Corp.					452	13225	54776	78
Brunswick Corp.	65677	77875	55436	66666	66665	76434	20554	78
Bucyrus Erie	77	77867	76664	66666	65768	77788	89988	88
Burndy Corp.								8
Burroughs Corp.	34333	33422	22245	66554	33213	67877	67677	88
The Marquardt Corp.								88
Carlisle Corp.								88
Carter-Wallace, Inc.							887	68
Chadbourn Gotham, Inc.	56433	33488	88877	75776	58789	88799	9 99	98
Chemetron Corp.			2	33434	55454	23544	56688	88
City Investing Co.	000	00000	00000	04678	74345	58888	98888	68
Conelco, Inc.	95477	67998	89888	88899	88888	99997	76777	78
Crescent Corp.					654	33100	00233	68

CLASS 9 (cont'd)	1935	'40	'45	'50	'55	'60	'65	
Crowell-Collier & Macmillan, Inc.							8	98
Cudahy Corp.	00011	11223	44455	56768	88899	99998	99999	98
Curtis Publishing Co.	3	44546	67899	99999	99987	71232	26877	88
Dayco Corp.					8888	87666	47888	88
Champlain National Corp.	11333	34378	99999	98754	55577	75666	55657	88
Walt Disney Productions Inc.							99	88
Duplan Corp.	3	34211	11125	67787	73456	57777	86656	58
Eastern Stainless Steel Corp.	9	99999	99999	99999	99999	99999	99999	98
Eltra Corp.						5656	68899	98
Endicott Johnson Corp.	00111	11112	22230	01111	10011	21000	11467	88
Minerals & Chemicals Philipp Corp.							88999	98
Factor (Max) and Co. (A)								8
Fairchild Hiller Corp.						998	89778	88
Financial Federation, Inc.								8
Florida East Coast Railway Company								8
Vanadium Corp. of America	99876	65568	88885	67788	88889	99999	98767	88
Foremost Dairies, Inc.							21456	68
Foster Wheeler	7	76788	88888	77889	99998	89966	75677	78
Foxbord Co.								8
General Precision Equipment Corp.			3236	56765	76534	35778	77898	98
General Signal Corp.	23654	55368	88887	77877	77476	55877	88888	78
Ginn and Co.								8
Glen Alden Corp.						4533	66899	78
Granby Mining Co., Ltd.	77788	77798	99866	68788	86765	67889	87555	68
Great Western Financial Corp.								98
Harvey Aluminum, Inc.								8
H. J. Heinz Co.					000	00113	35888	88
Helene Curtis Industries, Inc.								8
Hertz Corp.	66565	55534	34679	99823	22233	34543	22655	68
Hupp Corp.	98556	66897	54468	99999	99999	99999	99988	78
IPL, Inc.						34466	87877	78
IRC, Inc.								88
Jaeger Machine Co.					366	67688	77777	88
Kayser Roth Corp.	23544	44211	10024	56655	34565	66599	99999	98
Spartans Imyers, Inc. (New)							389	98
Lanvin-Charles of the Ritz, Inc.								8
Lear Siegler Corp.							98	88
Litton Industries							888	88
Lowenstein, M & Sons					8857	65899	88776	88
McCall Corp.	01	11121	22212	11354	45434	43453	67999	88
Metro-Goldwyn-Mayer, Inc.	66544	48221	22213	22221	12215	65765	68888	88
Loews Theatres, Inc.							8	88
Moore & McCormack Co.					4565	54543	34567	78
Motorola, Inc.					3354	44435	77899	88
North American Coal Corp.								8
Parke Davis			0111	10110	00001	25422	32787	78
Pittsburgh Coke & Chemical Co.			997	77777	88899	98887	77656	78
Revlon, Inc.							999	98
Ronson Corp.					242	11223	26888	98
St. Louis San Francisco Ry.					999	87999	99766	78
Imperial Corp. of America							9	88
Schenley Industries, Inc.		22	34456	65677	34446	87566	78888	88
Schick Electric, Inc.							999	98
Sharon Steel Corp.	7	77887	77777	87777	88999	97888	89999	98
A. O. Smith			6677	77799	89976	78857	76787	78
Wagner Electric Corp. (New)						657	86887	88
Texas Gulf Sulphur	23322	21102	21121	10011	13345	65677	78866	78
Texas Instruments	9999	99899	99984	36778	99886	12457	87888	88
Getty Oil Co.		33	33346	75445	45764	57888	88888	88
Twentieth Century Fox Film Corp.	68999	99742	22237	66453	34434	44457	77788	98
Ling-Temco Vought, Inc.							78766	78
U.S. Borax & Chemical							788	88
U.S. Freight	5	54557	89998	88744	55667	76776	78777	78
U.S. Smelting Refining and Mining	42232	22123	34443	44443	46678	88888	68554	78
Ward Foods, Inc.	99888	77877	76789	99988	02110	00233	45545	68
Warner Lambert						7632	45899	98
Western Union Telegraph Co.	01565	66558	88885	33345	78887	86687	88988	88
Xerox Corp.								8

TABLE IVc. Risk-Return Class 8

Morrell, John and Co., Inc.	0	01112	22230	01000	10013	46678	98887	67
Aeroquip Corporation							35898	87
Alcan Aluminum, Ltd.						67876	65567	77

CLASS 8 (cont'd)	1935	'40	'45	'50	'55	'60	'65	
American Broadcasting Paramount	37998	88775	55535	44544	33335	67788	75666	67
American Enka Corp.							98888	77
Anaconda Co.	67987	87456	56551	22233	35678	99988	88566	67
Arvin Industries, Inc.				34455	65433	33332	34677	77
Baltimore & Ohio RR.								87
Basic, Inc.								87
Baxtor Laboratories, Inc.								7
Blaw-Knox Co.		44556	77788	87777	89987	65668	99888	87
Fram Corp.								7
Bigelow-Sanford, Inc.		666	66554	33456	65566	66788	88766	67
Bliss, E. W.					7745	67999	99888	77
Budd Co.	8	88967	77788	99999	99887	67888	88877	77
Bulova Watch	5	55875	55535	33344	55553	31357	77665	67
Carborundum Co.						54	55456	67
Celanese Corp.		99966	77756	66576	75647	67799	99988	87
Chemway Corp.		3245	55566	77776	44456	58466	64777	77
Cincinnati Milling Machine					5451	20225	45566	77
Cleveland Cliffs Iron Co.								77
Clevite Corp.			55532	22344	43335	57778	87787	77
Combustion Engineering, Inc.		33467	77776	66743	33354	57656	75355	57
Cooper Tire & Rubber Co.								87
Corning Glass Works					23423	36645	63788	77
Crucible Steel Corp.	23455	55668	38875	45467	89999	99999	99988	87
Delta Air Lines, Inc.							788	77
Detroit Steel Corp.					799	99999	99999	87
Diamond Shamrock Corp.						656	76677	67
Diana Stores Corp.					4	43110	01678	87
Oxford Paper Co.							66666	67
Filtrol Corporation						76	43245	67
FMC Corp		2133	44432	10132	23434	47566	76667	77
Food Giant Markets, Inc.			24	42344	45678	75333	57989	87
General Dynamics Corp.	87667	76786	55565	66655	66666	75531	22556	67
General Tire & Rubber Co.			667	86788	89999	99867	87999	87
Georgia Pacific Corp.					9	99998	84777	77
Warner Brothers Pictures, Inc.	99	99775	54435	67754	11112	33434	52576	67
Grace, W. R. & Co.						43	37798	87
Grand Union Co.	66445	56785	44334	53566	66633	34322	34899	87
Great Northern Paper Co.						6	67678	77
Universal American Co.				5455	55567	66689	87734	67
Gulf, Mobile & Ohio R.R. Co.	64789	99997	77788	99999	99898	77899	98545	57
Paul Hardeman, Inc.	5	55667	88888	78888	88778	99863	33577	77
Hat Corporation of America	8	87955	56665	66767	64353	24568	87866	67
Hewlett Packard Company								7
Hotel Corp. of America	57777	88887	77768	86645	37799	99999	89866	77
Inspiration Consolidated Copper Co.	77877	77478	99876	67666	67899	99989	89888	77
International Business Machines Co.	22110	11000	00000	00001	11232	35444	42677	77
International Minerals & Chemical Co.	66988	88998	88897	88777	66654	44433	35566	77
International Silver Co.	444	43455	66655	33466	66545	56775	68677	77
Rayonier, Inc.			97	76578	76667	89999	99777	67
International Telephone & Telegraph	68887	77644	33458	88788	99999	99876	76888	87
Jones & Laughlin Steel Corp.				5677	88899	99987	88899	87
Kendall Company							8	87
Kerr McGee Oil							9898	87
KLM Royal Dutch Airlines							344	87
Mack Trucks, Inc.	56333	32346	66651	13466	88989	98877	88887	77
Magnavox Co.	5				7596	42436	79999	97
Mallory, P.R. and Co.							776	77
Mays, J. W., Inc.								97
McDermott (J. Ray) & Co.							99	87
McLean Trucking Co.							23	57
McNeil Corp.								7
Mohasco Industries, Inc.					4458	99999	99988	87
National Acme	88777	77868	78772	44456	77776	77888	87666	67
National Can Corp.	11	11125	67786	67789	99999	98753	46566	67
National Steel Corp.		55523	33342	21111	12336	88876	64678	77
Newmont Mining Corp.				46567	77887	78878	87677	67
Olin Mathieson Chemical Corp.	54332	22224	44453	35454	44556	76777	75677	77
Outboard Marine Corp.			213	23223	32220	00113	43545	67
Owens Corning Fiberglass Corp.						567	85777	77
Pan American Sulphur Co.								77
Perkin Elmer Corp.								7
Shattuck, Frank G.	5323	22232	22124	55653	22223	32111	22677	87
Pfizer, Chas. and Co.				6	75544	33233	55777	77
Pittson Co.		34998	87786	78889	98898	99987	89888	87

CLASS 8 (cont'd)	1935	'40	'45	'50	'55	'60	'65	
Publicker Industries					9988	98899	89977	87
Raymond International, Inc.								77
Reeves Brothers					4447	65673	48778	87
Reichhold Chemicals							88	87
Rheem Mfg.				67	76664	43468	99999	87
Ritter Pfaudler Corp.	3	32243	32222	57767	53443	22222	22567	67
Robertshaw Controls Co.					55	65776	77778	87
St. Regis Paper					988	89887	86878	77
Sun Chemical Corp.		54423	34445	66676	46544	65677	67666	67
Sunstrand Corp.							56	77
Superior Oil Company (Nev.)				89	77841	43446	66787	87
Texas Pacific Land Trust Cert.	88654	44333	43343	46535	63478	88787	78888	77
National General						333	35677	67
Varian Associates							7	77
Victor Comptometer Corp.					467	76899	99986	77
Wallace and Tiernan, Inc.							8	77
Western Air Lines					78899	99975	66778	77
Westinghouse Electric Corp.	77644	44333	33322	12233	44543	45434	41345	57
Radio Corp. of America	99877	76554	45568	88866	56644	68788	76777	67
Wheeling Steel		7778	88886	66688	99999	98888	88777	87
White Motor		178	88875	56788	88886	33446	88888	77
Zenith Radio Corp.	8	88898	77757	55656	67542	43346	88999	87

TABLE IVd. Risk-Return Class 7

A. J. Industries, Inc.	72000	00000	01247	87755	34357	76765	55333	46
Addressograph-Multigraph Corp.		11121	11112	35566	55423	45778	84654	56
Allegheny Ludlum Steel Corp.		55646	77763	46777	88888	89989	98788	86
Alpha Portland Cement	4	44653	33213	32243	23423	55566	55545	56
Amerace Corp.							444	56
American Consumer Industries, Inc.	11023	33742	22148	88973	22100	00114	31131	36
American Metal Climax, Inc.	56999	99843	33324	56677	75665	79888	77555	56
Armstrong Cork Co.			34446	43333	22331	22112	31566	56
Atlas Chemical Industries, Inc.	43343	34433	43321	12222	34576	78778	77877	76
Atlas Corp.			124	67744	22231	22245	67655	46
Bates Manufacturing Co. (Del.)					67	64454	43454	56
Callahan Mining Corp.	97999	99889	99999	99999	99999	99999	99866	66
Carpenter Steel Co.			670	23345	56767	78887	77767	76
Carrier Corp.					7765	46677	77455	66
Central Foundry			988	98999	87789	99985	57777	86
Central Soya Co., Inc.								56
Chock Full O Nuts Corp.							8	76
Chrysler Corp.	87676	65534	45433	23355	44442	43434	32366	46
Clark Equipment		55676	77763	22344	56677	77889	98655	56
Collins and Aikman Co.	8687	77887	78877	66776	77899	99765	41432	36
Columbia Pictures		323	44557	77787	77735	34576	76898	86
Consolidated Cigar Corp.	32356	67774	54444	44522	22233	51122	25777	66
Cooper Industries				8	76644	33579	99754	56
Copeland Refrigeration Corp.								76
Copperweld Steel				77666	78899	98999	99988	76
Crane Co.			6676	55444	45665	66565	75434	36
Cutler Hammer, Inc.	66	66665	55655	56676	76655	57768	85342	36
Cyclops Corp.			663	45655	45456	78999	99888	86
Dresser Industries, Inc. Del.		8887	87777	67754	66678	99986	66555	66
Elastic Stop Nut Corp. of America				6	75432	02332	56676	66
Electric & Musical Industries, Ltd.	5	54222	23559	88755	76666	26767	77875	66
Emerson Electric Co.				8	99886	66645	57888	86
Emhart Corp.							5644	56
Ferro Corp.				55566	67887	68889	99888	76
Flintkote Co.			6657	65677	67665	64333	44677	66
Food Fair Stores, Inc.				23466	75544	13121	12677	86
Ruberoid Co.			5532	11455	65445	55443	33355	56
New York Air Brake	14555	55468	88876	56644	66677	66665	44456	66
Stanley Warner Corp.						34	57677	76
Sheller-Globe Corp.							2	56
Grant, W.T.	7 11	11111	11101	10122	12100	00112	10011	56
South Puerto Rico Sugar Co.	35422	21012	33344	33111	13353	21110	12576	66
Harcourt Brace and World, Inc.								6
Harris Intertype Corp.							98888	66
Hart Schaffner & Marx					64456	67664	53245	46
Hayes-Albion, Inc.				888	87675	43311	12466	66
Hilton Hotels Corp.					332	11345	55523	66
Hoover Ball & Bearing Co.								56
Houdaille Industries, Inc.	8	88887	78766	66688	77774	42312	23356	66
Household Finance			0002	20000	00000	00000	00566	66

CLASS 7 (cont'd)	1935	'40	'45	'50	'55	'60	'65	
Hunt Foods & Industries, Inc.					8651	20102	24788	76
Illinois Central Industries, Inc.	01666	77668	88889	99999	98999	88888	88666	66
International Mining Corp. (New)	57999	99998	88877	77787	54435	75554	68878	66
Sheraton Corp. of America	55777	78798	89899	99996	55567	77774	33545	76
Island Creek Coal (Del.)	0222	22101	11230	00000	01255	56866	77677	66
Jonathan Logan, Inc. Del.								86
Kroehler Mfg. Co.							2544	56
Lehigh Valley Industries	8	88769	9 9	99999	99844	20389	79955	86
Manhatten Industries	54544	45453	22223	46554	43334	53343	35676	66
Mesta Machine Co.		344	44541	43333	33346	76876	67767	76
Midland Ross Corp.		88766	66667	77544	22232	44435	43343	56
Minnesota Mining & Mfg. Co.					3433	36656	64677	66
Montgomery Ward	88765	55344	44433	32223	34433	22245	66766	56
M.S.L. Industries, Inc.				2	45576	53343	27899	96
J.J. Newberry Co.		1	11001	23333	21111	11122	22677	76
Pitney Bowes, Inc.						14566	87888	86
Pullman, Inc.	23333	32236	66764	34321	22333	45667	54434	56
Raytheon Co.						996	77888	86
Republic Corp.					8887	76688	78766	76
Revere Copper & Brass, Inc.	9	99999	99887	88899	98886	78788	86433	46
Rex Chainbelt, Inc.			1	24466	63323	33456	75655	56
Rohm & Haas Co.					4	65545	43666	56
Rohr Corp.						5	56644	56
Roper Corp.			225	43332	33222	23001	13787	66
Royal Crown Cola				33445	35553	21100	21155	56
Sangamo Electric Co. Del.						5445	55565	56
Schlumberger, Ltd.	12889	99997	77778	88788	87778	88976	65566	56
Scovill Mfg. Co.						43333	36466	66
Screw and Bolt Corp. of America	4	54658	89986	88887	57778	64333	35656	76
Signode Corp.							63565	56
Smith Kline & French Laboratories							777	66
Sperry-Rand Corp.	89988	87564	44444	44566	67667	99989	88988	86
Stanray Corporation						7766	45576	76
Stauffer Chemical Co.						5	53676	66
Richardson Merrill, Inc.		00	00000	00133	31111	23122	22676	76
Stokely Van Camp, Inc.			687	88898	67766	74666	47688	86
Suburban Gas								86
TRW, Inc.		44455	55553	45577	87777	67878	77667	76
Tandy Corp.	7899	99979	99999	99887	64334	20233	58756	66
Tishman Realty & Construction Co.							88	86
Union Camp Corp.	75343	43447	78887	66666	66776	77655	44456	56
Wilson & Co.	73222	12357	78887	77778	77778	89653	32565	56
Boeing Co. (The)		6	65663	44533	46667	76752	22001	36
U.S. Steel	33333	33346	66662	23345	55667	88887	76778	76
Vulcan Materials Co.	99988	77522	12110	00000	00012	44657	88787	76
Welbilt Corp.					576	89989	66666	76
Wickes Corp.								6
Youngstown Steel Door			87	78876	77666	66787	65666	66

TABLE IVe. Risk-Return Class 6

Air Reduction Co., Inc.	33311	11013	33341	13343	34446	65555	64444	45
Allen Industries			767	76555	43434	45532	11122	35
American Home Products	1100	00010	00000	00122	11111	13323	42577	55
American Potash & Chemical Corp.						755	56555	65
American Seating Co.	799	99985	55544	33467	77886	66444	36666	65
American Smelting & Refining Co.	66876	66345	66642	23356	56778	89876	77245	55
Ametek, Inc.	78556	65688	88885	67589	99997	54546	78776	65
Arizona Public Service								5
ARC Corp.								45
Austin Nichols	98576	65854	55456	43688	88879	87563	67856	45
Babbitt, B.T., Inc.					126	88898	77745	55
Barber Oil Corp.	68566	65667	77776	74544	26776	85646	65232	25
Beaunit Corp.					588	87899	87411	25
Bliss & Laughlin, Inc.			4	32334	12221	50234	47766	55
Book of the Month Club, Inc.						0014	37887	85
Briggs & Stratton	3	33232	32212	24567	66652	45668	86776	65
Ceco Corp.								5
Chicago Pneumatic Tool Co.	77888	88888	88762	45578	88999	99988	75455	45
City Stores Co.	998	88676	77768	88888	41001	11221	00000	35
Holt Rinehart & Winston								55
Curtiss Wright Corp.	4	33376	66651	33333	45569	98975	56455	55
DeSoto, Inc.					9999	9997	69887	75
Nopco Chemical Co.				01245	65677	88776	68887	75
Symington Wayne Corp.	87999	99989	98998	88988	88888	88877	55455	55

CLASS 6 (cont'd)	1935	'40	'45	'50	'55	'60	'65	
Dunhill International, Inc.	999	99935	56668	88899	84300	00000	05777	65
Eastman Kodak	22111	10000	00000	01111	11223	45544	63444	35
Fawick Corp.	3266	66977	78777	88899	99999	99977	35443	55
Eaton Yale and Towne Co.	89777	66644	45431	12344	55563	34446	76454	45
Edison Bros. Stores			2	34566	32120	00123	46766	65
Engelhard Minerals and Chemicals								65
Eurofund, Inc.								5
Florida Power & Light Co.						34322	33677	55
Fruehauf Corp.				5777	76666	57999	99877	75
Gardner Denver Co.				4	22223	56654	43223	45
Gèneral Host		0122	22236	75410	00000	00001	10123	45
General Cable Corp.	89999	99999	99999	99998	78889	99976	54234	45
General Steel Industries, Inc.							6576	55
Goodrich, B.F.	78998	88776	77767	73533	35567	88654	54466	55
Gould National Batteries, Inc.					4442	34322	23677	75
Grumman Aircraft Engineering Corp.				66654	66676	54433	34232	25
Hamilton Watch Co.		34553	32235	65521	11124	46777	77644	55
Hammermill Paper Co.						898	76533	45
Harsco Corp.						5	56455	55
Walter E. Heller Co.							4777	75
Honeywell, Inc.	1	11233	33332	11122	33322	37767	86676	65
Ingersoll Rand Co.	34444	44432	33332	10011	23334	45656	43444	55
Interchemical Corp.	33	33444	45445	44565	55634	76445	53344	25
International Nickel Company of Canada	88654	44221	11113	24432	33455	66766	65566	45
International Paper Co., N.Y.				5566	57876	68766	64555	55
Kaiser Aluminum & Chemical Corp.						8999	98555	45
Kelsey Hayes Co.	878	88897	88877	77877	64345	66766	76454	45
Kennecott Copper	45765	65334	33320	12123	33556	78766	54222	35
Kern County Land					23	66677	67776	65
King Seeley Thermos Co.						3312	22365	65
Louisville and Nashville R.R.	01655	55235	44442	13333	44455	65566	55344	45
R.H. Macy and Co., Inc.	55544	44223	33446	65453	34457	75431	22555	55
Martin-Marietta			443	54566	58676	51201	22454	45
Masonite Corp.			312	22357	88877	68878	86333	35
Medusa Portland Cement							5	55
Merck & Co., Inc.					3346	67420	10345	55
Monarch Machine Tool Co.				2	33354	31123	34234	45
Natomas Co.			00002	33300	00148	99883	49888	75
Neptune Meter Co.							3	35
Norris Industries, Inc.								35
North American Car Corp.							5	55
Northwestern Steel & Wire Co.								65
Norwich Pharmacal Co.				11221	23344	65433	20344	45
Pet, Inc.	0	01111	11100	00012	12211	22244	46778	75
Philip Morris, Inc.	31111	00101	11111	01221	10001	22011	11344	45
Phillips Van Heusen Corp.	22000	11354	44467	76665	53322	56688	88766	65
Murphy (G.W.) Industries, Inc.					6	74543	25332	55
Reliance Electric Engineering							666	55
Republic Steel Corp.	89999	98768	88774	35566	77778	88876	77877	75
Reynolds Tobacco	10000	00000	00003	32100	00001	11001	11565	65
Rubbermaid, Inc.							3	45
Ryan Aeronautical Co.							5	35
Schering Corp.						65	64344	45
Warren Company								65
Seaboard Coast Line Railroad					99886	54666	66434	35
Seaboard Finance Co.					22	22111	12455	65
Seilon, Inc.					9999	85557	65200	15
Singer Co.								65
Square D Co.			5530	01134	46777	77767	88788	65
Tootsie Roll Industries	81756	66330	11015	34423	44563	20111	03446	75
Swift & Co.			11121	11112	12321	22112	21233	35
United Çarr, Inc.			33333	12111	21221	24334	33232	35
Textron, Inc.					89	88875	78665	55
United Artists Corp.							434	45
Transamerica Corp.		33122	22234	55555	43433	24354	56777	65
Uniroyal Corp.	88999	88755	66668	76655	57778	88887	87565	55
United States Shoe Corp.							1344	45
Universal Oil Products							8	85
Upjohn Company							3	45
Walgreen Co.		0	11011	12211	10000	00112	23555	55
Wallace-Murray Corp.	99899	99997	88878	88887	77655	65655	44111	35
Walworth Co.	67999	99999	88887	77888	88888	88733	46766	45
West Virginia Pulp and Paper				55553	32214	36564	64656	55
Whirlpool Corp.							88777	65
Youngstown Sheet and Tube Co.	24677	77767	77764	34466	77778	99998	98777	65

TABLE IVf. Risk-Return Class 5

	1935	'40	'45	'50	'55	'60	'65	
Abacus Fund				9999	98754	21111	11434	34
Ace Industries, Inc.	15677	77779	99984	46767	88887	77767	68566	54
American Bakeries Co.	6565	55642	22213	42322	12110	00000	00022	44
American Cyanamid Co.					445	66532	32245	44
American Distilling Co.	3	32446	67773	10078	78854	64222	35777	64
American Optical Co.						211	22365	44
Westinghouse Air Brake	23122	22346	56675	55544	45554	55789	99644	44
American Standard Corp.	45454	44554	45557	76544	34544	55677	67434	44
American Tobacco Co. (Com.)	00101	11000	00013	53311	00012	22010	00345	54
Armco Steel Corp.	8	87656	66776	66677	78888	99987	75666	44
Armstrong Rubber Co.								54
Atlantic Coast Line R.R.	12777	78567	77877	66566	77888	78899	98422	24
Avco Corp.		34567	76668	46788	88788	88888	88765	44
Babcock & Wilcox Co.						866	54334	44
Bendix Corp.	98655	55455	56540	02333	44554	55556	65555	44
Bethlehem Steel Corp.	55655	66556	55551	22234	57889	99985	44445	64
Black & Decker Mfg.			553	43344	56543	31434	45356	64
Bobbie Brooks								4
Borden, Inc.	11	11111	11010	00011	11100	00011	10455	44
Borman Food Stores, Inc.								64
Burlington Industries, Inc.			544	45666	76668	87787	67443	44
Canada Dry Corp.	5233	33432	22225	55565	54433	33222	11223	44
Champion Papers, Inc.			5665	66566	77775	45434	32233	44
Checker Motors Corp.	3	33599	99998	78889	98877	67899	99988	54
Consolidated Foods Corp.					7654	20002	22555	34
Continental Baking Co. (Del.)	5467	77996	55546	76632	12223	44344	55645	44
Continental Insurance Co.	45544	44332	22211	00001	11101	14222	22456	44
Continental Steel Corp.			6653	42111	24578	99988	88877	64
Corn Products Co.	23211	10000	00000	00000	00110	00001	22566	54
Crown Cork & Seal Co., Inc.	2	11545	56667	77666	46766	78577	65665	64
DWG Corp.			3324	54311	01112	31010	22577	64
Deere & Co. Del.		44	44454	66677	66643	32124	54565	44
Delmarva Power and Light					0	12111	10233	34
Dover Corp.							555	44
Dow Chemical Co.			100	01122	34555	55444	54444	34
Harbison Walker Refractories Co.	123	33556	77775	55443	54556	55432	24667	74
Eastern Gas & Fuel Associates							454	44
Ex-Cell-O Corp.			40	22355	45554	45556	66544	44
Fenestra, Inc.							2011	14
Fibreboard Corp.			3424	42133	23544	33477	99867	64
Firestone Tire & Rubber Co.		23332	22345	55456	67787	88655	64666	54
Franklin Stores					21	10001	12666	74
Freeport Sulphur Co.	23432	22114	45561	11123	35566	75545	65222	34
General Electric Co.	65433	33223	23332	22122	34532	46545	52222	24
Goodyear Tire Rubber	887	78555	56667	75644	56688	89754	53566	54
Granite City Steel	4	44468	88888	88888	98999	99999	98777	64
Greyhound Corp.			34445	54332	21111	11111	00133	44
Halliburton Co.					21	22445	46334	44
Hazeltine Corp.								4
Hooker Chemical Corp.					44	78889	87544	44
Howe Sound Co. (Del.)	34554	44344	55524	55432	22379	99999	99865	54
Interlake Steel Corp.	2566	77889	89887	78899	99988	77776	77433	44
Pennsylvania Glass Sand Corp.			2110	21100	00111	12444	44344	34
Johnson & Johnson				5	56764	44233	35455	54
Kansas City Southern Industries, Inc.	56767	77687	78889	99899	88766	66766	54344	24
Koppers Co.					55446	67776	66334	54
Lehigh Portland Cement Co.	44	44654	44323	33432	12245	67554	43455	54
Leonard Refineries, Inc.								4
Libby McNeill and Libby			55566	54523	23333	45678	77655	54
MacAndrews & Forbes Co.	011	11100	00001	12101	10000	00144	45543	34
Madison Square Garden Corp. (New)	95555	56787	66679	99999	99998	99999	99854	54
Maremont Corp.								64
Marine Midland Banks, Inc.		22122	11125	65521	11111	21000	01344	44
McCord Corp.						44445	43211	14
McDonnell Douglas Corp.							3	34
McGraw Edison Co.			224	44333	21221	24536	55554	54
McGraw-Hill, Inc.	1	12256	66676	56543	21111	24536	53344	44
Mead Corp.			8886	66766	78888	78653	31343	44
NVF Co.					5665	55579	87654	34
National Cash Register Co.		4	34324	43232	33423	45655	56777	64
Hudson Bay Mining & Smelting Co., Ltd.	•		15	43222	34476	54533	32000	34
Northern Natural Gas Co.					211	11012	12244	44
Northrop Corp.						653	45222	34
Otis Elevator	44322	22244	44445	55555	43211	25545	54544	44

CLASS 5 (cont'd)	1935	'40	'45	'50	'55	'60	'65	
Penn Fruit Co., Inc.								54
Pillsbury Co.	110	01100	00013	31101	12222	23234	65765	54
Pittsburgh Forgings				77667	88886	67534	22112	34
PPG Industries, Inc.					2232	34422	21344	44
Portec, Inc.	8	88989	99999	99988	78775	65788	88532	34
St. Joseph Lead	35665	55445	55555	65332	36778	76455	46555	54
Scott Paper	0	00000	00000	00000	01112	36443	22466	64
Simplicity Pattern							43	44
Sterling Drug, Inc.	22222	22100	00000	00111	11111	22122	43665	54
Bristol Myers Co.		10	00001	00133	45446	78865	64555	44
Stevens, J.P.					112	35466	67322	24
Storer Broadcasting							32010	24
Tidewater Oil Co.	444	43343	33333	33334	45553	36889	88534	64
Trane Co.							26777	74
Transwestern Pipeline Co.								4
Tri Continental Corp.		55567	77899	99999	99989	98764	54455	44
Unarco Industries, Inc.	0				7566	75689	99767	44
Union Oil of California	12111	11111	11123	44244	45655	66655	45466	54
Union Tank Car	00000	00101	00010	00000	01000	00001	12112	34
UTD Corp.							555	54
United Fruit	01332	22101	11110	00000	11222	32212	23366	64
United Merchants & Manufacturers			66	55677	77768	76566	57555	54
U.S. Pipe and Foundry Co.	66444	45663	33215	44444	43333	47767	75555	54
U.S. Plywood-Champion Papers, Inc.				2256	77856	58788	75210	14

TABLE IVg. Risk-Return Class 4

Allied Kid			321	22222	21121	12112	11110	23
Allied Stores Corporation	8	88677	77767	77776	54434	53354	45323	33
Allied Supermarkets, Inc.				8	99999	64533	23565	53
Aluminum Co. America						8888	86334	33
American Chain and Cable Company		88877	77763	23344	45656	66656	66322	23
American Commercial Lines Co.							1	13
American Crystal Sugar Co.	45654	43135	66775	24111	31121	00100	02344	43
American Hospital Supply								53
Amercon Corp.								3
American News Co. Del.		00011	10000	00110	00002	43567	87764	33
Conwood Corp.	00000	00000	00001	21100	00000	00000	00121	33
Amsted Industries, Inc.	47777	77668	88874	56667	87775	45566	66544	43
Anderson Clayton					01234	43332	22101	23
Baker Oil Tools, Inc.								3
Bath Industries, Inc.				3356	78977	43444	55322	33
Beatrice Foods Co.	2	33542	22221	11122	22213	43222	22455	43
Beneficial Finance Co.		00	00001	21111	10101	12233	23545	33
Bush Terminal Co.	53433	35599	99999	99986	54453	21112	21100	23
Campbell Soup Co.							23677	53
Carey (Philip) Mfg. Co.						56554	45444	33
Cluett, Peabody & Co., Inc.	12122	22444	33211	11223	44554	32244	56533	33
Cone Mills Corp.						464	46211	33
Container Corp.	88	78936	67776	44545	68888	86554	34544	43
Crown Zellerbach Corp.	6	77977	66665	42223	56676	57654	54456	33
Dan River Mills, Inc.							34110	23
Dana Corp.	86232	22466	66652	21256	68864	44556	65344	33
Denver & Rio Grande Western R.R. Co.					988	86765	44323	23
Diamond International Corp.	000	00001	11111	22122	22223	46564	56666	43
Eagle-Picher Industries, Co.	8			7	66887	77667	76322	23
Falstaff Brewing Corp.					10	00000	00222	23
Fedders Corp.					46	76677	77655	53
Federal-Mogul Inc.				42355	55333	24565	65555	43
Florida Power Corp.					0001	13433	32444	33
Link Belt	3	33433	33443	21011	12333	46676	66433	33
Ford Motor Co.							5555	43
General American Transportation Co.	32332	33234	44454	33221	21112	33322	20111	13
General Portland Cement					663	44567	65545	33
General Telephone & Electronics Co.			2	22311	00000	12223	42454	23
Gerber Products							7666	53
Gillette Co.	211	00011	12247	87764	44554	43322	23455	53
Gimbel Brothers, Inc.	88898	88888	88878	88899	65436	86575	65422	23
Harshaw Chemical Co.							5433	43
Hercules, Inc.	2	23312	22110	11111	12233	34324	54654	33
Hershey Foods	10	00000	00001	00001	10010	00000	02444	43
Holly Sugar Corp.			4563	34344	55435	55342	23444	53
Houston Lighting & Power Co.				00	00111	34443	31334	33
Ideal Basic Industries, Inc.							433	33

CLASS 4 (cont'd)	1935	'40	'45	'50	'55	'60	'65	
International Salt Co.	01111	21110	10000	00001	10000	03434	44445	43
Interco, Inc.	0	00101	10000	00000	00000	00000	00021	23
Jewel Companies, Inc.	43222	21110	10001	11253	22102	23222	21454	43
Kellogg Co.							5	53
Kimberly-Clark Corp.	3	33523	33342	21111	21244	48544	20233	33
Kresge, S.S.	31222	23211	11111	00000	00000	00012	21111	23
Lane Bryant		78553	34324	55689	76521	20123	37777	73
Lehman Corp.		11112	22233	23344	43322	23333	33333	33
P. Lorillard Co.	45222	21110	00002	33211	00001	12000	11666	53
Louisville Gas and Electric Co.					00	11000	01345	43
Lykes Corp.							23	33
Madison Fund, Inc.							4544	33
Marshall Field and Co.		66666	77656	56676	55544	33355	44312	23
May Department Stores	23233	33432	22212	11223	22222	33322	33322	13
McKesson & Robbins, Inc.				32212	21111	10100	23233	23
Mercantile Stores Co., Inc.					3235	74432	11223	23
Merritt Chapman and Scott Corp.					22	21356	57765	43
Mission Development Co.					5	67999	99532	33
National Distillers & Chemical Co.	75133	22421	11113	33333	22346	77543	33222	33
National Gypsum Co.			657	77788	87766	68755	52443	33
Neisner Bros.	7	78954	45545	53455	34322	21233	23111	23
Chesapeake & Ohio Ry.	11422	22023	33442	22110	00013	46654	43222	23
Northern Pacific Ry.	13656	66467	78899	99888	89999	99888	87655	33
Pacific Tin Consolidated Corp.			79	87555	88887	66766	57334	43
Penn Dixie Cement Corp.	799	99988	99999	99975	56455	76888	87656	33
Pennsault Chemicals Corp.					21211	34355	65434	33
Pepsico, Inc.	33222	22498	99866	32445	46777	87664	54555	33
Petroleum Corp. of America		33344	33333	56544	45677	76656	54444	43
Phelps Dodge	4	44355	55532	44355	44666	78765	54211	13
Phillips Petroleum	26454	43323	33331	11022	34665	67655	54333	33
Pittsburgh & West Virginia Railway	34777	88899	99999	99878	77878	78887	79878	63
Potomac Electric					00	00000	00244	33
Quaker Oats Co.						0000	00011	33
Ranco, Inc.	3						3433	33
Red Owl Stores, Inc.								3
Simmons Co.	77777	77776	66667	66766	65433	33456	57543	43
Sinclair Oil Corp.	68444	43433	22333	44344	56766	67766	54333	33
Sola Basic Industries					0000	10001	11000	23
Southern Co.	6	66565	55689	99999	84232	22212	21333	23
Southern Pacific	01656	66577	88887	77766	77776	76676	54323	33
Stewart Warner Corp.	67777	76566	67777	78877	77788	77655	55454	43
James Talcott	7		223	32211	11011	01123	33554	43
Toledo Edison Co.						0011	01122	33
Union Carbide Corp.	5322	21112	22220	00011	22343	34334	32133	43
United-Greenfield Corp.					455	52444	32000	03
United Park City Mines Co.						99	99987	73
Universal Leaf Tobacco	21	21100	01103	00000	00000	00000	02455	43
Virginia Electric and Power					122	33322	21244	33
Von's Grocery Co.								3
Western Pacific RR.					87686	33567	65433	33
Winn Dixie Stores, Inc.						000	00122	23
Woolworth, F.W.	21111	11010	00003	21210	00000	11133	33444	43

TABLE IVh. Risk-Return Class 3

Allied Chemical Corp.	33211	11012	22221	10011	11223	35556	76443	22
Abex	22233	34445	55654	34432	32335	54556	66211	12
American & Foreign Power	99999	99887	78899	99999	9988	57434	34111	22
Adams Express	78888	87767	77776	67787	75644	46554	43222	22
American Natural Gas Co.						11123	33432	22
American Zinc Co.	99998	88889	99998	99999	98887	89888	66100	12
Ashland Oil & Refining Co.						88654	54332	32
Associated Dry Goods Corp.	66787	77777	78778	88878	66666	75555	64322	22
Associated Investment			011	00000	01024	46431	21333	22
Atchison Topeka & Santa Fe Railway	11444	45245	66664	24334	45565	67678	76322	12
Baltimore Gas & Electric Co.						11000	11344	22
Bayuk Cigars	21333	33212	23323	31212	22133	33220	11445	42
Brown Shoe Co., Inc.	00000	00100	00011	23322	10000	12221	11122	32
Buffalo Forge				445	54331	00001	10001	12
Carriers & General Corp.		56565	56666	67777	53322	44444	32121	12
Caterpillar Tractor Co.		55545	55540	23332	32214	67777	77655	42
Central Ill. Light Co.					1	22122	22322	22
Champion Spark Plug Co.							3	22
Chesapeake Corp., Va.					1	23478	89774	32211	12
Columbia Broadcasting System, Inc.			214	44334	35552	32346	64544	32

CLASS 3 (cont'd)	1935	'40	'45	'50	'55	'60	'65	
Commercial Credit Co.	77344	43432	34423	22322	21111	12221	12222	32
Continental Can Co., Inc.	44211	10001	12245	64433	33222	23333	43112	12
Continental Motors Corp.	77555	55677	66665	88999	99999	98775	56433	32
Cunningham Drug Stores					42221	24222	21000	02
Dayton Power & Light Co.					1101	11010	01111	22
DeVilbiss Co.					1212	45541	11123	32
Shamrock Oil & Gas					55653	43456	55322	22
Distillers Corp. Seagrams, Ltd.			1102	23566	55444	22223	33223	32
Dr. Pepper Co.					5653	43366	56422	22
Dominick Fund, Inc.			122	43233	32211	22323	33554	32
Duke Power Co.								2
E. I. DuPont DeNemours & Co., Inc.	64332	22211	11110	11111	12223	45544	44333	12
Ebasco Industries, Inc.								2
ESB, Inc.	12222	22122	22222	23211	11256	88765	65332	02
Federated Department Stores, Inc.		33422	33335	44544	42223	35333	31223	22
General American Investors		88676	67767	76666	46545	54444	44432	22
General American Oil Co. of Texas							665	52
General Foods Corp.	100	00010	00000	00110	00000	11112	21344	22
General Mills	0	00000	00000	00000	00000	11123	33443	22
General Motors	54343	44433	34433	22233	33443	45544	43011	12
Glidden Co.	88666	55555	66756	67676	76777	76455	45433	22
Great Atlantic & Pacific Tea Co., Inc.							6	52
Great Northern Ry. Co.	12677	78766	67776	55555	56667	88787	75422	12
Green Shoe Manufacturing Co.								2
Hall, W.F. Printing Co.		34686	66654	55554	11100	10001	13343	32
Hammond Corp.							765	42
Helme Products, Inc.	00000	00000	00002	42100	00000	00000	01233	32
Udylite Corp.					453	44444	33000	12
Indianapolis Power & Light				65311	00111	00001	02233	22
Inland Steel Co.	33555	56523	22342	21022	34666	77665	66656	42
International Utilities Corp.					1	12578	77322	22
Johns Manville Corp.	65	55534	44443	11123	44332	14344	43333	32
Earl M. Jorgensen Co.								32
Keller Industries, Inc.								32
Lone Star Cement Corp.	35577	77754	44424	33332	22335	66554	33333	42
McIntyre Porcupine Mines, Ltd.	01000	00000	00001	00000	01135	76777	77332	22
Melville Shoe Corp.	22	22221	11100	00011	10011	11122	22100	12
Middle South Utilities					2	12111	11222	12
Mission Corp.			44544	54355	57767	88988	64111	22
Mississippi River Fuel Corp.						4445	44443	32
Missouri Portland Cement Co.							1	12
Montana Power Co.						22112	11322	22
Munsingwear, Inc.	12767	77565	55545	55777	66424	22110	12343	32
G.C. Murphy and Co.			1110	00000	01101	00121	10000	12
National Aviation		6	66776	77666	56677	63555	65321	12
National Starch and Chemical Corp.								2
Niagara Share Corp.							76443	32
North American Sugar Industries, Inc.	37999	98789	99998	77643	33366	52222	33433	12
Orange & Rockland Utilities, Inc.								32
Pacific Gas and Electric	43211	11000	00012	21100	01101	12212	11122	22
United Gas Corp.					3	32234	43111	12
Peoples Drug Stores		00111	11111	22211	00000	00000	01333	42
Quaker State Oil Refining Corp.			1133	32111	23432	20001	00000	02
Raybestos Manhattan	6	66422	11123	32322	23333	33211	14344	42
Riegel Paper Corp.							8622	12
Rochester Telephone							3	22
South Jersey Gas Co.							44	42
Southern Railway	13999	99898	99988	88888	88888	88887	75333	22
Southwestern Public Service Co.						0	00011	02
Stone & Webster	6	66687	78878	87888	78775	42445	55443	32
El Paso Natural Gas			112	21110	01112	32334	43221	12
Tenneco Corp.							21	22
Texas Gas Transmission Corp.							1	12
Texas Utilities Co.						3333	42222	12
Timken Roller Bearing	44333	33244	44432	12222	34555	45678	76212	22
Union Electric Co. of Missouri						11	01333	32
Union Pacific RR.	11433	33122	22221	12111	21233	45456	45222	22
United Aircraft Corp.	5	54233	22231	34422	34644	53433	44111	12
Keebler Co.	21	11111	11103	33345	42110	00000	00111	22
United Engineering & Foundry Co.			3321	34434	42333	45567	65311	22
Public Service Electric & Gas Co.					10	11111	11111	12
United Shoe Machinery							543	22
U.S. & Foreign Securities	8	88787	78889	99999	99999	98877	66333	32
United States Gypsum		3232	22214	31111	02222	36444	41111	12
Walker Hiram Gooderham & Worts, Ltd.			1102	12244	54444	33212	21112	22
Warner Co.							3	22
Wisconsin Electric Power					11	22111	00232	32
Wyandotte Industries, Inc.					99999	77787	77300	12

TABLE IVi. Risk-Return Class 2

Acme Markets, Inc.	0	00022	33323	34333	21100	10000	11333	11
Allegheny Power System, Inc.	77665	65556	67889	99998	64212	23333	33222	11
American Electric Power Co., Inc.					0	00002	21111	11
American International Corp.	89866	65467	77888	88777	66555	65543	43221	01
American Motors Corp.	34322	22234	45568	88877	77777	64165	55624	21
American Sugar Co. (N.J.)	43222	22114	44565	34421	22234	33211	11000	21
American Water Works Co.					21	10010	00000	11
Anchor Hocking Glass Corp.	3	33343	33312	13444	20113	56444	33321	21
Archer Daniels Midland Co.	33122	21222	33322	01121	22135	67564	44200	01
Atlantic City Electric Co.						11111	10111	11
Atlantic Richfield Co.	45222	21222	22232	34245	66756	67766	55232	21
Belding Heminway Co.	33132	22331	11100	24566	64434	35455	53210	01
Beco Industries Corp.	554	44332	33325	43322	22212	21121	11111	11
Bond Stores			013	21345	34435	64332	12111	11
Borg Warner Corp.	6	55444	55543	23355	55534	44555	66222	11
Brooklyn Union Gas	54100	00023	34557	87522	21111	01110	00000	01
Canadian Breweries, Ltd.					211	11122	33222	11
Canadian Pacific Ry.	01223	33335	67889	88788	79988	98887	66100	11
Central Ill. Public Service Co.						322	10111	21
Central Southwest Corp.					1	13322	31122	11
Cincinnati Gas & Electric					0001	11000	00223	21
Cleveland Electric Illuminating Co.					000	12121	10111	01
Coca Cola	11000	00000	00000	00000	01111	22111	11233	31
Colgate Palmolive Co.		34532	22212	11133	33333	43123	56777	41
Columbus & Southern Ohio Electric					0000	01100	00022	21
Commonwealth Edison Co.			01	10000	00000	11110	00011	11
Consolidated Edison Co. of New York	54211	11122	22224	43211	11110	00011	00100	11
Consolidated Laundries Corp.		2354	33437	64222	11110	01113	10311	11
Dentists Supply Co.								11
DiGiorgio Corp.								01
Empire District Electric Co.					0000	00011	22221	21
Fairmont Foods Co.							11	21
Family Finance Corp.					1	12221	12344	21
Federal Paper Board							32101	21
First National Stores, Inc.	43100	00011	11111	11000	00000	00000	00111	21
Gamble Skogmo, Inc.					25	44455	67533	21
General Cigar Co., Inc.	12111	00021	11113	32322	23223	21000	00112	11
General Contract Finance Corp.							2	11
Surveyor Fund, Inc.	8	88566	67999	999	88841	10101	00000	21
General Public Utilities					1100	01100	11122	11
Giant Portland Cement Co.								21
Gulf States Utilities Co.					012	13211	10011	11
Iowa Electric Light & Power Co.							22	21
Kansas City Power & Light						12111	00101	11
Kansas Gas & Electric Co.							10122	11
Kansas Power & Light					0	01100	00122	31
Peabody Coal Co.					9	99997	46644	41
Keystone Steel & Wire Co.			5550	00123	65565	44444	34223	21
Libby-Owens-Ford Glass Co.	7	67944	44433	12234	33323	77654	43233	21
Ligget and Meyers, Inc.	00111	11000	00001	21100	00000	11000	00000	01
Maytag Co.	45888	88753	34569	98865	66442	23236	76554	21
McCrory Corp.	2034	44864	44444	33443	21112	21222	14211	31
McGregor Doniger, Inc.							3000	01
McQuay Norris Mfg. Co.				3	22223	54444	34311	21
Mesabi Trust U.B.I.								1
Gulf Oil Corp.				11	12333	68754	42123	21
Missouri Public Service Co.							00	01
Monsanto Co.	1	10101	11110	01255	54544	56544	53233	01
Mountain Fuel Supply Company								1
Fuqua Industries, Inc.							100	11
National Biscuit	11211	11111	00102	32211	11111	11000	01122	11
National City Lines					5423	32243	12000	01
National Dairy Products	44222	22221	22224	32221	22211	13110	00112	21
National Standard Co.							1	01
National Sugar Refining Co.					00000	01211	12222	11
New York State Electric & Gas Corp.					1	00000	00112	21
Newport News Shipbuilding & Dry Dock				1111	25666	62210	02212	11
Pacific Telephone & Telegraph Co.	10000	00000	00000	00000	00000	00101	13354	41

CLASS 2 (cont'd)	1935	'40	'45	'50	'55	'60	'65	
J.C. Penney Co.	1	11111	11100	00012	21111	12111	20000	01
Pennsylvania Power & Light Co.					0111	10110	01222	21
Marquette Cement Mfg. Co.						2	21100	11
Procter and Gamble Co.	1	11100	11000	00000	12253	33100	00234	21
Public Service Co. of Colorado					0111	21012	22222	21
Public Service Co. of Indiana, Inc.						11100	00112	11
Rochester Gas and Electric Corp.						00000	10233	21
Rockwell Standard Corp.	7	77876	66541	13354	66668	88777	54321	11
Royal Dutch Petroleum Co.						5	44111	11
San Diego Gas and Electric Co.						1	11111	11
Sears, Roebuck & Co.	76543	44332	22212	11122	22211	13223	42334	21
Skelly Oil	57344	32445	66654	34355	66767	88877	54100	01
South Carolina Electric & Gas					221	21123	32432	11
Southern California Edison Co.	2100	00010	00001	11110	10111	12110	10012	11
Southern Indiana Gas & Electric Co.						22111	11011	01
Southern Natural Gas				1001	12221	21345	46211	11
Standard Brands	21110	01011	11125	54422	23323	32222	32322	11
Standard Oil Company (Indiana)		2	22222	11011	22434	67666	54233	11
Beech Nut Life Savers, Inc.	20000	00000	00000	00000	00010	00111	22012	11
Suburban Propane Gas Co.								1
Sucrest Corp.					2212	32333	32000	01
Sunbeam Corporation					6	44433	32000	01
Texas Eastern Transmission Corp.								1
Torrington Co.								21
Western Can Corporation							66	31
United Corp.	5	55355	66899	99999	86500	11111	01111	11
Consumers Power					000	00000	00011	11
U.S. Lines Co.	55767	77689	99998	78776	43434	34455	34100	01
U.S. Tobacco	00000	00000	00001	31100	00000	00000	00133	31
Van Raalte Co.	31333	34353	34311	12234	32321	12234	22000	01
Wayne-Gossard Corp.					4233	12334	42210	01

TABLE IVj. Risk-Return Class 1

Abbott Laboratories			111	11111	22244	54222	33232	10
Alabama Gas Corp.							00	00
Amalgamated Sugar Co.						2212	10000	00
Amerada Petroleum Corp.	2011	00222	22233	22255	56643	45867	55355	40
American Bank Note Co.	55766	68445	56678	88877	54322	22000	00000	00
American Can Co.	43221	11001	11112	10000	00122	22111	11000	00
American Investment Co.				21100	00011	12120	00101	10
American & South African Investment							0	00
American Telephone & Telegraph Co.	11100	00000	00000	00000	00000	00001	11222	10
Benquet Consolidated Inc.					9	89884	00000	00
Boston Edison						0	00000	00
C.I.T. Financial	76433	22222	23334	32322	22222	23210	00112	10
California Packing Corp.	12444	44324	56676	54333	44444	44432	23232	10
Campbell Red Lake Mines Ltd.							00000	00
Carolina Power & Light Co.					012	24222	21222	10
Central Aguirre Sugar Co.	0	00001	11233	33000	00000	00000	12121	00
Central Hudson Gas Electric Corp.					0000	00000	00000	00
Cities Service Co.						7866	54000	00
Coca Cola Bottling Co. of New York								10
Columbia Gas System Inc.	57766	65444	45578	88866	63422	11111	21000	00
Allied Mills Inc.			4321	01111	11133	33222	23211	10
Cuneo Press				43433	33344	54367	76300	00
Detroit Edison Co.	21000	01110	00000	00000	00000	00000	00001	00
Domes Mines Ltd.	11010	00100	00016	64200	01146	54342	10000	00
Duquesne Light Co.						11	21100	00
Equitable Gas Co.						20111	11000	00
GAC Corp.							11111	10
General Bancshares Corp.						1	12221	00
General Finance Corp.						1210	11201	00
Genesco Inc.			2	35555	41100	01135	43210	00
Great Northern Iron Ore Properties	21233	34534	33330	11100	00010	11214	33111	00
Great Western Sugar Co.	24443	32101	11231	11000	01012	10000	01111	00

CLASS 1 (cont'd)	1935	'40	'45	'50	'55	'60	'65	
Hackensack Water Co.	000	00000	00000	00000	00000	00000	00000	00
Homestake Mining Co.	00000	00000	00003	31000	00013	32221	00000	00
Idaho Power Co.				0	00000	13232	10000	00
Illinois Power Co.					01	12211	21111	00
Industria Electrica de Mexico S.A.					2348	88750	13000	10
International Harvester Co.	65543	44223	34454	33232	22344	55455	44211	10
Interstate Power Co.						000	01000	00
Iowa Illinois Gas & Electric Co.						00000	00000	00
Iowa Power & Light Co.						01000	00000	00
Kroger Co.	32	22211	11100	00011	11000	00001	21121	00
Laclede Gas Co.	00000	12255	56668	86643	31100	10111	22222	10
Lilly Tulip Cup Corp.		0111	11111	24456	43322	66321	21000	00
Lockheed Aircraft				65535	47776	54333	56432	10
Lone Star Gas Corp.						23	32000	00
Long Island Lighting Co.						00000	00010	00
Marathon Oil Co.	67233	22323	43454	55445	67875	55667	77110	00
Midwest Oil Corp.						444	33101	00
Continental Oil Co.	57444	43334	33442	43344	33434	57877	74221	00
Minnesota Enterprises, Inc.	25344	55796	55668	89999	98764	51332	21000	00
Minnesota Power & Light						00001	11000	00
Montana Dakota Utilities Co.					55	66434	82000	00
National Fuel Gas Co.							11110	00
National Lead Co.	22122	22224	44544	43332	22335	78877	65110	10
National Service Industries, Inc.				1	10000	00000	01111	00
National Tea Co.	55443 33223	44567	54545	66512	34222	34222	11233	20
New England Electric System					11	22221	11110	00
Norfolk & Western Ry.	00100	00011	11110	00000	01112	33344	43100	00
Northern States Power Co.					0	01000	11000	00
Oklahoma Gas and Electric Co.						12223	21211	00
Oklahoma Natural Gas Co.						2	21111	00
Outlet Co.	10000	00000	00000	00000	00000	01010	00000	00
Owens-Illinois, Inc.	32011	00222	22110	00122	32212	36444	42433	20
Pacific Lighting	11	11011	00112	20000	00000	00000	00000	00
Panhandle Eastern Pipe Line Co.				2	11211	33344	33100	00
Peoples Gas Light & Coke Co.	43322	22242	23212	00000	11121	11123	33332	10
Puget Sound Power and Light							01000	00
Reliable Stores			4332	32212	10000	11221	11000	00
Safeway Stores	1	11143	33311	00121	11110	01001	00112	10
St. Joseph Light and Power						00101	00000	00
Shell Oil Co.	16434	43355	55541	01244	45534	54522	22011	10
Shell Transport and Trading N.Y.S.							000	00
Mobil Oil Corp.	222	22222	22334	43223	23433	56533	22011	00
Southeastern Public Service								20
Ohio Edison Co.					1101	12212	11011	10
North American Rockwell Corp.		66576	66665	65545	45667	88766	54321	00
Standard Oil Co. of California	12111	11112	21223	32001	12344	46655	42000	00
Standard Oil Company (New Jersey)	22100	00012	22223	21111	12333	46644	32000	00
Consolidated Natural Gas. Co.				11	21111	01000	00011	00
Standard Oil of Ohio				0122	34566	76545	43000	00
Starrett L. S.	4	44354	44541	33122	24352	00001	10000	00
Sterchi Bros. Stores					3211	00000	00000	00
Sun Oil	21000	00001	11110	10000	01121	11100	00000	00
Sunray DX Oil Co.				77	64555	78777	54000	00
Texaco, Inc.	24222	22223	22231	10001	13444	56645	44222	00
LGI Corp.	1	11111	01124	54222	21100	00001	22221	10
Philadelphia Electric				00	00000	01011	01011	10
Niagara Mohawk Power						21111	00001	10
U.S. Playing Card Co.			1	21211	11010	00000	01112	00
Utah Power & Light						13223	32100	00
Washington Gas Light				32000	00000	00011	12221	00
Washington Water Power Co.						221	01111	10
Waukesha Motor			5555	66633	33356	55554	33111	10
Wheeling and Lake Erie Ry.	00000	00001	00110	10000	00000	00000	00000	00
Wisconsin Public Service						00	00111	10
Woodward Corp.			72	23333	33366	77883	77311	10
William Wrigley, Jr. Company	00000	00000	00001	10000	00000	00000	00000	00

Risk, Return and Yield:

New York Stock Exchange Common Stocks, 1928-1969

by William F. Sharpe and Howard B. Sosin

Because capital gains are taxed at lower rates, and only when realized, the difference between dividends and capital appreciation is important for many investors. Although there may thus be compelling reasons for "tilting" portfolio yield away from average levels, can tilting be effective, and at what cost? Using NYSE common stock data from 1928 to 1969, the authors demonstrate the feasibility of constructing well diversified portfolios whose yields differ from the market average by 100 basis points.

Reprinted from Financial Analysts Journal, March/April 1976—all rights reserved by William F. Sharpe and Howard B. Sosin

Risk, Return and Yield:

New York Stock Exchange Common Stocks, 1928-1969

Most studies of the risk and return on common stocks do not distinguish returns obtained via dividend payments (yield) from those resulting from changes in price (capital gains/losses). For many investors, this focus on *total return* is quite appropriate. Cash can be obtained by realizing capital gains (or losses) as well as by cashing dividend checks. Alternatively, dividends can be reinvested in additional stock.

For many U.S. investors, however, there is at least one important reason for considering the components of return separately: the differential tax treatment accorded yield and capital gain. Capital gains are taxed at lower rates and only when realized; moreover, by willing appreciated stock to a relative or donating it to a non-profit institution, an investor may avoid the payment of capital gains entirely. However, this does not imply that low yield, high capital gains stocks are to be preferred by any investor subject to the personal income tax. The relative attractiveness of a dollar of dividends versus a dollar of capital gains differs significantly among investors. A tax-exempt institution may be indifferent between the two. A corporate investor may prefer a dollar of dividends, since 85 per cent is not subject to the corporate income tax. This preference is likely to be shared by small investors, since $100 of dividend income per year per person is not subject to any personal income tax. Individual investors in high tax brackets will strongly prefer a dollar of capital gains to a dollar of dividends.

William F. Sharpe is Timken Professor of Finance, Stanford University. Howard B. Sosin is a Ph.D. Candidate at Stanford University. *This article draws on the results of research performed under a grant from the Eli Lilly Foundation. Thanks are due to John G. McDonald and Rodney Adams of Stanford University for valuable suggestions.*

Accordingly, one might expect that as he moves from high yield, low capital gains stocks to low yield, high capital gains stocks, holding risk constant, a dollar of dividends would trade for more or less than a dollar of expected capital gains. Those with preferences falling on one side of the dividing line may find it desirable to select portfolios with higher than average yields, while those on the other side select portfolios with lower than average yields. On the other hand, since any attempt to concentrate on particular kinds of stocks is likely to reduce portfolio diversification, with an attendant increase in risk, shifts away from market-based portfolios should be made with caution, and only if the offsetting benefits are reasonably likely to be obtained.

Attempts to find the rate at which yield may be traded for capital gains, holding risk constant, have met with limited success. Elton and Gruber, studying price behavior on the day after a stock goes ex-dividend, estimated that on average a dollar of yield could be traded for 78 cents of capital gain.[1] Subsequent work by Black and Scholes obtained similar results, but cast considerable doubt on the accuracy of the estimate.[2] In a detailed study of returns, yields and risk over time, Black and Scholes found that, within reasonable statistical boundaries, the tradeoff between dividends and capital gains could easily be any amount between one dollar for one dollar and one dollar for 50 cents.[3] The result led them to conclude that since any benefit a

1. Footnotes appear at end of article.

tax-exempt investor might obtain by switching to higher than average yield stocks is problematic, while the cost in loss of diversification is predictable, in the absence of special circumstances, concentration in high yield securities should not be recommended.

There are, of course, other reasons for differentiating between the components of return. Many trust agreements direct income to one or more beneficiaries, with the principal value at some specified date going to others. By choosing high yield, low capital gains stocks, a trustee can benefit the former group at the expense of the latter. By choosing low yield, high capital gains stocks, the latter group can benefit at the expense of the former. Yield is an important attribute of such an investment portfolio.[4]

Similar considerations may apply to the endowment funds of non-profit institutions where original donors of funds have specified that only "income" be spent, with the "corpus" left intact. Sometimes such a prescription is interpreted to allow expenditure of realized capital gains; in other cases, only dividends and interest payments may be spent. Despite legal decisions greatly enlarging the scope for spending out of capital in such situations, many officers and trustees of non-profit institutions insist that only "income" be spent. With this narrow definition of income, the yield of the stock portion of the institution's portfolio is likely to be of interest, apart from its contribution to total return.

Although there may be compelling reasons for "tilting" a portfolio to obtain a higher or lower than average yield, an empirical question remains: Can tilting be effective and if so at what cost? This article analyzes the historical record of several portfolios to determine some of the effects of managing a portfolio to obtain higher or lower than average yield. While the investment procedures employed are intentionally simple and easy to understand, in practice much more sophisticated methods could and perhaps should be used. Our figures should be interpreted as lower limits on the results obtainable for given yield levels.

Despite this qualification, examination of the record provides useful insights into the results that might be obtained in the future from portfolios with yields differing from the overall market average. The record suggests that within limits it may be possible to alter yield without excessive loss of diversification or change in sensitivity to market swings. However, a tax-exempt investor should not expect to obtain greater return relative to risk by doing so. On the other hand, *substantial* departures from market yield may entail serious loss of diversification and require a significant change in sensitivity to market swings, hence should be undertaken only under compelling circumstances.

Yield Groups

Our first step was to predict dividend yield for each common stock listed on the New York Stock Exchange. The second was to group these stocks into portfolios differing in predicted yield. We used only available historic data to predict yield in each case, although in practice investors might well use additional information to improve predictions. Our values were based on data compiled by the Center for Research in Security Prices at The University of Chicago (sponsored by Merrill Lynch, Pierce Fenner and Smith).

To begin, the dividends paid on a stock during 1927 were divided by the closing price of the stock at the end of the year to obtain a predicted yield for the year 1928.[5] The actual yield in 1928 was determined by dividing the sum of the actual dividends paid during 1928 by the price at the end of 1927. The total return for 1928 was then obtained by adding to the yield the percentage change in stock price from the end of 1927 to the end of 1928. This procedure was repeated, using dividends paid during 1928 and the price at the end of 1928 to obtain the yield predicted for 1929, etc. For each year from 1928 through 1969, three values were obtained in this manner for each stock listed on the New York Stock Exchange at the time: predicted yield, actual yield, and actual total return.

For some purposes these three measures suffice. However, it is often useful to consider *excess return,* obtained by subtracting the return on a default-free security from total return.[6] This measure, which will be used frequently in the analysis to follow, represents the return over and above that obtained from a default-free investment; such a return may reasonably be presumed to represent the reward for bearing risk.

At the beginning of each year, all available stocks were divided into 10 *yield deciles,* based on predicted yield. Decile 10 contains the 10 per cent of the stocks with the lowest predicted yield, Decile Nine the next 10 per cent, and so on, with Decile One containing the 10 per cent of the stocks with the greatest predicted yield.

An investor wishing to obtain a very low yield might consider holding all the stocks in yield Decile 10 to obtain as much diversification as possible. Although one wishing to obtain a somewhat higher yield could hold all the stocks in Decile Nine, he could obtain virtually the same yield with greater diversification by including stocks from

Deciles 10 and Eight as well. This suggests that *yield groups,* each including all the stocks in one or more deciles, held in equal dollar amounts, could better accomplish the goals than could the simple deciles. For this reason, 10 groups were constructed from the 10 deciles as follows:

group	deciles
10	10
9	10,9,8
8	10,9,8,7,6
7	10,9,8,7,6,5,4
6	10,9,8,7,6,5,4,3,2
5	9,8,7,6,5,4,3,2,1
4	7,6,5,4,3,2,1
3	5,4,3,2,1
2	3,2,1
1	1

Holdings in each group were readjusted at the beginning of each year to obtain equal dollar values of all stocks included in the relevant deciles at the time.

The yield, total return and risk of each of these groups will be compared with the yield, total return and risk of a "market portfolio" constructed to obtain a high degree of diversification, with no consideration paid to yield *per se*. This study used a portfolio including every stock in equal dollar values at the beginning of each year to represent the market.[7]

Yields

Figure 1 shows that our method for predicting yield works reasonably well. Figure 1a shows the average yields obtained over the full period for each of the 10 groups, while Figure 1b shows the values for the last 20 years for which data were available.[8] (Throughout, we will use these two periods to emphasize both longer-run and more recent experiences.) In each case, the results are in the predicted order and differ substantially among groups. The average yield on the market was 4.69 per cent for the first period and 4.36 per cent for the second. Clearly, it is possible to obtain above or below average yield, if desired.[9]

Figure 1. Yield (Percentage)

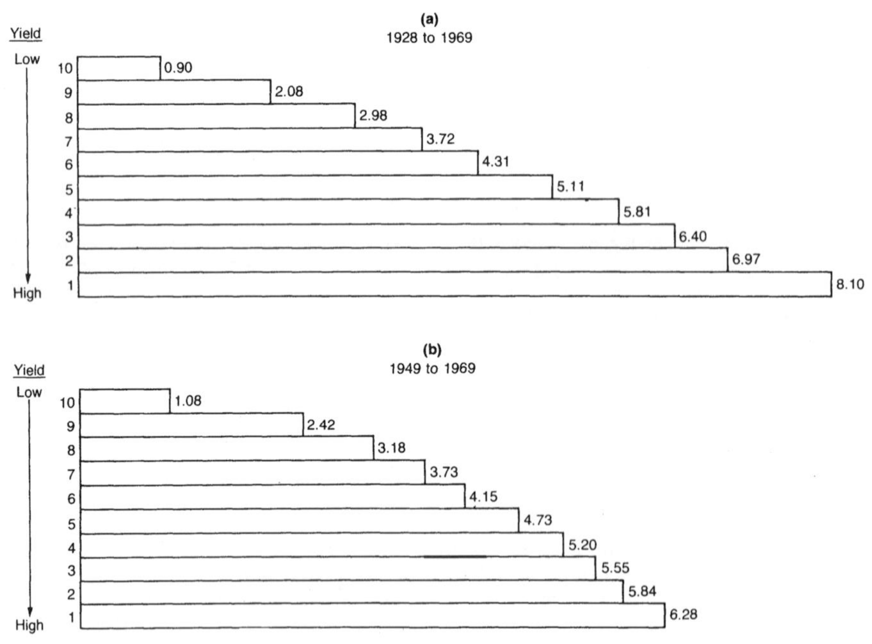

Average Excess Returns

Figure 2 shows the average excess returns for the 10 groups over the two periods.[10] In each case the lowest yield group (number 10) provided the greatest average excess return; moreover, the below average yield groups (6 through 10) generally provided higher average excess returns than the above average yield groups (1 through 5).[11] The average excess return for the market was 14.42 per cent during the first period and 14.25 per cent during the second.

Beta Vàlues

While low yield tends to be accompanied by high excess return, this does not necessarily suggest that the market shows a preference for dividends over capital gains. High return generally goes with high risk; differences in return of the type shown in Figure 2 might thus be due entirely to differences in risk. The most relevant aspect in this regard is *market risk*—that portion of the risk of a security or portfolio that cannot be diversified away by holding a broadly-based market portfolio. This is traditionally represented by *beta,* which measures sensitivity to changes in the overall market.[12] Of course, the beta for the market is equal to one.

Figure 3 shows the beta values for the 10 groups over the two periods. Each value was obtained by regressing the annual excess returns of the group in question on those of the market portfolio. In each case, there is a relationship between yield and market risk. This is most pronounced for group 10. A portfolio composed of very low yield stocks without regard for risk is very sensitive to market swings—an effect that may or may not be desirable, but should not be ignored.

The effect is not as pronounced for the other groups, especially in the postwar period. However, below average yield groups do tend to have above average beta values, while above average yield groups tend to have below average beta values.[13]

Non-market Risk

By definition, the market portfolio has only market risk. Other portfolios tend to have both market and non-market risk. Were there only the

Figure 2. Average Excess Return (Percentage)

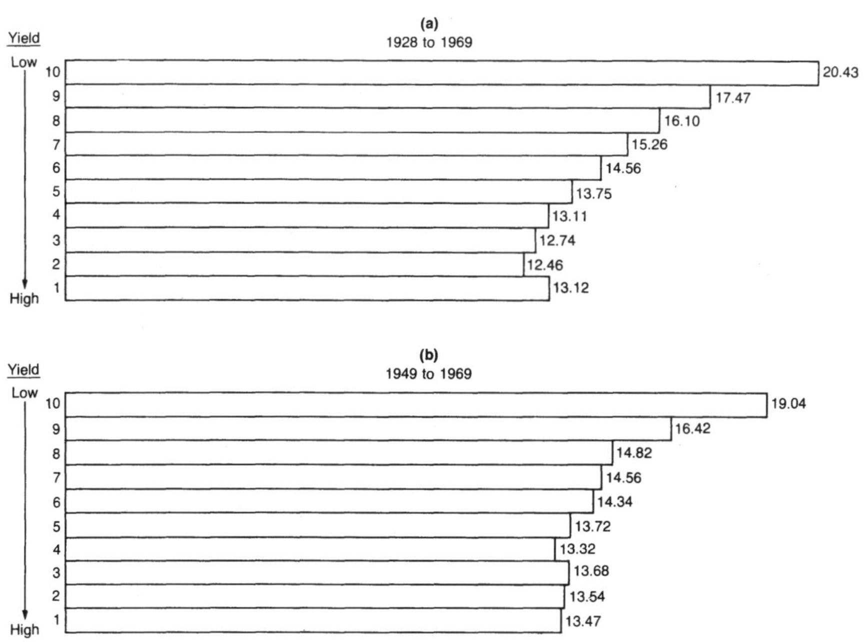

Figure 3. Beta Values

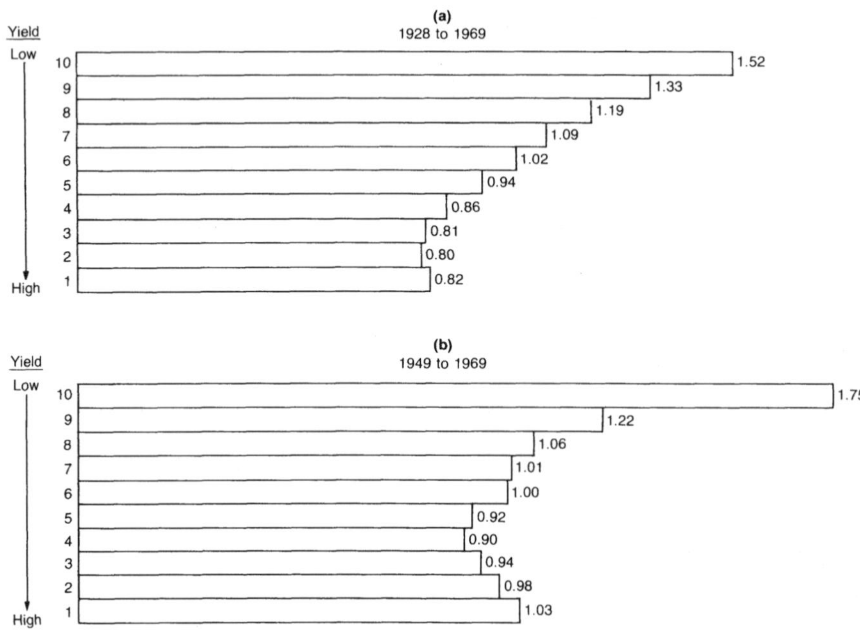

Figure 4. Non-market Risk

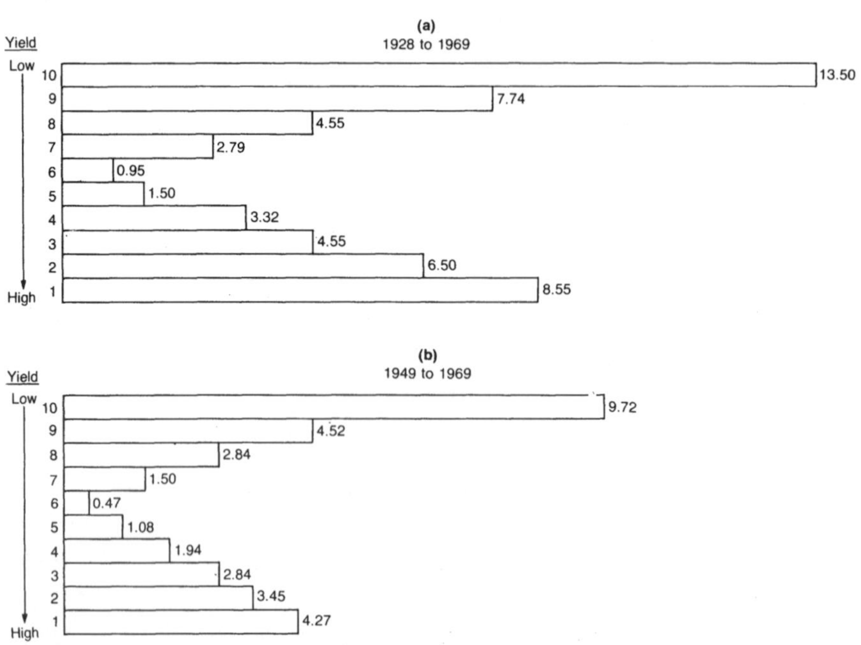

former, the excess return on a portfolio in any year would equal its beta value times the excess return on the market. The difference between this amount and the actual excess return can be attributed to non-market factors, and the typical magnitude of this difference can be termed non-market risk.

An historic measure of non-market risk is provided by the standard error of the regression equation used to estimate beta. A band two standard deviations wide that straddles the regression line running through the predicted values will encompass two-thirds of the actual values. If a portfolio's standard error is five per cent, one can assume there is one chance in three that its actual return in any given year will diverge from that expected, given the market's performance, by five per

Figure 5. Alpha Values

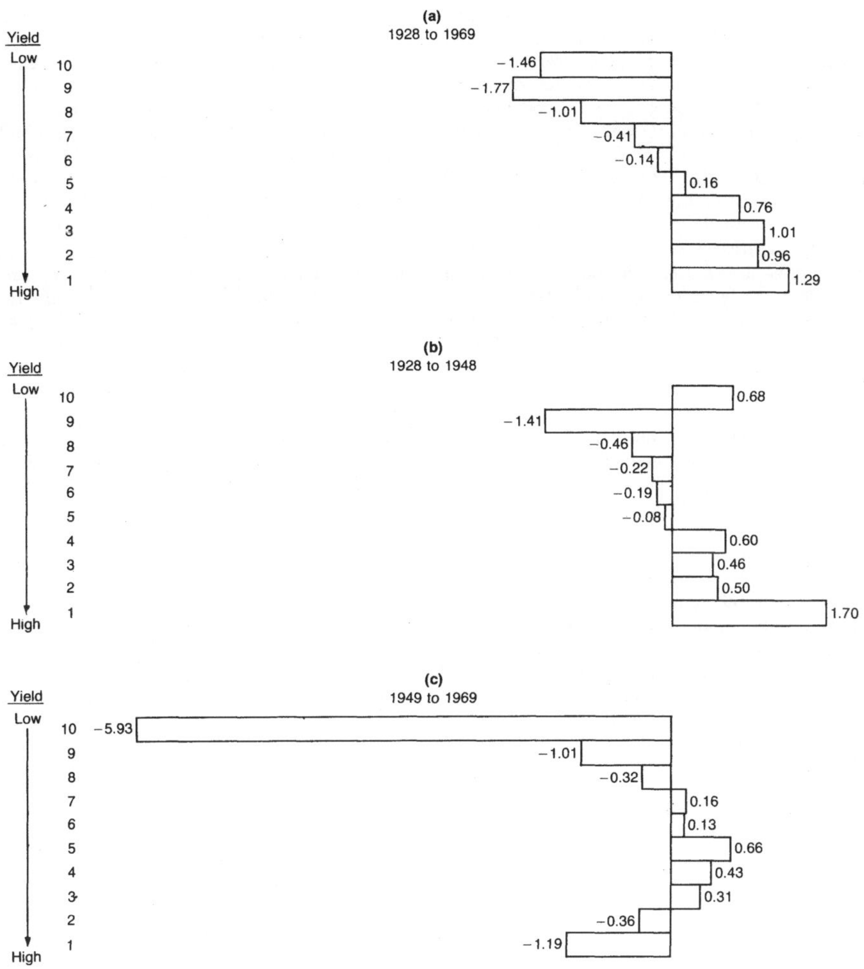

cent (500 basis points) or more.

Figure 4 shows the standard errors for each of the groups in the two time periods. The results are not surprising (although the magnitudes may be). Attempts to depart significantly in either direction from the market-average yield require the sacrifice of diversification, with a commensurate increase in non-market risk. Not surprisingly, the effect is most pronounced for group 10, which thus proves to be high in both market and non-market risk.

Alpha Values

A number of measures have been proposed to indicate the return on a portfolio after adjustment for the risk involved. One, the "alpha value," measures the difference between the average excess return on a portfolio and the excess return on the combination of the market portfolio and default-free short-term securities with the same beta value.[14]

Figure 5a shows the alpha values over the full period for the 10 groups. There appears to be a strong relationship: High-yield portfolios seem to offer higher returns after adjustment for risk, which might seem to suggest that one could gain more in yield than must be given up in capital gains by moving to a higher yield group. However, these results are deceptive. None of the alpha values is significantly different from zero in a statistical sense.[15] More importantly, the relationship is far from consistent over time.

Figure 5b shows the alpha values for the first half of the period. With the exception of group 1, the results are more or less in the order obtained for the overall period. An analyst considering these values in 1948 might have been tempted to recommend investment in group 1 or group 2 to a tax-exempt investor in the hope of obtaining a positive alpha value in subsequent years. But Figure 5c, which gives the results for the second 20 years, shows that such advice would have turned out badly. Not only would such a strategy have increased non-market risk (as shown in Figure 4b), it would have reduced return relative to market risk—i.e., produced a negative alpha value.

Figures 5b and 5c suggest that only groups 3 and 4 provided positive alpha values in both periods. However, this was most likely due to chance—any projection of such results into the future would be foolhardy. Moreover, one can assume that groups 4 through 7 are not likely to have alpha values that differ from zero by large amounts over an extended period of time. The extreme groups have more non-market risk than the others, and thus they have more room for superior or inferior performance. But as groups 1 and 10 demonstrate, such performance may be superior in one period and inferior in the next. Neither the magnitude nor the direction of performance measured by the alpha value can be predicted in advance—only its uncertainty.

Differential Return

For some purposes, a portfolio's alpha value may not be the most relevant measure of risk-adjusted performance. It compares returns after adjustment for differences in *market* risk. But if a group is to be used as a portfolio, and if the person or institution depending on the portfolio's return does not hold many other investments, both market *and* non-market risk will be relevant. A measure that adjusts for differences in *total risk* is thus needed.[16]

Figure 6 shows how this measure can be constructed. Point G plots the average excess return and total risk of a group, point M plots the performance of the market portfolio, and point Π that of default-free short-term securities. Point G′ represents the performance of a combination of group G and default-free securities, with the combination chosen to have the same total risk as the market portfolio. The difference in average excess return between this combination and the market portfolio is represented in the figure by the distance Δ. We will call it the *differential return*.

Figure 7a shows the differential returns over the full period for the 10 groups, while Figures 7b and 7c show the values for the two sub-periods. The relationships are similar to those shown in Figures 5a, b, and c for alpha values. For the overall period, higher yield groups provided greater differen-

Figure 6

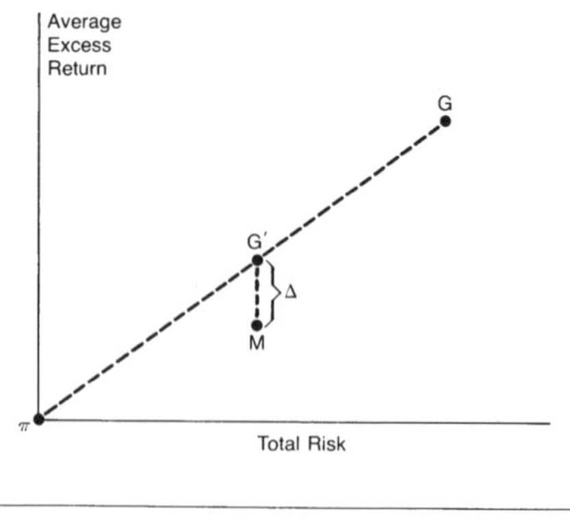

tial returns, although their advantage is relatively less than that shown in Figure 5a, due to high nonmarket risk. Here too, however, the relationship is unstable over time. Comparison of Figures 7b and 7c shows that one could easily be disappointed if past results were used to predict future differential returns for various yield groups.

Yield, Risk and Return

Figures 8a and 8b provide estimates of the possible results that might be obtained in the future with each yield group. All future alpha values are assumed to be zero. The values plotted in Figure 8a assume that the beta values and risks of the groups, as well as the risk and return of the market port-

Figure 7. Differential Returns

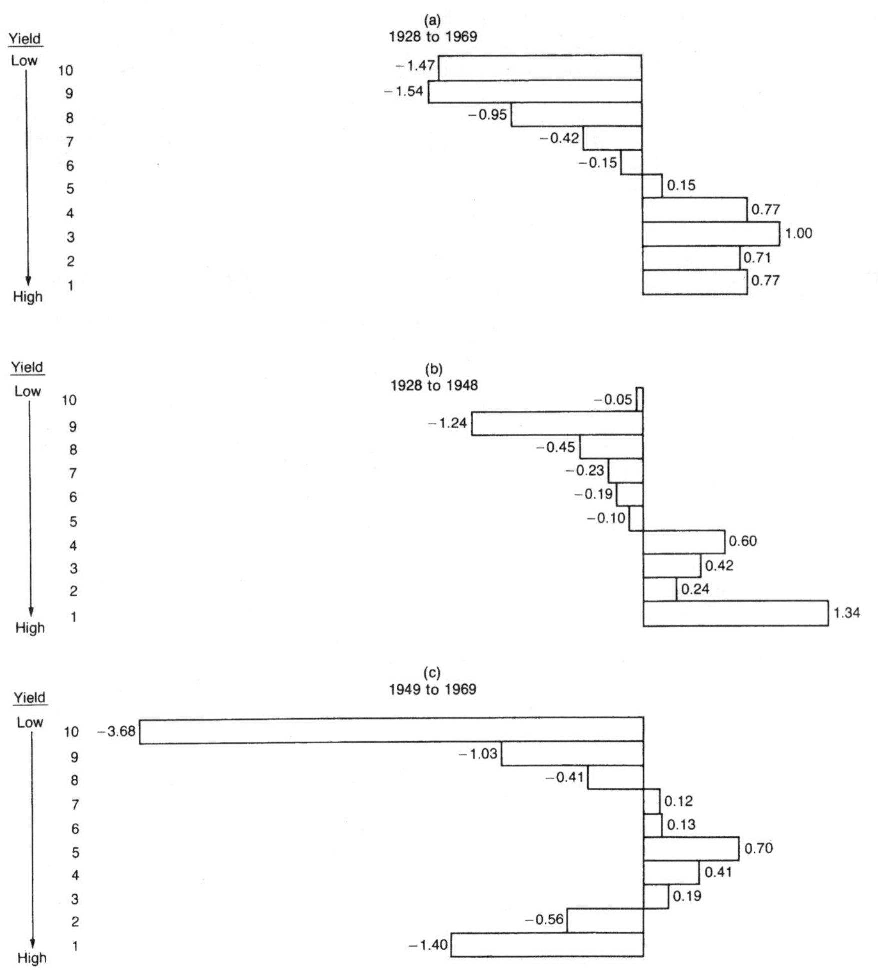

Figure 8.
Possible Future Differential Returns

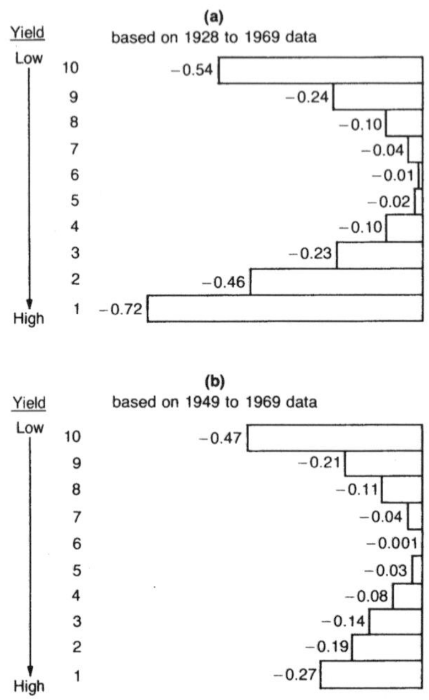

folio, will correspond to those experienced in the full period 1928 through 1969. Given these assumptions, the differential return for each group can be calculated directly.[17]

A comparison of Figures 1 and 8 suggests the extent to which a portfolio's yield may be altered without seriously affecting its overall performance. For example, within the range spanned by groups 4 to 7, the following values were obtained:

TABLE I

(a) based on 1928 to 1969 data

group	yield	possible future differential return
7	3.72 per cent	−0.04 per cent
4	5.81	−0.10

(b) based on 1949 to 1969 data

group	yield	possible future differential return
7	3.73 per cent	−0.04 per cent
4	5.20	−0.08

These values suggest that it should not prove difficult to construct a portfolio with relatively little non-market risk, average market risk (i.e., a beta value of 1.0), and yield differing from the market average by up to 100 basis points. Alternatively, total risk can undoubtedly be held constant and yield "tilted" to this extent with only a relatively small decrease in average return (e.g., from four to 10 basis points).

On the other hand, attempts to depart substantially from market average yield may seriously degrade risk-adjusted performance. The values obtained for the extreme groups illustrate this:

TABLE II

(a) based on 1928 to 1969 data

group	yield	possible future differential return
10	0.90 per cent	−0.54 per cent
1	8.10	−0.72

(b) based on 1949 to 1969 data

group	yield	possible future differential return
10	1.08 per cent	−0.47 per cent
1	6.28	−0.27

Holding total risk constant, any attempt to alter yield from the market average by 200 to 300 basis points may result in a decrease of 25 to 75 basis points in total return. This penalty may be necessary in some circumstances, but should not be borne lightly or unwittingly. ■

Footnotes

1. E.J. Elton and M.J. Gruber, "Marginal Stockholder Tax Rates and the Clientele Effect," *Review of Economics and Statistics* (February 1970).
2. Fischer Black and Myron Scholes, "The Behavior of Security Returns Around Ex-dividend Days," unpublished paper.
3. Black and Scholes, "The Effects of Dividend Yield and Dividend Policy on Common Stock Prices and Returns," *Journal of Financial Economics* (May 1974).
4. Dual Purpose Funds provide an institutional example of the same effect. These closed end mutual funds issue two types of shares (income and capital) and have a fixed termination date. The income shareholders receive all the income of the fund (dividend or interest income) as it accrues and the minimum of either their initial investment or the total assets of the fund when it terminates. The capital shareholders have a claim to any residual value (capital gains) left in the fund after the income shareholders have been paid off.
5. Dividends were considered to be "paid" on the ex-

dividend day; all splits on stock dividends were taken into account.

6. The values obtained by Ibbotson and Sinquefield were used for this purpose. See, R. Ibbotson and R. Sinquefield, "Stocks, Bonds, Bills and Inflation: The Past and the Future," paper presented at the Center for Research in Security Prices, The University of Chicago, May 1974.
7. On a theoretical basis a market portfolio in which stocks are represented in proportion to market value outstanding would be preferred. Correspondingly, yield groups in which stocks are represented in proportion to market values outstanding could be constructed. Unfortunately, the available data preclude the latter; an equal-dollar weighted market portfolio was thus utilized for consistency.
8. The yield for a group in a given year is a simple average of the yields of the included securities; the average yield for a group over a period of years is a simple average of the annual yields.
9. The pattern of average yield obtained for the simple deciles was very similar and had the same stairstep appearance.
10. The excess return for a group in a given year is a simple average of the excess returns of the included securities; the average excess return for a group over a period of years is a simple average of the annual excess returns.
11. As with average yield, the pattern of average excess return for the deciles was similar to that of the groups.
12. The approach is described by Vasicek and McQuown and Sharpe. See, O.A. Vasicek and J.A. McQuown, "The Efficient Market Model," *Financial Analysts Journal* (September/October 1971); see also, William F. Sharpe, *Portfolio Theory and Capital Markets* (New York: McGraw-Hill, 1971).

    Some empirical evidence on its relevance is given by Sharpe and G.M. Cooper, "Risk-return Classes of New York Stock Exchange Common Stocks," *Financial Analysts Journal* (March/April 1972).
13. Once again decile results and group results were similar.
14. Alternatively, alpha is the vertical intercept of the characteristic line obtained by regressing the excess return of a security or portfolio on the excess return of the market portfolio.
15. The highest t-value is 1.52.
16. The historic standard deviation of excess returns was used as a measure of total risk.
17. $$\Delta = \left(\frac{\beta_g \cdot A_m}{\sigma_g} \cdot \sigma_m \right) - A_m$$

    where Δ = the differential return;
    β_g = the beta of the group;
    A_m = the average excess return of the market portfolio;
    σ_m = the total risk (standard deviation of excess return) for the market portfolio; and
    σ_g = the total risk (standard deviation of excess return) for the group.

JOURNAL OF FINANCIAL AND QUANTITATIVE ANALYSIS
Proceedings Issue - November 1978

DURATION AND SECURITY RISK

*Ronald Lanstein and William F. Sharpe**

I. Introduction

Estimation and control of security risk are subjects of major theoretical and practical importance. Much of the literature in this area has focused on the risk associated with returns over a single holding period. Within this context, a great deal of attention has been devoted to estimation of security betas, which relate to coveriance with "the market," since the well-known Capital Asset Pricing Model implies that expected returns will, in equilibrium, be related to such values. However, a number of papers [3, 7, 14] have considered "extra-market covariances," i.e., covariances among security returns not due to common correlations with the market as a whole. Accurate estimates of such covariances are necessary for tailoring portfolios to account for differences in investors' circumstances (e.g., tax brackets) and, *a fortiori*, for active portfolio management designed to exploit any security mispricing.

Most discussions of return covariance focus on the stock market where risk has long been considered explicitly. Analyses of bond returns tend to be cast in a different framework, with risk assumed to arise from uncertainty concerning a single state variable, i.e., the "shift" in the term structure of interest rates. Many discussions of the concept of duration fall in this category.[1]

This paper deals explicitly with general structures of security return covariance and examines possible roles for the concept of duration in such an environment. However, only uncertainty about future discount rates for cash flows associated with different dates is considered. This form of uncertainty (often termed "interest rate risk") is the major source of risk for most bonds but only one of many such sources for most stocks. The theory is thus relevant for both bonds and stocks, but relatively more important for bonds. Nonetheless, we show that it has some predictive power for stocks.

The paper is divided into three parts. Section II discusses components of security risk. Section III uses this framework to examine the concept of duration and the related

---

**Respectively, consultant Barr Rosenberg Associates, and Tim Ken Professor of Finance, Stanford University.* *This study was performed with the support of the Investment Systems Group of Wells Fargo Investment Advisors. The authors wish to express their appreciation to Virginia Chung of Wells Fargo who did the empirical tests. The study was also sponsored by the Stanford Program in Finance. Major contributors to the Stanford Program in Finance are: BankAmerica Foundation, The First Boston Corporation, The Chase Manhattan Bank, Continental Bank Foundation, The Dean Witter Foundation, General Electric Company, Goldman, Sachs & Co., Morgan Guaranty Trust Company, Morgan Stanley & Co., Inc., Salomon Brothers, Security Pacific National Bank, and Wells Fargo Bank.*

[1]For excellent summaries of this literature, see [1] and [6].

idea of immunization. We conclude (as have others)[2] that duration provides at best a crude approach to determining and/or controlling risk. Nonetheless, in Section IV, when we test the ability of the traditional measure of duration to help predict extra-market covariances among the returns of common stocks, we obtain positive results. Our findings for the stock market complement those of others (e.g., [4] who found that, despite theoretical flaws, duration measures have useful empirical properties in explaining return covariances in the bond market.

II. Security Risk

Let security i provide cash flows $F_{i1}, F_{i2}, \ldots, F_{in}$ in years 1, 2,..., n (the term "year" will be used to represent any arbitrary period). Assume that the security's present price is determined by a series of market-wide discount factors $p_1, p_2, \ldots, p_n$ for years 1, 2,..., n. Letting P_i be security i's current price:

$$P_i = p_1F_{i1} + p_2F_{i2} + \ldots + p_nF_{in}. \quad (1)$$

We consider only uncertainty concerning return over a specified holding period of less than one "year." At the end of this holding period there will be a new (and probably different) set of discount rates and hence a new security price. Letting asterisks denote values at the end of this holding period:

$$P_i^* = p_1^*F_{i1} + p_2^*F_{i2} + \ldots + p_n^*F_{in}. \quad (2)$$

We assume that the projected cash flows $F_{i1}, F_{i2}, \ldots, F_{in}$ do not change during the holding period. This is obviously appropriate for default-free bonds, with the F_{it}'s interpreted as promised (certain) payments and $p_1, p_2, \ldots, p_n$ derived from the riskless term structure of interest rates. For risky assets such as stocks, the F_{it} values can be interpreted as certainty-equivalent flows[3] and the p_t's (as before) as discount rates appropriate for riskless investments. Now, define:

$$X_{it} \equiv \frac{p_tF_{it}}{P_i} \quad (3)$$

as the proportion of security i's present value attributable to the payment provided in year t.

Combining (1), (2) and (3) gives:

$$\frac{P_i^*}{P_i} = \frac{p_1^*}{p_1}X_{i1} + \frac{p_2^*}{p_2}X_{i2} + \ldots + \frac{p_n^*}{p_n}X_{in}. \quad (4)$$

Define:

$$R_i \equiv \frac{P_i^*}{P_i} - 1$$

as the holding-period return on security i and

$$R_t \equiv \frac{p_t^*}{p_t} - 1$$

---

[2] See [1] and [6].

[3] That is, F_{it} is a certain cash flow with the same market value as the distribution of uncertain cash flows $\tilde{F}_{it}$.

as the holding-period return on a security with a cash flow only in year t.

Then (4) can be written as:

(5) $$R_i = X_{i1}r_1 + X_{i2}r_2 + \ldots + X_{in}r_n.$$

Let m represent the market of all securities, with:

(6) $$X_{mt} = \sum_i M_i X_{it}$$

where

M_i = the proportion of the current value of all securities contributed by security i.

Similarly, let R_m represent the holding period return on the market.

Making the assumption that risk is to be characterized by the second moment of return distributions, all relevant elements can be summarized by the n x n covariance matrix:[4]

$$C = \left[c_{t\tau}\right]$$

where:

$$c_{t\tau} = \text{cov}(r_t, r_\tau).$$

Letting X_i represent the 1 x n vector $\left[X_{i1}, X_{i2}, \ldots\right]$ and X_j and X_m corresponding vectors for security j and the market:[5]

(7a) $$\text{Var}(R_i) = X_i C X_i'$$

(7b) $$\text{Var}(R_m) = X_m C X_m'$$

(7c) $$\text{Cov}(R_i, R_j) = X_i C X_j'$$

(7d) $$\text{Cov}(R_i, R_m) = X_i C X_m'$$

(7e) $$\beta_i \equiv \frac{C_{im}}{V_m} = \frac{X_i C X_m'}{X_m C X_m'}$$

where

β_i = security i's beta value, reflecting the contribution of the market to its total risk.

Now, define:

(8) $$\varepsilon_i \equiv R_i - \beta_i R_m$$

as the extra-market (or residual) return on security i. Then, the extra-market covariance

[4] For a related approach, see [12].

[5] The prime (') denotes a transpose.

between securities i and j is:

$$\text{cov}(\varepsilon_i,\varepsilon_j) = \text{cov}(R_i - \beta_i R_m, R_j - \beta_j R_m)$$

(9) $$= \text{cov}(R_i,R_j) - \beta_i\beta_j \text{ Var}(R_m)$$

Now, let:

$$b_t \equiv \frac{\text{cov}(r_t,R_m)}{\text{Var}(R_m)}$$

be the beta value of a security with a cash flow only in year t, and let B represent the 1 x n vector $\left[b_1, b_2,\ldots, b_n\right]$. Clearly,

(10) $$\beta_i = \sum_t X_{it}b_t = X_i B'.$$

Combining (7), (9) and (10):

$$\text{Cov}(\varepsilon_i\varepsilon_j) = X_i C X_j' - (X_i B')(X_j B')\text{Var}(R_m)$$

(11) $$= X_i \left[C - B'B\text{Var}(R_m)\right] X_j'$$

Define the n x n matrix of extra-market covariances for single period cash flow securities as:

$$E = \left[E_{t\tau}\right] = \left[C - B'B \text{ Var}(R_m)\right]$$

where

$$E_{t\tau} = C_{t\tau} - b_t b_\tau \text{Var}(R_m)$$

$$= \text{cov}(r_t - b_t R_m,\ r_\tau - b_t R_m)$$

$$= \text{cov}(\varepsilon_t,\ \varepsilon_\tau)$$

Then,

(12) $$\text{Cov}(\varepsilon_i,\ \varepsilon_j) = X_i E X_j'.$$

To summarize: holding-period risks due to interest rate uncertainty depend on:

C : covariances among returns on securities with cash flows in only one period,

X_i, X_j, X_m : proportions of current values of securities and of the market attributable to each year's cash flows.

From these can be derived:

B : betas for single period cash flow securities,

E : extra-market covariances for such securities,

and thus values of:

$\beta_i (=X_i B')$: security i's beta value,

$Cov(\varepsilon_i, \varepsilon_j)$ $(=X_i E X_j')$: the extra-market covariance between securities i and j.

III. Duration and Immunization

Duration

The concept of duration arises from a (perhaps unfortunate) concentration on interest rates rather than prices (discount factors).

Define the t-period interest rate i_t as the value that satisfies:

$$\frac{1}{(1+i_t)^t} = p_t. \tag{13}$$

Given this definition, it follows that:

$$\frac{dp_t}{p_t} = -t \frac{d(1+i_t)}{(1+i_t)} . \tag{14}$$

Define k_t as the elasticity of $(1+i_t)$ with respect to $(1+i_1)$:

$$k_t \equiv \frac{d(1+i_t)}{(1+i_t)} \Bigg/ \frac{d(1+i_1)}{(1+i_1)} . \tag{15}$$

Combining (13) and (14):

$$\frac{dp_t}{p_t} = -t\, k_t \frac{d(1+i_1)}{(1+i_1)} . \tag{16}$$

For t = 1:

$$\frac{dp_1}{p_1} = - \frac{d(1+i_1)}{(1+i_1)} .$$

Thus,

$$\frac{dp_t}{p_t} = tK_t \frac{dp_1}{p_1} . \tag{17}$$

Recall that r_t is the holding period return for a security with a single cash flow at time t:

For small changes:

$$r_t = \frac{p_t}{p_t} - 1 \simeq \frac{dp_t}{p_t}$$

Thus,

$$r_t \simeq t\, k_t\, r_1 . \tag{18}$$

Now, define:

(19) $$d_t \equiv tk_t.$$

Then, from (5), (18) and (19):

(20) $$R_i = (\sum_t X_{it}d_t)\ r_1$$

or

(21) $$R_i \simeq D_i\ r_1$$

where D_i, security i's *duration,* is defined as:

(22) $$D_i = \sum_t X_{it}d_t.$$

The original concept of duration, first obtained by MacAulay [11] is consistent with the assumption that $k_1 = k_2 = \ldots = 1$ (i.e., that [1 + interest rates] move proportionately). We will denote this "traditional" measure of duration D_i^*:

(23) $$D_i^* = \sum_t X_{it}t.$$

Note that D^* has the familiar intuitive interpretation of a weighted avarege of the cash flow dates, with relative proportions of value as weights (i.e., it is the "central tendency" of the cash flows).

Modified versions of duration have been proposed since empirical evidence suggests that $k_t > k_{t+1}$ (i.e., shorter interest rates vary more than longer ones). However, such discussions implicitly assume relationships more or less equivalent to (21).

Steps (13) through (22) appear to involve little more than definitions and an approximation for small changes. If the values of k_t are assumed to simply equal after-the-fact elasticities, (21) has virtually no economic content. But if restrictions are placed on the values of the k_t's, the situation is quite different. For example, the traditional assumption (23) gives (21) strong economic content.

A strict interpretation of (21) and (23) implies perfect correlation among all security returns, and some discussions of duration assume this, explicitly or implicitly. However, others tend to stop short of such a strong assumption. Rather, the impression is given that measures of duration (calculated *ex ante*) predict the *expected* reactions of security prices to unexpected changes in interest rates.

(24) $$E\left[(R_i - E(R_i) \mid r_1\right] = D_i\left[(r_1 - E(r_1)\right].$$

Equivalently,

(25a) $$R_i = a_i + D_i\ r_1 + e_i$$

(25b) $$E(e_i) = 0$$

(25c) $$\operatorname{cov}(e_i, r_1) = 0$$

where D_i is understood to be determinable *ex ante* in some manner (e.g., by (23)).

Given the measure chosen for D_i, a related measure can be determined for the market portfolio:

(26) $$D_m \equiv \sum_i M_i D_i .$$

While (25) is a strong statement, it falls short of the implications sometimes attributed to duration. For example, it implies that:

(27) $$\operatorname{cov}(R_i, R_j) = D_i D_j \operatorname{Var}(r_1) + \operatorname{cov}(e_i, e_j)$$

(28) $$\beta_i = \frac{D_i D_m \operatorname{Var}(r_1) + \operatorname{cov}(e_i, e_m)}{D_m^2 \operatorname{Var}(r_1) + \operatorname{Var}(e_m)}$$

where

(29) $$e_m \equiv \sum_i M_i e_i .$$

Relative duration is sometimes equated to a beta value.[6] For a one-to-one mapping, a much stronger assumption than (25) is required. An obvious case arises when all returns are perfectly correlated (i.e., for all i: $\operatorname{Var}(e_i) = 0$). A less extreme assumption would hold that "abnormal" changes in interest rates are uncorrelated across the term structure. That is:

(30) $$\operatorname{Cov}(e_i, e_j) = 0 \quad \text{for all } i \neq j.$$

This strong assumption implies that both $\operatorname{Var}(e_m)$ and $\operatorname{Cov}(e_i, e_m)$ will be small, and that:

(31) $$\beta_i \simeq \frac{D_i}{D_m} .$$

Assumption (30) elevates duration to an important role in determining the risk of a security. Market risk is then a direct function of duration:

(32) $$\beta_i^2 \operatorname{Var}(R_m) \simeq D_i^2 \operatorname{Var}(r_1)$$

and there are virtually no extra-market covariances among pairs of securities. From (9) and (31):

(33) $$\begin{aligned} \text{for } i \neq j: \quad \operatorname{Cov}(\varepsilon_i, \varepsilon_j) &= \operatorname{Cov}(R_i, R_j) - \beta_i \beta_j \operatorname{Var}(R_m) \\ &\simeq D_i D_j \operatorname{Var}(r_1) - \frac{D_i}{D_m} \frac{D_j}{D_m} D_m^2 \operatorname{Var}(r_1) \\ &\simeq 0. \end{aligned}$$

[6]For discussions of such relations, see [2], [9], [10], and [12].

Immunization

The assumption that extra-market covariances are negligible is central to traditional discussions of *immunization*. The idea is to find two sets of investments, one set to serve as assets and the other as liabilities, such that net worth (the difference) has zero risk over a specified holding period. That is:[7]

$$\text{(34)} \qquad \mathrm{Var(NW)} = (X_a - X_\ell)\ C\ (X_a - X_\ell)' = 0.$$

If all the r_t's are perfectly correlated:

$$\mathrm{cov}(r_t, r_\tau) = D_t D_\tau \mathrm{Var}(r_1)$$

and

$$\text{(35)} \qquad C = D\ \mathrm{Var}(r_1) D$$

where

$$D = \text{the nx1 vector } \left[D_1, D_2, \ldots, D_n \right].$$

Under these conditions, (34) can be written:

$$\mathrm{Var(NW)} = (X_a - X_\ell) D\ \mathrm{Var}(r_1)\ D'(X_a - X_\ell)'$$

$$\text{(36)} \qquad = (X_a D - X_\ell D)\ \mathrm{Var}(r_1)\ (X_a D - X_\ell D)'\ .$$

The necessary and sufficient condition for (36) to be zero is:

$$\text{(37)} \qquad X_a D = X_\ell D.$$

But $X_a D$ and $X_\ell D$ are the durations of the assets and liabilities, respectively. Given perfect correlation among the r_t's, immunization is always possible as long as asset and liability durations are equal, with duration defined appropriately, using the sensitivity coefficients D_1, D_2, ... of the assumed stochastic process for returns (or interest rates).

The strong assumption of perfect correlation among the r_t's is essential for complete immunization using only asset and liability durations. In the more realistic case in which there are extra-market covariances, matrix C cannot be decomposed as in (35) and immunization requires a more sophisticated matching of asset and liability cash flows.[8]

---

[7] Both X_a and X_ℓ should be expressed as proportions of the same base (e.g., the beginning value of net worth).

[8] For a discussion of such cases, see [1].

Extra-Market Covariance and Duration

In the stock market, extra-market covariances are substantial.[9] However, even bond returns are not perfectly correlated. Table 1 shows the correlation coefficients for monthly returns on portfolios of short-term (3- to 4-year), intermediate-term (6- to 9-year), and long-term (over 10-year), U.S. government bonds from January 1938 through December 1975.[10] The substantial departures from perfect correlation show that simple duration calculations will not suffice to completely immunize a bond portfolio.

TABLE 1

CORRELATION COEFFICIENTS, MONTHLY RETURNS 1938-1975, U.S. GOVERNMENT BONDS

	short-term	intermediate-term	long-term
short-term	1	.807	.677
intermediate-term		1	.742
long-term			1

For our purposes it is especially important to assume that (30) does *not* hold and thus that (31), (32), and (33) do not apply. In particular, we assume that there *are* significant extra-market covariances among securities and examine the role that the traditional measure of duration (23) can play in predicting such covariances.

As indicated earlier, the extra-market covariance between two securities depends on the respective patterns of value over time (X_i, X_j) and E, the covariance matrix of extra-market returns on securities with cash flows in only one period. Given X_i, X_j, and a prediction of E, formula (12) can be used to obtain a prediction of $cov(\varepsilon_i, \varepsilon_j)$.

Unfortunately, detailed predictions of E are difficult to make. As an alternative, one might begin by breaking covariance terms into standard deviations and correlation coefficients:

$$E_{t\tau} = \sigma(e_t)\ \sigma(e_\tau)\ \rho(e_t, e_\tau) \qquad (38a)$$

where

$e_t = r_t - b_t R_m$,

$\sigma(e_t)$ = the standard deviation of e_t, and

$\rho(e_t, e_\tau)$ = the correlation coefficient between e_t and e_τ.

One might then assume that:

---

[9] See [14].

[10] For details, see [5].

(38b) $$\sigma(e_t) = g(t)$$

where g(t) is an increasing function of t on the grounds that b_t is an increasing function of t and that empirically, securities with high betas tend also to have high residual variances.[11]

Further, one might assume that:

(38c) $$\rho(e_t, e_\tau) = f(|t - \tau|)$$

where

$f(|t - \tau|)$ is a decreasing function of $|t - \tau|$

on the grounds that securities of similar maturity are likely to move together when the term structure "swings," while those with very different maturities are likely to move in opposite directions.

Even if functions f and g were known, calculation of $cov(\varepsilon_i, \varepsilon_j)$ would still require the use of E. In particular, the relevant functions are not likely to be stable under addition, so that "central tendencies" (traditional durations) cannot simply be used in formulas (38) in lieu of t and τ to determine $cov(\varepsilon_i, \varepsilon_j)$.

As a practical matter, however, it may be possible to find related functions which take into account (at least partially) the effects of using a single central tendency to represent a full vector of relative values. While these will at best provide approximations, and will be of a different form, one might assume that they would retain the monotonic properties of f and g. We thus hypothesize that there exist functions F and G such that:

(39) $$\sigma(\varepsilon_i) \simeq G(D_i^*)$$

(40) $$\rho(\varepsilon_i, \varepsilon_j) \simeq F(|D_i^* - D_j^*|)$$

where

G is an increasing function of D_i^*, and

F is a decreasing function of $|D_i^* - D_j^*|$.

The final part of the paper provides a test of these hypotheses.

[11] As shown in, e.g. [8].

IV. Duration and Components of Extra-Market Covariance for Common Stocks

The data for our empirical tests were obtained from Wells Fargo Bank. In December 1972 the bank's analysts made detailed forecasts of expected future dividends for 262 stocks.[12] Of these, 220 remained on the bank's "covered list" for the next five years. The latter group constitutes our sample.[13]

For each stock, duration (D_i^*) was calculated using the traditional formula[14] (23) with proportionate values (X_{i1}, X_{i2}, ...) based on the internal rate of return ("yield-to-perpetuity") implied by the projected cash flows and the current price of the stock in question.[15] Figure 1 shows the distribution of the 220 values of D_i^*.

Monthly returns were calculated for the 220 stocks over the subsequent five years.[16] Using Standard and Poor's 500-stock index as a surrogate for the market, all extra-market covariances and correlations were calculated, giving a sample of:

24,090 different values of $\text{cov}(\varepsilon_i, \varepsilon_j)$ for $i \neq j$ [17]

220 values of $\sigma(\varepsilon_i)$

24,090 different values of $\rho(\varepsilon_i, \varepsilon_j)$ for $i \neq j$ [17]

These data allow us to investigate the ability of *ex ante* estimates of duration to predict some of the variation in the components of *ex post* extra-market covariance.

To test the hypothesis that residual risk increases with duration, a simple linear regression was run, giving:

$$\sigma(\varepsilon) = 7.561 + .009\, D^* . \qquad (41)$$

---

[12] For a description of the procedure, see [15, pp. 315-319]; such forecasts, made monthly, are summarized in [16].

[13] While this involves *ex post* selection, it is not clear that any bias is introduced for the purposes of this study.

[14] After a specified maturity date, the Wells Fargo analysts utilize a constant-growth model, making it possible to calculate finite duration estimates.

[15] This is, of course, a major compromise with the underlying theory, which suggests that the appropriate term structure of discount rates should be used, along with certainty-equivalent (not expected) cash flows. The procedure is defended here on grounds of practicality.

[16] For correlation coefficients, the period from the end of December 1972 through the end of December 1977 was used. For residual standard deviations, the period from the end of November 1972 through the end of November 1977 was used, due to a change in data sources. There is no reason to believe that significantly different results would have been obtained had the latter analysis utilized a period beginning at the end of December 1972.

[17] $= 1/2(220^2 - 220)$.

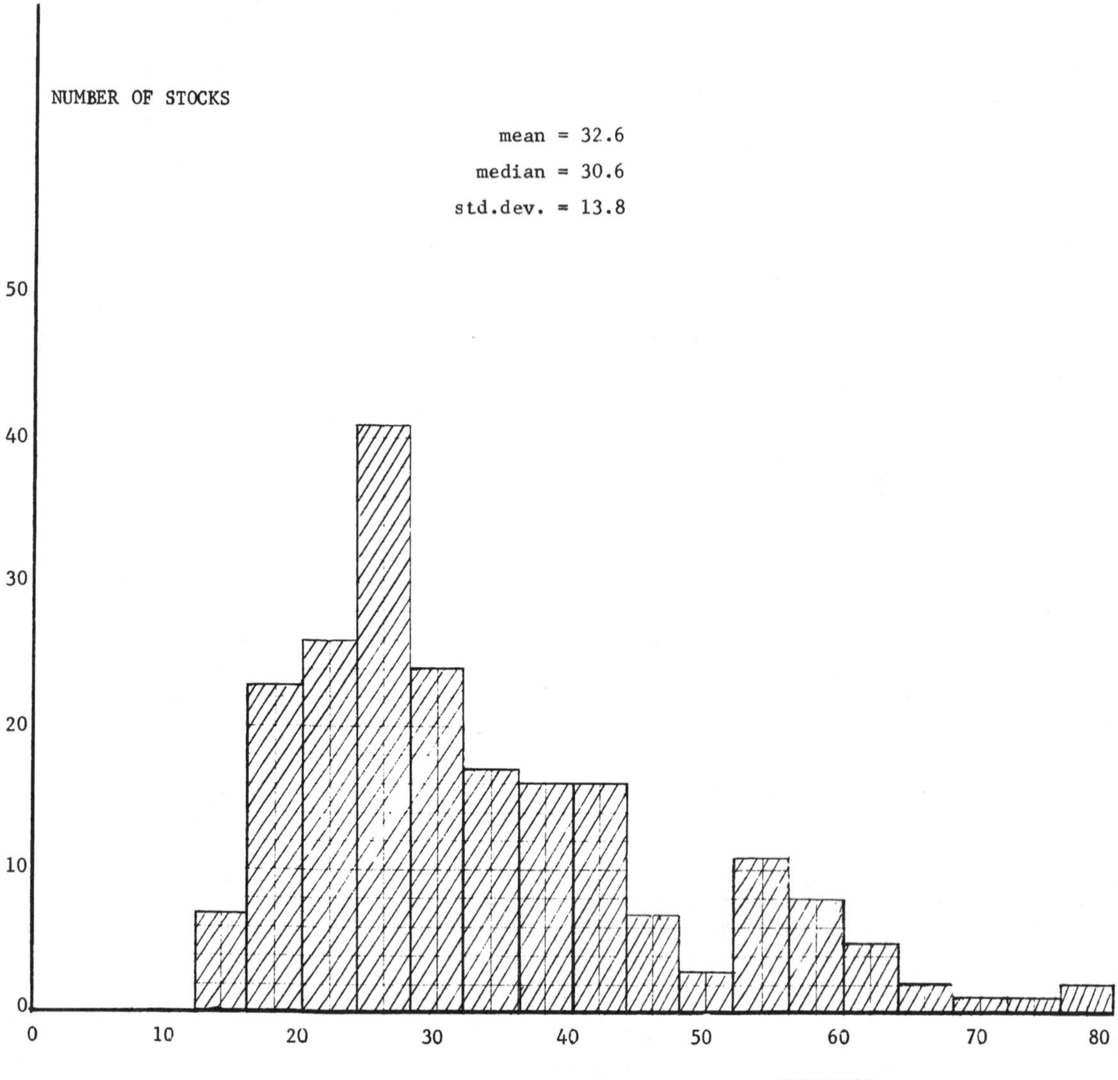
NUMBER OF STOCKS
mean = 32.6
median = 30.6
std.dev. = 13.8
50
40
30
20
10
0
0
10
20
30
40
50
60
70
80
DURATION

FIGURE 1

While the relationship is of the predicted type, it is not statistically significant: the t-value for the slope coefficient is .80.[18] Examination of the data suggests that the problem is not the use of an incorrect form for the equation. It is at least possible that factors associated with uncertainty concerning the cash flows may have dominated changes due to variations in discount rates.

When the relationship between residual correlation and duration difference was tested, the results were much more satisfying. Since there were over 24,000 different observations, the initial analysis was performed using grouped data. Each security was assigned to one of 15 groups, based on duration.[19] Each possible pair of groups was then analyzed. For every group pair the residual correlation of each security in the first group with each security in the second group[20] was calculated, and the average value found. Then the average difference in duration for the securities in the two groups was computed.[21] This procedure yielded two values for each group pair: an average residual correlation and an average duration difference. These 120[22] observations were reduced to 34 by combining all cases in which the duration difference fell within a range of one year.[23]

Figure 2 shows the results. There is a significant negative relationship between residual correlation and duration difference as hypothesized: the t-value for the slope coefficient is -15.97. Similar regressions using individual security pairs showed even more significant results.[24]

---

[18] There is also a positive relationship between beta and duration, but it is also insignificant (the t-value for the slope coefficient is 1.09).

[19] The groups were formed as follows:

	duration	
group	from	to
1	12.0	15.99
2	16.0	17.99
.	.	.
10	32.0	33.99
11	34.0	37.99
12	38.0	40.99
13	41.0	43.99
14	44.0	48.99
15	49.0	80.0

[20] Except that if the groups were the same, the residual correlation of each security with itself (which is, of course, always 1.0) was excluded.

[21] Assuming uniform distributions of durations over the ranges spanned by the two groups.

[22] $= \left[(15^2 - 15)/2\right] + 15.$

[23] The average residual correlations for the cases within a given range were averaged, using the original number of observations for each case as weights.

[24] When the 24,090 observations were partitioned into two groups, the t-values for the slope coefficients in the resulting equations averaged -24.7.

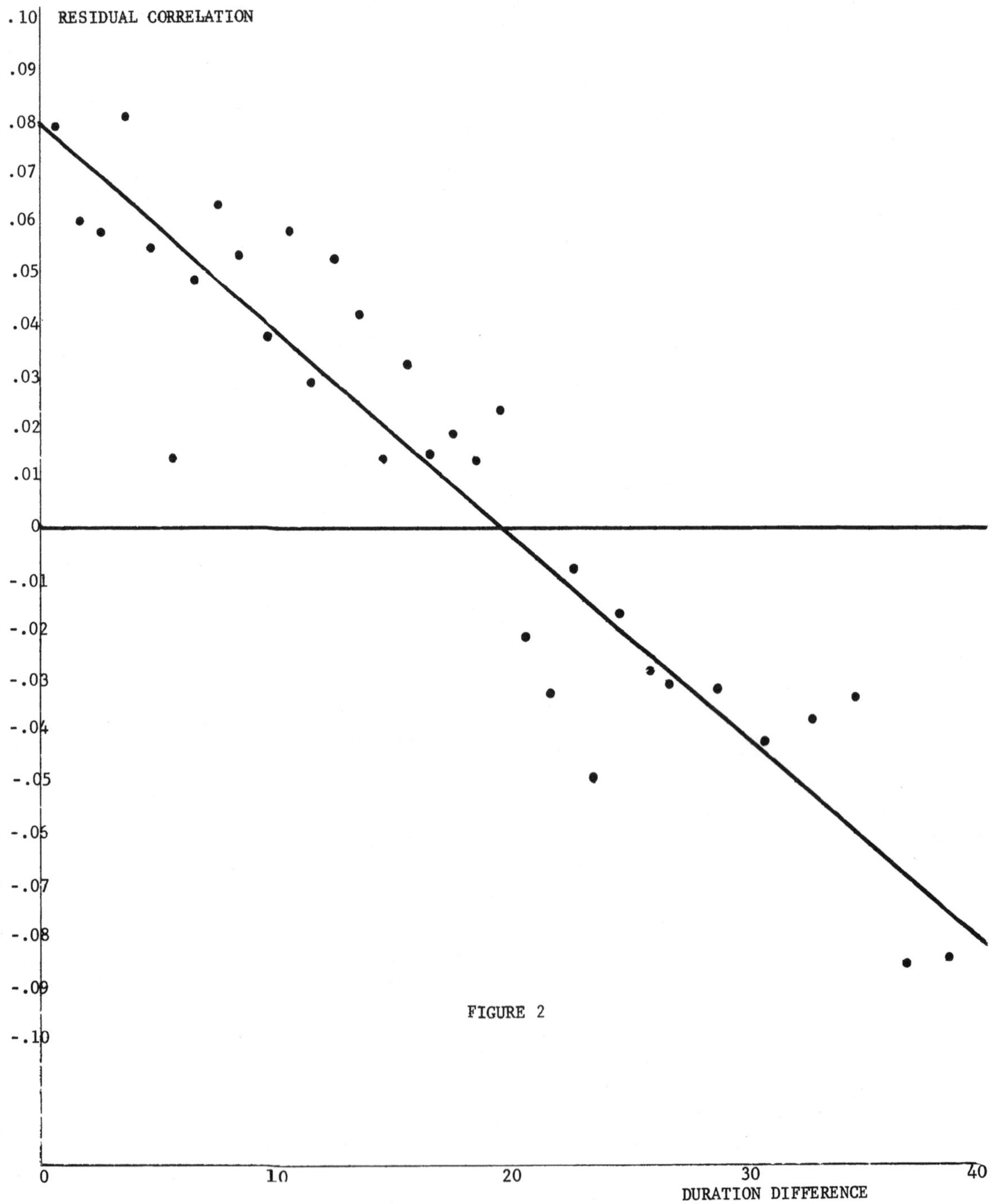
RESIDUAL CORRELATION
.10
.09
.08
.07
.06
.05
.04
.03
.02
.01
0
-.01
-.02
-.03
-.04
-.05
-.06
-.07
-.08
-.09
-.10
0
10
20
30
40
DURATION DIFFERENCE

FIGURE 2

V. Summary

In general, security returns are affected by changes in market-wide discount rates and by changes in certainty-equivalent cash flows. Roughly speaking, "normal shifts" in the term structure of discount rates contribute to market risk, while "swings" ("abnormal shifts") contribute to extra-market (residual) covariances. Securities whose cash flows are "centered" in nearby time periods tend to move together over and above any common response to the overall market. Securities whose cash flows are centered very far apart tend to move differently aside from market effects. The traditional concept of duration, which provides a measure of the central tendency of cash flows, can help predict such relationships. *Ceteris Paribus*, the greater the difference between two securities' durations, the smaller will be the correlation of their residual (extra-market) returns.

Interest rate risk is, of course, only part of the relevant risk for common stocks. Certainty-equivalent cash flows also change, and the sources of such changes can usefully be broken into market-wide, extra-market, and unique components. Moreover, cash flows may also be characterized as having a term structure with "normal shifts" and "swings." The theory presented here does not deal explicitly with such phenomena, but there is reason to believe that our empirical procedures capture reactions to both changes in discount rates and changes in certainty-equivalent cash flows. This does not lessen the importance of the finding that residual correlation is related to duration difference. But it suggests the need to extend the model to one including a wider range of sources of risk.

[1] Bierwag, G. O.; George G. Kaufman; and Chulsoon Khang. "Immunization Strategies and the Implications." The Center for Capital Market Research, University of Oregon (1978).

[2] Boquist, John A.; George A. Racette; and Gary G. Schlarbaum. "Duration and Risk Assessment for Bonds and Common Stocks." *Journal of Finance* (December 1975).

[3] Farrell, James L., Jr. "Analyzing Covariation of Returns to Determine Homogeneous Stock Groupings." *Journal of Business* (April 1974).

[4] Fisher, Lawrence, and Roman L. Weil. "Coping with the Risk of Interest Rate Fluctuations: Returns to Bondholders from Naive and Optimal Strategies." *Journal of Business* (October 1971).

[5] Goodman, Laurie, and William F. Sharpe. "Perspective on Bank Capital Adequacy: A Time Series Analysis." Working Paper, No. 247, National Bureau of Economic Research (May 1978).

[6] Ingersoll, Jonathan E., Jr.; Jeffrey Skelton; and Roman L. Weil. "Duration Forty Years Later." Graduate School of Business, University of Chicago (April 1978).

[7] King, Benjamin F. "Market and Industry Factors in Stock Price Behavior." *The Journal of Business* (January 1966).

[8] Klemkosky, Robert C., and John D. Martin. "The Effect of Market Risk on Portfolio Diversification." *Journal of Finance* (March 1975).

[9] Kaufman, George. "Duration, Planning Period, and Tests of the Capital Asset Pricing Model." Paper presented at the Eastern Finance Association Meeting (April 1978).

[10] Livingston, Miles. "Duration and Risk Assessment for Bonds and Common Stocks: A Note." *Journal of Finance* (March 1978).

[11] MacAulay, F. R. *Some Theoretical Problems Suggested by the Movements of Interest Rates, Bond Yields, and Stock Prices in the U.S. since 1856.* New York: National Bureau of Economic Research (1938).

[12] Oldfield, George S., Jr., and Richard S. Bower. "Returns on Government Securities." Unpublished Manuscript (August 1976).

[13] Oldfield, George S., Jr. "The Behavior of Default Free Spot Discount Rates." Paper presented at the Institute for Quantitative Research in Finance (April 1978).

[14] Rosenberg, Barr, and Vinay Marathe. "Common Factors in Security Returns: Microeconomic Determinants and Macroeconomic Correlates." University of California Berkeley Research Program in Finance Working Paper No. 44 (May 1976).

[15] Sharpe, William F. *Investments.* Englewood Cliffs, N.J.: Prentice-Hall (1978).

[16] Wells Fargo Investment Advisors. *Security Market Line Report.*

Factors in New York Stock Exchange security returns, 1931-1979*

The analysis calls into question naive applications of the Capital Asset Pricing Model.

William F. Sharpe

In some months, high-yield ("value"?) stocks seem to do better than low-yield ("growth"?) stocks. In other months, the opposite situation seems to occur. Occasionally there seems to be no difference.

FACTOR MODELS

Figure 1 illustrates one way of providing substance for such statements. Each point represents one security. On the horizontal axis is a measure of yield.[1] On the vertical axis is the excess return (i.e. the return over and above a riskless rate) of the security in the following month.[2]

FIGURE 1

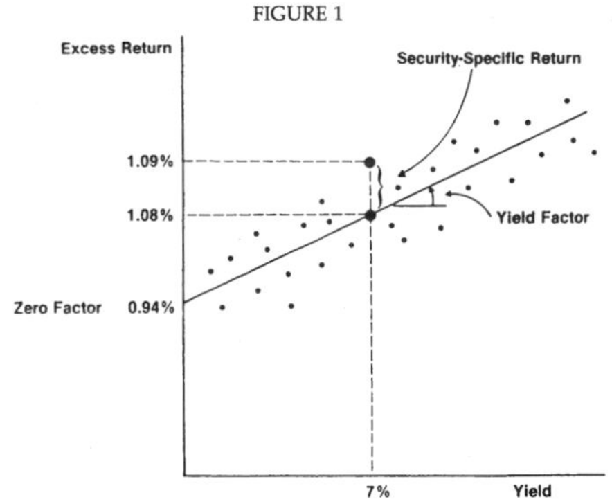

* An early version of this paper was presented at the Financial Analysts' Federation workshop at Princeton University in July 1981. Comments and suggestions from Peter Bernstein, Michael Gibbons, Robert Litzenberger, and Krishna Ramaswamy are gratefully acknowledged. This research was supported in part by the Stanford Program in Finance.

1. Footnotes appear at the end of the article.

In Figure 1, yield is an *attribute* of each security. The regression line fit to the data is an *ex post security market line* indicating the general relationship between this attribute and return over a subsequent period. We can describe the relationship as follows:

$$R_{it} - r_t = 1\,F_{zt} + b_{i1t}F_{1t} + e_{it}, \quad (1)$$

where:

R_{it} = the return on security i in period t;

r_t = the riskless interest rate for period t;

F_{zt} = the "zero" *factor* for period t;

b_{i1t} = the first *attribute* (here, yield) of security i at the beginning of period t;

F_{1t} = the first *factor* (here, the yield factor) for period t, and

e_{it} = security i's *security-specific* return in period t.

In Figure 1 the "zero" factor is .94% per month. This is the return on a "typical" security with zero yield. The "yield factor" is .02% per month. This indicates that, "in general," higher yield securities outperformed lower yield securities during the month, with (for example) the typical 4% yield stock outperforming the typical 3% yield stock by .02%. For the security plotted at point i, e_{it} was .01%: The stock's excess return was higher (by .01%) than the 1.08% "typical" for securities with its yield (b_{i1t}) of 7%.

In effect, Figure 1 and equation 1 *attribute* each security's excess return in each period to three elements:

$1\,F_{zt}$: an effect common to all securities,

$b_{i1t}F_{1t}$: an effect that differs among securities, depending on their yields, and

e_{it}: an effect specific to each security.

Two statistics associated with regression analysis provide added information.

The *t-statistic* for factor 1 (the yield factor) indicates the *significance* of the value: The larger its (absolute) value, the more likely the relationship is "real." Assume, for example, that there was no "true" relationship between yield and excess return during the period in question. By chance a majority of securities with high yields might have had positive "true" security-specific returns, and a majority of those with low yields might have had negative "true" security-specific returns. The regression analysis would thus produce an erroneous positive yield factor with a t value that could, by chance, be large. A rough rule of thumb holds that a t value with an absolute value greater than 2.0 will obtain in roughly 5% of the months in which there is no "true" relationship.

The other statistic of interest is the *R-squared* of the regression. This indicates the proportion of the variance in security returns attributed to the factors. The smaller the scatter of points around the line, the greater the R-squared.

Yield is, of course, only one attribute of a security that may be related to return. In some months, stocks of large companies seem to outperform those of small companies; in other months, the opposite seems to occur. While we could investigate this relationship by repeating the procedure illustrated in Figure 1 with some measure of size on the horizontal axis, this has some drawbacks: Larger firms tend to provide higher dividends. Thus an investigation of yield alone (as in Figure 1) may attribute to yield some effects related to size, while an investigation of size alone may attribute to size some effects related to yield.

A better procedure uses *multiple regression.* Figure 2 provides an illustration. Each point represents a security, plotting both its attributes (b_{i1t} = yield and b_{i2t} = size) and its subsequent excess return. Regression analysis is used to fit an *ex post security market plane.* Its slope in the yield direction is the *yield factor* (F_{1t}), and its slope in the size direction is the *size factor* (F_{2t}). The intercept (the *zero factor*) indicates the return on a hypothetical security with zero yield *and* zero size. The distance of a security's point from the plane indicates its *security-specific return* (e_{it}), i.e. the portion not attributed to either the yield effect or the size effect.

The equation of the plane in Figure 2 can be written as:

$$R_{it} - r_t = 1\,F_{zt} + b_{i1t}F_{1t} + b_{i2t}F_{2t} + e_{it}. \quad (2)$$

Multiple regression analysis produces t-statistics for each of the factors (which can be interpreted as before) and an R-squared value for the entire regression, indicating the proportion of the variance among security returns in the period that can be attributed to (all) the factors.

FIGURE 2

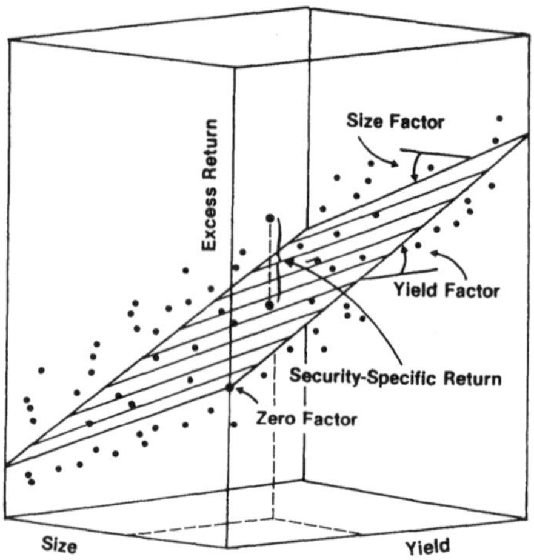

To extend the approach to more than two factors requires the abandonment of diagrams. Nevertheless, the concepts are the same. In effect, we fit an *ex post security market hyperplane* (the generalization of a plane) to the data using multiple regression analysis. If there are m attributes the equation can be written as:

$$R_{it} - r_t = 1F_{zt} + b_{i1t}F_{1t} + b_{i2t}F_{2t} + \dots + b_{imt}F_{mt} + e_{it}. \quad (3)$$

USES OF FACTOR MODELS

We can use a factor model for attribution of *ex post* portfolio performance. If X_{ipt} represents the proportion of portfolio p invested in security i at the beginning of period t, the return on the portfolio will be:

$$R_{pt} = X_{1pt}R_{1t} + X_{2pt}R_{2t} + \dots + X_{npt}R_{nt}, \quad (4)$$

where n = the number of securities.

A little manipulation of equations (3) and (4) provides a formula for breaking the return on a portfolio into components:

$$R_{pt} = r_t + 1\,F_{zt} + b_{p1t}F_{1t} + b_{p2t}F_{2t} + \dots + b_{pmt}F_{mt}$$
$$+ (X_{1pt}e_{1t} + X_{2pt}e_{2t} + \dots + X_{npt}e_{nt}), \quad (5a)$$

$$\text{where: } b_{pjt} = X_{1pt}b_{1jt} + X_{2pt}b_{2jt} + \dots + X_{npt}b_{njt}. \quad (5b)$$

As indicated in (5b), each attribute of the portfolio (b_{pjt}) equals a weighted average of the corresponding values of the attribute for the securities in the portfolio, using the values of portfolio holdings as weights.

The terms in parentheses in (5a) represent the

effects of security-specific returns; each depends on the joint effect of the amount held (X_{ipt}) and the performance of the security *per se* (e_{it}). The terms not in parentheses represent the effects of factors. The first (r_t) is the riskless rate and the second ($1\ F_{zt}$) an effect common to all securities. Each of the remaining terms involves the joint effect of an attribute of the portfolio (b_{pjt}) and the performance of the associated factor (F_{jt}).

Another use of factor models involves the comparison of two portfolios (e.g. an active portfolio and an index or an active portfolio and a "normal" set of holdings). Letting *q* represent a second portfolio, one can write an equation corresponding to (5a) for portfolio q, then subtract it from (5a) to get:

$$R_{pt} - R_{qt} = (b_{p1t} - b_{q1t})F_{1t} + (b_{p2t} - b_{q2t})F_{2t} + \ldots + (b_{pmt} - b_{qmt})F_{mt} + (X_{1pt} - X_{1qt})e_{1t} + (X_{2pt} - X_{2qt})e_{2t} + \ldots + (X_{npt} - X_{nqt})e_{nt}. \quad (6)$$

In this case the *difference* between the returns on the portfolios is broken into components. Each of the initial m terms indicates the joint effect of the *difference* in the portfolios' attributes ($b_{pjt} - b_{qjt}$) and the performance of the related factor (F_{jt}). Each of the last n terms indicates the joint effect of the *difference* in the portfolios' holdings of a security ($X_{ipt} - X_{iqt}$) and its security-specific return (e_{it}).

Performance attribution is *ex post* in nature — it deals with the past. For decision-making one is concerned with *ex ante* values — values that will be realized in the future but must be predicted now. We can use factor models for predictive purposes as well.

One application concerns *expected values*. For example, does one expect high-yield stocks to outperform low-yield stocks, and if so, by how much (i.e. what is the expected value of the yield factor)? Does one expect General Motors to do especially well (i.e. what is the expected value of its security-specific return)?

An investment organization with a "bottom-up" approach might produce estimates of expected returns for each of many securities (perhaps using a dividend discount model). They can then use these *ex ante* expected returns in a multiple regression analysis (instead of *ex post* actual returns) to find implicit expected values for the various factors. After review, the firm might change some of the values (i.e. employ a bit of "top-down" decision-making).

A firm with a totally top-down approach might make estimates of expected factor values directly, with security analysts focusing on security-specific return (e.g. making *conditional* forecasts). Whatever procedure is employed, the goal is to estimate the *expected* position of the security market hyperplane and the *expected* distances of the points from it.

Expected values are, however, only part of the story. The actual hyperplane will undoubtedly turn out to be somewhere other than in its expected position, and at least some of the points will be in positions relative to it that are different from the expected ones. One thus needs to estimate the likely range within which the hyperplane might lie and the likely range within which each security-specific return might fall. Such estimates constitute a *risk model*. The needed ingredients are:

1. a measure of risk for each factor,
2. measures of the extent to which each factor is likely to move with each of the other factors, and
3. a measure of security-specific risk for each security.[3]

In practice, estimates of this type are usually obtained by assuming that *variations* around *average* values in the *past* provide good estimates concerning *risk* relative to *expected values* in the *future*. This is indeed an heroic assumption. In fact, it is difficult to defend the common practice of primary reliance on judgment for estimating expected values and the almost exclusive reliance on econometric analysis of past data to estimate components of risk, since risk and expected return are simply two summary descriptions of a (subjective) probability distribution. In time, both judgmental and econometric inputs will undoubtedly be employed for both purposes.

CALCULATING THE FACTOR MODEL

How many factors affect security returns? How can they be identified? One approach (factor analysis) relies solely on historic security returns to answer these questions. Present practice uses other information to *preselect* a set of attributes and the associated attribute values for securities. Whatever method is used, the goal is to obtain a model that will prove helpful for making the *predictions* needed for investment decisions.

We do not attempt to answer the difficult questions concerning selection of attributes and factors. Our goal is much more modest. We provide historic data over a long period for a model intended to be as similar as possible to those currently provided by consultants[4] and used by a number of investment organizations.

We follow standard practice by selecting a list of attributes (more or less *ex cathedra*) and then fitting an *ex post* security market hyperplane[5] for each of many months. A check on our selection of attributes is provided by the t-statistics. If a factor is significantly different from zero (i.e. the absolute value of the associated t-statistic exceeds 2.0), then in substantially more than 5% of the months we have at least some evidence that its inclusion in the model is desirable. As will be shown, all of our factors pass this test.

Since we compute a value for each factor for each of many months, it is a simple matter to compute the *average* value of a factor over the period examined, as well as its *variation* around that average over time.[6]

Commercial services typically employ a few "common factors" and a number of "industry factors." Moreover, a common factor may be related to a *composite attribute* that is, in turn, a function of a number of (simple) attributes. Models of this type have been fitted to data only from the last two or three decades, since the required detailed information is not available in appropriate form for earlier years.

Our goal is to provide a long view reaching back several decades. This requires a more parsimonious model.[7] Accordingly, we employ five simple "common" attributes and eight attributes representing "sectors" of the economy. There is an intentional correspondence between our common factors and those of presently-available commercial services, but it is, of necessity, less than perfect.[8]

TABLE 1

Attributes as of Dec. 1979
(1325 NYSE Stocks)

Attribute	Mean	Std. Dev.
Beta	1.336	0.555
Yield	4.781	3.204
Size	−0.698	0.653
Bond beta	1.323	0.686
Alpha	0.819	1.112

Attributes

Dividend *yield* is the first of the attributes. It is simply the prior twelve months' dividends paid common stockholders divided by the market value at the end of the prior month (expressed as percent yield per year).

The second attribute measures *size*. The value used is the logarithm (to base 10) of the market value (in billions of dollars) of the firm's equity at the end of the prior month. Thus a firm with $1 billion of equity has a "size" of 0, one with $10 billion a size of 1, one with $100 billion a size of 2, etc., while one with a $100 million has a size of −1 and one with $10 million a size of −2. This measure was adopted because returns correlate more closely with it than with the market value of equity *per se*.[9]

TABLE 2

Sectors as of Dec. 1979
(1325 NYSE Stocks)

Sector	% of Stocks	% of Value
Basic Industries	9.97	9.34
Capital Goods	14.26	13.06
Construction	4.45	1.84
Consumer Goods	35.93	29.96
Energy	3.62	21.09
Finance	14.79	7.31
Transportation	5.66	3.47
Utilities	11.32	13.93

The remaining measures concern past performance. Following common practice, we regress the excess returns on a stock over the prior sixty months on those of Standard and Poor's stock index. The slope is the security's historic *beta* value; the intercept is its historic *alpha* value. Roughly, securities with high beta values were "aggressive" in the past, while those with low beta values were "defensive." Those with positive alpha values did well ("market-adjusted") and those with negative alpha values did poorly ("market-adjusted"). Alpha is measured in units of percent return per month.

The final attribute is obtained by regressing the excess returns on a stock over the prior sixty months on the excess returns on long-term government bond returns.[10] The slope coefficient is the security's historic *bond beta*. Roughly, securities with high bond betas were "bond-like" — due perhaps to the nature of their assets — while those with low bond betas were less "bond-like." Securities with negative bond betas tended to move counter to bonds in the past, perhaps because the firms had large amounts of financial leverage.

Significance of the Attributes

Are our attributes really relevant? Are security returns related to them often enough to warrant their examination (and prediction)? Tables 3 and 4 provide

TABLE 3

Percent of Months in Which a Common Factor Was Significant
[absolute value of t-statistic > 2]
1931-1979

Factor	% of Months
Beta	58.3
Yield	39.5
Size	56.5
Bond Beta	28.2
Alpha	43.5

TABLE 4

Percent of Months in Which a Sector was Significantly
Different from All Other Sectors
[absolute value of t-statistic > 2]
1931-1979

Sector	% of Months
Basic Industries	32.5
Capital Goods	18.7
Construction	15.3
Consumer Goods	39.3
Energy	36.9
Finance	16.3
Transportation	43.9
Utilities	35.0

some evidence. As described earlier, we would expect a truly irrelevant attribute to produce a t-statistic with an absolute value greater than 2.0 in about 5% of the 588 months. Every one of our attributes did so more often. While this is not a formal test, it provides presumptive evidence for including all our attributes in the analysis.[13]

Table 5 provides an indication of the extent to which the attributes "explain" the variance among security returns. As indicated earlier, when a factor model is fitted to the returns for a month, the resulting R-squared value indicates the proportion of variance in security returns attributed to the associated factors. For our model, this was done 588 times. The *average* of the 588 R-squared values obtained in this manner was .104, as shown at the bottom of Table 5. In a typical month, about 10% of the variation in returns on *individual* securities could be attributed to our factors. While this may seem discouraging,[14] recall that security-specific returns are much less important for *portfolios* than for individual securities, and that a much higher R-squared value would typically be obtained if we were analyzing a group of diverse portfolios.

TABLE 5

Average Cross-Section Fits of Models
588 Months, 1931-1979

Model	Average R^2	Diff.
Beta	.037	
		.042
Common Factors	.079	
		.025
Common and Sector Factors	.104	

Table 5 also reports results obtained with two other models. The first uses only one attribute — historic beta. As shown, it explained only about one-third of the variance explained by the full model. The second approach used all five common attributes, but no sector information. The four additional attributes collectively added 4.2% to the 3.7% explained by beta alone. The eight sector attributes added another 2.5%. Historic beta is clearly an important attribute, but it is not the only one worth considering.[15]

Regression Procedures

All the results presented thus far were based on monthly regressions, with each security given equal weight. This was done to insure that the tests of significance and explanatory power would be difficult to pass. Both theory and practice show that better estimates can be obtained if relatively more attention is paid to data less likely to be subject to error.

For the remainder of the paper, we report results using a simple procedure similar to that employed by some of the commercial services. As described earlier, for each month a regression of the excess returns on a security over the prior sixty months on those of Standard and Poor's stock index was performed. The *standard error* of this regression measures the scatter of points around the resulting regression line — this is often termed the security's historic "non-market risk." The larger this value, the more likely it is that a security's return will reflect security-specific returns rather than factor effects. In the regressions designed to estimate factor effects, it makes sense to pay more attention to securities with less non-market risk. To do this, we weight each security by the reciprocal of this measure of historic non-market risk.[16]

Table 6 reports one set of results based on this procedure. For each month, the excess return on a stock can be broken into two parts — that attributed to the factors and that not so attributed (i.e. the security-specific return). Over the course of many months the excess return on the security will vary, and that variance can be compared with the variance of the two components. For example, if the variance of a stock's security-specific returns is 60% as great as the variance of its overall excess return, we say that the chosen factors "explained" 40% of the variance in the stock's excess return.[17]

TABLE 6

Average Time-Series Fit of Models
2197 stocks, 1931-1979

Model	Average R^2	Diff.
All Beta = 1	.250	
		.089
Beta	.339	
		.043
Common Factors	.382	
		.021
Common and Sector Factors	.403	

The percent of variance of returns explained by factors varied from security to security. In all, 2,197 securities entered the analysis at various times from 1931 through 1979.[18] Table 6 shows average values for the 2,197 stocks.

It is important to emphasize the difference between Tables 5 and 6. The former averages the results of cross-section analyses over 588 months, while the latter averages the results of time-series analyses over 2,197 stocks. Thus, Table 5 indicates the extent to which differences *among* stocks are explained in a "typical" month, while Table 6 indicates the extent to which we can explain differences in the returns of a "typical" stock *over time.*

The bottom line in Table 6 indicates that we can attribute about 40% of the variance in return for the typical stock to our factors. The other lines report results for other factor models. A model using only historic beta explained about 34% of the average variance in return, while one with all five common factors explained about 38%.

The first line in the table reports results for a model in which each security was assigned a beta of 1.0.[19] As shown, the performance of the overall stock market is important, although differences in security attributes are well worth attention.

These values are larger than those in Table 5 and comparable values for most portfolios would typically be larger still.[20]

FACTOR PERFORMANCE

Table 7 provides summary data concerning the

TABLE 7

Annualized Values
588 Months: 1931-1979

Factor	Avg.	Std. Dev.
SP500 ER	8.295	20.969
LT Govt ER	0.518	5.760
Beta	5.355	18.376
Yield	0.237	1.043
Size	−5.563	7.804
Bond Beta	−0.118	2.719
Alpha	−2.001	4.639
Basic Industries	1.653	7.974
Capital Goods	0.155	5.720
Construction	−1.589	8.862
Consumer Goods	−0.180	5.173
Energy	6.282	11.042
Finance	−1.478	5.247
Transportation	−0.570	9.492
Utilities	−2.622	9.425

performance of the factors over time. In this case, each of the 588 months was given equal weight. The first column indicates the average value for a factor, the second its standard deviation over time. For comparison, two additional rows are included. The first summarizes the excess returns on Standard and Poor's stock index, the second the excess returns on long-term government bonds. For ease in interpretation the values in Table 7 are stated in terms of annualized monthly returns.[21]

As Table 7 shows, stocks outperformed Treasury bills by about 8.3% per year ("ER" means "excess returns"), but with considerable variability: The standard deviation was about 21% per year. Long-term government bonds outperformed Treasury bills by a much smaller amount, but with less variability.

Stocks with high historic betas outperformed those with low historic betas on average. Thus, stocks with betas of, say, 1.5 outperformed by over 5% per year other stocks similar in other respects but with betas of .5 — but not every year, as the standard deviation was over 18%.

High-yield stocks outperformed low-yield stocks by almost 24 basis points per year for each 1% difference in dividend yield. Nevertheless, the variability was substantial, with a standard deviation of over 100 basis points per year.

Large stocks underperformed smaller ones by a substantial amount. For each unit increase in size (i.e. ten-fold increase in market value of equity) average performance declined by 5.6% per year! While there was some variability — the standard deviation was 7.8% per year — the size factor was clearly negative most of the time.

The bond beta factor was relatively small and variable, but less important than the stock beta factor.

The alpha factor was negative on average, indicating that stocks with good historic non-market performance tended to do poorly (i.e. suffered a "reversal").[22] A portfolio of stocks with historic alphas of 1% per month might have underperformed, by about 2% per year on average, a portfolio similar in other respects but holding stocks with alphas of zero but with a standard deviation of more than 4%.

The sector factors indicate that, on average, energy stocks did especially well relative to the average sector (over 6% per year), and utility stocks did rather poorly (−2.6% per year). Although the energy sector factor showed the greatest variability, given the large average value, this sector clearly outperformed the average sector in most months.

Table 7 provides only one view of the data. To probe more deeply we need a method for displaying the behavior of a factor over time. To do so, we use the idea of the cumulative profit on a "factor play."

Figure 3 illustrates the procedure. Imagine that at the end of December 1930, one had purchased $1 worth of Standard and Poor's stock index and taken a short position in Treasury bills. At the end of January 1931, imagine that the long position outperformed the short position by $.02. The *cumulative profit* (undiscounted) would be $.02. Now imagine that, at the end of January 1931, the position was re-established, with $1 again invested in a long position in Standard and Poor's Index and a $1 short position taken in Treasury bills. Imagine that, at the end of February 1931, the long position underperformed the short position by $.05. The profit for the month would be −$.05 and the cumulative profit −$.03 (= $.02 − $.05).

Figure 3 shows the cumulative profit, month by month, for such a strategy with monthly adjustments in holdings. The curve goes up when Standard and Poor's index outperformed Treasury bills and goes down when Standard and Poor's index underperformed Treasury bills. Moreover, a given vertical distance represents the same magnitude in terms of the difference in returns, since the positions are revised to

FIGURE 3

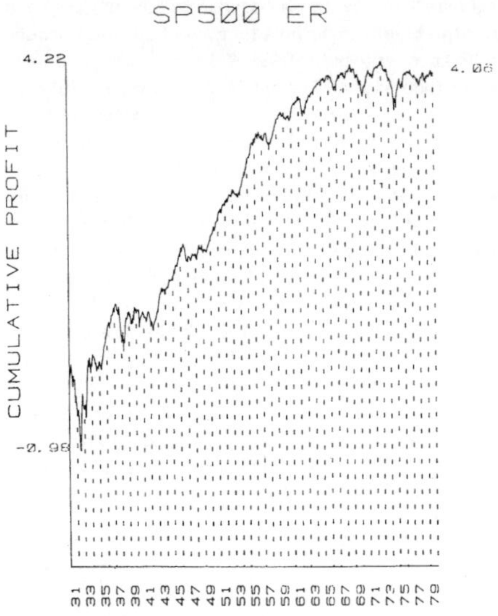

FIGURE 4

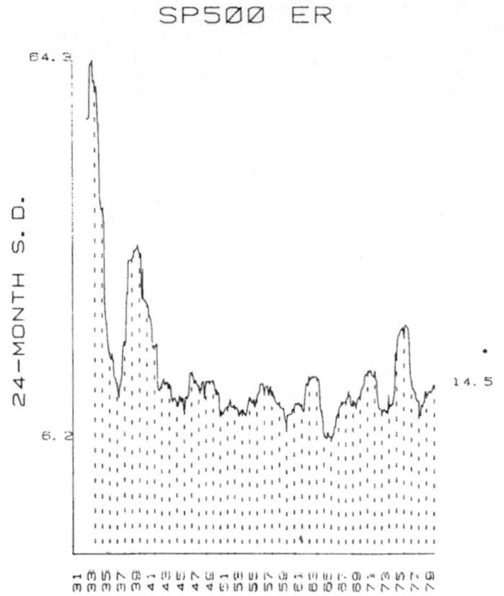

be worth $1 each month. Thus the greater the slope of the curve, the greater the average difference: The greater the variability around a trend, the greater the variability of the difference in the two returns around the average.

One can easily assess the nature of average returns in a graph such as the one shown in Figure 3. In this case the flattening out in the last two decades is depressingly obvious. Nevertheless, another representation is helpful to analyze changes in variability. Figure 4 plots the standard deviation of the difference in returns for the 24-month period from January 1931 through December 1932, then the standard deviation for the 24-month period from February 1931 through January 1933, etc. While the use of a 24-month "window" is arbitrary, the graph shows clearly that the stock market has been less variable in the last 40 years than it was in the 1930's.[23] A value-weighted index of all stocks on the New York Stock Exchange would show results close to those based on Standard and Poor's index.[24]

To display data efficiently, the figures have been scaled differently, so that vertical distances are not directly comparable from graph to graph. The range of values is shown on the left of each diagram and the ending value on the right to facilitate comparison.

Figures 5 and 6 are based on the difference between returns on long-term government bonds and those on Treasury bills. As Figure 5 shows, the first and second halves of the period were different, with government bonds outperforming Treasury bills during much of the former period and underperforming them during much of the latter period. As Figure 6 shows, bond returns have also become more variable (not less, as have stock returns) over time.

FIGURE 5

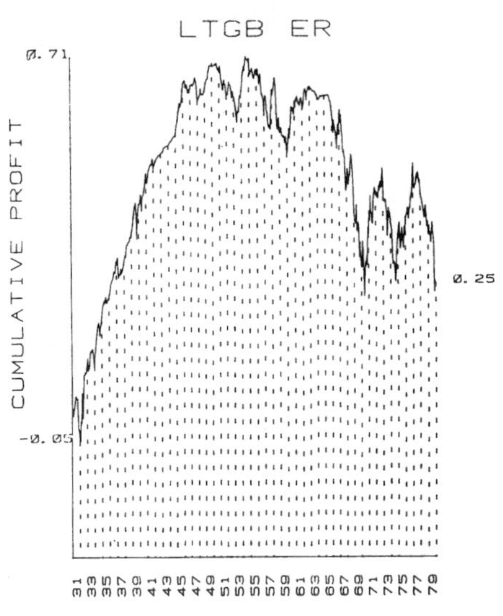

FIGURE 6

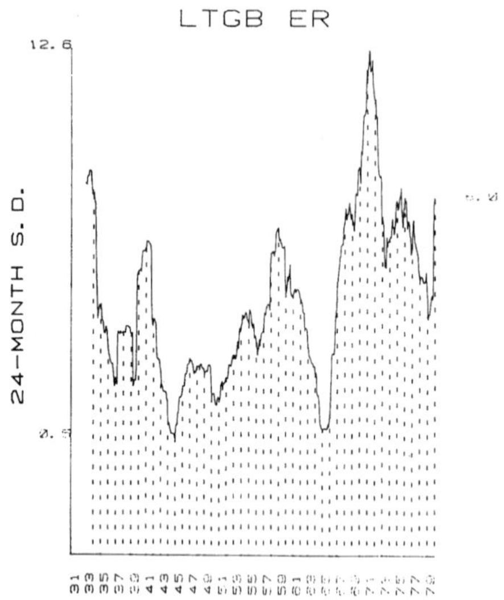

Figure 7 depicts the behavior of the beta factor. It is merely the cumulative value of the monthly factors; thus, the curve goes up in months when high-beta stocks outperformed low-beta stocks and down in months when high-beta stocks underperformed low-beta stocks. This graph can also be given a portfolio interpretation. Imagine a long position in a portfolio with an average beta of, say, 1.5 and a short position in a portfolio with an average beta of, say, .5, with each position worth $1. Assume that we construct these portfolios so that they are alike in all other attributes and that each is highly diversified.[25] The profit from such a strategy would be very close to the beta factor for the month. By re-adjusting the position each month, we could obtain a cumulative profit very close to that shown in Figure 7. A similar interpretation can be given for each of the other factors.

Not surprisingly Figure 7 bears a resemblance to Figure 3 — when the market went up, stocks with high historic betas tended to outperform those with low historic betas. The correlation between the beta factor and the excess return on Standard and Poor's stock index was in fact .814 over the period. This indicates that historic beta is a useful predictor of future beta. But it can be improved upon, as will be shown.

As Figure 8 shows, the pattern of the variability of the beta factor is similar to that of Standard and Poor's stock index.

Figures 9 and 10 provide information about the yield factor. As shown, high-yield stocks outperformed low-yield stocks on average, but there were extended periods during which they did not.

FIGURE 7

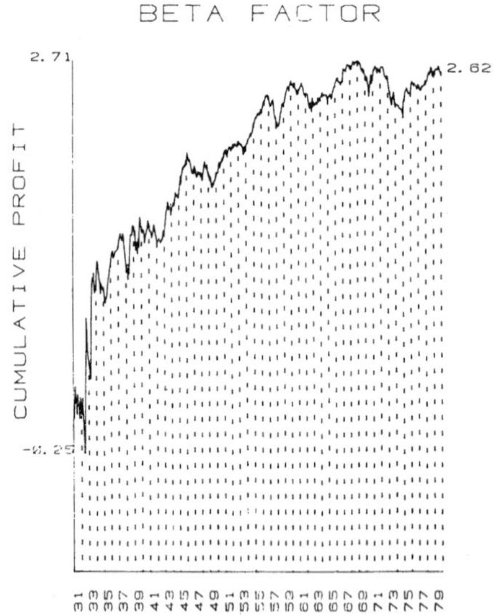

FIGURE 8

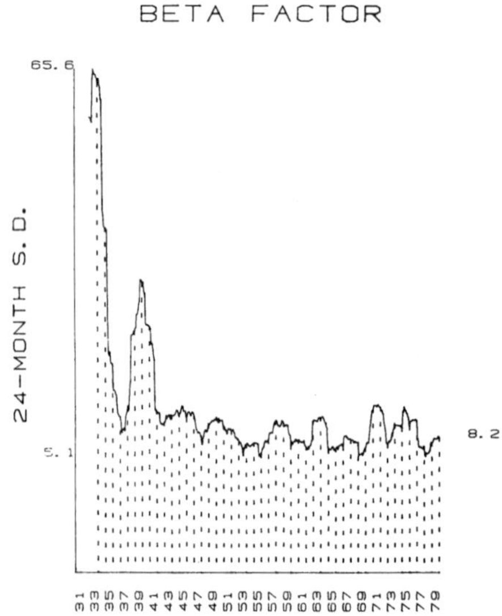

FIGURE 9

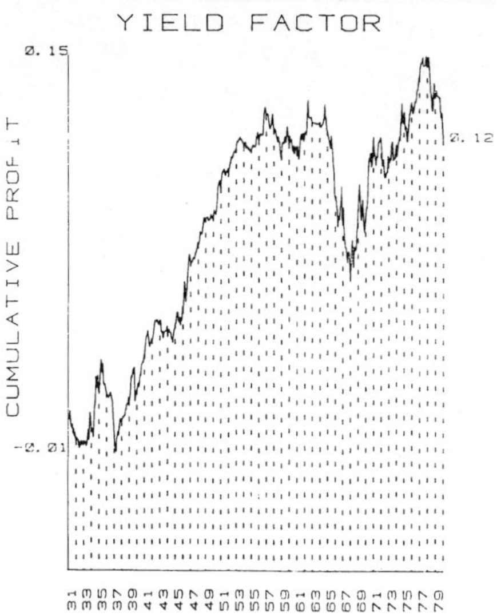

FIGURE 10

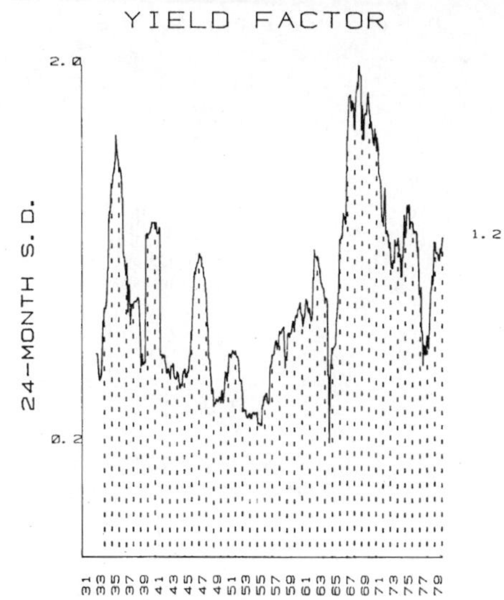

FIGURE 11

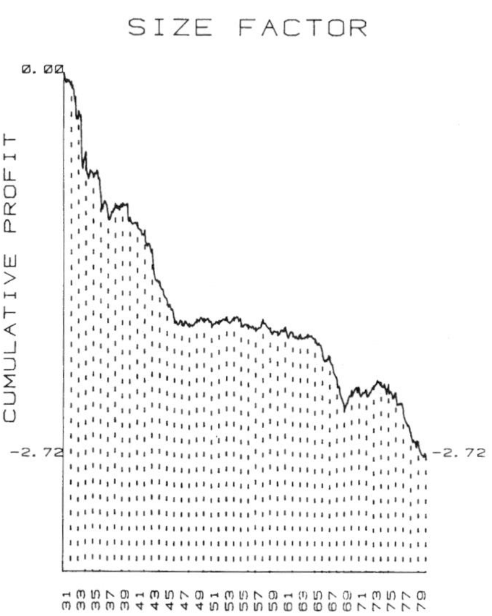

FIGURE 12

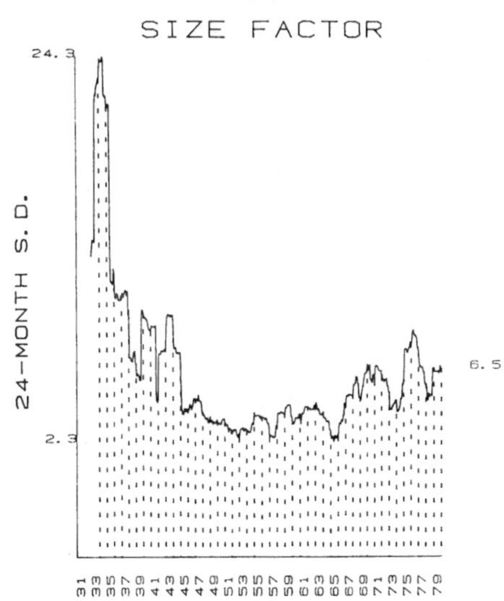

Figure 11 shows that the size factor has been negative most of the time. Moreover, the magnitudes are very large. Figure 12 shows the pattern of its variability.

Figures 13 and 14 show results for the bond beta factor. It is correlated with the excess return on government bonds, but not highly (the correlation coefficient was .154). Moreover, the magnitudes are relatively small.

FIGURE 13

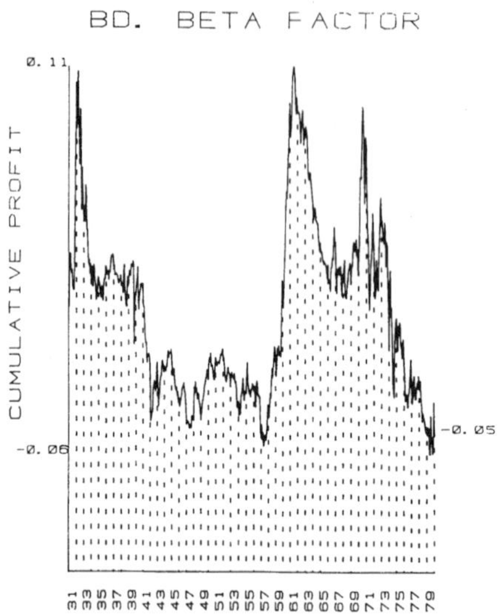

FIGURE 14

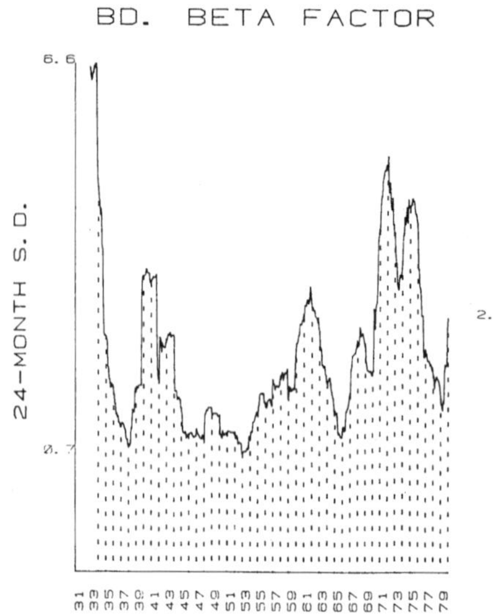

FIGURE 15

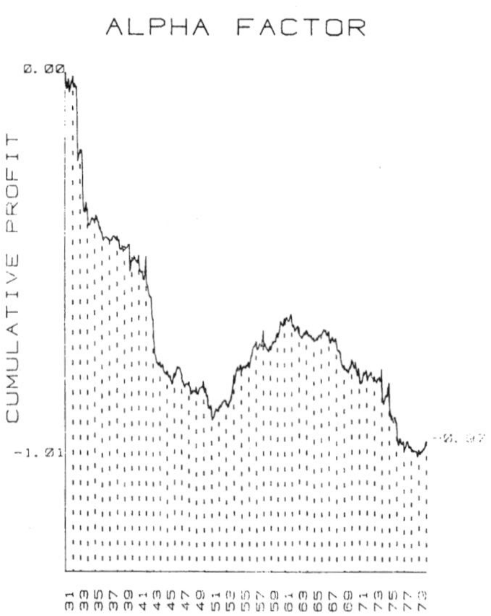

FIGURE 16

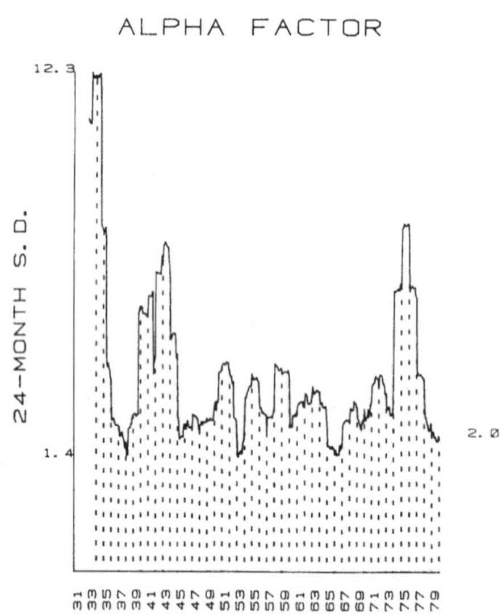

Figures 15 and 16 provide information about the alpha factor. Other things equal, an investor holding stocks with poor historic non-market performance would have done well overall except during the 1950's.

The remainder of the diagrams concern the sector factors (to save space, only the cumulative profit diagrams are shown). These results can also be given a portfolio interpretation. In this case, the strategy

FIGURE 17

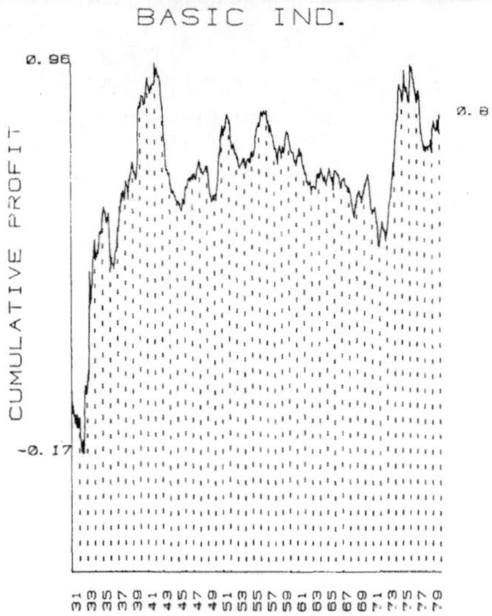

FIGURE 18

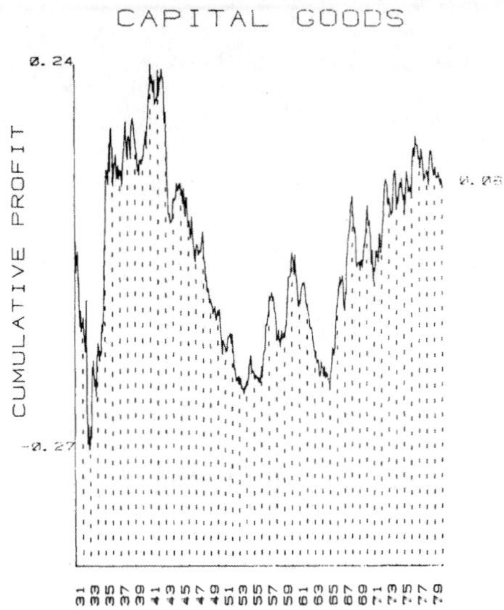

FIGURE 19

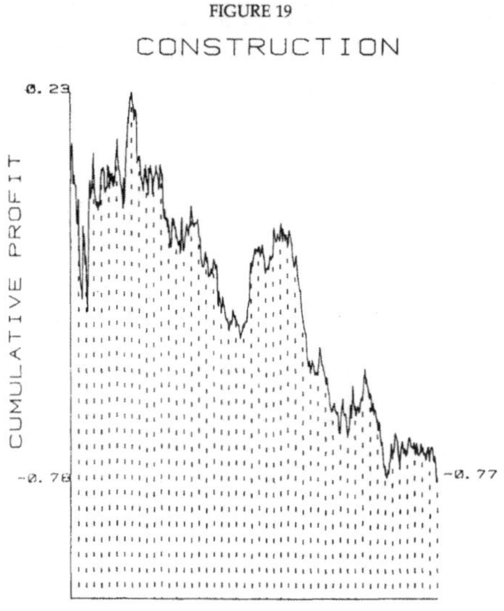

FIGURE 20

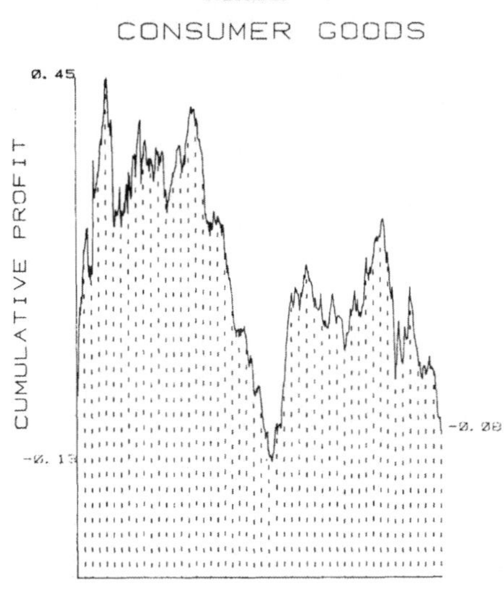

would involve a long portfolio of stocks in the sector in question and a short portfolio of stocks diversified across all sectors, with all other attributes equal in the two portfolios.

By far the most dramatic of these diagrams is that shown in Figure 21 for the energy sector. Not only is the magnitude large, but the graph is upward-sloping in most months.

FIGURE 21

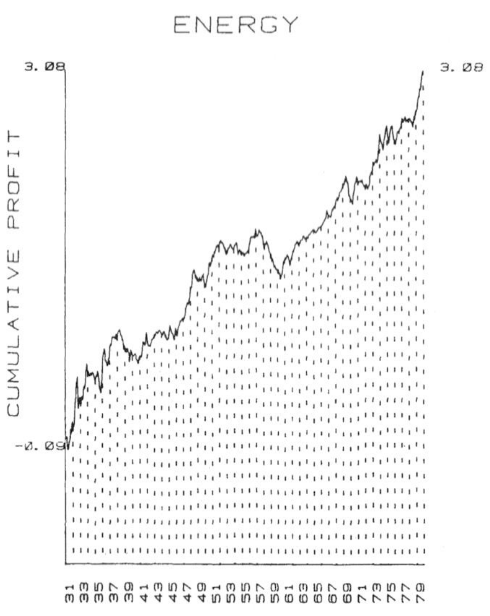

FIGURE 22

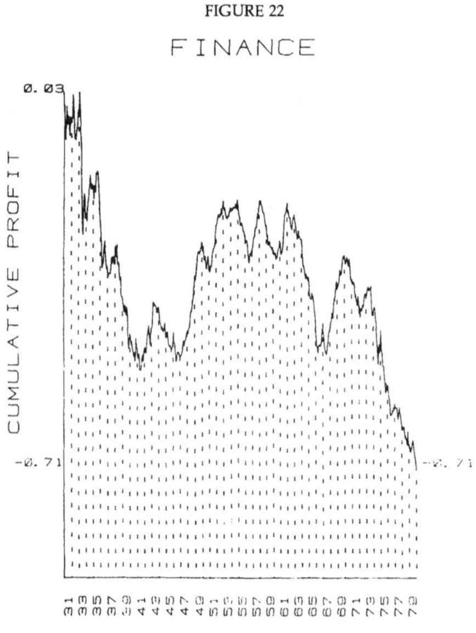

16 SUMMER 1982

PREDICTING FUTURE BETA

The correlation between the beta factor and the excess return on Standard and Poor's stock index shows that "future beta" is definitely related to historic beta. With a factor model, however, one can go further. In fact, equation (3) implies directly that:

$$\beta(R_{it}) = \beta(F_{zt}) + b_{i1t}\beta(F_{1t}) + b_{i2t}\beta(F_{2t}) + \ldots + b_{imt}\beta(F_{mt}) + \beta(e_{it}),$$

where (x) = the beta of x relative to some selected base (e.g. Standard and Poor's stock index). If the portfolio used as a base is well diversified, the betas of the security-specific returns will be very small. Thus:

$$\beta(R_{it}) \approx \beta(F_{zt}) + b_{i1t}\beta(F_{1t}) + b_{i2t}\beta(F_{2t}) + \ldots + b_{imt}\beta(F_{mt}). \qquad (7)$$

Equation (7) provides a recipe for estimating the future beta of a security, given its attributes ($b_{i1t}, \ldots, b_{imt}$). All one needs (!) is the set of numbers $\beta(F_{zt})$, $\beta(F_{1t}), \ldots, \beta(F_{mt})$ for the equation.

Table 8 provides one set of such numbers,

TABLE 8

Beta Relative to SP500

Factor	Beta
Z (intercept)	.303
Beta (historic)	.745
Yield	−.014
Size	−.062
Bond Beta	−.009
Alpha	−.086
Basic Industries	.074
Capital Goods	−.014
Construction	.103
Consumer Goods	−.028
Energy	−.057
Finance	−.023
Transportation	.065
Utilities	−.047

based on the betas of each of the factors relative to Standard and Poor's stock index over the 1931-1979 period.[26] These values suggest that, other things equal:

— the higher a security's historic beta, the greater its future beta;
— the higher its yield, the smaller its future beta;
— the larger its size, the smaller its future beta;
— the more bond-like a security, the smaller its future beta, and
— the better its past non-market performance, the smaller its future beta.

Also, other things equal, basic industry, construction, and transportation stocks have substantially larger than average betas, while energy and utility stocks have substantially smaller than average betas.

AVERAGE FACTOR VALUES AND THE CAPITAL ASSET PRICING MODEL

An investment organization should be concerned with the *future* values of factors and security-

FIGURE 23

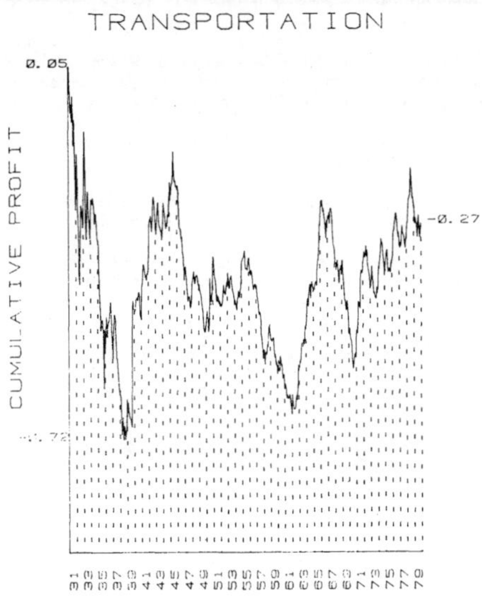

FIGURE 24

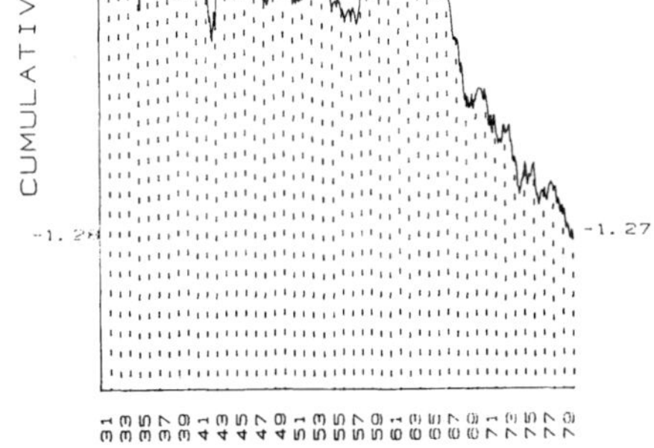

specific returns. For example, what should one *expect* the yield factor to be? How much *risk* is associated with the projection?

One theory of market equilibrium, the *Arbitrage Pricing Theory* of Ross [4], holds that the expected return on a security will be related only to its sensitivities to key factors (in our notation, the b_{11t}, b_{12t}, . . . values). This theory, however, implies nothing about the signs or magnitudes of the expected values of the factors. Another theory, the original Capital Asset Pricing Model of Sharpe [5], Lintner [2], and Mossin [3], implies that expected returns will be related to predicted future beta values. For example, it implies:

$$\bar{R}_p - r = \beta_p(\bar{R}_m - r), \tag{8}$$

where:

$\bar{R}_p$ = the expected return on portfolio or security p;

r = the riskless interest rate;

β_p = portfolio or security p's predicted beta relative to "the market portfolio," and

$\bar{R}_m$ = the expected return on the market portfolio.

As we have indicated, a "factor" can be thought of as the return on a portfolio. With this interpretation, the original Capital Asset Pricing Model implies that the expected value of each factor should equal its beta times the expected excess return on the market portfolio:

$$\bar{F}_{jt} = \beta(F_{jt})\,(\bar{R}_m - r), \tag{9}$$

where:

$\bar{F}_{jt}$ = the expected value of factor j at time t, and

$\beta(F_{jt})$ = the predicted beta of factor j at time t relative to the market portfolio.

A simple, though implausible, set of assumptions would hold that "true" expected returns and risks have been the same since 1931 and that the value-weighted index of New York Stock Exchange stocks is an adequate proxy for "the market portfolio." These assumptions, plus those of the original Capital Asset Pricing Model, would imply expected factor values equal to those shown in the second column of Table 9. For example, Table 8 showed that the yield

TABLE 9

Average Returns Versus CAPM Values

Factor	Avg.	CAPM	T-Diff
Z (intercept)	−0.24	2.51	−1.32
Beta	5.36	6.18	−0.31
Yield	0.24	−0.11	2.37
Size	−5.56	−0.51	−4.53
B. Beta	−0.12	−0.08	−0.11
Alpha	−2.00	−0.71	−1.94
Basic Ind.	1.65	0.61	0.91
Capital Gds.	0.16	−0.12	0.33
Construction	−1.59	0.85	−1.93
Consumer Gds.	−0.18	−0.23	0.07
Energy	6.28	−0.47	4.28
Finance	−1.48	−0.19	−1.72
Transptn.	−0.57	0.54	−0.82
Utilities	−2.62	−0.39	−1.66

factor had a beta of −.014, and Table 1 showed that the average excess return on the New York Stock Exchange index was 8.193% per year; the product, −0.11, is shown in Table 9.

The first column in Table 9 shows the actual average factor values. How significant are the differences from the values in the second column? The third column provides some answers. Given the variability of a factor, one can estimate the significance of the difference between actual and "expected" values. Using the usual standard (the absolute value of the t-statistic greater than 2.0), only three differences are large enough to command special attention. High-yield stocks did better, large stocks worse, and energy stocks better than would be expected, given these assumptions.

The data are thus inconsistent (but not pervasively so) with the *joint* hypothesis that includes (1) the original Capital Asset Pricing Model *and* (2) our very strong assumptions about stability of expected returns and risks and the adequacy of the New York Stock Exchange index to serve as as a market surrogate. Nevertheless, the data may be completely consistent with the implications of an expanded Capital Asset Pricing Model, a joint hypothesis involving changes in expectations and risks over time, or the use of an alternative measure of the return on the market portfolio.

Although these results do not confirm or reject the original Capital Asset Pricing Model as a description of reality, they do call into question naive applications in which expected returns are assumed to be related *only* to estimates of future betas based on past patterns of returns.

[1] E.g. dividends paid from March 1978 through February 1979, divided by the stock price at the end of February 1979.

[2] E.g. (1) the change in price from the end of February 1979 to the end of March 1979 plus dividends with ex-dates during March 1979, all divided by the price at the end of February 1979 minus (2) the return obtained by purchasing at the end of February a Treasury bill due to expire at the end of March.

[3] Factor models usually assume that security-specific returns are uncorrelated with the factors.

[4] In particular, Barra, Wells Fargo Investment Advisors, and Wilshire Associates.

[5] As indicated, this differs from factor analysis procedures that use return data to estimate (possibly unidentified) attributes directly. It also differs from procedures using forecasts (e.g. those employing scenarios).

[6] The correlation between the values of any two factors can be computed, as can the average value and variation in value for each security-specific return. These figures were computed but are not reported here.

[7] This may be desirable in its own right, since it may focus more on predictable regularities than on unpredictable anomalies.

[8] There are other differences between our approach and those of some of the commercial services. The relative merits of alternative procedures will not be considered here.

[9] Based on analyses not reported here; commercial services use a similar attribute.

[10] The Ibbottson/Sinquefield [1] data were used for bond, Treasury bills, and Standard and Poor's stock index returns.

[11] The codes used were those on the data base prepared by the Center for Research in Security Prices at the University of Chicago (this set of data was utilized for all the analyses). The ranges assigned to each of the eight sectors were:
Basic Industries:
1000-1299, 1400-1499, 2600-2699, 2800-2829, 2870-2899, 3300-3399
Capital Goods:
3400-3419, 3440-3599, 3670-3699, 3800-3849, 5080-5089, 5100-5129, 7300-7399
Construction:
1500-1999, 2400-2499, 3220-3299, 3430-3439, 5160-5219
Consumer Goods:
0000-0999, 2000-2399, 2500-2599, 2700-2799, 2830-2869, 3000-3219, 3420-3429, 3600-3669, 3700-3719, 3850-3879, 3880-3999, 4830-4899, 5000-5079, 5090-5099, 5130-5159, 5220-5999, 7000-7299, 7400-9999
Energy:
1300-1399, 2900-2999
Finance:
6000-6999
Transportation:
3720-3799, 4000-4799
Utilities:
4800-4829, 4900-4999

[12] In fact, the regression was actually performed using only seven of the eight attributes. The intercepts for the eight sectors were thus F_{zt}, $F_{zt} + F_{2t}$, $F_{zt} + F_{3t}$ . . . and $F_{zt} + F_{8t}$, where F_{zt} represents the intercept and F_{2t} etc. the factor values obtained in the regression. These eight values were then averaged, with the difference between each one and the average value used as the corresponding sector factor.

[13] In other words, given the inclusion of all but one of the attributes, we should add the remaining one. On the other hand, all our results concern the extent to which our model *fits* historic data. More important questions concern the ability of a procedure using such a model to *predict* future risk and return. For this, one needs to define the precise manner in which results such as ours would be used for prediction—a task beyond the scope of this paper.

[14] Some commercial services fail to report the corresponding value for their models, perhaps because their principals are discouraged by them.

[15] It is important to point out that there is no inconsistency between the importance of other factors in explaining differences among *actual* security returns and the implication of the original Capital Asset Pricing Model that only *predicted* beta is relevant for explaining differences among *expected* security returns. The relationship between our results and the implications of the original Capital Asset Pricing Model is explored later in the paper.

[16] In principle one should use an estimate of *security-specific risk* based on the use of the full factor model over a period for this purpose. However, this requires more than sixty months of

data before a security can be included in the analysis. The cruder method described in the text was employed to use more of the data for fitting the factor model.

[17] This assumes (as does the model) that the security-specific return is uncorrelated with the factor values. The procedure does not guarantee this, but is likely to give results that are relatively uncorrelated. Each value in Table 6 equals one minus the ratio of the security-specific variance to the variance of the security's excess return.

[18] All securities with adequate prior data were included. This criterion might introduce a small amount of *ex post* selection bias, but any effects are likely to be minor (and of undetermined sign).

[19] In this case security-specific return was measured as:

$$(R_{it} - r_t) - (R_{mt} - r_t),$$

where R_{mt} is the return on the value-weighted index of all NYSE stocks in month t. As before, the R-squared value equals one minus the ratio of the variance of this security-specific return to that of the security's excess return.

[20] The figures in Table 6 were also larger than comparable values obtained using unweighted cross-section regressions.

[21] I.e. the average of the monthly values was multiplied by 12 and the standard deviation by the square root of 12; this is equivalent to multiplying each monthly return by 12, then taking the average and standard deviation of the resulting values.

[22] This borders on providing a statistically significant challenge to certain notions of market efficiency. An alternative approach would make predictions employing any serial correlation in factor or security-specific returns or (better yet) provide a detailed model of the time-series behavior of such returns.

[23] Interestingly, many users of commercial risk models assume a standard deviation for the stock market of approximately 20% (consistent with our 49-year average) but employ estimates of other risks based on the last two or three decades when the stock market risk was closer to 15%.

[24] The correlation between the two indices was .993.

[25] The latter assumption implies that the portion of each portfolio's return due to security-specific effects is very close to zero. In practice such portfolios might well require extreme positions (both long and short), with proceeds from short sales used to finance some of the long positions. Since such procedures are not feasible for most investors, and since no transactions costs have been assessed, our "portfolio interpretations" should be considered simply useful abstractions, and the figures should not be regarded as records of directly attainable investment outcomes.

[26] An alternative (and logically superior) method would use the assumed factor covariances and the *current* attributes of the base (and also take security-specific risk into account).

REFERENCES

1. Roger C. Ibbotson and Rex A. Sinquefield. *Stocks, Bonds, Bills and Inflation: Historical Returns*. The Financial Analysts Research Foundation, 1979.
2. John Lintner. "The Valuation of Risk Assets and the Selection of Risky Investments in Stock Portfolios and Capital Budgets." *Review of Economics and Statistics*, February 1965, pp. 13-37.
3. Jan Mossin. "Equilibrium in a Capital Asset Market." *Econometrica*, October 1966, pp. 768-783.
4. Stephen A. Ross. "The Arbitrage Pricing Theory of Capital Asset Pricing." *Journal of Economic Theory*, December 1976, pp. 341-360.
5. William F. Sharpe, "Capital Asset Prices: A Theory of Market Equilibrium Under Conditions of Risk." *Journal of Finance*, September 1964, pp. 425-442.

by Blake R. Grossman and William F. Sharpe

Financial Implications of South African Divestment

The minimum financial costs associated with divesting a portfolio of stocks of companies doing business in South Africa include both direct and indirect costs of buying and selling securities plus effects on risk and expected return. The magnitude of these costs depends materially on the divestment strategy chosen. Divesting only the stocks of companies not complying with the Sullivan Principles results in the exclusion of a relatively small portion of an investment universe and has little effect on portfolio characteristics and returns. A complete divestment policy—selling all South Africa-related stocks—has more meaningful consequences.

The divested South Africa-free (SAF) universe consists of companies whose market capitalizations are significantly smaller than those of the total universe. The SAF universe is also relatively underweighted in technological capital goods and consumer growth stocks and overweighted in finance and utility stocks.

Analysis of a representative divestment strategy based on buying and holding a value-weighted portfolio of all the SAF stocks in the NYSE suggests that initial transaction costs for a $1 billion portfolio can be as low as 0.41 per cent of the overall portfolio value (assuming trades are not liquidity or information-motivated). Reinvestment of dividends and investment of additional funds after divestment should not substantially exceed those associated with an undivested portfolio.

Historical returns since 1959 indicate, further, that the SAF portfolio, diluted with Treasury bills to bring its risk in line with the NYSE, would have outperformed the NYSE by 0.187 per cent annually. Analysis of the factors contributing to the SAF portfolio's returns indicates that the exclusion of South Africa-related stocks hurt portfolio performance, on average, while the small stock bias of the SAF strategy greatly increased portfolio return.

IN REACTION TO the apartheid policies of the South African government, a number of public and private retirement funds have decided to divest their portfolios of stocks of companies that do business in that country. Many more are actively considering such a policy. Such a choice cannot, of course, be made lightly. Both benefits and costs must be carefully weighed.

Evaluation of the benefits involves complex political and social aspects. Most investors share with the U.S. government the goals of abolition of apartheid and improvement of the status of blacks in South Africa; there is disagreement,

Blake Grossman is a portfolio manager at Wells Fargo Investment Advisors. William Sharpe is Timken Professor of Finance, Stanford University, and a consultant to Wells Fargo Investment Advisors.

The authors thank Leslie Durschinger of Wells Fargo for providing much of the transaction costs analysis. Support from the Stanford Program in Finance is gratefully acknowledged.

however, about the effectiveness of divestment as a means to accomplish these ends. Can a single investor's sale of shares of a U.S. corporation influence that corporation? Does that corporation have sufficient influence to affect the policies of the South African government, either directly or via changes in the policies of the U.S. government toward South Africa? Even if many investors choose to divest, will the overall effect be sufficient?

Assessment of the costs is equally difficult. Some costs can be subjected to financial analysis; others involve legal and ethical considerations. In the final analysis, the attitudes of the ultimate beneficiaries for whom the funds are managed should be considered. What financial costs are such individuals *willing* to bear to meet political, moral or ethical objectives? Equally important, how large are the costs they *must* bear?

This article addresses the latter question. More specifically, we ask: How large are the *minimum* financial costs associated with divestment? We include both direct and indirect costs of buying and selling securities and effects on the risk and expected return of the overall portfolio. Armed with an assessment of such costs, one can better address the larger issue by weighing the benefits for the relevant beneficiaries against the relevant costs.

Previous Studies

In 1979, Andrew Rudd analyzed the impact of a particular divestment strategy on the projected risk and return of a portfolio.[1] In 1984, Wayne Wagner, Allen Emkin and Richard Dixon assessed the risk and return of a different strategy and also provided estimates of associated transaction costs.[2] Many subsequent studies have based their results on those of Rudd or Wagner; some have performed new analyses.

This article analyzes a new (and we believe more relevant) divestment strategy, one that differs from those of both Rudd and Wagner. We provide historical results covering a longer time period than analyzed in previous studies. We provide estimates of transaction costs more relevant for a divestment strategy than those presented by Wagner. We attempt to decompose historical performance into that attributable to familiar financial variables and that attributable to investors' attitudes toward operations in South Africa. Finally, we provide an upper bound on the future expected return premium for South Africa-related stocks.

Investment Universes

Any study of divestment must compare at least two security universes—one that would be utilized in the absence of a divestment policy and another that would be chosen if such a policy were adopted.

Many institutional portfolios comprise stocks similar to those included in Standard & Poor's (S&P) 500 stock index, which includes 500 large stocks, each in proportion to its outstanding market value. Even portfolios that differ significantly from the S&P 500 are often compared with it for performance evaluation.

Other institutional portfolios comprise stocks from larger universes than that represented by the S&P 500. For purposes of this article, we consider all stocks listed on the New York Stock Exchange (NYSE)—an investable universe that includes stocks of large and (moderately) small firms, and one from which a "South Africa-free" portfolio can be usefully constructed.

Divestment Candidates

In principle, appropriate "divestment candidates" cannot be determined without detailed consideration of the goals of a divestment program. In practice, however, one of two sets of "divestment" candidates is generally used. Since 1978, the Investor Responsibility Research Center (IRRC) has provided lists of companies with direct investments in South Africa and of some banks with loans to the South African public sector. Those advocating a *complete divestment strategy* usually adopt the IRRC list.

In 1977, the Reverend Leon Sullivan proposed a set of principles for companies doing business in South Africa. These principles include lack of segregation in the workplace and equal and fair employment practices for all races. Companies that sign the Sullivan Principles agree to have their performance evaluated by an outside agency (currently the Arthur D. Little organization), which classifies each firm into one of several compliance categories. Investors adopting a *Sullivan non-compliance divestment strategy* typically exempt companies ranked in either of the two top compliance categories from the list of divestment candidates.

1. Footnotes appear at end of article.

Figure A Divestment Candidates as Proportions of NYSE and S&P 500

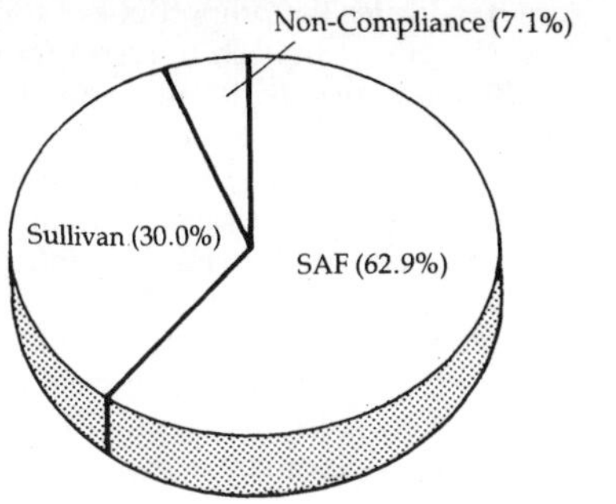

NYSE Market Values (December 1983)

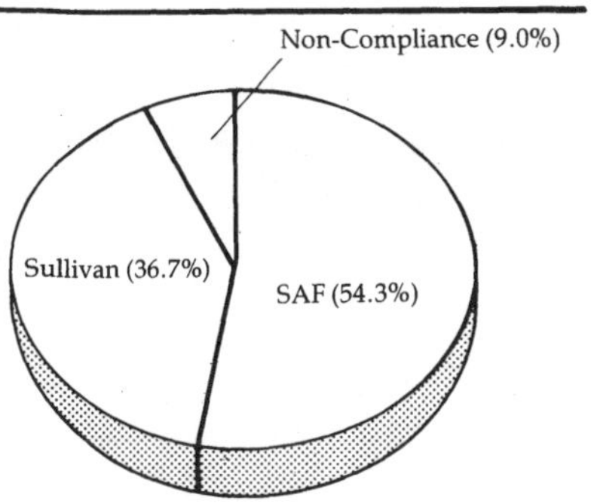

S&P 500 Market Values (December 1983)

Effects on Sizes of Universes

Figure A shows divestment candidates as proportions of both the NYSE and S&P 500 universes at the end of 1983. The South Africa-free ("SAF") component includes companies not found on the list compiled by the IRRC in 1984.[3] The "Sullivan" component includes companies identified by the IRRC in 1984 as doing business in South Africa but classified in Sullivan compliance categories 1 or 2. The "Non-Compliance" component includes the remaining companies doing business in South Africa. Some of these firms have refused to sign the Sullivan principles; others have refused to pay the costs of monitoring compliance; yet others have been monitored and classified in a category other than 1 or 2.

The 1984 IRRC list identified 205 NYSE-listed firms that had business operations in South Africa. At the end of 1983, such firms had a combined market value of $570 billion—37.1 per cent of the total value of stocks listed on the NYSE. Sullivan non-compliance companies accounted for only 7.1 per cent of the NYSE's total value.

Figure A also provides a comparable breakdown for the S&P 500. While approximately 63 per cent of the NYSE would have been available for investment after "total divestment," less than 55 per cent of the S&P 500 would have remained. Because most U.S. firms with operations in South Africa are large, hence likely to be included in the S&P 500, it is not surprising that narrowing the original investment universe increases the potential impact of divestment.

As Figure A indicates, divestment of stocks of Sullivan non-compliance companies results in the exclusion of a relatively small portion of an investment universe. Analysis of the effects of such a limited policy shows little effect on portfolio characteristics or historical performance. Furthermore, the number of such firms may be expected to decrease as corporate attitudes and the policies of the U.S. government change.

The remainder of the article considers the effects of the more stringent complete divestment policy. Statistics on the Sullivan non-compliance policy are presented in the appendix.

Characteristics of the SAF Universe

How might complete divestment affect the key characteristics of a relevant investable universe? To answer this question, we compared a universe comprising all NYSE stocks with a South Africa-free (SAF) universe including only NYSE-listed companies not shown on the 1984 IRRC list. Table I gives some key characteristics of these universes at the end of 1983.

Historical beta values for the individual companies were obtained by regression analysis using 60 monthly returns ending in December 1983. In the analysis, stock returns served as the dependent variable and S&P 500 returns as the independent variable. Universe beta values were computed by value-weighting those of the individual companies. As the table indicates, the two universes had similar beta values, which suggests that divestment need not significantly affect systematic risk.

Dividend yields were computed by dividing 1983 dividends by 1983 year-end prices. Uni-

Table I Universe Characteristics (December 1983)

	NYSE	*SAF*
Beta Relative to the S&P 500	1.03	1.05
Dividend Yield	4.07%	4.01%
Average Size (billions)	$1,116	$802

verse yields are value-weighted averages of the yields of the individual companies. The yields on the two universes were also similar.

The final row in Table I compares the average market capitalizations of the stocks in each universe at the end of 1983. These are simply equally weighted averages of the year-end outstanding values of the component securities. The largest U.S. firms tend to have operations in South Africa; the average SAF firm is thus nearly 30 per cent smaller than the average NYSE firm (and on a value-weighted basis, the difference would be even larger). Numerous studies have found size to be an important factor affecting stock returns.[4] The "small stock bias" of the SAF universe undoubtedly represents its most significant difference from the larger set of investable stocks.

Figure B indicates the proportions of the total values of the stocks in each universe found in various economic sectors. Relative to the NYSE universe, the SAF universe is underweighted in technological capital goods and consumer growth stocks and overweighted in finance and utility stocks. The underweighting of capital goods stocks stems primarily from the absence of a few very large firms, such as IBM and General Electric, while the overweighting of finance and utility stocks reflects the difficulty of international diversification in these sectors.

Selecting a Divestment Strategy

Studies of divestment usually begin with a *benchmark portfolio* that represents a typical investment policy in the absence of divestment. A *divestment universe* is then selected, and a *divestment strategy* chosen to determine a *divestment portfolio.*

Figure C shows the total values at the end of 1983 of (1) the S&P 500, (2) the SAF portion of the S&P 500 and (3) the SAF portion of the NYSE. While the S&P 500 might be an accept-

Figure B Economic Sector Representation in NYSE and SAF Portfolios

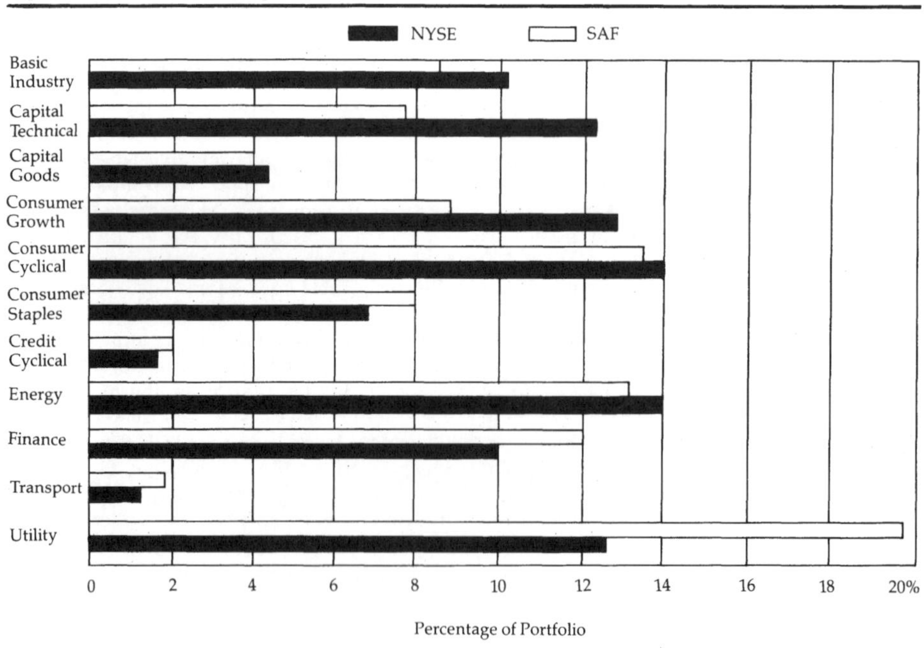

Figure C South Africa-Free Universes (December 1983)

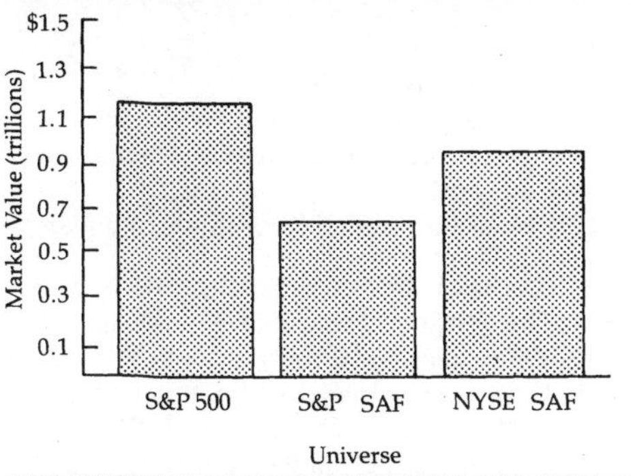

able portfolio for an institutional investor, implementation of a complete divestment strategy using only stocks included in the S&P 500 would be highly constraining. A much better strategy would employ the larger SAF NYSE universe.

Previous studies have considered divestment strategies designed to replicate the performance of a selected benchmark portfolio as closely as possible. Rudd used stocks from the SAF S&P 500 universe to create a portfolio that minimized predicted residual standard deviation from the S&P 500 index.[5] Both a detailed model of security risks and correlations and an optimization program were employed in the process.

Wagner also began with a SAF subset of the S&P 500.[6] Stocks from this universe were included in proportion to their outstanding values (as in the index). For each excluded stock, the largest available non-South Africa-related American company in the same industry was substituted. Substitute companies were also included in proportion to their outstanding values. Here, too, the goal was replication of the S&P 500's performance.

Each of these studies employed a risk model (Rudd explicitly, Wagner implicitly). For implementation, one approach used an optimization procedure, the other simple substitution. Ultimately, of course, the relative efficacies of such procedures in meeting the stated goal can only be adequately assessed using *ex post* performance data. Neither study included such an assessment.

More importantly, we believe there is reason to question the objective assumed in these (and other) previous studies. An investor's ultimate objective is to select a portfolio that maximizes utility, taking into account all assets and liabilities. Even if benchmark portfolio "B" accomplishes this objective in terms of one universe, it does not necessarily follow that the best portfolio to be chosen from another universe is the one with minimum residual risk measured relative to portfolio B. When selecting a portfolio, the objective should be the maximization of utility, without reference to the portfolio that maximizes utility in another setting.

In a larger context, the inputs used to solve such a problem should lead to results that are *macroconsistent*; that is, investors analyzing the situation should be able collectively to implement the strategy. If this is not the case, security prices can be expected to change until a new set of macroconsistent expected returns, risks and correlations is produced. In an equilibrium context, one would expect that the *average* investor who wishes to divest will find that the optimal portfolio includes *all* South Africa-free stocks, each held in proportion to its outstanding market value.

We thus analyze a *representative divestment strategy* using a value-weighted portfolio of all the SAF stocks on the NYSE. Because such a strategy is truly "buy and hold," it minimizes transaction costs. *Ex ante*, it is also likely to prove optimal for the average investor seeking complete divestment.

Data

We concentrated on the NYSE because of availability of monthly returns and valuations for all NYSE stocks from the Center for Research in Security Prices (CRSP) at the University of Chicago. At the time the study was begun, data were available through the end of 1983, so this formed the final date for the analysis. January 1960 was selected (more or less arbitrarily) as the beginning date for the investigation of historical performance.

For most of the analysis, we selected divestment candidates from the 1984 IRRC list of companies with business operations in South Africa (plus banks with outstanding loans to public agencies and no announced policy against future loans). Of course, such a procedure could not have been implemented during the 1960–83 period, because the list was not available prior to 1984. Moreover, this procedure could introduce a substantial *ex post* selection bias into the analysis. Successful firms might be expected to expand abroad, thus leading to a potentially erroneous conclusion that firms doing business in South Africa perform well, when cause and effect could be just the reverse.

Despite these drawbacks, we chose this approach because our ultimate interest concerns the effects of current divestment proposals on future risks and returns, and the 1984 IRRC list is representative of the companies included in such proposals. Fortunately, a cross-check reveals no significant *ex post* selection bias.

Divestment Costs

What might it cost an investor to move from a highly diversified portfolio to one composed only of SAF stocks? To answer this question, we assumed a transition from an initial value-weighted portfolio of all NYSE stocks to a value-weighted portfolio of all SAF NYSE stocks. We also estimated the additional transaction costs associated with subsequent investments in this restricted universe.

Wagner based his transaction cost estimates on results obtained by Loeb from a survey of brokers' estimates of the total costs associated with specified block trades, including the market-maker's spread, price concessions and brokerage commissions. Loeb tabulated trading costs for various combinations of security market capitalization and value of block size.[7] Wagner aggregated securities into Loeb's ranges, then assumed that an equally weighted portfolio of South Africa-related stocks was replaced with an equally weighted portfolio of substitute stocks. For a \$1 billion portfolio, Wagner estimated divestment transaction costs to be 6.0 per cent of the amount divested, or 2.28 per cent of overall portfolio value.

Because neither the Wagner strategy nor ours involves replacement of one equally weighted portfolio of securities with another, it is necessary to provide a more detailed set of estimates using the Loeb costs. Moreover, for greater generality, it is useful to replace Loeb's table of point estimates with a more general function. We attempted to represent the Loeb data with a relatively simple function that minimizes the sum of the squared deviations of predicted values from those presented by Loeb. The following function proved to be the most effective of those tried:

$$\ln C = \underset{(26.09)}{4.0368} + \underset{(18.30)}{0.6109} \ln P + \underset{(4.70)}{0.0227} (\ln P)^2 - \underset{(-9.69)}{0.1983} \ln B \quad (1)$$

where

ln = natural logarithm,
C = percentage transaction cost,
P = percentage of outstanding shares traded, and
B = block size traded (thousands of dollars).

The t-statistics are shown below each coefficient. The R-squared was 0.9293, indicating that almost 93 per cent of the variation in the values of ln C was explained by the function. (The comparable value for C itself was 0.8717.)

Figure D plots the points from Loeb's study, with P on the horizontal scale and C on the vertical scale (both axes are plotted in log scale). Also shown are values of the function for three values of B, representing mid-points of selected ranges from the Loeb table.

Loeb's estimates indicate that, holding block size equal, percentage transaction costs increase at an increasing rate as one attempts to buy or sell more of the outstanding shares of a company. This undoubtedly reflects price pressure, resulting from the fact that stocks are not perfect substitutes for one another. If one holds percentage of outstanding shares traded constant, however, percentage transaction costs *decrease* as block size increases, as fixed costs of trading are spread over a larger transaction.

Using this "Loeb function," we estimated the divestment cost for a \$1 billion portfolio on a stock-by-stock basis. The initial portfolio was assumed to be the value-weighted NYSE at the end of 1983 and the divestment portfolio to be the value-weighted SAF NYSE at the end of 1983. Thus divestment entailed selling 37.1 per cent of the value of the initial portfolio and reinvesting the proceeds on a value-weighted basis in the remaining (SAF) stocks. Estimated transaction costs were 2.57 per cent of the amount divested, or 0.95 per cent of the overall portfolio value.

Using the same initial estimates of transaction costs as Wagner, we obtained a significantly lower estimate for the costs of divesting a \$1 billion portfolio (0.95 per cent of the overall value versus 2.28 per cent). Because of the nonlinearities of Loeb's estimates, Wagner's assumption of equal-weighting appears to have produced an erroneously high estimate for any strategy (such as ours or his) in which stocks are

Figure D Transaction Costs vs. Percentage Traded for Various Block Sizes (thousands of dollars)

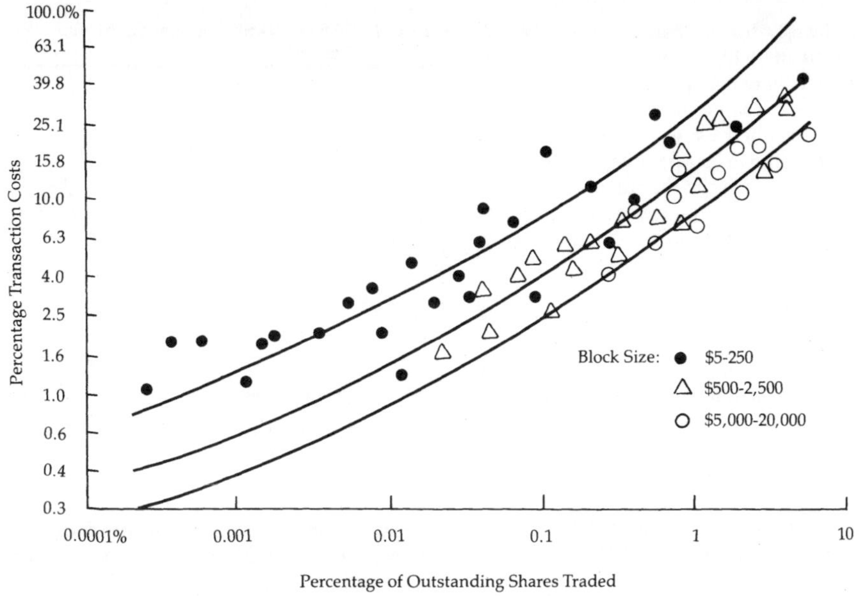

to be sold and purchased in proportion to their outstanding values.

Costs Under Passive Trading

Loeb's transaction cost estimates are widely used. However, they are not the most appropriate ones for estimating divestment costs. Brokers responding to Loeb's survey were not told why a trade was being made (nor whether it would in fact be made). It is thus likely that the responses incorporated price changes designed to insure the brokers against an "information-motivated" transaction. Moreover, the trades were to be executed on demand, rather than spread out over time.

Loeb's estimates thus reflect likely costs of immediate, active management trades. But divestment transactions reflect no new information and can be made over a period of at least several days. They are similar to passive, liquidity-motivated trades, which should entail significantly lower transaction costs than active, information-motivated trades.

To obtain better estimates of relevant divestment costs, we utilized an extensive data base of 36,463 actual transactions made between November 1984 and May 1985 by Wells Fargo Investment Advisors as part of their management of passive index funds. Both explicit (broker commissions) and implicit ("market impact") costs were included.

The market impact was computed as the difference between the return on the traded stock and the return on a selected proxy. Three different proxy returns were used—(1) the return on the stock's equal-weighted industry group, (2) the return on the S&P 500 multiplied by the traded stock's historical beta and (3) the return on stocks with characteristics similar to the traded stock (determined by a factor model similar to the one described below). The difference between the return on the traded stock and the return on each of these proxies provided three different measures of market impact; we used the average of these three estimates.

The actual commissions paid for each trade were added to this market impact measure to arrive at the total transaction cost. These costs were then grouped according to market capitalization and block size. Finally, a smooth function was fitted to the observations and detailed estimates of the divestment costs made on a stock-by-stock basis.

As expected, the resulting transaction costs

were considerably lower than those estimated by Loeb. Estimated divestment costs for a $1 billion portfolio were 0.41 per cent of the overall portfolio value, considerably lower than the 0.95 per cent obtained using the Loeb assumptions.[8] Figure E shows comparable estimates for portfolios of other sizes. Not surprisingly, the percentage cost of divestment increases as portfolio size increases, although at a decreasing rate.

Incremental Transaction Costs

In addition to one-time transaction costs, a divestment policy is likely to incur continuing incremental transaction costs associated with reinvestment of dividends and the investment of additional funds. Because funds will be invested in a smaller portion of the market, a typical purchase will involve a larger percentage of the outstanding shares of a security, hence higher percentage transaction costs.

Figure E Transaction Costs of Divestment for Passive Trading Techniques

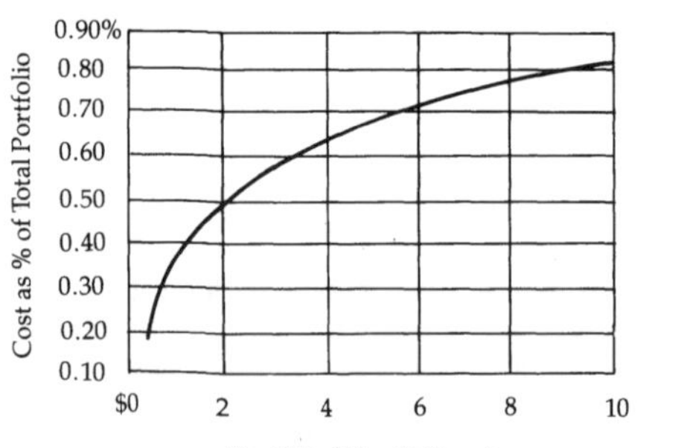

Figure F Incremental Transaction Costs, SAF vs. NYSE

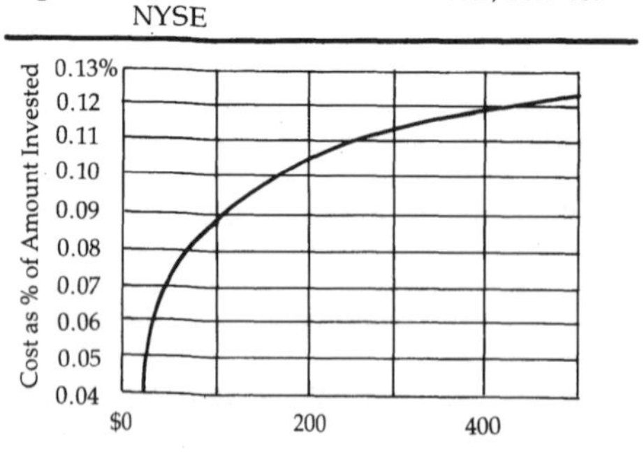

Figure G SAF vs. NYSE Cumulative Values, 1960-1983

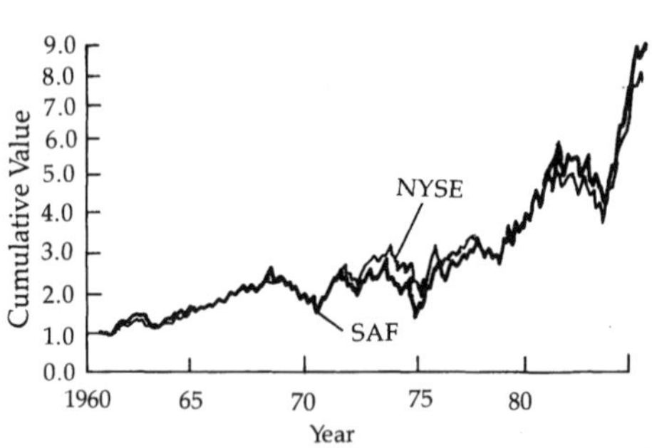

Our data suggest that this difference is likely to be very small for a representative passive strategy. A comparison of the transaction costs for a $100 million investment in a value-weighted portfolio of SAF NYSE stocks with those for a $100 million investment in a value-weighted NYSE portfolio indicates a differential cost of only 0.09 per cent of the amount invested. Figure F provides values for investments of other sizes.

Historical Performance

How would a divested portfolio have performed in the past? Figure G provides some evidence, graphing the cumulative values of $100 invested in the value-weighted NYSE and SAF NYSE portfolios in December 1959; all dividends are assumed to have been reinvested. Over this period, the SAF portfolio outperformed the NYSE. Table II provides summary statistics for the excess returns (actual returns minus Treasury bill rates) of the two portfolios. On average, the SAF excess return was 0.261 per cent higher than that of the NYSE. The standard deviation of the SAF portfolio's excess return was also slightly higher than that of the NYSE.

Table III provides a more direct performance comparison. It compares the NYSE performance

Table II 1960–1983 Performances of NYSE and SAF Portfolios

	Average Excess Return (%/year)	*Standard Deviation of Excess Return (%/year)*
SAF Portfolio	3.922	15.071
NYSE Portfolio	3.661	14.788
Difference	0.261	0.283

Table III 1960–1983 Performances of NYSE and Equal-Risk SAF Portfolios

	Average Excess Return (%/year)	*Standard Deviation of Excess Return (%/year)*
SAF Equal-Risk Portfolio*	3.848	14.788
NYSE Portfolio	3.661	14.788
Difference	0.187	0.000

* 98.12 per cent original SAF portfolio and 1.88 per cent Treasury bills.

with that of a portfolio consisting of Treasury bills and the SAF portfolio in a mix designed to have the same standard deviation as the NYSE. This "equal risk" SAF strategy outperformed the NYSE by 0.187 per cent annually over the period.

The SAF portfolio tracked the NYSE closely while achieving its higher returns. The correlation coefficient for the returns of the two portfolios was 0.986. The residual standard deviation of the SAF portfolio relative to the NYSE was 2.51 per cent per year—considerably higher than the "tracking error" of most index funds, but lower than that of a typical actively managed portfolio.

We have compared the SAF strategy with an investment in the entire NYSE to reduce the disparity between the two universes. Had the comparison been made with the S&P 500, the historical superiority of the SAF strategy would have been even greater. Figure H graphs the cumulative values of S&P 500 and NYSE portfolios from 1960 through 1983. Primarily because of its greater proportion of small-market-capitalization stocks, the NYSE outperformed the S&P 500 over this period. Inasmuch as the SAF strategy outperformed the NYSE, it would, *a fortiori,* have outperformed an investment in the S&P 500.

The South Africa Factor

History is, at best, an imperfect guide to the future. Before assuming that future results will conform to past results, we may find it useful to analyze the determinants of historical performance. Some of these influences may reasonably be projected into the future; others may not.

To estimate future results, we used a factor model and performed a cross-section regression for every month from January 1960 through December 1983.[9] Each regression included all stocks (with available data) that were listed on the NYSE at the beginning of the month. The dependent variable was the return on each stock during the month. We used 15 independent variables as "factors" in the attribution of returns. Information on key characteristics of each stock was provided by the first three variables—

- historical beta, based on a regression using 60 months' data ending one month prior to the regression month;
- dividend yield, based on the previous 12 months' dividends divided by month-end price, computed using data available one month prior to the regression month; and
- size, based on the logarithm (base 10) of the total value of the shares outstanding one month prior to the regression month.

The next 11 variables indicated the economic sector into which the company was classified, based primarily on its Standard Industry Classification (SIC) code. For each stock, one of these 11 variables equaled 1, while all others equaled 0. The sectors are shown in Figure B.

The final variable indicated whether or not the stock was South Africa-related. Stocks of companies shown on the 1984 IRRC list were assigned a value of 1; all other stocks were given a value of 0. We termed the regression coefficient obtained for this variable the *South Africa factor.* A positive value indicates that, during the month in question, stocks of South Africa-related (SAR) companies did better than stocks of SAF companies in the same economic sector with similar beta values, yields and market capitalizations. A negative value indicates that SAR stocks did worse than otherwise similar SAF stocks. A zero value indicates no difference in performance.

Figure H S&P 500 vs. NYSE Cumulative Values, 1960-1983

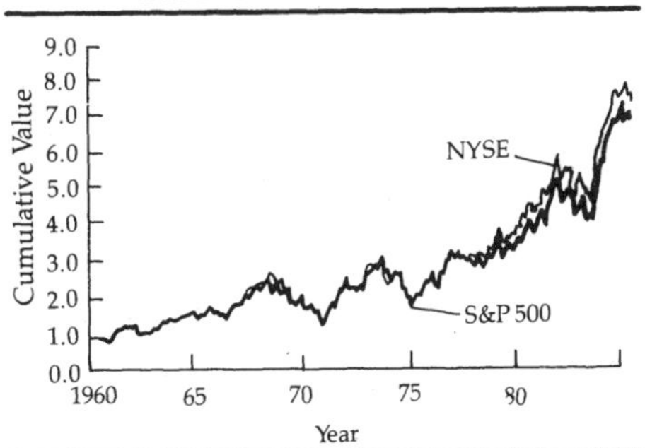

Figure I South Africa Factor, **Ex Ante** vs. **Ex Post** Estimation

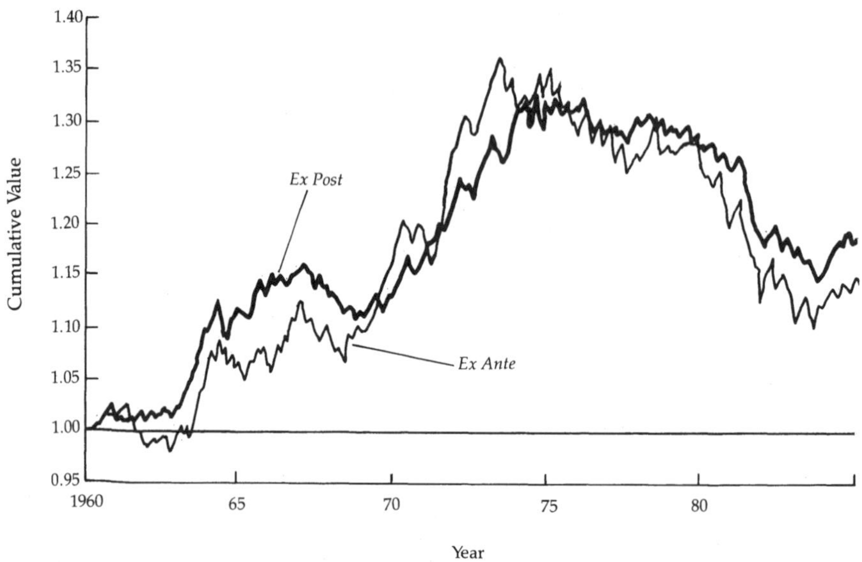

Figure I shows the *cumulative* value of the South Africa factor from 1960 through 1983, computed by summing the values for each of the months. The values shown on the vertical axis may be interpreted as the cumulative return to a hedged strategy in which a portfolio of SAR stocks is held "long" and an otherwise similar (in beta, yield, size and economic sector composition) portfolio of SAF stocks is held "short." An upward (downward) trend indicates those periods in which SAR stocks outperformed (underperformed) SAF stocks, other things equal.

As the figure indicates, the average South Africa factor over the 1960–83 period was positive. Its behavior was far from consistent, however. From 1960 through 1975, SAR stocks tended to outperform SAF stocks. From 1976 through 1979, the two groups performed approximately equally well. And from 1980 through 1983, SAR stocks *under*performed SAF stocks.

Table IV provides more detail, showing the average annualized value for each period (obtained by multiplying the average monthly value by 12). The t-statistic indicates the significance of the difference between this average and zero. A classical statistician using the rule of thumb that only values with absolute t-statistics greater than 2.0 warrant attention would conclude that the superior performance of SAR stocks was "statistically significant" only in the period prior to 1976. The underperformance of such stocks in the 1980s, while of less significance statistically, is nonetheless of sufficient magnitude to reject the hypothesis that SAR stocks have substantially outperformed SAF stocks with similar characteristics in the recent past.

Ex Post versus Ex Ante Selection

Each of the traditional attributes used in estimating the factor model was carefully measured

Table IV The South Africa Factor Percentage Return per Year

	Average Value	*t-statistic*
Overall period:		
1960–1983	0.77	1.31
Subperiods:		
1960–1975	2.05	2.99
1976–1979	−0.91	0.76
1980–1983	−2.69	1.55

using information that would have been available in advance. This was not the case, however, for the South Africa factor, which was based on the inclusion or exclusion of each stock in the 1984 IRRC list. As indicated earlier, this was done to reflect the incidence of a 1984-type divestment on historical returns.

Unfortunately, this approach raises the possibility of *ex post* selection bias. It is entirely possible that substantially different results would have been obtained had lists available in advance of each month been used.

To assess this possibility, we repeated the analysis using an alternative source. Approximately every four years since 1959, the World Trade Academy (WTA) has prepared lists of companies doing business in South Africa.[10] Although they are less carefully researched than those prepared by the IRRC, the WTA lists can provide the inputs needed for a truly *ex ante* factor model.

Figure I also shows the cumulative value of a South Africa factor derived from analyses in which the South Africa attribute of each stock was 1 if it appeared on the most recent WTA list available prior to the regression month and 0 if it did not appear on that list. Differences between the *ex ante* and *ex post* curves are small enough to allow us to reject the hypothesis of major *ex post* selection bias in the previous results.

Sources of Differences

A comparison of Tables III and IV provides useful evidence on the sources of differences in historical performance of the SAF and NYSE portfolios. There were two key differences between these portfolios. By design, the SAF strategy excluded SAR stocks. Over the 1960–83 period, this reduced the portfolio's performance, given the positive average South Africa factor. The SAF strategy also had, as a byproduct, a small stock bias; this greatly *increased* its returns over this period. The small stock effect was of much greater magnitude than the South Africa effect, causing the equal-risk SAF portfolio to outperform the NYSE by 0.187 per cent per year.

Had the average South Africa factor equaled *zero* during this period, the equal-risk SAF strategy would have outperformed the NYSE by more than 0.187 per cent annually. The South Africa factor averaged 0.77 per cent over the 1960–83 period, and an average of 42.3 per cent of the NYSE was invested in SAR stocks. It follows that the South Africa effect contributed roughly 0.326 per cent (=0.423 · 0.77%) per year to the NYSE's return over this period. Had the South Africa factor equaled zero, the SAF strategy would have beaten the NYSE by an additional 0.326 per cent, or a total of 0.513 per cent (=0.187% + 0.326%) per year.[11]

Likely Future Risks and Returns

Many studies of the small stock effect indicate that, on average, small stocks have outperformed otherwise similar large stocks over extensive periods of time. Although this empirical regularity is not well understood (especially its heavy concentration in the month of January), there is little reason to assume that its future behavior will differ significantly from that of the past. Because a representative SAF strategy will have a small stock bias, one would reasonably expect it to outperform the NYSE, were this the only difference of consequence. Based on our historical data, the magnitude of this difference might be projected to be approximately 0.51 per cent per year.

The more difficult question concerns the likely future value of the South Africa factor and its effect on the performance of a SAF strategy. Is the 1960–83 effect of +0.77 per cent relevant for the future? The 1980–83 effect of −2.69 per cent? Or neither?

Knowledge of the situation, and the statistics shown in Table IV, suggest that little reliance can be placed on history. Attitudes toward stocks of companies with business operations in South Africa have changed significantly in the past, and further change is almost certain. Present and future attitudes must be considered in projecting future returns, and even the recent past may prove a poor guide, given these attitudes' susceptibility to rapid change.

If some investors find it distasteful to hold South Africa-related stocks, while all other investors remain indifferent, security prices must adjust until such stocks have higher expected returns than those of otherwise similar SAF stocks. Under this situation, the expected South Africa factor will be positive. During the period in which investors begin to anticipate such a situation, however, prices of SAR stocks must fall relative to those of SAF stocks so that differential expected returns can obtain.

Eventually, SAR stocks should be expected to outperform otherwise similar SAF stocks. But during the transition period, they are likely to underperform SAF stocks. The length of the transition period will depend on the rapidity with which investors anticipate eventual attitudes toward South Africa. It is possible that the negative performance of the South Africa factor from 1980 through 1983 reflected some (relative) downward pricing of SAR stocks. This need not imply that the future value will be negative. Unless the transition is not yet complete, a positive future factor value should be expected.

Equilibrium Expected Returns

To assess the likely magnitude of an equilibrium difference in expected returns, we analyzed a case in which there is no small stock effect in order to estimate the likely difference in expected returns resulting solely from aversion to holding SAR stocks.[12]

Consider two portfolios—one composed entirely of SAR stocks, the other entirely of SAF stocks. Let the former have expected return E_s and variance V_s and the latter expected return E_f and variance V_f. Let C_{sf} represent the covariance between the returns of the two portfolios. An investor choosing a combination of these two portfolios may expect the following overall return:

$$E_P = X_sE_s + X_fE_f, \quad (2)$$

where

X_s = proportion invested in SAR stocks and
X_f = proportion invested in SAF stocks.

The overall variance of this portfolio may be calculated as follows:

$$V_P = X_s^2V_s + X_f^2V_f + 2\,X_sX_fC_{sf}. \quad (3)$$

We assumed that the investor's objective is the maximization of utility, or risk-adjusted expected return, defined as follows:[13]

$$U = E_p - \frac{V_P}{t}, \quad (4)$$

where

t = the investor's risk tolerance.

The principle of portfolio optimality implies that an investor with no aversion to holding SAR stocks will choose a mix (i.e., values of X_s and X_f) for which the marginal utilities of the two portfolios are the same. In this case the marginal utilities will be the following:

$$MU_s = \frac{\partial U}{\partial X_s} = E_s - \frac{2}{t}[X_sV_s + X_fC_{sf}] \quad (5)$$

and

$$MU_f = \frac{\partial U}{\partial X_f} = E_f - \frac{2}{t}[X_fV_f + X_sC_{sf}]. \quad (6)$$

Setting Equations (5) and (6) equal and substituting $(1 - X_s)$ for X_f implies that an optimal mix will satisfy the following condition:

$$E_s - E_f = \frac{2}{t}[C_{sf} - V_f] + \frac{2}{t}[V_s + V_f - 2\,C_{sf}]\,X_s. \quad (7)$$

Each investor takes security risks, expected returns and covariances as given, then selects an investment decision (X_s) for which Equation (7) holds. For there to be equilibrium in the capital markets, however, security risks, expected returns and covariances must be such that investors' collective choices equate the demand and supply of each security.

If some investors choose to divest SAR stocks, these stocks must be picked up by "neutral" investors (i.e., those with no aversion to holding SAR stocks). For equilibrium to obtain, then, neutral investors must be led—on purely economic grounds—to overweight their portfolios (in terms of market value proportions) with SAR stocks. Expected returns, risks and covariances must be such that the optimal value of X_s for a neutral investor with average risk tolerance will equal the ratio of the total value of SAR stocks to the total value of all stocks held by neutral investors.

Assume, for example, that the NYSE is representative of the overall market. For every \$100 of stock value, let \$37 be in SAR stocks and \$63 in SAF stocks. Table V shows required values of X_s for a neutral investor for three possible cases covering the range from no divestment to maximum possible divestment, given current security values. Clearly, the larger the value of the divested portfolios, the higher must be the proportion of SAR stocks in the neutral investor's portfolio.

Some idea of the magnitude of the expected return differential between the two portfolios required to induce these X_s holdings may be obtained by assuming that historical risks and correlations are representative of future values.

Table V Required Holdings for a Neutral Investor for Different Degrees of Divestment

(1) Degree of Divestment	(2) Value of Divested Portfolios	(3) Value of Neutral Portfolios	(4) Value of SAR Stocks	(5)* x_s
none	0.0	100.0	37.0	0.37
	31.5	68.5	37.0	0.54
maximum	63.0	37.0	37.0	1.00

* Column (5) equals Column (4) divided by Column (3).

Over the 1960–83 period, the historical statistics, in terms of return per month, were:

$$V_s = 18.5764,$$
$$V_f = 18.7543 \text{ and}$$
$$C_{sf} = 17.2864.$$

A typical current assumption among institutional investors holds that expected stock excess return (over the Treasury bill rate) is 4.5 per cent, with a standard deviation of 15 per cent. Assume that, given these assumptions, the average neutral investor faced with a choice between Treasury bills and a stock portfolio would invest entirely in stocks. This implies a risk tolerance of 100. Using this risk tolerance, and the risks and covariance given above, gives the expected return differentials shown in Table VI.

A comparison of the first and last rows in Table VI provides an estimate of the effect of maximum divestment on the difference in expected returns. As shown, the maximum likely divestment-induced change in the differential between E_s and E_f would be 0.310 minus 0.107, or 0.417 per cent per year.[14] This provides an estimate of the expected South Africa factor under conditions of maximum divestment. An expected South Africa factor of 0.417 per cent per year would increase the expected return on the NYSE by 0.155 per cent (= 0.371 · 0.417%) per year.

As noted earlier, had the average South Africa factor been zero during the 1960–83 period a SAF strategy would have outperformed the NYSE by 0.513 per cent per year. Assuming that the small stock effect persists, one might reasonably predict that a SAF portfolio will outperform the NYSE by at least 0.358 per cent (= 0.513% − 0.155%) per year, *even under conditions of maximum possible divestment.*

Table VI Expected Return Differentials for Different Degrees of Divestment

(1) Degree of Divestment	(2) x_s	(3) $E_s - E_f$ (%/month)	(4)* $E_s - E_f$ (%/year)
none	0.37	−0.009	−0.107
	0.54	0.000	0.005
maximum	1.00	0.026	0.310

* Column (4) equals Column (3) times 12.

Conclusions

It is a simple exercise in logic to demonstrate that any constraint placed upon a decision can only lower or leave unchanged the maximum utility that can be obtained. Thus the avoidance of SAR stocks cannot improve the financial situation of an investor who has previously made an optimal set of investment decisions.

On the other hand, some institutional investment portfolios appear to be suboptimal (at least after the fact). It may well be that substitution of an efficient, passive SAF strategy for an inefficient active strategy may lead to an overall improvement, although a smaller one than might have been obtained with an efficient unconstrained strategy.

We have focused on a representative, highly diversified investment strategy that excludes stocks of companies with operations in South Africa. Even after adjustment for risk, such a strategy would have outperformed the New York Stock Exchange index and, *a fortiori,* the S&P 500 and the majority of actively managed institutional portfolios. Moreover, it is not unreasonable to expect such performance to continue. Although SAR stocks may be expected to outperform otherwise similar SAF stocks, a SAF strategy is not "otherwise similar." In particular, a representative divestment strategy results in a portfolio with a small stock bias relative to the overall market. If the small stock effect persists, this bias can be expected to lead to superior performance for the divested portfolio.

Divestment of an existing portfolio will incur non-trivial transaction costs. However, such costs should be considerably less than previously estimated if a truly representative portfolio is selected and the appropriate trading procedures utilized. A $1 billion portfolio should incur initial transaction costs of approximately 50 basis points (i.e., 0.50 per cent of the value of the overall portfolio). Because its subsequent expected performance is likely to be at least 35 basis points above that of the NYSE index, its initial transaction costs could be recouped in less than two years.

These estimates are based only in part on historical values. They also take into account relations required for equilibrium to obtain in the capital markets. The superior performance predicted for a representative SAF policy is composed of a small positive component stemming from its small stock bias and an even smaller negative component from its concentration in more popular (hence lower expected return) SAF stocks.

Compared with a portfolio representing the overall stock universe, a representative, highly diversified SAF strategy can provide a slightly higher expected return with the same risk but considerably less liquidity (because of its concentration in small stocks). The relative importance of these two differences will, of course, depend on the circumstances of the fund in question, as will the assessment of the potential nonfinancial benefits of divestment, which have not been treated here. ■

Footnotes

1. A. Rudd, "Divestment of South African Equities: How Risky?" *The Journal of Portfolio Management*, Spring 1979.
2. W. Wagner, A. Emkin and R. Dixon, "South African Divestment: The Investment Issues," *Financial Analysts Journal*, November/December 1984.
3. A. Newman and C. Bowers, eds., "Foreign Investment in South Africa and Namibia" (Investors Responsibility Research Center, December 1984).
4. See, for example, R. W. Banz, "The Relationship Between Return and Market Value of Common Stocks," *Journal of Financial Economics* 9 (1981); D. B. Keim, "Size-Related Anomalies and Stock Return Seasonality," *Journal of Financial Economics* 12 (1983); and M. Reinganum, "Abnormal Returns in Small Firm Portfolios," *Financial Analysts Journal*, March/April 1981.
5. Rudd, "Divestment," *op. cit.*
6. Wagner *et al.*, "South African Divestment," *op. cit.*
7. T. Loeb, "Trading Cost: The Critical Link Between Investment Information and Results," *Financial Analysts Journal*, May/June 1983.
8. Part of the difference between these estimates is attributable to broker commissions. Loeb assumed a commission rate of 10 cents per share for his trades. In the sample of actual trades made by Wells Fargo, the average commission was significantly lower. If a commission rate of 10 cents per share is applied to these trades, the estimated divestment costs for a $1 billion portfolio would be approximately 0.55 per cent of the total portfolio value (versus 0.41 per cent obtained using actual commissions). This figure is still substantially less than the 0.95 per cent estimated from the Loeb costs.
9. The model we used is similar to that described in W. F. Sharpe, "Factors in New York Stock Exchange Security Returns, 1931–1979," *The Journal of Portfolio Management*, Summer 1982.
10. J. L. Angel, ed., *Directory of American Firms Operating in Foreign Countries* (New York: World Trade Academy Press), editions from 1959 to 1981.
11. This analysis assumes that the proportion of the NYSE invested in South Africa-related stocks was constant over the period. Taking into account the effect of the small changes in this proportion over the period would affect the solution only trivially.
12. We used an approach similar to that suggested in A. Rudd, "South Africa Revisited," *The Journal of Portfolio Management*, forthcoming.
13. This approach is described in Sharpe, *Investments* (New York: Prentice-Hall, 1985).
14. The difference in expected return premiums in the first and last rows of Table VI depends, of course, on both the simplifying assumptions and the numeric values assumed in the computations. For simplicity, we followed the common practice of considering only a stock-Treasury bill asset allocation decision. Similar magnitudes for this key value can be obtained in more general setting with additional asset classes.

Appendix

A Sullivan Compliance Portfolio

When a divestment proposal excludes only U.S. firms with South African operations not ranked in one of the top two Sullivan compliance categories, the investment problem becomes almost trivial. Because Sullivan non-compliance firms constitute only 7.1 per cent of the total value of the NYSE, their removal has only minor effects on the universe. This appendix examines the *Sullivan compliance* (SC) investable universe, consisting of all NYSE stocks either excluded from the 1984 IRRC list or included but with Sullivan compliance ratings of 1 or 2.

Table AI shows the (weighted) beta values, (weighted) yields and (unweighted) average size of the NYSE and SC universes. Figure AA breaks down the composition of each universe by economic sector. As indicated, the differences are very minor.

Table AII shows that, over the 1960–83 peri-

Figure AA Economic Sector Representation in NYSE and SC Portfolios

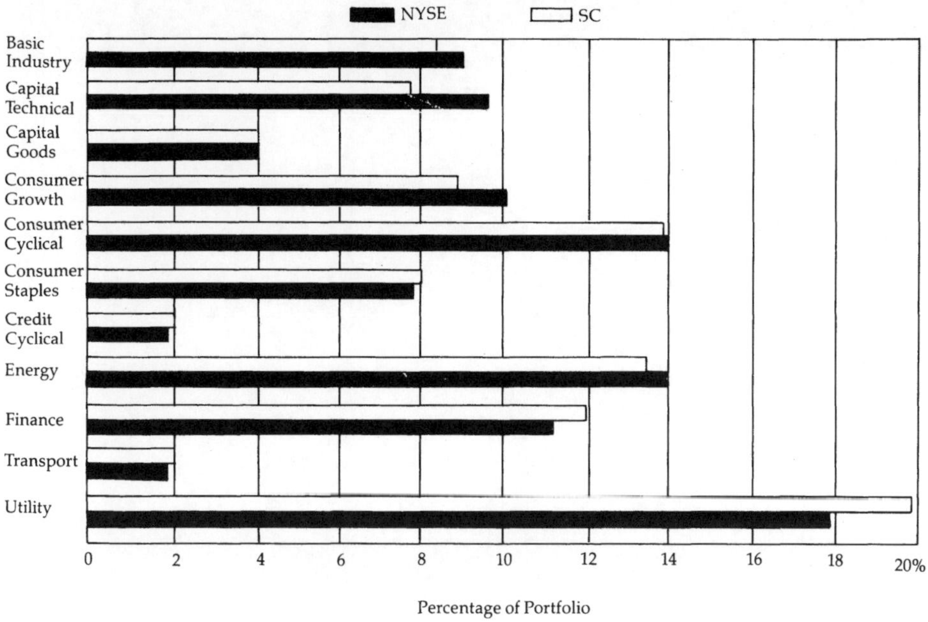

Table AI Universe Characteristics (December 1983)

	NYSE	*SC*
Beta Relative to the S&P 500	1.03	1.02
Dividend Yield	4.07%	4.10%
Average Size (billions)	$1,116	$1,193

Table AII 1960–1983 Performance, NYSE and SC Portfolios

	Average Excess Return (%/year)	*Standard Deviation of Excess Return (%/year)*
Sullivan Portfolio	3.715	14.675
NYSE Portfolio	3.661	14.788
Difference	0.054	−0.113

od, a value-weighted portfolio had slightly higher average excess returns than did the NYSE, with a slightly lower standard deviation, but the differences were hardly significant.

Compared with a complete divestment strategy, a decision to divest only stocks of companies with operations in South Africa not rated in the top two Sullivan compliance categories should incur small transaction costs and virtually insignificant changes in performance. ■

Investor Wealth Measures and Expected Return

William F. Sharpe

Over the past few years, a number of people have discovered that the premium in expected return for bearing risk changes in somewhat predictable ways. The studies on this subject differ in a number of respects. First, they differ in how they define the risk premium. Some studies focus on the risk premium for large stocks—e.g., the Standard & Poor's 500 (S&P 500); others analyze the risk premium for bonds. Some define a risk premium in terms of the spread between bond and stock expected returns; others define it in terms of the spread between the expected return of an asset class and the yield on Treasury bills. Several studies use forward-looking predictions as part of the information set from which risk premium predictions are made; others use only information concerning past results and current prices. Some use information from one market to predict the risk premium in that market; others use that information to predict the risk premium in other markets.

The studies also differ in method. Some fit procedures to one body of data and then estimate the statistical significance of the fitted relations. Others fit procedures to one set of data and then test the significance of the procedures in making predictions for another set of data. Some test the results that could have been obtained had the procedures been followed in practice. A small minority report actual results obtained by using their procedures.

Finally, the studies differ in their market efficiency premise. The differences here are rather subtle. Some assume that their procedures discover market inefficiencies that can be exploited by a suitable investment strategy. Others are agnostic concerning the efficiency or inefficiency of the markets in which risk premia appear to change. Some authors believe they have documented investor irrationality (which may or may not persist in the future). Others are not certain whether they have found inefficiencies, anomalies, or simply manifestations of a more complex efficient marketplace than typically envisioned.

The approach outlined in this presentation differs from the previous research in a number of respects. First, the definition of the relevant risk premium is different. This presentation investigates the premium for bearing risk in the U.S. security market as a whole. More precisely, we consider the "U.S. Mix," which represents the total holdings of market-valued securities by U.S. investors. Second, this study relies on predictive measures motivated by fundamental principles. In particular, we test the thesis that when investors are rich the risk premium is lower than when they are poor. Third, both in-sample fits of the hypothesized relation and out-of-sample tests of the investment performance of strategies based on this relation are provided. Finally, the method insures that the results are compatible with efficient securities markets. Investment strategies based on these relations need not carry the seeds of their own destruction: The relations derived here can exist even if everyone knows about them.

WEALTH AND THE RISK PREMIUM

The behavior of individual investors is an important consideration. A number of studies have shown that, other things being equal, the richer an investor is, the greater is his or her risk tolerance. Equivalently, it has been shown that the richer an investor is, the more aggressive is his or her investment portfolio.

If this is true for individuals, it can be expected to be true for investors as a whole. If a *society* becomes wealthier, the "average" investor's risk tolerance should increase. More precisely, societal risk tolerance may be defined as the weighted average of investors' risk tolerances, using their relative amounts of invested wealth as weights. Thus, one would expect societal risk tolerance to be greater when the society is significantly richer.

When an individual becomes more tolerant of risk, he or she simply chooses a riskier portfolio. When a society becomes more tolerant of risk, however, the result is that the prices of riskier securities increase because of "buying pressure" (an increase in demand). An increase in societal risk tolerance, therefore, should result in a decrease in the premium obtained for bearing risk. Conversely, a decrease in societal risk tolerance should lead to an increase in the premium for bearing risk.

These relations are summarized graphically in **Figure 1**. Note the use of the term "premium per unit of risk." It involves two components. Premium refers to the difference between the expected return on "the market" and the current short-term interest rate. Risk refers to uncertainty concerning the actual return on the market. In this context, risk is measured by the variance of the projected distribution of possible returns on the market portfolio. The resulting reward-to-variance ratio conforms to that obtained from standard portfolio theory. The focus of this presentation is on the extent to which it changes as investor wealth changes.

FIGURE 1. Wealth and the Risk Premium

INDIVIDUAL BEHAVIOR	
Wealth:	Poor ↔ Rich
Risk Tolerance:	Low ↔ High
SOCIETAL ANALOGUE	
Wealth:	Poor ↔ Rich
Societal Risk Tolerance:	Low ↔ High
Premium Per Unit of Risk:	High ↔ Low

Source: Sharpe-Tint, Inc.

It would be ideal to measure the entire wealth of a society for a study of this type. In practice, it is impossible to obtain up-to-date estimates of the values of real estate, human capital, and other major components of total wealth. Instead, we will consider two proxies for overall wealth: the real security value per capita (RSVPC) and the cumulative real return (CRR). RSVPC is particularly useful for "in-sample" tests because it has a secular trend that is small enough to be ignored for such purposes. The RSVPC is defined as the U.S. asset mix divided by the consumer price index. The cumulative real return measure has several desirable qualities. Its secular trend, however, is too large to be ignored, making this measure undesirable for in-sample tests. It will be used for out-of-sample tests.

The wealth measures focus on the set of all marketable securities held by U.S. investors. The market is defined as the 12 market-valued asset classes held by U.S. investors, including some foreign securities listed in **Exhibit 1**. Information on the proxies used to estimate total returns and outstanding market values from January 1980 to the present are also shown in Exhibit 1. Estimates for earlier periods were derived from these and other sources.

We call the total the "U.S. Mix." This presentation is concerned only with its return each month and with its total value each month. The former we consider the return on "the market." The latter we consider one possible measure of investor wealth.

EXHIBIT 1. Definition of the U.S. Mix

- Treasury Bills
  - Returns: Salomon Brothers 3-month U.S. Treasury Bill Index
  - Value: U.S. Treasury Department data
- Intermediate-term Government Bonds
  - Returns: Shearson Lehman Hutton Intermediate Government Bond Index
  - Value: Same
- Long-term Government Bonds
  - Returns: Shearson Lehman Hutton Long Term Government Bond Index
  - Value: Same
- Corporate Bonds
  - Returns: Shearson Lehman Hutton Corporate Bond Index
  - Value: Same
- Mortgages and Mortgage-backed Securities
  - Returns: Shearson Lehman Hutton Mortgage Backed Securities Index
  - Value: Same
- Large Value Stocks
  - Returns: BARRA S&P High Book/Price Index
  - Value: Same
- Large Growth Stocks
  - Returns: BARRA S&P Low Book/Price Index
  - Value: Same
- Medium-capitalization Stocks
  - Returns: BARRA Medium-Capitalization Index
  - Value: Same
- Small-capitalization Stocks
  - Returns: BARRA Small Capitalization
  - Value: Same
- Foreign Bonds
  - Returns: Salomon Unhedged Non-U.S. Dollar Bond Index
  - Value: U.S. Department of Commerce data
- European Stocks
  - Returns: FT-Actuaries Europe and Pacific ex Japan Index
  - Value: U.S. Department of Commerce data
- Japanese Stocks
  - Returns: FT-Actuaries Japan Index
  - Value: U.S. Department of Commerce data

VARIANCE RATIO TESTS

A number of studies have utilized variance ratios to assess the extent to which a set of returns follows a random walk. For example, if the ratio of the variance of two-year returns divided by 2 times the variance of one-year returns is 1.0, the returns do not have a tendency to follow trends or to show mean reversion. If, however, such a ratio is less than 1.0, above-average returns tend to be followed by below-average returns and vice-versa. This is typically termed mean reversion.

Figure 2 shows variance ratios for returns on the U.S. Mix from January 1946 through April 1989. For example, the second point shows the variance ratio for two-year returns, with all consecutive 12-month periods used to estimate the one-year variance and all consecutive 24-month periods used to estimate the two-year variance. Note that the ratio is considerably less than one. The other points in Figure 2 show comparable ratios for longer periods. The ratio for three years is the ratio of the variance of three-year returns to three times the variance of one-year returns. It is even smaller than that for two years. In fact, every ratio shown (except that for one year, which is 1.0 by construction) is less than 1.0. This suggests substantial mean reversion in the return on the market as a whole. Similar results have been found for sub-markets (e.g., stocks) over various periods in the United States and other countries.

FIGURE 2. Variance Ratios

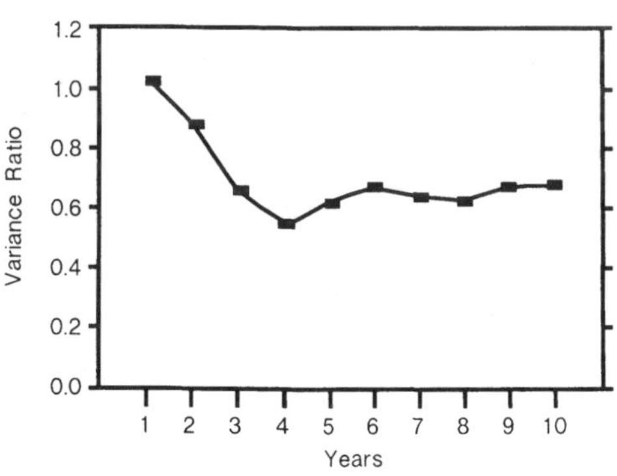

Source: Sharpe-Tint, Inc.

In analyses of this type, the use of overlapping periods makes standard statistical tests of significance inappropriate. We employed Monte Carlo analysis to assess the significance of these variance ratios. The actual returns were rearranged randomly and a new set of variance ratios was computed. Then the entire process was repeated over and over.

Figure 3 shows the results of 1,000 repetitions of this procedure. In roughly 18 percent of the 1,000 cases, the two-year variance ratio was lower than the one actually obtained (i.e., the 0.84 shown in Figure 2). Because the 1,000 cases came from a process in which the underlying return distribution was truly random (by construction), the probability is roughly 0.18 that the results actually obtained for the two-year variance ratio were due to chance and that the true process is in fact random.

FIGURE 3. Variance Ratio Monte Carlo Simulations: Percent of Cases with Lower Variance Ratios

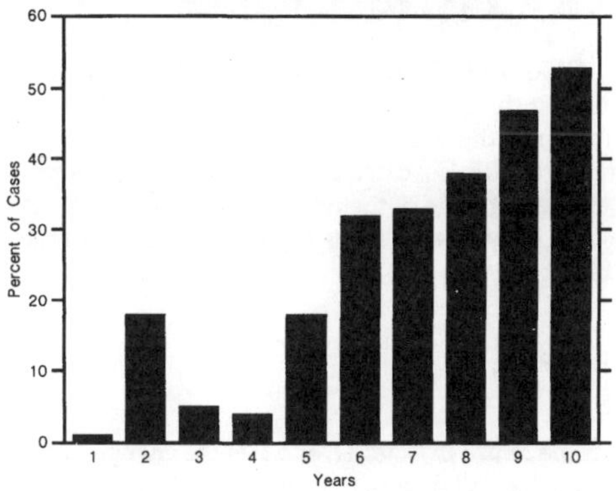

Source: Sharpe-Tint, Inc.

Although the two-year result is not highly significant, the results for three- and four-year intervals are more impressive. For example, Figure 3 indicates that there is only about a 5 percent chance (1 in 20) that the underlying process for market returns is truly random over periods as long as four years.

These results are highly suggestive of mean reversion in market returns over relatively long periods (e.g., of three or four years). We hypothesize that this can be attributed in part to the influence of wealth on investor risk tolerance.

PROXIES FOR WEALTH

Two proxies for wealth are utilized in our study. Each one is intended to serve as a proxy for the unattainable measure of choice—the real wealth of an average investor.

The first measure is the real security value per capita, or RSVPC. To begin, we estimate the total value of the U.S. Mix. Then we divide by the Consumer Price Index (CPI) to obtain a measure of real wealth. Finally, we divide by a measure of population to obtain an estimate of the real security value per capita.

RSVPC has substantial intuitive appeal. Moreover, its secular growth rate has been relatively small, averaging slightly over 1 percent per year in the period from 1946 through 1980. This makes it suitable for our in-sample tests.

The second measure is the cumulative real return, or CRR. To start, we assign a base value of 1.00 to the beginning of our sample period (December 1945). Then we cumulate the real return on the U.S. Mix each month:

$$CRR_t = CRR_{t-1}\,(1 + RR_t)\,.$$

CRR_t and CRR_{t-1} represent cumulative real return at the end of months t and t-1, respectively, and RR_t is the real return on the U.S Mix during month t. RR_t is calculated by taking a value-weighted average of the returns on the asset classes in the U.S. Mix, then adjusting for the change in the CPI:

$$1 + RR_t = \frac{1 + R_t}{1 + I_t}\,.$$

R_t is the return in month t, and I_t is the change in the level of the CPI during month t.

Unlike RSVPC, CRR is unaffected by transactions, such as leveraged buyouts, that alter the share of total wealth represented by marketable securities without changing total wealth. This property suggests that it may provide a better measure of changes in overall wealth. Its secular trend (approximately 3.5 percent from 1946 through 1980) is too large to be ignored, however. For this reason, we utilize it only for tests involving out-of-sample data.

WEALTH AND MARKET RETURNS

We hypothesize a relation between investor wealth and the market-wide premium per unit of risk, but we cannot measure either directly. Therefore, they must be approximated. Wealth is approximated by one of the two measures described in the previous section. The premium (an *ex ante* concept) is approximated using actual returns (i.e., *ex post* realizations).

Figure 4 shows RSVPC from January 1946 through May 1989 expressed in 1980 dollars per capita. Three observations are of particular interest: (1) the relatively rapid decline in the first half of the 1970s, (2) the very rapid increase during the bull market of the 1980s, and (3) the major decline in October 1987. Those more familiar with graphs plotting the level of the stock market may be somewhat surprised by these results. In particular, note that the overall market declined considerably less in October 1987 than did the stock market—primarily because bond prices rose in that period and partially offset the declines in stock prices.

FIGURE 4. Real Security Value Per Capita: January 1946-May 1989

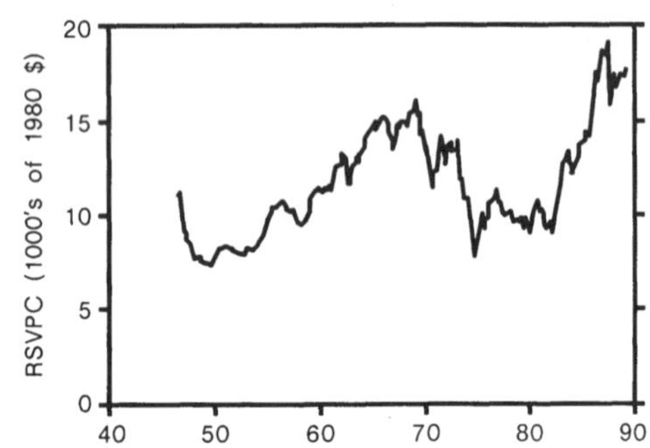

Source: Sharpe-Tint, Inc.

The hypothesized relation between investor wealth and the market-wide premium per unit of risk is tested using data from the post-war period through 1980; the period following 1980 is reserved for out-of-sample tests. RSVPC is the measure of wealth.

Standard mean-variance portfolio theory, coupled with market equilibrium theory (e.g., the Capital Asset Pricing Model), implies that market prices will adjust so that the following relation holds:

$$\frac{\text{Risk Premium}}{\text{Predictive Variance}} = \frac{2}{\text{Societal Risk Tolerance}} \tag{1}$$

Here risk premium refers to the difference between the expected return on the U.S. Mix and a riskless rate of interest, predicted variance denotes the uncertainty (measured by variance) concerning the return on the U.S. Mix, and societal risk tolerance refers to the wealth-weighted average of the risk tolerances of the investors who purchase the U.S. Mix.

Rearranging (1) gives:

$$\text{Risk Premium} = \frac{2 \times \text{Predicted Variance}}{\text{Societal Risk Tolerance}}. \quad (2)$$

This emphasizes the importance of both predicted risk and societal risk tolerance in determining the market risk premium.

We assume that societal risk tolerance is larger the greater the relevant measure of investor wealth. Specifically:

$$\text{Societal Risk Tolerance} = k \times \text{RSVPC}. \quad (3)$$

Combining (2) and (3) gives:

$$\text{Risk Premium} = \frac{2 \times \text{Predicted Variance}}{k \times \text{RSVPC}}. \quad (4)$$

A number of studies have found that near-term future risk tends to be somewhat more like recent risk than its long-term counterpart. Such a relation can be represented simply by:

$$\text{Predicted Variance} = a + b \times \text{Recent Variance}. \quad (5)$$

Combining (4) and (5) gives:

$$\text{Risk Premium} = \frac{2a}{k \times \text{RSVPC}} + \frac{2b \times \text{Recent Variance}}{k \times \text{RSVPC}}. \quad (6)$$

As noted earlier, the risk premium is an *ex ante* concept. One can only observe the *ex post* counterpart—e.g., the average excess return over some period following the determination of the risk premium. The realization is apt to differ from the expected—a relation that can be represented as:

$$\text{Average Excess Return} = \text{Risk Premium} + \text{Surprise}. \quad (7)$$

If expectations are unbiased, the "surprises" should be zero on average.

Combining (6) and (7) and representing groups of terms as parameters gives:

$$\text{Average Excess Return} = \alpha \frac{1}{\text{RSVPC}} + \beta \frac{\text{Recent Variance}}{\text{RSVPC}} + \varepsilon. \quad (8)$$

Multiple regression—with the average excess return as the dependent variable and the reciprocal of RSVPC and the ratio of recent variance to RSVPC as the independent variables—is used to test this relation.

The measure of recent variance is the actual variance over 12 months ending on the date at which RSVPC is measured. The measure of average excess return is the arithmetic average of the difference between the return on the U.S. Mix and the one-month U.S. Treasury-bill rate over a 12-month period subsequent to the date at which RSVPC is measured. To avoid biases, the average excess return is measured over a period starting one full month after the date at which RSVPC is measured. Thus, when RSVPC is measured at the end of December 1970, average excess return is measured over the 12 months from February 1971 through January 1972.

For the first observation used in the analysis, RSVPC is measured at the end of December 1945. For the last, it is measured at the end of December 1980. The results obtained from this analysis are consistent with the hypothesized relation. The multiple R^2 for the regression is 0.277 and the *t*-statistics for the two coefficients (alpha and beta) are 4.47 and 3.59, respectively. Moreover, the implied values for the underlying coefficients (k, alpha, and beta) are economically plausible.

Measures of statistical significance are not reported. There are two reasons for this. First, the use of overlapping periods provides an upward bias to standard measures of significance. Second, Monte Carlo methods are difficult to interpret when two dependent variables are utilized in the regression analysis. Our results, however, provide substantial presumptive evidence that the hypothesized relation is present. For a more robust test, the out-of-sample performance of strategies based upon the relation are considered.

MEAN REVERSION IN THE CUMULATIVE REAL RETURN

The next step is to look at the performance of investment strategies based on the relation between wealth and the market risk premium. Because this analysis focuses primarily on periods beginning in 1983, the CRR measure is utilized as the proxy for investor wealth. **Figure 5** shows the level of CRR from December 1945 through December 1979. To emphasize percentage changes, a logarithmic scale has been used for the Y-axis. A trend-line fit using standard regression analysis is also shown. In a diagram with a logarithmic scale such as this one, a straight line represents a constant growth rate throughout the period.

Although deviations from this trend line should not be used for in-sample tests, deviations of future values from the line (fit using data only through December 1979) may be used as "signals" concerning

FIGURE 5. Cumulative Real Return: 1946-79

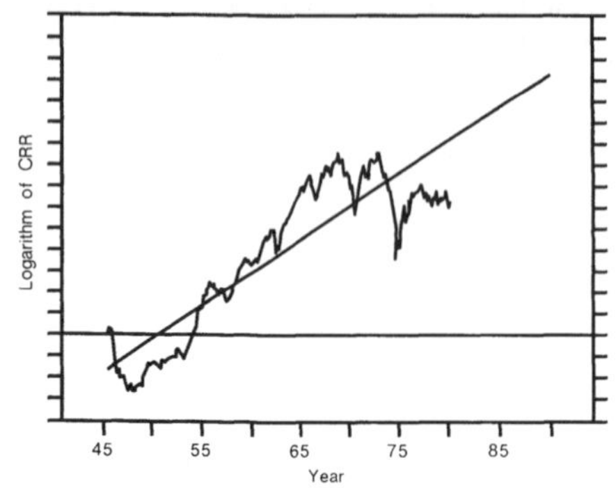

Source: Sharpe-Tint, Inc.

When wealth is below the trend line, we hypothesize that investors consider themselves poor (relative to expectations). Under such conditions, societal risk tolerance is low, and the market risk premium is high. There is, therefore, a tendency for wealth to increase at a greater-than-normal rate. Although actual results will differ from expectations, in the long run we anticipate reversion to the long-run trend.

The converse holds when wealth is above the trend line. In this case, investors are richer than expected, societal risk tolerance is high, and the premium per unit of risk is smaller than normal (although still positive). Under these conditions, there will be a tendency for wealth to increase at a smaller-than-normal rate, causing pressure for reversion to the trend line in the long run.

the level of investor wealth relative to its long-term trend.

Figure 6 extends the CRR through May 1989. The trend line is extended, not re-fit. As the points representing the actual levels of CRR indicate, during the 1980s market wealth reverted to its long-run trend, passed it, fell back to it in October 1987, and then rose above it.

Figure 7 portrays the mean-reversion hypothesis graphically. When wealth levels coincide with the long-run trend, the risk premium per unit of variance is at its "long-run normal" level. Under such conditions, when risk is normal, the market is expected to rise at a rate that will maintain wealth on its long-run trend line. Of course, actual returns will differ from expected returns. Nonetheless, when wealth is in line with long-run expectations, we hypothesize that there will be no net pressure for movement either above or below the trend line.

RISK PREMIUM-BASED INVESTMENT STRATEGIES

It is possible to predict the market risk premium using cumulative real return in a manner analogous to that used in the earlier in-sample tests. First, a long-run normal premium per unit of variance is estimated. The ratio of the average excess return on the U.S. Mix from 1946 through 1979 to the variance of this excess return over the same period is used in the tests reported here.

Next, a relative risk premium per unit of variance (RRP) as of the end of each month is computed. This is simply the inverse of the ratio of the CRR to its trend-line value:

$$RRP = \frac{\text{Trend–line CRR}}{\text{CRR}}.$$

FIGURE 6. Cumulative Real Return: 1946-89

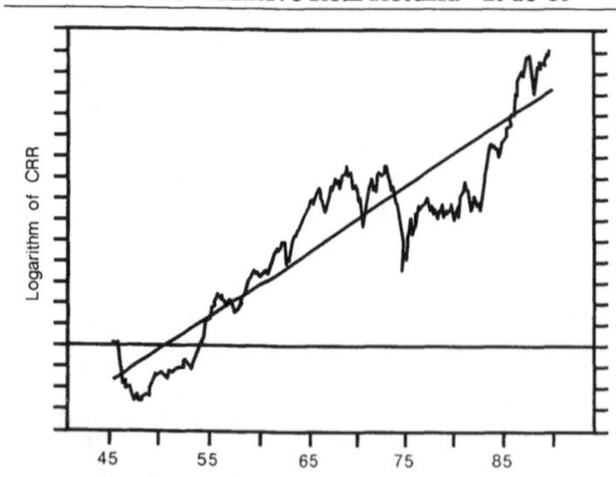

Source: Sharpe-Tint, Inc.

FIGURE 7. Mean Reversion in Cumulative Real Return

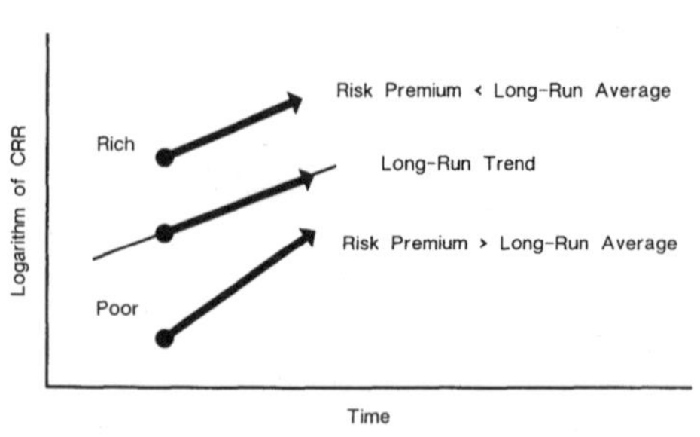

Source: Sharpe-Tint, Inc.

The predicted market risk premium per unit of variance at any time may then be computed by multiplying the long-run normal premium per unit of variance by the current relative risk premium per unit of variance.

We are now in a position to consider strategies in which RRP serves as a signal. In the first instance, the action item is the investor's choice of relative risk tolerance (RRT), defined as follows:

$$RRT = 100\left(\frac{\text{Investor Risk Tolerance}}{\text{Societal Risk Tolerance}}\right).$$

It is useful to think of RRT as a "knob" on an asset allocation optimizer. If the knob is set at 100 (percent) and a mix appropriate for the average investor will be produced. If it is set at a value greater than 100, a more aggressive mix will be obtained. If it is set at a value below 100, a more conservative mix will result.

I will concentrate on a set of possible "dynamic strategies" of the type shown in **Figure 8**. The relative risk premium serves as the signal, or trigger. The relative risk tolerance used to select an asset mix, shown on the vertical axis, is the decision variable. For simplicity, only strategies that plot as straight lines are considered.

Any strategy of this type may be described with two parameters. The first is the investor's policy or long-run normal relative risk tolerance. This represents his or her desired position under normal market conditions (i.e., when RRP = 100). The second parameter is the investor's response coefficient. This reflects the way in which the investor's desired position changes as market conditions (summarized by RRP) change. For ease of interpretation, we state this in terms related to the investor's long-run normal RRT:

$$RRT = RRT_{LR}\left(1 + c\,\frac{(RRP - 100)}{100}\right).$$

RRT_{LR} represents the investor's long-run normal relative risk tolerance, and c represents the investor's response coefficient. If, for example, an investor has a long-run normal RRT of 80 and a response coefficient of 1.0, an increase in the RRP from 100 to 110 would lead to an increase in RRT from 80 to 88 (each representing a change of 10 percent).

Figure 8 shows three different types of strategies. A flat line represents a constant-RRT strategy. Although not entirely passive, it is fairly close to a buy-and-hold approach (especially if the long-run normal position is close to 100). Downward-sloping lines represent "trend-following" or "portfolio insurance-like" strategies (strategies I1 and I2). They call for more aggressive stances when wealth is large (and the risk premium small) and more conservative strategies when wealth is small (and the risk premium large). Upward-sloping lines represent "contrarian" or "tactical asset allocation-like" strategies (strategies C1 and C2). They call for taking on added risk when wealth is small (and the risk premium large) and becoming more conservative when wealth is large (and the risk premium small).

It is important to note that only a minority of investors can adopt dynamic strategies such as tactical asset allocation. For such approaches to be feasible, there must be investors on the other side—i.e., "trend followers" to make trades with "contrarians." It is not possible for the average investor to follow either strategy.

This suggests that in an efficient market no dynamic strategy should be clearly better than any other. Some such strategies, however, may be more suitable for some groups of investors and other strategies more appropriate for other groups. Before we discuss these aspects further, let us examine the results that could have been obtained by following several alternative contrarian strategies.

FIGURE 8. Simple Dynamic Strategies

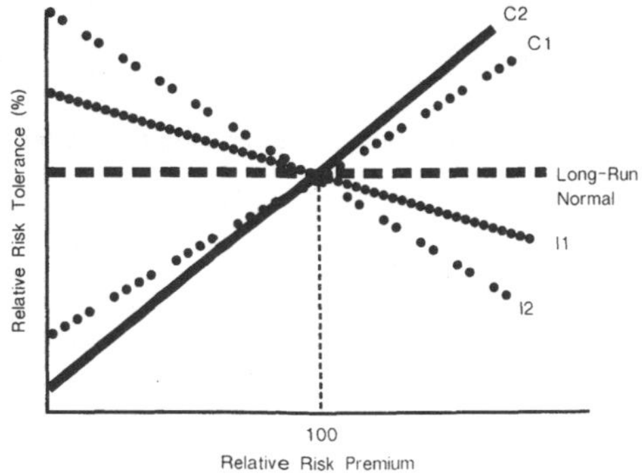

Source: Sharpe-Tint, Inc.

PERFORMANCE OF RISK PREMIUM-BASED STRATEGIES

Figure 9 summarizes performance over the 72 months from January 1983 through December 1988 for 15 strategies. The first group had a long-run normal RRT of 120; the second, 100; and the third, 80. Within each group, response coefficients of 0, 0.5, 1.0, 1.5, and 2.0 were investigated.

FIGURE 9. Alternative Optimized Strategies with 12-Way Allocation: 1983-88

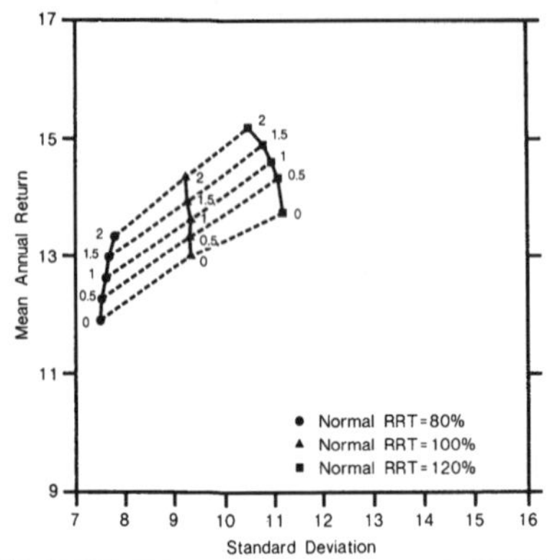

Source: Sharpe-Tint, Inc.

The annualized mean monthly returns are plotted on the vertical axis and the annualized standard deviation of monthly returns are plotted on the horizontal axis. The investment decision for each month is based on the RRP value computed using data as of the end of the prior month (i.e., one full month of data is assumed to be available for computations prior to each decision). Given an RRP value, the appropriate RRT value for the strategy is computed, then used as an input for a 12-way asset allocation optimizer. The asset classes employed are those listed earlier as components of the U.S. Mix. Risk and correlation estimates are based on monthly values provided by a model of the behavior of such attributes.[1] Asset expected returns are based on the risk premium implied by the overall model plus a model of equilibrium in the capital markets.[2] All estimates are updated each month using data applying to periods at least one month prior to the date at which each decision was made.

The results shown are computed before transaction costs and any possible market impacts. In practice, optimization models should take such costs into account. However, doing so here would make the results specific to initial funding, cash inflows and outflows, etc.

[1]The model, developed by Sharpe-Tint, Inc., uses a structure derived from analysis of the relation between historic risks, correlations, and corresponding future values. It was developed using data prior to 1983.

[2]The model used for this test was, in effect, the Capital Asset Pricing Model with the U.S. Mix serving as the market portfolio and the risks and correlations obtained from previous model taken as given.

In Figure 9, points representing strategies with similar response coefficients have been connected. The dotted line connecting the points marked "0" may be interpreted as the *ex post* risk-return trade-off using relatively static policies. The dotted line connecting the points marked "0.5" may be interpreted as the *ex post* risk-return trade-off using mildly contrarian strategies. The line connecting the points marked "1" indicates the trade-off using more reactive strategies, and soon.

Figure 9 shows that over this period contrarian (tactical) strategies provided added average returns relative to risk. Moreover, the more variable the investment mix, the better the results. Thus, the dotted line connecting the points marked "0.5" dominates that through the points marked "0." The line connecting the points marked "1" dominates that through the points marked "0.5," and so on.

It would appear that tactical strategies have offered something for nothing—results incompatible with efficient markets. But this is not necessarily the case. To obtain this added performance, the tactical asset allocator must take on added risk at the most difficult times, i.e. when most investors are poor. In an efficient market such behavior should be rewarded in the long run.

Six years is a very short time for a test of this sort, and one should be reluctant to conclude too much based on these results. Although data are not available to perform a truly out-of-sample test covering a longer period, we can offer some further presumptive evidence. To do so, we must switch from full optimization across 12 asset classes to a simple equity/cash strategy. In this analysis, the decision variable RRT is replaced by the direct action item: the percentage to be invested in equities. Long-run normal positions of 48 percent, 60 percent, and 72 percent (which correspond roughly to RRT values of 80, 100, and 120) are considered. **Figure 10** shows results for the 1983-88 period using this type of "two-way" asset allocation. Although each strategy underperforms its "12-way" counterpart, the basic relations are similar to those shown earlier, suggesting the relevance of such an analysis for comparative purposes.

Figure 11 shows the results obtained by following such two-way strategies over the 1973-88 period. The year 1973 has become a traditional starting date for studies of this type because the first formal tactical strategy was initiated then. Although part of this period overlaps part of the period used to fit the CRR trend line, the results are nonetheless likely to be representative of long-run expectations for such approaches.

Note that within a group of strategies with the

FIGURE 10. Alternative Optimized Strategies with Equity/Cash Allocation: 1983-88

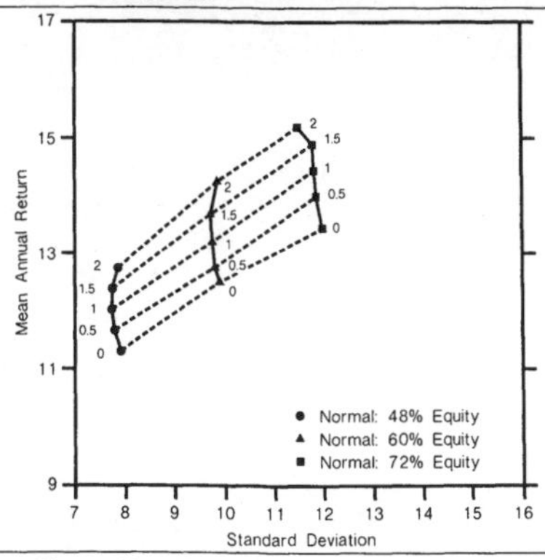

Source: Sharpe-Tint, Inc.

FIGURE 11. Alternative Optimized Strategies with Equity/Cash Allocation: 1973-88

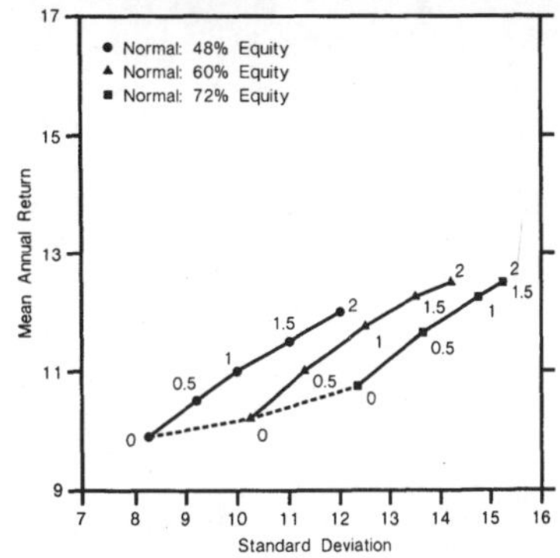

Source: Sharpe-Tint, Inc.

same long-run normal RRT (i.e., those connected by a solid line), those with greater response coefficients generally provided both higher average returns and greater standard deviations. This is more in line with theoretical expectations, suggesting that the behavior of the market in the 1983-88 period may have provided somewhat better results for tactical strategies than should be expected in the long run.

TACTICAL ASSET ALLOCATION: PROSPECTIVE RETURNS

In the approach described in this presentation, a tactical asset allocation strategy is simply a dynamic strategy with a positive response coefficient. Both fundamental principles and the empirical results obtained here suggest that an approach with a response coefficient of 1.0 might be expected to add 60 to 100 basis points per year to return for a given level of risk. Such an estimate, however, ignores transaction costs. In practice, asset allocations (and re-allocations) should be analyzed taking such costs into account. If this is done carefully with an asset allocation optimizer, tactical moves will be made more often when there are net cash flows into or out of a fund (requiring transaction costs in any event) than when there are no net cash flows.

Does this imply that tactical strategies offer something for nothing? Not necessarily. Such approaches require an investor to take on added risk at the hardest times—such as when investors are poorer than usual. In an efficient market, the willingness and ability to do so should be rewarded. The reward (added return), however, is by no means sure, and it may take years to obtain.

For all these reasons, a tactical asset allocation strategy would appear to be appropriate only for a relatively small minority of investors. In particular, it should appeal to those who (personally or organizationally) can take a truly long-run view. It appears to be a desirable strategy for those long-run investors who can "take the heat" when it is most uncomfortable to do so. Although the added returns may be modest, in the long run their cumulative effect may be substantial.

International Value and Growth Stock Returns

Carlo Capaul,
Ian Rowley and
William F. Sharpe

The returns obtained from portfolios of stocks with high price/book ratios ("growth" stocks) and those obtained from portfolios of stocks with low price/book ratios ("value" stocks) were analyzed for six countries over the period from January 1981 through June 1992. Results suggest the existence of a significant "value–growth factor" in each country. The returns on portfolios formed according to the value–growth factor differ far more from month to month than would be expected if the securities had been selected randomly.

Value stocks outperformed growth stocks on average in each country during the period studied, both absolutely and after adjustment for risk. Cross-country correlations of monthly value–growth spreads were small, suggesting that any decision to "tilt" a portfolio toward value stocks would have been more effective if done globally.

For decades, analysts of investment fund policies have used classifications such as "growth funds," "income funds" and "growth and income funds." Growth fund managers tend to concentrate their holdings in "growth stocks," while income fund managers favor securities that provide high current income and/or appear to be inexpensive relative to some measure of fundamental value.

One school of thought holds that the securities of companies with substantial growth prospects will provide high returns to investors over the long run. Another holds that the best investment strategy involves selecting companies whose securities can be purchased for prices that are low relative to the companies' estimated underlying values. There are many approaches to implementing these notions of growth and value. Those who advocate growth investing, for example, estimate companies' future earnings growth rates, but differ in the manner in which they make such predictions. Those who look for underpriced stocks compare current security prices with various indicators of value.

While it is possible to find "cheap" high-growth stocks and "expensive" low-growth stocks, most classification schemes find few securities fit such categories. Far more commonly, "growth" and "value" lie at opposite ends of the classification spectrum.

Several investigators have recently adopted a simple classificatory scheme to categorize securities or portfolios along a value/growth dimension. This scheme uses only one classificatory measure—the current price per share divided by the most recently reported book value per share. The intuition is straightforward: A security's price represents investors' assessments of future prospects, while its book value represents accountants' representation of its past costs; the greater a company' prospects for future growth, the greater should be the ratio of its future prospects to its embedded costs.

A number of objections can be made to this relatively simple interpretation. Growth in earnings *per se* should not provide added value unless it is expected to result from abnormally profitable investment opportunities. Moreover, book values based on accrual accounting may themselves reflect accountants' assessments of a firm's prospects. Nonetheless, a number of researchers have shown the simple price/book (P/B) measure to be especially useful for U.S. equities.[1]

Studies have shown that, in the U.S., returns on value and growth stocks can differ significantly, in either direction, from month to month, quarter to quarter or year to year; that many investment managers concentrate in predictable ways on value or growth stocks; and that value stocks have outperformed growth stocks over the long run. More precisely:

1. The difference between the return on a portfolio of value stocks and the return on a portfolio of growth stocks varies substantially from month to month—much more so than the difference between two otherwise similar portfolios holding randomly chosen securities.[2]
2. The "style" of an investment fund can be determined by analyzing the historical covariance of the fund's returns with those of portfolios of value stocks and

Glossary

►***Efficient Market:***
A market in which security prices are the same as they would be if everyone was aware of a specified, common set of information.

►***Excess Return:***
The difference between the return on an asset or portfolio and the nominal riskless rate for the same period and currency.

►***Monte Carlo Simulation:***
A procedure in which a set of simulated histories is created by using random numbers to draw values from probability distributions representing underlying processes. Ranges of relevant outcomes across the simulated histories provide estimates of the likelihood of various values being produced, given the assumptions used to characterize the overall process.

►***Sharpe Ratio:***
A measure of the reward obtained per unit of risk. For an investment, reward is measured by the average excess return (return minus a riskless rate) and risk by the standard deviation of excess returns. For a zero-investment strategy, reward is measured by the average return and risk by the standard deviation of returns.

►***S&P/BARRA Value Stock Index:***
An index of stocks within the S&P 500 universe with low ratios of price per share to book value per share. Every six months, a "breakpoint" price/book ratio is selected such that roughly half the market capitalization of the S&P 500 consists of stocks with ratios below the breakpoint and the other half of stocks with ratios above the breakpoint. The Value Stock Index is a market-capitalization-weighted index of the stocks in the set with low price/book ratios.

►***S&P/BARRA Growth Stock Index:***
An index of stocks within the S&P 500 universe with high ratios of price per share to book value per share. Every six months, a "breakpoint" price/book ratio is selected such that roughly half the market capitalization of the S&P 500 consists of stocks with ratios below the breakpoint and the other half of stocks with ratios above the breakpoint. The Growth Stock Index is a market-capitalization-weighted index of the stocks in the set with high price/book ratios.

►***t-statistic:***
The ratio of (1) the difference between an observed and an hypothesized value to (2) the standard error of that value. The greater the absolute value of the t-statistic, the greater the probability that the "true" value differs from the hypothesized value.

►***Value–Growth Factor:***
A factor representing differences in returns of securities with different price/book ratios.

►***Value–Growth Spread:***
The difference between the return on a portfolio of "value" (low-price/book-ratio) stocks and the return on a portfolio of "growth" (high-price/book-ratio) stocks.

growth stocks (plus other major asset classes). A large part of the variance of a fund's future return can be attributed to the return on its style, determined in advance using such "style analysis."[3]

3. Over the period from July 1963 through December 1990, value stocks significantly outperformed growth stocks in the United States.[4]

Measuring Growth

While the ratio of a security's price to its book value has substantial intuitive appeal, it is only one of many measures of growth used by investors. However, stocks with high price/book ratios also tend to have high values for other popular measures of growth. This can be seen in Table I, which reports the average values of several measures for the securities held by groups of U.S. mutual funds based on classifications by Morningstar, a major publisher of analytic information on such funds.[5] With one exception, the differences conform to popular notions of growth and value and to traditional classifications, as implemented by Morningstar.

Index Construction

We analyzed returns from six countries—France, Germany, Switzerland, the United Kingdom, Japan and the United States. For the U.S., we used the **S&P/BARRA Value Stock Index** and the **S&P/BARRA Growth Stock Index**, produced by BARRA for Standard & Poor's. For the other five countries, we used indexes produced by the Union Bank of Switzerland's Institutional Investment Management Group (Zurich).

The S&P/BARRA indexes are constructed by dividing all the stocks in the Standard & Poor's 500 stock index into two groups. The division is performed every six months. At each "division point," stocks are ranked on the basis of the ratio of a recent price to the most recently released book value per share. A dividing line is drawn so that the total market capitalization of the stocks "above the line" is as close as possible to that "below the line."[6] The stocks are then placed accordingly in value (low price/book) and growth (high price/book) portfolios. The monthly return for each portfolio is computed by taking a weighted average of the total returns on the underlying stocks, using outstanding total market

Table I Characteristics of Types of Mutual Funds

Fund Objective	*Price/Earnings Ratio*	*Price/Book Ratio*	*Earnings Growth Rate*	*Return on Assets*
Aggressive Growth	22.8	4.6	17.8%	8.6%
Growth	20.4	4.0	14.0%	7.9%
Growth and Income	18.7	3.3	9.3%	6.8%
Equity-Income	18.9	2.8	6.3%	5.8%

Source: *Morningstar Mutual Funds*, August 1, 1992.

capitalizations (price per share times number of shares) as weights.

Between the division points, the stocks in the assigned portfolios remain the same unless stocks are added to the S&P 500 or removed from it. When this happens, stocks added to the index are simply placed in one portfolio or the other, based on the price/book ratios that would have been computed at the prior division point, using the previously determined dividing line. In every month, the return on each index is simply the return on the corresponding portfolio.

The S&P 500 covers approximately 75% of the market capitalization of traded equity securities in the U.S. The underlying stocks tend to be larger and more liquid than stocks not included in the index. The other five country indexes are constructed by the Union Bank of Switzerland (UBS). The goal is to subdivide indexes published by Morgan Stanley Capital International (MSCI) in a manner similar to that employed for the S&P/BARRA indexes. This has been done explicitly for the months from July 1990 onward. Unfortunately the exact composition of the MSCI indexes prior to that time was not recorded. However, the lists of stocks covered by MSCI (which include all those used for their indexes) are available. Using a relatively simple rule, the USB has constructed indexes highly correlated with the published MSCI indexes from the MSCI data base, using only data that would have been available at the time.[7] In most countries the companies included in the MSCI indexes account for approximately 60% of the total market value of all relatively liquid traded equity securities.

The UBS indexes are constructed using the same procedures employed for the S&P/BARRA indexes. Because only annual dividend income figures are available from MSCI, security returns are computed by adding 1/12th of the previous 12 months' dividends to the relevant monthly percentage price changes. As with the S&P/BARRA indexes, index returns are computed by taking a weighted average of the total returns on the underlying stocks, using outstanding total market capitalizations (price per share times number of shares) as weights.

We believe that the methods used to construct the indexes used for this study are free from *ex post* selection biases. More precisely, the portfolios underlying the indexes each month could have been constructed well beforehand.

Data Coverage

Monthly returns and values were available for both value and growth indexes for all six countries from January 1981 (8101) through June 1992 (9206) inclusive. For each of the six countries, we used three indexes—the value stock index, the growth stock index and a market index. The latter was constructed by taking a market-value-weighted combination of the two former indexes. In the U.S., the market index is the S&P 500. For the other countries, it is either the MSCI index or a close approximation.

We constructed two additional indexes. First, we converted country returns to dollar returns, using exchange rates in effect at the beginning and end of each month.[8] Returns for our Europe index were computed by taking a value-weighted average of the dollar returns for France, Germany, Switzerland and the U.K. Returns for our global index were computed by taking a value-weighted average of the dollar returns for all six countries. Table II shows the composition of each index at the end of May 1992.

Excess Returns

Some of the analysis that follows uses **excess returns.** By definition, excess return equals the difference between the return on a security or portfolio and that of a "riskless asset." Since we employ monthly returns, we selected proxies for one-month interest rates for the latter. For the U.S., we used Ibbotson Associates' one-month U.S. Treasury bill returns. For the other countries, we employed short-term interest rates, also provided by Ibbotson Associates.

To compute excess returns within each country, we subtracted the proxy for the riskless rate in the country from the returns in question. For the Europe and global indexes, we first converted each country's excess return to a dollar equivalent, then computed a market-value-weighted average of the resulting dollar excess returns.

Table II Composition of Europe and Global Indexes, Month-End, May 1992

	Europe	*Global*
France	17.3%	3.9%
Germany	19.2%	4.4%
Switzerland	10.0%	2.3%
U.K.	53.5%	12.2%
Japan		24.5%
U.S.		52.7%
	100.0%	100.0%

Table III Correlations of Value and Growth Indexes: Actual and Simulated

	Actual Correlation	*Simulation: Mean Correlation*	*Simulation: Standard Deviation of Correlations*	*Number of Simulated Cases with lower Correlations*
France	.8245	.8526	.0202	9
Germany	.8847	.9205	.0128	0
Switzerland	.8461	.9078	.0169	0
U.K.	.8203	.9082	.0170	0
Japan	.8448	.9431	.0099	0
U.S.	.9196	n/a	n/a	n/a

Value–Growth Factors

Before proceeding, it is important to determine whether the **value–growth factor** truly affected security returns in the countries studied. To evaluate this, we analyzed the returns for the five countries for which we had sufficient data. The second column of Table III shows the correlation of each of these countries' value index with the corresponding growth index over the period studied. Not surprisingly, each coefficient was less than 1.00. However, this would be expected, even if the underlying portfolios were chosen at random.

To evaluate the correlations, we performed 100 **Monte Carlo simulations** for each of the five countries. Each simulation involved the creation of a set of indexes (one "value," one "growth") using precisely the method employed to construct the real indexes, with one key exception: Instead of using price/book ratios at the division points, we relied on a set of random numbers. Thus, in any one simulation, the correlation between the "value" and "growth" indexes would be due only to the use of subsets of the overall set of securities, as the underlying portfolios were not selected on the basis of a true factor.

The third column of Table III shows the mean correlation obtained in each set of 100 simulations. The fourth column shows the standard deviation across the 100 cases for each country, while the final column shows the number of simulations (out of 100) in which the simulated correlation between the two randomly selected indexes was less than that shown in the preceding column. The latter can be interpreted as a rough estimate of the probability that our results are simply due to chance—i.e., that there was ***not*** a value–growth factor in the country in question.

The results in Table III provide strong evidence that value–growth factors measured using price-to-book ratios caused substantial differences in security returns in the five countries studied. Only for France did any of the simulated cases produce a correlation coefficient as low as that actually experienced. While no results are available for the U.S., the fact that the U.S. value and growth indexes include a great many securities strongly suggests that the correlation shown (although higher than those obtained for the other countries) is also significantly below that which would be obtained were such a factor not at work.

Value–Growth Spreads

We computed each **value-growth spread** by subtracting the return on a growth index from that on the corresponding value index. Several interpretations are possible. The result can be considered the return advantage (if positive) or disadvantage (if negative) resulting from holding value stocks rather than growth stocks. It can also be considered the return "pick-up" (if positive) or "drop" (if negative) associated with a prior decision to switch from growth to value stocks. It can also be regarded as the net return on a swap, whereby an investor agrees to receive the return on value stocks in return for a promise to pay the return on growth stocks. Finally, it can be considered the net re-

Figure A Global Cumulative Value-Growth Spread

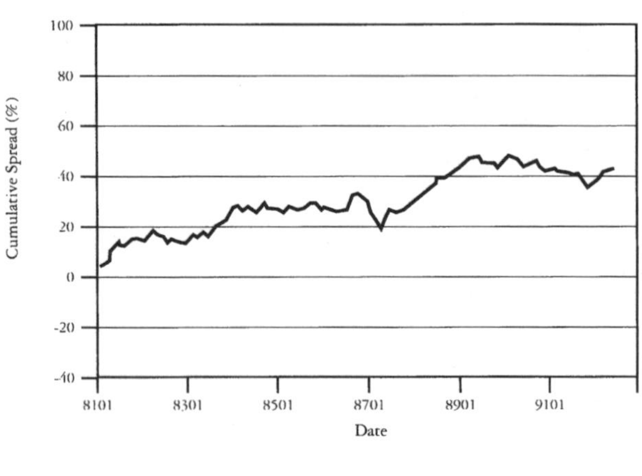

Figure B Japanese Cumulative Value-Growth Spread

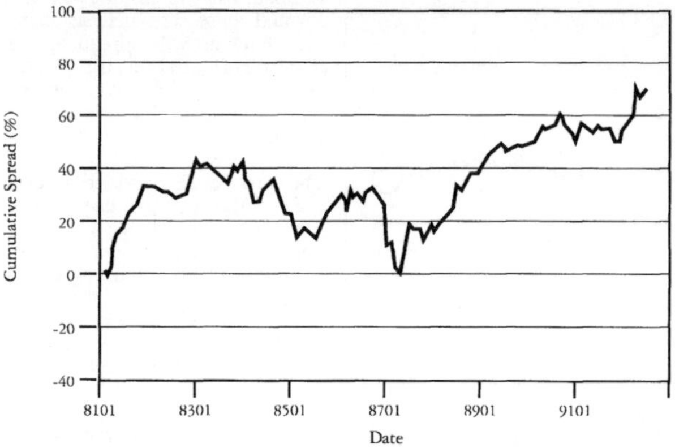

turn from a strategy in which growth stocks are sold short and value stocks purchased (i.e., held long).

Figures A through H show the cumulative values of the value–growth spread for each of our eight sets of indexes.[9] For ease of comparison, all are plotted using the same scale. Increases indicate periods in which the value index outperformed the growth index; decreases indicate periods in which the value index underperformed the growth index.

Figure A shows that, over the 11½ years, global value stocks outperformed global growth stocks by almost 40% (the actual figure was 39.54%), or somewhat over 3.3% per year. Figures B, C and D show that the three regions (Japan, the U.S. and Europe) contributed quite differently to the global results. The cumulative outperformance of value stocks over growth stocks was 69.5% for Japan, 15.6% for the U.S. and 31.9% for Europe. Note that the U.S. turned in the lowest figure.

Figures E, F, G and H show that value stocks outperformed growth stocks on a cumulative basis in every one of the four European countries. Cumulative spreads were 73.7% for France, 17.7% for Germany, 42.7% for Switzerland, and 31.5% for the U.K. Here, too, every value exceeded that for the U.S.

Value stocks did indeed outperform growth stocks over this period in the U.S., but by very small amounts relative to the historical differences found over longer periods by prior researchers.[10]

Figure C U.S. Cumulative Value-Growth Spread

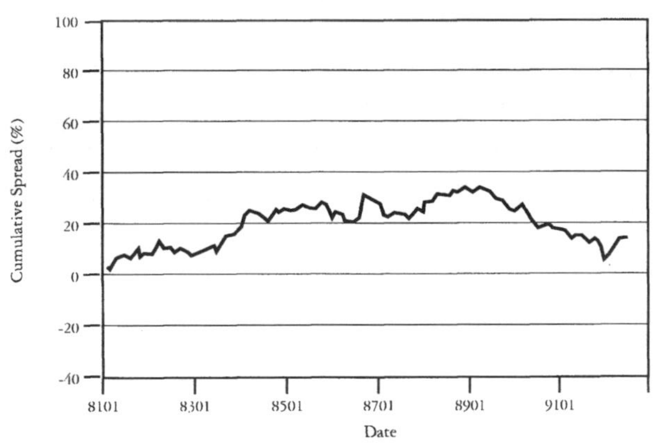

Value stocks also outperformed growth stocks in every one of the other five countries analyzed, and most of the differences were substantially larger than that for the U.S. But were they significantly so?

Table IV provides some evidence on this point. The initial columns show the average monthly return spread and standard deviation of monthly return spreads for each of the eight series. The next column shows the **t-statistic** associated with each of the average returns.[11] The final columns re-express the information in the initial columns in more familiar units: The annualized average return spread is simply 12 times the average monthly return spread; the annualized standard deviation is simply the square root of 12 times the monthly standard deviation.[12]

The results show that the global spread was significantly different from zero in both an economic and a statistical sense, with a t-statistic close to 2.0. The t-statistics were somewhat lower, but still relatively high, for France, Switzerland, Japan and Europe. In contrast, they were low for Germany, the U.K. and the U.S.

Figure D European Cumulative Value-Growth Spread

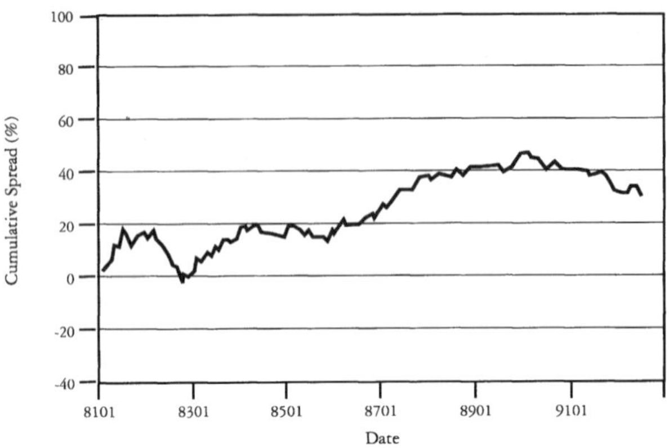

Table IV also shows that the standard deviation of the value–growth spread was lowest for the global series. This suggests that there were diversification benefits associated with global "value tilting," given the low correlations across the spreads in different countries.

Table V confirms that this was the case. It shows that spreads were positively correlated for some pairs of countries, negatively correlated for others and close to zero for yet others. The average of the (off-diagonal) values in the table was only 0.071.

To summarize: Value stocks outperformed growth stocks over the period covered, and the difference in performance was significant on a global basis. Thus the phenomenon operated to a greater or lesser extent in every country, but in different ways in different places at different times. Thus, while the differences were statistically significant on a global basis, they were less significant for some countries and insignificant for others. This suggests that an investor considering a "tilt" toward value stocks would be well advised to implement the policy globally, rather than within a single country or even a single region.

Value–Growth Spreads and Market Returns

The period from January 1980 through July 1992 saw generally upward movements in stock markets worldwide. Hence it is at least possible that some or all of the superior performance of value stocks might have been due simply to their greater sensitivities to market movements compared with growth stocks. To evaluate this possibility, we performed regression analyses using the value–growth spread as the dependent variable and the excess return of the corresponding market index as the independent variable.

This procedure provided an estimate of the "beta" of each value–growth spread relative to a "market" made up of the two indexes in question. The resulting coefficients, in turn, equaled the differences in the corresponding beta values of the two indexes. In cases in which the beta of the value–growth spread was positive, value stocks were indeed more sensitive to market moves than growth stocks. In cases in which the beta of the spread was negative, value stocks were less sensitive to such moves than growth stocks.

Table VI reports the results of the analysis. For each case, we show both the beta value and the associated t-statistic. For Germany, Japan and the U.S., the beta values were statistically significantly different from zero. For the global index, the absolute value of the t-statistic was well above 2.0,

Figure E French Cumulative Value-Growth Spread

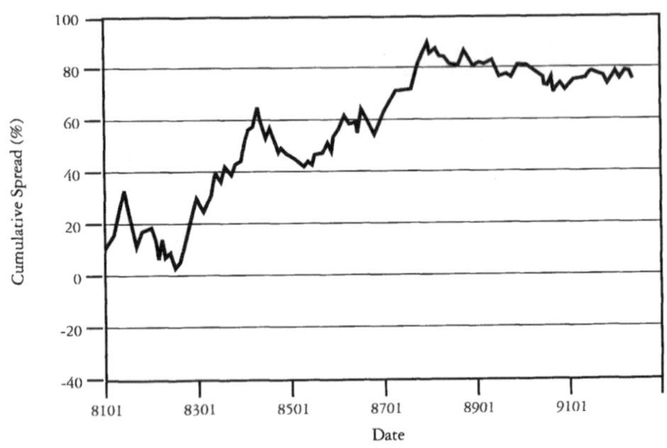

Figure F German Cumulative Value-Growth Spread

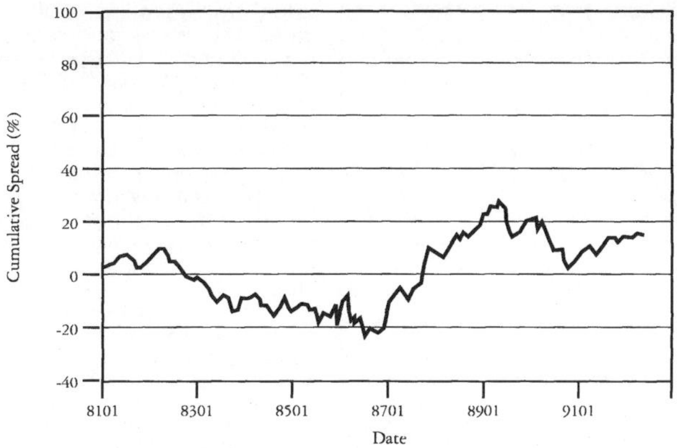

hence also significantly different from zero. Note, however, that all these values were negative. In the case of France, the beta value was positive, but not significantly so. Only for Switzerland was the beta value significantly positive.

These results provide evidence that the superior performance of value stocks found earlier does not merely reflect differences in the beta values of value and growth stocks. In most cases, value stocks had *lower* beta values than growth stocks. In a period such as the one covered in this study, one would expect the lower beta values of value stocks to cause them to *under*perform growth stocks. But just the reverse was the case.

Portfolio Risk and Return

We turn next to an examination of historical returns and variabilities of return. We measured variability by the annualized standard deviation of the excess return for each index. We measured return by the annualized average excess return. The return provided per unit of risk is summarized by the **Sharpe ratio**—the ratio of the average excess return to the standard deviation of excess return.[13]

Assuming that it is possible to borrow or lend at the riskless rate, a portfolio with a higher Sharpe ratio can be said to have dominated one with a lower Sharpe ratio. To be more specific, let X have a higher Sharpe ratio than Y. Then, for any specified level of variability, the appropriate combination of X plus borrowing or lending would have produced a greater average return than the appropriate combination of Y plus borrowing or lending. More simply, the Sharpe ratio indicates the return achieved per unit of risk borne, hence summarizes in one number two crucial aspects of total performance.

Table VII shows the Sharpe ratios for the indexes. In every case, the value index provided the best results. Moreover, each value index provided results superior to those of the corresponding market index.[14]

While the Sharpe ratio summarizes performance in a useful manner, the magnitudes are not especially intuitive. To indicate the practical implications of the differences in Table VII, we computed the differences in return between two equal-variability strategies—one involving a value index, the other the corresponding market index. In each case, the value-index-based strategy used a combination of the value index in question and borrowing or lending at the riskless rate. Each such combination was constructed to have precisely the same variability as the market index in question. The difference between the return on such a strategy and that of the market

Figure G Swiss Cumulative Value-Growth Spread

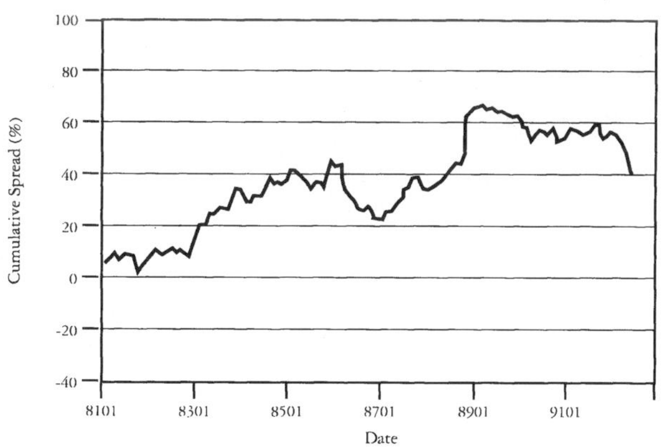

Figure H U.K. Cumulative Value-Growth Spread

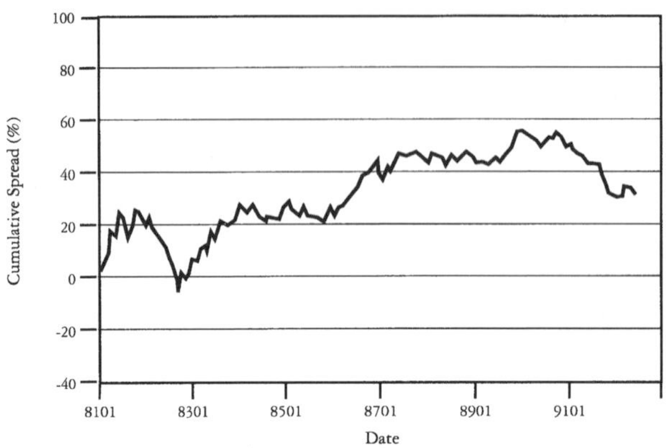

index can thus be interpreted as the added return that could have been achieved had an investor switched from the market index to a combination of the value index plus borrowing or lending in the amount required to achieve the same risk. Table VIII shows the results.

During this period, a strategy that included *no* growth stocks could have added substantially to overall performance. At a global level, a "return pick-up" of 1.88% per year could have been achieved without an increase in variability. Overall, the differences ranged from 1% to over 3%.

Needless to say, to achieve the results in Table VIII one would have had to construct strategies having at least one characteristic (the appropriate amount of borrowing or lending) not fully known in advance. Nonetheless, the record indicates that portfolios with significant value tilts could have provided substantial improvements over those more representative of the markets in question.

Optimal Value Tilts

Tables VII and VIII show that, over the period studied, each value index provided more return per unit of risk than the corresponding growth index. In fact, in every case the returns provided by the value index were sufficiently superior to those provided by the growth index that a strategy of investing 100% of one's funds in the value index dominated *any* combination of the two indexes except those involving short positions in the growth index.

In an **efficient market,** one might expect that a portfolio of securities based on market values would prove superior to one involving "tilts" away from such values. However, it is important to take a broad view when interpreting such statements. A significant number of investors may be concerned with aspects other than before-tax risk and return. If value stocks are inferior to growth stocks in some respect (such as greater taxes owing to higher dividends), one could well expect them to offer greater expected return per unit of risk on a before-tax basis.[15] Moreover, investors may prefer to hold securities of companies with good records and superior growth prospects. For personal and institutional reasons, a portfolio of "household names" may be considered better than one of "fallen angels"—enough so as to offset the prospect that the former may provide less return per unit of risk than the latter.

What of the future? To the extent that the historical superiority of value stocks over growth stocks resulted from investors' errors in pricing, the publication of papers such as this one might be expected to alter the relationship, thereby reducing the benefits associated with value tilts. Nonetheless, some advantages might still remain. An interesting question concerns the relationship between the future magnitude of such advantages and optimal investment policy.

To provide a context in which to evaluate this issue, we performed one last set of calculations for each country and for our Europe and global composites. Given the standard deviations of the excess returns on the value and growth indexes for an area, and the cor-

Table IV Monthly Value–Growth Spread Statistics

	Average	*Standard Deviation*	*t-statistic for Average*	*Annualized Average*	*Annualized Standard Deviation*
France	0.53	3.86	1.62	6.41	13.38
Germany	0.13	3.14	0.48	1.54	10.88
Switzerland	0.31	2.90	1.26	3.71	10.03
U.K.	0.23	3.32	0.81	2.74	11.50
Japan	0.50	3.76	1.57	6.04	13.03
U.S.	0.11	1.99	0.67	1.35	6.89
Europe	0.23	2.18	1.24	2.77	7.57
Global	0.29	1.70	1.98	3.44	5.89

Table V Correlations of Value–Growth Spreads

	France	*Germany*	*Switzerland*	*U.K.*	*Japan*	*U.S.*
France	1.00	−0.07	0.08	0.34	0.03	0.24
Germany	−0.07	1.00	0.20	−0.13	−0.20	0.08
Switzerland	0.08	0.20	1.00	0.08	0.06	0.03
U.K.	0.34	−0.13	0.08	1.00	0.07	0.26
Japan	0.03	−0.20	0.06	0.07	1.00	0.01
U.S.	0.24	0.08	0.03	0.26	0.01	1.00

relation between the excess returns, we computed alternative values for the corresponding average returns. These alternative, equilibrium values had the same average as that of the actual values but were consistent with the optimality of a 50/50 mix of the two indexes. More specifically, had these returns been obtained on average, a 50/50 combination would have had the greatest Sharpe ratio of any possible combination of the two indexes.

Let A equal the set of actual average excess returns and E the set of "equilibrium" average excess returns constructed in the manner described. Assume that one projects future expected excess returns to equal kA + (1 − k)E, with risks and correlations equal to historical values. What is the lowest value of k for each area that would make an all-value stock portfolio superior to any combination of the value and growth stock indexes with no short positions? Table IX provides the answers.

These results indicate that, even if the future superiority of the global value index is as little as 10.1% (0.101) as great as it was in the period covered by our study, a 100% value tilt would prove desirable for an investor concerned only with maximum before-tax expected excess return per unit of risk. Note that, while all the values in Table IX are substantially less than 1.0, the value for the global index is the smallest, as one would expect, given the earlier conclusion that the advantages of value tilting are greatest on a global basis.

Table IX can also be used to estimate the optimal mix of value and growth indexes if the future values of k are less than those shown. Assume, for example, that one anticipates that the future value of k for the global indexes will be 0.0606—60% of the threshold value of 0.101. Then the optimal policy would be to allocate 60% of an investor's funds to the value index and the remaining 40% to a 50/50 combination of the value and growth indexes, giving a total mix with 80% in the value index and 20% in the growth index.

Table VI Beta Values of Value–Growth Spreads

	Beta	*t-statistic for Beta Value*
France	0.01	0.15
Germany	−0.17	−4.21
Switzerland	0.10	2.03
U.K.	−0.02	−0.31
Japan	−0.18	−3.63
U.S.	−0.14	−3.96
Europe	−0.01	−0.37
Global	−0.09	−2.72

Conclusions

We have documented the existence of a value–growth factor related to the ratio of stock price-to-book value per share over the period from January 1981 through June 1992 in six major security markets. We have shown that this factor contributed significantly to variations in security prices, hence returns. Moreover, we have shown that, during this period, portfolios of stocks with low price-to-book ratios ("value" stocks) provided risk-adjusted performance superior to that of portfolios of stocks with high price-to-book ratios ("growth" stocks).

Ignoring transaction costs, taxes and potential principal–agent problems associated with holding stocks with bad records, a substantial tilt towards value stocks would have been attractive during the period of our study, especially if implemented on a global basis. This may or may not mean that such a policy will prove desirable over, say, the next 10 years. We have not taken into account the fact that the maintenance of an index fund of value stocks utilizing our methods would require substantial turnover and would thus incur higher transaction costs than a fund including both value and growth stocks in market proportions. More importantly, lacking a well articulated theory to explain the superior performance of such stocks, we are unable to predict whether the phenomenon will continue, diminish or entirely disappear. Suffice it to say that the ubiquitous nature of the phenom-

Table VII Index Sharpe Ratios

	Value	*Growth*	*Market*
France	0.53	0.26	0.38
Germany	0.47	0.33	0.40
Switzerland	0.43	0.25	0.36
U.K.	0.47	0.32	0.41
Japan	0.39	0.08	0.23
U.S.	0.50	0.36	0.44
Europe	0.50	0.33	0.42
Global	0.46	0.21	0.33

Table VIII Annualized Return Difference: Value Index at Market Risk Minus Market Index

	Added Return
France	3.26%
Germany	1.39%
Switzerland	1.17%
U.K.	1.09%
Japan	3.43%
U.S.	1.06%
Europe	1.30%
Global	1.88%

Table IX Values of k for which 100% Value Tilts are Optimal

	k
France	0.273
Germany	0.383
Switzerland	0.313
U.K.	0.537
Japan	0.133
U.S.	0.269
Europe	0.272
Global	0.101

enon in recent years suggests that investors pay serious attention to the extent to which their holdings tilt towards either value or growth stocks.

Footnotes

1. *See B. Rosenberg, K. Reid and R. Lanstein, "Persuasive Evidence of Market Inefficiency,"* Journal of Portfolio Management *9 (1985), pp. 18–28; W. F. Sharpe, "Asset Allocation: Management Style and Performance Measurement,"* Journal of Portfolio Management *18:2 (1992), pp. 7–19; W. F. Sharpe, "Determining a Fund's Effective Asset Mix,"* Investment Management Review, *September/October 1988; and E. F. Fama and K. R. French, "The Cross-Section of Expected Stock Returns,"* Journal of Finance *47 (1992), pp. 427–65.*
2. *Rosenberg, Reid and Lanstein, "Persuasive Evidence,"* op. cit. *and Fama and French, "The Cross-Section,"* op. cit.
3. *Sharpe, "Determining a Fund's Effective Asset Mix,"* op. cit. *and "Asset Allocation,"* op. cit.
4. *Fama and French, "The Cross-Section,"* op. cit.
5. *Data are composites for 44 aggressive growth funds, 254 growth funds, 125 growth and income funds and 34 equity income funds.*
6. *In practice, the division is based on the ratio of book value to price, so that stocks with negative or zero book values fall in the growth category.*
7. *It was assumed that the largest-capitalization stocks comprising 80% of the value of the stocks covered by MSCI at the time were used for each of the indexes. For a typical country, the MSCI universe covers 75% of the total value of traded equities, while the MSCI index covers 60% of such value. Thus the ratio of the value of securities in a country's index to those in the MSCI universe for the country is 0.80. Analyses of the relationships between the returns on our proxy indexes and the actual MSCI indexes provide evidence of the validity of our procedures. The correlations of the returns on our proxy indexes with those of the published MSCI indexes from January 1981 through June 1990 were as follows: France 0.967, Germany 0.991, Switzerland 0.989, Japan 0.982 and the U.K. 0.992.*
8. *Throughout we used exchange rates provided by Ibbotson Associates.*
9. *Note that the cumulative values represent the sums of the monthly spreads; no compounding is employed. Thus a given vertical distance has the same meaning at each point in the graph.*
10. *Fama and French, "The Cross-Section,"* op. cit. *In the period from January 1973 through December 1980, the annualized U.S. value–growth spread using our indexes was 5.67% per year—considerably greater than the 1.36% per year during the period from January 1981 through June 1992.*
11. *This is equal to the average return divided by the standard deviation of returns divided by the square root of the number of observations (138 months).*
12. *Both calculations indicate the annual values that would be predicted under the assumption that returns are uncorrelated from month to month.*
13. *Termed the reward-to-variability ratio by its originator, but widely referred to in this manner by others.*
14. *This need not be the case, even if the value index has outperformed the growth index. In particular, even though a value index may have had a higher average return than the corresponding market index, it may have also had sufficiently greater risk, owing to a lower degree of diversification, for its Sharpe ratio to be less than that of the market index.*
15. *For an early suggestion that this might be the case, see R. H. Litzenberger and K. A. Ramaswamy, "Dividends, Short Selling Restrictions, Tax-Induced Investor Clienteles and Market-Equilibrium,"* Journal of Finance *35 (1980), pp. 469–85.*

Section 6: Lifetime Finance

6-1 "Financial Planning in Fantasyland," www.wsharpe.com, October 1997.

When I returned to Stanford in 1992, I turned my research focus from the problems faced by managers of large institutional pension, endowment and foundation funds to the decisions made by individuals saving and investing for their retirement. It seemed to me that the shift from traditional defined benefit pension plans to defined contribution plans would continue and accelerate, due to the changing demographics of most developed economies. My reasoning was that as the percentages of the populations over the traditional age for retirement continued to increase due to lower fertility rates and greater longevity, optimal generational risk-sharing would require some mechanisms that would allow and encourage people to share in overall societal risk when saving for retirement and when spending such savings in later life. In the United States, the primary vehicles used by lower and middle income people for doing this were (and still are) defined contribution plans which require individuals to make crucial and complex decisions for which many are ill equipped.

This paper, based on a dinner speech given at a conference sponsored by the University of California Davis Graduate School of Management and posted on my website in the fall of 1997, reflected my dismay with the approach many in the financial industry were taking to help people make such decisions. Projections were computed without even recognizing the uncertainty associated with equity investments. The extensive theoretical work in portfolio choice and asset pricing was virtually ignored, as was almost all the empirical research on asset risks, returns and correlations and on mutual fund performance. As I indicated in the final paragraph of the paper: "We need to devise software that recognizes that investment returns are not certain, that conveys risk/return tradeoffs in ways that are relevant and understandable by the user and that projects mutual fund characteristics as carefully as possible."

I had held many of the views and desires reflected in the paper for some time. In early 1996, I shared such ideas with Joseph Grundfest, a good friend who teaches securities law at the Stanford Law School. Joe suggested that we talk with Craig Johnson, a lawyer who headed a firm that helped start idea-based companies in Silicon Valley. The result was the founding of Financial Engines, Inc. — a firm dedicated to trying to meet the needs outlined in the paper and to do so at a sufficiently low marginal cost to make good advice and/or investment management available to every employee in a defined contribution plan. For a number of years I served as a board member, advisor and consultant to the company. With substantial capital provided by local venture capital firms and the hard work of many highly skilled professionals (a number from Stanford) the goals were met. Over the years, the firm has applied, implemented and extended much of the research done in the field of Financial Economics, including a number of the ideas and results included in this volume. In 2010, the company's shares were listed on the NASDAQ exchange, providing measures of the market's views of its accomplishments.

6-2 "Retirement Financial Planning: A State/Preference Approach," www.wsharpe.com, February 2006.

This paper, posted to my web site, reflected my shift from a focus on pre-retirement savings and investing to the problems faced by individuals and families after retirement. My goal was to describe a framework for deriving strategies for spending, investing and annuitizing retirement savings. To do so, I drew heavily on the material in my 2007 book that was nearing completion when I wrote this in early 2006. Given the framework, I then presented some possibilities for efficient algorithms for deriving optimal strategies.

The structure is one of discrete times and states, with complete markets provided by explicit time/state securities, other types of derivatives, standard securities or dynamic strategies. The goal is to maximize a function equivalent to the measure of expected utility used in standard economic models of multi-period decision-making. I called this function desirability to emphasize that it measures the expected utility assessed today by an individual for contingent amounts of consumption at future dates when he or she may be in significantly different mental states.

A key assumption is that the expected contributions of consumption in each of the states to this measure can be computed separately, then aggregated to obtain the overall measure of desirability. This corresponds to the assumption of time-separable utility functions used in a number of economic models. Importantly, it rules out phenomena such as "habit formation" in which the utility of consumption in one period is in part a function of consumption in one or more prior periods. Behavioral studies have shown that many people exhibit such preferences. In a Naval Postgraduate School Masters Thesis for which I served as an advisor, Issac Gonzales conducted experiments that found evidence for such behavior although the influence of prior consumption was the often opposite that often assumed. Hopefully future experimental work will shed more light on this key aspect of individual preferences.

The latter part of the paper proposes an algorithm that can be used to efficiently find a post-retirement financial strategy, given the characteristics of an individual's preferences. Unfortunately it does not generalize to cases in which utility functions are not separable in the assumed manner. John Watson, a close friend and long-time

Financial Engines employee, has now developed an algorithm that can efficiently solve such problems when returns follow a binomial process. For another Master's Thesis at the Naval Postgraduate School, Wesley Johnson, working with John as an advisor, implemented and tested the algorithm. While programs for efficiently solving larger problems with more complex return-generating processes and investor preferences are not available at present, it appears that the more vexing problems in this domain are those associated with building adequate representations of investors' true preferences. There is a great need for more behavioral research in this area.

6-3 "Financing Retirement: Saving, Investing, Spending and Insuring," www.wsharpe.com, October 2006.

This is based on a talk I gave at Middlebury College, outlining some of the issues associated with the current regime in which individuals bear much of the responsibility for financing their lives.

The first section spells out the arguments for the need to have broader risk-sharing across generations than was possible with earlier retirement systems, but cautions that individuals and governments need to do a much better job of implementing social and private programs to facilitate this. I then outline some of the problems with the U.S. Social Security and Medicare programs. Both had huge unfunded liabilities but differed in an important respect. The Trustees' reports indicate that for future participants, the present value of contributions to Social Security will be virtually equal to the present value of benefits paid. Almost all the unfunded liability in that program is associated with those currently in the program. On a prospective basis, Social Security is not "broken", as many politicians have argued. Not so for Medicare, which had (and still has) a much greater unfunded liability, including that associated with the costs and benefits for future participants. I then suggested that it might be best to leave the Social Security system alone, funding the shortfalls arising from the past with general tax revenues (a policy that I still consider worthwhile).

Next, I discuss defined benefit pension plans, deploring accounting and actuarial approaches frequently used to hide their true funding status. In the U.S. legislation and accounting rulings had reduced the latitude for corporate sponsors of such plans to discount liabilities at, say, 8% when government bonds were yielding 4%, thus "wildly understating the economic value of liabilities". Unhappily, this practice continues with most pension plans for state and local government employees. As I write this, the Government Accounting Standards Board (GASB) has just confirmed that it will in large part continue to condone the practice (over the objections of almost all economists familiar with the subject).

I next turn to issues surrounding defined contribution plans. As before, I decry some of the advice formerly given to participants in such plans and hope that the trend toward the provision of better advice will continue. I conclude with some comments on the problems faced by individuals in their retirement years, indicating my increasing interest in such issues. I suggest that it will be important to combine actuarial science with investment expertise, since mortality and economic uncertainty both play important roles in later life. I mention, but do not solve, the "annuity puzzle" — the fact that when social norms change to allow people to avoid annuitization, they generally do so in whole or large part, The final portion of the talk includes a broad-brush description of the possible use of models designed to select post-retirement financial strategies that maximize expected utility and an example involving the integration of long-term care insurance with a variable annuity (a possibility I had explored in some detail a year earlier in a talk at an industry conference).

6-4 "Lockbox Separation," www.wsharpe.comm, June, 2007.

This paper, posted to my web site, serves two purposes. First, it shows that in a complete market the relationship between a consumption plan and an investment plan will conform to a simple matrix equation: Mx = c, where c is a vector representing consumption over times and states, x is a vector representing a dynamic investment strategy and M is a matrix representing the opportunities provided by purchasing and selling securities at various dates. Given such a relationship, it is straightforward to show that any optimal strategy can be decomposed into a series of static or dynamic strategies, each of which is designed to provide the desired state-contingent consumptions in a single time period. The funds for any such strategy can, in principle, be placed in a lockbox, with the proceeds to be spent only at the designated maturity date.

Some approaches proposed or implemented within the investment industry can be easily decomposed into lockbox strategies. In many cases, doing this makes it possible to better evaluate the characteristics of the overall strategy. More broadly, it may be fruitful to use lockbox equivalents to evaluate aspects of the optimal strategies obtained when maximizing expected utility for different classes of investor utility functions in more complex capital market settings than those employed in the simple examples used in this paper. It remains to be seen whether or not there are behavioral arguments for implementing a strategy with soft or hard lockboxes for a particular individual or family.

6-5 "Efficient Retirement Financial Strategies," (with Jason S. Scott and John G. Watson), John Ameriks and Olivia Mitchell, *Recalibrating Retirement Spending and Saving*, Oxford University Press, 2008.

This paper was written with Jason Scott, an economist, and John Watson, a mathematician — both good friends and long-time employees of Financial Engines. I have worked with Jason and John on many research projects over the years, including the one that resulted in this paper and the subsequent paper on the 4% rule reprinted later in this section. We presented a summary of the work covered here in April, 2007 at a symposium sponsored by the Pension Research Council of the Wharton School at the University of Pennsylvania. This paper and others presented at the symposium were subsequently published in a book edited by John Ameriks and Olivia Mitchell who organized the conference.

A goal of the conference was to establish a dialogue about retirement financial strategies between academic economists and investment professionals. Nowhere is this more needed than in the area of post-retirement investment and spending strategies. To frame the issues we introduced the economists' standard assumptions of complete markets and time separable utility functions with the goal of maximizing expected utility, given an investor's specific preferences. For our illustrations, we utilized a standard binomial model of independent and identically distributed market returns and a setting in which the investor can choose any combination of the market portfolio and a riskless asset, adjusting holdings over time dynamically, depending on the state of the world, if desired. With these simplifying assumptions it is straightforward to evaluate any proposed financial strategy to determine whether or not it is efficient in the sense that for some possible set of investor preferences, the approach will provide the maximum expected utility. If a strategy passes this test it is then possible to infer some or all of the characteristics of the utility function for which it is optimal (in our terns, the "revealed" utility function).

For much of the analysis we utilized the lockbox equivalents that can be constructed for any strategy in a complete market. We showed that for a strategy to be efficient, the terminal payment for any lockbox should be a monotonic decreasing function of the price per chance of the terminal states and, more pragmatically, a monotonic increasing function of the cumulative market return to that date. We showed that buy-and-hold and constant mix strategies meet these tests, hence are efficient and have revealed utilities of, respectively, constant relative risk aversion and hyperbolic absolute risk aversion. We then turned to two approaches popular among practitioners. The first involves a "glide path" investment policy in which the risk of the overall portfolio decreases through time and is unaffected by asset returns. We showed that given such an investment strategy, there is an accompanying spending strategy that will be efficient (equation 9–12c) but it is highly complex and we were unaware that any advisors had advocated adjusting spending in this manner.

Finally, we discussed the widely-advocated "4% rule" in which a retiree is counseled to spend a given percentage of his or her savings (often 4%) in the first year, then an amount equal in real value every year thereafter (until, perhaps, the money runs out). In our setting, this is efficient only if paired with an investment strategy in which all funds are invested in a riskless real investment that will last until the designated horizon (often 30 years). However, financial planners usually pair the constant real spending rule with advice to hold both bonds and stocks, resulting in an overall plan that is inefficient under our assumptions. This suggests that, no matter what the investor's preferences, a better combination of investment and spending strategy can almost certainly be found.

As we indicated, in the area of retirement financial strategies there was clearly a "gulf" between economists and financial advisors. We wondered if this might be due to explicit or implicit assumptions by practitioners that their clients have more complex utility functions than we assumed, that they believe security returns do not follow random walks and/or that some forms of non-market risk may be rewarded. This said, we agreed with many from both sides of the aisle that in this area, practitioners and economists can and should learn from one another.

6-6 "Choosing Outcomes Versus Choosing Products: Consumer-focused Retirement Investment Advice," (with D.G. Goldstein and E.J. Johnson), *Journal of Consumer Research*, Vol. 35, No. 5, October, 2008, pp. 440–456.

Some time in 1998 I received a call from Daniel Goldstein who was then a Visiting Scholar in the psychology department at Stanford. Dan asked if he could chat with me about some projects that we might undertake. He had earned his PhD from the University of Chicago, was very interested in financial decisions and had a deep background in cognitive psychology. We met and soon after began constructing a series of experiments designed to infer some of the characteristics of investors' preferences.

The work proceeded in fits and starts over the years. The first serious experiment was performed at the Max Planck Institute in Berlin where Dan was a Research Scientist in 1999. I subsequently conducted a very amateur experiment in 2001 but the serious work was done later when Dan was a Research Scientist at Columbia and then on the marketing faculty at the London Business School. Eric Johnson, a marketing professor at Columbia, joined the effort when Dan was at Columbia. I coauthored the initial paper on the work, describing the software and the underlying financial models, with Dan and Philip Blythe in 2000. It is available on my web site, as is a 2001 paper about the experiment that I conducted. Due to the exigencies of our other duties and the editorial process at the journal for which it was written, the final paper, reprinted here, was not published until 2008. Given the interests of the majority of the authors, it was written for and published in a leading marketing journal, thereby meeting the professional standards of both that field and financial economics.

The fundamental tool that we developed for this work we called the Distribution Builder. It is a graphic interface that allows the user to create a probability distribution of outcomes subject to a budget constraint, with the alternatives priced using an underlying model of the capital markets. In the experiments reported in this paper, we used a discrete approximation to a lognormal probability distribution for a multi-year holding period, assuming that the riskless real return is 2% per year and that stocks have an expected return of 8% per year with a standard deviation of 18%. The approximation provided 100 different states of the world and a state price for each. For any distribution of outcomes chosen by an investor, the software computes the least-cost investment plan by assigning each of the 100 "markers" to a state, with markers in higher rows (representing larger payoffs) assigned to cheaper states. The lowest cost for any selected distribution is then shown as a percentage of the user's total budget. The goal is for the user to select his or her most preferred distribution subject to the requirement that its cost not exceed the budget.

Given a user's chosen distribution, it is straightforward to estimate his or her marginal utility function. Since each of the 100 states is equally probable, the state price of each is proportional to its price per chance and, assuming the distribution is optimal, equal to the investor's marginal utility times a constant. For an investor with constant relative risk aversion, a plot of the logarithms of state prices and payoffs will be linear. Fitting regression lines to the two variables showed that a number of investors made choices highly consistent with CRRA preferences. The median R-squared value was 0.90. For the half of the subjects with R-squared values greater than 0.90 the aggregated distributions were consistent with an average risk-aversion coefficient close to that of a CRRA investor holding a typical mix of bonds and stocks. On the other hand, those for whom the CRRA function fit less well tended to exhibit "reference dependence", consistent with behavioral models such as the prospect theory of Kahneman and Tversky. The aggregated distributions chosen by the two groups are summarized in Figure 5.

While the paper focused on the use of the Distribution Builder as a research tool, we suggested that it might be used directly to help individuals choose investment strategies by focusing on prospective outcomes, not product offerings — an approach well worth pursuing.

6-7 "The 4% Rule — At What Price?", (with Jason S. Scott and John G. Watson), *Journal of Investment Management*, Vol. 7, No. 3, Third Quarter 2009, pp. 31–48.

After writing our paper on efficient retirement financial strategies (reprinted in this section), Jason, John and I continued to research the characteristics of the 4% rule. In particular, we wanted to estimate the costs of its inefficiencies and provide new estimates of other aspects that had been studied by previous authors. To do so we utilized the pricing kernel model of capital markets described in the Appendix. As in previous papers in this section, the model assumes complete markets and investment in a riskless real security and/or a market portfolio. We assumed typical parameters: a riskless real return of 2% and a market portfolio with an expected real return of 6% and a standard deviation of 12%. The costs shown in the paper were obtained using this model with very large numbers of Monte Carlo simulations.

For each of 30 combinations of initial withdrawal rates and portfolio risk, we estimated two costs. The first, shown in Tables 2 and 5, are the present values of funds remaining at the end of the usually-assumed 30-year period. For a typical rule with constant portfolio risk this ranged between 10% and 20% of the portfolio's initial value. The second costs, shown in Tables 3 and 6, are associated with inefficiently providing returns in periods in which funds could be insufficient to make scheduled payments. As illustrated in Figure 1, the rule can lead to scenarios in which payment is uncertain but is not an increasing function of cumulative market return. The same probability distribution could be obtained at lower cost with a strategy that has this property, as illustrated in Figure 2. In effect, we estimate the cost of obtaining the same distribution of portfolio returns by eliminating unrewarded non-market risk and replacing it with rewarded market risk. For a typical rule with constant portfolio risk this ranged between 2% and 4% of the initial portfolio value. We also showed that for strategies that include glide path investment policies the inefficiencies can be even larger.

Our overall view was that despite the widespread recommendation documented in the paper, the 4% rule has one of two serious flaws. If implemented as stated, it is likely to waste a considerable portion of an investor's funds. If, as is likely the case, a financial planner would plan to recommend future changes in real spending if the portfolio value increases or decreases by unexpectedly large amounts, the rule is insufficiently specified, cannot be adequately evaluated, and is subject to added uncertainty. As in our earlier paper, we called for a better approach than one that combines a desire for constant real spending with a prescription for risky investment.

Shortly after this paper was published, we received several comments from financial planners, many of whom took issue with our conclusions. Initially the paper was downloaded only a modest number of times from the Social Sciences Research Network site. Subsequently, the Stanford Graduate School of Business was kind enough to feature our paper in the school's magazine. This elicited newspaper columns, comments on investment blogs and over 2,000 downloads of the paper. Hopefully this attention will accelerate the search for better retirement financial strategies — an task in which I hope to participate.

Financial Planning in Fantasyland

William F. Sharpe
STANCO 25 Professor Finance, Stanford University

Note: this paper is an expanded version of a dinner speech presented at a conference sponsored by the University of California, Davis Graduate School of Management on October 17, 1997

There is a world-wide trend away from **defined benefit** pension plans, in which workers make no decisions about savings and investment, to **defined contribution** plans, in which they make such decisions. For example, twenty years ago, 70% of U.S. corporate retirement assets were in defined benefit plans; the proportion is now 50% and falling, as the following figure shows..

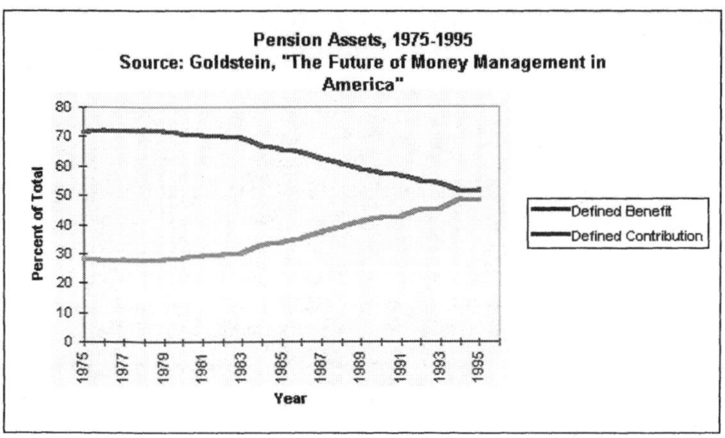

This sea change in retirement savings is creating an unprecedented need for ordinary human beings to make informed decisions about investing their retirement savings -- a task for which most are currently ill-equipped. Most participants in defined contribution plans don't know what they are doing and desperately need help.

Since such help must be provided at low cost, we are seeing a plethora of computer-based procedures for such "financial planning". One assumes that the approaches typically implemented in such software reflect the traditional practice of human financial planners, but of course it is difficult to know what goes on between two consenting adults when a financial planner meets a client in the privacy of the planner's office.

I have been studying software provided by major mutual fund and software companies and have found that it reflects remarkably few of the lessons learned after decades of the development of financial theory and its implementation by and for large institutional investors.

Participants in defined contribution plans need economic science, but what they are getting at present is bookkeeping and pseudo-science.

Here is an example of the kind of information that drives such analyses.

Current Age	**50**
Current Savings	**$ 100,000**
Annual Savings (today's $)	**$ 12,000**
Retirement Age	**65**
Annual Retirement Spending (today's $)	**$ 70,000**
Years in Retirement	**20**
Investment Return (%)	**10.5 %**
Inflation (%)	**3.5 %**

In some cases, questions of mortality are left to the user. In others, the age at death is provided by the software, presumably from a mortality table. But it is always a single number. One dies right on schedule. So much for actuarial science.

Note that the investment return is specified by the user, although most software provides some historic perspective as background for the decision. Imagine complaining about a stomach ache only to have the doctor respond: "Well, do you think it is indigestion, an ulcer or cancer?". If there is an investment expert lurking behind the software, it is one reluctant to give opinions.

Also note that the investment return is summarized with one number. So much for Markowitz's notion of risk.

The implications of these inputs are shown in a graph of one's savings account, produced in living color by virtually all the software packages. Here is an example:

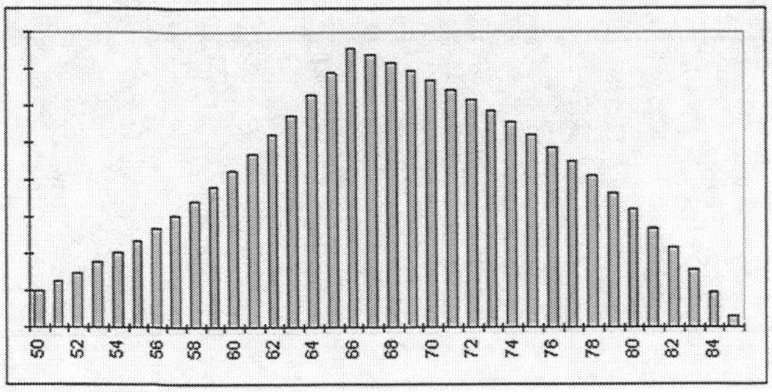

Prior to retirement the account grows regularly, due to new contributions and the unvarying rate of return on assets. After retirement the account eventually begins to diminish as spending overtakes the rate of return, which remains resolutely constant.

Eventually one of two things happens. Either you die (right on schedule) with money in the bank or you run out of money before you die. This case above is one of the happier ones. The user has a bit left at death.In such instances, the software will usually issue a message such as:

CONGRATULATIONS
You have a surplus and will meet or exceed your goal

or:

CONGRATULATIONS
Your plan works

or the like.

Such messages are usually delivered in green to indicate that everything is a go.

In many cases, however, the situation may be ugly. Here is a case in point:

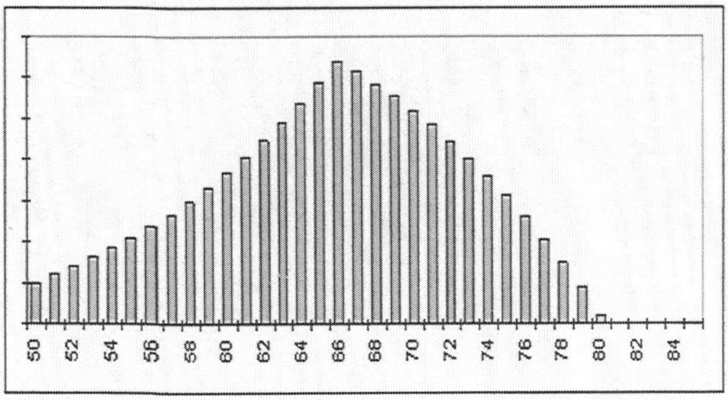

This poor soul will run out of money before the appointed date with the grim reaper. The software will issue a message such as:

YOU HAVE A SHORTFALL

or:

WARNING
Your plan does not work

Such messages are usually delivered in **red**, indicating the need to stop and reconsider.

When there is a shortfall, the software packages will generally suggest changes in one or more of four key inputs. To improve the situation, the user is urged to:

- save more,
- retire later,
- spend less, or
- increase investment return

The first three choices are, of course, rather painful. But the last one seems easy. Why not choose investments with a higher rate of return? That will clearly improve things. And the software makes it easy to determine the magnitude of the improvement.

What we have here is a return/return tradeoff, rather than the risk/return tradeoff that our textbooks describe. So much for portfolio theory.

To be fair, the software will probably point out that higher returning investments may bring higher "short-term risk". But there is no sign of this in the savings graph. Moreover, such risk has no effect on the deliverance or withholding of congratulations. One is left with the impression that a high-risk investment may go down every so often, but that it will kindly go up subsequently by a large enough amount to get the account back on its appointed track -- mean-reversion with a vengeance.

Of course, one must eventually invest in order to achieve return, and the software packages generally provide advice on this front, although it is sometimes limited to allocation among major asset classes. Here are two examples:

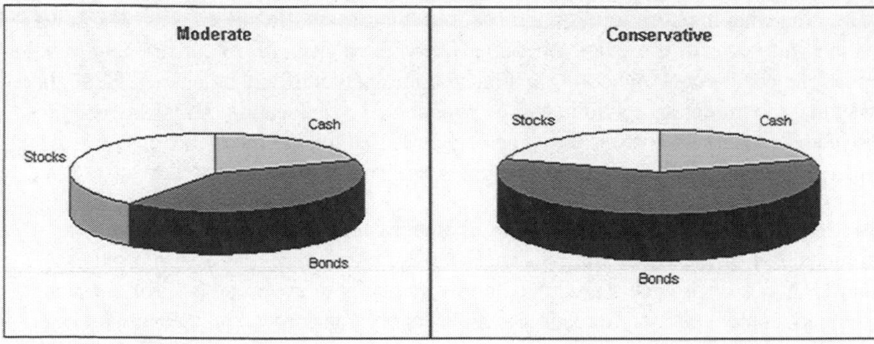

Diagrams of this sort are rather like dinner plates, with the sections indicating proportions of three major food groups. Typically, 6 to 10 such standard menus are offered. At one end is the all-cash, or granola diet, which provides small pleasure but is unlikely to cause much in the way of gastric distress. At the other end is the all-stock, or classic French diet, which will taste delicious but may cause a heart attack or two. While the pain (risk) is sometimes indicated only the pleasure (return) affects the savings account projections.

One might imagine that asset allocations suggested in such software packages conform to the prescriptions of Markowitz, representing points along an efficient risk/return frontier, with each one optimal for a different degree of risk tolerance. However, this seems unlikely. In this case the "moderate" portfolio has 20% in cash and equal parts of bonds and stocks. This would suggest that a 50/50 bond/stock portfolio has the greatest excess return Sharpe ratio. But if this is the case, why is the "conservative" portfolio not a combination with equal parts of bonds and stocks and more cash rather than a mix with the same amount of cash and three times as much in bonds as in stocks.

Here is another example:

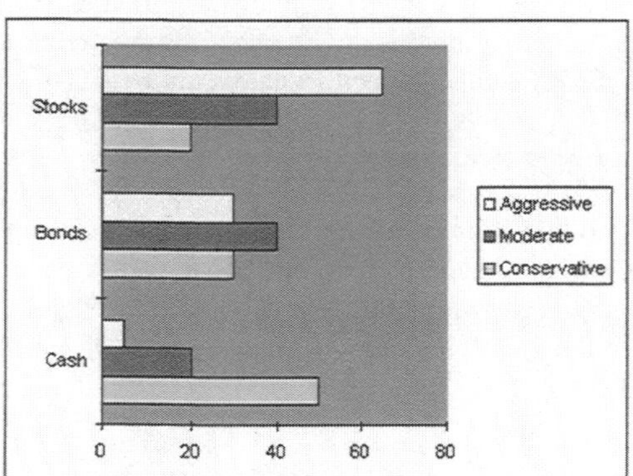

As one goes from the "aggressive" to the "moderate" and on to the "conservative" portfolio, the amount invested in stocks declines and the amount invested in cash increases. So far so good. But note what happens to the bond portion. It increases, then decreases. Markowitz showed that in regions of the efficient frontier for which a given set of constraints is binding, every portfolio can be constructed using a linear combination of any other two. Here, there is no way that the moderate portfolio can be constructed by allocating funds between the aggressive and conservative portfolios. The principles that guided the dietitians constructing these menus were not the ones typically taught in business schools.

However important asset allocation may be, ultimately the investor must select specific mutual funds. For this task, software packages tend to either leave the user in a sea of thousands of funds or provide a crude taxonomy involving a few broad categories (such a "growth and income") with all funds in a given category considered equivalent. The latter approach flies in the face of numerous studies that have found the standard fund classifications to be inaccurate in almost every case and intentionally misleading in some.

At this point it is useful to recount the key ingredients of portfolio theory. In the diagram below, each point in blue plots the risk and expected return for a specific portfolio composed in a more or less traditional way from 1 to 18 different asset classes. The points in red represent portfolios that are efficient in the sense of Markowitz. Collectively, they form the efficient frontier of risk/return opportunities. For any given level of risk, the efficient portfolio is the one with the greatest expected return.

Estimation of the risk and return of a portfolio and determination of the set of efficient portfolios requires knowledge of financial markets and hence is properly the task of an expert investment advisor.

The curves in green in the diagram represent the attitudes of a particular investor towards risk and return. This investor considers all points on a given green curve to be equally desirable -- that is, he or she is indifferent among them. Points on higher curves are preferred to points on lower curves. There are, of course, many such indifference curves, only a few of which have been shown. Note that the curves slope upward, indicating that the investor will only be willing to take on more risk if there is the prospect for greater expected return. The shape of the curves reflects the investor's degree of tolerance for risk.

Ultimately, only the investor knows his or her risk tolerance.

The goal, of course, is to find the portfolio that will be best for the investor in question. Formally, this lies at the point on the efficient frontier at which one of the investor's indifference curves just touches the frontier -- shown by the yellow point in the figure. To determine this, the information known to the investment advisor must be brought together with the information known to the investor.

There are two ways to do this.

First, the investment advisor can help the investor understand the implications of each of a number of alternative efficient portfolios, letting the investor choose among them. This is almost universally done in institutional investment practice. However, to do this the investment advisor must admit that there is risk and help the investor understand the implications of both risk and return.

Since the typical software package fails to quantify the efficient investment opportunity set in meaningful risk and return terms, a different other approach is taken. The investor is asked a series of questions that attempt to elicit information about his or her preferences (the green curves in the figure). Then the software suggests a portfolio that seems appropriate. Unfortunately, such questions often leave a great deal to be desired. Two types of questions recur.First there are those that try to assess the respondent's willingness to take risk in other contexts -- for example: "Do you like to jump out of airplanes?". The presumption is that those who answer in the affirmative are prime candidates for all-stock portfolios. The second type of question probes the respondent's current investment positions -- for example: "True or False: I have a lot of stocks and am comfortable with the risk." Not surprisingly, those who answer such an inquiry in the affirmative are counseled to have a stock-heavy portfolio. There are other types of questions, such as those that ask about short-term needs for cash, and so on. There may or may not be some sort of science behind such procedures but it seems unlikely that the leap from answers to such questions to a recommended portfolio is a sound one.

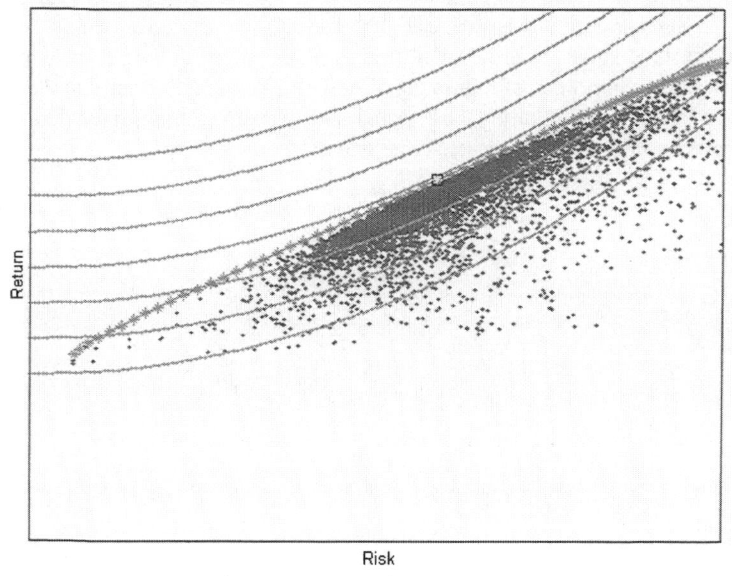

Enough bashing of software that is, for all its substantive failings, often aesthetically pleasing and fun to use. It is time to address the two obvious questions. First, why this state of affairs? Second, what might be done instead?

I think there are two major reasons for this situation.

First, there is a perfectly well-placed concern that ordinary human beings just can't understand and process uncertainty. It is thought that probability distributions may be fine in the MBA classroom, but not in the factory. At the very least, it will be a challenge to educate large numbers of people to think probabilistically.

Second, there are the ever-present legal and regulatory constraints. Many believe that it is safer to give no advice than to give good advice. Just as the threat of medical malpractice suits may severely constrain even the most dedicated physician, the threat of fiduciary suits may constrain the most dedicated investment advisor, whether operating in person or via software. To take a key example, it should be the case that a plan sponsor is more likely to be sued for providing little advice or overly simplistic advice than for providing realistic projections that take uncertainty into account. If this is not the case, we need to change public policy so that it will be.

Finally, what should be done? Here the answer is reasonably obvious. We need to devise software that recognizes that investment returns are not certain, that conveys risk/return tradeoffs in ways that are relevant and understandable by the user and that projects mutual fund characteristics as carefully as possible. There is ample experience on this front from institutional practice, in particular pension fund asset allocation studies. But such studies typically cost tens to hundreds of thousands of dollars. We need to bring such technology to individuals for a tiny fraction of that cost. A number of people, myself included, believe that with today's technology this is possible. Time will tell.

Retirement Financial Planning: A State/Preference Approach

William F. Sharpe[1]
February, 2006

Introduction

This paper provides a framework for analyzing a prototypical set of decisions concerning spending, investment and insurance made by or for an individual or family following retirement. While the structure is formal it is designed to be used eventually for actual decisions. Hence attention will be paid not only to the overall structure but also to the design of algorithms and approximation methods that can facilitate low-cost determination of desirable strategies.

We utilize the discrete-time, discrete-state approach of [Arrow 1953] and [Debreu 1959] as well as a number of the concepts in [Sharpe 2007]. In this paper we also assume that markets are sufficiently complete in the sense defined in the latter. Hopefully, subsequent papers will cover cases in which markets are incomplete and/or there are costs associated with some or all financial products.

The Retirement Financial Planning Problem

For convenience we will focus on a single individual whom we will call "the investor". In practice decisions are often made for two or more people, acting as a family unit, however our approach can easily be adapted to handle such cases by expanding the number of personal states considered. We will not differentiate between cases in which the investor selects his or her own retirement financial plan and those (more likely) instances in which a professional advisor provides assistance.

[1] This paper has benefited greatly from comments and suggestions provided by Wei Hu, Jason Scott, Jim Shearer and John Watson of Financial Engines, Inc., Steve Grenadier of Stanford University and Geert Bekeart of Columbia University

The investor begins with a set of state-dependent "outside sources" of income such as social security, a defined benefit retirement plan, etc. He or she also has a given amount of *investable wealth* that can be used to provide additional spending in different states of the world. A retirement financial plan is a set of state-dependent amounts of spending with a present value equal to the initial investable wealth.

The investor's goal is to select the most desirable feasible financial plan. We operationalize this concept with the notion of a measure associating a level of *desirability* with any financial plan. Desirability depends on the total amount to be spent in each state and the probability of each state. For simplicity we assume that the contribution of each state to total desirability can be computed separately, with the overall desirability of a plan equal to the sum of the desirabilities associated with the states.

As will be seen, our concept of desirability is formally identical to the economist's standard construct of expected utility. However, we adopt a different nomenclature to reflect a salient characteristic of the retirement financial planning problem. There are states of the world for an individual (for example, 90 years old, in a skilled nursing home with Alzheimer's disease) in which the concept of utility at the time is fanciful at best. For this reason it is best to interpret the utility associated with a state-contingent amount to be spent in such a state as the utility that the individual associates with knowing today that this will be the situation in that future state if it comes to pass. For this reason we term the probability-weighted sum of state-dependent "utilities" the investor's assessment of the desirability (today) of the specific set of amounts to be spent in possible future states of the world.

Market and Personal States

A key aspect of the retirement financial planning problem is the identification and analysis of states of the world that differ in ways relevant for many people from those that differ in ways relevant for the investor in question. We illustrate this and other aspects of our approach with a simple two-date example.

There are two dates: Now and Next Year. There is one state this year. The market next year can be in one of three possible *market states*: Bear, Normal or Bull. The investor can be in one of two possible *personal states*: Alive or Dead. Thus there are 7 states in all. Diagramatically:

		Next Year	
Now		Alive	Dead
	Bear	x_2	x_5
x_1	Normal	x_3	x_6
	Bull	x_4	x_7

Each x value indicates an amount available to be spent in the state in question. The total amount spent in state s, denoted by z_s will equal this amount (x_s) and the amount, if any, from outside sources which we will denote y_s:

$$z_s = x_s + y_s$$

The complete set of x values will be denoted X, the complete set of y byY and the complete set of z values by Z. Y is taken as given; the only decision variables are the values in X.

The Optimal Retirement Financial Plan

The investor's preferences are reflected in a series of utility functions, one for each state. We denote the utility function for state s as u_s. The utility associated with total spending in state s is thus $u_s(z_s)$.

We impose some restrictions on the utility functions. For each one, marginal utility ($u'_s(z_s)$) must be continuous and decrease with total spending (z_s). As shown in [Sharpe 2007] this allows a wide range of representations of investor preferences, including quadratic utility, constant relative risk aversion utility, HARA utility and piecewise marginal utility functions reflecting some of the characteristics of behavioral models of investor preferences.

Importantly, the utility functions for all states that occur at the same date (year) and reflect the same personal state will be the same (for example, u_2, u_3, and u_4 in the example).

Associated with each state is a probability, π_s. The set of all such probabilities will be denoted Π. The probability for a state will equal the product of the probability of the associated market state times the associated personal state. The probability of the present state is, of course, 1. The sum of the probabilities of all possible states at a given date will also equal 1.

Associated with each state is a *state price*, p_s. This is an amount that can be paid today to provide 1 unit of spending in state s (but only in state s). We assume that the market is sufficiently complete that any desired amount x_s can be provided in state s for an expenditure from investable wealth equal to $p_s x_s$. The set of all state prices will be denoted P. The cost of a retirement plan X is thus:

$$c = \sum_s p_s x_s$$

The desirability of retirement plan X is given by:

$$d = \sum_s \pi_s u_s(z_s)$$

Or:

$$d = \sum_s \pi_s u_s(x_s + y_s)$$

Given an amount of investable wealth w, the goal is to select X to maximize d subject to the constraint that c = w. More simply put, we want to find the most desirable plan the investor can afford. We will term the solution to this problem the *optimal retirement financial plan.*

Credit Constraints

We allow negative x values representing agreements that require payment in some states of the world. This is feasible if the total consumption in each state (z_s) is positive, since the payment (x_s) can be made from income (y_s) in the state.

Rather than impose a constraint that no elements of Z can be negative we require utility functions for which marginal utility is infinite for zero consumption (or, possibly, a positive feasible level of consumption). In this way the marginal utility acts as a barrier or penalty function that guarantees that the optimal plan will not violate credit constraints in any state.

Efficient Plans

For a given cost c there will be an optimal plan X. We term such a plan an *efficient plan*, since it provides the maximum desirability (d) for the specified cost (c).

Now consider the set of efficient plans, one for each possible level of cost c. Given the restrictions we have imposed, there will be a monotonic and increasing relationship between d and c: more expensive efficient plans will be more desirable.

The figure below provides an hypothetical example.

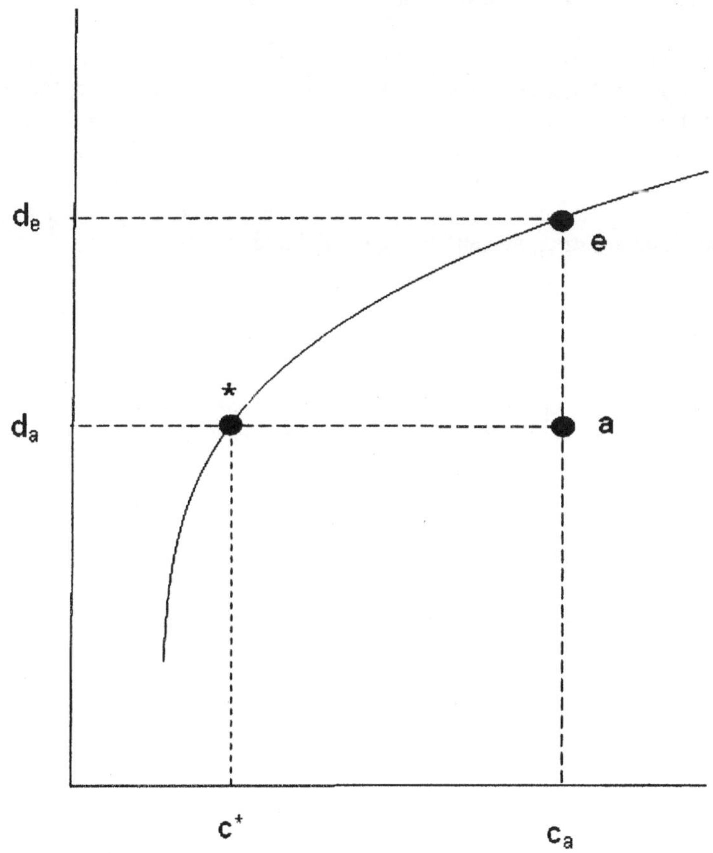

In this case the investor's wealth equals c_a. The current actual (suboptimal) plan provides a desirability of d_a. However, an optimal plan could provide a desirability of d_e. It would be tempting to consider the ratio d_a/d_e or the difference d_e-d_a as a measure of the relative efficiency of the current plan. However, this would be based on the premise that the measure of desirability represents some fundamental aspect of the investor's happiness. This is far too much to assume. We use the concept only as a means to summarize the investor's willingness to substitute consumption in one state of the world for consumption in another. In this context, any linear transform of all the utility functions would lead to the same choice of a retirement financial plan. Thus we could multiply every utility function by one positive constant and add another constant to each function without changing the representation of the investor's preferences. However, the former would change the difference d_e-d_a and the latter the ratio d_a/d_e.

For this reason we choose monetary measures of the relative efficiency of a plan. We find the efficient plan (*) that provides the same level of desirability (d_a) as the actual plan, then determine its cost (c*). The ratio of the cost of an equally desirable efficient plan to the cost of the actual plan (c^*/c_a) or the difference between the costs of the plans (c_a-c^*) can then serve as measures of relative efficiency. Clearly these will be unaffected by any linear transformation of the utility functions. They also have the advantage of being based on monetary measures and being easily understood.

Marginal Utility Functions

Key to choices made under uncertainty are the investor's *marginal utility functions* for each of the states. The marginal utility for consumption in a state is the change in utility per unit change in consumption:

$$m_s(z_s) \equiv du_s(z_s)/dz_s$$

In our setting the investor's decisions depend only on the marginal utility functions. Of course the marginal utility of consumption in a state will depend on the amount consumed in that state.

A common assumption is that the investor's preferences display constant relative risk aversion:

$$m_s = a_s z_s^{-b_s}$$

Such a function is infinite at $z_s = 0$ which meets our requirements for credit constraints. However, other marginal utility functions can be used including HARA functions of the form:

$$m_s = a_s(z_s - q_s)^{-b_s}$$

In this case, q_s, the minimum acceptable consumption in the state must be non-negative and only plans for which z_s exceeds q_s in each state can be considered. As can be seen, when q_s=0, this becomes a constant relative risk aversion function. For positive values of q_s, it exhibits decreasing relative risk aversion.

It is entirely possible to represent an investor's preferences for consumption in a given state with a marginal utility function composed of a series of pieces, one for each of several ranges of consumption in that state. We require only that marginal utility be infinite at a non-negative level of consumption, that marginal utility be continuous and that it decrease as consumption increases. These conditions can be satisfied by, for example a series of connected HARA functions which can reflect at least some of the characteristics found in experimental studies of choice under uncertainty, as discussed in [Sharpe 2007].

Finally, preferences in one state can be represented with functions that differ in type as well as in specifics (parameters) from those in another state at the same or at a different date.

Investor Reservation Prices

Given a plan, it is straightforward to compute an investor's *marginal rate of substitution* for consumption in one state vis-a-vis consumption in another. This is the rate at which he or she could substitute consumption in one state for the other without changing the overall desirability of the plan. Of particular interest is the rate at which the investor would substitute consumption in a future state for present consumption. We term this his or her *reservation price* for the state. Since the present is state 1, the reservation price for state s will equal:

$$\frac{\pi_s m_s(z_s)}{\pi_1 m_1(z_1)}$$

Of course the probability of the present equals 1 so only the marginal utility of present consumption need be included in the denominator.

Optimality Conditions

A plan will be inefficient if the investor's reservation price for any state differs from the price for that state. If the reservation price is higher, the investor can obtain a more desirable plan by increasing consumption in the future state and reducing present consumption. If the reservation price is lower, the investor can obtain a more desirable plan by decreasing consumption in the future state and increasing it in the present. A necessary condition for a plan to be efficient is for the investor's reservation price to equal the actual price for every state:

$$\frac{\pi_s m_s(z_s)}{m_1(z_1)} = p_s$$

These are often termed the *first-order conditions* for optimality. In our setting these conditions are both necessary and sufficient for a plan to be optimal.

Finding an Efficient Plan

Finding an efficient plan would appear to require solving a complex nonlinear optimization problem. In our setting, however, a much simpler procedure can be utilized.

Consider an efficient plan Z'. It will have cost c' and desirability d'. The first element z_1' will indicate the amount to be spent in the present period. Now consider the set of all efficient plans. Efficient plans with greater cost will have greater desirability. They will also provide more consumption in the present period.

Now assume that we know the amount of present consumption z_1' for an efficient plan. The amount to be consumed in state s can then be determined using the first order conditions. Rearranging the prior expression gives:

$$m_s(z_s') = m_1(z_1')p_s/\pi_s$$

This can be solved for z'_s (and hence x'_s). For example, with a HARA marginal utility function:

$$a_s(z_s' - q_s)^{-b_s} = m_1(z_1')p_s/\pi_s$$

Taking the logarithms of both sides provides a simple equation that can be solved for z'_s. Subtracting y_s gives x'_s.

With piecewise marginal utility functions a solution can be obtained for each marginal utility function, then the one with a value falling within the relevant range utilized.

Given z_1, the set of first order conditions for all future states can be solved to find the other elements of the efficient plan with initial consumption equal to z_1. The cost of the plan can then be computed. This provides one point on the efficient frontier shown in the earlier graph.

Finding the Optimal Plan

The optimal plan for the investor will be the efficient plan with a cost equal to his or her wealth. Since efficient plans can be computed quickly, it is computationally efficient to find as many such plans as required to determine the optimal plan. First an initial consumption z_1 is selected, the corresponding efficient plan determined and its cost computed. If the cost equals the investor's wealth, this is the optimal plan. Otherwise a different value is selected for z_1 and a new efficient plan and corresponding cost determined. The process is continued until an efficient plan with a cost equal to the investor's wealth is found.

In some special cases only one iteration will be required. For example, if all the marginal utility functions are of the HARA type with the same risk aversion coefficient (b_s), the cost of an efficient plan will be proportional to the initial consumption z_1. Any arbitrary value of z_1 can be selected for the first solution and the corresponding cost computed. Then every value of z_s can be set to equal the ratio of the investor's wealth to the cost of the initial plan.

For cases with greater variation in marginal utility functions, efficient iteration methods can be used to home in on the optimal portfolio. To begin, a low value of z_1 is used to find a plan with a cost below the investor's wealth and then a high value of z_1 is used to find a plan with a cost above the investor's wealth. Next an intermediate value of z_1 is selected and a new plan determined. It then replaces either the low or high plan, depending on the relationship of its' cost to the investor's wealth. The process continues until a plan with a cost sufficiently close to the investor's wealth is found.

Parsimony

Clearly there are many possible market states, many personal states and, as a result, a great many specific states.

As a practical matter it is important to reduce the dimensionality of the retirement financial plan as much as possible. To see how this can be accomplished consider the first order condition for the optimal amount to be consumed in state s:

$$m_s(z_s') = m_1(z_1')p_s/\pi_s$$

Now, consider two states with the same marginal utility function and the same ratio of price to probability (termed price per chance in [Sharpe 2007]). Clearly the optimal plan will require the same level of consumption in each of the states. Suppose that we choose to combine the two states into a single new state. The new state will have a price equal to the sum of the prices of the initial states and a probability equal to the sum of the probabilities of the initial states. Moreover, it will have the same ratio of price to probability as each of the original states. An optimal plan determined using this new state instead of the two original states will correctly call for the same amount of consumption as was originally indicated for each of the component states. The amount to be spent from investable assets in each of the component states can then be determined by subtracting the outside income from the total amount to be spent.

This example provides the basis for aggregation of "sub-states" into a smaller number of more aggregate states. For purposes of finding the total amount to be consumed, two or more states can be combined if the states:

1. have the same marginal utility functions, and
2. have the same ratios of state price to state probability

Note that both these conditions must hold to allow states to be aggregated.

If market returns are unrelated to an investor's marginal utility functions it may be possible to aggregate security market outcomes into a series of overall market states (the *superstates* proposed initially by [Hakansson 1976]), greatly reducing the dimensionality of the retirement financial planning problem. Moreover, it may be plausible to assume that the market is sufficiently complete if dynamic strategies can be used to obtain payments contingent on the realizations of such superstates, making the approach described here relevant.

As a practical matter, of course, there could still be far too many states for practical solution since the overall market portfolio's return can take on many different values. However, in many cases discrete approximations can be utilized effectively. For example, one could approximate a lognormal distribution of return and derive a set of state prices using the approach in [Sharpe 2001] or an alternative procedure. Importantly, this should suffice in cases in which the goal is to select a strategy that will provide payments related to overall market performance in some relatively simple manner.

Of course the solution to any retirement financial planning problem will be only as good as the assumptions about capital markets that underlie it. The better the assumptions about the determinants of asset prices, the better will be the recommended plan.

Incomplete Markets

Unfortunately, in many cases markets may not be sufficiently complete to allow the fully optimal solutions of the type derived here for many investors' retirement financial planning problems. However, a great deal can be learned about such strategies by assuming such perfect and frictionless conditions. Moreover, some aspects of incomplete markets can be accommodated by aggregating states for which detailed markets do not exist.

When there is no way to obtain different amounts of spending in states with different marginal utility functions, it may be possible to reformulate the problem to determine a plan that will be optimal, given such a constraint. Consider, for example, a case in which annuities are infeasible or unduly expensive so that the same amount must be spent in the states "alive" (a) and "dead" (d). The expected marginal utility for an expenditure of z' conditional on one of the two states being realized will thus be:

$$\pi_a m_a(z') + \pi_d m_d(z')$$

This can be regarded as the marginal utility function for a single aggregate state that combines the two personal states. Given such aggregation, a set of constrained efficient plans can be found. The efficient frontier will generally fall below that for unconstrained solutions, providing a lower desirability (d) for any given cost (c). The inefficiency of the resulting plans can provide a measure of the value of new personalized financial instruments that could help complete the markets.

solutions, providing a lower desirability (d) for any given cost (c). The inefficiency of the resulting plans can provide a measure of the value of new personalized financial instruments that could help complete the markets.

Further Research and Application

This paper is intended to provide a framework for examining aspects of retirement financial planning. At best it is only a first step towards helping individuals make efficient decisions concerning this stage of their financial and personal lives. Hopefully, much more research will build on this base leading in time to applications of significant practical value.

References

Arrow, Kenneth J., 1953, "Le Rôle de valeurs boursières pour la répartition le meillure des risques," Econométrie, Colloques Internationaux du Centre National de la Recherche Scientifique 11, pp.41-47.

Debreu, Gerard, 1959, *The Theory of Value*, Wiley and Sons, New York.

Hakansson, Nils, 1976, "The Purchasing Power Fund: A New Kind of Financial Intermediary," *Financial Analysts Journal*, December 1976.

Sharpe, William F,. 2001, "Individual Risk and Return Preferences: A Preliminary Survey," September, 2001, www.stanford.edu/~wfsharpe/art/rrsurvey/vienna2001.htm

Sharpe, William F., 2007, *Investors and Markets: Portfolio Choices, Asset Prices and Investment Advice*, Princeton University Press, November.

Financing Retirement: Saving, Investing, Spending and Insuring

William F. Sharpe
STANCO 25 Professor of Finance, Emeritus, Stanford University

Based on a public lecture given at Middlebury College, Vermont on Oct 6, 2006

Today I'm going to talk about something that used to be a problem primarily for the rich. In my generation, average people had very few decisions to make about financing their retirement. You worked for an employer, retired, got your checks from the government and the employer until you died. And, if your partner outlived you, he or she got checks after you were gone. No risk, no decisions. And, of course, no upside potential.

How times change. In my children's generation, average people, like academics such as myself before them, now have to decide how much to save for retirement and how to invest it, within the limits provided by their employer. When they retire they have to decide whether or not to buy an annuity from an insurance company that will pay them until they and/or their partner die and, if they do so, whether the annuity payments will be fixed or will vary with the level of the stock market. If they don't use all their money to buy an annuity (and most don't), they have to decide how much to spend each year and how to invest the rest. Social security remains as it was, but proposals to change it resurface periodically – usually in years in which no one is running for office.

Not surprisingly, many average people are ill-prepared to make the complex financial decisions that are now required. There are two reasons. First, most lack sufficient information about financial risks and returns. And second, many lack sufficient foresight and/or self-control. Those who practice and study finance need to provide all the help they can. And there is a key role for sensible social policy in this crucial area.

Today I would like to talk about some of the issues associated with this sea change. Why has it happened? What does the future hold? What are some of the public policy issues? What can financial economics contribute? And what new products and services can financial institutions provide? Of course I can only skim the surface but hopefully this will provide a framework as you think about these issues.

Why has this happened?

My answer -- demographics.

In a given year, a country, region or the world produces a set of goods and services. Think of this as a pie that is divided among young people (say, under 20), working age people (say 20 to 64) and elderly people (65 and older). The rest of the pie is used for productive investment that will hopefully make future pies larger.

The key fact is that the ratio of elderly people to working age people has increased and is projected to increase even more. Here are some numbers from the U.S. Census Bureau. For every 100 working age people in the more developed countries there were 14 elderly people in 1950. There are 25 now. This is projected to rise to 50 by 2050.

These numbers vary considerably across countries. At present, for every 100 working age people there are 9 elderly in India, 12 in China, 20 in the US, 29 in Western Europe and 31 in Japan. Not surprisingly, the rate of growth in GDP per capita has been greater in the countries in which the working age people have fewer elderly people to support.

By 2050 all these ratios are projected to increase. At that time the ratio in China will be 42-- considerably greater than the ratio in the US. Some have said that China's biggest task is to get rich before it gets old.

The graying of the population is not limited to more developed countries. For the world as a whole, the ratio of elderly to working age people is now only 13 but by 2050 it is expected to be to 30. There will still be substantial disparities among countries. For the now more developed countries the ratio will be 50 while it will be only 27 in the now less developed countries. The good news is that global trade and immigration can mitigate the problem. The bad news is that it can't solve the problem completely.

The causes of these changes are obvious. We have fewer children and we live longer. We are going to have to work longer, save more while we are working, or both. But why do we need to save in the new way rather than the old?

My answer -- economic uncertainty.

If we knew the size of each year's total output pie there might be no reason to change. But we don't know it. There is always the risk of a downturn, a recession or worse. Now consider what happens in such a case under the old system. The pie gets smaller but the elderly have a fixed claim on output. Therefore the amount going to the working age and young people has to decrease by a greater percentage than does the total output. All the risk is borne by the young and those of working age. This may have been sensible when there were 14 elderly people for every 100 of working age but almost certainly is not the best way to allocate risk when there are 25, let alone 50.

In short, we need to be able to share risk to at least some extent between the young and the old, and the old system did not do this. We need mechanisms so at least some people can take at least some financial risk.

Newer social retirement savings plans in some countries tie retirement checks to current national income or earnings. In the U.S., private plans such as 401(k) plans allow each worker to decide how much risk to bear before retirement and after.

Looking at this from an investment viewpoint, in the older private retirement plans, workers in effect got bonds both before and after retirement. But in some of the newer plans a worker can invest retirement savings in bonds, stocks and/or other assets. Under the pressure of changing demographics, retirement systems are changing to permit more efficient sharing of overall economic risk.

But allowing for better risk sharing doesn't mean that we will get it. If individuals are to make their own financial decisions they need to know what they are doing and to make rational decisions that are in their long-run best interests. Moreover, governments need to design efficient social programs and operate them responsibly. On both fronts reality falls far short of the ideal.

Retirement Savings in the U.S.

A traditional pension plan is termed a *defined benefit plan* since the amount to be received by the employee in retirement is specified, with the employer left to make investments, take the associated risk and get the associated return. According to EBRI, the Employee Benefit Research Institute, at the end of 2004 the assets in such plans were somewhat under 1.9 trillion dollars.

A 401(k) plan is termed a *defined contribution plan* since the amount contributed each year by the employee and employer is specified but the amount available during retirement depends on investment performance. At the end of 2004 EBRI estimates that these and other such plans had over 2.5 trillion dollars of assets.

There are even more assets in so-called IRA (individual retirement) accounts, many having been rolled over from defined contribution plans. At the end of 2004 these assets amounted to approximately $3.5 trillion dollars, according to EBRI.

The ratio of assets in defined contribution plans to those in defined benefit plans has been increasing for a decade and shows every sign of continuing to increase in the future.

In the United States, Social Security will provide a large part of most peoples' retirement income. Moreover, it serves as a safety net since it is a defined benefit plan. But its liabilities greatly exceed its assets. According to the 2005 report of the Trustees of the system, to be able to pay benefits to current participants (working and retired), in addition to the future payroll taxes to be paid by those still working, almost 14 trillion dollars in government bonds would have to be in the famous lockbox. Unfortunately, less than 2 trillion dollars worth were there at the time. The unfunded liability was thus 12 trillion dollars – roughly equal to the annual gross domestic product of the U.S.,

This is certainly bad news. But in an important sense, the Social Security system is not broken. The 2005 Trustees report also shows that for future participants from now to infinity, the present value of future payroll taxes actually exceeds the present value of future benefit payments (but only by a tiny amount). And an actuarial report issued by the Social Security system in 2004 showed that stopping the program at that time, so that no further benefits would be accrued would have required over 13 trillion additional dollars. The problem is thus the past, not the future.

This is discouraging, but there are worse bills to be paid. In 2005 Kent Smetters and his colleagues estimated that the present value of the shortfall for Medicare parts A and B was approximately 39 trillion dollars. To this, an additional shortfall of 24 trillion dollars was added when Medicare part D was passed. Only in Washington can folks vote for a new benefit underfunded by 24 trillion dollars then complain that an old one underfunded by 12 trillion dollars is unsustainable.

Let me note in passing that just changing part or all of Social Security to a defined contribution system will not help solve this problem. One way or other benefits must be reduced and/or taxes must be increased. Moreover, although we need some way to allow more risk-sharing between the old and the working age population this does not mean that we have to have the social safety net vary with economic conditions and/or investment results. It may be good social policy to leave the Social Security system alone, with general tax revenues funding future shortfalls, and allow supplemental savings to be invested individually.

The Pension Protection Act of 2006

While on the subject of Washington I should say a few words about the recently passed Pension Protection Act. It is long (over 900 pages) and complex but appears to be well-intentioned. Many of the provisions concern defined contribution plans but there is considerable emphasis on defined benefit plans. Recall that such plans promise workers specific payments in retirement paid by the employer. To guarantee such payments the employer is supposed to put an adequate amount of money in a separate trust fund. Then the money can be invested in bonds, stocks, hedge funds, or whatever.

One might imagine that an employer would put aside enough money each year to buy bonds that would fund the benefits earned that year, then invest the money in such bonds. But most employers do otherwise. The amounts contributed each year are determined by a mixture of regulations, accounting procedures and actuarial analyses. In many cases the contributions are much less than required to guarantee all the accrued benefits. To take an egregious example, when government bonds were yielding 4%, some plans computed the present value of future benefit payments by discounting the payments using an interest rate of 8% or more. This wildly understated the economic value of liabilities, making such funds appear to be well funded when in fact they were significantly underfunded. Other procedures were used to smooth asset values, so that a fall in the value of a portfolio would be reflected in full only over several years. And in the first years of this century there was a perfect storm, with stock prices falling and bond values rising as interest rates decreased. For many funds the true economic value assets fell just when the economic value of liabilities was rising. In too many cases only actuarial and accounting legerdemain kept the reported numbers from reflecting this reality.

For these and other reasons, employees in many private pension plans had claims that were more like bonds issued by their employer than default-free government bonds. In 1974, Congress tried to mitigate this by providing that in the event of a corporate bankruptcy a quasi-government agency, the Pension Benefit Guaranty Corporation (or PBGC) would take on a plan's assets and liabilities. However, not all benefits are covered in full, as the pilots of United Airlines recently discovered. And in September, 2005 the PBGC reported that it had assets of 57.6 billion and liabilities of 80.7 billion and was thus 23 billion dollars in the hole.

The Pension Protection Act improves this situation in a number of ways. It increases the insurance premiums that must be paid by corporations who sponsor defined benefit plans, it mandates better funding of such plans and requires valuation more in line with the true economics of the situation. But it goes only part way. And there are the usual exceptions intended to make it easier on some corporations -- in particular the airlines.

A cynic might say that a traditional corporate defined benefit plan was a ruse that allowed an employer to get workers to accept lower wages and salaries in return for a benefit that appeared to be like a portfolio of long-term government bonds, but was instead a portfolio of corporate bonds, some of which were actually junk bonds. The recent legislation, along with planned changes in the same direction by the Financial Accounting Standards Board may make such a game harder and more expensive to play. This is a serious step forward although it may lead to an acceleration in the demise of defined benefit plans.

For good or ill, the provision of a traditional defined benefit pension plan appears to be on the way out in corporate America. However, it may remain the preferred vehicle for many employees of governments and government agencies for which taxpayers are the ultimate source of benefit payments. In any event, the defined contribution plan is here to stay in corporate America. We had better find a way to make it work.

Saving, Investment, Spending and Insuring Decisions

The first step is to acknowledge that uncertainty abounds. We don't know what most investments will return. We don't know when we will die. We don't know the magnitudes of future medical expenses. And so on. Individuals can mitigate or even avoid some uncertainty but not all. Societies can reduce overall economic uncertainty but they cannot eliminate it. They can, however, assist in allocating societal risk among people efficiently.

Fortunately financial economists spend much of their lives dealing with decisions in a world of uncertainty.

Pre-Retirement Saving and Investment

In the early 1990's I looked at the retirement saving and investment advice being offered by financial institutions, mutual funds and others. Much of it was fantastic -- as in "fantasy". Calculations were based on saving a specified amount each year until retirement, earning a constant percent return each year on investments, spending a specified percent of total savings each year after retirement, then dying at an appointed hour. The typical output graph showed the total value of savings, growing steadily until retirement then decreasing steadily until the grim reaper's prearranged arrival date. As long as there was something left, the individual would be congratulated on having a "plan that works".

Not surprisingly this didn't seem adequate to financial economists. Hence a number of us went to work to see if we couldn't find a better approach. My own efforts have included academic research and the founding of a firm that provides investment advice and management. An employee in a plan for which we give advice is given estimates of the likelihood of meeting certain retirement financial goals, not a single number purporting to be his or her retirement income. The portfolios that we recommend or manage provide ranges of retirement outcomes that are efficient, taking into account not only the middle of the range but also its width. In short, we quantify risks, make the best estimates we can of those risks, and select investment strategies that are projected to get the best possible return for the amount of risk appropriate for the investor in question. Our goal is to bring the results of decades of theoretical and empirical research in financial economics plus some of our own work to bear on the retirement financing decisions made in the working phase of one's life.

The Pension Protection Act contains some provisions that help in this regard. Employers are encouraged to adopt provisions which specify that by default a new employee is automatically included in a 401(k) plan, with a minimal amount to be saved each year and invested in a reasonable default option such as diversified portfolio or a personalized managed account. The employee can choose to not be included but this takes explicit action. Research by behavioral economists has shown that participation rates are significantly higher when inertia leads to participation rather than non-participation. In a relatively short time, research conducted in the academy has led to good legislation.

The Act also widens the scope for the provision of financial advice to those in 401(k) plans. Previously only a non-conflicted firm could provide such advice. Now firms that stand to make more money if, for example, an employee invests in mutual fund A rather than mutual fund B can provide advice on investing in such funds, but only if the advice is produced by a computer model that has been certified as unbiased by an appropriate third party. The practical implications of this provision are unclear at present, but the intent is to help people who are not investment professionals make the best decisions about their retirement savings and investment.

Post-Retirement Spending, Investment and Insuring

Until fairly recently, the majority of the activity devoted to bringing financial economics to individuals in this domain focused on those who were still some years from retirement. But here too the inevitable force of demographics has been at work. The oldest baby boomers have now turned 60. A huge wave of retirees is coming. As a result financial economists and financial institutions have begun to focus serious resources on the problems associated with spending, investing and insuring in the retirement years.

Not surprisingly, given my age, I am keenly interested in these problems and I am devoting much of my research to them.

Here too, uncertainty is central. But there are two equally important types of uncertainty. We don't know what most investments will return and we don't know how long we will be around. In the academy we need to combine actuarial science with financial economics. In the financial industry we need to combine insurance expertise with investment expertise.

Consider this prototypical example. You retire with one million dollars in your 401(k) account. You could go to your favorite life insurance company and buy an annuity. You give them the million dollars and they promise to pay you X dollars per year as long as you live and to pay your partner one-half X dollars per year for every year thereafter that he or she is alive. This totally removes the financial uncertainty associated with mortality.

With social security and many traditional defined benefit plans everyone receives an annuity. In many corporate plans the checks were for the same dollar amount each year. In many government plans and for social security payments the amounts were adjusted to take inflation into account. In any event, individuals didn't have to worry about outliving their savings.

But now many people have a choice. The early evidence in this country and longer-term evidence in other countries suggests that given such a choice, most people reject annuities. Instead they invest their savings, spend an amount each year that they think may be appropriate, then accept the risk that they may outlive their money or have to drastically cut their spending.

This seems puzzling. In the old system did we force people to accept an inferior alternative? Or are people now taking far too shortsighted a view? Are the annuity terms offered by insurance companies to individuals so much worse than those offered for group policies that it is better to avoid insuring against the financial costs of long life? These and other questions are the subjects of much current research.

Maximizing Expected Utility

The annuity puzzle is part of a bigger question. How should one approach the problem of selecting an appropriate post-retirement spending, investing and insuring policy? We have many tools that served us well when considering pre-retirement decisions, including mean/variance portfolio optimization, equilibrium models such as the capital asset pricing model, Monte Carlo simulation and others. But these do not appear to be completely adequate for this new task. My view, and that of a number of others doing research in this area, is that we need to first return to fundamentals, viewing the goal as one of maximizing an individual's expected utility, taking into account the amounts that can be spent in different years under different circumstances and the available set of financial and insurance alternatives.

This is not the place to go into specifics but this broader view allows one to consider many aspects of these decisions in a unified and consistent manner, although at the cost of considerable complexity, heavy informational and computational demands and the need to seriously study each individual's preferences.

A particularly important aspect of individual preference is this: The utility that I get from a particular amount of spending depends on the amount I spend, when I spend it, and my circumstances at the time. For example, how do I think about taking risk that will affect my income ten years from now? Let's say that I can choose to have \$100,000 for certain or a 50/50 chance of getting either \$80,000 or \$150,000. Which will I choose? If I knew that I would be alive and well at the time I might well take the gamble. But if I knew that I would be in a skilled nursing home and that the cost would be \$100,000 I would very like take that sure thing. In economists' jargon, my utility is state-dependent.

If we can obtain valid information about such preferences as well as the investment and insurance alternatives, we know how to find a spending, investment and insurance strategy that will maximize an individual's expected utility. But many PhD dissertations and extensive research in the financial industry will be required before there will be widespread practical use of such an approach. In the meantime, parts of the overall intellectual structure can be used to help solve some immediate problems.

Here is a brief example.

Integrating Long-term Care Insurance with a Variable Annuity

Today it is possible to buy a variable annuity that will pay an amount each year that will be greater, the better the performance of an associated investment portfolio. It is also possible to buy a long-term-care insurance policy that will pay a fixed amount each year while the holder is infirm. One can, of course, put some money in one of these policies and the rest in the other. But these policies can't be used to accomplish the goals of the person for whom the best choice is to guarantee a given amount (say \$100,000) when sick and to take an attractive gamble that will pay an uncertain amount that may be less or more (say, $80,000 or $150,000) when well. To my knowledge, payoffs of this sort are not possible with present financial products. But if I am right, demand will create the needed supply. Insurance companies take note.

Conclusion

It is time to conclude.

These are exciting times for financial economists, for people in the financial services industry and for those seriously concerned with good social economic policy. We need to figure out how much to entrust individuals with their lifetime financial decisions and then constrain them, cajole them and/or assist them so they may make decisions that will truly increase their personal welfare.

A tall order, but financial economists can help. Of course you would expect me to say this.

Lockbox Separation

William F. Sharpe
June, 2007

Introduction

This note develops the concept of *lockbox separation* for retirement financial strategies in a complete market. I show that in such a setting any strategy can be implemented by dividing initial wealth among a series of "lockboxes", each designed to fund spending at a particular date using a predetermined investment strategy for managing the funds until that date. Such an approach allows a retiree to pre-commit to follow spending and investment rules throughout the remainder of his or her life. This may have significant advantages since the decisions can be made prior to future reductions in reasoning ability, cognition, etc.. In effect, the current person can act in *loco parentis* for a potentially diminished future person.

To keep the exposition simple I omit issues associated with additional sources of income, mortality, annuities, health insurance etc.. The approach can, however, be extended to cover many of these and other aspects of the real-world problems associated with financial planning in retirement.

The approach utilizes the formulation developed in my on-line textbook, *Macro-Investment Analysis*. For details, see the section on Dynamic Strategies, (last revised in April 1999) at www.wsharpe.com/mia/prc/mia_prc3.htm#dynamic.

A Binomial Example

For simplicity I utilize a three-date example in which security returns follow an independent and identical binomial process. In particular, at each date there are two one-period securities. A riskless bond (B) has a total real return of 1.02 – that is, for each dollar invested at a date the security provides 1.02 real dollars at the next date. A security invested in all the risky securities in the market (S) provides a total real return of 0.94 if the market is "down" and 1.18 if the market is "up". These two states are equally likely.

The retiree has W0 dollars to finance spending at the three dates. There are seven possible states of the world, shown by the following tree.

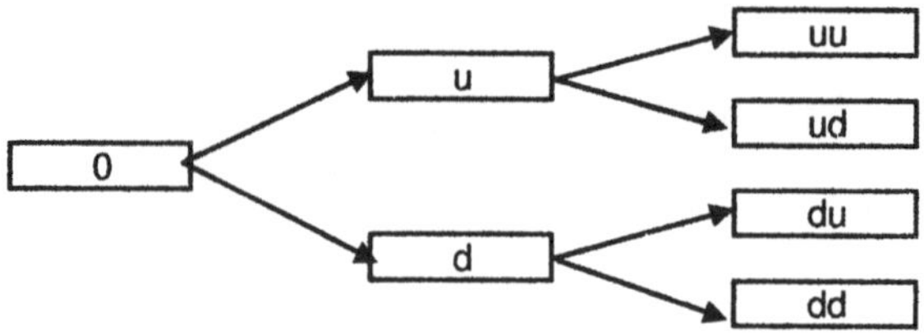

Retirement Financial Plans

A *retirement financial plan* assigns an amount to be spent (consumed) at each node on such a tree. The amounts to be spent must be obtained by investing W0 dollars in available capital market instruments. The retiree's goal is to maximize the expected utility of the amounts to be spent subject to the constraint that the total cost equal the initial wealth W0.

The capital market conditions can be summarized in a square matrix **M** which will have as many rows and columns as there are states. The matrix for this example is shown below.

	W0	B0	S0	Bd	Sd	Bu	Su
0	1	-1	-1	0	0	0	0
d	0	1.02	0.94	-1	-1	0	0
u	0	1.02	1.18	0	0	-1	-1
dd	0	0	0	1.02	0.94	0	0
du	0	0	0	1.02	1.18	0	0
ud	0	0	0	0	0	1.02	0.94
uu	0	0	0	0	0	1.02	1.18

Each row represents a state, or node on the tree. The columns represent decision variables. W0 can be considered a security that pays $1 at the initial date. B0 represents a decision to invest $1 at date 0 in a riskless bond, which will provide $1.02 at date 1 whether the market is up or down. S0 represents a decision to invest $1 in the risky security at date 0, which will pay $0.94 at date 1 if the market is down and $1.18 if the market is up. Bd represents a decision to invest in a riskless bond at date 1 if the market is down at that time. It will provide payments at date 2 in the two states that are subsequently possible. The remaining variables are similar, with each representing a decision made initially to take an action contingent on the occurrence of a particular state of the world.

A financial plan can be characterized in two ways. The first is represented by a vector **x**, which shows the values assigned to each of the decision variables. For example[1]:

W0	100.00
B0	1.96
S0	59.68
Bd	1.32
Sd	25.70
Bu	1.64
Su	31.92

This plan requires an initial wealth of $100, since it calls for the purchase of 100 units of security W0, which costs $1 per unit. However, no additional wealth is required, since each of the other decision variables represents a "zero-investment strategy". For example, the value of 1.96 for B0 indicates that $1.96 is to be invested at date 0 in riskless bonds. This will result in a payment of 1.02*1.96 at date 1 if the market is down or a payment of 1.02*1.96 at date 1 if the market is up. No initial funds are required. Each of the other decision variables has this property. In general, the cost (initial wealth required) for a financial plan will equal x(1).

The other way to characterize a financial plan focuses on the amounts to be spent in each possible state. We denote this vector **c** (for consumption). For the plan shown by x, the amounts spent will be as follows:

0	38.36
d	31.08
u	38.86
dd	25.51
du	31.67
ud	31.67
uu	39.34

Clearly there is a close relationship between **x** and **c**. Importantly:

$$Mx = c$$

Thus capital market conditions (**M**) as well as wealth and the contingent decisions to be taken (**x**) determine consumption (**c**). The process can also be reversed. Assume that one wishes to obtain a particular set of amounts to be consumed (**c**). Then the required decision variables (**x**) will given by:

$$x = M^{-1}c$$

Where M^{-1} is the inverse of M.

---

[1] All values in this paper are rounded to the number of decimal places shown.

For this example, M^{-1} (rounded to four places) is:

1.0000	0.6536	0.3268	0.4272	0.2136	0.2136	0.1068
0.0000	4.8203	-3.8399	3.1505	1.5752	-2.5097	-1.2549
0.0000	-4.1667	4.1667	-2.7233	-1.3617	2.7233	1.3617
0.0000	0.0000	0.0000	4.8203	-3.8399	0.0000	0.0000
0.0000	0.0000	0.0000	-4.1667	4.1667	0.0000	0.0000
0.0000	0.0000	0.0000	0.0000	0.0000	4.8203	-3.8399
0.0000	0.0000	0.0000	0.0000	0.0000	-4.1667	4.1667

There is an important economic meaning associated with each column of this matrix. Consider a desired plan to spend $1 in state u. Vector **c** will thus be:

0	0.00
d	0.00
u	1.00
dd	0.00
du	0.00
ud	0.00
uu	0.00

The required set of decision variables is:

W0	0.3268
B0	-3.8399
S0	4.1667
Bd	0.0000
Sd	0.0000
Bu	0.0000
Su	0.0000

This is the third column of the inverse of M. It shows the cost of a "state claim" to receive $1 in state u and nothing otherwise is $0.3268. This is defined as the "state price" for the state. The remainder of the column shows the strategy required to obtain the desired outcome: buy $4.1667 of stocks and sell $3.8399 of bonds. The net cost of these two transactions is, of course, $0.3268.

Each column of the inverse of M provides the cost of a state claim (in the top row) and the strategy that can produce the desired payment.

Our example is one in which there is a complete market, in the sense that it is possible to obtain any one of N state claims by following a strategy using currently available securities. Key to this is the existence of a set of N decision variables using available securities that provide payments in an NxN matrix that can be inverted.

Expected Utility Maximization

The consumption amounts **c** used in our example were not chosen casually. Rather, they represent an optimal solution for a retiree who wishes to maximize expected utility, given an initial wealth of 100, in the manner described in my working paper *Retirement Financial Planning: A State Preference Approach* (February 2006) at www.wsharpe.com/wp/rfp.pdf. In this case the utility functions were time-varying with constant relative risk aversion at each date. Specifically, for each date, $U = a(C^{1-g})/(1-g))$ where the values were as follows:

Date	a	g
0	1.00	3.00
1	0.98	3.10
2	0.96	3.20

The optimal values for **c** for such an investor can be found using the state prices obtained from the inverse of matrix **M**, as described in the referenced working paper. Then the required decision variables can be found by multiplying the inverse of M by vector **c**.

An alternative approach uses the matrix **M** directly. Construct an excel spreadsheet with **M**, **x** and **c**, where **c** is obtained by multiplying **M** by **x**. For every value in **c** provide a formula that computes the associated utility. Finally, multiply each utility by the probability of the associated state and sum the products to obtain the overall expected utility. The goal is to find a vector **x** with the initial value equal to initial wealth that will maximize expected utility. This can be accomplished using Excel's *solver* program (available as an add-in). The resulting vectors **c** and **x** will provide the overall investment and spending rules constituting the optimal retirement financial plan. If the optimization is successful[2] the results will be the same as those obtained using the prior procedures.

Lockbox Separation

I turn now to the issue of lockbox separation. Recall the relationship between the vector of desired consumption c and the associated financial strategy:

$$x = M^{-1}c$$

[2] It may be necessary to experiment with the solver settings to obtain sufficient precision and avoid numeric problems.

Now, divide **c** into a number of desired consumption vectors $\mathbf{c}_0$, $\mathbf{c}_1$ and $\mathbf{c}_2$, which sum to the overall vector **c**:

$$c = c_0 + c_1 + c_2$$

The optimal strategy x will be:

$$x = M^{-1} (c_0 + c_1 + c_2)$$

or:

$$x = M^{-1}c_0 + M^{-1}c_1 + M^{-1}c_2$$

But this can be implemented using a series of strategies $\mathbf{x}_0$, $\mathbf{x}_1$ and $\mathbf{x}_2$ where:

$$x_i = M^{-1}c_i$$

This relationship can be used for any partition of c but our interest is in a partition in which all the states at a given date are included in one such vector. For our example:

	C0	C1	C2
0	38.36	0.00	0.00
d	0.00	31.08	0.00
u	0.00	38.86	0.00
dd	0.00	0.00	25.51
du	0.00	0.00	31.67
ud	0.00	0.00	31.67
uu	0.00	0.00	39.34

The required strategies are:

	X0	X1	X2
W0	38.36	33.01	28.63
B0	0.00	0.57	1.40
S0	0.00	32.44	27.23
Bd	0.00	0.00	1.32
Sd	0.00	0.00	25.70
Bu	0.00	0.00	1.64
Su	0.00	0.00	31.92

Each of these can be implemented with a separate lockbox.

The first lockbox will begin with $38.36, which will be used for immediate consumption.

The second lockbox will begin with $33.01 which will be used to purchase $0.57 of bonds and $32.44 of stocks. At date 1 the box will be opened. If the market is down there will be $31.08 to spend; if the market is up there will be $38.86.

The third lockbox will begin with $28.63 that will be used to purchase $1.40 of bonds and $27.23 of stocks. At date 1 the portfolio will be changed. If the market is down, the holdings will be revised so that $1.32 is invested in bonds and $25.70 in stocks. If the market is up the holdings will be altered so that $1.64 is invested in bonds and $31.92 in stocks. When the box is opened at date 2 there will be $25.51, $31.67 or $39.34 to be spent, depending on the course of the market moves up to that date.

Asset Allocations

It is straightforward to compute the percentage of total value invested in stocks at each time and state for any given strategy. For, example, at date 0 lockbox 1 has $32.44 invested in stocks and $0.57 in bonds. Thus 98.28% or 0.9828 is invested in stocks. Lockbox 2 has 95.12% (0.9512) invested in stocks at date 0 and also at date 1, whether the market is up or down. This is not surprising, since in our setting maximization of expected utility with a constant relative risk aversion function requires a constant asset allocation in value terms.

It is important to note, however, that the overall asset allocation does change through time. Performing the same calculations for the vector c shows that the overall percentage invested in stocks is initially 96.81%, falling to 95.12% at date 1, whether the market is down or up. This is not surprising, since the overall asset allocation can be thought of as a type of average of the asset allocations in the remaining unspent lockboxes. Since the retiree's risk-aversion is greater for consumption at later dates, lockboxes designed for later consumption have lower percentages of stock. As time goes on, the remaining lockboxes collectively provide a more conservative overall investment strategy.

Extensions and Applications

Our example has utilized a highly simplified model of security returns, with only two states of the world at each date as well as security returns that are the same in each period. Moreover, for our expected utility optimization we assumed that up and down moves were equally probable and that each of the retiree's utility functions exhibited constant relative risk aversion. Some of our results were dependent on one or more of these assumptions. However, the lockbox separation property is quite general. As long as the capital market is complete, our basic equation relating M, x and c will hold. This in turn will permit separation of an overall optimal investment strategy into a series of strategies, one to finance spending for each date, with each such strategy implemented in a lockbox to be used for that date, with an initial amount invested and a designated investment strategy to be followed until the date in question.

But why utilize a lockbox strategy? An overall strategy with the appropriate spending and investment rules will provide the same outcomes. The answer hinges on assumptions about the ability of the retiree to make optimal decisions in later years. Consider, for example, a person who is now 65 years old. She could leave investment and spending decisions 20 years hence to her "future self". But there is a possibility that at that point she might not be capable of making decisions that are truly in her best interests. One alternative would be to have a wise counselor make her financial decisions at the time. Another would be for her "present self" to make decisions now for her "future self." A lockbox strategy would facilitate this. As a practical matter, of course, there would almost certainly need to be provisions that would allow changes if certain unanticipated events transpired. But it could be advantageous to make plans now, when one has one's faculties, that at least specify appropriate reactions to future market moves.

For these reasons it appears that additional research in this area is warranted. Possible extensions could cover mortality, insurance vehicles, incomplete markets and transactions costs (broadly construed). Applications could investigate typical retiree preferences and other relevant behavioral aspects. Clearly, more research is needed.

Chapter 9
Efficient Retirement Financial Strategies

William F. Sharpe, Jason S. Scott, and John G. Watson

Today's retirees are making increasingly complex financial decisions. Gone are the days when one could rely solely on government or corporate pensions. The freezing or elimination of pension plans, combined with the rapid introduction of defined contribution plans, has forced retirees to rely more and more on their own investments to fund their retirement spending. Retirees are not only expected to fund a larger portion of their retirement spending, but early retirement and increased longevity imply their assets must support potentially longer retirements as well. To address this responsibility, a retiree has either implicitly or explicitly adopted an *investment strategy* to govern his investment decisions and a *spending strategy* to govern his spending decisions. A pair of investment and spending strategies constitutes a *retirement financial strategy*.

Economists have long explored the issue of optimal spending and investment strategies (Merton 1971). A major theme of their work is that optimal or *efficient* solutions are only achieved when investment and spending decisions are made in tandem as part of a complete retirement financial strategy. Economists use a standard framework in which the retiree's goal is to maximize expected utility in a *complete market*. However, solving such a utility maximization problem requires detailed knowledge about the retiree's preferences. Moreover, one must make assumptions about the trade-offs available in capital markets. Not surprisingly, financial advisers rarely embrace this approach; rather they rely on 'rules of thumb'. For example, one popular rule suggests annually spending a fixed, real amount equal to 4 percent of initial wealth and annually rebalancing the remainder to a 40–60 percent mix of bonds and stocks. The goal of this chapter is to consider whether the advice suggested by financial planners is consistent with the approach advocated by financial economists. More specifically, we examine some rules of thumb to see if they are consistent with expected utility maximization, for at least some investor in a standard market setting. If a rule is consistent, we say it is efficient and refer to the underlying utility as the investor's *revealed* utility.

In what follows, we make several key assumptions—the assumptions of our *canonical setting*. Regarding retiree preferences, we assume they are well modeled by additively separable utility functions.[1] Moreover, we assume that spending preferences take into account mortality estimates and the retiree's attitudes concerning his spending relative to that of any beneficiaries, and that the amounts to be spent under the plan will go either to the retiree or to beneficiaries. Further, we assume, as do many rules advocated by financial planners, that no annuities are purchased. Our assumptions about asset prices are consistent with a condition associated with models of asset pricing such as the Capital Asset Pricing Model and a number of Pricing Kernel Models—only risk associated with the overall capital market is compensated. More specifically, we assume that there is no compensation in higher expected return from taking nonmarket risk (Cochrane 2005; Sharpe 2007). Further, to keep the mathematics as simple as possible, we will develop our results using a simple *complete market* consisting of a riskless asset and a risky asset. Our risky asset tracks the market portfolio, which is assumed to follow a *binomial* process.

In the remainder of this chapter, we first provide the details of our canonical setting and formulate the financial economist's problem—find the investment and spending strategies that maximize a retiree's expected utility. We then develop conditions and tests to determine whether an arbitrary retirement strategy is optimal or efficient, and the equations for its revealed utility, when it exists. We then introduce the simple complete market to be used for illustrative purposes. Next we describe a fundamental spending strategy that employs *lockboxes.* We discuss three efficient lockbox strategies and their revealed utilities. We next look at two popular rules of thumb used by financial planners. We show that the first rule, the investment *glidepath* rule, is efficient provided it is paired with a very specific spending rule. We show that the second rule, the constant 4 percent spending rule, is only efficient when all investments are in riskless securities. Finally, we conclude with a summary of results and some topics for further investigation.

Revealed Utility and Retirement Spending

A retiree, who maximizes his expected utility, is faced with the following problem. For each year in the future, and for all states of the world in each year, our investor must optimally choose how much to consume and an investment policy to support that consumption. If markets are complete, our retiree can purchase contingent claims on the future states, and cash in these securities to pay for consumption. We assume that markets are complete, so that the investment alternatives are known, and only the consumption values are to be determined. Let 't' index future years, 's' index future states, and the pair 't, s' index a state that occurs at time 't'. We denote consumption by $C_{t,s}$, the probability that a state occurs by $\pi_{t,s}$, the current price of a contingent claim by $\psi_{t,s}$, utility from consumption at time t by $U_t(C)$, and initial wealth by W_0. Our investor must choose consumption values that maximize the function:

$$\max \sum \pi_{t,s} \cdot U_t(C_{t,s}) \tag{9-1a}$$

and also satisfy the budget constraint:

$$W_0 = \sum C_{t,s} \cdot \Psi_{t,s} \tag{9-1b}$$

In Equation (9-1), the summations are with respect to all states and times. Note that we have assumed that all states occurring at time t have the same utility function U_t, and that this utility is only a function of consumption at time t. The maximand in Equation (9-1a) is the expected utility of the consumption plan, which is assumed to be time separable. We assume that the utility functions $U_t(C)$ are increasing and concave, that is, $U_t'(C) > 0$ and $U_t''(C) < 0$. In other words, we assume that investors always prefer more to less and are risk averse. We term this the *canonical retiree problem*: given an initial wealth, to find the set of consumptions at every time and state in the future that will maximize expected utility, where these consumptions are provided by investments in state-contingent claims. Throughout, we assume that the retiree has a known separable utility function, knows the probabilities of future states, and knows the prices of contingent claims.

Many economists will find our canonical retiree problem both familiar and sensible, though most practitioners are likely to consider it beyond the pale. How many retirees know their utility functions? Very few, at best. But by choosing a particular retirement financial strategy, a retiree has either made a mistake or revealed something about his preferences. When we examine some popular strategies, in each case we seek to determine (a) whether the strategy is consistent with expected utility maximization; and (b) if so, what the characteristics are of the associated utility function. A strategy that meets condition (a) will be said to *reveal utility* in the sense that we can, if desired, answer question (b)—that is, determine the characteristics of the utility function for which the strategy would be optimal.

The relevant equations for this task are derived from the first order equations for the maximization problem. The full set of such equations includes the budget constraint and the following equations for each time t and state s:

$$U_t'(C_{t,s})/U_0'(C_{0,0}) = \Psi_{t,s}/\pi_{t,s} \tag{9-2}$$

In Equation (9-2), the right-hand side is the ratio of the state-price to state-probability, sometimes termed the state's price-per-chance (PPC).[2] For any given time in the future, a retirement strategy prescribes a set of consumption values—one for each state. Using these choices and a model that specifies the PPC for each state, we can infer the marginal utility function $U_t'(C)$ for that time period, if it exists. Such a function exists if two conditions are met. First, the strategy must provide a single consumption value for each time and state. Second, in order to recover a concave utility function, consumption must be higher in states with lower PPC and the same in all states with the same PPC. More succinctly, if for a given time we rank the states in order of increasing consumption, this must be equivalent to ranking the states in order of decreasing PPC. If such an ordering is possible, we can then integrate the marginal utility function to get a revealed utility function. We note that the revealed utility functions $U_t(C)$ are not completely unique; for each time we can add an arbitrary integration constant, and all times can have a common positive multiple, namely $U_0'(C_{0,0})$. Fortunately this nonuniqueness is economically immaterial.

A key ingredient in our analyses is a model of the characteristics of asset prices. Since contingent claims prices are not observable, we need to make an assumption about the nature of equilibrium in capital markets. We adopt a multiperiod generalization of the results obtained with several standard models of asset pricing, such as the Capital Asset Pricing Model, some Pricing Kernel models, and the binomial model employed below. In particular, we assume that the explicit or implicit contingent claim prices at any given time t are a decreasing function of the cumulative return on the overall market portfolio from the present time to that time period. Equivalently, if for a given time we rank the states in order of increasing market return, this must be equivalent to ranking the states in order of decreasing PPC. This is the market setting for our canonical retiree problem.

For the remainder of the chapter, we will consider a state 's' at time 't' to be synonymous with cumulative market return at time 't'. So a retirement strategy must predict a single consumption value for any particular market return and be independent of prior market returns, that is, the particular *paths* that lead to the final cumulative return. Further, since we assume that the PPC is a decreasing function of market returns, the existence of a revealed utility requires that consumption be an increasing function of market return. Although our illustrations utilize a binomial process, the results apply in other settings as well.

Not all retirement strategies have revealed utilities. Three straightforward tests can be used to identify obvious violators. First, the retirement strategy cannot lead to multiple values of consumption for the same cumulative market return. Consumption must be path independent. Second, the present level of wealth for every state (before or after consumption) must also be path independent. If not, either consumption will ultimately be path dependent (a violation of the first test), or it must be the case that for one or more paths not all wealth will have been spent (a violation of optimality).

The third test used to identify violators is nonobvious, subtle, and exceedingly powerful. We term it the principle of *earmarking*. If knowledge of a state provides knowledge of consumption, and state prices exist, then at any point in time, the retiree's portfolio can be subdivided into assets that are earmarked for consumption in that state and time. It follows that assets allocated to all states at a given time can be aggregated so that our retiree can also identify the assets earmarked to support spending in any given year. Maximizing expected utility implies that our retiree knows at any point in time how much wealth is currently earmarked for consumption at each future date. If the wealth allocated to consumption at a specific time is uncertain, this uncertainty must translate to uncertainty regarding consumption in at least one state at that time, which necessarily violates maximizing expected utility.

A Simple Complete Market

In this section, we describe the simple *complete market* we use in the remainder of this chapter. Generally, a market is complete if the set of all contingent claims can be constructed using its assets. Our simple market has just two assets, a deterministic risk-free asset and a stochastic risky asset. The yearly returns on the risk-free asset are assumed constant, while the returns on the risky asset will track the returns of the total market portfolio. We assume that in any year the market is equally likely to move up or down, that the characteristics of the movements in each year are the same, and that the movement in any year is independent of the actual movements in prior years. More succinctly, the market moves are independent and identically distributed coin-flips, and thus the total number of up-moves (or down-moves) over a span of years has a *binomial distribution*.[3]

Given the above assumptions, our complete market is specified by three parameters: (*a*) the total annual market return R_u for an up-move; (*b*) the total annual market return R_d for a down-move; and (*c*) the total annual return R_f on a risk-free asset. All three of these annual returns are assumed to be real. For example, the values $R_u = 1.18$, $R_d = 0.94$, and $R_f = 1.02$ give a market portfolio with an annual expected real-rate of return of 6 percent, a volatility of 12 percent, and a Sharpe Ratio of 1/3. These values roughly correspond to an aggregate market portfolio made up of 40 percent bonds and 60 percent equities.

We take the initial value of the market portfolio to be 1, which is the value at the root of the binomial tree. After one year, the market value is equal to $\mathbf{V}_{m,1} = \mathbf{R}_{m,1}$. This value, the random total market return for the first

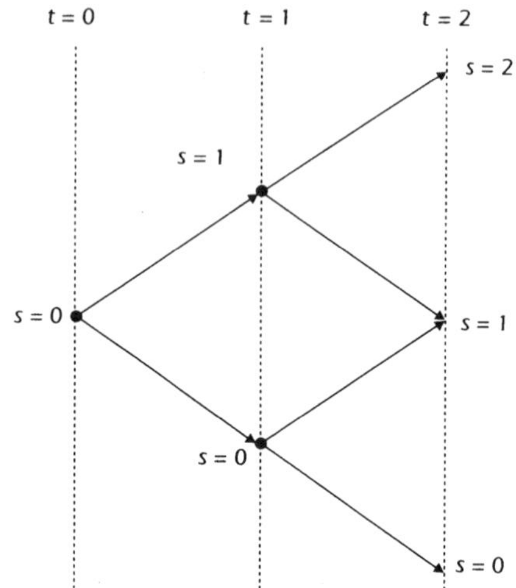

Figure 9-1. An illustration of a two-year binomial tree. *Source*: Authors' conception. *Note*: Each successive year (t) has one more possible market state (s). In the second year ($t = 2$) the middle state ($s = 1$) can be reached by either following the up-down path or down-up path.

year, can equal either R_u or R_d. In Figure 9-1, we draw two paths emanating from the initial market value, one up and one down, that connect the initial value to the two possible values at $t = 1$. After two years, the market value is equal to the random product $\mathbf{V}_{m,2} = \mathbf{R}_{m,1} \cdot \mathbf{R}_{m,2}$. It can have one of three possible values $\{R_u^2, R_u \cdot R_d, R_d^2\}$, but there are now four different, equally likely paths, {up-up, up-down, down-up, down-down} connecting the initial value with the three final values. The up-down path and the down-up path lead to the same market return, namely $R_u \cdot R_d$, and this value is twice as likely as either of the two possible paths that lead to it. After t years, the market value $\mathbf{V}_{m,t} = \mathbf{R}_{m,1} \cdot \mathbf{R}_{m,2} \cdots \mathbf{R}_{m,t}$ can have one of $(t + 1)$ possible values, $\{V_{t,s} = R_u^s \cdot R_d^{t-s} | 0 \leq s \leq t\}$, where the parameter '$s$' is the total number of 'up-moves'—a useful parameter for indexing the market values. On the other hand, there are 2^t paths between the initial state and the final states. The number of paths that have the market value indexed by s at time t will equal the binomial coefficient for 't-choose-s.' Hence, the state probability $\pi_{t,s}$, the probability that the market's value is equal to $V_{t,s}$, is given by the expression:

$$\pi_{t,s} = \frac{t!}{s! \cdot (t-s)!} \cdot 2^{-t} \tag{9-3}$$

In Equation (9-3), an exclamation point is used to denote a factorial.

Associated with every path of the binomial tree is the price today of a security that pays \$1 if and only if that path is realized. We term these securities path-contingent claims. We can use standard arbitrage pricing techniques to compute any such price. The price of a claim to receive \$1 at a given time and state is the cost of a dynamic strategy using the market and the risk-free asset that will provide this amount and nothing at any other time and state. For example, the current option price f_u for the first period up-move path and the current option price f_d for the first period down-move path are the following functions of R_f, R_u, and R_d:

$$f_u = \frac{R_f - R_d}{R_f \cdot (R_u - R_d)} \tag{9-4a}$$

$$f_d = \frac{R_u - R_f}{R_f \cdot (R_u - R_d)} \tag{9-4b}$$

The inequality $R_d < R_f < R_u$ is a necessary condition for positive prices. The prices for the two period paths can be written in terms of the one-period prices: $f_{uu} = f_u^2$, $f_{ud} = f_{du} = f_u \cdot f_d$, and $f_{dd} = f_d^2$. More generally, for a t-year path, the price is equal to $(f_u^s \cdot f_d^{t-s})$, where s is the number of up-moves. Hence, the option price for all paths that end at the market state 's' are the same, and depend only on the total number of up-moves and down-moves, not on the particular sequence of up-moves and down-moves. Thus today's price $\psi_{t,s}$ of a state claim that pays \$1 if and only if state s occurs is equal to the number of paths to the state times the price of each path:

$$\psi_{t,s} = \frac{t!}{s! \cdot (t-s)!} \cdot f_u^s \cdot f_d^{t-s} \tag{9-5}$$

We assume that markets are complete, or at least sufficiently complete, so dynamic strategies involving the market and the risk-free asset can replicate any state-claim. Finally for a fixed value of t, the sum of all the state prices is equal to $1/R_f^t$, the price of a risk-free dollar, t-years from now. This must be the case, since purchasing all the state claims available at year t guarantees the investor a dollar in year t, no matter which state is realized.

We are now in a position to show that for our binomial model, the PPC is a decreasing function of cumulative market return. First, the PPC and the cumulative market value are given by the formulas:

$$\psi_{t,s}/\pi_{t,s} = 2^t \cdot f_u^s \cdot f_d^{t-s} \tag{9-6a}$$

$$V_{t,s} = R_u^s \cdot R_d^{t-s} \tag{9-6b}$$

If we take the logarithm of each equation, we obtain two equations that are linear in s. After we eliminate the parameter s from this pair, we get the following simple relation between PPC and cumulative market return:

$$\psi_{t,s}/\pi_{t,s} = a^t / V_{t,s}^p \tag{9-7a}$$

In Equation (9-7a), the power p and time-factor a are constants defined by:

$$p = \ln\left(\frac{R_u - R_f}{R_f - R_d}\right) \div \ln(R_u/R_d) \tag{9-7b}$$

$$a = 2 \cdot f_d \cdot R_d^p \tag{9-7c}$$

Generally, p and a are positive, and so PPC is a decreasing function of total cumulative market return. In our numeric example, $p = 3.05$ and $a = 1.08$.

Lockbox Spending Strategies

Next, we introduce and illustrate *lockbox* strategies, an approach to spending which divides a retiree's initial wealth among separate accounts, one account for each future year of spending. The assets in each account are dynamically managed according to the account's exogenous investment rule. When an account reaches its target year, our retiree cashes out its investments, closes the account, and spends all of its proceeds. The accounts can be real or virtual, and we collectively call them lockboxes—a term that emphasizes the retiree's implicit obligation to yearly spend all the assets from the target account and to never comingle or spend the assets of any of the remaining accounts.

All efficient strategies adhere to the earmarking principle and have a lockbox formulation; however, there are inefficient lockbox strategies. The test for efficiency is simple: each lockbox's value must be a path-independent, increasing function of the cumulative market. For example, lockboxes that alternate investments in the risk-free and market assets are obviously path dependent and inefficient. In the remainder of this section, we pair three different investment strategies with lockbox spending. For each pair, we show that the resulting retirement strategy is efficient and derive its revealed utility.

Consider the lockbox strategy where each lockbox is invested in the market portfolio. Suppose our retiree has a planning horizon of T years, and has assigned F_0 dollars for today's consumption, placed F_1 dollars in the first lockbox, F_2 in the second and, more generally, F_t in the tth year lockbox. The total assigned dollars will sum to the initial wealth, that is, $W_0 = F_0 + F_1 + \ldots + F_T$. At the end of each year, the consumption from the *t*th lockbox will equal F_t times the cumulative return of the market:

$$C_{t,s} = F_t \cdot V_{t,s} \tag{9-8a}$$

Note that for each state at each time there will be a unique amount of consumption, and this will be an increasing function of the market value. We see immediately that this investor has a revealed utility. The revealed marginal utility follows from Equations (9-2) and (9-7):

$$U_t'(C) = a^t \cdot (F_t/C)^p \tag{9-8b}$$

To obtain Equation (9-8b), we set $U_0'(C_{0,0})$ equal to 1, since the entire set of an investor's utility functions can be multiplied by a constant without changing the implied optimal strategy. This strategy is thus optimal for an investor with a utility function that exhibits constant relative risk aversion, generally abbreviated as constant relative risk aversion (CRRA), with risk-aversion parameter p. Further, our investor's attitudes toward consumption in future states relative to the present are revealed by the dollars assigned to the lockboxes.

Now, suppose that instead of investing solely in the market, our retiree invests $F_{m,t}$ dollars of lockbox t in the market and $F_{f,t}$ dollars in the risk-free asset, with the sum of the dollars invested equal to W_0. Once the initial allocation is made, our investor adopts a buy and hold investment strategy. In practice, this investment strategy could be implemented by purchasing a zero-coupon bond and a market exchange-traded fund for each lockbox. When the *t*th lockbox is opened and cashed out, the consumption will be:

$$C_{t,s} = F_{f,t} \cdot R_f^t + F_{m,t} \cdot V_{t,s} \tag{9-9a}$$

As long as at least some dollars are allocated to the market, consumption will be an increasing function of market returns. Solving for the revealed marginal utility we obtain:

$$U_t'(C) = a^t \cdot \left(\frac{F_{m,t}}{C - F_{f,t} \cdot R_f^t} \right)^p \tag{9-9b}$$

In this case, the strategy is optimal for an investor with a HARA utility function—one that exhibits hyperbolic absolute risk aversion. In effect, the investor requires a minimum subsistence level equal to the amount provided by the allocation to the risk-free asset and has CRRA with respect to the amount provided by the allocation to the market.

Our third example has lockboxes invested in constant-mix, constant-risk portfolios. Specifically, we annually rebalance a lockbox's assets so that a fraction β is invested in the market portfolio and the remaining fraction $(1 - \beta)$ is invested in the risk-free asset. We impose a no-bankruptcy condition; hence the total return must be positive in either an up or down state.

and so β is limited to the range:

$$-R_f/(R_u - R_f) = \beta_{\min} < \beta < \beta_{\max} = +R_f/(R_f - R_d) \qquad \text{(9-10a)}$$

For our parameter choices, the bounds are $\beta_{\min} = -6.38$ and $\beta_{\max} =$ 12.75. The total annual returns of the mix follow a binomial model, and the cumulative return $M_{t,s}(\beta)$ of the mix at time t and in state s is given by:

$$\mathbf{M}_{t,s}(\beta) = \left[(1-\beta)\cdot R_f + \beta\cdot R_u\right]^s \cdot \left[(1-\beta)\cdot R_f + \beta\cdot R_d\right]^{t-s} \qquad \text{(9-10b)}$$

Again, s denotes the number of up-moves in the path to time t.

As before, we let F_t's be the amounts of initial wealth allocated to the lockboxes, and we introduce β_t's as the constant mixes for the lockboxes. Although the risk in any given lockbox is constant, the risks among all the lockboxes are allowed to vary. It follows that the spending from a constant-mix lockbox is given by:

$$C_{t,s} = F_t \cdot \mathbf{M}_{t,s}(\beta_t) \qquad \text{(9-11a)}$$

We see from the previous equations that consumption will be an increasing function of s, provided the market exposures are nonnegative. But Equation (9-6a) showed that PPC is a decreasing function of s. Thus for a constant mix strategy, consumption at time t will be a decreasing function of PPC. Therefore the investor's utility function for that period will be revealed. Moreover, Equation(9-6b) showed that market return is an increasing function of s. Thus a constant-mix strategy will have no nonmarket risk and will be efficient.

Using Equations (9-6b) and (9-10b), we can eliminate the parameter s from Equation (9-11a) and write $C_{t,s}$ as an increasing function of $V_{t,s}$. The revealed marginal utility then follows:

$$U_t'(C) = a_t^t \cdot (F_t/C)^{\gamma_t} \qquad \text{(9-11b)}$$

$$\gamma_t = \ln\left[\frac{R_u - R_f}{R_f - R_d}\right] \div \ln\left[\frac{(1-\beta_t)\cdot R_f + \beta_t \cdot R_u}{(1-\beta_t)\cdot R_f + \beta_t \cdot R_d}\right] \qquad \text{(9-11c)}$$

$$a_t = 2 \cdot f_d \cdot \left[(1-\beta_t)\cdot R_f + \beta_t \cdot R_d\right]^{\gamma_t} \qquad \text{(9-11d)}$$

Again, our retiree has a CRRA utility, but in this case, the retiree's choice for the exposures β_t determines the risk-aversions γ_t. Both the exposures β_t and initial allocations F_t determine the retiree's relative preference for consumption today, versus the future. We note if all the exposures are equal to one, the market exposure, then Equation (9-11b) reduces to Equation (9-8b), the result for the market only strategy.

The above three examples illustrate efficient financial retirement strategies and their revealed utility functions. Since financial economists often use CRRA or HARA models for utility, they may likely suggest one of our example strategies to a retiree. On the other hand, financial planners, who tend to rely on rules of thumb for investing and spending, would rarely advise one of the above combinations of investing and spending strategies. In the next two sections, we evaluate the efficiency of two of the most common rules.

Glide-Path Investment Strategies

Many advisers recommend that retirees annually adjust their portfolios by decreasing their exposure to equities, and thus reducing their overall risk. This rule of thumb, often called a *glide-path* strategy, is an age-based investment strategy. A classic example is the oft-quoted 100 – age rule for the percentage of assets allocated to equities, for example, 60-year-olds should hold 60 percent of their assets in bonds and 40 percent of their assets in equities. Many retirees follow a glide-path strategy by investing in *life-cycle funds*—age-targeted, managed funds intended to serve as the sole investment vehicle for all of a retiree's assets. In recent years, interest in life-cycle funds has exploded. Jennings and Reichenstein (2007) analyzed the policies of some leading life-cycle funds and found that a 120 – age equity allocation describes the typical management rule. An earlier chapter by Bengen (1996) suggested that the target equity allocation should equal 128 – age for clients up to age 80 and 115 – age afterward. The advocates of glide-path strategies often pair this investment rule with one or more options for a spending rule. However, there is only one spending rule that makes the complete retirement strategy efficient, and that rule is the focus of this section.

The investing rules described above specify equity percentages, but our market model deals more conveniently with market fractions. However, there is a simple linear relationship between the two descriptions. For example, our sample parameters roughly correspond to a market of 60 percent equities. In this case, the equity mix is 0 percent when $\beta = 0$, is 60 percent when $\beta = 1$, and is 100 percent when $\beta = 5/3$. Now, consider a 65-year-old retiree following the 120 – age rule. This retiree has the annual equity percentage targets of 55, 54, 53 percent, etc., and the annual market fraction targets of 55/60, 54/60, 53/60, etc. Because age-based rules are easily translated into a market-fraction time series, we generally use the latter to describe a glide path.

Consider the generic glide-path investment and spending strategy. At the beginning of each year, some portion of the portfolio is spent; the fraction β_t of the remainder is invested in the market, and the rest is invested in the risk-free asset. When this total portfolio strategy is efficient, it has a lockbox equivalent. We use this equivalence principle to derive the optimal spending rule. We start by choosing any one of the lockboxes, say the jth box, and virtually combine its contents and the contents of all succeeding lockboxes. Initially, the jth combined portfolio will have value $F_j + \ldots + F_T$, where the F_t's are again the initial lockbox allocations. The future values of a combined portfolio must satisfy two requirements. First, they must evolve in a path-independent manner, just like the values of the constituent lockboxes. Second, since the jth combined portfolio *is* the total portfolio for the jth year, this combined portfolio must have the glide path's market fraction β_j in the jth year, independent of the market state. Now, as we saw in the previous section, a constant-mix portfolio with market exposure β_j satisfies both of these requirements; in fact, it can be shown that every combined portfolio is a constant-mix portfolio. If we let the random variable $\Sigma_{j,t}$ be the value of the jth combined portfolio at year $0 \leq t \leq j$, then we have:

$$\Sigma_{j,t} = \left(F_j + \ldots + F_T\right) \cdot \mathbf{M}_t\left(\beta_j\right) \tag{9-12a}$$

where $\mathbf{M}_t(\beta)$ is the random cumulative return at year t for the constant-mix portfolio with market weight β; its value in state s at time t is given by Equation (9-10a).

Given the combined portfolios for an efficient glide path, the individual lockbox holdings follow immediately. First, the lockbox for T is just the combined portfolio for T; a constant-mix portfolio with exposure β_T and initial allotment F_T. The remaining lockbox portfolios are obtained by differencing successive combined portfolios. Let the random variable $\mathbf{\Lambda}_{j,t}$ be the value of jth lockbox at time t:

$$\begin{aligned}\mathbf{\Lambda}_{j,t} &= \Sigma_{j,t} - \Sigma_{j+1,t} \\ &= \left(F_j + \ldots + F_T\right) \cdot \mathbf{M}_t\left(\beta_j\right) - \left(F_{j+1} + \ldots + F_T\right) \cdot \mathbf{M}_t\left(\beta_{t+1}\right) \\ &= F_j \cdot \mathbf{M}_t\left(\beta_j\right) + \left(F_{j+1} + \ldots + F_T\right) \cdot \left[\mathbf{M}_t\left(\beta_j\right) - \mathbf{M}_t\left(\beta_{t+1}\right)\right]\end{aligned} \tag{9-12b}$$

The initial lockbox holds cash, the last lockbox holds a constant-mix portfolio, and the middle lockboxes hold a combination of assets; the first is a constant-mix asset, and the second is a 'swap' between two constant-mix assets. Finally, the efficient spending is given by $\mathbf{C}_t = \mathbf{\Lambda}_{t,t}$, or in terms of states:

$$C_{t,s} = \begin{cases} F_0, & t = 0 \\ F_t \cdot \mathbf{M}_{t,s}\left(\beta_t\right) + \left(F_{t+1} + \ldots + F_T\right) \cdot \left[\mathbf{M}_{t,s}\left(\beta_t\right) - \mathbf{M}_{t,s}\left(\beta_{t+1}\right)\right], & 0 < t < T \\ F_T \cdot \mathbf{M}_{T,s}\left(\beta_T\right), & t = T \end{cases} \tag{9-12c}$$

It is tedious, but straightforward, to directly verify that the above spending rule, coupled with its glide-path investment rule, is efficient. Further, though there is no simple function to describe the revealed utility, its values can be easily computed numerically.

Glide paths may well reflect the desires of many retirees to take less risk concerning their investments as they age, but these retirees' retirement strategies will be inefficient unless spending follows Equation (9-12c). Glide-path rules are ubiquitous, but their complementary spending rules are rare. In fact, we are unaware of any retiree that computes his annual spending according to the above rule. As an alternative to the glide-path strategy, we recommend the constant-mix lockbox strategy discussed in the previous section. If a retiree decreases the market fractions for successive lockboxes, then his total portfolio risk will tend to decrease over time. Thus, a retiree can retain the desired feature of the glide path, but can have a much simpler spending rule.

The Four Percent Rule

Many recent articles in the financial planning literature have attempted to answer the question: 'How much can a retiree safely spend from his portfolio without risking running out of money?'. Bengen (1994) examined historical asset returns to determine a constant spending level that would have had a low probability of failure. He concluded that a real value equal to ~4 percent of initial wealth could be spent every year, assuming that funds were invested with a constant percentage in equities within a range of 50–75 percent. Cooley, Hubbard, and Walz (1998) used a similar approach and found that a 4 percent spending rule with inflation increases had a high degree of success assuming historical returns and at least a 50 percent equity allocation. Later, Pye (2000) concluded that with a 100 percent allocation to equities, the 4 percent rule would be safe enough if equity returns were log-normally distributed with a mean return of 8 percent and a standard deviation of return equal to 18 percent.[4] Based on this research, there is a growing consensus that newly retired individuals with funding horizons of 30–40 years can safely set their withdrawal amount to 4 percent of initial assets and increase spending annually to keep pace with inflation. This is the foundation for the now common *4 percent rule* of thumb for retirement spending.

An efficient retirement strategy must be totally invested in the risk-free asset to provide constant spending in every future state.[5] However, the generic 4 percent rule couples a risky, constant-mix investment strategy with a riskless, constant spending rule. There is a fundamental mismatch between its strategies, and as a result it is inefficient. The following simple example illustrates these points. Consider a retiree who, whether the market goes up or down, wants to spend only $1 next year. He can achieve this goal by investing $1/R_f$ dollars in the risk-free asset. On the other hand, if he uses the market asset, he must increase his investment to $1/R_d$dollars, so that if the market goes down, the investment pays the required \$1. However, if the market goes up, the investment pays (R_u/R_d) dollars, and there is an unspent surplus. So, if our retiree truly requires just \$1, then investing in the market is less efficient than investing in the risk-free asset because of the greater cost and the potential unspent surplus.

We can use the above argument to investigate a more general case. Suppose a retiree wants to support a constant spending level $C_{t,s} = f \cdot W_0$ for T years from a portfolio with initial wealth W_0 that is invested in a possibly, time-dependent strategy, for example, a glide path. Further, let D_t equal the minimum total return of the portfolio in year t. These minimums will correspond to down (up) moves for portfolios with positive (negative) market fractions β_t. Then to insure against the worst-case scenario, a safe spending fraction f must satisfy the equation:

$$\frac{1}{f} = 1 + \frac{1}{D_1} + \frac{1}{D_1 \cdot D_2} + \ldots + \frac{1}{D_1 \cdot D_2 \cdot \ldots \cdot D_T} \tag{9-13}$$

The most efficient investment will yield the largest spending fraction f, which corresponds to maximizing the minimum returns D_t. However, in any period, the best of the worst is achieved by investing in the risk-free asset, and thus $\beta_t = 0$. For example, suppose a retiree has a planning horizon of 35 years and invests in the risk-free asset, then $D_t = R_f = 1.02$ and $f = 3.85$ percent. On the other hand, if the retiree insists on investing in the market portfolio, then $D_t = R_d = 0.94$ and $f = 0.77$ percent, a fivefold decrease in spending. For the risk-free asset $(D_t > 1)$, each successive year is cheaper to fund, but for the market portfolio $(D_t < 1)$, each successive year is more costly.

The safe spending fraction satisfies Equation (9-13). With this spending level, all scenarios, other than the worst-case scenario, will have an unspent surplus. If we raise the spending fraction just a bit, then the worst-case scenario will be underfunded and the spending plan will collapse if this path is realized. As we continue to raise the level, more and more scenarios will be underfunded, a few may be spot on, and the remaining will have a surplus. If our example retiree insists both on investing in the market and increasing his spending fraction to 4 percent, then ~10 percent of scenarios will be underfunded and the remaining 90 percent of scenarios result in an unspent surplus. Further, more than 50 percent of the scenarios will have a surplus more than twice initial wealth! It is very unlikely that this retiree, who desired a riskless spending plan, would find such an eschewed-feast or -famine plan acceptable.

This type of analysis generalizes to any given desired spending plan. With complete markets, any given spending plan has a unique companion investment plan that delivers the spending at minimum cost. With state-contingent securities, the minimum cost investment plan involves simply purchasing the contingent claims that deliver the desired spending. Given our simple complete market, the contingent claims must be translated into dynamic strategies utilizing the market and riskless assets. Deploying this minimum required wealth using any other investment strategy necessarily results in surpluses and deficits relative to the desired spending plan. Extra wealth must then be introduced to eliminate all deficits.

The preceding assumed individual preferences were consistent with a fixed spending plan and demonstrated the inefficiency of a market investment plan. If we instead assume the investment plan is indicative of preferences, then we need to find a spending plan consistent with a market portfolio investment plan. This problem was previously analyzed, and the spending solution is reported in Equation (9-8a). If a market investment plan is indicative of preferences, then all efficient spending plans require spending that is proportional to cumulative market returns.

The 4 percent rule does not generate a revealed utility because the investment and spending rules do not correspond to an efficient retirement strategy. Retirees interested in fixed retirement spending should invest in the risk-free asset. Anyone who chooses to invest in the market should be prepared for more volatile spending. Either can adopt an efficient strategy. However, a retiree who plans to spend a fixed amount each period, while investing some or all funds in the market, faces a very uncertain future. Markets could perform well, and his wealth would far exceed the amount needed to fund his desired spending, or they could perform poorly, and his entire spending plan would collapse.

Conclusion and Discussion

Virtually all retirees have an explicit or implicit retirement spending and investment strategy. What is striking is the gulf that exists between how financial economists approach the problem of finding optimal retirement strategies and the rules of thumb typically utilized by financial advisers. Aside from identifying this gap, our objective with this chapter has been to evaluate the extent to which several popular retirement spending and investment strategies are consistent with expected utility maximization. This evaluation has two stages. First, is the given rule of thumb consistent with expected utility maximization for *any* investor? Second, if it is, how must the rule's investment and spending strategies be integrated to achieve and maintain efficiency?

By and large, we find that the strategies analyzed fail one or more of our tests. Investment rules suggesting risk glide paths pass the first assessment in that they are not per se inconsistent with expected utility maximization. However, the conditions on the implied spending rule required by efficiency seem onerous and unlikely to be followed by virtually any retirees. While risk glide paths only specify suggested investments, the 4 percent rule is fairly explicit about both the recommended spending and investment strategy. Unfortunately, the 4 percent rule represents a fundamental mismatch between a riskless spending rule and a risky investment rule. This mismatch renders the 4 percent rule inconsistent with expected utility maximization. Either the spending or the investment rule can be a part of an efficient strategy, but together they create either large surpluses or result in a failed spending plan.

While most of our results are obtained using a simple binomial model of the evolution of asset returns, many hold in more general settings, as we intend to show in subsequent research. Our results suggest a reliance on lockbox spending strategies, a very different type of retirement financial strategy than those currently advocated by practitioners. To an extent, this may be attributable to the assumptions we have made concerning both the nature of the capital markets and the objectives of the retiree. It is at least possible that one or more of the standard rules may be appropriate if prices are set differently in the capital markets and/or the investor has a different type of utility function. For example, one might posit that returns are not independent, but negatively serially correlated. Or one might focus on the efficiency of a strategy for an investor whose utility for consumption at a given time depends on both the consumption at that time and the consumption in prior periods. However, we suspect that it may be difficult to prove that the practitioner rules we have analyzed are efficient even in such settings.

Much of the analysis in this chapter relates to identifying problems with existing rules of thumb, but thus far, we have only hinted at ways to remedy the situation. An interesting line of inquiry would address this gap by finding an efficient strategy that strictly dominates an inefficient strategy such as one of those advocated by practitioners. There are two types of inefficiencies that could be introduced. First, a given retirement strategy could inefficiently allocate resources. That is, the same set of outcomes could be purchased with fewer dollars.[6] Given this inefficiency, a revised strategy could be constructed that strictly dominates the original strategy in that the revised strategy would increase spending in at least one state without decreasing spending in any state. A second type of inefficiency occurs when a strategy entails multiple spending levels for a given market return. If the total present value allocated to purchase the multiple spending levels were instead used to purchase a single spending amount, then as long as the expected returns in all such states are the same, any such replacement would be preferred by any risk-averse investor (formally, the revised set of spending amounts would exhibit second-degree stochastic dominance over the initial set). By making all such possible replacements, an inefficient strategy could be converted to a dominating efficient strategy. Another line of inquiry involves the examination of the properties of the revealed utility function associated with any efficient strategy, whether advocated initially or derived by conversion of an inefficient strategy. Such examination might reveal preferences that are inconsistent with those of a particular retiree and hence the strategy, while efficient, would not be appropriate in the case at hand.

Overall, our findings suggest that it is likely to be more fruitful to clearly specify one's assumptions about a retiree's utility function than to establish the optimal spending and investment strategy directly. Of course, one should take into account more aspects of the problem than we have addressed in this chapter. Annuities should be considered explicitly, rather than ruled out *ex cathedra*. Separate utility functions for different personal states (such as 'alive' and 'dead') could be specified rather than using a weighted average using mortality probabilities, as we have assumed here. Yet our analysis suggests that rules of thumb are likely to be inferior to approaches derived from the first principles of financial economics.

Acknowledgments

The authors thank John Ameriks, Olivia S. Mitchell, and Stephen Zeldes for many valuable comments on an early draft of this chapter. We also thank our colleagues at Financial Engines Wei Hui and Jim Shearer for their insights and support.

Notes

[1] We are assuming that for each time period, there is a utility function that gives the utility *measured today* as a function of the amount consumed in that period. Moreover, we assume that the investor prefers more to less and is risk-averse, so the utility function for a time period increases with consumption at a decreasing rate. The expected utility of consumption in a time period is simply the probability-weighted average of the utilities of the amounts consumed in different scenarios at the time. Finally, the expected utility of the retirement plan is the sum of the expected utilities for each of the time periods.

[2] Sharpe uses the term price-per-chance or PPC for the ratio of a state's price to its probability (Sharpe 2007). As discussed by Cochrane (2005), this quantity is also called the marginal rate of substitution, the pricing kernel, a change of measure, and the state-price density.

[3] Although our binomial model for annual market returns may appear highly restrictive, similar models using shorter time periods are often used in both the

academy and financial sector for pricing options and predicting the results of investment strategies.

[4] Pye (2000) also shows that a 60 percent initial allocation to Treasury Inflation Protected Securities (TIPS) improves the allowable withdrawal to 4.5 percent, while simultaneously lowering the measured downside-risk.

[5] As the market fraction β approaches zero, constant-mix lockboxes are invested in just the risk-free asset and provide constant spending. Further, the risk-aversion parameter of the underlying CRRA utility approaches infinity in this limit. Alternatively, state-independent spending can be viewed as the limit of the buy and hold lockbox for which all wealth is allocated to the risk-free asset and none in the market asset. Here, the subsistence levels of the underlying HARA utility exhaust the budget.

[6] Dybvig (1988*a*, 1988*b*) explored inefficient portfolio strategies in a pair of chapters. His approach is very useful for analyzing retirement strategies such as the 4 percent rule.

References

Bengen, William P. (1994). 'Determining Withdrawal Rates Using Historical Data,' *Journal of Financial Planning*, 7(4): 171–80.

—— (1996). 'Asset Allocation for a Lifetime,' *Journal of Financial Planning*, 9(4): 58–67.

Cochrane, John H. (2005). *Asset Pricing: Revised Edition.* Princeton, NJ: Princeton University Press: 3–147.

Cooley, Phillip L., Carl M. Hubbard and Daniel T. Walz (1998). 'Retirement Savings: Choosing a Withdrawal Rate That Is Sustainable,' *The American Association of Individual Investors Journal*, February: 16–21.

Dybvig, Phillip H. (1988*a*). 'Distributional Analysis of Portfolio Choice,' *Journal of Business*, 61: 369–93.

—— (1988*b*). 'Inefficient Dynamic Portfolio Strategies or How to Throw Away a Million Dollars in the Stock Market,' *Review of Financial Studies*, 1:67–88.

Jennings, William W. and William Reichenstein (2007). 'Choosing the Right Mix: Lessons From Life Cycle Funds,' *The American Association of Individual Investors Journal*, January: 5–12.

Merton, Robert C. (1971). 'Optimum Consumption and Portfolio Rules in a Continuous-Time Model,' *Journal of Economic Theory*, 3: 373–413.

Pye, Gordon B. (2000). 'Sustainable Investment Withdrawals,' *The Journal of Portfolio Management*, 26(4): 73–83.

Sharpe, William F. (2007). *Investors and Markets: Portfolio Choices, Asset Prices, and Investment Advice.* Princeton, NJ: Princeton University Press: 74–100.

Choosing Outcomes versus Choosing Products: Consumer-Focused Retirement Investment Advice

DANIEL G. GOLDSTEIN
ERIC J. JOHNSON
WILLIAM F. SHARPE*

Investing for retirement is one of the most consequential yet daunting decisions consumers face. We present a way to both aid and understand consumers as they construct preferences for retirement income. The method enables consumers to build desired probability distributions of wealth constrained by market forces and the amount invested. We collect desired wealth distributions from a sample of working adults, provide evidence of the technique's reliability and predictive validity, characterize individual- and cluster-level differences, and estimate parameters of risk aversion and loss aversion. We discuss how such an interactive method might help people construct more informed preferences.

In this article, we present an approach for gaining insight about consumers' preferences for investments. Because it is based on both normative and behavioral views of investment decision making, the approach may also help financial services firms better meet consumers' needs. Unlike current practice, the approach does not attempt to match people to products or to reduce risk to a unidimensional construct. The key idea is enabling consumers to explore probability distributions of prospective outcomes, which are constrained by market forces and the amount invested.

To begin, imagine an employee on the first day of a new job. He or she is taken down the hall to Human Resources, is told about the retirement plan, and is shown a catalog of investments consisting of stocks, bonds, and money market funds.

At this juncture, the retirement investment decision is a product-selection task. The products are funds. The prices are the fees, which are usually 1%–3%, with lifetime costs that can reach tens of thousands of dollars. The product attributes are the funds' performance history, composition, brand image, and so on (Capon, Fitzsimons, and Prince 1996). To help make this decision, investment management firms provide brochures describing product attributes and so-called risk-tolerance quizzes. While commonly used, these quizzes do not appear to be the result of extensive evaluation; we are aware of only one published study on them, which shows that the various quizzes used by different fund providers have at best modest intercorrelations (Yook and Everett 2003).

There are many potential sources of information. Employees may take the provided quiz, do their own research over the course of several days, or talk to an advisor. However, there is some evidence that people do not do much research. One study of university employees found that the majority spent less than an hour deciding and did not consult with anyone other than family members (Benartzi and Thaler 1999). The short time spent on the initial allocation is not troubling if employees later revise their choice. But for many, this allocation rarely changes (Agnew, Balduzzi, and Annika 2003). An early study found that 100% of employees did not change their initial allocation in their entire tenure of employment (Samuelson and Zeckhauser 1988), and a

*Daniel G. Goldstein is an assistant professor of marketing, London Business School, London, NW1 4SA, United Kingdom (dgoldstein@london.edu). Eric J. Johnson is Norman Eig Professor of Business, Columbia University, New York, NY 10027 (ejj3@columbia.edu). William F. Sharpe is the STANCO 25 Professor of Finance, Emeritus, Stanford University Graduate School of Business, 518 Memorial Way, Stanford, CA 94305-5015 (wfsharpe@stanford.edu). This research has been supported by the Columbia Center for Excellence in E-Business and by National Science Foundation grant SES-0352062 to Eric J. Johnson. The authors thank the editors and reviewers, in addition to the following people, for help in developing this article: Beatrice Belizaire, Shlomo Benartzi, Phil Blythe, Noel Capon, Isaac Dinner, Emel Filiz, Wendy Garrido, Dominique Goldstein, John Hauser, Bruce Hardie, Peggy Hu, Raghu Iyengar, Anja Lambrecht, John Payne, Margaret Pierson, Drazen Prelec, Duncan Simester, Richard Thaler, Elke Weber, Martijn Willemsen, and Besir Wrayet.

John Deighton served as editor and Ann McGill served as associate editor for this article.

Electronically published August 21, 2008

 0093-5301/2008/3503-0010$10.00. DOI: 10.1086/589562

later one found that 87% made one or zero reallocations (Ameriks and Zeldes 2004). Thus, retirement investing has similarities with the purchase of subscription services in which initial decisions exhibit inertia.

The decision space faced by the consumer is large. A recent study of hundreds of retirement plans showed that they offered as many as 59 funds, with most offering between six and 22 (Huberman and Jiang 2006). Assuming a plan presents 10 funds, our employee must make three main decisions: how much to contribute, which funds to invest in, and how much to allocate to each of the funds.

If we use the United States as an example, the first decision—contribution level (the amount of money to invest each year)—can range from $0 to a maximum of $16,000. While this is an important decision, it is not the main focus of this article, in part because various companies and countries are experimenting with the introduction of auto-enrollment, linking retirement investing to the marketing literature on defaults (e.g., Madrian and Shea 2001). We focus on the second and third decisions.

The second question—how many different funds to select—could be simple. An investor might dedicate 100% of his contribution to a single fund. However, if he seeks further diversification, this is followed by a third decision—how to allocate the contribution across funds (asset allocation). Allocating between funds A and B, he could split the contribution many different ways: 5% to fund A and 95% to fund B, 10% to A and 90% to B, and so on. To compute the size of the decision space, we can assume that a person may choose a portfolio of between 1 and 10 funds—this would cover nearly all the plan participants studied by Huberman and Jiang (2006)—and make allocations in units no smaller than five percentage points. Assuming 16 possible contribution levels from $1,000 to $16,000 per year, this yields a choice set over 160 million possibilities.[1] In practice, the decision space is much larger, since employees may be presented with dozens of funds and can deal in units as small as 1% and $1. Though the options are numerous, somehow they are whittled down to one in as little as an hour. These rapid decisions can lead to outcomes that differ by large amounts over the course of a lifetime. This is obvious for the case of saving something versus saving nothing, but even a reallocation of a few hundred dollars per year from a fund returning 7% to a fund returning 3% can make tens of thousands of dollars of difference over the years.

This decision is also marked by uncertainty at multiple levels. For instance, there are at least two levels of risk at play in fund investing: risk between portfolios and risk within portfolios. Choosing a portfolio, as shown above, is risky because it involves choosing one option from a large and varied set. Once a portfolio is selected, however, each component fund or stock is a risk on its own, taking on many possible values over time. The risk of a portfolio also involves changing interfund correlations, interest and inflation rate fluctuations, currency risk, and beyond. In defined-contribution plans, a person is not signing up for a guaranteed level of income in retirement, as in defined-benefit plans. Rather, the income in retirement is essentially a random draw from a probability distribution of wealth. The three decisions we have discussed thus far affect the distribution, not the outcome. While marketers have modeled uncertainty (see Woodruff [1972] for an early example), it is usually uncertainty in the beliefs of the consumer about product attributes, not uncertainty in the realized outcome.

Forecasting a portfolio's outcome is difficult. Experts do so with Monte Carlo simulations and still miss the mark when fundamental assumptions are wrong. Research from behavioral finance suggests that people either do not know or do not like how their investments will translate into probability distributions of wealth in retirement. Benartzi and Thaler (2002) used financial techniques to forecast the retirement wealth distributions resulting from people's own investment choices and those resulting from two alternatives (based on the mean and median choices of other plan participants). Only 20% of people preferred the outcome distributions arising from their own investment choice over those of the median plan participant, which suggests that people could not forecast how their choices would translate into outcomes or that people had not rebalanced in a while, or both. These findings suggest that consumers have significant room for improvement when making retirement investment decisions.

Economic theory (Hakansson 1970; Merton 1969, 1971; Samuelson 1969), investment advice (Perold and Sharpe 1988), and the marketing collateral of mutual fund vendors often recommend that people divide their contributions between a risky and risk-free (or very low-risk) asset and perform periodic rebalancing to fixed proportions by dollar value. These recommendations are based on the assumption that people's risk preferences are described by constant relative risk aversion (CRRA). If returns are uncorrelated over time, such an investment strategy yields a roughly log-normal distribution of long-term returns.[2] If consumers follow this strategy, their wealth at retirement will effectively be drawn from a log-normal distribution. This raises a key question: How many investors prefer a log-normal distribution of wealth? Is a log-normal distribution the most suitable alternative given most people's stated preferences? Some investors may desire more downside protection or more upside potential. If it turns out that a substantial number of people are loss averse (Benartzi and Thaler 1995; Kahneman and Tversky 1979) and reference dependent, they would prefer non-log-normal distributions. Following standard investment advice would produce outcomes inconsistent with such nontraditional stated preferences.

In what follows, we describe a method for gaining insight

[1] There are 20 units of 5% to be allocated and 10 possible funds in which to place them, and there are $\binom{N+r-1}{r-1}$ ways to partition N objects into r categories.

[2] If returns are independent, the ending value for such a strategy will converge to log-normality as the number of periods increases. If r is the rate of return, the ending value is the product of $1 + r$, its log is the sum of the logs of $1 + r$, and the central limit theorem holds that the sum of uncorrelated random variables converges to normality.

FIGURE 1

THE DISTRIBUTION BUILDER INTERFACE

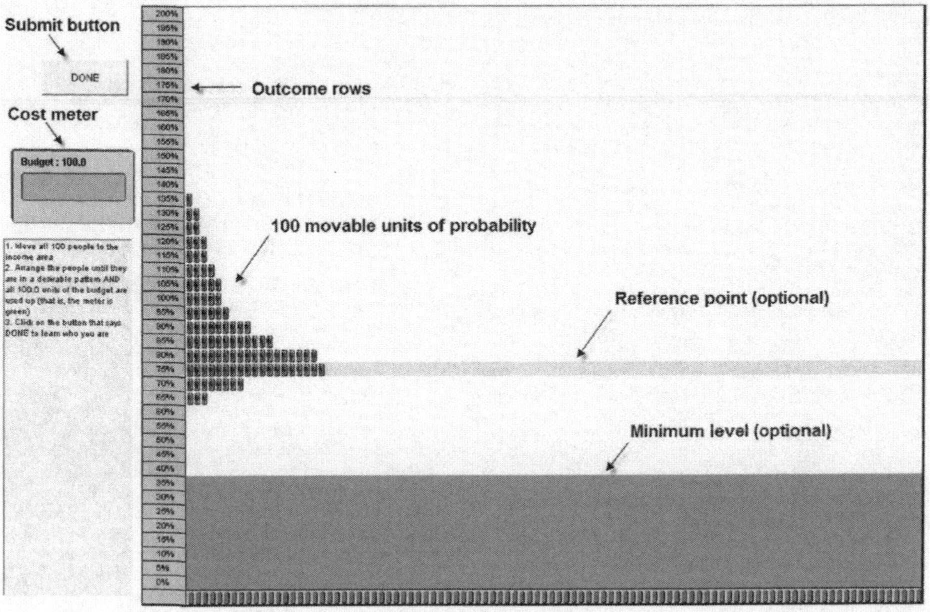

NOTE.—Using movable units of probability, participants can create arbitrarily shaped discrete probability distributions over numerous outcomes (on the vertical axis). Between two and 40 outcomes and one and 100 units of probability can easily be displayed on a standard-size monitor. The 40-outcome/100-unit case provides over 10^{34} unique distributions to choose among. A cost meter (upper left) can be used to constrict the space of allowable distributions, for example, to those that have a particular risk-return relationship. The cost meter functions by not allowing one to submit a distribution (using the submit button on the upper left) until it satisfies an arbitrary cost function. Users can see how every change to the distribution affects the cost meter numerically and graphically. All movements are seen in the context of their effects on the system as a whole. Color version and video demonstration available as online enhancements.

into investor preferences and use it to elicit desired wealth distributions from a sample of working adults who have been saving for retirement for 5–30 years. The method passes tests of reliability and validation and allows us to characterize individual differences in both risk attitude and loss aversion. We conclude by discussing how this method—exploring probability distributions of potential outcomes—might serve as a market research tool and might benefit consumer welfare by helping people construct, as opposed to state, preferences.

THE DISTRIBUTION BUILDER

The Distribution Builder (DB) is a market research tool that has been used to estimate the coefficient of constant relative risk aversion (CRRA parameter) from user-constructed probability distributions of desired outcomes (Sharpe 2006; Sharpe, Goldstein, and Blythe 2000). In this article, we describe a version of the tool created to elicit preferred probability distributions of retirement income.

Figure 1 shows the interface of the DB. On the vertical axis are outcome rows, percentages ranging from 0% to 200%. These represent income in retirement expressed as a percentage of preretirement income. If a person earned $100,000 in the year before retirement, the 75% row would represent $75,000 annual income in retirement. In the experiments described below, participants were told that 75% of preretirement income is a typical goal for income in retirement, and the 75% row was highlighted as a reference point. Indeed, popular investment advice, such as that given in *Ernst and Young's Retirement Planning Guide*, lists income-replacement ratios ranging from 68% to 80% (Arnone et al. 2002).

The interface has 100 markers forming a probability distribution against its left vertical axis. At the beginning of a session, the markers sit at the bottom of the screen and are dragged up into the square exploration area with the mouse. Clicking and dragging one marker moves it and all the markers on its right. Each of the 100 markers has an image of a person drawn on it. The participant is told that just one of the 100 markers represents her and that the others are just placeholders. Importantly, she is told that the marker representing her was chosen at random by the computer, and there is no way to tell which one it is before submitting a distribution. The participant arranges the markers into a probability distribution of her pleasing—that is, one she would be happy to have determine her own wealth in retirement. When finished, she clicks the "Done" button to simulate observing a randomly determined investment outcome. Clicking "Done" causes 99 randomly chosen markers to disappear slowly, one by one, until only one marker is left standing on its respective row. This relates a draw from a probability distribution to the amount of wealth one might have in retirement. For a demonstration of the DB, see video 1 (6.4 MB) in the online edition of the *Journal of Consumer Research*.

One obvious question is why, if higher rows represent more retirement wealth, do participants not move all 100 markers up to the top row, giving a 100% chance of enjoying 200% of preretirement income in retirement? The answer is that distributions are cost constrained, and participants may only submit a distribution of a given cost. The cost of each distribution is represented by the cost meter (the "Budget" reading on the left in fig. 1). As markers are moved upward, the cost goes up, and as markers are moved downward, the cost goes down. In retirement decision making, the DB uses a cost function that estimates the cost of obtaining each distribution in financial markets. The details of the cost function are beyond the scope of this article but may be found in Sharpe et al. (2000) and in Sharpe (2006). This type of cost function works by weighting each of the 100 markers by a unique state price and only allowing the submission of distributions in which the sum of the 100 chosen outcome rows (each weighted by its state price) is roughly equal to a given budget. In intuitive terms, with the DB, the participant is given a budget and state prices (weights) and is asked to create a distribution of outcome values that satisfies a cost constraint. We use the distribution of markers to make inferences about the person's utility for outcome levels, as will be shown.

In our studies, participants can only submit distributions that cost between 99 and 100 units of a hypothetical budget. We used a budget that was large enough such that participants could obtain 75% of their preretirement income risk free. That is, they could put all 100 markers on the 75% row and satisfy the cost meter. The 75% row is important because it serves as a reference point for three reasons: First, participants are told that 75% is a typical goal. Second, it stands out from the background. Third, it is the risk-free alternative that participants can discover, although they are not told about it. Figure 2 shows that the risk-free alternative satisfies the cost meter (i.e., all 100 units of the budget are used).

In the studies that follow, we have configured the DB so that it allows a user to trade off risk and return. People can decide to accept a certain amount of downside loss to provide an even greater possible amount of upside gain. For instance, in figure 1, a person taking 11 chances in 100 of ending up below 75% is rewarded with 70 chances in 100 of ending up above 75%.

At this point, we briefly provide technical details of how the DB allows for the estimation of utility functions. Readers less interested in these specifics might wish to skip ahead to the description of the experiments.

USING COST-CONSTRAINED DISTRIBUTIONS TO MAKE INFERENCES ABOUT UTILITY FUNCTIONS

Our goal is to use the cost-constrained placement of markers on the DB interface to estimate utility functions and parameters at an individual level. As a practical consumer concern, we can test whether participants' utility is consistent with advice often given to retirement investors.

Distributions are constrained by cost according to the function $\sum_{i=1}^{N} o_i s_i = B$, where the budget B is the exact enough amount of money needed to retire at 75% of preretirement income if only a risk-free investment is used, o_i is the outcome row associated with the ith marker, and s_i is the Arrow-Debreu state price (or weight) of the ith marker (Arrow 1964; Debreu 1959). The outcome rows are indexed in increasing (or nondecreasing) order, but the state prices are indexed in decreasing (or nonincreasing) order. The least-cost way to obtain a distribution of outcomes is thus $\sum_{i=1}^{N} o_i s_i$, which is the cost associated with the distribution and is shown as a percent of the budget (B) on the cost meter.

A key attribute of this procedure is that taking on downside risk allows for proportionally more upside gain, as in real markets. The intuition for this is as follows. The markers at the bottom of the distribution are more heavily weighted than those at the top. Each time a marker is moved, the state prices are reassigned so that this relative weighting holds. Since lower markers have more impact on the cost function than do higher markers, the result is a risk-return trade-off, which can be seen by comparing figure 1 with figure 2. Both figures satisfy the cost meter, but figure 1 clearly has the higher expected value.

While any set of unique state prices could provide useful information about utility functions, it is desirable to choose trade-offs that are similar to those in actual capital markets. We provided the DB with a set of state prices that, given assumptions, made the budget meter readout proportional to the cost of obtaining the distribution with a least-cost investment strategy (Dybvig 1988; Sharpe et al. 2000).

Inferring utility: The DB can be used to infer utility functions from distributions instead of from choices between simple two-alternative gambles, as was the dominant paradigm in the twentieth century. In order to do this, we assume that a person building a distribution is maximizing

FIGURE 2

LOWEST-RISK ALTERNATIVE

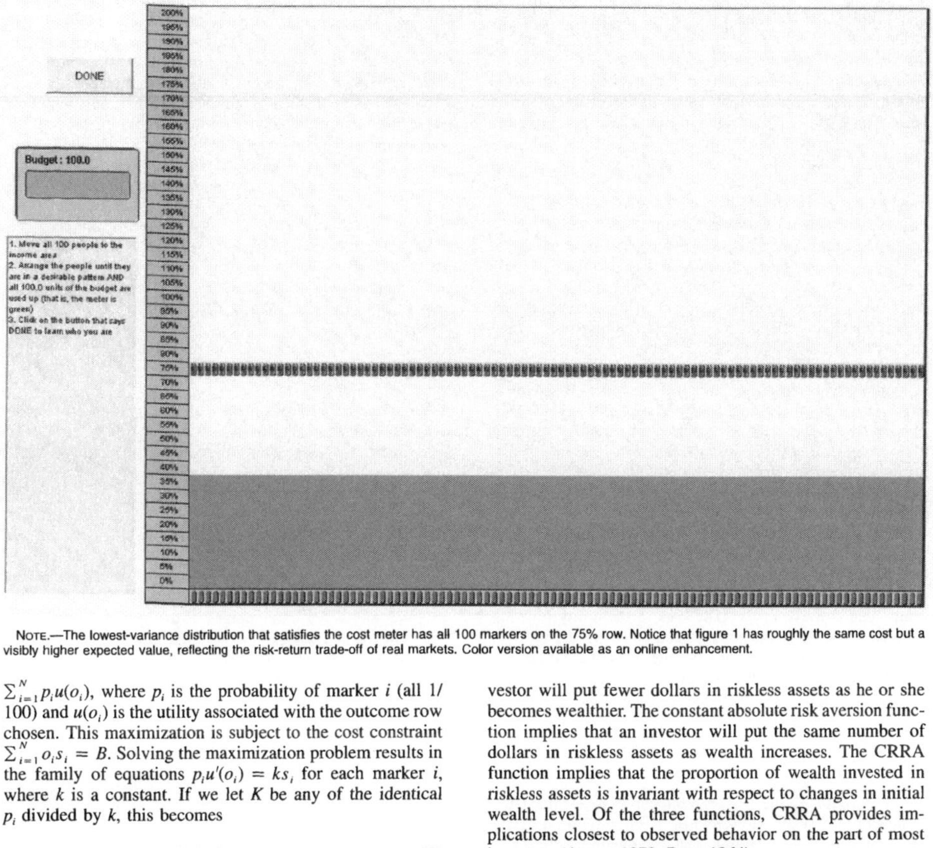

NOTE.—The lowest-variance distribution that satisfies the cost meter has all 100 markers on the 75% row. Notice that figure 1 has roughly the same cost but a visibly higher expected value, reflecting the risk-return trade-off of real markets. Color version available as an online enhancement.

$\sum_{i=1}^{N} p_i u(o_i)$, where p_i is the probability of marker i (all 1/100) and $u(o_i)$ is the utility associated with the outcome row chosen. This maximization is subject to the cost constraint $\sum_{i=1}^{N} o_i s_i = B$. Solving the maximization problem results in the family of equations $p_i u'(o_i) = k s_i$ for each marker i, where k is a constant. If we let K be any of the identical p_i divided by k, this becomes

$$Ku'(o_i) = s_i. \quad (1)$$

That is, the slope of the utility function at marker i is proportional to the ith state price. This key result can be used to make inferences about individual utility functions and to assess reference dependence (loss aversion).

Predictions of CRRA: A common classical assumption is that investors' risk preferences possess a property called constant relative risk aversion, or CRRA (Arrow 1970; Barberis 2000; Pratt 1964; Safra and Segal 1998). The three most commonly used utility functions in financial economic models are the quadratic, the constant absolute risk aversion, and the CRRA. The quadratic function implies that an investor will put fewer dollars in riskless assets as he or she becomes wealthier. The constant absolute risk aversion function implies that an investor will put the same number of dollars in riskless assets as wealth increases. The CRRA function implies that the proportion of wealth invested in riskless assets is invariant with respect to changes in initial wealth level. Of the three functions, CRRA provides implications closest to observed behavior on the part of most investors (Arrow 1970; Pratt 1964).

People with CRRA utility functions should prefer a constant mix of assets if returns are uncorrelated over time, resulting in log-normally shaped distributions of terminal wealth. A typical CRRA utility function is the power utility function $u(o) = (o^{1-\alpha})/(1-\alpha)$. An investor with such a function will have a marginal utility of $u'(o) = o^{-\alpha}$. Combining this with equation 1 and taking logarithms gives

$$\ln(s_i) = \ln(K) - \alpha \ln(o_i). \quad (2)$$

In the finance literature, this is commonly referred to as the coefficient of CRRA. If most people's risk preferences are well fit by CRRA, standard investment advice should help them select investment products. If not, then many people who follow the standard advice could be holding portfolios that violate their expressed preferences. In the experiment that follows, we fit equation 2 at an individual level by plotting the log state prices of the markers against the log outcome row levels and computing the regression line. If the relationship is not linear (low R^2), it would suggest that investor preferences may be better described by a model other than CRRA. If the relationship is linear, we assume that CRRA fits well and would expect estimates of the coefficient of relative risk aversion α to fall in the range commonly found by other means.

Alternatives to the traditional CRRA model are loss-averse utility functions such as that in prospect theory (Kahneman and Tversky 1979), which have received recent attention in the marketing domain (Ariely, Huber, and Wertenbroch 2005; Camerer 2005; Novemsky and Kahneman 2005). In loss-averse utility functions, losses have a higher impact than gains due to a loss-aversion parameter λ, which applies on one side of a reference point perceived to be the border between gains and losses. One means of estimating λ is taking the ratio of the slopes of the utility function on opposite sides of this border (Köbberling and Wakker 2005). The loss-aversion parameter has been empirically estimated to be around 2.25 (Tversky and Kahneman 1992). Note that we do not concern ourselves with fitting various parameters of prospect theory in this article; we only estimate the loss-aversion parameter.

Predictions of loss aversion: As mentioned, the participants in our experiment had a reference point: the 75% row. Recall that from equation 1, the state price s_i of the ith marker equals the slope of the utility function times a constant—that is $Ku'(o_i) = s_i$. The kink in the utility function parameterized by λ can thus be estimated by the ratio of state prices of the markers on opposite sides of the reference point (loss side divided by gain side). From the distributions submitted, we will estimate λ at an individual and group level.

Experiment 1

The purpose of the first experiment is to estimate the parameters of risk aversion and loss aversion for preferences concerning wealth in retirement and to obtain a descriptive overview of data gathered with DB.

Method and Participants. Experimentation was carried out online. Participants were 152 geographically diverse U.S. citizens who were randomly selected from our participant pool on the basis of age and citizenship and who were paid for their participation. Participants had an average age of 42 years with a standard deviation of 8 years. All have been saving for retirement for 5–30 years. Of the participants, 76% were married, 12% were single, and 12% were divorced or widowed; 71% were female, in line with the gender ratio of the entire subject pool at the time. Median income was $50,000 with a standard deviation of about $33,000. Average net worth was estimated to be about $200,000, and average amount saved toward retirement was about $110,000.

Participants were instructed to think about income in retirement as a percentage of preretirement income. They were told that 75% of preretirement income was a typically recommended goal. An extensive training session explained how to interact with the DB. Participants created one practice distribution that did not have any budget constraint (cost meter) but that did demonstrate the one-by-one random selection of markers once the distribution was submitted. After this, users were instructed on the role of the cost meter. They were told their task was to find a pattern of markers that they would like to have apply to their own income in retirement and that uses between 99% and 100% of the budget. The importance of treating the task as if it concerned their own income in retirement was emphasized. Participants were strongly advised against taking a chance of going below 25% of preretirement income, and, for this reason, as seen in figures 1 and 2, the bottom rows of the DB are shaded. Participants created two distributions, one after the other, and then went on to answer a survey containing demographic questions.

One year after submitting their first two distributions with DB, 85 participants from the above described set and 73 participants from a similar DB experiment completed a follow-up study, for a total of 158 year 2 respondents. This other experiment, which we do not analyze here, was the same as the reported one, except that the budget constraint had been set such that the risk-free level was 60% instead of 75% in the first session. Jumping ahead, there is no significant difference in year 2 risk-tolerance estimates between participants from two different year 1 experiments (t ratio −.4688, 144 df). Demographics of this group are naturally very close to the first-year set: average age 41 years, median income $50,000, 68% female.

As in year 1, participants submitted two distributions concerning desired income in retirement. To provide criteria for validation, respondents were then presented a DB on which they were asked to play two small-stakes gambles for a gain of up to $1.25 or a loss of up to $.75, with a risk-free alternative of $0 and outcome row increments of $.05. The stakes were real: money was added or subtracted to the participants' payments on the outcome of these gambles. Outside of the axis labeling, the mechanics of the DB were exactly the same as in the retirement scenarios. After submitting the two retirement and two gamble distributions, participants engaged in additional validation tasks, described in experiment 2.

Distributions. Figure 3 shows the aggregate distribution based on the number of markers at each wealth level from both distributions, averaged across all participants in the first year. Note that the composite distribution is roughly log-normal in shape, as CRRA would predict, but exhibits a peak at the reference point at 75%, congruent with loss-averse preferences, as will be discussed. Later, we will break apart this aggregate distribution into the clusters it com-

FIGURE 3

AGGREGATE DISTRIBUTION

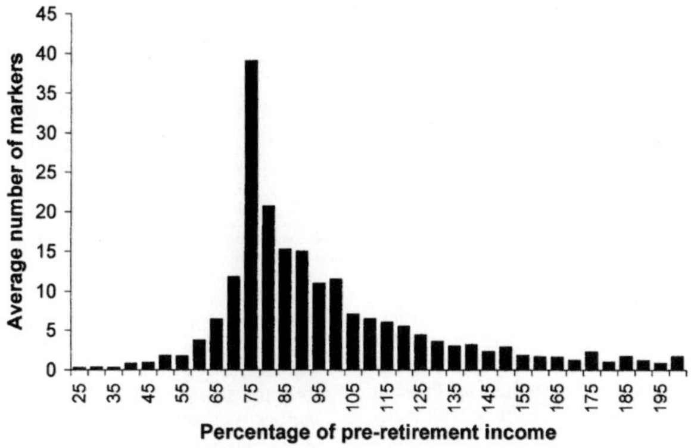

NOTE.—The distribution of the average investor, created by combining the number of markers at each wealth level in both distributions and averaging across all participants. The distribution is right skewed and shows a peak of twice the next highest level at the reference point. The 75% row served as a reference point because participants were told it is a typically recommended goal level for income in retirement and because 75% was the outcome that could be obtained without taking any risk (placing all 100 markers at 75% would satisfy the budget meter).

prises. Looking across the retirement distributions individually, the most common modes of the distributions are the 75%, 80%, 85%, 90%, and 100% wealth levels, which describe 55%, 11%, 7%, 6%, and 3% of distributions, respectively. Clearly, the intended reference point of 75% was a popular choice. Since we could have chosen 70% or 80% as the reference point, and distributions would presumably have shifted accordingly, these data show the reference-dependent nature of preferences. For instance, in the previously mentioned experiment in which the risk-free level was 60% but the recommended level was 75%, we observed aggregate distributions that peaked in both places.

Aggregate Model Fit. We fit a power function $u(o) = (o^{1-\alpha})/(1-\alpha)$, which is a CRRA utility function, to each participant's first and second distributions. Since the state prices (s_i values) were given and the participants chose a distribution of outcome (o_i) values, we treated the logarithm of the former as the independent variable and the logarithm of the latter as the dependent variable in our regressions. Rearranging equation 2 shows that the slope in such a regression provides an estimate of $-1/\alpha$, which can be easily transformed into the coefficient of relative risk aversion α.

The loss-aversion parameter λ was estimated by taking a ratio of the state prices (which are multiples of the slope of the utility curve) of the markers on either side of the reference point, namely the 75% row. Since this row is a bin that could be seen as ranging from 72.5 to 77.5, one cannot say which markers would sit just above and below 75. We take as a proxy the two most differing state prices in this row, which should reflect the change in slope experienced when moving across the reference row. Because of this issue of granularity, and because this estimate of loss aversion is not independent of risk aversion (someone who places many markers at 75 may simply be expressing a preference for a low-variance distribution), we consider our estimates to be somewhat rough approximations. We have tested a more complex model-based method to estimate loss aversion while accounting for risk aversion and find its estimates to correlate highly (>.9) with the estimates we provide here. For the sake of simplicity, we stick with the straightforward method.

Table 1 provides estimates of α, λ, and R^2 for the six individual distributions and for all retirement distributions together. We exclude cases in which CRRA and loss-aversion parameters cannot be estimated because no markers were placed below the reference point. This excludes 50 of the 620 retirement distributions we collected, a sizable exclusion that in the future can be avoided by altering the tool's submission constraints. Apart from these cases, the CRRA model tended to fit the data well, with median R^2 values around .9. The difference between the medians and means, as well as figure 4, shows skewness in both parameters, with most individual distributions having rather low risk and loss aversion. When the tool was used to engage in two small-stakes gambles for real money, risk aversion was less than when retirement was contemplated, as would be expected for smaller stakes. The first distribution from the first session stands out with its low risk- and loss-aversion estimates, possibly due to learning effects.

TABLE 1

PARAMETER ESTIMATES

	Risk aversion		Loss aversion		R^2	
	Median	Mean	Median	Mean	Median	Mean
Year 1 distribution 1	4.3	5.8	1.3	2.4	.91	.88
Year 1 distribution 2	6.1	10.6	1.8	4.7	.89	.85
Year 2 distribution 1	6.3	8.8	1.8	3.9	.90	.86
Year 2 distribution 2	8.3	10.7	2.2	4.9	.88	.84
Year 2 gamble distribution 1	4.9	8.5	1.4	4.4	.88	.82
Year 2 gamble distribution 2	4.1	6.8	1.5	4.6	.88	.81
All retirement distributions	6.1	9.0	1.8	4.0	.90	.86

NOTE.—Estimates of coefficient of constant relative risk aversion α and loss-aversion parameter λ, as well as R^2, for the six types of distributions and for all retirement distributions together.

For all retirement distributions, median α is 6.1, consistent with economic estimates in the range from 1 to 10 or higher (Blake 1996; Brav, Constantinides, and Geczy 2002; Campbell 1996; Friend and Blume 1975; Mehra and Prescott 1985). The median λ is 1.8, which is consistent with many other estimates (Tversky and Kahneman 1992). While this might be considered to indicate widespread occurrences of kinked utility curves (i.e., loss aversion), it is important to recall the limitations of our estimate of λ given earlier and to recall that figure 4 shows that many individuals are not loss averse.

Individual Differences. Do these aggregate parameter estimates mask variation across people? In other words, are there subpopulations of people with different risk preferences? Are participants who are not well fit by CRRA loss averse, or do they deviate in some other way from the CRRA model?

When fitting the CRRA model, median R^2 in the experiment centers around .9. If we perform a median split and categorize participants with $R^2 \geq .9$ as CRRA and $R^2 < .9$ as non-CRRA, the difference in the distributions between the two subpopulations of participants is easily visually observed. Figure 5 shows the composite distributions of high and low R^2 participants. The average R^2 was computed per participant on the basis of his or her two submitted distributions. Both distributions went into either the high or low R^2 composite histogram depending on this average. The distribution of the high R^2 group is roughly log-normal in shape, skewed to the right. The low R^2 distribution deviates from this smooth form in a very specific way, consistent with reference dependence. To understand why this shape suggests loss aversion, recall that the loss-aversion parameter is estimated by comparing the state prices of the two most differing markers at the reference row. As the number of markers at the reference row increases, so does this loss-aversion ratio. Note that this relationship between R^2 and loss aversion is not obvious. It is possible to create low R^2 distributions with low loss aversion, as is the case with a bimodal distribution or a distribution with probability massed around a point other than the reference point.

Summarizing experiment 1, we have estimated risk- and loss-aversion parameters on six distributions, obtaining estimates that fall into the expected ranges. The DB technique captures 100 points of a distribution that can be used to infer the slopes on a utility curve and can be analyzed by various means to gain insight into individual differences. While this may be a useful tool, practical applications depend upon establishing the reliability and validity of the method. Our data also suggest that there are important individual differences, which we explore later. In experiment 2 we go beyond face validity to demonstrate reliability and examine predictive validity.

FIGURE 4

RISK-AVERSION AND LOSS-AVERSION PARAMETER ESTIMATES

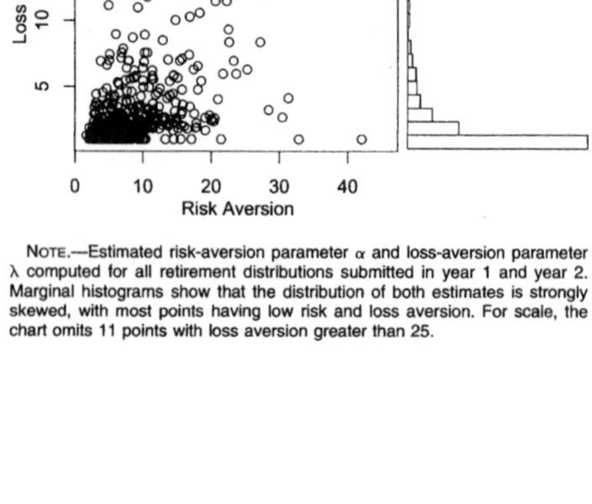

NOTE.—Estimated risk-aversion parameter α and loss-aversion parameter λ computed for all retirement distributions submitted in year 1 and year 2. Marginal histograms show that the distribution of both estimates is strongly skewed, with most points having low risk and loss aversion. For scale, the chart omits 11 points with loss aversion greater than 25.

FIGURE 5

POPULATION SPLIT BY FIT TO CRRA MODEL

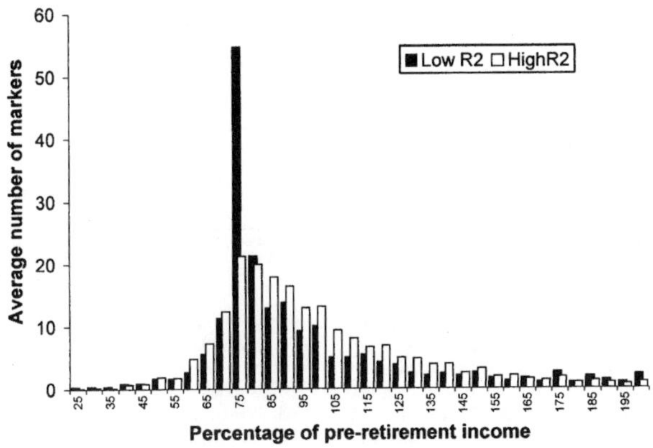

NOTE.—Composite distribution of participants who are well (high R^2) and poorly (low R^2) fit by the constant relative risk aversion (CRRA) model. The low R^2 people do not deviate arbitrarily, but rather in a systematic way, from CRRA (log-normality). The massing of probability at the reference point (here 75%) is a property of a loss-averse distribution. The bars of each color sum to 200 because each participant submitted two 100-marker distributions.

Experiment 2

Method. In order to assess individuals on covariate measures of risk preference, participants from the year 1 study completed the following validation tasks after creating their two distributions.

Outcome Preferences Task. In this task, participants were shown histograms representing distributions of returns resulting from portfolios holding 0%, 10%, 20%, 30%, 40%, 50%, or 60% in stock and the rest in a risk-free asset and were asked which pattern of investment results they would like to apply to their own retirement. Graphs were made with the same assumptions about budget, holding period, and stock returns as those used for the DB. Histograms of returns were chosen as a validating measure for four reasons: they have been shown to facilitate estimates of volatility (Ibrekk and Morgan 1987), they have been favored by people assessing risks (Thompson and Bloom 2000), they are commonly used in financial prospectuses and studies of financial risk perception (Siebenmorgen, Weber, and Weber 2000), and, finally, unlike asset allocation tasks, they preclude application of the 1/*N* heuristic (Benartzi and Thaler 2001), which can bias responses. Because the histograms we present consist of a constant mix of stocks and a risk-free asset, they are log-normal in shape and thus approximate the options available to people who follow the constant-mix investment advice.

Gamble Choice Task. To validate DB in comparison with a dominant form of risk-assessment task, participants were presented with three choices between sure amounts and gambles. The first item was "Which would you prefer if offered right now 1) $4.50 for certain 2) A 50% chance of getting $1 and a 50% chance of getting $15." The choices in the other items were "1) $1 for certain 2) A 10% chance of getting $12 and a 90% chance of getting nothing" and "1) $8 for certain 2) A 90% chance of getting $10 and a 10% chance of getting nothing." The number of risky choices (0–3) was computed for each participant.

Risk-Tolerance Scales. Participants completed two risk-tolerance scales. The first was the gambling and investment subscale of the Weber-Blais-Betz Domain Specific Risk Attitude Scale (Weber, Blais, and Betz 2002). Participants also completed a reworded variant of an actual risk-tolerance self-assessment scale used by one of the world's largest providers of retirement investment products.

Reliability, Validation, and Predictive Validity

Reliability. To assess the reliability of the risk measures collected with DB, we computed the reliability coefficient as the Pearson correlation between parameters estimated from two distributions submitted one after the other, as shown in table 2. Within the first session in year 1, the two measurements of the transformed CRRA model-based risk parameter $-1/\alpha$ have a Pearson correlation of .700 (Spearman .702). In the year 2 session, this correlation reached .803 (Spearman .793). Note that the respondents started with a cleared screen for each distribution, so these high corre-

TABLE 2

TEST-RETEST RELIABILITY

Component	Pearson correlation	Spearman correlation	Count
Within year 1	.700	.702	152
Within year 2	.803	.793	148
Between year 1 and year 2:			
Averages:			
Uncorrected	.431	.454	75
With correction for attenuation	.575		75
With ≥$25,000 savings:			
Uncorrected	.583	.559	57
With correction for attenuation	.778		57

NOTE.—Test-retest correlations of the constant relative risk aversion (CRRA) parameter computed within years, between years, with and without correction for test-retest attenuation, and with the exclusion of those who have little or nothing saved toward retirement.

lations are not due to merely resubmitting the previous response. To look at reliability over time, the average $-1/\alpha$ value from year 1 is correlated with its corresponding value in year 2, giving a Pearson correlation of .431 (Spearman .454). As Ghiselli, Campbell, and Zedek (1981) point out, the between-year reliability measure $r_{12(\text{true})}$ must take into account the attenuation due to within-year reliabilities and is $r_{12}/\sqrt{r11r12}$, where r_{11} and r_{22} are the respective reliabilities within year 1 and year 2. Using the Pearson correlations as reliabilities, here $r_{12(\text{true})}$ is equal to .575. Reasoning that participants with little or no experience in investing for retirement may provide less reliable data, we reran the analysis, excluding those with the lowest level of retirement savings ($0–$24,999). The uncorrected across-year correlations were higher at .583 (Spearman .559), and with the correction they reached .778.

Validations

Because the validations span two dependent variables (outcome preferences and gamble choice) and two types of estimates of $-1/\alpha$ (from retirement distributions and small-stakes gamble distributions) across two years, figure 6 is provided to serve as a visual guide. The goal of the validations is to show that the risk-aversion parameter, as estimated by DB, is a valid predictor of preferences even in the presence of numerous traditional predictors of risk attitude. In addition to the psychological and industry scales described, we look at the demographic variables of age, income, and gender, which have long been studied as covariates of risk preference. In general, younger people, wealthier people, and males are found to exhibit less risk aversion (for a review, see Bajtelsmit and Bernasek [2001]).

Predicting Outcome Preferences. The variance of the distribution of returns in the outcome preferences task is a common measure of risk attitude: greater variance implies greater risk tolerance. We modeled the standard deviation of the histogram chosen in the outcome preference task with six predictors: (1) $-1/\alpha$, the average transformed coefficient of relative risk aversion as estimated by DB, thus transformed to make it amenable to regression analysis; (2) age in years; (3) income, log-transformed; (4) gender, coded 1 for male and 2 for female; (5) industrial risk profile; and (6) psychological risk profile, the participant's score on the gambling and investment subscales of the Weber-Blais-Betz Domain Specific Risk Attitude Scale (Weber et al. 2002).

Regressions 1–4 in table 3 show the results of predicting preferred outcomes. Note that N varies from regression to regression because not all participants in a given year are able to be predicted with data from another year. For instance, only 85 participants from experiment 1 participated

FIGURE 6

GUIDE TO THE EIGHT VALIDATION REGRESSIONS

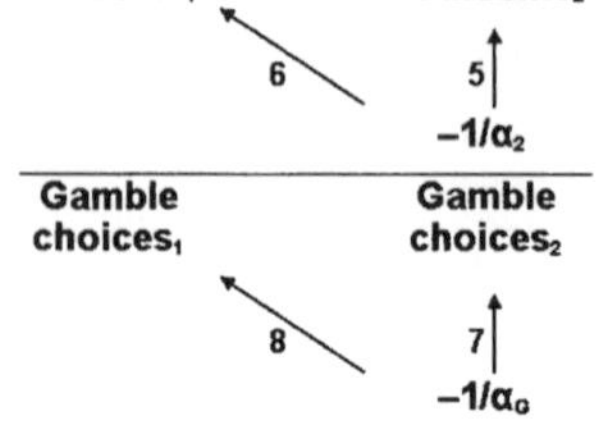

NOTE.—Guide to the eight validation regressions. α_1 and α_2 are based on the retirement distributions in years 1 and 2. α_G is based on the small-stakes gamble distribution, which was made in year 2 only.

TABLE 3

VALIDATIONS

	Year 2 retirement distributions[a]						Year 1 retirement distributions[a]					
	Year 2 outcome preference[b] (1)			Year 1 outcome preference[b] (2)			Year 2 outcome preference[b] (3)			Year 1 outcome preference[b] (4)		
	Estimate	SE	*t*-ratio	Estimate	SE	*t*-ratio	Estimate	SE	*t*-ratio	Estimate	SE	*t*-ratio
Intercept	−4.072	9.841	−.41	−5.484	14.856	−.37	−7.230	10.891	−.66	−8.537	12.281	−.7
$-1/\alpha$	−52.490	8.252	−6.36***	−50.613	13.818	−3.66***	−35.643	9.029	−3.95***	−19.390	10.104	−1.92*
Age	−.069	.112	−.62	.046	.163	.28	−.058	.129	−.45	.079	.142	.56
Income	.965	1.634	.59	1.840	2.519	.73	1.420	1.815	.78	.551	2.008	.27
Gender	.359	.961	.37	3.043	1.463	2.08**	.669	1.089	.61	1.653	1.212	1.36
Industry risk scale	.380	.390	.97	.526	.617	.85	.648	.431	1.5	.932	.512	1.82*
Psychological risk scale	.352	.134	2.62**	−.032	.189	−.17	.336	.161	2.09**	.270	.160	1.68*
R^2		.322			.224			.199			.115	
% of explained variance due to $-1/\alpha$		61.68			64.55			46.83			22.08	
No. of observations		145			79			141			136	

	Year 2 gamble distributions[a]											
	Year 2 outcome preference[b] (5)			Year 1 outcome preference[b] (6)			Year 2 gamble choice[b] (7)			Year 1 gamble choice[b] (8)		
	Estimate	SE	*t*-ratio	Estimate	SE	*t*-ratio	Estimate	SE	*t*-ratio	Estimate	SE	*t*-ratio
Intercept	12.028	9.703	1.24	−2.575	14.075	−.18	1.844	.708	2.61**	1.692	.739	2.29**
$-1/\alpha$	−21.622	6.536	−3.31***	−16.514	9.249	−1.79*	−.977	.477	−2.05**	−.939	.498	−1.89*
Age	−.130	.128	−1.02	−.009	.174	−.05	.002	.009	.26	−.025	.010	−2.6**
Income	1.926	1.878	1.03	3.950	2.749	1.44	−.142	.137	−1.04	.104	.143	.73
Gender	1.150	1.097	1.05	1.699	1.513	1.12	.295	.080	3.69***	.093	.083	1.11
R^2		.124			.117			.120			.109	
% of explained variance due to $-1/\alpha$		56.40			33.05			22.53			21.32	
No. of observations		142			78			142			142	

NOTE.—Predicting preferred outcome distributions and gamble choices based on estimates of the constant relative risk aversion (CRRA) parameter obtained with the DB method. The parameter accounts for 22%–65% of explained variance, even when predicting ahead or back one year in time. Income is log of income in U.S. dollars. α is the coefficient of CRRA, a transformation of which is used to improve suitability for regression analysis. Outcome preference is the standard deviation of the participant's choice in a task that presented participants with seven log-normal distributions of terminal wealth corresponding to a 0%, 10%, . . . , 60% investment in stock and the rest in a risk-free asset.

[a] Source of $-1/\alpha$.

[b] Dependent variable.

* $p<.1$.

** $p<.05$.

*** $p<.01$.

in experiment 2, and 79 of these participants provided usable parameter estimates by submitting two non-zero-variance distributions in year 2. The transformed risk-aversion parameter α accounts for 22%–65% of variance explained by the various models and is particularly predictive in tests that involve year 2. Remarkably, the DB estimate of risk aversion predicts outcome preferences expressed one year later and one year earlier than the time it is measured, and it does so in the presence of five explanatory variables.

Regressions 5 and 6 provide a validation across tasks (gambles versus retirement distributions) and years. Since the gamble distributions were presented only in year 2, there are two regressions of this type instead of four. In both cases, the risk-aversion parameter is significant and accounts for roughly 56% and 33% of explained variance. No other predictor is significant.

Predicting Gamble Choices. Regressions 7 and 8 provide a validation entirely in the much-investigated domain of small-stakes gambles. Here, the risk-aversion parameter predicts the number of risky gambles chosen both within year 2 and from year 2 to year 1 and accounts for 23% and 21% of explained variance, respectively. It is interesting to note that when regressions 1 and 4 are compared, R^2 is higher within year 2 than within year 1, and, similarly, table 2 shows greater reliability within year 2, which is suggestive of practice or learning effects.

In regressions 5–8, models were built with four predictors: $-1/\alpha$, age, log-transformed income, and gender. We ran four additional regressions numbered 9–12, which correspond to models 5–8 but with two additional predictors: the industrial and psychological scales. In models 10, 11, and 12 (but not

TABLE 4

DEMOGRAPHICS AND RISK AVERSION

Condition and variable	Pearson correlation	p	Spearman correlation	p	N
All participants:					
Years 1 and 2 α:					
Age	.286	.013**	.261	.024**	75
Income	−.215	.066*	−.109	.354	74
Gender	−.013	.909	−.001	.991	75
Year 2 α:					
Age	.182	.028**	.200	.016**	146
Income	−.062	.456	−.081	.335	145
Gender	.022	.794	.040	.630	146
Year 2 gamble α:					
Age	.238	.004***	.211	.011**	143
Income	−.170	.042**	−.123	.145	142
Gender	.071	.397	.040	.639	143
Year 1 α:					
Age	.175	.040**	.154	.070*	139
Income	−.174	.043**	−.159	.065*	136
Gender	.056	.512	.074	.389	139
≥$25,000 retirement savings:					
Years 1 and 2 α:					
Age	.301	.030**	.261	.062*	52
Income	−.333	.016**	−.269	.054*	52
Gender	.042	.769	.094	.506	52
Year 2 α:					
Age	.243	.015**	.238	.017**	100
Income	−.190	.059*	−.214	.033**	100
Gender	.135	.181	.147	.144	100
Year 2 gamble α:					
Age	.313	.002***	.268	.008***	98
Income	−.195	.055*	−.186	.067*	98
Gender	.179	.079*	.170	.094*	98
Year 1 α:					
Age	.131	.208	.127	.222	94
Income	−.249	.017**	−.234	.025**	92
Gender	.065	.534	.076	.467	94

NOTE.—Relationship between transformed risk-aversion parameter and demographic covariates age, income, and gender.
*$p<.1$.
**$p<.05$.
***$p<.01$.

9) the coefficient on $-1/\alpha$ falls below conventional levels of significance with t-values of −1.6, −1.48, and −1.11. Thus, in models with many predictors, parameters estimated from DB gamble distributions seem to be less predictive of retirement outcomes and of two-alternative gambles. The industrial scale turns out to predict the small-stakes two-alternative gambles quite well—its t-values in models 11 and 12 are 3.15 and 5.00, respectively.

Demographic Analysis. Correlating the DB estimate of risk aversion with age, income, and gender provides indirect validations. If DB provides sensible estimates, we would expect to find significant correlations (though typically low in the literature) and consistent directional relationships between these variables and the risk-aversion parameter. Table 4 shows these correlations for all estimates of $-1/\alpha$ discussed so far, in addition to an average of all four estimates. Looking at both Pearson and Spearman correlations, age and income are related to $-1/\alpha$ in 12 of 16 cases ($p < .1$) spanning the year of measurement and type of distribution (retirement or gamble). As with table 2, results are shown excluding the lowest retirement savings group, and slightly stronger relationships are seen (14 of 16 significant relationships). Notably, in all 32 cases involving age and income, the correlation is in the expected direction (age increases risk aversion; income decreases it).

Equally notable is that in 14 of 16 cases, there is no relationship between gender and risk aversion, and in two cases only modest relationships are found (Pearson correlation .179, Spearman .17). However, in 14 of 16 cases, the expected sign is observed (being female predicts greater risk aversion). Though many studies have found relationships between gender and risk aversion, few offer ideas on why this relationship might exist, with one exception of those in evolutionary psychology (Low 2000). For a review and

FIGURE 7

CLUSTERING ANALYSIS

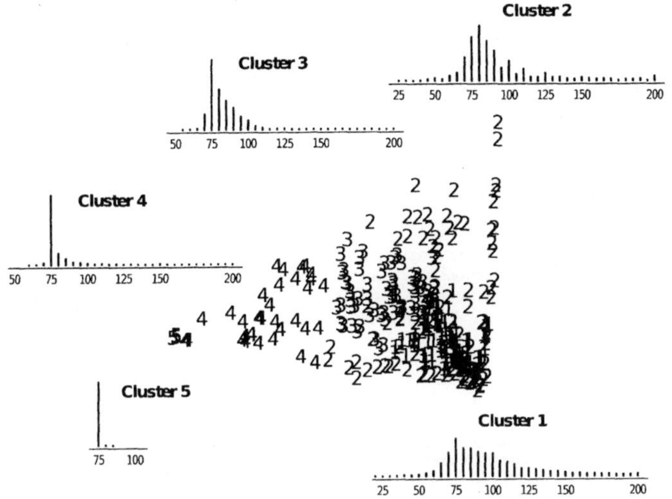

NOTE.—Cluster membership and location of distributions in principal components space. Data are retirement distributions submitted in year 2. The horizontal and vertical axis frames, representing the first and second principal components, respectively, are omitted for clarity. The number of distributions in clusters 1 through 5 is 100, 98, 66, 32, and 20, respectively. The five inset histograms are the aggregated markers within each cluster, plotted with vertical axes of the same scale.

some pointers to a conceptual framework, see Bajtelsmit and Bernasek (2001).

Describing Individual Differences: Cluster Analysis

We have seen that when segmenting distributions by their fit to the classic CRRA model, the well-fitting distributions appeared log-normal, while those poorly fit by the model were peaked at the reference point. Just as the overall distribution in figure 3 masked the two interesting subpopulations in figure 5, insight into individual differences may be gained by segmenting even more finely. To avoid seeing the world only through the lens of utility models, we now cluster distributions in a model-free way. Clustering requires the specification of variables that will be used to judge similarity between histograms. Recall that the distributions consist of 100 markers placed in 41 bins (wealth levels 0–200). We clustered two ways, using either 41 variables (the number of markers in each bin) or 100 variables (the wealth level of the marker associated with each of the 100 markers). Since similar results were found with both approaches, we present the first here because we find it simpler and more intuitive. An optimal model-based clustering routine that uses the Bayesian Information Criterion to choose among models (Fraley and Raftery 2003) was applied to both retirement distributions built in the second year. The procedure was constrained to fit up to five spherical, variable-shaped, equal-sized mixture components after determining them to have the best Bayesian information criterion values of 10 candidate component shapes. The procedure suggested five clusters we refer to as 1–5, comprising 100, 98, 66, 32, and 20 distributions, respectively.

To visualize the relationships between clusters, a principal components analysis was performed on the same 41 variables. The first two components accounted for 74% of the total variance, allowing for the construction of an informative two-dimensional representation. In figure 7, the cluster label of each point is plotted at its location in principal components space. The five inset histograms show the aggregated number of markers in each bin of each distribution making up each cluster, plotted with a common vertical axis scale. The points fall into a triangular shape. At the left corner, clusters 4 and 5 comprise narrow distributions peaked at the reference point, 75. Moving right, cluster 3 has higher variance and still peaked at 75. Cluster 2 takes up more area than the others and, interestingly, peaks at 80, not 75. Finally, cluster 1, which is roughly log-normal and

TABLE 5

CLUSTER PROFILES

Cluster	Size	Age	Income	Preretirement income	% Female	% College
1	100	39.7	57,400	77,600	65.0	66
2	98	40.5	68,776	96,289	68.4	76
3	66	42.9	61,212	78,154	74.2	54
4	32	41.3	53,333	70,938	71.9	72
5	20	39.9	53,000	59,500	60.0	60
Overall	316	40.8	61,083	81,656	68.4	67

NOTE.—Mean values by cluster of age in years, present income in U.S. dollars, participant estimates of preretirement income, percentage of female participants, and percentage with a college education or beyond. The bottom row is the mean for all year 2 retirement distributions.

highest in spread, takes up a small area in the lower right corner but contains about as many distributions as cluster 2. When we inspect the loadings, the first principal component is most influenced by the 75 bin, and the second principal component mostly by the 80 and 85 bins. As a robustness check, we have repeated the clustering analysis on each of the four retirement distributions individually. The principal components plot maintains a similar triangular shape, and the inset histograms showing cluster composition bear a strong visual similarity to those presented here.

Table 5 shows mean demographics by the clusters in figure 7. Values were computed by averaging the demographic values of the person who built each distribution within the cluster. Since each participant made two distributions for this analysis, one person's demographics may appear in the means of one or two clusters. Unlike those in table 4, these data are thus not useful in significance testing. However, when this technique is applied to a large number of distributions, one per individual, it is a promising way to segment people. We repeated this analysis separately for each of the six distribution types, in which one person could belong to only one cluster. The two lowest-variance clusters in each analysis (e.g., clusters 4 and 5 in fig. 7) tended to have a lower income than the others. When collapsing these two low-variance clusters into one, it had the lowest mean income (and lowest mean estimated retirement income) in five of the six distribution types, a finding that accords with the correlation between income and risk aversion reported in table 4.

Summary of Experiments

In retirement investing, an important determinant of consumer welfare, we estimated the coefficient of relative risk aversion and the loss-aversion parameter, using the Distribution Builder, and plotted the marginal distributions of these parameters based on several hundred observations. Parameter estimates fell within ranges observed in the literature, providing a first level of validation of the tool. Two correlation metrics were calculated within sessions and between years showing significant long-term reliability, particularly for those actively saving more for retirement. Stronger validation tests used DB estimates of risk aversion to predict preferred investment outcomes both within and across years and in the presence of five additional predictors known to correlate with risk preferences. Crossing domains, a DB designed for a small-stakes gamble task provided risk-aversion estimates that significantly predicted both preferred investment outcomes and choices between gambles. Correlations with age and income provided an indirect validation of the method, while correlations with gender were for the most part not observed in these domains.

In addition to parameter estimation and validation, an interesting finding of this investigation was that the CRRA preferences, a common assumption in financial engineering and prescriptive advice, did not describe all participants' data well. Estimating a loss-aversion parameter, we found that participants who were not well fit by CRRA were more loss averse (reference dependent) than the rest. One group of investors that had CRRA preferences may be satisfied with the investment advice of maintaining a constant asset allocation between a risky and risk-free asset. The group with loss-averse preferences might be more concerned about the likelihood that their investments could go below a reference level. Interestingly, in recent years, investment and insurance firms have offered products that offer upside gain when the market goes up and absolute downside protection when the market goes down. The latter group of consumers might well be the intended audience for these products.

Two points are relevant in this connection. First, the investors in the experiments described here, as in the real world, could only obtain upside gain (results greater than 75%) by accepting some downside loss (results less than 75%). Hence they were limited to strategies that would provide the reference return over a range of market outcomes, with lower returns in very bad markets and higher returns in very good markets. The second point is that in real markets, for every investor with a strategy that essentially buys protection against falling below certain reference wealth levels, there must be one or more with a strategy that sells this insurance. There has been speculation that loss aversion addresses why stocks, which provide better returns over the long run, seem to be underpriced relative to bonds, an observation called the equity premium paradox (Benartzi and

Thaler 1995). For a discussion of equilibrium in a capital market with investors who have kinked utility curves, see the recent work of Sharpe (2006).

Segmenting the population of distributions more finely, a clustering analysis uncovered subpopulations of distributions differing on variance, location of mode, and peakedness consistent with reference-dependent preferences.

DISCUSSION

Financial Services Marketing

The presumption of efficient markets would seem to render marketing irrelevant to understanding financial markets. However, developments in behavioral finance suggest that marketing may be quite relevant. Recent research has started to emphasize differences in preferences for investments (Wilcox 2003) or trading style (Dhar and Zhu 2002). In addition, behavioral finance has started to characterize psychological differences among investors. By asking about differences in needs in investing, finance is asking the same question that motivates much of marketing research: how do consumer needs differ? We have begun to answer this question by identifying two main preference segments, one well described by standard theory, the other more reference dependent. An important next step would be to examine these differences more closely and determine the correlates and causes of the differences.

Beyond financial services, the basic DB framework could be used to study other consumer choices in which there is a risk-reward trade-off, including waiting times at health clinics (or on customer support lines), delivery times of packages, and overage charges for mobile phone plans. In a sense, this research extends Woodruff's (1972) investigations of eliciting distributions of beliefs about product attributes to eliciting preferences for distributions of prospective outcomes.

Constructing Constructive Preferences

Many tools in marketing research presume to measure existing preferences. The DB suggests a revised view: market research can help people construct preferences in a way that increases their welfare. We do not, for example, believe that consumers of investment products hold ideal probability distributions of retirement income in their heads. Income distributions are likely to be something they have never thought about before. However, each of the millions of employees who specify a fixed asset allocation for their 401(k) plan is indeed signing their name to a probability distribution of wealth, a distribution of which they may never even learn the mean or standard deviation. Since most investors must actively make decisions, consumers can benefit from a tool such as the DB to help them explore the costs and benefits of downside protection and upside gain. We suggest three aspects of the DB that might facilitate better preference construction.

Focusing on Prospective Outcomes, Not Product Offerings. In the world of behavioral research, much attention is paid to choices between gambles, and not on the overall risk that results from considering all these gambles jointly. In the world of investment advice, the same is true—not about gambles, but about choices of multiple funds. Risk-tolerance questionnaires like the one we tested ask how people would feel about a single investment product that could lose varying percentages of its worth overnight, but not about shocks to overall net worth, which could affect well-being not just overnight, but over a lifetime. The actual investment products in a portfolio should largely be irrelevant to the consumer. What matters is how investments combine to give an overall distribution of possible outcomes. With DB we have an efficient method for constructing and exploring complex outcome distributions.

Simulating Experienced Outcomes. The DB can be run in a repeated mode to cycle through the process of building distribution and drawing from a distribution many times. The current study used only two iterations through this cycle, but in other research we are beginning to explore the effect of repeated trials. Early results suggest that extensive experience systematically changes the preferences people construct about risk. In this way we think that the DB can function like a flight simulator, allowing investors to explore the outcomes of their decisions with only virtual outcomes.

More Realistic Utility Functions. The DB can fit not only standard CRRA utility functions but also exotic variants incorporating, for example, loss aversion. We do not take a position on whether or not reference dependence is a mistake in retirement settings. After all, reference wealth does matter—one must continue to make mortgage payments, for instance. However, we do point out that the DB makes explicit the trade-off resulting from buying downside protection. It is possible that, with sufficient experience with the DB, the desired level of insurance against losses might decrease, suggesting an exciting direction for future research. The unfortunate alternative, which exists currently in financial services, is to sell overpriced products that cater to loss-averse consumers, offering full downside protection at the cost of significantly reduced upside potential.

CONCLUSION

Employees making retirement investment decisions are likely to have inchoate preferences over the dizzying number of possibilities before them. Since well-defined preferences are necessary to guide the reasoned selection of investments, it is not clear how employees choose products. Experimental evidence suggests that many could be unsatisfied with the probable outcomes of their choices (Benartzi and Thaler 2002). We suggest an alternative approach in which consumers can explore candidate wealth distributions and, in so doing, construct informed preferences for outcomes instead of products. The idea that marketing could help people construct better preferences is a shift away from the view that stable preferences exist and that it is the job of marketing to uncover them.

REFERENCES

Agnew, Julie, Pierluigi Balduzzi, and Sunden Annika (2003), "Portfolio Choice and Trading in a Large 401(K) Plan," *American Economic Review*, 93, 193–215.

Ameriks, John and Stephen Zeldes (2004), "How Do Household Portfolio Shares Vary with Age?" Working paper, Economics Department, Columbia University Graduate School of Business.

Ariely, Dan, Joel Huber, and Klaus Wertenbroch (2005), "When Do Losses Loom Larger than Gains?" *Journal of Marketing Research*, 42 (2), 134–38.

Arnone, William J., Freida Kavouras, Glenn M. Pape, Martin Nissenbaum, Charles L. Ratner, Kenneth R. Rouse, David C. Voss, and Patricia A. Wiley (2002), *Ernst and Young's Retirement Planning Guide*, New York: Wiley.

Arrow, Kenneth J. (1964), "The Role of Securities in the Optimal Allocation of Risk-Bearing," *Review of Economic Studies*, 91–96.

——— (1970), *Essays in the Theory of Risk-Bearing*, Amsterdam: North-Holland.

Bajtelsmit, Vickie L. and Alexandra Bernasek (2001), *Risk Preferences and the Investment Decisions of Older Americans*, AARP Public Policy Institute report no. 2001–11, Washington DC: American Association of Retired Persons.

Barberis, Nicholas (2000), "Investing for the Long Run When Returns Are Predictable," *Journal of Finance*, 55 (1), 225–64.

Benartzi, Shlomo and Richard H. Thaler (1995), "Myopic Loss Aversion and the Equity Premium Puzzle," *Quarterly Journal of Economics*, 110 (1), 73–92.

——— (1999), "Risk Aversion or Myopia? Choices in Repeated Gambles and Retirement Investments," *Management Science*, 45 (3), 364–81.

——— (2001), "Naive Diversification Strategies in Retirement Saving Plans," *American Economic Review*, 91 (1), 79–98.

——— (2002), "How Much Is Investor Autonomy Worth?" *Journal of Finance*, 57 (4), 1593–1616.

Blake, David (1996), "Efficiency, Risk Aversion and Portfolio Insurance: An Analysis of Financial Asset Portfolios Held by Investors in the United Kingdom," *Economic Journal*, 106 (438), 1175–92.

Brav, Alon, George M. Constantinides, and Christopher C. Geczy (2002), "Asset Pricing with Heterogeneous Consumers and Limited Participation: Empirical Evidence," *Journal of Political Economy*, 110 (4), 793–824.

Camerer, Colin (2005), "Three Cheers—Psychological, Theoretical, Empirical—for Loss Aversion," *Journal of Marketing Research*, 42 (2), 129–33.

Campbell, John Y. (1996), "Understanding Risk and Return," *Journal of Political Economy*, 104 (2), 298–345.

Capon, Noel, Gavan J. Fitzsimons, and Russ Alan Prince (1996), "An Individual Level Analysis of the Mutual Fund Purchase Decision," *Journal of Financial Services Research*, 10 (1), 59–82.

Debreu, Gerard (1959), *Theory of Value*, New York: Wiley.

Dhar, Ravi and Ning Zhu (2002), "Up Close and Personal: Investor Sophistication and the Disposition Effect," *Management Science*, 52 (5), 726–40.

Dybvig, Philip H. (1988), "Inefficient Dynamic Portfolio Strategies or How to Throw Away a Million Dollars in the Stock Market," *Review of Financial Studies*, 1 (1), 67–88.

Fraley, Chris and Adrian E. Raftery (2003), "Enhanced Software for Model-Based Clustering, Discriminant Analysis, and Density Estimation: Mclust," *Journal of Classification*, 20 (2), 263–86.

Friend, Irwin and Marshall E. Blume (1975), "The Demand for Risky Assets," *American Economic Review*, 65 (December), 900–922.

Ghiselli, Edwin E., John P. Campbell, and Sheldon Zedeck (1981), *Measurement Theory for the Behavioral Sciences*, San Francisco: Freeman.

Hakansson, Nils H. (1970), "Optimal Investment and Consumption Strategies under Risk for a Class of Utility Functions," *Econometrica*, 38 (September), 587–607.

Huberman, Gur and Wei Jiang (2006), "Offering vs. Choice by 401(K) Plan Participants: Equity Exposure and Number of Funds," *Journal of Finance*, 61 (2), 763–801.

Ibrekk, Harald and M. Granger Morgan (1987), "Graphical Communication of Uncertain Quantities to Nontechnical People," *Risk Analysis*, 7 (4), 519–29.

Kahneman, Daniel and Amos Tversky (1979), "Prospect Theory: An Analysis of Decisions under Risk," *Econometrica*, 47 (2), 263–91.

Köbberling, Veronika and Peter P. Wakker (2005), "An Index of Loss Aversion," *Journal of Economic Theory*, 122 (1), 119–31.

Low, Bobbi S. (2000), *Why Sex Matters: A Darwinian Look at Human Behavior*, Princeton, NJ: Princeton University Press.

Madrian, Brigitte C. and Dennis F. Shea (2001), "The Power of Suggestion: Inertia in 401(K) Participation and Savings Behavior," *Quarterly Journal of Economics*, 116 (4), 1149–87.

Mehra, Rajnish and Edward C. Prescott (1985), "The Equity Premium: A Puzzle," *Journal of Monetary Economics*, 15 (2), 145–61.

Merton, Robert C. (1969), "Lifetime Portfolio Selection under Uncertainty: The Continuous Time Case," *Review of Economics and Statistics*, 51, 247–57.

——— (1971), "Optimum Consumption and Portfolio Rules in a Continuous Time Model," *Journal of Economic Theory*, 3, 373–413.

Novemsky, Nathan and Daniel Kahneman (2005), "Boundaries of Loss Aversion," *Journal of Marketing Research*, 42 (2), 119–28.

Perold, Andre F. and William F. Sharpe (1988), "Dynamic Strategies for Asset Allocation," *Financial Analysts Journal*, 44 (1), 16.

Pratt, John W. (1964), "Risk Aversion in the Small and the Large," *Econometrica*, 32 (1/2), 122–36.

Safra, Zvi and Uzi Segal (1998), "Constant Risk Aversion," *Journal of Economic Theory*, 83 (1), 19–42.

Samuelson, Paul A. (1969), "Lifetime Portfolio Selection by Dynamic Stochastic Programming," *Review of Economics and Statistics*, 51 (3), 239–46.

Samuelson, William and Richard Zeckhauser (1988), "Status Quo Bias in Decision-Making," *Journal of Risk and Uncertainty*, 1 (1), 7–59.

Sharpe, William F. (2006), *Asset Prices and Portfolio Choice*, Princeton, NJ: Princeton University Press.

Sharpe, William F., Daniel G. Goldstein, and Phil W. Blythe (2000), "The Distribution Builder: A Tool for Inferring Investor Preferences," Working paper at http://www.stanford.edu/~wfsharpe/art/qpaper/qpaper.html.

Siebenmorgen, Niklas, Elke U. Weber, and Martin Weber (2000), "Communicating Asset Risk: How the Format of Historic Volatility Information Affects Risk Perception and Investment Decisions," Sonderforschungsbereich 504 Publication no. 00-38, University of Mannheim, Mannheim.

Thompson, Kimberly M. and Diane L. Bloom (2000), "Communication of Risk Assessment Information to Risk Managers," *Journal of Risk Research*, 3 (4), 333–52.

Tversky, Amos and Daniel Kahneman (1992), "Advances in Prospect Theory: Cumulative Representation of Uncertainty," *Journal of Risk and Uncertainty*, 5 (4), 297–323.

Weber, Elke U., Ann-Renee Blais, and Nancy E. Betz (2002), "A Domain-Specific Risk-Attitude Scale: Measuring Risk Perceptions and Risk Behaviors," *Journal of Behavioral Decision Making*, 15 (4), 263–90.

Wilcox, Ronald T. (2003), "Bargain Hunting or Star Gazing: Investors' Preferences for Stock Mutual Funds," *Journal of Business*, 76 (4), 645–64.

Woodruff, Robert B. (1972), "Measurement of Consumers' Prior Brand Information," *Journal of Marketing Research*, 9 (August), 258–63.

Yook, Ken C. and Robert Everett (2003), "Assessing Risk Tolerance: Questioning the Questionnaire Method," *Journal of Financial Planning*, 18 (8), 48–55.

Journal Of Investment Management, Vol. 7, No. 3, (2009), pp. 31–48

JOIM
www.joim.com

THE 4% RULE—AT WHAT PRICE?

Jason S. Scott, William F. Sharpe*[a] *and John G. Watson*[b]

The 4% rule is the advice many retirees follow for managing spending and investing. We examine this rule's inefficiencies—the price paid for funding its unspent surpluses and the overpayments made to purchase its spending policy. We show that a typical rule allocates 10–20% of a retiree's initial wealth to surpluses and an additional 2–4% to overpayments. Further, we argue that even if retirees were to recoup these costs, the 4% rule's spending plan remains wasteful, since many retirees actually prefer a different, cheaper spending plan.

1 Introduction

Retirees must annually decide how to invest their retirement portfolios and how much to withdraw from them to cover their living expenses. Some retirees turn to financial planners for advice, whereas others consult brokers, investment publications, or web sites. Although these sources are quite different, their spending and investment advice is consistently the same—the 4% rule. This rule of thumb originated in the financial planning literature, and it was quickly adopted by many financial firms to advise their retail customers. Much of the financial press and many investor web sites now embrace the rule, and hence now it is the most endorsed, publicized, and parroted piece of advice that a retiree is likely to hear. Therefore, it behooves readers of this journal to be familiar with the rule's approach, features, and flaws.

A typical rule of thumb recommends that a retiree annually spend a fixed, real amount equal to 4% of his initial wealth, and rebalance the remainder of his money in a 60–40% mix of stocks and bonds throughout a 30-year retirement period. For example, a retiree with a $1MM portfolio should confidently spend a cost of living adjusted $40K a year for 30 years, independent of stock, bond, and inflation gyrations. Confidence in the plan is often expressed as the probability of its success, for example, in nine of ten scenarios, our retiree will sustain his spending. Modifications to this basic example include

*Corresponding author. Managing Director, Retiree Research Center at Financial Engines, Financial Engines, Inc., 1804 Embarcadero Road, Palo Alto, CA 94303, USA. Tel.: 650-565-4925; fax: 650-565-4905; e-mail: jscott@financialengines.com

[a]STANCO 25 Professor of Finance, Emeritus Graduate School of Business, Stanford University.

[b]Fellow, Retiree Research Center at Financial Engines, Financial Engines, Inc., 1804 Embarcadero Road, Palo Alto, CA 94303, USA.

changing the amount to withdraw, the length of the plan, the portfolio mix, the rebalancing frequency, or the confidence level. However, all these variations have a common theme—they attempt to finance a constant, non-volatile spending plan using a risky, volatile investment strategy. For simplicity, we refer to this entire class of retirement strategies as 4% rules, the sobriquet of its first and most popular example.

Supporting a constant spending plan using a volatile investment policy is fundamentally flawed. A retiree using a 4% rule faces spending shortfalls when risky investments underperform, may accumulate wasted surpluses when they outperform, and in any case, could likely purchase exactly the same spending distributions more cheaply. The objective of this study is to price these inefficiencies—we want to know how much money a retiree wastes by adopting a 4% rule. In the next sections, we review the 4% rule's history and examine its popularity. We then present a financial parable featuring two aging boomers and the single spin of a betting wheel. Our parable illustrates the flaws of the 4% rule, both qualitatively and quantitatively. Next, we use standard assumptions about capital markets and show that the approach of the 4% rule to spending and investing wastes a significant portion of a retiree's savings and is thus *prima facie* inefficient. Finally, we argue that a better solution can be obtained by formulating the retirement problem as one of maximizing the retiree's expected utility, an approach advocated by financial economists.

2 History

Not long ago, many financial planners estimated a retiree's annual spending budget using a mortgage calculator, an estimate of the average rate of return on the retiree's investments, and the retiree's horizon—the number of years that a retiree's investments had to support his spending.[1] Further, to include a cost of living increase, the planner would adjust the average nominal investment return downward by an estimate of the average inflation rate and compute the real spending. This method is only valid when all the future yearly investment returns and inflation rates are nearly equal to their estimated averages, and hence non-volatile.

First Larry Bierwirth (1994), and then William Bengen (1994) argued that since actual asset returns and inflation rates were historically quite volatile, retirement plans based on their averages were unrealistic. Bengen proposed an alternative strategy that retained the basic investment and spending strategies inherent in the mortgage calculation. In particular, he assumed that a retiree's assets were invested in a mix of stocks and bonds and annually rebalanced to fixed percentages. Further, he assumed that in terms of real dollars, a retiree's annual spending was constant and financed by a year-end, inflation-adjusted withdrawal from the portfolio. Hence, choosing a stock-bond mix and a withdrawal rate—the ratio of annual, real spending to initial wealth—specified a retirement plan. Now, for a given horizon, some of these plans would have historically performed better than all the other possibilities. Therefore, Bengen collected scenarios of past asset returns and inflation rates, simulated a number of plans under these scenarios, and identified the best performers.

Although a retiree wants the highest withdrawal rate possible, he also wants to sustain his spending throughout his retirement years. Bengen required that all his recommended plans be historically sustainable—the investments had to support all scheduled withdrawals for every historical scenario. Further, he sought the sustainable plans with the largest withdrawal rates. For example, using a portfolio mix consisting of between 50% and 75% stocks, Bengen (1994, 172) reported:

> Assuming a minimum requirement of 30 years of portfolio longevity, a first-year withdrawal of 4 percent, followed by inflation-adjusted withdrawals in subsequent years, should be safe.

Larger (smaller) withdrawal rates were recommended for shorter (longer) horizons. However, the horizons of most interest were in the 30–40-year range and had withdrawal rates that were near 4%. For this reason, Bengen's approach is now commonly called the 4% rule.

In his original article, Bengen did not give a confidence level for his rule—he deemed it safe, since it had never historically failed. However, in a similar study, Cooley *et al.* (1998, 20, Table 3) reported a 95% historical success rate for a 30-year horizon, a 4% withdrawal rate, and 50–50% mix of stocks and bonds. This success rate increased to 98% when the percentage of stocks was increased to 75%. This study is often cited as the Trinity Study (all three authors are finance professors at Trinity University in San Antonio, Texas).

Bengen (1996, 1997, 2001, 2006a) extended his approach in a series of articles. For example, Bengen (1996) treats both tax-deferred and taxable accounts, and recommends that conservative clients reduce their risk with age by yearly decreasing their percentage of stocks by 1%. Bengen (1997) extends the investment choices to include Treasury Bills and small-cap stocks. For a summary of Bengen's work, we recommend his recent review (Bengen, 2006b). Cooley *et al.* (1999, 2001, 2003a) also continued to analyze withdrawal rates. Cooley *et al.* (1999) focuses on monthly versus annual withdrawals, and Cooley (2003a) concludes that investors "would benefit only modestly in the long run from international diversification."

When estimates of success rates are based on a small number of scenarios, they are prone to estimation error. This is particularly true for estimates that use overlapping historical scenarios. This problem led some investigators to develop market models—stochastic models of asset returns and inflation rate processes. A model's parameters are chosen so that the joint probability distribution of the processes reflects the average values, variances, and correlations commonly observed. An unlimited supply of scenarios can be numerically generated from these models, and then statistics, such as the success rate, can be computed using Monte Carlo methods. Further, in a few cases, estimates can be derived analytically.

George Pye (2000) simulated all-equity portfolios whose real returns were log-normally distributed with a mean return of 8% and a standard deviation of 18%. Pye concluded that his modified 4% rule would be safe for a 35-year horizon. Pye's strategy increases a portfolio's longevity by ratcheting down spending when markets perform poorly. We include his rule in the 4% class since its "focus is on sustaining the initial withdrawal" (Pye, 2000, 74) and invests in a volatile asset.

Most of the withdrawal rate research ignores a retiree's mortality and assumes a fixed planning horizon. An exception is the series of articles by Ho *et al.* (1994a, 1994b), Milevsky *et al.* (1997), and Milevsky and Robinson (2005). In particular, Milevsky and Robinson (2005) chose simple models for both the markets and mortality and developed estimates of success rates without using simulation. We recommend the article by Milevsky and Abaimova (2006) for a summary of this approach and its application to retirement planning.

Cooley *et al.* (2003b) compared the results obtained using historical data and market models, but their study "does not take sides on which methodology is better." Finally, in another approach, Spitzer *et al.* (2007) generate scenarios using a bootstrap algorithm to resample historical data with replacement.

3 Popularity

The authors conducted an informal survey of retiree guidance sources and their recommendations on spending and investment strategies. We were struck by the universal popularity of the 4% rule—retail brokerage firms, mutual fund companies, retirement groups, investor groups, financial websites, and the popular financial press all recommend it. Sometimes the guidance explicitly references Bengen's work, the Trinity Study, or related research, but more often, it is presented as the perceived wisdom of unnamed experts. In this section, we report a sample of our findings.

Vice President of Financial Planning Rande Spiegelman of the Schwab Center for Financial Research wrote an article on retirement spending, subtitled "The 4% Solution", for the August 17, 2006 issue of *Schwab Investing Insights®*, a monthly publication for Schwab clients. In this article, he recommends the basic 4% rule that we used in the introduction to this study (30-year horizon, 4% withdrawal rate, 60–40% mix of stocks and bonds, and 90% confidence level).

T. Rowe Price's web site (2008a) suggests, "If you anticipate a retirement of approximately 30 years, consider withdrawing no more than 4% of your investment balance, pretax, in the first year of retirement. Each year thereafter, you'll want to increase that dollar amount 3% every year to maintain your purchasing power." A popular feature of this web site is the "Retirement Income Calculator" (T. Rowe Price, 2008b) that simulates 500 scenarios of returns for seven asset classes, where the monthly returns are assumed to be jointly normal. The calculator automatically accounts for minimum required distributions after age $70^1/_2$, attempts to decrease equity exposure every five years, and yearly inflates withdrawals by 3%. For a single retiree starting retirement at age 65, having a 30-year horizon, beginning with a $1MM portfolio, investing initially in a 60% equity mix (portfolio E), and withdrawing $3.3 K per month, the withdrawal rate is 3.96%, and the calculator predicts a 90% success rate.

The Vanguard Group (2008) advises "making withdrawals at rates no greater than 3% to 5% at the outset of your retirement..." They also provide a tool for retirees to determine how much they can annually withdraw in real dollars. The tool uses 81 historical scenarios, and "the monthly withdrawal amount shown by the tool is the highest level of spending in which 85% of these historical paths would have left you with a positive balance at the end of your chosen investment horizon." A retiree with a 30-year horizon is advised to withdraw at a rate of 3.75%, 4.75%, or 5.25%, if he is invested in a conservative (less than 35% equities), moderate (between 35% and 65% equities), or aggressive (higher than 65% equities) portfolio, respectively.

AARP (2008) indicates that "most experts" recommend 4% spending and that stocks should be added to the portfolio to "help your money last." Jane Bryant Quinn echoes Bengen's recommendations in the June 2006 *AARP Bulletin.* John Markese (2006), President of the American Association of Individual Investors (AAII), writes, "Most research and simulation studies conclude that portfolios with annual withdrawal rates of 4% or less and greater than 50% in stock are most likely to last throughout retirement."

Liz Weston (2008), writing for MSN Money Central, refers to Bengen and the T. Rowe Price Retirement Income Calculator (2008b) and recommends a 3–4% withdrawal rate for retirees with horizons of 30 or more years. Scott Burns (2004), business columnist for the *Dallas Morning News,* was an early champion of the Trinity Study. Also, Walter Updegrave (2007), *Money Magazine* senior editor, often fields questions on the 4% rule in his "Ask the Expert" forum. In his *CNN Money* article, "Retirement: The 4 Percent Solution", he recommends that a 65-year-old person withdraw money at the 4% rate, invest in a 50–50% mix of stocks and bonds, and shift gradually more to bonds with age. Further, he adds, "The reason many pros recommend this rate is because studies show that it provides a high (but not absolute) level of assurance that your savings will last 30 years or more.

The explanation of the 4% rule's popularity is its simplicity—it is easy to understand and implement. Many of today's retirees use the rule and have benefited from its disciplined approach to spending and investment. However, as we shall see, that benefit comes with a price.

4 The parable of two boomers[2]

A simple example often yields insights that extend to more complicated venues—this is true in our case. In this section, we present a parable about two boomers, who share similar spending goals, but have radically different investment strategies. One of their strategies wastes money, and we will show that it can be replicated by a series of less-expensive strategies. In later sections, we use this same approach to show that the 4% rule wastes money.

Our two boomers, Eric and Mick, want to hear Bob Dylan in concert. Dylan's next concert has three-ticket tiers: floor pass ($125), general admission ($75), and pay-per-view ($50). Although both boomers would prefer a floor pass, unfortunately, each boomer has only $100 to spend. Fortunately, the concert promoters have set up a betting wheel and will allow Eric and Mick to each wager on a single spin. The betting wheel has three sectors of equal area that are equally likely to be selected. If a sector is selected, a chance on that sector will pay $1; otherwise the price of the chance is lost. Our boomers can purchase chances on any or all of the wheel's sectors. However, the promoters have contrived to make the costs of the three sectors differ[3]—they are 10 ¢, 30 ¢, and 40 ¢ for sectors one, two, and three, respectively, or in vector short hand (10 ¢, 30 ¢, and 40 ¢).

Eric decides to purchase 125 chances on each sector. He allocates his $100 wager as follows ($12.50, $37.50, and $50.00) to receive the payouts ($125, $125, and $125). Eric's can't-lose, no-blues strategy is guaranteed to have a 25% return, and he will be enjoying the concert from the floor. However, Eric's friend Mick, who briefly attended the London School of Economics, likes high-return, high-risk gambles. Mick makes the purchases ($35.00, $15.00, and $50.00) and will receive the payouts ($350, $50, and $125). This strategy has a 75% expected return and a 127% standard deviation.

Mick has focused on his betting strategy and has lost sight of his quest, a concert ticket. In fact, if you take his goal into account, Mick is actually wasting money in three ways. First, Mick is paying for a surplus he is not planning to spend. If sector one occurs, Mick will get $350, buy a floor pass for $125, and be left with a $225 surplus. At the rate of a dime for a dollar, Mick is wasting $22.50 on the surplus, or alternatively, he has wagered only $77.50 of his $100 toward his ticket.

Second, Mick is also overpaying for his ticket chances—even if the surplus is eliminated. Mick's payouts without the surplus are ($125, $50, and $125). He has a two-third chance of a floor pass and a third chance of watching on pay-per-view. However, consider the alternative strategy that wagers ($12.50, $37.50, and $20.00) and costs just $70. It has the payouts ($125, $125, and $50) and would give Mick the same ticket chances as his current strategy and the same concert experience.[4] The alternative plan is less expensive because it pairs payouts and sectors so that the largest payouts correspond to the cheapest sectors.

Third, suppose that Mick ranks his ticket preferences using *Billboard* bullets: a floor-pass gets five bullets, a general admission ticket gets four bullets, and pay-per-view gets just one bullet. It is clear that Mick loves a live concert (he often performs himself). Further, he would prefer (as measured in expected bullets) a guaranteed general admission ticket (4 bullets) to a two-third chance at a floor pass and a third chance for pay-per-view ($3^2/_3$ bullets).

The betting strategy ($7.50, $22.50, and $30.00) would pay ($75, $75, and $75) and would guarantee a general admission ticket. Since Mick prefers the ticket chances of this $60 alternative strategy, he is wasting an additional $10 by following his current plan.

Our parable illustrates a number of key points. Eric wanted a floor pass to the concert, and he placed bets that paid $125 no matter what the wheel's outcome. Eric's fixed spending was paired with a risk-free strategy. On the other hand, Mick's wager has volatile payouts that overshoot the $125 goal when sector one is the outcome, but fall short for the remaining sectors. Generally, fixed spending is best supported by fixed payouts—volatile payouts lead to surpluses and deficits. In fact, Mick required $22.50 of his original stake to fund his surplus—wasted money. Further, Mick's particular strategy has wasted an additional $7.50 by overpaying for his spending distribution. Generally, when payouts are volatile, there may be alternative wagers that generate the same payout distribution, and some will be cheaper than others. Lastly, Mick arguably wasted another $10.00 by subscribing to an inferior ticket plan. More generally, when wagers and preferences are at odds, even more money can be wasted.

5 An experiment

Unfortunately, if a retiree adopts a 4% rule, he faces outcomes much like Mick's—he will waste money by purchasing surpluses, will overpay for his spending distribution, and may be saddled with an inferior spending plan. In this section, we describe a numerical experiment that demonstrates the first two problems. For simplicity, we limit our analysis to the specific, but representative, planning horizon of 30 years.[5]

Our experiment uses a simple market model—an economy with just two basic assets. The first is a one-year bond that pays a guaranteed annual 2% real return. A multiyear, risk-free bond can be replicated by purchasing a series of these one-year bonds. The second asset is a market portfolio consisting of all other bonds and all stocks, held in market proportions. The annual real returns on our market portfolio are independent and log-normally distributed with an expected value of 6% and a standard deviation of 12%. Because the returns are independent, they are serially uncorrelated. We note investors can create portfolios with any desired volatility by purchasing a mix of the two basic assets.

Our market model is similar to those used by investment consultants for asset allocation and asset liability studies. A 2% risk-free real rate is broadly consistent with the historical record for U.S. Treasury STRIPS and TIPS investment returns. In addition, our market portfolio assumptions imply a Sharpe ratio of a third, a fairly typical choice. While the actual market values of bonds and stocks vary over time, on average, bonds contribute about 40% of the value of the market portfolio and stocks 60%. Thus, a strategy that invests 100% in the market portfolio can be thought of as a 60% equity strategy.

An investor can guarantee a real dollar every year for 30 years by purchasing a series of zero-coupon, risk-free bonds. The cost of this investment is the sum of the discounted prices[6] $\$1/(1.02) + \$1/(1.02)^2 + \cdots + \$1/(1.02)^{30}$, which amounts to a little less than $22.40. Alternatively, if a retiree invests in a risk-free bond portfolio, he can safely withdraw at a yearly rate that is a bit more than $\$1.00/\$22.40 \approx 4.46\%$. This withdrawal rate—the guaranteed rate—is the maximum withdrawal rate that can be guaranteed to never fail. This risk-free strategy is analogous to Eric's strategy and is a special case of the 4% rule—the limit of zero investment volatility. This version of the 4% rule never has a surplus, never has a shortfall, and is the cheapest way to receive a constant, guaranteed payout every year. If a cheaper investment were to exist, then there would be an arbitrage opportunity.

The risk-free strategy supports constant spending using the constant-return, risk-free bond—a perfect match. However, a typical 4% rule advises supporting constant spending using a volatile-return, stock, and bond mix—a mismatch. Our first set of experiments will analyze constant mix portfolios with six volatility levels, evenly spaced from 0% to 15%. These levels correspond to market exposures from 0% to 125%, or alternatively, equity exposures of from 0% to 75%.[7] We pair each of these portfolios with a range of withdrawal rates that brackets the guaranteed rate—4.0%, 4.25%, 4.46%, 4.75%, and 5.0%. Except for the pair that corresponds to Eric's strategy, our benchmark, these pairs will all exhibit at least one of Mick's problems.

We will report three metrics for each pair of investment and spending strategies: the failure rate, the cost of the surplus, and the overpayment for the spending distribution. A strategy's failure rate is the probability that the actual spending in the last year is less than the spending goal; in other words, the probability of a shortage. Failure rates (and success rates or confidence levels) have been the main focus of previous investigators, and we include them here for comparison. The final portfolio value, the surplus, is a function of random market returns. Hence, we can use the machinery of derivative pricing to find its fair price, the cost of funding the surplus. Similarly, we can compute the present value of the actual spending and the price of an alternative investment that delivers the same spending distribution, but at the cheapest price. The difference in these prices is the overpayment for the spending strategy. We refer the reader to Appendix A for more details.

For each pair of investment and spending strategies, we numerically simulated many equally probable, 30-year-long, scenarios. The portfolio value for each scenario was initially set to $100, without loss of generality, and the annual spending goal was set to the withdrawal rate times $100. We began each scenario by drawing a random real market return from its lognormal probability distribution, and recorded its value. Given the investment strategy and the returns on the risk-free bond and the market, we determined the real value of the portfolio at the end of the first year. Next, we computed the first year's actual real spending—the smaller of the portfolio's value and the spending goal—and deducted it from the portfolio. The actual spending amount and the portfolio's post-withdrawal value were recorded. This process was then repeated for the remaining 29 years. We then computed the metrics of our experiment using Monte Carlo estimates, for example, the failure rate was approximated by the percentage of scenarios for which there was a spending shortage. Again, we refer the reader to Appendix A for more details.

5.1 Failure rates

Table 1 summarizes the failure rates for our first set of experiments. The columns in Table 1 correspond to constant mix investment strategies (labeled with the strategy's volatility), and its rows to constant real spending strategies (labeled with the strategy's withdrawal rate). The investment portfolios are annually rebalanced to maintain a constant risk level. The numbers in the body of the table are the estimated failure rates, the percent of scenarios that fell short of the spending goal. For example, with 12% portfolio volatility and a 4.25% withdrawal rate, spending had a shortfall in 8.1% of cases. The standard errors of the estimates reported in this table are less than 0.01%. The failure rates reported in Table 1 are consistent with the previous studies.

Table 1 illustrates several key features of the 4% rule. First, the influence of portfolio risk depends critically on the spending level. For rates less than or equal to the guaranteed rate, adding risk necessarily introduces the possibility of failure. Moreover, the chance of failure increases with portfolio volatility.

Table 1 Failure rates for constant-mix portfolios.

Withdrawal rate	Constant-mix volatility 0%	3%	6%	9%	12%	15%
4.00%	0.0%	0.3%	1.9%	3.9%	5.7%	7.6%
4.25%	0.0%	1.9%	4.4%	6.3%	8.1%	9.9%
4.46%	0.0%	6.8%	7.9%	9.2%	10.6%	12.1%
4.75%	100.0%	22.5%	15.0%	14.0%	14.5%	15.4%
5.00%	100.0%	44.2%	23.4%	19.2%	18.4%	18.7%

Table 2 Cost of surpluses as a percentage of initial wealth for constant-mix portfolios.

Withdrawal rate	Constant-mix volatility 0%	3%	6%	9%	12%	15%
4.00%	10.4%	10.8%	13.0%	15.8%	18.8%	21.8%
4.25%	4.8%	6.3%	9.3%	12.5%	15.7%	19.0%
4.46%	0.0%	3.4%	6.8%	10.1%	13.5%	16.8%
4.75%	0.0%	1.2%	4.2%	7.5%	10.8%	14.2%
5.00%	0.0%	0.4%	2.7%	5.7%	8.9%	12.2%

However, for withdrawal rates above the guaranteed rate, investing in the risk-free asset is guaranteed to fail, so adding risk to the portfolio is the only possible hope for success. For example, by increasing the portfolio volatility from 0% to 3%, the 4.75% spending plan's failure rate drops from 100% to 22.5%. However, beyond a certain level, additional risk begins to increase the chances of failure. For example, with the 4.75% withdrawal rate, a portfolio volatility of 9% has the smallest failure rate, that is, 14.0%.[8] It is this pattern that led some researchers to devise strategies that minimize the failure rate and the risk of ruin.

5.2 Cost of surpluses

Retirees who follow a 4% rule will often generate portfolio surpluses that waste money. In Table 2, we report the results for our numeric experiment. The layout of Table 2 is the same as Table 1; however, the values in its body are estimated percentages of initial wealth that are spent on funding surpluses. The standard errors of all estimates are uniformly less than 0.05%. Clearly, withdrawing less (more) than the guaranteed rate and investing in the risk-free bond always (never) generates surpluses. However, for all rates, volatility adds significantly to the surplus and shifts money away from retirement spending. In particular, an investor withdrawing at the guaranteed rate (4.46%) and investing in the market portfolio (12% volatility) has allocated 13.5% of his portfolio to surpluses, and only 86.5% to actual spending. Strikingly, the surplus from this strategy could be used to increase *every* retirement payout by nearly 16% ($\approx$ 13.5%/86.5%).

5.3 Spending overpayments

In Table 3, we present our third metric—the spending overpayment. This table's structure is the same as its two predecessors, but the values in its body are

Table 3 Spending overpayments as a percentage of initial wealth for constant-mix portfolios.

Withdrawal rate	Constant-mix volatility					
	0%	3%	6%	9%	12%	15%
4.00%	0.0%	0.2%	1.1%	1.9%	2.5%	3.0%
4.25%	0.0%	0.7%	1.6%	2.4%	3.0%	3.5%
4.46%	0.0%	1.2%	2.1%	2.8%	3.4%	3.8%
4.75%	0.0%	1.7%	2.6%	3.3%	3.8%	4.2%
5.00%	0.0%	1.9%	2.9%	3.6%	4.1%	4.5%

the estimated percentages of initial wealth wasted by obtaining the spending distribution using the 4% rule versus a more cost-effective strategy. The standard errors of all estimates are uniformly less than 0.05%. The waste increases with increasing withdrawal rate, since relatively more money goes toward spending, and also increases with portfolio volatility. With a market portfolio investment (12% volatility), spending overpayments claim an additional 2–4% of a retiree's initial portfolio wealth. In the next section, we shall look at least cost strategies in greater detail and see how to eliminate overpayments.

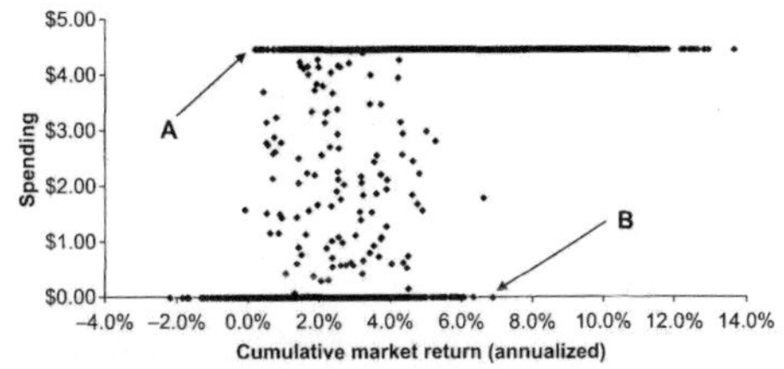

Figure 1 Spending versus cumulative market return in year 30 for a 4.46% withdrawal rate and the market portfolio.

6 Least cost spending strategies

We have identified and quantified the 4% rule's first two sources of waste—funding unspent surpluses and overpaying for spending. However, what investment strategy can a retiree use to recoup these losses? In this section, we answer that question and also demonstrate a useful diagnostic tool for discovering spending overpayments. For concreteness, we consider a retiree that has a 30-year horizon, starts with \$100, withdraws at the 4.46% guaranteed rate, and invests in the market portfolio.

Figure 1 is a scatter plot of our retiree's last year of spending versus the cumulative market return over the 30-year period since his retirement began. For convenience, the cumulative market return has been annualized. Each point on the plot represents a scenario. As shown in Table 1, our retiree spent less than his \$4.46 goal in 10.6% of the scenarios, and in fact, he spent nothing at all in 9.6% of them. The remaining 89.4% of the scenarios had sufficient funds to fully support the \$4.46 spending goal. The Monte Carlo estimate of the cost of purchasing the last year's payout is 96¢. Note that if our retiree had invested in the risk-free bond, he would have been guaranteed a \$4.46 payout in the last year. The cost of the bond investment would have been $\$4.46/1.02^{30} \approx \$2.46$. Hence what happened to the \$1.50 saved by allowing deficits? It was wasted on funding surpluses.

Our retiree spent 96¢ to fund the last year of his plan, but he could have obtained its spending distribution more cheaply.[9] To see why, consider points A and B in Figure 1. Point A is a scenario for which spending was \$4.46 and the market averaged a mere 21 basis point increase over 30 years—times

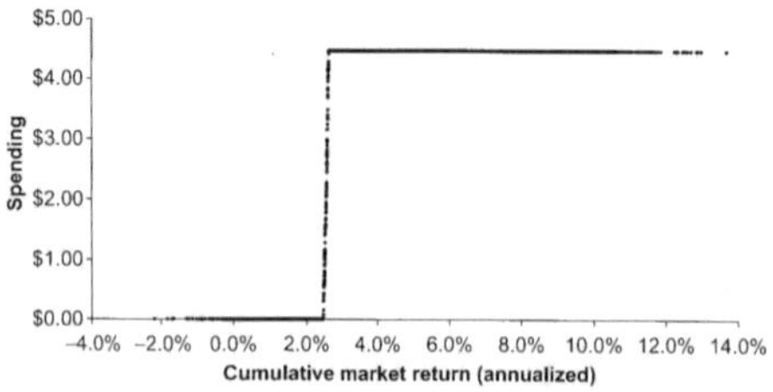

Figure 2 Spending versus cumulative market return in year 30 for the least cost-spending strategy.

were tough. In contrast, point B is a scenario for which spending completely disappeared, and yet the market averaged a hefty 6.92% real, annualized increase. Since the cost of money is cheaper in good times than it is in bad times, our retiree could have saved money by finding an alternative investment that paid nothing in scenario A, \$4.46 in scenario B, and kept the payouts in all the remaining scenarios unchanged. If our retiree exploited all these money-saving swaps, he would have a least cost strategy (Dybvig, 1988a, 1988b). Figure 2 is a scatter plot of the least cost-spending strategy versus the cumulative market return. The spending distributions of Figures 1 and 2 are the same—the spending amounts have the same values and frequency—however, the spending amounts have been reassigned to different market returns and have different underlying investment strategies. Our estimated price to implement the least cost strategy is 69 ¢, a savings of 27 ¢ over the 4% rule.[10]

Generally, scatter plots of spending versus the cumulative market return can identify overspending. A least cost strategy will plot as a smooth non-decreasing curve (see Figure 2), and spending will be higher when prices are cheaper. For example, the plot of constant, risk-free spending versus the market is a horizontal line, is non-decreasing, and is a least cost strategy. Inefficient strategies will either exhibit scatter (see Figure 1) or, if they are smooth, have a region where spending decreases with cumulative market return.

What investments should our retiree make to get the least cost? Because the shape of Figure 2 is approximately flat–ramp–flat, a financial engineer would suggest a strategy of buying and selling 30-year, European call options on the market portfolio. Our retiree would purchase calls with an exercise price equal to the rightmost value for which the payouts are zero. Simultaneously, he would sell an equal number of calls with an exercise price equal to the leftmost value for which the payouts equal \$4.46. By adjusting the numbers of calls purchased and sold, a payoff diagram very similar to that shown in Figure 2 would be obtained. Specifically, suppose that N calls are bought at the strike price $K_b = F(P_0)$ and sold at $K_s = F(P_F)$, where P_0 and P_F (the failure rate) are the probabilities of a zero withdrawal and a shortage, respectively, and the function $F(\cdot)$ is the inverse cumulative probability distribution for the (log-normal) cumulative market return. The number of calls to buy and sell is $N = \delta \cdot W_0/(K_s - K_b)$, where δ is the withdrawal rate and W_0 is the initial portfolio value. The prices of the calls are easily determined from the Black–Scholes formula. For our example, $P_0 \approx 9.56\%$, $P_F \approx 10.58\%$, and $\delta \cdot W_0 = \$4.46$, and we get the values $K_b \approx \$2.12$ (2.53% annualized), $K_b \approx \$2.19$ (2.65% annualized), and $N = 57.97$. The net cost of the replicating call options is 68.5 ¢, which equals our Monte Carlo price to three digits.

The above analysis could be repeated to cover all 30 years of spending. Efficient strategies for each year would entail the purchase and sale of call options with different exercise prices. The total cost would equal the cost of all the options purchased minus the proceeds from selling all the options written. For this particular investment and spending combination, our retiree would save 3.4% of his initial portfolio by adopting the least cost strategy, where 0.27% of the savings can be attributed to the last year.

It is, of course, possible that no counterparty would offer the multiyear options necessary for a retiree to replicate the 4% rule's spending distribution. If not, it is still possible to replicate the least cost strategy by following a dynamic strategy using the riskless bond and the market portfolio. Further, if enough retirees wanted the 4% rule's spending distribution and the least cost-investment strategy was sufficiently below other readily available investment options, then financial institutions would be motivated to offer new products and services that replicated the spending distribution at a cheaper price for the retiree, but at a profitable price for the institution.

The key to recouping surpluses is to just not fund them—just fund spending. The key to recouping overpayments is to spend relatively large amounts when payouts are cheap and to spend relatively small amounts when payouts are expensive. A retiree can get the 4% rule's spending distribution at a much cheaper cost by buying and selling call options or by implementing a dynamic strategy. However, does he really want this spending distribution or is there a cheaper distribution he would prefer?

7 Spending preferences and expected utility

Mick wagered \$100 and had a two-third chance of winning a floor pass and a third chance of watching Dylan on pay-per-view ($3^2/_3$ bullets). Mick's gamble can be replicated for just \$70 by eliminating a surplus and using a least cost strategy, but this is still wasteful, since Mick would have preferred a guaranteed general admission ticket (4 bullets), which he could have had by wagering just \$60. In our parable, the money spent on surpluses and overpayments is only a lower bound on waste; choosing a strategy whose payouts are inconsistent with preferences wastes even more. In this section, we argue that this result is also true for a retiree who follows a 4% rule, but prefers a different spending plan.

Does a retiree really want the spending distribution of a 4% rule strategy? Consider a retiree who is planning on spending \$40K a year for the next 30 years. Now, suppose that after the first year, his portfolio suffers a 20% loss. Without knowing much about our retiree, what would you expect him to do? Would he continue spending \$40K, cut his spending by 20% to \$32K, or do something in between? We might reasonably expect him to spread the pain of his loss across all his remaining years, and adopt one of the latter two options. However, if our retiree were a strict follower of the 4% rule, he will continue spending \$40K a year, until his portfolio is exhausted.[11] It seems unlikely that a retiree would prefer fixed dependable spending in his early retirement years and the volatile spending of Figures 1 and 2 in his late retirement years. Our retiree could have addressed this issue much earlier, when he created his plan, either by investing in a riskless bond or by relaxing his requirement for fixed spending. However, without knowing more about his preferences, we do not know which option would have been more appropriate.

Financial economists advocate a very different approach toward retirement spending and investing. Building on the seminal work of Hakansson (1970), they suggest that a retiree's preferences concerning different amounts of income in different years be represented with a set of utility functions. Then they determine an integrated investment and spending policy that can be funded with the retiree's initial wealth and that will maximize the expected value of his overall utility.

Figure 3 places our earlier analysis in the context of retiree preferences and utility. Each point on the plot is a retirement strategy. The vertical axis plots the expected utility of a strategy, and the horizontal axis plots the cost of the strategy. The strategies that maximize the expected utility plot on the solid curve. The strategy labeled A represents the traditional 4% rule—an initial portfolio value of \$100, withdrawal rate of 4.0%, and 60–40% stock-bond mix (i.e., the market portfolio). This strategy does not maximize expected utility—it has

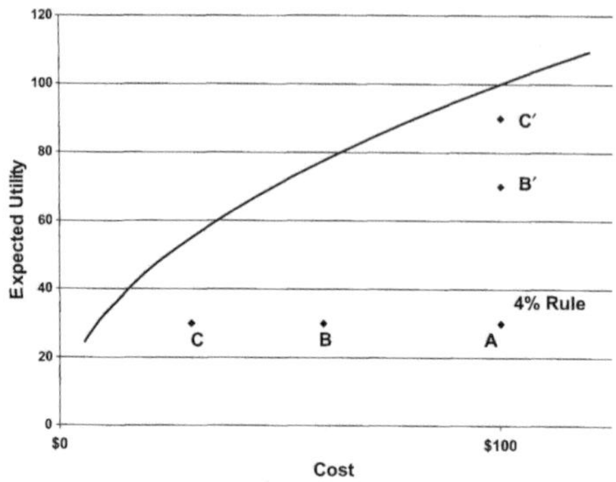

Figure 3 Expected utility versus cost for various retirement strategies.

unspent surpluses and overpays for spending—and must plot below the curve. The least cost-spending strategy has the same spending distribution as the 4% rule, and therefore the same expected utility. However, this strategy recoups the $18.80 spent on surpluses (Table 2) and the $2.50 spent on overpayments (Table 3), and can be purchased for $78.70. The least cost-spending strategy (labeled B) plots to the left of the 4% rule strategy (labeled A) on Figure 3.

Generally, we do not expect strategy B to maximize a retiree's expected utility, and therefore, there may be many strategies that deliver the same benefit as A, but at a lower cost than B's. For example, suppose a retiree truly prefers constant spending—even a 1% chance of failure makes him extremely uncomfortable. He might be equally happy if he traded his current strategy that targets a $4 withdrawal, but has a chance of shortfalls, for a new strategy, which pays half as much, but is guaranteed. In Figure 3, we have labeled this case as C—it invests in the risk-free bond and costs $44.80. By knowing this retiree's preferences, we can make him just as happy as he was with the 4% rule, but at less than half the cost.

Of course, no advisor would recommend strategy B or C, since they both cost less than the available $100 and would leave money on the table. One strategy, labeled B′, fully funds the least cost-spending strategy, but uses the savings on surpluses and overpayments to increase all the payouts. This strategy costs $100, increases all payouts by more than 27%, and plots directly above the 4% rule in Figure 3. It is unlikely that this strategy would maximize the expected utility, unless our retiree enjoys the 4% rule's occasional spending shortages and his only mistake is failing to find the least cost way of achieving them. Hence, typically, there are many strategies with higher expected utility than B′ that cost the same. If C′ is one of these preferred strategies, it will plot above B′ in Figure 3. As an example, consider a retiree who has no tolerance for risk and prefers investing in the risk-free bond. He would use his full $100 to get a guaranteed $4.46 annual payout. This strategy's payout is at a minimum 10% higher than any payout of the 4% rule, and never fails to pay. It clearly dominates the 4% rule for all retirees, will not dominate the least cost strategy for a few retirees, and will be likely dominated itself for retirees who have a modest tolerance for risk.[12]

To actually reach the efficient curve on our figure, we need to know a retiree's utility function. However, much of the gap between the efficient curve and the 4% rule can be closed with a less formal description of a retiree's preferences. Basically, retirees need to understand that the cost of providing spending when markets perform poorly is often substantially greater than when they perform well.[13] If this point is well understood, then most retirees are likely to choose to spend less in bad scenarios in order to be able to spend more in good scenarios, versus spending the same amount in all scenarios. The willingness to make these spending tradeoffs and to assume the investment volatility needed to implement them will differ among investors, and therefore so should their retirement strategies.

8 Glide-path investment strategies

Our first set of experiments focused on constant-mix investment strategies—portfolios are annually rebalanced to maintain a constant volatility level. This was the original approach of Bengen (1994), and it is often recommended. Recently, however, *glide-path* investment strategies have experienced a surge in popularity. These strategies systematically reduce portfolio volatility as a retiree gets older, and several authors, including Bengen, have suggested that retirees adopt this alternative. Two years after his original article, Bengen (1996) concluded that, "All things considered, I recommend that you adopt a phase-down of one percent of your stock allocation each year . . ." Jennings and Reichenstein (2007) analyzed a number of lifecycle mutual funds and found that these funds, even when intended for post-retirement use, generally follow an investment glide path, averaging an equity percentage equal to approximately 120 less the target investor's age.

We have argued that the major flaw of the 4% rule is its attempt to support nonvolatile spending with volatile investing. Perhaps a glide path that systematically reduces risk could cause less inefficiency and reduce failure rates? Using our previous withdrawal rates and our previous volatility levels, we ran a numeric experiment to test this hypothesis. However, this time the volatility level was only used as the initial level for the first year's investments, and thereafter, the level was decreased each year so that in the 30th year the volatility was zero, and the portfolio was invested in just the risk-free bond.

The results of our glide-path experiments are reported in Tables 4–6, which correspond to Tables 1–3 of our constant-mix experiments. Comparing the failure rate tables, we notice that except possibly for the lowest volatilities, the glide-path rates are worse—even though the glide-path portfolios were on average less risky than the corresponding constant mix portfolios. The reason for this behavior is that glide-path strategies are just as likely as constant-mix strategies to have a series of poor early returns and run out of money. However, the glide-path strategy tends to lock-in these poor returns, decreasing the likelihood that future good returns allow the portfolio to recover and sustain spending.

A comparison of Tables 5 and 2, the cost of surpluses tables, shows that glide-path strategies do a bit better than constant-mix strategies in this category. Basically, a glide-path strategy generates a smaller surplus. For the market portfolio, the glide-path strategy spent approximately 2.5% less on surpluses than the corresponding constant-mix portfolio. However, a comparison of Tables 6 and 3, the overpayment tables, shows that the savings on surpluses are offset by higher overpayments. For the market portfolio, the glide-path strategy spent approximately 1–2% more on overpayments

Table 4 Failure rates for glide-path portfolios.

Withdrawal rate	Initial-mix volatility 0%	3%	6%	9%	12%	15%
4.00%	0.0%	0.2%	2.0%	4.1%	6.0%	7.7%
4.25%	0.0%	2.1%	5.3%	7.4%	9.1%	10.6%
4.46%	0.0%	9.8%	10.6%	11.5%	12.5%	13.5%
4.75%	100.0%	35.0%	21.6%	18.6%	17.9%	17.9%
5.00%	100.0%	63.9%	34.2%	26.2%	23.3%	22.3%

Table 5 Cost of surpluses as a percentage of initial wealth for glide-path portfolios.

Withdrawal rate	Initial-mix volatility					
	0%	3%	6%	9%	12%	15%
4.00%	10.4%	10.6%	11.9%	14.0%	16.3%	18.7%
4.25%	4.8%	5.7%	8.1%	10.6%	13.2%	15.8%
4.46%	0.0%	2.7%	5.4%	8.1%	10.8%	13.5%
4.75%	0.0%	0.7%	3.0%	5.6%	8.2%	10.9%
5.00%	0.0%	0.2%	1.6%	3.9%	6.4%	9.0%

Table 6 Spending overpayments as a percentage of initial wealth for glide-path portfolios.

Withdrawal rate	Initial-mix volatility					
	0%	3%	6%	9%	12%	15%
4.00%	0.0%	0.2%	1.5%	2.7%	3.7%	4.5%
4.25%	0.0%	0.9%	2.4%	3.5%	4.4%	5.1%
4.46%	0.0%	1.8%	3.1%	4.1%	5.0%	5.6%
4.75%	0.0%	2.5%	3.8%	4.8%	5.6%	6.2%
5.00%	0.0%	2.6%	4.2%	5.3%	6.0%	6.7%

than the corresponding constant mix strategy. In total, the surpluses and overpayments of glide-path strategies are comparable to constant mix strategies. Further, since we expect that the spending distributions generated by glide-path strategies are likely at odds with a retiree's true preferences, the costs of surpluses and overpayments are again only a lower bound on the total money wasted by adopting these strategies.

9 Conclusion

The 4% rule and its variants finance a constant, nonvolatile spending plan using a risky, volatile investment strategy. Two of the rule's inefficiencies—the price paid for funding its unspent surpluses and the overpayments for its spending distribution—apply to all retirees, independent of their preferences. For a typical rule, we used a market model to estimate that between 10% and 20% of a portfolio's initial wealth is being allocated to surpluses, and an additional 2–4% is going toward overpayments. If the spending distribution of the 4% rule were inconsistent with a retiree's preferences, then the costs can be much higher. All in all, any retiree who adopts a 4% rule pays a high price.

Our approach can be easily extended to investigate other retirement rules of thumb and to use alternative market models. If a retirement plan generates unspent surpluses then our approach can price the surplus. A scatter plot of spending amount versus cumulative market return will quickly reveal whether a strategy is of least cost type. Strategies with overpayments will often generate a cloud of points (Figure 1), whereas least cost strategies will generate a non-decreasing curve (Figure 2).

Many practical issues remain to be addressed before advisors can hope to create individualized retirement financial plans that maximize expected utility for investors with diverse circumstances, other sources of income, and preferences. While we still may be far away from such an ideal, there appears to be no doubt that a better approach can be found than that offered by combinations of desired constant real spending and risky investment. Despite its ubiquity, it is time to replace the 4% rule with approaches better grounded in fundamental economic analysis.

Appendix A. Pricing

Our simple two-asset economy is complete—any series of payouts, volatile or nonvolatile, can be dynamically replicated using just the risk-free bond and the market portfolio. Further, we can assign a fair, no-arbitrage price to the payouts using the economy's state price density function or pricing kernel (refer to Cochrane (2005) and Sharpe (2007) for a full discussion). This approach is often used to price derivative securities, and we use it in this study to price portfolio withdrawals for spending and surpluses. In this framework, the current price P of an asset that pays a random amount $\mathbf{C}_t$ in t years is equal to the expected value:

$$P = E[\mathbf{C}_t \cdot \mathbf{M}_t] \tag{A.1}$$

where the random variable $\mathbf{M}_t$ is the pricing kernel. Generally, both $\mathbf{C}_t$ and $\mathbf{M}_t$ are functions of the random market returns $\mathbf{R}_1, \mathbf{R}_2, \ldots, \mathbf{R}_t$, and the expected value $E[\cdot]$ in the above equation is with respect to the joint-density distribution of these returns.

Equation (A.1) can be used to price the surplus at the horizon $t = T$ and to price each annual spending withdrawal at years $t = 1, 2, \ldots, T$. The price of all withdrawals is equal to the sum of the prices for these annual withdrawals. Note that in our analysis, the total of all prices (withdrawals and surplus) will equal the initial portfolio value.

Usually, the pricing kernel $\mathbf{M}_t$ depends on the annual market returns via the cumulative market return $\mathbf{V}_t$. In this Appendix, we assume that all returns are gross returns (ratios of ending value to beginning value) so that in particular, the cumulative market return is just the product of consecutive annual market returns (i.e., $\mathbf{V}_t = \mathbf{R}_1 \cdot \mathbf{R}_2 \cdots \mathbf{R}_t$). Hence, whereas the payout often depends on the order of the returns, the pricing kernel's value is independent of order—a low return followed by a high return is equivalent to the high return followed by the low return. When the annual market returns have identical log-normal distributions and are independent, the pricing kernel is simply:

$$\mathbf{M}_t = A^t / \mathbf{V}_t^b \tag{A.2}$$

The positive parameters A and b are given by the formulas:

$$A = (\sqrt{E_m \cdot R_f})^{b-1} \tag{A.3a}$$

$$b = \frac{\ln (E_m / R_f)}{\ln (1 + S_m^2 / E_m^2)} \tag{A.3b}$$

In the above equations, R_f is the total risk-free return, $E_m = E[\mathbf{R}_t]$ is the yearly expected total market return, and $S_m = (\mathrm{Var}[\mathbf{R}_t])^{1/2}$ is the annual market volatility. For our experiments, we use the values $R_f = 1.02, E_m = 1.06$, and $S_m = 0.12$, and so we get the approximate values $A \approx 1.08$ and $b \approx 3.02$ for the two kernel parameters.

Because the exponent on the cumulative market return in Eq. (A.2) is positive, payouts are relatively cheap to secure when the market has high returns. This is a standard result of asset pricing theory: market prices must adjust until the total demand for claims paying off in states of scarcity will be less than that for claims paying off in times of plenty. To the extent that cumulative market returns serve as adequate proxies for overall consumption (scarcity or plenty), we expect the pricing kernel to be a monotonically decreasing function of cumulative market return.

Our Monte Carlo simulation generates a number of equally likely random paths, where each path is a scenario of annual market returns of length T. For each path, we compute sample values for the payout and the pricing kernel. In particular, let $C_t^{(i)}$ and $M_t^{(i)}$ be the payout and kernel values for the ith path. Using N of these paths, we can estimate the expected value of Eq. (A.1) with a sample mean and get the following approximate price:

$$P \approx \frac{1}{N} \sum_{i=1}^{N} C_t^{(i)} \cdot M_t^{(i)} \qquad \text{(A.4)}$$

The error of this approximation can be made as small as we want by choosing the number of paths N to be sufficiently large.

For complete markets, Dybvig (1988a, 1988b) derived an elegant formula for computing the minimum price for receiving any payout distribution. Dybvig creates a dynamic investment strategy that replicates the payout distribution, but purchases payouts most efficiently—the highest payout is purchased at the cheapest price (when markets perform the best), the next highest is purchased at the next cheapest price, and so on. More formally, let $F_t(c) = P(\mathbf{C}_t \leq c)$ and $G_t(v) = P(\mathbf{V}_t \leq v)$ be the cumulative probability densities for the random payout $\mathbf{C}_t$ and market value $\mathbf{V}_t$, respectively. We can implicitly define the random payout $\mathbf{X}_t$ as a function of the cumulative market value $\mathbf{V}_t$ using the following equation:

$$F_t(\mathbf{X}_t) = G_t(\mathbf{V}_t) \qquad \text{(A.5)}$$

For any percentile, let us say the 75th, the 75th percentile of the market value will be paired with the 75th percentile of the payout distribution of $\mathbf{C}_t$, which becomes the 75th percentile of the payout $\mathbf{X}_t$. Hence, $\mathbf{X}_t$ increases with market value, decreases with pricing kernel, and has the same distribution as $\mathbf{C}_t$. Finally, if we replace $\mathbf{C}_t$ by $\mathbf{X}_t$ in Eq. (A.1), we obtain the formula for the minimum price.

The Monte Carlo simulation is easily modified to estimate the minimum price. After simulating N pairs of payouts and pricing kernels, each variable is separately sorted. The payouts are sorted in ascending order, the kernel values in descending order. The sorted values are re-paired and fed into Eq. (A.4). The result is an estimated minimum price. In practice, we generated a large number of paths (N = 50,000) for our estimates, and then further refined the results by averaging a large number (500) of independent estimates. For the results we present in this study, the standard deviation of the estimated prices was uniformly less than 5¢ for an initial wealth of $100.

Acknowledgments

The authors thank Robert L. Young, CFA of Financial Engines for suggesting the title of this study and Wei-Yin Hu, Ph.D. of Financial Engines for careful reviews of earlier drafts and a number of helpful comments.

Notes

1 For brevity, we will refer to the typical retiree in the singular and use the male pronoun. However, all our arguments apply equally well to single females, a married couple, and partnerships.

2 The author who is actually a member of the baby boom generation wrote this section. He assures his younger and older colleagues that the parable will have deeper meaning for readers of his cohort.

3 The betting wheel's sectors have the same $1 payout, have the same chance of occurrence, but have different costs. Similarly, in an economy, a boom and a recession may have the same chance of occurring, but the cost of a $1 in the former state is typically much cheaper than in the latter state.

4 We assume that Mick only cares about the distribution of tickets and not on the sector chosen by the wheel. More formally, Mick's utility is not state dependent.

5 Modeling mortality is a very important aspect of retirement planning, and by assuming a fixed retirement period, we have made an extreme simplification—retirees drop dead at a specific, deterministic, future date. Further, we are implicitly assuming that any remaining portfolio value at that date is wasted. That said, any serious attempt to include mortality would introduce at a minimum annuities and bequest motives—two complexities that we defer

to another investigation. Annuities allow retirees to pool mortality risk, and bequests allow retirees to transfer surpluses to heirs.

6 This is the formula for the present value of an ordinary simple annuity paying a dollar at the end of each year for 30 consecutive years.

7 We included the leveraged market portfolio (125%) in the analysis to match the volatility of the oft-recommended 75% equity strategy. This implicitly assumes that investors can borrow at the risk-free rate. If borrowing costs are higher, the expected return for this portfolio can be adjusted downward.

8 More simulations could be run to refine the estimate of the volatility that minimizes the failure rate for this, and any other, withdrawal rate.

9 We assume that our retiree does not have state-dependent utility, cares only about the probability distribution of spending in each year, and does not care about his spending sequences.

10 An alternative way to view the inefficiency with the payout plan shown in Figure 1 is to recognize that our retiree is exposed to two sources of risk. He does not know where on the horizontal axis the market's cumulative return will plot. This is market risk, for which an investor can expect to be rewarded in an efficient capital market. But even if the market's cumulative return were known, there may still be uncertainty concerning his payout, since there are multiple payouts for many of the vertical slices. Our retiree's payouts are not only dependent on the cumulative return on the market, but also on the order of the returns; that is, the market *path*. It is this path dependency that causes the observed multiplicity and creates additional risk. This additional risk, called *path risk* or *sequence risk*, is not rewarded in a capital market conforming to the standard assumptions of most asset pricing theories.

11 Many devotees of the 4% rule recommend adjusting spending and investment after a dramatic market move, but some are strict adherents. For example, Guyton (2004) describes a retired couple, who after the bear market of 2000–2002, wonder if they "should reduce their withdrawals to keep their rate at roughly four percent" (of their depressed 2002 portfolio values). He advised them "that—on the contrary—it was fine if their current withdrawal rates approached six percent or even seven percent!"

12 We can also plot Mick's gambles on Figure 3. The points A, B, and C, correspond to his original gamble ($100), the equivalent least cost gamble ($70), and the preferred guaranteed general admission ticket ($60), respectively. In Mick's case, the point B′ may correspond to a strategy that has a third chance of a general admission ticket and a two-third chance of a floor pass versus his original gamble that has a third chance of pay-for-view and a two-third chance of a floor pass. For Mick, the point C′ would be Eric's gamble, the guaranteed floor pass, and since this gamble is optimal for Mick, C′ would plot on the curve.

13 In Section 6, we estimated that the price of the least cost strategy for the 4% rule's spending distribution in year 30 was 69¢. This spending distribution pays $4.46 in over 89% of the top performing market scenarios. A risk-free bond would cover all market scenarios, pay $4.46, and cost $2.46. Hence, it costs another $1.97 to cover the bottom 11% of market scenarios; that is, almost three times as much to cover one-ninth of the scenarios.

References

AARP. (2008). "Managing Money in Retirement: Make Your Money Last." Availabe at: http://www.aarp.org/money/financial_planning/sessionseven/managing_money_in_retirement.html (accessed September 22, 2008).

Bengen, W. P. (1994). "Determining Withdrawal Rates Using Historical Data." *Journal of Financial Planning* 7(4), 171–180.

Bengen, W. P. (1996). "Asset Allocation for a Lifetime." *Journal of Financial Planning* **9**(4), 58–67.

Bengen, W. P. (1997). "Conserving Client Portfolios during Retirement, Part III." *Journal of Financial Planning* **10**(6), 84–97.

Bengen, W. P. (2001). "Conserving Client Portfolios during Retirement, Part IV." *Journal of Financial Planning* **14**(5), 110–119.

Bengen, W. P. (2006a). "Baking a Withdrawal Plan 'Layer Cake' for Your Retirement Clients." *Journal of Financial Planning* **19**(8), 44–51.

Bengen, W. P. (2006b). "Sustainable Withdrawals." In: Evensky, H. and Katz, D. B. (eds.), *Retirement Income Redesigned: Master Plans for Distribution*. NewYork: Bloomberg Press.

Bierwirth, L. (1994). "Investing for Retirement: Using the Past to Model the Future." *Journal of Financial Planning* 7(1), 14–24.

Burns, S. (2004). "Portfolio Survival: The Trinity Study." *Dallas Morning News*. December 7, 2004. Available at: http://www.dallasnews.com/sharedcontent/dws/bus/scottburns/readers/stories/SBportfoliosurvival.f5a90da.html (accessed September 22, 2008).

Cochrane, J. H. (2005). *Asset Pricing: Revised Edition*. Princeton, NJ: Princeton University Press.

Cooley, P. L., Hubbard, C. M. and Walz, D. T. (1998). "Retirement Savings: Choosing a Withdrawal Rate That Is Sustainable." *American Association of Individual Investors Journal* **20**(2), 16–21.

Cooley, P. L., Hubbard, C. M. and Walz, D. T. (1999). "Sustainable Withdrawal Rates from Your Retirement Portfolio." *Financial Counseling and Planning* **10**(1), 39–47.

Cooley, P. L., Hubbard, C. M. and Walz, D. T. (2001). "Withdrawing Money from Your Retirement Portfolio Without Going Broke." *CCH Journal of Retirement Planning* 4(4), 35–41, 48.

Cooley, P. L., Hubbard, C. M. and Walz, D. T. (2003a). "Does International Diversification Increase the Sustainable Withdrawal Rates from Retirement Portfolios?" *Journal of Financial Planning* **16**(1), 74–80.

Cooley, P. L., Hubbard, C. M. and Walz, D. T. (2003b). "A Comparative Analysis of Retirement Portfolio Success Rates: Simulation Versus Overlapping Periods." *Financial Services Review* **12**(2), 115–129.

Dybvig, P. H. (1988a). "Inefficient Dynamic Portfolio Strategies or How to Throw Away a Million Dollars in the Stock Market." *Review of Financial Studies* **1**(1), 67–88.

Dybvig, P. H. (1988b). "Distributional Analysis of Portfolio Choice." *Journal of Business* **61**(3), 369–393.

Guyton, J. T. (2004). "Decision Rules and Portfolio Management for Retirees: Is the 'Safe' Initial Withdrawal Rate Too Safe?" *Journal of Financial Planning* **17**(10), 54–62.

Hakansson, N. H. (1970). "Optimal Investment and Consumption Strategies Under Risk for a Class of Utility Functions." *Econometrica* **38**(5), 587–607.

Ho, K., Milevsky, M. A. and Robinson, C. (1994a). "How to Avoid Outliving Your Money." *Canadian Investment Review* 7(3), 35–38.

Ho, K., Milevsky, M. A. and Robinson, C. (1994b). "Asset Allocation, Life Expectancy and Shortfall." *Financial Services Review* **3**(2), 109–126.

Jennings, W. W. and Reichenstein, W. (2007). "Choosing the Right Mix: Lessons From Life Cycle Funds." *American Association of Individual Investors Journal* **29**(1), 5–12.

Markese, J. (2006). "Developing a Withdrawal Strategy for Your Fund Portfolio." *American Association of Individual Investors Journal* **28**(11), 13–16.

Milevsky, M. A. and Abaimova, A. (2006). "Risk Management during Retirement. Retirement." In: Evensky, H. and Katz, D. B. (eds.), *Retirement Income Redesigned: Master Plans for Distribution*. NewYork: Bloomberg Press.

Milevsky, M. A., Ho, K. and Robinson, C. (1997). "Asset Allocation via the Conditional First Exit Time or How to Avoid Outliving Your Money." *Review of Quantitative Finance and Accounting* **9**(1), 53–70.

Milevsky, M. A. and Robinson, C. (2005). "A Sustainable Spending Rate without Simulation." *Financial Analyst Journal* **61**(6), 89–100.

Pye, G. B. (2000). "Sustainable Investment Withdrawals." *Journal of Portfolio Management* **26**(4), 73–83.

Quinn, J. B. (2006). "Get Smart with Your Money." *AARP Bulletin* 47(6), (June). Reprinted and available at: http://bulletin.aarp.org/yourmoney/retirement/articles/simple_money_steps.html (accessed September 22, 2008).

Sharpe, W. F. (2007). *Investors and Markets: Portfolio Choices, Asset Prices and Investment Advice*. Princeton, NJ: Princeton University Press.

Spiegelman, R. (2006). "Retirement Spending: The 4% Solution." *Schwab Investing Insights®*, August 17, 2006. Available at: http://www.schwab.com/public/schwab/research_strategies/market_insight/retirement_strategies/planning/retirement_spending_the_4_solution.html (accessed September 22, 2008).

Spitzer, J. J., Strieter, J. C. and Singh, S. (2007). "Guidelines for Withdrawal Rates and Portfolio Safety during Retirement." *Journal of Financial Planning* **20**(10), 52–59.

T. Rowe Price (2008a). "Investment Guidance and Tools: Retirement Planning: Living in Retirement: A Withdrawal Rule of Thumb." Available at: http://www.troweprice.com/common/index3/0,3011,lnp%253D10014%2526cg%253D12 210%2526pgid%253D7549,00.html (accessed September 22, 2008).

T. Rowe Price (2008b). "Investment Guidance and Tools: Retirement Planning: Retirement Income Calculator." Available at: http://www3.troweprice.com/ric/RIC/ (accessed September 22, 2008).

Updegrave, W. (2007). "Retirement: The 4 Percent Solution." *CNNMoney.com*. August 16, 2007. Available at: http://money.cnn.com/2007/08/13/pf/expert/expert.moneymag/index.htm (accessed September 22, 2008).

Vanguard Group. (2008). "Planning and Education: Retirement: Managing Your Retirement: Tap Your Assets: Determine How Much You Can Withdraw." Available at: https://personal.vanguard.com/us/planningeducation/retirement/PEdRetTapDetermineWDContent.jsp (accessed September 22, 2008).

Weston, L. P. (2008). "Make Your Money Last in Retirement; 5 Keys." Available at: http://articles.moneycentral.msn.com/RetirementandWills/RetireEarly/MakeYourMoneyLastInRetirement5keys.aspx (accessed September 22, 2008).

Keywords: Retirement economics; expected utility; fixed withdrawals